October 28-30, 2015
Tokyo, Japan

Association for Computing Machinery

Advancing Computing as a Science & Profession

IMC'15

Proceedings of the 2015 ACM Conference on Internet Measurement Conference

Sponsored by:

ACM SIGCOMM and ACM SIGMETRICS

Supported by:

NSF, Akamai, MLAB, Internet Initiative Japan, Internet Society, facebook, technicolor, ThousandEyes and Keio University

Association for
Computing Machinery

Advancing Computing as a Science & Profession

The Association for Computing Machinery
2 Penn Plaza, Suite 701
New York, New York 10121-0701

ISBN: 978-1-4503-3848-6 (Digital)

ISBN: 978-1-4503-4101-1 (Print)

Additional copies may be ordered prepaid from:

ACM Order Department
PO Box 30777
New York, NY 10087-0777, USA

Phone: 1-800-342-6626 (USA and Canada)
+1-212-626-0500 (Global)
Fax: +1-212-944-1318
E-mail: acmhelp@acm.org
Hours of Operation: 8:30 am – 4:30 pm ET

Printed in the USA

General Chairs' Welcome

Welcome to ACM IMC 2015 in Tokyo!

We are proud to host IMC in Japan, for the first time in Asia, and we thank you for being part of it. IMC is a highly-regarded conference, co-sponsored by ACM SIGCOMM and ACM SIGMETRICS, that brings together networking researchers to advance the current state-of-the-art in the measurement and characterization of the Internet.

This exciting conference would not have been possible without the extensive effort by many individual volunteers. Specifically, we acknowledge the efforts of the technical program committee, led by Vivek Pai and Neil Spring, for their thorough paper review process. We hope that you enjoy the talks and have many stimulating discussions during your three days at the conference.

We would like to thank the IMC Steering Committee (Mark Allman, Ratul Mahajan, Renata Teixera, and Darryl Veitch) for talking us into this role, and for handling industry sponsorships and the student travel grant program. Their collective knowledge provides an endless source of wisdom on conference finances and organizational logistics.

IMC is encouraging student participation by providing a travel grant program, and by reduced registration fees. We are grateful to NSF, SIGCOMM and corporate supporters for their generous funds leading to 32 travel grant awards (30 students and 2 GeoDiversity applicants) to attend the conference. Our supporters are NSF, Akamai, MLab, IIJ, Internet Society, Facebook, Technicolor, and ThousandEyes. Their commitments to this event and the IMC conference series are highly appreciated. We are also grateful to Keio University for hosting the conference, and assistance on logistics.

Our thanks to our local team members: Hajime Tazaki as Web Chair, Shigeya Suzuki as Local Arrangements Chair, Romain Fontugne as Publications Chair, and our student volunteers. Special thanks to Carey Williamson, last year's General Chair, who has provided invaluable assistance from his experiences.

We hope you will find this conference and your visit to Tokyo exciting and enjoyable!

Kenjiro Cho
IMC 2015 General Co-chair
IIJ / Keio University, Japan

Kensuke Fukuda
IMC 2015 General Co-chair
NII / Sokendai, Japan

Welcome from the Program Co-Chairs

It is our pleasure to welcome you to the 2015 Internet Measurement Conference. IMC has become the premier venue for measurement-based research into all kinds of networks that comprise the Internet ecosystem, and this year's program reflects that diversity of the IMC community.

IMC 2015 received 169 papers of which 96 were long and 73 were short. As usual, we solicited both long papers with deep treatment of topics and short papers that convey exciting work in progress, offer high-level visions, or present more succinct viewpoints. We accepted 43 papers, comprising 31 long papers and 12 short papers. As usual, we used a single-blind reviewing process, conducted over two rounds. In the first round, each paper was reviewed by three program committee (PC) members. The 90 papers selected for the second round were reviewed by at least two more PC members. In a few cases, we solicited an extra review from outside experts. The final decisions were based on all the reviews, extensive online discussions, and a day-long meeting.

We wish to thank our talented, committed and hardworking PC. Their rigorous reviewing and detailed insights were invaluable in this process. Many of our PC members made great efforts to attend the PC meeting, such as taking long international/overnight flights.

After slowly building for some time, this year saw a new change, with ethical concerns explicitly mentioned as reviewing criteria in the call for papers, and many papers responded appropriately and explained any ethical issues that arose in their data collection and methodology. As more measurements move away from network-level activities and toward more explicit human-level behaviors, we can expect more of these kinds of issues to arise going forward.

We adopted the change made in last year's IMC of discontinuing review summaries of the papers, and we also continued with the change made in 2012 of having separate awards for the best paper and releasing the best public datasets. We thank our general chairs, Kenjiro Cho and Kensuke Fukuda, for all of their organization and for making the process run more smoothly, and the IMC Steering Committee for their advice during the entire process starting with assembling the PC. Importantly, this conference is indebted to our generous sponsors whose contributions greatly benefit the experience of all participants.

Vivek Pai
Google
vivekpai@google.com

Neil Spring
University of Maryland
nspring@cs.umd.edu

Table of Contents

Session: WiFi and Mobile

Session Chair: Ben Zhao *(University of California, Santa Barbara)*

Session: What's in a Name?

Session Chair: Alan Mislove *(Northeastern University)*

Session: Measurement and/or Platforms Deux

Session Chair: Renata Teixeira *(INRIA)*

Session: China and Cuba

Session Chair: Phillipa Gill *(Stony Brook University)*

Session: Analyses

Session Chair: Vivek Pai *(Google)*

IMC 2015 Conference Organization

General Chairs: Kenjiro Cho (IIJ/Keio University)
Kensuke Fukuda (NII/Sokendai)

Program Chairs: Vivek Pai (Google)
Neil Spring (University of Maryland)

Web Chair: Hajime Tazaki (University of Tokyo)

Proceedings Chair: Romain Fontugne (NII)

Local Arrangements Chair: Shigeya Suzuki (Keio University)

Steering Committee: Mark Allman (ICSI)
Ratul Mahajan (Microsoft Research)
Renata Teixeira (INRIA)
Darryl Veitch (University of Technology Sydney)

Program Committee: Paul Barford (University of Wisconsin)
Robert Beverly (Naval Postgraduate School)
Fabian Bustamante (Northwestern University)
Mark Crovella (Boston University)
Jon Crowcroft (University of Cambridge)
Xenofontas Dimitropoulos (University of Crete & ETH Zurich)
Anja Feldmann (Technische Universität Berlin)
Phillipa Gill (Stony Brook University)
Alex Halderman (University of Michigan)
Mohamed Ali (Dali) Kaafar (NICTA Australia)
Ethan Katz-Bassett (University of Southern California)
Balachander Krishnamurthy (AT&T Labs -- Research)
Yao Liu (Binghamton University)
Matthew Luckie (CAIDA)
Bruce Maggs (Duke University & Akamai)
Ratul Mahajan (Microsoft Research)
Evangelos Markatos (University of Crete & ICS FORTH)
Marco Mellia (Politecnico di Torino)
Alan Mislove (Northeastern University)
Erich Nahum (IBM Research)
Vivek Pai (Google)
Dina Papagiannaki (Telefonica Research)
Aiko Pras (University of Twente)
Vyas Sekar (Carnegie Mellon University)
Georgios Smaragdakis (MIT & TU Berlin)

Program Committee (continued):

Neil Spring (University of Maryland)
Renata Teixeira (INRIA)
Don Towsley (University of Massachusetts)
Arun Venkataramani (University of Massachusetts)
Nicholas Weaver (International Computer Science Institute)
Walter Willinger (NIKSUN)
Christo Wilson (Northeastern University)
Ben Zhao (UC Santa Barbara)
Heather Zheng (UC Santa Barbara)

Additional reviewers:

Giovanni Comarela (Boston University)
Ben Wu (Princeton University)

Sponsors:

Platinum Supporter:

Gold Supporters:

Silver Supporters:

Measurement and Analysis of Traffic Exchange Services

Mobin Javed
U.C. Berkeley
mobin@cs.berkeley.edu

Cormac Herley
Microsoft Research
cormac@microsoft.com

Marcus Peinado
Microsoft Research
marcuspe@microsoft.com

Vern Paxson
U.C. Berkeley, International Computer Science Institute
vern@cs.berkeley.edu

Abstract

Traffic exchange services enable members to bring traffic to their websites from a diverse pool of IP addresses, in return for visiting sites of other members. We examine the world of traffic exchanges to characterize their makeup, usage, and monetization. We find that the ecosystem includes a range of services, from manual exchanges where participants must solve CAPTCHAs between successive page views, to exchanges that provide tools that automatically surf without requiring any user action. By "milking" a sample of these exchanges, we analyze month-long datasets to examine the nature of URLs that members submit to them. We find a wide prevalence of URLs for services that pay users in return for views to their content, and at least 30% of the requested impressions are for pages that clearly participate in a class of impression fraud called *referrer spoofing*. We also analyze the size and composition of a sample of these exchange networks by making purchases, finding that the exchanges delivered visits from roughly 200K unique IP addresses, and that in some exchange networks, the majority of visits came from cloud hosting services.

Categories and Subject Descriptors

C.2.0 [**General**]: Security and protection

General Terms

Measurement; Advertising fraud

Keywords

Traffic exchanges; Impression fraud; Click fraud

1. INTRODUCTION

An eco-system has arisen to provide free traffic from a diverse pool of IP addresses using the principle of *exchange*: members visit each other's websites, in return receiving visits to their own websites. Exchanges of significant size can potentially enable members to effectively "launder" clicks to their sites, making them appear of a much richer nature than in reality.

IMC'15, October 28–30, 2015, Tokyo, Japan.

ACM 978-1-4503-3848-6/15/10 ...$15.00.
DOI: http://dx.doi.org/10.1145/2815675.2815708.

Understanding the significance and likely evolution of such exchanges requires identifying the motives of the participants. One obvious motive—though not the only one, it turns out—concerns forms of advertising fraud. Internet advertisers generally desire "organic" visitors, i.e., truly engaged users. Unscrupulous publishers of Internet content, however, can seek to receive cheap inorganic traffic in order to fraudulently earn from purported impressions and clicks received on the advertisements they display. Advertisers can identify simple forms of bogus traffic by observing impressions or clicks disproportionately due to the same IP addresses over a short period of time. Fraudsters in turn will seek ways to spread out the apparent pool of users visiting their pages to thwart such detection.

Indeed, over the past decade different schemes for generating fraudulent traffic from a diverse pool have arisen. By their sheer size, botnets are well suited to generate traffic from disparate sources, as evidenced by impression and click-fraud botnets such as ZeroAccess, Fiesta, and 7cy [31, 33]. Another approach, *pay-per-view networks*, embeds websites as pop-unders in other websites, seemingly delivering the visitors of one website to another [34].

A third approach, one that our study examines in detail, is the use of traffic exchanges to pool clicks, allowing participants to bring disparate traffic to their sites on-the-cheap. In such exchange networks, participants performing N clicks for the exchange, all coming from the participant's IP address, in return reap credits to receive a different N visits (or somewhat fewer, depending on the exchange's structure) delivered to URLs of their choosing. Since the exchange has many members, the traffic arriving at each member's target site appears quite dispersed.

More broadly, we examine the world of traffic exchanges, finding a wide variety of offerings, and usage paradigms beyond just ad fraud. The offerings range from manual exchanges, where participants must solve CAPTCHAs between successive clicks, to exchanges that provide tools that automatically surf without requiring any user action, and allow customization of time-on-page, User-Agent, and Referer fields. Some exchanges are free, while others charge for certain levels of service. We study several prominent exchanges in each category, casting light on this little-studied phenomenon and the monetization it supports.

By lurking as a non-active exchange participant, we observe both the origin (which IP addresses) and the destination (what websites) of traffic in circulation. This allows us to estimate the size of exchanges and understand the strategies pursued by those using them. We find that some exchanges deliver traffic from tens of thousands of IP addresses. A large fraction of the traffic that flows through the *autosurf* exchanges is generated by bots running in cloud hosting services, and terminates on websites that generate a multitude of impression requests to ad networks. Such *referrer spoofing* ad fraud makes up one of the major categories we observed [35, 25]. In contrast, members of the *manual* exchanges appear to indeed reflect the sought-after demographic of the ads displayed there.

Two factors distinguish our work from previous studies on traffic generation. First, while there have been studies of services that deliver bulk traffic for money, ours is the first large-scale examination of exchange networks primarily designed for *free* exchange of traffic amongst participants, though they also offer traffic for purchase. Second, the targets of traffic exchanges potentially differ in character from those for paid sites; since participants barter for their traffic with reciprocal traffic, they may pursue different monetization strategies from those who pay for traffic.

The rest of this paper proceeds as follows: § 2 covers related work and § 3 provides basic background on the different categories of exchanges. § 4 describes the characteristics of the exchanges we study. § 5 describes our measurements of popular target websites in the exchanges. In § 6 we measure the size of the exchanges in terms of unique participants and provide estimates of the impressions these exchanges serve per day. In § 7 we discuss our findings and provide rough estimates of the volume of money flowing through the exchanges.

2. RELATED WORK

Traffic generation and advertising fraud have received considerable study. Work on advertising fraud lies in three categories: (i) impression fraud and markets for buying traffic, (ii) characterization studies on click fraud, and (iii) detection of fraudulent clicks.

Zhang et al. study the quality of traffic delivered by traffic providers who promise bulk visitors for a monthly cost, and compare that to the traffic obtained from traditional keyword auctions and sponsored banner ads in search results [37]. They purchase traffic from these providers, and based on characterization of mouse activity, sub-page views, and timing of visits on their websites, find that these providers mostly deliver inorganic/automated traffic; only one of the providers delivered seemingly organic traffic via a paid-to-view scheme for recruiting visitors.

The work of Springborn et al. on impression fraud appears most relevant to our paper [34]. The authors bought views from multiple traffic sources and studied how the traffic is delivered to their honeypot websites by investigating the referer field. They identify various pay-per-view (PPV) networks, in which participating websites load multiple other websites as pop-unders, i.e., in windows hidden behind the active browser window. This way, whenever a legitimate user arrives at the participating website, they unknowingly also visit the websites loaded as pop-unders. By mining the publicly available Common Crawl Dataset [7], the authors identify $\approx$ 11K unique domains that embed PPV tags, similar to standard ad tags, from the ten networks they study. By looking at the traffic statistics of these websites at MuStat [19], they estimate that these networks deliver on the order of 150M impressions per day to websites, which in turn load up $\approx$ 500M ad impressions per day. Based on this analysis, the authors suggest simple countermeasures, to the effect of checking the referer against a blacklist of PPV networks/publishers that participate in these networks, and checking the viewport dimensions to make sure that the ad is indeed displayed in a visible area in a browser. Pay-per-view networks differ from traffic exchange networks in how they generate traffic and their business model. While traffic exchange networks often offer free traffic using the principle of exchange, pay-per-view networks generate traffic using participating websites, to whom they pay cheap CPM (cost per thousand impressions) rates, and then sell the generated traffic at a profit.

We are unaware of any work on view-fraud botnets in the academic literature. However, at least two botnets intended for view fraud have received blogging attention: (i) The Chameleon botnet estimated to consist of $\approx$ 120K machines targeted a set of 200 websites, and repeatedly cleared cookies on the victim's browser to appear as a new user on every visit to the website [9]; (ii) The TDSS botnet, which leveraged the ClickIce Ad Exchange to deliver bot traffic to various publishers, who in turn defrauded display advertisers [8]. This botnet utilized the pay-per-click model of the ClickIce Exchange to request *text ads* that contained a clickable publisher link. TDSS bots have the following capabilities: (i) deliver traffic to publishers by visiting the clickable link; some publishers optimize their webpages for this bot traffic—if a real user visits, they are shown pages with content, but if the bot requests the same page, a page with only ads is displayed, (ii) use the browser cookies of the infected user to make the ad networks on the publisher's website believe that the ad-slot is for a high-value user, and (iii) spoof mouse, scroll, and click events on the target webpages.

Recent years have seen characterization studies of click fraud bots. Miller et al. studied the Fiesta and 7cy clickbot families to understand the click fraud techniques they employ [31]. For Fiesta, they observe that, similar to TDSS, the pay-per-click model is used to deliver traffic to publishers rather than directly to the advertisers in order to serve as an intermediary layer; the publishers act in an advertiser role on *obscure* ad exchanges in order to capture the traffic generated from the bots. For 7cy, they find traffic directly delivered to the publishers, with the bots mimicking human browsing behavior closely and acting upon C&C instructions to click on ads. Pearce et al. examine the activities of the ZeroAccess botnet, and estimate that it plausibly induced losses of $100K per day until Microsoft's takedown operation in late 2013 [33]. Finally, Stone-Gross et al. document the fraudulent activities in online ad exchanges, as observed from the perspective of a participating ad network [35].

Detection of fraudulent traffic has received less attention in the literature, primarily due to the lack of access to data from advertising networks. Haddadi proposed a technique to fight click fraud using "bluff" ads—ads having content that a normal human user is highly unlikely to click, but click-bots would click since they do not base clicking on comprehensibility of the content [27]. Based on this idea, Dave et al. developed a technique to estimate the fraction of click spam from the perspective of an advertiser, independently from the estimates of the ad network [24]. They signed up as an advertiser on ten different networks and collected click data for their ads (26M impressions over a period of 50 days). Analyzing this data, they identified click spam delivered using malware, parked domains, and arbitrage.

Lewis and Rao point out the difficulty of measuring the Return on Investment for advertising campaigns; the noisiness of the efficacy signals available to advertisers makes fraud hard to detect [29].

Click fraud is but one web-based fraud phenomenon that has surged in recent years. Careful measurements have played a large part in furthering our understanding of different types of fraud and abuse. Kanich et al., for example, study the returns from several large spam campaigns [28]. Grier et al. characterize the spam found on Twitter [26]. Christin details activity found on a large underground market for illicit goods [23]. McCoy et al. study the affiliate programs that are commonly used in selling medications online [30]. These measurement studies reveal phenomena that are more complex than they first appear and inform efforts to combat the fraud.

3. BACKGROUND

We surveyed the landscape of traffic exchanges by performing online web searches. We compiled a list of 50 such exchanges, and manually investigated them to understand the features they offer. In our analysis, we observed two categories of traffic exchanges: (i) generic, and (ii) social media promotion, where *generic* refers to an exchange which offers traffic exchange service for any website, whereas *social media promotion* refers to an exchange designed specifically for increasing views, likes, comments, and/or subscribers/friends/followers on social platforms such as Twitter, Facebook and YouTube. The latter category often requires members to use their social network accounts for participation in the exchange.

In this paper, we focus on *generic* exchanges as the destinations to which the participants direct *free* traffic. Determining their reasons for doing so presents interesting puzzles.

We further classify the *generic* exchanges into the following categories based on the quality of traffic they offer:

(i) Manual: Manual surf exchanges require an exchange member to solve a CAPTCHA for each website view. This check allows the exchange to claim that it offers human surfers for website views.

(ii) Basic Autosurf: Basic autosurf exchanges provide the members a surf link that they can open in a browser for autosurf. Javascript on this page automatically fetches the next site to be viewed periodically and opens it inside an iframe within the surf page.

(iii) Advanced Autosurf: Advanced autosurf exchanges provide the members a tool/plugin, that they can download and run on their machines. In addition to automatically fetching and loading the next page to be viewed, this tool can generate webpage view requests with custom *Referer* and *User-Agent*.

We look at a sample of nine exchanges in this paper, which we chose according to their popularity in Google search results, the Internet marketing underground forum *Black Hat World* [5], and various traffic exchange ranking lists. We picked two manual exchanges: EasyHits4U [10] and HitSafari [15]; two basic autosurf exchanges: 247AutoHits [2] and 10Khits [1]; and four advanced autosurf exchanges: HitLeap [14], eBesucher [11], Jingling [16], Otohits [20]. We also look at one of the social media promotion exchanges, EnhanceViews Autowatcher [12], for the purpose of comparing view traffic characteristics.

4. EXCHANGE CHARACTERISTICS

In this section we provide an overview of the characteristics of the exchanges, such as account pricing and the configuration options that each exchange provides for the traffic it delivers. Table 1 summarizes the characteristics of the exchanges we studied. We discuss these in detail below.

4.1 Earning and using traffic exchange credits

All exchanges, with the exception of Jingling, require a user to sign up for an account on their website. The sign-up process is simple, requiring only a valid email address. Some of the exchanges offer premium memberships, which cost extra, but provide a better exchange ratio (of sent to received views), monthly bonus points, or enhanced functionality (see Table 1). The exchanges provide a link or tool to the registered members, which they can view/run on their machine(s) to earn exchange credits. The autosurf link/tool communicates with the exchange Command & Control server periodically to get the list of URLs to view, whereas the manual exchanges require the user to solve a CAPTCHA for each URL fetch from the server. The following are some of the features that differentiate exchanges and membership levels.

- **Account-to-Machine Ratio**: The manual surf exchanges enforce that one account be used only from one IP address at a time. On the other hand, all the autosurf exchanges we studied allow an account to be used from multiple IP addresses simultaneously.

- **Exchange Ratio**: For free accounts, most exchanges offer an exchange ratio of less than 1 (often in the range 0.5–0.7). This means that free members do not receive the same number of visits to their own websites as the number of websites they view. Instead, the exchange takes a cut, thereby enabling it to sell views directly for money. One autosurf exchange offers a ratio greater than 1 for premium levels of membership. The high premium membership cost at this exchange presumably allows the exchange to generate the extra clicks for premium members using its own infrastructure if the order cannot be fulfilled using the exchange members.

- **Credits/Cash-Out**: All the exchanges we investigated offer traffic exchange credits as a reward for surfing/running their autosurf tool. Only EasyHits4U and eBesucher offer a conversion of the credits to cash pay-out (via Paypal). EasyHits4U pays \$0.30 per 1,000 website views, and has a minimum cash-out of \$3. eBesucher pays \$0.02 per 1,000 views, and has a minimum cash-out of $\approx$\$3 as well. To the best of our knowledge, cashing out on eBesucher involves an identity check, requiring a scanned copy of a valid photo identity document. This means that anyone who wishes to remain anonymous must find an indirect path to monetize their credits. We did not try to cash-out from EasyHits4U, since that would have required significant effort (solving 10K CAPTCHAs).

4.2 Controls offered for views

The exchanges offer a range of capabilities to make the traffic resemble that of an organic user population. Some of these are offered only to premium members, which comes at a monthly membership price of 3–7€, depending on the exchange and the service level (see Table 1).

- **Website Slots:** Website slots are the number of URLs that a member can have simultaneously active for viewing in the exchange (the URLs can be pages of the same website or different websites). The number of slots vary with membership level on most exchanges, with a free account offering between 3–15 slots depending on the exchange, and paid accounts offering a higher number of slots—unlimited in some cases. Some exchanges offer the same number of slots regardless of membership level. For example, Jingling offers 400 slots, and Otohits and EnhanceViews Autowatcher offer unlimited slots for all tiers.

  An exchange user who wishes to direct traffic at a small number of URLs might manage with few slots; however, a user who wishes to generate views to a large number of URLs (for example, different videos on a YouTube channel) might need more than what the free tiers offer.

- **Views Timing**: This refers to how long a website will be viewed for, which can affect whether the view is credited for view count and payment purposes on the target website. Manual and basic autosurf exchanges offer fairly short views

Exchange	Requires Account?	Earning Credits		Delivering Traffic								
		Machines Per Account	Cash Payout	Account Level	Cost	Website Slots	Exchange Ratio	Geo Targeting	Referer: Anonymous	Referer: Custom	Randomize View Time	Pageview Time
Manual												
HitSafari	Yes	1	No	I	Free	10	0.5	-	-	-	No	6s
				II	$5	30	1.0	-	-	-		
				III	$9.99	40	1.0	-	-	-		
EasyHits4U	Yes	1	Yes	I	Free	15	1.0	✗	-	-	No	10–40s
				II	$7.95	UL	1.0	✓	-	-		
				III	$19.95	UL	1.0	✓	-	-		
Basic Autosurf												
10Khits	Yes	UL	No	I	Free	3	0.5	-	-	-	No	10s
				II	$10	10	1.2	-	-	-		
				III	$29	45	2.0	-	-	-		
247AutoHits	Yes	UL	No	I	Free	5	0.7	-	-	-	No	30s
				II	$6.99	10	0.8	-	-	-		
				II	$9.99	100	1.0	-	-	-		
Advanced Autosurf												
HitLeap	Yes	UL	No	I	Free	3	0.7	-	✗	✗	Yes	10–60s
				II	3€	5	0.8	-	✓	✗		
				III	7€	15	1.0	-	✓	✓		
eBesucher	Yes	UL	Yes	I	Free	15	1.0	✓	✗	✗	No	15s–10m
				II	2.90€	50	1.0	✓	✓	✓		
				III	5.90€	150	1.0	✓	✓	✓		
Jingling	No	UL	No	I	Free	400	1.0	✓†	✓	✗	Yes	20s–40s
				II	6.34€	400	1.0	✓†	✓	✓		20s–2m
Otohits	Yes	UL	No	-	Free	UL	Variable ∓	-	✓	✓	Yes	10s–10m
EnhanceViews	Yes	UL	No	-	Free	UL	1.0	-	-‡	-‡	No	30s–2m

Table 1: The different traffic exchanges offer different levels of service. For example, the Basic service at eBesucher is free, allows geo-targeting, but will not allow anonymous or custom referer-fields, while the premium service costs 2.90€ per month and allows custom and anonymous referers. † indicates that the exchange offers geo-targeting at the granularity of China vs. Non-China. ‡ indicates the exchange does not offer setting a referer value, and we lack visibility to comment on the default value. ∓ indicates the exchange ratio decreases with the number of website "slots" used (see below). UL indicates Unlimited. '–' indicates that the exchange does not offer the feature at any membership level.

(6–20s) for all service levels, and do not offer randomizing the length of the views. Among the advanced autosurf exchanges, Jingling offers the shortest views (view-length of 20–40s) for a free account, but offers longer views at an additional cost. HitLeap offers a maximum of 60s view time, and provides the option of randomizing the time for each view. eBesucher, Otohits and EnhanceViews Autowatcher offer longer views (2m–10m), but all views are of the same length. Longer views cost more on all exchanges.

- **User-Agent**: This option is only offered by advanced autosurf exchanges. Both Otohits and Jingling offer configuring a custom User-Agent. Others do not specifically offer this option. However, based on the traffic we bought (which we discuss later in Section 6), we observe HitLeap and eBesucher, by default, use a variety of User-Agents, whereas Jingling, by default, provides only various versions of Internet Explorer. We lack visibility for EnhanceViews Autowatcher; we did not buy any traffic from this exchange because directing autosurf traffic to YouTube potentially raises ethical concerns.

- **Anonymous/Custom Referer**: This option is also only offered by advanced autosurf exchanges; the manual and basic autosurf exchanges send the link of the exchange itself as referer. All advanced autosurf exchanges except EnhanceViews Autowatcher offer sending a custom *referer* for the view requests at an additional cost (see Table 1 for details). HitLeap and eBesucher also charge for hiding the default referer which indicates the views come from the traffic exchange. Jingling by default does not send a referer. Obviously a user-agent or referer field that indicates the click comes from a traffic exchange would allow a website to easily filter the autosurf traffic.

- **Geo-Targeting**: Geo-targeting refers to advertising the page for viewing to exchange members residing in a specific location. eBesucher and EasyHits4U offer geo-targeting at the country-level as well as at a coarser granularity of continents. Jingling offers geo-targeting at a coarse granularity of China and Non-China, and city-level granularity within China. Others do not offer any geo-targeting.

4.3 Buying views from the exchange

The exchanges also sell traffic views directly, i.e., one can get traffic by paying, instead of by earning exchange credits via surfing/running their autosurf tool. The price per 100K views with a view-length of 15s ranges between $2–60 for the generic autosurf exchanges. Views on manual and social media promotion exchanges cost more; 100K views cost $450 on EasyHits4U, and $1,000 on HitSafari. Similarly, the cost for 100K 15s-long YouTube views on EnhanceViews Autowatcher is $375. (The exchanges sell views in bulk, with discounts for packages with higher views).

5. POPULAR TARGETS IN THE EXCHANGES

In order to develop insight into the popular domains in these exchanges, we captured a snapshot of the websites in circulation in the exchanges. We did so by *milking*: retrieving the instructions from the exchanges on the URLs to view, but not performing the action. In this section, we discuss our milking infrastructure, the

Exchange	Time Span	Milkers	Requested Page Impressions		
			Total	Unique URLs	Unique Domains
EasyHits4U	3 d	-	210	125	121
HitSafari	3 d	-	210	152	141
247AutoHits	30 d	25	0.7 M	3,632	2,195
10Khits	30 d	25	0.2 M	7,209	3,436
HitLeap	30 d	50	5.5 M	98,243	28,734
Jingling	30 d	25	104 M	337,829	61,727
eBesucher	30 d	25	0.6 M	7,323	1,431
Otohits	30 d	50	5.2 M	2,708	1,409
EnhanceViews Autowatcher	7 d	5	8.5 K	2,772	1

Table 2: Dataset obtained by milking the autosurf traffic exchanges, i.e., collecting the lists of URLs to be clicked but not sending clicks. We collected the data for manual exchanges manually, solving CAPTCHAs.

datasets we collected, and analysis on the popular categories of monetization observed in these exchanges.

5.1 Dataset

In all the autosurf exchanges we study, the communication with the exchange is unencrypted, enabling us to easily write our own milker bots that replicate this communication and receive instructions from the exchange. The instructions contain the URL(s) to be viewed, visit-length, and the referer to use in the view request (if offered by the exchange). We ran these milker bots from 25–50 different IP addresses per exchange via a proxy.

Using the above infrastructure, we collected month-long datasets for all autosurf exchanges, except for EnhanceViews Autowatcher. Since the latter only offers visits to a pre-defined list of social networks/user-content websites, we do not carry out the domains analysis for this exchange. Instead, we collected a week-long dataset for EnhanceViews Autowatcher's YouTube Watcher tool to compare the characteristics of video URLs in this exchange with those in the other generic exchanges we study. For the manual exchanges, which require a CAPTCHA to be solved between consecutive page views, we collected smaller datasets by manually surfing on the exchanges.

Table 2 describes the datasets we collected. For the manual exchanges, EasyHits4U and HitSafari, we solved 70 CAPTCHAs each. Each click resulted in the display of the main target page, as well as one display and one text ad. We also manually clicked on the display and text ads (see below), resulting in a total of 210 web page visits on each of the two exchanges. For autosurf exchanges, our milker bots recorded between 8.5K–104M page impression requests per exchange. The average rate of requests and the median view length varies across the exchanges, resulting in a difference in the scale of datasets.

We processed the raw URLs dataset to expand any URLs in the following set of popular URL shortening services: {bit.ly, goo.gl, ow.ly, t.co}.[1] We further processed the URLs to extract the "registered domains", according to the public suffix list maintained by Mozilla [18]. The numbers listed in Table 2 are for the processed dataset. It contains 2.7–337K unique URLs, and 1.4–61K unique domains per exchange. For the rest of the analysis, we work at the granularity of registered domains.

[1]We compiled this list based on their high frequency in our dataset, and unshortened the URLs belonging to them because the shortened versions hide the intended destination. We also observed URLs shortened using paid shortening services in our dataset, but did not unshorten them since they present an interesting monetization avenue, as we sketch later in § 5.3.1.

Category	EasyHits4U	HitSafari
Web traffic	38%	30%
Affiliates and marketing	35%	48%
Other products and services	27%	22%

Table 3: Distribution of website and ad categories we observed on EasyHits4U and HitSafari.

Ethical Considerations: We were cautious to not participate in view/click fraud when collecting our datasets. For the manual exchanges, we collected small-scale datasets by hand. We observed no indication of ad fraud. In addition, since during the process we ourselves viewed the websites circulating in the exchanges—as expected by the exchange and a website owner/advertiser—we view our actions as not contributing to view fraud.

For autosurf exchanges, we only collected the associated URLs, and did not view them in an automated fashion. Our milker bots emulated the timing patterns of requests from the autosurf tools—except for Jingling, for which we could request URLs at a rate five times greater than what a Jingling bot would do. (For other exchanges, requesting at a higher rate did not return any new URLs). We did so after determining, as best as we could from inspecting Jingling's website, that doing so did not violate any terms-of-service.

We note that none of our actions underlied intent to fraudulently earn credits, as prohibited by some of the exchanges in their terms-of-service, though such crediting did occasionally occur as a by-product of milking. The exchanges varied in their detection of milking: HitLeap imposed a penalty on our account after about an hour of milking. They continued to provide us with URLs to view, but we did not earn any credits for those URLs (as in fact, we were not viewing them). eBesucher temporarily blocked our accounts. Milking Jingling did not require accounts, hence we did not earn any credits. Others showed no indications of detection.

5.2 Analysis: Manual Exchanges

For manual exchanges, our datasets are small enough that categorizing them manually was viable. Table 3 summarizes the results.

The first category, web traffic, comprises traffic-related websites. This included other manual exchanges as well as sellers of web traffic and offers of cash for manual clicks (paid-to-promote sites).

The second category, affiliates and marketing, comprises websites that target persons attempting to earn money by selling over the Internet. Many ads offered commissions to affiliates for sale of various products and services. Some websites offered tools and infrastructure for affiliates such as email advertising. Others offered classes and manuals on how to become a successful Internet marketer. For example, one site offered a system for earning $10,000 per month as a Clickbank affiliate for a fee of $37 per month [6].

The large majority of the websites in these two categories appeared to be directly targeted at users of manual traffic exchanges, offering the prospect of cash in exchange for small fees or various types of simple online tasks. Websites of this type made up about three quarters of the total on both exchanges.

The third category, other products and services, contains ads for products and services outside the affiliate marketing and web traffic ecosystem itself. These ranged from web hosting services to legitimate niche products, such as self-published children's ebooks or special chocolate bars, to miracle weight loss programs and supplements, to formulas for large profits in currency and options trading,

Exchange	Top domains by views	Top domains by URLs
247AutoHits	*twistrix.com* (10%) *hitlink.com* (6 %) *paragonmailer.com* (4%) *paragontraffic.com* (4%) vitality.ws (4%)	trck.me (1%) trafficadbar.com (1%) wordpress.com (1%) weebly.com (1%) **adf.ly** (1%)
10Khits	kpopselca.com (10%) reportershub.com (2%) ebay.co.uk (2%) *hitleap.com* (2%) apkmodder.com (1%)	apkmodder.com (3%) **ziddu.com** (2%) **youtube.com** (2%) ebay.co.uk (2%) seoad.in (1%)
Jingling	**adf.ly** (6%) saringan.net (5%) wonosobo.in (4%) trifter.com (2%) gameolosophy.com (2%)	**adf.ly** (10%) taobao.com (10%) baidu.com (8%) **ziddu.com** (5%) user.qzone.qq.com (3%)
HitLeap	**youtube.com** (8%) **ziddu.com** (4%) ads-host-media.com (2%) ijgbiorjg.com (2%) 4554fdd56f4.com (2%)	**ziddu.com** (20%) **youtube.com** (11%) **adfoc.us** (1%) **adf.ly** (1%) **sh.st** (1%)
eBesucher	mustbuysneakers.com (13%) planetfem.com (10%) admg.info (6%) genevaforever.com (6%) feltdizzy.com (4%)	admg.info (3%) dhush.com (3%) trends-beauty.de (3%) softskills24.eu (2%) job-market24.com (2%)
Otohits	health-spiritual.net (13%) healthspiritual.net (13%) *zenbux.co* (10%) planete-carpe.com (4%) menintown.net (4%)	nomeimporta.es (1%) herreiroimoveis.com.br (1%) *tripleclicks.com* (1%) weebly.com (1%) my-style.in (1%)

Table 4: Popular domains of the milked URLs in the autosurf traffic exchanges. Bold domains represent direct monetization avenues: the service offers pay-per-view for user content/sharing links. Italic domains are traffic exchanges; members promote exchanges in order to earn activity points, as top 25 active members get a share in the monthly cash pot (worth $\approx$ \$10). Domains colored light-green are backed by a blogging service `triond` that pays users for views to their blog posts. Domains colored red do not have any real content and participate in ad placement fraud via *referer spoofing* on the AppNexus ad exchange.

to a manual on how to fuel cars with water. This category makes up about one quarter of the URLs on each exchange.

The target web sites were mostly free of external ads. We did not observe any indication of ad fraud.

5.3 Analysis: Autosurf Exchanges

For autosurf exchanges, we focus our analysis on the popular domains by views and URLs, since our datasets for this category are extensive. A domain can receive a high number of views from the exchange under three scenarios: (i) popular Internet service domains having a large user base (for example, YouTube), (ii) domains belonging to exchange participants, who are able to earn a large number of exchange credits using a number of machines, and in return direct huge volume of traffic to their own domains, or (iii) someone buying bulk views to a domain from the exchange. We can identify the first of these, but it is hard to differentiate between the latter two, and we treat these as equally interesting as potential targets for monetization/SEO/Alexa rank increase.

We characterize the top five domains by views and URL counts for each exchange in Table 4. We observe four categories of popular domains: (i) direct monetization avenues, (ii) ad fraud domains, (iii) legitimate looking domains, and (iv) traffic exchanges.

5.3.1 *Direct Monetization Avenues*

This category comprises domains that pay users for views to content they upload, such as YouTube. YouTube inserts video advertisements when playing user videos, and pays the user in proportion to the legitimate views their videos receive. In recent years, another category of services has emerged that does not require users to provide their own content in order to earn. Rather, users can get paid for linking and sharing existing content on the Internet. For example, URL shortening services such as `adf.ly` pay users for visits to their shortened URLs. A visitor to a URL shortened using such a service is first shown an advertisement, and then redirected to the URL that was shortened. Hence, money enters the eco-system from advertisers and flows to the users of the URL shortening services. We next discuss examples of both these monetization avenues as observed in the exchanges we studied.

The URL shortening services `adf.ly`, `adfoc.us`, and `sh.st` are among the top five domains in HitLeap, Jingling and 247AutoHits. Manually inspecting several requested `adf.ly` URLs reveals that 90% of the time the intermediate link solicits downloading a video player. It is possible that in addition to legitimate advertising, some of the malicious advertisers attempt to install malware on user machines. Our observation of malicious advertisements is consistent with the findings of Nikiforakis et al., who investigated malicious aspects of paid URL shortening services [32].

Another domain in this category popular on HitLeap, Jingling, and 10Khits is `ziddu.com`, a content distribution platform that pays for file downloads and sharing news links hosted on its platform [22]. Users with their own content can upload their files and earn for downloads of those files. An alternative (and lower effort) way to earn is to share existing content on Ziddu and direct views to it. Manually analyzing some of the `ziddu.com` URLs in our dataset, we observed that they contain news content lifted from other news websites under the title "Sponsored news", and generate impression requests to multiple ad networks. Further inspecting Ziddu's website, we found that it also offers desktop and mobile apps to *"turn idle cycles into money"*. The app displays advertisements (rather than websites) automatically, indicating that Ziddu apparently defrauds advertisers. In a manual investigation, we found the majority of the advertisements to be malicious, requesting to upgrade a media player or download a software. Ziddu does not list pay rates on its website.

We observe another model for the domains `trifter.com` and `gameolosophy.com`, popular in Jingling. These are niche sites dedicated to travel and online games respectively. The content hosted on these websites is not generated by the website owners. Instead, these websites are backed by `triond.com`, a blogging service, which automatically shares the content submitted by its bloggers to the most relevant site out of the pool of sites it supports. Triond then pays the blogger for views to their content.

YouTube receives the highest percentage of view requests (8%) in HitLeap, and has the second-highest percentage of URLs in this exchange. Note that YouTube *video watch* URLs[2] play videos automatically upon opening the link in a browser or an autosurf tool. Hence, directing exchange traffic to YouTube videos results in the videos being auto-watched. We investigated whether sending exchange traffic from HitLeap to YouTube videos results in increasing video view counts, and consequently provides a monetization avenue. We extracted the list of YouTube videos from our dataset ($\approx$ 10K unique videos) and queried the YouTube API to get their view counts. Per Figure 1, approximately 24% of the videos in circulation on the HitLeap exchange were no longer available on YouTube at the time of querying; they were either taken down by YouTube or the user themselves. 25% had a view count frozen at

[2]These URLs have the form: http://www.youtube.com/watch?v=VIDEOID.

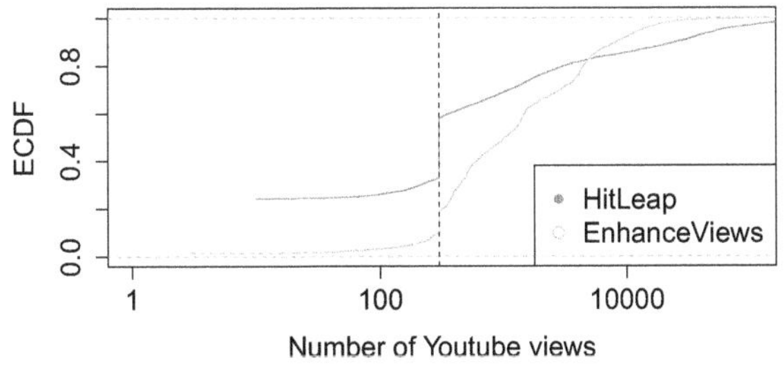

Figure 1: Distribution of view counts of the YouTube video URLs obtained by milking traffic exchanges. We obtained the view counts of the videos by querying the YouTube API provided by Google. The size of the discontinuity at 301 views indicates the fraction of videos stuck at that view count. Note that about 25% of HitLeap but only 10% of EnhanceViews Autowatcher videos are stuck there. The discontinuity at 301 views suggests that YouTube's fraud detection prevents many videos from advancing beyond this point, even if they receive many more clicks.

301 (indicating that YouTube had identified something suspicious with the views [13]). However, ≈ 42% of the videos on HitLeap had view counts above 301, with a maximum of 18 million views.

Recall from Table 1 that HitLeap views are short-lived (60s at maximum), which possibly could be a factor in the detection of its fraudulent traffic. For comparison, we look at the view counts of YouTube videos in the EnhanceViews Autowatcher exchange, which plays the full video for each view. We observe in Figure 1 that EnhanceViews Autowatcher does better than HitLeap, with a frozen view count for only 10% of the videos.

We also queried the YouTube API to get the channel ID and the categories of the videos in our HitLeap dataset. The 10K videos were associated with ≈ 2,500 channels—8% of the videos came from a single channel. The videos in this dominant channel belonged to the categories *Gaming*, *Shows*, and *Film/Animation*, with none of the videos stuck at a view count of 301. Inspecting this channel, we found that the latest video gathered 25K views in one day, though we lack visibility into what fraction of these were fraudulently generated. Generally, we find that 26% of the videos in our dataset belong to the *Gaming* category and 23% in the category *People and Blogs*, with the former mainly screen-captures of people playing video games, and the latter primarily comprising tutorials.

5.3.2 Ad Placement Fraud

We also observed websites that show clear evidence of impression/click fraud. For example, *ads-host-media.com*, *ijgbiorjg.com*, and *4554fdd56f4.com* in HitLeap do not display any content to a visiting user.[3] But these sites generate dozens of ad requests with varying referrers to the AppNexus ad exchange [4]. The URL requests are of the format: `ib.adnxs.com/tt?ttjb=1&bdc=1&bdh=CQLrezBk2vGyQNA7G5993lyZhww.&id=3445029&size=300x250&referrer=carpreserve.com`, with varying referrers sent on each request.

Others have documented this *referrer* spoofing fraud [35, 25]. Stone-Gross et al. observed it in the context of the Yahoo Right-Media exchange in their study of fraudulent activities in online ad exchanges. The convoluted online advertising ecosystem fosters this kind of fraud. In particular, the exchange/advertisers take the referrer in the URL parameters at face value. Although the impression requests to an ad exchange contain an `id` value that determines which party gets credited when an ad is displayed on the site in the *referrer* field, the need for reaching broad audiences in online advertising complicates its use for fraud detection. Since impressions can be bought through an intermediary (rather than directly from publishers) to enable wider reach, an ad exchange cannot employ an exclusive website-owner-specific `id` to be credited on impression requests for the particular website [25].

Exchange	URLs	Impressions
HitLeap	2,606 (2.7%)	1,231,027 (23%)
Jingling	2,571 (0.8%)	10,426,448 (11%)
eBesucher	230 (3.1%)	59,410 (9%)
Otohits	50 (1.9%)	336,634 (6%)
247AutoHits	27 (0.7%)	5,398 (1%)
10Khits	28 (0.4%)	494 (0.2%)

Table 5: Percentage of milked URLs and corresponding impressions served by sites exhibiting referrer-spoofing ad placement fraud in various exchanges.

Given that we observed *referrer spoofing* fraud as one of the major categories in multiple exchanges, we fingerprinted this behavior in order to classify the number of URLs in our dataset that participate in this fraud. We crawled the entire datasets using a distributed infrastructure, recording all the web requests that each URL generates.[4] We then identified the URLs that generate requests to `adnxs.com` with *spoofed* referrers. We identified *spoofed* referrers as those that are for a domain other than on which the ad is actually displayed. Table 5 summarizes our findings. We find ≈ 2.5K URLs in HitLeap and Jingling that participate in this ad fraud, respectively accounting for 23% and 11% of the total impression requests we milked for these exchanges. Other exchanges have fewer URLs, accounting for 1–9% of their impression requests.

5.3.3 Legitimate looking domains

We find some of the other websites harder to judge. While essentially all of them bear advertisements, some of these appear to be niche websites targeted at topics such as cars, sneakers, workout, and news specific to a particular location.

The most popular domain in eBesucher, `mustbuysneakers.com`, is a legitimate-looking niche website, with an '*Advertising: Starboyant Media*' tag in the website footer. Investigating the Starboyant Media website, we found that it offers advertising on three other niche websites: `onlyhiphop.com`, `workouteveryday.com`, and `stylishceleb.com`. We find all of these in our eBesucher dataset, accounting for 22% of the total impression requests we milked on eBesucher.

We find ourselves unable to judge whether these and other legitimate-looking domains are websites with considerable legitimate traffic to which a fraudster also directs traffic, or they have been crafted to make judgment difficult and have little traffic beyond that automatically generated.

5.3.4 Traffic Exchanges

Surprisingly, most of the top domains in the basic autosurf exchange 247AutoHits are other traffic exchanges. On closer inspec-

[3]We confirmed that we had not been cloaked against by visiting these domains in the autosurf tool in addition to the browser; we configured a proxy to allow the autosurf tool to visit these domains for a short amount of time.

[4]We opened each website in a browser instance until the browser indicated that the page had finished loading.

tion, we find that these are *splash pages* provided to the users by an exchange itself for circulation in other exchanges. The four exchanges that appear in the top domains—*twistrix.com*, *hitlink.com*, *paragonmailer.com*, and *paragontraffic.com*—were not included in our study. Looking through their websites, we find that these exchanges offer a share in a *cash pot* (worth ≈ \$10) at the end of every month to the top 25 active users. Submitting the member-specific exchange promotion link on other exchanges is one of the ways in which members can earn activity points towards a share in the *cash pot*.

6. TRAFFIC QUALITY & SIZE OF EXCHANGE NETWORKS

In this section we study the quality of traffic that the exchange networks deliver, and measure the scale and characteristics of the IP address population that participates in these exchanges. We base our observations on buying bulk views from the exchanges for five consecutive days and recording the characteristics of the visitors.

Infrastructure: We set up eight websites, one per exchange, on Amazon EC2, configured to auto-scale in order to handle large peaks of traffic. The websites themselves were fairly simplistic, and identical in content, appearing to be a photo blog. We employed Javascript instrumentation on the websites to detect (i) mouse movement, and (ii) whether at the time of visit the visitor was logged into any of Google, Twitter, or Facebook.[5] While not perfect, this instrumentation gives us a sense of organic (real) users participating in these exchanges. Where possible, we requested views for a view-length of 30s or greater, in order to allow enough time for the instrumentation Javascript to execute. We also set cookies to study the behavior of returning visitors.

We signed up for two premium accounts on each exchange, and purchased views from the exchanges alternating between the accounts every other day. Premium accounts gave us access to more website slots on the exchanges, enabling us to submit multiple pages of our websites in order to get bulk traffic. Making purchases from two accounts arguably enables us to collect *independent* samples of the IP addresses in an exchange.

Purchases: Table 6 lists the breakdown of traffic we bought from each exchange. For each exchange, we started with a pilot measurement of 100K visitors per day for autosurf and 10K visitors per day for manual exchanges,[6] and scaled down the number of visitors in subsequent purchases, requesting at least twice as many visitors as the number of unique IP addresses observed in the pilot measurement.

Purchase Order Completion: For each purchase, we requested visitors distributed across multiple pages of our corresponding website (at a maximum rate of 250 visitors per hour per page),[7] so that the expected completion time for the purchase order was one day. The exchanges varied in the completion of purchase order. HitSafari, 247AutoHits, and 10Khits on average fulfilled only 50/63/68% of the order, and charged us only for what they were able to fulfill. Our measurements indicate that these three are the smallest of the eight exchanges we measured (on the order of a thousand IP addresses), explaining the inability to fulfill larger orders within a day. Others claimed to fulfill the complete orders, but had some losses—the instrumentation reported by the exchange did not match that recorded by our web server logs. Specifically, Jingling fulfilled only 61% of the order on average; others had a loss in the range 2–12%.

[5]We used the methodology described at http://www.tomanthony.co.uk/blog/detect-visitor-social-networks/.

[6]We made smaller purchases from manual exchanges due to higher cost of manual traffic.

[7]The exchanges set upper bounds on the number of visits per URL per hour, e.g., 500 for HitLeap and 1,000 for eBesucher. We requested a limit lower than the upper bound based on a pilot run that found the upper bound did not get delivered in a timely fashion.

Exchange / IP Addresses	Popular ASNs
eBesucher (33,749)	**Google, US (15%)** Hetzner Online AG, DE (5%) Scana, UA (5%)
Jingling (110,641)	CHINANET-BACKBONE No.31, CN (26%) **Amazon, US (12%)** China169 Backbone, CN (10%) **Google, US (7%)** HINET, TW (7%)
HitLeap (72,135)	**Amazon, US (35%)** **Google, US (19%)** OVH SAS, FR (10%)
Otohits (3,931)	**Amazon, US (26%)** **Google, US (24%)**

Table 7: ASNs having at least 5% representation in the exchanges. We highlight major cloud hosting providers in bold. A significant percentage of the IP addresses in the advanced autosurf exchanges comes from Google and Amazon.

6.1 Quality of delivered views

The views were delivered from a variety of User-Agents by default, on the order of several hundred for most of the exchanges. Most notably, Jingling delivered traffic from ≈ 33K different user-agents (dominated by different versions of Internet Explorer). Since we did not request a custom `Referer`, the `Referer` we received was the link of the traffic exchange for all the exchanges except Jingling, for which it was not present.

The page components (stylesheet, Javascript) hosted on the same domain were fetched for 92–100% of IP addresses of the different exchanges. An image embedded from a different domain was fetched for 86–100% of IP addresses for all exchanges except Jingling, for which only 1% of the IP addresses fetched the image.

We found that Javascript was executed for 83–97% of the IP addresses on six of the exchanges. On Jingling, the number is much lower (37%)—this could be due to high load on the machines that run Jingling, because it initiates multiple threads and views multiple websites in parallel. For 10Khits, the Javascript instrumentation fired for only 20% of the IP addresses. Further, upon investigation, our web logs indicated that for the IP addresses where it did fire, the POST request paths were malformed, hence no data was logged in our database for the mouse movement and social-network login instrumentation. This is presumably because at the time of our data collection, the 10Khits website indicated it was in a transitional phase, soon to launch their own autosurf tool. Perhaps the hits to our websites were delivered by a buggy version of the tool.

6.2 Characterization of View Sources/IP addresses

Over the five days, we received visits to our websites from ≈ 204K unique IP addresses across the eight exchanges, corresponding to ≈ 93K unique /24 network prefixes. 77–95% of the /24 prefixes have only one IP address, suggesting that a significant fraction of these IP addresses belong to individual machines (or NATs), with little IP aliasing.

6.2.1 Manual Exchanges

We recorded 1K IP addresses on HitSafari from 73 countries, and 6K on EasyHits4U from 128 countries. Of these, 40% on HitSafari

Exchange	Purchase Order (Per Day)				Avg. Order Fulfilled	Exchange Size & Characteristics Of IP Addresses (Measured over five days)						
	Views	Cost	Duration	CPM		IP Addresses	User Agents	Page Component Fetches		Javascript Executed	Social Network Logins	Mouse Movement
								Same Domain	Other Domain			
HitSafari	2.5K	$25	6s	$10	50%	1,018	179	92%	86%	84%	40%	10%
EasyHits4U	10K	$75	30s	$7.5	98%	6,191	699	99%	96%	96%	65%	21%
10Khits	10K	$10	30s	$1	68%	1,578	260	99%	95%	20%	–	–
247AutoHits	10K	$7	30s	$0.7	63%	1,420	219	95%	85%	83%	43%	6%
Otohits	50K	$3	30s	$0.06	98%	3,931	336	100%	97%	97%	13%	4%
eBesucher	100K	$17	30s	$0.17	88%	33,749	1,752	96%	95%	95%	12%	3%
HitLeap	100K	$44	30s	$0.44	97%	72,135	871	100%	100%	97%	–	0.1%
Jingling	100K	$41	40s	$0.41	61%	110,641	33,222	99%	1%	37%	0.1%	–

Table 6: Our purchases from various exchanges to study the quality of traffic. We purchased traffic in varying quantities, and recorded the HTTP requests, page rendering, and organic-visitor instrumentation over five days.

and 65% on EasyHits4U had an account logged into a social network, indicating that a significant fraction of views came from real users (or compromised machines). Our instrumentation recorded mouse movements for 10% and 21% of IP addresses on HitSafari and EasyHits4U respectively. The low percentage is presumably because the users do the bare minimum required to get paid.

Finding these organic visitor indicators, we next investigate whether this traffic comes from real users in low-wage countries who click intentionally in the hope of earning money. We looked at the top ASNs, and find that the traffic mostly comes from residential networks, with no single dominant contributor. Surprisingly, geo-location (using the MaxMind database) indicates that 52% of the IP addresses in EasyHits4U come from Europe, with Asia the second major contributor (25%). The IP addresses from Europe are dominated by Russia, Romania, and Ukraine with each having 5–6% representation. IP addresses from Asia are dominated by India and Indonesia. In HitSafari, North America has a 40% contribution, followed by Europe (31%), and Asia (22%). We find that the country distribution in HitSafari differs from that in EasyHits4U, with UK and Germany having the top representation (but only 4–5% each) in Europe, and China and Singapore dominating IP addresses from Asia.

In light of this geographic diversity and the significant contributions from North America and Western Europe, click farms in low-wage countries do not appear to be the principal source of clicks on manual exchanges.

6.2.2 *Autosurf Exchanges*

Our measurements find that the basic autosurf exchanges, 247AutoHits and 10Khits, are small in size, on the order of 1.5K IP addresses each. However, in the advanced autosurf category Otohits has $\approx$ 4K IP addresses, while the other three are an order of magnitude larger.

Geolocation: We received hits from 80–147 different countries across the various autosurf exchanges. The spread over countries for the smaller networks differed from that of the larger ones: eBesucher is highly concentrated (80%) in Europe, with Russia, Ukraine and Germany predominant. Jingling has the highest representation in Asia (70%), with China contributing 56% of the IP addresses. The second major contributor in both eBesucher and Jingling is North America, with 15% and 28% representation respectively. HitLeap's network is predominantly based in North America (63%), with 60% of IP addresses from the US. 20% of HitLeap's IP address space is based in Europe, with Italy and Germany the top contributors (but only 4–5% IP addresses each). Similar to HitLeap, Otohits has representation in North America (47%) and Europe (26%), with the US predominant (45%), and Taiwan, Vietnam and Germany each at 5%.

For the smaller networks, 247AutoHits and 10Khits, Asia and Europe have 74% representation. The country distribution is dispersed, with Vietnam, Indonesia, India, Germany, and the UK as the popular countries (4–8% representation).

Organic Visitors: The traffic recorded from 247AutoHits had the highest percentage of visitors from machines where a user was logged in to a social network (43%), but only 6% indicated a mouse movement. For the advanced autosurf exchanges, it is possible that the user uses a browser different than that used by the autosurf tool. Hence we treat the estimates we discuss below as a lower bound. We find that on average $\approx$ 12% of the visitors from eBesucher, and $\approx$ 13% on Otohits, were from machines where a user was logged in to a social network.[8] In contrast, the number is much lower for Jingling; only 0.1% of the visitors appear organic. We recorded mouse movement for only 1–4% of IP addresses on these exchanges.

We could not carry out this analysis for HitLeap and 10Khits, because (i) HitLeap's autosurf tool uses a built-in browser rather than a browser on the user's machine, and thus none of the visitors appeared to have logged in, when in fact they might have been, and (ii) as described in Section 6.1, the 10Khits surf tool had malformed URL request paths, due to which we did not log any data in our database.

Popular ASNs: We next take a look at the popular entities/organizations to which the IP addresses of exchange networks belong. We obtain the ASNs of the IP addresses via Team Cymru's IP-to-ASN mappings database [36]. Table 7 lists the popular ASNs (those having at least a 5% representation), and the corresponding percentage of IP addresses observed for each exchange. We find that a striking percentage of the IP addresses in the HitLeap and Jingling exchanges belong to Amazon, totaling $\approx$ 38K IP addresses. Similarly, a significant portion of IP addresses in the autosurf exchanges comes from Google's cloud, totaling $\approx$ 27K IP addresses.

We also observe other smaller cloud providers and Internet hosting/data centers in the top five ASNs. For example, the second-highest contribution in eBesucher's network comes from Hetzner Online (5%), an Internet hosting provider and data center operator based in Germany. Similarly, HitLeap addresses also appear from other smaller cloud providers such as Limestone Networks [17] and OVH [21].

6.2.3 *Overlap across exchanges*

We find very little overlap across the IP address space of the manual and autosurf exchanges. However, within these categories, we observe significant overlaps. 17% of HitSafari's IP address space

[8]Conceivably, there is a small chance that there is a fraudster running social media promotion tools in parallel; we do not have a method for verifying whether the user on a machine is genuine.

Exchange	% Overlap with other exchanges	Top overlap contributors (≥ 5% contribution)
HitSafari	17%	EasyHits4U
EasyHits4U	9%	–
10Khits	43%	HitLeap, 247AutoHits, eBesucher
247AutoHits	43%	HitLeap, 10Khits, eBesucher
Otohits	74%	HitLeap, Jingling
eBesucher	8%	HitLeap
HitLeap	31%	Jingling
Jingling	18%	HitLeap

Table 8: Overlap of IP address space across various exchanges.

Exchange	IP addresses		Impressions per bot	Estimated total impressions
HitSafari	329	(σ=94)	–	–
EasyHits4U	1,786	(σ=414)	–	–
10Khits	483	(σ=109)	359	173 K
247AutoHits	507	(σ=376)	1,420	719 K
Otohits	2,178	(σ=378)	3,654	7.9 M
eBesucher	18,164	(σ=707)	1,066	19 M
HitLeap	41,711	(σ=507)	3,607	150 M
Jingling	40,227	(σ=5,200)	19,630	789 M

Table 9: Impression estimates per day. σ represents standard deviation across five days of measurements.

overlaps with that of EasyHits4U. 43–74% of the address space of smaller autosurf networks is also seen in other exchanges. For the larger networks, 31% of HitLeap's space overlaps with that of Jingling.

6.3 Impressions Per Day Estimates

In this section we develop a handle on the number of impressions these exchanges serve per day. We base our estimates on the daily number of IP addresses recorded in our logs. However, we note that two factors can lead to overestimating/underestimating these numbers: (i) IP address aliasing (the same machine switching IP addresses), and (ii) multiple machines behind NATs.

We analyzed cookie data recorded in our web logs to potentially adjust for these two factors. For multiple visits from the same IP address, we find that 85–95% of IP addresses in manual exchanges, 80–85% in basic autosurf, and 20–45% in advanced autosurf returned the same cookie set on the first visit. Others request and return multiple cookies. Investigating this further, we find that a high fraction of the IP addresses in advanced autosurf exchanges clear cookies after every visit.

Due to the limitation of the cookie data, we report our population estimates at the granularity of IP addresses. We use these population sizes to estimate the total number of impressions the exchanges serve per day. To this end, we compute the average number of impression requests that our milker bots received on average per day,[9] and multiply it by the population size of the exchange. Table 9 lists the impressions per day estimates. On the lower end, we estimate that 10Khits serves 173K impressions per day, and on the higher end Jingling serves on the order of 789 M impressions per day.

7. DISCUSSION

In the previous sections we measured a number of facets of traffic exchanges. In this section, we attempt to draw plausible inferences based on what we observed.

7.1 Selection pressure

We find evidence of traffic fraud responding to selection pressure. The very existence of exchanges, a tool to disperse the originating IP addresses of traffic, indicates that advertisers actively look for fraud; clearly, clicking endlessly from a single IP address seldom achieves the desired result. The differences between the free and premium versions of the advanced autosurf tools (shown in Table 1) largely reflect the ability to target certain geographic locations, and to set custom User-Agent and Referer fields. There would be little reason for exchange participants to pay for this functionality if it did not bring meaningful advantage. It seems likely that these fields are used by sites to detect fraudulent traffic, and the ability to vary them will increase profits. The large fraction of YouTube videos stuck at 301 credited views in Figure 1 strongly suggests a fraud-detection barrier that blocks a large fraction of the YouTube-bound traffic from two autosurf networks.

[9]Since we milked Jingling at a higher rate, we use the number obtained from running the original bot through the Fiddler proxy, configured to only allow communication with the exchange.

7.2 Manual vs. Autosurf exchanges

A common property of the exchanges is that they facilitate dispersion of traffic; indeed the need for dispersion is likely the factor that has led to their popularity. Beyond this common point, we found little similarity between the manual and autosurf exchanges. Table 4 shows that the most popular destinations for traffic from the autosurf exchanges have ad-bearing properties, and ad-fraud of some kind dominates their traffic. By contrast, Table 3 shows that traffic from the manual exchanges is predominantly directed at sites that advertise affiliate programs, other manual traffic exchanges, or pages advertising goods sold by the participants themselves. In other words, pages visited in the manual exchanges appear directed at luring humans (the exchange participants) to upgrade, join other exchanges or affiliate programs, or purchase products that do not have mainstream appeal. Our inspection of manual exchange traffic turned up numerous examples of what appear to be implausible propositions and get-rich-quick schemes. For example, one site asks $9.99 for a pamphlet explaining how to "run your car on water." A number of destinations of the manual exchange traffic appear to be Ponzi or multi-level marketing schemes. For example, at http://imarketingfasttrack.com/ new entrants invest $25 and recruit four newcomers who do similarly; while participants are promised an easy $1,700, there is no mention of any product beyond participant recruitment. Another, http://www.theleadmagnet.com/, is a viral email lead-generation tool that offers commissions if members get others to purchase the tool.

7.3 Monetization

Monetization clearly poses a significant problem even if one can generate volumes of well-dispersed traffic. The direct cash-out payments offered by the exchanges are low: $0.30 per thousand manual clicks for EasyHits4U, and $0.02 per thousand automated clicks at eBesucher (though getting paid requires a photo ID, as noted in Section 4.1). Note that, based on Table 9, this amounts to 2 cents per machine per day, or $7.30 per machine per year.

For fraudsters, exploiting sites such as YouTube, which offer to pay for traffic delivered, represents an appealing approach. This has the benefit of low start-up costs: the fraudster simply sets up a channel with some content to which they direct the traffic, avoiding costs associated with registering a domain and hosting. Moreover, the content does not have to be of a quality sufficient to attract actual human viewers. If the fraud is discovered and the channel blocked, one can simply start over by setting up a new channel.

Figure 1 suggests that services such as YouTube successfully detect a good percentage of inorganic traffic, making it hard to linearly translate automatically generated views to money. Perhaps participants direct traffic to YouTube primarily for increasing view counts to gain popularity, rather than monetization.

7.4 Lack of sophistication

Some of our data supports the view that many traffic exchange participants lack technical sophistication and struggle to monetize their efforts, particularly on the manual exchanges. At first sight, the manual exchanges operate as web traffic brokers, offering free traffic/advertising in exchange for clicks. The exchange extracts money from participants via the exchange ratio (i.e., exchanging clicks at less than a 1–1 ratio so that the excess can be sold) or monthly fee. But this explanation does not seem satisfactory. A participant who seeks traffic for their product receives clicks only from others similarly motivated to sell their products. Since the average quality of clicks received is the same as those delivered, the average participant should lose in expectation once the exchange's cut is removed, unless outside money enters the exchange. It is also hard to believe that cash-out rates of $0.30 per 1,000 clicks (about $0.05 per hour of clicking) could be a long-term incentive for participants.

The emphasis on affiliate programs and related tools and services among the exchange ads points to a different explanation. These ads appear targeted at an unsophisticated user group lured by the prospect of easy money and a career in "Internet marketing". This description may well be representative of a large fraction of the actual manual exchange users. In this case, the sites advertising on the exchanges might be receiving quality traffic for their offers with acceptable conversion rates, even if they buy traffic from the exchange rather than clicking.

7.5 Revenue estimates

Table 6 gives the prices at which we bought clicks from various exchanges. The cost per thousand (CPM) ranges from $0.06 at Otohits to $10 at HitSafari. Obviously, the clicks are not all of the same quality, and some may suit far better than others for a particular purpose. For comparison, we compute the cost of generating clicks if one rented the cheapest instance of a virtual machine from a cloud hosting service. A micro-instance from Amazon AWS costs $0.013 per hour [3]; setting such a machine to click twice per minute would cost $\$0.013 \times 1000/(2 \times 60) \approx \$\ 0.11$ per thousand. Of course these clicks would offer no IP address dispersion. However, these clicks can be dispersed by using the free service of one of the autosurf exchanges. Thus, we calculate that dispersed clicks can be produced at about $0.11 per thousand. If one needed the customization that the premium services offer, then at 2.9€≈ $3.5 per month the cost becomes $\$\ (0.013 \times 24 \times 30 + 3.5) \times 1000/(30 \times 24 \times 60 \times 2) \approx \$\ 0.15$ per thousand (i.e., renting the instance for a month at the hourly rate plus the cost of premium exchange membership). Note that this is significantly lower than several of the auto exchanges charge; e.g., HitLeap charges $0.44 and Jingling $0.41 per thousand. The fact that dispersed customized clicks can be produced at significantly lower cost than the exchanges charge suggests an inefficient market. It could be that the exchanges price optimistically and sell very little at the advertised rates, or it could be that there are unsophisticated buyers for whom the task of setting up an AWS instance represents a barrier. Note that the manual exchanges ask more than 10× more per click. A possible explanation is that proposed in Sections 7.2 and 7.4: it is the participants themselves rather than an ad network who are the targets, and sending Ponzi and get-rich-quick schemes at this population is more profitable on a per-click basis than sending inorganic traffic to YouTube. Our measurements (and the requirement to perform a CAPTCHA between clicks) suggest that a large fraction of traffic on the manual exchanges is in fact organic.

It is hard to pin down definitive stable numbers for how much one can expect to earn from inorganic traffic. Some URL shortening sites post their current payout rates: `adf.ly` pays $3.96, `adfoc.us` pays $5.50, and `sh.st` pays $4.03 per thousand. YouTube does not post payout rates, and discussion forums seem to indicate it is a complex function of channel subscribers and number of "likes" that a video receives; between $0.50 and $4 per thousand appears to be a commonly mentioned range. (The need for "likes" and subscribers to help monetize views suggests a market for those commodities also).

If clicks can be produced at $0.15 per thousand (or bought at the rates shown in Table 6) and sold for $4 or so per thousand to URL shortening services, the opportunity is very profitable. At the two clicks per minute rate this would produce $\$\ (4.03 - -0.15) \times 30 \times 24 \times 60 \times 2/1000 \approx \$\ 335.2$ profit per machine per month. It seems very likely however that URL shortening services detect (and refuse to credit) a large volume of inorganic traffic (e.g., in its TOU `adf.ly` forbids publishers from "advertising their adf.ly URL links directly on any form of traffic exchange/PTC website", and other services use similar wording). Equally, even the lower of YouTube payout rates would appear profitable if detection has negligible effect. Ethical considerations prevent us from sending automated traffic to any of these services to probe their detection rates. It is thus difficult to estimate the true return on inorganic traffic. We note, however, that even if only 5% of the inorganic traffic is credited (≈ $17 per machine per month), the ability to scale up by adding more machines would still allow healthy returns.

Table 9 gives our estimate of the number of impressions per day from each of the autosurf exchanges. Again, we caution that the fraction of exchange traffic that is detected (and thus not credited) is unknown. Nonetheless it is interesting to get rough ideas of the economic damage inorganic traffic might be causing. HitLeap, at 150M impressions per day, would cost $66K per day to advertisers *if all exchange participants managed to monetize at $0.44 per thousand impressions* (i.e., the rate the exchange charges for clicks as shown in Table 6). Similarly, the figures for eBesucher and Jingling would be $3,230 and $323K respectively. These can be considered somewhat loose upper bounds.

8. CONCLUSION

We examined several manual and automated traffic exchange services, which enable dispersion of traffic origins. We found that these exchanges range across three orders of magnitude in diversity of IP addresses and impressions served per day, and appear to differ significantly in the monetization strategies of participants. Our results shed light on a previously poorly understood part of the traffic and ad-fraud ecosystem.

Acknowledgments

Our thanks to Ben Edelman, Paul England, Mariusz Jakubowski, and Gloria Mainar-Ruiz for discussions on various aspects of this work.

This work was supported by the U.S. Army Research Office under MURI grant W911NF-09-1-0553, and by the National Science Foundation under grant CNS-1237265. Any opinions, findings, and conclusions or recommendations expressed in this material are those of the authors and do not necessarily reflect the views of the sponsors.

9. REFERENCES

[1] 10khits. http://www.10khits.com. Online. Mar, 2015.

[2] 247autohits. http://www.247autohits.com. Online. Mar, 2015.

[3] Amazon ec2 pricing. http://aws.amazon.com/ec2/pricing/. Online. Mar, 2015.

[4] Appnexus. http://www.appnexus.com. Online. Mar, 2015.

[5] Black hat world. http://www.blackhatworld.com. Online. Mar, 2015.

[6] Clickbank. http://www.clickbank.com. Online. Mar, 2015.

[7] Common crawl. http://commoncrawl.org/the-data/. Online. Mar, 2015.

[8] Cyber criminals defraud display advertisers with tdss. http://goo.gl/e1dcsj. Mar, 2015.

[9] Discovered: Botnet costing display advertisers over six million dollars per month. http://www.spider.io/blog/2013/03/chameleon-botnet/. Online. Mar, 2015.

[10] Easyhits4u. http://www.easyhits4u.com. Online. Mar, 2015.

[11] Ebesucher. http://www.ebesucher.com. Online. Mar, 2015.

[12] Enhanceviews autowatcher. http://www.enhanceviews.com. Online. Mar, 2015.

[13] Frozen view count - youtube. https://support.google.com/youtube/troubleshooter/2991876?hl=en-GB/. Online. Mar, 2015.

[14] Hitleap. https://hitleap.com. Online. Mar, 2015.

[15] Hitsafari. http://www.hitsafari.com. Online. Mar, 2015.

[16] Jingling. http://service.spiritsoft.cn. Online. Mar, 2015.

[17] Limestone networks. https://www.limestonenetworks.com. Online. Mar, 2015.

[18] Mozilla public suffix list. http://wiki.mozilla.org/Public_Suffix_List. Online. Mar, 2015.

[19] Mustat. http://www.mustat.com. Online. Mar, 2015.

[20] Otohits. http://www.otohits.net. Online. Mar, 2015.

[21] Ovh - webhosting, cloud and dedicated servers. https://www.ovh.com/. Online. Mar, 2015.

[22] Ziddu. http://www.ziddu.com. Online. Mar, 2015.

[23] N. Christin. Traveling the silk road: A measurement analysis of a large anonymous online marketplace. In *Proceedings of the 22nd international conference on World Wide Web*, pages 213–224. International World Wide Web Conferences Steering Committee, 2013.

[24] V. Dave, S. Guha, and Y. Zhang. Measuring and fingerprinting click-spam in ad networks. In *Proceedings of the Special Interest Group on Data Communication (SIGCOMM)*, August 2012.

[25] B. G. Edelman. Accountable? the problems and solutions of online ad optimization. In *IEEE Security & Privacy 12, no. 6 (November–December 2014): 102–107.*

[26] C. Grier, K. Thomas, V. Paxson, and M. Zhang. @spam: The underground on 140 characters or less. In *Proceedings of the 17th ACM conference on Computer and communications security*, pages 27–37. ACM, 2010.

[27] H. Haddadi. Fighting online click-fraud using bluff ads. *SIGCOMM Comput. Commun. Rev.*, 40(2):21–25, Apr. 2010.

[28] C. Kanich, C. Kreibich, K. Levchenko, B. Enright, G. M. Voelker, V. Paxson, and S. Savage. Spamalytics: An empirical analysis of spam marketing conversion. In *Proceedings of the 15th ACM conference on Computer and communications security*, pages 3–14. ACM, 2008.

[29] R. A. Lewis and J. M. Rao. On the near impossibility of measuring the returns to advertising. *Unpublished paper, Google, Inc. and Microsoft Research. http://justinmrao.com/lewis_rao_nearimpossibility.pdf*, 2013.

[30] D. McCoy, A. Pitsillidis, G. Jordan, N. Weaver, C. Kreibich, B. Krebs, G. M. Voelker, S. Savage, and K. Levchenko. Pharmaleaks: Understanding the business of online pharmaceutical affiliate programs. In *Proceedings of the 21st USENIX conference on Security symposium*. USENIX Association, 2012.

[31] B. Miller, P. Pearce, C. Grier, C. Kreibich, and V. Paxson. What's clicking what? techniques and innovations of today's clickbots. In *Proceedings of the 8th International Conference on Detection of Intrusions and Malware, and Vulnerability Assessment*, DIMVA, pages 164–183. Springer-Verlag, 2011.

[32] N. Nikiforakis, F. Maggi, G. Stringhini, M. Z. Rafique, W. Joosen, C. Kruegel, F. Piessens, G. Vigna, and S. Zanero. Stranger danger: Exploring the ecosystem of ad-based url shortening services. In *Proceedings of the 23rd international conference on World wide web*, pages 51–62. International World Wide Web Conferences Steering Committee, 2014.

[33] P. Pearce, V. Dave, C. Grier, K. Levchenko, S. Guha, D. McCoy, V. Paxson, S. Savage, and G. M. Voelker. Characterizing large-scale click fraud in zeroaccess. In *Proceedings of the 21st ACM Conference on Computer and Communications Security (CCS)*. ACM – Association for Computing Machinery, November 2014.

[34] K. Springborn and P. Barford. Impression fraud in on-line advertising via pay-per-view networks. In *Proceedings of the 22nd USENIX Security Symposium*, pages 211–226, Washington, D.C., 2013. USENIX.

[35] B. Stone-Gross, R. Stevens, A. Zarras, R. Kemmerer, C. Kruegel, and G. Vigna. Understanding fraudulent activities in online ad exchanges. In *Proceedings of the eleventh ACM SIGCOMM Conference on Internet Measurement Conference*, pages 279–294, New York, NY, USA, 2011. ACM.

[36] TeamCymru. IP to ASN Mapping. http://tinyurl.com/5dtp78. Online. Mar, 2015.

[37] Q. Zhang, T. Ristenpart, S. Savage, and G. M. Voelker. Got traffic?: An evaluation of click traffic providers. In *Proceedings of the Joint WICOW/AIRWeb Workshop on Web Quality*, pages 19–26, New York, NY, USA, 2011. ACM.

Resilience of Deployed TCP to Blind Attacks

Matthew Luckie
University of Waikato
mjl@wand.net.nz

Robert Beverly
Naval Postgraduate School
rbeverly@nps.edu

Tiange Wu
CAIDA / UC San Diego
tiangewu@caida.org

Mark Allman
ICSI
mallman@icir.org

kc claffy
CAIDA / UC San Diego
kc@caida.org

ABSTRACT

As part of TCP's steady evolution, recent standards have recommended mechanisms to protect against weaknesses in TCP. But adoption, configuration, and deployment of TCP improvements can be slow. In this work, we consider the resilience of *deployed* TCP implementations to blind in-window attacks, where an off-path adversary disrupts an established connection by sending a packet that the victim believes came from its peer, causing data corruption or connection reset. We tested operating systems (and middleboxes deployed in front) of webservers in the wild in September 2015 and found 22% of connections vulnerable to in-window SYN and reset packets, 30% vulnerable to in-window data packets, and 38.4% vulnerable to at least one of three in-window attacks we tested. We also tested out-of-window packets and found that while few deployed systems were vulnerable to reset and SYN packets, 5.4% of connections accepted in-window data with an invalid acknowledgment number. In addition to evaluating commodity TCP stacks, we found vulnerabilities in 12 of 14 of the routers and switches we characterized – critical network infrastructure where the potential impact of any TCP vulnerabilities is particularly acute. This surprisingly high level of extant vulnerabilities in the most mature Internet transport protocol in use today is a perfect illustration of the Internet's fragility. Embedded in historical context, it also provides a strong case for more systematic, scientific, and longitudinal measurement and quantitative analysis of fundamental properties of critical Internet infrastructure, as well as for the importance of better mechanisms to get best security practices deployed.

Categories and Subject Descriptors

C.4 [**Performance of Systems**]: Measurement techniques; C.2.0 [**Computer-communication Networks**]: Security

Keywords

TCP; security; blind attacks; middleboxes

IMC'15, October 28–30, 2015, Tokyo, Japan.
© 2015 ACM. ISBN 978-1-4503-3848-6/15/10 ...$15.00.
DOI: http://dx.doi.org/10.1145/2815675.2815700.

1. INTRODUCTION

Despite the rich history of attacks against TCP [40, 38, 31, 14], and subsequent counter-measures [6, 36, 32, 15], little recent empirical data exists on the current resilience of *deployed* TCP implementations on the Internet. In this paper, we focus on attacks against TCP by a "blinded" attacker, i.e. an attacker that is off-path and does not observe the TCP connection. Of particular interest is the vulnerability of critical infrastructure, including web servers, routers, and switches. For example, long-lived BGP and OpenFlow TCP sessions are well-known to be vulnerable [8, 12], while recent work [14] demonstrated new blinded attacks that pollute web caches. As connection speeds increase and TCP receive windows grow, other long-lived TCP applications such as file transfers, ssh, and rsync may become vulnerable.

We therefore take a multi-faceted measurement examination of both commodity operating system TCP stacks as well as proprietary TCP implementations in routers and switches. We adopted an oracle-based approach by simulating a variety of blinded attacks. Our simulated exploits sent packets (RST, SYN, data, both in and out of window) that a blinded attacker might send as part of a brute-force attack. We also examined ephemeral port selection strategies in the wild, which impact the feasibility of blind attacks.

To test commodity TCP stacks as deployed in the wild, we established connections to websites in the Alexa list [2], and observed the behavior of their TCP implementations in response to our oracle's probing packets. We do not claim that our results are representative of any particular population; we tested websites to understand properties of currently deployed web operating systems and middleboxes. Nevertheless, we consider our results indicative of current likely behavior in other populations, including systems that support long-lived protocols including ssh and rsync.

In this population as measured in September 2015, we found: (1) 38.4% of systems tested were vulnerable to at least one blind in-window attack; (2) the in-window data attack is the most significant vulnerability, as 29.6% of systems accepted data with inadequate validation of the acknowledgment number; (3) systems that advertised a maximum segment size (MSS) of 1380 were almost never vulnerable to in-window reset and SYN packets (suggesting that middleboxes with this feature correctly filtered those suspicious packets) but incorrectly passed invalid in-window data packets, (4) in response to an in-window SYN, 1.1% of hosts established a parallel TCP connection using the same 4-tuple, which is unexpected behavior as a 4-tuple can only support a single TCP connection at any one time.

We also investigated the TCP behavior of 14 network infrastructure devices (BGP routers and OpenFlow switches) in a laboratory setting to assess their resilience to these same off-path attacks. Of the devices we tested, 12 of 14 had some vulnerability in their handling of packets that could have been sent by a blinded attacker. In particular, 10 of 14 devices accepted data that could have been sent by a blinded attacker.

Finally, in addition to these active tests, we used passive captures of TCP connections to understand deployed ephemeral port selection algorithms. Within a March 2015 packet trace from an internal 10Gbps link between Chicago and Seattle belonging to a Tier-1 ISP, we observed 50% of selected ports within a 2K range – a fraction of the available ephemeral port range. Longitudinal analysis of an enterprise trace suggests that the slow adoption of new operating systems is slowly increasing the range of ports used in the wild.

We begin by describing blind in-window attack methods and defenses in section 2, and present our active measurement techniques to test for the vulnerability in section 3. In section 4 we present our findings from using our method to test TCP stacks deployed in a webserver environment; we found 22% of connections vulnerable to blind in-window SYN and reset packets, and 30% vulnerable to in-window data packets. In section 5 we report our findings from testing embedded TCP stacks in routers and switches; we found that while more recent stacks were not vulnerable to blind in-window SYN and reset attacks, they have not deployed best practices when validating data packets. In section 6 we explore deployed port selection algorithms over time using longitudinal connection summary logs from a campus intrusion detection system, and using a packet capture from a Tier-1 ISP backbone link. We end with a brief discussion on the current difficulty of mounting a blind attack in section 7, a comparison with related work in section 8, and conclude in section 9. We make our code publicly available as part of scamper [24], allowing vendors to test their deployed implementations of TCP for the mitigations recommended by RFC 5961 [32].

2. BACKGROUND

A TCP connection is defined by a four-tuple consisting of source and destination IP addresses, and source and destination port numbers. To interfere with a TCP connection, a "blinded" attacker (i.e. an attacker that is off-path and does not observe the TCP connection) has to guess (or infer) all four tuple values, as well as valid sequence (and sometimes acknowledgment) numbers for the connection. The TCP protocol has evolved, and vendors have strengthened implementations over time, to better resist attack. For example, the initial sequence number (ISN) was once predictable – allowing an attacker to infer acknowledgment numbers and forge entire TCP connections [6]. Modern TCPs instead generate unpredictable ISN values using a cryptographic hash function.

Despite unpredictable ISNs, Paul Watson demonstrated in 2004 that a blinded attacker could reset TCP connections by: (1) guessing a sequence number within the receive window; and (2) leveraging the small range of likely source port values [38]. Not only did operating systems at the time typically choose source ports from within a small range (1024-5000), they were selected sequentially. Watson noted two possible solutions. First, a host should choose an ephemeral port value randomly when it initiates a new TCP connection to increase the difficulty of blind-attacking a TCP connection by a factor of up to 2^{16}. Second, hosts should strictly validate the sequence and acknowledgment values, so that rather than requiring the packet to be merely in-window, it has to be exactly congruent with the receiver's position in the connection's window space. RFC 4953 [36], published in 2007, described blinded attack vectors in TCP known at that time. RFC 5961 [32], published in 2010, described attacks that a blinded attacker could conduct in addition to the well-known reset attack, and recommended that receivers strictly validate received packets for their position in the receive window.

Blind attackers rely on brute force to attack TCP connections, and are therefore constrained by network capacity. With the exponential growth of network capacity, attacks become easier. For example, a 100Mbps network link is capable of carrying 148,410 minimum-sized frames per second, and can be rented from some hosting networks for less than $100 per month. A blind attacker needs only small packets that fit entirely inside the minimum-sized Ethernet frame. Therefore, an attack that requires 2^{17} (131,072) packets to succeed can complete in less than one second at 100Mbps.

2.1 Slipping in the window

Operating systems retain myriad state about each active TCP connection. Beyond the source and destination IP addresses and port numbers that represent the 4-tuple, each end of the TCP connection has a 32-bit number corresponding to the next sequence number value it will use to send new data (*snd.nxt*), a 32-bit number recording the next in-order sequence number expected from the receiver (*rcv.nxt*), a 32-bit number recording the last sequence number for which it received an acknowledgment (*snd.una*), as well as a 16-bit number the receiver advertises which represents the amount of data it can accept (*rcv.wnd*). This 16-bit number can be scaled by up to 14-bits with the TCP window scale option, so that a TCP sender can have up to 1GB of data in flight provided the receiver advertises a sufficient window size [20].

The blind in-window reset attack described by Watson [38] relies on the victim's TCP stack following the original TCP specification from 1981, RFC 793 [30], which says that "a reset is valid if its sequence number is in the window." To reset a TCP connection with a given four tuple, a blinded attacker only has to try one packet in each possible window. Therefore, the number of packets required to complete the attack is inversely proportional to the size of the advertised window, i.e. the difficulty of an attack reduces the larger the receiver's window becomes.

RFC 5961 [32] suggests TCP should tighten the original specification's notion of an acceptable sequence number from "in the window" to exactly the next expected sequence number (*rcv.nxt*). Otherwise, the victim must send a *challenge ACK*, which is an acknowledgment reporting the current values of *snd.nxt* and *rcv.nxt*. The purpose of this ACK is to double check that the sender of the reset actually intended to reset the connection. If so, it will send a second reset packet, with the challenge ACK's *rcv.nxt* value copied into the sequence number space, confirming the reset and providing a valid reset that the receiver will act on. This approach increases the number of guesses the attacker must make from 2^{32} / *rcv.wnd* to 2^{32}.

RFC 5961 describes two additional attack vectors similar in nature to the well-known reset attack: a blind reset attack using the SYN bit, and a blind data injection attack. The SYN attack is similar to the reset attack, and relies on similar language in RFC 793 [30], which says that if a SYN is received in the window it is an error, and to send a reset. As with the reset attack, RFC 5961 says the receiver must send a *challenge ACK* to confirm the loss of the previous connection; this challenge ACK must be sent regardless of the sequence number in the SYN packet.

In a blind data injection attack, an attacker tries to inject data into an existing TCP connection by guessing a sequence number within the victim's receive window. Unlike the reset and SYN attacks, an attacker should also have to guess an acknowledgment value that is acceptable to the receiver. RFC 793 states that an acknowledgment number is acceptable as long as it is not acknowledging data that has not yet been sent. In practice, this means that the acknowledgment number in the packet can be any value less than the victim's *snd.nxt*, which is a range of nearly 2^{31} values. To reduce the likelihood of success, RFC 5961 introduces a variable to represent the maximum receive window the peer has advertised to the victim (*max.rcv.wnd*) and limits the acceptable acknowledgment range to lie between *snd.una* - *max.rcv.wnd* and *snd.nxt*.

RFC 5961 explicitly states that these mitigations are not required of TCP stacks – the mitigations to the blind reset and SYN attacks are recommended, and the mitigation to the blind data attack is optional because the attack is perceived to be twice as difficult (a blind attacker has to send the data twice, with two different acknowledgment values). However, RFC 5961 also notes that all three mitigations increase the robustness of TCP in general.

Finally, some connections are subject to a trivial blind attack that does not require an in-window packet. Until September 2014, all supported versions of FreeBSD were susceptible to an attacker being able to tear down any TCP connection by sending two packets with the SYN flag set that shared the same 4-tuple as an ongoing connection [1]. If an attacker has reason to believe there are connections between two IP addresses and a destination port, and the FreeBSD system has not been patched [1], the attacker could tear down all connections with 2^{17} packets (two packets for all 2^{16} ephemeral ports). While this vulnerability was fixed in all supported versions of FreeBSD, the recommendations in RFC 5961 have only been added to the development version of FreeBSD, and all supported versions of FreeBSD as of August 2015 are still vulnerable to some blind attacks.

2.2 Defenses to blind in-window attacks

Beyond strictly checking incoming packets per the advice in RFC 5961, there are several mitigations to blind in-window attacks that vendors can implement, ranging from those that make the problem harder to cryptographic solutions that make successful attacks practically impossible. The simplest approach is for a host to choose a random source port when establishing a TCP connection. Operating systems select port values from a configurable ephemeral range. Historically, versions of Windows and BSD used the range 1024 to 5000 – a range of 3976 port values. IANA now recommends the range 49152 to 65535 [10, 19] be used by all transport protocols – a range of 16K port values. Table 1 summarizes the ephemeral port ranges used by popular operating systems.

Port Range	Size	Operating System
1024–5000	3976	Windows XP and earlier
		FreeBSD $\leq$ 4.11 (Jan 2005)
		Linux $\leq$ 2.2
49152–65535	16384	FreeBSD $\geq$ 5.0 (Jan 2003)
		Windows Vista (Jan 2007)
		Apple MacOS X
		Apple IOS
32768–61000	28232	Linux $\geq$ 2.4
10000–65535	55535	FreeBSD $\geq$ 8.0 (Nov 2011)

Table 1: Port ranges and sizes used by common operating systems to select ephemeral ports. Port selection strategies differ among systems; Windows and Apple currently assign ephemeral TCP ports sequentially, FreeBSD randomly, and Linux uses hash-based port selection.

It is tempting to believe that operating systems choose ports at random from within these ranges, making it difficult to guess which port values are likely to be used. This was one of the pieces of advice made by Paul Watson in 2004 when he reported on the feasibility of blind in-window attacks [38]. Researchers have since studied ephemeral port selection strategies [3] and port randomization is IETF best current practice [23] as of 2011.

Implementers made the well-known Kaminsky DNS cache poisoning attack [21] much more difficult to mount by using a random ephemeral port value selection strategy. However, for expediency, implementers made this fix in DNS server software, not in the operating systems, and while some operating systems have chosen ports at random since at least 2004 (FreeBSD, OpenBSD) current popular operating systems (Windows and MacOS) choose TCP ports sequentially from the global range of ephemeral ports. Linux kernels since version 2.6.15 choose ports sequentially from an offset in the ephemeral range based upon a cryptographic hash of the destination address and port with a secret, per [23].

Some protocols, such as BGP, typically operate between topologically adjacent systems. Because they are adjacent, the TTL value contained in the IP header will not be decremented by outside routers before packets arrive at the peer. The Generalized TTL Security Mechanism [15] relies on this fact; if the peer requires the received IP TTL to be 255 (the largest TTL value possible) then it will discard attack packets from outside the network because outside routers will have decremented the TTL and therefore the packets' TTL value cannot be 255. This mitigation does not protect Internet applications in the general case, though it does help in some situations.

It is also possible to protect TCP sessions by using a cryptographic authentication protocol between the hosts, to allow a receiver to validate that the packet must have come from its peer and not a third-party attacker. The three most common authentication options are the TCP MD5 option [16], the TCP authentication option [37], and the IP authentication option [22]. In all cases, the peers must establish a shared secret, or deploy certificates, before establishing a TCP connection. This approach is feasible for BGP, where sessions are configured between known endpoints, but

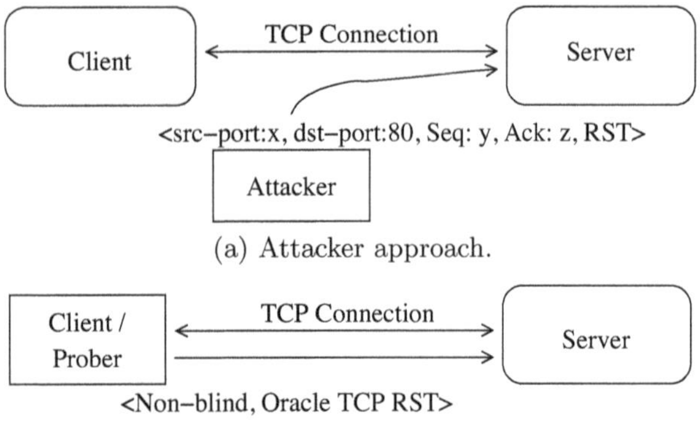

(a) Attacker approach.

(b) Our oracle approach.

Figure 1: Comparing our oracle approach with that of an attacker. We do not attempt to disrupt third-party connections, rather we establish our own TCP connection and send test packets with perfect knowledge of the connection.

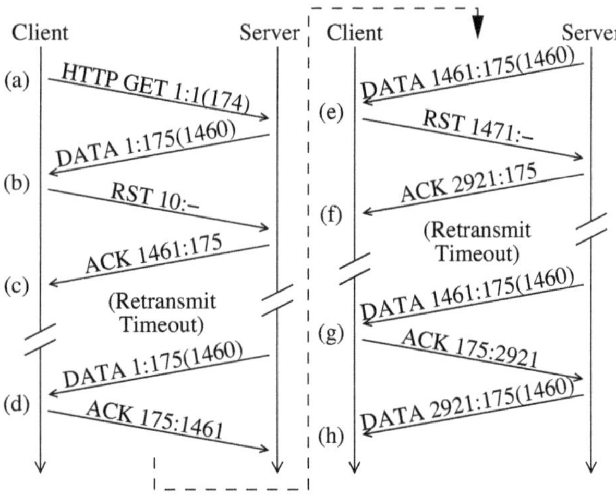

Figure 2: Overview of our blind reset and SYN test. After the TCP (and TLS) handshake, we send an HTTP request (a) to solicit a response to which we send a reset packet (b). If the server follows RFC 5961, it will send a challenge ACK (c, f) with the expected sequence number in the acknowledgment field. When the server re-transmits the unacknowledged data, we send an acknowledgment (d, g) and send the next blind reset (e) when the server sends new data. This method allows the TCP connection to progress while we send our three reset attempts; only two reset attempts (b, e) are shown.

is more difficult in the general transport protocol case between arbitrary endpoints.

Application-layer encryption, such as that provided by TLS, does not prevent an attacker from disrupting a TCP session. A blind in-window reset, SYN, or piece of data can still cause the connection to terminate; the only advantage of TLS is that, in the case of the blind data attack, an attacker's accepted data will cause the application-layer decryption software to note the error and abort the TLS connection rather than corrupting the transmitted data.

Some TCP stacks use automatic buffer tuning [35] and increase the receive window (and *max.rcv.wnd*) when they infer the sender's transmission rate is receive window limited. A TCP stack that uses automatic buffer tuning can reduce their attack surface by using small initial receive windows, and only increase the window when they detect the sender is receive window limited. A study of TCP performance on a fiber-to-the-home network during 2011 and 2012 found that 20%-41% of TCP connections increased their window during the connection's lifetime [34], suggesting modest use of automatic buffer tuning.

Finally, since blind attacks require the attacker to use the source IP address of an ongoing TCP connection, blind attacks are possible because there is inadequate source address validation and hence IP address spoofing is allowed. RFC 2827 [13] describes best current practices for filtering spoofed packets, however previous work has found filtering not well deployed in the Internet [7] so blind attacks are unfortunately still possible.

3. ACTIVE MEASUREMENT METHOD

Our general approach is to actively open a normal TCP connection with some server and then simulate an attack on this connection. Our attacks were confined to our own experimental connections and at no point did we attempt to disrupt production traffic. Figure 1 compares our approach to that of a blind attacker. This methodology gives us perfect knowledge of the precise packets to use to determine if the TCP connection was susceptible to packets from a blind attacker who knows the four tuple of the target connection. Our specific tests follow from RFC 5961 [32]: we sent packets that have a sequence or acknowledgment number that should cause the receiver to reject or challenge the packet.

3.1 Blind Reset and SYN Tests

Figure 2 illustrates our blind reset and SYN tests. Our tests began by establishing a TCP connection without the use of any TCP options. We established a TLS session in the HTTPS case, and sent a HTTP GET request specifying the HTTP "Host" header for the server. From there, we sent reset (or SYN) packets as if we were a blind attacker by using a sequence number 10 greater than the first byte of data the receiver is expecting from our client. We sent up to three reset (or SYN) packets to account for packet loss, interspersing each with an ACK that acknowledged a new segment of data to encourage the server to keep the TCP connection alive. If the server sent multiple packets, we used the first to trigger our test, and subsequent packets to send duplicate acknowledgments as if we had lost the first.

If we received a reset packet in response to a duplicate acknowledgment we sent, then we classified the server as vulnerable because it reset the connection in response to the reset or SYN. Likewise, if we received no other packets after sending the first reset packet, then we inferred the server reset the connection and was also vulnerable. If we received a challenge ACK, or the server ignored the packets and continued to send data, then we classified the server as not vulnerable because it ignored the packets. Otherwise, if we received a FIN before we could send all three packets, or the server went silent before we could send all three packets, then we classified the test as being inconclusive.

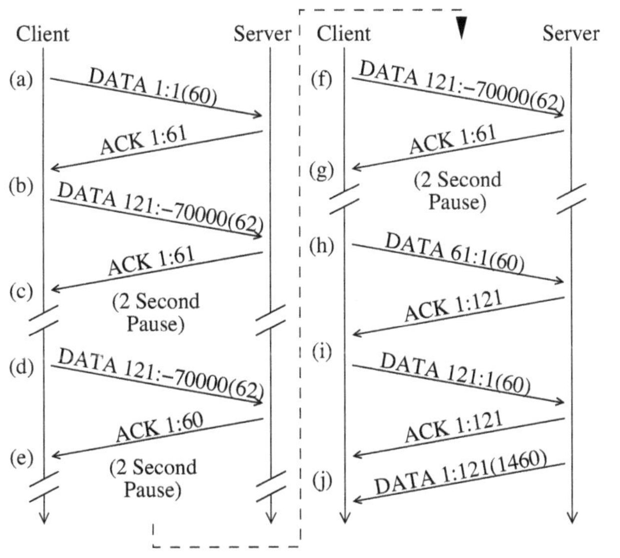

Figure 3: Overview of our blind data test. We break the first segment of data for the connection into three pieces. After the TCP handshake, we send the first piece (a) with an expected acknowledgment number, and then send the third piece (b) with an invalid acknowledgment number. We send the third piece twice more to account for potential packet loss (d, f), and then the second piece (h) with an expected acknowledgment number. If the server rejected the third piece, then we will not receive an ACK for it after the hole is filled by the second piece. We then send the third piece with an expected acknowledgment number (i) to allow the connection to complete (j). The acknowledgment packets (c, e, and g) are recommended by RFC 5961 though they are not challenge ACKs because they are not used by the server to confirm the loss of the connection.

The blind SYN test can reveal two additional behaviors. First, if the server sent a reset packet in response to the SYN (identified by the acknowledgment number in the reset being one greater than the sequence number in our reset packet) we inferred these systems were vulnerable. We confirmed these systems reset the original TCP connection, as any subsequent duplicate acknowledgments also solicited a reset. Second, if the server sent a SYN/ACK packet acknowledging the new sequence number, we classified these systems as establishing a parallel TCP connection using the same 4-tuple. This behavior was an unexpected finding; we confirmed that data continued to flow in the original TCP connection, and that the new TCP connection re-transmitted the SYN/ACK as if the server had state for both connections. We were able to associate most of the systems that established a parallel connection with a large content distribution network.

Finally, we also tested if the sequence number even had to be in-window for the reset or SYN packet to cause the connection to be reset. We begin a new test by sending packets with a sequence number 70,000 earlier than would be required for the packet to be in-window. We chose this value arbitrarily but it is a value that is outside the window and represents a position in the stream that our connection has not covered.

3.2 Blind data test

Devising a realistic methodology to test for vulnerability to the blind in-window data attack was not straight forward. In our testing, if we sent the first data packet for a connection with an unexpected acknowledgment number, we elicited a reset from 22% of the tested webserver population, regardless of the sequence number chosen. The same systems did not send a reset if the packet with an unexpected acknowledgment number was not the first data packet for the connection. In addition, we did not want to send the first segment with the exact sequence number expected by the receiver, in case the receiver's TCP has a special case for that specific segment.

Therefore, we chose a slightly complicated approach where we broke the first segment of data (the HTTP GET or the first packet in the TLS handshake) into three equal-sized pieces, and then sent the pieces as follows: (1) we sent the first piece with an acknowledgment number expected by the receiver, (2) we sent the third piece with a sequence number ahead of the receiver's *rcv.nxt* (leaving a hole for the second piece) and an acknowledgment number outside of the acceptable range defined by RFC 5961, and (3) we sent the second piece with an acknowledgment number expected by the receiver.

If the receiver accepted the third piece with an invalid acknowledgment number, the second piece will fill a hole and the receiver will send an acknowledgment for both pieces. We inferred the receiver is vulnerable to blind data attacks if we receive an acknowledgment for the third piece. Otherwise, we sent the third piece with the acknowledgment number expected by the receiver to avoid conflating an unresponsive TCP with a system that was ignoring our segments. Figure 3 illustrates our approach. We sent the third piece three times, and with a two second delay, regardless of the presence or absence of acknowledgments, and sent the first and second pieces up to three times each, to account for transient packet loss.

If we received an acknowledgment for any of the third pieces with an incorrect acknowledgment number, we classified these systems as not vulnerable and report them in the challenge ACK category, though these ACKs were not challenge ACKs because the sender was not using them to confirm the loss of the connection. If we did not receive an acknowledgment for any of the third pieces we sent with an incorrect acknowledgment number, we also classified these systems as not vulnerable because they ignored the data. If we received a reset quoting our invalid acknowledgment number, we classified these systems as vulnerable because they reset the connection, rather than discard the data packet.

Finally, we also tested if the acknowledgment number even had to acknowledge previously sent data for a blind data attack to be successful. We sent the third piece with an acknowledgment number 70,000 ahead of the receiver's position in the sequence number space, which we know from the SYN, and is beyond the feasible range of sequence numbers it could have sent given our advertised receive window.

3.3 Fingerprinting test

We completed probing with a test that established a TCP connection advertising support for TCP window scaling [20], timestamps [20], and Selective Acknowledgments [26]. We used this test to infer the normal behavior of a TCP connection with a peer, as well as to fingerprint the peer's operat-

Methods	Parameters
Blind reset: in window	Host's snd.nxt + 10
Blind reset: out of window	Host's snd.nxt - 70,000
Blind SYN: in window	Host's snd.nxt + 10
Blind SYN: out of window	Host's snd.nxt - 70,000
Blind data: behind	Peer's snd.una - 70,000 Host's snd.nxt + x
Blind data: ahead	Peer's snd.una + 70,000 Host's snd.nxt + x

Table 2: Summary of blind tests we conducted. We chose different sequence and acknowledgment values to test for different checks made by the receiver.

ing system with p0f [39]. p0f can infer the operating system using features found in the SYN/ACK packet, such as the ordering of TCP options, the window size advertised, and the IP-TTL value.

3.4 Implementation

Table 2 summarizes the blind TCP tests we implemented in scamper, an open-source parallelized packet prober [24]. For each measurement, our tool records, in a single data unit, meta-data about the test such as the URL and the server MSS seen, and all packets sent and received for that test. We also implemented a driver to coordinate scamper's measurements. Our driver first performs the sequence of blind tests towards the webserver one at a time, in random order, waiting at least one minute between tests to each unique IP address to avoid being a nuisance. Our driver concludes with the null test to fingerprint the operating system of the host. Our code is publicly available and available in scamper [24].

4. WEBSERVER VULNERABILITY

4.1 Targets

The first step in our methodology was to choose a list of web servers to test. We derived our targets from the Alexa Top 1,000,000 websites list [2]. Each of our measurement vantage points (see 4.2) independently chose 50K random web sites from the Alexa list. We sent a DNS query for each web site and used the first returned IPv4 address for the duration of our probing. Further, if multiple sites shared an IP address, we only probed the IP address once. This process yielded roughly 41K target IP addresses per vantage point. Additionally, some of our tests require a transfer to last long enough to conduct the test and therefore we must find a URL within each site that returns an object of at least 25KB. Therefore, we run a pre-probing step with wget against each IP address, as follows. If the default page for the given site is at least 25KB, we use that for our tests. Otherwise, we retrieved all objects required to display the default page and used the first that was at least 25KB in size in our tests.

4.2 Vantage Points

We used two of CAIDA's Archipelago vantage points (VPs) to conduct measurements [18]: cld-us, hosted by CAIDA in San Diego, and hlz-nz, hosted by the University of Waikato in New Zealand. We used a third machine hosted by the Massachusetts Institute of Technology (MIT) in Cambridge. We used three VPs to attempt to avoid an undetected middlebox in the hosting network from impacted our measurements by manipulating our test packets before they reached the destination network. We obtained permission from the operators of these three VPs to conduct our measurements from their network.

4.3 Results

Table 3 summarizes the results of our testing the webserver population from cld-us. The columns labeled in/out represent SYN and reset tests where the sequence numbers were in or out of window as per table 2, and the ahead/behind represent data tests where the acknowledgment number was behind or ahead of the range acceptable by RFC 5961. We found 22.2% of the connections tested were vulnerable to an in-window reset packet. Of these, most (18.8%) sent a reset in response to duplicate acknowledgments, while 3.4% went silent after we sent the reset packet. An additional 76.5% of the connections were not vulnerable to the in-window reset attack, with 71.4% issuing a challenge ACK as required by RFC 5961, and the remaining 5.1% simply ignoring the reset packets rather than confirming the loss of the connection.

22.4% of the connections we tested were vulnerable to an in-window SYN packet, with 17.1% sending a reset that acknowledged the in-window sequence number, and 5.3% sending a reset after we sent a duplicate acknowledgment. Interestingly, 35.9% of the connections we tested did not send a challenge ACK as required by RFC 5961, to confirm the loss of the previous TCP connection. Additionally, 1.1% of TCP connections acted in an unexpected way by appearing to create a second parallel TCP connection in response to the in-window SYN packet. These TCP connections were mostly with a large CDN provider, who appeared to terminate TCP connections on their systems, and relayed data from their customer's webserver obtained over a separate TCP connection.

30.3% of connections we tested were vulnerable to data injection attacks. In most of the cases (29.6%) the injected data was accepted by the stack, while the receiver sent a reset in the remaining cases. Most of the systems that reset the connection confirmed that they reset in response to the data packet because they quoted the invalid acknowledgment value in the reset packet. We also found that in the majority of the non-vulnerable connections, the server sent an ACK to the packets (37.1%) rather than just ignore the packets (29.3%).

Table 4 shows the overall results collected from the VPs we used to test webservers. Quantitatively, the results are similar, with overall classifications from each VP usually within 1% of each other, despite each VP testing a different set of random webservers. However the results of the blind in-window SYN tests were impacted by a stateful on-campus router at hlz-nz, which silently discarded outgoing SYN packets belonging to an existing connection. Because our results for each VP are quantitatively similar, we believe the behaviors observed occur close to the webserver end of the TCP connection.

Overall, 38.4% of the webservers tested from cld-us were vulnerable to at least one blind in-window attack. Figure 4 shows the overlap of vulnerability to blind in-window tests between tested systems. 12.4% of the webservers tested were vulnerable to all three blind in-window attacks tested. The vector with the largest exposure was the blind data injection

Result	Blind reset		Blind SYN		Blind data	
	in	out	in	out	behind	ahead
Accepted	3.4%	0.4%	-	-	29.6%	5.4%
Reset (ack-blind)	-	-	17.1%	0.0%	0.6%	0.6%
Reset (dup-ack)	18.8%	0.6%	5.3%	1.2%	0.1%	0.2%
Vulnerable	22.2%	1.0%	22.4%	1.2%	30.3%	6.2%
Challenge ACK	71.4%	1.1%	37.7%	57.0%	37.1%	8.1%
Ignored	5.1%	91.8%	35.9%	38.3%	29.3%	81.3%
Not Vulnerable	76.5%	93.0%	73.6%	95.3%	66.4%	89.4%
Parallel TCP	-	-	1.1%	1.1%	-	-
Early FIN	0.3%	3.3%	1.5%	1.6%	3.2%	3.7%
No Result	1.0%	2.7%	1.3%	0.9%	0.1%	0.7%
Other	1.3%	6.0%	4.0%	3.6%	3.3%	4.4%

Table 3: Overview of results for the webserver population testing from cld-us VP in September 2015. In our data, 22% of connections were vulnerable to in-window reset and SYN packets, and 30% of connections were vulnerable to an in-window data packet. A further 6.2% of connections were vulnerable to data packets with an acknowledgment ahead of the receiver's window; 5.4% accepted the data without correctly validating the acknowledgment number, and 0.8% reset the connection.

	cld-us	MIT	hlz-nz
Blind reset (in):			
Vulnerable	22.2%	22.1%	21.9%
Not Vulnerable	76.5%	76.0%	76.5%
Other	1.3%	1.9%	1.6%
Blind SYN (in):			
Vulnerable	22.4%	22.2%	0.3%
Not Vulnerable	73.6%	73.2%	94.2%
Other	4.0%	4.6%	5.5%
Blind data (behind):			
Vulnerable	30.3%	30.3%	30.3%
Not Vulnerable	66.4%	66.5%	66.2%
Other	3.3%	3.3%	4.5%

Table 4: Summary of the blind tests conducted from three VPs. Overall results are quantitatively similar, apart from the SYN tests from hlz-nz, which were blocked by a stateful campus router.

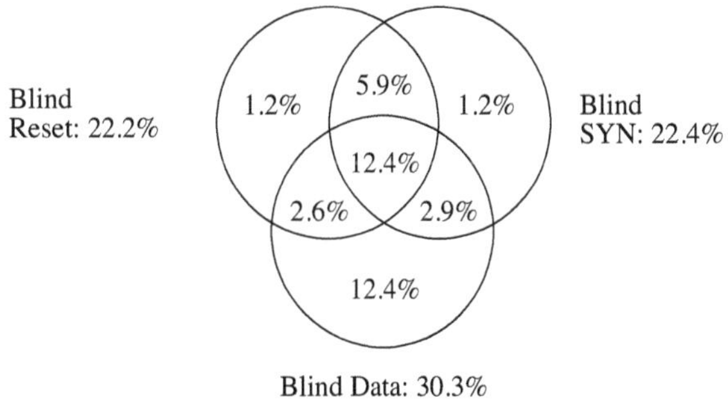

Figure 4: Overlap of vulnerability to blind in-window attacks of systems tested from cld-us. 38.4% of servers tested were vulnerable to at least one in-window attack, with 12.4% of the servers tested only vulnerable to the blind in-window data attack.

attack, with 12.4% of the webservers tested (32.3% of the vulnerable population) only vulnerable to that vector.

4.3.1 Out-of-window tests

Table 3 also contains the results of our out-of-window tests. In our experiments, we found that 1.0% of tested systems incorrectly processed the reset and 1.2% incorrectly processed the SYN even though the sequence number we included was outside of the window. We are encouraged that most TCP connections were not falsely reset, though these represent systems where a blinded attacker with knowledge of the use of an application port between two IPs only has to brute force up to 65,536 ports to reset the connection, i.e. on average a successful attack requires 2^{15} packets.

More problematic is the in-window data attack, where 6.2% showed a vulnerability to packets containing an acknowledgment value ahead of the peer's send window that the peer could not have sent. In fact, 5.4% of servers acknowledged the data we sent, and sent a response anyway. A further 0.6% of connections were reset, quoting the invalid acknowledgment number we sent in our data packet. If an attacker's goal is simply to reset an arbitrary connection, then the attacker merely has to brute force a packet into the receive window, acknowledging data that has not been sent yet, a range of up to 2^{31} values, or half the sequence number space. Most (81.3%) systems simply ignored the data packet with an acknowledgment value ahead of their window, and 8.1% sent an acknowledgment before discarding the packet.

4.3.2 Middlebox behavior

In our previous 2010 work examining the behavior of Path MTU discovery (PMTUD) in the context of TCP [25], we found that servers that advertised an MSS of 1380 bytes were much more likely to fail PMTUD, suggesting a middlebox was interfering with PMTUD. We were curious if we could find evidence of middleboxes defending webservers from blind attacks. Table 5 shows the five server MSS values most frequently observed in our data and their vulnerability to blind attack. Because most (87.2%) of the TCP connections involved an MSS of 1460, the failure rate of these systems is within 2-3% of that observed for all connections.

However, systems with an MSS of 1380 were almost never vulnerable to blind in-window reset (2.0%) and SYN (0.5%) packets, but were vulnerable to in-window data packets in roughly half the cases. We found that 85.6% of TCP connections with an MSS of 1380 sent an ACK in response

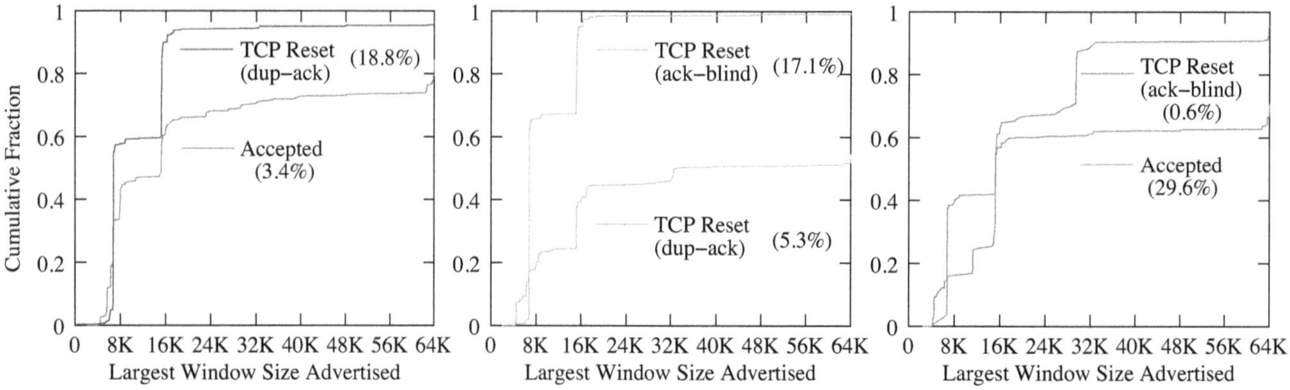

(a) Blind Reset (b) Blind SYN (c) Blind Data

Figure 5: Largest window sizes observed for systems vulnerable to blind in-window attacks and their failure modes. A larger receive window makes it easier for an attacker to disrupt a connection. The small (8K) receive window we observed for most systems vulnerable to blind reset and SYN attacks makes it more difficult to attack those connections (2^{19} packets), but 40% of the systems vulnerable to accepting in-window data advertised a window of at least 64K.

Server MSS	Vulnerable Portion		
	Blind reset	Blind SYN	Blind data
1460 (87.2%)	23.9%	24.7%	28.1%
1380 (5.4%)	2.0%	0.5%	58.8%
8961 (2.3%)	2.3%	2.3%	4.7%
1440 (0.8%)	5.9%	4.7%	57.5%
1436 (0.7%)	22.2%	5.8%	32.5%

Table 5: Top five server MSS values advertised and the corresponding portion that were vulnerable to in-window reset, SYN, and data packets. Servers that advertised an MSS of 1380 were much less likely to be affected by in-window reset and SYN packets than the general population (MSS 1460), but were affected by in-window data packets.

to data with an acknowledgment ahead of the receiver's window, representing 57.6% of all connections that did so yet only 5.4% of the population; only 3.3% of connections with an MSS of 1460 behaved this way. Similarly, we observed 96% of TCP connections with an MSS of 1380 to send challenge ACKs to in-window SYNs and resets, and out of window resets; interestingly, 1380-MSS connections behaved identically to the general population, as 80% ignored out-of-window resets. We further investigated for the presence of middleboxes by searching for TCP connections where we received packets with different TTL values for the blind in-window tests, but not for the null test. We found that we received challenge ACKs with a different TTL value than the rest of the packets in the TCP flow where a 1380 byte MSS value was advertised, indicating that a middlebox intercepted the attack packets and correctly stopped them. Challenge ACKs with different TTL values were absent almost entirely from the other MSS values in table 5.

Systems with an MSS of 8961 were hosted by Amazon, which likely had a middlebox rewriting the server MSS value. It is unclear if this middlebox protected the TCP connections involved, or if the homogeneous nature of operating systems images is responsible for the low vulnerability rate.

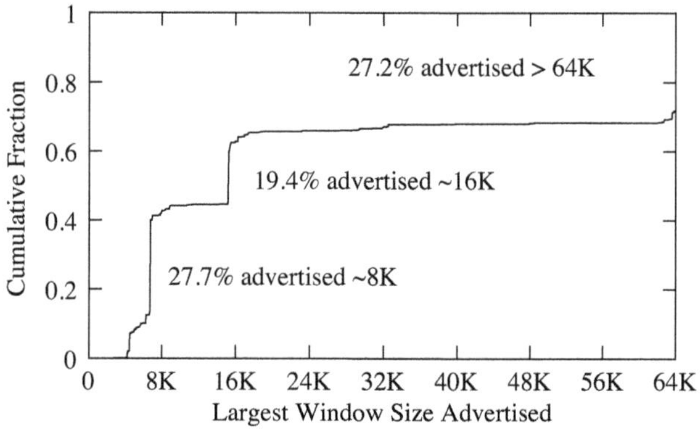

Figure 6: Largest window sizes observed for systems vulnerable to any blind in-window attack. 27% advertise a window of at least 64K, so an attacker requires a maximum of 2^{16} packets to disrupt a corresponding 4-tuple (twice as many in the data case).

4.3.3 Window sizes observed

The ease at which a blind attacker can inject a packet into a window depends on the size of the receiver's window. Figure 5 shows the largest window sizes observed to be advertised for the blind reset, SYN, and data tests. The blind in-window reset and SYN attacks appear to be the most difficult of the three attacks to accomplish, as most (60%) of potential victims used a receive window less than 8K bytes. A blind attacker would have to send more than 2^{19} packets to successfully disrupt a TCP connection that is using a receive window less than 8K bytes. However, a blind attacker might have more luck using data packets, as 50% of potential victims will accept data into a receive window of 64K. Because an attacker has to try each segment twice, with different acknowledgment values in different halves of the receiver's sequence number space, an attacker would require 2^{17} packets to successfully disrupt these TCP connections.

Figure 6 shows the landscape for systems vulnerable to any of the blind attacks tested. Because of the prevalence

Operating System	Blind reset		Blind SYN		Blind data		Total
	in	out	in	out	behind	ahead	
FreeBSD 8.x	19.2%	0.5%	**93.8%**	56.5%	**83.9%**	None	193 (0.5%)
FreeBSD 9.x	18.8%	1.0%	**88.1%**	22.2%	54.7%	None	612 (1.5%)
Linux 2.4-2.6	**87.4%**	3.0%	**83.6%**	0.4%	54.3%	40.5%	269 (0.6%)
Linux 2.6.x	**90.1%**	0.9%	**84.1%**	None	63.2%	35.8%	4903 (11.8%)
Linux 3.x	15.3%	0.6%	14.0%	0.1%	11.6%	0.6%	18021 (43.4%)
Windows 7 or 8	5.1%	2.1%	0.3%	0.3%	**88.7%**	0.9%	3877 (9.3%)
Windows XP	7.9%	6.1%	3.0%	1.8%	6.3%	3.5%	838 (2.0%)
Unknown	9.6%	0.8%	12.7%	1.4%	23.9%	3.2%	12543 (30.2%)

Table 6: Vulnerability to blind attacks based on operating system inferred by the p0f tool for the cld-us VP. Most vulnerable connections were Linux-based, and running older kernel releases. Many operating systems handled in-window data incorrectly by accepting the data that could have come from a blind attacker. We excluded operating systems that each accounted for fewer than 0.5% of observed connections (HP-UX, Linux 2.4, MacOS, OpenBSD, and Solaris).

of systems that will accept in-window data from a blind attacker and advertise a receive window of at least 64KB, 23% of tested connections could be disrupted with 2^{17} packets.

4.3.4 *Operating systems inferred*

Table 6 correlates the behavior inferred for each TCP connection with the OS inferred by the Passive OS Fingerprinting (p0f) tool [39] for data collected by the cld-us VP. The most vulnerable populations were inferred to be running Linux 2.6, with nearly all tested systems (84–90%) vulnerable to blind in-window reset and SYN attacks, and more than half vulnerable to in-window data attacks. The results for FreeBSD correlate with what is publicly known about their vulnerability to SYN packets matching an existing connection [1].

Table 6 only lists operating systems that made up at least 0.5% of the population. Beyond the operating systems in table 6, we also observed: (1) 0.3% of systems p0f classified were HP-UX 11.x, most of which were not vulnerable to blind reset or SYN attacks, but were vulnerable to blind data; (2) 3 Mac OSX systems that were vulnerable to the three blind in-window attacks tested, but not to the out/ahead of window tests; (3) 6 OpenBSD systems that were not vulnerable to any blind attacks.

4.3.5 *Summary of findings for webservers*

We found that 38.4% of currently deployed TCP stacks that support popular websites were vulnerable to at least one blind in-window attack, with the data attack the least well defended. Most TCP stacks correctly ignored reset and SYN attacks for out-of-window packets, but some incorrectly established a parallel TCP connection (1.1%) and some incorrectly reset the connection (1.0–1.4%). Perhaps most troubling was the 6.2% of tested systems whose connections were vulnerable to a blind data attack with an acknowledgment value ahead of the receiver's send window.

Systems advertising an MSS of 1380 were almost never vulnerable to in-window reset and SYN packets, because they represented TCP connections likely protected by a middlebox that sent challenge ACKs on their behalf. It is likely that the attack surface will reduce as the fraction of systems running older versions of Linux are upgraded. For example, we found approximately 3% fewer hosts vulnerable to in-window SYN and reset attacks in September 2015 than we found in April 2015.

5. INFRASTRUCTURE VULNERABILITY

Blind attacks have the potential to disrupt not just end stations, but also core infrastructure [8, 12]. For example, both BGP-speaking routers and OpenFlow-speaking switches establish TCP connections to exchange routing information. BGP and OpenFlow connections are especially susceptable to brute forcing, as they are long-lived. Long-lived flows permit the attacker to feasibly probe the entire sequence and portions of the tuple space. Furthermore, the four-tuples of control-plane flows may be easier to discover as BGP peers are well-known. An off-path attacker that is able to successfully disrupt a BGP or OpenFlow TCP connection can induce significant harm. When a BGP session with a peer that has advertised a large number of prefixes terminates, significant route recomputation and announcements may occur while the routers involved reconverge.

In recognition of the dangers of blind attacks on infrastructure TCP stacks, several mechanisms have been developed to protect TCP sessions. First, the generalized TTL mechanism (GTSM) [15] only accepts packets with a TTL of 255 (the maximum value), such that any packets not on the local subnetwork will arrive with a lower TTL and will not be accepted. While GTSM works for point-to-point eBGP sessions, it does not generalize. Second, TCP MD5 [16] and TCP-AO [37] options provide cryptographic authentication. Unfortunately, these strong authentication mechanisms require configuration of a shared secret, a manual and complex process that can discourage use. Finally, best common practices [12] dictate filtering of control plane messages via access control lists that admit only traffic from trusted networks. However, attackers able to employ IP source address spoofing [7] can circumvent such filtering.

5.1 Testing infrastructure stacks

Because routers and switches frequently use specialized operating systems, we sought to better understand the behavior of these non-commodity TCP stacks. We chose not to probe BGP or OpenFlow devices in the wild for several reasons. First, we did not want our probing to be perceived as an active attack by operators. In private discussions with a network operator, we were strongly discouraged from attempting to probe BGP routers in the wild. Second, many BGP routers employ source address filtering, yet may still be vulnerable to spoofed-source attacks, which we did not want to mount.

Device	OS date	Blind reset in	Blind reset out	Blind SYN in	Blind SYN out	Blind data behind	Blind data ahead	Port range
Cisco 2610 12.1(13)	2002-01	× (A)	✓ (I)	× (R)	✓ (C)	× (A)	✓ (C)	seq.
Cisco 2610 12.2(7)	2002-01	× (A)	✓ (I)	× (R)	✓ (C)	× (A)	✓ (C)	seq.
Cisco 2650 12.3(15b)	2005-08	✓ (C)	✓ (I)	✓ (C)	✓ (C)	× (A)	✓ (C)	40785
Cisco 7206 12.4(20)	2008-07	✓ (C)	✓ (I)	✓ (C)	✓ (C)	× (A)	✓ (C)	54167
Cisco 2811 15.0(1)	2010-10	✓ (C)	✓ (I)	✓ (C)	✓ (C)	× (A)	✓ (C)	46166
Cisco 2911 15.1(4)	2012-03	✓ (C)	✓ (I)	✓ (C)	✓ (C)	× (A)	✓ (C)	39422
Juniper M7i 8.2R1.7	2007-01	× (A)	✓ (I)	× (R)	✓ (I)	× (A)	✓ (C)	181
Juniper EX9208 14.1R1.10	2014-06	✓ (C)	✓ (I)	✓ (C)	✓ (I)	× (A)	✓ (C)	13769
Juniper MX960 13.3	2015-05	✓ (I)	✓ (I)	✓ (C)	✓ (I)	× (A)	✓ (C)	13033
Juniper J2350 12.1X46-D35.1	2015-05	✓ (I)	✓ (I)	✓ (C)	✓ (I)	× (A)	✓ (C)	12481
HP 2920 WB.15.16.0006	2015-01	✓ (C)	✓ (C)	✓ (C)	✓ (C)	✓ (I)	✓ (I)	14273
HP e3500 K.15.16.0007	2015-06	× (A)	✓ (I)	× (R)	✓ (C)	✓ (I)	✓ (I)	15611
Brocade MLX-4 5.7.0bT177	2014-10	✓ (I)	✓ (I)	✓ (C)	✓ (C)	✓ (C)	✓ (C)	const.
Pica8 Pronto3290 v2.6	2015-05	× (A)	✓ (I)	× (R)	✓ (C)	× (A)	× (A)	HBPS

Table 7: Laboratory testing of blind TCP attacks against BGP-speaking router and OpenFlow-speaking switches. A cross-mark means the TCP connection accepted (A) or reset (R) in response to the packet that it should have rejected. A tick-mark means the TCP connection challenged (C) or ignored (I) the packet. The port range is reported from ten ephemeral port selections made by the device. Over time, implementations have generally become more resilient to blind reset and SYN attacks, but not to blind data attacks.

We therefore used our oracle approach on a variety of routers and switches available to us in a controlled laboratory environment. To perform this testing, we added a basic BGP application protocol [33] to scamper that sends a valid BGP OPEN message with the correct autonomous system number and no BGP options. We ensured that the BGP keepalive time was large enough so that the router under test did not prematurely terminate the TCP connection during testing. Similarly, we implemented the basic OpenFlow application protocol by sending an OpenFlow HELLO message. We further explicitly configured each device we tested to recognize our prober as a peer so that it would establish a BGP or OpenFlow session, allowing the prober to test the underlying TCP behavior. Concurrent to our probing, we captured packets from the device under test so that we could assess the device's choice of ephemeral ports from ten port selections, as we explain in the appendix.

Table 7 shows that while the overall protection mechanisms within Cisco devices improved across subsequent releases of the operating system, even versions released post RFC 5961 exhibit weakness to the blind in-window data attack. In fact, only 2 of 14 devices we tested were not vulnerable to any of the blind attacks tested (the HP 2920 and the Brocade MLX-4 switches). All of the Cisco and Juniper devices we tested accepted the data with an acknowledgment number behind the range recommended by RFC 5961.

Relatively obsolete operating systems (Cisco 12.1, 12.2, Juniper 8.2) used sequential or a small range of ephemeral ports, making these more predictable. While modern Cisco devices used a much wider ephemeral port range, modern Juniper and HP systems drew from a 16k range.

All systems we tested correctly ignored or challenged reset and SYN packets that were out of window, and all but one (the Pica8 switch) correctly rejected the data that used an acknowledgment value ahead of the sender's send window. The Pica8 OpenFlow switch was built on a Linux 2.6.27 kernel and selected ephemeral ports using a hash-based ephemeral port selection (HBPS) algorithm, but was vulnerable to four of the six tests.

5.2 Implications

Most devices we tested correctly ignored SYN and reset packets that could have come from a blind attacker, but few rejected data with a behind-window acknowledgment value. We encourage operators to remain vigilant in deploying available defense mechanisms such as GTSM [15] and TCP authentication options [16, 37] to ensure the security of their infrastructure, as well as ingress filter packets with a source address purporting to be from their infrastructure but arriving from outside of their network [4, 12].

6. PORT SELECTION OBSERVATIONS

Finally, we used passive network traces to infer current ephemeral port selection algorithms in deployed TCP stacks. Our goal was to understand the current degree to which TCP endpoints use an ephemeral port selection algorithm that is predictable, i.e. selecting ports in sequence using a central counter; as discussed in section 2.2, a predictable port selection algorithm can make a blind attacker's job easier. However, gaining an accurate picture of the deployment of port selection algorithms using passive data is difficult for a number of reasons. Figure 7 summarizes the two largest challenges. First, multiple devices may share a single global IP address if they are behind a router that does network address translation. In figure 7, hosts X and Y are selecting ephemeral port values sequentially in the range 1024–5000; X selects 1050 at time T-1, and Y selects 1030 at time T-2. Because these devices are behind a NAT device that rewrites their source IP addresses, the port sequence observed begins 1050, 1030, i.e. goes backwards and therefore although not predictable is not random.

Second, consider a passive tap at the edge of a network. If we include the internal population of the edge network, then we risk observing trends that do not hold in the general population. However, if we use only the external population who establish TCP connections to the internal population, we can only observe an unknown fraction of the TCP connections that each external host establishes. In figure 7, the passive tap does not observe connections from Y using

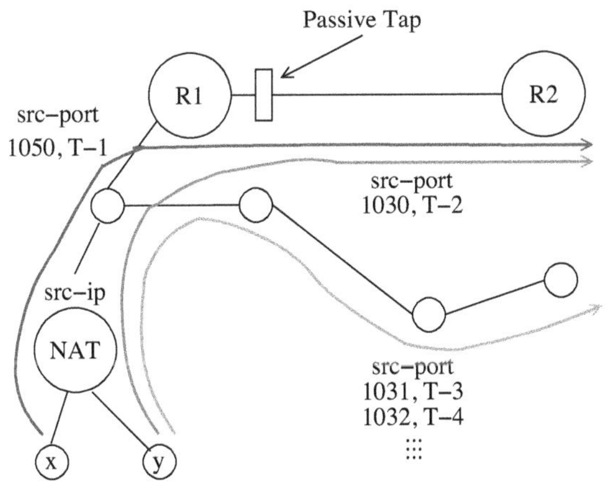

Figure 7: Challenges in using passive data to infer port selection algorithms. A passive tap topologically distant from the sources it measures observes an unknown fraction of the TCP connections established by hosts X and Y. Further, X and Y might use a predictable ephemeral ports assignment scheme, but be behind a NAT that rewrites the source address, which makes the predictable assignments indistinguishable from a hash-based counter.

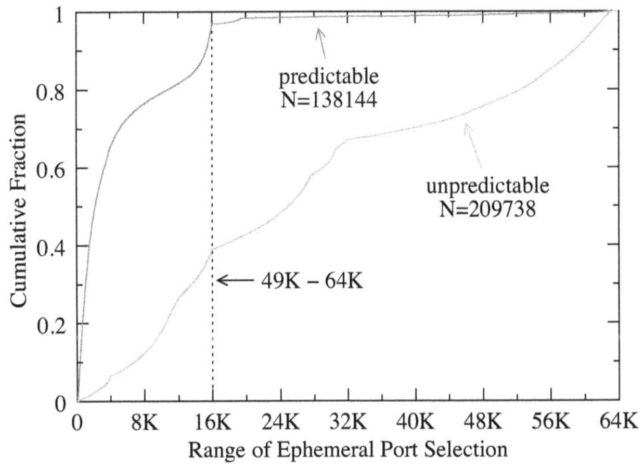

Figure 8: Range of ports observed (max - min) for one hour packet trace collected on 19th March 2015 at 1pm UTC from a Tier-1 ISP link between Chicago and Seattle. We observed that most port selections used a fraction of the available port space, especially the predictable port selections, where 50% of selections were in a range of 2K ports.

source ports 1031, 1032, and so on. If the passive tap later observes a connection established by Y, there may be a large gap in the source port values chosen by Y.

Third, Linux hosts use a simple hash-based port selection technique to generate ephemeral ports, so the sequence of ephemeral port values chosen by Linux systems may appear predictable, yet an attacker would have to know the randomly-generated secret the system uses to select ephemeral port values to any given destination. To address this concern, we only considered a source if we observed it establishing connections to multiple destinations.

In this section, we consider two sources of passive data: (1) a passive tap operated by CAIDA on a Tier-1 ISP's backbone link between Chicago and Seattle, which periodically records 1-hour packet header traces, and (2) longitudinal data recorded by a Bro intrusion detection system (IDS) instance at ICSI containing logs of TCP flows since 2005.

6.1 Equinix Chicago Passive Header Trace

CAIDA operates a passive monitor located at Equinix Chicago, which since 2008 has captured a one-hour packet header trace per-month from a Tier-1 ISP's 10Gig Ethernet backbone link between Chicago and Seattle (there was an 18-month outage due to hardware failure from September 2011 to March 2013). From these files, we extracted ephemeral ports with the following algorithm.

For each SYN packet, we created a 4-tuple containing the source (the active opener) and destination IP addresses and ports, as well as a flag that records if the flow carried data. After two minutes had elapsed in the trace, we discarded the flow to allow for 4-tuple reuse. At this point we included the flow for further processing if we observed data transmission and discarded it if no data was observed (i.e. the SYN was a result of a scan or other anomalous behavior). Finally, we grouped the 4-tuples by source IP address, and only considered sources that established at least ten TCP connections.

For each active opener, we classified the sequence of ports as predictable (derived from a central counter) by consulting a sliding windows of 3 ports at a time. We used windows of 3 ports at a time because these are the shortest window for which we can test for an unpredictable sequence. We deemed a single window to be "predictable" when ephemeral ports were generally increasing – with the possibility of a single wrap per window. For example, if we observed the ports [1, 2, 3], [2, 3, 1], or [3, 1, 2], then we would infer the use of a counter, but if we observed [2, 1, 3], [3, 2, 1] or [1, 3, 2] then we would infer the ports were selected unpredictably. Note that this method would have incorrectly inferred some busy active openers as unpredictable if we only observed a fraction of their SYNs on the Chicago-Seattle link. We also allowed for a small amount of packet reordering and SYN loss: enough to allow for the first retransmission of a SYN which was previously lost before the SYN could have crossed the link where we collected the passive header trace. Specifically, if the difference between two port values was less than 15 (a nominal value which is 0.4% of the smallest ephemeral range in the operating systems listed in table 1) and the difference in time was less than three seconds – then we assumed the port values were generated in order and the out-of-order observation was an artifact introduced by the network. For a source IP address with 10 port observations, we tested 8 windows; we inferred the address as generating a predictable ephemeral port sequence if all windows were inferred to be predictable.

Figure 8 shows the observed range (maximum - minimum) of ephemeral ports for each source that established at least 10 connections over this link over the course of an hour on 19 March 2015 to at least two destinations. As shown in the appendix, the expected port range given a host selecting ephemeral ports at random from the entire 2^{16} space given 10 observations is approximately 53,620. Of the hosts we inferred to select predictable ephemeral ports, 50% established all ports within a 2K port range – 3% of the total range of

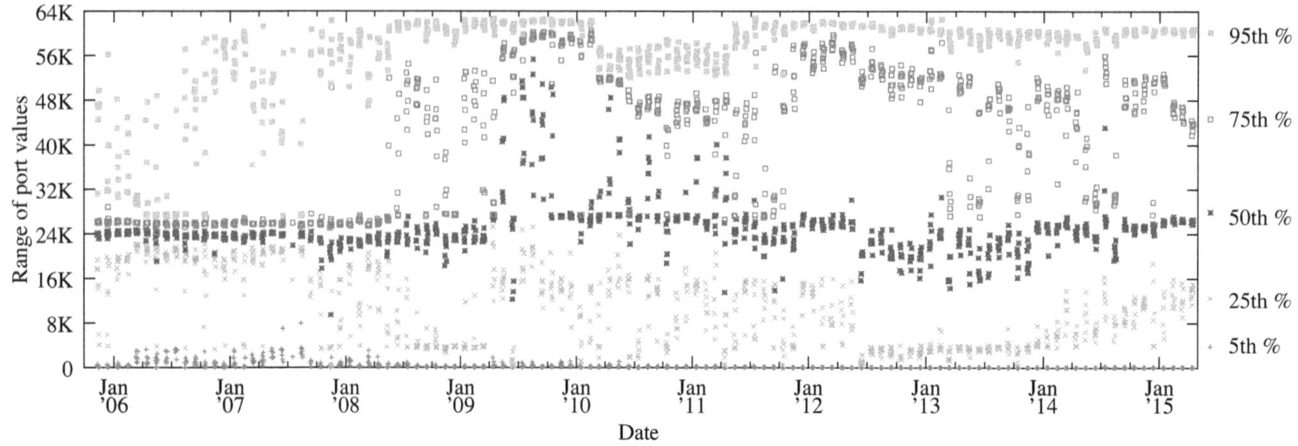

Figure 9: Range of ports observed (max - min) for one day of Bro logs collected one week per month since October 2005 at ICSI. The points represent the 5th, 25th, 50th, 75th, and 95th percentiles for one day's traffic within each week. Beginning January 2014, the range of ports selected for the 25th percentile has begun to widen.

port values potentially available, and 12% of the ephemeral port range recommended by IANA. Of the hosts we inferred to use an unpredictable strategy, a third chose ports from at least a range of 32K ports; a blind attacker would have to use other sophisticated means to infer port selection behavior of these hosts [14]. These results are consistent with the known port selection strategies of modern operating systems shown in table 1. We conclude that some operating system vendors continue to not follow best practices in ephemeral port selection [23].

6.2 Longitudinal ICSI Trace

Finally, we investigated longitudinal patterns in port selection using Bro logs collected at ICSI. We focused on inbound connections from external hosts, from sources that established at least 10 data-carrying TCP connections to internal hosts. Because of the sparsity of the data over the course of a day, rather than try to infer whether or not port selection is predictable or not, we instead focused on the ranges observed to have been used by individual IP addresses. Figure 9 plots the ranges of ports selected from October 2005 until May 2015. While the data is noisy, we can see two encouraging shifts in port selection behavior. First, between January 2006 and January 2008, the 95th percentile range rose from 32K to 62K, suggesting that systems were gradually upgraded to choose ephemeral ports from a larger range. Second, between October 2013 and May 2015, the 25th percentile of port ranges gradually increases from 4K to 12K, suggesting a different set of systems were gradually upgraded to choose ephemeral port ranges from a larger range. We conjecture this trend is due to the well-publicized end-of-life date for Windows XP systems, which chose port values between 1024–5000 (see table 1).

6.3 Implications

Beyond these trends, it is difficult to distill insight on port selection algorithms from either passive data source (CAIDA or ICSI) owing to many conflating factors. However, our experimental data indicates that as of March 2015 that most operating systems are choosing ports from a small fraction of the ephemeral port ranges (figure 8) which is consistent with MacOS and Windows operating systems choosing TCP ephemeral ports sequentially (table 1).

7. DISCUSSION

Holistically, the ability of an attacker to mount a blind attack is more difficult than it was 2004, as there has been some deployment of RFC 5961 into TCP stacks, and operating systems have been upgraded over time. In addition, some operating systems are using automatic TCP buffer tuning [35, 34] to increase the receive window as required, and using small receive windows by default (figure 5). Nevertheless, we found a surprising fraction of webservers acted inappropriately when they received a packet that could have come from a blind attacker. In particular, defenses to blind attackers forging data packets are less deployed than defenses to reset and SYN packets, suggesting further implementation and deployment effort is required. For example, middleboxes that correctly challenged reset and SYN packets did not discard invalid data packets (section 4.3.2). In addition, some popular operating systems (Windows and MacOS) are choosing ephemeral ports from a 16K range in a predictable fashion, allowing a blind attacker to optimize their efforts in relatively narrow port ranges.

8. RELATED WORK

Previous active measurement of TCP has focused on the deployment and behavior of features that improve the performance of TCP, such as algorithms used for congestion control and slow-start [29, 28]. In addition, there has been particular focus on the role that middleboxes play in hampering deployment and use of TCP features (e.g. [27, 25, 5, 17, 11]). Our work focuses on active measurement of TCP features that enhance TCP's resilience to blind attack.

More recently, researchers have shown it is possible for unprivileged malware deployed on a victim's computer to learn information that can help an otherwise blind attacker to focus their efforts [31], or even by visiting a malicious website that uses a script to predict TCP parameters, including source port values in the face of simple hash-based port selection algorithms [14]. While dangerous and similar to the attack we investigated, arguably the attackers in these cases are not completely blind, which aids the attacker. Our work holistically examines the state of TCP vulnerability to blind attackers, in terms of TCP implementation, port selection, and middlebox protections.

Convery and Franz examined the behavior of BGP speaking routers in the wild in 2003 [9]. They encouraged operators to deploy ingress filtering for router address space to make blind attacks impossible from outside of the network, and reported TCP enhancements (choosing ephemeral ports unpredictably, and requiring the reset to exactly match the receiver's position in the sequence number space) made TCP highly resistant to attacks. Our work examined the degree to which TCP enhancements that make blind attacks difficult have been deployed.

9. CONCLUSION

TCP is the most important transport protocol in the Internet, carrying the vast majority of the traffic volume on the Internet, including web browsing, streaming video (e.g., YouTube and Netflix), email, and BGP. Because of its importance, researchers and vendors are constantly developing and deploying features to improve the security and performance of TCP. However, for at least three reasons, little is empirically known about the current state of TCP deployment: TCP features have evolved over time, there are many vendors of operating systems and middleboxes, and there is no dedicated instrumentation or sustained effort to gather longitudinal measurements on the deployed ecosystem.

Complicating the situation is the fact that TCP was implemented with limited security functionality, and although several RFCs have recommended modifications to improve the security defenses of TCP, the adoption, configuration, and deployment of fielded TCP improvements can be slow. In this study we empirically assessed the resilience of *deployed* commodity TCP implementations to blind in-window attacks, where an off-path adversary can disrupt an established connection, causing data corruption or connection reset. We also characterized router and switch behavior – critical infrastructure where the impact of any TCP vulnerabilities is particularly acute. We tested operating systems (and middleboxes deployed in front) of webservers in the wild and found 22% of connections vulnerable to in-window SYN and reset packets, 30% vulnerable to in-window data packets, and 38.4% vulnerable to at least one of the three in-window attacks we tested. This surprisingly high level of extant vulnerabilities we found in the most mature Internet transport protocol in use today is a perfect illustration of the Internet's fragility. Given the largely unregulated and insecure TCP/IP network architecture society relies on for most of our communications, it also provides a strong case for more systematic, scientific, and longitudinal measurement and quantitative analysis of fundamental properties of critical Internet infrastructure, as well as for the importance of better mechanisms to get best security practices deployed.

Acknowledgments

We thank the UCSD systems and networking research group for early feedback. Special thanks to John Gibson, Tom Hutton, Bill Owens, and Brad Cowie for providing operational routers to test against. This work was supported in part by U.S. NSF grants CNS-1111449, ACI-1127506, and CNS-1237265, and by DHS S&T Cyber Security Division BAA 11-02 and SPAWAR Systems Center Pacific via N66001-12-C-0130 and Defence Research and Development Canada (DRDC) pursuant to an Agreement between the U.S. and Canadian governments for Cooperation in Science and Technology for Critical Infrastructure Protection and Border Security. This work represents the position of the authors and not of NSF, DHS, DRDC, or the U.S. government. Matthew Luckie conducted this work while at CAIDA, UC San Diego.

Appendix

In our analysis of ephemeral ports, we restricted our analysis to only those sources that established 10 or more connections and reported on the ephemeral port range. For the set of observed ephemeral ports $S = \{\}$, we compute $range = max(S) - min(S)$. In this appendix, we derive the expected value of *range* given a source that chooses ports from a uniform random distribution over the interval $(0, high)$. (The following trivially extends to a non-zero starting port range; we omit this detail for clarity). Given n flows from a source, the probability that the largest port observed is k is given by:

$$P\left(max(S) = k\right) = \frac{k^n - (k-1)^n}{high^n}$$

while the probability that the smallest port observed is k is:

$$P(min(S) = k) = P(max(S) = high - k)$$

Thus, the expected range is:

$$\begin{aligned} E[range] &= E[max(S)] - E[min(S)] \\ &= \sum_{k=1}^{high} k\Big(P\big(max(S) = k\big) - P\big(min(S) = k\big)\Big) \end{aligned}$$

For $n = 10$, we find (corresponding to ranges of ephemeral port numbers of operating systems in Table 1):

$$\begin{aligned} E[range|high = 2^{16}] &\simeq 53620 \\ E[range|high = 3976] &\simeq 3253 \\ E[range|high = 16384] &\simeq 13404 \\ E[range|high = 28232] &\simeq 23098 \\ E[range|high = 55535] &\simeq 45438 \end{aligned}$$

10. REFERENCES

[1] FreeBSD-SA-14:19.tcp: Denial of service in TCP packet processing. https://www.freebsd.org/security/advisories/FreeBSD-SA-14:19.tcp.asc.

[2] Alexa. Top 1,000,000 sites. http://www.alexa.com/topsites.

[3] M. Allman. Comments on selecting ephemeral ports. *ACM SIGCOMM Computer Communication Review*, 39(2):14–19, 2009.

[4] F. Baker and P. Savola. Ingress filtering for multihomed networks. RFC 3704, Mar. 2004.

[5] S. Bauer, R. Beverly, and A. Berger. Measuring the state of ECN readiness in servers, clients, and routers. In *IMC*, Nov. 2011.

[6] S. Bellovin. Defending against sequence number attacks. RFC 1948, May 1996.

[7] R. Beverly, A. Berger, Y. Hyun, and k claffy. Understanding the efficacy of deployed Internet source address validation. In *IMC*, pages 356–369, Nov. 2009.

[8] Cisco. TCP Vulnerabilities in Multiple IOS-Based Cisco Products, 2004. http://tools.cisco.com/security/center/content/CiscoSecurityAdvisory/cisco-sa-20040420-tcp-ios.

[9] S. Convery and M. Franz. BGP vulnerability testing: separating fact from FUD. In *Blackhat*, 2003.

[10] M. Cotton, L. Eggert, J. Touch, M. Westerlund, and S. Cheshire. Internet assigned numbers authority (IANA) procedures for the management of the service name and transport protocol port number registry. RFC 6335, Aug. 2011.

[11] R. Craven, R. Beverly, and M. Allman. A middlebox-cooperative TCP for a non end-to-end Internet. In *SIGCOMM*, pages 151–162, 2014.

[12] J. Durand, I. Pepelnjak, and G. Doering. BGP Operations and Security. RFC 7454 (Best Current Practice), Feb. 2015.

[13] P. Ferguson and D. Senie. Network ingress filtering: Defeating denial of service attacks which employ IP source address spoofing. RFC 2827, May 2000.

[14] Y. Gilad and A. Herzberg. Off-path TCP injection attacks. *ACM Transactions on Information and System Security*, 16(4), Apr. 2014.

[15] V. Gill, J. Heasley, D. Meyer, and P. Savola. The generalized TTL security mechanism (GTSM). RFC 5082, Oct. 2007.

[16] A. Heffernan. Protection of BGP sessions via the TCP MD5 signature option. RFC 2385, Aug. 1998.

[17] B. Hesmans, F. Duchene, C. Paasch, G. Detal, and O. Bonaventure. Are TCP extensions middlebox-proof? In *HotMiddlebox*, pages 37–42, 2013.

[18] Y. Hyun and k. claffy. Archipelago measurement infrastructure, 2015. http://www.caida.org/projects/ark/.

[19] Internet Assigned Numbers Authority (IANA). Service name and transport protocol port number registry. http://www.iana.org/assignments/port-numbers.

[20] V. Jacobson, R. Braden, D. Borman, and R. Scheffenegger. TCP Extensions for High Performance. RFC 7323, Sept. 2014.

[21] D. Kaminsky. Black Ops 2008: It's the end of the cache as we know it. *Black Hat USA*, 2008.

[22] S. Kent. IP authentication header. RFC 4302, Dec. 2005.

[23] M. Larsen and F. Gont. Recommendations for transport-protocol port randomization. RFC 6056, Jan. 2011.

[24] M. Luckie. Scamper: a scalable and extensible packet prober for active measurement of the Internet. In *IMC*, pages 239–245, Nov. 2010.

[25] M. Luckie and B. Stasiewicz. Measuring path MTU discovery behaviour. In *IMC*, pages 102–108, Nov. 2010.

[26] M. Mathis, J. Mahdavi, S. Floyd, and A. Romanow. TCP selective acknowledgment options. RFC 2018, Oct. 1996.

[27] A. Medina, M. Allman, and S. Floyd. Measuring interactions between transport protocols and middleboxes. In *IMC*, pages 336–341, Oct. 2004.

[28] A. Medina, M. Allman, and S. Floyd. Measuring the evolution of transport protocols in the Internet. *ACM SIGCOMM Computer Communication Review*, 35(2):37–52, 2005.

[29] J. Pahdye and S. Floyd. On inferring TCP behavior. In *SIGCOMM*, pages 287–298, 2001.

[30] J. Postel. Transmission control protocol. RFC 791, Sept. 1981.

[31] Z. Qian and Z. M. Mao. Off-path TCP sequence number inference attack: How firewall middleboxes reduce security. In *IEEE Symposium on Security and Privacy*, pages 347–361, May 2012.

[32] A. Ramaiah, R. Stewart, and M. Dalal. Improving TCP's robustness to blind in-window attacks. RFC 5961, Aug. 2010.

[33] Y. Rekhter, T. Li, and S. Hares. A Border Gateway Protocol 4 (BGP-4). RFC 4271 (Draft Standard), Jan. 2006.

[34] M. Sargent and M. Allman. Performance within a fiber-to-the-home network. *ACM SIGCOMM Computer Communication Review*, 44(3), July 2014.

[35] J. Semke, J. Mahdavi, and M. Mathis. Automatic TCP buffer tuning. In *SIGCOMM*, pages 315–323, Sept. 1998.

[36] J. Touch. Defending TCP against spoofing attacks. RFC 4953, July 2007.

[37] J. Touch, A. Mankin, and R. Bonica. The TCP authentication option. RFC 5925, June 2010.

[38] P. Watson. Slipping in the window: TCP reset attacks, Apr. 2004.

[39] M. Zalewski. p0f v3 (version 3.08b). http://lcamtuf.coredump.cx/p0f3/.

[40] M. Zalewski. Strange attractors and TCP/IP sequence number analysis, 2002.

Neither Snow Nor Rain Nor MITM . . . An Empirical Analysis of Email Delivery Security

Zakir Durumeric[†] David Adrian[†] Ariana Mirian[†] James Kasten[†] Elie Bursztein[‡]
Nicolas Lidzborski[‡] Kurt Thomas[‡] Vijay Eranti[‡] Michael Bailey[§] J. Alex Halderman[†]
[†] University of Michigan [‡] Google, Inc. [§] University of Illinois, Urbana Champaign
{zakir, davadria, amirian, jdkasten, jhalderm}@umich.edu
{elieb, nlidz, kurtthomas, vijaye}@google.com
mdbailey@illinois.edu

ABSTRACT

The SMTP protocol is responsible for carrying some of users' most intimate communication, but like other Internet protocols, authentication and confidentiality were added only as an afterthought. In this work, we present the first report on global adoption rates of SMTP security extensions, including: STARTTLS, SPF, DKIM, and DMARC. We present data from two perspectives: SMTP server configurations for the Alexa Top Million domains, and over a year of SMTP connections to and from Gmail. We find that the top mail providers (e.g., Gmail, Yahoo, and Outlook) all proactively encrypt and authenticate messages. However, these best practices have yet to reach widespread adoption in a long tail of over 700,000 SMTP servers, of which only 35% successfully configure encryption, and 1.1% specify a DMARC authentication policy. This security patchwork—paired with SMTP policies that favor failing open to allow gradual deployment—exposes users to attackers who downgrade TLS connections in favor of cleartext and who falsify MX records to reroute messages. We present evidence of such attacks in the wild, highlighting seven countries where more than 20% of inbound Gmail messages arrive in cleartext due to network attackers.

Keywords

SMTP, Email, Mail, TLS, STARTTLS, DKIM, SPF, DMARC

1. INTRODUCTION

Electronic mail carries some of a user's most sensitive communication, including private correspondence, financial details, and password recovery confirmations that can be used to gain access to other critical resources. Users expect that messages are private and unforgeable. However, as originally conceived, SMTP—the protocol responsible for relaying messages between mail servers—does not authenticate senders or encrypt mail in transit. Instead, servers support these features through protocol extensions such as STARTTLS, SPF, DKIM, and DMARC. The impetus for mail servers to adopt these features is entirely voluntary. As a consequence, gradual rollout has led to a fractured landscape where mail servers must tolerate unprotected communication at the expense of user security. Equally problematic, users face a medium that fails to alert clients when messages traverse an insecure path and that lacks a mechanism to enforce strict transport security.

In this work, we measure the global adoption of SMTP security extensions and the resulting impact on end users. Our study draws from two unique perspectives: longitudinal SMTP connection logs spanning from January 2014 to April 2015 for Gmail, one of the world's largest mail providers; and a snapshot of SMTP server configurations from April 2015 for the Alexa Top Million domains. We use both perspectives to estimate the volume of messages and mail servers that support encryption and authentication, identify mail server configuration pitfalls that weaken security guarantees, and ultimately expose threats introduced by lax security policies that enable wide-scale surveillance and message forgery.

From Gmail's perspective, incoming messages protected by TLS have increased 82% over the last year, peaking at 60% of all inbound mail in April 2015. Outgoing messages similarly grew by 54%, with 80% of messages protected at the conclusion of our study in April. This improvement was largely fueled by a small number of popular web mail providers, including Yahoo and Outlook, enabling security features mid-year. However, such best practices continue to lag for the long tail of 700,000 SMTP servers associated with the Alexa Top Million: only 82% support TLS, of which a mere 35% are properly configured to allow server authentication. We argue that low adoption stems in part from two of the three most popular SMTP software platforms failing to protect messages with TLS by default.

A similar split-picture emerges for the adoption of technologies such as SPF, DKIM, and DMARC that authenticate senders and guard against message spoofing. In terms of sheer volume, during April 2015, Gmail was able to validate 94% of inbound messages using a combination of DKIM (83%) and SPF (92%). However, among the Alexa Top Million mail servers, only 47% deploy SPF policies and only 1% provide a DMARC policy, the absence of which leaves recipients unsure whether an unsigned message is invalid or expected. When mail servers specify SPF policies, 29% are overly broad (covering tens of thousands of addresses.)

This security patchwork—paired with opportunistic encryption that favors failing open and transmitting messages in cleartext, so as to allow incremental adoption—enables network attackers to intercept and surveil mail. In one such attack, network appliances corrupt STARTTLS connection attempts and downgrade messages to non-encrypted channels. We identify 41,405 SMTP servers in 4,714 ASes and 193 countries that cannot protect mail from passive eavesdroppers due to STARTTLS corruption on the network. We analyze the mail sent to Gmail from these hosts and find that in seven countries, more than 20% of all messages are actively prevented

IMC'15, October 28–30, 2015, Tokyo, Japan.
ACM 978-1-4503-3848-6/15/10.
DOI: http://dx.doi.org/10.1145/2815675.2815695.

from being encrypted. In the most severe case, 96% of messages sent from Tunisia to Gmail are downgraded to cleartext.

In the second attack, DNS servers provide fraudulent MX records for the SMTP servers of common mail providers. We searched for DNS servers that provide fraudulent addresses for Gmail's SMTP servers, and we find 14,600 publicly accessible DNS servers in 521 ASes and 69 countries. We investigate the messages that Gmail received from these hosts and find that in 193 countries more than 0.01% of messages from each country are transited through these impostor hosts. In the largest case, 0.08% of messages from Slovakia are relayed from a falsified IP, which can intercept or alter their contents.

Drawing on our measurements, we discuss various challenges and attacks, present current proposals for securing mail transport, and propose directions for future research. We hope that our findings can both motivate and inform further work to improve the state of mail security.

2. BACKGROUND

Simple Mail Transfer Protocol (SMTP) is the Internet standard for sending and relaying email [34,40]. Figure 1 illustrates a simplified scenario: a client sends mail by transmitting it to its local outgoing SMTP server, which relays each message to the incoming SMTP server for the recipient's domain. In practice, mail forwarding, mailing lists, and other complications result in messages traversing multiple SMTP relays before arriving at their final destination.

As originally conceived in 1981, SMTP did not support protecting the confidentiality of messages in transit or authenticating messages upon receipt. Due to these shortcomings, passive observers can read message content on the wire, and active attackers can additionally alter or spoof messages. To address this gap in security, the mail community developed protocol extensions, such as STARTTLS, DKIM, DMARC, and SPF, to encrypt message content and authenticate senders.

2.1 Protecting Messages in Transit

STARTTLS is an SMTP extension introduced in 2002 that encapsulates SMTP within a TLS session [28]. In a typical STARTTLS session, a client first negotiates an SMTP connection with the server, after which the client sends the command `STARTTLS`, which initiates a standard TLS handshake. The client then transmits mail content, attachments, and any associated metadata over this cryptographically protected channel.

STARTTLS aims to protect the individual hops between SMTP servers, primarily protecting messages from passive eavesdroppers. As we will discuss in Section 4, STARTTLS is typically not used to authenticate destination mail servers, but rather provides opportunistic encryption. (This differs from the behavior of HTTPS clients, which strictly require TLS.) In almost all cases, mail servers do not validate presented certificates and will relay messages over cleartext if STARTTLS is not supported. Because STARTTLS only protects hops between individual relays, each relay still has access to messages and can freely read and modify message content.

The STARTTLS RFC [28] does not define how clients should validate presented certificates. While it suggests that the recipient's domain (e.g., `gmail.com`) should be present in the certificate, it also permits checking the fully qualified domain name (FQDN) of the MX server. This removes the need for third-party mail servers (e.g., shared hosting like Google Apps for Work) to present a trusted certificate for each hosted domain. However, it also enables network-level attackers to falsely report MX records that point to an attacker-controlled domain. Without additional security add-ons (e.g., DANE [14]), this attack remains a real threat.

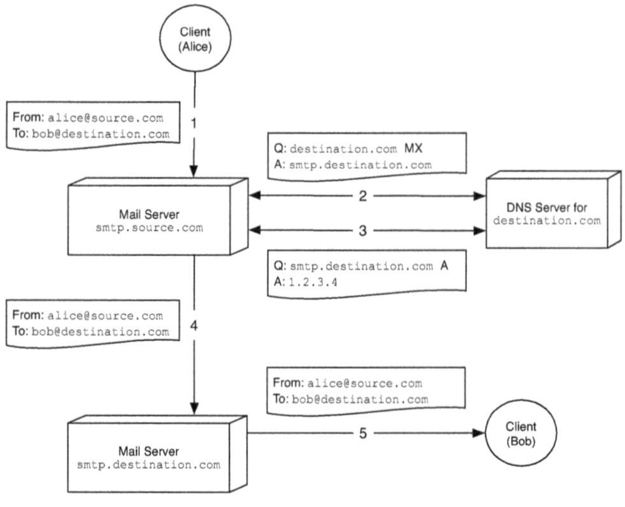

Figure 1: **SMTP Protocol**—A client sends outgoing mail by connecting to its organization's local SMTP server (❶). The local server performs a DNS lookup for the mail exchange (`MX`) record of the *destination.com* domain, which contains the hostname of the destination's SMTP server, in this case *smtp.destination.com* (❷). The sender's server then performs a second DNS lookup for the destination server's IP address (❸), establishes a connection, and relays the message (❹). The recipient can later retrieve the message using a secondary protocol such as POP3 or IMAP (❺).

2.2 Authenticating Mail

Mail servers deploy several complementary mechanisms for authenticating and verifying the integrity of received mail. While STARTTLS protects individual hops between servers, these additional protocols allow recipients to verify that messages have not been spoofed or modified, and they provide a mechanism to report forged messages. A more detailed discussion of each protocol and its limitations is available from MAAWG [12]. We depict the interplay between these mechanisms in Figure 2.

DKIM DomainKeys Identified Mail (DKIM) lets SMTP servers detect whether a received message has been spoofed or modified during transit (RFC 6376 [11]). To utilize DKIM, a sender appends the `DKIM-Signature` field to the message header. This header contains a digital signature of the message signed with the private key tied to the sender's domain. Upon delivery, the recipient can retrieve the sender's public key through a DNS request and verify the message's signature. DKIM does not specify what action the recipient should take if it receives a message with an invalid or missing cryptographic signature. Instead, the organization must have a predetermined agreement with the sender.

SPF Sender Policy Framework (SPF) allows an organization to publish a range of hosts that are authorized to send mail for its domain (RFC 7208 [33]). To deploy SPF, the organization publishes a DNS record that specifies which hosts or CIDR blocks belong to the organization. Upon receiving mail, the recipient performs a DNS query to check for an SPF policy and can choose to reject messages that do not originate from the specified servers. SPF further allows organizations to delegate a portion or the entirety of their SPF policy to another organization, and they commonly delegate SPF settings to a cloud provider (e.g., Google Apps for Work.)

DMARC Domain-based Message Authentication, Reporting, and Conformance (DMARC) builds upon DKIM and SPF and allows senders to suggest a policy for authenticating received mail

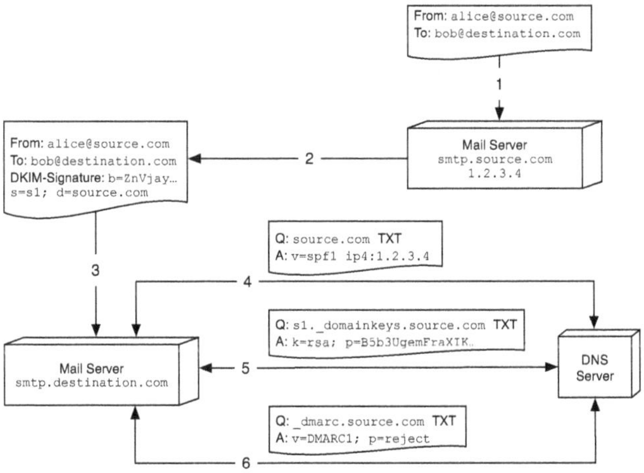

Figure 2: **Mail Authentication**—SPF, DKIM, and DMARC are used to provide source authentication. The outgoing server digitally signs the message (❷). The receiving mail server performs an SPF lookup (❹) to check if the outgoing server is whitelisted, a DKIM lookup (❺) to determine the public key used in the signature, and a DMARC lookup (❻) to determine the correct action should SPF or DKIM validation fail.

(RFC 7489 [35]). Senders publish a DNS TXT record (named `_dmarc.domain.com`) that indicates whether the sender supports mail authentication (i.e., DKIM and/or SPF), and what action recipients should take if authentication fails (e.g., the DKIM signature is missing or invalid). DMARC further allows organizations to request daily reports on spoofed messages that other servers receive.

3. DATASET

Our study is based on two unique datasets: logs of the SMTP handshakes negotiated for mail sent to and from Gmail from January 2014 to April 2015, and a snapshot of SMTP server configurations from April 2015 for the Alexa Top Million domains.

Gmail Inbound and Outbound Messages Google publicly reports statistics about encrypted inbound and outbound messages via its Transparency Report.[1] This dataset explicitly excludes spam messages as not to conflate user security with bulk automated messages. We obtain a companion dataset via a collaboration with Google that contains the set of all ciphers negotiated with external SMTP servers during the same period, as well as any authentication performed on behalf of the sending party. We rely on this dataset for making observations about the volume of mail protected by encryption and authentication. We note that this dataset is noticeably skewed towards a handful of large web mail providers, including Yahoo and Outlook, as well as personal mail accounts provided by local ISPs that relay the bulk of the mail.

Alexa Top Million Mail Servers For a second perspective on organizational support for mail security, we examine the SMTP security features enabled by mail servers belonging to the Alexa Top Million ranked websites [1]. On April 26, 2015, we performed `MX` record lookups for the Alexa Top Million domains. For domains with mail servers, we followed up with a DNS query to identify supported SMTP security extensions (i.e., SPF and DMARC) and attempted an SMTP and STARTTLS handshake using ZMap [16, 19] to identify whether the mail servers support encryption. Our previous work [17, 19] describes our scanning methodology and ethical considerations involved and the practices we use to minimize potential harms.

[1]Data is available at http://www.google.com/transparencyreport/safermail.

Status	Top Million Domains	
No MX records	152,944	(15.29%)
No resolvable MX hostnames	5,447	(0.55%)
No responding SMTP servers	49,125	(4.91%)
SMTP Server	792,494	(79.25%)

Table 1: **Organizational SMTP Deployment**—We investigate how domains in the Alexa Top Million have deployed SMTP.

In total, 792,494 domains (79.2% of the Alexa Top Million) have operational mail servers, as detailed in Table 1. The remaining domains include sites such as `t.co`, `googleusercontent.com`, and `blogspot.com` that do not need incoming mail servers.

4. CONFIDENTIALITY IN PRACTICE

We measure the state of mail confidentiality based on the volume of messages protected by STARTTLS that are sent and received by Gmail, and the fraction of mail servers that support and correctly configure encryption.

4.1 Gmail

As of April 26, 2015, Gmail successfully initiated STARTTLS connections for 80% of outgoing messages, while 60% of incoming connections initiated a STARTTLS session. This represents a 54% increase (52% to 80%) in outbound and an 82% increase (33% to 60%) in inbound connections that utilize STARTTLS since January 2014. While this growth is encouraging, overall gains arrived in bursts rather than consistent growth, as shown in Figure 3. We point out two periods of immediate interest. Between May 10 and 30, 2014, outbound encryption jumped from 47% to 71%. This was likely due to Yahoo and Outlook deploying STARTTLS. Second, between October 8 and 17, outbound STARTTLS dropped from 73% to a low of 50%. The lowest point occurred on October 14, which corresponds with the public disclosure of the POODLE vulnerability [15]. We suspect the correlated drop was a result of mail server misconfigurations introduced by administrators attempting to disable SSLv3.

Influence of Major Mail Providers Major mail providers, such as Gmail, Yahoo, and Outlook, heavily skew the apparent adoption of STARTTLS in contrast to the long tail of organizations that run their own mail servers. Of the 877 most common domains that Gmail transited mail to on April 26, 2015, only 58% accepted 100% of messages over TLS. Similarly, only 29% of 26,406 inbound mail domains encrypted 100% of messages. We explore this skew further in Section 4.2 from the perspective of the Top Million domains.

Along these same lines, we argue that the periodicity present in Figure 3 stems from users sending less business mail on weekends and instead relying on personal accounts provided by major providers. In particular, on weekdays between April 1 and 26, 2015, Gmail encrypted 79.8% of outbound messages, while mail servers encrypted 53.7% of incoming connections. Weekends during this same period saw an average 7.2% increase in the number of secured messages. As we discuss in Section 4.4, major mail providers support encryption by default.

Negotiated Cipher Suites We analyzed the cipher suites chosen by incoming Gmail connections on April 30, 2015, and found that 84.2% of TLS connections (45.2% of all incoming connections) chose a perfect forward secret cipher suite. However, similar to HTTPS, 45.63% of clients continue to prefer RC4 despite its known

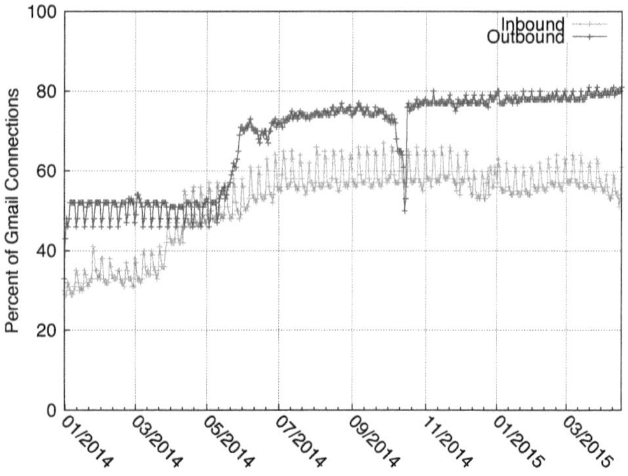

Figure 3: **Historical Gmail STARTTLS Support**—Inbound connections that utilize STARTTLS increased from 33% to 60% for weekdays between January 2014 and April 2015. Weekends consistently have close to 10% more connections that support STARTTLS than weekdays. Support for outgoing STARTTLS increased from 52% to 80% during this period.

TLS Version	Key Exchange	Symmetric Cipher	HMAC	Inbound Traffic
TLSv1.2	ECDHE	AES-128-GCM	SHA-256	51.500%
TLSv1	ECDHE	RC4	SHA-1	29.225%
TLSv1	RSA	RC4	SHA-1	14.403%
TLSv1.2	ECDHE	AES-128	SHA-1	1.586%
TLSv1.2	RSA	RC4	SHA-1	1.147%
TLSv1	ECDHE	AES-128	SHA-1	0.999%
TLSv1.1	ECDHE	RC4	SHA-1	0.723%
TLSv1.2	RSA	AES-128-GCM	SHA-256	0.203%
SSLv3	RSA	RC4	SHA-1	0.060%
TLSv1.2	ECDHE	RC4	SHA-1	0.060%
TLSv1	RSA	AES-128	SHA-1	0.050%
TLSv1.1	RSA	RC4	SHA-1	0.024%
TLSv1.1	ECDHE	AES-128	SHA-1	0.011%
TLSv1.1	ECDHE	AES-256	SHA-1	0.004%
TLSv1.2	RSA	AES-256	SHA-1	0.003%
TLSv1.2	RSA	AES-128	SHA-1	0.001%
TLSv1	RSA	RC4	MD5	0.001%

Table 2: **Cipher Suites for Inbound Gmail Traffic**—80% of inbound Gmail connections are protected by TLS. Here, we present the selected cipher suites for April 30, 2015.

weaknesses [2,45]. For the remaining connections, 95% utilized AES-128-GCM and 5% used AES-128 (Table 2). We note that while this perspective does not show any known-broken ciphers (e.g., EXPORT suites), these may still occur between other mail servers. These do not appear in our dataset because Google does not support these ciphers, and if a client does not support any modern ciphers the TLS handshake will fail.

Comparison With Prior Estimates We compare Gmail's perspective with prior estimates published by Facebook [23]. During May 2014, Facebook—which sends mail notifications for friend requests and new user activity—successfully encrypted 58% of outbound messages. Of the mail servers contacted, 76% supported STARTTLS. By August 2014, Facebook successfully encrypted 95% of outbound notifications after several large webmail providers, notably Microsoft and Yahoo, deployed STARTTLS.

During this same time period, outbound encrypted messages for Gmail increased from 47% to 74%. Despite the same opportunistic STARTTLS policy, we find Gmail generally has a lower percentage of outgoing mail protected by STARTTLS than Facebook. We believe this stems from Facebook primarily communicating with personal mail accounts provided by major providers (e.g., Gmail, Yahoo, and Outlook) as opposed to businesses. We note that our Gmail measurements may have similar but less pronounced biases towards large providers, which we investigate further in the next section.

4.2 Organizational Deployment

Given the skew present in Gmail's message volume towards major mail providers, we provide an alternate perspective by analyzing STARTTLS support for the 792,494 Alexa Top Million domains that advertise mail servers. In total, 648,030 (81.8%) of mail-enabled domains supported STARTTLS, as shown in Table 3. Only 5 domains within the Alexa Top 50 did not: `wikipedia.org`, `vk.com`, `weibo.com`, `yahoo.co.jp`, and `360.cn`. Support for encrypted mail was bolstered in part by 25% of domains outsourcing their mail servers to common third-party providers, such as Gmail, GoDaddy, Yandex, QQ, and OVH, all of which support STARTTLS. We give more details about these providers and their popularity in Table 4.

Key and Cipher Suites With the exception of two mail servers, all present certificates with RSA keys: 10.0% of domains use 1024-bit keys, 86.4% use 2048-bit keys, and 3% use 4096-bit or larger keys. Only 316 domains present 512-bit RSA certificates (which provide little to no security in 2015 [26]). We found 25.3% of domains support perfect forward secrecy and completed an ephemeral Diffie-Hellman key exchange. In addition, 59.2% of domains use RC4 and 40.8% use AES; only 25 domains select 3DES. In summary, most domains that deploy STARTTLS also deploy secure certificates. However, as in the HTTPS ecosystem, domains are slow in deploying modern, secure cipher suites.

Certificate Validity As part of the STARTTLS handshake, each mail server presents an X.509 certificate. While RFC 3207 [28] suggests that certificates match the mail domain (e.g., `gmail.com`), it also permits certificates that only match the name of the server in the domain's MX record (e.g. `aspmx.1.google.com`). However, certificates that match the MX server do not provide true authentication unless the MX records for the domain are cryptographically signed. Otherwise, an active attacker can return the names of alternate, attacker-controlled MX servers in the initial MX query. In practice, DNSSEC has not been widely deployed—recent studies have found that less than 0.6% of `.com` and `.net` domains have deployed DNSSEC [46]—and so operators cannot rely on this protection.

In our scan, 414,374 Top Million domains (52% of domains with valid SMTP servers, and 64% of domains that support STARTTLS) present certificates that validate against the Mozilla NSS root store [38], as detailed in Table 5. However, only 0.6% of domains present trusted certificates that match their domain name, while 34.2% present trusted certificates that match their MX server.

Surprisingly, 18.1% of domains present trusted certificates that match neither. These are primarily due to several mail hosting providers, including `psmtp.com` and `pphosted.com`, that incorrectly deployed wildcard certificates. In the remaining cases, certificates were simply for different domains. Another 33,281 domains present expired certificates, 60 certificates are signed by unknown CAs, and 55 certificates are invalidly signed by a parent certificate whose type mismatched the child certificate.

In summary, the certificates used by mail servers are in disarray. Less than 35% of mail servers with STARTTLS can be authenticated in any form, and a sender can only confirm that their connection had

Status	Top Million Domains	
SMTP Server—No STARTTLS support	144,464	(18.2%)
SMTP Server—STARTTLS support	648,030	(81.8%)

Table 3: **STARTTLS Deployment by Top Million Domains**—Our scan results show that 79% of Alex Top Million domains have incoming SMTP servers, of which 81.8% support STARTTLS.

Mail Provider	Domains	STARTTLS	Trusted Certificate	Certificate Matches
Gmail	126,419 (15.9%)	Yes	Yes	server
GoDaddy	36,229 (4.6%)	Yes	Yes	server
Yandex	12,326 (1.6%)	Yes	Yes	server
QQ	11,295 (1.4%)	Yes	Yes	server
OVH	8,508 (1.1%)	Yes	Yes	mismatch
Other	597,717 (75.4%)	–	–	–

Table 4: **Top Mail Providers for Alexa Top Million Domains**—Five providers are used for mail transport by 25% of the Top Million domains. All five support STARTTLS for incoming mail.

	Matches Domain	Matches Server	Matches Neither
Trusted	4,602 (0.6%)	270,723 (34.2%)	143,113 (18.1%)
Untrusted	4,345 (0.6%)	21,057 (2.7%)	181,242 (22.9%)
Total	8,947 (1.1%)	291,780 (36.8%)	324,355 (41.0%)

Table 5: **Certificates for Top Million Domains**—While 52% of domains' SMTP servers present trusted certificates, only 34.2% of trusted certificates match the MX server, and only 0.6% are valid for the recipient domain.

not been intercepted by an active attacker for 0.6% of domains. This has likely occurred because, as we discuss in the next two sections, common SMTP implementations and popular mail providers do not validate certificates, so server operators have little incentive to purchase and maintain a certificate.

4.3 Common Software Implementations

In order to understand why such a large number of organizations have not deployed STARTTLS and why only half of inbound connections to Gmail initiate a STARTTLS connection, we investigated the five most popular SMTP implementations, which account for 97% of identifiable mail servers for the Top Million domains. We tested whether each implementation initiated STARTTLS connections, whether it supported STARTTLS for incoming connections, and how it validated certificates. We installed the latest version of each SMTP server on an Ubuntu 14.04.1 LTS system, except for Microsoft Exchange, which was readily documented online [37]. The results are summarized in Table 6.

By default, Microsoft Exchange, Exim, and Sendmail initiate STARTTLS connections when delivering messages. Postfix and qmail—which together account for nearly 35% of all identifiable mail servers on the public IPv4 address space—send all messages over cleartext unless explicitly configured to use STARTTLS. All of the servers we tested fail open and send mail in cleartext if STARTTLS is not available.

Postfix and Microsoft Exchange Server support inbound STARTTLS connections by default by generating a self-signed certificate upon installation. This provides immediate protection against passive attacks without user configuration. The remaining servers do not accept TLS connections without manual configuration. Postfix and Exchange—the two servers that have confidentiality protection enabled by default—account for 22% of servers associated with Top Million domains.

Postfix was the only server capable of performing both server-based and domain-based certificate validation, although its documentation specifically recommends *against* enabling validation when interacting with the greater Internet [41]. Exim, qmail, Sendmail, and Microsoft Exchange do not support validating the destination domain when relaying mail.

4.4 Popular Mail Providers

Since a large fraction of mail is transited through a small number of popular providers, a single change can have a large impact on the entire ecosystem, as previously demonstrated in Figure 3. We measured inbound and outbound STARTTLS support for 19 common webmail providers and Internet service providers. We created an account on each provider and then sent mail to a Postfix server that we configured to support STARTTLS with a self-signed certificate. To test incoming STARTTLS support, we connected to the mail servers listed in each domain's MX record and initiated a STARTTLS handshake.

We summarize our results in Table 7. Only one provider, Lycos, did not support inbound STARTTLS. Two providers—facebookmail and OVH—presented certificates that matched neither their domain nor the hostname of their MX server. *None* of the providers presented a certificate that matched their domain, and thus none could have provided strong authentication in the presence of an active attacker who falsified the service's MX records.

Less than half of the providers negotiated a perfect-forward-secret cipher suites. When sending mail, three of the providers—Lycos, GoDaddy, and OVH—did not initiate STARTTLS connections. The remaining providers initiated STARTTLS connections but did not validate certificates; in effect, this provides opportunistic encryption but no authentication.

4.5 Takeaways

Our results show that there has been significant growth in STARTTLS adoption over the past year. However, much of this growth can be attributed to a handful of large providers. In contrast, as seen in our scans, smaller organizations continue to lag in deploying STARTTLS, and as of March 2015 nearly half of inbound weekday connections remain unencrypted. This may be due, in part, to several popular implementations failing to initiate STARTTLS connections by default.

In the cases where encryption is present, messages are protected opportunistically. Connections fail open to cleartext if any issues arise during the handshake or if STARTTLS is not supported. None of the popular providers and implementations we tested use TLS for authentication, and only one common implementation supports validating a certificate against the destination domain.

Unfortunately, in the protocol's current form, mail providers cannot fail closed in the absence of STARTTLS until there is near total deployment of the extension, and until organizations deploy valid certificates, relays will be unable to automatically authenticate destination servers.

5. THREATS TO CONFIDENTIALITY

As deployed in practice, STARTTLS protects connections against passive eavesdroppers but does not protect against active man-in-the-middle attacks. We examine two types of network attacks that this enables—downgrading STARTTLS sessions to insecure channels and falsifying MX records to re-route messages—and measure the prevalence of both methods in the wild.

Mail Software	Top Million Market Share	Public IPv4 Market Share	STARTTLS Incoming	STARTTLS Outgoing	Server Validation	Domain Validation	Reject Invalid Certificates	TLS Version
exim 4.82	34%	24%	◐	●	○	○	○	1.2
Postfix 2.11.0	18%	21%	●	◐	◐	◐	◐	1.2
qmail 1.06	6%	1%	◐	◐	○	○	○	1.2
sendmail 8.14.4	5%	4%	◐	●	○	○	○	1.2
Exchange 2013	4%	12%	●	●	◐	○	◐	1.0
Other	3%	<1%						
Unknown	30%	38%	● default behavior | ◐ supported but not default | ○ no support					

Table 6: **Popular Mail Transfer Agents (MTA)**—We investigated the default behavior for five popular MTAs. By default, Postfix and qmail do not initiate STARTTLS connections. All five MTAs we tested fail open to cleartext if the STARTTLS connection fails.

Provider	Incoming TLS Version	Incoming Key Exchange	Incoming Cipher	Certificate Matches	Outgoing TLS Version	Outgoing Key Exchange	Outgoing Cipher
Gmail	1.2	ECDHE	AES-128-GCM	server	1.2	ECDHE	AES-128-GCM
Yahoo	1.2	ECDHE	AES-128-GCM	server	1.0	ECDHE	RC4-128
Outlook	1.2	ECDHE	AES-256-CBC	server	1.2	ECHDE	AES-256
iCloud	1.2	ECDHE	AES-128-GCM	server	1.2	DHE	AES-128-GCM
Hushmail	1.2	RSA	RC4-128	server	1.2	ECDHE	AES-256-GCM
Lycos	–	–	–	–	–	–	–
Mail.com	1.2	ECHDE	AES-256-CBC	server	1.2	DHE	AES-256-GCM
Zoho	1.0	RSA	RC4-128	server	1.0	RSA	RC4-128
Mail.ru	1.2	RSA	RC4-128	server	1.2	ECDHE	AES-256-GCM
AOL	1.0	RSA	RC4-128	server	1.0	DHE	AES-256-CBC
QQ	1.1	RSA	RC4-128	server	1.0	DHE	AES-256-CBC
Me.com	1.2	ECHDE	AES-128-GCM	server	1.2	DHE	AES-128-GCM
facebookmail	1.0	RSA	AES-128-CBC	mismatch	1.0	ECDHE	AES-128
GoDaddy	1.2	RSA	RC4-128	server	–	–	–
Yandex	1.2	RSA	AES-128-GCM	server	1.2	ECDHE	AES-256-CBC
OVH	1.2	RSA	AES-128-GCM	mismatch	–	–	–
Comcast	1.2	RSA	RC4-128	server	1.2	DHE	AES-128-CBC
AT&T	1.2	ECDHE	AES-128-GCM	server	1.0	ECDHE	RC4-128
Verizon	1.2	RSA	AES-128-GCM	server	1.0	DHE	AES-128-CBC

Table 7: **Encryption Behavior of Mail Providers**—We measured support for incoming and outgoing STARTTLS among various popular mail providers. While most providers supported STARTTLS, *none of them* validated our certificate, which was self-signed.

Provider	Servers Providing Invalid MX Answers	Servers Providing Invalid IP Answers	Unique Invalid MX Servers	Unique Invalid IPs	Responsive Invalid Mail Servers
Gmail	30,931	23,134	146	1,150	144
Yahoo	31,219	55,459	130	1,117	114
Outlook.com	29,618	23,145	117	1,059	110
Mail.ru	31,214	25,796	97	1,053	110
QQ	30,091	55,467	122	1,171	111

Table 8: **Fraudulent DNS Responses**—We scanned the public IPv4 address space for DNS servers that returned falsified MX records or SMTP server IP addresses for five popular mail providers. This data excludes loopback addresses and obvious configuration errors.

	Nov. 2013	Apr. 2015	Change
Overall failure rate	10.65%	6.14%	−4.42%
Crypto failures:			
Weak crypto key (<1024 bits)	21.00%	15.08%	−5.92%
Key is revoked	0.02%	0.01%	−0.01%
Signature algorithm not supported	0.27%	0.26%	−0.02%
Key is expired		0.06%	
Body hash doesn't match signature		18.66%	
Protocol version incorrect	0.59%	3.32%	+2.73%
Some DKIM tags are duplicated		0.05%	
Other error	77.91%	62.55%	−15.36%

Table 9: **Gmail DKIM Errors**—We present the breakdown of Gmail DKIM validation failures for November 2013 and April 2015.

Scan Result	IPv4 Hosts
TCP port 25 open	14,131,936
Responsive SMTP server	8,850,664
Successful STARTTLS handshake	4,620,561

Table 10: **IPv4 SMTP Scan Results**—We could perform a STARTTLS handshake with 52% of the SMTP servers that our IPv4 scans identified.

Category	IPv4 Hosts	
Command not echoed	3,606,468	(85.26%)
STARTTLS echoed correctly	617,093	(14.59%)
STARTTLS replaced	5,756	(0.14%)
Command truncated to four characters	786	(0.02%)

Table 11: **Detecting STARTTLS Manipulation**—We could extract an echoed command from 14.75% of servers that sent errors in response to our STARTTLS command. 0.14% of these responses indicate that the command was tampered with before reaching the server.

Type	ASes	
Corporation	182	(43.0%)
ISP	74	(17.5%)
Financial	57	(13.5%)
Academic	35	(8.3%)
Government	30	(7.1%)
Healthcare	14	(3.3%)
Unknown	12	(2.8%)
Airport	9	(2.1%)
Hosting	7	(1.7%)
NGO	3	(0.7%)

Table 12: **ASes Stripping STARTTLS**—We categorize the 423 ASes for which 100% of SMTP servers showed behavior consistent with STARTTLS stripping.

	Top Million Domains	IPv4 Hosts
Cisco-style tampering	2,563	41,405
BLUF tampering	0	6

Table 13: **Styles of STARTTLS Stripping**—The most prominent style of manipulation matches the advertised behavior of Cisco security devices and affects 41K SMTP servers.

Category	IPv4 Hosts
DNS servers	13,766,099
Responsive DNS servers	8,860,639
Any invalid MX responses	234,756
Class of invalid behavior:	
Identical response regardless of request	131,898
Returns loopback address	16,015
Returns private network address	7,680
Flipped bits in response	56,317
Falsified DNS record	178,439

Table 14: **Invalid or Falsified MX Records**—We scanned the IPv4 address space for DNS servers that provided incorrect entries for the MX servers for five popular mail providers.

5.1 STARTTLS Corruption

An active attacker—or a legitimate organization with a vested interest in snooping mail—can prevent mail encryption by tampering with the establishment of a TLS session. In this attack, a network actor takes advantage of the fail-open design of STARTTLS—where SMTP servers fall back to cleartext if any errors occur during the STARTTLS handshake—to launch a downgrade attack. A network actor can manipulate packets containing the `STARTTLS` command to prevent mail servers from establishing a secure channel, or alter a mail server's `EHLO` response to remove `STARTTLS` from the list of server capabilities. To measure whether STARTTLS sessions are being downgraded in the wild, we attempted to initiate STARTTLS connections with SMTP servers throughout the public IPv4 space and looked for evidence of tampering.

Scanning Methodology To find servers where STARTTLS is blocked, we build on the fact that SMTP servers frequently report back invalid commands they receive—which would include any corrupted `STARTTLS` command. We performed a TCP SYN scan of the public IPv4 address space on port 25 and attempted to perform an SMTP and STARTTLS handshake with responsive hosts. We performed this scan on April 20, 2015, from the University of Michigan campus using ZMap [19].

We found 14.1M hosts with port 25 open, 8.9M SMTP servers, and 4.6M SMTP servers that supported STARTTLS (see Table 10). Of the 4.2M hosts that failed to complete a TLS handshake, 623,635 (14%) echoed back the command they received. We classify these responses in Table 11. 617,093 (98.95%) of the responding hosts returned `STARTTLS` (and indeed do not to support it), 5,750 (0.92%) returned `XXXXXXXX`, 786 (0.14%) responded with `STAR` or `TTLS`, and 6 responded with `BLUF`.

The `STAR` and `TTLS` commands are four-character command truncations and are likely not due to an attack. Prior to ESMTP, SMTP commands were all four characters, and we were able to confirm that all commands were truncated to four characters on these servers. However, the `XXXXXXXX` and `BLUF` commands appear due to the `STARTTLS` command being altered to prevent the establishment of a TLS session.

Affected Servers Excluding four-character truncations, our scan found 5,756 servers that display evidence of a corrupted `STARTTLS` command. However, given that only 14% of servers reported back the received command, this is likely an underestimate. We extended our search for servers where the `STARTTLS` command was corrupted in the server's list of advertised features, which is returned in response to the `EHLO` command. This identified an additional 35,649 servers. When combined with the initial set, this yields a total of 41,405 servers that apparently have `STARTTLS` messages corrupted. These 41K servers are located in 4,714 ASes (15% of all ASes with an SMTP server) and 191 countries (86% of countries with SMTP servers). They transit mail for 2,563 domains in the Top Million.

In 423 ASes (736 hosts), 100% of SMTP servers are affected by STARTTLS stripping. The AS performing stripping on 100% of the inbound and outbound mail with the most SMTP servers (21) belongs to Starwood Hotels and Resorts (AS 13401). We show the classification of ASes with 100% stripping in Table 12. Overall, no single demographic stands out; the distribution is spread over networks owned by governments, Internet service providers, corporations, and financial, academic, and health care institutions. We note that several airports and airlines appear on the list, including an AS belonging to a subsidiary of Boingo (AS 10245), a common provider of in-flight and airport WiFi.

Our scanning methodology does not comprehensively find all servers where STARTTLS is blocked. Local SMTP servers may not be accessible from the University of Michigan, STARTTLS might only be stripped for outgoing messages, or the command might be removed altogether instead of being corrupted in place. However, it appears that the practice is widespread.

Possible Causes The `XXXXXXXX` replacements are likely caused by security products that intercept and strip the command. In one prominent example, Cisco Adaptive Security Appliances (ASA) [7] and Cisco IOS Firewalls [8] both advertise replacing the `STARTTLS` command with `Xs` to facilitate mail inspection as part of their *inspect smtp* and *inspect esmtp* configurations. By inspecting messages, Cisco advertises that their products are capable of searching for and dropping messages with invalid characters in mail addresses, invalid SMTP commands, and long commands that may be attempting to exploit buffer overflows [9]. Table 13 shows the prominence of this style of tampering. While Cisco advertises this functionality, we cannot necessarily attribute every instance seen in the wild to Cisco devices, since others could implement stripping the same way.

We are unable to attribute the `BLUF` replacement to any commonly known security software. The six hosts affected by this replacement also had the `PIPELINING` and `CHUNKING` capabilities in the `EHLO` response masked to `HIPELINING` and `PHUNKING`, respectively. Only those six hosts displayed this behavior; all were located in Ukraine.

Impact on Transited Mail To understand the volume of mail affected by STARTTLS corruption, we measure the number of messages transited to/from these devices from Gmail's perspective. The overall fraction of mail affected is small, but a handful of countries have a high local stripping rate (see Table 15). In the most extreme example, 96.13% of mail transited from Tunisia to Gmail is affected by STARTTLS stripping. Another 8 countries experience over 10% stripping, and 16 experience more than 5% stripping.

It is important to note that the devices that are stripping TLS from SMTP connections are not inherently malicious, and many of these devices may be deployed to facilitate legitimate filtering. Regardless of the intent, this technique results in messages being sent in cleartext over the public Internet, enabling passive eavesdropping and other attacks. Furthermore, the Cisco documentation does not discuss the downsides of enabling this functionality, and administrators may not be aware that the setting puts users at risk. Instead of stripping TLS, manufacturers should consider deploying in-line devices that accept and initiate STARTTLS connections, allowing them to inspect messages before securely forwarding them.

5.2 DNS Hijacking

Mail security, like that of many other protocols, is intrinsically tangled with the security of DNS resolution. Rather than target the SMTP protocol, an active network attacker can spoof the DNS records of a destination mail server to redirect SMTP connections to a server under the attacker's control. We investigated the prevalence of DNS servers that provide false MX records or SMTP server IP addresses for: gmail.com, yahoo.com, outlook.com, qq.com (a popular Chinese webmail provider), and mail.ru (a popular Russian webmail provider). We find evidence that 178,439 out of 8,860,639 (2.01%) publicly accessible DNS servers provided invalid IPs or MX records for one or more of these domains (see Table 8).

Scanning Methodology We identified servers responding with falsified DNS records by scanning the IPv4 address space ten times with ZMap in search of open resolvers and subsequently requesting the MX and A record of gmail.com, yahoo.com, outlook.com, qq.com, and mail.ru. We performed these scans on April 25, 2015, from the University of Michigan. In total, we identify 13.8 million DNS servers, of which 8.9 million resolved at least one query and 235K provide an invalid or falsified MX record (see Table 14).

Tunisia	96.13%	Reunion	9.28%
Iraq	25.61%	Belize	7.65%
Papua New Guinea	25.00%	Uzbekistan	6.93%
Nepal	24.29%	Bosnia and Herzegovina	6.50%
Kenya	24.13%	Togo	5.45%
Uganda	23.28%	Barbados	5.28%
Lesotho	20.25%	Swaziland	4.62%
Sierra Leone	13.41%	Denmark	3.69%
New Caledonia	10.13%	Nigeria	3.64%
Zambia	9.98%	Serbia	3.11%

Table 15: **Countries Affected by STARTTLS Stripping**—We measure the fraction of incoming Gmail messages that originate from the IPs that we found were stripping TLS from SMTP connections. Here, we show the countries with the most mail affected by STARTTLS stripping and the affected percentage of each country's incoming mail between April 20 and 27, 2015.

Slovakia	0.08%
Romania	0.04%
Bulgaria	0.03%
India	0.02%
Israel	0.01%
Switzerland	0.01%
Poland	0.01%
Ukraine	0.01%

Table 16: **Countries Affected by Falsified DNS Records**—We measure the fraction of mail received by Gmail on May 21, 2015 from IP addresses pointed to by false Gmail DNS entries. Here, we show the breakdown of mail from each country that originates from one of these addresses for the countries with the most affected mail.

We then performed a secondary scan, in which we repeated the same queries as well as performed A record lookups for a domain unrelated to mail transit (umich.edu) and a nonexistent domain. Of the 235K servers that provided invalid responses in our first scan, 56K supplied correct results in the secondary scan and were incorrectly flagged due to erroneous bit flips. Excluding those hosts, 132K provide the same publicly accessible address for every DNS query regardless of the domain, 7.7K provide reserved or private addresses, 16K respond with a loopback address, and 17.2K did not appear to spoof answers but were missing at least one of the MX servers. The devices that provided identical responses to every query or were missing an MX server appeared to be improperly configured embedded devices rather than malicious. After removing these hosts, we were left with 14.6K hosts that provided invalid responses for mail servers. These hosts pointed to 1,150 unique falsified mail servers, of which 144 (12.5%) completed an SMTP handshake.

Our scans do not provide an exhaustive list of hosts that might be intercepting mail. Since open resolvers are frequently used to launch DDoS attacks, most recursive DNS resolvers are not externally accessible and will not appear in our scans. Similarly, many of the addresses we recorded are private, non-routable addresses, so we are unable to test whether mail transits through these hosts. However, our scan still finds upwards of 15K open resolvers that provide fraudulent responses when queried about mail providers and 1.2K false mail servers, which allows us to determine whether mail server DNS hijacking occurs in the wild.

Responsible Networks The DNS servers that provide fraudulent responses are located in 521 ASes. 83.6% of the hosts were located in five ASes: 62% Unified Layer (American Hosting Provider), 11.7% ChinaNet, 5.3% Telecom Italia (Italian ISP), 2.4% SoftLayer Technologies, and 2.0% eNom. In the case of Unified Layer, 9K

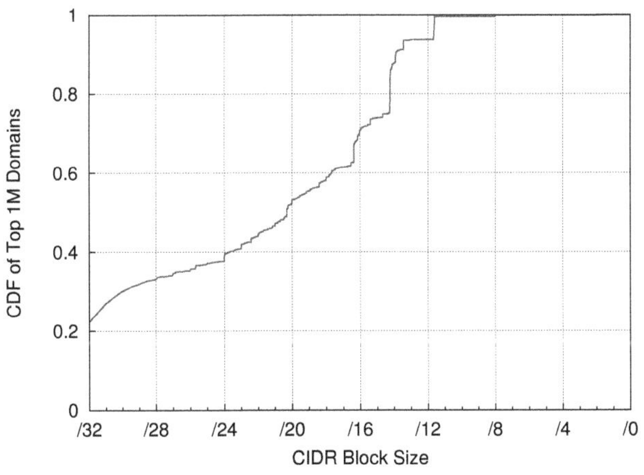

Figure 4: **Size of SPF Permitted Networks**—We show the CDF of the number of addresses whitelisted in a recursive resolution of the SPF records for Top Million domains.

hosts point back to seven servers, of which two completed SMTP handshakes. The hosts in the ChinaNet AS point to a range of loopback and private addresses and to 42 publicly routable servers, of which one completed an SMTP handshake. The devices in the Telecom Italia AS returned monotonically increasing IP addresses within 198.18.1.0/24 for all queries and do not appear to be specifically intercepting mail queries. The SoftLayer hosts respond with one of 18 addresses, of which 10 were SMTP servers. All eNom hosts point to a single IP, which did not accept SMTP connections. The remaining 2,386 DNS servers are located in 533 ASes and in 69 countries.

Impact on Transited Mail While a number of servers appear to be intercepting mail, the impact on transited messages is unclear. We estimate the amount of mail affected by measuring the number of inbound messages that Gmail received from each of the servers. The vast majority of mail that transits from these hosts is spam, but a small number of non-spam messages are sent through these servers. As shown in Table 16, in the most extreme case, upwards of 0.08% of mail transited from Slovakia came from falsified servers.

Whether malicious or well-intentioned, STARTTLS stripping and falsified DNS records highlight the weakness inherent in the fail-open nature and lack of authentication of the STARTTLS protocol. These attacks are both readily found in the wild and pose a real threat to users, with more than 20% of mail being sent in cleartext within seven countries.

6. AUTHENTICATION IN PRACTICE

While STARTTLS protects messages against passive eavesdropping, it does not provide authentication. Mail can be modified or spoofed altogether, even in the presence of STARTTLS. As described in Section 2, SPF, DKIM, and DMARC have been developed to authenticate incoming mail. In this section, we measure how these protocols have been deployed in practice. We summarize the deployment of all three protocols in Table 18.

6.1 SPF

When supported, SPF allows recipients to check that incoming messages from a domain (e.g., gmail.com) originate from an IP range authorized by that organization. From Gmail's perspective, Google successfully authenticated 92% of inbound messages during April 2015 using SPF, as detailed in Table 19. Of the unauthenticated

Provider	SPF Policy	DMARC Policy
Gmail	soft fail	none
Yahoo	neutral	reject
Outlook	soft fail	none
iCloud	soft fail	none
Hushmail	soft fail	–
Lycos	soft fail	–
Mail.com	fail	–
Zoho	soft fail	–
Mail.ru	soft fail	none
AOL	soft fail	reject
QQ	soft fail	none
Me.com	soft fail	none
Facebook	fail	reject
GoDaddy	fail	none
Yandex	soft fail	–
OVH	neutral	–
Comcast	neutral	none
AT&T	–	–
Verizon	neutral	–

Table 17: **SPF and DMARC Policies**—The majority of popular mail providers we tested posted an SPF record, but only three used the "strict fail" policy. Even fewer providers posted a DMARC policy, of which only three used "strict reject."

messages, Gmail fails to validate 0.42% due to failures fetching the domain's SPF record; all other messages come from domains without an SPF policy.

Similar to STARTTLS deployment, the servers associated with the Top Million domains show significantly slower adoption with only 401,356 domains—47% of the Top Million domains with MX records—publishing an SPF policy (see Table 20). Of those, 255,867 domains allow mail to be sent if the server has an MX record on the domain, and 104 domains allow mail from hosts with reverse DNS names that match the domain.

Record Delegation Of the Top Million domains, 10,432 redirect (or fully delegate their SPF policy) to another provider, and 213,464 (53.2%) include records from one or more other domains' SPF policies. While this could potentially open an attack vector if multiple organizations specified the same IP blocks, we find that this was not the case. Instead, domains commonly include records from or redirect to a few well-known cloud mail providers. In the case of redirection, 35.7% delegate to Yandex (a Russian mail provider), 16.7% to mailhostbox.com, 8.0% to nicmail.ru, 3.9% to serveriai.lt, and 3.5% to mail.ru. 3,813 (36.6%) of all redirects point to a Russian mail service. For includes, 136,473 domains (64% of domains with includes) include one of five large mail providers: Gmail (59,660), Outlook (44,216), websitewelcome.com (20,291), mandrillapp.com (16,606), and SendGrid (10,700).

SPF Policy Coarseness For the domains that specify SPF policies, we find evidence that some report overly broad IP ranges that potentially enable an attacker to spoof mail origins, as shown in Figure 4. We find that 133,490 domains (60.9%) specify SPF CIDR ranges larger than a /24, 99,698 (29.2%) specify CIDR ranges larger than or equal to a /16, and 1,333 (0.4%) specify more than a /8. The vast majority of the domains that include a /8 mistakenly allowed messages from 10.0.0.0/8. In rarer cases, we find evidence of blatant misconfiguration: 62 domains specify network ranges akin to 255.255.255.255/8, and 20 domains specify ranges larger than a /8.

Policy Types Of the domains that deploy SPF, 21.7% adopt hard-failure policies, where recipients should reject mail from outside of the specified network. Another 58.0% adopt soft-failure policies, where recipients should accept the mail but consider it suspect (e.g., mark as spam), and 20.3% set no policy. If we restrict our analysis to the top mail providers, we find that most publish SPF records with a soft-fail policy (see Table 17). Exceptions include Facebook Mail, Mail.com, and GoDaddy, all of which have hard-fail policies. AT&T was the only provider we checked that does not have a valid SPF policy. We note that soft-fail policies allow more leeway for the destination domain to decide how to process a message, such as considering other spam indicators instead of downright rejecting messages.

6.2 DKIM

As a complement or alternative to SPF, DKIM allows a recipient to confirm the integrity and authenticity of inbound messages, even in the presence of a man-in-the-middle attack. In April 2015, 83.0% of the messages that Gmail received contained a DKIM signature. Of the signed messages, 6.14% failed to validate due to weak cryptographic keys, revoked keys, or protocol errors (see Table 9). This represents a 4.42% decrease in invalid signatures when compared to two years prior. We specifically call attention to the fact that 18.7% of failures in April 2015 arose due to DKIM signatures not matching a message's content. While we cannot distinguish between malice and misconfiguration, such failures reflect the importance of authentication to alert mail servers to potential tampering, and they emphasize the imperative for the remaining 17% of unauthenticated inbound Gmail messages to adopt DKIM signatures. Unfortunately, due to the nature of the DKIM protocol, we cannot directly measure how many domains in the Alexa Top Million have deployed DKIM.

6.3 DMARC

DMARC policies allow sending mail servers to alert recipients that they support DKIM and SPF and then inform recipients how to handle incoming messages that fail to validate or that lack a DKIM signature. In contrast to the 90% of the messages that Gmail can validate with SPF or DKIM, only 26.1% of all inbound Gmail messages come from domains with a published DMARC policy. This discrepancy limits the effectiveness of DKIM as, absent a publicized policy, recipients cannot determine whether the lack of a signature is intended or is an indication of spoofing. For those messages with a policy, we provide a detailed breakdown in Table 22. We found that the majority of policies favored rejection (13%), though a significant fraction did not specify any action (11%).

A similarly pessimistic picture emerges for the Alexa Top Million, for which only 1.1% of domains with MX records published DMARC policies. We provide a breakdown of all the policies in Table 22 and the policies of top mail providers in Table 17. Even when DMARC is present, the majority of Alexa domains and even the top mail providers specified an empty policy. Only Yahoo, AOL, and Facebook advertised DMARC reject policies.

We suspect that many organizations have yet to deploy DMARC due its relatively young age—RFC 7489 was first introduced in March 2013 and was last updated in March 2015, one month prior to our measurements. However, we note its necessity in enforcing SPF and DKIM policies, and we hope it will see increased deployment moving forward.

7. DISCUSSION

The mail community has retroactively applied several security measures to SMTP. Nearly 60% of incoming connections to Gmail are encrypted and 94% of messages are authenticated with DKIM or SPF. In many ways, this is a feat, given that SMTP did not originally provide any support for transport security. However, our two perspectives paint drastically different pictures of how mail security

Authentication Method	Nov. 2013	Apr. 2015	Change
DKIM & SPF	74.66%	81.01%	+6.31%
DKIM only	2.25%	1.98%	−0.27%
SPF only	14.44%	11.41%	−2.99%
No authentication	8.65%	5.60%	−3.00%

Table 18: **Gmail Incoming Mail Authentication**—During April 2015, 94.40% of incoming Gmail messages were authenticated with DKIM, SPF, or both.

SPF Policy	Gmail Messages
DNS timeout	<0.001%
Temporary error	0.184%
Permanent error	0.141%
Invalid record	0.098%

Table 19: **SPF Errors for Incoming Gmail Traffic**—We show the breakdown of errors fetching SPF records for incoming mail. Temporary errors can be fixed by retrying later; permanent errors mean the record was unable to be fetched.

Policy	Top Million Domains	Recursive Top Million
SPF policy	401,356	401,356
Hard fail	84,801 (21.13%)	86,919 (21.65%)
Soft fail	226,117 (56.34%)	232,736 (57.99%)
Neutral	80,394 (20.03%)	81,701 (20.36%)
Redirect	10,045 (2.50%)	0 (0.00%)

Table 20: **SPF Policies for Top Million Domains**—We queried the SPF policies for the Top Million domains for both the top-level record and for full recursive resolution.

Record Type	Top Million Domains	Recursive Top Million
IPv4	200,976 (33.08%)	344,844 (40.22%)
IPv6	6,862 (1.13%)	108,086 (12.61%)
A	139,979 (23.04%)	148,688 (17.34%)
MX	249,345 (41.04%)	255,867 (29.84%)
REDIRECT	10,432 (1.72%)	0 (0.00%)

Table 21: **SPF Record Types for Top Million Domains**—We show how hosts are whitelisted within an SPF record for both the top-level SPF record and for full recursive resolution.

Published Policy	Gmail Messages	Top Million Domains
Quarantine	1.34%	709 (0.09%)
Empty	11.66%	6,461 (0.82%)
Reject	13.08%	1,720 (0.22%)
Not published	73.92%	783,851 (98.9%)

Table 22: **DMARC Policies**—We categorize DMARC policies for incoming Gmail messages from April 2015 and for Top Million domains with MX records on April 26, 2015.

has been deployed. As can be seen by the 51% jump in encrypted inbound messages when Microsoft and Yahoo deployed STARTTLS, much of this success can be attributed to large mail providers that are pushing security forward. Unfortunately, as our scans demonstrate, smaller organizations lag in deploying security mechanisms correctly. While mail delivery security is rapidly improving, there are several structural problems that the mail community must address to guarantee the confidentiality and integrity of mail.

7.1 Challenges for Confidentiality

There are several challenges to guaranteeing the confidentiality of mail in transit. First, unlike HTTPS, there is no mechanism in SMTP for servers to indicate that mail should be protected by TLS. Further, users cannot indicate that mail should only be transited securely nor can they detect whether a message traversed a secure path.

In HTTPS, users can choose not to communicate over an insecure channel, and HSTS allows sites to indicate that future connections must use HTTPS. However, in SMTP, messages are relayed in cleartext if TLS cannot be negotiated. As we showed in Section 5.1, this has led to organizations corrupting the STARTTLS negotiation to force mail to be sent in the clear. Whether this is being done for legitimate or nefarious purposes, it illustrates that STARTTLS provides no protection against frequently occurring man-in-the-middle (MITM) attacks.

Second, even when TLS is used, there is no robust way for a sender to verify the authenticity of the recipient mail server. Common MTAs can validate that a server's certificate matches the destination domain's MX record, but not the destination domain name itself. Unfortunately, this still leaves the server open to impersonation unless the DNS responses are separately authenticated. As we showed in Section 5.2, certain entities are using this weakness to redirect the flow of messages.

One potential option for preventing MITM attacks is to create a mechanism similar to HTTP Public Key Pinning [21] for SMTP. This would allow a mail server to indicate whether future connections should require TLS and specify a public key. Other protections being adopted for the HTTPS PKI might also be considered for STARTTLS, such as the use of Certificate Transparency [6] to guard against dishonest or compromised certificate authorities.

Finally, we note that end-to-end mail encryption, as provided by PGP [4] and S/MIME [42], does not address many of the challenges we discuss in this work. While these solutions do safeguard message content, they leave metadata, such as the subject, sender, and recipient, visible everywhere along the message's path. This information is potentially exposed to network-based attackers due to the lack of robust confidentiality protections for SMTP message transport. Although greater adoption of end-to-end encryption would undoubtedly be beneficial, for now, the overwhelming majority of messages depend solely on SMTP and its extensions for protection.

7.2 Challenges for Integrity

A major open question surrounding mail integrity is how to authenticate mail sent through mailing lists. Mailing lists frequently modify messages in transit, and DKIM signatures are invalidated by these modifications, which prevents large mail providers from publishing a DMARC reject policy. When Yahoo deployed a reject policy in 2014, it resulted in a heavy number of complaints and service malfunctions [10].

A second challenge is ensuring strong integrity as organizations move to cloud providers, where mail infrastructure and IP address blocks may be shared with other organizations. This infrastructure sharing is challenging in two respects. First, SPF has become less relevant, since, as explained in Section 6.1, SPF records tend to be overly broad. Second, DKIM becomes threatened by massive key compromises, as was the case for the SendGrid leak [5]. Overall, these two issues are part of a larger open question: How do we reliably establish the legitimacy of senders—whether for spam prevention or for integrity purposes—when many senders, good and bad, share common infrastructure?

The issue of shared infrastructure also affects mail confidentiality, as third-party providers would need to have certificates containing their clients' domains to allow strict certificate verification. This is problematic, as it opens the door to attacks where the third-party mail provider—or an attacker who breaches their systems—uses these certificates to impersonate the clients' domains, either for mail delivery or for HTTPS connections. This threat might be mitigated with a scope-reducing X.509 extension or through some other mechanism not yet devised.

8. RELATED WORK

There has been little formal measurement of the public key infrastructure that supports mail transport until recently. There are three works similar to ours.

The first is a set of Facebook blog posts [22, 23] that describe the STARTTLS configurations seen from the perspective of Facebook notifications. In May 2014, Facebook found that 28.6% of notification emails are transported over a STARTTLS connection with strict certificate validation, 28.1% are protected with opportunistic encryption (indicating a misconfigured STARTTLS server), and 41.0% of notifications are sent in cleartext. In August 2014, Facebook posted follow-up statistics in which they note that 95% of notification emails are sent over STARTTLS with strict certificate validation. Facebook further notes that this rise is primarily due to two major mail providers, Yahoo and Microsoft, deploying STARTTLS. The jump of encrypted messages from 28.6% to 95% is incredibly exciting. However, as noted by Facebook, their notification emails are skewed towards personal addresses and large hosting providers, such as Gmail and Yahoo Mail.

Concurrently with our work, Foster et al. [24] performed a similar study on the deployment of SMTP extensions for the Top Million domains present in the 2013 Adobe data breach [3] (ranked by number of accounts) and investigated how different types of senders (e.g., popular banks and e-commerce sites) protect mail. They found that 89% of popular mail providers deploy STARTTLS, 85% have SPF records, and 68% have DMARC policies. In comparison, at the termination of our study in April, 54% of incoming messages to Gmail were protected by STARTTLS, and 82% of the domains to which Gmail transited mail supported inbound STARTTLS. While protocol deployment appears higher in their work, this falls in line with the trends we see: popular providers have deployed security extensions more comprehensively than smaller organizations.

In June 2014, Sean Rijs [43] published a measurement study on the use of STARTTLS among 116 Dutch organizations which found that: 55% of their domains used STARTTLS, 34% did not support STARTTLS, and 11% could not be tested. Our results provide another perspective, including how incoming messages are protected, mail is authenticated, and organizations deploy STARTTLS .

Mail Redirection There is a large corpus of work on DNS servers that provide false responses in order to facilitate content filtering [13, 36, 39, 47]. However, our study is the first to measure the extent to which DNS servers are falsifying MX records for mail providers and the amount of mail sent through these servers. In 2014, the Electronic Frontier Foundation (EFF), Golden Frog, and Telecom Asia posted anecdotal evidence of several ISPs blocking STARTTLS sessions in the United States and Thailand [25, 29, 44]. The EFF proposed STARTTLS Everywhere, an open source project that contains a public list of domains that support STARTTLS and scripts for generating configuration files for common MTAS that require STARTTLS for those domains [30]. Our work provides an additional perspective and estimates the amount of mail affected by STARTTLS stripping.

Internet-wide Scanning While Internet-wide scanning has not previously been used to measure the mail security ecosystem, it has become a standard practice for measuring the HTTPS ecosystem. In 2010, the EFF performed a distributed scan [20] of the IPv4 address space to identify certificate authorities. Later, in 2011, Holz et al. [31] scanned the Alexa Top Million in order to measure HTTPS deployment and commonly used CAs. In 2012, Heninger et al. [27] performed comprehensive scans of HTTPS servers and detected wide use of weak cryptographic keys. Again in 2013, Durumeric et al. [18] completed daily scans in order to identify weaknesses in the HTTPS CA ecosystem. In 2014, Huang et al. [32] scanned the Top Million to measure the deployment of Forward Secrecy.

9. CONCLUSION

While electronic mail carries some of users' most sensitive correspondence, SMTP did not originally include support for message confidentiality or integrity. Over the past fifteen years, the mail community has retrofitted SMTP with several security mechanisms, including STARTTLS, SPF, DKIM, and DMARC. In this work, we analyzed the global adoption of these technologies using data from two perspectives: Internet-wide scans and logs of SMTP connections to and from one of the world's largest mail providers over a sixteen month period. Our measurements show that the use of these secure mail technologies has surged over the past year. However, much of this growth can be attributed to a handful of large providers, and many smaller organizations continue to lag in both deployment and proper configuration. The fail-open nature of STARTTLS and the lack of strict certificate validation reflect the need for interoperability amidst the gradual rollout of secure mail transport, and they embody the old adage that "the mail must go through." Unfortunately, they also expose users to the potential for man-in-the-middle attacks, which we find to be so widespread that they affect more than 20% of messages delivered to Gmail from several countries. We hope that by drawing attention to these attacks and shedding light on the real-world challenges facing secure mail, our findings will motivate and inform future research.

Acknowledgments

The authors thank Vern Paxson, Paul Pearce, Niels Provos, Eric Wustrow, and our shepherd, Alan Mislove, for their help and feedback. We thank the exceptional sysadmins at the University of Michigan for their help and support, including Chris Brenner, Kevin Cheek, Laura Fink, Dan Maletta, Jeff Richardson, Donald Welch, Don Winsor, and others from ITS, CAEN, and DCO. This material is based upon work supported by the National Science Foundation under grants CNS-1111699, CNS-1255153, CNS-1345254, CNS-1409505, CNS-1409758, and CNS-1518741, by the Google Ph.D. Fellowship in Computer Security, by the Morris Wellman Faculty Development Assistant Professorship, and by an Alfred P. Sloan Foundation Research Fellowship.

10. REFERENCES

[1] Alexa Internet, Inc. Alexa Top 1,000,000 Sites. http://s3.amazonaws.com/alexa-static/top-1m.csv.zip.

[2] N. J. AlFardan, D. J. Bernstein, K. G. Paterson, B. Poettering, and J. C. Schuldt. On the security of RC4 in TLS. In *22nd USENIX Security Symposium*, pages 305–320, Aug. 2013.

[3] B. Arkin. Adobe important customer security announcement, Oct. 2013. http://blogs.adobe.com/conversations/2013/10/important-customer-security-announcement.html.

[4] J. Callas, L. Donnerhacke, H. Finney, D. Shaw, and R. Thayerj. OpenPGP message format. RFC 4880, 2007. https://www.ietf.org/rfc/rfc4880.txt.

[5] D. Campbell. Update on security incident and additional security measures, 2015. https://sendgrid.com/blog/update-on-security-incident-and-additional-security-measures/.

[6] Certificate Transparency, 2015. http://www.certificate-transparency.org/.

[7] Cisco. Cisco ASA 5500-X series next-generation firewalls, 2015. http://www.cisco.com/c/en/us/products/security/asa-5500-series-next-generation-firewalls/index.html.

[8] Cisco. Cisco IOS Firewall, 2015. http://www.cisco.com/c/en/us/products/security/ios-firewall/index.html.

[9] Cisco. SMTP and ESMTP inspection overview, 2015. http://www.cisco.com/c/en/us/td/docs/security/asa/asa93/configuration/firewall/asa-firewall-cli/inspect-basic.html#pgfId-2490137.

[10] L. Constantin. Yahoo email anti-spoofing policy breaks mailing lists, 2014. http://www.pcworld.com/article/2141120/yahoo-email-antispoofing-policy-breaks-mailing-lists.html.

[11] D. Crocker, T. Hansen, and M. Kucherawy. DomainKeys Identified Mail (DKIM) signatures. RFC 6379, Sept. 2011. https://tools.ietf.org/html/rfc6376.

[12] D. Crocker and T. Zink. M3AAWG trust in email begins with authentication, 2015. https://www.m3aawg.org/sites/maawg/files/news/M3AAWG_Email_Authentication_Update-2015.pdf.

[13] H. Duan, N. Weaver, Z. Zhao, M. Hu, J. Liang, J. Jiang, K. Li, and V. Paxson. Hold-on: Protecting against on-path DNS poisoning. In *Workshop on Securing and Trusting Internet Names*, 2012.

[14] V. Dukhovni and W. Hardaker. SMTP security via opportunistic DANE TLS, July 2013. http://tools.ietf.org/html/draft-ietf-dane-smtp-with-dane-12.

[15] Z. Durumeric, D. Adrian, J. Kasten, D. Springall, M. Bailey, and J. A. Halderman. POODLE attack and SSLv3 deployment, 2014. https://poodle.io.

[16] Z. Durumeric, D. Adrian, A. Mirian, M. Bailey, and J. A. Halderman. A search engine backed by Internet-wide scanning. In *22nd ACM Conference on Computer and Communications Security*, Oct. 2015.

[17] Z. Durumeric, M. Bailey, and J. A. Halderman. An Internet-wide view of Internet-wide scanning. In *23rd USENIX Security Symposium*, Aug. 2014.

[18] Z. Durumeric, J. Kasten, M. Bailey, and J. A. Halderman. Analysis of the HTTPS certificate ecosystem. In *13th ACM Internet Measurement Conference*, Oct. 2013.

[19] Z. Durumeric, E. Wustrow, and J. A. Halderman. ZMap: Fast Internet-wide scanning and its security applications. In *22nd USENIX Security Symposium*, Aug. 2013.

[20] P. Eckersley and J. Burns. An observatory for the SSLiverse. Talk at Defcon 18 (2010). https://www.eff.org/files/DefconSSLiverse.pdf.

[21] C. Evans, C. Palmer, and R. Sleevi. Public key pinning extension for HTTP. RFC 7469, 2015. http://tools.ietf.org/html/rfc7469.

[22] Facebook. The current state of SMTP STARTTLS deployment, May 2014. https://www.facebook.com/notes/protect-the-graph/the-current-state-of-smtp-starttls-deployment/1453015901605223/.

[23] Facebook. Massive growth in SMTP STARTTLS deployment, Aug. 2014. https://www.facebook.com/notes/protect-the-graph/massive-growth-in-smtp-starttls-deployment/1491049534468526.

[24] I. Foster, J. Larson, M. Masich, A. Snoeren, S. Savage, and K. Levchenko. Security by any other name: On the effectiveness of provider based email security. In *22nd ACM Conference on Computer and Communications Security*, Oct. 2015.

[25] Golden Frog. The FCC must prevent ISPs from blocking encryption. http://www.goldenfrog.com/blog/fcc-must-prevent-isps-blocking-encryption.

[26] N. Heninger. Factoring as a service. Rump session talk, *Crypto* 2013.

[27] N. Heninger, Z. Durumeric, E. Wustrow, and J. A. Halderman. Mining your Ps and Qs: Detection of widespread weak keys in network devices. In *21st USENIX Security Symposium*, Aug. 2012.

[28] P. Hoffman. SMTP service extension for secure SMTP over transport layer security. RFC 3207, Feb. 2002. http://www.ietf.org/rfc/rfc3207.txt.

[29] J. Hoffman-Andrews. Isps removing their customers' email encryption. https://www.eff.org/deeplinks/2014/11/starttls-downgrade-attacks.

[30] J. Hoffman-Andrews and P. Eckersley. STARTTLS everywhere, June 2014. https://github.com/EFForg/starttls-everywhere.

[31] R. Holz, L. Braun, N. Kammenhuber, and G. Carle. The SSL landscape: A thorough analysis of the X.509 PKI using active and passive measurements. In *11th ACM Internet Measurement Conference*, 2011.

[32] L.-S. Huang, S. Adhikarla, D. Boneh, and C. Jackson. An experimental study of TLS forward secrecy deployments. In *Web 2.0 Security and Privacy (W2SP)*, 2014.

[33] S. Kitterman. Sender policy framework (SPF) for authorizing use of domains in email. RFC 7208, Apr. 2014. http://tools.ietf.org/html/rfc7208.

[34] J. Klensin. Simple mail transfer protocol. RFC 5321, Oct. 2008. http://tools.ietf.org/html/rfc5321.

[35] M. Kucherawy and E. Zwicky. Domain-based message authentication, reporting, and conformance (DMARC). RFC 7489, Mar. 2015. https://tools.ietf.org/html/rfc7489.

[36] G. Lowe, P. Winters, and M. L. Marcus. The great DNS wall of China. Technical report, New York University, Dec. 2007. http://cs.nyu.edu/~pcw216/work/nds/final.pdf.

[37] Microsoft. TLS functionality and related terminology, June 2014. http://technet.microsoft.com/en-us/library/bb430753%28v=exchg.150%29.aspx.

[38] Mozilla Developer Network. Mozilla Network Security Services (NSS). http://www.mozilla.org/projects/security/pki/nss/.

[39] Z. Nabi. The anatomy of web censorship in Pakistan. *arXiv preprint arXiv:1307.1144*, 2013.

[40] J. B. Postel. Simple mail transfer protocol. RFC 821, Aug. 1982.

[41] http://www.postfix.org/postconf.5.html#smtp_tls_security_level.

[42] B. Ramsdell and S. Turner. Secure/multipurpose Internet mail extensions (S/MIME) version 3.2 message specification. RFC 5751, 2010. https://tools.ietf.org/html/rfc5751.

[43] S. Rijs and M. van der Meer. The state of StartTLS, June 2014. https://caldav.os3.nl/_media/2013-2014/courses/ot/magiel_sean2.pdf.

[44] Telecom Asia. Google, Yahoo SMTP email severs hit in thailand. http://www.telecomasia.net/content/google-yahoo-smtp-email-severs-hit-thailand.

[45] M. Vanhoef and F. Piessens. All your biases belong to us: Breaking RC4 in WPA-TKIP and TLS. In *24th USENIX Security Symposium*, Aug. 2015.

[46] Verisign Labs. DNSSEC scoreboard, 2015. http://scoreboard.verisignlabs.com/.

[47] J.-P. Verkamp and M. Gupta. Inferring mechanics of web censorship around the world. *3rd USENIX Workshop on Free and Open Communications on the Internet (FOCI)*, Aug. 2012.

Affiliate Crookies: Characterizing Affiliate Marketing Abuse

Neha Chachra
nchachra@cs.ucsd.edu

Stefan Savage
savage@cs.ucsd.edu

Geoffrey M. Voelker
voelker@cs.ucsd.edu

Department of Computer Science and Engineering
University of California, San Diego

ABSTRACT

Modern affiliate marketing networks provide an infrastructure for connecting merchants seeking customers with independent marketers (affiliates) seeking compensation. This approach depends on Web cookies to identify, at checkout time, which affiliate should receive a commission. Thus, scammers "stuff" their own cookies into a user's browser to divert this revenue. This paper provides a measurement-based characterization of cookie-stuffing fraud in online affiliate marketing. We use a custom-built Chrome extension, AffTracker, to identify affiliate cookies and use it to gather data from hundreds of thousands of crawled domains which we expect to be targeted by fraudulent affiliates. Overall, despite some notable historical precedents, we found cookie-stuffing fraud to be relatively scarce in our data set. Based on what fraud we detected, though, we identify which categories of merchants are most targeted and which third-party affiliate networks are most implicated in stuffing scams. We find that large affiliate networks are targeted significantly more than merchant-run affiliate programs. However, scammers use a wider range of evasive techniques to target merchant-run affiliate programs to mitigate the risk of detection suggesting that in-house affiliate programs enjoy stricter policing.

Categories and Subject Descriptors

K.4 [**Computers and Society**]: Electronic Commerce—*Security*

Keywords

Measurement; Online Advertising; Affiliate Marketing; Security

1. INTRODUCTION

Affiliate marketing is a popular form of pay-per-action or pay-per-sale advertising whereby independent marketers are paid a commission on "converting traffic" (e.g., clicks that culminate in a sale). Heralded as the "the holy grail" of online advertising a decade ago [17], affiliate marketing has become prevalent across the Web, complementing more traditional forms of display advertising.

Often described as a "low-risk" proposition for merchants who pay out only upon successful completion of sales, affiliate marketing attracts significant investment from almost every major online retailer, some of whom also invest in multiple third-party affiliate advertising programs. Similarly, it is an attractive proposition for independent marketers as they can create online content (e.g., book reviews) that can be monetized simultaneously as a means to attract likely converting traffic and to host contextual advertising. Of the two approaches, affiliate marketing is frequently the more profitable option with earnings typically between 4 and 10% of sales revenue [2, 18].

Like almost all economic activity on the Web, affiliate marketing also attracts the attention of fraudsters looking to make easy cash. Affiliate fraud garnered widespread media attention in 2013 with the indictment of Shawn Hogan, an EBay affiliate indicted for wire fraud of $28M through the use of a technique called *cookie-stuffing* [8] whereby the Web cookies used to determine the likely source of user traffic are overwritten without the user's knowledge. There have been multiple similar legal disputes over affiliate marketing since then [6]. Besides media attention, affiliate marketing has also been a subject of academic research to understand the incentives in the ecosystem and the extent of affiliate fraud [7, 16]. In this paper, we characterize popular cookie-stuffing techniques. From crawling likely sources of cookie-stuffing, we find that large affiliate networks such as CJ Affiliate (formerly Commission Junction) and Rakuten LinkShare (recently renamed to Rakuten Affiliate Network) are implicated in cookie-stuffing orders of magnitude more than affiliate programs run by merchants themselves, such as the Amazon Associates Program. Lower attempted fraud coupled with the much higher use of evasive cookie-stuffing techniques against in-house affiliate programs suggests that such programs enjoy stricter policing, thereby making them difficult targets of fraud.

We also find that retailers in the *Apparel*, *Department Stores*, and *Travel and Hotels* sectors of e-commerce are disproportionately targeted by affiliate fraud, usually through domains typosquatted on the merchant's trademarks. Finally, we evaluate data from a two-month *in situ* user study with 70+ users and find that affiliate marketing is dominated by a small number of affiliates while cookie-stuffing fraud is rarely encountered. Overall, our targeted crawl and user study both suggest that the problem, while real, appears to be less prevalent than suggested by previous reports.

IMC'15, October 28–30, 2015, Tokyo, Japan.

DOI: http://dx.doi.org/10.1145/2815675.2815720.

2. BACKGROUND

Online merchants benefit from affiliate marketing through customized and targeted advertising for their products. For example, when an affiliate reviews a bicycle on a blog dedicated to biking, the bicycle merchant can receive sales from the readers of the blog without the merchant having to produce an advertising creative or directly advertise to the blog subscribers. Instead, the merchant pays a commission to the affiliate for each such sale made.

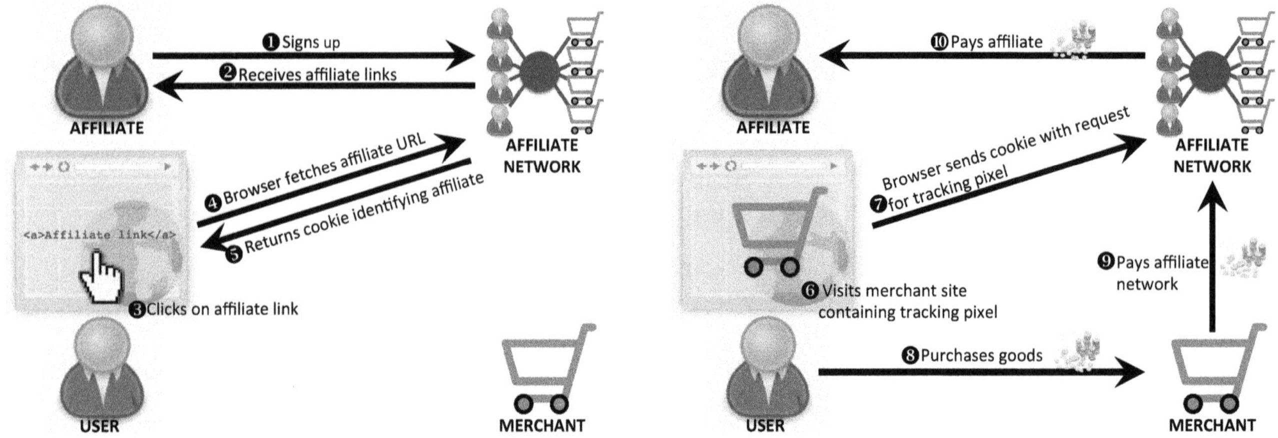

Figure 1: Different actors and revenue flow in the affiliate marketing ecosystem. The left half of the figure depicts a potential customer receiving an affiliate cookie, while the right half shows the use of the affiliate cookie to determine payout upon a successful transaction.

To recruit *affiliates* for advertising goods and services, an online merchant can either run its own *affiliate program* or join one run by a larger *affiliate network*. While some merchants like Amazon and HostGator run their own affiliate programs, most online retailers (particularly those whose expertise is on the brick-and-mortar side of the business) market through large affiliate networks such as CJ Affiliate and Rakuten LinkShare. Figure 1 provides an overview of the affiliate marketing ecosystem where a merchant is part of a large affiliate network that acts as a link between *affiliates*, who are typically content *publishers*, and *merchants*.

Affiliates who sign up for an affiliate network can choose to market for one or more merchants who are members of the network. Affiliate networks generally assign unique identifiers to all affiliates (*affiliate IDs*) and merchants (*merchant IDs*). Upon signup, affiliates receive special links from the affiliate network that encode the identifiers for the affiliate and the merchant for whom the affiliate is advertising. An affiliate includes these *affiliate links* in published content (e.g., a product review site) such that, when a potential buyer visits an affiliate's Web site and clicks on the link, it redirects the visitor to the merchant site via the affiliate program. The affiliate link `GET` request to the affiliate program returns an HTTP cookie (i.e., an *affiliate cookie*) that associates the user's visit with the corresponding affiliate. These cookies uniquely identify the referring affiliate for up to a month after the initial visit. If the user visits the merchant site during this period and completes a transaction, the affiliate network can identify the referral using the affiliate program's tracking pixel on the merchant's site. The referring affiliate usually earns between 4 and 10% on a completed transaction as a commission from the affiliate network who, in turn, is paid by the merchant for sourcing the sale.[1] In-house programs work similarly, with the network replaced by infrastructure maintained by the merchant itself.

Affiliate cookies remain in a user's browser until they expire, are overwritten by a different affiliate's cookie, or the user deletes them manually. If a user clicks on links for the same merchant from multiple affiliates in the same affiliate program, the cookie is overwritten and only the last affiliate to refer the user earns a commission.

These behaviors — that the presence of a cookie determines payout and that the most recent cookie "wins" — are at the core of the *cookie-stuffing* technique that allows fraudulent affiliates to obtain illicit commissions. In Figure 1, instead of using the affiliate URL as a clickable link, a fraudulent affiliate may cause the browser to directly fetch her affiliate URL on a page controlled by her without any explicit clicks from the user, thereby tricking the affiliate program into returning a cookie that then identifies the fraudulent affiliate as the referrer for the user's transactions. As a result, not only does an affiliate program pay a non-advertising affiliate, but the fraudulent cookie overwrites any existing affiliate cookie that may have already been present, thereby potentially stealing the commission from a legitimate affiliate. Furthermore, cookie-stuffing fraud is typically completely opaque to an end user and goes against the advertising guidelines issued by the Federal Trade Commission for marketers, which require declaration of any financial relationship with advertisers [9]. As a result, most affiliate programs explicitly forbid cookie-stuffing. For instance, the HostGator affiliate program states that "sales made through cookie stuffing methods will be considered invalid" [10].

In prior work, Moore et al. found several typosquatted domains that belong to fraudulent affiliate marketers [13]. Kapravelos et al. also found popular browser extensions that were cookie-stuffing major affiliate networks like the Amazon Associates Program [11]. Snyder et al. studied the extent to which users encountered affiliate fraud from the HTTP request logs for a public university [16]. In another study, Edelman et al. explored the incentives of different players in the affiliate marketing ecosystem, and also used crawling to identify affiliate programs defrauded through adware, typosquatting, and search engine optimization (SEO) [7]. Our work furthers this line of work by characterizing cookie-stuffing techniques and the range of targeted networks and retailers. In addition, we perform a user study to characterize the prevalence of affiliate marketing and cookie-stuffing fraud.

3. METHODOLOGY

In this section we describe how we measure cookie-stuffing fraud against six large affiliate programs: CJ Affiliate, Rakuten LinkShare, ShareASale, ClickBank, Amazon Associates Program, and HostGator Affiliate Program. While Amazon and HostGator run their own affiliate programs, the remaining four are consistently top-rated affiliate networks [15], which include well known merchants such as Nordstrom, Lego Brand, GoDaddy, etc. First, we study the structures of affiliate URLs and cookies used by these programs

[1]This is a general description. The details of the commission, the allowed duration for conversion and the implementation details (including the affiliate URL and cookie structures) can vary considerably among affiliate programs.

so that we can identify the affiliate network, the targeted merchant, and the affiliate's ID. We then use a custom-built browser extension to identify affiliate cookies received while browsing, and use it for the large scale crawling and the user study.

3.1 Identifying Affiliate URLs and Cookies

Broadly, we identified affiliate URLs and cookies either by signing up for these programs ourselves, or by finding this information online. Table 1 shows how we parse out affiliate and merchant IDs from some example affiliate URLs and cookies. For CJ Affiliate, we only show how we identify the publisher ID because we are unable to identify the corresponding affiliate ID. Every CJ affiliate can have multiple publisher IDs, one for each site used for publishing affiliate marketing creatives. However, every publisher ID is uniquely associated with a single affiliate. As a result, we use the terms publisher ID and affiliate ID interchangeably when discussing CJ Affiliate in the following sections.

Finally, the merchant is easy to identify because an affiliate URL eventually redirects to the merchant domain.

3.2 User Study

In our user study, we examine how often users click on affiliate links while browsing the Web, and identify affiliate cookies using a custom-built browser extension for Google Chrome called AffTracker.[2]

AffTracker gathers information about every single affiliate cookie it observes in the `Set-Cookie` HTTP response headers while a user is browsing. Upon detection of an affiliate cookie, AffTracker parses out the affiliate and merchant identifiers and the rendering information, including size and visibility, for the DOM element that initiated the affiliate URL request. AffTracker also records the redirect chain for the requests that result in affiliate cookies. Besides notifying the user about the cookie, AffTracker also submits this information to our server which stores it in a Postgres database.

By advertising to friends and colleagues, we obtained browsing data from 74 installations between March 1, 2015 – May 2, 2015. Using a locally generated unique ID, we can attribute affiliate cookies to specific users without collecting any personally identifiable information (PII).

While we can identify final attributes of DOM elements that cause a browser to fetch the affiliate links, we cannot automatically determine how such DOM elements are generated. Upon manual inspection we came across several affiliates who use JavaScript or Flash to dynamically generate hidden images and iframes that then request affiliate URLs. However, we are unable to quantify this phenomenon. Also, our user study does not have a completely random sample of users, and is likely biased towards savvy computer users. We discuss the results of our user study in Section 4.3.

3.3 Crawling

To characterize cookie-stuffing at scale, we visited over 475K domains to search for stuffed cookies. As described in Section 2, a user should only receive an affiliate cookie upon clicking on an affiliate URL. While crawling we do not click on any links and therefore every affiliate cookie we receive is deemed fraudulent. Since it is infeasible to crawl every Web page, we narrowed our visits to four different sets of URLs where we expected to come across affiliate fraud.

For every crawl we used a slightly modified version of our publicly available extension, AffTracker, which automatically grabs a new URL from a queue on Redis, a persistent key-value store. Upon completion of a visit, the extension submits results to our server and purges the crawler browser of all history, cookies, and local storage. We purge the browser because we found affiliates who save state in browsers to rate-limit their cookie-stuffing to evade detection by affiliate programs. For example, an affiliate, *jon007*, who controls `bestwordpressthemes.com`, sets a custom cookie called `bwt` which is valid for a month. As long as this cookie remains valid in a browser, `bestwordpressthemes.com` does not request HostGator affiliate cookies for the user. Also, inspired by Shawn Hogan who, according to EBay, rate-limited his cookie-stuffing by only requesting an affiliate cookie once per IP [4], we use 300 proxies to mitigate IP based detection by fraudulent affiliates.

We crawled the following four sets of domains to gather affiliate cookies. Except Alexa top domains set, the remaining three sets are purposely biased towards domains where we expect to find higher concentration of cookie-stuffing.

Alexa Top Domains. We crawled the Alexa [1] top 100K domains as of April 16, 2015 to find popular domains stuffing cookies.

Reverse Cookie Lookups. After identifying the cookie names used by different affiliate programs, we performed reverse lookups on the cookie-search interface [5] on `digitalpoint.com`, a webmaster community that indexes all of the cookies its crawler encounters. Overall, we gathered 9.5K domains that the Digital Point crawler observed performing cookie-stuffing over the last 2 years.

Reverse Affiliate ID Lookup. Using the cookie-stuffing affiliate IDs discovered from our Digital Point domain crawl, we queried an aggregator site, `sameid.net`, that indexes domains by Amazon and ClickBank affiliate IDs seen on a domain. By iteratively crawling domains queried from the newly discovered cookie-stuffing affiliate IDs, we visited a total of 74.5K domains.

Typosquatted Domains. In our first three sets we observed that much of the cookie-stuffing fraud was on domains typosquatted on merchant domains names. Thus, we crawled all typosquatted `.com` domains for over 7K domains belonging to major e-retailers. Similar to Edelman et al. [7], we interpret the use of typosquatting to redirect users to merchant sites without any explicit clicks as cookie-stuffing, and therefore, fraudulent. Typically users visiting typosquatted domains intend to visit the merchant site rather than the typosquatted domain itself. Thus, typosquatting a domain does not bring new customers to merchant sites via direct affiliate marketing of products. Therefore, we recognize cookie-stuffing via typosquatted domains as fraudulent.

We acquired the set of domains belonging to e-retailers from a public API offered by Rakuten Popshops.[3] The downloaded data includes merchant lists for Commission Junction, ShareASale, and Rakuten LinkShare affiliate networks. By calculating the Levenshtein distance [12] for merchant domains against all `.com` domains in a zone file from April 19, 2015, we found over 300K typosquatted domains with an edit distance of one. We visited this set of domains as well.

We gather the same features about affiliate cookies through crawling as from the user study because we use the same browser extension, AffTracker, in both cases. Furthermore, we only visit top-level pages of domains and therefore miss any cookie-stuffing in domain sub-pages. Also, Google Chrome disables popups by default, a feature we left unchanged because it emulates a user's browser more faithfully. However, this behavior likely caused our

[2]affiliatetracker.ucsd.edu

[3]`https://www.popshops.com`

Affiliate Program	URL	Cookie
Amazon Associates Program	http://www.amazon.com/dp/tag=**<aff>**&...	UserPref=.*
CJ Affiliate	http://www.anrdoezrs.net/click-**<pub>**-...	LCLK=.*
ClickBank	http://**<aff>**.**<merchant>**.hop.clickbank.net/	q=.*
HostGator	http://secure.hostgator.com/~affiliat/...	GatorAffiliate=.*.**<aff>**
Rakuten LinkShare	http://click.linksynergy.com/fs-bin/click?...	lsclick_mid**<merchant>**=".*|**<aff>**-.*"
ShareASale	http://www.shareasale.com/r.cfm?...	MERCHANT**<merchant>**=**<aff>**

Table 1: Examples of affiliate URLs and cookies for different affiliate programs.

crawler to miss any affiliate fraud where a fraudster opens a popup to load an affiliate URL.

Finally, while we can detect fraudulent affiliates stuffing cookies, we are unable to discern whether an affiliate network has already identified the fraudster. We have seen examples of ClickBank and LinkShare affiliate sites where affiliate links show an error message about affiliates having been banned, but some networks do not break banned affiliate links to prevent bad end-user experience for their URLs.

4. RESULTS

In this section we first analyze the affiliate networks and merchants most impacted by cookie-stuffing fraud. Next, we survey various cookie-stuffing techniques used by affiliates, and then present the results from our user study on the prevalence of affiliate marketing and cookie-stuffing fraud.

4.1 Networks Affected by Cookie-Stuffing

Using data collected from our crawls, we identify the affiliate networks most targeted by cookie-stuffing. Overall, we received 12,033 affiliate cookies from 11.7K domains. Table 2 summarizes our results.

We found that CJ Affiliate and Rakuten LinkShare are the most targeted programs, comprising 85% of all fraudulent cookies we observed. We identified affiliate IDs for all but 1.6% of these cookies. Every fraudulent CJ affiliate stuffed almost 50 cookies, while every LinkShare affiliate stuffed 41 cookies. However, fraudulent affiliates in Amazon and HostGator affiliate programs only stuffed 2.5 cookies per affiliate on average, the fewest of all affiliate programs in our study, suggesting that fraudulent affiliates target networks much more than they target in-house affiliate programs.

Generally, affiliate networks present greater cookie-stuffing opportunity to fraudulent affiliates because a single affiliate can simultaneously defraud multiple merchant members of the network. Our data from the Popshops API (Section 3.3) contains almost 2.4K merchants in CJ Affiliate, and 1.3K merchants in Rakuten LinkShare, and as Table 2 shows, each fraudulent affiliate targeted more than three merchants in LinkShare on average. We received 10 and 15 cookies on average for every targeted merchant in CJ Affiliate and Rakuten LinkShare, respectively.

Using the Popshops data as ground truth, we classified the defrauded merchants in all of the major networks (Figure 2) in our study except ClickBank and 420 CJ Affiliate cookies. We found that on the whole, *Apparel and Accessories* e-retailers are targeted the most across all three affiliate networks while the second most impacted group of merchants are *Department Stores*, again abused in all three networks but to a greater extent in LinkShare. *Travel and Hotel* sites were the third-most defrauded group. These three sectors have a large number of merchants and we found almost 11 stuffed cookies on average for every targeted merchant. On the other hand, the *Tools and Hardware* category only contains four impacted merchants but we observed almost 45 cookies for each of

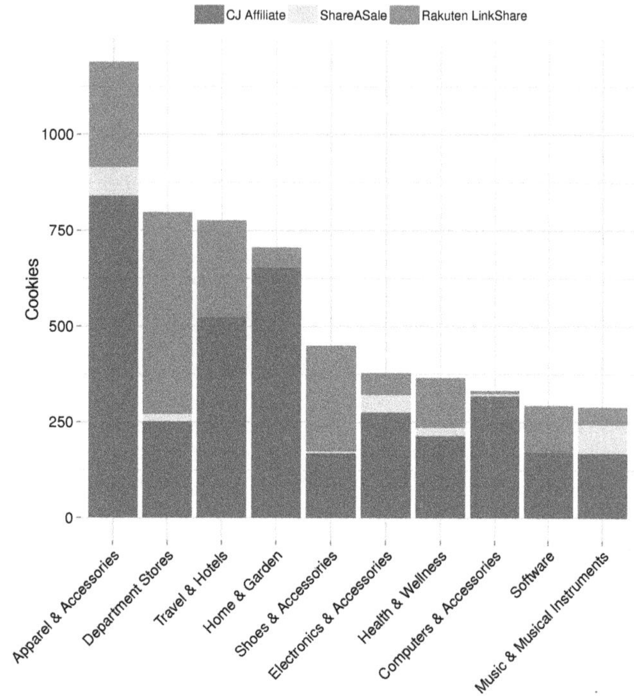

Figure 2: Stuffed cookie distribution for top 10 categories of impacted merchants.

them on average, the highest of any category. Home Depot, a CJ Affiliate member, was the most impacted merchant in this category with 163 stuffed cookies.

We also found 107 merchants who were defrauded across two or more networks. *Chemistry.com*, a member of CJ Affiliate and LinkShare, was the most targeted merchant participating in more than one affiliate program.

4.2 Prevalence of Cookie-Stuffing Techniques

We use the collected data to characterize the use of various cookie-stuffing techniques against each of the affiliate programs under consideration. As described in Section 3, whenever the browser requests an affiliate URL, our extension finds the DOM element that caused the fetch. Visiting a fraudulent affiliate's Web page can cause the user's browser to fetch an affiliate URL without any explicit click from the user by setting it as the src attribute of images, iframes, or script tags. All of these DOM elements can request third-party content on a Web page. Our extension is able to detect all affiliate cookies by observing the Set-Cookie HTTP headers, and distinguish between these techniques automatically.

Affiliate Program	Cookies	Domains	Merchants	Affiliates	Techniques			Avg. Redirects
					Images	*Iframes*	*Redirecting*	
Amazon Associates Program	170 (*1.41%*)	122	1	70	28.8%	34.1%	37.0%	1.64
CJ Affiliate	7344 (*61.0%*)	7253	725	146	0.29%	2.46%	97.2%	0.94
ClickBank	1146 (*9.52%*)	1001	606	403	34.4%	13.5%	52.0%	0.68
HostGator	71 (*0.59%*)	63	1	29	43.7%	19.7%	35.2%	0.87
Rakuten LinkShare	2895 (*24.1%*)	2861	188	57	0.28%	0.41%	99.3%	1.01
ShareASale	407 (*3.38%*)	404	66	34	0.25%	0.0%	99.8%	0.74

Table 2: Affiliate Programs affected by cookie-stuffing.

Table 2 shows the percentage of cookies corresponding to each of these techniques for every affiliate program.

At a high level, we observe that fraudulent affiliates use a much larger variety of techniques uniformly for affiliate programs run by the merchants themselves compared with larger affiliate networks, which are targeted primary via redirects to merchant sites without user clicks. Table 2 also shows the average number of intermediate domains requested after the initial page visit but before the affiliate URL, i.e., a value of zero means that an affiliate URL was directly requested from the crawled page. Intermediate referrers can be used to obfuscate the original source of a fraudulent affiliate URL request because an affiliate program only sees the final referrer when determining the legitimacy of such a request. Affiliates defrauding Amazon Associates Program use more intermediate domains on average. Since the cost of getting intermediate domains is higher, it is likely more expensive for fraudulent affiliates to defraud Amazon Associates Program presumably due to stricter policing by Amazon.

Redirecting. Fraudulent affiliates redirect users to affiliate URLs without any clicks by either using 301 or 302 HTTP response status codes, or using Flash or JavaScript to redirect the browser to the affiliate URL. In each of these cases, the original page we crawled only resulted in one stuffed cookie per visit. Such redirects delivered over 91% of all stuffed cookies, most of which resulted from typosquatted domains. In fact, we received 84% of all affiliate cookies from 10.1K typosquatted domains.

Of the 10.1K cookies from typosquatted domains, 93% (9.4K cookies) are from domains typosquatting on merchant domain names while 1.8% resulted from typosquatting on subdomains. For example, `liinensource.com` redirects to Rakuten LinkShare merchant `linensource.blair.com`. We manually inspected 30 of the remaining 520 typosquatted domains that resulted in affiliate cookies and found that these domains can be broadly classified into three types. One-third of these domains are contextually related to the final landing page. For example, `0rganize.com` redirects to CJ merchant `shopgetorganized.com`, and `bhealthypets.com` and `healthypts.com` redirect to CJ merchant `entirelypets.com`. Another third appear to be expired CJ offers, and thus did not redirect to any merchant site. The remaining one-third cookies result from typosquatted domains selling traffic to traffic distributors like `pureleads.com`, `7search.com`, and `blendernetworks.com` that eventually redirect through an affiliate URL. We revisit traffic distributors in our discussion on referrer obfuscation in this section.

Iframes. Iframes are often used to render third-party content on a Web page, which is otherwise forbidden by the Same-Origin policy implemented by browsers. Most major affiliate programs disallow the use of iframes, as it is a commonly used mechanism to facilitate cookie-stuffing. For example, HostGator explicitly prohibits iframes: "iframes may not be used unless given express permission by HostGator, sales made through hidden iframes or Cookie-stuffing methods will be considered invalid" [10]. Similarly, Amazon Associates Program prohibits framing any Amazon link on a page [3].

We received 420 cookies from content rendered in iframes on third-party sites. Generally, a server can prevent a Web site from framing its content on a page by using the `X-Frame-Options` HTTP header with its value set to `SAMEORIGIN` to only allow rendering content on a page with the same origin as the frame, or `DENY` to completely disallow framing content on any Web site [14]. We determined that Google Chrome and Firefox browsers honor the `X-Frame-Options` header and do not render the iframe content, but both browsers save the cookies nonetheless. Thus, iframe based stuffing is effective despite the use of `X-Frame-Options` header.

We found that 17% of the cookies received from iframes set `X-Frame-Options` to either `SAMEORIGIN` or `DENY`, including every Amazon Associates Program cookie. Table 2 shows that iframes still accounted for over a third of the stuffed Amazon cookies. Unlike Amazon, only 2% of CJ cookies and 50% of LinkShare cookies were accompanied by a restrictive `X-Frame-Options` header.

We also used the style and size information gathered in our crawl to determine how, if at all, a user would have seen the corresponding iframe on the crawled page. We gathered this information for 46% of the iframes. Of the 191 iframes, 64% explicitly set the height or width to either 0 or 1px; 49 (25%) iframes have `visibility:hidden` or `display:none` set, thereby making the iframe invisible to an end user. Additionally, seven iframes use CSS classes to hide the iframe DOM element. Of these, three have the same affiliate ID *kunkinkun* and the CSS class `rkt` specifies `left:-9000px`, which positions the iframe outside the viewport, and therefore invisible to the user. The same affiliate also defrauds Amazon Associates Program using the same technique and ID *shoppertoday-20*. We also found two examples where iframes were made invisible by setting the `visibility` CSS property on their parent DOM elements. The 49 remaining iframes were not hidden, and most of them correspond to ClickBank.

Images. Images can also be used to fetch third-party content on a Web page. 504 cookies in our data set were requested as images. Of these we have recorded rendering information for 91% cookies. Unlike our iframe data, we found that every single DOM element either had width or height set to 0 or 1px, or style set to `display:none`, effectively hiding the image from the end user.

We also found six cookies were requested by hidden `img` elements embedded within `iframe` elements. For example, `bestblackhatforum.eu`, a domain with Alexa rank 47,520, stuffs cookies for three different LinkShare merchants (`UDemy.com`, `microsoftstore.com`, `origin.com`), one CJ merchant (`GoDa ddy.com), and Amazon. All of these affiliate URLs are requested as hidden images of height and width zero pixels *inside* iframes with `src` set to `lievequinp.com`, which is then observed by affiliate programs as the referrer. As a result, the affiliate programs do not observe the actual cookie-stuffing `bestblackhatforum.eu` domain in the request for affiliate URLs thereby making detection of cookie-stuffing difficult. As shown in Table 3, fraudulent affiliates use iframes to defraud Amazon and HostGator more often than affiliate networks, suggesting greater difficulty in evading detection by these in-house programs.

Scripts. Even though `script` tags can be used to fetch third-party content from affiliate URLs by setting the `src` attribute, we only found two such stuffed cookies. However, upon manual inspection of several cookie-stuffing domains we found that scripts are often used for dynamic generation of hidden images and iframes that then request the affiliate URLs.

Referrer Obfuscation. Next, we analyze the extent to which fraudulent affiliates hide the actual cookie-stuffing domain behind innocuous domains. Referrer obfuscation is used to make cookie-stuffing via any technique, such as images, opaque to the affiliate programs.

Of the 12K cookies we gathered in our crawl, 84% were fetched via at least one intermediate domain. In fact, 77% of all cookies were fetched via a single redirect, 4.5% via two redirects, and another 2% via three or more redirects. Only the last redirect is seen by the affiliate program in the HTTP `Referer` header.

We analyzed the intermediate domains, and found that a significant portion of the redirects go through a very small variety of domains. The most common intermediate domains we observed are `cheap-universe.us`, `flexlinks.com`, `dpdnav.com`, `pgpartner.com`, `7search.com` and `pricegrabber.com`. Of these, `flexlinks.com` belongs to an affiliate program called FlexOffers, while the other domains are likely traffic distributors buying traffic and then monetizing via affiliate fraud. Over 25% of the cookies in our data contain a redirect through at least one of these traffic distributors. In fact, 36% of all CJ cookies contain at least one of these domains.

4.3 Prevalence of Affiliate Marketing

As described in Section 3, we gathered affiliate cookie data from 74 users over a two month period to study how often users click on affiliate links and how often they receive stuffed cookies. Only 12 users received any affiliate cookie, encountering a total of 61 cookies for 23 distinct merchants. Over a third of these cookies resulted from affiliate links on `dealnews.com` and `slickdeals.net`. Thus, while almost 84% of the users did not receive any cookie at all, 12 users received an average of 5 cookies per user. Table 3 shows the high level results.

Amazon Associates Program was the most popular affiliate program in our study, accounting for almost 51% of the cookies. As shown in Table 3, CJ Affiliate was the second most popular affiliate program, followed by Rakuten LinkShare. Our users did not receive any affiliate cookies from the ClickBank or HostGator affiliate programs. This distribution is different from the networks targeted by cookie-stuffers, where CJ Affiliate is targeted significantly more than Amazon.

Notably, none of these affiliate cookies were rendered within hidden DOM elements. We manually inspected all of them and verified that none of the source affiliate Web sites are stuffing cookies. To rule out the possibility that users were protected by ad-blocking extensions that often disallow third-party cookies, we gathered the lists of extensions on their browsers and found that only four users use any such extension. From our user study we found that users rarely encounter cookie-stuffing fraud, and affiliate marketing is dominated by a small number of affiliates. While the set of participants of our user study is likely biased towards technologically savvy users, our results are consistent with Snyder et al. [16] who found that cookie-stuffing was a very small percentage of the HTTP traffic of a large public university.

Affiliate Network	Cookies	Users	Merchants	Affiliates
Amazon Associates Program	31	9	1	16
CJ Affiliate	18	5	2	7
ClickBank	0	0	0	0
HostGator	0	0	0	0
Rakuten LinkShare	9	3	6	5
ShareASale	3	2	3	2

Table 3: Affiliate Programs that AffTracker users received cookies for.

5. CONCLUSION

In this study we characterized the abuse of affiliate marketing for monetary gains through the use of techniques broadly classified as *cookie-stuffing*. Overall, even through targeted crawling of domains with higher likelihood of encountering affiliate fraud, we observed only a limited amount cookie-stuffing in our study.

Most merchants interested in affiliate marketing have a choice to either run their own affiliate programs, or join a large affiliate network with thousands of other merchants and affiliates. Since affiliate networks have a larger number of merchants, they provide greater opportunity to fraudulent affiliates to simultaneously target multiple merchants. In fact, of the affiliate fraud we did identify, we observed that large affiliate networks are targeted disproportionately more compared to the merchant-run affiliate programs who are targeted to a smaller extent, but through more sophisticated and costly cookie-stuffing techniques such as the use of intermediate domains to obfuscate the cookie-stuffing domains. These results suggest that the in-house affiliate programs are better placed to police their affiliate programs due to greater visibility into the affiliate activities and the revenue flow, and possibly shorter turnaround time to take action against a fraudulent affiliate upon detection. However, running an in-house affiliate program requires expertise and cost investment not necessary for outsourcing the logistics of running an affiliate program to an existing network.

Finally, we conducted a user study to determine the extent of affiliate marketing encountered by users during their daily Web browsing. We found that a small number of affiliates dominate affiliate marketing, and, as with the crawling results, our users rarely encountered cookie-stuffing fraud.

Acknowledgements

We thank our shepherd Paul Barford for his help with improving the paper, and the anonymous reviewers for their valuable feedback. We are also grateful to all the users of the AffTracker extension without whom our user study would not have been possible. We are in debt to Cindy Moore for her help in setting up the `affiliatetracker.ucsd.edu` domain, and to Tristan Halvorson for managing the .COM zone file data. This work was supported by National Science Foundation grant NSF-1237264 and by generous research, operational and/or in-kind support from Google, Microsoft, Yahoo, and the UCSD Center for Networked Systems (CNS).

6. REFERENCES

[1] Alexa. Does Alexa have a list of its top-ranked websites? https://support.alexa.com/hc/en-us/articles/200449834-Does-Alexa-have-a-list-of-its-top-ranked-websites-.

[2] Amazon. Associates Program Advertising Fee Schedule. https://affiliate-program.amazon.com/gp/associates/help/operating/advertisingfees.

[3] Amazon. Associates Program Participation Requirements. https://affiliate-program.amazon.com/gp/associates/help/operating/participation/.

[4] Civil Cover Sheet. http://www.benedelman.org/affiliate-litigation/ebay-digitalpoint-hogan-kessler-thunderwood-dunning-complaint.pdf#page=8, 2008.

[5] Digital Point. Cookie Search. https://tools.digitalpoint.com/cookie-search.

[6] B. Edelman. Affiliate fraud litigation index. http://www.benedelman.org/affiliate-litigation/, 2015.

[7] B. Edelman and W. Brandi. Risk, Information, and Incentives in Online Affiliate Marketing. In *Journal of Marketing Research*, 2014.

[8] J. Edwards. How eBay Worked With The FBI To Put Its Top Affiliate Marketers In Prison. http://finance.yahoo.com/news/ebay-worked-fbi-put-top-120500693.html, 2013.

[9] Federal Trade Commission. Guides Concerning the Use of Endorsements and Testimonials in Advertising. https://www.ftc.gov/sites/default/files/attachments/press-releases/ftc-publishes-final-guides-governing-endorsements-testimonials/091005revisedendorsementguides.pdf.

[10] HostGator. Affiliate Terms of Service. http://www.hostgator.com/tos/affiliate-tos.

[11] A. Kapravelos, C. Grier, N. Chachra, C. Kruegel, G. Vigna, and V. Paxson. Hulk: Eliciting Malicious Behavior in Browser Extensions. In *Proceedings of the 23rd USENIX Security Symposium*, 2014.

[12] V. I. Levenshtein. Binary Codes Capable of Correcting Deletions, Insertions, and Reversals. In *Soviet Physics Doklady*, 1966.

[13] T. Moore and B. Edelman. Measuring the perpetrators and funders of typosquatting. In *Financial Cryptography and Data Security*, 2010.

[14] Mozilla Developer Network. The X-Frame-Options response header. https://developer.mozilla.org/en-US/docs/Web/HTTP/X-Frame-Options.

[15] mThink. The Top 20 Affiliate Networks 2014. http://mthink.com/the-top-20-affiliate-networks-2014.

[16] P. Snyder and C. Kanich. No Please, After You: Detecting Fraud in Affiliate Marketing Networks. In *Proceedings of the Workshop on the Economics of Information Security (WEIS)*, 2015.

[17] The Economist. Pay Per Sale. http://www.economist.com/node/4462811.

[18] The New York Times. Surviving the Dark Side of Affiliate Marketing. http://www.nytimes.com/2013/12/05/business/smallbusiness/surviving-the-dark-side-of-affiliate-marketing.html.

MPLS Under the Microscope: Revealing Actual Transit Path Diversity

Yves Vanaubel
Université de Liège
Belgium
yves.vanaubel@ulg.ac.be

Pascal Mérindol
Université de Strasbourg
France
merindol@unistra.fr

Jean-Jacques Pansiot
Université de Strasbourg
France
pansiot@unistra.fr

Benoit Donnet
Université de Liège
Belgium
benoit.donnet@ulg.ac.be

ABSTRACT

Traffic Engineering (TE) is one of the keys for improving packet forwarding in the Internet. It allows IP network operators to finely tune their forwarding paths according to various customer needs. One of the most popular tool available today for optimizing the use of networking resources is MPLS. On the one hand, operators may use MPLS and label distribution mechanisms such as RSVP-TE in conjunction with BGP to define multiple transit paths (for a given edge pair) verifying different constraints on their network. On the other hand, when operators simply enable LDP for distributing MPLS labels in order to improve the scalability of their network, another kind of path diversity may appear thanks to the ECMP feature of IGP routing.

In this paper, using an MPLS labels analysis, we demonstrate that it is possible to better understand the transit path diversity deployed within a given ISP. More specifically, we introduce the Label Pattern Recognition (LPR) algorithm, a method for analyzing `traceroute` data including MPLS information. LPR reveals the actual usage of MPLS according to the inferred label distribution protocol and is able to make the distinction between ECMP and TE multi-path forwarding. Based on an extensive and longitudinal `traceroute` dataset obtained from CAIDA, we apply LPR and find that each ISP behavior is really specific in regard to its MPLS usage. In particular, we are able to observe independently for each ISP the MPLS path diversity and usage, and its evolution over time. Globally speaking, the main outcomes of our study are that (*i*) the usage of MPLS has been increasing over the the last five years with basic encapsulation being predominant, (*ii*) path diversity is mainly provided thanks to ECMP and LDP, and, (*iii*), TE using MPLS is as common as MPLS without path diversity.

IMC'15, October 28–30, 2015, Tokyo, Japan.
 ISBN 978-1-4503-3848-6/15/10 ...$15.00.
DOI: http://dx.doi.org/10.1145/2815675.2815687.

Categories and Subject Descriptors

C.2.1 [**Network Architecture and Design**]: Network topology

General Terms

Measurements

Keywords

network discovery; MPLS; ECMP; multipath; LDP; RSVP-TE; traffic engineering; traceroute

1. INTRODUCTION

One of the cornerstones of the Internet is the way data is forwarded through routing paths. Typically, most of the IP flows are treated the same way whatever their specific Quality of Service (QoS) needs, their destination, or their origin. This absence of privileges and flow distinction is called *best effort routing* or *Internet neutrality*. Tools allowing operators to easily enable path diversity and, so, to perform *Traffic Engineering* (TE) are *Equal Cost MultiPath* (ECMP) load balancers [1] at the IP level and *Multiprotocol Label Switching* (MPLS [2]).

Historically, MPLS has been designed to reduce the time required to make forwarding decisions thanks to the insertion of *labels* before the IP header. Nowadays, it is commonly believed that MPLS is mainly used for providing additional virtual private networks (VPN) services [3] and TE capabilities [4, 5]. Recently, a few studies focused on MPLS, explaining essentially how to reveal its presence and its deployment level [6, 7, 8] or studying its impact on packet forwarding [9]. However, to the best of our knowledge, none of them evaluated how MPLS is actually used in today's Internet.

Two label distribution protocols are used to construct tunnels, according to the intended MPLS usage. On the one hand, the *Label Distribution Protocol* (LDP) [10] on top of IGP enables inter-domain routing stability and extensibility but also preserves ECMP features of the underlying IGP, if any. On the other hand, distributing labels with the *Resource Reservation Protocol TE* (RSVP-TE) [11] allows operators to enable service differentiation (i.e., TE) through the use of multiple *forwarding equivalent classes* (FEC – i.e., a set of packets a given hop forwards to the same next hop,

0 … 19	20 … 22	23	24 … 31
Label	TC	S	LSE-TTL

Figure 1: The MPLS label stack entry (LSE) format. An LSE is made of four fields, the *label*, the *traffic class*, the *bottom of the stack*, and the *time-to-live*.

via the same interface with the same treatment). In practice the same ISP may use concurrently both types of label distribution protocols depending on the tunnel usage. Usually, LDP seems to be deployed as a default protocol (to build a full-mesh between edge routers) on MPLS enabled networks. This observation is aligned with our findings presented in this paper as we observe more LDP than RSVP-TE.

Note that VPN based on MPLS may rely either on LDP or RSVP-TE depending on the QoS requirements. Since our study focuses on transit traffic in the public Internet, and since we did not observe many tunnels through VPNs, we will not consider VPNs in the following.

In this paper, in order to differentiate standard IP equal cost paths (that LDP allows) from tunnels built with RSVP for actual TE purposes, we present the *Label Pattern Recognition* (LPR) algorithm. LPR is a passive algorithm in the sense that it does not require any additional probing to standard `traceroute`. It must be applied once the data has been collected, as long as this data contains information related to MPLS tunnels [7, 8]. Briefly, LPR classifies each <Entry point; Exit point> pair of a tunnel into one particular class according to the recognition of the standard behaviors of RSVP-TE versus LDP in terms of label distribution.

We apply LPR on an extensive dataset obtained from CAIDA. Running LPR on five years of data, we find that the usage of MPLS has increased over this period, and that the use of the basic encapsulation method (i.e., LDP for enabling IGP/BGP routing scalability) seems predominant, with or without path diversity. Further, we are able to observe the evolution of each Autonomous System (AS) independently and understand whether it enables path diversity, how, and when it evolves (e.g., from almost no path diversity to a wide deployment of TE). Finally, when TE is deployed, in many cases, the different MPLS paths between endpoints often take the same IP path. We thus observe that TE using MPLS is as common as MPLS without path diversity. This seems to imply that bandwidth is often sufficiently abundant for allowing all tunnels to follow the same route in practice.

The remainder of this paper is organized as follows: Sec. 2 provides the required background for this paper. In particular, it describes MPLS, label distribution, and how MPLS tunnels can be revealed using `traceroute`; Sec. 3 presents the main contribution of this paper with the Label Pattern Recognition (LPR) algorithm; Sec. 4 applies LPR on an extensive and longitudinal CAIDA dataset; Sec. 5 discusses the limits of LPR and of the dataset we used as well as potential future research directions; Sec. 6 positions this paper regarding the state of the art; finally, Sec. 7 concludes this paper by summarizing its main achievements.

2. BACKGROUND

In this section, we provide the required background for the remainder of the paper. In Sec. 2.1, we discuss generalities about MPLS. In Sec. 2.2, we explain the mechanisms for distributing labels in an MPLS network. Finally, Sec. 2.3 explains how MPLS tunnels can be revealed through basic `traceroute` measurements.

2.1 MPLS Overview

The *Multiprotocol Label Switching* (MPLS) [2] was originally designed to speed up the forwarding process. In practice, this was done with one or more 32 bits *label stack entries* (LSE) inserted between the frame header (Data-link layer) and the IP packet (Network layer). A given packet can manage several LSEs at the same time. In this case, the packet is said having a *stack of labels.* Each LSE is made of four fields, as illustrated in Fig. 1: a 20-bit label value used for forwarding the packet to the next router, a 3-bit Traffic Class field for quality of service (QoS), priority, and Explicit Congestion Notification (ECN) [12], a 1-bit bottom of stack flag (when set the current label is the last in the stack [13]), and an 8-bit time-to-live (LSE-TTL) field having the same purpose as the IP-TTL field [14].

MPLS routers, called *Label Switching Routers* (LSRs), exchange labelled packets over *Label Switched Paths* (LSPs). The first MPLS router (*Ingress Label Edge Router*, or Ingress LER, i.e., the tunnel entry point) adds the label stack, while the last MPLS router (*Egress Label Edge Router*, or Egress LER, i.e., the tunnel exit point) removes the label stack. In some cases, for performance reasons, the LSE stack may be removed by the penultimate MPLS router (*penultimate hop popping*, PHP). The Egress LER then performs a classic IP lookup and forwards the traffic, reducing so the load on the Egress LER (specially if the Egress LER is shared among several LSPs). This means that, when using PHP, the tunnel exit is one hop before the Egress LER. Fig. 2 illustrates the main vocabulary associated to MPLS tunnels.

Historically, MPLS has been designed to reduce the time required to make forwarding decisions (an exact match in a LSE Label Information Base – LIB – is faster than a longest prefix match in a trie). Nowadays, MPLS has two main usages: (*i*) a basic encapsulation technique allowing to transparently transmit packets through an MPLS domain using best effort IP routes computed by an IGP, and (*ii*) a traffic engineering (TE) tool allowing to better control routing and resources used by some flows [4, 5]. These two different usages leverage two different signalling protocols to allocate and distribute labels, as we will see in more details in Sec. 2.2.

Moreover, note that there exist other kinds of usage such as MPLS fast reroute [15] to enable faster reaction to network failures with backup LSPs that are computed in a proactive way. Eventually, one really promising MPLS usage, known as *segment routing* [16], will enable in a near future the possibility to easily define routing paths that are orthogonal to those "forced" by the IGP. Indeed, one may be able to recompose IGP paths as a collection of routing segments to deal with numerous interesting use cases such as load balancing, routing policies, or fast-rerouting [17].

2.2 Label Distribution and Usage

In practice, it is worth to notice that, while label distribution protocols are standardized in several RFCs (e.g., [10, 11]), some of their characteristics are specific to router vendors, e.g., the labels range and the default configuration modes. Consequently, some of the following descriptions and statements come from manufacturers' documentation

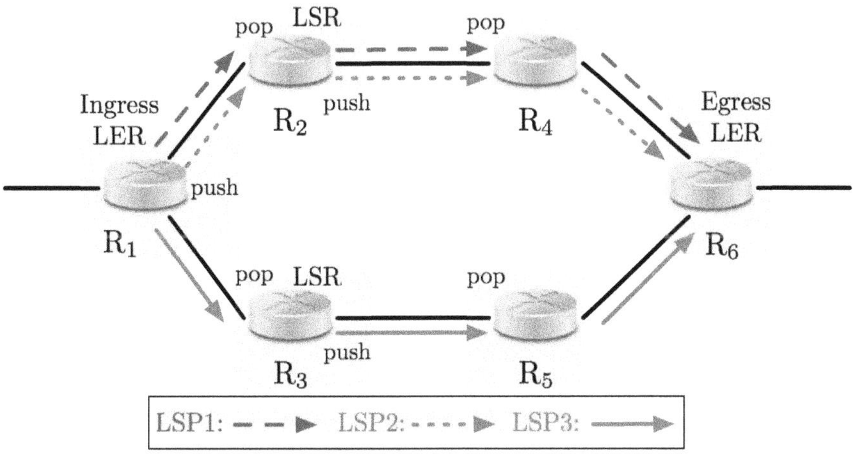

Figure 2: General overview of MPLS (with PHP enabled). Here, there are three different LSPs between the Ingress LER and the Egress LER. LSPs between the Ingress LER and the Egress LER might be physically different (i.e., different IP addresses, as LSP1 and LSP3) or logically different (i.e., same IP addresses but different labels, as LSP1 and LSP2).

(instead of RFCs). Those descriptions have been experimentally verified in our labs, with different configurations and pieces of equipment.

2.2.1 Basic Encapsulation and LDP

The basic encapsulation method cited in Sec. 2.1 is mainly used in two common scenarios. First, in the BGP transit scenario, a transit network using BGP as an inter-domain routing protocol and an IGP (e.g., IS-IS or OSPF) as an intra-domain routing protocol may use MPLS tunnels between its border routers to transparently carry packets between them. This way, intermediate routers do not need to know about external destinations[1], only the incoming border routers need to know the outgoing one (by the BGP decision process, it is the BGP next-hop) and the corresponding LSP. Such an MPLS usage may prevent routing loops and other kinds of anomalies [18] and, mostly, enables scalability. Another similar usage is for basic BGP MPLS VPN (Virtual Private Networks [19]). Again LSPs are constructed between the provider equipment (PE) of the VPN and, this way, packets belonging to a VPN may transparently cross the MPLS domain. In both cases, the objective pursued is to separate routing within the domain from routing outside (inter-domain routing or routing in the VPN), not to select routes in the network.

For this basic encapsulation method, labels are allocated through the *Label Distribution Protocol* (LDP) [10]. A router announces to its MPLS neighbors the association between a prefix in its routing table and a label it has chosen. Therefore, labels are allocated from downstream and, for a given prefix, a router advertises the same label to all its neighbors. Depending on the implementation, LDP may advertise a label for all prefixes in its IGP routing table (default case for Cisco routers) or only for loopback addresses (default case for Juniper routers). For transit traffic, LSPs are constructed by LDP towards loopback addresses of the exit border router. The IP route followed by the LSP is the best effort IP route(s) computed by the IGP. If there is no IGP load balancing in the network, there is only one route between the two endpoints (for instance, only LSP1 in Fig. 2 between the Ingress and the Egress LERs). On the other hand, if load balancing is used there may be several routes (usually with equal cost: ECMP Equal Cost Multipath – for instance LSP1 and LSP3 on Fig. 2 between the Ingress and the Egress LERs): the load balancing is generally performed using a hash function on particular IP and transport header fields. Note that LDP builds an LSP-tree towards the destination prefix. Note also that, while the prefix used to build this tree may be very specific (i.e., a single IP loopback address), the *Forwarding Equivalence Class* (FEC – i.e., a set of packets a single router forwards to the same next-hop, via the same interface with the same treatment) may be very large, e.g., all traffic exiting a Tier1 AS from the same border router. On the contrary, using access control list for instance, it is also possible that the FEC is defined at a finer grain (by considering other fields than the IP destination).

2.2.2 Traffic Engineering and RSVP-TE

Another quite different usage of MPLS is TE, where the goal is to tune the routes used by flows either to give them requested QoS, or to optimize the network usage. In this case, it is expected that different flows entering the MPLS domain at the same Ingress LER and leaving at the same Egress LER may use different routes (for instance, LSP2 and LSP3 on Fig. 2). Therefore, an IGP adapted for TE

[1]It has been shown [8] that, in practice, there exists a significant difference between the share of routers unable to reply to `ping` if they are involved in an LSP (without being LER). It means that many LSRs do not have a global IP routing plan (no BGP redistribution within the IGP). Instead, IGP routers may then use a default route via a route server for example.

(e.g., OSPF-TE [20] or ISIS-TE [21]) is in charge of computing routes satisfying the TE constraints, while the *Resource Reservation Protocol TE* (RSVP-TE) [11] is the signaling protocol in charge of reserving resources and allocating labels along the route. Note that it is expected that several LSPs can be built between the same pair of LERs. Their label sequences are completely different while their IP path may or may not be distinct (for instance, LSP1 and LSP2 on Fig. 2). One can also define source routed MPLS tunnels to tune its network "manually". In such a case, the label sequences among LSPs are likely to be also specific for each LSP.

Note that the RSVP-TE signalling protocol may be used conjointly with LDP or not. These two protocols are independent even if there is no reason to use only RSVP-TE for specific purposes without using LDP globally within the network.

2.3 Revealing MPLS Tunnels

MPLS routers may send ICMP `time-exceeded` messages when the LSE-TTL expires. In order to debug networks where MPLS is deployed, routers may also implement RFC 4950 [22], an extension to ICMP allowing a router to embed an MPLS LSE in an ICMP `time-exceeded` message. In that case, the router simply quotes the MPLS LSE (or the LSE stack) of the received packet in the ICMP `time-exceeded` message. RFC4950 is particularly useful for operators as it allows them to verify the correctness of their MPLS tunnels and TE policy. This extension mechanism has been implemented by router manufacturers since 1999 [23], and is displayed by modified versions of `traceroute` [24] that report the LSE returned by each hop in addition to RTT values currently displayed.

If the Ingress LER copies the IP-TTL value to the LSE-TTL field rather than setting the LSE-TTL to an arbitrary value such as 255, LSRs along the LSP will reveal themselves via ICMP messages even if they do not implement RFC4950. Operators can configure this action using the `ttl-propagate` option provided by the router manufacturer [14] (while, to the best of our knowledge, the RFC4950 is just a matter of implementation and cannot be deactivated on recent routers supporting it).

Donnet et al. [8] have discussed in detail the impact of those two features (i.e., RFC4950 and `ttl-propagate`) on MPLS tunnel discovery based on `traceroute`. In particular, they show that it is possible to reveal *implicit MPLS tunnels* (i.e., MPLS tunnels with `ttl-propagate` enabled but RFC450 disabled) because core LSRs do not reply to `ping` by themselves but rather forward the reply to their Egress LER (because they do not necessarily benefit from BGP route redistribution).

In this paper we focus on *explicit MPLS tunnels*, i.e., tunnels that can be fully revealed via `traceroute` as they implement both TTL propagation (they are seen in traces) and RFC4950 (they are seen as LSRs providing their LSE). Indeed, mechanisms developed in the following need to interpret the displayed labels to classify MPLS usages, so that we cannot consider implicit MPLS tunnels.

3. LABEL PATTERN RECOGNITION ALGORITHM

In this section, we discuss the *Label Pattern Recognition* (LPR) algorithm, our solution for classifying MPLS tunnels according to their usages and the path diversity they bring. LPR is a passive algorithm in the sense that it does not require any additional probing to standard `traceroute`. It must be applied once the data has been collected. Briefly, our algorithm classifies each <Ingress LER; Egress LER> pair into one of several classes according to the recognition of the standard behaviors of RSVP-TE versus LDP in terms of label distribution. Those behaviors have been experimentally tested and validated in our lab (using both routing emulators and real routers) with different configurations and pieced of equipment.

The whole classification process is illustrated at Fig. 3. Once the `traceroute` data has been collected, we retrieve from the raw dataset MPLS explicit tunnels[2]. Next, our algorithm can be applied. It works in two fundamental steps. First, it filters the MPLS explicit tunnels in order to remove noise and ensure we only focus on transit tunnels diversity (see Sec. 3.1). Once the data has been sanitized, the classification itself is performed. At the end, each considered *In-Out Transit Pair* (IOTP) is assigned to one of the defined classes. In the remainder of this paper, when we talk about "IOTP", we refer to a <Ingress LER; Egress LER> pair, i.e., a set of explicit MPLS tunnels having the same IP entry and exit points. This means that this IOTP may have several branches, each one corresponding to a particular LSP (as illustrated on Fig. 2, where the IOTP <R_1; R_6> has three branches).

3.1 Filtering

The first step consists in the filtering and sanitizing of the set of LSPs and/or IOTPs. This step is done through four different filters sequentially applied.

First, based on our observations, using inter-domain MPLS tunnels for transit traffic is negligible[3]. We therefore chose to not consider them in our study. As a consequence, IP addresses involved in a given LSP must belong to the same AS, otherwise it is rejected. This first filtering step is done by the `IntraAS` filter (see Fig. 3).

The objective of the `TargetAS` filter is to ensure that the `traceroute` destination is in a different AS than the tunnel itself. Indeed, imagine a situation in which the tunnel and the `traceroute` destination belong to the same domain. In that case, we are not in a scenario in which the tunnel is used for carrying transit traffic and, so, unlikely to be used for TE purpose.

[2]Any `traceroute` dataset can serve as input to LPR. The only condition is to be able to retrieve MPLS explicit tunnels from the `traceroute`, as explained in Sec. 2.3.

[3]Note that the observed rise in remote peering [25] does not contradict this measurement statement for several reasons. First, remote peering are made of invisible MPLS tunnels (i.e., no RFC4950 and no `ttl-propagate`– see Sec. 2.3) such that our measurement methodology is unable to retrieve them. Second, the purpose of remote peering is to avoid transit through another network while the scope of our study is the transit traffic. Eventually, remote peering consists in MPLS tunnels that belong to the remote peering provider, not tunnels going through several subsequent ASes

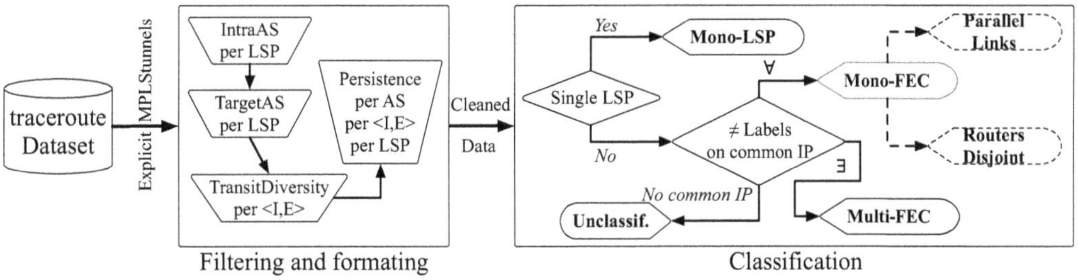

Figure 3: Overview of the LPR algorithm. LPR is divided in two important steps: (*i*) data filtering and (*ii*) MPLS tunnels classification.

To have a better view of the routing diversity, we next want to keep only IOTPs that are used to reach at least two destinations belonging to different ASes (`TransitDiversity` filter). The idea here is to capture multiple FECs (*multi-FEC* – remind that a FEC refers to a set of packets a single router forwards to the same next hop, via the same interface with the same treatment) scenarios based on IP destination prefixes that, by definition of IP routing, represent the more classical practice of TE. It is worth to notice that, even with that filter, we may underestimate the transit tunnel diversity (and, so, TE usage).

Finally, we verify the persistence in time of the LSPs to remove noise due to routing changes (`Persistence` filter). We keep LSPs encountered in measurement cycle X only if they are also seen in measurement cycle $X+1$, $X+2$, ..., or $X+j$ (the impact of the number of additional cycles j is evaluated in Sec. 4.2). In this case, the j cycles are consecutive and taken in the same month as cycle X. Note that we keep track of dynamics as it can represent in itself a TE usage rather than routing changes. In practice, if the vast majority of LSPs disappear for a given AS, we reinject the whole set of its LSPs to perform a standard classification on a given snapshot[4]. That is, we do not remove such an AS and continue to process it as the others but adding a dynamic tag to it.

The resulting set of IOTPs can then be classified with LPR whose pseudo-code is given in Algorithm 1. Those subsets of LSPs are robust, i.e., they are persistent in time, possibly diverse in targets, and focus on transit traffic through a single ISP. In the following, for each LSP falling within the same AS and the same couple of border edge routers <Ingress LER, Egress LER>, we compare their content both in terms of IP addresses and labels in order to determine the actual usage of the tunnel.

Algorithm 1 Classification step of the LPR algorithm.

Require: $\mathbb{T}$, the set of IOTPs after filtering

```
1: function LPR_CLASSIFICATION(T)
2:     /* creating resulting classes */
3:     MonoLSP ← ∅
4:     MultiFEC ← ∅
5:     MonoFEC ← ∅
6:     Unclassified ← ∅
7:     for IOTP_i in T do
8:         /* obtaining all LSPs of a given tunnel */
9:         LSPs ← IOTP_i.getLSPs()
10:        if |LSPs| == 1 then
11:            /* class 1 (Mono-LSP) */
12:            MonoLSP ← MonoLSP ⋃ IOTP_i
13:            continue
14:        /* checking for common IP addresses */
15:        CIP_i ← IOTP_i.getCommonIP()
16:        if |CommonIP| == 0 then
17:            /* class 4 (Unclassified) */
18:            Unclassified ← Unclassified ⋃ IOTP_i
19:            continue
20:        for IP_j in CIP_i do
21:            if |IP_j.getLabels()| > 1 then
22:                /* class 2 (Multi-FEC) */
23:                MultiFEC ← MultiFEC ⋃ IOTP_i
24:                IOTP_i_ismFEC = TRUE
25:                continue
26:        if ¬IOTP_i_ismFEC then
27:            /* class 3 (ECMP) */
28:            MonoFEC ← MonoFEC ⋃ IOTP_i
29:    /* returning all tunnel classes */
30:    return MonoLSP, MultiFEC, MonoFEC, Unclassified
```

3.2 Classification

The first class, illustrated in Fig. 4(a), is called *Mono-LSP*. That is, for a given IOTP, there exists only a single LSP (i.e., same IP addresses and same labels) for different destination ASes. This means we do not observe transit tunnel diversity, the same LSP being always used whatever the destination. As a consequence, for this tunnel, we are not able to reveal ECMP load balancing (by definition of the class) or the deployment of several FECs used to reach different ASes with different routing constraints (although we consider at least two destination ASes as stated in the filtering subsection). The condition to reveal such a class is described at line 10 of Algorithm 1.

The second class, illustrated in Fig. 4(b), is called *Multi-FEC*. That is, for a given IOTP, there exists at least one convergence point, i.e., a *common IP* interface belonging to an LSR where at least two LSPs converge. This convergence occurs on a given IP address of the LSR but we observe that the different LSPs use different MPLS labels at that convergence point. For instance, on Fig. 4(b), the first LSP (plain line) considers labels (L_3, L_1), while the second (dashed line) considers labels (L_4, L_2). Labels L_1 and L_2 being used on

[4] In this paper, the reinjection is realized only if the whole set of LSPs is deleted by the filter.

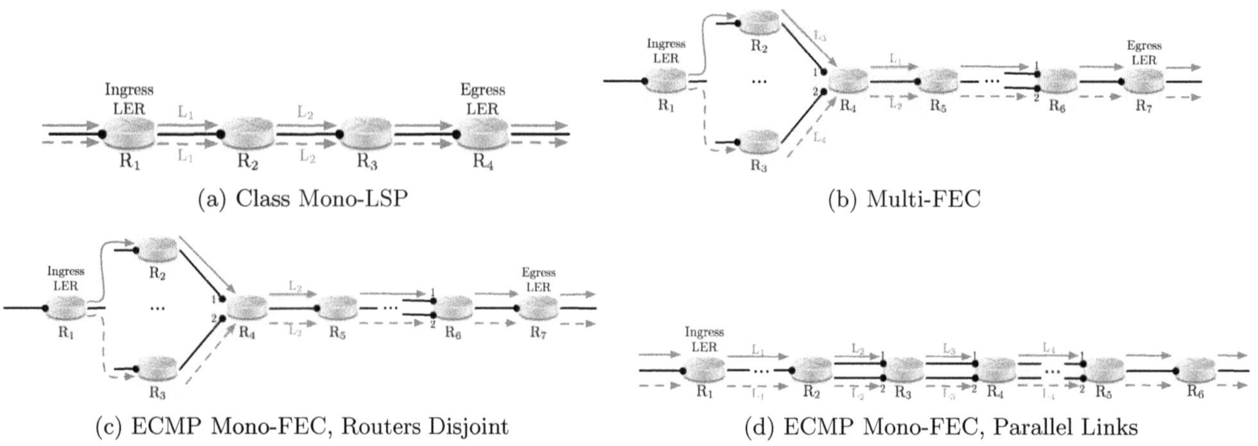

(a) Class Mono-LSP

(b) Multi-FEC

(c) ECMP Mono-FEC, Routers Disjoint

(d) ECMP Mono-FEC, Parallel Links

Figure 4: Typical MPLS Label Based Patterns. Note that big dots refer to a router IP interface.

the same IP address, thus on the same router, this case suggests the use of multiple FECs for that tunnel. On the contrary to the use of standard LDP where, by default, labels have a router scope (i.e., each LSR proposes the same label for a given destination to all its upstream routers[5]), distinct labels proposed by the same LSR for a given Egress LER, indicate distinct FECs. This use of multi-FEC suggests TE practice for that particular tunnel. In order to provide an upper bound of TE usage, we classify an IOTP as multi-FEC as soon as distinct labels appear on a given common IP address as described at lines 20–25 of Algorithm 1.

Note that the concept of common IP address is fundamental for the classification as we cannot conclude anything if there does not exist any of them for a given IOTP. Fortunately, most LSPs of a given IOTP converge at some point[6], such that we can distinguish the label distribution protocol in use. In practice, we introduce the notion of common IP address sets computed independently for each IOTP (line 15 of Algorithm 1). It simply consists of all IP addresses belonging to LSRs that are traversed by at least two distinct LSPs of a given IOTP. The two LSPs may differ at a given hop either in terms of IP addresses (this hop is then not included in the common IP set by definition) or in terms of labels (at any hop, including a common IP one).

The third class, shown in Fig. 4(c) and Fig. 4(d), refers to IOTPs that perform load balancing between their LSPs. More specifically, this class implies that, for all LSPs of a given IOTP traversing a common LSR, labels are identical (on the contrary to the Multi-FEC class where there exists at least one difference). Therefore, this class refers to the use of a single FEC between the Ingress and the Egress LERs. It typically corresponds to the use of MPLS load balancing on the top of IP thanks to ECMP. Note that an IOTP falls in this class if and only if all its common IP addresses verify this behavior as stated at lines 26–28 of Algorithm 1. This class, that we call *ECMP Mono-FEC* (or *Mono-FEC* on Fig. 3 for readability reasons because it consists in Multi-LSP Mono-FEC), may be divided into two subclasses. First, if labels are the same all along the LSPs but IP addresses differ, we believe IP addresses at a given hop are aliases. Indeed, recalling that the scope of LDP labels is local to the LSR, it is unlikely that two distinct LSRs will propose the same label. We thus conclude, in this case, that the IOTP only uses parallel links to perform ECMP load balancing (Fig. 4(d)). On the contrary, if LSPs differ both in labels and IP addresses on, at least, a given hop, the IOTP seems to perform ECMP load balancing through disjoint routers (Fig. 4(c)). This distinction is of the highest interest: we do not require the use of an active resolution probing to show that a large portion of ECMP load balanced paths relies actually only on parallel links.

Finally, when PHP is used, the common IP set for a given IOTP may be empty if the LSPs converge only at the Egress LER. In this situation, we arbitrarily tag this IOTP as *Unclassified*, as indicated at lines 16–18 of Algorithm 1. Sec. 5 proposes an alternative method to avoid this limitation, but in practice, it rarely occurs as demonstrated in Sec. 4.

[5]In practice, such destinations are generally loopback addresses of BGP edges routers. It is used here for scalability reasons and refers to the use of the BGP next-hop feature: it does not distinguish FECs for a given edge router.

[6]It is not necessarily at the Egress LER since the use of PHP does not exhibit labels at this last hop in practice.

4. EVALUATION

In this section, we use our LPR algorithm in order to evaluate and understand the usage of MPLS. We first describe the considered dataset (Sec. 4.1). Next, we evaluate the impact of the filtering steps on the dataset and the classification (Sec. 4.2). We also focus on several IOTPs properties in Sec. 4.3. Then we focus on a subset of five large ASes (mainly Tier-1) whose MPLS deployment is characteristic and discuss how it is used and deployed over the five years of data (Sec. 4.4). Finally, we discuss some properties of MPLS label dynamics on a specific AS (Sec. 4.5).

4.1 Dataset

In order to evaluate how MPLS is used and how its usage has evolved over time, we apply LPR on an extensive dataset obtained from the CAIDA Archipelago infrastructure [26], a distributed infrastructure in which teams of monitors perform Paris traceroute [27] to all routed /24 prefixes in a short amount of time. Currently, the Archipelago infrastructure is made of more than 100 monitors scattered around the world.

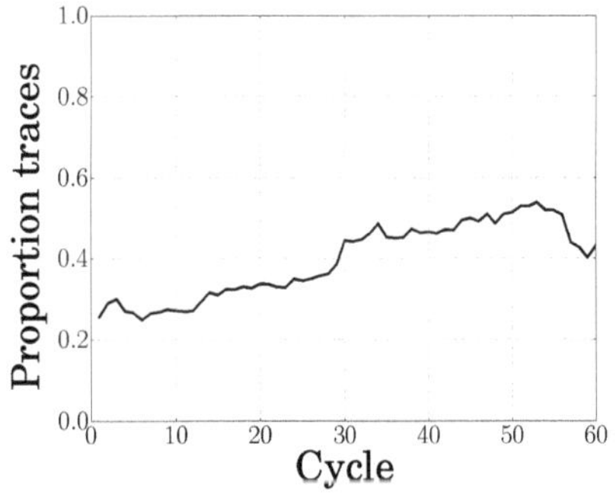

(a) Proportion of traceroutes traversing at least one MPLS explicit tunnel

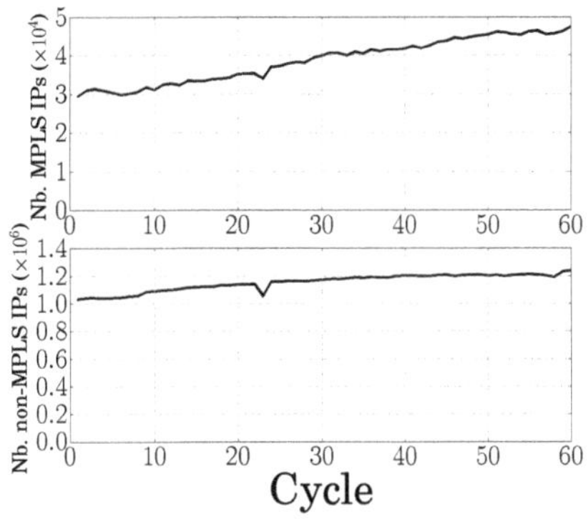

(b) MPLS usage in IP addresses

Figure 5: Global deployment of MPLS in our dataset.

For our needs, we download data collected between January 2010 and December 2014. For each month in that period, we consider the first run of each team and call such a data a *cycle*. We therefore work on 60 cycles. For each cycle, we perform IP2AS mapping using Routeviews data [28] collected the same day as the considered cycle. Next, for each cycle, we extract all explicit tunnels, i.e., MPLS tunnels that exhibit the `ttl-propagate` option and ICMP extension (see Sec. 2.3).

Fig. 5(a) shows, for each cycle, the proportion of `traceroute` that traverse at least one explicit tunnel (before any kind of filtering performed by our cleaning stage). During the five years of data, we observe a significant increase in the deployment of MPLS. Around the 30th cycle, we see an increase of roughly 10% in the traces showing at least one MPLS tunnel. Similarly, at the end, we observe a decrease. This phenomenon is due to the rise and fall of MPLS usage inside AS3356 (see Sec. 4.4, and Fig. 16 in particular, for details about AS3356 – a Tier-1 whose name is Level3). Fig. 5(b) shows the raw number of unique IP addresses used in MPLS (upper graph) and those not used in MPLS (lower graph) for each cycle. If we see a slight increase in the number of IP addresses observed in the data collected (21% over the five years), we observe a much larger increase in the number of IP addresses used for MPLS (60%). Further, two drops are observed in Fig. 5(b): at cycle 23 and 58. Those drops are caused by measurements issues in the Archipelago infrastructure.

Filter	Average	
Incomplete LSPs	0.853	± 0.01
`IntraAS`	0.844	± 0.01
`TargetAS`	0.717	± 0.009
`TransitDiversity`	0.644	± 0.009
`Persistence`	0.534	± 0.007

Table 1: Cumulative average (and confidence interval), over the 60 cycles, of the proportion of tunnels remaining after applying each filter. On average, a cycle contains 14×10^6 LSPs before filtering.

Globally speaking, and as already stated previously [7, 8], this evolution shows operators seem to deploy more and more MPLS tunnels during the last decade. This increase confirms the interest of many operators for MPLS and opens the question of its actual usage.

4.2 Filtering Impact

In this section, we evaluate the impact of the first step of LPR, i.e., the filtering process (see Sec. 3.1). Table 1 gives a first overview of filtering effects on LSPs. It provides the cumulative average (with confidence intervals) over the 60 cycles of the LSPs proportion remaining after applying each filter. The "Incomplete LSPs" line refers to LSPs that are incomplete in the `traceroute` sense, i.e., at least one of the LSRs composing the LSP did not reply to probes (i.e., anonymous router). In that case, the whole LSP is removed from the dataset. We see that the strongest filter (i.e., the one that removes most of tunnels) is the Incomplete LSPs as it removes, on average, 14.7% of tunnels. There is nothing surprising here as it is very common to have incomplete `traceroute` due to anonymous routers [29]. This filter impact is also considerable relatively to others because this is the first one being applied.

In Sec. 3.1, we claimed that using inter-domain MPLS tunnels is negligible. This is confirmed by statistics associated to the `IntraAS` filter as only a low 0.9% of LSPs concerns inter-domain tunnels. Further, on average, 12.7% of the tunnels concern a destination located in the same AS as the tunnel itself (`TargetAS`) while 7.3% were used for reaching a single destination (`TransitDiversity`). Finally, 10% of remaining tunnels are removed due to routing noise (`Persistence`). This filter keeps LSPs encountered in measurement cycle X only if they are also seen at least once in measurement cycle $X+1$, $X+2$, ..., or $X+j$. Here, the j cycles are taken consecutively in the same month as cycle X. For Table 1, we fixed $j = 2$.

To evaluate the impact of the `Persistence` filter and, in particular, the impact of the number of subsequent snapshots considered for applying the filter, we focus on the 29 snapshots composing the whole December 2014 Archipelago dataset. We vary the parameter j between 0 (no `Persistence` filter) and 29 (the whole month is used for the persistence analysis but a few measurement campaigns last a bit more than one day). Results are shown in Fig. 6.

Fig. 6(a) shows the amount of tunnels kept after `Persistence` filtering. We observed that increasing the parameter j does not affect that much the number of tunnels. When $j \geq 2$, the amount of tunnels remains mostly stable. A drop is observed compared to when $j = 0$. This is expected as, by definition, when $j = 0$, no `Persistence` filter is applied.

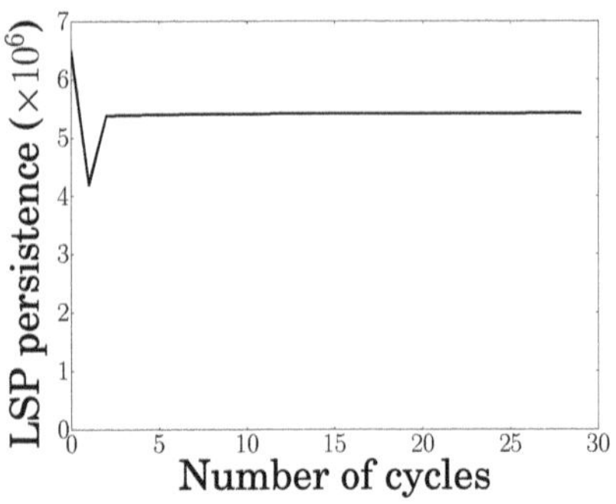

(a) Number of tunnel kept

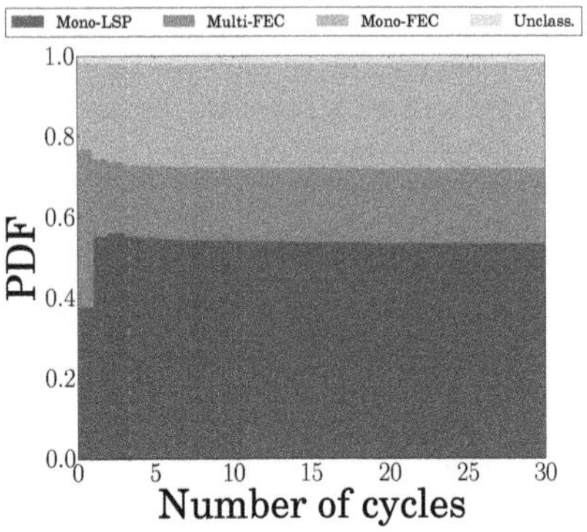

(b) Impact on classification

Figure 6: Impact of `Persistence` filter on the December 2014 dataset.

In the same fashion, the large drop at $j = 1$ is due to the necessity to retrieve the LSP in two subsequent snapshots while the condition is, by definition, more relaxed for $j \geq 2$. Fig. 6(b) shows the impact of the `Persistence` filter on the classification at a global scale. It would be a matter of concern if the persistence had a strong impact on the classification. We observe that when $j \geq 2$, the classification remains stable. The impact, for $j \leq 1$ is to trade Mono-LSP tunnels with Multi-FEC tunnels and is partially explained by the use of dynamic Multi-FEC LSPs (see Sec. 4.5).

In the remainder of this paper, we consider the value $j = 2$ for the `Persistence` filtering, meaning that an LSP observed in cycle X will be considered for classification if it is also encountered in measurement snapshot $X+1$ or $X+2$ of the same month.

4.3 Tunnel Length, Width, and Symmetry

In order to describe observed IOTPs at a high level, we adapt metrics proposed by Augustin et al. [1] for load balanced paths. Recall that an IOTP is defined as an <Ingress LER; Egress LER> pair corresponding to a set of explicit MPLS tunnels having the same entry and exit points.

We first define an IOTP *length* as the number of LSRs in the longest LSP of that IOTP without counting the Ingress and Egress LERs, i.e. the number of intermediate LSRs in the longest LSP. Fig. 7 provides the length distribution of IOTPs for the last cycle of our data set (i.e., December 2014). We observe that, in most cases (i.e., > 65%), tunnels

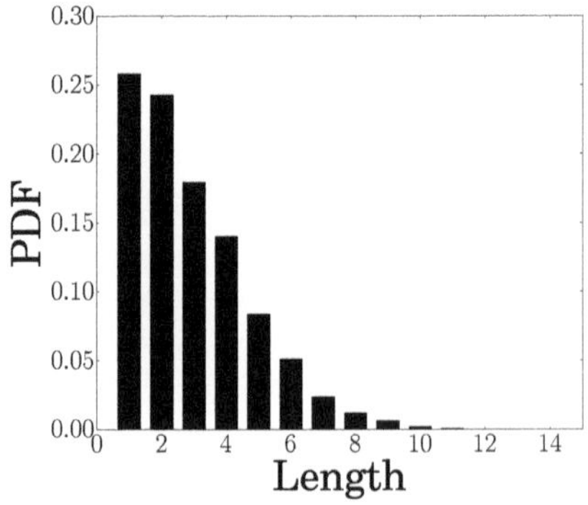

Figure 7: IOTP length distribution (Cycle 60).

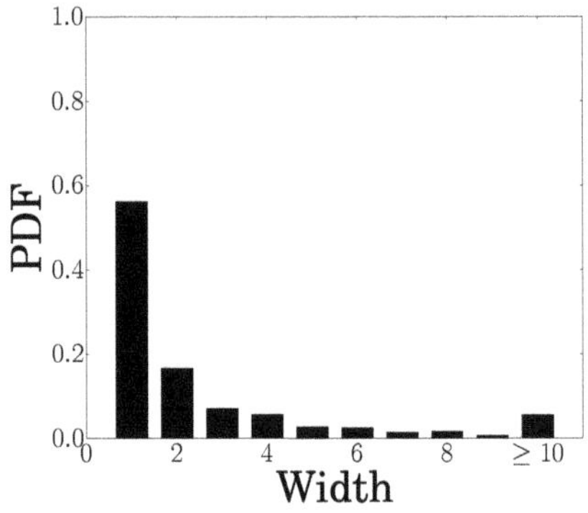

(a) All classes

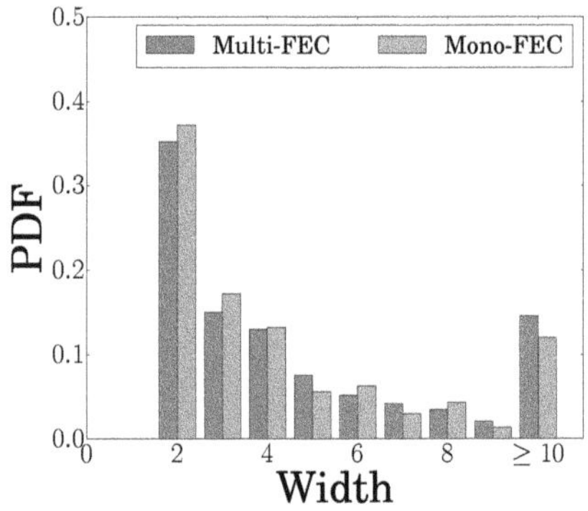

(b) Mono-FEC and Multi-FEC

Figure 8: IOTP width distribution (Cycle 60).

are rather short, i.e., ≤ 3 LSRs[7], although a very low proportion of them can be quite long. This property is related to the short diameter of many ASes [30].

Fig. 8(a) provides IOTPs' *width* distribution, i.e., the number of "branches" between the Ingress LER and the Egress LER. Branches may differ physically (i.e., IP addresses) or logically (i.e., MPLS labels). It is worth to notice that, by definition, only tunnels falling in the Mono-LSP class will have a width of 1. Although a very low proportion of the IOTPs are very large (up to 236 branches in our dataset),

[7]To which one has to add the LERs to obtain the complete LSP.

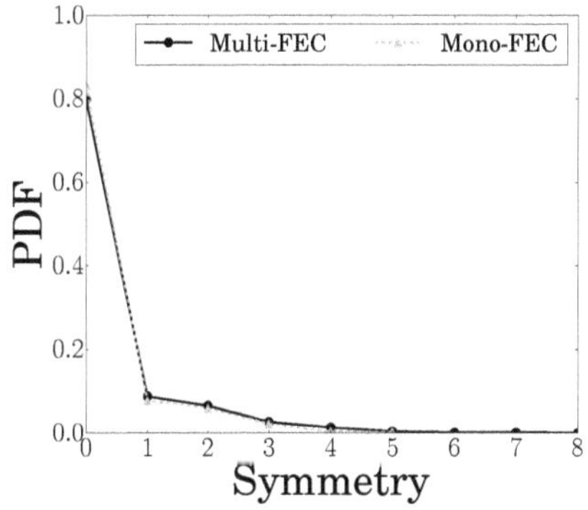

Figure 9: IOTP symmetry distribution (Cycle 60) for Multi-FEC and Mono-FEC classes.

most of them (56%) are narrow, i.e., a width of 1. This reveals that, in our dataset, the observed IOTPs are mainly Mono-LSP. It is worth to notice that this result is consistent with Fig. 6(b) in which the majority of IOTPs are indeed Mono-LSP. Additionally, Fig. 6(b) also reveals how tunnels are used in general. The usage of RSVP-TE (and thus TE) is limited (roughly 20% of the IOTPs), leading thus to the conclusions that tunnels are essentially built based on LDP.

Fig. 8(b) shows the width distribution for each class separately, except the Mono-LSP one[8]. The key point here is that Mono-FEC and Multi-FEC tunnels have nearly the same distribution. Although the tail of the distribution is slightly dominated by Multi-FEC, this result is quite surprising as it tends to indicate that TE-based LSPs do not use much more path diversity than basic ECMP (with a different way to perform load balancing though). Since such a property is biased by the measure itself (it is a lower bound as it does not provide a complete exploration, see Sec. 5), the following property may be useful to better understand structural differences between this two kinds of path diversity.

Finally, an IOTP *symmetry* is defined as the difference between that IOTP length and the number of LSRs in the smallest LSP of that IOTP. If the symmetry equals 0, we say that the IOTP is *balanced* (or *symmetrical*). Otherwise, it is said to be *unbalanced* (or *asymmetrical*) and the value obtained gives an idea of the imbalance. Obviously, by definition, an IOTP that would fall in the Mono-LSP class is balanced. Therefore, the distribution given in Fig. 9 does not show the Mono-LSP case[9]. The first observation is that balanced paths represent 80% of the distribution (for both classes). This property is derived from two facts: ECMP forwarding paths are often similar in terms of hop count (80% of Mono-FEC IOTPs are balanced) and many multi-FEC LSPs actually go through the same path, they only differ in terms of labels – note that it is the main cause of the 80% share of the balanced Multi-FEC IOTPs. The second one is, again, that there are no significant differences between the two classes. This similarity is really surprising as one may speculate that TE paths may completely

[8]Unclassified tunnels (not shown on Fig. 8(b) as they are marginal – see Fig. 6(b)) are mainly narrow.

[9]Unclassified IOTPs are marginal and, thus, not shown on Fig. 9.

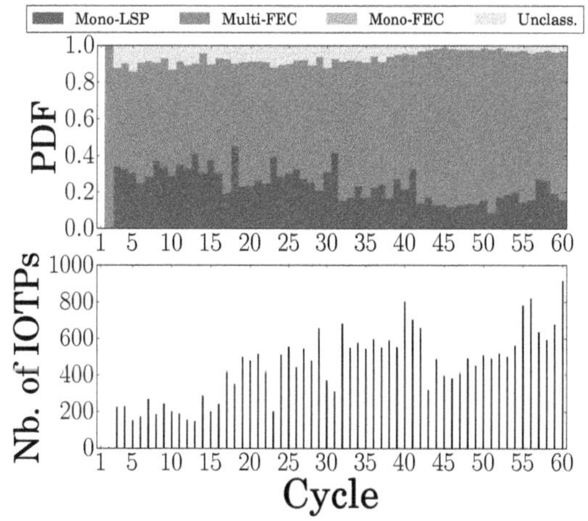

Figure 10: Tunnels classification for AS1273 (Vodafone). We observe mainly a Multi-FEC usage of MPLS.

differ among themselves according to each FEC constraint. In practice, constraints seem to be satisfied by a unique IP path in most cases, meaning that reserving bandwidth in an over-provisioned network is equivalent to using resource pooling mechanisms such as ECMP.

4.4 IOTPs Classification

Fig. 10, 11, 12, 14 and 15 present the IOTPs classification for several ASes. We selected this set of five ASes as they are representative of typical MPLS behaviors across the whole dataset. It is worth to notice that they are all Tier-1 ASes except Vodafone (AS2173), a Transit network. Each of those figures is made of two parts:

- The lower part gives, for each cycle (X-Axis), the number of IOTPs that were considered for classification.
- The upper part provides, for each cycle (X-Axis), the proportion of tunnels in each of the four classes.

Empty zones in both parts of the graph refer to cycles where no MPLS tunnel was encountered. Finally, note that those figures must be read conjointly with Table 2 that provides the name and statistics about all analyzed network infrastructures (i.e., minimum/maximum/average number of IP addresses, tagged as MPLS or not, observed over a year).

Fig. 10 gives the classification for AS1273 (Vodafone, large Transit ISP). AS1273 is interesting in several points of view. First, as we notice in Table 2 and in Fig. 10 (below part), the usage of MPLS (for transit traffic) within this AS has increased over time. Second, AS1273 seems to deploy MPLS mostly for TE reasons (the Multi-FEC class usage also grows with time to the detriment of Mono-LSP usage). Moreover Mono-FEC (ECMP) is almost invisible.

Fig. 11 presents tunnels classification for AS7018 (AT&T, Tier-1 ISP). The usage of MPLS relatively decreases over time while the Multi-FEC class is more and more used in place of Mono-FEC tunnels. There is a drop in the number of IOTPs around cycle 22, that seems to correspond to a transition in MPLS usage.

Fig. 12 presents tunnels classification for AS6453 (Tata Communications, Tier-1 ISP). This AS has almost no Multi-FEC and a strong (although declining) usage of Mono-FEC

		2010			2011			2012			2013			2014		
		min	max	avg	min	max	avg	min	max	avg	min	max	avg	min	max	avg
AS1273 (Vodafone)	non MPLS	796	1097	887	828	914	871	901	993	950	918	1,014	971	928	1,088	990
	MPLS	0	160	115	108	192	147	149	230	199	134	234	178	147	222	171
AS7018 (AT&T)	non MPLS	36,614	37,656	36,984	34,537	39,988	37,874	40,022	48,839	45,764	48,946	57,995	50.597	50,518	57,403	52,489
	MPLS	379	588	493	555	775	663	608	701	655	554	648	605	486	554	508
AS6453 (Tata)	non MPLS	2,099	2,269	2,181	1,896	2,209	2,043	1,883	2,118	2,005	2,017	2,165	2,084	2,054	2,162	2,099
	MPLS	435	513	463	326	454	380	291	334	308	260	336	298	268	314	293
AS2914 (NTT)	non MPLS	2,760	3,061	2,884	3,138	3,368	3,243	3,293	3,429	3,349	3,349	3,641	3,490	3,652	4,116	3,885
	MPLS	191	247	216	226	270	248	243	293	262	283	314	300	308	328	316
AS3356 (Level3)	non MPLS	9,121	9,417	9,253	9,245	9,775	9,503	9,464	10,033	9,700	9,434	9,997	9,708	9,342	11,108	10,162
	MPLS	0	14	1	0	0	0	0	646	369	570	726	676	3	776	518

Table 2: Statistics about IP addresses for some ASes of interest (after filtering).

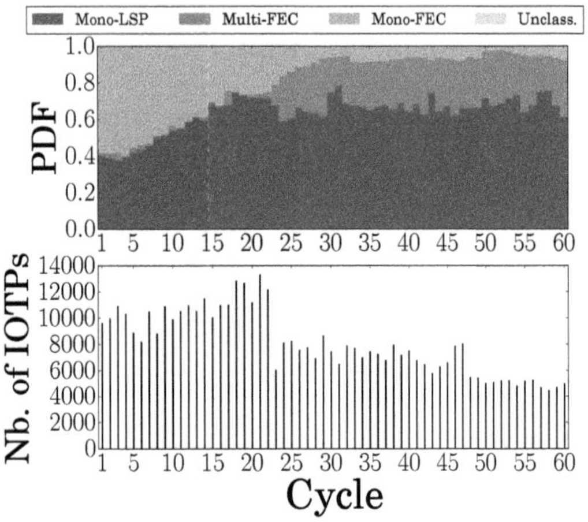

Figure 11: Tunnels classification for AS7018 (AT&T).

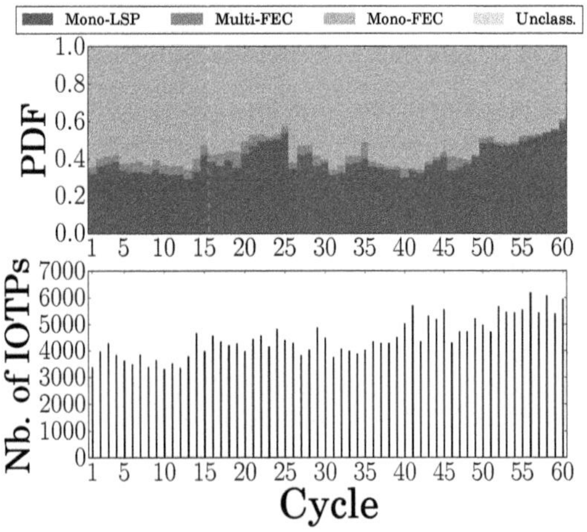

Figure 12: Tunnels classification for AS6453 (Tata Communications). We observe mainly a Mono-FEC usage of MPLS.

that exhibit topology logical properties enabling a large use of ECMP.

Fig. 13 deepens the Mono-FEC class for AS6453 (Tata Communications). Indeed, this class can be split into "Routers Disjoint" (i.e., LSPs in a given IOTP differ both in labels and

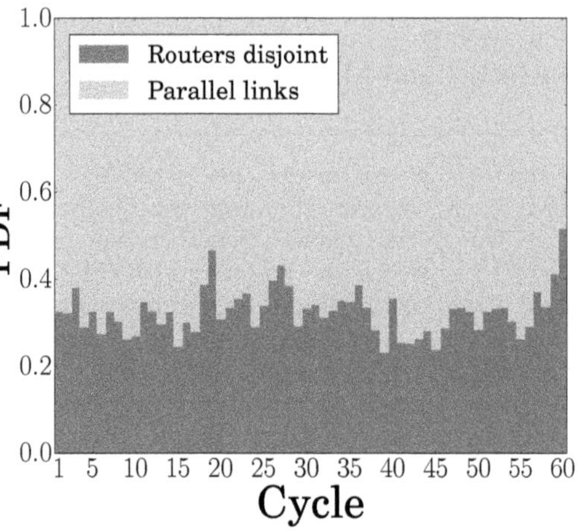

Figure 13: Split between "Routers Disjoint" and "Parallel Links" for Mono-FEC class of AS6453 (Tata Communications).

IP addresses on at least a given hop) and "Parallel Links" (i.e., LSPs in a given IOTP in which labels are the same all along the LSPs while the corresponding IP addresses are different). Over time, AS6453 has deployed Mono-FEC tunnels mostly based on parallel links (between 60 and 70% of tunnels belong to the Parallel Links subclass).

Fig. 14 presents the tunnel classification for AS2914 (NTT, Tier-1 ISP. This AS shows an increase in MPLS usage. The number of IOTPs observed during the period of interest has been multiplied by three, which is consistent with the fact that the number of IP addresses used in MPLS has also increased (see Table 2), while the usage of MPLS has remained mostly stable over time: Mono-LSP. We, however, see that, with time, the usage of Mono-LSP slightly and relatively decreases in favor of Mono-FEC.

Fig. 15 presents tunnels classification for AS3356 (Level3, Tier-1 ISP), which has a quite curious shape: MPLS appears during the 29th cycle, observes a period of stability, and, finally, presents a sharp decrease starting at cycle 55.

We investigated the data before cycle 29, in order to determine whether the rise of MPLS during that cycle matches with new hardware (or IP addresses) deployment that is dedicated to MPLS or a dramatic change in routing. Looking at the Archipelago files, we find that, in an infrastructural point of view, nothing has changed between Cycle 28 and Cycle 29, i.e., we observe mostly the same set of IP addresses. This

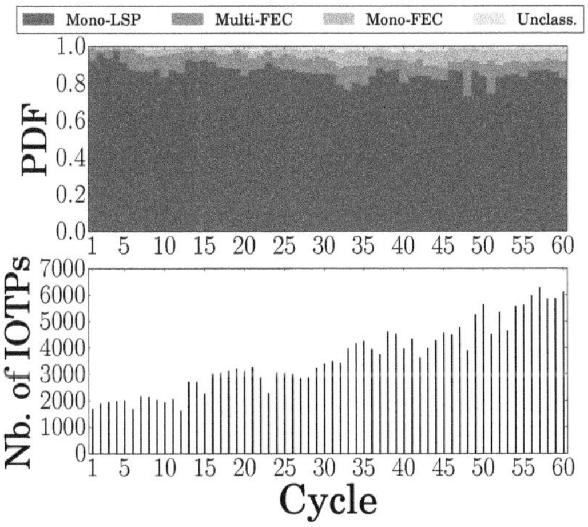

Figure 14: Tunnels classification for AS2914 (NTT). We observe mainly a Mono-LSP usage of MPLS.

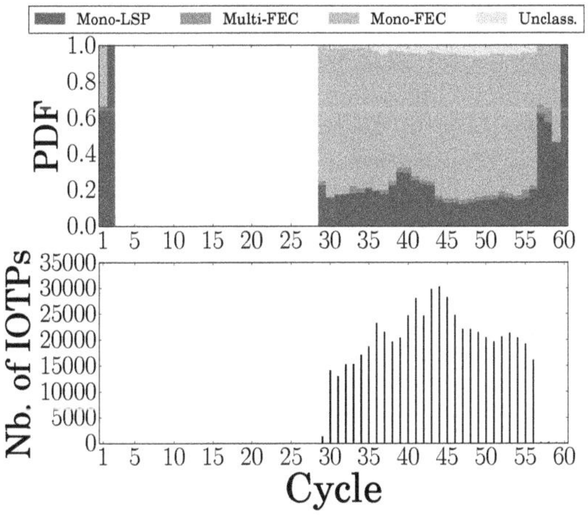

Figure 15: Tunnels classification for AS3356 (Level3). We mainly observe a Mono-FEC usage of MPLS.

means that only the usage of the existing infrastructure has been modified between cycle 28 and cycle 29.

To investigate further, Fig. 16 presents the state of MPLS deployment the month prior to the 29th cycle (April 2012). To do so, we downloaded all daily Archipelago data dumps for April 2012, without respecting the probing cycle (as described in Sec. 4.1). This means that the number of considered Archipelago vantage points differs from one day to another. Fig. 16 provides two pieces of information: (*i*) the number of encountered IOTPs each day before and after the filtering steps (upper part of Fig. 16) and (*ii*) the number of LSPs identified each day, again before and after the filtering steps (lower part of Fig. 16). Peaks and drops observed in the number of IOTPs identified after April 25th are due to the variations in the number of considered Archipelago vantage points.

We observe that the deployment of MPLS has started around April 15th, and it took a half month to fully deploy MPLS in AS3356. It exhibits an incremental MPLS

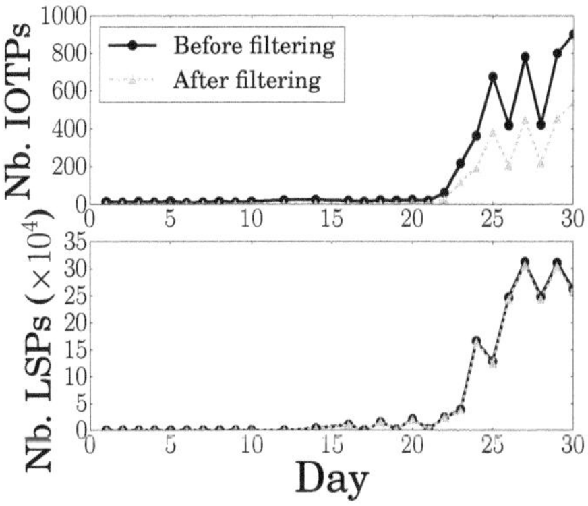

Figure 16: The rise of MPLS deployment in AS3356 (Level3), focus on April 2012.

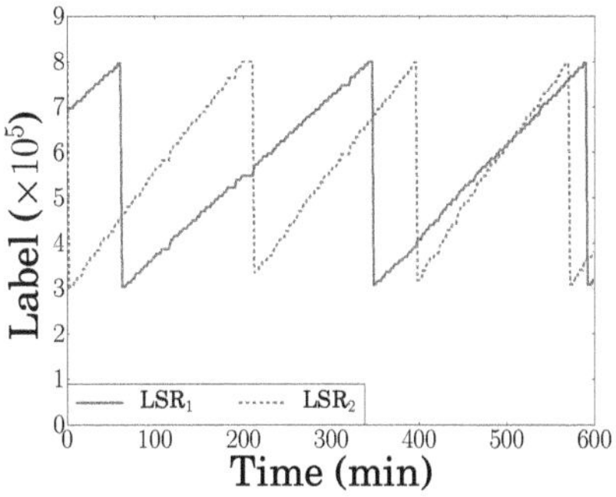

Figure 17: Label range evolution in case of Multi-FEC tunnels, belonging to AS1273 (Vodafone), as seen from a vantage point located in Strasbourg.

deployment rather than an abrupt transition. Further, the number of LSPs does not differ before and after filtering (the `Persistence` filter is not used here), while it does for IOTPs. It is due to the fact that most LSPs are "shared" by several IOTPs, i.e., only one of the two LSP extremities (the LER) differ among a subset of them in many cases (see Sec. 5 for discussions about LPR limitations and alias resolution in particular).

Generally speaking, we observe in this section that using LDP is the rule (with – Mono-FEC – or without ECMP – Mono-LSP) while RSVP-TE seems to be more marginal both in terms of deployment and, more surprisingly, in terms of the structural path diversity it enables compared to ECMP.

4.5 Multi-FEC and Label Dynamics

The `Persistence` filter (see Sec. 4.2) was introduced to remove side effects of routing dynamics. For example, we could infer two LSPs in a given IOTP (hence a Multi-LSPs IOTP in theory) while these two LSPs were not simultaneously used in practice. It may be due to a routing change during the measurement. However we found that in some (rare) cases this filter could hide an interesting phenomenon, namely LSPs that change their labels very frequently. This type of LSPs is filtered out by the `Persistence` filter so that we study those ASes in a different way (in practice, they are easily retrievable since all or almost all LSPs disappear with the filter)[10].

To investigate this a little bit further, we selected a small number of ASes exhibiting this behavior (this was the case for AS1273 we discussed in Sec. 4.4), and launched an additional `traceroute` campaign from a unique vantage point located in Strasbourg, the purpose being to monitor the label changes frequency. So for each destination, the route was traced at a very high sampling rate, i.e., a `traceroute` was sent to each destination every two minutes. The results for a single LSP made of two LSRs is given in Fig. 17. The Y axis represents the labels (labels range from 300,000 to 800,000) and each line represents the label evolution. When a label reaches its maximum, it starts again from the minimum).

Fig. 17 shows that the LSP is reconstructed at a high frequency and almost periodically. Our interpretation is that this LSP is built by RSVP-TE and that the Ingress LER is configured to "re-optimize" frequently the LSP (although in practice it follows the same IP route). Moreover, we point out three interesting findings. First, this systematic temporal-based behavior seems to be mainly related to Juniper hardware [31]. Second, we also observe on Fig. 17 that label changes seem to be also performed on a factual basis (on each curve, some step durations differ at some points). Eventually, the shape of the curve resulting from LSR_2 evolves more quickly than the one of LSR_1: it suggests that LSR_2 is more solicited than LSR_1 in terms of number of LSPs going through it.

5. DISCUSSION

In this section, we discuss possible extensions of our works. While the core mechanism of LPR, i.e., the inference technique that allows for distinguishing among LDP and RSVP-TE, has been experimentally tested and validated, our work can be improved in two directions to extend its scope and to increase its accuracy. We first discuss potential measurement improvements (the active campaign) and then consider possible LPR extensions (the passive analysis).

The first hypothesis we need to verify and explore is about the way MPLS TE is deployed and used by today's operators. In particular, we considered that the traffic differentiation is performed according to destination prefixes (as in standard IP forwarding), i.e., distinct FECs are set up on this basis. Some operators may consider other ways for distinguishing types of services: the source IP prefix, the incoming AS, or even other fields from both the IP and the transport headers for setting FECs at the flow grain. Instead of simply optimizing their own resources according to the entry point in their networks, some operators may enable multipath forwarding for more specific objectives (using complex access control lists – ACLs – rather than standard commands). In this paper, as a first global study on the MPLS usage, we mainly rely on an extensive and longitudinal existing dataset that provides historical traces. The main purpose of this dataset being to provide topology discovery data for helping researchers to understand IP network properties, it does not bring enough information for such a specific study. However, based on a dedicated and finely calibrated probing campaign, we should better understand whether such practices are common or not.

Second, as an ongoing work for providing ground truth results, we currently check if our distinction between IP and MPLS multipath routing is valid. One way to do that would be to launch an extensive Paris traceroute [27] campaign to understand if the LSPs we tag as Mono-FEC ECMP (and so using LDP) are actually also visible with such a tool. Beside, we also plan to check whether Multi-FEC LSPs are, indeed, not visible through Paris traceroute. If those two properties are correct, we argue that it would be a ground proof of our label-based analysis done through LPR. We believe that such a validation campaign will also provide us the ability to state if IP-only (i.e., not using TCP or UDP ports) load balancers actually exist for standard traffic. Indeed, the study of Augustin et al. [1] mentions this possibility while we suspect it is likely to be rather due to multi-LSP deployed on a destination basis.

Third, in this paper, we decided not to rely on any alias resolution mechanisms [32] to avoid well known biases that they may induce. However, it can be interesting to define an IOTP at the router level rather than at the IP level. Such a consideration should provide more refined data for distinguishing our MPLS classes. In particular, it will reduce the number of IOTPs and so provide more consistent results that may be closer to the actual MPLS usage.

On the LPR algorithm itself, we may modify two main aspects. As a future work, we envision to extend our analysis in order to take into account *LSP-trees* (i.e., the capability of forwarding packets belonging to the same FEC but issued from several Ingress LER, and so arriving from distinct IP addresses – but with the same LSE label considering LDP – using the same outgoing label [2]). It may allow for a better understanding of the underlying use of LDP and so improve the applicability of our classification. Indeed, using such an extension, more LSPs will be classified with LPR because they will be indexed only through the Egress LER. Note that, in practice, we will have to consider DAGs rather than trees due to the use of ECMP. This study is in the same vein as the one that envisions to use preliminary alias resolution techniques as it can provide more consistent data.

Finally, if PHP is used (i.e., the LSE is removed by the penultimate LSR – see Sec. 2.1), the Egress LER generally does not exhibit labels. In such a situation, LSPs within a given tunnel may never reach a common IP address providing labels[11]. To avoid such a limitation and so achieve a complete classification, we can rely on a simple heuristic for alias resolution mechanism. In a usual situation with a series of point-to-point links inferred thanks to a `traceroute` path, all previous IP level interfaces of a given common IP address should belong to the same router. Indeed, if we assume that a router answers to `traceroute` probes using the incoming interface of the probe and there is no layer-two device connected to this interface, then such IP addresses are aliases of the same router (since to enter a router through the same IP interface, it is necessary to use the same point-to-point link on the same upstream router). In the case of Mono-FEC, we should thus observe the same label on previous IP addresses while we should observe distinct ones in case of Multi-FEC case. This simple mechanism reen-

[10]Remind that if the vast majority of LSPs disappear for a given AS (due to the `Persistence` filter, we reinject the whole set of its LSPs in order to perform the classification. The difference with the standard classification is that those particular ASes are tagged as dynamic.

[11]By definition, the Egress LER is a convergence point while intermediate LSRs are not necessarily traversed by multiple LSPs.

forces the analysis by ensuring that any set of common IP addresses cannot be empty. Indeed, even in a worst case situation, at least the penultimate hop of an IOTP (the upstream of the Egress LER) can serve as a common IP. We already observed that results seem to be robust in this regard since they do not significantly change the classification except by removing the *Unclassified* class. Again, we preferred to work without relying on other hypothesis than the ones about MPLS label distribution and so did not present those results in this paper.

6. RELATED WORK

During the last years, MPLS has been more and more investigated by the research community. However, all the work performed up to now focuses on MPLS tunnels identification. For instance, Sherwood et al. investigated the presence of anonymous and hidden routers as part of DisCarte [6] using the IP Record Route option. However, they note that routers involved in an MPLS LSP do not record any IP address in the provided IP option space, and so, the record route option is not able to identify hidden routers. More recently, Sommers et al. [7] examined the characteristics of MPLS deployments that are explicitly identified using RFC4950 extensions, as observed in CAIDA's topology data. They also developed a methodology to infer MPLS tunnels in archived data where ICMP extensions are not recorded. Donnet et al. [8] provided algorithms for detecting MPLS tunnels depending on the way LSRs react to the `ttl-propagate` and RFC4950 options.

It has also been demonstrated that MPLS tunnels may have an impact on Internet topology discovery tools. For instance, the presence of MPLS tunnels may interfere with load balancing detection [1] or violate the destination-based forwarding [9].

On the contrary to this paper, none of these studies discussed the actual usage of MPLS tunnels by operators, neither investigated the dynamic of labels.

7. CONCLUSION

In this paper we presented a classification algorithm, LPR, that takes as input data obtained from `traceroute` campaigns, and produces a classification of MPLS paths used for transit traffic. This gives some insights on the different usages of MPLS, either as a basic encapsulation technique allowing, through LDP, scalability and independence between routing/forwarding in the ISP network and outside, or, as a more refined technique, allowing, through RSVP-TE and Traffic Engineering (TE), extended routing protocols to differentiate traffic and finely tune network usage.

We gave results based on the classification by LPR over five years of data collected by Archipelago. As a result, we found that the usage of MPLS is increasing over this period, and that the use of the basic encapsulation method seems predominant, with or without path diversity. Although the use of RSVP-TE is less common, traffic engineering is also well represented in some Autonomous Systems (ASes). Another (not so surprising) lesson, is that the use of MPLS varies greatly depending on the considered AS, from almost all mono-path (no diversity) to a wide deployment of traffic engineering. For a given AS, class distribution may also vary greatly over time.

Since most major vendor routers implement MPLS capabilities, deploying (or removing) MPLS is mainly a system configuration process. Similarly deploying LDP, RSVP-TE, or both is a matter of configuration. A last lesson is that when TE is deployed, in many cases, different LSPs between the same endpoints take the same IP path (TE using MPLS is almost as common as MPLS without path diversity). This seems to imply that bandwidth is sufficiently abundant for allowing all LSPs to share the same physical route. We aim at investigating the traffic distribution among MPLS tunnels in future works.

Acknowledgments

This work is partially funded by the European Commission funded mPlane ICT-318627 project.

8. REFERENCES

[1] B. Augustin, R. Teixeira, and T. Friedman, "Measuring load-balanced paths in the Internet," in *Proc. ACM Internet Measurement Conference (IMC)*, November 2007.

[2] E. Rosen, A. Viswanathan, and R. Callon, "Multiprotocol label switching architecture," Internet Engineering Task Force, RFC 3031, January 2001.

[3] K. Muthukrishnan and A. Malis, "A core MPLS IP VPN architecture," Internet Engineering Task Force, RFC 2917, September 2000.

[4] C. Srinivasan, L. P. Bloomberg, A. Viswanathan, and T. Nadeau, "Multiprotocol label switching (MPLS) traffic engineering (TE) management information base (MIB)," Internet Engineering Task Force, RFC 3812, June 2004.

[5] X. Xiao, A. Hannan, and B. Bailey, "Traffic engineering with MPLS in the Internet," *IEEE Network Magazine*, vol. 14, no. 2, April 2000.

[6] R. Sherwood, A. Bender, and N. Spring, "Discarte: a disjunctive Internet cartographer," in *Proc. ACM SIGCOMM*, August 2008.

[7] J. Sommers, B. Eriksson, and P. Barford, "On the prevalence and characteristics of MPLS deployments in the open Internet," in *Proc. ACM Internet Measurement Conference (IMC)*, November 2011.

[8] B. Donnet, M. Luckie, P. Mérindol, and J.-J. Pansiot, "Revealing MPLS tunnels obscured from traceroute," *ACM SIGCOMM Computer Communication Review*, vol. 42, no. 2, pp. 87–93, April 2012.

[9] T. Flach, E. Katz-Bassett, and R. Govindan, "Quantifying violations of destination-based forwarding on the Internet," in *Proc. ACM Internet Measurement Conference (IMC)*, November 2012.

[10] L. Andersson, I. Minei, and T. Thomas, "LDP specification," Internet Engineering Task Force, RFC 5036, October 2007.

[11] D. Awduche, L. Berger, D. Gan, T. Li, and G. Srinivasan, V. ans Swallow, "RSVP-TE: Extensions to RSVP for LSP tunnels," Internet Engineering Task Force, RFC 3209, December 2001.

[12] L. Andersson and R. Asati, "Multiprotocol label switching (MPLS) label stack entry: EXP field renamed to traffic class field," Internet Engineering Task Force, RFC 5462, February 2009.

[13] E. Rosen, D. Tappan, G. Fedorkow, Y. Rekhter, D. Farinacci, T. Li, and A. Conta, "MPLS label stack encoding," Internet Engineering Task Force, RFC 3032, January 2001.

[14] P. Agarwal and B. Akyol, "Time-to-live (TTL) processing in multiprotocol label switching (MPLS) networks," Internet Engineering Task Force, RFC 3443, January 2003.

[15] P. Pan, G. Swallow, and A. Atlas, "Fast reroute extensions to RSVP-TE for LSP tunnels," Internet Engineering Task Force, RFC 4090, May 2005.

[16] C. Filsfils, S. Previdi, A. Bashandy, B. Decraene, S. Litkowski, M. Horneffer, R. Shakir, J. Tantsura, and E. Crabbe, "Segment routing with MPLS data plane," Internet Engineering Task Force, Internet Draft (Work in Progress) draft-ietf-spring-segment-routing-mpls-00, November 2014.

[17] C. Filsfils, P. Francois, S. Previdi, B. Decraene, S. Litkowski, M. Horneffer, I. Milojevic, R. Shakir, S. Ytti, W. Henderickx, J. Tantsura, S. Kini, and E. Crabbe, "Segment routing use cases," Internet Engineering Task Force, Internet Draft (Work in Progress) draft-filsfils-spring-segment-routing-use-cases-01, October 2014.

[18] S. Vissicchio, L. Vanbever, C. Pelsser, L. Cittadini, P. Francois, and O. Bonaventure, "Improving network agility with seamless BGP reconfigurations," *IEEE/ACM Transactions on Networking*, vol. 21, no. 3, pp. 990–1002, June 2013.

[19] E. Rosen and Y. Rekhter, "BGP/MPLS IP virtual private networks (VPNs)," Internet Engineering Task Force, RFC 4364, February 2006.

[20] D. Katz, K. Kompella, and D. Yeung, "Traffic engineering (TE) extensions to OSPF version 2," Internet Engineering Task Force, RFC 3630, September 2003.

[21] T. Li and H. Smit, "IS-IS extensions for traffic engineering," Internet Engineering Task Force, RFC 5305, October 2008.

[22] R. Bonica, D. Gan, D. Tappan, and C. Pignataro, "ICMP extensions for multiprotocol label switching," Internet Engineering Task Force, RFC 4950, August 2007.

[23] ——, "Extended ICMP to support multi-part messages," Internet Engineering Task Force, RFC 4884, April 2007.

[24] "NANOG traceroute," ftp://ftp.netbsd.org/pub/NetBSD/packages/distfiles/traceroute-nanog/traceroute.c.

[25] I. Castro, J. C. Cardona, S. Gorinsky, and P. Francois, "Remote peering: More peering without internet flattening," in *Proc. ACM CoNEXT 2014*, December 2014.

[26] k. claffy, Y. Hyun, K. Keys, M. Fomenkov, and D. Krioukov, "Internet mapping: from art to science," in *Proc. IEEE Cybersecurity Applications and Technologies Conference for Homeland Security (CATCH)*, March 2009.

[27] B. Augustin, X. Cuvellier, B. Orgogozo, F. Viger, T. Friedman, M. Latapy, C. Magnien, and R. Teixeira, "Avoiding traceroute anomalies with Paris traceroute," in *Proc. ACM Internet Measurement Conference (IMC)*, October 2006.

[28] University of Oregon, "Route views, University of Oregon Route Views project," see http://www.routeviews.org/.

[29] M. H. Gunes and K. Sarac, "Resolving anonymous routers in the Internet topology measurement studies," in *Proc. IEEE INFOCOM*, April 2008.

[30] D. Magoni and J.-J. Pansiot, "Analysis of the autonomous system network topology," *ACM SIGCOMM Computer communication Review*, vol. 31, no. 3, pp. 26–37, July 2001.

[31] Y. Vanaubel, J.-J. Pansiot, P. Mérindol, and B. Donnet, "Network fingerprinting: TTL-based router signature," in *Proc. ACM Internet Measurement Conference (IMC)*, October 2013.

[32] K. Keys, "Internet-scale IP alias resolution techniques," *ACM SIGCOMM Computer Communication Review*, vol. 40, no. 1, pp. 50–55, January 2010.

Is Explicit Congestion Notification usable with UDP?

Stephen McQuistin
School of Computing Science
University of Glasgow
sm@smcquistin.uk

Colin Perkins
School of Computing Science
University of Glasgow
csp@csperkins.org

ABSTRACT

We present initial measurements to determine if ECN is usable with UDP traffic in the public Internet. This is interesting because ECN is part of current IETF proposals for congestion control of UDP-based interactive multimedia, and due to the increasing use of UDP as a substrate on which new transport protocols can be deployed. Using measurements from the author's homes, their workplace, and cloud servers in each of the nine EC2 regions worldwide, we test reachability of 2500 servers from the public NTP server pool, using ECT(0) and not-ECT marked UDP packets. We show that an average of 98.97% of the NTP servers that are reachable using not-ECT marked packets are also reachable using ECT(0) marked UDP packets, and that ~98% of network hops pass ECT(0) marked packets without clearing the ECT bits. We compare reachability of the same hosts using ECN with TCP, finding that 82.0% of those reachable with TCP can successfully negotiate and use ECN. Our findings suggest that ECN is broadly usable with UDP traffic, and that support for use of ECN with TCP has increased.

Categories and Subject Descriptors

C.2.5 [**Local and Wide-Area Networks**]: Internet

Keywords

Explicit congestion notification; network measurement; UDP

1. INTRODUCTION

Explicit congestion notification (ECN) is a mechanism that allows Internet routers to signal the presence of congestion to end systems without packet drops. The current ECN standard for TCP/IP [10] was published in 2001, and has seen wide implementation, but only moderate use, in part due to concerns about compatibility with firewalls and other middleboxes. Recent work [14] has eased those concerns, and use of ECN is growing. With this growth, we are now starting to see broader interest in using ECN, including use with transport protocols that layer above UDP.

ECN can be used with UDP to support interactive multimedia systems, such as those using the WebRTC framework [5]. WebRTC uses RTP [13] over UDP for media transport, and RTP extensions to support ECN feedback in this environment have recently been defined [15]. Congestion control algorithms for interactive video using RTP over UDP are under development in IETF, and one of the candidates, NADA [17], makes extensive use of ECN. This is desirable for interactive video, since ECN support in the network allows for lower queue occupancy, hence lower latency, and because the ability to react to congestion without packet loss avoids visible disruption to the video, improving the user experience.

Other cases where ECN is potentially helpful for UDP-based transports include congestion feedback for tunnelled pseudo-wire traffic, and when UDP is used as a substrate for new transport protocol development. Examples of the latter include Google's QUIC protocol [12], SPUD [3], and various proposals for IP stack evolution discussed at the recent IAB workshop on Stack Evolution in a Middlebox Internet [4].

In this paper, we present results of an initial measurement study to determine the impact of ECN on UDP reachability. Based on a study of the servers in the NTP pool, we show that the presence of ECN marks has a small, but non-zero, impact on reachability of UDP servers, with an average of 98.97% of the NTP servers that are reachable without ECN also being reachable when ECN is used, and ~98% of network hops passing ECN marks. For comparison, we find that 82.0% of the servers that are reachable using TCP will successfully negotiate ECN.

To the best of our knowledge, ours is the first study to measure the impact of ECN on reachability of UDP servers, and to offer a comparison with the ability to negotiate ECN for TCP connections. Our results, should they be replicated in larger studies, demonstrate that ECN is generally safe to enable for UDP traffic on the Internet. Furthermore, we show that ECN is increasingly usable with TCP, with greater willingness of TCP servers to negotiate and use ECN.

We structure the remainder of this paper as follows. We begin by reviewing the ECN standards and their use with different transport protocols in Section 2. Our experimental methodology is discussed in Section 3, and we present our measurement results in Section 4. We discuss related work in Section 5, and conclude in Section 6.

2. BACKGROUND

The Internet relies on packet loss as a congestion signal. Routers queue packets on their outgoing links, and congestion results in queue overflow and packet loss. The transport detects this loss, and sends feedback to the sender to reduce its transmission rate, completing the feedback loop. The addition of ECN allows routers to mark packets as a signal that queues are growing, indicating the presence of congestion before it becomes necessary to discard packets. The receiver detects marked packets, and informs the sender, which reacts to the indication as it would react to loss.

IMC'15, October 28–30, 2015, Tokyo, Japan.

ACM 978-1-4503-3848-6/15/10 ...$15.00.
DOI: http://dx.doi.org/10.1145/10.1145/2815675.2815716.

ECN takes two bits from the IP header to indicate if a packet belongs to an ECN capable transport (ECT) flow (00 = not ECT, 01 = ECT(1), and 10 = ECT(0), where ECT(0) and ECT(1) are equivalent). Routers that receive packets marked ECT(0) or ECT(1), and that are experiencing congestion, remark some of those packets by setting the ECT bits to 11 (ECN-CE), indicating congestion on the path. When ECN is used with TCP transport, that feedback is provided by use of two previously reserved bits in the TCP header: ECE (ECN-Echo) and CWR (Congestion Window Reduced). On receipt of an IP packet marked ECN-CE, TCP sets the ECN-Echo bit in the corresponding ACK packet. The sender, on receipt of an ACK with ECN-Echo set, reacts to congestion as if the packet were dropped, and sets the CWR flag in the TCP header of its next outgoing TCP segment to acknowledge its response to the congestion. Since ECN for TCP uses two previously reserved bits of the TCP header, and requires active participation from the receiver, it must be negotiated before use. The initiator of a TCP connection signals its desire to use ECN by setting both ECE and CWR on the SYN packet; if the receiver also understands and desires to use ECN, it will set ECE on the SYN-ACK.

UDP provides no feedback, so cannot directly be used with ECN. Rather, ECN is used in the context of a higher layer transport that runs over UDP and provides the necessary feedback. One such protocol is RTP [13], for which ECN feedback is defined in [15]. The use of ECN with RTP is negotiated using a non-RTP signalling channel, such as SIP [11] or WebRTC [5], and both endpoints need to agree to its use before data is sent with ECT markings. Other transports layered on UDP can support ECN in a similar way, with an initial ECN capability negotiation phase while the communication session is being set-up, before ECT-marked UDP packets are sent.

Since ECN has not been used with UDP until recently, it is possible that some firewalls, or other middleboxes, will regard the presence of ECN marked UDP as suspicious, and discard the traffic. The goal of this work is to determine the extent to which that happens, and understand whether ECN is usable with UDP in the Internet.

3. METHODOLOGY

To determine if ECN affects reachability when using UDP over the public Internet, we need a set of publicly available UDP-based servers to test against. To allow us to compare against TCP usability with ECN, it's desirable if those servers are also reachable using TCP. A set of servers that meet these constraints are the network time protocol (NTP) pool servers (DNS servers could also be used, and may be more representative of core infrastructure; we believe NTP pool servers better represent servers for other UDP applications).

NTP is a UDP-based client-server protocol that can be used for precision timekeeping. The NTP server pool is a worldwide, volunteer operated, virtual cluster of NTP servers that provide a publicly available time service. Servers in the pool are assumed to have stable IP addresses, and clients lookup an appropriate server with a DNS query for the `pool.ntp.org` domain. The pool operates round-robin DNS that returns a different answer every few minutes, to ensure clients are load-balanced across the servers in the pool. In addition to the UDP-based NTP service, each host in the pool is encouraged to run a web server providing a redirect to the main NTP pool website at `www.pool.ntp.org`. This combination gives us access to a worldwide pool of servers, accessible using both UDP and TCP, against which we can test ECN reachability.

To discover servers in the NTP pool, we wrote a script to perform a DNS query for `pool.ntp.org` and each of its country- and region-specific sub-domains in turn, with a one second gap between each query. This script was run at approximately ten minute intervals for a period of several weeks in March/April 2015, and discovered the addresses of a total of 2500 servers out of the NTP pool. These servers form the measurement targets in our study.

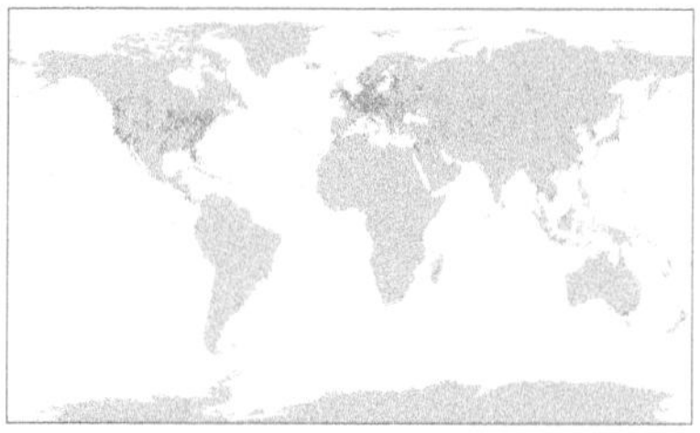

Figure 1: Geographic locations of NTP pool servers

Region	NTP Server Count
Africa	22
Asia	190
Australia	68
Europe	1664
North America	522
South America	32
Unknown	2
Total	2500

Table 1: Geographic distribution of NTP pool servers

The approximate locations of these NTP servers were found using the MaxMind GeoLite2 City database, as of 25 April 2015, and are shown in Figure 1 and summarised in Table 1. The servers under study are distributed around the world, albeit with strongest coverage in Europe and North America, moderate coverage in parts of Asia and Australia, and only limited coverage in South America and Africa. While broader coverage in those regions would be desirable, we believe this set of servers does have sufficient reach to give meaningful results regarding ECN usability.

We conduct measurements against each discovered server, to evaluate its reachability with UDP (NTP) and TCP (HTTP), with and without ECN. In total, we perform 210 traces, where each trace tests both protocols, with and without the use of ECN, against each of the 2500 servers. Traces were collected from the authors' homes (connected via two different UK ISPs), from the University of Glasgow (using both wired and wireless connections), and using virtual machines running on each of the nine regions of the Amazon EC2 service (N. Virginia, Oregon, N. California, Ireland, Frankfurt, Singapore, Tokyo, Sydney, and Sao Paolo). These measurement points give broad geographical reach, albeit from a small number of networks. The data was collected in two batches: initial traces from the authors' homes and the University of Glasgow wireless in April/May 2015, with further traces from those locations and from EC2 in July/August 2015. Traces were collected using a custom measurement application. For each of the 2500 servers in turn, this application probes reachability for UDP and TCP based services, with and without use of ECN.

To probe reachability of UDP based services, our measurement application implements a custom NTP client. An NTP request is sent in a not-ECT marked UDP packet, and the response, if any, is recorded using a parallel `tcpdump` session. If no response is received, the request is retransmitted up to five times, with a one second timeout for each retransmission. If an NTP response is received after any request, we mark the server as reachable without ECN; otherwise it is marked as unreachable after five requests have

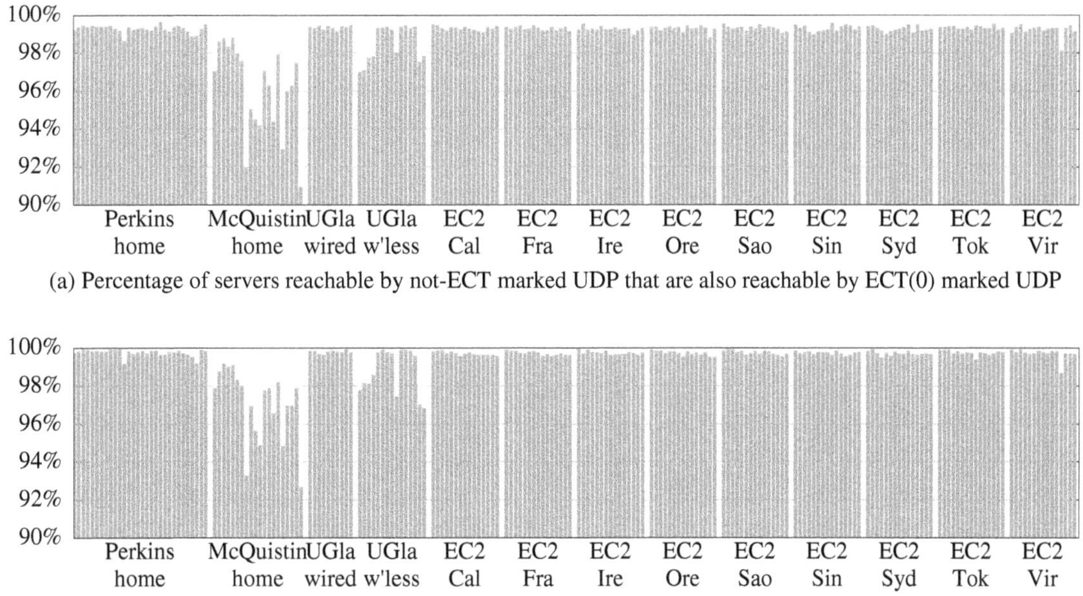

(a) Percentage of servers reachable by not-ECT marked UDP that are also reachable by ECT(0) marked UDP

(b) Percentage of servers reachable by ECT(0) marked UDP that are also reachable by not-ECT marked UDP

Figure 2: Reachability of NTP servers using UDP and UDP with ECT(0) marks for all traces, one bar per trace

timed out. The process is then repeated using NTP requests sent in an ECT(0) marked UDP packet, to determine reachability of that server with ECN (we use ECT(0) rather than ECT(1), to match the typical marking used with ECN for TCP). This allows us to check if the path from client to server passes ECT(0) marked UDP packets. Since we test against unmodified NTP servers, we cannot probe the return path from server to client.

To test reachability using TCP, we make an HTTP GET request for the root page of the server, without attempting to negotiate ECN, and record if the server responds to HTTP, and what HTTP response is received. We repeat the HTTP request, this time with ECN enabled, using an ECN-setup SYN packet to negotiate the use of ECN for the HTTP connection to the server. A parallel `tcpdump` session records the response, and is used to determine whether the returned SYN-ACK packet is an ECN-setup SYN-ACK packet.

Each of the four measurements (UDP, UDP with ECN, TCP, and TCP with ECN) is done for each of the 2500 servers in turn, to form a complete trace. Our data set comprises 210 such traces. It is available at http://dx.doi.org/10.5525/gla.researchdata.207.

4. RESULTS

We present four sets of results. Section 4.1 reports on the impact of ECN on reachability of UDP servers, and is supplemented in Section 4.2 with a discussion of whether and where ECN marks are stripped from UDP packets. Section 4.3 presents results on the fraction of TCP servers that will negotiate ECN, and we compare reachability between the two protocols in Section 4.4.

4.1 Reachability using ECN with UDP

We consider reachability of NTP servers using requests sent in not-ECT marked UDP packets, and in UDP packets sent with an ECT(0) mark. The goal is to characterise differences in server reachability when using ECN, to determine if the presence of an ECT(0) mark on UDP packets makes them more likely to be discarded than not-ECT marked packets. In contrast, Section 4.2 presents a path-based analysis, showing where ECT marks are modified in the network.

Across all traces, an average of 2253 servers from the set of 2500 tested are reachable using not-ECT marked UDP packets. This varies somewhat across traces. The early traces taken in the authors' homes, and the early University of Glasgow wireless traces, show higher reachability than the later traces. These are the traces taken in April/May 2015, whereas those collected in July/August 2015 had lower overall reachability. We believe this is due to servers leaving the NTP pool between the two sets of measurements. We note poor reachability from McQuistin's home, perhaps due to congestion in the access network. We also see more variation in the wireless traces than those collected on wired networks. That some servers are unreachable is not surprising. The NTP pool is operated by volunteers, and offers no service guarantee, so some servers can be expected to be unavailable. Further, UDP is unreliable, and while we retry requests to compensate for packet loss, it can be expected to result in a small number of servers being falsely found unreachable.

Our reachability results are summarised in Figure 2. For each of the 210 traces, we plot a vertical bar in Figure 2a showing the percentage of NTP servers that respond to requests sent in not-ECT marked UDP packets that are also reachable using ECT(0) marked UDP packets. In Figure 2b, we plot the corresponding percentage of servers that respond to requests sent in ECT(0) marked UDP packets that are also reachable using not-ECT marked UDP packets.

The impact of ECT(0) marks on reachability of UDP servers is shown in Figure 2a. Of those servers that respond to not-ECT marked requests, an average of 98.97% also respond to requests sent in ECT(0) marked packets, although this fraction varies somewhat (but is always above 90%) depending on the location from which data is collected. It can be expected that some of these reports are false positives, due to packet loss unrelated to the use of ECN, but some will be caused by middleboxes dropping ECT(0) marked packets. By this measure, and on this dataset, the use of ECT(0) marks generally has a small, but measurable, impact on the reachability of UDP servers (although McQuistin's home network shows that the impact can be larger in some cases).

We also consider the converse, in Figure 2b, where we see that an average of 99.45% of the servers that are reachable with ECT(0)

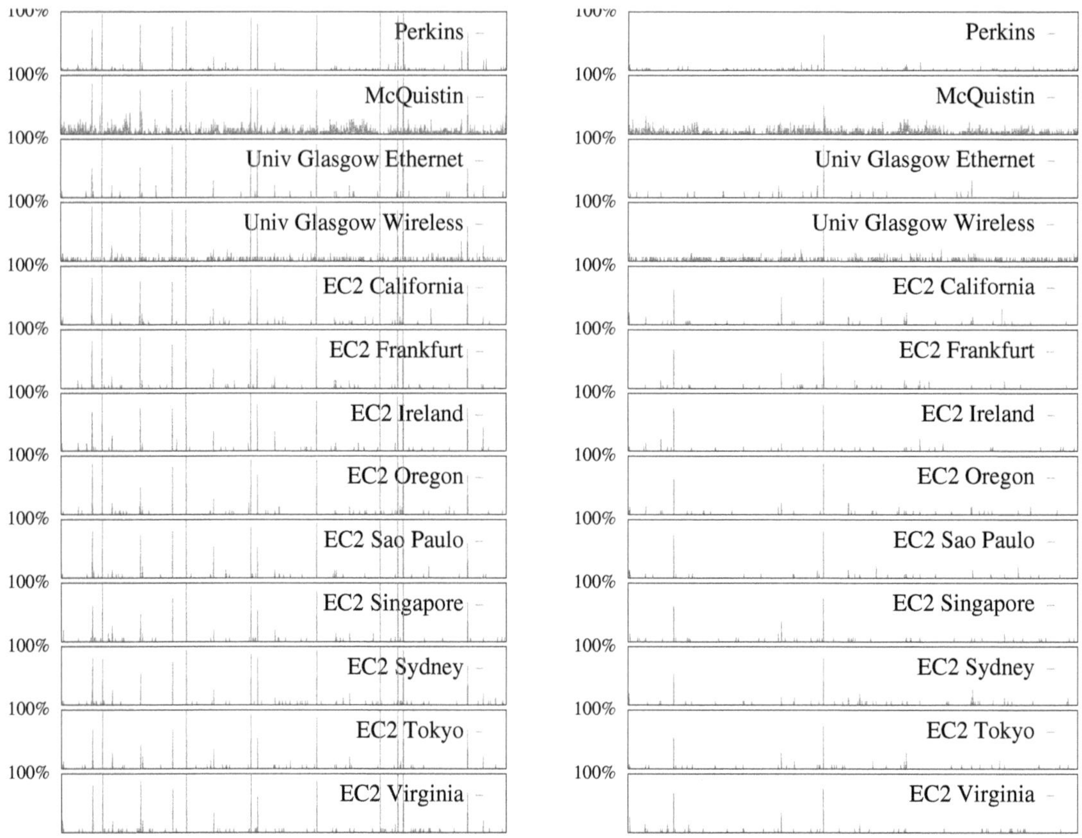

(a) Reachable by not-ECT but not ECT(0) marked packets (b) Reachable by ECT(0) but not by not-ECT marked packets

Figure 3: Differential reachability of each server using ECT(0) and not-ECT marked packets

marked packets are also reachable using not-ECT marked packets. NTP does not use ECN in its normal operation, so NTP servers configured to drop not-ECT marked UDP packets in this manner, or behind middleboxes with this behaviour, would not be usable for their intended purpose. Accordingly, we believe the unreachable reports for these servers are false, and are due to packet loss that is unrelated to ECN.

To better understand differential reachability when ECN is used, Figure 3a plots, for each server, and from each location, the fraction of traces in which that server is reachable using not-ECT marked packets but not using ECT(0) marked packets. Each vertical bar represents one of the 2500 servers tested. If the server is always reachable with ECT(0) marked packets when reachable with not-ECT marked packets, it will show 0% differential reachability; if it is never reachable using ECT(0) marked packets when reachable using not-ECT packets, it will show 100% differential reachability. Ideally, all servers will be reachable using both ECT(0) and not-ECT marked UDP packets, and hence will show 0% differential reachability.

In practice, the majority of servers have near zero differential reachability. However, a small number of servers (between 9 and 14, depending on the location from which measurements are taken) have differential reachability >50% (these are the tall vertical spikes in Figure 3a). This shows that some servers are generally not reachable with ECT(0) marked UDP packets, but are reachable with not-ECT marked packets, presumably due to firewalls or other middleboxes that drop ECT-marked packets. Visual inspection of Figure 3a shows that it is usually the same set of servers having high differential reachability from every location, suggesting that the ECT(0) marked packets are being dropped near to the destination (we revisit this in Section 4.2).

We note that the differential reachability is high, but not 100%, for some servers. This indicates servers that are usually, but not always, reachable using not-ECT marked packets but not using ECT(0) marked packets. Possible reasons for this might be route changes, causing the middlebox that drops ECT(0) marked packets to be bypassed in some cases, or routers treating the ECN bits as part of the type-of-service field and preferentially dropping such packets. Further study is needed.

Figure 3b shows differential reachability for servers that can be reached using ECT(0) marked packets but not with not-ECT marked packets. As expected, differential reachability is less in this case, with at most 3 servers having differential reachability >50%. Of those, one has high differential reachability from every location tested, while the other two (pool NTP servers run by Phoenix Public Library) seem to be affected in the traces taken from EC2 only. The reasons for the differential reachability of these servers when ECN is not used are unclear.

Overall, we see high reachability of UDP servers with ECT(0) marked packets. While a small number of servers are (sometimes) reachable using not-ECT marked UDP packets but never reachable using ECT(0) marked UDP packets, there are around 4× more servers that are transiently unreachable. Indeed, for the subset of the NTP server pool that we probe, persistent failures due to use of ECN appear to be the least significant cause of reachability problems, behind transient packet loss, and servers that are off-line.

Figure 4: Sample traceroutes, showing hops where ECN is missing

4.2 Are ECN marks stripped from UDP?

The results in Section 4.1 show that use of ECT(0) marks on request packets has only a small impact on reachability of UDP servers. There are two possible reasons why this could be: either the presence of such marks does not significantly affect reachability, or the marks were stripped by a router near the sender and so were not visible to the wider network.

To determine whether the ECT(0) marks were actually traversing the network, we ran traceroutes from each measurement location to each of the NTP servers we identified. The traceroute was configured to send TTL limited ECT(0) marked UDP packets, and we captured returning ICMP responses. We then compared the UDP/IP header encapsulated in the ICMP response with the UDP/IP header sent, to determine whether the ECT(0) mark was present at each hop. This is the same technique used in [1], [2], and [8].

In total, our traceroute data covers 155439 IP level hops in 1400 ASes (subject to the usual limitations of IP to AS mapping accuracy [16]). Representative sample results are presented graphically in Figure 4. The source of the traceroute requests is in the centre of the figure, with the destination servers located at the edges. The path to each server is shown with a dot representing each hop, and lines showing the connections between the hops. IP addresses are omitted, for readability reasons. Hops that return an unmodified ECN field are drawn in green; those where the returned ECN field differs from that sent are shown in red. In all cases, observed changes to the ECN field were to set it to not-ECT, hence we see runs of red in the figure, after the ECT mark has been stripped. We did not see any ECN-CE marks. Traces stop at the point where a traceroute to the server stops; this is generally one hop before the destination.

It is clear that ECT(0) marked packets do traverse the network with their marking intact, in the majority of cases. Of the 155439 hops measured, 154421 pass the ECT(0) mark unmodified, and the mark is stripped at 1143 hops (125 hops only sometimes strip the ECN mark). Regions where ECT marks have been removed, shown in red in Figure 4, are few, widely scattered, and not located near the sender. 59.1% of the locations where ECT(0) marks are stripped, where we were able to determine the AS, were at AS boundaries (again, subject to the limitations of inferring AS number from traceroute IP addresses). This data does not tell us whether marked packets reach their destination with the ECT(0) mark intact, since firewalls that block traceroute might also strip ECN marks, but it does indicate that the marks traverse the wide-area network.

4.3 Reachability using ECN with TCP

We also consider the reachability of the web servers co-located with the NTP pool servers when making HTTP requests using TCP with ECN. Our goals are to determine the fraction of web servers in the pool that successfully negotiate and use ECN, and to compare this to reachability of UDP servers with ECN-marked traffic.

Results are shown in Figure 5. For each trace, the figure shows the number of web servers that respond to requests sent via TCP without using ECN, and the number that successfully negotiate ECN when requested (i.e., the number of servers that respond to an ECN-setup SYN with an ECN-setup SYN-ACK packet). On average, we are able to reach 1334 web servers from the 2500 hosts studied. This is significantly less than the 2253 servers that are reachable on average using UDP. Operators of hosts in the NTP pool are encouraged to run a web server, but it is clear that many do not. As expected, there is little variation in reachability between traces. For those hosts that run web servers, the servers are generally available, and TCP retransmits conceal the impact of packet loss.

Across all traces, the average number of web servers that negotiate ECN support with TCP when requested was 1095 (82.0% of those reachable using TCP). This is considerably lower than the fraction of NTP servers in the pool that were reachable with ECT(0) marked UDP packets, but the results are not directly comparable, since to be recorded as reachable with TCP using ECN, the server needs to actively respond with an ECN-setup SYN-ACK, whereas the UDP reachability test didn't require active participation of the server.[1]

A better comparison is with previous studies of TCP use with ECN. For example, Trammell *at el.* [14] conducted active probes of the Alexa Top million web servers list in 2014 and found 56.17% negotiated ECN when requested. Similar studies by Kühlewind *et al.* [6] found 29.48% would negotiate ECN in 2012, while [1] found 17.2% would negotiate ECN. Langley [7] and Medina *et al.* [9] present earlier data, showing negligible deployment.

Plotting these previous measurements in a time series, along with our new data, gives the result shown in Figure 6. Our results show a significant increase in willingness to negotiate ECN, when compared to the previous measurements, but on a growth curve that looks to be in line with previous results.

Overall results are encouraging, showing successful ECN negotiation with TCP for a high fraction of the servers. We see significantly higher reachability than previous studies, but further work is needed to determine whether the increase is due to measuring against a different set of servers, or whether it is a general increase in TCP ECN reachability.

4.4 UDP and TCP reachability correlation

We compare the servers reachable using unmarked UDP packets but not using ECT(0) marked packets, with the set of servers that do not successfully negotiate the use of ECN with TCP. The goal is to determine if the same servers are unreachable with ECN for both UDP and TCP.

Results are shown in Table 2. There is only weak correlation between servers that are unreachable using UDP with ECT(0), and those that refuse to negotiate ECN with TCP. The majority of servers that cannot be reached using ECN with UDP *can* be reached using ECN with TCP (that is, they will negotiate ECN, then send and receive ECT-marked packet with TCP, but not respond to ECT-marked UDP). This is evidence of middleboxes that discard ECT marked IP packets when the payload is UDP, but not when the payload is TCP.

[1]The ECN-setup SYN is sent in a not-ECT marked packet, so it's also not possible to compare response rates for ECT and not-ECT SYN packets with those for ECT and not-ECT UDP.

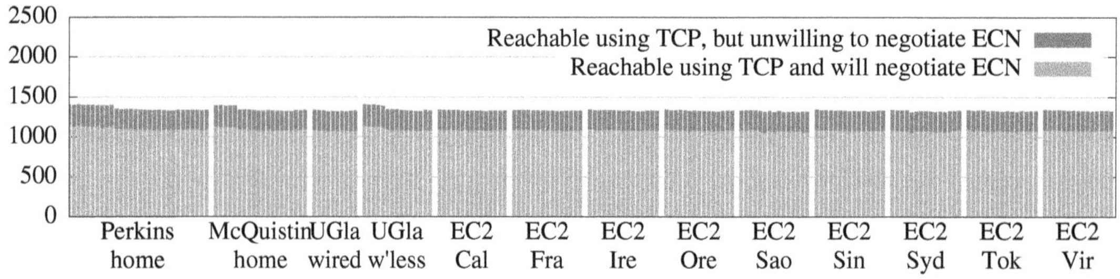

Figure 5: Reachability of web servers using TCP and TCP with ECN, one bar per trace

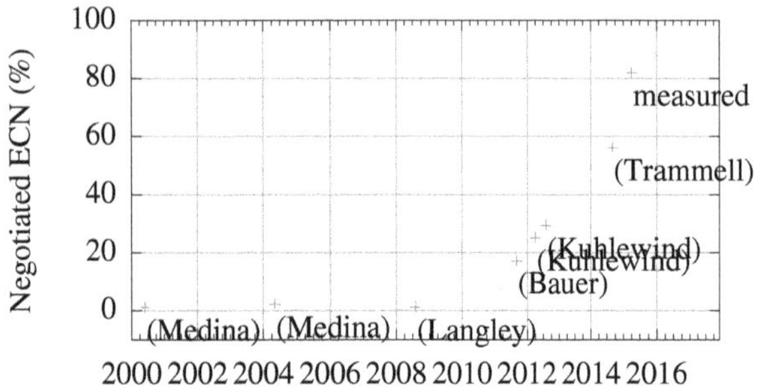

Figure 6: Trends in ECN TCP capability

Location	Avg. unreachable UDP with ECT	Num of those that fail to negotiate ECN w/TCP
Perkins home	8	3
McQuistin home	160	20
U. Glasgow wired	10	2
U. Glasgow w'less	43	4
EC2 California	10	3
EC2 Frankfurt	14	5
EC2 Ireland	11	4
EC2 Oregon	14	2
EC2 Sao Paulo	16	3
EC2 Singapore	10	3
EC2 Syndey	11	5
EC2 Tokyo	13	2
EC2 Virginia	16	3

Table 2: Correlation between UDP and TCP reachability

5. RELATED WORK

Trammell *et al.* [14] probed the Alexa top web servers list, finding 56.17% of IPv4 servers tested in August-September 2014 were willing to negotiate ECN, rising to 65.41% of IPv6 servers. They also studied ECN-dependent connectivity, finding 0.42% of servers showed differences in connectivity when ECN was requested for TCP; this is comparable to our results for UDP.

Kühlewind *et al.* [6] also studied the Alexa top web servers, finding ECN support in 25.16% of servers tested in April 2012, rising to 29.48% in August 2012. Tests conducted against IPv6 hosts show 48.56% successfully negotiating ECN. We find a higher fraction of servers negotiating ECN with TCP, as discussed in Section 4.3. Kühlewind *et al.* also test ECN usability with hosts that negotiate ECN, by sending ECN-CE marked segments and checking whether the returned ACK includes has the ECE flag set, showing approximately 90% usability. We do not perform such a test with TCP, but this result is comparable to our results using UDP in Section 4.2.

Bauer *et al.* [1] performed similar measurements of ECN usability with TCP, testing against both the Alexa server list, and against other University and College web servers, and against mobile sites. The results are broadly comparable to those of Kühlewind *et al.*, although being older, they show less ECN support. Bauer *et al.* also perform traceroute-based probes, similar to those we describe in Section 4.2 although using a larger set of destinations, to determine where ECN marks are modified or stripped in the network. Their results show approximately 82% of traces preserving the ECT bits for the entire path. This is a noticeably lower fraction than we observe, perhaps due to increased awareness of ECN in the operational community.

Langley [7] probed 1,445,303 web servers in 2008, finding approximately 1% negotiated ECN support, and around 0.5% ignored SYN packets sent with ECE and CWR set, but these were not uniformly distributed, with a few providers being responsible for the majority of failures. Medina *et al.* [9] conducted tests of ECN reachability using TCP in 2000 and 2004, with similarly low success.

6. CONCLUSIONS

We present initial results showing how use of ECN affects reachability of UDP servers, testing against 2500 servers from the NTP pool. An average of 98.97% of those reachable with not-ECT marked UDP packets were also reachable using ECT(0) marked packets. The remaining servers were unreachable using ECT(0) marked packets, often persistently so. The use of ECN has a small negative impact on reachability of UDP servers (Section 4.1). Further measurements show that ECT(0) marks successfully traverse most (~98%) reachable network hops unmodified, but have the ECT mark set back to not-ECT in the remaining cases (Section 4.2).

We test reachability of the same servers using TCP with ECN, finding 82.0% of those reachable with TCP will negotiate ECN support (Section 4.3). This is higher than previous studies, and indicates that ECN is becoming usable with TCP. Comparison of TCP and UDP reachability when using ECN (Section 4.4) shows poor correlation between servers unreachable using ECT(0) marked UDP and servers that refuse to negotiate ECN with TCP. Some paths allow ECT(0) packets when the payload is TCP, but not for UDP.

While our dataset is comparatively small, and our measurements were taken from a small number of locations, the servers we probe are located at a wide range of locations around the world, and in many different network environments. Ongoing studies, to verify our results in more environments, would be welcome. To the extent that they are representative, though, our results show that marking UDP packets with ECT(0) will not, in general, harm reachability. Whether the use of ECN with UDP offers any benefit has not been determined, but it seems to cause no significant harm.

Acknowledgements: We thank the anonymous reviewers, and our shepherd, Matthew Luckie, for their feedback.

7. REFERENCES

[1] S. Bauer, R. Beverly, and A. Berger. Measuring the state of ECN readiness in servers, clients, and routers. In *Proceedings of the Internet Measurement Conference*, Berlin, Germany, November 2011. ACM.

[2] G. Detal, B. Hesmans, O. Bonaventure, Y. Vanaubel, and B. Donnet. Revealing middlebox interference with tracebox. In *Proceedings of the Internet Measurement Conference*, Barcelona, Spain, October 2013. ACM.

[3] J. Hildebrand and B. Trammell. Substrate protocol for user datagrams (SPUD) prototype. Internet Engineering Task Force, March 2015. Work in progress (draft-hildebrand-spud-prototype).

[4] Internet Architecture Board. Workshop on stack evolution in a middlebox Internet, January 2015. https://www.iab.org/activities/workshops/semi/.

[5] C. Jennings, T. Hardie, and M. Westerlund. Real-time communications for the web. *IEEE Communications Magazine*, 51(4):20–26, April 2013.

[6] M. Kühlewind, S. Neuner, and B. Trammell. On the state on ECN and TCP options on the Internet. In *Proceedings of the Passive and Active Measurement Conference*, Hong Kong, China, March 2013. Springer.

[7] A. Langley. Probing the viability of TCP extensions. https://www.imperialviolet.org/binary/ecntest.pdf, September 2008.

[8] D. Malone and M. Luckie. Analysis of ICMP quotations. In *Proceedings of the Passive and Active Measurement Conference*, Louvain-la-neuve, Belgium, April 2007.

[9] A. Medina, M. Allman, and S. Floyd. Measuring the evolution of transport protocols in the Internet. *ACM Computer Communication Review*, 35(2):37–52, April 2005.

[10] K. K. Ramakrishnan, S. Floyd, and D. L. Black. The addition of ECN to IP. Internet Engineering Task Force, September 2001. RFC 3168.

[11] J. Rosenberg et al. SIP: Session initiation protocol. Internet Engineering Task Force, June 2002. RFC 3261.

[12] J. Roskind. Experimenting with QUIC, June 2013. https://blog.chromium.org/2013/06/experimenting-with-quic.html.

[13] H. Schulzrinne, S. Casner, R. Frederick, and V. Jacobson. RTP: A transport protocol for real-time applications. Internet Engineering Task Force, July 2003. RFC 3550.

[14] B. Trammell, M. Kühlewind, D. Boppart, I. Learmonth, G. Fairhurst, and R. Scheffenegger. Enabling Internet-wide deployment of explicit congestion notification. In *Proceedings of the Passive and Active Measurement Conference*, New York, NY, USA, March 2015.

[15] M. Westerlund, I. Johansson, C. S. Perkins, P. O'Hanlon, and K. Carlberg. ECN for RTP over UDP. Internet Engineering Task Force, August 2012. RFC 6679.

[16] Y. Zhang, R. Oliveira, H. Zhang, and L. Zhang. Quantifying the pitfalls of traceroute in AS connectivity inference. In *Proceedings of the Passive and Active Measurement Conference*, Zurich, Switzerland, April 2010.

[17] X. Zhu et al. NADA: A unified congestion control scheme for real-time media. Internet Engineering Task Force, March 2015. Work in progress (draft-ietf-rmcat-nada).

Investigating Interdomain Routing Policies in the Wild

Ruwaifa Anwar
Stony Brook University
manwar@cs.stonybrook.edu

Haseeb Niaz
Stony Brook University
mniaz@cs.stonybrook.edu

David Choffnes
Northeastern University
choffnes@ccs.neu.edu

Ítalo Cunha
Universidade Federal de Minas Gerais
cunha@dcc.ufmg.br

Phillipa Gill
Stony Brook University
phillipa@cs.stonybrook.edu

Ethan Katz-Bassett
University of Southern California
ethan.kb@usc.edu

Abstract

Models of Internet routing are critical for studies of Internet security, reliability and evolution, which often rely on simulations of the Internet's routing system. Accurate models are difficult to build and suffer from a dearth of ground truth data, as ISPs often treat their connectivity and routing policies as trade secrets. In this environment, researchers rely on a number of simplifying assumptions and models proposed over a decade ago, which are widely criticized for their inability to capture routing policies employed in practice.

In this study we put Internet topologies and models under the microscope to understand where they fail to capture real routing behavior. We measure data plane paths from thousands of vantage points, located in eyeball networks around the globe, and find that between 14-35% of routing decisions are not explained by existing models. We then investigate these cases, and identify root causes such as selective prefix announcement, misclassification of undersea cables, and geographic constraints. Our work highlights the need for models that address such cases, and motivates the need for further investigation of evolving Internet connectivity.

Categories and Subject Descriptors

C.2.2 [Computer-Communication Networks]: Network Protocols

Keywords

Network Measurement; BGP; routing

1. INTRODUCTION

Research on existing and new protocols on the Internet is challenging because key aspects of the network topology are hidden from public view by interdomain routing protocols. Further, deploying new protocols at Internet scale requires convincing large numbers of autonomous networks to participate. As a result, networking researchers rely on assumptions, models, and simulations to evaluate new protocols [13, 26], network reliability [20, 41], and security [1, 16, 24].

IMC '15 October 28 - 30, 2015, Tokyo, Japan

ACM 978-1-4503-3848-6/15/10 ...$15.00.
DOI: http://dx.doi.org/10.1145/2815675.2815712.

Our existing models of interdomain routing [11], however, have important limitations. They are built and validated on the same incomplete topology datasets, typically routes observed via route monitors such as RouteViews and RIS [33, 39]. These vantage points expose a large fraction of paths from global research & education networks (GREN) and core networks, but they are incomplete in two keys ways. First, they expose few paths to and from eyeball and content networks. Second, they do not expose less preferred paths that would be used if the most preferred path was not available. As a result, they do not capture partial peering, more complex routing policies based on traffic engineering, or load balancing and the rich peering mesh which exists near the edge of the network [35].

While limitations of our existing models are well known [27, 29, 35]–and are even being addressed in recent work [15]–we lack a solid understanding of how much these limitations impact our ability to accurately model the interdomain routing system. Recent work has attempted to address this issue by observing destination-based routing violations in control plane data [28] and by surveying a population of network operators about their policies [12]. However, these approaches are limited in terms of scale and their ability to observe behavior at the network edge.

In this paper, we take a systematic approach to understand how our models of routing policies [11] hold in practice. We leverage a combination of data plane measurements covering the network edge (Section 3.1) and control plane experiments which allow us to directly measure relative preference of routes (Section 3.2). We create a methodology that accounts for numerous potential causes of violations to our assumptions including sibling ASes [4], complex AS relationships [15], prefix-specific routing policies, and the impact of geography. We investigate the prevalence of each of these causes in AS-level paths observed via measurements of the data and control planes.

We revisit generally held assumptions and models of Internet routing. Our goal is *not* to measure a complete Internet topology; rather, we seek to improve our understanding of routing decisions made by ASes when routing their traffic. Towards this goal we make the following observations for our measured paths:

- Known hybrid and partial transit relationships (*e.g.*, those explored in [15]) contribute a surprisingly small amount to unexpected routing decisions.
- Per-prefix routing policies appear to explain 10-20% of unexpected routing decisions, where an AS chooses a longer or more expensive path than our model predicts.
- We find that some large content providers like Akamai and Netflix are destinations for a large fraction of unexpected routing decisions (21% and 17%, respectively).

- Routing decisions vary based on geography. We find that paths traversing multiple continents deviate from our models more, owing to undersea cable ASes which are not accounted for in our models. We also observed a tendency for ASes to prefer non-international paths when endpoints are in the same country.

Our results highlight areas where more investigation would yield the largest payoff in terms of improving our accuracy when modeling AS relationships and routing policies. We also identify key areas, specifically investigating prefix-specific routing policies, where additional vantage points and looking glass servers could improve the fidelity of our AS topology data.

2. MODELING INTERDOMAIN ROUTING

The now standard model of routing policies was developed by Gao and Rexford [10, 11] based on seminal work by Griffin, Sheppard, and Wilfong [17] and Huston [18, 19]. In this model, ASes connect to each other based on business relationships: (1) customer-provider, where the customer pays the provider, and (2) peer-to-peer, where the ASes exchange traffic at no cost. This model gives the following view of local preferences and export policies, based on the economic considerations of ASes:

Local Preferences. An AS will prefer routes through a neighboring customer, then routes through a neighboring peer, and then routes through a provider. In other words, an AS will prefer cheaper routes.

Export Policy. A customer route may be exported to all neighboring ASes. A peer or provider route may only be exported to customers.

This model is sometimes augmented with the assumption that ASes only consider the next hop AS on the path when making their routing decisions. This simplifies analysis and makes debugging more tractable [20]. Simulation studies also often restrict path selection to the shortest among all paths satisfying Local Preference and use tie-breakers to induce unique routing decisions when AS path lengths are same [13, 14].

While the above model and variations thereof have been used in many studies (*e.g.*, [1, 13, 16, 21, 41]), it is well known that this model fails to capture many aspects of the interdomain routing system [27, 29, 35]. These aspects include AS relationships that vary based on the geographic region [15] or destination prefix, and traffic engineering via hot-potato routing or load balancing.

Prior work has used traceroute measurements and BGP data to address some of these issues (*e.g.*, [27, 29]); however, these measurements only offer a glimpse into ASes' routing preferences. Namely, they expose only the set of paths that are in use at the time of measurements. In contrast, we use active control plane experiments (PEERING [37]) to expose less preferred paths. Further, these datasets have poor or no coverage of paths used by edge networks [7]. On a smaller scale, network operators were surveyed about their routing policies to better understand how our models correspond to practice [12], but the scale and representativeness of a survey approach makes generalizing these observations infeasible.

3. METHODOLOGY

We aim to understand the gap between interdomain routing models and empirically observed behavior on the Internet. Our methodology combines two measurement techniques to gain better visibility into interdomain routing policies. First, we passively observe routing decisions on paths towards popular content networks (Section 3.1). We leverage the RIPE Atlas platform which provides a large collection of vantage points located around the world for our traceroute measurements. We thus observe routing decisions for broad range of hosts from variety of vantage points. One limitation of this approach lies in its passiveness as it only provides information about paths that are in use at the time of measurements. We do not get any information about the alternate paths available to an AS. Our second technique (Section 3.2) overcomes the above mentioned limitation and exposes less preferred paths for different ASes. We use PEERING [2, 37, 40] to selectively poison BGP announcements and force ASes to choose an alternate path, then we use RIPE Atlas probes as vantage points to run traceroutes towards poisoned prefixes to observe these alternate paths. This approach of actively probing routing decisions enables us to discover less preferred paths and also reverse engineer the BGP decision process. However, the PEERING platform is currently limited to few locations from which we can send poisoned announcements.

3.1 Passively observing route decisions

It is well known that a disproportionately large amount of Internet traffic originates from a few popular content providers [23, 36]. However, there is little empirical data about the paths this traffic takes [23]. We target these paths with our measurements. Note that it is not our goal to observe routing decisions for the entire Internet. Rather, we focus on the more tractable task of measuring a subset of important Internet paths (those carrying most traffic) from a diverse set of vantage points, and putting those paths under the microscope to understand how and why they differ from paths predicted by routing models.

Selecting content providers. We consider a list of the top applications from Sandvine [36] and top Web sites from Quantcast [31]. From these lists, we isolate top HTTP and non-HTTP hosts in terms of number of downstream bytes and number of visits. Finally, we arrive at a list of 34 DNS names representing 14 large content providers.

AS type	Probes	Distinct ASes	Distinct Countries
Stub-AS	787	333	106
Small ISP	581	188	78
Large ISP	56	109	51
Tier 1	69	8	3

Table 1: Distribution of selected RIPE Atlas probes.

Vantage points (VPs). RIPE Atlas has broad global coverage, but is known to have a disproportionate fraction of probes skewed towards Europe. To avoid a bias towards European ASes, we picked equal number of probes from each continent. For every continent, we picked probes in a round robin fashion from different countries and ASes so that selected probes cover a wide range of ASes. Table 1 summarizes the location of these probes in terms of AS type using the categorization method of Oliveira *et al.* [30]. The bulk of the probes are located near the network edge in stub and small ISP networks. To measure paths to content providers, each RIPE Atlas node performs a DNS lookup for each of the 34 content DNS names, and then performs a traceroute to the resolved IP. We use 1,998 RIPE Atlas probes located in 633 ASes, distributed according to our sampling methodology.

Data set. We used maximum probing rate allowed by RIPE Atlas to perform 28,051 traceroutes towards selected hosts. These traceroutes ended up in a total of 218 destination ASes. The number of destination ASes is large relative the number of content providers because large numbers of content servers are hosted outside the provider's network (*e.g.*, inside ISPs) [5]. We convert the traceroute-based IP-level paths into AS paths using the method described by Chen et al. [7]. Since interdomain routing is destination-based, we can observe routing decisions for all ASes along the path to a given destination. We thus observe routing decisions for a total of 746 ASes.

3.2 Actively probing route decisions

Passive measurements observe only the most preferred route for an AS toward a destination. We use PEERING [2,37,40] to expose alternate, less preferred routes and to attempt to reverse engineer BGP decisions.

PEERING operates an ASN and owns IP address space that we can announce via several upstream providers. PEERING allows us to manipulate BGP announcements of its IP prefixes and observe how ASes on the path react. We used PEERING to announce prefixes using six US universities (Georgia Tech, Clemson, University of Southern California, Northeastern, Stony Brook, and Cornell) and one Brazilian university as providers. We change announcements at most once per 90 minutes to allow for route convergence and avoid route flap dampening. We use prefixes allocated to the PEERING research testbed reserved for our experiments; these prefixes carry no real traffic beyond our measurements.

Discovering alternate routes. We start announcing an IP prefix from all PEERING locations in an anycast announcement. At each round, we observe the preferred route at a target AS T and the next-hop neighbor N that T is using to route toward our prefix. We then poison N, *i.e.*, add N's AS number to the path [3, 9], to trigger BGP loop prevention at N and cause N to no longer have a path to our prefix (and stop announcing a route to T). This forces T to choose a different route, through a different neighbor N'. We repeat this process in consecutive rounds, poisoning the newly-discovered neighbor, to identify all neighbors and routes T can use toward our prefixes. When we observe different routes at the target AS T (through different neighbors) from multiple vantage points (*e.g.*, due to different routing preferences at different geographic locations), we run the algorithm for each vantage point separately. We can potentially execute this algorithm for each AS in the topology as the target AS. A similar experiment was performed by Colitti [9]; here, we use the same mechanism with a more diverse set of providers and with a different goal.

We insert all poisoned ASes into a single AS-set, and surround the poisoned AS-set with PEERING's AS number. This limits AS-path length, prevents inference of non-existent inter-AS links, and allows operators to identify the poisoning.

Reverse engineering BGP decisions. In addition to the experiment to discover alternate routes, we conduct a complementary experiment to infer BGP decision triggers. We first announce an IP prefix from one PEERING location (called the *magnet*), wait five minutes to allow for route convergence, then announce (*anycast*) the same IP prefix from all other PEERING locations. After we anycast the prefix, an AS may change to a new route with higher LocalPref, shorter AS-path length, or better intradomain tie-breakers, as specified in the BGP decision process [8]. If an AS x keeps using the route toward the magnet after we anycast the prefix, we check if the magnet route is cheaper according to the Gao-Rexford model or has shorter AS-path length than all other routes we observed from x. If none of these checks are satisfied, we infer AS x is using intradomain costs or route age (the last tie-breaker before router ID) as a tie-breaker. If AS x did not choose the route to the magnet, we check if the chosen route is cheaper or shorter than the route to the magnet. If none of these checks are satisfied, we infer AS x is using intradomain costs as a tie-breaker.

We repeat this process using each PEERING location as the magnet. We also check whether the route chosen after we anycast the prefix is more expensive according to the Gao-Rexford model or is the same cost but has longer AS-path length than other routes we observed, which is a violation of the model. The route to the magnet may become unavailable when a downstream AS receives and chooses a more preferred route; in these cases we consider the downstream AS's decision.

Vantage points (VPs). We perform traceroutes from 96 RIPE Atlas probes and approximately 200 PlanetLab nodes every 20 minutes, and collect BGP feeds every 15 minutes from RouteViews and RIPE RIS to monitor paths toward PEERING prefixes. We use the maximum number of RIPE Atlas probes allowed within daily probing budget limits. We implement a greedy heuristic that picks probes to maximize the number of ASes traversed on the default paths toward PEERING locations.

Data set. We needed a total of 188 distinct poisoned announcements to infer preferences for all 360 target ASes we observe on paths toward PEERING (some poisonings are useful for multiple target ASes). We observe 739 inter-AS links. We find 45 inter-AS links that are not in CAIDA's AS-relationship database, 10 of which (22.2%) can only be observed with poisoned announcements.

3.3 Comparison with existing models

We compare paths observed in our passive and active measurements with CAIDA's topology of inferred inter-AS relationships. We aggregate five topologies (Oct. 14 to Feb. 15) inferred using the method presented by Luckie *et al.* [25]. We aggregate these snapshots to mitigate the impact of transient link failures on the topology used in our analysis. When inferences conflicted, we took the majority poll of inferred relationships while assigning higher weight to more recent inferences, *i.e.*, if the latest two months had the same inference, we used that inference regardless of the first three months. We use this topology to compute all paths that satisfy the Gao-Rexford (GR) model described in Section 2.

We compare the measured paths with all paths satisfying the GR model computed using CAIDA's inferred relationships. We consider two properties: (1) whether the measured path satisfies the GR model of local preference, and (2) whether the measured path has the same length as the shortest paths satisfying the GR model of local preference. Based on this we classify routing relationships as either obeying GR local preference; *i.e.*, using the neighbor with the Best Relationship type (**Best**), routing based on shortest path (**Short**), or a combination of the two.

For our active probing measurements, we consider the order in which the target AS T chooses paths. Again, we consider two properties: (1) whether the relationship between T and the next-hop on the first path is equal or better than the relationship with the next-hop on the second path, and (2) whether the first path is shorter or equal in length as the second path. We similarly label the observed decisions which obey property (1) as **Best**, and those that obey (2) as **Short**. We have limited visibility on what path the second neighbor exported to T when T chose the first path. When labeling decisions, we assume the second neighbor exported the second path to T when T chose the first path. We verified this assumption holds for the results we report.

In both cases, the sets should be treated as disjoint, with ASes that obey both Best and Short path policies appearing only in the **Best/Short** category. Observations which follow **neither** of these properties are considered inconsistent with existing models (*i.e.*, **NonBest/Long** category). There can be, however, some cases when a path suggested by CAIDA's inferences might not exist in practice. One of the reasons can be incomplete or erroneous inferences in the topologies. In addition, an AS might apply more complex filters than suggested by Gao-Rexford model when deciding which paths to advertise to neighbors (Section 4.3 discusses this in more detail).

4. HOW OFTEN DO MODELS HOLD?

We now consider how empirically observed AS paths compare with those predicted by GR model. We then investigate how often deviations can be explained by known sources of inaccuracies.

Encouragingly, we find that a majority of routing decisions (64.7%) for passively observed measurements are correctly inferred by the commonly used GR model; however, a significant fraction (34.3%) do not follow that model. Figure 1 (Simple) characterizes the observed routing decisions based on whether the path chosen is Best or Short. We find only a small number of cases (8.3%) where decisions can neither be explained by Best nor by Short path selection. In the following sections, we explore the reasons behind these decisions that differ from model-based predictions.

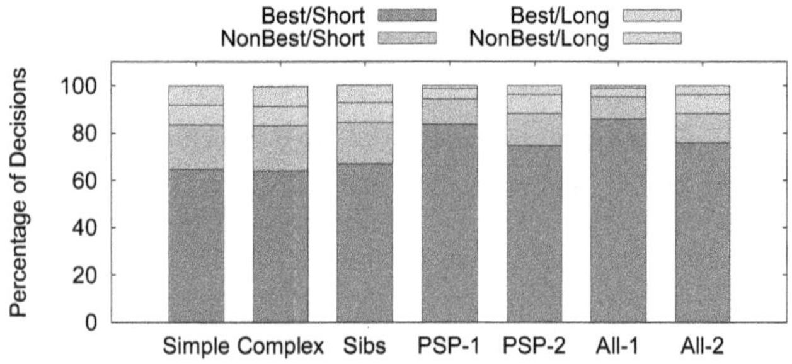

Figure 1: Breakdown of routing decisions observed by taking into account complex relationships (Complex), siblings (Sibs), prefix-specific policies (PSP-1, PSP-2) and by combining complex and siblings relationships with both criteria of prefix-specific policies (All-1, All-2).

4.1 Complex routing relationships

A well known limitation of existing routing policy models is the simplification of relationships into either customer-provider or settlement-free peering relationships. Recent work by Giotsas *et al.* addresses this limitation by augmenting relationship inferences with cases of hybrid relationships (*i.e.*, ASes whose arrangements vary based on location) and partial transit relationships (*i.e.*, ASes who will behave as providers, but only for a subset of prefixes) [15]. The hybrid relationship dataset contains pairs of ASes and the corresponding cities where relationships differ for a given AS pair. To use this dataset, we use the geolocation data from [6], which offers good coverage of infrastructure IPs such as routers. For each pair of ASes in each AS path, we geolocate corresponding IP addresses and if the geolocation data points to the same city as mentioned in hybrid relationship dataset for that AS pair, we use the hybrid relationship. Figure 1 (Complex) shows the breakdown of routing decisions observed taking into account these complex relationships. Interestingly, we find that taking these relationships into account has nearly no impact on the classification in our dataset (less than 1% change).

4.2 Sibling ASes

The mapping between AS numbers and organizations is not one-to-one [4]. Many organizations manage multiple AS numbers, either for geographic regions (e.g., Verizon with ASNs 701, 702, and 703) or due to mergers (e.g., Level 3 (AS 3356) and Global Crossing (AS 3549)).

Cai et al. [4] present a technique to map organizations to ASes by using attributes like organization IDs, email addresses and phone numbers found in `whois` information of ASes. We take a similar approach to identify AS siblings, but our approach differs in two key ways. First, we focus only on e-mail addresses in `whois` data, which previous work identified as the field with best precision and recall [4]. Second, we use DNS SOA records to identify different e-mail domains that belong to the same organization. For example, dish.com and dishaccess.tv share the dishnetwork.com authoritative domain. We also remove groups where the e-mail address is hosted by a popular e-mail provider (*e.g.*, hotmail.com), or regional Internet registry (*e.g.*, ripe.net). This results in a total of 94 sibling groups identified in our traceroute data set.

For every non GR decision that an AS makes, we check whether the AS chooses a path via a sibling. If the path is via a sibling, we mark this decision as satisfying the Best condition. Figure 1 (Sibs) shows the result of this change—3.9% more decisions are classified as Best/Short.

4.3 Prefix-specific policies

Interdomain routing is often abstracted to the level of a destination AS. However, in practice routing is based on IP prefixes which may be subject to different export policies by their originating AS (*e.g.*, forwarding prefixes hosting enterprise-class services to a more expensive provider). While Giotsas *et al.* consider partial transit [15], which is a type of prefix-specific policy, they do not explicitly consider per-prefix policies as implemented by origin ASes.

We use two criteria to identify prefix-specific policies based on correlation with BGP data obtained from Routeviews/RIPE [34, 39]. Given an origin AS (O), a neighbor N and a prefix P: **Criteria 1** do not assume the edge $N - O$ exists for prefix P unless we observe O announcing P to N in the BGP data. **Criteria 2** is similar to Criteria 1, except that we require that we observe at least one prefix announced from O to N before applying Criteria 1. The first criteria can be seen as being more aggressive whereas the second aims to ensure that our observation is actually caused by selective prefix announcement and not poor visibility.

Figure 1 (PSP-1, PSP-2) shows the breakdown of routing decisions using Criteria 1 and 2 above, respectively. We find that prefix-specific policies account for a significant fraction (10-19%) of unexpected routing decisions. Combining Criteria-1 and Criteria-2 separately with simple, complex and siblings relationships, yields 85.7% and 75.7% of decisions for Best/Short category respectively (Figure 2, All-1, All-2). One limitation of these approaches is that we only check prefix-specific policies for origin ASes. Other limitation is incomplete visibility in BGP control plane data.

Validation. In order to validate the cases of prefix-specific policies, we try to find a Looking Glass server hosted by the neighboring AS of the AS originating the prefix being examined. There were a total of 630 cases of prefix-specific policies involving 149 unique neighboring ASes. We were able to find looking glass servers in 28 of the neighboring ASes. Using these looking glass servers we manually verify 100 cases of prefix-specific policies and confirm that applying Criteria 1 was correct 78% of the time.

4.4 Active BGP Measurements

Using our active BGP measurements, we discover alternate routes. We study whether the sequence of alternate route choices match existing models and infer which step of the BGP decision

BGP DECISION	BGP FEEDS		TRACEROUTES	
Best relationship	435	(46.0%)	228	(42.4%)
Shorter path	152	(16.0%)	158	(29.4%)
Intradomain tie-breaker	155	(16.4%)	84	(15.6%)
Oldest route (magnet)	24	(2.5%)	9	(1.6%)
Violation	179	(18.9%)	58	(10.8%)
Total	**945**	(100%)	**537**	(100%)

Table 2: BGP decisions observed after we anycast a prefix previously announced from a single (magnet) location.

process led to each route. We report results for experiments performed between Feb. 25th and Apr 27th, 2015.

Alternate routes. We analyze AS routing choices when we use PEERING to discover alternate, less preferred routes. We compare the sequence of routes chosen by target ASes with CAIDA's AS-relationships database. Out of the 360 ASes we targeted, 310 (86.1%) chose routes following both Best and Shortest (as defined in Sec. 3.3); 29 (8.0%) chose routes following Best only; 18 (5.0%) following Shortest only; and 3 (0.8%) did not follow either property. We discuss the three observations that did not satisfy either property to illustrate limitations of current models.

One violation occurs for a European network E that routes via OpenPeering (AS20562)–a transit relationship identified from RPLS entries in public routing databases. After poisoning OpenPeering, E routes through (a likely peer-to-peer relationship) with AMPATH (AS20080) at AMS-IX. We list this as a violation because CAIDA identifies OpenPeering as a provider for E and AMPATH as a peer of E. Interestingly, the second route is the suffix of the first route (*i.e.*, the route through OpenPeering also reaches PEERING through AMPATH at AMS-IX), indicating the first route includes an unnecessary detour. Relationships are complex; transit and peering relationships may be preferred one over the other. Models with finer granularity for ranking neighbors of an AS may resolve these issues [27].

Another violation occurs at a US university U. The university first routes through Internet2 (AS11537) toward one of the PEERING locations in the US. After we poison Internet2, U routes through AMPATH (AS20080) toward the PEERING location in Brazil. We list this as a violation because CAIDA identifies Internet2 as a provider and AMPATH as a settlement-free peer of U. Our last observed violation is similar, where a European network first routes through Switch (AS559, identified as a provider) and then routes through NCSA (AS10764, identified as a settlement-free peer) to reach PEERING after we poison Switch. These violations indicate that identifying links used as back-up might improve our routing models.

Reverse engineering BGP decisions. We now turn to our second control plane experiment, where we use anycast to explore considerations such as route age on routing decisions. Table 2 shows the root cause behind BGP routing decisions. Although most decisions are made based on relationship and path length, more than 17% of decisions are made based on intradomain tie-breakers and route age, which are not considered in and could improve current models.

Limitations. BGP poisoning does not work when BGP loop prevention is disabled or when ASes filter poisoned announcements [20,22]. Intermediate ASes between PEERING locations and target ASes may prevent us from controlling routes exported to the target AS. These factors limit our ability to identify all routes available to and neighbors of target ASes. We consider the subset of routes we observed and neighbors we identified. Moreover, our results for these experiments cover a small fraction of the Internet and are probably biased toward academic and research networks. Our control plane techniques, however, are general and could be used by other networks to cover different portions of the Internet. We believe better coverage and visibility would result in discovering more violations. To this end, we are working to extend the PEERING platform and RIPE has configured periodic measurements from a diverse set of Probes toward all PEERING prefixes.

5. SKEWNESS BY SOURCE AND DESTINATION

We now investigate which source and destination ASes account for most of the routing decisions which deviate from our model. Figure 2 (a) and (b) shows the cumulative fraction of routing decisions which violate either the Best or Short condition (*i.e.*, the AS chooses a path that is longer or more expensive than we would expect). If violations were evenly distributed across ASes, the curves would fix $y = x$; otherwise, some ASes are responsible for a disproportionately larger (or smaller) fraction of violations. We find this effect is present in both plots, but more prominently for destination ASes. We focus on the latter.

Destination ASes owned by Akamai account for 21% of violations. Of these, Cogent (AS174) is the most common source, responsible for 3.4% of these Akamai related violations. These Cogent-Akamai violations tend to occur when Cogent prefers a peer-to-peer path through a Tier-1 AS over a longer customer route towards Akamai. Netflix's AS is the destination on 17% of paths with violations. Of these, nearly a quarter (24%) are due to a stale inter-AS link in CAIDA's topology, which included a direct link between AS3549 and Netflix that no longer exists according to RIPE ASN Neighbor History [32]. For source ASes, the distribution is less skewed. Cogent and Time Warner are the top two sources, responsible for 4.1% and 2.2% of violations, respectively.

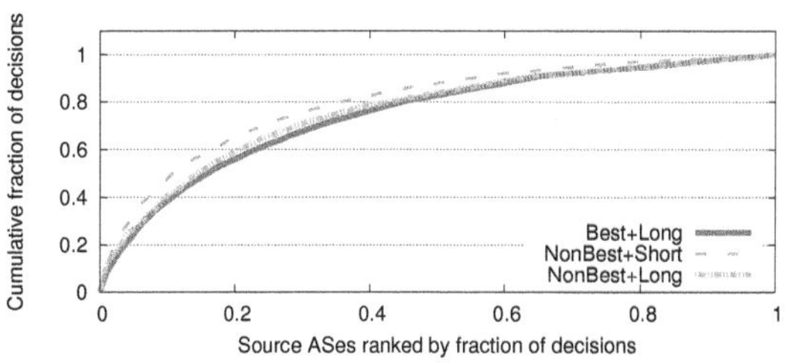

(a) Distribution of violations across source ASes.

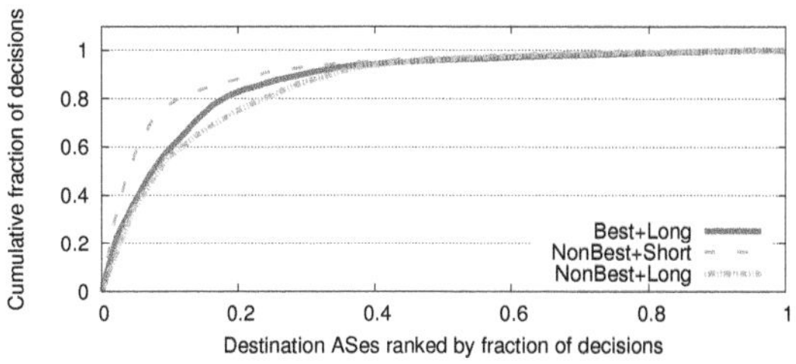

(b) Distributions of violations across destination ASes.

Figure 2: CDF plot of the fraction of violations (x-axis) explained by source and destinations ASes (y-axis). Violations observed in our dataset are skewed significantly toward Akamai and Netflix (21% and 17% of total NonBest/Short violations respectively). The skew for source ASes is less prominent.

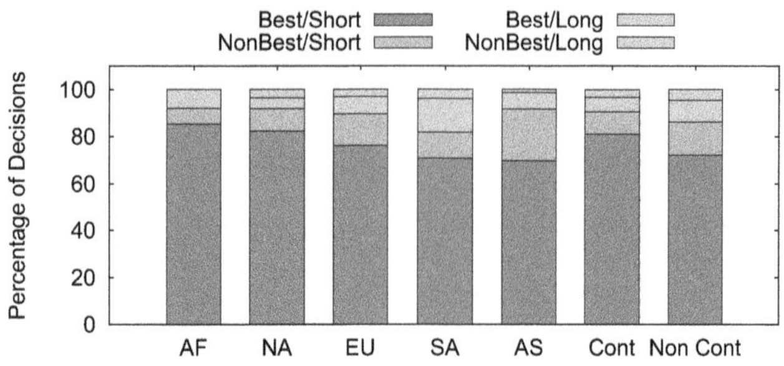

Figure 3: Breakdown of routing decisions for traceroutes that stay within continents of Africa (AF), North America (NA), Europe (EU), South America (SA), Asia (AS) and all continents combined (Cont), and for intercontinental traceroutes (Non Cont).

Continent	Non-Best/Short Decisions explained
Asia	40.1%
Africa	62.5%
Europe	64.3%
N. America	10.9%
Oceania	62.9%
S. America	66.6%

Table 3: Summary of Non-Best/Short decisions explained by ASes preferring intra-country routes.

6. IMPACT OF GEOGRAPHY

We next consider the role of geography on routing decisions. First, we isolate traceroutes that stay within a continent (Continental traceroutes), *i.e.*, all hops stay inside a given continent based on geolocating router IP addresses. Figure 3 shows the breakdown of decisions in the continental traceroutes (45% of our dataset). The fraction of decisions explained by GR for continental traceroutes is significantly greater than for intercontinental ones.

Domestic paths. Next we focused on traceroutes where we infer that the entire traceroute stayed within a single country, but there is a better *multinational Best/Short path* (in the CAIDA data), which we define to be a path with at least one AS registered (via `whois` data) in a country outside the source and destination AS's country. We find that more than 40% of non-Best/Short decisions can be explained by avoiding alternative multinational paths. One limitation of this approach is that even for the ASes that reside in multiple countries, `whois` data still points to just one country or when an AS spans across multiple regional internet registries then each RIR shows different country as the origin of that AS. Table 3 details the non-Best/Short decisions explained by ASes preferring domestic routes.

Undersea cables. Undersea cable ASes are a critical component of Internet topologies that previous works overlook [15,25]. While some cables are jointly owned by large ISPs, e.g., Pan-American Crossing, Americas-II (owned by AT&T, Sprint, and many others), we observed that others, e.g., EAC- C2C (PACNET), are operated by independent organizations using their own allocated ASNs and IP prefixes. Because these cable operators only provide point-to-point transit along the cables (i.e., they do not originate traffic and peer in locations proportional to cable landings), they resemble high-latency, high-cost IXPs and thus confuse existing AS relationship models. As such, we need techniques to identify cable ASes and correct their relationships in inferred topologies.

We use a list of undersea cables from the TeleGeography Submarine Cable Map [38] to identify ASes for undersea cable operators. Overall, cable-ASes appear on less than 2% of paths but most of the decisions (51.2%) involving cable-ASes caused deviations from Best/Short paths. Table 4 shows fraction of each type of decision explained by undersea cable ASes.

Violation type	Pct. of decisions explained
Non-Best & Short	3.0%
Best & Long	6.5%
Non-Best & Long	4.5%

Table 4: Fraction of decisions of each type that can be attributed to undersea cables.

7. CONCLUSION

In this work, we investigated how interdomain paths predicted by state-of-the-art routing models differ from empirically observed routes. We found that while a majority of paths in our dataset agree with models, more than a third do not. We explained a significant fraction of these differences due to factors such as sibling ASes, selective prefix announcements and undersea cables. Further, we investigated how the models hold up when comparing with ground-truth routing preferences revealed using PEERING announcements, and identified AS behavior that is not included in existing models. As part of future work, we are continuing to investigate cases of routing decisions that violate today's models, and we aim to incorporate our findings into new models of Internet routing.

Acknowledgments

Research in this paper was funded by NSF grants CNS-1422566, CNS-1351100, CNS-1413978; CNPq grant PU-477932; a Comcast TechFund Award; and a Google Faculty Research Award. The PEERING testbed was partially funded by NSF CNS-1406042. We gratefully acknowledge GENI for support of an early incarnation of PEERING. We also thank RIPE Atlas for help with traceroute measurements.

8. REFERENCES

[1] H. Ballani, P. Francis, and X. Zhang. A study of prefix hijacking and interception in the Internet. In *SIGCOMM*, 2007.

[2] M. Berman, J. S. Chase, L. Landweber, A. Nakao, M. Ott, D. Raychaudhuri, R. Ricci, and I. Seskar. GENI: A Federated Testbed for Innovative Network Experiments. *Computer Networks*, 61:5–23, 2014.

[3] R. Bush, O. Maennel, M. Roughan, and S. Uhlig. Internet optometry: Assessing broken glasses in internet reachability. In *ACM IMC*, 2009.

[4] X. Cai, J. Heidemann, B. Krishnamurthy, and W. Willinger. Towards an AS-to-organization map. In *ACM IMC*, 2010.

[5] M. Calder, X. F. Z. Hu, E. K.-B. J. Heidemann, and R. Govindan. Mapping the Expansion of Google's Serving Infrastructure. In *Proceedings of the ACM Internet Measurement Conference (IMC '13)*, October 2013.

[6] B. Chandrasekaran, M. Bai, M. Schoenfield, A. Berger, N. Caruso, G. Economou, S. Gilliss, B. Maggs, K. Moses, D. Duff, K. NgâĂă, E. G. Sirer, R. WeberâĂă, and B. Wong. Alidade: Ip geolocation without active probing. *Department of Computer Science, Duke University, Technical Report*, 2015.

[7] K. Chen, D. Choffnes, R. Potharaju, Y. Chen, F. Bustamante, D. Pei, and Y. Zhao. Where the sidewalk ends: Extending the internet AS graph using traceroutes from P2P users. In *CoNEXT '09*, 2009.

[8] Cisco. BGP Best Path Selection Algorithm: How the Best Path Algorithm Works. Document ID: 13753, May 2012.

[9] L. Colitti. *Internet Topology Discovery Using Active Probing*. Ph.D. thesis, University di Roma Tre, 2006.

[10] L. Gao, T. Griffin, and J. Rexford. Inherently safe backup routing with BGP. *IEEE INFOCOM*, 2001.

[11] L. Gao and J. Rexford. Stable Internet routing without global coordination. *Trans. Netw.*, 2001.

[12] P. Gill, S. Goldberg, and M. Schapira. A survey of interdomain routing policies. *ACM CCR*, 2014.

[13] P. Gill, M. Schapira, and S. Goldberg. Let the market drive deployment: A strategy for transistioning to BGP security. *SIGCOMM'11*, 2011.

[14] P. Gill, M. Schapira, and S. Goldberg. Modeling on quicksand: dealing with the scarcity of ground truth in interdomain routing data. *SIGCOMM Comput. Commun. Rev.*, 42(1):40–46, Jan. 2012.

[15] V. Giotsas, M. Luckie, B. Huffier, and K. Claffy. Inferring Complex AS Relationships. In *ACM IMC*, November 2014.

[16] S. Goldberg, M. Schapira, P. Hummon, and J. Rexford. How secure are secure interdomain routing protocols? In *SIGCOMM'10*, 2010.

[17] T. Griffin, F. B. Shepherd, and G. Wilfong. The stable paths problem and interdomain routing. *Trans. Netw.*, 2002.

[18] G. Huston. Peering and settlements - Part I. *The Internet Protocol Journal (Cisco)*, 2(1), March 1999.

[19] G. Huston. Peering and settlements - Part II. *The Internet Protocol Journal (Cisco)*, 2(2), June 1999.

[20] U. Javed, I. Cunha, D. R. Choffnes, E. Katz-Bassett, T. Anderson, and A. Krishnamurthy. Poiroot: Investigating the root cause of interdomain path changes. In *SIGCOMM*, 2013.

[21] J. Karlin, S. Forrest, and J. Rexford. Nation-state routing: Censorship, wiretapping, and BGP. *CoRR*, 2009.

[22] E. Katz-Bassett, C. Scott, D. R. Choffnes, I. Cunha, V. Valancius, N. Feamster, H. V. Madhyastha, T. Anderson, and A. Krishnamurthy. LIFEGUARD: Practical repair of persistent route failures. In *SIGCOMM*, 2012.

[23] C. Labovitz, S. Iekel-Johnson, D. McPherson, J. Oberheide, and F. Jahanian. Internet inter-domain traffic. In *SIGCOMM'10*, 2010.

[24] M. Lad, D. Massey, D. Pei, Y. Wu, B. Zhang, and L. Zhang. PHAS: A prefix hijack alert system. In *Proc. USENIX Security Symposium*, 2006.

[25] M. Luckie, B. Huffaker, A. Dhamdhere, and V. Giotsas. AS relationships, customer cones, and validation. In *ACM Internet Measurement Conference*, 2013.

[26] R. Lychev, S. Goldberg, and M. Schapira. Is the juice worth the squeeze? BGP security in partial deployment. In *SIGCOMM'13*, 2013.

[27] H. Madhyastha, E. Katz-Bassett, T. Anderson, A. Krishnamurthy, and A. Venkataramani. iPlane Nano: Path prediction for peer-to-peer applications. In *Usenix NSDI*, 2009.

[28] R. Mazloum, M. Buob, J. Auge, B. Baynat, D. Rossi, and T. Friedman. Violation of Interdomain Routing Assumptions. In *Passive and Active Measurement Conference*, March 2014.

[29] W. Mühlbauer, A. Feldmann, O. Maennel, M. Roughan, and S. Uhlig. Building an AS-topology model that captures route diversity. In *SIGCOMM*, 2006.

[30] R. Oliveira, D. Pei, W. Willinger, B. Zhang, and L. Zhang. Quantifying the completeness of the observed internet AS-level structure. *UCLA Computer Science Department - Techical Report TR-080026-2008*, Sept 2008.

[31] Quantcast. `http://www.quantcast.com`.

[32] RIPE ASN Neighbor History. `https://stat.ripe.net/widget/asn-neighbours-history`.

[33] RIPE RIS raw data. `http://www.ripe.net/data-tools/stats/ris/ris-raw-data`.

[34] RIPE Network Coordination Center. RIPE Routing Information Service. http://www.ripe.net/data-tools/stats/ris/routing-information-service.

[35] M. Roughan, W. Willinger, O. Maennel, D. Perouli, and R. Bush. 10 lessons from 10 years of measuring and modeling the Internet's autonomous systems. *JSAC*, 2011.

[36] Sandvine. Fall 2012 global internet phenomena, 2012.

[37] B. Schlinker, K. Zarifis, I. Cunha, N. Feamster, and E. Katz-Bassett. PEERING: An AS for Us. In *Proc. ACM HotNets*, Los Angeles, CA, October 2014.

[38] TeleGeography Submarine Cable Map. `http://www.submarinecablemap.com/`.

[39] University of Oregon Route Views Project. `http://www.routeviews.org/`.

[40] V. Valancius, N. Feamster, J. Rexford, and A. Nakao. Wide-area route control for distributed services. In *USENIX ATC*, 2010.

[41] J. Wu, Y. Zhang, Z. M. Mao, and K. Shin. Internet routing resilience to failures: Analysis and implications. In *CoNEXT*, 2007.

Empirical Analysis of Search Advertising Strategies

Bhanu C. Vattikonda
University of California, San Diego
bvattikonda@cs.ucsd.edu

Saikat Guha
Microsoft Research, Bangalore, India
saikat@microsoft.com

Vacha Dave
Microsoft, Mountain View, California
vachad@microsoft.com

Alex C. Snoeren
University of California, San Diego
snoeren@cs.ucsd.edu

ABSTRACT

Top search ad placement is the coin of today's Internet services realm. An entire industry of search engine marketing companies have emerged to help advertisers optimize their ad campaigns to deliver high returns on investment, peddling a plethora of advertising strategies. Yet, very little is publicly known about the effectiveness of online search advertising, especially when trying to compare the various campaign strategies used by advertisers.

This paper presents the first large-scale measurement of the effectiveness—measured in terms of incremental conversion gains—of online search ads. We develop a simple metric called net acquisition benefit (NAB) that admits comparisons between the efficacy of different ad campaign strategies without access to advertisers' private financial information. We study three common campaign strategies used by advertisers on a large search ad network: cannibalization, poaching, and ad extensions. Considering data from a month in the last two years, we employ NAB to identify cases where these campaign strategies are justified. Advertisers and ad agencies can replicate our methodology to apply it to other strategies of interest.

Categories and Subject Descriptors

C.4 [**Performance of Systems**]: Measurement Techniques; H.3.5 [**Online Information Services**]: Web-based services

General Terms

Measurement

Keywords

Sponsored search; advertising effectiveness;

IMC'15, October 28–30, 2015, Tokyo, Japan.

ISBN 978-1-4503-3848-6/15/10$15.00
DOI: http://dx.doi.org/10.1145/2815675.2815694.

1. INTRODUCTION

Measuring the effectiveness of advertising is, in general, a hard problem. As John Wanamaker famously quipped, "half the money I spend on advertising is wasted; the trouble is I don't know which half." Online search advertising holds out the promise of addressing this longstanding challenge by focusing spend on the right consumers at the right time. The sheer scale of fine-grained, user-activity data that can be brought to bear (e.g., tracking every ad click and every user action on advertisers' site) allows advertisers to reach populations of particular interest. Moreover, search queries capture the intent of the user allowing more direct connections between the ad and the user action [26]. This tight relationship contrasts with traditional brand advertising where connections between ads and purchases are more nebulous. Hence, it is no surprise that search advertising accounts for over 40% of the $42 billion spent in online ads in the US alone, and is growing at 18% annually [25].

Despite its ever-increasing prevalence, very little is publicly known about the effectiveness of online search advertising. Indeed, large advertisers have presented conflicting anecdotal evidence. As recently as in April 2013, a study claimed that the estimated $51 million eBay spends on search ads is ineffective since they essentially cannibalize clicks from organic search results: in the absence of eBay's ad the user would have clicked the eBay page in the organic results [10]. Similarly, three Indian online apparel retailers found that poaching each other's users by advertising on their competitors' brand names was counterproductive; while they might succeed in getting their competitors' customers to click their ad, the customers would typically not convert. For the few customers who do end up making a purchase, the cost paid by the advertiser is too high [7]. Despite these reports, ad networks and ad agencies maintain that poaching and cannibalizing organic clicks both have a net positive return on investment [7]. Opinions are similarly mixed in the mobile space, where many advertisers complain about accidental clicks while ad networks defend the effectiveness of mobile search ads [4, 6].

One factor contributing to these seemingly contradictory reports is the current inability of anyone other than the advertisers themselves to determine if a particular advertising campaign is effective. Publishers and marketing firms deal in terms of metrics like click-through ratio (CTR), which reports the number of clicks on an ad as a fraction of the number of times the ad is shown, and cost per acquisition (CPA), which reports an advertiser's total spend divided by the number of resulting purchases. Unfortunately, neither of these metrics lends insight to the key question—namely whether a particular advertising campaign is *profitable* for the advertiser or not, which is captured by the metric profit per impression (PPI). However, determining an ad campaign's PPI fundamentally requires knowledge of an advertiser's cost and revenue structure—

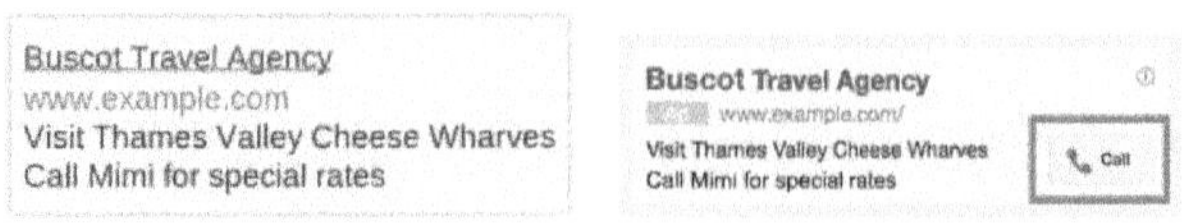

(a) Traditional search ad (b) Ad with call extension

Figure 1: Examples of search ad types.

information they are likely loathe to share, even with their marketing agencies.

Instead, we present a simple metric—net acquisition benefit (NAB)—that leverages information about how much an advertiser bids for ad placement (which, for rational advertisers, is a lower bound on the profit they expect) to estimate profit per impression (PPI). Using data about billions of clicks from a large search ad network we conduct a month-long measurement study of the effectiveness of three search ad campaign strategies—cannibalization, poaching, and ad extensions—that are widely employed by advertisers today.

We find that the advertising landscape is quite nuanced: a given campaign strategy may be effective for some advertisers but not others. For instance, advertisers with well-established brands may find little benefit in advertising on search queries mentioning their brand, while less well-known brands may need to do so to protect themselves from competitors looking to poach their customers. Similarly, ads on mobile devices may be more effective for businesses with brick-and-mortar storefronts than for businesses with purely online presence. We hope that NAB will allow not only advertisers but ad agencies and other third parties to replicate our methodology to measure and compare other advertising strategies.

2. BACKGROUND

This section provides a brief overview of search advertising and related concepts. Readers already familiar with search ads may prefer to skip ahead and refer back to this section as needed.

Search ads and organic results. When a user types a search query into a search engine like Google, Bing, or Yahoo!, the resulting page contains two types of listings. Organic search results—traditionally understood to be the search results—are determined by the search engine through proprietary heuristic algorithms; the listed websites do not pay the search engine for placement or click-throughs. Paid search results, on the other hand, which we refer to as search ads, are typically sold by the search engine through an auction mechanism where the destination website (i.e., advertiser) bids for inclusion. The top paid search results are typically displayed alongside organic search results and formatted to look similar except for, e.g., a slightly different background shade, or a 'Sponsored' or 'Ad' label.

Content. The content of an ad includes at a minimum a title, the advertiser's domain name, and two short lines of descriptive text, typically rendered in blue, green, and black, respectively as illustrated in Figure 1. The advertiser also provides the URL the user should be directed to if the ad is clicked. Search engines increasingly support ad extensions that allow advertisers to include additional information or actions in the rendered ad. The call extension, for instance, allows an advertiser to provide a phone number; when the ad is shown on a mobile phone, the extension is rendered as a button that invokes the dialer as shown in Figure 1(b).

Targeting. Advertisers select individual keywords or phrases that must be present in the (normalized) user search query for the ad to be included in the ad auction. User search queries are normalized to fix misspellings, stem words, and resolve ambiguities using various heuristics. The advertiser may further target their ad by device type, geographic region, time of day, and user demographics. Targeting is often quite fine-grained in practice, with top advertisers managing tens of millions of keywords [10].

Campaigns and pricing. Ads are priced through an auction mechanism that is designed to encourage advertisers to bid the maximum amount they are willing to pay for a click. The amount the advertiser is charged if the ad is clicked is based on the next-lower-ranked bid in a form of generalized second-price auction [20]. The position of the ad on the results page is based on some function of the bid and the probability the ad will be clicked (e.g., based on historical click-through rates). Advertisers typically manage bids for a group of related keywords and targeting criteria through a logical construct called a campaign. Each bid is associated with a particular ad campaign, which can specify fine-grained bid modifications based upon device type and individual keywords.

Conversion. The purpose of an ad is obviously to drive revenue to the advertiser. Conversion (or equivalently, acquisition) refers to the user performing some desirable action on the advertiser's site after clicking the ad, e.g., signing up for a newsletter, purchasing a product, or subscribing to a service. Sophisticated search-ad networks assist advertisers in monitoring the effectiveness of their campaigns by providing support for analytics. In particular, the advertiser can inform the search-ad network of a conversion event by placing JavaScript code provided by the search-ad network on the page on which the conversion happens. The JavaScript directs the browser to contact the search-ad network's server with a user cookie which can then be used to link the conversion event to any previous user actions performed on the search-ad network. The advertiser can track campaign performance along different types of conversions by passing an opaque tag to the conversion JavaScript; the search-ad network typically does not learn the semantics of the tag or the value of the conversion and simply tallies the counts of these opaque tags for the campaign.

3. METRIC

In this section we present NAB, a simple metric we use for measuring the effectiveness of online search ads. Our primary goal is to design a metric that can be used by ad networks, ad agencies, or any entity that manages large search advertising campaigns. We discuss the challenges in choosing the right metric to measure the performance of ad campaigns. In particular, we address the fact that details of customer transactions (e.g., profit margins) may not be available to the entities running the search engine marketing campaigns for the advertisers.

3.1 Challenges

Our choice of metric for comparing the performance of different advertising strategies is driven by the following challenges.

3.1.1 Advertiser diversity

Advertisers on our partner ad network span orders of magnitude in terms of their scale. The effective cost per acquisition (CPA) for an advertiser, computed as the total amount charged divided by the total number of conversions, is a rough proxy for the monetary utility the advertiser expects to derive from advertising [21]. Figure 2 plots the normalized CPA for advertisers reporting at least 10 conversion events in our dataset vs. the total normalized money spent by the advertiser; the values are normalized to the median value along each axis. (Because each advertiser has at least 10 conversions, there can be no points above the $\text{CPA} = \text{TotalSpend}/10$ diagonal.) As one might expect, different advertisers have vastly different budgets. Both the total money spent by advertisers (x-axis domain) and effective cost-per-acquisition (y-axis range) span

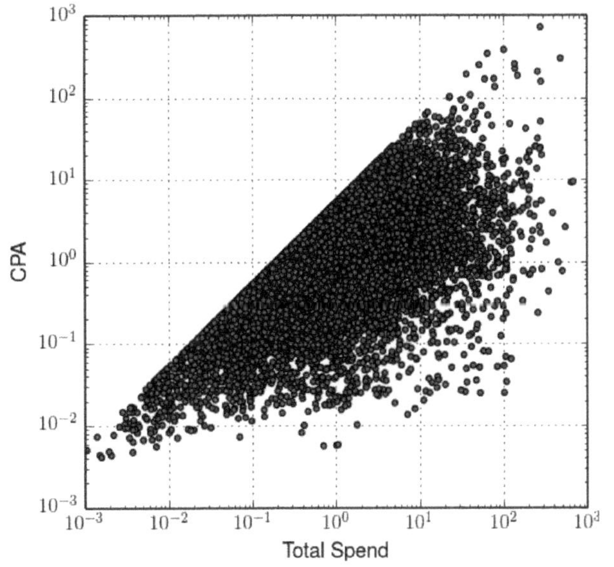

Figure 2: Large spread in the normalized advertiser ad spend and the normalized price they pay per conversion.

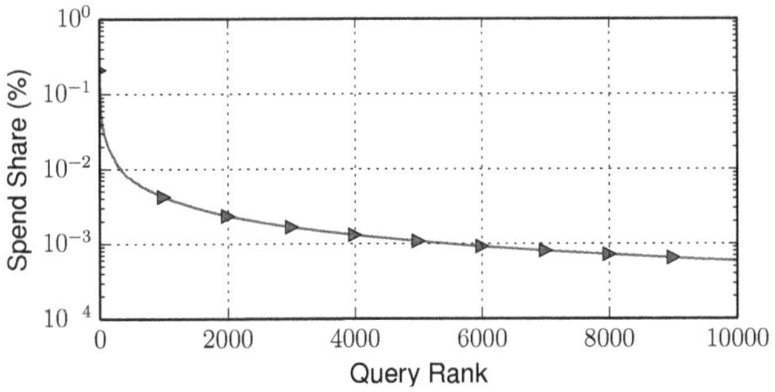

Figure 3: Top queries account for a small share of overall spend illustrating the query diversity.

almost six orders of magnitude. Thus, our metric must take into account an advertisers' target cost per acquisition and allow comparison between different advertising strategies of an advertiser.

3.1.2 Statistical significance

As mentioned, ad targeting can be extremely fine-grained focusing on specific keywords, device types, geographic regions, etc. Figure 3 plots the probability density function of the share of total advertising money spent on a sampling of the most popular keywords (ordered by the amount of money spent on them). To illustrate, note that the top keyword contributes to less than 0.2% of the total spend. There is a heavy tail of keywords with the top 200 most-popular together accounting for less than 7% of the total spend in the sample. Performing analysis at keyword granularity results in poor statistical significance. The statistical significance is lower still if the data is further sliced by user, device type, advertiser and other targeting parameters.

Hence, any useful metric must be defined over traffic aggregates, which we refer to as slices of search requests. The dimensions along which the data should be aggregated depends upon the strategy being evaluated. In general, we will consider slices that capture a particular advertising campaign. For instance, aggregating data by device type may help evaluate the effectiveness of advertising on mobile devices, while aggregating data by query classification to, e.g., consider only ads placed on competitors' brand names, may help evaluate the impact of poaching.

3.2 Net acquisition benefit (NAB)

Intuitively, the net acquisition benefit (NAB) is the conversion probability of a traffic slice adjusted by its cost. We define NAB for a traffic slice x as follows:

$$\text{NAB(x)} = \pi_x - \frac{\nu_x}{\lambda},$$

where:

x, n : Traffic slice x consisting of n impressions
π_x = Conversion probability, i.e., $\frac{\#conversions}{n}$
ν_x = Average cost, i.e., $\frac{cost}{n}$
λ = Advertiser's target cost-per-acquisition

λ is the maximum amount an advertiser would be willing to pay for a conversion, which is well captured, for example, by their bid in an ad auction (see Section 2). Obviously, a rational advertiser would not want to pay more for an ad than they stand to make in profit on the conversion, so we argue that λ serves as a lower bound for the profit an advertiser expects to capture from a conversion. Note that if λ precisely equals the advertiser's profit margin, then NAB is proportional to profit per impression (PPI).

NAB $= 1$ for an optimally beneficial traffic slice — where every case results in a conversion ($\pi = 1$) and there is no cost ($\nu = 0$). NAB $= 0$ for traffic slices that have no net benefit, e.g., where the traffic slice is so expensive that the advertiser is willing to forgo every conversion and save the entire cost (i.e., effective cost-per-acquisition is λ and $\nu = \lambda\pi$). For detrimental traffic slices, e.g., there are no conversions ($\pi = 0$) and the advertiser is losing money ($\nu > 0$), NAB is negative. In practice, NAB is on the order of 10^{-2} in our real-world dataset. (Intuitively, this makes sense, as CTRs are typically of the same order.)

3.3 Incremental NAB

The incremental net acquisition benefit (INAB) measures the relative improvement in NAB of one traffic slice over another, i.e., the effectiveness of one ad campaign vs. another. Intuitively, it is the change in conversion probability ($\Delta\pi$) adjusted by the change in cost ($\Delta\nu$). We define INAB for traffic slice x over slice y as follows:

$$\text{INAB(x | y)} = \frac{\text{NAB(x)} - \text{NAB(y)}}{|\text{NAB(y)}|}$$

INAB is defined only for two comparable traffic slices. That is, INAB can be computed for two traffic slices x and y belonging to the same advertiser but not across advertisers. Traffic slice x is more beneficial than y if and only if x has more net acquisition benefit than y, i.e., INAB(x | y) is positive. Slice x is less beneficial than y if INAB(x | y) is negative (or equivalently, INAB(y | x) is positive). Both are equivalent if INAB(x | y) is zero.

3.4 Discussion

NAB approximates profit per impression (PPI) when λ is equal to profit margin on conversion. But, unlike profit per impression, NAB does not require information about revenue derived and cost of the products. This allows ad networks and ad agencies to use the NAB metric to compare effectiveness of advertising campaigns. Note that both NAB and PPI, being impression based, can be sensitive to impression counts (impressions are cheap, one may argue). However, an impression represents the most basic intervention to user experience on behalf of advertisers, and in absence of a better denominator, impression-based metrics are still considered industry standard [2, 38].

CTR and CPA. Click-through ratio (CTR) and cost per acquisition (CPA) are the two most commonly used metrics to evaluate effectiveness of ad campaigns. CTR captures the effectiveness of a campaign in attracting users but does not capture the benefit of attracting those users. It also does not capture the price that the advertiser has to pay for the clicks. While CPA captures the quality of users being attracted, it does not capture the efficiency of the campaign in attracting users overall, something that CTR captures.

We find that NAB captures the performance of a campaign better than both CTR and CPA. In particular, NAB is robust to the diversity of advertisers and sparsity of query-level data found in our dataset. It has been observed [12, 24] that even large search engines have very sparse data when aggregated by user queries. NAB allows comparisons between different advertising strategies of a given advertiser and can be applied to any slice of traffic with sufficient data.

Target cost per acquisition. One subtlety with NAB is that advertisers could have different target costs per acquisition for different ad campaigns. We discuss our methodology for inferring target cost per acquisition in next section.

4. DATA AND METHODOLOGY

This section describes the dataset we use and the methodology we follow for measuring effectiveness of various ad campaign strategies in the subsequent sections.

4.1 Dataset

Our dataset sample is several terabytes in size, consisting of billions of search and ad clicks on a large search ad network in the United States English language market. We report upon clicks capturing all actions taken by hundreds of millions of users who issue hundreds of millions of unique English-language queries over a period of four contiguous weeks within the last two years. (Analysis of a different four-week time period obtains qualitatively similar results.) The dataset contains a representative sample of clicks from desktops, tablets and phones. Our dataset sample covers many millions of dollars in advertising spend[1] by hundreds of thousands of advertisers. Our dataset does not cover specialized search verticals like image, video and map, or product listings.

For each click our dataset includes the following anonymized information: *i*) the normalized search query issued by the user and the search ad network's internal query classification; *ii*) information about the browser including version and operating system, device form factor *iii*) the list of organic search results and paid search ads that were presented to the user; *iv*) the details of the associated ad campaign including bid amounts, keywords targeted, and ad extensions; *v*) the organic search results or paid search ads on which the user actually clicked (if any) including clicks on multiple results and ads; and, lastly, for ads clicked, *vi*) the second-price bid charged to the advertiser along with any advertiser-reported conversion event(s) for that click along with the URL of the pages for which the user conversion was reported and the (opaque) conversion types.

Along with click data, the analytics system collects user activity data on advertiser websites to track the performance of their ad campaigns. Whenever a user performs an action that the advertiser wants to track, JavaScript embedded in the page sends information about the action—along with a user cookie allowing the data to be connected to the user's search behavior—to the ad network. This system allows advertisers to declare which user actions constitute conversions.

[1]We are obliged to report only the magnitude or normalized values for some sensitive quantities when doing so does not compromise the scientific value of our results.

4.2 Methodology

In order to compute NAB we infer target cost per conversion (λ) and conversion rate of traffic acquired organically from the data. We aggregate data over queries that identify traffic representing different advertising strategies.

Conversions. In order to identify the conversions that an advertiser obtains from a slice of traffic we have to attribute the conversion to a specific prior search. For this, we identify the user actions on the search engine prior to the conversion event on the advertiser website. We then attribute the conversion to the latest user click (regardless of whether the click was on an organic result or a search ad) that led the user to the advertiser's website—as long as the click happened in the 24 hours prior to the conversion event.

Not all advertisers report conversion signals, or not in significant numbers. Unless otherwise mentioned, we omit advertisers for whom we have less than 30 conversion reports in our dataset sample.

Inferring target cost per acquisition. Recall from Section 2 that advertisers place a bid which is the maximum amount they are willing to pay for a click. We infer the maximum amount the advertiser is willing to pay for a conversion (λ) by dividing their total bid amount for the ads clicked by the number of conversions they received. Since the bid values are always more than the actual cost of advertising, overall NAB for any advertiser is always positive. Note that by making this choice we consider all conversions that the advertiser receives in US English market—irrespective of campaign—equivalent.

Aggregating queries. NAB must be computed over a significant aggregation of traffic. As mentioned earlier, individual search queries are too granular. We follow the search-ad network's internal classification scheme [41] to aggregate queries into the following four classes of particular interest: navigational, local, commercial, and other, which includes informational queries.

Since the ad network's internal query classifier uses heuristics, we verify the correctness of classification by manually investigating a representative sample. In all we manually verify 200 queries and find that in the large majority of cases (94%) our manual label matches the classifier's; in the remaining 6% of the cases we believe the classifier misclassified the query. We compute the sensitivity and specificity measures for classification of navigational queries and find that that 77% of the time, a navigational query is classified as navigational, whereas 4% of the time, a non-navigational query is classified as navigational. Overall, the query classification—while not perfect—seems sufficiently accurate for the purposes of our study.

Traffic slices. In subsequent sections we compare the effectiveness of various campaign strategies used by advertisers by comparing the benefits across different traffic slices. Each slice of traffic is defined by the query classification, device type, the position of the advertiser in the organic results (if at all), whether the advertiser's ad is shown or not, and whether the call button was present for the ad or organic result (in the case of mobile devices). Table 1 lists these features and describes the values they take. Table 2 labels the various combinations of these features with a name that we use to refer to that traffic slice in subsequent sections. We discuss our choice of the traffic slices in Section 8.

Query	
nav	Navigational query; user seeks specific site
com	Commercial query; user has purchase intent
all	All queries
Device	
phone	Mobile smartphones
pc	Desktops and laptops
all	All devices
Organic	
yes	Present in first page of results
no	Not in first page of results
top	Top-most organic search result
poor	Ranked 2 or worse, or not on first page
n	Ranked n
$n+$	Ranked n or worse
all	All cases whether present or not
Ad	
yes	Ad present
no	Ad not present
Ext. (set)	
ad:call	Ad has call button
org:call	Organic result had call button
ad:comp	Competitor has an ad

Table 1: Traffic features used to define traffic slices

Slice	Query	Device	Org.	Ad	Ext.
Section 5: Cannibalizing Organic					
org-n-noad	all	pc	n	no	
org-n-ad	all	pc	n	yes	
nav-noad	nav	pc	top	no	
nav-ad	nav	pc	top	yes	
nav-comp-noad	nav	pc	top	no	ad:comp
nav-comp-ad	nav	pc	top	yes	ad:comp
noorg-ad	all	pc	no	yes	
Section 6: Poaching					
poach-ad	nav	pc	poor	yes	
poach-noad	nav	pc	poor	no	
commerce-ad	com	pc	all	yes	
Section 7: Ad Extensions					
phone-orgcall	all	phone	yes	no	org:call
phone-org	all	phone	yes	no	
phone-ad	all	phone	all	yes	
phone-adcall	all	phone	all	yes	ad:call
phone-noorg-ad	all	phone	no	yes	
phone-noorg-adcall	all	phone	no	yes	ad:call
phone-orgcall-adcall	all	phone	all	yes	org:call, ad:call

Table 2: Traffic slices used in this paper

5. CANNIBALIZING ORGANIC TRAFFIC

We refer to the scenario where advertisers show ads for queries where they have an organic presence as cannibalization: in the absence of ads, users could have navigated to the advertiser using organic results. We consider three particular scenarios of cannibalization and use NAB to measure the benefits of each. We find that, *i)* for queries where the advertiser is the top result 56% of the advertisers derive no benefit from advertising, *ii)* the incremental benefit of advertising increases as the organic rank of advertiser decreases and *iii)* over 61% of the advertisers achieve limited benefit by advertising on navigational queries.

5.1 Improving visibility

In this section we consider the general case of searches where the user does not already have a particular destination website (advertiser) in mind. In such an instance, even though an advertiser's site appears in the organic search results, the advertiser may wish to increase its visibility to induce the user to visit its site as opposed to a competitor's. We consider an advertiser to be attempting to improve their visibility if the advertiser chooses to display an ad despite already being included in the organic results likely to be considered by the user (i.e., ranked in the top ten organic results which are chosen based on their relevance to the user query).

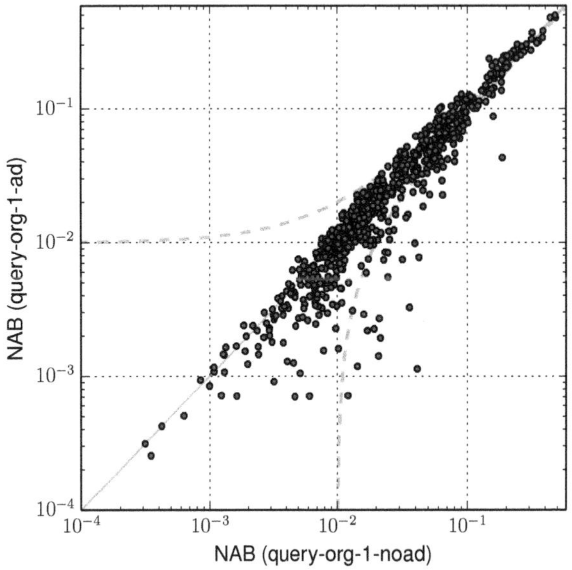

Figure 4: Most advertisers see little to no benefit in advertising for queries where they are the top result.

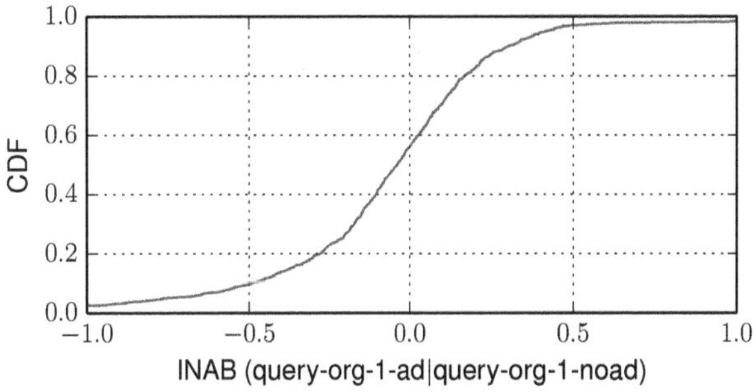

Figure 5: 56% advertisers achieve zero or negative INAB by advertising on queries where advertiser is the top result.

5.1.1 *Same-query visibility*

The main challenge in measuring the impact of advertising is obtaining comparable search impressions. In the ideal scenario we would compare user actions in the presence and absence of an ad while everything else remains the same. Since we do not have such data, we compare the performance of ads by comparing benefits of advertising over two sets of impressions for the same query, one with ads and one without ads. Comparing user actions over impressions for the same query ensures that the most significant variable—the user query—remains the same in both sample sets.

We begin by considering the effectiveness of advertising when an advertiser is already the top organic search result. For each (advertiser, query) pair, where advertiser is the top organic result for that

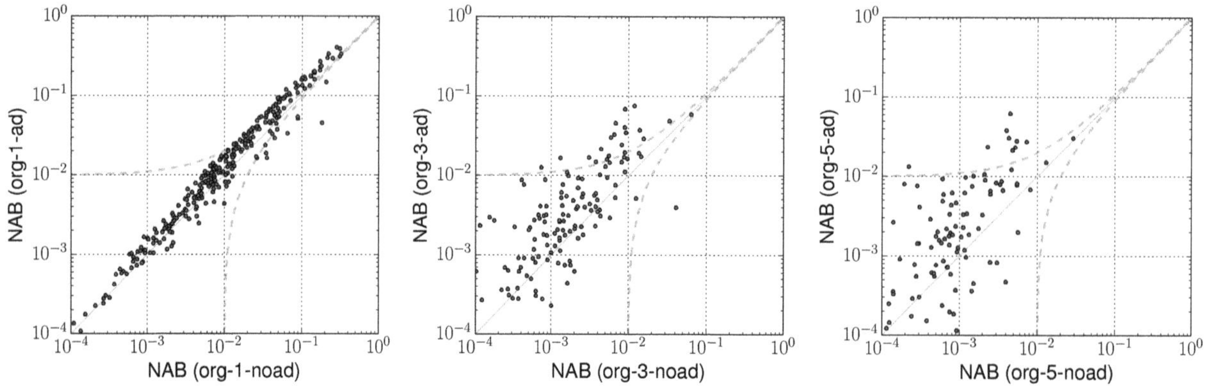

(a) Rank 1 (b) Rank 3 (c) Rank 5

Figure 6: The benefits of cannibalizing organic clicks increase with decreasing organic search ranking.

query, we identify impressions with and without ads by the advertiser. I.e., a single advertiser may be considered multiple times if they are the top search result for more than one query. Figure 4 plots the NAB of advertising (query-org-1-ad) vs. not advertising (query-org-1-noad) for all (advertiser, query) pairs where we have more than 30 conversions (as discussed in Section 4). In our dataset, we have 824 (advertiser, query) pairs covering 345 distinct advertisers. The diagonal line represents an INAB of zero, i.e., the effectiveness of advertising is equivalent to the effectiveness of not advertising for that advertiser. Advertising is more effective than not for advertisers above the diagonal. A slight majority are below the line where the inverse is true—i.e., it is not worth advertising for that query. The dashed red curves above and below the diagonal are intended to aide comparison as the graph spans four orders of magnitude on each axis: they represent a ΔNAB (NAB(ad) - NAB(noad)) of $+0.01$ and -0.01 respectively.

As an alternative representation of the same data, Figure 5 plots the CDF of the corresponding INAB metric. Recall that INAB is normalized to the NAB of the base strategy, so a value of 1.0 represents a $2\times$ improvement. For 56% of the (advertiser, query) pairs the corresponding advertiser gets zero or negative incremental benefit by advertising on the query (i.e., fall below the diagonal in Figure 4). Again, this means that these advertisers should reconsider advertising on those queries.

5.1.2 Over all queries

The constraint of comparing the benefits of advertising by holding the user query a constant limits our analysis to a few advertisers who have significant number of conversions for the same query. Even for those advertisers, these few queries contribute to a small proportion of their entire ad spend. Hence, there is reason to believe the same-query results may not be representative. By design, we can apply our metric to measure effectiveness of ads on an arbitrary slice of traffic. Here we expand our analysis to compare traffic slices where the advertiser has a particular rank in organic results, irrespective of user query.

Figure 6 considers only non-navigational queries (i.e., those where the user likely does not have a particular destination website in mind) and plots NAB of advertising (org-n-ad) vs. not advertising (org-n-noad) aggregated across all queries for each advertiser (i.e., each advertiser is a single data point) where we have sufficient data as described in Section 4. We separate campaigns based upon their rank in organic results. Figure 6(a) considers the aggregate performance of all non-navigational queries for which an advertiser

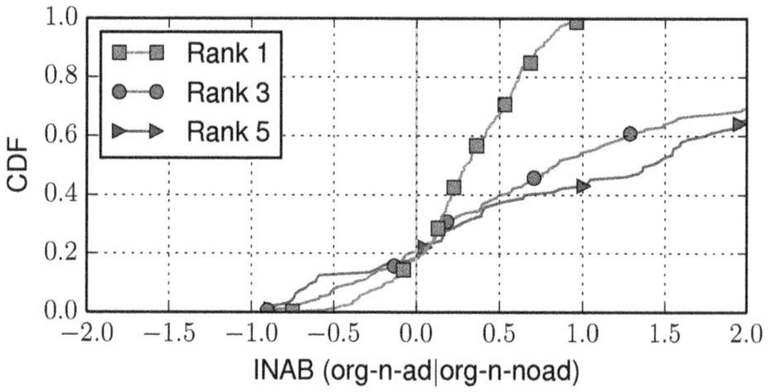

Figure 7: As rank increases in organic results benefits of cannibalistic advertising turn positive, albeit only slightly.

anyway obtains the top organic result (c.f. Figure 4 which shows a distinct point for each unique top-result-producing query an advertiser may obtain). Figures 6(b) and 6(c) show the same comparison for campaigns where the advertiser appears third or fifth in organic search results, respectively.

Figure 7 plots the CDFs of the corresponding INAB metrics for each of the three classes of campaign considered in Figure 6. In contrast to the same-query results above, most of the advertisers gain by advertising for non-navigational queries despite being present in the organic results. This is likely because non-navigational queries tend to be competed for more aggressively and users are flexible with choosing any business that meets their needs. Also, while the relative benefit (i.e., INAB) of advertising increase as the organic rank drops, the absolute benefits (i.e., NAB) of advertising are very low.

Interestingly, for 32% of the top-ranked websites, there appear to be significant benefits to advertising (INAB $> 50\%$). Manual investigations find that these advertisers belong to two categories. One set of advertisers have less-well-recognized brands. If a more well recognized brand advertises for the query, and is thus placed above the top-ranked organic result, the latter lose out. The other category of advertisers who gain are those who share their brand with other advertisers. For example, car manufacturers lose potential converting users to competing ads placed by car dealers trying to attract the same users. For 19% of the top-ranked websites, advertising is a drain on their ad spend (INAB < 0) since they end up competing on hotly contested queries resulting in higher cost per acquisition than their overall average.

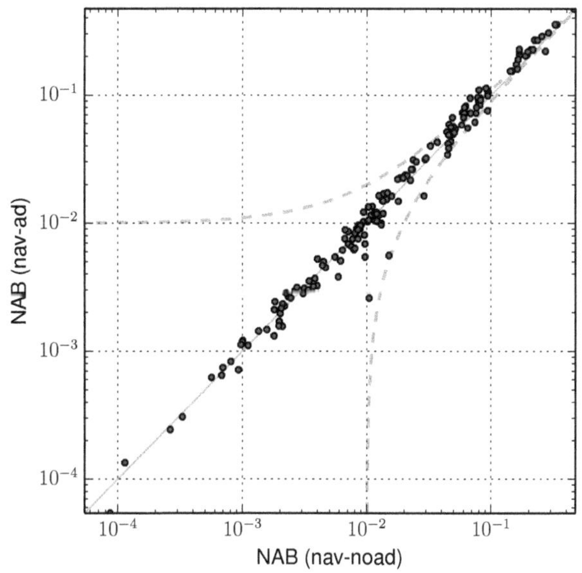

(a) Advertising for navigational queries.

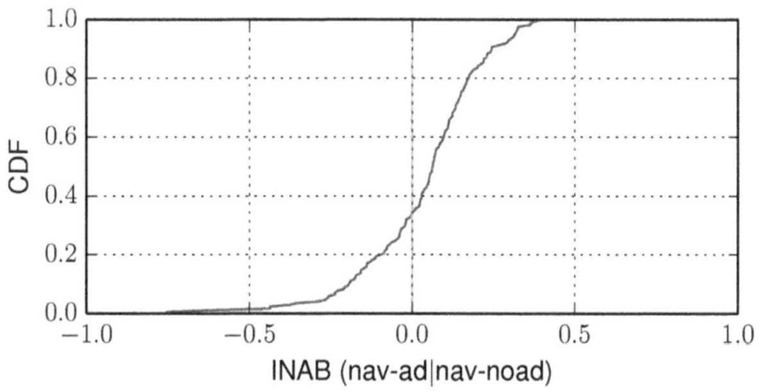

(b) INAB of navigational queries.

Figure 8: The incremental benefit of advertising for navigational queries is very small for most advertisers.

5.2 Navigational queries

A subset of queries (explicitly excluded above) for which an advertiser is the top organic result is known as navigational queries—i.e., the user is using the search engine as a way to navigate to the advertiser's site. We consider a given query navigational for an advertiser if: *i)* the search query is classified by the search ad network as navigational, i.e., the user query includes branded terms or keywords (e.g., Amazon or Facebook) that suggests the user is seeking a specific website, and *ii)* the advertiser is the top-most organic result for that query. Here, we consider whether it is effective for a website to advertise for queries where the user is explicitly seeking to navigate to the advertiser website.

Figure 8(a) plots the NAB of advertising (nav-ad) versus not advertising (nav-noad) for all advertisers where we have at least 30 conversions attributed to clicks following queries matching the above criteria. Figure 8(b) plots the same data as a CDF of the INAB of advertising over not advertising on these queries. As is evident from points clustering along the diagonal in the scatter plot, the majority of advertisers (61%) receive very little incremental benefit (less than 10%) from advertising on navigational queries where they are the top organic result. Moreover, for 32% of advertisers, advertising on navigational queries for which they are the top organic result is a net loss when compared to not advertising (i.e., INAB is < 0). In 9% of the cases, however, such advertising bears significant fruit (INAB is $> 25\%$).

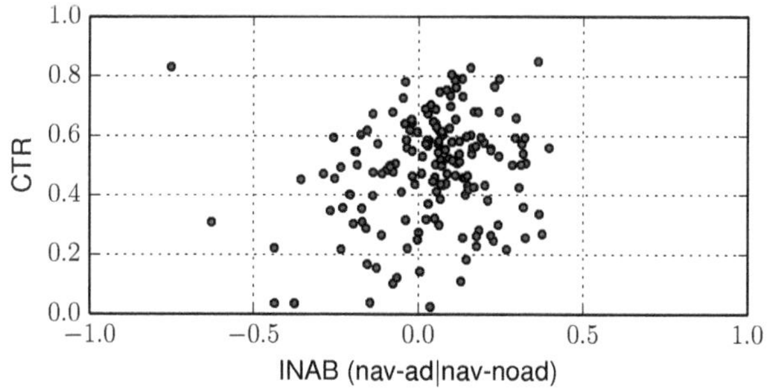

Figure 9: INAB has no correlation with CTR and most advertisers receive a high click through rate on navigational queries.

Our finding that 61% of advertisers receive limited benefit (INAB approximately zero) from advertising on navigational queries vs. not advertising squarely contradicts reports from other ad networks that suggest 89% of ad clicks are incremental, and would be lost without advertising [13]. We reconcile these results by observing that the previous study [13] does not consider conversions and focuses solely on clicks. Indeed, the study's authors explicitly state that advertisers should consider conversions since relying on clicks alone may be misleading. We show below that advertising on navigational queries does, in fact, inflate click counts without increasing conversions for the vast majority of advertisers. Another reason for the divergent result is that the previous study considers campaigns that are paused due to budget shortage. This would bias the choice of campaigns towards very small advertisers who would not have strong presence for navigational queries.

For advertisers that value conversions, however, our data discredits conventional wisdom that promotes advertising on navigational queries for which the advertiser is the top organic result. Finally, while our general finding is consistent with experimental evidence from large advertisers including eBay [10], we nevertheless encourage advertisers to conduct their own experiments and track conversions to determine if they belong to the small (9%) set of advertisers for whom advertising on navigational queries brings significant benefits. These advertisers, as we discussed in Section 5.1.2, either have a weaker brand or are competing against other advertisers who can legitimately advertise on their brand.

5.3 Click count inflation

Many advertisers appear to optimize for clicks rather than conversions. While we can only speculate as to why they choose to do so, anecdotal evidence ranges from naïveté, e.g., unawareness of metrics other than the click-through rate, to financial, e.g., ad agencies that collect commission per-click and advertisers that specify CTRs and minimum click counts (rather than conversions) in contracts with such agencies [3]. One of the easiest ways for advertisers to inflate ad click counts is to cannibalize the advertiser's own navigational queries.

Figure 9 plots achieved click-through rate of campaigns that advertise on an advertiser's own navigational queries as a function of their INAB. While the INAB of such a strategy is close to zero for the vast majority of campaigns as one would expect, the click-through rate for these campaigns is extremely high as compared to typical search ad CTRs of around 1-2% [5]. Advertisers should run

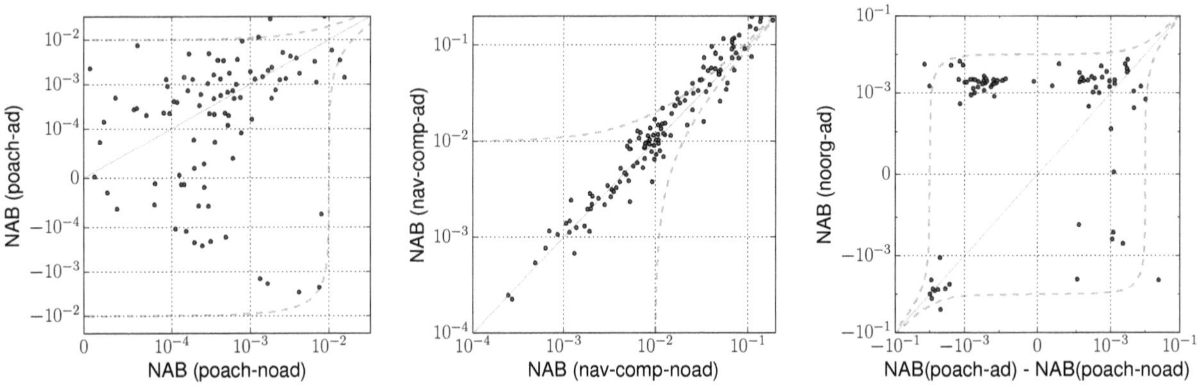

(a) Poaching offense. (b) Poaching defense. (c) Alternative to poaching.

Figure 10: Poaching often leads to wasteful spend and defending against it is not worthwhile either. A better alternative is to try to gain users on commercial queries where there is no organic presence.

carefully calibrated A/B tests to determine the incremental benefit of advertising for queries where the user is already looking to navigate to the advertiser.

6. POACHING COMPETITOR TRAFFIC

Poaching refers to advertising strategies that involve bidding on navigational queries specifically seeking a competitor's website (e.g., queries with competitor's trademarked terms or brand names). Initially, Google's trademark usage policy prevented advertisers from bidding on trademarked keywords they did not own or from using them in their ad content; the restriction of bidding on competitors' trademarked keywords was relaxed in 2004—even if the trademark owner explicitly objected—and restrictions on using them in ad content were relaxed in 2009 [1, 2]. The relaxed policy effectively increased the cost per click of trademarked keywords by allowing competition from third parties, thereby increasing trademark owners' costs by compelling them to bid defensively to protect their trademark.

We find that poaching may help smaller advertisers get users who would not navigate to the advertiser in the absence of ads. But, the costs of attempting to gain such users may be too high for some advertisers when compared to the cost they pay for an average conversion. Moreover, given the varied effectiveness of poaching, defending against poaching has uneven results and can, in fact, occasionally lead to negative results due to the high cost of defense.

6.1 Offense

Here, we analyze the benefit of trying to poach users seeking to navigate to a competitor. Figure 10(a) compares the NAB for poaching ads (poach-ad, i.e., ads on navigational queries where the advertiser is not the top-most organic search result) against the NAB of not advertising on the same queries (poach-noad, i.e., navigational queries where the advertiser has an organic presence but is *not* the top-most organic result, and does not display an ad). Each data point represents an advertiser where we have sufficient conversion data. About half the advertisers fall below the diagonal showing that poaching is actually detrimental. For the half that do see relative gains over not advertising, the absolute benefits are negligible (note the absolute value of NAB is generally below 0.01).

Figure 11 plots the CDF of the INAB for these advertisers. For 50% of advertisers, poaching is of negative value—likely due to few conversions and high costs associated with such ads. There

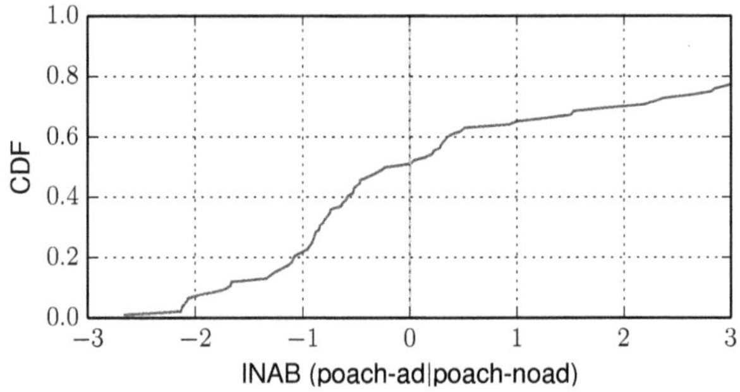

Figure 11: For most advertisers, poaching competitor's navigational queries yields little benefit, while some see extreme gains.

are however, a minority that see significant gains relative to their performance when ads are not shown. This is due to the very poor rate at which they obtain traffic when they do not show ads; said another way, while the relative gains are substantial, in absolute terms they still do not receive many conversions.

6.2 Defense

Regardless of how effective poaching is for the advertiser, competitors may still be harmed because they value lost conversions more dearly. Here, we consider whether it is useful for an advertiser to defend against potential poaching by out-bidding competitors for ad space despite being the top organic result for a navigational query. This data represents a specific scenario of advertising for navigational queries (discussed in Section 5.2) where a competitor ad is also present. We consider an advertiser a potential victim of poaching for a given query if: *i*) the search query is classified as navigational, i.e., the user query includes branded terms (e.g., Amazon or Macys) that suggests the user is seeking a specific website, *ii*) the advertiser is the top-most organic result for that query, and *iii*) another advertiser advertises on the query.

Figure 10(b) compares the NAB of defensive ads (nav-comp-ad, i.e., ads on navigational queries where the advertiser is the top-most organic search result) against the NAB of not advertising on the same queries (nav-comp-noad). Figure 12 plots the CDF of the INAB for these advertisers. The results are mixed: 20% of advertisers realize significant (INAB $>$ 25%) benefits, while a 32% are negatively impacted by attempting to defend these queries.

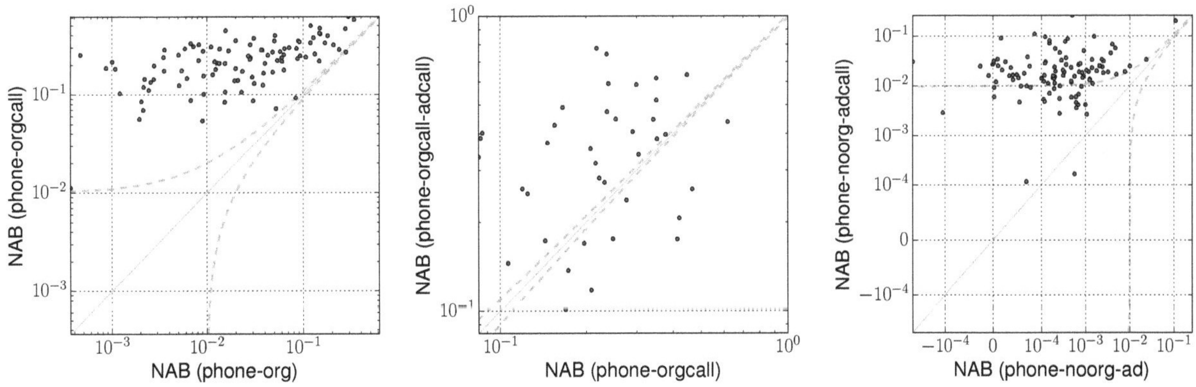

(a) Benefit of listing. (b) Ad call when organic call is present. (c) Benefit of call ad over regular ad.

Figure 13: Listing business details benefits advertisers and in the presence of organic call options, ad call extensions yield mixed results. But, showing an ad with extension is more beneficial than a regular ad.

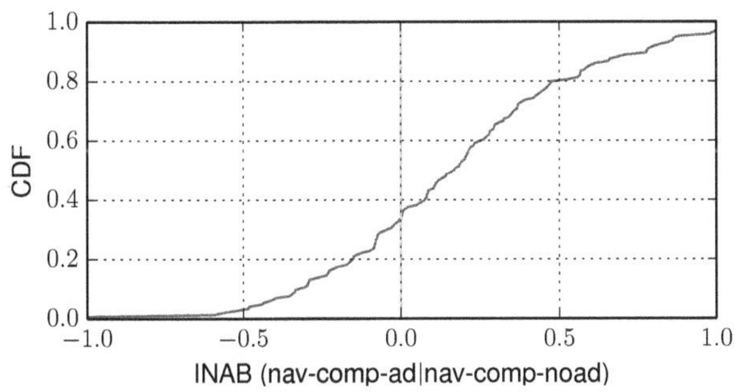

Figure 12: The benefits of defending against poaching vary dramatically across advertisers.

6.3 Spending smarter

As an alternative to poaching a competitor's customers (i.e., users who have issued a navigational search query for a competing website), an advertiser might try instead to recruit customers who are likely to convert somewhere, but have not yet decided on a particular vendor. Here we consider an advertiser deciding between spending money on poaching ads vs. spending that money to compete on commercial queries (i.e., those that are likely to lead to conversions) where they may not be prominently ranked in the organic results, Figure 10(c) plots the additional benefit of advertising on commercial queries where the advertiser does not have an organic presence i.e. NAB(noorg-ad) vs. the benefit of poaching ads over not poaching (NAB(poach-ad) - NAB(poach-noad)). For 78% of the advertisers, advertising on commercial queries where the advertiser has no organic presence dominates poaching by a wide margin (i.e., the are significantly above the diagonal).

7. DISPLAYING AD EXTENSIONS

Call extensions allow advertisers to explicitly add a call button to their ads when rendered on mobile phones. Call buttons are also shown for business listings in the organic search results. These features are provided by our partner ad network for no additional cost to the advertisers. We have limited data for different advertising strategies on mobile devices. However, our preliminary results show that creating a business listing, which would allow the ad network to show a call button in organic results, is beneficial to the advertisers. The effect of adding a call button to an ad when an organic result with call button is already present is mixed.

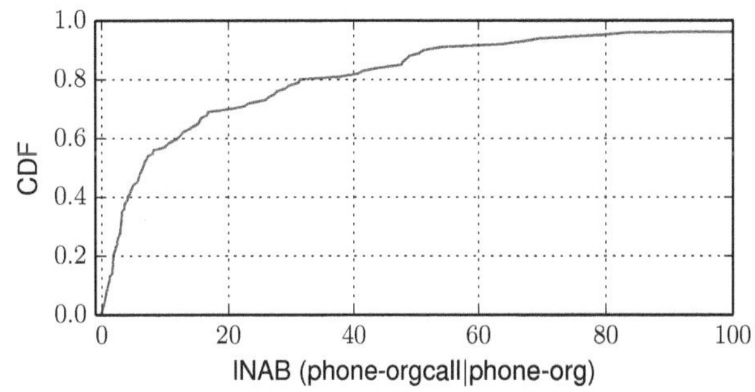

Figure 14: Listing a business in local results brings clear benefit to advertisers.

7.1 Organic business listings

Businesses can create a (free) listing that includes their location, phone number, store hours, parking information, and payment methods accepted through the network's "Places for Business" portal or third-parties like Yelp. The ad network uses this structured information to enhance the presentation of organic results including showing the call button, map directions, and so on.

We first look at the effectiveness of the call button for organic business listings vs. plain search results. It is challenging, however, to define conversion rates in these scenarios. We obviously have no way of knowing from the search logs how many users that call the business end up converting in a way that is equivalent to the conversions in previous sections; here, we consider the simple act of a user contacting the business by clicking the call button as a conversion event for the purposes of computing the NAB. For organic listings without call buttons, however, no similar data is available. Instead, we substitute the conversion rate the advertisers obtain when they advertise on local queries. While conversions are potentially an undercount when compared to calls, we hope that using the conversion rate for ads as opposed to organic clicks restores some of the balance, offering a reasonable baseline of user engagement.

Figure 13(a) plots the NAB of having an organic call button (phone-orgcall) vs NAB of plain search results (phone-org) for searches performed on mobile phones. Note that since both NABs

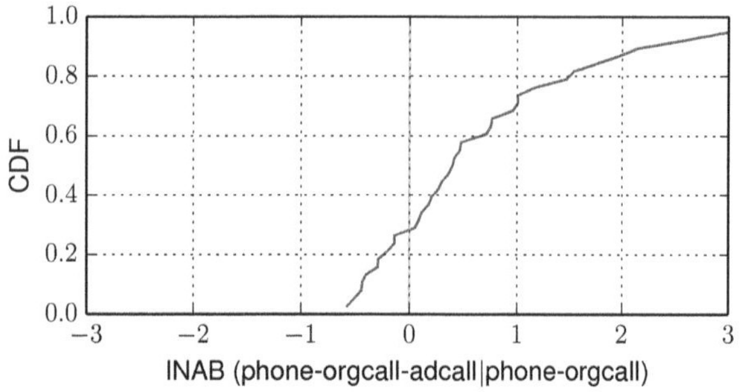

Figure 15: When organic call is already listed, advertising with a call ad has mixed results.

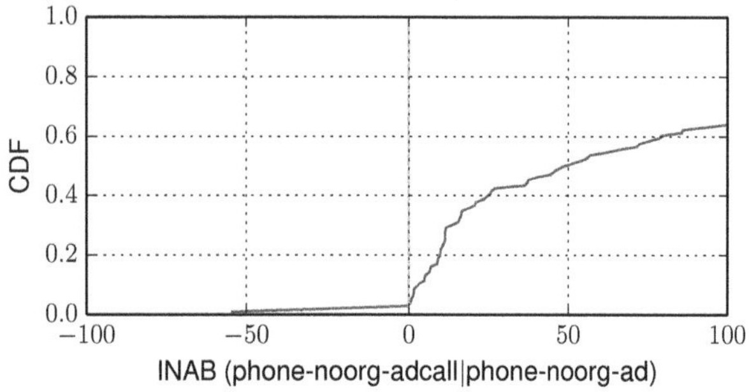

Figure 16: When advertiser does not have organic presence, advertising with a call button is more beneficial.

are for organic results—for which businesses do not pay—the cost term in the NAB computation is zero, and NAB reduces to conversions per impression. Figure 14 plots the CDF of the INAB of call button over plain results. As evident from the figures, median conversions per impression increases by a factor of 10 when a organic call result is present.

7.2 Ads with call extensions

When an advertiser chooses to place a call button in an ad, it is possible the ad results in a conversion off-line; i.e., rather than navigating to the website and converting, the user may instead call the advertiser and "convert" by making a purchase or similar analogous activity without further web interaction. Hence, when considering conversions for ads with call extensions, we define a conversion event to be either a call or an advertiser-reported conversion. For the very few impressions that result in both, we report only one conversion.

Figure 13(b) compares the NAB of mobile search ads with call extensions (phone-orgcall-adcall) vs. the NAB of organic business listings with call buttons (phone-orgcall) for the very few businesses in our dataset that both advertise call extensions as well as created an organic listing, as well as reported a sufficient number of conversion events. Figure 15 plots the CDF of the corresponding INAB. We find that even if organic search results contain a call button extension, ads employing the same are effective for 74% of advertisers, but ineffective for the remaining 26%. The orders-of-magnitude larger NAB (and INAB) values in this section can be attributed to the relative paucity of data for results using the call extension.

For businesses that do not have a rank high enough to be listed in the organic results, Figure 13(c) compares the NAB of mobile search ads with call extensions (phone-noorg-adcall) vs. the NAB of ads without the call extension (phone-noorg-ad). Figure 16 plots the CDF of the corresponding INAB. We find that ads with a call extension are universally more effective.

Preliminary data suggests that there are mixed benefits to using call extensions for businesses where organic listings include call button. For businesses that do not have a high-enough organic rank for their listing to appear in the first page of ads, however, there is a consistent boost from call extensions in search ads. That being said, since call extensions and business listings are both recent features and very few advertisers have opted-in to both, our results are preliminary and we encourage advertisers to conduct their own experiments and compute their respective INABs to assess the effectiveness of the call extension in their specific case.

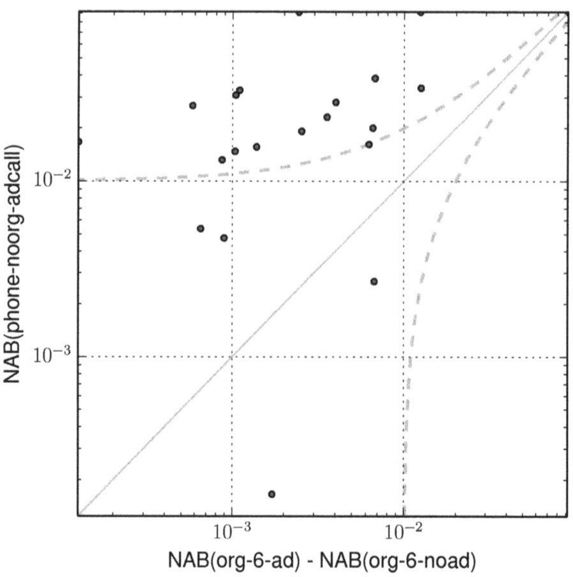

Figure 17: Call ads on mobile are better than regular desktop ads in the absence of organic presence.

7.3 Spending smarter

In closing, we compare the marginal benefit of call extensions in mobile ads to the benefit of traditional advertising on computers. As we discussed previously, the benefit of the latter depends tremendously on the position of the advertiser in the organic search results. As an optimistic estimate, we focus on an advertiser who appears sixth in the organic search results. Specifically, Figure 17 plots the marginal benefit of running mobile ads with call extension over organic business listings with call button (phone-noorg-adcall) vs. advertising on desktops and laptops. For 75% of the advertisers in our dataset, it is (modestly) more beneficial to focus on mobile call ads vs. desktop ads.

While we have limited data in our dataset, our initial assessment indicates greater benefits can be obtained by adding call buttons to ads on mobile compared to traditional advertising on desktop when organic presence is poor.

8. DISCUSSION

In this section, we discuss our choice of using aggregated traffic slices and the underlying systemic bias that exists in the way the traffic slices are chosen for comparison.

8.1 Choosing traffic slices

The techniques that we use in this paper can be applied to estimate the profitability achieved by an advertiser over an arbitrary slice of traffic that is representative of a particular advertising strategy. To measure the effectiveness of advertising, we identify similar search impressions with and without ads. For this, an ideal comparison would require impressions where the presence of an ad is the only distinguishing attribute. However, even the largest search engines have only sparse data when aggregated at the query level [24]. In order to have reasonable samples of impressions, we aggregate impressions by the category of user query. Note that the techniques we discuss in this paper can however be applied to traffic slices aggregated on other attributes like geography or user characteristics.

8.2 Systemic biases

A source of bias in our analyses is that queries for which ads are shown are often more representative of the advertiser than queries where ads are not shown for comparable traffic slices. This is because whenever ads are shown, both the ad network and advertiser find the query relevant. But, when ads are not shown, the ad network finds query relevant to advertiser but advertiser does not. So, whenever results returned by the ad network are poor, users are less likely to choose the advertiser from organic results hence lowering NAB for the traffic slice without ads.

An exception to this rule is when the advertiser tries to poach users looking for a competitor (Section 6.1). This is because in case of poaching, while the impressions with advertiser ad are likely to be more attractive to the advertiser, they also cost more.

Finally, in Section 7 queries for which the ad network presents a result with a call button are often more relevant to a mobile user than queries where a web result is delivered; hence, the NAB for organic search results with call buttons may be overstated.

9. RELATED WORK

Measuring ad effectiveness. There have been a number of studies measuring the effectiveness of display advertising ad campaigns [27, 29]. These studies measure the incremental impact of advertising by creating a treatment and a control group. We take a similar approach by identifying comparable traffic slices and then measuring the incremental impact of advertising.

Reiley, Lewis and Rao have also highlighted the challenges in conducting such studies [30, 31] and how the benefits of advertising can be overestimated. They highlight this by studying the impact of display ads on user activity. They show that presence of display ads is not necessarily correlated with subsequent user activity. A key reason is that display ads are expected to perform by their mere presence in the absence of explicit expression of intent by the user. In case of web search, however, advertiser pays the search engine only when there is an ad click and user intent is captured through the query made by the user. So, a subsequent conversion can be attributed to a click performed by the user on search engine results — sponsored or organic.

Absolute metrics. Advertising effectiveness has traditionally been measured in absolute terms, e.g., click through rates [14, 22, 37, 40] or conversion rates [11, 36]. Other work focuses on prevalence [9] or effectiveness of different advertising strategies like mobile advertising [18, 39] or the interaction between ads and organic search results [10, 44]. Since different metrics focus on different dimensions of the campaign, comparing them is not straightforward. NAB is also an absolute metric, however it explicitly addresses the multi-dimensional comparison problem by converting other dimensions (i.e., cost) into the primary dimension (conversion probability) through a conversion factor (λ) that explicitly tracks the advertiser's relative utility across dimensions.

Incremental metrics. The Incremental Ad Clicks metric [13] and the related one for mobiles [32] take a novel approach by proposing a way to compare two traffic slices. We were inspired by IAC but ultimately identified the severe limitations in the general approach relating to: i) ignoring conversions, ii) being ill-conditioned to noise; and iii) not scaling to the orders of magnitude difference in advertiser scale. NAB and INAB are designed to address these challenges. We were also inspired by work in cost-effectiveness analysis in the health sector [43].

Other use cases. Our work complements the large body of work in the space of ad optimizations. Researchers have described a methodology for A/B testing in context of controlled experiments online for fairer comparisons [19]. INAB complements this work by providing a metric that enables direct comparison of the relative effectiveness of the two tests. [8] develops strategies that advertisers may use to modify bid amounts. Incorporating NAB in the bidding strategy may allow for joint optimizations in cost and conversions. A large body of work has looked at identifying fraud in online ads [15, 16, 17, 23, 28, 33, 34, 35, 42]. NAB of various suspicious traffic slices may be used as an additional signal in these techniques.

10. FUTURE WORK

In this section we discuss areas where the NAB metric can be refined and outline future work.

Multiple types of conversions. In this paper we treat all the conversion events of an advertiser equivalently. If an advertiser has multiple types of conversions she is interested in, she would need to compute the NAB for each type of conversion, and those NABs would not be mutually comparable. One approach would be to allow the advertiser to specify the relative value of each conversion and extend NAB to allow different types of conversions to be traded off against one another to arrive at the net NAB across all conversion types.

Probabilistic NAB and brand advertising. As defined NAB can be applied most readily to search ads since every impression, click and conversion can be tracked precisely and with certainty. In traditional brand advertising, simply estimating impression counts is a hard problem (e.g., TV viewers going to the restroom during commercial breaks), let alone tracking conversions. It may, however, be possible to arrive at probabilistic estimates of impressions, and conversions. One approach could be to extend NAB to incorporate probabilistic inputs and output the expected NAB with confidence intervals.

What-if analysis. In our design of NAB we consider only point-in-time values and do not leverage the longitudinal perspective our historical data provides. While one could compute NAB at different points in the past to extrapolate into the future, a better approach may be to directly incorporate time-series data as input and output a time-parameterized NAB function.

11. CONCLUSION

In this paper we develop the net acquisition benefit (NAB) metric to approximate profit per impression in order to measure the effectiveness of an ad campaign, and the incremental net acquisition benefit (INAB) to measure the marginal benefit of one ad strategy over another. Using these metrics and extensive search and ad click data from a major search-ad provider, we find that cannibalizing organic traffic and poaching a competitor's traffic are frequently ineffective while call extensions on mobile phones show promise.

Acknowledgments

We thank the anonymous reviewers for their valuable feedback. This work was funded in part by the National Science Foundation through grant CNS-1237264.

12. REFERENCES

[1] Google Settles With Rosetta Stone Over Trademark Infringement Within Search And Ads Lawsuit. http://techcrunch.com/2012/10/31/google-settles-with-rosetta-stone-over-trademark-infringement-within-search-and-ads-lawsuit/.

[2] Google:Update to U.S. ad text trademark policy. http://adwords.blogspot.com/2009/05/update-to-us-ad-text-trademark-policy.html.

[3] Search Marketing Agency Price Models. http://searchengineland.com/search-marketing-agency-pricing-models-11039.

[4] Smartphone user study shows mobile movement under way. http://googlemobileads.blogspot.com/2011/04/smartphone-user-study-shows-mobile.html.

[5] What average Ads click through rate (CTR) is good for text ad? https://www.en.adwords-community.com/t5/Tracking-Reporting/What-average-Ads-click-through-rate-CTR-is-good-for-text-ad/td-p/150054.

[6] Will 'Useless' Clicks Really Cost Mobile Advertisers $6 Billion+ by 2016? http://searchenginewatch.com/article/2207164/Will-Useless-Clicks-Really-Cost-Mobile-Advertisers-6-Billion-by-2016.

[7] Is Google Gobbling Up the Indian Internet Space? http://forbesindia.com/article/real-issue/is-google-gobbling-up-the-indian-internet-space/35641/1, July 2013.

[8] M. Babaioff, N. Nisan, and R. Paes Leme. Price Competition in Online Combinatorial Markets. In *Proceedings of the 23rd International Conference on World Wide Web*, 2014.

[9] P. Barford, I. Canadi, D. Krushevskaja, Q. Ma, and S. Muthukrishnan. Adscape: Harvesting and Analyzing Online Display Ads. In *Proceedings of the 23rd International Conference on World Wide Web*, 2014.

[10] T. Blake, C. Nosko, and S. Tadelis. Consumer Heterogeneity and Paid Search Effectiveness: A Large Scale Field Experiment. *NBER Working Paper*, pages 1–26, 2013.

[11] L. Blumrosen, J. Hartline, and S. Nong. Position auctions and non-uniform conversion rates. In *ACM EC Workshop on Advertisement Auctions*, 2008.

[12] A. Z. Broder, P. Ciccolo, M. Fontoura, E. Gabrilovich, V. Josifovski, and L. Riedel. Search Advertising Using Web Relevance Feedback. In *Proceedings of the 17th ACM Conference on Information and Knowledge Management*, CIKM '08, pages 1013–1022, New York, NY, USA, 2008. ACM.

[13] D. Chan, Y. Yuan, J. Koehler, and D. Kumar. Incremental Clicks Impact Of Search Advertising. Technical report, Google, Inc., 2011.

[14] Y. Chen and T. W. Yan. Position-normalized Click Prediction in Search Advertising. In *Proceedings of the 18th ACM SIGKDD International Conference on Knowledge Discovery and Data Mining*, 2012.

[15] N. Daswani and M. Stoppelman. The Anatomy of Clickbot.A. In *Proceedings of the first conference on First Workshop on Hot Topics in Understanding Botnets*, 2007.

[16] V. Dave, S. Guha, and Y. Zhang. Measuring and Fingerprinting Click-Spam in Ad Networks. *SIGCOMM Comput. Commun. Rev.*, 42(4):175–186, August 2012.

[17] V. Dave, S. Guha, and Y. Zhang. ViceROI: Catching Click-spam in Search Ad Networks. In *Proceedings of the ACM SIGSAC Conference on Computer & Communications Security*, 2013.

[18] M. de Sa, V. Navalpakkam, and E. F. Churchill. Mobile Advertising: Evaluating the Effects of Animation, User and Content Relevance. In *Proceedings of the SIGCHI Conference on Human Factors in Computing Systems*, 2013.

[19] A. Deng, T. Li, and Y. Guo. Statistical Inference in Two-stage Online Controlled Experiments with Treatment Selection and Validation. In *Proceedings of the 23rd International Conference on World Wide Web*, 2014.

[20] B. Edelman, M. Ostrovsky, and M. Schwarz. Internet advertising and the generalized second price auction: Selling billions of dollars worth of keywords. Technical report, National Bureau of Economic Research, 2005.

[21] Google. AdWords Help – Measuring return on investment (ROI). https://support.google.com/adwords/answer/1722066?hl=en.

[22] T. Graepel, J. Q. Candela, T. Borchert, and R. Herbrich. Web-Scale Bayesian Click-Through Rate Prediction for Sponsored Search Advertising in Microsoft's Bing Search Engine. In *Proceedings of the 27th International Conference on Machine Learning ICML 2010, Invited Applications Track (unreviewed, to appear)*, June 2010. Invited Applications Track.

[23] H. Haddadi. Fighting Online Click-Fraud Using Bluff Ads. *SIGCOMM Comput. Commun. Rev.*, 40(2):21–25, Apr. 2010.

[24] D. Hillard, S. Schroedl, E. Manavoglu, H. Raghavan, and C. Leggetter. Improving Ad Relevance in Sponsored Search. In *Proceedings of the Third ACM International Conference on Web Search and Data Mining*, WSDM '10, pages 361–370, New York, NY, USA, 2010. ACM.

[25] IAB. Internet advertising revenue report. http://www.iab.net/media/file/IAB_Internet_Advertising_Revenue_Report_FY_2013.pdf.

[26] B. J. Jansen and S. Schuster. BIDDING ON THE BUYING FUNNEL FOR SPONSORED SEARCH AND KEYWORD ADVERTISING. *Journal of Electronic Commerce Research*, 12(1):1–18, 2011.

[27] G. A. Johnson, R. A. Lewis, and D. H. Reiley. Location, Location, Location: Repetition and Proximity Increase Advertising Effectiveness. *Available at SSRN 2268215*, 2014.

[28] A. Juels, S. Stamm, and M. Jakobsson. Combating Click Fraud via Premium Clicks. In *Proceedings of 16th USENIX Security Symposium on USENIX Security Symposium*, 2007.

[29] R. Lewis and D. Reiley. Online Ads and Offline Sales: Measuring the Effect of Retail Advertising via a Controlled Experiment on Yahoo! *Quantitative Marketing and Economics*, 12(3):235–266, 2014.

[30] R. A. Lewis and J. M. Rao. On the Near Impossibility of Measuring the Returns to Advertising. 2013.

[31] R. A. Lewis, J. M. Rao, and D. H. Reiley. Here, There, and Everywhere: Correlated Online Behaviors Can Lead to Overestimates of the Effects of Advertising. In *Proceedings of the 20th International Conference on World Wide Web*, WWW '11, pages 157–166, New York, NY, USA, 2011. ACM.

[32] S. Lysen. Incremental Clicks Impact of Mobile Search Advertising. Technical report, Google, Inc., 2013.

[33] A. Metwally, D. Agrawal, and A. El Abbadi. DETECTIVES: DETEcting Coalition hiT Inflation attacks in adVertising nEtworks Streams. In *Proceedings of the 16th International Conference on World Wide Web*, WWW '07, pages 241–250, New York, NY, USA, 2007. ACM.

[34] A. Metwally, F. Emekçi, D. Agrawal, and A. El Abbadi. SLEUTH: Single-pubLisher attack dEtection Using correlaTion Hunting. *PVLDB*, 1(2):1217–1228, Aug. 2008.

[35] B. Miller, P. Pearce, C. Grier, C. Kreibich, and V. Paxson. What's Clicking What? Techniques and Innovations of Today's Clickbots. DIMVA, pages 164–183, 2011.

[36] B. Rey and A. Kannan. Conversion Rate Based Bid Adjustment for Sponsored Search. In *Proceedings of the 19th International Conference on World Wide Web*, 2010.

[37] M. Richardson, E. Dominowska, and R. Ragno. Predicting Clicks: Estimating the Click-through Rate for New Ads. In *Proceedings of the 16th International Conference on World Wide Web*, 2007.

[38] D. Sculley, R. G. Malkin, S. Basu, and R. J. Bayardo. Predicting Bounce Rates in Sponsored Search Advertisements. In *Proceedings of the 15th ACM SIGKDD International Conference on Knowledge Discovery and Data Mining*, KDD '09, pages 1325–1334, New York, NY, USA, 2009. ACM.

[39] V. Shankar and S. Balasubramanian. Mobile Marketing: A Synthesis and Prognosis. *Journal of Interactive Marketing*, 23(2):118 – 129, 2009. Anniversary Issue.

[40] E. Sodomka, S. Lahaie, and D. Hillard. A Predictive Model for Advertiser Value-Per-Click in Sponsored Search. In *Proceedings of the 22nd international conference on World Wide Web*, 2013.

[41] Y. Song, H. Ma, H. Wang, and K. Wang. Exploring and Exploiting User Search Behavior on Mobile and Tablet Devices to Improve Search Relevance. In *Proceedings of the 22Nd International Conference on World Wide Web*, 2013.

[42] K. Springborn and P. Barford. Impression Fraud in Online Advertising via Pay-per-view Networks. In *Proceedings of the 22Nd USENIX Conference on Security*, 2013.

[43] A. A. Stinnett and J. Mullahy. Net health benefits a new framework for the analysis of uncertainty in cost-effectiveness analysis. *Medical Decision Making*, 18(2):S68–S80, 1998.

[44] S. Yang and A. Ghose. Analyzing the Relationship Between Organic and Sponsored Search Advertising: Positive, Negative, or Zero Interdependence? *Marketing Science*, 29(4):602–623, 2010.

Annoyed Users: Ads and Ad-Block Usage in the Wild

Enric Pujol
TU Berlin
enric@inet.tu-berlin.de

Oliver Hohlfeld
RWTH Aachen
oliver@comsys.rwth-aachen.de

Anja Feldmann
TU Berlin
anja@inet.tu-berlin.de

ABSTRACT

Content and services which are offered for free on the Internet are primarily monetized through online advertisement. This business model relies on the implicit agreement between content providers and users where viewing ads is the price for the "free" content. This status quo is not acceptable to all users, however, as manifested by the rise of ad-blocking plugins which are available for all popular Web browsers. Indeed, ad-blockers have the potential to substantially disrupt the widely established business model of "free" content—currently one of the core elements on which the Web is built.

In this work, we shed light on how users interact with ads. We show how to leverage the functionality of AdBlock Plus, one of the most popular ad-blockers to identify ad traffic from passive network measurements. We complement previous work, which focuses on active measurements, by characterizing ad-traffic in the wild, i.e., as seen in a residential broadband network of a major European ISP. Finally, we assess the prevalence of ad-blockers in this particular network and discuss possible implications for content providers and ISPs.

Categories and Subject Descriptors

C.2.2 [**Computer-Communication Networks**]: Network Protocols; H.5.4 [**Information Interfaces and Presentation**]: Hypertext/Hypermedia

Keywords

Web; Advertising; AdBlock Plus; Residential Broadband Traffic

1. INTRODUCTION

The World Wide Web has fueled an unprecedented commercialization of the Internet by turning a system designed for academic data exchange into a widely used social medium. The economic foundation of many services in this medium is online advertisements (ads) which allow content and services to be offered free of charge to users.

IMC'15, October 28–30, 2015, Tokyo, Japan.

ACM 978-1-4503-3848-6/15/10 ...$15.00.
DOI: http://dx.doi.org/10.1145/2815675.2815705.

The history of this business model goes back to the first clickable Web ads, which emerged around 1993 with the first commercial Web sites. HotWired was among the first to sell banner ads to companies such as AT&T and Coors. The first central ad servers emerged in 1995 to enable the management, targeting, and tracking of users and online ads. This started the proliferation of Web ads, which brought with it an increasingly complex infrastructure to serve these advertisements. DoubleClick introduced the process of online behavioral advertising in the late 1990s which used 3rd party cookies to track users across sites and present ads based on the users' browsing patterns. Today, online advertisement has become a large and complex industry where entire exchanges trade user-specific information for the purpose of better ad placements [58].

This user specific profiling has raised many privacy and security concerns in particular among privacy and consumer advocacy groups. The debate has, for instance, led to agreements about the expiration dates of *cookies* as well as clear statements regarding the collection of user information [8]. While the Federal Trade Commission (FTC) identifies problems with online behavioral advertisement, it allows advertisers to continue this practice with some safeguards such as greater transparency, provisions for consumers to opt out, and special handling of sensitive data, e.g., those related to health and financial information [13]. The motivation underlying the FTC's position is that the FTC views online advertisements as the key enabler for "free" content on the Web.

However, to Web users, online advertisements can be perceived as being not only invasive to privacy, but also annoying, since they can distract them from the primary content they wish to consume. This situation has resulted in a proliferation of tools to evade or block the ads. We refer to these tools as *ad-blockers*. Among the most convenient and popular ad-blockers are extensions for Web browsers like *Adblock Plus* and *Ghostery*. According to Google and Mozilla usage statistics of browser add-ons, *Adblock Plus* is among the most popular. More than 30M users surf the Web daily using a browser with this extension enabled [18, 15].

The use of ad-blockers is, however, perceived by the advertisement industry and content publishers as a growing threat to their business model [6, 19]. Their rationale is that ad-blockers provide users a way to "evade paying" for the content they consume. Thus, some players try to put pressure on the developers of ad blocking browser extensions in order to be excluded from the blocking. This exclusion is envisioned to be implemented by *i)* removing them from the filter lists, or *ii)* by adding them to a whitelist [6]. Others also try to detect ad-blockers and explicitly appeal these users to either whitelist their site or completely disable the ad-blocker.

Another claim regarding the rise of ad-blockers is that "as more end users adopt them, revenues decline and the number of obnoxious advertisements increases" [3]. To break this vicious cycle some players in this domain encourage advertisers to adopt "acceptable ads" as a compromise. The most important implication of this initiative is that advertisements that conform to these guidelines are by default whitelisted by *Adblock Plus* [5], a setting that end users can still override.

Moreover, the ad-blocking debate is not uniquely centered on ad-blockers like *Adblock Plus*. In fact, some Internet Service Providers (ISPs) have already stated their intention to block advertising on their networks and thereby, force some companies in the advertising business to share their revenues [12]. In light of this tussle between users, advertisers, publishers, and ISPs, we inform the ongoing debate with a passive measurement study about the "ad-scape" and how end users interact with it.

Our work: We complement previous work with a passive measurement study on advertisements. Namely, we collect traces from a residential broadband network (RBN) of a major European ISP to *i)* elaborate on the prevalence of ad-blockers in this vantage point, and *ii)* characterize ad traffic in the wild. The contributions of this paper are as follows:

- We present a methodology to extract structural Web site information from packet header traces. With this methodology at hand, we can use the *Adblock Plus* functionality to classify ad traffic in passive measurements. We validate the effectiveness of this methodology with an active measurement study based on different configurations of an instrumented browser, e.g., running *Adblock Plus*.
- We leverage two indicators to infer *Adblock Plus* usage: *i)* low ratio of ad requests, and *ii)* connections to the *Adblock Plus* servers. Based on these metrics we estimate that 22% of the most active users likely use this extension. Moreover, we have indications that, perhaps, most *Adblock Plus* users do neither subscribe to *EasyPrivacy* (the list that protects them from trackers), nor opt out from the list of *non-intrusive* ads.
- We find that advertisement traffic contributes to a significant percentage of requests, roughly 18% in both of the studied traces. We dissect ad requests by type and find that 11% of them match the list of *non-intrusive ads*, while the rest is distributed among advertisers and trackers. Given the prevalence of this traffic in terms of requests, we also characterize various aspects thereof, including object types, server-side infrastructure as well as back-end functionality, i.e., real-time bidding.

The remainder of this paper is structured as follows: we first discuss the basic functionality of *Adblock Plus* and the corresponding filter lists in §2. We then describe in §3 our measurement methodology and its subsequent evaluation in §4. Section §5 summarizes the two data sets as well as the involved vantage points. We present our first results about *Adblock Plus* usage in §6. We then elaborate on traffic- and infrastructure-centric aspects of advertisements in §7 and §8. Section §9 presents the related work. We discuss the limitations of our methodology in §10 and present our conclusions in §11.

2. AD BLOCKERS – A SHORT REVIEW

There is a wide range of browser extensions available to end-users who want to evade or protect themselves from the *ad-scape*. *Adblock Plus* is arguably among the currently most popular ad-blockers [17]. Users can configure this browser extension to *i)* block or hide advertisements, and to *ii)* protect their privacy by blocking trackers. Another popular tool is *Ghostery*, which mainly focuses on protecting end-users' privacy. The Electronic Frontier Foundation's *Privacy Badger* [10] shares the same objective; but in contrast to *Ghostery*, which is proprietary software, *Privacy Badger* is open source—and based on *Adblock Plus*. Another option is the *NoScript* plugin which is designed to interactively disable executable Web content such as JavaScript, which is often used by advertisers and trackers.

To assess the popularity of these extensions we can refer to statistics reported by popular browsers or to recent work by Metwalley et al. [46]. They report, relying on a passive measurement study, that 80% of the households visible at their vantage point do not use any of these popular plugins. Among those that do, *Adblock Plus* dominates, i.e., *Adblock Plus* is installed at 10%-18% of the households. Indeed, less than 3% of the households exhibit evidence of other installed plugins. Given the popularity of *Adblock Plus*, we next describe how this particular extension operates.

Adblock Plus. At the heart of *Adblock Plus* is the mechanism to filter adverts based on *filter rules* that appear in *filter lists*. The regular expressions that form the set of filter rules follow a specific syntax, which is described in detail in [4, 21]. If a filter rule matches a URL that is not otherwise whitelisted, *Adblock Plus* will prevent the Web browser from requesting the URL. Hence, this extension reduces network traffic as it averts undesired ad-related objects from being fetched.

However, some Web pages embed advertisements into the (main) HTML document, e.g., textual advertisements. Since this document is required to render the page, the tool does not block the download of these HTML documents. However, *Adblock Plus* includes functionality to hide such—otherwise displayed— embedded ads via CSS modification. Note that these ads are still transferred over the network even though they will not be displayed in the browser to the user.

Filters Lists. *Adblock Plus* users can obtain various lists of filter rules via a subscription mechanism. There are several filter lists available for different purposes. When an end user installs the *Adblock Plus* extension for the first time, the plugin subscribes itself to two filter lists. The first one is named *EasyList* and its goal is to remove ads from English Web pages. The second list is called *non-intrusive advertisements* (acceptable ads) and its purpose is to whitelist the advertisements that are blacklisted by *EasyList* but comply with the directives summarized in [5].

This list and, in particular, its activation by default is most likely the origin of the controversy described in [6] (i.e., advertisers paying to be whitelisted). Note that users may still opt to deactivate this list with a single click. There are additional lists to which *Adblock Plus* users can subscribe. Examples include *i)* customizations of *EasyList* to non-English Web pages, or *ii)* *EasyPrivacy*, which aims to protect the end users' privacy by blocking Web trackers.

Measurement challenges. At first glance, given that this ad-blocker only uses filter lists, it should be easy to emulate its behavior on a passively collected network trace. However, this is not that simple as *Adblock Plus* relies on the information contained in the DOM tree of the Web site to classify Web elements as adverts. For example, the classification can be based on whether an image is displayed in an iframe, which cannot be detected by inspecting the URL. Thus, this ad-blocker relies on the entire structure of a Web page rather than purely the URLs.

To reconstruct the entire structure of the Web page one needs parse the payload part of the traces. For privacy reasons we cannot and do not have access to this part. Our traces only include HTTP header information (see §5). Hence, our methodology has to rely on the information available in the HTTP headers. How we tackle this challenge is discussed in the next section. Our methodology enables us to *approximately* reconstruct the Web page meta-data from the HTTP headers.

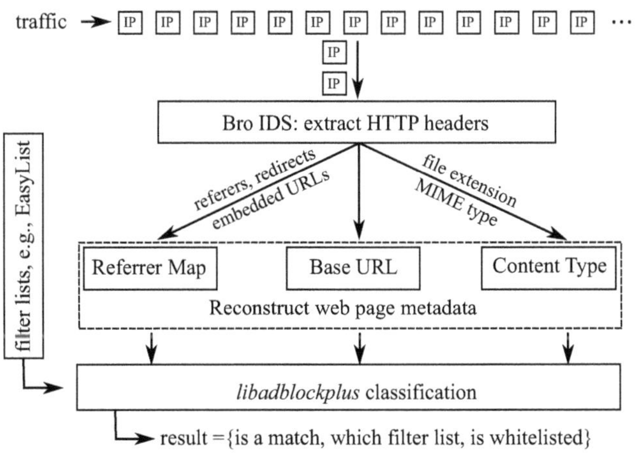

Figure 1: Approach to classify ad requests.

3. METHODOLOGY

In this section we describe our approach for identifying ad-blocker users from passive traces. The premise is that ad-blocker users access fewer ads than non ad-blocker users. Thus, we need a methodology for identifying Web objects and separating them into ad or non-ad objects. This is where we rely on *Adblock Plus*.

3.1 Identifying ad traffic

The goal of our methodology is to classify ad traffic in TCP/HTTP header traces captured via passive measurements. For this classification we rely on *Adblock Plus* functionality as it is the most popular ad-blocker to date. But rather than using a *Adblock Plus* browser directly we use *libadblockplus* [16], a C++ wrapper around *Adblock Plus*, developed by the same project. This allows us to classify Web objects from the traces in an off-line fashion without the need to operate a full browser. A summary of the classification methodology is shown in Figure 1.

We use *Bro* [48] HTTP analyzer to extract information about all HTTP transactions in network traces. This information includes *i)* both the `Host` and the `URI` fields in the request header, *ii)* the `referer` field in the request, *iii)* the `Content-Type` field in the response, and *iv)* the `Content-Length` field present in HTTP responses. We also extended the *Bro* analyzer to parse and include *v)* the `Location` header field present in response headers that relate to HTTP redirections.

Processing passive traces with *Bro* gives us a list of Web objects. We then invoke *libadblockplus* to classify each of these objects into ad and non-ad objects. However, *libadblockplus* cannot properly classify a URL as an advert using only the information that is self-contained in the URL's string. Many rules in the filter lists apply to specific combinations of domains, i.e., a Web object hosted in a specific (advertiser) domain from a specific (publisher) domain. Thus, *libadblockplus* requires the following information to properly classify a URL: *i)* the requested URL itself, *ii)* the rest of URLs in the Web page that triggered the request that is currently processed, and *iii)* the type of the content that is being requested e.g., `document`, `script`, `stylesheet`, `image`, `media` or `object`.

As mentioned above, the *Adblock Plus* browser extension relies on information contained in the DOM tree. We, in contrast, have only the information available in the HTTP headers. However, we can still use this information to obtain a *partial view* of the relationships between the Web objects in a Web page. We tackle this challenge in the following way. See the middle boxes in Figure 1 for an illustration of the approach.

Referrer Map. First, we extract the set of related URLs for a given request. To this end we construct a *referrer map* that approximates the set of URLs in a Web page based on the chain of observed HTTP referrers. Our approach is based on the *StreamStructure* and *ReSurf* methods discussed in [38, 56]. We also use these methods to obtain the Web site that triggered the request. We construct the referrer map out of the values in the `referer` header fields in the requests. However, there are a few cases in which this chain may be "broken". One typical example is when the request following a redirection to a new URL has no `referer`. This is the reason why we extend *Bro* to also parse the `Location` response headers. With this small modification we can add this type of missing referrers to the map of referrers. Furthermore, we also insert the URLs that we can find embedded within the URL of a request into the referrer map.

Content Type. Second, we infer the type of the content in the following way: one of the pitfalls in HTTP traffic analysis are mismatches between the `Content-Type` of the request and the actual content. Schneider et al. [52] showed that while mis-matches often occur due to the format (e.g., `jpeg` vs. `png`), they actually agree on the general category (e.g., `image`). In these cases the mismatch does not impair our classification because *libadblockplus* relies on general categories. For other mismatches we parse the URL to map the following file extensions to content types: i) *.png*, *.gif*, *.jpg*, *.svg*, *.ico* (`image`) ii) *.css* (`stylesheet`) iii) *.js* (`script`) iv) *.mp4* and *.avi* (`media`). As a rule of thumb, we rely on the `Content-Type` field when the file extension does not yield a type. Some redirections may lead to mis-classifications. For instance, there are cases where a URL within an `<img>` HTML tag results in a redirection. Suppose there exists an exception filter for that URL and its content type is `image`. To *Adblock Plus* this request is an image, since it can glean this information from the tag. We, on the other hand, would filter it because we do not have access to this information. Here, the referrer map helps us to set the appropriate content type for the URL that is being redirected by inspecting the type of the consequent request.

Base URL. Third, we process the URLs to avoid conflicts with the filter lists. Namely, we noticed that *libadblockplus* mis-classifies some requests because they include parts of the URL of a previous request in the query string. While the *Adblock Plus* plugin does not filter the second request, *libadblockplus* does. To prevent this type of mis-classifications we normalize the query strings by removing dynamic values. However, there are some filters in these lists that specify values for the fields in the query strings of a URL, e.g., @@*jsp?callback=aslHandleAds*, where * represents a wild-card. If we would normalize this string to *jsp?callback=X*, it would not match anymore the previous *exception filter* and thereby we would mis-classify the corresponding URL. Hence, we take care not to overwrite the values in the query strings that appear in the filter lists.

Finally, recall that *Adblock Plus* also includes functionality to block text advertisements that are included in the HTML itself. Quite a number of HTML documents embed these advertisements, which means that the browser extension will not block the associated request because blocking it would also imply blocking non-ad content. Instead, the browser plugin hides this ad content during the rendering phase of the page, in a process called *element hiding*. Since we cannot and do not have access the packet payload we cannot parse the Web page's content and thereby, can neither detect nor comment on this type of advertisements.

3.2 Identification of ad-blocker users

To identify if an end user has installed an ad-blocker we rely on the following observation: a browser with such an extension should issue less ad requests than a browser without any ad-blocker. In other words, a low number of ad requests is a strong indicator for the presence of an ad-blocker.

Hence, we have to identify all requests of a particular end user and compute the ratio of ad requests. The ratio for an end user depends on *i)* the browser configuration, i.e., whether there is an ad-blocker installed and, if so which ad-blocker with which configuration, and *ii)* which sites the user visits. Given that many of the most popular sites do indeed have extraneous content [42, 27, 25], the likelihood that an active user visits such a site is substantial. Thus, we can use an active measurement study (see §4) to find ad-ratio thresholds that distinguish between ad-blocker and non ad-blocker users.

Although our primary goal is to identify *any* ad-blocker user, we can additionally rely on plugin updates to identify specific ad-blockers like *Adblock Plus* or *Ghostery*. For instance, the former plugin regularly checks for updates of the filter lists to which the user has subscribed. The update frequency is driven by the expiration time specific to each list, e.g., *EasyList* has a soft expiration date of 4 days [1] and *EasyPrivacy* soft-expires already after a single day [2]. In fact, the *Adblock Plus* contact frequency is quite high: typically upon browser bootstrap or once per day [46]. Hence, monitoring connections to *Adblock Plus* servers is a good indicator for the presence of *Adblock Plus*. To identify *Adblock Plus* servers in the traces we rely on multiple DNS resolvers to obtain an up-to-date list of *Adblock Plus* server IPs.

4. METHOD EVALUATION & VALIDATION

We complement our passive analysis with an active measurement study that has two goals *i)* validate that our methodology can classify ad traffic, and *ii)* identify ad-ratio thresholds to differentiate between end users that browse the Web with an ad-blocker and those who do not.

Accordingly, we instruct a popular Web browser to fetch Web sites using different configuration modes, e.g., with *Adblock Plus* enabled or disabled. In parallel we capture the browsers network traffic with *tcpdump* and apply the above methodology to the passive traces.

4.1 Active measurement setup

We instrument the widely used browser Chromium with Selenium [20] to crawl the Alexa top 1000 sites. We run the browser in a virtual frame-buffer on a dedicated GNU/Linux machine connected to a university campus network. For each URL in the Alexa top list we start a new browser instance with an empty cache, wait 5 seconds before starting a *tcpdump* traffic trace, load the URL and wait another 5 seconds before closing the browser and *tcpdump*. For each URL we repeat this process 7 times, once for each of the following browser profiles:

Vanilla: We do not activate any plugin.

AdBP-{Ads|Privacy|Paranoia}: We activate the *Adblock Plus* plugin and configure three separate profiles using the following lists i) the *EasyList* and *non-intrusive advertisements* (Ads), ii) *EasyPrivacy* (Privacy), and iii) *EasyList* and *EasyPrivacy* (Paranoia).

Ghostery-{Ads|Privacy|Paranoia}: We activate the *Ghostery* plugin and configure three separate profiles, which block the following object categories i) Advertisements (Ads), ii) Privacy (Privacy), and iii) all categories, including Analytics, Beacons and social media widgets (Paranoia).

Browser Mode	#HTTPS	#HTTP	#EL$_{hits}$	#EP$_{hits}$
Vanilla	7,263	57,862	4,738	4,807
AdBP-Pa	4,287	48,599	**6** *	**6** *
AdBP-Ad	5,254	53,435	**10** *	4,279
AdBP-Pr	5,189	55,717	3,627	**7** *
Ghostery-Pa	2,908	48,765	940	624
Ghostery-Ad	5,734	57,425	1,326	4,668
Ghostery-Pr	6,902	55,394	4,514	2,865

Table 1: Active measurements: Aggregate results for the Alexa top 1K list. Browser modes include Paranoia (Pa), Ad-blocker (Ad) and Privacy (Pr). Classification of URLs based EasyList (EL)and EasyPrivacy (EP). Ad-blockers lessen the total number of requests and lower the ratio of ad requests.

This experiment results in seven sets of passive traces for each of the top-1000 Alexa Web sites corresponding to the seven different browser profiles viz., with and without *Adblock Plus* and/or *Ghostery* enabled. With this information—the configuration of the Web browser that produced the network trace—we can apply our methodology to each set of traces and, thereby, assess the accuracy of our methodology.

4.2 Impact of ad-blockers on traffic

As described in §3, we use *Bro* HTTP analyzer to extract the HTTP information from the set of traces collected during the experiment. We then classify the requests using *libadblockplus*. Table 1 summarizes the total number of HTTP(S) requests in the traces and the corresponding classification of requests according to the filters of *EasyList* and *EasyPrivacy*.

Our first observation is that ad-blockers indeed significantly reduce the number of HTTP and HTTPS requests. For instance, in the *AdBP-Paranoia* mode the browser issues 9K less HTTP requests than in the *Vanilla* mode. The number of HTTP requests issued by a browser configured with *Adblock Plus* in the most aggressive mode is roughly 80% of the corresponding value for the *Vanilla* mode. In this context, 6% of the ad requests in the trace for the *Vanilla* mode either match a filter in *EasyList* (8.1%) or one in *EasyPrivacy* (8.3%). These observations are consistent with those reported in related work, e.g., see [42, 27]. The number of HTTPS connections follows likewise this trend, i.e., 2.9K connections less. This implies that browsers and servers also exchange ad traffic over HTTPS, a case not covered by our methodology.

The number of requests for both plugins configured in the *Paranoia* mode also differs. We remark that the numbers reported in Table 1 are subject to configurations and do not strictly reflect the actual filtering performance of each plugin; rather, they reflect the existence of the filtering process.

Nonetheless, Table 1 shows that the number of objects classified as ad requests is a strong indicator for the presence of an ad-blocker. As expected, ad-blockers hinder many requests from being issued and thus, the number of identified ads with our methodology is small (indicated in bold numbers in the table). In the absence of an ad-blocker, the number of ad requests is significantly larger (see the vanilla browser configuration row).

We note that our approach mis-classifies a small number of requests. We indicate *false positives* with a $*$ in Table 1. *False positives* are requests that the *Adblock Plus* browser plugin does not block but our methodology classifies as ad-related objects. We manually investigate these cases and offer the following explana-

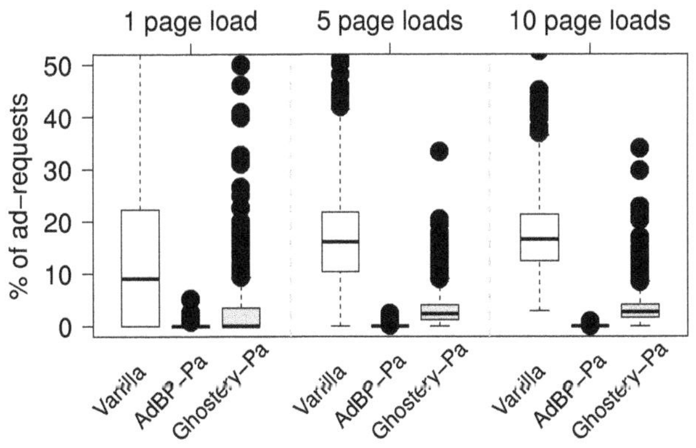

Figure 2: Active measurements: ratio of ad-requests per browser configuration. Comparison among 1K iterations of 1, 5, 10 randomly selected page loads. The presence of an ad-blocker is more evident when the user becomes more active.

tion: some are due to inconsistent `Content-Type` values in the responses. For instance, in one case *Bro* reports the MIME *text/x-c*. Our methodology maps this request to the content type `object`, but a manual inspection of the object reveals that this object is in reality a JavaScript object. Remapping the content type to `script` triggers an exception filter that prevents the mis-classification. In fact, the main source of mis-classifications are URLs to JavaScript objects where the `Content-Type` field is set to *text/html*. Modern browsers circumvent this problem since they infer the type of the object without relying on the HTTP headers. Our methodology has to rely on the HTTP headers and thereby is affected by such inconsistencies.

4.3 Identifying ad-blocker users

Table 1 illustrates the effectiveness of our approach for classifying ad requests in a network trace in a fashion similar to an ad-blocker. Next, we tackle the question from §3.2: what ratio of ad to non-ad requests is a useful indicator to infer ad-blocker usage? To answer this question we show in Figure 2 a series of box-plots for the ratio of ad requests across browser configurations (for space reasons we only include the results for *Vanilla*, *AdBP-Pa* and the *Ghostery-Pa* configuration modes). For each of these three modes we execute three experiments. We randomly select 1, 5 and 10 sites of the Alexa top 1K list, and compute three ratios of ad requests. Our motivation for choosing different number of sites is to represent users with different levels of activity. We repeat this 1K times. When comparing the box plots we can see that the ad-ratios differ significantly if the number of page loads is sufficiently large, i.e., when users are active. Accordingly, we use a discrimination threshold of 5% when the number of requests is sufficiently large, e.g., 10 page loads or 1K requests. Using a slightly higher or lower threshold does not alter the results significantly.

5. DATA SETS

We had access to two anonymized traces from a Residential Broadband Network (RBN) of a large European ISP. These two traces were collected within two customer aggregation networks in the same city. The first trace was captured at a low level which carries the traffic of about 7.5K DSL customers to the Internet. The second trace was captured at the next higher level, which carries the traffic of about 19.7K DSL customers. The up-link speeds are 3 and 10 Gbps, respectively. Table 2 reports the dates when the traces were collected.

Trace	RBN-1	RBN-2
Date	11th Apr. 2015	11th Aug. 2015
Time	00:00	15:30
Duration	4 days	15 and ½ hours
Subscribers	7.5K	19.7K
HTTP$_{bytes}$	18.8T	11.4T
HTTP$_{reqs}$	131.95M	85.09M

Table 2: Passive measurements: Data sets

The monitoring infrastructure uses Endace DAG network monitoring cards [11]. These cards support a port-based classification, which is appropriate for HTTP(S) traffic (see [44, 51]). Hence, HTTP traffic can be associated to TCP traffic from (or to) port 80. Likewise, HTTPS traffic relates to *EasyList* downloads can be associated to TCP traffic from (or to) port 443 from (or to) IPs in the list of *Adblock Plus* servers that host these lists. We obtained this list with active measurements (see §3.2) before and after the trace was captured. They did not exhibit differences.

Like many other ISPs, most of the customers of this ISP have a home gateway at their premises that performs Network Address Translation (NAT). These gateways multiplex many user devices, and thereby also browsers, to a single IP address. To report the prevalence of ad-blockers in residential broadband networks we have to identify unique devices and more specifically Web browsers. Maier et al. [45] showed that a good indicator for separating HTTP traffic from multiple devices behind the same NAT is the HTTP `User-Agent` strings of the browsers (in contrast to the strings used, e.g., by software update tools or media players). The rationale behind it is that the `User-Agent` string includes information about the operating system, browser version, etc. Thus, we use the pair end-host `IP` and `User-Agent` to separate our data by end device. Given that most ISPs assign addresses to their customers dynamically, we can only associate an IP address to a household for traces with short duration.

Table 2 gives an overview of the two traces collected in this ISP. The first data set corresponds to a 4-day long trace of the smallest set of customers for which we only capture HTTP traffic, i.e., 7.5K . The second trace is a shorter trace, but it captures peak time traffic for a larger number of end users, i.e., 19.7K . In the remainder of this work we use the latter trace to elaborate on ad-blocker usage, and the former to describe general characteristics of ad traffic.

We pay careful attention to respect and preserve the privacy of end users in our study. First and foremost, we process, aggregate, and analyze the data on a private and secured infrastructure. Second, the IP addresses of the end users are anonymized at the time of the packet capture, i.e., the real IP addresses of the end users were never stored to disk and are unknown to us. Third, we automate the ad classification process which, when completed, truncates every URL in the logs to a fully qualified domain name (FQDN), thereby removing sensitive information.

6. AD-BLOCKER USAGE IN THE WILD

Using the methodology from §3 we can proceed to assess ad-blocker usage in the residential broadband network trace `RBN-2`. To infer if an end user[1] is using an ad-blocker, we use the following two indicators: i.e., *i)* the ratio of ad to non-ad requests, and *ii)* automatic *EasyList* downloads by *Adblock Plus* (see §3.2).

[1]We use term "user" to refer to the pair formed by an `IP` address and a browser's `User-Agent` string.

To this end, we have first to identify browsers in the trace. Along with browsers, residential broadband networks indeed manifest a rich and complex mix of other HTTP-based applications. To illustrate this mix, we show in Figure 3 the total number of retrieved HTTP objects vs. the number of retrieved ads[2,3] for each `IP` address and `User-Agent` pair on a log-log scale. Due to the large number of data points, we use a heat map to capture the density within each area of the plot. We find in total 508.7K tuples of `IP` and `User-Agent` in `RBN-2`. We see the whole range: some pairs only account for a few requests while others issue orders of magnitude more requests. Overall, we observe 18.89% ad requests in this data set.

Most relevant for us is that there is a substantial number of pairs that request many Web objects but hardly any ads. These are the ones in the lower right hand side of Figure 3. They are most likely browsers that have an ad-blocker installed or visit only sites without advertisements.

However, there are many more points in this plot than we would have expected given the number of monitored DSL-lines (19.7K different households); more than 25 different `User-Agent` strings per household in average. Upon closer manual inspection we find pairs that identify devices like consoles and Smart TVs. On the other hand, given that most modern end-user devices run many HTTP-based applications in parallel, we also find pairs that correspond to desktop-based gaming applications or mobile apps (these applications use custom `User-Agent` strings). Since advertisements typically appear within Web sites and mobile applications, we can discard `User-Agent` strings that do not correspond to this type of applications. Moreover, since in-app ads differ substantially from browser ads, we limit our analysis to Web browsers in this paper. Namely, we restrict our analysis to sessions for which we can associate the `User-Agent` either to a well-known desktop browser or to a mobile device browser. Indeed, a manual inspection of the pairs shows that some of the points on the right hand side of Figure 3 correspond to mobile apps, which we do not want to consider. Thus, we next use the `User-Agent` strings to identify popular Web browsers.

6.1 Annotation of active users

Our approach is to manually label the `User-Agent` strings in a subset of the data. We use this as a starting point to subsequently classify the entire data set. Our starting subset is the active users. More precisely, we select tuples that issue more than 1K requests (the heavy hitters) e.g., those corresponding to a few page retrievals. As a result, we obtain a more tractable set of 15.2K pairs, with 1.6K unique `User-Agent` strings. Among this set of strings, we are able to manually annotate 601, which appear in 9.6K of the heavy-hitter tuples.

With this set of annotated strings, we proceed to classify browsers in the entire set of pairs. We identify 44.1K additional browsers. All these browsers generate 57.2% of the observed requests and 82.2% of the ad requests in the `RBN-2` trace. As expected, the heavy hitters issue most of these requests, i.e., 50.6% requests and 72.5% ad requests. We thus continue our study with the set of heavy hitters, i.e., the most active browsers.

[2]We use term "ad", "ad object" and "ad request" interchangeably in this paper to refer to a request that is blacklisted by *EasyList* and its derivatives, as well as those that are blacklisted by *EasyPrivacy*. We also use this term to refer to requests that are whitelisted by the list of *non-intrusive advertisements*.

[3]Note that fetching and displaying an advert can involve several executions and thereby multiple requests [25].

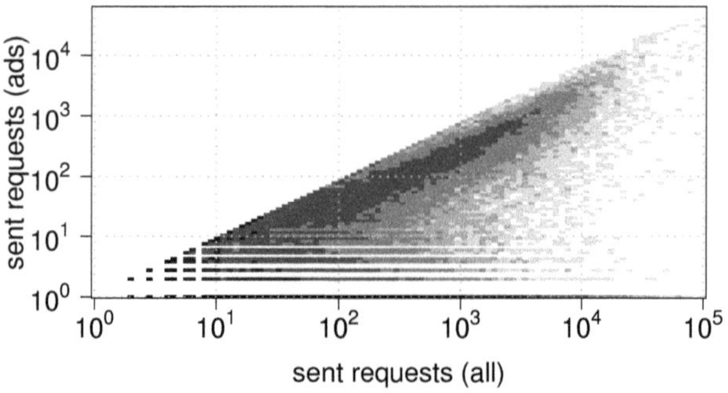

Figure 3: RBN-2 heat map: Number of total requests (x-axis, log-scale) vs. ad-requests (y-axis, log-scale) per IP, User-Agent pair. Darker points indicate more pairs. Most pairs issue a significant number of ad requests. Other pairs issue many requests but just a few ad requests.

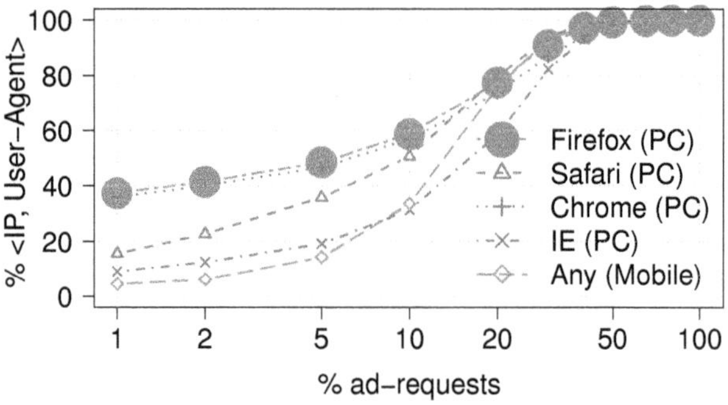

Figure 4: RBN-2 ECDF: Percentage of ad-requests (x-axis, log-scale) per active browser (those sending more than 1K requests). Many of the Firefox and Safari instances have a low ratio of ad requests.

We separate these browsers into *i)* mobile and *ii)* desktop versions. We identify 1.9K browsers in the mobile category. They correspond to iPhone and Android phones. These browsers issue 5.9% of both the ad and the total number of requests in the `RBN-2` trace. The desktop category accounts for the rest of requests and it is constituted by 7.7K browsers which we further separate into Firefox (3,423), Chrome (2,267), Internet Explorer (654) and Safari (1,324) browsers.

6.2 Inferring ad-blocker usage

With this set of annotated browsers, we continue our analysis of ad-blocker usage at our vantage point. We use two indicators: (a) ratio of ad requests, which applies to any ad-blocker, and (b) HTTPS connections to check for filter updates, which is specific to *Adblock Plus*.

First indicator: low ratio of ad requests. We use this indicator to detect the presence of an ad-blocker from the HTTP requests. Our motivation for this indicator stems from the insights of the active measurement study (see §4). The rationale is that users that installed an ad-blocker retrieve significantly smaller number of ads than those that have not.

Figure 4 shows the empirical cumulative distribution function (ECDF) of the percentage of ad requests per browser for the annotated set of active browsers. Since not all filter lists are installed by default, e.g., the *EasyPrivacy* list, we only consider ads classified by *EasyList*, which indeed is installed by default. In this context, 40% of the Firefox and Chrome active browsers issue less than 1% ad-requests; they qualify as ad-blocker candidates. By contrast, only for 18% of the Safari and 8% of the IE instances the ratio of ad requests is below the threshold. This can be due to the fact that installing and ad-blocker like *Adblock Plus* in these browsers is a bit more cumbersome and thus might deter their usage. Based on these observations and the results from the active measurement study (see §4), we set the threshold for identifying ad-blocking browsers to 5%, to *i)* tolerate mis-classifications due to content type (see §4.2), and *ii)* take into consideration users that disable blocking for specific sites.

Second indicator: downloads of filter lists. As mentioned above, *Adblock Plus* frequently checks for updates to the filter lists. These updates typically occur during browser bootstrap or when a list soft-expires (see §3.2). Thus, we can estimate the number of *Adblock Plus* users by monitoring *EasyList* downloads. However, the *Adblock Plus* browser extension uses HTTPS to download the lists. Hence, we cannot differentiate between multiple browsers hidden behind a single IP (e.g., in the presence of a NAT), since the `User-Agent` is not visible. Instead, we can only report the number of households in which there is at least one device with an *Adblock Plus* installation.

We find several thousands of HTTPS connections to *Adblock Plus* servers in the `RBN-2` trace. These connections are issued from 19.7% of the households in this data set. This number is slightly larger than what has been previously reported. Metwalley et al. [46] reports that the fraction of households with at least one device using an *Adblock Plus* plugin is between 10% and 18%. As stated previously, this information is not sufficient to discern browsers that likely run an ad-blocker, but we can leverage it as indicator and correlate it with the ad-ratio indicator.

Correlation of indicators to assess *Adblock Plus* usage. We proceed to correlate the ad-ratio with the *EasyList* downloads indicator. We obtain four classes as the cross product corresponding to a combination of the two indicator values. We summarize these 4 classes along with their corresponding traffic statistics in Table 3. We find that 46.8% of the 9.6K active browsers neither classify as an ad-blocker candidate nor contact *Adblock Plus* servers (denoted in the table with the type name A). The orthogonal case, i.e., those annotated with type C, constitute 22.2% of the active browsers population. As expected, this class is dominated by Firefox and Chrome browser `User-Agents`. These two types of browsers represent 51% and 32% of the occurrences respectively. Safari on the other hand accounts for 11%. In practice 31% of the Firefox and Chrome instances fall into this class and thereby they probably have *Adblock Plus* installed. This share is slightly larger than the official statistics [18, 15]. This difference could be explained by a permissive threshold value or by a bias due to the population at our vantage point.

There are many browsers for which the download information and the ratio of ad requests produce inconsistent outcomes (types B and D). Type-D browsers exhibit ad-blocker-like behavior, albeit they did not attempt to download *EasyList*. Browsers in this category sum up to 15.3% of the active browser population. There are two possible explanations for this apparent inconsistency. The end users might *i)* have installed a different plugin, e.g., *Ghostery* or *NoScript*, or *ii)* have requested content from sites with few advertisements. Based on the observation that other ad-blockers are much less prevalent than *Adblock Plus* [46], we speculate that the most likely cause for this inconsistency is the latter scenario.

The second type of inconsistency relates to type-B browsers. They add up to 15.7% of the active browser population. For these instances we observe an *EasyList* download but the ratio of ad requests is higher than 5%. The most plausible explanation for this contradictory information is that there may be many users in the same household, some of them using *Adblock Plus* and others not.

Type	Ratio	EasyList	Instances	% requests	% ad reqs.
A	X	X	46.8%	22.5%	46.3%
B	X	✓	15.7%	8.1%	15.8%
C	✓	✓	22.2%	12.9%	6.5%
D	✓	X	15.3%	7.1%	4.0%
Any	-	-	9.6K	50.6%	72.5%

Table 3: Ad-blocker usage: classification and statistics for the annotated set of active browsers using the indicators *i) Ratio:* low ratio of ad requests, i.e., $\leq$5%, and *ii) EasyList*: HTTPS connections to an *Adblock Plus* server.

6.3 Adblock Plus configurations

There are various filter lists with different objectives available for *Adblock Plus* users. Most notably, there are lists to *i)* block and hide adverts (e.g., *EasyList*), *ii)* whitelist adverts (list of *non-intrusive ads*), and *iii)* protect user privacy by blocking Web trackers (e.g., *EasyPrivacy*). To further elaborate on ad-blocker usage we dissect our corpus of adverts by the list that triggered the classification.

Our first observation is an unexpected high share of ad requests among the likely *Adblock Plus* users (type-C). For this observation, we refer to Table 3, which reports the contribution of each user category to the total number of ad requests in `RBN-2`. One would expect the relative share of ad requests for *Adblock Plus* users to be close to 0%. Instead, we find a share of 6.5% ad requests. The explanation for this high percentage is that our threshold-based classification is based on *EasyList* hits. We use this list because it is by default activated upon *Adblock Plus* installation; along with the list of *non-intrusive* advertisements whitelist. However, the numbers that we report in Table 3 correspond to all hits, including those triggered by the other lists, i.e., *EasyList* derivatives and *EasyPrivacy*. Indeed, we observe that 82.3% and 11.1% of the positive classifications for *Adblock Plus* users relate to filters in *EasyPrivacy* and in the list of *non-intrusive ads* respectively. This observation motivates the consequent analysis about the lists that *Adblock Plus* users subscribe to.

EasyPrivacy. Metwalley et al. [46] report that 77% of the users contact a tracker immediately after they start browsing the Web. We can leverage this observation to estimate the extent to which (if at all) an *Adblock Plus* user interacts with a tracker. Our assumption is that such interactions should only occur for those users who do not install the *EasyPrivacy* list. We observe that only 0.1% of the *non-adblock* users do not issue requests matching *EasyPrivacy* filter rules, i.e., almost every user contacts a tracker. By contrast, the corresponding fraction for *Adblock Plus* users is 5.1%. If we use a more permissive value, i.e., 10 requests to account for misclassifications, then the percentage of *Adblock Plus* users that likely installed *EasyPrivacy* is 13.1%. Overall, we see a consistent difference around 15% using different values.

In light of these observations, we speculate that most *Adblock Plus* users, i.e., more than 85%, do not subscribe to *EasyPrivacy* but just to *EasyList*. In fact, this argument is supported by a blog post from the *EasyList* maintainers, which reported back in 2011 that only 4.1% of their 12 million users subscribed to *EasyPrivacy* [9]. The key take-away is that it seems that *Adblock Plus* users install this software to block annoying advertisements but do not configure it to protect their privacy.

Non-intrusive adverts. We conduct a similar analysis to elaborate on the prevalence of the *non-intrusive ads* list. We find that *Adblock Plus* users issue 7.9% of the total number of whitelisted requests. In comparison, *non-adblocker* users generate 37.9% of this type of requests, despite the fact that the population of this set is almost twice the population of the former set. This first observation highlights the importance of this list for advertisers and publishers alike, i.e., *Adblock Plus* users still generate a significant fraction of ad requests.

When trying to elucidate whether an *Adblock Plus* user opts out of this whitelist, we find that 11.8% of the *Adblock Plus* users issue no requests of this kind. The corresponding percentage for *non-adblock* users is 6.1%. The reason why many *non-adblock* users do not issue ad requests of this kind is because this type of adverts are less prevalent (see §7). At less than 10 issued whitelisted requests, the difference between both groups is roughly 20%, a pattern that is repeated across different values. This is, perhaps, an indication that at most 20% of the users actually deactivate this list, thus disabling the whitelisting of adverts that conform the non-intrusive ads guidelines. We emphasize a word of caution on this last statement and remark that corroborating this observation would require to conduct an analysis of the browsing patterns of *Adblock Plus* users.

Summary: Our main observation is that a significant fraction of the most active users in our traces browse the Web with *Adblock Plus*, i.e., 22.2% of the active users. This extension is especially popular among Chrome and Firefox users, i.e., 30%; and less popular among Safari and Internet Explorer users. We find that most *Adblock Plus* users do not install the *EasyPrivacy* list that protects them from trackers. Hence, it seems that *Adblock Plus* users are mostly interested in blocking ads rather than protecting their privacy. However, this might be an awareness problem. We also find that most *Adblock Plus* users probably do not opt out from the list of acceptable ads (*non-intrusive ads*) which is enabled by default. In fact, we find that the set of heavy-hitter *Adblock Plus* users still generates a substantial number of such ads, even when compared to *non-adblock* users. This observation suggests that conforming to the acceptable ads guidelines may benefit some players in the advertising domain.

7. ADS IN THE WILD

One under-explored aspect of the ad-scape is the prevalence of ads that end users experience during *regular browsing sessions*. Most previous work (see e.g., [25, 42]) has relied on active measurements and therefore cannot capture how the average user interacts with the *ad-scape* while browsing the Web. Thus, in this section we use our passive measurement methodology to study basic properties of ad traffic in the wild. Concretely, we investigate *i)* basic ad-traffic properties, *ii)* content-related properties of the observed ads, and *iii)* whitelisted ads.

7.1 Ad-traffic characterization

To comment on the temporal characteristics of the ad-traffic we conduct our analysis on the RBN-1 trace, as it spans a longer period than RBN-2. We find that 17.25% and 1.13% of the requests and bytes respectively correspond to ad objects in the RBN-1 trace. To put these numbers into perspective, we refer to our active measurement results (see Section 4). For the Alexa top 1K sites we classified 16.4% of the total requests as adverts (see Table 1).

We highlight the variability of ad traffic in Figure 5(a), where we depict a time series for the number of requested Web objects vs. the number of ad requests using bins of 1 hour. The non-ad requests manifest the characteristic time of day and of week pattern of residential networks. During the night there are relatively fewer requests and the busy time is in the evenings, right before midnight. On the weekend there are fewer requests than during the week, in particular on Saturday. Moreover, the lunch break is also clearly visible. Surprisingly, the ad-related requests do not show the same pattern. To visualize these differences we plot in Figure 5(b) the percentages of ad requests and ad bytes over time. Here we only consider ads reported by filters in *EasyList* and *EasyPrivacy* (excluding *non-intrusive ads*). The figure reveals that, surprisingly, the ratio of ad requests also manifests a diurnal pattern, ranging from 6% up to 12%, instead of having a constant rate.

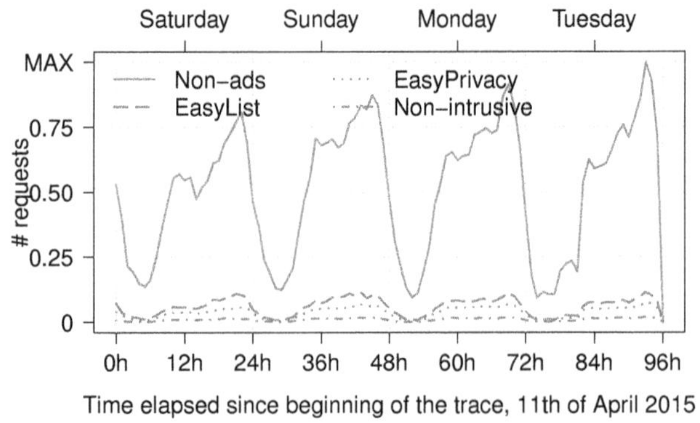

(a) # of ad requests vs. non-ad requests

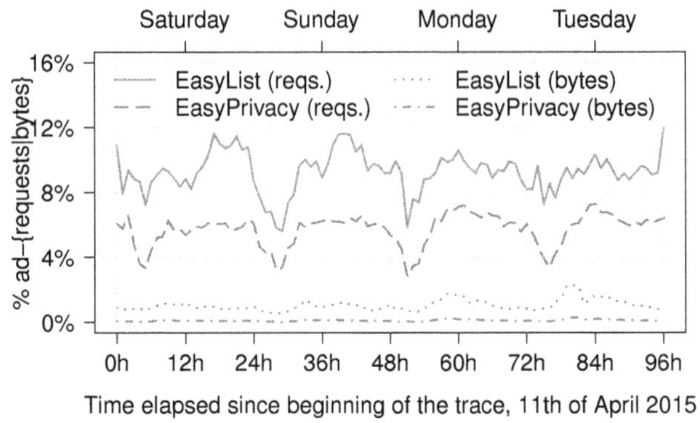

(b) % of ad requests and ad bytes according to *EasyList* and *EasyPrivacy*

Figure 5: Time series for ad and non-ad traffic (1h time bins, RBN-1 trace). Ad traffic exhibits a daily pattern, both in terms of number of requests and in terms of its ratio to all requests in the trace.

To explain this surprising diurnal pattern we offer two possible explanations. The first one is that users request different content and that the pages that serve this content have a different ratio of advertisements. For example, streaming video chunks might result in a very low ratio of ads. Another example are Web site categories, e.g., the *news* category has more objects than other categories (see [27] for a detailed study about the complexity of popular Web sites). Our second explanation for the diurnal pattern is that the share of ad-blockers users varies at different times of the day. We leverage the classification described in §6.1 to investigate this for RBN-2. Our finding is that at peak time the number of *non-adblocker* active users is twice the number of active *Adblock Plus* users. By contrast, during the off hours the number of active *Adblock Plus* and *non-adblocker* users is roughly the same.

Content-type	Ads		Non-Ads	
	Reqs	Bytes	Reqs	Bytes
image/gif	35.1%	14.1%	3.5%	0.7%
text/plain	28.7%	34.2%	14.3%	2.1%
text/html	14.4%	11.8%	7.6%	1.1%
-	11.8%	5.4%	28.7%	63.4%
app./xml	4.5%	2.2%	1.8%	0.2%
image/png	1.9%	1.6%	5.1%	0.8%
image/jpeg	1.8%	5.2%	19.8%	3.4%
app./x-shock.	1.4%	8.1%	0.2%	0.1%
video/mp4	0.0%	10.9%	0.3%	8.6%
video/x-flv	0.0%	5.4%	0.1%	3.1%

Table 4: Trace RBN-1: ad traffic by *Content-type*.

Our next question relates to the type of adverts that we see. To answer it we dissect the ad requests by the list that triggers the classification. *EasyList* causes significantly more hits than *EasyPrivacy*, which in turn triggers more classifications than the *non-intrusive ads* list. More precisely, *EasyList* classifies 55.9% of the ad requests in RBN-1. The *EasyPrivacy* is responsible for 35.1% of the requests. The *non-intrusive ads* list triggers the remaining matches. We observe the same trend in RBN-2.

7.2 Ad-related objects by Content-Type

Next, we consider the types of the requested ads (e.g., image vs. video ads) and their prevalence. Therefore, we analyze the *Content-Type* of the Web objects in RBN-1. Table 4 shows the most prevalent objects according to the MIME type reported by *Bro* HTTP analyzer along with their corresponding contribution to the total traffic and to the ad traffic in terms of requests and bytes. Most ads are either *image/gif*, *text/html*, or *text/plain*. The fraction of bytes is dominated by *text/html* objects, while the fraction of bytes for the type *image/gif* is relatively small. The latter is not surprising given that many of the ad objects used to track users are small, i.e., 43 bytes. At the other extreme are videos (i.e., *video/mp4, video/x-flv*), flash objects (i.e., *x-shockwave*), and non-*gif* images such as *image/jpg*. All these types contribute a higher fraction of bytes than requests.

To highlight the different distributions, we show in Figure 6(a) the density of the ad-object size on a log scale separated by the Content-Type. We consider four different classes: images (*gif, jpeg*, and *png*), text (*html, plain*), video (*mp4, flv*), and applications (*xml, flash*). The density of the logarithm highlights that most images are very small (43 bytes), while most videos are rather large (> 1 MByte). If we compare these values to the typical object size of non-ad objects, see Figure 6(b), we notice significant differences. Most non-ad videos are smaller than ad videos, while most non-ad images are larger. One of the reasons is that most video-streaming providers split regular videos into multiple chunks and each chunk corresponds to one Web object. Since most video ads only last for 15-45 seconds and advertisers expect end users to see the complete video stream, chunking may be considered to be unnecessary. Moreover, most ad videos typically have a length in the same order of magnitude. Surprisingly, we see that non-ad text objects are likely to be smaller. These are likely requests involving high-interactive sites, e.g., for auto-completion or for suggestions.

7.3 Non-intrusive advertisements

Next, we look at the relevance of the list of *non-intrusive ads*. On the one hand, ad-blockers threaten the financial backbone of the Web. On the other hand, they also ensure some balance by

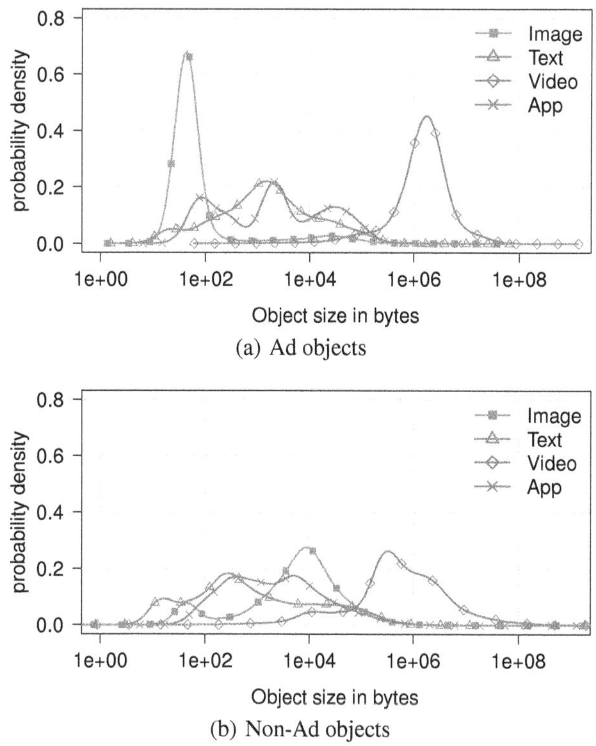

Figure 6: PDF of the object size distribution of the requests according to their MIME type (RBN-1). Ad-related objects exhibit characteristic sizes.

preventing ads from becoming too intrusive [19]. The result is the *non-intrusive ads* list which whitelists adverts and is enabled by default. Indeed, according to Financial Times [6] some companies including Google, Microsoft and Amazon, pay money to *Adblock Plus* to be whitelisted. But what is the effect of this list? Given our vantage point and our ability to classify traffic the same way *Adblock Plus* does, we can investigate the impact of the whitelist using the RBN-2 trace.

We first ask how many of the ad-related requests match the whitelist. This is the case for 9.2% of the ad requests. While this number may seem low at first, we calculated it using also the hits triggered by an *EasyPrivacy* filter. If we restrict ourselves to ad requests identified by *EasyList* and *non-intrusive ads*, then the percentage that is subject to whitelisting grows up to 15.3% viz., these adverts would not be blocked by the default *Adblock Plus* installation.

List accuracy. However, these numbers likely *overestimate* the real impact that this list has. We manually inspected the filter rules and found some anomalies: some rules are overly general, e.g., they whitelist an entire domain rather than specifically addressing ad-related parts. For example, many requests match the `@@||gstatic.com^$document` filter rule, which whitelists the entire `gstatic.com` domain. This domain hosts unsuspected fully qualified domain names (FQDNs) e.g., `fonts.gstatic.com` and services such as *Street View*. Hence, this filter list may also whitelist non-ad-related traffic. On the other hand, and referring to the previous example, font objects may very well be necessary to display an advertisement e.g., *Google's AdSense*.

Therefore, we ask how much of the whitelisted traffic would have been otherwise blocked by a blacklist, i.e., when *Adblock Plus* users choose to stop allowing *non-intrusive* advertisements. The ratio is surprisingly small: only 57.3% of the whitelisted requests would have been blacklisted. Moreover, 23.2% of those would be filtered by *EasyPrivacy*. These observations highlight that the list of *non-intrusive ads* should be handled with caution when trying to identify adverts. In the remainder of this subsection we consider only those whitelisted requests which "match the blacklist".

Publishers. Recall, we can identify the main page that originated the request using the methodology described in [56]. We find 991 unique FQDNs with more than 1K blacklisted requests to which we can associate 84.0% of the total requests blacklisted by *EasyList* and its language derivatives. The *non-intrusive ads* list whitelists 8.6% of these requests.

We find that some sites in the *dating*, *shopping*, *translation*, *audio and video streaming* categories, as well as some sites in the *mixed content* categories benefit the most from the whitelist[4]. On the other side, we find that most of the sites without whitelisted requests belong to the *adult content* category, followed by Webs in the *mixed content* category. Here, we also find another one in the *file sharing / video streaming* category. It is not surprising to see that these sites are not whitelisted. However, it is surprising to find a few instances of popular sites in the *news* category (in fact they appear in the Alexa top 1K). Thus, an *Adblock Plus* user would block every ad-related request related to these sites. We manually checked these sites with *Adblock Plus* to corroborate this observation.

Ad-tech companies. We repeat the same analysis to shed light on how the *non-intrusive ads* list affects ad-tech companies. We select FQDNs with more than 10K blacklisted requests. These domains sum up to 82.1% of the total blacklisted requests, from which 11.1% are whitelisted.

Like in the publisher case, we see a mix. The list of *non-intrusive ads* whitelists 47.9% of Google's requests (recall we exclude HTTPS traffic). Some of its services do get most of their requests through (e.g., analytics, ad-services) while others do not. While the bulk of these requests corresponds to Google, we also see other companies benefiting from the *non-intrusive ads* list. One particular example is a *technology/Internet* Web site that operates its own ad-platform, for which the *non-intrusive ads* list whitelists 94% of the otherwise blacklisted requests.

Summary. Our main observation is that a significant share of the requests and bytes in a residential broadband network are due to online advertising e.g., 17.25% and 1.13% of the requests and bytes respectively for trace `RBN-1`. We observe that ad-related traffic exhibits a different diurnal pattern than regular traffic. Moreover, ad objects have more characteristic sizes than non-ad objects. In ads *gif* images dominate in terms of number of requests, followed by *text/plain* objects, which in turn dominate the share of ad traffic in terms of bytes.

Moreover, our analysis of the potential benefits of whitelisting i.e., the list of *non-intrusive ads*, shows that some content publishers substantially benefit from this list, while others not. Among the latter are sites in the *adult* category. However, we also find popular sites in the *news* category among them. Some ad-tech companies also benefit from this list; for instance Google, which carries the bulk of the whitelisted traffic and for which 47.9% of the ad-related traffic is whitelisted. Another example is a popular *technology/Internet* Web site. This site operates its own ad-platform, for which the *non-intrusive ads* list whitelists 94% of the otherwise blacklisted ad traffic.

[4]We use `http://sitereview.bluecoat.com` to classify Web sites into categories.

8. ADVERTISEMENT INFRASTRUCTURE

Next, we turn our attention to the infrastructure that serves ad-related objects. This study is motivated by the need to better understand the ad-scape [7], a complex and diverse ecosystem composed by hundreds of companies that provide numerous services and closely interact with each other, e.g., ad-networks and exchanges. In this section we study the server-side infrastructure from the perspective of an end user using *Adblock Plus*. Namely, which infrastructures end users contact, how often and how many, and if we can find signs of real-time bidding.

8.1 Server side ad infrastructure

The first aspect of the *ad-scape* infrastructure are the characteristics of the Web servers that deliver ad objects to the end users. We use the term server to refer to an IP address. Note, that any of these addresses may on the one hand be only a front-end of a large server farm or on the other hand a server that is co-located with other virtual servers. We find 29.0K and 19.6K servers in `RBN-1` that serve ad objects according to *EasyList* and respectively *EasyPrivacy*. Some servers (i.e., 5.2K) serve objects matching both lists. As one may expect—like almost every other distribution in the Internet—the distribution of requests per server is heavy-tailed (not shown). If we use only *EasyList* driven classification, the median number of ad objects per server is 7, the mean is 438, and the 90th / 95th / 99th percentiles are respectively 320 / 1.1K / 6.8K ad objects. The busiest server in the `RBN-1` trace, which is operated by Liverail, received 312.3K ad requests in total.

The second aspect relates to the objects served by these servers: do they exclusively serve ad-related objects or do they serve regular content as well? One argument for the first case is that by now there is a separate infrastructure and market dedicated to the ad-tech ecosystem. The opposing argument is that one can take advantage of synergy effects by delivering ads via the same infrastructure as regular content. We find 222.2K servers in `RBN-1`. For 21.1% of them we classify at least one request as an ad object. These IPs serve 54.3% of the total number of non-ad objects in `RBN-1`. However, about 6.9K servers deliver exclusively ad objects. Here, we consider that a server is exclusively dedicated to deliver ad objects if our methodology identifies more than 90% of its requests as adverts. We consider this reasonable since our methodology may not be able to identify all ads and thus provides only a lower bound. We use the previous threshold to find 10.1K ad servers, which altogether deliver 32.7% of the adverts. Likewise, we define the notion of "tracking server" to refer to the set of servers that only serve ad-related objects identified using *EasyPrivacy*. We find 3.3K of these servers, which deliver 18.8% of all the ad-related objects reported by *EasyPrivacy*.

Next, we consider the Autonomous Systems (ASes) which host the ad servers since we want to understand if ad traffic is highly concentrated in a few large infrastructures. To this end we use the global routing information in order to determine the AS that is responsible for the IPs of the servers. The top-10 ASes contribute to the majority of the ad objects in the `RBN-1` trace, namely 56.8%. Among these ASes, see Table 5, we find four categories of players: search engines, cloud providers, CDNs and two ad-tech ASes, i.e., AppNexus and Criteo. Google leads this ranking with 21.0% and 33.9% of all ad requests and bytes, respectively. The relative ratio of ad objects for Google traffic is 50.7% and 15.9% of the total ad requests and bytes to this AS. This ratio may at first seem large and one may ask if our methodology is sound. However, recall that Google switched many of its services to HTTPS—apparently mostly for their "core" content, i.e., search results and video streaming.

AS	%ads relative to ad objects in trace		% ads relative to all objects per AS	
	Requests	Bytes	Requests	Bytes
Google	21.0%	33.9%	50.7%	15.9%
Am.-EC2	7.0%	4.6%	19.8%	2.8%
Akamai	6.5%	19.0%	6.4%	1.0%
Am.-AWS	5.5%	1.1%	45.9%	16.6%
Hetzner	3.4%	1.4%	23.4%	3.5%
AppNexus	3.1%	0.4%	32.9%	50.2%
MyLoc	2.9%	3.0%	64.0%	14.9%
SoftLayer	2.8%	0.4%	48.5%	1.9%
AOL	2.7%	0.3%	74.7%	25.4%
Criteo	1.9%	1.1%	78.1%	88.2%

Table 5: Trace `RBN-1`: Ad traffic by AS for top-10 ASes.

Among the other top contributors are also cloud providers, including Amazon, Hetzner, and MyLoc. Finding cloud providers in the list of top contributors highlights that clouds are also used by the advertisement industry. While some companies opt to manage their own AS to better control and operate their ad infrastructure, others opt to take advantage of the massive amount of resources and flexibility that cloud providers offer. Finally, CDNs like Akamai (which deploys caches within ISPs or within their own address space) and SoftLayer form the third category of ASes that serve ad objects. The presence of CDNs in this list of top contributors supports the argument that the same infrastructure that serves regular content delivers also ad objects.

The last category of ASes in Table 5 includes the relatively unknown ASes AppNexus and Criteo. These are companies whose main business is online advertising. They operate just a few servers (those visible in our traces), e.g., 39 for Criteo. Excluding the landing pages of these companies, we expect these ASes to mostly serve adverts, which is not strictly the case. While we classify 50.2% of the AppNexus bytes as advertisement traffic, the ratio of the requests is much lower (32.9%). Hence, our methodology probably underestimates the number of ad requests for this AS. One possible explanation for this mismatch is that the lists are conservative and do not address all possible URLs to prevent blacklisting desired traffic. Another possible explanation is that fetching an advert can require several JavaScript executions (see [25]) and thereby involve multiple non-ad requests as well. If we do not classify all requests in this chain as ad objects, except for one, the ratio of adverts per AS may decrease. In contrast to AppNexus, the percentage of ad traffic for Criteo in terms of requests and bytes is as high as 78.1% and 88.2%, respectively.

8.2 Ad-exchanges and real-time bidding

Real-time bidding (RTB) refers to the process of *selling* advertisement space on a per-impression basis, i.e., per user. This is a standard process in today's Internet (see [23, 53, 25]). The process works as follows. When a user requests an advert from an ad exchange, this exchange contacts multiple advertisers and the highest bidder among them wins the right to display the ad to the user. Advertisers can use many pieces of information to decide on their bid, including but not limited to geographical location, age, or gender. Usually, exchanges wait for around 100 ms before closing the auction [14]. Earlier work revealed the complexity of the ad-ecosystem which involves multiple players [23, 58, 49].

With our traces we can identify real-time bidding in the wild by leveraging a threshold of 100 ms for answering a request. The key observation here is that the bidding threshold adds extra delay to the *HTTP hand-shake* i.e., the time difference between the first HTTP response and the first HTTP request packet. If the delay is larger than 100 ms it may be due to RTB. However, it may also be due to large network delays. To avoid mis-classifications we use the TCP hand-shake time—the difference between the TCP SYN-ACK and the TCP SYN packets—as a proxy for the network round trip time (RTT) to the server. Note, that given the location of our monitor within the aggregation network, the TCP hand-shake time only captures the wide area delays and thus automatically removes access network variations. Likewise, we remove biases due to the servers' locations viz., otherwise data in Europe can be expected to be served faster than that in the US or even Asia. Finally, if the HTTP object is fetched via a persistent connection we still use the TCP hand-shake time from this connection as the delays usually do not vary that significantly within a few seconds—the expected durations of these persistent connections.

Figure 7 shows the *density of the logarithm* of the difference between the HTTP and TCP hand-shake times for the `RBN-2` trace, dissected into ad and non-ad HTTP transactions. The first observation is that most of the hand-shake time differences are small, i.e., 1 ms. They relate to noise on the network path or to the processing overhead at the server to determine the HTTP response. The second observation is that while most of the non-ad objects have a short hand-shake time, namely less than 10 ms, ads have—more often than non-ads—larger hand-shake times. This can be seen from the three clear modes at 1 ms, 10 ms and 120 ms in Figure 7. Compared to the non-ad objects a much larger share of ad objects exhibit a time difference between hand-shakes of more than 100 ms. This suggests the presence of *back-offices*, which include ad-exchanges to enable RTB and CDN to fetch objects from other distant servers [49].

In fact, a manual inspection of the fully qualified domain names with such large hand-shake time differences (≥90 ms) reveals that these host names belong to ad-tech companies. To give an example, Google's DoubleClick, which offers RTB, contributes to 14.5% of the ads in this range. We also find other organizations offering RTB, e.g., Mopub (an RTB exchange for mobile in-app ads), the Rubicon project, Pubmatic or Criteo. Each of these organizations contributes roughly 5% to the total number of ads in this range. We also find Web tracking companies here, e.g., AddThis.

Summary: The ad infrastructure is mostly concentrated in a few ASes. Along with the expected players, e.g., Google, we observe that some ad-tech companies opt to either deploy their infrastructure in clouds or rely on CDNs, while others choose to manage their own AS, e.g., AppNexus and Criteo. Moreover, our data suggests that often the same infrastructure serves ad content as well as regular content, although some servers do indeed only serve ad-related content. Finally, we show that ad requests typically involve more back-end functionality, i.e., RTB, than non-ad requests, which again highlights the complexity underlying this ecosystem.

9. RELATED WORK

Content and services which are offered for free on the Internet are primarily monetized through online advertisement. A rich body of literature seeks to broadly understand the scale, dynamics, mechanisms, economics and general interest concerns related to advertisements on the Web. In this section we provide a summary of the most relevant lines of research concerning our work.

Privacy and security aspects. The first and largest line of research includes studies that investigate the extent to which advertisements violate or are in conflict with end users' privacy [35, 40,

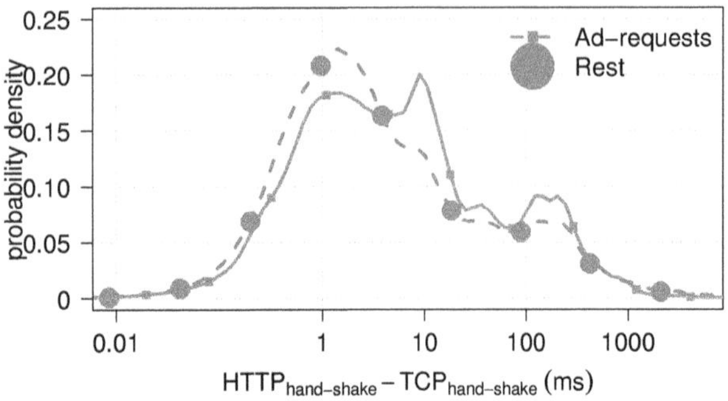

Figure 7: Real time bidding in RBN-2: difference between the HTTP and TCP hand-shake latencies dissected by type of request. The more pronounced modes at 10 ms and 100 ms suggest that ad requests typically involve more back-end functionality than non-ad requests.

36]. Other studies propose to address these issues with privacy-aware ad technologies [37]. Security-centric studies report the prevalence and properties of malicious ads [59, 43] and how to detect them [54, 53]. Another related study concerns ad injecting browser extensions [57]. Other studies in this area paid special attention to targeted advertisements. The goal of these advertisements is to improve the effectiveness of the displayed ads to the user by matching the users' interest. Farahat et al. [31] report an empirical evaluation and confirm the effectiveness of such advertisements. However, they also outlined ways in which more sophisticated targeting algorithms can cause harm. A large body of related work investigates privacy issues related to such user profiling, e.g., [35, 40, 36, 37, 30]. Gill et al. conducted a passive measurement study to quantify the information that is aggregators collect and assess, at the same time, the value of this data [32]. Balebako et al. propose tools to mitigate behavioral advertisements [24]. Krishnamurthy and Wills [41] investigate privacy diffusion in a longitudinal study, where they report about the increasing aggregation of user-related information by a few companies, as well as the limitations of existing protection techniques.

Ad content and traffic characterization. Another notable line of research concerns the empirical characterization of the online advertisement landscape as well as its impact on Web site complexity. Guba et al. [34] and Barford et al. [25] characterize the ad-scape and highlight its underlying complexity. For instance, how ad exchanges enable real-time bidding to sell advert placements on a per user basis. Pujol et al. [49] report the scale of such "hidden" interactions in a passive measurement study. However, advertising has also a very visible and pronounced influence on today's Web site complexity. Krishnamurthy and Wills [42] report that 25–30% of the Web objects in the Alexa most popular sites are extraneous.

Mobile ads. There is one branch of related studies that focuses on advertising in the mobile domain. For example, Rodríguez et al. [55] quantify empirically mobile ad traffic via passive measurements. They reveal insights in the delivery mechanisms and outline means for optimized ad delivery. Targeting mechanisms used in the mobile world (e.g., location-based or user-based targeting) are not rare in today's Internet [26]. In this regard, Nath [47] characterizes the ads displayed in mobile applications and reports about the information that these apps collect for targeted advertising. Moreover, energy consumption is an important topic in the mobile domain. Thus, some studies also devoted their attention to quantify the energy consumed by mobile advertisements [22, 29, 28, 55]. In this regard, energy savings can be achieved by either pre-fetching ads [28], or by blocking them to reduce radio traffic [50].

Ad-blocking tech and tracking services. Butkiewicz et al. [27] report the share of extraneous content like ads in Web pages, and conclude that an ad-blocker can reduce the median number of requested objects per site by up to 75%. Guglemann et al. [33] investigate how to detect privacy-intrusive trackers and services from passive measurements. Kontaxis and Chew [39] describe a tracking protection mechanism for the Mozilla Firefox browser. Metwalley et al. [46] contribute to this line of research with a passive measurement study about the extent to which Web trackers follow users in a residential broadband network. One of their findings is that while many users install *Adblock Plus* (roughly 18% of the households), most of them do not install an extension to protect their privacy.

Previous research on online advertisements mainly focused on the empirical classification and characterization of advertisements via active measurement studies. In the passive measurement domain, related work has mostly focused on assessing privacy issues. Our work complements this body of work with a passive measurement study about advertisement traffic and ad-blocker usage in a residential broadband network.

10. DISCUSSION

Our methodology leverages *Adblock Plus* functionality to provide insights into how ad-blockers may influence ad traffic dynamics and thereby, Web traffic. Although we show that the proposed methodology is capable of classifying ad requests in HTTP header traces, the classification approach comes at a price.

First of all, the classification of ad requests in header traces is complicated by the lack of structural information in the absence of the HTML payload; individual HTTP requests cannot be associated with Web objects (e.g., if an image is embedded in an iframe). This structural information is leveraged by *Adblock Plus* to improve the ad detection.

To tackle this challenge, we propose a methodology to partially reconstruct the Web page structure. Our methodology mainly employs the construction of a referrer map which associates individual requests (e.g., images, video, CSS, or JavaScript) with the accessed page. While this approach allows us to cluster related requests by page, it cannot reconstruct the entire Web page structure as needed by *Adblock Plus* to achieve higher detection accuracy. We suggest that a complete reconstruction is only possible by accessing the payload and executing the embedded JavaScript code, which might further manipulate the Web page structure.

Moreover, ad and non-ad objects can be transferred over HTTPS, or a mixture of HTTP and HTTPS (e.g., the landing page over HTTPS and the ads over HTTP). Since URLs in HTTPS transfers cannot be analyzed, we cannot always associate all requested objects with a page when constructing the referrer map of such a page. We are, thus, also unable to reason about the prevalence of ad traffic carried over HTTPS connections.

Second of all, our methodology can underestimate the volume of ad traffic in the presence of *hidden ads*, i.e., ads embedded in the main HTML of the page whose retrieval cannot be blocked. To identify these kind of ads we would require access to the entire HTML document (i.e., packet payload), which is not possible in our study. In cases where the payload can be analyzed, our methodology can be extended to detect *hidden ads* and address the challenges discussed above.

Lastly, we remark that there are many other ad-blockers available to end users besides *Adblock Plus*. We may not be able to detect users with different extensions (or even *Adblock Plus* with custom configurations) if they are tailored to block different objects than those affected by *EasyList*.

Furthermore, analyzing the number of ad requests (indicator 1, see §6.2) involves a set of potential biases: *i)* custom configurations and different filter lists (e.g., Web site whitelisting), *ii)* cascaded effects in which the blocked ad request who have triggered subsequent requests, or *iii)* the interaction of *Adblock Plus* with other blocking extensions. The immediate consequence of such biases is that we may *underestimate* the overall usage of ad blocking browser extensions. Moreover, caches and ad blocking middle-boxes or proxies can also decrease the number of observed ad requests. Consequently, confusing *Adblock Plus* instances with ad blocking proxies will lead to *overestimation* of the number of *Adblock Plus* users. To limit the effect of these biases, we introduced the filter list download indicator (§6.2) which monitors updates triggered by *Adblock Plus*. However, since such updates are fetched via HTTPS, we cannot observe the *User-Agent* string required to differentiate different browsers behind a NAT.

We point out that this is a general limitation of the presented *results*, which we produced using the lists mentioned in Section 2, rather than of the applied *methodology*. We selected *Adblock Plus* based on its popularity among end users and note that our approach can be extended to consider other ad-blockers.

11. CONCLUSION

The goal of our work is to elucidate the interactions between the end users and the ad ecosystem. We conduct a passive measurement study using traces collected at a residential broadband network of a major European ISP with two objectives in mind. First, elaborate on the prevalence of ad-blockers to inform the ongoing debate regarding these tools. Second, complement related work by characterizing ad traffic at this vantage point using *Adblock Plus* functionality.

Our main observation is that a significant fraction (22%) of the most active users in our traces browse the Web with *Adblock Plus*. Surprisingly, we find little evidence that *Adblock Plus* users install the *EasyPrivacy* list of filters, which aims to protect end users' privacy by blocking trackers. Likewise, our results suggest that most *Adblock Plus* users do not opt out from the list of acceptable ads that is enabled by default in *Adblock Plus*. Based on these observations we conjecture that *Adblock Plus* users are mostly interested in blocking annoying ads rather than protecting their privacy, or that they are not aware of these options or how to change them.

Motivated by these observations, we also investigate the potential benefits of whitelisting, i.e., the list of *non-intrusive ads*. This list can be tremendously beneficial to some content publishers and ad-tech companies given the number of *Adblock Plus* users. We find that 9% of the ad-related requests are whitelisted by this list, while 56% and 35% of the ad-related requests are blacklisted by *EasyList* and *EasyPrivacy*, respectively.

Overall, we find that 18% and 1% (requests and bytes) of the total traffic at our vantage point relates to ad traffic. This share of ad traffic is distributed across different infrastructures, including content and cloud providers and CDNs. However, these infrastructures are concentrated in a few ASes. The top 10 ASes include the expected players, e.g., Google (which dominates the list in terms of requests and bytes). We further observe that some ad-tech companies opt to either deploy their infrastructure in clouds or rely on CDNs, while others choose to manage their own AS, e.g., AppNexus and Criteo. Moreover, our data suggests that often the same infrastructure serves ad content as well as regular content, although some servers do indeed only serve ad-related content.

We also show that ad-related requests typically involve more back-end functionality than non-ad requests. This complexity results in higher observed response times for ad objects than non-ad objects. These latency inflations suggest the presence of real-time bidding within ad exchanges.

This paper takes a first step towards understanding how users employ ad-blockers and what advertisement traffic is potentially affected by this software. Yet, our study also poses new questions. In future work we plan to extend our analysis to better understand the reasons that drive end users to use ad-blockers. Moreover, we also plan to explore the economic impact and implications that *ad-blocking* tech has for the "free" Web.

Acknowledgments

We would like to thank the anonymous reviewers and Philipp Richter for their constructive feedback. This work was supported by the German Ministry for Education and Research project BBDC (Berlin Big Data Center; funding mark 01IS14013A).

12. REFERENCES

[1] https://easylist-downloads.adblockplus.org/easylist.txt.
[2] https://easylist-downloads.adblockplus.org/easyprivacy.txt.
[3] Acceptable Ads Manifesto. https://acceptableads.org/en/.
[4] Adblock Plus Filters Explained. hhttps://adblockplus.org/en/filter-cheatsheet.
[5] Allowing Acceptable Ads in Adblock Plus. https://adblockplus.org/en/acceptable-ads.
[6] Amazon, Google and Microsoft Escape Adblock Plus, for a Price. http://www.engadget.com/2015/02/03/amazon-google-microsoft-adblock-plus/.
[7] Display LUMAscape. http://www.lumapartners.com/lumascapes/display-ad-tech-lumascape/.
[8] DoubleClick Nearing Privacy Settlements. http://news.cnet.com/2100-1023-871654.html.
[9] EasyList Statistics: August 2011. https://easylist.adblockplus.org/blog/2011/09/01/easylist-statistics:-august-2011.
[10] Electronic Frontier Foundation's Privacy Badger. https://www.eff.org/privacybadger.
[11] Emulex Endace DAG technology. http://www.emulex.com/.
[12] EU Carriers Plan to Block Ads, Demand Money from Google. http://arstechnica.com/business/2015/05/eu-carriers-plan-to-block-ads-demand-money-from-google/.
[13] FTC Staff Report: Self-regulatory Principles for Online Behavioral Advertising. www.ftc.gov/opa/2009/02/behavad.shtm.
[14] Google AdExchange. http://developers.google.com/ad-exchange/rtb/getting_started.
[15] Google Chrome Store AdBlock Plus Statistics. https://chrome.google.com/webstore/detail/adblock-plus/cfhdojbkjhnklbpkdaibdccddilifddb.
[16] libadblockplus: A C++ Library Offering the Core Functionality of Adblock Plus. https://github.com/adblockplus/libadblockplus.
[17] Most Popular Extensions :: Add-ons for Firefox. ttps://addons.mozilla.org/en-us/firefox/extensions/?sort=users.
[18] Mozilla AdBlock Plus Statistics. https://addons.mozilla.org/en-US/firefox/addon/adblock-plus/statistics/usage/?last=30.
[19] Publishers Watch Closely as Adoption of Ad Blocking Tech Grows. http://adage.com/article/digital/adoption-ad-blocking-tech-grows/297101/.
[20] Selenium: Web Browser Automation. seleniumhq.org.
[21] Writing Adblock Plus Filters. https://adblockplus.org/en/filters.

[22] Abdurhnam Albasir, Kshirasagar Naik, Bernard Plourde, and Nishith Goel. Experimental Study of Energy and Bandwidth Costs of Web Advertisements on Smartphones. In *IEEE MobiCASE*, 2014.

[23] Sebastian Angel and Michael Walfish. Verifiable Auctions for Online Ad Exchanges. In *ACM SIGCOMM*, 2013.

[24] Rebecca Balebako, Pedro Leon, Richard Shay, Blase Ur, Yang Wang, and L. Cranor. Measuring the Effectiveness of Privacy Tools for Limiting Behavioral Advertising. In *IEEE W2SP*, 2012.

[25] Paul Barford, Igor Canadi, Darja Krushevskaja, Qiang Ma, and S. Muthukrishnan. Adscape: Harvesting and Analyzing Online Display Ads. In *WWW*, 2014.

[26] Theodore Book and Dan S Wallach. An Empirical Study of Mobile Ad Targeting. *arXiv 1502.06577*, 2015.

[27] Michael Butkiewicz, Harsha V. Madhyastha, and Vyas Sekar. Understanding Website Complexity: Measurements, Metrics, and Implications. In *ACM IMC*, 2011.

[28] Xiaomeng Chen, Abhilash Jindal, and Y. Charlie Hu. How Much Energy Can We Save From Prefetching Ads?: Energy Drain Analysis of Top 100 Apps. In *ACM HotPower*, 2013.

[29] S. D'Ambrosio, S. De Pasquale, G. Iannone, D. Malandrino, A. Negro, G. Patimo, A. Petta, V. Scarano, L. Serra, and R. Spinelli. Mobile Phone Batteries Draining: Is Green Web Browsing the Solution? In *IEEE IGCC*, 2014.

[30] Amit Datta, Michael Carl Tschantz, and Anupam Datta. Automated Experiments on Ad Privacy Settings: A Tale of Opacity, Choice, and Discrimination. *IEEE PETS*, 2014.

[31] Ayman Farahat and Michael C Bailey. How Effective is Targeted Advertising? In *WWW*, 2012.

[32] Phillipa Gill, Vijay Erramilli, Augustin Chaintreau, Balachander Krishnamurthy, Konstantina Papagiannaki, and Pablo Rodríguez. Follow the Money: Understanding Economics of Online Aggregation and Advertising. In *ACM IMC*, 2013.

[33] David Gugelmann, Markus Happe, Bernhard Ager, and Vincent Lenders. An Automated Approach for Complementing Ad Blockers Blacklists. In *IEEE PETS*, Jul 2015.

[34] Saikat Guha, Bin Cheng, and Paul Francis. Challenges in Measuring Online Advertising Systems. In *ACM IMC*, 2010.

[35] Saikat Guha, Bin Cheng, and Paul Francis. Privad: Practical Privacy in Online Advertising. In *USENIX NSDI*, 2011.

[36] Hamed Haddadi, Pan Hui, Tristan Henderson, and Ian Brown. Targeted Advertising on the Handset: Privacy and Security Challenges. In *Pervasive Advertising*, pages 119–137. 2011.

[37] Michaela Hardt and Suman Nath. Privacy-aware Personalization for Mobile Advertising. In *ACM CCS*, 2012.

[38] Sunghwan Ihm and Vivek S. Pai. Towards Understanding Modern Web Traffic. In *ACM IMC*, 2011.

[39] Georgios Kontaxis and Monica Chew. Tracking Protection in Firefox for Privacy and Performance. *arXiv 1506.04104*, 2015.

[40] Aleksandra Korolova. Privacy Violations Using Microtargeted Ads: A Case Study. In *IEEE PADM*, 2010.

[41] Balachander Krishnamurthy and Craig Wills. Privacy Diffusion on the Web: A Longitudinal Perspective. In *WWW*, 2009.

[42] Balachander Krishnamurthy and Craig E. Wills. Cat and Mouse: Content Delivery Tradeoffs in Web Access. In *WWW*, 2006.

[43] Zhou Li, Kehuan Zhang, Yinglian Xie, Fang Yu, and XiaoFeng Wang. Knowing Your Enemy: Understanding and Detecting Malicious Web Advertising. In *ACM CCS*, 2012.

[44] Gregor Maier, Anja Feldmann, Vern Paxson, and Mark Allman. On Dominant Characteristics of Residential Broadband Internet Traffic. In *ACM IMC*, 2009.

[45] Gregor Maier, Fabian Schneider, and Anja Feldmann. NAT Usage in Residential Broadband Networks. In *PAM*, 2011.

[46] Hassan Metwalley, Stefano Traverso, Marco Mellia, Stanislav Miskovic, and Mario Baldi. The Online Tracking Horde: A View From Passive Measurements. In *Traffic Monitoring and Analysis*, 2015.

[47] Suman Nath. MAdScope: Characterizing Mobile In-App Targeted Ads. In *ACM MobiSys*, 2015.

[48] Vern Paxson. Bro: A System for Detecting Network Intruders in Real-Time. *Computer Networks*, 31(23-24):2435–2463, 1999.

[49] Enric Pujol, Philipp Richter, Balakrishnan Chandrasekaran, Georgios Smaragdakis, Anja Feldmann, Bruce Maggs, and K. C. Ng. Back-Office Web traffic on the Internet. In *ACM IMC*, 2014.

[50] Kent Rasmussen, Alex Wilson, and Abram Hindle. Green Mining: Energy Consumption of Advertisement Blocking Methods. In *ACM GREENS*, 2014.

[51] Philipp Richter, Nikolaos Chatzis, Georgios Smaragdakis, Anja Feldmann, and Walter Willinger. Distilling the Internet's Application Mix from Packet-Sampled Traffic. In *PAM*, 2015.

[52] Fabian Schneider, Bernhard Ager, Gregor Maier, Anja Feldmann, and Steve Uhlig. Pitfalls in HTTP Traffic Measurements and Analysis. In *PAM*, 2012.

[53] Kevin Springborn and Paul Barford. Impression Fraud in Online Advertising via Pay-Per-View Networks. In *USENIX Security*, 2013.

[54] Brett Stone-Gross, Ryan Stevens, Apostolis Zarras, Richard Kemmerer, Chris Kruegel, and Giovanni Vigna. Understanding Fraudulent Activities in Online Ad Exchanges. In *ACM IMC*, 2011.

[55] Narseo Vallina-Rodríguez, Jay Shah, Alessandro Finamore, Yan Grunenberger, Konstantina Papagiannaki, Hamed Haddadi, and Jon Crowcroft. Breaking for Commercials: Characterizing Mobile Advertising. In *ACM IMC*, 2012.

[56] Guowu Xie, Marios Iliofotou, Thomas Karagiannis, Michalis Faloutsos, and Yaohui Jin. Resurf: Reconstructing Web-Surfing Activity from Network Traffic. In *IEEE IFIP*, 2013.

[57] Xinyu Xing, Wei Meng, Byoungyoung Lee, Udi Weinsberg, Anmol Sheth, Roberto Perdisci, and Wenke Lee. Understanding Malvertising Through Ad-Injecting Browser Extensions. In *WWW*, 2015.

[58] Shuai Yuan, Jun Wang, and Xiaoxue Zhao. Real-Time Bidding for Online Advertising: Measurement and Analysis. In *ACM ADKDD*, 2013.

[59] Apostolis Zarras, Alexandros Kapravelos, Gianluca Stringhini, Thorsten Holz, Christopher Kruegel, and Giovanni Vigna. The Dark Alleys of Madison Avenue: Understanding Malicious Advertisements. In *ACM IMC*, 2014.

Measuring the Impact and Perception of Acceptable Advertisements

Robert J. Walls Eric D. Kilmer Nathaniel Lageman Patrick D. McDaniel
Department of Computer Science and Engineering
Pennsylvania State University, University Park, PA, USA
{rjwalls, ekilmer, njl5114, mcdaniel}@cse.psu.edu

ABSTRACT

In 2011, Adblock Plus—the most widely-used ad blocking software—began to permit some advertisements as part of their *Acceptable Ads* program. Under this program, some ad networks and content providers pay to have their advertisements shown to users. Such practices have been controversial among both users and publishers. In a step towards informing the discussion about these practices, we present the first comprehensive study of the Acceptable Ads program. Specifically, we characterize which advertisements are allowed and how the whitelisting has changed since its introduction in 2011. We show that the list of filters used to whitelist acceptable advertisements has been updated on average every 1.5 days and grew from 9 filters in 2011 to over 5,900 in the Spring of 2015. More broadly, the current whitelist triggers filters on 59% of the top 5,000 websites. Our measurements also show that the program allows advertisements on 2.6 million parked domains. Lastly, we take the lessons learned from our analysis and suggest ways to improve the transparency of the whitelisting process.

Categories and Subject Descriptors

H.3.5 [**On-line Information Services**]: Web-based services; K.4.4 [**Computers and Society**]: Electronic Commerce

General Terms

Acceptable Ads; Adblock Plus; Ad Avoidance

1. INTRODUCTION

Over 144 million users employ ad blocking software [27]. Users are motivated by a desire to hide intrusive ads, increase their privacy, or protect themselves from malicious adverts [34]. Yet, some claim ad blocking threatens the Web's business model. Indeed, Google lost an estimated $887 million in revenue to blocking in Q2 2013 [26,31].

In 2011 Eyeo GmbH—the maker of the most popular ad blocker, Adblock Plus—introduced their *Acceptable Ads* program. Through this program, Adblock Plus allows some "non-intrusive" ads that satisfy a set of community-driven guidelines, such as "ads should never obscure page content." According to Eyeo, their goal is to strike a balance between the needs of users and publishers, and they emphasize *transparency* as key to the program's success [6, 22]. However, Eyeo drew strong criticism when they confirmed some companies—including Google, Microsoft, and Amazon—paid undisclosed amounts to be included in the whitelist [9,32]. Some view this arrangement as a conflict of interest; the organization that provides blocking software is in a position to indirectly profit from ads being shown.

The Acceptable Ads program impacts millions of users and billions of dollars,[1] but little is known about the whitelisting process or how it impacts users. In this paper, we provide the first comprehensive study of the Acceptable Ads program. We identify how the users experience the Web under this program by exploring the use of ad policies (called filter lists, or just whitelists). We develop tools and techniques to explore and correlate information from Internet measurements, a complete history of the program's whitelist, instrumented browser behavior, and user surveys. In this, we have focused on the following questions:

1. *What is in the whitelist and how has it changed over time?* We find that at the current revision, Rev. 988, the whitelist contains 5,936 filters and is updated every 1.5 days to add or modify 11.4 filters on average.
2. *Who benefits from the whitelist?* We find that the whitelist identifies 3,545 unique explicitly listed publisher domains (including 15 of the top 100), and that five general-purpose filter types are responsible for allowing content on 2,676,165 parked domains.
3. *How do we measure the impact of the whitelist?* We survey whitelist use in the Alexa top 5,000 most popular websites as well as 5,000 sites from the 5k to 1 million most popular. The current whitelist triggers filters on 59% of the top 5,000 websites but explicitly whitelist only a few percent of less popular sites.
4. *How do users perceive acceptable advertisements?* A survey of over 300 users showed wide dissension on many advertisements that were judged as being invasive. One area of agreement was clear: advertisements interspersed with and largely indistinguishable from web content were deemed as undesirable.

Our study is motivated by other large-scale Web and security measurement studies, including those characterizing SPAM [14, 17], affiliate programs [20], domain abuse [4,7], and malicious advertising [19,34]. We begin by detailing the operation of Adblock

IMC'15, October 28–30, 2015, Tokyo, Japan.

ACM 978-1-4503-3848-6/15/10 ...$15.00.
DOI: http://dx.doi.org/10.1145/2815675.2815703 .

[1]The Internet Advertising Bureau reported a record high of $12.4 billion in U.S. advertising revenue for Q3 2014, breaking the previous record of $12.1 billion in Q4 of 2013 [13].

```
<iframe id="ad_main" frameborder="0" scrolling="no" name="ad_main" src="http://static.adzerk.
    net/reddit/ads.html?sr=-reddit.com,loggedout&amp;bust2#http://www.reddit.com"></iframe>
```

Figure 1: Sample ad code from Reddit. This code displays an `iframe` for an Adzerk advertisement on the right side of the page. Similar code constructions are common across different sites using the same ad network. This allows Adblock Plus to use a single filter to block ads on multiple domains.

Plus and the Acceptable Ads program. We then characterize how the program works in practice. Finally, we offer suggestions for improving the transparency of the whitelisting process.

2. ADBLOCK PLUS

Adblock Plus is the most widely used browser extension with over 50 million users across all major browsers.[2] In 2014, the extension's Firefox version was downloaded 68 million times and boasted 19.2 million users daily.[3] Adblock Plus is open source and available free of charge.

Adblock Plus was created by Michael McDonald's as a fork of Henrik Aasted Sørensen's Adblock project. In January 2006, Wladimir Palant rewrote the code and released it as a separate project for Firefox. Since then, Adblock Plus has been ported to run on all major browsers: Chrome (Dec. 2010 [28], formerly AdThwart [3]), Opera (Nov. 2012 [10]), Internet Explorer (Aug. 2013 [29]), and Safari (Jan. 2014 [25]). Eyeo offers an Android version, but it is not available in the Google Play store [30].

Adblock Plus uses textually encoded *filters* to determine the content shown on a page. *Blocking filters* restrict page content, while *exception filters* override any matching blocking filters to allow the content. Filter definitions generally consist of: *(i)* a *matching expression* that specifies what content to block (or allow), e.g., the URL of an advertising network; and *(ii)* a set of filter options, e.g., the `image` option applies the filter to image requests. A detailed description of the filter syntax is included in Appendix A.

Adblock Plus users rarely write their own filters. Instead, they subscribe to regularly published text-based *filter lists*. By default, Adblock Plus subscribes users to two filter lists: the first, *EasyList*, contains tens of thousands of filters to block advertisements and covers most common ad networks. Other blocking extensions also use EasyList, including the second most popular blocker, AdBlock. The second default filterlist—which we refer to as the *Acceptable Ads whitelist*—is used to implement the Acceptable Ads program. In short, this list overrides the user's other filter lists allowing certain publishers to show advertisments. We characterize the scope and impact of the whitelist in later sections.

Users can subscribe to additional filter lists that provide functionality beyond blocking advertisements including: disabling tracking, allowing the user to "browse the web truly anonymously", blocking known malicious domains, and removing social media buttons, such as the Facebook Like button.[4] We defer analysis of these lists to future work.

2.1 Filter Matching

Broadly, individual filters match one of two types of content: *Web requests* or *page elements*. We briefly describe each below.

2.1.1 Matching Web Requests

Publishers often rely on third-party ad networks, such as Adzerk or Google Adsense, to display advertisements on their site. These

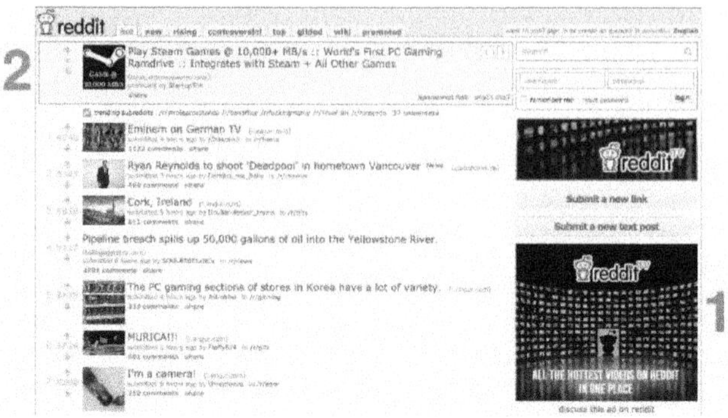

Figure 2: Acceptable ads on `Reddit.com`. Reddit is a member of the Acceptable Ads program. Consequently, Adblock Plus allows both of the ads on this page. A third-party network, Adzerk, serves the ad on the right side (labeled **1**). The sponsored link (labeled **2**) is embedded directly into the page.

networks make it possible for publishers to show ads by simply including a small snippet of code provided by the ad network. This straightforward interface also simplifies the blocking process by allowing a single filter to block ads on multiple sites.

For example, `reddit.com` uses the code in Figure 1 to show Adzerk advertisements. When an Adblock Plus user visits the page, their browser will make a *third-party* web request to fetch the advertisement from Adzerk. Adblock Plus will preempt this request to check if the request URL matches any filters. If the match is for a blocking filter, such as the following, Adblock Plus will cancel the request, stopping the browser from fetching the ad.

```
||adzerk.net^$third-party
```

In short, the above filter will block all third-party requests to `adzerk.net` or any of its subdomains. For a more complete explanation of filter syntax see Appendix A.

If the request matches an exception filter,[5] then Adblock Plus allows it, *regardless of any blocking filter matches*. The advertisement is then shown as an image on the right of the page—denoted by the bold **1** in Figure 2.

2.1.2 Matching Page Elements

Adblock Plus uses different filter syntax for matching advertising elements embedded directly into the page. Similar to how request filters match URLs, element filters use CSS Selectors[6] to identify elements based on attributes such as the element's `class` or `id`.

The following filter blocks the "sponsored link" at the top of Reddit's front page (bold **2** in Figure 2) by matching elements with an `id` attribute of `siteTable_organic`.

```
reddit.com###siteTable_organic
```

However, Adblock Plus does not block either of the advertisements in our example. It allows these ads because Reddit is a part of the Acceptable Ads program.

[2] `https://adblockplus.org/en/about`
[3] `https://addons.mozilla.org/en-US/firefox/addon/adblock-plus/statistics/`
[4] `https://adblockplus.org/en/features`
[5] Request exception filters are denoted by the `@@` prefix.
[6] `http://www.w3.org/TR/CSS21/selector.html`

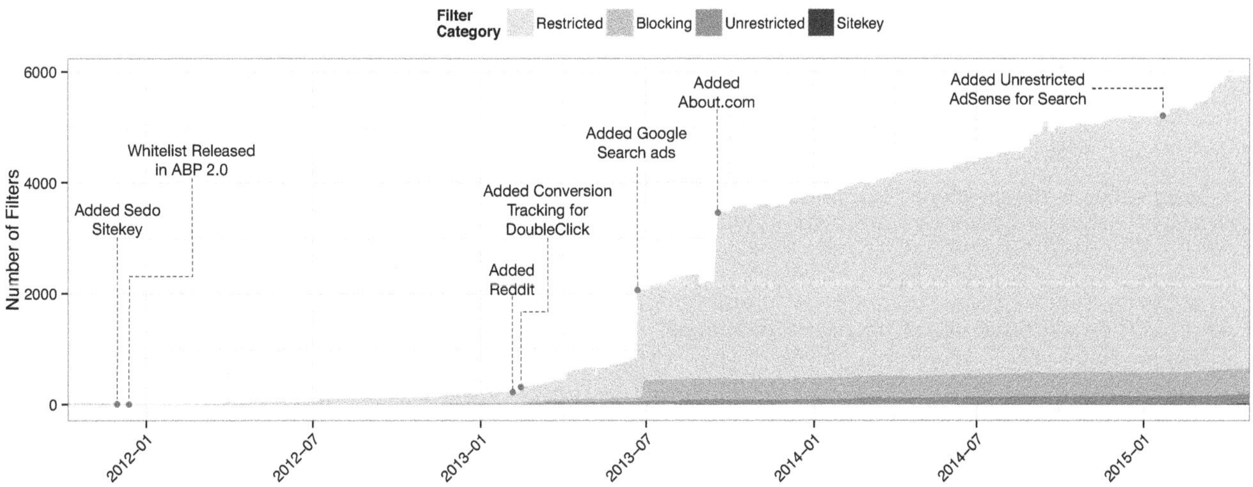

Figure 3: The growth of the Acceptable Ads whitelist. The whitelist has grown steadily since its introduction in 2011. On average, this filter list is updated every 1.5 days, adding or modifying 11.4 exception filters. The most recent version (Rev. 988 on April 28, 2015) includes 5,936 filters. Among these are exceptions for domain parking services, conversions tracking, and third-party ad networks.

3. ACCEPTABLE ADS

In May 2011, Adblock Plus's creator, Wladimir Palant, outlined the criteria for Acceptable Ads with the goal of "encourag[ing] websites to use advertising that users don't perceive as annoying."[7] These guidelines have been refined multiple times based on feedback from the community. Whitelisted sites are required to adhere to these guidelines. To paraphrase the most recent criteria [1], sites must ensure that:

1. Advertisements cannot contain animations, sounds, or "attention-grabbing" images.
2. Advertisements cannot obscure page content or obstruct reading flow, i.e., the ad cannot be placed in the middle of a block of text.
3. Advertisements must be clearly distinguished from the page content and must be labeled using the word "advertisement" or equivalent terms.
4. Banner advertisements should not force the user to scroll down to view page content.

After publishing the initial Acceptable Ads requirements, Palant and his partner, Till Faida, created Eyeo GmbH in August 2011. Their goal was to make the Adblock Plus project "more sustainable" [8]. The following month, the company began surveying users about their willingness to allow advertising in some form.[8] By the year's end released Acceptable Ads as an opt-out feature in Adblock Plus version 2.0.[9]

The program has been controversial. Eyeo drew criticism from both users and publishers when they confirmed that some companies—including Google, Microsoft, and Amazon—paid undisclosed amounts to be included in the whitelist [9,32]. Eyeo has stated that received funds are used to sustain the program. Further, they state that whitelisting is free for smaller sites and *all* participants of the program must abide by the acceptable ads criteria.

Eyeo's practices have incensed some publishers to such a degree that they have accused the company of "extortion" and "shaking down" websites [23]. Recently, this criticism has escalated to the courtroom, and Eyeo is facing lawsuits in France and Germany [11, 12,16]. In Germany, publishers filed suit against Eyeo claiming that their product is anti-competitive and threatens their ability to generate revenue. The regional court in Hamburg ruled in favor of Eyeo after a four month trial [15,33].

3.1 Filter List Maintenance

Eyeo regularly updates the whitelist. On average, the company adds or modifies 11.4 filters every 1.5 days, and has a documented process for requesting new whitelist filters to be added. The process of adding new sites to the Acceptable Ads program comprises four steps: contact, application, agreement, and inclusion.

The first step, *contact*, consists of communication between Eyeo and a perspective publisher. Either party may initiate this dialog [24]. Next, Eyeo works with the publisher to ensure their site follows the Acceptable Ads guidelines (the *application* step). Once Eyeo confirms the site's advertisements adhere to their policy, they establish a private *agreement* with the publisher. These agreements may involve a fee, but Eyeo does not currently disclose the fee structure, monetary value, or list of paying publishers. However, anecdotal sources claim the company has requested up to 30% of recovered revenue [5], and Eyeo acknowledges they have experimented with both flat and performance-based fees [24]. After reaching an agreement, Adblock Plus adds the filter to the list and solicits community feedback on the application via an online forum.[10] Forum posts made after Nov. 2014 include links to the whitelist revision and optional sample screenshots.

4. WHITELIST ANALYSIS

In the following sections, we examine the complete history of Eyeo's Acceptable Ads program. Our analysis combines whitelist changes with public disclosures and empirical observations of browser behavior. We focus on answering the following broad questions.

[7] https://adblockplus.org/forum/viewtopic.php?f=4&t=7551

[8] https://adblockplus.org/releases/adblock-plus-1310-released

[9] https://adblockplus.org/releases/adblock-plus-20-released

[10] https://adblockplus.org/forum/viewforum.php?f=12

Year	Revisions	Filters Added	Filters Removed	Domains Added	Domains Removed
2011	26	25	17	5	1
2012	47	225	30	59	4
2013	311	5152	1555	2248	73
2014	386	2179	775	859	125
2015	219	1227	495	371	207
Total	989	8808	2872	3542	410

Table 1: Yearly activity for the Acceptable Ads whitelist. This table shows the year, number of revisions, number of first-party domains, and number of changes to exception filters—modifications are counted as new filters. The data covers changes up to Apr. 28, 2015 (Rev. 988).

1. How has the whitelist changed over time? We analyze all revisions of the whitelist to quantify the number of domains and filters. Section 4.1.
2. Who benefits explicitly from the whitelist? We first characterize the whitelist filters based on their scope and target content. Then, we parse the whitelist filters to extract explicitly listed publisher domains and group these domains based on popularity and category. Section 4.2.
3. How do we measure the impact of the whitelist? We run an automated survey across the top 5,000 most popular websites and 5,000 additional sites from the 5K to 1M top sites. Section 5.
4. How do users perceive acceptable advertisements? We survey 305 users on Amazon's Mechanical Turk platform and ask them to rate 15 "acceptable" advertisements. Section 6

4.1 Whitelist History

Eyeo tracks all whitelist changes in a public Mercurial repository.[11] Using this repository, we extracted 988 versions of the whitelist dating from the start of the whitelist in Oct. 2011 to Apr. 2015. The most recent version (Rev. 988) comprises 5,936 distinct filters. The majority of these exceptions allow advertisements and other advertising functionality such as conversion tracking.

Figure 3 shows the growth of the Acceptable Ads whitelist over time. There are two large jumps visible in the figure. The first corresponds to Google's official addition to the whitelist on June 21, 2013 (Rev. 200).[12] In total, this revision added 1,262 filters for Google search advertisements on `google.com` and other variations of this URL, e.g., `google.co.uk`. The second jump was caused by filters for `ask.com`, `about.com`, and related subdomains, e.g., `cars.about.com`. These additions are discussed in Section 7.

Table 1 summarizes the yearly changes. The second full year of the whitelist (2013) saw the list grow by an order of magnitude over the previous year: Eyeo made 4,633 filter changes, bringing the total to 2,319 publisher domains compared to just 60 domains in 2012. However, as we discuss below, these numbers belie the actual scope of the whitelist.

4.2 Whitelist Scope

In order to understand who benefits from the Acceptable Ads program, we need to first understand the *scope* of a whitelist filter, i.e., the set of domains that can activate the filter. For some filters, this list of applicable domains is explicitly enumerated in the filter's definition. We call these *restricted* filters. For others—namely *unrestricted* and *sitekey* filters—the filter can apply to *any* domain. The implication here is that it is impossible to determine the actual impact of these filters using filter definitions alone. Instead, we can only empirically estimate this value through site surveys (Section 5).

[11] `https://hg.adblockplus.org/exceptionrules`

[12] `https://hg.adblockplus.org/exceptionrules/rev/8bdf815a5291`

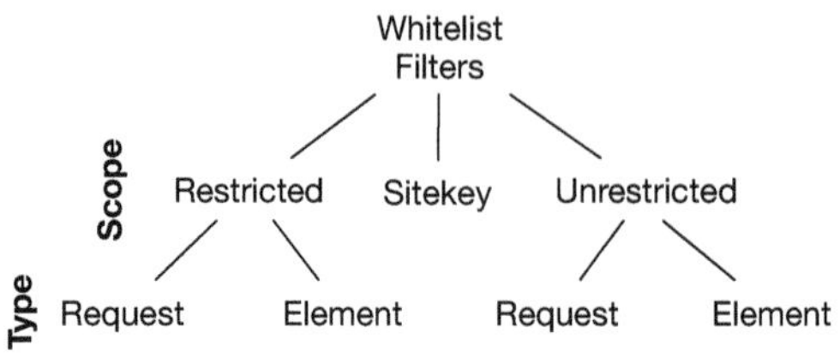

Figure 4: Hierarchy of Filter Types in the Whitelist.

Figure 4 illustrates a hierarchy of whitelist filter types and their scope. We discuss each class in detail below.

4.2.1 *Restricted Exception Filters*

A *restricted* exception filter explicitly defines the first-party domains for which it activates, i.e., the filter will only match when the user is browsing a page on one of these domains. The syntax for defining the domain list depends on the filter's type. For example, the following are two of the whitelist's restricted exceptions for `reddit.com`.

```
reddit.com#@##ad_main
@@||adzerk.net/reddit/$subdocument,
    document,domain=reddit.com
```

The first filter—an element exception—instructs Adblock Plus to allow any `reddit.com` elements with the `ad_main` identifier. For element filters, restricted domains are prepended to the start. The second filter allows requests to `adzerk.net`, the ad provider for `reddit.com`. In this case, the filter is restricted via the `domain` option.

Restricted exception filters make up 89% of the whitelist and cover 3,545 fully qualified domains, including search engines (Microsoft, Yahoo, Google), commercial sales (Walmart, Amazon), content publishers (Reddit, About.com, Cracked), and ISPs (Comcast, Time Warner), amongst others. Many of the fully qualified domains appearing in the whitelist map to the same publisher. For instance, the whitelist includes over 1,044 subdomains for `about.com`, including `cars.about.com` and `food.about.com`. Additionally, there are 919 country-based domains for Google properties included in the whitelist, e.g., `google.co.uk` and `google.de`. Table 2 shows the respective count and Alexa rankings for fully qualified domains.

4.2.2 *Unrestricted Exception Filters*

An *unrestricted* exception filter applies to all first-party domains, i.e., these exceptions can match on any site. The whitelist uses unrestricted exceptions primarily for two purposes. First, many of these filters enable conversion tracking. Broadly, conversion tracking is used to measure if an advertisement resulted in some user action, e.g., user purchased the product after clicking on the ad. Second, unrestricted filters are used to whitelist specific ad networks.

Alexa Partition	Fully Qualified Domains
All	1,990
Top 1,000,000	1,286 (0.12%)
Top 5,000	316 (6.32%)
Top 1,000	167(16.70%)
Top 500	112(22.40%)
Top 100	33(33.00%)

Table 2: Domains explicitly included in the whitelist. The whitelist contains restricted exception filters for 3,544 fully qualified publisher domains. This corresponds to 1,990 effective second-level domains, e.g., `google.com` is the effective second-level domain of `maps.google.com`. Percentages are on the total number of domains within the particular Alexa partition.

This practice allows the ad network to show advertisements across multiple domains without having to explicitly include these domain in the whitelist. PageFair is an example of the latter.

PageFair. While PageFair is oft-quoted for their reports on the prevalence of ad blocking and its monetary costs—in fact, we cite one in the introduction—the company is also an ad network involved in the Acceptable Ads program.[13]

```
@@||pagefair.net^$third-party
@@||tracking.admarketplace.net^$third-party
@@||imp.admarketplace.net^$third-party
```

These unrestricted exception filters allow PageFair to show advertisements on any partnered website without needing a separate exception for each domain. The company takes a "minority share of the additional advertising revenue" that they provide publishers. PageFair also pays Eyeo to participate in the Acceptable Ads program.

Another advertising network, Influads, has similar unrestricted exceptions.

```
@@||influads.com^$script,image
#@##influads_block
```

The second of these filters—an element exception—is not actually limited to Influads advertisements; instead, this filter will match any element on any site as long as the element's id is `influads_block`. This is the only example of an unrestricted element filter in the whitelist, and possibly an oversight by the whitelist's authors.

In Section 5, we further explore the impact of the 156 unrestricted exception filters using a survey of popular domains.

4.2.3 Sitekey Exception Filters

A *sitekey* exception filter includes a DER-encoded, base-64 representation of an RSA public key.

```
! Text ads on Sedo parking domains
@@$sitekey=MFwwDQYJK...wEAAQ,document
```

Adblock Plus allows advertisements on *any* domain that presents a valid signature signed with a current sitekey. Effectively, sitekeys delegate the task of whitelisting to the publisher.

Adblock Plus calculates the signature by signing a string containing the URI, hostname, and user-agent string of the HTTP request. Adblock Plus then compares the result with the signature returned by the server in: *(i)* the `X-Adblock-key` header of the HTTP response, and *(ii)* the `data-adblockkey` attribute of the returned page.

The first sitekey—added to the whitelist before its release—belongs to Sedo, a domain parking and hosting company based in Cologne,

[13] `https://pagefair.com/about/`

Company	Whitelisted	Domains (.com)
Sedo	2011-11-30	1,060,129
ParkingCrew	2013-05-27	368,703
RookMedia	2013-07-31	949
Uniregistry	2013-09-25	1,246,359
Digimedia	2014-07-02	25
		2,676,165

Table 3: Domain statistics for the five parking services whitelisted by Adblock Plus. RookMedia was removed from the whitelist on Sept. 16, 2014 (rev. 656); all others remain active.

Germany (the same city as Eyeo). The company's founder, Tim Schumacher, is also Eyeo's chief investor and participated in the initial development of the Acceptable Ads program [24].

Currently, there are 4 sitekeys and 25 sitekey filters in the whitelist, all belonging to domain parking services. They are, in order of introduction, Sedo, ParkingCrew, Uniregistry, and Digimedia. A fifth sitekey (for Rook Media) was removed from the whitelist in Sept. 2014.

Parked domains typically exist to show advertisements (and sell domains), usually in the form of links to pages related to the domain name. Misspellings of popular sites are also frequently parked. For example, `reddit.cm` is a parked domain that advertises dating services and photos of celebrities; this domain is whitelisted under the Acceptable Ads program using a sitekey. For a more complete treatment of domain parking, see the recent work by Alrwais et al. [4].

Using the top-level domain zone file for `.com` domains, we identified approximately 3 million parked domains managed by one of the parking services listed in Table 3. Specifically, we focused on those domains whose name servers belong to one of the sitekey parking services. For example, Sedo domains use the `ns1.sedoparking.com` and `ns2.sedoparking.com` nameservers. The list of parking name servers, in part, was derived from the example sites given in Adblock Plus online forums. We used automated tools to visit each suspected domain and only recorded those that presented a sitekey signature.

Table 3 provides a lower bound on the number of domains for each parking service. In total, we find the four active sitekeys account for at least 2,676,165 distinct whitelisted domains.

Finally, some of the above sites required special accommodations to scrape. For example, ParkingCrew domains employ countermeasures to prevent scraping, returning a `403` response if the user-agent string matches that of a tool like `curl`. Further, some domains, e.g., Uniregistry, behave differently given the presence or absence of specific cookie values. For instance, when a user visits a Uniregistry domain for the first time, the site will return a page that first generates a cookie and then redirects the user to another page with advertisements (and the sitekey signature).

Factoring Sitekeys. All current sitekeys use 512 bit RSA keys (RSA-155). Such small key sizes are well within the factoring capabilities of an individual or publisher with modest hardware resources. To demonstrate this, we constructed a cluster comprising 8 desktop computers running Ubuntu 14.04, each with an Intel Xeon E5-2630 clocked at 2.30GHz and 32 GB of memory. We used the CADO-NFS[14] implementation of the Number Field Sieve algorithm. This setup took approximately one week on average to factor each sitekey.

In Figure 5, we demonstrate how an adversarial publisher could use a factored sitekey to show intrusive or malicious advertising.

[14] `http://cado-nfs.gforge.inria.fr/`

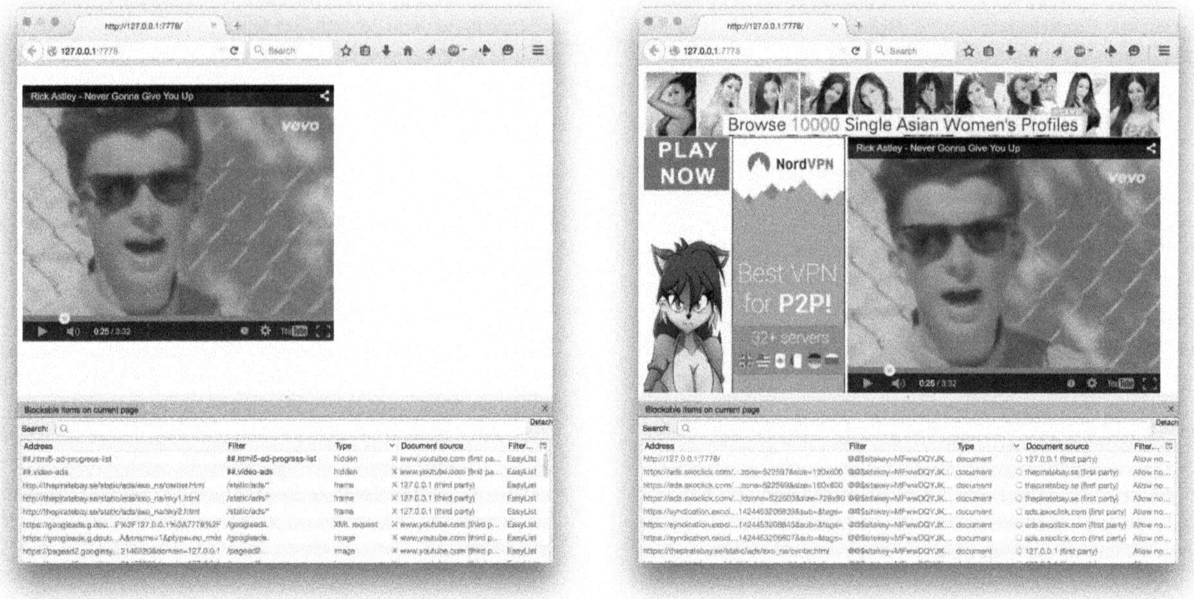

(a) Without sitekey. (b) With sitekey.

Figure 5: Exploiting sitekeys. Using a cluster of desktop computers, we were able to factor one of the whitelist sitekeys in five days. The derived key allowed our test site to bypass Adblock Plus's blocking entirely.

For our proof of concept, we used Adblock Plus's default settings with both the EasyList blacklist and the Acceptable Ads whitelist enabled. The figure shows our test site before and after adding the sitekey. In short, our test site bypassed all blocking filters.

5. MEASURING FILTER BEHAVIOR

Our previous analysis—focusing on the content of the whitelist—provides a necessary but incomplete picture of the whitelist's behavior. For instance, the whitelist includes an exception filter for PageFair advertisements, but it does not list any of the domains that use PageFair.

Complicating matters, whitelist behavior also depends on a myriad of more subtle factors including filter ambiguity, unpredictable website behavior, and complex interactions between different filters and filter lists. In this Section, we expand on our previous analysis using empirical measurements of filter activation.

Methodology. We instrument Adblock Plus to measure filter activations on domains drawn from four sample groups: *(i)* the 5,000 most popular domains,[15] *(ii)* 1,000 domains randomly sampled from the rank 5K–50K popularity strata, *(iii)* 1,000 domains randomly sampled from the rank 50K–100K popularity strata, *(iv)* 1,000 domains randomly sampled from the rank 100K–1M popularity strata.

We instrumented Adblock Plus to record filter activations and used Selenium[16] to visit each domain. We surveyed only the landing page of each site. By limiting our visit to the first page, our survey produces a lower bound on the number of matching filters as some filters will not activate without user interaction. For instance, Google search ads only appear after a search.

Figure 6 shows the filter activations on the top 50 sites with at least one filter activation. We show the number and type of filter matches by the height and color of the bars, respectively. Domains explicitly included in the whitelist are shown in bold along the x-axis.

This figure illustrates a number of subtle issues when measuring filter behavior. First, 12 domains not explicitly included in the whitelist nevertheless activate whitelist filters, e.g., `youtube.com`. Second, whitelist filters activate needlessly. That is, the filter matches content that would not have otherwise been blocked by the EasyList blacklist. Third, sites may behave differently based on browser state and configuration. For example, `ask.com` will activate more filters if the user does not have specific cookies in the browser cache. Further, some sites will show different advertisements if the sites detects the presence of Adblock Plus, e.g., `imgur.com`.

Finally, not all whitelist filters are directly responsible for displaying advertisements, e.g., `gstatic` exceptions. Many common exceptions are for conversion tracking and do not visually impact the website.

These results suggests the need for more complex analysis techniques to fully characterize the whitelist's behavior. We leave such explorations for future work.

5.1 Active Filters on the Top 5K Domains

Of the Top 5,000 domains, 3,956 activated at least one Adblock Plus filter from either the EasyList blacklist or the Acceptable Ads whitelist. The remaining 1,044 domains were largely non-English (and thus out of the purview of Easylist) or required additional user interaction to trigger filters, e.g., logins, search queries, etc.

Figure 7 shows the distribution of the total and distinct whitelist filter matches per surveyed site. We include only domains with at least one whitelist filter activation (2,934 sites). `Toyota.com` saw the most filter activations with 83 total matches for 8 distinct filters, 5% of the surveyed sites activated at least 12 exception filters (non-distinct), and, on average, each site activated 2.6 distinct whitelist filters.

[15]Website popularity was based on Alexa rankings from Apr. 2015. `http://www.alexa.com/topsites`
[16]`http://www.seleniumhq.org/`

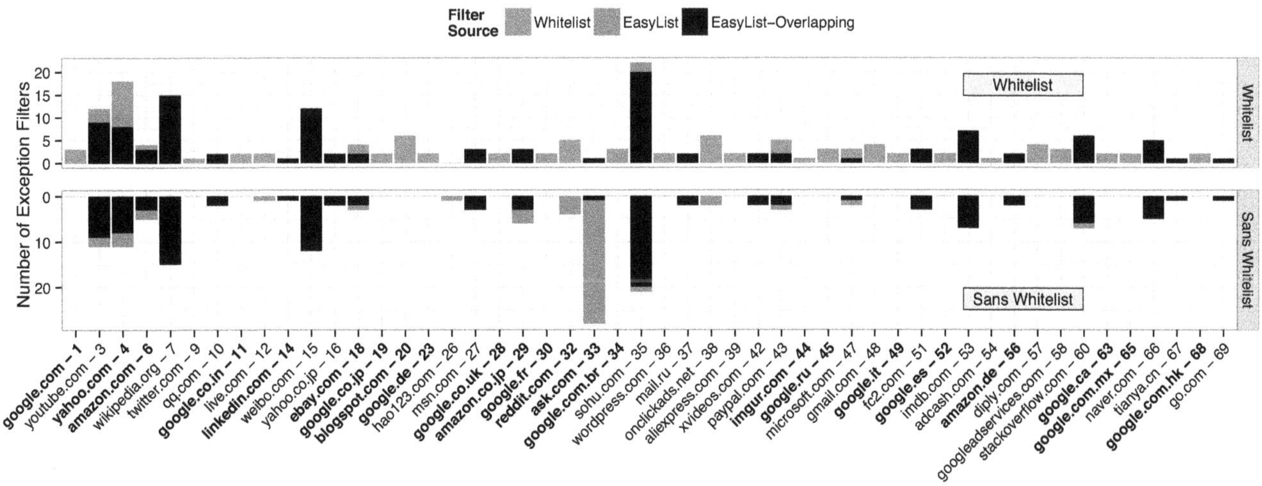

Figure 6: Filter matches with and without the whitelist enabled. The upper panel shows the filter matches when both the whitelist and EasyList are enabled, the bottom shows matches when just EasyList is enabled. We limit this figure to sites that match at least one filter from either the whitelist or EasyList (and elide `sina.com.cn` for ease of presentation). Each bar is labeled with the domain and rank. **Bold** denotes domains explicitly included in a whitelist filter definition. The height of the bar represents the number of matches and the fill specifies the filter's source. Filters that match in both configurations are shown in black.

	Filter (Truncated)	Domains	Modified	Purpose
1	`@@||stats.g.doubleclick.net^$script,image`	1,559	2013-02-21	Conversion tracking.
2	`@@||googleadservices.com^$third-party`	1,535	2013-06-21	Google search ads.
3	`@@||gstatic.com^$third-party`	1,282	2013-06-21	Google search ads.
4	`@@||googleads.g.doubleclick.net/pagead/view...`	929	2013-08-08	Experimental.
5	`@@||google.*/ads/user-lists/$image,subdoc...`	892	2013-05-31	Conversion tracking.
6	`@@||googletagmanager.com/gtm.js`	746	2013-08-08	Experimental.
7	`@@||fls.doubleclick.net^$subdocument,image`	300	2013-03-20	Conversion tracking.
8	`@@||doubleclick.net/activity*$subdocument,i...`	135	2013-08-08	Experimental.
9	`@@||google.com/adsense/search/*.js$domain=~...`	78	2015-01-22	*Google Adsense(A-filter)*
10	`@@||google.*/ads/conversion`	69	2014-11-28	Conversion tracking.
11	`@@||p.skimresources.com/px.gif?ch=1&rn=`	53	2013-11-07	Text to affiliate links.
12	`||p.skimresources.com/px.gif?ch=2&rn=`	53	2013-11-07	Blocking, text to affiliate links.
13	`@@||r.skimresources.com/api/?$script`	48	2013-08-27	Text to affiliate links.
14	`@@||s.skimresources.com/js/*.skimlinks.js^$...`	48	2013-08-14	Text to affiliate links.
15	`@@||t.skimresources.com/api/track.php?$script`	47	2013-08-27	Text to affiliate links.
16	`@@||pagefair.net^$third-party`	31	2014-01-30	PageFair ads.
17	`#@##influads_block`	30	2012-11-08	Influads ads.
18	`||viglink.com/images/pixel.gif?ch=2$third-party`	25	2014-06-02	Blocking, text to affiliate links.
19	`@@||doubleclick.net/json`	22	2013-08-08	Experimental.
20	`@@||google.com/gen_204`	20	2013-08-08	Experimental.

Table 4: Most common whitelist filters in the survey. This table displays the 20 most common exception filters from our survey of Alexa's top 5,000 websites. Number 9 on this list was added without community vetting; it allows Google's AdSense for search on nearly *all* domains.

Table 4 shows the 20 most common whitelist exception filters in the Top 5,000 group. As expected, all of these filters are unrestricted. As we discussed previously, unrestricted filters can trigger on any site.

The most activated filter, `@@||stats.g.doubleclick.net^$script,image`, triggered on 1,559 domains (31.2%). This filter is used to allows conversion tracking. The second-most popular filter, `@@||googleadservices.com^$third-party`, was observed on 1,535 domains, and allows advertisements from Google's AdSense network. The third-most popular filter, `@@||gstatic.com^$third-party`, occurred on 1,282 domains. This filter does not appear to contribute to the visibility of advertisements. Instead, the Google-owned `gstatic.com` serves fonts, scripts, images, and other resources to sites to increase browsing performance. The necessity of the `gstatic.com` filter is unclear to us, given that EasyList does not currently contain any filters that would block the observed `gstatic.com` requests.

We observed one unrestricted element exception filter, `#@##influads_block`, which activated on 30 different domains. As discussed in Section 4.2.2, this filter prevents the blocking of content contained within any element with an id of `influads_block`.

5.2 Filter Activations Across Categories

Figure 8 shows the number of filters triggered by domains in each group. The top portion shows categorical filter activation frequencies while the lower portion shows filter activation frequency

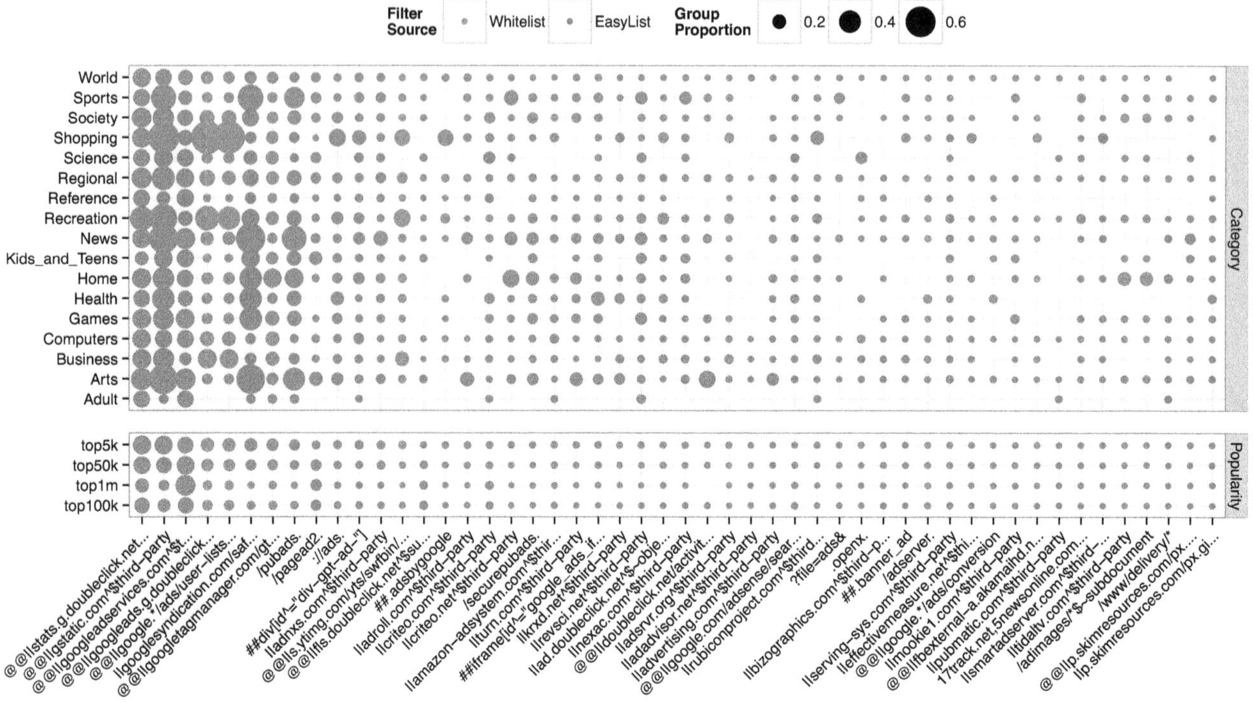

Figure 8: Filter matches per group ranking. Each row represents 1,000 domains within the respective Alexa ranking group. For each group we plot the frequency each filter is triggered by domains in that group.

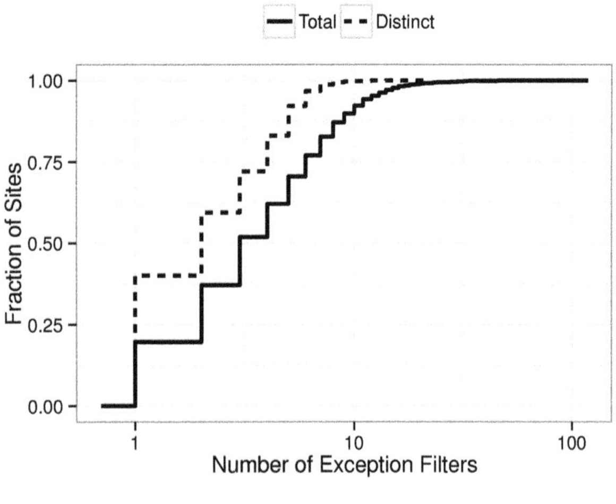

Figure 7: ECDF of filter matches per surveyed domain. We only include domains with at least one match. A single filter may match multiple elements (or requests) on a single domain; the solid line represents the total number of matches while the dashed line is the number of unique matching filters.

for the most popular sites taken from Alexa. We chose the top 50 most frequently activated filters and found that the 5 most activated filters out of both the EasyList and Whitelist were all filters from the whitelist. These filters also related to Google. This implies that these filters may be more broad than necessary.

We find that the whitelist filters are skewed more towards shopping websites, which we can attribute to the filter's purpose.

We also find that 4 of these filters were triggered more often by the top 5,000 websites than by any of the other groups. There is one filter that was used most often by the group of domains consisting from Alexa rank 100,000 to 1,000,000. This particular filter is used for conversion tracking.

6. USER PERCEPTION

Underlying the Acceptable Ads program is the goal that both publishers and users find the whitelisted ads to be acceptable. There have been many studies of how users perceive Web advertisements (e.g., [21]), and the degree to which they intrude on the user experience (e.g., [18]). In this section, we build on these efforts to survey user perception of advertisements on popular websites based on the criteria stated in Eyeo's Acceptable Ads guidelines [1]. We used Amazon's Mechanical Turk [2] to solicit participation, limiting our pool to workers with at least 5,000 approved submissions and at least 98% approval rate. Each of the 305 respondents were paid 1$US and completed the 72 question survey in about 10 minutes. 50% of the users used some form of ad blocking software before, with 61% using the Google Chrome browser, 28% using FireFox, 9% Safari, and 1% each for Opera and Internet Explorer. The results of the survey are discussed below and shown in Figure 9.

The online survey showed eight different sites, each containing one or more advertisements allowed by Adblock Plus. The eight sites were selected based on their popularity and diversity of ad placement. Specifically, we choose a search engine (Google), an image hosting service (Imgur), an online retailer (Walmart), a Web service (IsItUp.com), an online game forum (Utopia-game.com), a humor website (Cracked.com), a viral content curator (ViralNova), and a user-submitted content site (Reddit).

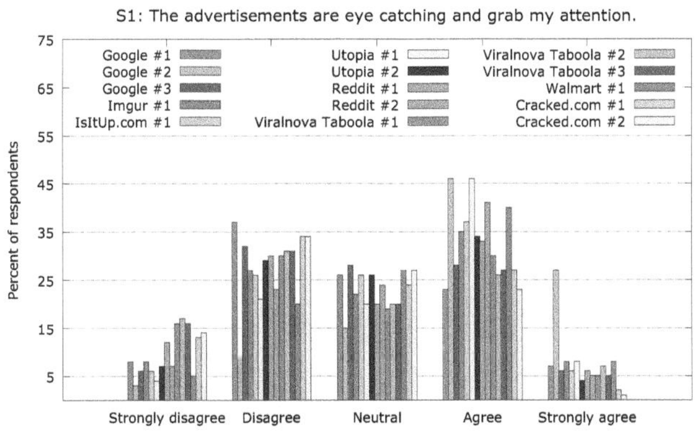

(a) Attention grabbing advertisements

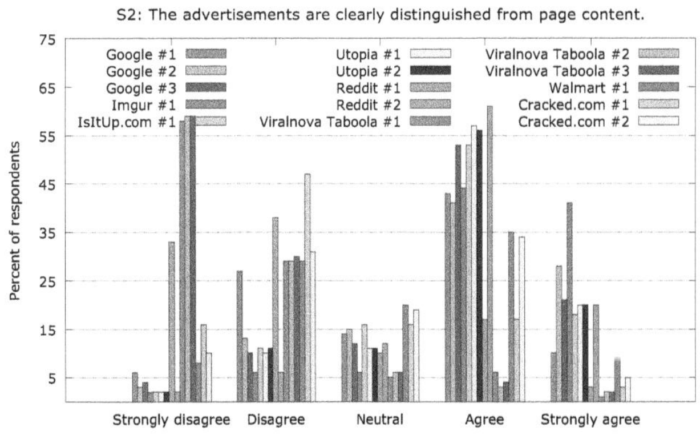

(b) Advertisement distinguished from content

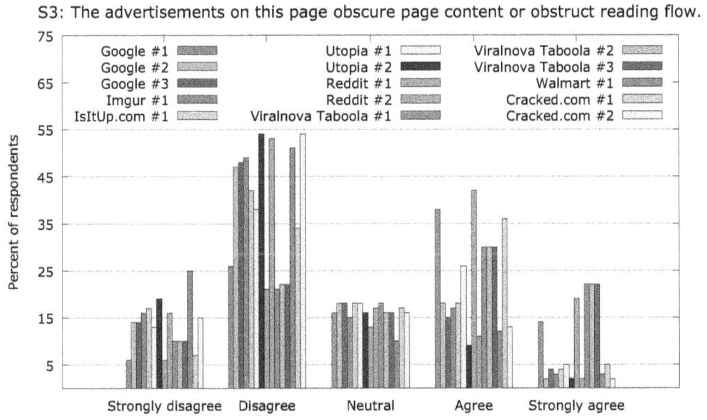

(c) Advertisement obscuring content

	Attention	Distinguished	Obscuring
Search Engine Marketing Advertisements			
μ	0.217	0.597	-0.260
$VAR(X)$	0.304	0.095	0.219
Banner Advertisements			
μ	0.152	0.755	-0.613
$VAR(X)$	0.015	0.131	0.042
Content Advertisements			
μ	-0.247	-0.935	0.125
$VAR(X)$	0.009	0.305	0.178

(d) Mean and variance of the survey responses. Calculated by assigning integer values [-2, 2] to the Likert scale, e.g., strongly disagree was given -2.

Figure 9: User perception survey results.

For each whitelisted advertisement, we asked the participants to rate their level of agreement with statements relating to acceptability on a Likert scale, e.g., "Strongly Disagree," "Disagree," "Neutral," "Agree," or "Strongly Agree." Each statement is a direct transcription from the Adblock Plus policy (with minor adjustments for clarity) and states characteristics that must or must not be true for an advertisement to be "acceptable". Ideally, Adblock Plus should only allow advertisements that meet these criteria.

Statement 1: **The advertisements are eye catching and grab my attention.** - This first statement measures the level of distraction that the advertisement has on the user. There were two types of advertisements that many users found to be attention grabbing or distracting. Figure 10 shows two examples of the advertisements deemed most attention getting, (10*a*, Google Ad #2, with 73% agreeing or strongly agreeing) the image-based sales advertisements displayed with search results on engines and, (10*b*, Utopia Ad #2, 45%) the advertising bar next to navigation buttons on many websites.

Statement 2: **The advertisements are clearly distinguished from page content.** - This statement is designed to measure how well the user can distinguish the advertisements from page content. Illustrated in Figure 10, the mixed content/advertising grid images used in curator websites such as ViralNova appears to intentionally blur the lines between advertisement and content. Almost 90% of users viewing all grid-layout ads stated that they were not distinguished from the content. Hence the allowance by Adblock Plus seems to be in conflict with the program's stated policies.

Statement 3: **The advertisements on this page obscure page content or obstruct reading flow.** - This last statement measures the degree to which users feel the ads are intrusive on content use. While the mixed content/advertising grids seem to inhibit some content use, other ad strategies were viewed as more invasive. In particular, a little more than a third of users viewed sidebar advertisements (e.g., Reddit #1, not shown), first search results (Google #1), and top bar advertisements (Cracked.com #1) as inhibiting.

Summary. While the above results are instructive, one must be careful not to over-read the meaning of one survey. A summary of the survey results in Figure 9(d) shows that there is broad dissension amongst the participants about what was acceptable, confusing, or inhibiting. However, this reenforces our experience; we have observed that each person views advertisements differently—often vastly so. Therefore, any single policy of whitelisting is unlikely to serve the needs of a large and diverse user community well. Developing deeper and larger studies of user desires is needed to develop a better understanding of user preferences and ultimately a more precise and flexible advertisement blocking policy.

7. UNDOCUMENTED FILTERS

Over the course of our analysis outlined in the previous sections, we discovered several instances where filters were added without

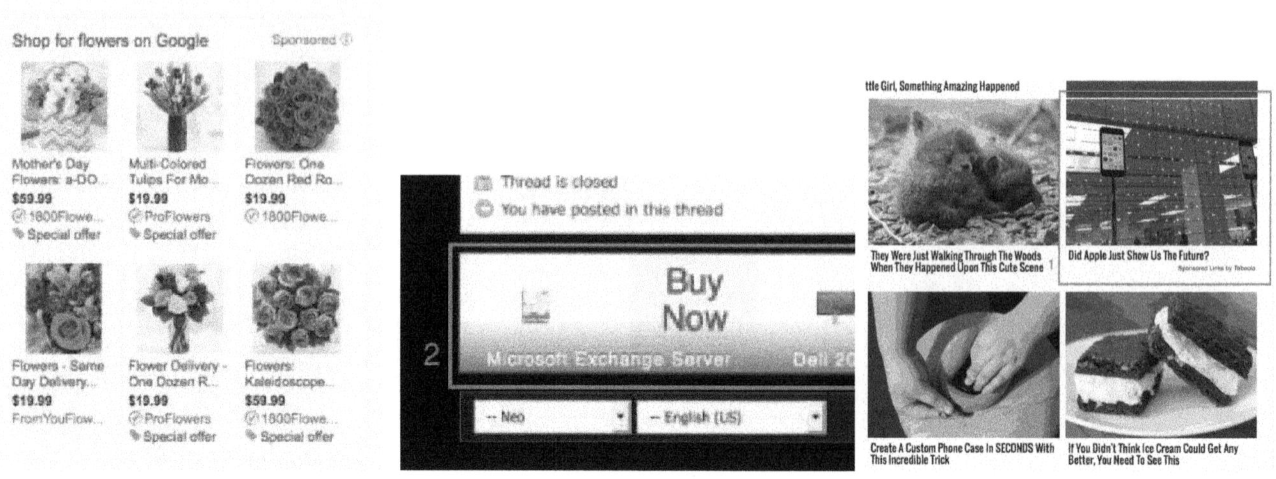

(a) Google Ad#2 **(b)** Utopia Ad#2 **(c)** ViralNova Ad#1

Figure 10: Survey advertisement examples.

community vetting or public disclosure. For completeness, we discuss two representative instances here.

Google's introduction. Google was officially added to the whitelist on June 21, 2013 (Rev. 200).[17] Prior to this, Eyeo allowed some publishers (but not all) to show Google AdSense for search ads on their own search pages. Of particular note among these exceptions are the two filters added for `golem.de` (Rev. 67, Dec. 2012).[18]

```
@@||google.com/ads/search/module/ads/*/
    search.js$domain=suche.golem.de|www.
    google.com
www.google.com#@##adBlock
```

These exception filters are structured differently than previous AdSense filters. Namely, the first exception specifies both `golem.de` and `www.google.com` in the domain list. This is unusual as the addition of Google in the first-party `domain` option is not necessary for showing search advertisements on `golem.de`. Rather, this option makes the filter active on `www.google.com`. The second filter is even more unusual as it unblocks the `adBlock` element on `www.google.com`, i.e., the filter does not make any reference to `golem.de`. None of the previous AdSense exceptions included analogous filters.

Roughly two weeks later, Eyeo modified these filters[19] to match other restricted AdSense exceptions. In particular, they removed `www.google.com` from the domain list in the first filter and deleted the second filter entirely.

```
@@||google.com/ads/search/module/ads/*/
    search.js$domain=suche.golem.de
```

The forum post for the `golem.de` filters does not provide any rationale for the initial dissimilarities between these other AdSense exceptions, nor does it indicate the purpose of the later changes (or even mention such changes were made). However, during the two weeks the original filters were active, Google could conceivably have used the filters (especially the element filter) to measure the impact of whitelisting by adding an element with id `adBlock`. This element would be active via the whitelist when normal ads were not.

[17] hg.adblockplus.org/exceptionrules/rev/8bdf815a5291
[18] hg.adblockplus.org/exceptionrules/rev/feb913d65a21
[19] hg.adblockplus.org/exceptionrules/rev/9c5f8032d88b

```
!A6
@@||Ask.com^$elemhide
@@||us.ask.com^$elemhide
@@||uk.ask.com^$elemhide

!A29
@@||google.com/adsense/search/ads.
    js$domain=search.comcast.net
@@||google.com/ads/search/module/ads/*/
    search.js$script,domain=search.
    comcast.net
@@||google.com/afs/$script,subdocument,
    document,domain=search.comcast.net

!A46
@@||kayak.com.au^$elemhide
@@||kayak.com.br^$elemhide
@@||checkfelix.com^$elemhide

!A50
@@||twcc.com^$elemhide
@@||google.com/adsense/search/ads.
    js$domain=twcc.com
@@||google.com/ads/search/module/ads/*/
    search.js$script,domain=twcc.com
```

Figure 11: Subset of A-filter groups. In contrast to typical filters, A-filter groups do not contain a comment with a link to the forum. Insofar as we can determine, none of these filters were publicly disclosed by Eyeo. In total, we uncovered 59 A-filter groups.

A-List filters. There are 61 instances of Eyeo adding whitelist filters without community vetting—many of which are exceptions for large companies. We refer to these as *A-filters* because of the nondescript comments preceding each group in the whitelist, e.g. `!A1`. Figure 11 shows four example sets. Insofar as we can determine, none of these filters were publicly disclosed. In other words, none of the A-filter groups appear in Eyeo's notification forum. Nearly all A-filter additions use the same repository commit message, "Updated whitelists."[20] In contrast, for other filters, Eyeo includes a link to the appropriate forum post in both the commit message and with a comment in the whitelist itself.

Eyeo first added A-filters in Rev. 287[21], with sets A1 and A2. Since the addition of these first filters, Eyeo has continued to add A-filters to the whitelist. The most recent one being A61 in Rev. 955.[22] Over time they have also removed 5 A-filter groups; one of these was re-added as a different A-filter, i.e. A7 as A28 in Rev. 625.[23] Among the filters added are exceptions for large companies such as Walmart and Time Warner Cable. Domains within an A-filter group appear to be closely related, possibly under the same parent organization, e.g., media company IAC owns both `about.com` and `ask.com`.[24]

In Rev. 789[25] Eyeo added A59. This filter group includes an *unrestricted* filter for Google's AdSense for search service. Specifically, this filter allows nearly *all* domains to show Google search ads.[26] As we see in Table 4, this AdSense exception was the ninth most popular filter in our survey, having been observed on 78 distinct domains.

8. INCREASING TRANSPARENCY

Acceptable Ads can benefit both users and publishers. Users are no longer subjected to annoying and intrusive advertising, while publishers—who use advertising as the primary means to support their work—can avoid erecting paywalls or reducing content. However, our analysis suggests several program areas in need of improvement. Namely, the current process lacks full transparency. Such transparency is essential for this laudable tradeoff between user desires and economic needs to become reality.

We largely agree with the Acceptable Ads criteria, but recommend that Eyeo take additional steps to reassure users that the company is acting in good faith. We recommend the following for improving the whitelisting process and policies.

Disclose financial entanglements. Other than a few isolated examples, users must guess at which filters and domains originate from a paid agreement. Eyeo claims that roughly 90% of those companies added to the list did not have to pay, however full disclosure of these statistics would strengthen public trust in the Acceptable Ads initiative.

Eyeo should clearly identify why certain sites have to pay and others do not. Eyeo states that whitelisting is free for small and medium-sized sites, but they do not say how they make this determination or if this is the only criterion. For instance, Alexa ranks `reddit.com` higher than Microsoft's Bing search; however, the former has stated they do not pay for their whitelist exceptions, while the latter does. Further, do all whitelisted ad networks pay Eyeo?

Public disclosure of whitelist agreements is especially important when one considers that a single company may own multiple domains. For instance, both `ask.com` and `about.com` are in the whitelist, and both are owned by the same parent company, IAC.[27]

Document *all* whitelist modifications. Currently, Eyeo notifies their users of whitelist changes through their online forum. However, as we discussed in previous sections, Eyeo does not give all filters the chance to be publicly vetted, e.g. `kayak.com`. It is unclear why some proposals are included in the forums and others are not.

The inclusion of forum links and a short description for groups of filters contained in the whitelist allow users to easily find relevant information. However, filter groups with nondescript titles, e.g. `A3`, are opaque.

Avoid overly general filters. A single unrestricted (or sitekey) filter in the whitelist may apply to any number of domains, making it impossible for a user to determine the filter's full scope. Overly general filters obscure whitelist understanding.

Identify whitelisted advertisements. In Google Chrome, the Adblock Plus extension logo includes a number indicating the number of blocked elements on the page. Moreover, a greyed-out logo appears when the user manually disables Adblock Plus on a page. However, there is no visible indication as to the number of whitelisted elements. Conversely, the Firefox version includes a "Blockable Items" toolbar that displays a list of page objects along with any triggered filters and the list from where the filter originates: EasyList, whitelist, etc. All Adblock Plus versions would benefit from such functionality by allowing interested users to determine which page elements were blocked and which ones were allowed (and why).

Practice good whitelist hygiene. The whitelist contains redundant, obsolete, and malformed filters. In addition to 35 duplicate filters, we observed at least 8 malformed exception filters, all of which appear to have been erroneously truncated (in Rev. 326) at a max length of 4095 characters. Similarly, AdSense for search exceptions are no longer required for individual domains. A process for retiring needed filters should be created and documented; and superfluous, malformed, and outdated filters should be purged.

9. CONCLUSIONS

This paper provides an analysis of Acceptable Ads: a program with the goal of changing Internet advertising for the better by allowing non-intrusive ads. Our study shows that the program has grown aggressively over the last four years. There is a diversity of sites being whitelisted, but a seeming (and understandable) concentration of whitelisting on popular sites. Yet, the complexity of the lists and their interaction with other web systems makes a full understanding difficult.

To us, the way forward seems clear. Public disclosures of financial relationships and more process transparency will foster trust and allow users to make informed choices about how they use blocking and ultimately what sites they visit. This community voice is essential because an open discussion is perhaps the only means of reaching a universally acceptable resolution in the blocking/whitelisting debate.

10. ACKNOWLEDGMENTS

Research was sponsored by the Army Research Laboratory and was accomplished under Cooperative Agreement Number W911NF-13-2-0045 (ARL Cyber Security CRA). The views and conclusions contained in this document are those of the authors and should not be interpreted as representing the official policies, either expressed or implied, of the Army Research Laboratory or the U.S. Government. The U.S. Government is authorized to reproduce and distribute reprints for Government purposes notwithstanding any copyright notation here on.

[20] Rev. 304 used the message "Added new whitelists."

[21] `hg.adblockplus.org/exceptionrules/rev/b60864b2ab92`

[22] `hg.adblockplus.org/exceptionrules/rev/5a666fbe3612`

[23] `hg.adblockplus.org/exceptionrules/rev/8a9d97588927`

[24] `http://iac.com/brands`

[25] `hg.adblockplus.org/exceptionrules/rev/c182d9dc5600`

[26] The filter defines a set of 43 domains for which the AdSense filter will **not** apply.

[27] `http://iac.com/brands`

11. REFERENCES

[1] Allowing acceptable ads in adblock plus. https://adblockplus.org/en/acceptable-ads. Accessed Sept. 2014.

[2] Amazon mechanical turk. https://www.mturk.com/mturk/welcome. Accessed April, 2015.

[3] Is adblock plus for chrome (formerly adthwart) superior... https://adblockplus.org/forum/viewtopic.php?f=10&t=6509, Dec. 2010.

[4] S. Alrwais, K. Yuan, E. Alowaisheq, Z. Li, and X. Wang. Understanding the dark side of domain parking. In *Proceedings of the 23rd USENIX Security Symposium*, 2014.

[5] B. Brinkmann. Wie adblock plus mit werbung geld verdient. http://www.sueddeutsche.de/digital/browsererweiterung-in-der-kritik-wie-adblock-plus-mit-werbung-geld-verdient-1.1715051, July 2013. Accessed Oct. 2014.

[6] H. Cett. Adblock founder faida calls for transparency in ad industry. http://www.gomonews.com/adblock-founder-faida-calls-for-transparency-in-ad-instustry/, Dec. 2013. Accessed Feb. 2015.

[7] N. Chachra, D. McCoy, S. Savage, and G. Voelker. Empirically characterizing domain abuse and the revenue impact of blacklisting. In *Proceedings of the Workshop on the Economics of Information Security (WEIS)*, 2014.

[8] N. Cohen. An ad blocker opens the gate, ever so slightly. http://www.nytimes.com/2012/01/02/business/media/adblock-plus-allowing-some-online-advertisements.html?pagewanted=all&r=1&_r=0, Jan. 2012.

[9] R. Cookson. Google, microsoft and amazon pay to get around ad blocking tool. http://www.ft.com/intl/cms/s/0/80a8ce54-a61d-11e4-9bd3-00144feab7de.html#axzz3QbaQtkaZ, Feb. 2015. Accessed Feb. 2015.

[10] F. Dahlke. Adblock plus 1.3.3 for opera released. https://adblockplus.org/releases/adblock-plus-133-for-opera-released, Nov. 2012.

[11] M. Ermert. First court hearing of broadcasters and adblock plus. http://policyreview.info/articles/news/first-court-hearing-broadcasters-and-adblock-plus/347, Dec. 2014. Accessed Dec. 2014.

[12] S. Gandhe. Adblock plus sued by german marketing companies. http://www.neowin.net/news/adblock-plus-sued-by-german-marketing-companies, July 2014. Accessed Jan. 2015.

[13] IAB. Q3 2014 internet advertising revenues hit $12.4 billion, making it the highest quarter on record. http://www.iab.net/about_the_iab/recent_press_releases/press_release_archive/press_release/pr-121814, Dec. 2014.

[14] C. Kanich, N. Weaver, D. McCoy, T. Halvorson, C. Kreibich, K. Levchenko, V. Paxson, G. M. Voelker, and S. Savage. Show me the money: Characterizing spam-advertised revenue. In *USENIX Security Symposium*, pages 15–15, 2011.

[15] L. Kelion. Adblock plus defeats german publishers in court. http://www.bbc.com/news/technology-32409952, April 2015. Accessed April, 2015.

[16] L. Leong. Adblock plus responds to german lawsuit. http://news.en.softonic.com/adblock-plus-responds-to-german-lawsuit, July 2014. Accessed Jan. 2015.

[17] K. Levchenko, A. Pitsillidis, N. Chachra, B. Enright, M. Félegyházi, C. Grier, T. Halvorson, C. Kanich, C. Kreibich, H. Liu, et al. Click trajectories: End-to-end analysis of the spam value chain. In *Security and Privacy (SP), 2011 IEEE Symposium on*, pages 431–446. IEEE, 2011.

[18] H. Li, S. M. Edwards, and J.-H. Lee. Measuring the intrusiveness of advertisements: Scale development and validation. *Journal of advertising*, 31(2):37–47, 2002.

[19] Z. Li, K. Zhang, Y. Xie, F. Yu, and X. Wang. Knowing your enemy: understanding and detecting malicious web advertising. In *Proceedings of the 2012 ACM conference on Computer and communications security*, pages 674–686. ACM, 2012.

[20] D. McCoy, A. Pitsillidis, G. Jordan, N. Weaver, C. Kreibich, B. Krebs, G. M. Voelker, S. Savage, and K. Levchenko. Pharmaleaks: Understanding the business of online pharmaceutical affiliate programs. In *Proceedings of the 21st USENIX conference on Security symposium*, pages 1–1. USENIX Association, 2012.

[21] S. McCoy, A. Everard, P. Polak, and D. F. Galletta. The effects of online advertising. *Commun. ACM*, 50(3):84–88, Mar. 2007.

[22] M. McHugh. Media mafiosos: Is adblock plus shaking down websites for cash to let ads through? http://www.digitaltrends.com/web/adblock-plus-accused-of-shaking-down-websites/, Feb. 2013.

[23] M. McHugh. Media mafiosos: is adblock plus shaking down websites for cash to let ads through? http://www.digitaltrends.com/web/adblock-plus-accused-of-shaking-down-websites/, Feb. 2013. Accessed Jan. 2015.

[24] R. L. Mitchell. The business of ad blocking: A q&a with adblock plus lead investor tim schumacher. http://www.computerworld.com/article/2475721/desktop-apps/the-business-of-ad-blocking--a-q-a-with-adblock-plus-lead-investor-tim-schumacher.html, Jan. 2014.

[25] S. Noack. Adblock plus for safari beta released. https://adblockplus.org/releases/adblock-plus-for-safari-beta-released, Jan. 2014.

[26] PageFair. Acceptable ads soothe google pain. http://blog.pagefair.com/2013/acceptable-ads-soothe-google-pain/?cmp=17, Aug. 2013. Accessed Oct. 2014.

[27] PageFair and Adobe. Adblocking goes mainstream 2014 report. http://downloads.pagefair.com/reports/adblocking_goes_mainstream_2014_report.pdf, Sept. 2014. Accessed Oct. 2014.

[28] W. Palant. Adblock plus for google chrome (beta) 1.0.22 released. https://adblockplus.org/releases/adblock-plus-for-google-chrome-beta-1022-released, Dec. 2010.

[29] W. Palant. Adblock plus 1.0 for internet explorer released. https://adblockplus.org/releases/adblock-plus-10-for-internet-explorer-release, Aug. 2013.

[30] W. Palant. Adblock plus for android removed from google play store. https://adblockplus.org/blog/adblock-plus-for-android-removed-from-google-play-store, Mar. 2013.

[31] L. Stampler. Google saved an estimated $887 million by paying adblock plus to show its ads. http://www.businessinsider.com/google-saved-an-estimated-887-million-by-paying-adblock-plus-to-show-its-ads-2013-8, Oct. 2013. Accessed Oct. 2014.

[32] J. Steinschaden. Google ist geldgeber von adblock plus. http://www.horizont.at/home/detail/google-ist-geldgeber-von-adblock-plus.html, July 2013. Accessed Oct. 2014.

[33] B. Williams. Restating the obvious: adblocking declared legal. https://adblockplus.org/blog/restating-the-obvious-adblocking-declared-legal, April 2015.

[34] A. Zarras, A. Kapravelos, G. Stringhini, T. Holz, C. Kruegel, and G. Vigna. The dark alleys of madison avenue: Understanding malicious advertisements. In *Proceedings of the 2014 Conference on Internet Measurement Conference*, pages 373–380. ACM, 2014.

APPENDIX

A. FILTER SYNTAX

A filter is structured like a regular expression with additional modifiers and options for changing action and scope. A blocking filter prevents web content from loading or showing, and an exception filter overrides blocking filters to allow content. Options and modifiers adjust the scope of filters to affect only specific content or domains.

Adblock Plus provides documentation for the syntax of filters on its website.[28] Although Adblock Plus uses regular expressions to parse filters, we provide a BNF grammar in Figure 12, which can be used to understand how filters are created.

A.1 Blocking Filters

The simplest blocking filter is ⟨*request*⟩ with just ⟨*request-match*⟩. The ⟨*request-match*⟩ is made primarily of a regular expression that defines the path to be blocked, ⟨*regex-URL-path*⟩. The filter expression

```
|| http://example.com/ads/advert777.gif
```

will block the specified `gif` advertisement loaded from the given address. The use of wildcards can increase the effectiveness of a single filter. For convenience, each filter regular expression has an implicit wildcard operator at the beginning and end of the filter expression. For instance, the filter expression, `/ad-frame/`, will affect any domain and will block all page elements that are requested from the `ad-frame` subdirectory.

A '`|`' can be added at the beginning or end of ⟨*regex-URL-path*⟩ to override the implicit wildcard operators. Additionally, the '`||`' string appears before a domain to allow subdomains and multiple protocols, such as `http://` and `https://`. The following filter

```
|| ||example.com/ad.jpg|
```

matches both `http://good.example.com/ad.jpg` and `https://example.com/ad.jpg`, but not `https://example.com/ad.jpg.exe`.

Moreover, the '`^`' character matches any and all separator characters within a URL, and may be placed at the beginning or end of ⟨*regex-URL-path*⟩. Separator characters appear as "anything but a letter, a digit, or one of the following: `_ - . %`."[29] For example, the filter

[28] https://adblockplus.org/en/filters

[29] https://adblockplus.org/en/filters#separators

```
⟨filter⟩ ::= ⟨blocking⟩
  | ⟨exception⟩

⟨blocking⟩ ::= ⟨request⟩
  | ⟨element-hide⟩

⟨exception⟩ ::= '@@'⟨request⟩
  | ⟨element-exception⟩
  | ⟨sitekey⟩

⟨sitekey⟩ ::= '@@$sitekey='⟨pub-key⟩∗('|'⟨pub-key⟩)#(['∼']⟨option⟩)

⟨request⟩ ::= ⟨request-match⟩['$'1#(⟨no-neg-opt⟩ | ['∼']⟨option⟩)]

⟨element-hide⟩ ::= #(['∼']⟨page-domain⟩)'##'⟨elem-selector⟩

⟨elemhide-except⟩ ::= #(['∼']⟨page-domain⟩)'#@#'⟨elem-selector⟩

⟨request-match⟩ ::= ['||' | '|' | '^']⟨regex-URL-path⟩['|' | '^']

⟨option⟩ ::= 'script'
  | 'image'
  | 'stylesheet'
  | 'object'
  | 'xmlhttprequest'
  | 'object-subrequest'
  | 'subdocument'
  | 'document'
  | 'elemhide'
  | 'other'
  | 'third-party'
  | 'collapse'

⟨no-neg-opt⟩ ::= 'domain='['∼']⟨page-domain⟩
      ∗('|'['∼']⟨page-domain⟩)
  | 'sitekey='⟨pub-key⟩ ∗('|'⟨pub-key⟩)
  | 'match-case'
  | 'donottrack'
```

Figure 12: Adblock Plus Filter Syntax BNF Grammar.

```
|| ^www.google.com^
```

will match `http://www.google.com/#q=foo`, where the separator characters are bolded, but this expression will not match `http://scholar.google.com` due to the replacement of `www` with `scholar`.

Request Filters and Options. While a request filter can consist of only a regular expression with modifiers, the addition of options can tune the scope of a request filter. The '`$`' character is placed after ⟨*request-match*⟩ to indicate the start of an option list. An option list consists of 1 or more ⟨*option*⟩s or ⟨*no-neg-opt*⟩s separated by a comma. A '∼' character is the negation operator, and it can be coupled with an ⟨*option*⟩ to apply the inverse. However, there are some options that cannot be negated: ⟨*no-neg-opt*⟩. Refer to Section A.4 for more information on each filter option.

Element Hiding. Elements refer to text or page areas embedded into the web page itself through the source code. An element hiding filter is required to hide and block these elements. The element hiding filter requires at least '`##`' followed by ⟨*elem-selector*⟩ to match the target page elements.

The ⟨*elem-selector*⟩ is most commonly a CSS element selector,[30] however this is not always the case.[31] Selectors can name the element explicitly, as `##.ButtonAd`, or just specify the `id` attribute to hide, `###sideads`, which is a more general match. Like ⟨*regex-URL-path*⟩, selectors may contain regular expressions.

In the current implementation of Adblock Plus, restricting element hiding filters to a certain domain requires the use of full domain names.[32] Multiple domains are separated by a comma and apply to the same selector:

```
mnn.com,streamtuner.me###adv
```

A negation operator, '~', may also be applied to domain names to create an exception for element hiding filter.

A.2 Exception Filters

An exception filter allows the user to view page content that would otherwise be blocked by one or more blocking filters. Exception filter syntax is very similar to that of blocking filters. An ⟨*exception*⟩ can be either a ⟨*request*⟩ or an ⟨*element-exception*⟩, like blocking filters. The main differences are found at the beginning of request filters and in the middle of element filters.

Request Filters. An exception ⟨*request*⟩ filter takes the form of '`@@`'⟨*request*⟩, where '`@@`' must prefix all ⟨*request*⟩s. Refer to Section A.1 and the formation of ⟨*request*⟩ for further details. If only ⟨*request*⟩ appears in the filter (no options), then the string acts like a regular expression and matches all requests containing that string.

The following example appears in the whitelist allowing DoubleClick advertisements on `references.net`:

```
@@||g.doubleclick.net/pagead/$subdocument
    ,domain=references.net
```

The '`domain`' option specifies the domain for which this filter applies, and the '`subdocument`' option indicates that the DoubleClick advertisement will be embedded in the '`references.net`' page.

Element Filters. Element exception filters allow page elements to be viewed. An ⟨*elemhide-except*⟩ is very similar in form to ⟨*elem-hide*⟩. However, instead of the string '`##`' for element hiding, an ⟨*elemhide-except*⟩ uses '`#@#`' to denote that it is an exception. Refer to Section A.1 for more information on element hiding.

The next example also appears in the whitelist and is an element hide exception that allows `references.net` to show the above DoubleClick ad example on the page.

```
references.net#@#.adunit
```

Without this filter, a request to DoubleClick is established and the ad is loaded, but an element hiding filter hides it from view. The structure of this filter includes ⟨*page-domain*⟩ first, and the element's `class` name, '`.adunit`', second.

A.3 Sitekey Filters

Sitekey filters primarily occur as exception filters with '`document`' as ⟨*option*⟩, to allow *all* advertisements. These filters cover all sites that return a valid public key and signature. Section 4.2.3 explains how sitekeys work.

The syntax for ⟨*sitekey*⟩ is an exception ⟨*request*⟩ without a ⟨*request-match*⟩ and only specifying '`sitekey`' and '`document`' as ⟨*option*⟩s:

```
@@$sitekey=MFwwDQYJK...wEAAQ,document
```

The '`sitekey`' option is given an RSA public key created by a multi-domain owner, e.g., Sedo. The filter matches all domains that have the same public sitekey and return a signature signed with the private RSA key. The '`document`' option indicates that the entire page is permitted to show ads; even allowing third-party requests.

A.4 Filter Options Explained

Filters may include a number of options to further specify their effects on page elements and scope.[33] An overview of these filters is presented in the following text.

Some options can be grouped by the specific type of element loaded from the request. For instance, '`script`' limits the filter to block (or whitelist for exception filters) the HTML script tag that loads external scripts. Other similar options include '`image`', '`stylesheet`', '`object`' (where browser plugins like Flash or Java handle page content), '`xmlhttprequest`' (for requests by the XMLHttpRequest object[34]), '`object-subrequest`' (for requests started by browser plugins), and '`subdocument`' (for pages that are embedded within the page, usually through HTML frames). The '`other`' option covers requests that are absent from the previous list.

Additional options specify a broader content selection. The '`document`' option may only be included in an exception filter and disables all blocking filters on affected domains and requests. Similarly, '`elemhide`' also only applies to exception filters and disables all element-hiding filters. In contrast, the '`third-party`' option limits a filter only to external requests from a different origin than the current web page. These and all previous options can be prefixed with '~' to invert their original meaning.

Further, the '`domain`' option restricts the filter to certain domains, which are separated by commas. To *not* apply the filter on a certain domain, the domain can be prefixed with the negation operator. If the '`domain`' option is not specified, the request filter applies to all domains.

More options are also included in the filter syntax. The option '`match-case`' ensures that the request is matched on a case-sensitive basis. A '`collapse`' option will guarantee that the element is hidden.[35] The '`collapse`' option can also be negated. A '`donottrack`' option will send a Do-Not-Track header[36] to the web page as long as there is no matching exception rule with a '`donottrack`' option on the same page.

Finally, there are deprecated options that still exist for backwards compatibility, but their use is discouraged: '`background`', '`xbl`', '`ping`', and '`dtd`'.[37]

[30] http://www.w3.org/TR/css3-selectors/
[31] See https://adblockplus.org/en/filters#elemhide for more details.
[32] https://adblockplus.org/en/filters#elemhide_domains
[33] https://adblockplus.org/en/filters#options
[34] http://www.w3.org/TR/XMLHttpRequest/
[35] This option is only found once in EasyList and might be deprecated.
[36] http://donottrack.us/
[37] https://adblockplus.org/en/filters#options

Location, Location, Location: The Impact of Geolocation on Web Search Personalization

Chloe Kliman-Silver
Brown University
chloe@cs.brown.edu

Aniko Hannak
Northeastern University
ancsaaa@ccs.neu.edu

David Lazer
Northeastern University
d.lazer@neu.edu

Christo Wilson
Northeastern University
cbw@ccs.neu.edu

Alan Mislove
Northeastern University
amislove@ccs.neu.edu

ABSTRACT

To cope with the immense amount of content on the web, search engines often use complex algorithms to personalize search results for individual users. However, personalization of search results has led to worries about the *Filter Bubble Effect*, where the personalization algorithm decides that some useful information is irrelevant to the user, and thus prevents them from locating it.

In this paper, we propose a novel methodology to explore the impact of location-based personalization on Google Search results. Assessing the relationship between location and personalization is crucial, since users' geolocation can be used as a proxy for other demographic traits, like race, income, educational attainment, and political affiliation. In other words, *does location-based personalization trap users in geolocal Filter Bubbles?*

Using our methodology, we collected 30 days of search results from Google Search in response to 240 different queries. By comparing search results gathered from 59 GPS coordinates around the US at three different granularities (county, state, and national), we are able to observe that differences in search results due to personalization grow as physical distance increases. However these differences are highly dependent on what a user searches for: queries for local establishments receive 4-5 different results per page, while more general terms exhibit essentially no personalization.

Categories and Subject Descriptors

H.3.3 [**Information Storage and Retrieval**]: Information Search and Retrieval; H.3.5 [**Information Systems**]: Online Services—*web-based services*

Keywords

Search; Personalization; Geolocation; Internet Filter Bubble

IMC'15, October 28–30, 2015, Tokyo, Japan.

ACM 978-1-4503-3848-6/15/10 ...$15.00.
DOI: http://dx.doi.org/10.1145/2815675.2815714.

1. INTRODUCTION

Search engines are the primary gateway to information in the developed world. Thus, it is no surprise that Google has been the most visited site on the Internet for several years now [1]; it receives more than 48,000 queries every second [2]. The importance of content and ordering in search results is exemplified by Europe's recent Right to be Forgotten ruling [21], as well as the thriving Search Engine Optimization (SEO) industry [23].

To cope with the immense amount of content on the web, search engines use complex algorithms to *personalize* search results for individual users [9]. In many cases, personalized search results are useful: if two people on opposite ends of the US search for "coffee shop" they should probably be shown search results for local cafés.

However, personalization of search results has also led to worries about the *Filter Bubble Effect*, where the algorithm decides that some useful information is irrelevant to the user, and thus prevents them from locating it [19]. This issue is particularly concerning in the context of political and news-related information: personalization based on a user's political preferences may trap them in an "echo-chamber" where their pre-existing beliefs are constantly reinforced.

Motivated by concerns about Filter Bubbles, our prior work set out to explore which factors triggered personalization in Google Search [11]. We found that Google infers users' geolocation based on their IP address, and that *location-based personalization* caused more differences in search results than any other single feature. However, while these initial findings are intriguing, many questions remain, such as: does location-based personalization impact all types of queries (e.g., politics vs. news) equally? At what distance do users begin to see changes in search results due to location? Answering these questions is crucial, since users' geolocation can be used as a proxy for other demographic traits, like race, income-level, educational attainment, and political affiliation. In other words, *does location-based personalization trap users in geolocal Filter Bubbles?*

In this paper, we propose a novel methodology to explore the impact of location on Google Search results. We use the JavaScript `Geolocation` API [12] to present arbitrary GPS coordinates to the mobile version of Google Search. Google personalizes the search results based on the location we specified, giving us the ability to collect search results from any location around the globe. Although we focus on

Progressive Tax
Impose A Flat Tax
End Medicaid
Affordable Health And Care Act
Fluoridate Water
Stem Cell Research
Andrew Wakefield Vindicated
Autism Caused By Vaccines
US Government Loses AAA Bond Rate
Is Global Warming Real
Man Made Global Warming Hoax
Nuclear Power Plants
Offshore Drilling
Genetically Modified Organisms
Late Term Abortion
Barack Obama Birth Certificate
Impeach Barack Obama
Gay Marriage

Table 1: Example *controversial* search terms.

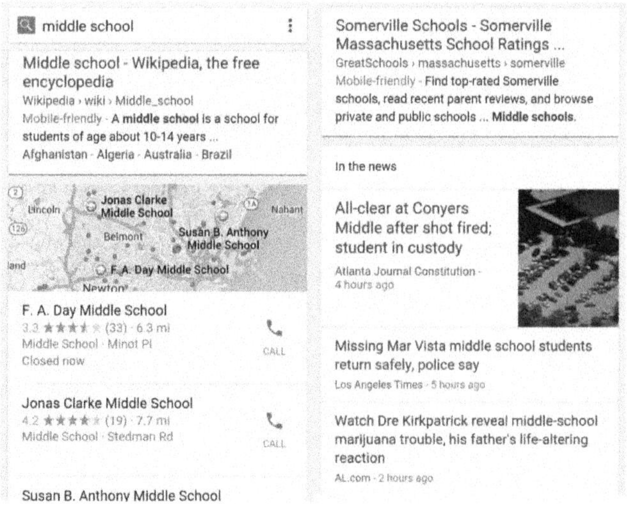

Figure 1: Example search results from the mobile version of Google Search.

Google Search in the US, our methodology is general, and could easily be applied to other search engines like Bing.

Using our methodology, we collected 30 days of search results from Google Search in response to 240 different queries. By selecting 75 GPS coordinates around the US at three granularities (county, state, and national), we are able to examine the relationship between distance and location-based personalization, as well as the impact of location-based personalization on different types of queries. We make the following observations:

- As expected, the differences between search results grows as physical distance between the locations of the users increases.
- However, the impact of location-based personalization changes depending on the query type. Queries for *politicians'* names (e.g., "Joe Biden") and *controversial* topics ("abortion") see minor changes, while queries for *local* terms ("airport") are highly personalized.
- Surprisingly, only 20-30% of differences are due to Maps embedded in search results. The remainder are caused by changes in "normal" search results.
- Also surprisingly, the search results for *local* terms are extremely noisy, i.e., two users making the same query from the same location at the same time often receive substantially different search results.

Outline. The rest of the paper is organized as follows: in Section 2, we give an overview of our data collection methodology, and then present analysis and findings in Section 3. We discuss related work in Section 4 and conclude in Section 5.

2. METHODOLOGY

Our goal is to explore the relationship between geolocation and personalization on Google Search. Thus, we require the ability to send identical queries to Google Search, at the same moment in time, from different locations. In this section, we explain our methodology for accomplishing these goals. First, we introduce the locations and search terms used in our study. Next, we explain our technique for querying Google Search from arbitrary locations, and how we parsed Google Search results. Finally, we discuss how we quantify differences between pages of search results.

2.1 Locations and Search Terms

Locations. First, we must choose the locations in which to execute queries. We decided to focus our study on Ohio, since it is known to be a "battleground" state in US politics. This property is important, since we want to examine whether demographics like political affiliation correlate with location-based personalization.

Overall, we picked 66 locations for our study spread across three *granularities*. For *nation*-level, we chose the centroids of 22 random states in the United States. For *state*-level, we chose the centroids of 22 random counties within Ohio. On average, these counties 100 miles apart. Finally, for *county*-level, we chose the centroids of 15 voting districts in Cuyahoga County, which is the most populous county in Ohio. On average, these voting districts are 1 mile apart. By examining locations in different granularities, we will be able to observe changes in search results across small, medium, and large-scale distances. This also gives us the ability to compare search results served in places with different demographics characteristics.

Search Terms. Next, we must select search terms for our study. We built a corpus of 240 queries that fall into three categories: 33 *local* queries, 87 *controversial* queries, and 120 names of *politicians*. *Local* queries correspond with physical establishments, restaurants, and public services such as "bank", "hospital", and "KFC". We chose these terms because we expect them to produce search results that are heavily personalized based on location, i.e., we treat them as an upper-bound on location-based personalization.

For *politicians*, we selected 11 members of the Cuyahoga County Board, 53 random members of the Ohio House and Senate, all 18 members of the US Senate and House from Ohio, 36 random members of the US House and Senate not from Ohio, Joe Biden, and Barack Obama. For national figures like Barack Obama, we do not expect to see differences in search results due to location; however, it is not clear how

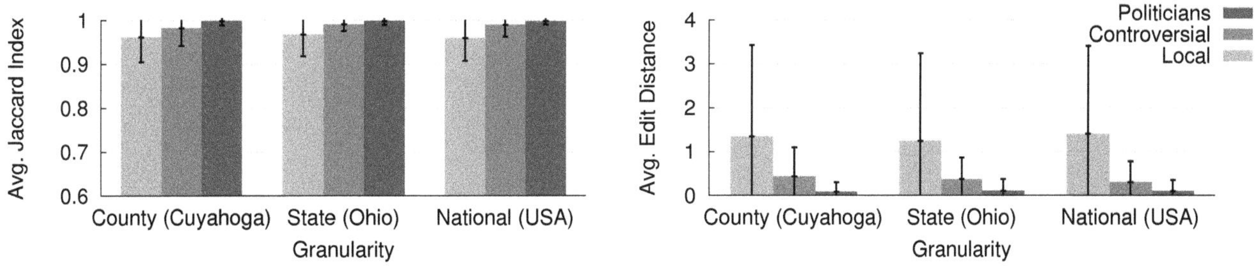

Figure 2: Average noise levels across different query types and granularities. Error bars show standard deviations.

Google Search handles queries for state- and county-level officials inside and outside their home territories.

Finally, our *controversial* terms are news or politics-related issues like those shown in Table 1. We chose these terms because it would be concerning if Google Search personalized search results for them based on location. To avoid possible external bias, we picked search terms that, to the best of our knowledge, were not associated with specific news-worthy events at the time of our experiments. Although we cannot completely rule out the possibility that exonegous events impacted the search results, we note that such an event would impact each treatment equally, and thus would likely not impact our findings.

2.2 Data Collection and Parsing

Our methodology for gathering data from Google Search is based on the techniques presented in our prior work et al. [10,11], with one key difference. As in prior work, we use PhantomJS [20] to gather data, since it is a full implementation of a WebKit browser. We wrote a PhantomJS script that takes a search term and a latitude/longitude pair as input, loads the mobile version of Google Search, executes the query, and saves the first page of search results.

Unlike prior work [11], we targeted the mobile version of Google Search because it uses the JavaScript `Geolocation` API [12] to query the user's precise location. By overriding the `Geolocation` API in our PhantomJS script, we can feed the coordinates specified on the command line to Google Search, thus giving us the ability to run queries that appear to Google as if they are coming from any location of our choosing. We distributed our query load over 44 machines in a single /24 subnet to avoid being rate-limited by Google. Finally, all of our experimental treatments were repeated for 5 consecutive days to check for consistency over time.

Validation. To make sure that Google Search personalizes search results based on the provided GPS coordinates rather than IP address, we conducted a validation experiment. We issued identical controversial queries with the same exact GPS coordinate from 50 different Planet Lab machines across the US, and observe that 94% of the search results received by the machines are identical. This confirms that Google Search personalizes search results largely based on the provided GPS coordinates rather than the IP address. Furthermore, Google Search reports the user's precise location at the bottom of search results, which enabled us to manually verify that Google was personalizing search results correctly based on our spoofed GPS coordinates.

Browser State. To control for personalization effects due to the state of the browser, all of our treatments were configured and behaved identically. The script presented the User-Agent for Safari 8 on iOS, and all other browser attributes were the same across treatments, so each treatment should present an identical browser fingerprint. Furthermore, we cleared all cookies after each query, which mitigates personalization effects due to search history, and prevents Google from "remembering" a treatments prior location. Lastly, we note that prior work has shown that Google Search does not personalize search results based on the user's choice of browser or OS [11].

Controlling for Noise. Unfortunately, not all differences in search results are due to personalization; some may due to noise. As in our prior work [10,11], we take the following precautions to minimize noise:

1. All queries for term t are run in lock-step, to avoid changes in search results due to time.
2. We statically mapped the DNS entry for the Google Search server, ensuring that all our queries were sent to the same datacenter.
3. Google Search personalizes search results based on the user's prior searches during the last 10 minutes [11]. To avoid this confound, we wait 11 minutes between subsequent queries.

However, even with these precautions, there may still be noise in search results (e.g., due to A/B testing). Thus, for each search term and location, we send two identical queries at the same time. By comparing each result with its corresponding *control*, we can measure the extent of the underlying noise. When comparing search results from two locations, any differences we see above the noise threshold can then be attributed to location-based personalization.

Parsing. As shown in Figure 1, Google Search on mobile renders search results as "cards". Some cards present a single result (e.g., "Somerville Schools"), while others present a meta-result (e.g., locations from Google Maps or a list of "In the News" articles). In this study, we parse pages of search results by extracting the first link from each card, except for Maps and News cards where we extract all links. Thus, we observe 12–22 search results per page.

2.3 Measuring Personalization

As in our prior work [11], we use two metrics to compare pages of search results. First, we use *Jaccard Index* to examine the overlap: a Jaccard Index of 0 represents no overlap between the pages, while 1 indicates they contain the same search results (although not necessarily in the same order). Second, we use *edit distance* to measure reordering of search

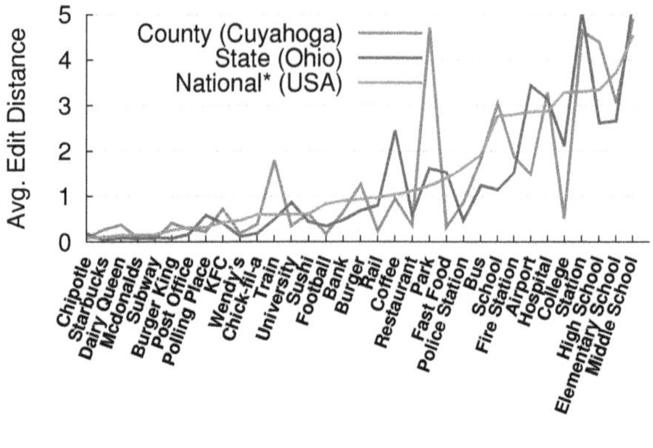

Figure 3: Noise levels for local queries across three granularities.

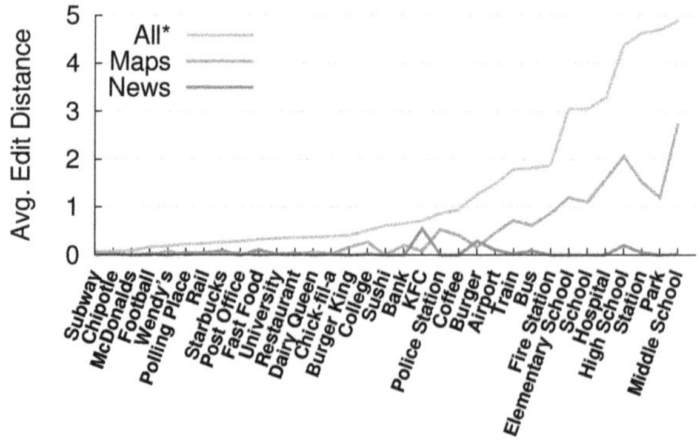

Figure 4: Amount of noise caused by different types of search results for *local* queries.

results. Edit distance calculates the number of additions, deletions, and swaps necessary to make two lists identical.

3. ANALYSIS AND FINDINGS

Using the methodology described in Section 2, we collected 30 days of data from Google Search. We executed the 120 *local* and *controversial* queries once per day for five straight days in the county, state, and national locations (so, 15 days total). We then repeated this process with the 120 *politicians*. Using this dataset, we analyze the impact of location-based personalization on Google Search results.

3.1 Noise

To start, we examine whether there is noise in our search results. To calculate noise, we compare the search results received by treatments and their controls, i.e., two browsers that are running the same queries at the same time from the same locations.

Unlike prior work [11], we find that Google Search results are noisy. Figure 2 shows the average Jaccard Index and edit distance for all treatment/control pairs broken down by granularity and query types (values are averaged over all queries of the given type over 5 days). We make three observations. First, we see that *local* queries are much noiser than *controversial* and *politician* queries, in terms of result composition (shown by Jaccard) and reordering (shown by edit distance). Second, not only do *local* queries have more differences on average, but we also see that they have more variance (indicated by the standard deviation error bars). Third, we observe that noise is independent of location, i.e., the level of noise is uniform across all three granularities.

Search Terms. Given the high standard deviations for *local* queries, we pose the question: *do certain search terms exhibit more noise than others?* To answer this, we calculate the Jaccard Index and edit distance for each search term separately. Figure 3 shows the *local* queries along the x-axis, with the average edit distance for each query along the y-axis. The three lines correspond to search results gathered at different granularities; for clarity, we sort the x-axis from smallest to largest based on the *national* locations.

Figure 3 reveals a divide between the queries: brand names like "Starbucks" tend to be less noisy than generic terms like "school". We observe similar trends for Jaccard Index. We examine this observation further next, when we look at the impact of different types of search results.

Search Result Types. To isolate the source of noise, we analyze the types of search results returned by Google Search. As described in Section 2.2, Google Search returns "typical" results, as well as Maps and News results. We suspect that Maps and News results may be more heavily impacted by location-based personalization, so we calculate the amount of noise that can be attributed to search results of these types separately. Intuitively, we simply calculate Jaccard and edit distance between pages after filtering out all search results that are not of type t.

Figure 4 shows the amount of noise contributed by Maps and News results for each query, along with the overall noise. Figure 4 focuses on the edit distance for *local* queries at *county* granularity, but we see similar trends at other granularities, and for Jaccard values. We observe that Maps results are responsible for around 25% of noise (calculated as the total number of search result changes due to Maps, di-

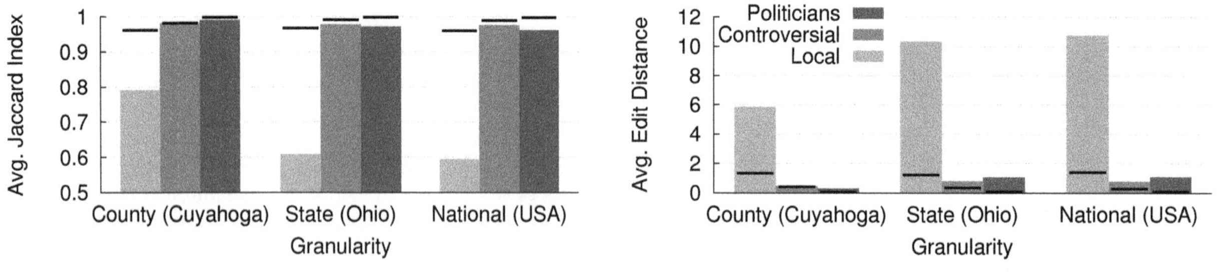

Figure 5: Average personalization across different query types and granularities. Black bars shows average noise levels from Figure 2.

vided by the overall number of changes), while News results cause almost zero noise. After some manual investigation we found that most differences due to Maps arise from one page having Maps results and the other having none. However, we also found cases where both queries yield Maps that highlight a different set of locations. Surprisingly, searches for specific brands typically do not yield Maps results, hence the low noise levels for those search terms.

Although we do not show the findings here due to space constraints, we observe the reverse effect for *controversial* queries: 6-17% of noise in such queries is due to News, while close to 0 is due to Maps. However, as Figure 2 shows, the level of noise in *controversial* queries is low overall.

3.2 Personalization

Now that we have quantified the noise in our dataset, we focus on answering the following two questions. First, *do certain types of queries trigger more personalization than others?* Second, *how does personalization change as the distance between two locations grows?*

Figure 5 shows the average Jaccard Index and edit distance values for each query category at each granularity. Values are averaged across all queries of the given types across 5 days. Recall that in the previous section, we were comparing treatments to their controls in order to measure noise; in this section, we are comparing all pairs of treatments to see if search results vary by location. For the sake of comparison, the average noise levels seen in Figure 2 are shown as horizontal black lines in Figure 5.

The first takeaway from Figure 5 is that *local* queries are much more personalized than *controversial* and *politicians* queries. The Jaccard index shows that 18-34% of the search results vary based on location for *local* queries, while the edit distance shows that 6-10 URLs are presented in a different order (after subtracting the effect of noise). *Controversial* and *politician* queries also exhibit small differences in Figure 5, but the Jaccard and edit distance values are very close to the noise-levels, making it difficult to claim that these changes are due to personalization.

The second takeaway from Figure 5 is that personalization increases with distance. The change is especially high between the *county-* and *state*-levels, with 2 additional search results changed and 4 reordered. As expected, this indicates that differences due to location-based personalization grow with geographic distance.

Search Terms. Our next step is to examine how personalization varies across search terms. As before, we focus on *local* queries since they are most impacted by personalization. Figure 6 shows the edit distances for each *local* search term at each granularity (with the x-axis sorted by the *national*-level values). The significant increase in personalization between *county-* and *state*-level search results is again apparent in this figure.

Overall, we see that location-based personalization varies dramatically by query. The number of search results that change is between 5 and 17, where 17 is essentially all search results on the page. We also notice that (similar to our observations about noise) general terms such as "school" or "post office" exhibit higher personalization than brand names.

The analogous plots for *politicians* and *controversial* queries show similar trends as Figure 6, but with much lower overall personalization. However, there are a few exceptional

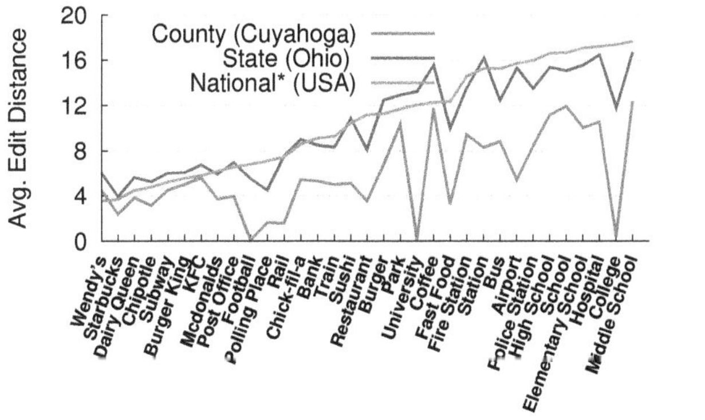

Figure 6: Personalization of each search term for *local* queries.

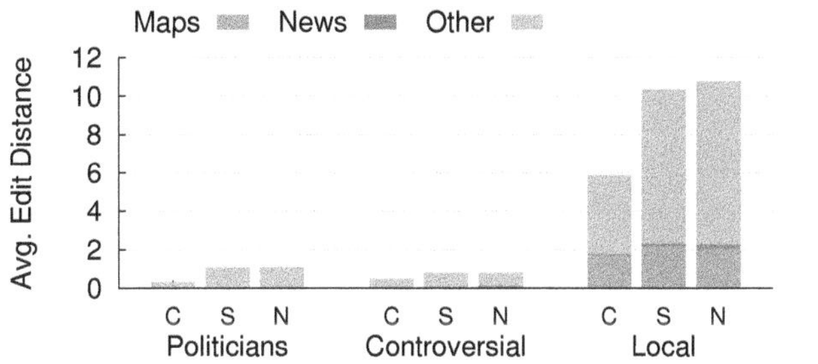

Figure 7: Amount of personalization caused by different types of search results.

search terms. In the case of *politicians*, these exceptions are common names such as "Bill Johnson" or "Tim Ryan", so it is likely that the differences stem from ambiguity. In the case of *controversial* terms, the most personalized queries are "health", "republican party", and "politics".

Search Result Types. It is not terribly surprising that Google personalizes Maps and News results based on location. However, we find that personalization of Maps and News results only explains a small portion of the differences we observe.

Figure 7 breaks down the overall edit distance values into components corresponding to News, Maps, and all other search results, for each granularity and query type. For *controversial* queries, 6-18% of the edit distance can be attributed to News results, and interestingly, this fraction increases from *county* to *nation* granularity. A different composition is seen for *local* queries: 18-27% of differences are caused by Maps results. The takeaway is that, surprisingly, the vast majority of changes due to location-based personalization impact "typical" results.

Consistency Over Time. Thus far, all of our plots have presented values averaged over 5 days. To determine whether personalization is consistent over time, we plot Figure 8. In this figure, we choose one location in each granularity to serve as the *baseline*. The red line plots the average edit distance when comparing the baseline to its control (i.e., the red line shows the noise floor); each black line is a comparison between the baseline and another location at that granularity. We focus on *local* queries since they are most heavily personalized.

Figure 8 shows that the amount of personalization is stable over time. *Politicians* and *controversial* terms show the

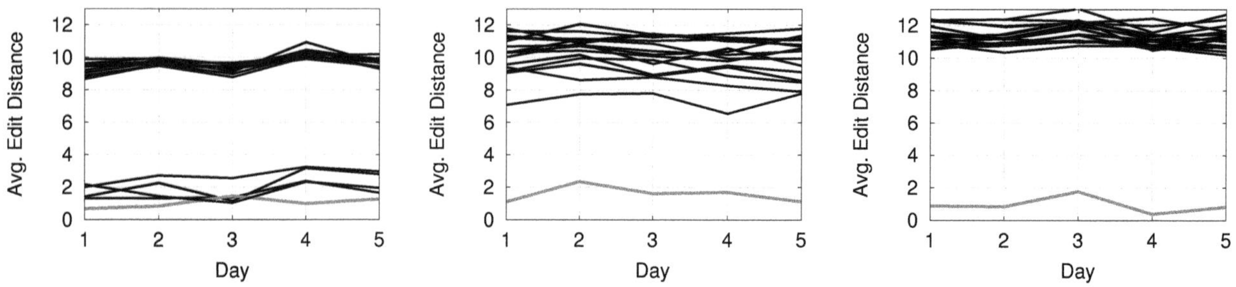

(a) County (Cuyahoga)

(b) State (Ohio)

(c) National (USA)

Figure 8: Personalization of 25 locations, each compared to a baseline location, for *local* queries. The red line compares two treatments at the baseline location (i.e., the experimental control), and thus shows the noise floor.

same trend but with lower personalization overall (findings not shown). As expected, we see a wide gulf between the baseline and other locations at *state* and *nation* granularity, since search results are extremely different at these long distances. However, interestingly, we see that some locations "cluster" at the *county*-level, indicating that some locations receive similar search results to the baseline.

Demographics. To investigate why certain locations cluster at the *county*-level, we examined many potential correlations between all pairs of *county*-level locations. This included correlations based on distance (i.e., do closer locations tend to cluster), as well as 25 demographic features like population density, poverty, educational attainment, ethnic composition, English fluency, income, *etc.* Unfortunately, we were unable to identify any correlations that explain the clustering of locations. Based on this analysis, it appears that Google Search does not use demographic features to implement location-based personalization.

4. RELATED WORK

Search Personalization. Many researchers have investigated strategies for personalizing search engines in order to increase the quality of results [8, 17, 18]. Dou et al. and Micarelli et al. survey several different personalization techniques [4, 14] to determine what features improve search results the most. Several studies have specifically focused on the importance of location in search personalization: [3, 26] use linguistic tools to infer geo-intention from search queries, while [25, 26] focuses on location relevance of webpage content to the given search query.

Auditing Algorithms. In contrast to studies that aim to develop new personalization algorithms, a recent line of work measures deployed personalization systems to understand their impact on users. Latanya Sweeney examined Google Adsense and uncovered that the system serves ads in a racially biased manner [22]. Our prior work [11] as well as Bobble [24] examine how Google Search personalizes search results, and find that geolocation is one of the features used by the algorithm. However, these studies only examine the impact of IP address geolocation, and only at course-grained locations (e.g., different states and countries). Other studies have examined the effects of algorithmic personalization on the Facebook News Feed [5, 6], e-commerce [10, 15, 16], and online ads [7, 13].

5. CONCLUDING DISCUSSION

In this paper, we present a detailed analysis of location-based personalization on Google Search. We develop a novel methodology that allows us to query Google from any location around the world. Using this technique we sent 3,600 distinct queries to Google Search over a span of 30 days from 59 locations across the US.

Our findings show that location does indeed have a large impact on search results, and that the differences increase as physical distance grows. However, we observe many nuances to Google's implementation of location-based personalization. First, not all types of queries trigger the algorithm to the same degree: *politicians* are essentially unaffected by geography; *controversial* terms see small changes due to News; and *local* terms see large differences due to changes in Maps and normal results. Second, not all queries expected to trigger location-personalization do: for example, search results for brand names like "Starbucks" do not include Maps.

Finally, and most surprisingly, we also discover that Google Search returns search results that are very noisy, especially for *local* queries. This non-determinism is puzzling, since Google knows the precise location of the user (during our experiments), and thus should be able to quickly calculate the closest set of relevent locations.

Much work remains to be done. Our methodology can easily be extended to other countries and search engines. We also plan on further investigating the correlations between demographic features and search results. Additional content analysis on the search results may help us uncover the specific instances where personalization algorithms reinforce demographic biases.

The full list of query terms, as well as our source code and data, are all open-source and available at our website:

`http://personalization.ccs.neu.edu`

Acknowledgements

We thank the anonymous reviewers and our shepherd, Matthew Luckie, for their helpful comments. We also thank Arash Molavi Kakhki for developing the JavaScript reimplementation of the Geolocation API used in this project. This research was supported in part by NSF grants CNS-1054233, CNS-1319019, and CHS-1408345. Any opinions, findings, and conclusions or recommendations expressed in this material are those of the authors and do not necessarily reflect the views of the NSF.

6. REFERENCES

[1] Alexa Top 500 Global Sites. http://www.alexa.com/topsites.

[2] J. Burn-Murdoch. US web statistics released for May 2012: which sites dominate, and where do we go for online news? *The Guardian*, 2012.

[3] P. N. Bennett, F. Radlinski, R. W. White, and E. Yilmaz. Inferring and Using Location Metadata to Personalize Web Search. *SIGIR*, 2011.

[4] Z. Dou, R. Song, and J.-R. Wen. A Large-scale Evaluation and Analysis of Personalized Search Strategies. *WWW*, 2007.

[5] M. Eslami, A. Aleyasen, K. Karahalios, K. Hamilton, and C. Sandvig. FeedVis: A Path for Exploring News Feed Curation Algorithms. *CSCW*, 2015.

[6] M. Eslami, A. Rickman, K. Vaccaro, A. Aleyasen, A. Vuong, K. Karahalios, K. Hamilton, and C. Sandvig. "I always assumed that I wasn't really that close to [her]": Reasoning about invisible algorithms in the news feed. *CHI*, 2015.

[7] S. Guha, B. Cheng, and P. Francis. Challenges in Measuring Online Advertising Systems. *IMC*, 2010.

[8] S. Gauch, J. Chaffee, and A. Pretschner. Ontology-based personalized search and browsing. *Web Intelligence and Agent Systems*, 1, 2003.

[9] Google. Personalized Search Graduates from Google Labs. *News From Google Blog*, 2005. http://googlepress.blogspot.com/2005/11/personalized-search-graduates-from_10.html.

[10] A. Hannak, G. Soeller, D. Lazer, A. Mislove, and C. Wilson. Measuring Price Discrimination and Steering on E-commerce Web Sites. *IMC*, 2014.

[11] A. Hannak, P. Sapiezyński, A. M. Kakhki, B. Krishnamurthy, D. Lazer, A. Mislove, and C. Wilson. Measuring Personalization of Web Search. *WWW*, 2013.

[12] HTML5 Geolocation API. http://dev.w3.org/geo/api/spec-source.html.

[13] M. Lecuyer, G. Ducoffe, F. Lan, A. Papancea, T. Petsios, R. Spahn, A. Chaintreau, and R. Geambasu. XRay: Enhancing the Web's Transparency with Differential Correlation. *USENIX Security*, 2014.

[14] A. Micarelli, F. Gasparetti, F. Sciarrone, and S. Gauch. Personalized Search on the World Wide Web. *The Adaptive Web*, Peter Brusilovsky, Alfred Kobsa, and Wolfgang Nejdl, eds., Springer-Verlag, 2007.

[15] J. Mikians, L. Gyarmati, V. Erramilli, and N. Laoutaris. Detecting Price and Search Discrimination on the Internet. *HotNets*, 2012.

[16] J. Mikians, L. Gyarmati, V. Erramilli, and N. Laoutaris. Crowd-assisted Search for Price Discrimination in E-Commerce: First results. *CoNEXT*, 2013.

[17] M. G. Noll and C. Meinel. Web Search Personalization via Social Bookmarking and Tagging. *Proc. of The Semantic Web and 2nd Asian Conference on Asian Semantic Web Conference*, 2007.

[18] A. Pretschner and S. Gauch. Ontology based personalized search. *ICTAI*, 1999.

[19] E. Pariser. *The Filter Bubble: What the Internet is Hiding from You*. Penguin Press, 2011.

[20] PhantomJS. 2015. http://phantomjs.org.

[21] Right to be Forgotten ruling. http://ec.europa.eu/justice/data-protection/files/factsheets/factsheet_data_protection_en.pdf.

[22] L. Sweeney. Discrimination in Online Ad Delivery. *SSRN*, 2013.

[23] D. Y. Wang, M. Der, M. Karmai, L. Saul, D. McCoy, S. Savage, and G. M. Voelker. Search + Seizure: The Effectiveness of Interventions on SEO Campaigns. *IMC*, 2014.

[24] X. Xing, W. Meng, D. Doozan, N. Feamster, W. Lee, and A. C. Snoeren. Exposing Inconsistent Web Search Results with Bobble. *PAM*, 2014.

[25] B. Yu and G. Cai. A query-aware document ranking method for geographic information retrieval. *GIR*, 2007.

[26] X. Yi, H. Raghavan, and C. Leggetter. Discovering Users' Specific Geo Intention in Web Search. *WWW*, 2009.

Reliable Recon in Adversarial Peer-to-Peer Botnets

Dennis Andriesse
VU University Amsterdam
The Netherlands
d.a.andriesse@vu.nl

Christian Rossow
Saarland University, Germany
crossow@mmci.uni-saarland.de

Herbert Bos
VU University Amsterdam
The Netherlands
h.j.bos@vu.nl

ABSTRACT

The decentralized nature of Peer-to-Peer (P2P) botnets precludes traditional takedown strategies, which target dedicated command infrastructure. P2P botnets replace this infrastructure with command channels distributed across the full infected population. Thus, mitigation strongly relies on accurate reconnaissance techniques which map the botnet population.While prior work has studied passive disturbances to reconnaissance accuracy —such as IP churn and NAT gateways—, the same is not true of active anti-reconnaissance attacks. This work shows that active attacks against crawlers and sensors occur frequently in major P2P botnets. Moreover, we show that current crawlers and sensors in the Sality and Zeus botnets produce easily detectable anomalies, making them prone to such attacks. Based on our findings, we categorize and evaluate vectors for stealthier and more reliable P2P botnet reconnaissance.

Categories and Subject Descriptors

D.4.6 [**Operating Systems**]: Security and Protection—*Invasive Software*; C.2.0 [**Computer-Communication Networks**]: General—*Security and Protection*

General Terms

Security

Keywords

Peer-to-Peer Botnet, Crawling, Reconnaissance

1. INTRODUCTION

The decentralized nature of Peer-to-Peer (P2P) botnet architectures eliminates the need for centralized Command-and-Control (C2) servers. As a result, P2P botnets are immune to traditional takedown strategies, designed to disrupt centralized C2 channels. Instead, takedown efforts against P2P botnets require large-scale distributed attacks, such as sinkholing, which target all bots in the network [28]. Due to the high resilience of P2P botnet architectures, many high-profile botnets have migrated from centralized to P2P networks. Among the most resilient of these are Sality [10] and P2P (GameOver) Zeus [2].

The recent takedown of GameOver Zeus underscores the resilience of botnets like these. This notorious banking trojan has been active since 2011, and has survived despite multiple intensive sinkholing efforts [28, 4], until finally being crippled in May 2014, following a massive collaboration between the FBI, VU University Amsterdam, Saarland University, Crowdstrike, Dell SecureWorks, and other agencies, universities and malware analysis labs [5, 3].

Attacks against botnets like these are fundamentally based on knowledge about the composition of the botnet [28]. For instance, sinkholing attacks disrupt C2 connections between bots, and thus require a view of the botnet connectivity graph. Similarly, banks use P2P botnet mappings to identify infected customers, and several nations are currently setting up centralized repositories for reporting infected IPs [31].

Knowledge about the nodes in a botnet and the connections between them is obtained using intelligence gathering (reconnaissance/recon) techniques. Reliable recon techniques for P2P botnets are thus crucial for both invasive attacks (e.g., sinkholing) and non-invasive countermeasures (e.g., infection notifications). *All* recent P2P botnet takedowns required accurate recon, including the ZeroAccess and GameOver Zeus attacks [5, 3, 22, 35, 19]. Note that connectivity graph-agnostic Sybil attacks, which could effectively disrupt early DHT-based P2P botnets [6], are not effective against modern unstructured networks like Sality and Zeus, which use dense, dynamic connectivity graphs to propagate signed commands between bots.

To maximize the reliability of reconnaissance results, prior work has studied a myriad of passive disruptive factors, such as bots behind NAT gateways and IP address aliasing [28, 17]. In contrast, very little attention has been devoted in the literature to the hardening of recon against active disruption by botnet operators.

We believe this issue calls for closer analysis, as botmasters increasingly implement active anti-recon strategies in P2P botnets, largely in response to recent successful takedowns. These upcoming anti-recon strategies are aimed at compromising the intelligence gathered by malware analysts in P2P botnets, using attacks such as (automatic) blacklisting [2], reputation schemes [10], and even DDoS against recon nodes [4]. Botmasters use anti-recon strategies to augment previously disabled botnets, and redeploy hardened

IMC'15, October 28-30 2015, Tokyo, Japan

ACM 978-1-4503-3848-6/15/10 ...$15.00.
DOI: http://dx.doi.org/10.1145/2815675.2815682.

versions of them, which are more difficult to take down. For instance, the Hlux botnet has already respawned three times, each time with additional hardening strategies [35, 19, 11]. These patterns suggest that next-generation P2P botnets will incorporate stronger anti-recon techniques. Because takedown and disinfection efforts against P2P botnets hinge on reliable reconnaissance, our work is aimed at proactively investigating the full extent of anti-recon implemented by P2P botmasters, and the range of possible defenses to safeguard reconnaissance in next-generation botnets.

We show that recon tools used by malware analysts to monitor high-profile botnets suffer from serious protocol deficiencies, making them easily detectable. Specifically, we infiltrate the Sality v3 and GameOver Zeus botnets by inserting passive sensors, which scan incoming traffic for anomalies and deviations from the botnet protocol. Additionally, we use active peer list requests to locate sensor nodes which do not actively initiate communication. (At the time of our analysis, the attack against GameOver Zeus had not yet been launched.) We identify 21 Zeus crawlers, 10 distinct Zeus sensors, and 11 Sality crawlers belonging to well-known malware analysis laboratories, network security companies, and CERTs. We find that all of these have shortcomings which make them easy to identify among the bot populations (200.000 bots for Zeus, and 900.000 for Sality) [28].

At first glance, it may seem that the situation could be remedied by eliminating syntactic protocol deficiencies in crawlers and sensors. We show that this is not so; even syntactically sound recon tools can be detected by anomalous in- or out-degrees. This is commonly true especially for crawlers, as they strive to contact as many bots in as short a time span as possible. To evaluate the magnitude of this problem, we design and implement a novel distributed crawler detection model, and show that it can automatically detect all crawlers in GameOver Zeus without false positives. We illustrate that the algorithm is applicable not only to Zeus, but also to other P2P botnets, including Sality. Based on these results, we propose and evaluate techniques to evade out-degree-based detection, such as rate limiting and distributed crawling, and we measure the impact of these techniques on crawling accuracy and completeness.

We also discuss an alternative reconnaissance strategy which has been widely proposed for use in P2P botnets, namely Internet-wide scanning [9]. We show that it is applicable to some P2P botnets, but is unfortunately not compatible with all P2P botnet protocols.

Summarizing, our main contributions are:

1. We identify and classify anti-recon attacks taking place in current P2P botnets, and generalize to potential attacks which could be implemented in future botnets.

2. We categorize recon strategies and their susceptibility to passive and active disruption.

3. We analyze the quality of crawlers and sensors used in Sality and Zeus, and classify major shortcomings.

4. We design and implement a syntax-agnostic crawler detection algorithm, and use it to analyze tradeoffs between reconnaissance stealthiness versus speed, accuracy, and completeness.

5. We discuss strategies for covert P2P botnet recon based on our results.

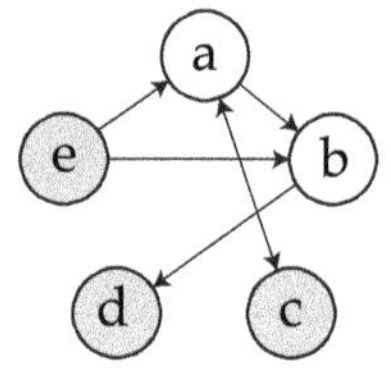

Figure 1: An example botnet connectivity graph. An arrow from node a to node b indicates that a knows b. Non-routable nodes are shaded.

2. RECON IN P2P BOTNETS

Reconnaissance methods for P2P botnets can be divided into two classes, namely crawler-based and sensor-based methods (though hybrids are feasible [28]). This section introduces both of these classes, and compares their tradeoffs and resilience to passive disruption. We discuss active recon disruption in Section 3.

Throughout this paper, we consider a botnet to be a digraph $G = (V, E)$, where V is the set of vertices (e.g. bots), and E is the set of edges (e.g. is-neighbor connections between bots). We refer to the number of outgoing edges from a bot v as its out-degree $deg^+(v)$, and the number of incoming edges as in-degree $deg^-(v)$.

2.1 Crawlers

Crawler-based reconnaissance relies upon the peer list exchange mechanism available in all P2P botnets [28, 2, 10, 13, 33, 35]. In P2P botnets, every bot maintains a list of addresses of other peers it has been contacted by or has learned about from other bots. To maintain connectivity with the network despite the constant churn of bots that join and leave the botnet, peers regularly exchange (parts of) their peer list with their neighbors. Support for peer list exchanges is typically implemented through special request messages included in the botnet protocol, called peer list requests, which each bot can use to request a set of peer addresses from another. Crawlers abuse this mechanism by recursively requesting peer lists from all bots they learn about, starting from an initial bootstrap peer list (usually obtained from a bot sample).

Due to its simplicity and ability to rapidly request peers from many bots, crawling is a highly popular intelligence gathering method used by malware analysts [15, 28]. Nevertheless, crawlers have been reported to suffer from a myriad of inaccuracy problems. For instance, address aliasing can occur with bots that use dynamic IP addresses, leading to significant botnet size overestimations if the crawling period is too long [17]. In addition, crawlers cannot contact and verify the liveness of non-externally reachable (non-routable) bots, such as bots protected by a firewall or NAT gateway [17, 28]. This is a significant shortcoming, since the percentage of non-routable bots can range up to 60–87% [28].

Figure 1 shows the inaccuracy that may result from the inability of crawlers to verify non-routable bots. The figure depicts a connectivity graph containing bots $a, \ldots, e$, of which bots $c, \ldots, e$ are non-routable (shaded). A crawler can only directly contact the externally reachable (routable) bots a and b; non-routable bots are only discoverable if they actively advertise themselves.

The only way for a crawler to learn about bots $c, \ldots, e$ is by relying on the peer lists returned by a and b. The addresses returned in these peer lists may be outdated, and the lists may include multiple aliases for bots with dynamic IPs. The crawler cannot be sure of this, and cannot actively establish contact with bots $c, \ldots, e$ to verify their existence. On the other extreme of the scale, the botnet protocol may not allow non-routable bots to push themselves into the peer lists of other bots at all, making it impossible for crawlers to find non-routable bots. As an example, node e in Figure 1 has no incoming edges from any routable bot, making it undetectable to crawlers regardless of the protocol.

2.2 Sensors

In contrast to crawlers, sensors are largely passive. When injecting a new sensor node into a botnet, its address is actively announced (as is done for new bots joining the network) until a sufficient number of bots learn about the existence of the sensor. After that, the active announcement is ceased, and the sensor relies upon peer list exchanges between bots to propagate its address. Sensors map the network by waiting for bots to contact them, instead of actively contacting bots.

Compared to crawlers, sensors achieve better coverage of routable bots [28]. In addition, sensors can find and verify all non-routable bots which contact them after learning the sensor addresses from other bots. This allows sensors to more precisely and reliably map the nodes in the botnet than crawlers [28].

Sensors are currently not as widely used by malware analysts as crawlers are. In part, this is due to the larger implementation and reverse engineering effort required to build and maintain a sensor. Since most botnets have mechanisms to evict unresponsive or incorrectly responding peers from peer lists, sensors must implement most or all of the botnet protocol to avoid being evicted. In contrast, crawlers only need support for peer list requests and responses. Furthermore, sensor injection can be complicated by botnet resilience measures like reputation schemes [10] and non-persistent peer list entries [36].

In contrast to crawlers, sensors map only the nodes in a botnet, but not the connectivity information. However, since sinkholing attacks overwrite peer list entries, they require connectivity information to determine which entries to target. To obtain this information, sensors must be expanded to request peer lists from bots which contact them. Compared to crawlers, sensors which are augmented with active peer list requests have the advantage that they can even reach the majority of non-routable bots through NAT punch holes.

3. ANTI-RECON ATTACKS

Recon tools like crawlers and sensors are open to a range of attacks which impair intelligence gathering. This section categorizes the anti-recon measures which we have observed in the wild in all major P2P botnets since 2007 [28]. We summarize these in Table 1, and categorize anti-recon into four categories: (1) deterrence, (2) passive attacks (i.e., blacklisting), (3) active disinformation, and (4) retaliation attacks.

3.1 Deterrence

Deterrence encompasses P2P botnet protocol characteristics designed to complicate recon. This includes measures meant to deter crawling or sensor injection.

As shown in Table 1, deterrence is currently the most common class of anti-recon: all major P2P botnets include some form of recon deterrence. Specifically, all botnets except Storm include an IP filter which prevents the injection of multiple sensors on a single IP [10, 25, 35, 19, 6, 13, 34, 33]. Zeus goes further than this, disallowing more than a single peer list entry per /20 subnet [2].

All botnets also include a form of information limiting designed to slow crawling, usually by returning only a small set of peer list entries at once. This is most extreme in Hlux, where at any moment there is only a small list of around 500 relay nodes (externally reachable bots) circulating in the network [19]. Another form of information limiting is clustering, observed in Zeus, Storm, and Hlux [2, 13, 35]. Zeus and Storm restrict the returned peer list entries based on a (Kademlia-like) XOR metric, returning only entries "close" to the requester according to this metric. Hlux clusters the bot population around a small core of relay bots shared in peer lists.

Finally, some bots also feature more specialized recon deterrence. For instance, Sality actively tries to prevent sensor injection by using a reputation scheme based on a goodcount, which reflects how well-behaved peers have been in the past [10]. Sensors are only propagated to other bots if they achieve a high goodcount first. Additionally, ZeroAccess prevents injection of persistent links to sensors by pushing a continuous flux of peer list updates, constantly overwriting the full peer list of each routable bot [25].

3.2 Blacklisting

Blacklisting is a passive attack, designed to starve crawlers and sensors of information by prohibiting bots from communicating with them. It is already used in ZeroAccess, and in particular also in GameOver Zeus, which features two distinct blacklisting mechanisms [2]. (1) Each bot binary is shipped and periodically updated with a hardcoded blacklist of IPs which the botmasters identified on the network due to anomalous behavior. (2) In recent versions of Zeus, an automatic blacklisting mechanism was introduced, which is a rudimentary approach to identify and block crawlers and nodes attempting to poison the network. Each bot tracks the request frequencies of its peers, and blocks peers sending many requests in quick succession. To prevent blocking of multiple NATed bots using the same IP, the maximum frequency is high enough to be circumventable by relatively efficient crawlers. Nevertheless, this mechanism is sufficient to thwart naive crawlers, and could be more finely tuned. Blocked IPs become unusable for malware analysis not only on the botnet in question, but also on other botnets, as (hardcoded) blacklists are often publicly visible.

3.3 Disinformation

Disinformation attacks actively supply crawlers and sensors with spurious peer list entries containing forged addresses, in order to divert them from the main bot population. This is problematic especially for crawlers, as they lack the ability to verify non-routable bot addresses. The attack can be expanded to thwart sensors by leading them into a "shadow botnet", containing a set of responsive peers which are isolated from the main bot population. Disinformation attacks can cause collateral damage by polluting lists of infected addresses reported to ISPs, and even rerouting sinkholing attacks to shadow nodes or uninfected hosts.

We have observed (possibly unintended) disinformation in ZeroAccess, where peer lists frequently include junk ad-

	Deterrence					Blacklisting		Disinformation	Retaliation
	IP filter	Reputation	Info limit	Flux	Clustering	Auto	Static	Spurious IPs	DDoS
Zeus	By /20	-	Peer list	-	XOR metric	By rate	Manual	-	After attack
Sality	By IP	Goodcount	Peer list	-	-	-	-	-	-
ZeroAccess	By IP	-	Peer list	Peer push	-	-	Manual	Junk	-
Kelihos/Hlux	By IP	-	Relay list	-	Relay core	-	-	-	-
Waledac	By IP	-	Relay list	-	-	-	-	-	-
Storm	-	-	Proximity	-	XOR metric	-	-	Rogue	After attack

Table 1: Anti-recon measures observed in P2P botnets.

dresses, such as reserved or unused IP addresses. In addition, Storm is known to have contained many rogue nodes, which also served to pollute exchanged peer lists [6]. Overall, current P2P botnets do not yet engage in disinformation on a large scale, but there is a real risk that future P2P botnets may engage in this strategy, especially as it has already been explored in detail in prior work [37]. We believe recon tools should implement measures to prevent this kind of attack, as it is quite difficult to detect once deployed in full-scale.

3.4 Retaliation

Retaliation is another category of active attack, in which botmasters take action to disable or compromise hosts used for reconnaissance. Retaliatory actions include denial-of-service attacks, as used by the GameOver Zeus botmasters in response to sinkholing attempts [4], and active infiltration or exploitation of hosts used for recon. Repeated denial-of-service attacks have also been observed in the Storm botnet, in response to takedown/infiltration attempts [6].

4. RECON ANOMALIES

This section analyzes the stealthiness of crawlers and sensors used in GameOver Zeus and Sality v3. Unstealthy reconnaissance tools expose themselves to an increased risk of the attacks discussed in Section 3. Section 4.1 discusses protocol anomalies found in crawlers, while Section 4.2 discusses sensor anomalies. In Section 4.3, we design a syntax-agnostic algorithm to detect crawlers based only on network coverage.

4.1 Crawler Protocol Anomalies

We base our crawler analysis on data gathered by 512 sensor nodes in the Zeus network (before it was sinkholed), and 64 sensors in Sality (the number is limited by Sality's peer management scheme and our IP range). We announced these sensors for two days, and then ran them passively for three weeks, until the combined sensor in-degrees matched botnet size estimates [28], ensuring reachability by all crawlers. Our sensor implementations included only protocol logic, and no malicious logic, and we verified the legality of our tactics with law enforcement officials.

We identified crawlers using protocol-specific anomaly detection on our sensor data, looking for peers with deviations from normal bot behavior. To define normal behavior, we reverse engineered Zeus and Sality to establish a ground truth. Next, we cross-verified our list of detected crawlers to ensure that crawlers from our anti-malware industry contacts were all correctly detected. While it is impossible to obtain a complete ground truth of crawlers in a live botnet, we established the significance of our results by attributing analyzed crawlers to large malware analysis companies, network security companies, CERTs, and (academic) researchers. We attributed crawlers using WHOIS data, protocol-specific information (such as bot IDs revealing company names), and inquiries with contacts in the community. We informed affected parties via closed mailing lists.

	c1	c2	c3	c4	c5	c6–c11
LOP range	✓	✓	✓	✓	✓	✓
Port range		✓	✓	✓	✓	✓
Random ID						
Version		✓	✓	✓		✓
Hard hitter	✓	✓	✓	✓	✓	✓
Protocol logic	✓	✓			✓	✓
Encryption						
Coverage (%)	69	100	100	100	100	100

Table 2: Defects found in Sality crawlers.

We study only well-functioning crawlers which cover at least 1% of the bot population (≥ 50 messages to our sensors), with the addition of one open-source Zeus crawler belonging to a large network security company. The resulting list of crawlers found by our anomaly detection includes 21 Zeus crawlers and 11 Sality crawlers. We summarize the defects found in these crawlers in Table 2 for Sality, and Table 3 for Zeus (anonymized to avoid revealing IPs used by malware analysts). Note that 6 of the 11 Sality crawlers are grouped together into a single column, as these were all running in the same subnet and exhibited the same characteristics (i.e., multiple instances of the same crawler).

The rest of this section discusses the results from Tables 2 and 3 in detail. We organize the results into several classes of common defects, each of which undermines crawler stealthiness, and increases attack vulnerability.

4.1.1 Range Anomalies

Crawlers with range anomalies exhibit static or constrained values for message fields that should be randomized. Additionally, range anomalies can occur when crawlers use random values for non-random fields. Our results show that range anomalies are the most common class of defects in Zeus crawlers. We found at least one range anomaly in 20 of the 21 analyzed crawlers.

The Zeus message header contains several fields which are normally randomized. These include a random byte at the beginning of each message, the Time to Live (TTL) field which is randomized when unused, and the Length of Padding (LOP) field, which indicates the length of the random padding at the end of the message. Furthermore, a random session ID is generated for each request-response pair. In 14 crawlers, the padding length was constrained, possibly to reduce bandwidth usage by limiting the number of padding bytes at the end of each message. Additionally, static or constrained random bytes and TTL values each occurred in 10 crawlers, and 11 crawlers used static session IDs, or rotated between a small number of session IDs.

	c1	c2	c3	c4	c5	c6	c7	c8	c9	c10	c11	c12	c13	c14	c15	c16	c17	c18	c19	c20	c21
RND range	✓	✓	✓	✓	✓	✓	✓	✓	✓	✓											
TTL range	✓	✓	✓	✓	✓	✓	✓	✓	✓	✓											
LOP range	✓	✓	✓	✓	✓	✓	✓				✓	✓	✓	✓	✓	✓	✓				
Session range	✓	✓	✓	✓	✓	✓	✓	✓	✓		✓	✓									
Session entropy	✓	✓								✓											
Random source																		✓	✓	✓	
Source entropy		✓									✓	✓	✓				✓				
Padding entropy	✓	✓	✓	✓	✓																
Abnormal lookup	✓	✓	✓	✓	✓			✓			✓	✓				✓	✓				
Hard hitter	✓							✓			✓	✓	✓	✓	✓			✓	✓		
Protocol logic	✓	✓	✓	✓	✓	✓	✓	✓	✓				✓	✓	✓						✓
Encryption	✓										✓	✓	✓	✓	✓	✓					
Coverage (%)	90	82	85	75	84	20	53	62	1	8	92	44	85	92	92	88	54	87	86	2	27

Table 3: Defects found in GameOver Zeus crawlers.

On the other hand, we found that 3 Zeus crawlers used random values for the source ID field on each message, which indicates the unique identifier of the bot that sent the message. Although a small variation in source ID per IP address is normal, and can indicate multiple bots behind a NAT gateway, these crawlers used over 1000 different source IDs, making them highly detectable.

Just as in Zeus, normal Sality messages end in a random amount of padding. Nevertheless, in all but one of the analyzed Sality crawlers, the padding length was set to a fixed value, and in the remaining crawler the padding length was constrained to reduce bandwidth usage. Additionally, 10 of the 11 analyzed crawlers sent messages from a fixed port, while ordinary Sality bots use a randomized port per message exchange.

Some types of Sality messages include a bot identifier, which normally does not change while the bot remains up. All of the crawlers we analyzed adhered to these semantics, and did not change their identifiers between messages exchanged with our sensors.

4.1.2 Entropy Anomalies

Entropy anomalies occur when multi-byte fields that normally contain high-entropy content are set to non-random values. In the Zeus protocol, such fields include the source ID and session ID, which are SHA-1 hashes, and the random padding bytes at the end of a message. We found 3 crawlers with low-entropy session IDs, 5 crawlers with non-random padding bytes, and 5 crawlers with low-entropy source IDs. The crawlers with low-entropy source IDs occasionally used identifiers with ASCII bytes representing the name of the company or individual running the crawler.

In contrast to Zeus, Sality uses randomly chosen integers instead of hashes as (non-global) bot identifiers. While Zeus crawlers often use low-entropy identifier strings, all Sality crawlers use seemingly random integer IDs, without any entropy anomalies.

4.1.3 Invalid Encryption

In 7 of the analyzed Zeus crawlers, we encountered corrupted messages that contained irrational data for all message fields. These corrupted messages were interspersed with correctly encoded messages. It appears that these crawlers occasionally select incorrect keys to encrypt outgoing messages, preventing our sensors from decrypting these messages. In GameOver Zeus, the unique identifier of each bot is used as the key to encrypt messages towards that bot. Thus, we suspect that the crawlers in question do not correctly keep track of the identifier of each bot they find. We did not encounter any invalid encryption in Sality crawlers.

4.1.4 Protocol Logic Anomalies

As mentioned in Section 2, an advantage of crawlers is that they avoid the need to implement the full P2P protocol. However, taking this simplification too far results in crawlers that manifest incorrect protocol logic. This was the case for 17 of the analyzed Zeus crawlers. In most cases, these crawlers simply sent large amounts of peer list requests, without regard for any other message types used by normal bots, such as messages used to exchange commands and binary/configuration updates.

Additionally, many crawlers used abnormal values for the lookup key field used in Zeus peer list requests. This field includes a Zeus identifier which is used by the receiving peer as a metric to determine which peers are sent back in the peer list response. Normal bots always set this field to the identifier of the remote peer. In contrast, many crawlers randomize the lookup key on each peer list request to increase the range of crawled peers.

Similarly to Zeus, most Sality crawlers (9 out of 11) used incorrect message sequences. Typically, these crawlers sent repeated peer list requests to the same bot, without interspersing any of the other normal message types, such as URL pack exchanges. Another common defect is the use of incorrect version numbers in the Sality message headers sent by crawlers. While all of the crawlers used a correct major version number, only 2 of them also used a valid minor version number.

4.1.5 Request Frequency Anomalies

In an effort to rapidly gather as much intelligence as possible about the botnet connectivity graph, 9 of the analyzed Zeus crawlers sent repeated peer list requests at high frequencies. These hard-hitting crawlers clearly contrast with real bots, which exchange only one peer list request per neighbor before returning to a suspended mode. Such request-suspend behavior is seen in many botnets [28], with a suspend period of 30 minutes for Zeus and 40 minutes for Sality, making hard-hitting crawlers highly anomalous.

In Sality, request frequency anomalies are even more common than in Zeus, occurring in all of the analyzed crawlers. This is because Sality bots only support the exchange of a single peer list entry at once, while Zeus bots return up to 10 entries in a single peer list response. Additionally, Sality peer lists are much larger than Zeus peer lists, typically containing around 1000 entries, while Zeus peer lists are limited to 150 entries (and rarely contain over 50 entries). To obtain a reasonable coverage of a bot's peer list, Sality crawlers are therefore obliged to send this bot multiple peer list requests. Sending these in quick succession, as all of the analyzed crawlers do, results in clear request frequency anomalies.

4.2 Sensor Protocol Anomalies

In addition to our crawler analysis from Section 4.1, we also analyzed the sensors active in GameOver Zeus and Sality during our monitoring. We found Zeus sensors belonging to 10 organizations (grouped by subnet) by analyzing the GameOver Zeus connectivity graph, and looking for nodes with high in-degrees. Since sensors aim to attract as many bots as possible, they are expected to have high in-degrees. To create a view of the connectivity graph and node in-degrees, our sensors sent active peer list requests to every bot that contacted them. After identifying high in-degree nodes, we probed each of these for anomalous responses to identify (defective) sensors. This is necessary as, unlike high out-degrees, our data shows that high in-degrees occur in hundreds of apparently legitimate bots. As in our crawler analysis, we cross-verified the identified sensors with a list of sensors known from industry contacts.

Our results show that the Zeus sensors suffer from the same shortcomings as current crawlers, including range anomalies, entropy anomalies, and protocol logic anomalies. In addition to these anomalies, we identified several sensor-specific anomalies. Specifically, all of the analyzed sensors failed to return the protocol-mandated list of proxy bots (used as data drops in GameOver Zeus) when requested. In addition, all but 3 of the sensors responded to peer list requests with empty peer lists, which is highly unusual behavior. Furthermore, all of the sensors which returned non-empty peer lists served duplicate peers in order to promote sinkholes or sensors, a behavior never displayed by legitimate bots. Finally, none of the sensors provided a correct implementation of the Zeus update mechanism; only 3 sensors reported valid and recent version numbers, and none of the sensors responded to update requests used to exchange binary and config files.

Although these anomalies allow current sensors to be detected, sensors are not inherently detectable. Specifically, although sensors generally have high in-degrees, our data shows that equally high in-degrees also occur for well-reachable legitimate bots, making high in-degree alone an insufficient metric for reliable sensor detection. Furthermore, P2P botnet protocols cannot be easily designed to expose sensors by limiting the in-degree of bots. This is because, by the degree sum formula[1], limiting the in-degree of bots implies limiting the out-degree as well, thus impairing the connectivity of the bots. In our analysis, we were unable to identify any sensors in Sality, precisely because no nodes with unusually high in-degree were present, and all high in-degree nodes responded correctly to probes for all packet types, including URL pack exchanges and peer exchanges. Thus, if any sensors are present in the Sality network, these cannot be detected in any straightforward way. In contrast, efficient crawlers tend to have unusually high out-degrees, as we show in Section 4.3, requiring special measures to avoid detection. To further investigate the detectability of crawlers by out-degree, we design a distributed crawler detection model in Section 4.3. Subsequently, we categorize crawling techniques to evade this model in Section 5, and implement and evaluate our detection model and evasive techniques in Section 6.

[1]In a directed graph $G = (V, E)$, with V the set of nodes and E the set of edges, the degree sum formula states that $\sum_{v \in V} deg^+(v) = \sum_{v \in V} deg^-(v) = |E|$, where $deg^+(v)$ and $deg^-(v)$ are the out-degree and in-degree of node v.

4.3 Network Coverage Anomalies

Even syntactically sound crawlers are detectable due to their tendency to contact many peers in a short timespan, in an attempt to quickly map the network. This behavior is visible in Tables 2 and 3. Sality and Zeus crawlers cover up to 100% and 92% of our sensors, respectively. Furthermore, nearly all crawlers cover at least 20% of our sensors, and most crawlers cover 50% or more. In contrast, ordinary bots cover only a small fraction of the botnet, due to their limited peer list sizes and evolution rates [10, 2, 28].

To evaluate the extent of this problem, and the effectiveness of our proposed countermeasures, we design and implement a syntax-agnostic crawler detection algorithm that identifies crawlers based on their network coverage. We chose to implement a distributed version of the algorithm to show that crawler detection is possible even without requiring centralized components in P2P botnets. The algorithm is scalable and Byzantine-tolerant, to allow crawler detection even in the presence of adversarial nodes (which malware analysts may inject to subvert the algorithm). To prevent impersonation attacks, the algorithm assumes a non-spoofable transport layer, such as TCP. This section provides an overview of our algorithm, while Sections 5 and 6 discuss improved crawling techniques and their effectiveness in evading our detection algorithm, respectively.

Note that this is just one from a range of out-degree-based crawler detection methods. Alternative implementations, even centralized ones, can equally well detect crawlers with anomalous out-degrees, and completely circumvent the risk of subversion by Sybils. Centralized implementations fit well with the hybrid structure of many current P2P botnets, such as Zeus and Kelihos, where bots periodically report to a higher layer of centralized servers [2, 35, 19]. Therefore, this paper focuses on our findings regarding the efficacy of stealthy crawling techniques, rather than technical details of our particular detection algorithm. Due to space limitations, we defer a discussion of such details, and the Byzantine-tolerance of our algorithm, to a technical report [1].

Our algorithm is based on periodic crawler detection rounds, with the period depending on the time needed to comprehensively crawl the botnet. This time depends on the botnet architecture, diurnal pattern, and protocol, and is 24 hours for Zeus and Sality, as shown in Section 6 and prior work [28]. Crawling for less than 24 hours misses part of the population, while crawling longer pollutes results due to infection churn and IP churn [28]. Our tests in Section 6 use hourly detection rounds to detect crawlers well before they cover a full diurnal period. The algorithm assumes that each bot has a random identifier, generated at infection time. Each round consists of the following operations.

Detection round announcement The botmaster pushes a round announcement (signed and timestamped to prevent replays) to a random bot, which then propagates to all bots using gossiping (a technique also used in Zeus and ZeroAccess [28]). We use push-based gossiping to reach only routable peers, excluding non-routable bots (never reached by crawlers) for scalability. The bots partition themselves into 2^g groups by sampling g bit positions (specified in the announcement) from their identifiers. Each group contains the bots with identical bit values at these g positions, and a per-group leader is assigned in the announcement, creating 2^g tree-shaped overlay networks rooted at the group leaders.

Hardhitter aggregation Every bot contacts its leader and reports all IPs that requested its peer list within a configurable history interval. This interval must cover multiple detection rounds, or else crawlers can avoid detection by contacting only a limited set of bots per round (see Section 6). Leaders aggregate the IPs (including their own history), and flag IPs reported by at least a configurable threshold fraction of the group as suspicious. Section 6 discusses how to set the threshold to minimize false positives/negatives.

Crawler voting Leaders collectively vote for suspected crawler IPs, and classify those IPs which receive a majority vote as crawlers. Majority voting makes the algorithm tolerant of adversarial leaders which unjustly blacklist non-crawler IPs, or whitelist true crawlers [1]. As leader selection is random, adversarial nodes are unlikely to dominate the leader population unless a large fraction of the bot population consists of Sybils (anti-Sybil strategies are discussed in prior work [29, 7]).

Crawler propagation All bots retrieve the list of crawlers from n randomly chosen leaders, and filter crawlers reported by a majority of the leaders. This limits the scope of faulty results reported by adversarial leaders. Bots can expect reliable results if $|A| < n \times m$, where $|A|$ denotes the number of adversarial leaders and m the fraction of leaders required in a majority.

5. STEALTHY CRAWLING TECHNIQUES

In this section, we propose methods to improve the reliability and stealthiness of P2P botnet crawling. These strategies are specifically aimed at evading out-degree- or request-frequency-based detection, as described in Sections 4 and 4.3. We measure the efficacy of these strategies, and their impact on crawling efficiency, in Section 6. The methods proposed in this section apply to all variants (distributed and centralized) of out-degree-based crawler detection algorithms.

5.1 Contact Ratio Limiting

A straightforward way to limit the out-degree of crawlers is to limit the set of bot IPs they contact. For instance, crawlers which contact only half of the bots (a contact ratio of 1/2) are expected to still obtain a reasonably complete view of the network, as the addresses of the excluded bots are returned in the peer list responses of the remaining bots. A limitation of this approach is that it further exaggerates the node verification problem described in Section 2. Contact ratio-limited crawlers are not only unable to verify the authenticity of non-routable nodes, but also cannot verify the excluded routable bots. Furthermore, we show in Section 6 that to evade detection using contact ratio limiting, crawlers must use very low contact ratios of 1/16, or even 1/32. As we show, this reduces the completeness of the gathered intelligence.

5.2 Request Frequency Limiting

As described in Section 4.1, many crawlers send multiple peer list requests in quick succession to maximize their coverage of each bot's peer list. Stealthy crawlers should limit their request frequencies to avoid being identified as hard hitters (see Section 4.1.5). We measure the impact of request frequency limiting in Section 6, and show that the crawling efficiency obtained by frequency-limited crawlers depends on protocol-specific factors, like the selection strategy for returned peers, and the number of entries per peer list response.

5.3 Distributed Crawling

By distributing their egress traffic over multiple source addresses, crawlers can reduce the risk of detection by IP-centric sensors. This strategy encompasses several techniques. (1) Crawlers can be (virtually) distributed over multiple addresses, crawling only a limited subset of bots per source address. (2) Addresses used for crawling can be rotated periodically, with a rotation frequency configured such that a new address is selected before exceeding the per-address detection threshold.

As we show in Section 6, distributed crawlers must use IPs from distinct subnets to reliably avoid detection. The crawler detection algorithm in our experiments can reliably detect crawlers with IPs distributed over a /20 subnet, or with per-address crawling traffic limited by a factor of up to 1/32. Thus, distributed Zeus or Sality crawlers require addresses from at least 32 distinct /20 subnets, or a single /16 network block.

5.4 Anonymizing Proxies

Crawlers could attempt to evade detection by using proxy servers or an anonymizing network such as Tor [8] to obtain rapidly changing IP addresses. This approach can be effective, but unfortunately does not blend well with current anonymizing services, due to several issues. (1) Effective crawlers simultaneously open thousands of connections, causing connection tracking and scalability problems with non-dedicated proxy services. Furthermore, the bandwidth and latency performance of the Tor network is known to be constrained, resulting in slowly converging, and thus inaccurate, crawling results [8, 26]. (2) The IPs used by anonymizing proxies and Tor exit nodes are often publicly known, and can thus be easily blocked by botmasters [12, 23]. A more effective option might be to set up a dedicated anonymizing proxy service, though this would require one or more large dedicated network address blocks as well as strong secrecy measures to avoid these from leaking out.

6. STEALTHY CRAWLING EVALUATION

In this section, we evaluate the detectability of in-the-wild Zeus crawlers by network coverage, using the crawler detection algorithm introduced in Section 4.3. Furthermore, we measure the effectiveness of the evasive crawling techniques introduced in Section 5, and their tradeoffs in crawling speed and completeness. We do this by simulating (to ensure repeatability) the effects of these evasive strategies on traffic we logged from real-world Sality and Zeus crawlers.

6.1 Crawler Detection Accuracy

A full-scale crawler detection algorithm would run distributed over all routable nodes in a botnet. Since we cannot deploy such an experimental setup, we instead ran our crawler detection experiments on the 512 sensor nodes which we injected into the GameOver Zeus botnet. As mentioned in Section 4.1, none of the sensors contained any malicious logic. We performed all our experiments before the recent

t	$\|G\|$	#FP	$D_{1/1}$	$D_{1/2}$	$D_{1/4}$	$D_{1/8}$	$D_{1/16}$	$D_{1/32}$	$D_{1/64}$	$D_{1/128}$	$D_{1/256}$
1	8	119	100	100	100	94	89	83	39	28	0
2	8	13	100	100	89	89	83	44	6	0	0
5	8	0	100	89	89	72	50	0	0	0	0
C_{Zeus}	N/A	N/A	100	80	52	42	38	2			
C_{Sality}	N/A	N/A	100	90	74	44	27	16			

Table 4: False positives vs. detected crawlers for $|G| = 8$ and $t \in \{1\%, 2\%, 5\%\}$.
D_c = % detected crawlers for contact ratio c. C = % bots covered by crawler using contact-ratio limiting (relative).

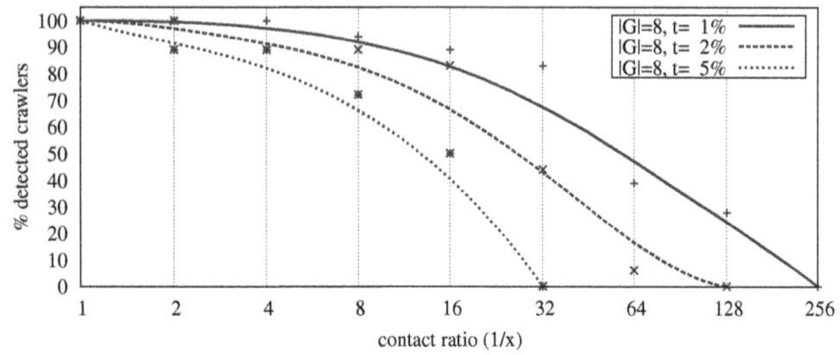

Figure 2: Crawlers detected in 24 hours for $|G| = 8$ and $t \in \{1\%, 2\%, 5\%\}$. The contact ratio simulated on the crawler traffic varies over x.

GameOver Zeus takedown. Our sensor nodes logged all received requests over a total test period of 24 hours. We chose a 24-hour period to account for a full diurnal cycle without suffering from duplicate results due to address aliasing caused by dynamic IP addresses. We then performed our experiments with varying configuration parameters on the logged traffic, to ensure that any detection differences were a result of the configuration parameters rather than churn in the bot and crawler populations. During our test period, 18 of the crawlers from Table 3 (Section 4.1) were active, which we used as a ground truth. The rest of this section describes our measurements of the effectiveness of the crawling techniques proposed in Section 5 to evade out-degree-based detection: (1) contact ratio limiting, and (2) address distribution. (We do not evaluate frequency limiting here as it does not pertain to the out-degree of crawlers.)

6.1.1 Contact Ratio Limiting

The detection results of our GameOver Zeus tests are shown in Figure 2 (detected crawlers) and Table 4 (detection rate vs. false positives). We used a per-bot request history of 24 hours, meaning that crawlers are detected if they cover a significant fraction of the bot population in 24 hours. In our experiments, we randomly partitioned our sensors into 8 groups per detection interval. In a full-scale implementation, this arrangement would split the Zeus population of 200.000 bots [2] into groups of 25.000 bots (including non-routable bots) per leader. We denote the number of groups as $|G|$ (the magnitude of the set of groups G) in Figure 2. We vary the per-group detection threshold, denoted as t in the figure, to illustrate the tradeoffs between detection accuracy and false positives. This threshold is the percentage of bots per group that a crawler must cover to receive a vote from that group. We simulated the detection performance for contact ratio-limited crawlers by excluding crawler requests to a varying subset of our sensors (the x-axis in Figure 2).

As shown in Figure 2, a per-group detection threshold of 1% allows 28% of crawlers to be detected even if these limit their contact ratio to only 1/128 bots. However, this comes at a cost of 119 falsely identified crawlers (denoted #FP in Table 4), most of which are actually sets of NATed bots sharing a single IP. Increasing the threshold to 2% reduces the number of false positives to 13, but also limits the detection accuracy to 44% for a 1/32 contact ratio, and 6% for a 1/64 contact ratio. In our tests, the ideal threshold is 5%, allowing 100% of crawlers to be detected without false positives if no contact ratio limiting is used in the crawlers. The accuracy degrades gracefully to 50% for crawlers with a 1/16 contact ratio, meaning that stealthy crawlers may contact at most 1 in every 16 bots to evade detection with 50% probability. When increasing the threshold further to 10%, the detection rate degrades to 89% (2 false negatives) if no contact ratio limiting is used, and to 50% when a contact ratio of 1/8 is applied.

6.1.2 Address Distribution

To determine the range of addresses needed by distributed crawlers, we also measured the effectiveness of crawler detection using subnet aggregation. Using the ideal detection threshold of 5%, our experiments show that crawlers can be detected with 100% accuracy (no false positives) using subnet aggregation ranging from /32 (per-IP detection) to /20 (aggregation per subnet of 4096 hosts). Starting from a /19 filter, the crawler detector reports 110 false positives, caused by multiple infections within the same subnet. This indicates that to evade detection, address-distributed crawlers for Zeus must take each address from at least a distinct /20 subnet. As shown by our contact ratio experiments, a coverage reduction of a factor 32 is required for Zeus crawlers to avoid detection, so that the address-distributed crawlers must take their addresses from 32 distinct /20 subnets, or alternatively from a single /16.

6.1.3 Sality Crawler Detection

To complement our Zeus experiments, we attempted to repeat our crawler detection tests in the Sality network. Unfortunately, the peer list size and peer exchange properties of Sality prohibit small-scale tests of our algorithm.

In Sality, bots maintain a peer list of 1000 entries, and exchange peers based on a responsiveness-based reputation metric, as documented by Falliere [10]. To obtain meaningful evaluation results, it is necessary to run significantly more sensors than fit in a Sality peer list. Otherwise, sensors are highly likely to be present in the peer lists of many legitimate bots, making these bots indistinguishable from crawlers.

While our 512 sensor nodes were sufficient to prototype our algorithm for Zeus, where typical bots only maintain around 50 peer list entries [2], a Sality prototype would require several thousand IP addresses, which we were unable to obtain for our experiments. Nevertheless, because Sality's reputation mechanism and limit of a single entry per peer exchange significantly restrict the out-degree of Sality bots,

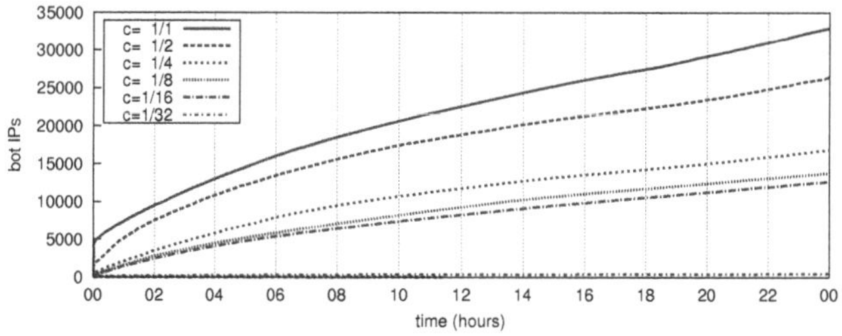

(a) Zeus.

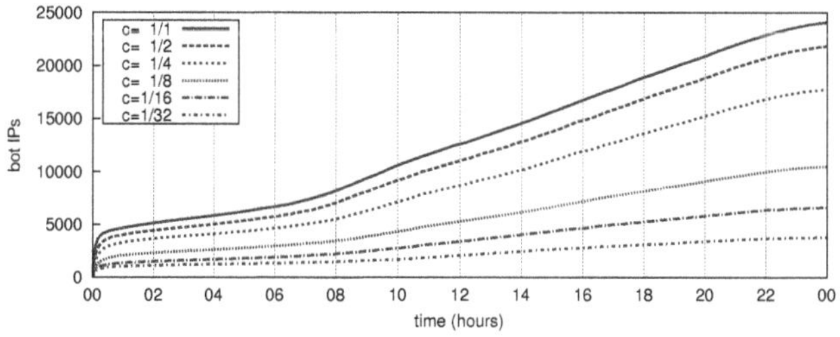

(b) Sality.

Figure 3: Bots crawled in 24 hours for varying contact ratio.

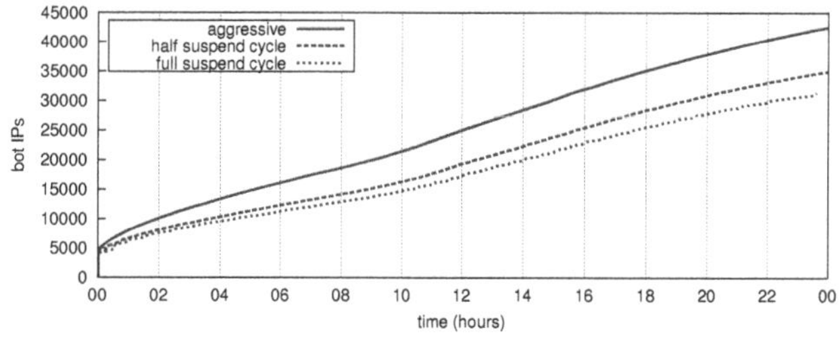

(a) Zeus.

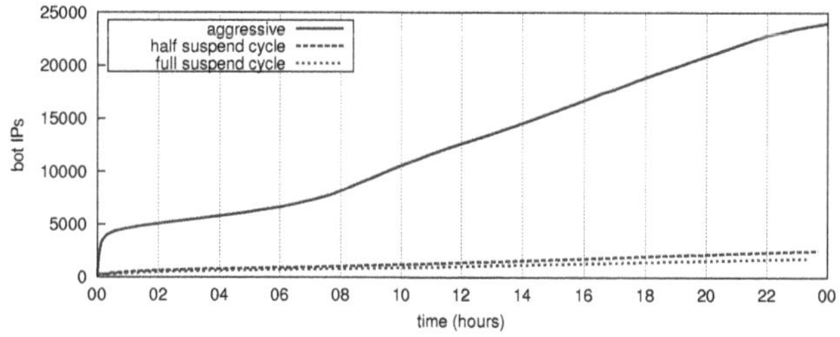

(b) Sality.

Figure 4: Bots crawled in 24 hours for varying request frequency.

we expect that Sality crawlers are highly susceptible to full-scale crawler detection (as could be implemented by the Sality botmasters).

6.2 Stealthy Crawling Performance

To evaluate the reconnaissance performance of the stealthy crawling techniques proposed in Section 5, we implemented contact ratio and frequency-limited crawlers for both GameOver Zeus and Sality. (We do not evaluate address-distributed crawlers, as these should suffer no degradation in crawling performance.) For both Zeus and Sality, we ran all of the crawling tests in parallel for 24 hours, to ensure that performance differences did not result from churn in the bot population. The contact ratio-limited crawlers only contacted a deterministically restricted fraction of bots, based on the bot identifier. Figure 3 graphs the number of bots detected over time by contact ratio-limited crawlers, while Figure 4 shows the results for frequency-limited crawlers.

6.2.1 *Contact Ratio Limiting*

As shown in Figure 3 and Table 4, the number of peers found steadily drops as the crawler contact ratio decreases. At a contact ratio of 1/2, crawling performance is still good, finding 80% of the Zeus peers found in a full crawl, and 90% of the Sality peers. However, as can be seen in Figure 2, this contact ratio still allows 89% of the crawlers to be detected. Reducing the contact ratio further causes a rapid decline in completeness. At a contact ratio of 1/4, our crawler finds 74% of Sality peers, and only 52% of Zeus peers. When reducing the contact ratio to 1/16, only 38% of the Zeus bots, and 27% of the Sality bots are found by our crawler, while this contact ratio still leads to a probability of 50% that crawlers are detected. These results show that contact ratio limiting achieves crawler stealthiness only at a high cost in crawling completeness. Note that it is not relevant whether or not our initial crawls reached the full bot population. Rather, the results serve only to show the relative coverage degradation which results from contact ratio limiting.

6.2.2 *Frequency Limiting*

Figure 4 shows crawling results for aggressive crawling, where the suspend-request cycle used by normal bots is not respected, as well as for crawls adhering to the suspend period between requests. We show results for crawlers using a full suspend cycle (30 minutes for Zeus and 40 minutes for Sality), as well as a half suspend cycle. The results are highly dependent on the protocol of the crawled botnet. For Zeus, even crawlers adhering to a full suspend cycle achieve reasonable efficiency, finding 74% of the bots found by the aggressive crawler. There are two main reasons for this. (1) Zeus returns 10 peers per peer list response, and the peer lists of typical bots contain only around 50 entries. This makes it possible to cover a larger fraction of each bot's peer list in a single suspend-request cycle than for Sality, which features more stringent constraints. (2) Due to the frequency-based automatic blacklisting mechanism used in Zeus, even our aggressive crawler is rate limited to avoid being blacklisted. This reduces the gap between the aggressive crawling results and the suspend cycle-adherent results. For Sality, the impact of frequency limiting is severe. Only 11% of the bots are found using a half suspend cycle, and only 7% when adhering to a full suspend cycle. This is because the peer lists of Sality bots contain up to 1000 entries, while only one entry is returned per peer list response. Note that even frequency-limited crawlers are prone to out-degree based detection. Thus, frequency limiting must always be used in unison with out-degree limiting.

7. INTERNET-WIDE SCANNING

Recent advances have enabled fast Internet-wide scanning in practical tools such as ZMap [9]. These tools work by probing large subsets of the public IP address space, in order to find hosts that have a particular property (i.e., a security vulnerability, OS version, etc.), as evidenced by their response to the probes. Internet-wide scanning has been proposed as an alternative reconnaissance method for finding botnet servers and bots [24]. Additionally (though

	Fixed port	Probe msg	Susceptible
Zeus	✗	✗	✗
Sality	✗	✓	✗
ZeroAccess	✓	✓	✓
Kelihos/Hlux	✓	✓	✓
Waledac	✗	✓	✗
Storm	✗	✓	✗

Table 5: Susceptibility of P2P botnets to Internet-wide scanning.

not strictly necessary), it has been used in practice to discover bots in the ZeroAccess P2P botnet [20].

Internet-wide scanning can be an efficient approach to node discovery in P2P botnets, but unfortunately it does not generalize well to all protocols. This is due to several factors. (1) Many P2P botnets use a large port range, where each bot listens on only a single port from this range. For instance, Zeus bots choose ports in the range 1024-10000 [2]. This makes Internet-wide scanning intrusive and inefficient, as thousands of ports must be scanned per host. Internet-wide scanning is a feasible reconnaissance method for ZeroAccess only because it runs on a single fixed port (depending on the version) [25, 36]. (2) Some botnets, like Zeus, use a different encryption key for packets destined to each bot, based on the node ID of the receiving bot. This makes it impossible to probe bots without a-priori knowledge of their node ID. Consequently, Internet-wide scanning is inherently incompatible with botnets like Gameover Zeus which use this tactic. (3) Like crawling, Internet-wide scanning cannot learn about non-routable nodes that remain hidden behind a firewall or NAT gateway.

Table 5 summarizes the susceptibility of all major P2P botnets active since 2007 to Internet-wide scanning [28]. We consider two prerequisites for Internet-wide scanning in P2P botnet reconnaissance: (1) the bot protocol must run on a known port (or small port range), and (2) it must be possible to construct a probe message to determine if a host is infected or not. As shown in Table 5, only two of the analyzed botnets run on a sufficiently small port range, namely ZeroAccess and Kelihos. Probe construction is possible for all botnets, except Zeus, which requires a-priori knowledge of the node ID in order to contact a bot. These results show that Internet-wide scanning is not a full-fledged alternative to crawling or sensor injection. Moreover, there are serious scalability issues in very large address spaces like IPv6, which is expected to become ubiquitous within a relatively short timeframe. Still, for susceptible P2P botnets in IPv4 networks, Internet-wide scanning is a valid recon alternative if no bootstrap peer list is available for crawling.

8. DISCUSSION

This section discusses tradeoffs of the various P2P botnet reconnaissance methods, given the stealthiness and coverage of the various alternatives as studied in this paper. We summarize tradeoffs and recon characteristics in Table 6.

8.1 Automating Protocol Logic Extraction

Current crawlers and sensors have many protocol-specific shortcomings which make them very easy to detect. On the other hand, protocol-adherent recon tools inherently require more implementation effort. To reduce this implementation effort, part of the botnet protocol state machine can be extracted from bot samples using tools like Inspector Gadget [21]. This leaves only particular message types, such as peer list requests and responses, in need of special handling and manual implementation.

8.2 Crawling vs. Sensor Injection

To detect syntactically sound reconnaissance implementations, botmasters must rely on semantic anomalies such as in-degree or out-degree fluctuations. Our results have shown that crawlers are inherently more prone to this than sensors, as they strive to actively contact all or most of the bot population. At the same time, high in-degrees are not uncommon in legitimate super-peers, and are thus not an effective metric for detecting sensors. This means that sensors are a more naturally stealthy reconnaissance method than crawlers. Moreover, properly announced sensors can be used as a launchpad for more invasive botnet takedown efforts, for instance by serving as sinkholes [28]. Data gathered by sensors also lends itself well to mapping infected IPs for subsequent cleanup actions. This applies even more to sensors than crawling and Internet-wide scanning, as sensors can find the expected 60–87% of NATed hosts [28].

On the downside, sensors cannot gather data about the edges between bot nodes. As shown in Table 6, this data can only be gathered by crawlers. In sinkholing attacks, edge data is crucial in determining which peer list entries to poison [28]. While it is possible to augment sensors with active peer list requests to gather edge data, this effectively adds a crawling component to them. Thus, both dedicated crawlers and augmented sensors require defenses against out-degree-based detection.

8.3 Stealthy Crawling Strategies

In Section 6, we have evaluated multiple stealthy crawling strategies in the wild. As we have shown, individual crawlers which limit the contact ratio or restrict the request frequency have a strongly reduced network coverage. A more promising method is distributed crawling. Given a large network address block (at least a /16 for the botnets we studied), or several smaller blocks, it is relatively painless to implement, and has no negative impact on crawling coverage. A possible caveat is that it is still an open problem to determine whether detection techniques for distributed network scanning generalize to distributed crawling [16]. Additionally, to prevent request frequency-based detection, crawlers must limit the per-address request rate, reducing network coverage. Coverage can be improved by running multiple rate-limited crawlers in parallel (each with a different node ID, if applicable), effectively masquerading as a set of bots behind a NAT gateway.

8.4 Internet-Wide Scanning

We have also investigated Internet-wide scanning as a reconnaissance alternative in Section 7, and found it unsuitable as a generic reconnaissance strategy. Whether or not it can be used depends on the port range, bot protocol, and IP address space (i.e., IPv4 vs. IPv6) used by the target botnet. Moreover, Internet-wide scanning from a limited address range is prone to IP-based detection. The nature of Internet-wide scanning is to quickly cover large network blocks by sending stand-alone lightweight probes. Implementing a full bot protocol makes no sense, as this defeats the simplicity of Internet-wide scanning. This means that scanners inherently do not behave like normal bots. Therefore, Internet-wide

Method	Generic	Mapping	Attacks	Stealth strategies	Advantages	Disadvantages
Crawling	✓	Edges	I, P, S	• Protocol adherence • Address distribution • Rate limiting	• Find edges • Fast deployment	• Cannot find NATed nodes • Need out-degree limiting
Sensor injection	✓	Nodes	I, P, S	• Protocol adherence • Announcement rate limiting	• Find NATed nodes • Support sinkholing • Node verification	• Cannot find edge data • Need announcements
Internet-wide scanning	✗	Nodes	I	• Sound probe syntax • Address distribution • One-time usage	• Fast deployment • No bootstrap list	• Cannot find NATed nodes • Cannot find edge data • Not generic • Only probes

Table 6: Tradeoffs of P2P botnet reconnaissance methods. Attacks: I = Infection reporting, P = Partitioning, S = Sinkholing.

scanning should be used only as a one-time measure, to bootstrap conventional crawling if no bootstrap peer list can be obtained. We stress that Internet-wide scanning of botnets should be used with extreme care, as by emulating the botnet protocol it may trigger IDS signatures even in uninfected networks. Unlike crawling, Internet-wide scanning cannot gather edge data, and it also cannot find non-routable bots.

8.5 Backbone-Based Sensors

An approach orthogonal to the recon methods we have studied uses sensors placed on Internet backbone systems. Given access to such systems and a suitable signature for a particular family of bot traffic, this allows for completely passive botnet recon, which cannot be detected or blocked by botmasters. While potentially highly efficient, an obvious caveat is that this method requires the cooperation of backbone operators. Moreover, completely passive detection may be difficult for botnets like GameOver Zeus, which take active measures to thwart signature-based detection systems and encrypt traffic using destination-based keys.

9. RELATED WORK

To the best of our knowledge, our work is the first systematic study of anti-recon in P2P botnets. Prior work has hardened theoretical P2P botnets against recon, and provided anecdotal evidence of anti-recon in practice. Our work expands on these results to provide a more complete picture of anti-recon, and how to overcome it.

Early experiments with crawler-based node enumeration in P2P botnets were performed by Holz et al. in the Storm botnet [13]. At the same time, passive crawling inaccuracies due to address aliasing, firewalls, NAT gateways and churn were studied by Rajab et al. [27] and Kanich et al. [17]. Recent work has studied the completeness and accuracy of sensors compared to crawlers in P2P botnets, showing that sensors can discover up to two orders of magnitude more peers, while also verifying their authenticity [28, 15]. Additionally, technical reports on specific P2P botnets have presented evidence of anti-recon in the wild [10, 25, 35, 19, 6, 13, 34, 33, 2, 4]. Our work systematizes this anecdotal evidence, and performs the first in-depth study of the susceptibility of current and future recon tools to active disruption.

Theoretical work has studied the design of botnet protocols which inherently complicate crawling. Such designs were proposed by Hund et al. [14], who use proof-of-work schemes to prevent efficient crawling, and by Starnberger et al., who use asymetrically encrypted bot IDs to prevent node discovery [32]. Additionally, Yan et al. propose a botnet design which spreads disinformation to thwart crawlers [37]. These methods cannot be directly applied to current botnets, and require botmasters to implement complex and radically different P2P protocols. Moreover, the approach of Starnberger et al. hides bots within legitimate P2P networks which botmasters cannot control. To the best of our knowledge, there are currently no real-world botnets implementing these or similar designs.

Sarat et al. detect sensors with faulty protocol implementations in structured P2P networks [30], but do not investigate crawlers or protocol-agnostic anti-recon. Our work studies protocol-specific weaknesses in both crawlers and sensors, as well as protocol-agnostic crawler detection. Moreover, in contrast to prior work, we evaluate improved recon strategies in practice.

Karuppayah et al. propose to reduce the set of crawled nodes by approximating a minimum vertex cover of the botnet graph [18]. However, their results are based on simulations of Zeus which assume that all bots are simultaneously reachable, peer lists can be fully retrieved using only a small number of requests, and peer addresses are distributed relatively uniformly over the peer lists. In contrast, our own experience based on non-simulated observations is that Zeus crawling coverage decreases rapidly as the set of crawled nodes is reduced (as it would be in a minimum vertex cover).

10. CONCLUSION

We have systematically analyzed anti-recon in P2P botnets, showing that current botnets already take active measures to discourage and retaliate against crawlers and sensors, and that future recon tools are at risk of more invasive attacks. Moreover, we have shown that current recon tools suffer from a myriad of shortcomings, which significantly increase their susceptibility to subversion. Crawlers are especially prone to protocol-agnostic detection, due to their tendency for out-degree explosion. We have investigated several stealthier crawling strategies, of which distributed crawling is the most promising — it does not negatively impact crawling coverage, and is straightforward to implement given a large network address block. Alternatively, sensor injection supports node verification and improved network coverage, and can be augmented with graph connectivity information.

Acknowledgements

This work was supported by the European Research Council through project ERC-2010-StG 259108 "Rosetta". We also thank the anonymous reviewers for their insightful comments, which helped improve this work.

11. REFERENCES

[1] D. Andriesse, C. Rossow, and H. Bos. Distributed Crawler Detection in Peer-to-Peer Botnets, 2015. `http://www.few.vu.nl/~da.andriesse/papers/imc-2015-addendum.pdf`.

[2] D. Andriesse, C. Rossow, B. Stone-Gross, D. Plohmann, and H. Bos. Highly Resilient Peer-to-Peer Botnets Are Here: An Analysis of Gameover Zeus. In *MALWARE'13*, 2013.

[3] Brian Krebs. Operation Tovar Targets GameOver Zeus, CryptoLocker, 2014. `http://krebsonsecurity.com/2014/06/operation-tovar-targets-gameover-zeus-botnet-cryptolocker-scourge/`.

[4] CERT.pl. Zeus P2P Monitoring and Analysis, 2013. Tech report. `http://www.cert.pl/PDF/2013-06-p2p-rap_en.pdf`.

[5] CrowdStrike. GameOver Zeus and CryptoLocker Takedown, 2014. Tech report. `http://www.crowdstrike.com/blog/gameover/index.html`.

[6] C. Davis, J. Fernandez, S. Neville, and J. McHugh. Sybil Attacks as a Mitigation Strategy Against the Storm Botnet. In *MALWARE'08*, 2008.

[7] J. Dinger and H. Hartenstein. Defending the Sybil Attack in P2P Networks: Taxonomy, Challenges, and a Proposal for Self-Registration. In *ARES'06*, 2006.

[8] R. Dingledine, N. Mathewson, and P. Syverson. Tor: The Second-Generation Onion Router. In *USENIX Sec'04*, 2004.

[9] Z. Durumeric, E. Wustrow, and J. A. Halderman. ZMap: Fast Internet-Wide Scanning and its Security Applications. In *USENIX Sec'13*, 2013.

[10] N. Falliere. Sality: Story of a Peer-to-Peer Viral Network, 2011. Tech report, Symantec.

[11] M. Garnaeva. Kelihos/Hlux Botnet Returns with New Techniques, 2012. Tech report, SecureList. `http://securelist.com/blog/virus-watch/32021/`.

[12] Hide My Ass. List of Proxy Addresses. `https://www.hidemyass.com/proxy-list/`.

[13] T. Holz, M. Steiner, F. Dahl, E. Biersack, and F. Freiling. Measurements and Mitigation of Peer-to-Peer-based Botnets: A Case Study on Storm Worm. In *LEET'08*, 2008.

[14] R. Hund, M. Hamann, and T. Holz. Towards Next-Generation Botnets. In *EC2ND'08*, 2008.

[15] B. B. H. Kang, E. Chan-Tin, C. P. Lee, J. Tyra, H. J. Kang, C. Nunnery, Z. Wadler, G. Sinclair, N. Hopper, D. Dagon, and Y. Kim. Towards Complete Node Enumeration in a Peer-to-Peer Botnet. In *ASIACCS'09*, 2009.

[16] M. G. Kang, J. Caballero, and D. Song. Distributed Evasive Scan Techniques and Countermeasures. In *DIMVA'07*, 2007.

[17] C. Kanich, K. Levchenko, B. Enright, G. M. Voelker, and S. Savage. The Heisenbot Uncertainty Problem: Challenges in Separating Bots from Chaff. In *LEET'08*, 2008.

[18] S. Karuppayah, M. Fischer, C. Rossow, and M. Mühlhäuser. On Advanced Monitoring in Resilient and Unstructured P2P Botnets. In *ICC'14*, 2014.

[19] Kaspersky Lab. How Kaspersky Lab and CrowdStrike Dismantled the Hlux Botnet: Success Story, 2012. `http://newsroom.kaspersky.eu/en/texts/detail/article/how-kaspersky-lab-and-crowdstrike-dismantled-the-second-hluxkelihos-botnet-success-story/`.

[20] P. Kleissner. Me Puppet Master: Behind the Scenes of Crawling P2P Botnets, 2014. Tech report. `http://blog.kleissner.org/?p=455`.

[21] C. Kolbitsch, T. Holz, C. Kruegel, and E. Kirda. Inspector Gadget: Automated Extraction of Proprietary Gadgets from Malware Binaries. In *S&P'10*, 2010.

[22] Microsoft Digital Crimes Unit. Microsoft, the FBI, Europol and industry partners disrupt the notorious ZeroAccess botnet, 2013. `http://www.microsoft.com/en-us/news/press/2013/dec13/12-05zeroaccessbotnetpr.aspx`.

[23] S. Murdoch and G. Danezis. Low-Cost Traffic Analysis of Tor. In *S&P'05*, 2005.

[24] A. Nappa, Z. Xu, J. Caballero, and G. Gu. CyberProbe: Towards Internet-Scale Active Detection of Malicious Servers. In *NDSS'14*, 2014.

[25] A. Neville and R. Gibb. ZeroAccess In-Depth, 2013. Tech report, Symantec.

[26] A. Panchenko, L. Pimenidis, and J. Renner. Performance Analysis of Anonymous Communication Channels Provided by Tor. In *ARES'08*, 2008.

[27] M. A. Rajab, J. Zarfoss, F. Monrose, and A. Terzis. My Botnet is Bigger Than Yours (Maybe, Better Than Yours): Why Size Estimates Remain Challenging. In *HotBots'07*, 2007.

[28] C. Rossow, D. Andriesse, T. Werner, B. Stone-Gross, D. Plohmann, C. Dietrich, and H. Bos. P2PWNED: Modeling and Evaluating the Resilience of Peer-to-Peer Botnets. In *S&P'13*, 2013.

[29] H. Rowaihy, W. Enck, P. McDaniel, and T. la Porta. Limiting Sybil Attacks in Structured P2P Networks. In *INFOCOM'07*, 2007.

[30] S. Sarat and A. Terzis. On Tracking Peer-to-Peer Botnets. In *LEET'08*, 2008.

[31] SIDN. AbuseHUB Launched to Tackle Botnets, 2013. `https://www.sidn.nl/en/news/news/article/abusehub-van-start-botnets-aangepakt-1/`.

[32] G. Starnberger, C. Kruegel, and E. Kirda. Overbot: A Botnet Protocol Based on Kademlia. In *SecureComm'08*, 2008.

[33] B. Stock, M. Engelberth, F. C. Freiling, and T. Holz. Walowdac – Analysis of a Peer-to-Peer Botnet. In *EC2ND'09*, 2009.

[34] G. Tenebro. W32.Waledac Threat Analysis, 2009. Tech report, Symantec.

[35] T. Werner. Botnet Shutdown Success Story: How Kaspersky Lab Disabled the Hlux/Kelihos Botnet, 2011. Tech report, Kaspersky Lab. `http://www.securelist.com/en/blog/208193137/`.

[36] J. Wyke. ZeroAccess, 2012. Tech report, SophosLabs.

[37] G. Yan, S. Chen, and S. Eidenbenz. RatBot: Anti-Enumeration Peer-to-Peer Botnets. In *Lecture Notes in Computer Science, vol. 7001*, 2011.

The Doppelgänger Bot Attack: Exploring Identity Impersonation in Online Social Networks

Oana Goga
MPI-SWS

Giridhari Venkatadri
MPI-SWS

Krishna P. Gummadi
MPI-SWS

ABSTRACT

People have long been aware of malicious users that impersonate celebrities or launch identity theft attacks in social networks. However, beyond anecdotal evidence, there have been no in-depth studies of impersonation attacks in today's social networks. One reason for the lack of studies in this space is the absence of datasets about impersonation attacks. To this end, we propose a technique to build extensive datasets of impersonation attacks in current social networks and we gather 16,572 cases of impersonation attacks in the Twitter social network. Our analysis reveals that most identity impersonation attacks are not targeting celebrities or identity theft. Instead, we uncover a new class of impersonation attacks that clone the profiles of ordinary people on Twitter to create real-looking fake identities and use them in malicious activities such as follower fraud. We refer to these as the *doppelgänger bot attacks*. Our findings show (*i*) that identity impersonation attacks are much broader than believed and can impact any user, not just celebrities and (*ii*) that attackers are evolving and create real-looking accounts that are harder to detect by current systems. We also propose and evaluate methods to automatically detect impersonation attacks sooner than they are being detected in today's Twitter social network.

1. INTRODUCTION

Today, users sign on to most online social networks like Facebook and Twitter via *weak identities*, i.e., unverified identities (accounts) that do not require users to prove that their online identities match their offline, real world, personalities. Weak identities lower the sign-on barriers for users, offer users a certain level of anonymity, but they leave the sites vulnerable to a variety of fake identities or *Sybil* attacks. Malicious attackers are known to use Sybil identities to post spam content [31] and to tamper with the popularity of content on these sites [33]. Consequently, a number of prior works have focussed on understanding and detecting Sybil attacks in online social networks [20, 25, 21, 14].

IMC'15, October 28–30, 2015, Tokyo, Japan.
 ISBN 978-1-4503-3848-6/15/10 ...$15.00.
DOI: http://dx.doi.org/10.1145/2815675.2815699.

In this paper, we focus on a special class of Sybil (fake identity) attacks known as *identity impersonation attacks*, where the attacker *spoofs or assumes* the identity of another real-world user, *the victim*. As more and more personal data about users becomes publicly available on the Web, impersonation attacks become easier to carry out. For instance, an attacker can easily copy public profile data of a Facebook user to create an identity on Twitter or Google+.

There are many different types of impersonation attacks based on the attacker's motivation. (*i*) In a *celebrity impersonation attack*, the attacker exploits or maligns the public reputation of the victim, whose identity she impersonated. Popular and celebrity users are often targets for such impersonation attacks [19, 26]. (*ii*) In a *social engineering attack*, the attacker abuses victim's identity to trick the victim's friends into revealing sensitive information or providing services (e.g., transfer money to the attacker) [30, 22]. (*iii*) In a *doppelgänger bot attack*, the attacker is simply interested in evading detection by the Sybil or Spam defenses deployed by site operators. As Sybil detectors are often trained to detect non-real-looking identities (e.g., lacking profile photos or location information or bio), attackers could create more real-looking fake identities by copying the attributes of a real user.

Regardless of the attacker's motivation, identity impersonation attacks could seriously damage the victim's online reputation. As people's online data is increasingly aggregated by people's search engines [28] and used for a variety of purposes including evaluating their suitability for employment [27], impersonation attacks, particularly those that go undetected, can have serious adverse consequences for the victims, even in the offline world.

Despite the serious threat posed by impersonation attacks, few studies, to date, have systematically studied impersonation attacks in online social networks. Beyond a few anecdotal examples that are reported in the popular press, we lack large datasets about real-world impersonation attacks. Perhaps, not surprisingly, most social networking sites today lack frameworks to automatically detect impersonators. Instead, they rely on manual reports from victims about accounts that are impersonating them [32], which can be risky as victims usually become aware of their attackers after their online reputation has already been damaged.

Against this background, this paper presents, to the best of our knowledge, the first extensive study of real-world impersonation attacks in online social networks. Specifically, it makes the following contributions:

1. Methodology for gathering data about impersonation attacks. We identify the fundamental challenges associated with gathering data about impersonation attacks and propose practical methods to circumvent the challenges. Our method, as described in §2, consists of two steps: (1) identify doppelgänger accounts in a social network that *portray* the same person/entity; and (2) out of the doppelgänger accounts that portray the same entity, label which accounts are legitimate and which accounts are impersonators.

The second step is complicated by the fact that people can maintain multiple legitimate accounts in a social network. We applied our method to gather data on Twitter. We identified 54,304 doppelgänger pairs of Twitter identities that portray the same person. We successfully labelled 16,572 of the doppelgänger pairs as resulting from impersonation attacks and 3,639 pairs as cases when a person maintains two legitimate accounts in the Twitter network.

2. Characterizing impersonation attacks. Our analysis of the data we gathered reveals many interesting facts about identity impersonation attacks, including some that contradicted our expectations.

(1) Contrary to our expectation that most impersonation attacks would largely target celebrity / popular user identities, we discovered that many impersonation attacks target ordinary users. (2) Additionally, many impersonation attacks do not seem to attempt social engineering attacks or even try to exploit the public reputation of their victims. They appear to have been created by attackers looking to create real looking fake accounts that could pass undetected by current Sybil detection systems. We call these attacks as the doppelgänger bot attacks. Despite their motivation, doppelgänger bot attacks can still harm the online reputation of the victim identity. (3) We found that it takes Twitter on average 287 days to suspend the impersonating accounts from our dataset. The long delay in detecting the attacks call for developing methods to detect such attacks sooner.

3. Methods to automatically detect impersonation attacks. Our analysis characterizing impersonation attacks yield novel insights for detecting impersonation attacks. First, given a pair of doppelgänger identities, we could determine whether the identity-pair is managed by the same person or whether it is the result of an impersonation attack, by comparing the social network neighborhood and interests of the user. In the former scenario, the pair of doppelgänger identities share considerable overlap in network neighborhood and interests, while in the latter, they are considerably more dissimilar. Furthermore, we find that we can infer which of the pair of doppelgänger identities is legitimate (victim) and which is the impersonator (attacker), by comparing various reputation metrics, such as creation date, number of followers etc. We find that victim identities almost always have higher reputation and older creation dates than impersonating identities.

We leverage these insights to propose automatic methods (based on machine learning techniques) to detect impersonation attacks in §4. We detect 10,894 more cases of impersonation attacks and 9,354 cases of accounts managed by the same person when we test the scheme on the 34,091 unlabeled pairs of accounts that portray the same person. More than half of the impersonating accounts detected by our method were subsequently suspended by Twitter (over a 6 month period), which shows the effectiveness of our method at detecting impersonating accounts sooner than Twitter.

In summary, our paper proposes methods to gather data about a large number of real-world impersonation attacks in online social networks. Although our method does not capture all impersonation attacks, the resulting dataset allows us to do an insightful exploration of impersonation attacks, and to build an automatic detector that is not only able to detect more such attacks, but also detect them sooner. Our work represents a useful step towards enabling users to better protect their online reputation from identity impersonation attacks.

2. DATA GATHERING METHODOLOGY

In this section, we first propose a methodology for gathering data about impersonation attacks in real-world social networks. Later, we apply our methodology to gather data about impersonation attacks on Twitter.

Intuitively, an identity impersonation attack involves an attacker creating an account (identity) *pretending* to be some other real-world user (victim), i.e., the attacker's identity mimics or copies the features of the victim's identity. However, gathering data about such attacks is surprisingly difficult in practice (which might explain why few prior studies, if any, have successfully analyzed real-world impersonation attacks).

2.1 Challenges

To understand why identifying impersonation attacks is hard, consider the real-world example attack shown in Fig. 1. We discovered this attack on "Nick Feamster", a computer science researcher, during the course of our study. We alerted Nick, who confirmed the attack, and the impersonating account has since been suspended by Twitter. We realized three challenges in the process:

Figure 1: Example of impersonation attack.

1. How do we determine which identities are attempting to *portray or represent* the same user? For instance, there are many Twitter identities with the same user name "Nick Feamster", but we felt that *only* the account that shared similar bio and photo as Nick's original account, is attempting to pretend to be Nick. Our intuitive decision raises the question: how similar should the profiles of two identities be to qualify as portraying the same user?

2. After determining that a pair of identities portray the same user, how do we determine whether the identity-pair is the result of an impersonation attack or the

result of a user simply creating multiple (duplicate) accounts for herself? For instance, users on Twitter are permitted to create multiple identities, including pseudonymous identities. To determine the shared ownership of identities, we would need to contact and obtain confirmation from the identities' owners themselves (e.g., by sending messages to the identities). However, such confirmations are not only hard to obtain for a large-scale study, but also when we attempted it on Twitter, the Twitter identity we created to contact other Twitter users for the study got suspended for attempting to contact too many unrelated Twitter identities.

3. After determining that a pair of identities portraying the same user is the result of an impersonation attack (i.e., they are not duplicate accounts owned by the same user), how do we determine which identity is legitimate and which is the impersonating identity? In our attack example, we were lucky to know the person portrayed, Nick Feamster, in the offline world. This knowledge enabled us to differentiate the legitimate identity from the attacker's identity. But, in practice, the offline user portrayed by the online identities is often unknown, i.e., it is unclear how to contact the offline user. In these scenarios, it is unclear how to differentiate the legitimate identity from the impersonating identity, as both may claim to be the legitimate identity.

Below we propose a practical methodology that tackles some of these fundamental challenges and circumvents others. We applied it on Twitter to gather data about several hundreds to thousands of real-world impersonation attacks. Our methodology does not guarantee that we would discover all or even a representative sample of all impersonation attacks occurring in Twitter. Nevertheless, given the inherent difficulty in collecting any data about impersonation attacks, we feel that our work represents a first step in the direction of addressing these challenges.

2.2 Terminology

We introduce some terminology to both simplify and clarify our discussion in the rest of the paper. (i) **doppelgänger identities:** We refer to identities as doppelgänger identities when they are determined to be portraying or representing the same user. (ii) **avatar-avatar pair:** A pair of doppelgänger identities is referred to as an avatar-avatar pair when both identities are managed by the same owner. (iii) **victim-impersonator pair:** A pair of doppelgänger identities is referred to as a victim-impersonator pair when one of the identities is legitimate (victim identity) and the other is created by an attacker (impersonating identity). Using our terminology, the above challenges can be rephrased as follows:

1. How do we identify doppelgänger identities?

2. How do we determine that a pair of doppelgänger identities is an avatar-avatar pair or a victim-impersonator pair?

3. How do we determine which of the victim-impersonator identity-pair is the victim and which is the impersonator?

2.3 Data gathering strategy

In this section, we discuss our strategy to tackle the above challenges when gathering data. We defer a detailed discussion of the collected data to the next section. At a high-level, our strategy involves first automatically identifying a large number of pairs of doppelgänger identities and then differentiating them into avatar-avatar and victim-impersonator pairs.

2.3.1 *Identifying doppelgänger pairs*

The ideal way to determine if a pair of identities is a doppelgänger pair would be to ask human workers if both identities portray the same user. Unfortunately, such an exercise would be very expensive to scale to millions of potential doppelgänger pairs. So we built an *automated* rule-based matching scheme that is trained on human-annotated data to determine when the profile attributes of two identities match sufficiently for humans to believe that they portray the same user.

More concretely, in the Twitter social network, every identity is associated with a set of profile attributes, such as *user-name, screen-name, location, photo, and bio.* We collected pairs of identities with different levels of profile attribute matching. Specifically, we collected three-levels of matching profile pairs: (i) *Loosely matching identities:* pairs of identities that have similar *user-name or screen-name*;[1] Starting from an initial set of Twitter profiles (see §2.4), we discovered these identity pairs via the Twitter search API that allows searching by names. (ii) *Moderately matching identities:* pairs of identities that, in addition to sharing a similar user-name or screen-name, also share one additional similar profile attribute be it *location or photo or bio.*[2] In practice, we found that location information is often very coarse-grained, at the level of countries, so we defined a tighter matching scheme ignoring location information. (iii) *Tightly matching identities:* pairs of identities that in addition to sharing a similar user-name or screen-name also share similar *photo or bio.*

For each level of matching profile pairs, we estimated the fraction of profile pairs that humans would believe as portraying the same user as follows: We selected between 50 to 250 pairs of matching profiles at each level and setup an Amazon Mechanical Turk experiment, where we gave AMT workers two links corresponding to the two Twitter accounts and we asked them to choose between three options: *'the accounts portray the same person'*, *'the accounts do not portray the same person'*, or *'cannot say'*. For each assignment we asked the opinion of three different AMT workers and only consider the *majority agreement*, i.e., when at least two AMT workers choose the same answer.

We find that, by majority agreement, AMT workers believe that 4% of loosely matching, 43% of moderately matching, and 98% of tightly matching identity-pairs portray the same user. Thus, by selecting a more conservative matching scheme, we would increase precision (i.e., be more certain) of detecting doppelgänger pairs. But, in the process, we

[1]Determining attribute similarity is a challenging task in and of itself. There is a lot of prior work, including our own, on this topic [10]. We summarize the relevant details in the Appendix.

[2]Twitter accounts that do not have profile information available such as bio, locations and photos will be automatically excluded.

would be sacrificing recall – for instance, we found that the tightly matching identity scheme captures only 65% of the doppelgänger pairs caught by moderately matching identity scheme. Since our goal is to correctly identify a large set of impersonating attacks, even if it comes at the cost of not identifying all possible impersonation attacks, we propose to use the conservative tightly matching identity scheme to detect doppelgänger pairs in Twitter.

Potential limitations: While our scheme represents a first step in the direction of scalable automated detection of doppelgänger pairs in social networks like Twitter, currently, we apply it only within a single social network. So we miss opportunities to detect doppelgänger pairs across multiple social networking sites, e.g., when an attacker copies a Facebook user's identity to created a doppelgänger Twitter identity. While our basic scheme could be extended to match identities across sites, it is beyond the scope of this work.

2.3.2 *Identifying victim-impersonator pairs*

As discussed earlier, the ideal way to determine whether a doppelgänger pair is a victim-impersonator pair requires contacting the real offline user represented by the identity to inquire about the ownership of the identities. However, this approach is infeasible in practice. When we attempted this approach, our Twitter identity got quickly suspended as indulging in potentially spam activity. So we instead rely on a signal from Twitter, when it officially suspends *one, but not both,* of the doppelgänger identities. We crawled the doppelgänger identities periodically (once a week) over an extended period of time (a three month period) to look for identity suspensions. We treat the suspended identity of the doppelgänger pair as the impersonating identity and the other identity as the victim.

Our hypothesis is that at least some fraction of the impersonating identities would be eventually detected and reported to Twitter (either by the victim herself or some other users that know the victim), which would result in Twitter suspending the identity. One concern with our approach is that we may be detecting impersonating attacks that are being caught by some automated Twitter spam defense system (as opposed to reports filed by victims or other Twitter users). In this case, we would essentially be reverse-engineering Twitter's impersonation detection system rather than study impersonation attacks in the wild. We address this concern in §4.2, where we show that the analysis of the impersonation attacks gathered using our methodology can help us design new automated detectors that in turn could be used to detect a large number of yet undiscovered impersonation attacks in Twitter. Had the identities been suspended by an automated impersonation detection framework in Twitter, it is unlikely that we would have succeeded in designing significantly better performing detection systems.

Potential Limitations: Our victim-impersonator pair detection strategy allows us to detect large numbers of such pairs, but it likely captures only those impersonation attacks that have been detected by Twitter's reporting system. We would be under-sampling clever attacks that have not yet been detected.

2.3.3 *Identifying avatar-avatar pairs*

As discussed earlier, the ideal way to determine whether a doppelgänger pair is avatar-avatar by contacting the owners of the identities is unfeasible in practice. So we instead rely on observing interactions between the doppelgänger identities that clearly indicate that each identity is aware of the presence of the other identity. Specifically, we check whether one of the doppelgänger identity follows or mentions or retweets the other doppelgänger identity. If it is the case, it is very likely that the identities are managed by the same user. Otherwise, the legitimate identity would have reported the impersonating identity and have it suspended by Twitter.

Potential Limitations: Our avatar-avatar pair detection strategy under-samples scenarios where a user maintains multiple identities but keeps them distinct, i.e., does not link the identities and use them for very different purposes. However, we suspect that in such scenarios, users would likely assume different pseudonymous identities and would avoid providing the same profile information. Such identities would not be matched as doppelgänger identities in the first place.

2.4 Data gathered

In this section, we describe how we applied our above data gathering strategy to collect information about real-world impersonation attacks in the Twitter social network at scale.

We begin by selecting 1.4 million *random* Twitter accounts – the initial accounts.[3] We call the dataset we generate starting with these random Twitter accounts the RANDOM DATASET. For each account a in the RANDOM DATASET, we gather a set of up to 40 accounts in Twitter that have the most similar names as the account (using the Twitter search API). We call the resulting 27 million name-matching identity-pairs initial accounts. From these pairs, we identify doppelgänger pairs, victim-impersonator pairs, and avatar-avatar pairs as described in §2.3. Table 1 summarizes the dataset. Note that a significant fraction of doppelgänger identities are not labeled as either avatar-avatar or victim-impersonator pairs.

While our strategy for detecting doppelgänger and avatar-avatar pairs yielded sizable numbers, our strategy for detecting victim-impersonator pairs proved quite time consuming. It took a 3 months waiting time to discover 166 victim-impersonator pairs amongst the 18,662 doppelgänger pairs and few tens of identities keep getting suspended every passing week. To quickly identify more victim-impersonator pairs, we resorted to a focussed crawl in the neighborhood of the detected impersonating identities. Specifically, we conducted a breadth first search crawl on the followers of four seed impersonating identities that we detected. Our intuition is that we might find other impersonating accounts in the close network of an impersonating account.

We collected 142,000 accounts with the breadth first search crawl and we call the dataset generated from this biased set of initial accounts the BFS DATASET. We repeated the same analysis on the BFS DATASET that we conducted on RANDOM DATASET. We report the results in Table 1. In the same amount of time, we discovered 16,408 victim-impersonator pairs out of the 35,642 doppelgänger pairs, suggesting that our focussed crawl succeeded in identifying a large number of real-world impersonation attacks.

[3]Twitter assigns to every new account a numeric identity that allows random sampling.

Table 1: Datasets for studying impersonation attacks.

	RANDOM DATASET	BFS DATASET
initial accounts	1.4 millions	142,000
initial accounts	27 millions	2.9 millions
doppelgänger pairs	18,662	35,642
avatar-avatar pairs	2,010	1,629
victim-impersonator pairs	166	16,408
unlabeled pairs	16,486	17,605

For each Twitter identity in doppelgänger pairs, we use the Twitter API to collect detailed information about a variety of their features. They include features related to:

1. Profile of the identity: We gather the data about the identity's *user-name, screen-name, location, photo, and bio.*

2. Activity of the identity: We gather data about the *creation date of the account, timestamp of the first tweet, timestamp of the last tweet, number of followings (the number of accounts a user follows), number of tweets posted, number of retweets posted, number of tweets favorited* and *number of mentions.*

3. Reputation of the identity: We collect data about the *number of followers* of an account, the *number of expert lists where the user appears* and the *klout score* [16] as metrics to measure the influence of an account. The *klout score* is a widely used metric to measure the social influence of an account.

3. CHARACTERIZING IMPERSONATION ATTACKS

In this section, we analyze the datasets we collected to characterize identity impersonation attacks in Twitter. We begin by investigating the different types of impersonation attacks found in our RANDOM DATASET. Our analysis reveals the prevalence of a new type of impersonation attack that we call **doppelgänger bot** attack. We then explore the features of doppelgänger bot attacks and the potential for detecting such attacks.

3.1 Classifying impersonation attacks

Based on conventional wisdom and anecdotal evidence, we were expecting to discover two types of impersonation attacks in our RANDOM DATASET: (i) *Celebrity impersonation attacks,* where attackers impersonate celebrities and popular Twitter users to either post untrustworthy information maligning the celebrity's reputation or take advantage of the celebrities' offline popularity to increase the visibility of their own posts (e.g., product promotions) or (ii) *Social engineering attacks* also known as identity theft attacks, where the attacker creates a fake account that clones the information of a victim account and then uses the fake account to connect and communicate with the victim's friends [5]. The ultimate goal here is to launch phishing attacks to harvest sensitive information about the victim or to trick the victim's friends into sending money to the attacker (that claims to be the victim).

We attempted to map the 166 victim-impersonator pairs in our dataset to these two types of attacks. In the process, we discovered that many of the victim-impersonators pairs corresponded to a small number of victims. Specifically, there were 6 different Twitter victims that in total accounted for half (83) of the victim-impersonator pairs. One hypothesis is that these six victims discovered multiple fake identities that were impersonating them and reported all such identities, leading them to be detected in our methodology. To avoid over-sampling these identities in our dataset, we only consider one pair of victim-impersonating identities for each of the 6 victims, which reduces our dataset to 89 victim-impersonator pairs.

3.1.1 Celebrity impersonation attacks

Twitter allows users to create accounts that are fan pages of celebrities, however, users have to specifically declare this in their bios. Our method to collect data about impersonation attacks in the previous section is consistent with Twitter's terms of service. If the fan account mentions or interacts in any way with the celebrity, it will be identified as an avatar, and if not, it will be identified as impersonator.

To identify celebrity impersonation attacks we simply check for victim-impersonator pairs where the victim is either a verified Twitter account [4] or has a popular following amongst Twitter users, i.e., it has more than 1000 or 10,000 followers.[5] Out of the 89 victim-impersonator pairs, we found *only three* are celebrity impersonation attacks out of which one is a impersonator of a football player and one of a journalist. In fact, 70 of the 89 victims have less than 300 followers, suggesting that most victims of impersonation in our dataset are not highly popular celebrities.

3.1.2 Social engineering attacks

While it is impossible to exactly know the intentions of the attacker, we could attempt to infer if an impersonating identity is attempting to launch a social engineering attack, by exploiting the observation that attackers try to contact the friends of the victims. So we select all victim-impersonator pairs where the impersonating account had *any interaction* with users that know the victim account, i.e., the impersonating account is friend of, follows, mentions or retweets people that are friends of or follow the victim account.

Our hypothesis is that it is unlikely that accounts that do not fall in the candidate set would try to mount social engineering attacks since they do not show any intent of contacting the people that know the victim. Out of the 89 victim-impersonator pairs in our dataset, *only two* accounts met our test for potentially being social engineering attacks.

3.1.3 Doppelgänger bot attacks

Our analysis of impersonation attacks above suggests that most attacks are not directed towards popular celebrities or attempting to trick a victim's friends. This observation raises the question: *What then might be motivating an attacker to launch an impersonation attack targeting non-celebrity users?*

One hypothesis is that these impersonation attacks are merely an attempt by attackers creating fake identities to evade detection by Twitter Sybil and spam defense systems. By simply copying the profile attributes of existing Twitter users, attackers could create new real-looking fake Twitter identities that might escape traditional spam defenses

[4]Twitter has an account verification program for highly popular users of its service.

[5]Less than 0.01% (0.007%) of Twitter users have more than 1000 (10,000) followers.

that analyze features of individual identities. Such identities could be used profitably to promote other Twitter users and content in the system (selling fake followers and fake content promotions is a growing business in Twitter). We refer to such attacks as **doppelgänger bot** attacks.

To check our hypothesis that many impersonating accounts are involved in follower fraud we analyzed whom they are following. Since the number of doppelgänger bots in our Random Dataset is limited to less than a hundred, we investigated the doppelgänger bots in the BFS Dataset, where we have identified tens of thousands of victim-impersonator pairs using a BFS crawl of the Twitter network starting with four seed doppelgänger bot accounts (see Table 1). We found that the impersonating accounts in the BFS Dataset follow a set of 3,030,748 distinct users. Out of the users followed, 473 are followed by more than 10% of all the impersonating accounts. We checked if the 473 most followed accounts are suspected of having bought fake followers in the past using a publicly deployed follower fraud detection service [34]. Among those users for which the service could do a check, 40% were reported to have at least 10% fake followers. [6] The fact that a large fraction of impersonating accounts follow the same small set of users and that the users they follow are suspected of having bought fake followers strongly points to the possibility of impersonating accounts being involved in follower fraud.

3.2 Analyzing doppelgänger bot attacks

In this section, our goal is to better understand doppelgänger bot attacks with the ultimate goal of detecting doppelgänger bots. To this end, we focus on understanding the characteristics (i.e., various reputation metrics and activities) of doppelgänger bots and their victims. Our investigation reveals important differences between the characteristics of victim accounts and doppelgänger bots, which we leverage in a later section to detect doppelgänger bots. The doppelgänger bot attacks analyzed in this section are from the BFS Dataset.

3.2.1 Characterizing victim accounts

To understand who the doppelgänger bot attacks are targeting we proceed by asking several questions related to the reputation and activity of victim accounts. We focus our analysis on the differences in the statistical distributions of properties of victim accounts and randomly chosen Twitter users.

Reputation of victim accounts.

How popular are the victim accounts? Figure 2a shows the CDF of the number of followers of victim accounts. The median number of followers is only 73, which shows that most doppelgänger bots do not target famous people but ordinary users.

How influential are the victim accounts? Figures 2b and 2c show the CDF of klout scores and the number of expert lists where a victim account appears in, respectively. 40% of victim accounts appear in at least one list

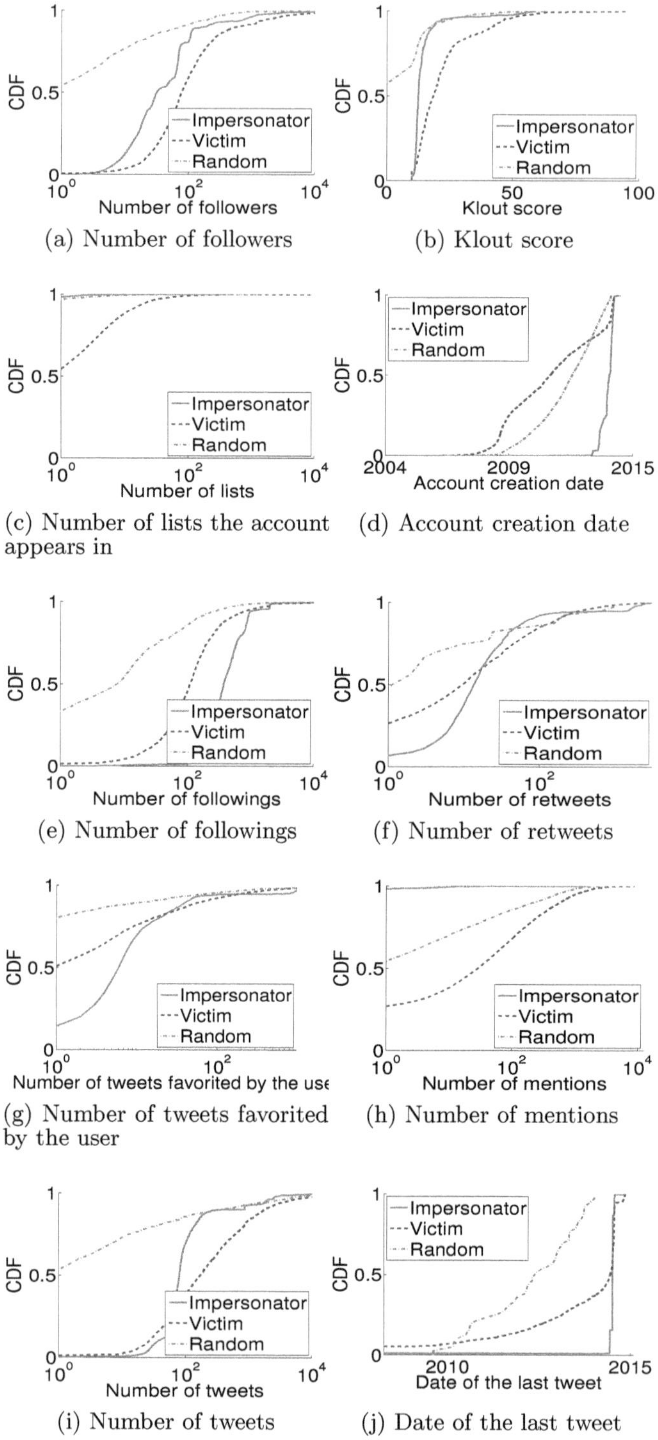

(a) Number of followers (b) Klout score

(c) Number of lists the account appears in (d) Account creation date

(e) Number of followings (f) Number of retweets

(g) Number of tweets favorited by the user (h) Number of mentions

(i) Number of tweets (j) Date of the last tweet

Figure 2: CDFs of different features for characterizing the reputation and activity of impersonating and victim accounts as well as Twitter accounts picked at random.

[6]For a point of comparison, we also checked whom the avatar accounts from avatar-avatar pairs follow. There are only four accounts followed by 10% of the avatar accounts and they correspond to Justin Bieber, Taylor Swift, Katy Perry and Youtube, all of which are well-known celebrity / corporate accounts followed widely on Twitter.

and 30% of victim accounts have klout scores higher than 25 (For comparison purposes, researchers like Dina Papagiannaki – @dpapagia – and Jon Crowcroft – @tforcworc – have klout scores of 26 and 45 respectively, while Barack Obama –@barackobama–has a klout score of 99). The figures also show that the influence scores of victims are noticeably higher than those of random Twitter users, which indicates that many victim accounts, while not exactly celebrities, correspond to professional users with good reputation in Twitter.

How old are the victim accounts? Figure 2d shows that victims have generally older accounts than random Twitter users. The median creation date for victim accounts is October 2010 while the median creation date for random Twitter users is May 2012. Attackers target users that have been for a long time in the system.

Activity of victim accounts.

How active are the victim accounts? Figures 2e through 2j show the CDFs of various activity metrics for victims. They show that victims are considerably more active than random Twitter users. For instance, Figure 2i shows the CDF of the number of tweets per victim account. The median number of tweets is 181. In contrast, the median number of tweets for random users is 0, while the median number of tweets for random users that have at least one post is 20. Similarly, Figure 2j shows that 75% of victim accounts posted at least one tweet in 2013, while only 20% of random Twitter users posted at least one tweet in 2013. So the victims tend to be fairly active Twitter users that have been active recently too.

In summary, the victims of doppelgänger bot attacks are active users with a level of reputation and influence that is significantly higher than a random Twitter user (though they are not necessarily celebrities). Our finding shows that attackers target, inadvertently or not, users who put a significant amount of effort into building an online image with a good reputation.

3.2.2 Characterizing doppelgänger bot accounts

To understand how doppelgänger bot impersonating accounts behave we analyze their reputation and activity.

Reputation of doppelgänger bot accounts.

Figures 2a through 2d compares the CDFs of different reputation metrics for doppelgänger bots, their victims, and random Twitter accounts. The plots show that: (1) the *number of followers* and *klout score* of impersonating accounts is lower than the number of followers and klout score of victim accounts but higher than the ones of random accounts (Figures 2a and 2b); (2) impersonating accounts do not appear in any *lists* of other accounts (Figure 2c); and (3) most impersonating accounts were *created* recently, during 2013 (Figure 2d). At a high level, the reputation of doppelgänger bots is clearly lower than the reputation of victim accounts, however, it is higher than the reputation of random Twitter users. In the next section, we will show that these differences have important implications for the detectability of doppelgänger bots. Thus, impersonating accounts do not have suspicious markers of reputation.

Activity of doppelgänger bot accounts.

We refer again to Figures 2e through 2j. The plots show that: (1) the *number of followings, retweets* and *favorites* of impersonating accounts is higher than victim and random accounts (Figures 2e, 2f, and 2g). This finding is consistent with our hypothesis that these accounts are involved in illegal promotion of content and users; (2) However, the number of times doppelgänger bots *mention* other users is unusually low, which is consistent with the intuition that doppelgänger bots would not not wish to draw attention to themselves and their activities (Figure 2h); and (3) impersonating accounts do not show excessive markers of activity: the median number of users an impersonating account follows is 372, which is not very high compared with the median number a victim account follows which is 111 and impersonating accounts do not tweet excessively (Figure 2i), but are very active, i.e. their *last tweet* is in the month we crawled them (Figure 2j). These markers of activity not only support our hypothesis that doppelgänger bots might be involved in illegal promotion of content, but they also suggest that attackers may be trying to emulate normal user behavior and avoid being detected with abnormal (excessive) tweeting or following behavior.

3.3 Detecting doppelgänger bot attacks

Even if doppelgänger bots do not seem to intentionally want to harm their victims, they can still harm unintentionally the online image of their victims. For example, in our dataset a doppelgänger bot of a tech company tweeted "I think I was a stripper in a past life", which is clearly not the image the tech company wants to promote. Even worse, Twitter took in average 287 days to suspend these accounts.[7] Thus, the online image of victims was potentially harmed for several months.

The natural question that follows is *why do these accounts go undetected for such long periods of time?* In this section, we analyze the challenges in detecting doppelgänger bots; in particular our analysis shows that traditional sybil detection schemes are not able to accurately detect them. The low accuracy can be potentially explained by the fact that doppelgänger bots operate under the radar and the accounts do not have any characteristics that makes them look suspicious in *absolute*. We show that the key to detect doppelgänger bots is to study their characteristics *relative* to their corresponding victim accounts.

Using traditional sybil-detection schemes: reasoning about the absolute trustworthiness of accounts.

Doppelgänger bots are a special type of sybil accounts, thus we investigate whether we can detect them using existing methods to detect sybil accounts. At a high level, many traditional sybil-detection schemes exploit ground truth about good and bad users to create patterns of good and bad behavior. The schemes then decide whether an account is sybil or not by comparing its behavior to these patterns [3, 40, 29]. We emulate such behavioral methods by training a SVM classifier with examples of doppelgänger bots (bad behavior) and random Twitter accounts (good behavior) using the methodology in [3].

[7]We know with an approximation of one week when Twitter suspended the impersonating accounts and we know from the Twitter API when the account was created.

We consider all doppelgänger bots from the BFS DATASET as positive examples (16,408 accounts), and we pick 16,000 random Twitter accounts as negative examples. We use 70% of examples for training and 30% for testing and we train the classifier with all features that characterize the reputation and the activity of a single account we presented in §2.4.

Because doppelgänger bots are only a small fraction of all accounts in Twitter, our classification problem has a high class imbalance (i.e., there are many more negative examples than positive examples). Such scenarios require classifiers that can operate at a very low false positive rate. The smallest false positive rate our SVM classifier achieves is 0.1% for a 34% true positive rate (the true positive rate drops to zero for lower false positive rates). A 0.1% false positive rate is, however, very high in our scenario. For example, if we take the 1.4 million random accounts (in the RANDOM DATASET), a classifier with 34% true positive rate for a 0.1% false positive rate will detect 40 actual doppelgänger bots (34%×122) while mislabeling 1,400 legitimate accounts as doppelgänger bots. This accuracy is clearly unsatisfying.

A plausible reason why these schemes are not optimal is precisely because attackers intentionally create real-looking accounts and emulate the behavior of legitimate users so that they are harder to detect by current sybil account detection systems.

Distinguish doppelgänger bots from victim accounts: reasoning about the relative trustworthiness of accounts.

The previous section showed that, given a set of accounts, it is hard to detect which ones are doppelgänger bots. Here we try to approach the problem from a different perspective and we ask a different question: *given a victim-impersonator pair can we pinpoint the impersonating account?* Our intuition is that, if it is too hard to reason about the trustworthiness of an account in absolute, it might be easier to reason about its trustworthiness relative to another account.

To answer the question we refer back to Figure 2 that presents the CDFs for different features of impersonating, victim and random accounts. We can see that the characteristics of victim accounts in aggregate are very different from the characteristics of impersonating accounts. More precisely, victim accounts have a much higher reputation (number of followers, number of lists and klout scores) than impersonating accounts and they have a much older account creation date. In fact, in all the victim-impersonator pairs in the BFS DATASET and RANDOM DATASET, none of the impersonating accounts have the creation date after the creation date of their victim accounts and 85% of the victim accounts have a klout score higher than the one of the impersonating accounts. Thus, to detect the impersonating account in a victim-impersonator pair with no miss-detections, we can simply take the account that has the more recent creation date. This reasoning opens up solutions to detect doppelgänger bots, however, it does not solve the whole problem because we still have to detect whether a pair of accounts is a avatar-avatar pair or victim-impersonator pair. This is the focus of section §4.

How well humans can detect doppelgänger bots.

In this section, we investigate how well humans are able to detect doppelgänger bots. We focus on two questions: (1) *If humans stumble upon a doppelgänger bot, are they able to detect that the account is fake?* (i.e., the question of assessing the absolute trustworthiness of accounts) – this scenario is specific to a recruiter that knows the name of the person and searches for his accounts in different social networks to learn more about him and stumbles upon the doppelgänger bot; and (2) *If humans have access to both the impersonating and the victim account, are they able to detect the impersonating account better?* (i.e., the question of assessing the relative trustworthiness of accounts). The first question will show the severity of the doppelgänger bot attacks problem by analyzing whether humans are tricked into believing the doppelgänger bots represent the real person. The second question will show whether humans are also better at detecting impersonating accounts when they have a point of reference.

We build two AMT experiments to answer these questions. For the first AMT experiment, we select 50 doppelgänger bot accounts and 50 avatar accounts from the victim-impersonator pairs and avatar-avatar pairs. In each assignment, we give AMT workers a link to a Twitter account and we ask them to choose between three options: *'the account looks legitimate'*, *'the account looks fake'* and *'cannot say'*. We mix doppelgänger bot accounts and avatar accounts in the experiments to force users to examine each case afresh. In all experiments we ask the opinion of three AMT workers and we report the results for majority agreement. In this experiment, AMT workers are able to only detect 18% of the doppelgänger bots as being fake (9 out of 50). Thus, most AMT workers get tricked by doppelgänger bots.

In the second experiment we show AMT workers two accounts that portray the same person. We picked the same 50 impersonating accounts (and their corresponding victims) and the same 50 avatar accounts (and their corresponding avatar doppelgänger) as in the previous experiment.[8] In each assignment, we give AMT workers two links corresponding to the two Twitter accounts and we ask them to choose between five options: *'both accounts are legitimate'*, *'both accounts are fake'*, *'account 1 impersonates account 2'*, *'account 2 impersonates account 1'*, and *'cannot say'*. In the second experiment, AMT workers were able to correctly detect 36% doppelgänger bots as fake. The experiment shows that there is a 100% improvement in their detection rate when they have a point of reference.

The results in this section have implications on both how to design automatic techniques to detect doppelgänger bots as well as how to design systems that better protect users from being deceived online by impersonation attacks.

4. DETECTING IMPERSONATION ATTACKS

The previous section showed that given a victim-impersonator pair of accounts, we can fairly accurately detect the impersonating account by comparing their account creation times and reputations. In this section, we investigate the extent to which we can detect whether a pair of accounts that portrays the same person (a doppelgänger pair) is a victim-impersonator pair or an avatar-avatar pair. We start by analyzing features that can signal the existence of an impersonation attack and we then propose a method to automatically detect such attacks.

[8]The AMT workers were different in the two experiments.

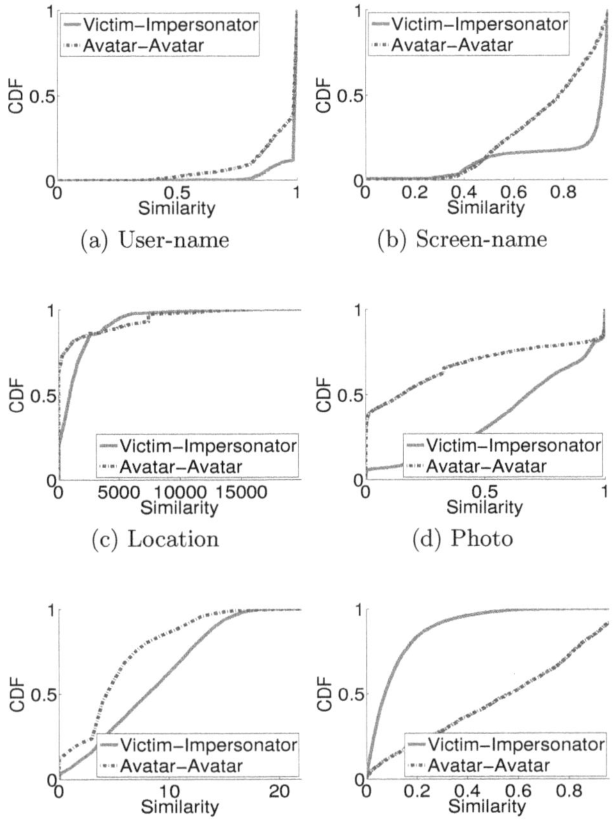

(a) User-name (b) Screen-name (c) Location (d) Photo (e) Bio (f) Interests similarity

Figure 3: CDFs of the similarity between accounts in victim-impersonator pairs and avatar-avatar pairs.

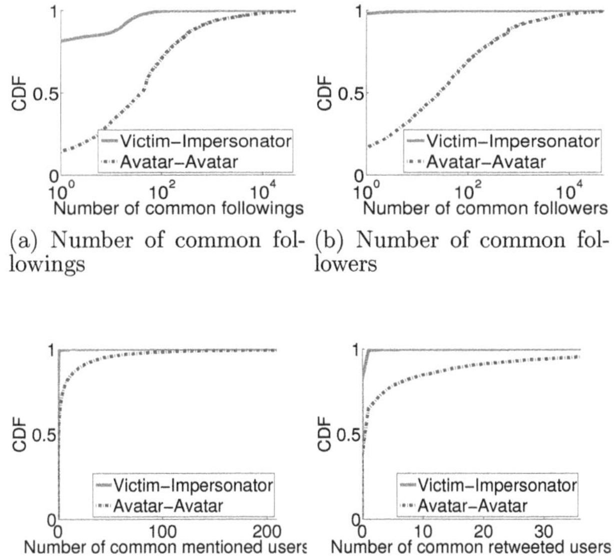

(a) Number of common followings (b) Number of common followers (c) Number of common mentioned users (d) Number of common retweeted users

Figure 4: CDFs of the social neighborhood overlap between accounts in victim-impersonator pairs and avatar-avatar pairs.

Twitter suspension signals and direct account interactions are very good signals to create a dataset to study impersonation attacks, however, there are still many doppelgänger pairs that are not yet labeled (e.g., there are 16,486 unlabeled pairs in the RANDOM DATASET). Thus, a secondary goal of this section is to investigate whether we can detect additional victim-impersonator pairs and avatar-avatar pairs in the doppelgänger pairs in our dataset.

4.1 Features to detect impersonation attacks

To detect impersonation attacks we consider features that characterize pairs of accounts and that can potentially differentiate victim-impersonator pairs from avatar-avatar pairs. We consider all victim-impersonator pairs and avatar-avatar pairs from the RANDOM DATASET and BFS DATASET combined (we call the combined dataset the COMBINED DATASET) to analyze how well the features distinguish between the two kinds of pairs of accounts.

Profile similarity between accounts.

We first analyze the similarity between profile attributes such as *user-names, screen-names, locations, profile photos* and *bios* (refer to the Appendix for details on how we compute the similarity scores for different attributes). Even if these features were used to collect the dataset of doppelgänger pairs we can still use them to distinguish between avatar-avatar pairs and victim-impersonator pairs. In addition, we measure the similarity between the *interests* of two accounts. We use the algorithm proposed by Bhattacharya et al. [4] to infer the interests of a user.

Figure 3 compares the CDFs of the pairwise profile similarity between accounts in avatar-avatar pairs and victim-impersonator pairs. For user-names, screen-names, photo and interests similarity, a value of zero means no similarity while one means perfect similarity. For the location, the similarity is the distance in kilometers between the two locations, thus a value of zero means the locations are the same. For bio, the similarity is the number of common words between two profiles, the higher the similarity the more consistent the bios are.

We observe that the similarity between user-names, screen-names, profile photos and bios is higher for victim-impersonator pairs than avatar-avatar pairs. Thus, users that maintain multiple avatar accounts do not spend the effort to make their accounts look similar, while impersonators do. On the other hand, the similarity between the *interests* of avatar-avatar pairs is higher than the victim-impersonator pairs. We did not expect such high similarity between avatar-avatar pairs because we believed that people maintain distinct accounts to promote different sides of their persona.

Social neighborhood overlap.

We call the set of users an account interacts with in a social network the *social neighborhood* of the account. On Twitter, the social neighborhood of an account *a* consists of the followings and followers of *a* as well as the users mentioned by *a* and the users retweeted by *a*. An overlap in the social neighborhood suggests that two accounts are positioned in the same part of the social network graph. This can be in-

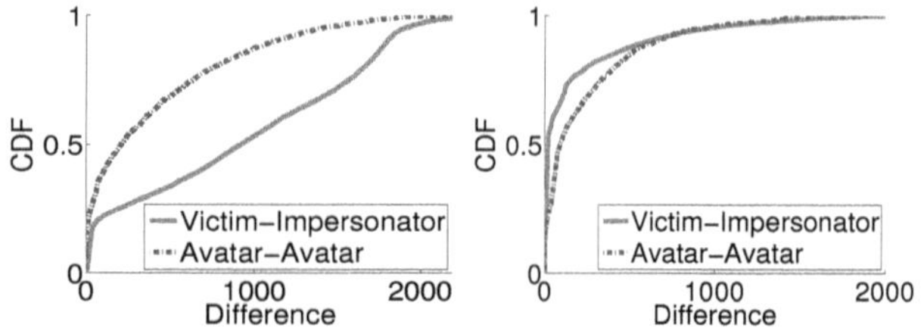

(a) Time difference between creation dates (b) Time difference between the last tweet

Figure 5: CDFs of the time difference in days between accounts in victim-impersonator pairs and avatar-avatar pairs.

dicative of two things: (1) the two accounts correspond to avatars managed by the same user; or (2) potential evidence of social engineering attacks. We use four features to measure the social neighborhood overlap: the *number of common followings*, the *number of common followers*, the *number of overlapping users mentioned* and the *number of overlapping users retweeted* by both accounts, which we present in Figure 4.

There is a striking difference between avatar-avatar pairs and victim-impersonator pairs: while victim-impersonator pairs almost never have a social neighborhood overlap, avatar accounts are very likely to have an overlap. Social neighborhood overlap is also indicative of social engineering attacks but there are not many such attacks in our dataset to be visible in the plots.

Time overlap between accounts.

We add features related to the time overlap between two accounts: *time difference between the creation dates*, *time difference between the last tweets*, *time difference between the first tweets* and whether one account stopped being active after the creation of the second account (we call this feature *outdated account*). Figure 5 compares the difference between creation dates and the date of the last tweet. Figure 5a shows that there is a big difference between account creation times for victim-impersonator pairs while for avatar-avatar pairs the difference is smaller.

Differences between accounts.

Finally, we consider a set of features that represent the *difference* between different numeric features that characterize individual accounts: *klout score difference*, *number of followers difference*, *number of friends difference*, *number of tweets difference*, *number of retweets difference*, *number of favorited tweets difference*, *number of public list difference*. Our intuition was that the difference between numeric features of accounts in avatar-avatar pairs will be smaller than for victim-impersonator pairs, e.g., a small klout score difference between two accounts could be indicative of avatars of the same person while a large klout score difference could be indicative of an impersonation attack. To our surprise, the difference is generally slightly smaller for victim-impersonator pairs.

Overall, the best features to distinguish between victim-impersonator pairs and avatar-avatar pairs are the interest similarity, the social neighborhood overlap as well as the difference between the creation dates of the two accounts.

4.2 Automated detection method

To build an automated method to detect impersonation attacks we build a SVM classifier, with linear kernel, that distinguishes victim-impersonator pairs from avatar-avatar pairs. We use, from the COMBINED DATASET, the victim-impersonator pairs as positive examples, and avatar-avatar pairs as negative examples to train the classifier. We use *all* the features presented in §4.1 as well as *all* the features that characterize individual accounts presented in §2.4 for the training. Since the features are from different categories and scales (e.g., time in days and distances in kilometers), we normalize all features values to the interval [-1,1].

We use 10-fold cross validation over the COMBINED DATASET to train and test the classifier. The SVM classifier, for each pair of accounts, outputs a probability of the pair to be a victim-impersonator pair. To perform the detection of victim-impersonator pairs and avatar-avatar pairs, we then proceed as follows. If the probability is higher than a certain threshold $th1$ we conclude that the pair is a victim-impersonator pair and if the probability is lower than a certain threshold $th2$ (different than $th1$) the pair is a avatar-avatar pair. Note that if $th1 > th2$, some pairs may remain unlabeled. This is done on purpose here because it is preferable in our problem to leave a pair unlabeled rather than wrongly label it (i.e., label avatar-avatar pairs as victim-impersonator pairs or vice versa). We therefore select thresholds $th1$ and $th2$ such that there are very few false positives (i.e., few victim-impersonator pairs mislabeled as avatar-avatar pairs or vice versa). The resulting classifier is able to achieve a 90% true positive rate for a 1% false positive rate to detect victim-impersonator pairs and a 81% true positive rate for a 1% false positive rate to detect avatar-avatar pairs.[9] Thus, we can detect a significant fraction of victim-impersonator pairs using only features that compare the reputation and activity of accounts in a doppelgänger pair. Therefore, it is possible to detect impersonation attacks automatically rather than wait for victims to report them or wait for the accounts to do something clearly malicious in order to be suspended by Twitter.

Potential limitations: Our detection method above, while quite effective today at detecting whether a doppelgänger pair is the result of an impersonation attack, is not necessarily robust against adaptive attackers that might change their strategy to avoid detection in the future. Similar to spam detection, system operators to constantly retrain the detectors (classifiers) to account for new attacker strategies. Also note that the accuracy percentages above only refer to the accuracy of detecting whether a doppelgänger pair is a victim-impersonator pair and does not include the accuracy of detecting a doppelgänger pair or the accuracy of detecting the doppelgänger bot account within a victim-impersonator pair of accounts.

4.3 Classifying unlabeled doppelgänger pairs

We apply the classifier over the 17,605 unlabeled pairs from the BFS DATASET and the 16,486 unlabeled pairs from the RANDOM DATASET. With a threshold corresponding to 1% false positive rate (for both detecting victim-impersonator pairs and avatar-avatar pairs) the classifier is able to identify 4,390 avatar-avatar pairs and 1,863 victim-impersonator

[9]Since there is little to no class imbalance in this classification problem, contrary to §3.3, a 1% false positive rate is low enough.

Table 2: Unlabeled doppelgänger pairs in our dataset that we can labeled using the classifier.

	BFS DATASET (17,605 unlabeled)	RANDOM DATASET (16,486 unlabeled)
victim-impersonator pairs	9,031	1,863
avatar-avatar pairs	4,964	4,390

pairs in the RANDOM DATASET (see Table 2). Thus, the classifier can identify a large additional number of avatar-avatar pairs and victim-impersonator pairs that were not caught in the initial dataset. For example, on top of the 166 examples of victim-impersonator pairs we initially labeled, the classifier labels 1,863 additional victim-impersonator pairs.

We re-crawled all doppelgänger pairs (from both datasets) in May 2015 (the initial crawl ended in Dec 2014), and 5,857 out of the 10,894 victim-impersonator pairs detected by our classifier were suspended by Twitter. This result shows the effectiveness of our method at detecting victim-impersonator pairs sooner than Twitter.

5. RELATED WORK

The closest to our work are a few studies on social engineering attacks which we will review in more detail. Also related are studies of matching accounts across social networks and sybil account detection techniques that we review at a more higher level.

Social engineering attacks.

We focus in this paper on a broader set of attacks that impersonate people, of which, social engineering attack are a subclass. Bilge et al. [5] demonstrated the feasibility of automatically creating cloned profiles in social networks, however, they did not propose techniques to detect the attacks. The closest to our work are three studies [17, 13, 15] that made some initial investigations toward detecting profile cloning. The studies hinted at the fact that cloned profiles can be identified by searching for profiles with similar visual features, but they either stopped at returning a ranked list of accounts that are similar with the victim account [17, 13], or to just test their technique on simulated datasets [15]. In contrast, we actually detect accounts that portray the same person in real-world social networks with high accuracy and we also detect whether they are involved in an impersonation attack or they are legitimate. Furthermore, we propose a technique to gather data about impersonation attacks in real-world social networks and we do the first, to our knowledge, characterization of impersonation attacks in Twitter. On the protection part, He et al. [11] proposed ways to protect against friend requests coming from cloned profiles by using adjacent mediums such as instant chats to verify if the request comes from the real person. To protect users we showed that humans are much better at detecting impersonating accounts when they can also see the victim account. Thus a system that protect users from friend requests coming from cloned profiles could simply just show the user all the accounts that portray the same person with the account that is requesting the friendship.

Account matching.

There are a number of works that propose methods to match the accounts a user has on multiple social networks that are related to our techniques to detect doppelgänger pairs. Note, however, the subtle difference, our goal is to find accounts that people think they *portray* the same person which is slightly different than detecting accounts that *belong* to the same user. To detect doppelgänger pairs we firstly have to only rely on visual features of accounts and then understand when humans get confused.

While there are several studies that exploited visual features similar to the features we use in this paper to match accounts (refer to [9] for an overview), none of these studies applied their methods to detect impersonation attacks. Most of the studies build classifiers that are able to detect whether two accounts belong or not to the same person. We drew inspiration from these works, however, we could not directly apply these techniques to gather doppelgänger pairs because we could not estimate their accuracy as there is no existing ground truth of accounts that portray the same person in the same social network.

Sybil account detection.

One of the most widely used approach today to detect fake accounts is to build behavioral profiles for trusted and untrusted users [3, 40, 29]. The behavioral profile can include, for example, the act of sending messages to other identities, following identities, or rating a particular piece of content. We showed that behavioral profiles are not optimal for detecting impersonating accounts and that we have to exploit features that characterize pairs of identities to identify impersonating accounts.

To assess the trustworthiness of identities, another type of information typically available on social networks is trust relationship *between* identities (e.g., friendship relationship between identities). Researchers have proposed a variety of schemes such as SybilGuard [39] and SybilRank [6] that analyze trust networks between identities to assess the trustworthiness of identities and thus identify Sybil attackers [39, 36, 35]. The key assumption is that an attacker cannot establish an arbitrary number of trust edges with honest or good users in the network. This assumption might break when we have to deal with impersonating accounts as for them it is much easier to link to good users, but it would be interesting to see whether these techniques are able to detect doppelgänger bots.

A third approach to identify suspicious identities is to crowdsource this task to experts who are familiar with identifying suspicious profiles or actions. Social networking services typically have a tiered approach where suspicious profiles reported by end users are further verified by a group of experts before taking a decision to suspend the account or show Captchas to those suspicious users [6]. In fact, researchers recently explored the possibility of using online crowdsourcing services such as Amazon Mechanical Turk (AMT) to crowdsource the task of detecting sybil identities in a social network [37]. Our AMT experiments showed, however, that such techniques are not optimal for detecting impersonating accounts because AMT workers get tricked easily to believe that impersonating accounts are legitimate.

6. CONCLUSION

We conducted the first study to characterize and detect identity impersonation attacks in Twitter. The key enabler of this study is our method to gather data of impersonation attacks. Our method is general and can be used to gather data in other social networks such as Facebook and LinkedIn.

Besides celebrity impersonators and social engineering attacks, we discovered a new type of impersonation attacks where attackers copy the profiles of legitimate users to create real-looking fake accounts that are used to illegally promote content on Twitter. Our analysis revealed that attackers target a wide range of users and anyone that has a Twitter account can be victim of such attacks.

Finally, we proposed an automated technique to detect impersonation attacks, that is able to detect 1,863 more impersonation attacks in our dataset (up from 166).

Our findings reveal a new type of privacy threat against the online image of users. Many surveys [12, 38] state that U.S. firms do background checks for job applicants that involve mining data from their online profiles. In this scenario, the doppelgänger bot attacks can potentially have a significant negative impact on the online image of users if the employer stumbles by mistake across the impersonating account.

7. REFERENCES

[1] Bing Maps API. http://www.microsoft.com/maps/developers/web.aspx.

[2] Get better results with less effort with Mechanical Turk Masters – The Mechanical Turk blog. http://bit.ly/112GmQI.

[3] F. Benevenuto, G. Magno, T. Rodrigues, and V. Almeida. Detecting spammers on Twitter. In *CEAS'10*.

[4] P. Bhattacharya, M. B. Zafar, N. Ganguly, S. Ghosh, and K. P. Gummadi. Inferring user interests in the twitter social network. In *RecSys '14*.

[5] L. Bilge, T. Strufe, D. Balzarotti, and E. Kirda. All your contacts are belong to us: Automated identity theft attacks on social networks. In *WWW'09*.

[6] Q. Cao, M. Sirivianos, X. Yang, and T. Pregueiro. Aiding the detection of fake accounts in large scale social online services. In *NSDI'12*.

[7] W. W. Cohen, P. Ravikumar, and S. E. Fienberg. A comparison of string distance metrics for name-matching tasks. In *IJCAI'03*.

[8] S. Corpus, 2015. http://anoncvs.postgresql.org/cvsweb.cgi/pgsql/src/backend/snowball/stopwords/.

[9] O. Goga. *Matching User Accounts Across Online Social Networks: Methods and Applications*. PhD thesis, Université Pierre et Marie Curie, 2014.

[10] O. Goga, P. Loiseau, R. Sommer, R. Teixeira, and K. Gummadi. On the reliability of profile matching across large online social networks. In *KDD*, 2015.

[11] B.-Z. He, C.-M. Chen, Y.-P. Su, and H.-M. Sun. A defence scheme against identity theft attack based on multiple social networks. *Expert Syst. Appl.*, 2014.

[12] Internetnews. Microsoft survey: Online 'reputation' counts, 2010. http://www.internetnews.com/webcontent/article.php/3861241/Microsoft+Survey+Online+Reputation+Counts.htm.

[13] L. Jin, H. Takabi, and J. B. Joshi. Towards active detection of identity clone attacks on online social networks. In *CODASPY '11*.

[14] A. M. Kakhki, C. Kliman-Silver, and A. Mislove. Iolaus: Securing online content rating systems. In *WWW'13*.

[15] M. Y. Kharaji, F. S. Rizi, and M. Khayyambashi. A new approach for finding cloned profiles in online social networks. *International Journal of Network Security*, 2014.

[16] Klout. Klout, 2014. http://klout.com/.

[17] G. Kontaxis, I. Polakis, S. Ioannidis, and E. Markatos. Detecting social network profile cloning. In *PERCOM'11*.

[18] D. G. Lowe. Distinctive image features from scale-invariant keypoints. *Int. J. Comput. Vision*, 2004.

[19] Mediabistro. Was twitter right to suspend 'christopher walken'?, 2009. https://www.mediabistro.com/alltwitter/was-twitter-right-to-suspend-christopher-walken_b5021.

[20] A. Mislove, A. Post, K. P. Gummadi, and P. Druschel. Ostra: Leveraging trust to thwart unwanted communication. In *NSDI'08*.

[21] M. Mondal, B. Viswanath, A. Clement, P. Druschel, K. P. Gummadi, A. Mislove, and A. Post. Defending against large-scale crawls in online social networks. In *CoNEXT'12*.

[22] Nairobiwire. Sonko's facebook impersonator arrested, 2014. http://nairobiwire.com/2014/07/mike-sonko-arrested-swindling-public.html?utm_source=rss&utm_medium=rss&utm_campaign=mike-sonko-arrested-swindling-public.

[23] D. Perito, C. Castelluccia, M. Ali Kâafar, and P. Manils. How unique and traceable are usernames? In *Proceedings of the 11th Privacy Enhancing Technologies Symposium (PETS)*, 2011.

[24] Phash. http://www.phash.org.

[25] A. Post, V. Shah, and A. Mislove. Bazaar: Strengthening user reputations in online marketplaces. In *NSDI'11*.

[26] Seattlepi. Racism and twitter impersonation prompt lawsuit for kirkland teen, 2010. http://www.seattlepi.com/local/sound/article/Racism-and-Twitter-impersonation-prompt-lawsuit-893555.php.

[27] Social Intelligence Corp. http://www.socialintel.com/.

[28] Spokeo. http://www.spokeo.com/.

[29] T. Stein, E. Chen, and K. Mangla. Facebook immune system. In *SNS'11*.

[30] Turnto23. Impersonator continuously creating fake facebook profiles of a well known bakersfield pastor. http://www.turnto23.com/news/local-news/impersonator-continuously-creating-fake-facebook-profiles-of-a-bakersfield-pastor.

[31] Twitter. Explaining twitter's efforts to shut down spam. https://blog.twitter.com/2012/shutting-down-spammers, 2012.

[32] Twitter. Twitter reporting impersonation accounts, 2014. https://support.twitter.com/articles/20170142-reporting-impersonation-accounts.

[33] B. Viswanath, M. A. Bashir, M. Crovella, S. Guha, K. Gummadi, B. Krishnamurthy, and A. Mislove. Towards detecting anomalous user behavior in online social networks. In *USENIX Security'14*.

[34] B. Viswanath, M. A. Bashir, M. B. Zafar, L. Espin, K. P. Gummadi, and A. Mislove. Trulyfollowing: Discover twitter accounts with suspicious followers. http://trulyfollowing.app-ns.mpi-sws.org/, April 2012. Last accessed Sept 6, 2015.

[35] B. Viswanath, M. Mondal, A. Clement, P. Druschel, K. Gummadi, A. Mislove, and A. Post. Exploring the design space of social network-based sybil defenses. In *COMSNETS'12*.

[36] B. Viswanath, A. Post, K. P. Gummadi, and A. Mislove. An analysis of social network-based sybil defenses. In *SIGCOMM '10*.

[37] G. Wang, M. Mohanlal, C. Wilson, X. Wang, M. J. Metzger, H. Zheng, and B. Y. Zhao. Social turing tests: Crowdsourcing sybil detection. In *NDSS'13*.

[38] Wikibin. Employers using social networks for screening applicants, 2008. http://wikibin.org/articles/employers-using-social-networks-for-screening-applicants.html.

[39] H. Yu, M. Kaminsky, P. B. Gibbons, and A. Flaxman. Sybilguard: Defending against sybil attacks via social networks. In *SIGCOMM '06*.

[40] C. M. Zhang and V. Paxson. Detecting and analyzing automated activity on twitter. In *PAM'11*.

APPENDIX

Here we first explain how we computed similarity between various attribute values (e.g., names and photos) of accounts and then describe the procedure we used to determine when two attribute values (e.g., two names or two photos) are "similar enough" to be deemed to represent the same entity.

A. SIMILARITY METRICS

Name similarity Previous work in the record linkage community showed that the *Jaro string distance* is the most suitable metric to compare similarity between names both in the offline and online worlds [7, 23]. So we use the Jaro distance to measure the similarity between user-names and screen-names.

Photo similarity Estimating photo similarity is tricky as the same photo can come in different formats. To measure the similarity of two photos while accounting for image transformations, we use two matching techniques: (*i*) *perceptual hashing*, a technique originally invented for identifying illegal copies of copyrighted content that works by reducing the image to a transformation-resilient "fingerprint" containing its salient characteristics [24] and (*ii*) *SIFT*, a size invariant algorithm that detects local features in an image and checks if two images are similar by counting the number of local features that match between two images [18]. We use two different algorithms for robustness. The perceptual hashing technique does not cope well with some images that are resized, while the SIFT algorithm does not cope well with computer generated images.

Location similarity For all profiles, we have the textual representations of the location, like the name of a city. Since social networks use different formats for this information, a simple textual comparison will be inaccurate. Instead, we convert the location to latitude/longitude coordinates by submitting them to the Bing API [1]. We then compute the similarity between two locations as the actual geodesic distance between the corresponding coordinates.

Bio similarity The similarity metric is simply the number of common words between the bios of two profiles after removing certain frequently used *stop words* (as is typically done in text retrieval applications). As the set of stop words, we use a popular corpus available for several languages [8].

B. SIMILARITY THRESHOLDS

Clearly the more similar two values of an attribute, the greater the chance that they refer to the same entity, be it a user-name or photo or location. To determine the threshold similarity beyond which two attribute values should be considered as representing the same entity, we rely on *human* annotators. Specifically, we attempt to determine when two attribute values are similar enough for humans to believe they represent the same entity.

We gathered human input by asking Amazon Mechanical Turk (AMT) users to evaluate whether pairs of attribute values represent the same entity or not. We randomly select 200 pairs of profiles and asked AMT users to annotate which attribute values represent the same entity and which do not. We followed the standard guidelines for gathering data from AMT workers [2].

For each attribute, we leverage the AMT experiments to select the similarity thresholds to declare two values as representing the same entity. Specifically, we select similarity thresholds, such that more than 90% of values that represent the same entity (as identified by AMT workers) and less than 10% of the values that represent different entities (as identified by AMT workers) have higher similarities. Consequently, we determine that two user-names or screen-names represent the same name if they have a similarity higher than 0.79, and 0.82 respectively. Two locations represent the same place if they are less than 70km apart. Two photos represent the same image if their SIFT similarity is higher than 0.11 and two bios describe the same user if they have more than 3 words in common.

Dissecting UbuntuOne: Autopsy of a Global-scale Personal Cloud Back-end

Raúl Gracia-Tinedo
Universitat Rovira i Virgili
raul.gracia@urv.cat

Yongchao Tian
Eurecom
yongchao.tian@eurecom.fr

Josep Sampé
Universitat Rovira i Virgili
josep.sampe@urv.cat

Hamza Harkous
EPFL
hamza.harkous@epfl.ch

John Lenton
Canonical Ltd.
john.lenton@canonical.com

Pedro García-López
Universitat Rovira i Virgili
pedro.garcia@urv.cat

Marc Sánchez-Artigas
Universitat Rovira i Virgili
marc.sanchez@urv.cat

Marko Vukolić
IBM Research - Zurich
mvu@zurich.ibm.com

ABSTRACT

Personal Cloud services, such as Dropbox or Box, have been widely adopted by users. Unfortunately, very little is known about the internal operation and general characteristics of Personal Clouds since they are proprietary services.

In this paper, we focus on understanding the nature of Personal Clouds by presenting the *internal structure* and a *measurement study* of UbuntuOne (U1). We first detail the U1 architecture, core components involved in the U1 metadata service hosted in the datacenter of Canonical, as well as the interactions of U1 with Amazon S3 to outsource data storage. To our knowledge, this is the first research work to describe the internals of a large-scale Personal Cloud.

Second, by means of tracing the U1 servers, we provide an extensive analysis of its *back-end activity* for one month. Our analysis includes the study of the *storage workload*, the *user behavior* and the performance of the U1 *metadata store*. Moreover, based on our analysis, we suggest improvements to U1 that can also benefit similar Personal Cloud systems.

Finally, we contribute our dataset to the community, which is the first to contain the back-end activity of a large-scale Personal Cloud. We believe that our dataset provides unique opportunities for extending research in the field.

Categories and Subject Descriptors

C.4 [**Performance of Systems**]: Measurement techniques; K.6.2 [**Management of Computing and Information Systems**]: Installation management–Performance and usage measurement

Keywords

Personal cloud; performance analysis; measurement

IMC'15, October 28–30, 2015, Tokyo, Japan.

ACM 978-1-4503-3848-6/15/10 ...$15.00.
DOI: http://dx.doi.org/10.1145/2815675.2815677.

1. INTRODUCTION

Today, users require ubiquitous and transparent storage to help handle, synchronize and manage their personal data. In a recent report [1], Forrester research forecasts a market of $12 billion in the US related to personal and user-centric cloud services by 2016. In response to this demand, Personal Clouds like Dropbox, Box and UbuntuOne (U1) have proliferated and become increasingly popular, attracting companies such as Google, Microsoft, Amazon or Apple to offer their own integrated solutions in this field.

In a nutshell, a Personal Cloud service offers automatic backup, file sync, sharing and remote accessibility across a multitude of devices and operating systems. The popularity of these services is based on their easy to use Software-as-a-Service (SaaS) storage facade to ubiquitous Infrastructure-as-a-Service (IaaS) providers like Amazon S3 and others.

Unfortunately, due to the proprietary nature of these systems, very little is known about their performance and characteristics, including the workload they have to handle daily. And indeed, the few available studies have to rely on the so-called "black-box" approach, where traces are collected from a single or a limited number of measurement points, in order to infer their properties. This was the approach followed by the most complete analysis of a Personal Cloud to date, the measurement of Dropbox conducted by Drago et al. [2]. Although this work describes the overall service architecture, it provides no insights on the operation and infrastructure of the Dropbox's back-end. And also, it has the additional flaw that it only focuses on small and specific communities, like university campuses, which may breed false generalizations.

Similarly, several Personal Cloud services have been externally probed to infer their operational aspects, such as data reduction and management techniques [3, 4, 5], or even transfer performance [6, 7]. However, from external vantage points, it is impossible to fully understand the operation of these systems without fully reverse-engineering them.

In this paper, we present results of our study of U1: the Personal Cloud of Canonical, integrated by default in Linux Ubuntu OS. Despite the shutdown of this service on July 2014, the distinguishing feature of our analysis is that it has been conducted using data collected by the provider itself. U1 provided service to 1.29 million users at the time of the study on January-February 2014, which constitutes the first complete analysis of the performance of a Personal Cloud in

UbuntuOne Analisys	Finding	Implications and Opportunities
Storage Workload (§ 5)	90% of files are smaller than 1MByte (**P**).	Object storage services normally used as a cloud service are not optimized for managing small files [8].
	18.5% of the upload traffic is caused by file updates (**C**).	Changes in file metadata cause high overhead since the U1 client does not support delta updates (e.g. `.mp3` tags).
	We detected a deduplication ratio of 17% in one month (**C**).	File-based cross-user deduplication provides an attractive trade-off between complexity and performance [5].
	DDoS attacks against U1 are frequent (**N**).	Further research is needed regarding secure protocols and automatic countermeasures for Personal Clouds.
User Behavior (§ 6)	1% of users generate 65% of the traffic (**P**).	Very active users may be treated in an optimized manner to reduce storage costs.
	Data management operations (e.g., uploads, file deletions) are normally executed in long sequences (**C**).	This correlated behavior can be exploited by caching and prefetching mechanisms in the server-side.
	User operations are *bursty*; users transition between long, idle periods and short, very active ones (**N**).	User behavior combined with the user per-shard data model impacts the metadata back-end load balancing.
Back-end Performance (§ 7)	A 20-node database cluster provided service to 1.29M users without symptoms of congestion (**N**).	The *user-centric data model* of a Personal Cloud makes relational database clusters a simple yet effective approach to scale out metadata storage.
	RPCs service time distributions accessing the metadata store exhibit long tails (**N**).	Several factors at hardware, OS and application-level are responsible for poor tail latency in RPC servers [9].
	In short time windows, load values of API servers/DB shards are very far from the mean value (**N**).	Further research is needed to achieve better load balancing under this type of workload.

C: Confirms previous results, **P**: Partially aligned with previous observations, **N**: New observation

Table 1: Summary of some of our most important findings and their implications.

the wild. Such a unique data set has allowed us to reconfirm results from prior studies, like that of Drago et al. [2], which paves the way for a general characterization of these systems. But it has also permitted us to expand the knowledge base on these services, which now represent a considerable volume of the Internet traffic. According to Drago et al. [2], the total volume of Dropbox traffic accounted for a volume equivalent to around one third of the YouTube traffic on a campus network. We believe that the results of our study can be useful for both researchers, ISPs and data center designers, giving hints on how to anticipate the impact of the growing adoption of these services. In summary, our contributions are the following:

Back-end architecture and operation of U1. This work provides a comprehensive description of the U1 architecture, being the first one to also describe the back-end infrastructure of a real-world vendor. Similarly to Dropbox [2], U1 decouples the storage of *file contents* (data) and *their logical representation* (metadata). Canonical only owns the infrastructure for the metadata service, whereas the actual file contents are stored separately in Amazon S3. Among other insights, we found that U1 API servers are characterized by long tail latencies and that a sharded database cluster is an effective way of storing metadata in these systems. Interestingly, these issues may arise in other systems that decouple data and metadata as U1 does [10].

Workload analysis and user behavior in U1. By tracing the U1 servers in the Canonical datacenter, we provide an extensive analysis of its *back-end activity* produced by the *active user population* of U1 for one month (1.29M distinct users). Our analysis confirms already reported facts, like the execution of user operations in long sequences [2] and the potential waste that file updates may induce in the system [4, 5]. Moreover, we provide new observations, such as a taxonomy of files in the system, the modeling of burstiness in user operations or the detection of attacks to U1, among others. Table 1 summarizes some of our key findings.

Potential improvements to Personal Clouds. We suggest that a Personal Cloud should be aware of the *behavior of users* to optimize its operation. Given that, we discuss the implications of our findings to the operation of U1. For instance, file updates in U1 were responsible for 18.5% of upload traffic mainly due to the lack of delta updates in the desktop client. Furthermore, we detected 3 DDoS attacks in one month, which calls for further research in automatic attack countermeasures in secure and dependable storage protocols. Although our observations may not apply to *all* existing services, we believe that our analysis can help to improve the next generation of Personal Clouds [10, 4].

Publicly available dataset. We contribute our dataset (758GB) to the community and it is available at `http://cloudspaces.eu/results/datasets`. To our knowledge, this is the first dataset that contains the back-end activity of a large-scale Personal Cloud. We hope that our dataset provides new opportunities to researchers in further understanding the internal operation of Personal Clouds, promoting research and experimentation in this field.

Roadmap: The rest of the paper is organized as follows. § 2 provides basic background on Personal Clouds. We describe in § 3 the details of the U1 Personal Cloud. In § 4 we explain the trace collection methodology. In § 5, § 6 and § 7 we analyze the storage workload, user activity and back-end performance of U1, respectively. § 8 discusses related work. We discuss the implications of our insights and draw conclusions in § 9.

2. BACKGROUND

A Personal Cloud can be loosely defined as a unified digital locker for users' personal data, offering at least three key services: *file storage*, *synchronization* and *sharing* [11]. Numerous services such as Dropbox, U1 and Box fall under this definition.

From an architectural viewpoint, a Personal Cloud exhibits a 3-tier architecture consisting of: *(i) clients*, *(ii) synchronization* or *metadata service* and *(iii) data store* [2, 10]. Thus, these systems explicitly decouple the management of file contents (data) and their logical representation (metadata). Companies like Dropbox and Canonical only own the infrastructure for the metadata service, which processes requests that affect the virtual organization of files in user volumes. The contents of file transfers are stored separately in Amazon S3. An advantage of this model is that the Personal Cloud can easily scale out storage capacity thanks to the "pay-as-you-go" cloud payment model, avoiding costly investments in storage resources.

In general, Personal Clouds provide clients with 3 main types of access to their service: Web/mobile access, Representational State Transfer (REST) APIs [7, 12] and *desktop*

API Operation	*Related RPC*	*Description*
ListVolumes	dal.list_volumes	This operation is normally performed at the beginning of a session and lists all the volumes of a user (root, user-defined, shared).
ListShares	dal.list_shares	This operation lists all the volumes of a user that are of type *shared*. In this operation, ther field shared by is the owner of the volume and shared to is the user to which that volume was shared with. In this operation, the field shares represents the number of volumes type *shared* of this user.
(Put/Get)Content	see appendix A	These operations are the actual file uploads and downloads, respectively. The notification goes to the U1 back-end but the actual data is stored in a separate service (Amazon S3). A special process is created to forward the data to Amazon S3. Since the upload management in U1 is complex, we refer the reader to appendix A for a description in depth of upload transfers.
Make	dal.make_dir dal.make_file	This operation is equivalent to a "touch" operation in the U1 back-end. Basically, it creates a file node entry in the metadata store and normally precedes a file upload.
Unlink	dal.unlink_node	Delete a file or a directory from a volume.
Move	dal.move	Moves a file from one directory to another.
CreateUDF	dal.create_udf	Creates a user-defined volume.
DeleteVolume	dal.delete_volume	Deletes a volume and the contained nodes.
GetDelta	dal.get_delta	Get the differences between the server volume and the local one (generations).
Authenticate	auth.get_user_id_from_token	Operations managed by the servers to create sessions for users.

Table 2: Description of the most relevant U1 API operations.

clients. Our measurements in this paper focus on the desktop client interactions with U1. Personal Cloud desktop clients are very popular among users since they provide automatic synchronization of user files across several devices (see Section 3.3). To achieve this, desktop clients and the server-side infrastructure communicate via a *storage protocol*. In most popular Personal Cloud services (e.g., Dropbox), such protocols are proprietary.

U1 Personal Cloud was a suite of online services offered by Canonical that enabled users to store and sync files online and between computers, as well as to share files/folders with others using file synchronization. Until the service was discontinued in July 2014, U1 provided desktop and mobile clients and a Web front-end. U1 was integrated with other Ubuntu services, like Tomboy for notes and U1 Music Store for music streaming.

3. THE U1 PERSONAL CLOUD

In this section, we first describe the U1 storage protocol used for communication between clients and the server-side infrastructure (Sec. 3.1). This will facilitate the understanding of the system architecture (Sec. 3.2). We then discuss the details of a U1 desktop client (Sec. 3.3). Finally, we give details behind the core component of U1, its metadata back-end (Sec. 3.4).

3.1 U1 Storage Protocol

U1 uses its own protocol (`ubuntuone-storageprotocol`) based on TCP and Google Protocol Buffers[1]. In contrast to most commercial solutions, the protocol specifications and client-side implementation are publicly available[2]. Here, we describe the protocol in the context of its *entities* and *operations*. Operations can be seen as end-user actions intended to manage one/many entities, such as a file or a directory.

3.1.1 Protocol Entities

In the following, we define the main entities in the protocol. Note that in our analysis, we characterize and identify the role of these entities in the operation of U1.

Node: Files and directories are *nodes* in U1. The protocol supports CRUD operations on nodes (e.g. list, delete, etc.). The protocol assigns Universal Unique Identifiers (UUIDs) to both node objects and their contents, which are generated in the back-end.

[1]`https://wiki.ubuntu.com/UbuntuOne`

[2]`https://launchpad.net/ubuntuone-storage-protocol`

Volume: A volume is a container of node objects. During the installation of the U1 client, the client creates an initial volume to store files with id=0 (root). There are 3 types of volumes: i) *root/predefined*, ii) *user defined folder* (UDF), which is a volume created by the user, and iii) *shared* (sub-volume of another user to which the current user has access).

Session: The U1 desktop client establishes a TCP connection with the server and obtains U1 storage protocol session (not HTTP or any other session type). This session is used to identify a user's requests during the session lifetime. Usually, sessions do not expire automatically. A client may disconnect, or a server process may go down, and that will end the session. To create a new session, an OAuth [13] token is used to authenticate clients against U1. Tokens are stored separately in the Canonical authentication service (see § 3.4.1).

3.1.2 API Operations

The U1 storage protocol offers an API consisting of the *data management* and *metadata operations* that can be executed by a client. Metadata operations are those operations that do not involve transfers to/from the data store (i.e., Amazon S3), such as listing or deleting files, and are entirely managed by the synchronization service. On the contrary, uploads and downloads are, for instance, typical examples of data management operations.

In Table 2 we describe the most important protocol operations between users and the server-side infrastructure. We traced these operations to quantify the system's workload and the behavior of users.

3.2 Architecture Overview

As mentioned before, U1 has a 3-tier architecture consisting of *clients*, *synchronization service* and the *data/metadata store*. Similarly to Dropbox [2], U1 *decouples* the storage of *file contents* (data) and *their logical representation* (metadata). Canonical only owns the infrastructure for the metadata service, which processes requests that affect the virtual organization of files in user volumes. The actual contents of file transfers are stored separately in Amazon S3.

However, U1 treats *client requests* differently from Dropbox. Namely, Dropbox enables clients to send requests *either to the metadata or storage service* depending on the request type. Therefore, the Dropbox infrastructure only processes metadata/control operations. The cloud storage service manages data transfers, which are normally orchestrated by computing instances (e.g. EC2).

In contrast, U1 receives *both metadata requests and data transfers* of clients. Internally, the U1 service discriminates client requests and contacts either the metadata store or the storage service. For each upload and download request, a new back-end process is instantiated to manage the data transfer between the client and S3 (see appendix A). Therefore, the U1 model is simpler from a design perspective, yet this comes at the cost of delegating the responsibility of processing data transfers to the metadata back-end.

U1 Operation Workflow. Imagine a user that initiates the U1 desktop client (§ 3.3). At this point, the client sends an `Authenticate` API call (see Table 2) to U1, in order to establish a new session. An API server receives the request and contacts to the Canonical authentication service to verify the validity of that client (§ 3.4.1). Once the client has been authenticated, a persistent TCP connection is established between the client and U1. Then, the client may send other management requests on user files and directories.

To understand the synchronization workflow, let us assume that two clients are online and work on a shared folder. Then, a client sends an `Unlink` API call to delete a file from the shared folder. Again, an API server receives this request, which is forwarded in form of RPC call to a RPC server (§ 3.4). As we will see, RPC servers translate RPC calls into database query statements to access the correct metadata store shard (PostgreSQL cluster). Thus, the RPC server deletes the entry for that file from the metadata store.

When the query finishes, the result is sent back from the RPC server to the API server that responds to the client that performed the request. Moreover, the API server that handled the `Unlink` notifies the other API servers about this event that, in turn, is detected by the API server to which the second user is connected. This API server notifies via push to the second client, which deletes that file locally. The API server finishes by deleting the file also from Amazon S3.

Next, we describe in depth the different elements involved in this example of operation: The desktop client, the U1 back-end infrastructure and other key back-end services to the operation of U1 (authentication and notifications).

3.3 U1 Desktop Client

U1 provides a user friendly desktop client, implemented in Python (GPLv3), with a graphical interface that enables users to manage files. It runs a daemon in the background that exposes a message bus (DBus) interface to handle events in U1 folders and make server notifications visible to the user through OS desktop. This daemon also does the work of deciding what to synchronize and in which direction to do so.

By default, one folder labeled `~/Ubuntu One/` is automatically created and configured for mirroring (root `volume`) during the client installation. Changes to this folder (and any others added) are watched using `inotify`. Synchronization metadata about directories being mirrored is stored in `~/.cache/ubuntuone`. When remote content changes, the client acts on the incoming unsolicited notification (push) sent by U1 service and starts the download. Push notifications are possible since clients establish a TCP connection with the metadata service that remains open while online.

In terms of data management, Dropbox desktop clients deduplicate data at chunk level [2]. In contrast, U1 resorts to file-based cross-user deduplication to reduce the waste of storing repeated files [5]. Thus, to detect duplicated files, U1 desktop clients provide to the server the SHA-1 hash of a file prior to the content upload. Subsequently, the system checks if the file to be uploaded already exists or not. In the affirmative case, the new file is *logically linked* to the existing content, and the client does not need to transfer data.

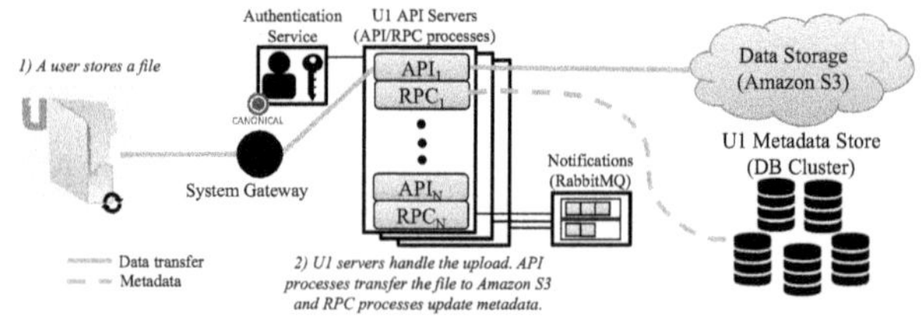

Figure 1: Architecture and workflow of U1 back-end.

Finally, as observed in [5], the U1 client applies compression to uploaded files to optimize transfers. However, the desktop client does not perform techniques such as file bundling[3], delta updates and sync deferment in order to simplify its design, which may lead to inefficiencies.

3.4 U1 Metadata Back-end

The entire U1 back-end is all inside a single datacenter and its objective is to manage the metadata service. The back-end architecture appears in Fig. 1 and consists of *metadata servers* (API/RPC), *metadata store* and *data store.*

System gateway. The gateway to the back-end servers is the load balancer. The load balancer (HAProxy, ssl, etc.) is the visible endpoint for users and it is composed of two racked servers.

Metadata store. U1 stores metadata in a PostgreSQL database cluster composed of 20 large Dell racked servers, configured in 10 shards (master-slave). Internally, the system routes operations *by user identifier* to the appropriate shard. Thus, metadata of a user's files and folders reside always in the same shard. This data model *effectively* exploits sharding, since normally there is no need to lock more than one shard per operation (i.e. lockless). Only operations related to shared files/folders may require to involve more than one shard in the cluster.

API/RPC servers. Beyond the load balancer we find the API and RPC database processes that run on 6 separate racked servers. API servers receive commands from the user, perform authentication, and translate the commands into RPC calls. In turn, RPC database workers translate these RPC calls into database queries and route queries to the appropriate database shards. API/RPC processes are more numerous than physical machines (normally $8-16$ processes per physical machine), so that they can migrate among machines for load balancing. Internally, API and RPC servers, the load balancer and the metadata store are connected though a switched 1Gbit Ethernet network.

Data storage. Like other popular Personal Clouds, such as Dropbox or SugarSync, U1 stores user files in a separate cloud service. Concretely, U1 resorts to Amazon S3 (`us-east`) to store user data. This solution enables a service to rapidly scale out without a heavy investment in storage hardware. In its latests months of operation, U1 had a $\approx$ 20,000$ monthly bill in storage resources, being the most important Amazon S3 client in Europe.

[3]Li et al. [5] suggest that U1 may group small files together for upload (i.e. bundling), since they observed high efficiency uploading sets of small files. However, U1 does not bundle small files together. Instead, clients establish a TCP connection with the server that remains open during the session, avoiding the overhead of creating new connections.

With this infrastructure, U1 provided service to 1.29 million users traced in this measurement for one month.

3.4.1 Authentication Service

The authentication service of U1 is shared with other Canonical services within the same datacenter and it is based on OAuth [13]. The first time a user interacts with U1, the desktop client requires him to introduce his credentials (email, password). The API server that handles the authentication request contacts the authentication service to generate a new token for this client. The created token is associated in the authentication service with a new user identifier. The desktop client also stores this token locally in order to avoid exposing user credentials in the future.

In the subsequent connections of that user, the authentication procedure is easier. Basically, the desktop client sends a connection request with the token to be authenticated. The U1 API server responsible for that requests asks the authentication service if the token does exist and has not expired. In the affirmative case, the authentication service retrieves the associated user identifier, and a new session is established. During the session, the token of that client is cached to avoid overloading the authentication service.

The authentication infrastructure consists of 1 database server with hot failover and 2 application servers configured with crossed stacks of Apache/Squid/HAProxy.

3.4.2 Notifications

Clients detect changes in their volumes by comparing their local state with the server side on every connection (generation point). However, if two related clients are online and their changes affect each other (e.g. updates to shares, new shares), API servers notify them directly (push). To this end, API servers resort to the TCP connection that clients establish with U1 in every session.

Internally, the system needs a way of notifying changes to API servers that are relevant to simultaneously connected clients. Concretely, U1 resorts to RabbitMQ (1 server) for communicating events between API servers[4], which are subscribed in the queue system to send and receive new events to be communicated to clients.

Next, we describe our measurement methodology to create the dataset used in our analysis.

4. DATA COLLECTION

We present a study of the U1 service back-end. In contrast to other Personal Cloud measurements [2, 7, 5], we did not deploy vantage points to analyze the service externally. Instead, we inspected directly the U1 metadata servers to measure the system. This has been done in collaboration with Canonical in the context of the FP7 CloudSpaces[5] project. Canonical anonymized sensitive information to build the trace (user ids, file names, etc.).

The traces are taken at both *API* and *RPC* server stages. In the former stage we collected important information about the storage workload and user behavior, whereas the second stage provided us with valuable information about the requests' life-cycle and the metadata store performance.

We built the trace capturing a series of service *logfiles*. Each logfile corresponds to the entire activity of a single API/RPC process in a machine for a period of time. Each logfile is within itself strictly *sequential and timestamped*. Thus, causal ordering is ensured for operations done for the same user. However, the timestamp between servers is not dependable, even though machines are synchronized with NTP (clock drift may be in the order of ms).

To gain better understanding on this, consider a line in the trace with this logname: `production-whitecurrant-23-20140128`. They will all be `production`, because we only looked at production servers. After that prefix is the name of the physical machine (`whitecurrant`), followed by the number of the server process (`23`) and the date. The mapping between services and servers is dynamic within the time frame of analyzed logs, since they can migrate between servers to balance load. In any case, the identifier of the process is unique within a machine. After that is the date the logfile was "cut" (there is one log file per server/service and day).

Database sharding is in the metadata store back-end, so it is behind the point where traces were taken. This means that in these traces any combination of server/process can handle any user. To have a strictly sequential notion of the activity of a user we should take into account the U1 *session* and sort the trace by timestamp (one session/connection per desktop client). A session starts in the least loaded machine and lives in the same node until it finishes, making user events strictly sequential. Thanks to this information we can estimate system and user service times.

Approximately 1% of traces are not analyzed due to failures parsing of the logs.

Trace duration	30 days (01/11 - 02/10)
Trace size	758GB
Back-end servers traced	6 servers (all)
Unique user IDs	1, 294, 794
Unique files	137.63M
User sessions	42.5M
Transfer operations	194.3M
Total upload traffic	105TB
Total download traffic	120TB

Table 3: Summary of the trace.

4.1 Dataset

The trace is the result of merging all the logfiles (758GB of `.csv` text) of the U1 servers for 30 days (see Table 3).

The trace contains the API operations (request type `storage/storage_done`) and their translation into RPC calls (request type `rpc`), as well as the session management of users (request type `session`). This provides different sources of valuable information. For instance, we can analyze the *storage workload* supported by a real-world cloud service (users, files, operations). Since we captured file properties such as file size and hash, we can study the storage system in high detail (contents are not disclosed).

Dataset limitations. The dataset only includes events originating from desktop clients. Other sources of user requests (e.g., the web front-end, mobile clients) are handled by different software stacks that were not logged. Also, a small number of apparently malfunctioning clients seems to continuously upload files hundreds of times —these artifacts have been removed for this analysis. Finally, we detected that sharing among users is limited.

5. STORAGE WORKLOAD

First, we quantify the storage workload supported by U1 for one month. Moreover, we pay special attention to the behavior of files in the system, to infer potential improvements. We also unveil attacks perpetrated to the U1 service.

[4]If connected clients are handled by the same API process, their notifications are sent immediately, i.e. there is no need for inter-process communication with RabbitMQ.

[5]`http://cloudspaces.eu`

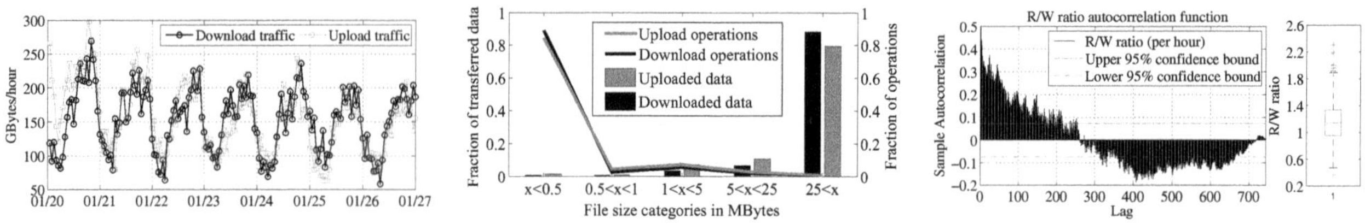

(a) Transferred traffic time-series. (b) Traffic vs file size category. (c) R/W ratio analysis.

Figure 2: Macroscopic storage workload metrics of U1.

5.1 Macroscopic Daily Usage

Storage traffic and operations. Fig. 2(a) provides a time-series view of the upload/download traffic of U1 for one week. We observe in Fig. 2(a) that U1 exhibits important *daily patterns*. To wit, the volume of uploaded GBytes per hour can be up to 10x higher in the central day hours compared to the nights. This observation is aligned with previous works, that detected time-based variability in both the usage and performance of Personal Cloud services [2, 7]. This effect is probably related to the working habits of users, since U1 desktop clients are by default initiated automatically when users turn on their machines.

Another aspect to explore is the relationship between file size and its impact in terms of upload/download traffic. To do so, in Fig. 2(b), we depict in relative terms the fraction of transferred data and storage operations for distinct file sizes. As can be observed, a very small amount of large files ($>$ 25MBytes) consumes 79.3% and 88.2% of upload and download traffic, respectively. Conversely, 84.3% and 89.0% of upload and download operations are related to small files ($<$ 0.5MBytes). As reported in other domains [14, 15, 16], we conclude that in U1 the workload in terms of *storage operations* is dominated by small files, whereas a small number of large files generate most of the *network traffic*.

For uploads, we found that 10.05% of total upload operations are *updates*, that is, an upload of an existing file that has distinct hash/size. However, in terms of traffic, file updates represent 18.47% of the U1 upload traffic. This can be partly explained by the lack of delta updates in the U1 client and the heavy file-editing usage that many users exhibited (e.g., code developers). Particularly for media files, U1 engineers found that applications that modify the metadata of files (e.g., tagging `.mp3` songs) induced high upload traffic since the U1 client uploads again files upon metadata changes, as they are interpreted as regular updates.

To summarize, Personal Clouds tend to exhibit daily traffic patterns, and most of this traffic is caused by a small number of large files. Moreover, desktop clients should efficiently handle file updates to minimize traffic overhead.

R/W ratio. The read/write (R/W) ratio represents the relationship between the downloaded and uploaded data in the system for a certain period of time. Here we examine the variability of the R/W ratio in U1 (1-hour bins). The boxplot in Fig. 2(c) shows that the R/W ratio *variability can be important*, exhibiting differences of 8x within the same day. Moreover, the median (1.14) and mean (1.17) values of the R/W ratio distribution point out that the U1 workload is *slightly read-dominated*, but not as much as it has been observed in Dropbox [2]. One of the reasons for this is that the sharing activity in U1 was much lower than for Dropbox.

We also want to explore if the R/W ratios present patterns or dependencies along time due to the working habits of users. To verify whether R/W ratios are independent along time, we calculated the autocorrelation function (ACF) for each 1-hour sample (see Fig. 2(c)). To interpret Fig. 2(c), if R/W ratios are completely uncorrelated, the sample ACF is approximately normally distributed with mean 0 and variance $1/N$, where N is the number of samples. The 95% confidence limits for ACF can then be approximated to $\pm 2/\sqrt{N}$.

As shown in Fig. 2(c), R/W ratios are not independent, since most lags are outside 95% confidence intervals, which indicates long-term correlation with alternating positive and negative ACF trends. This evidences that the R/W ratios of U1 workload are not random and follow a pattern also guided by the working habits of users.

Concretely, averaging R/W ratios for the same hour along the whole trace, we found that from 6am to 3pm the R/W ratio shows a linear decay. This means that users download more content when they start the U1 client, whereas uploads are more frequent during the common working hours. For evenings and nights we found no clear R/W ratio trends.

We conclude that different Personal Clouds may exhibit disparate R/W ratios, mainly depending on the purpose and strengths of the service (e.g., sharing, content distribution). Moreover, R/W ratios exhibit patterns along time, which can be predicted in the server-side to optimize the service.

5.2 File-based Workload Analysis

File operation dependencies. Essentially, in U1 a file can be *downloaded (or read)* and *uploaded (or written)* multiple times, until it is eventually *deleted*. Next, we aim at inspecting the dependencies among file operations [17, 18], which can be *RAW* (Read-after-Write), *WAW* (Write-after-Write) or *DAW* (Delete-after-Write). Analogously, we have *WAR*, *RAR* and *DAR* for operations executed after a read.

First, we inspect file operations that occur after a write (Fig. 3(a)). We see that *WAW* dependencies are the most common ones (30.1% of 170.01M in total). This can be due to the fact that users *regularly update synchronized files*, such as documents of code files. This result is consistent with the results in [17] for personal workstations where block updates are common, but differs from other organizational storage systems in which files are almost immutable [18]. Furthermore, the 80% of WAW times are shorter than 1 hour, which seems reasonable since users may update a single text-like file various times within a short time lapse.

In this sense, Fig. 3(a) shows that *RAW* dependencies are also relevant. Two events can lead to this situation: (i) the system synchronizes a file to another device right after its creation, and (ii) downloads that occur after every file update. For the latter case, reads after successive writes can be optimized with sync deferment to reduce network overhead caused by synchronizing intermediate versions to multiple devices [5]. This has not been implemented in U1.

Second, we inspect the behavior of X-after-Read dependencies (Fig. 3(b)). As a consequence of active update patterns (i.e., write-to-write) and the absence of sync deferment, we see in Fig. 3(b) that *WAR* transitions also occur

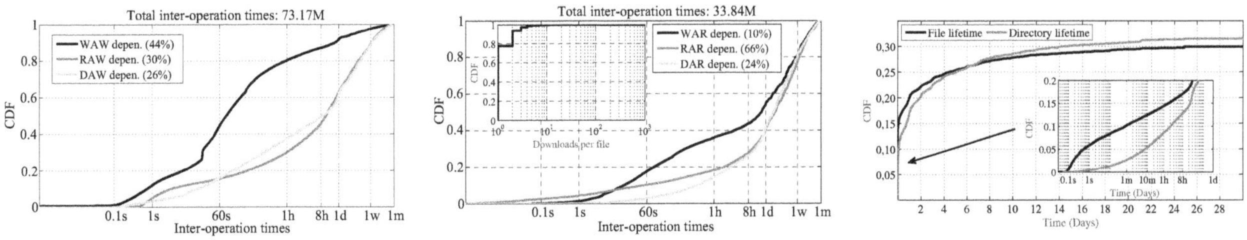

(a) X-after-Write inter-arrival times. (b) X-after-Read inter-arrival times. (c) File/directory lifetime.

Figure 3: Usage and behavior of files in U1.

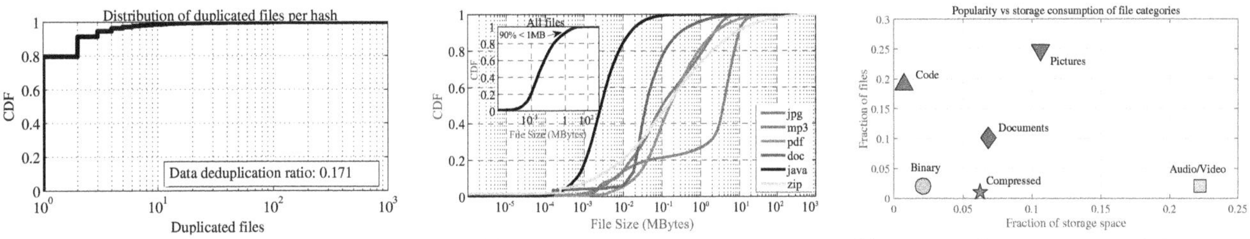

(a) Duplicated files per hash. (b) Size of files per extension. (c) Number/storage share of file types.

Figure 4: Characterization of files in U1.

within reduced time frames compared to other transitions. Anyway, this dependency is the least popular one yielding that files that are *read tend not to be updated again.*

In Fig. 3(b), 40% of RAR times fall within 1 day. RAR times are shorter than the ones reported in [18], which can motivate the introduction of *caching mechanisms* in the U1 back-end. Caching seems specially interesting observing the inner plot of Fig. 3(b) that reveals a long tail in the distributions of reads per file. This means that a small fraction of files is very popular and may be effectively cached.

By inspecting the Delete-after-X dependencies, we detected that around 12.5M files in U1 were *completely unused* for more than 1 day before their deletion (9.1% of all files). This simple observation on dying files evidences that *warm and/or cold data exists* in a Personal Cloud, which may motivate the involvement of warm/cold data systems in these services (e.g., Amazon Glacier, f4 [19]). To efficiently managing warm files in these services is object of current work.

Node lifetime. Now we focus on the lifetime of user files and directories (i.e., nodes). As shown in Fig. 3(c), 28.9% of the new files and and 31.5% of the recently created directories are deleted within one month. We also note that the lifetime distributions of *files and directories are very similar*, which can be explained by the fact that deleting a directory in U1 triggers the deletion of all the files it contains.

This figure also unveils that a large fraction of nodes are deleted within *a few hours after their creation*, especially for files. Concretely, users delete 17.1% of files and 12.9% of directories within 8 hours after their creation time.

All in all, in U1 files exhibit similar lifetimes than files in local file systems. For instance, Agrawal et al. in [15] analyzed the lifetimes of files in corporative desktop computers for five years. They reported that around 20% to 30% of files (depending on the year) in desktop computers present a lifetime of one month, which agrees with our observations. This suggests that *users behave similarly deleting files* either in synchronized or local folders.

5.3 File Deduplication, Sizes and Types

File-based deduplication. The deduplication ratio (dr) is a metric to quantify the proportion of duplicated data. It takes real values in the interval $[0, 1)$, with 0 signaling no file deduplication at all, and 1 meaning full deduplication. It is expressed as $dr = 1 - (D_{unique}/D_{total})$, where D_{unique} is the amount of unique data, and D_{total} is equal to the total storage consumption.

We detected a dr of 0.171, meaning that 17% of files' data in the trace can be deduplicated, which is similar (18%) to that given by the recent work of Li et al. [5]. This suggests that file-based cross-user deduplication could be a practical approach to reduce storage costs in U1.

Moreover, Fig. 4(a) demonstrates that the distribution of file objects w.r.t unique contents exhibits a long tail. This means that a small number of files accounts for a very large number of duplicates (e.g., popular songs), whereas 80% files present no duplicates. Hence, files with many duplicates represent a *hot spot* for the deduplication system, since a large number of logical links point to a single content.

File size distribution. The inner plot of Fig. 4(b) illustrates the file size distribution of transferred files in the system. At first glance, we realize that the *vast majority of files are small* [14, 15, 16]. To wit, 90% of files are smaller than 1MByte. In our view, this can have important implications on the performance of the back-end storage system. The reason is that Personal Clouds like U1 use object storage services offered by cloud providers as data store, which has not been designed for storing very small files [8].

In this sense, Fig. 4(b) shows the file size distribution of the most popular file extensions in U1. Non-surprisingly, the distributions are very disparate, which can be used to model realistic workloads in Personal Cloud benchmarks [3]. It is worth noting that in general, incompressible files like zipped files or compressed media are larger than compressible files (docs, code). This observation indicates that compressing files *does not provide much benefits* in many cases.

File types: number vs storage space. We classified files belonging to the 55 most popular file extensions into 7 categories: Pics (`.jpg`, `.png`, `.gif`, etc.), Code (`.php`, `.c`, `.js`, etc.), Docs (`.pdf`, `.txt`, `.doc`, etc.), Audio/Video (`.mp3`, `.wav`, `.ogg`, etc.), Application/Binary (`.o`, `.msf`, `.jar`, etc.) and Compressed (`.gz`, `.zip`, etc.). Then, for each cat-

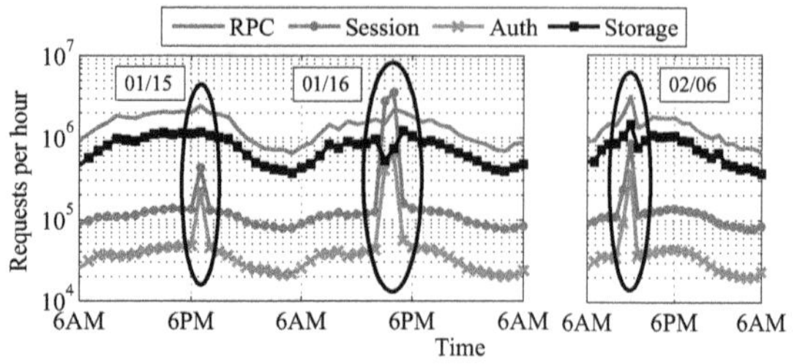

Figure 5: DDoS attacks detected in our trace.

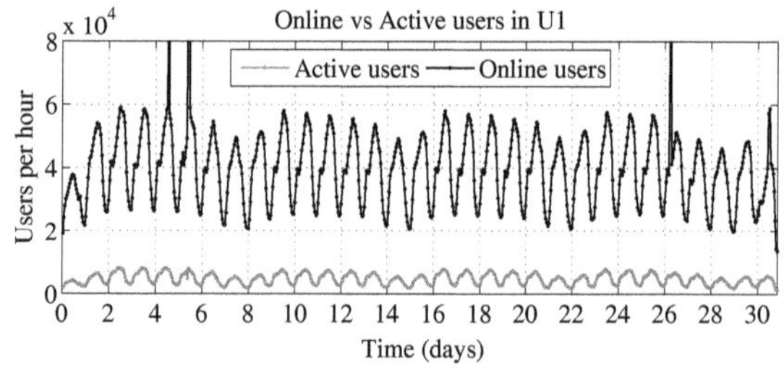

Figure 6: Online vs active users per hour.

egory, we calculated the ratio of the number of files to the total in the system. We did the same for the storage space. This captures the relative importance of each content type.

Fig. 4(c) reveals that Audio/Video category is one of the most relevant types of files regarding the share of consumed storage, despite the fraction of files belonging to this class is low. The reason is that U1 users stored `.mp3` files, which are usually larger than other popular text-based file types.

Further, the Code category contains the highest fraction of files, indicating that many U1 users are code developers who frequently update such files, despite the storage space required for this category is minimal. Docs are also popular (10.1%), subject to updates and hold 6.9% of the storage share. Since the U1 desktop client lacks delta updates and deferred sync, such frequent updates pose a high stress for desktop clients and induce significant network overhead [5].

5.4 DDoS and Abuse of Personal Clouds

A Distributed Denial of Service (DDoS) can be defined as the attempt to disrupt the legitimate use of a service [20]. Normally, a DDoS attack is normally accompanied by some form of fraudulent resource consumption in the victim's side.

Surprisingly, we found that DDoS attacks to U1 are *more frequent* than one can reasonably expect. Specifically, we found evidence of three such attacks in our traces (January 15, 16 and February 6)[6]. These DDoS attacks had as objective to *share illegal content* through the U1 infrastructure.

As visible in Fig. 5, all the attacks resulted in a dramatic increase of the number of session and authentication requests per hour —both events related to the management of user sessions. Actually, the authentication activity under attack was 5 to 15 times higher than usual, which directly impacts the Canonical's *authentication subsystem.*

The situation for API servers was even worse: during the second attack (01/16) API servers received an activity 245x higher than usual, whereas during the first (01/15) and last (02/06) attacks the activity was 4.6x and 6.7x higher than normal, respectively. Therefore, the most affected components were the API servers, as they serviced both *session and storage operations.*

We found that these attacks consisted on sharing a *single user id* and its credentials to distribute content across thousands of desktop clients. The nature of this attack is similar to the *storage leeching problem* reported in [12], which consists of exploiting the freemium business model of Personal Clouds to illicitly consume bandwidth and storage resources.

Also, the reaction to these attacks was not automatic. U1 engineers manually handled DDoS by means of deleting fraudulent users and the content to be shared. This can be easily seen on the storage activity for the second and third attack, which decays within one hour after engineers detected and responded to the attack.

These observations confirm that Personal Clouds are a suitable target for attack as other Internet systems, and that these situations are indeed common. We believe that further research is needed to build and apply secure storage protocols to these systems, as well as new countermeasures to automatically react to this kind of threats.

6. UNDERSTANDING USER BEHAVIOR

Understanding the behavior of users is a key source of information to optimize large-scale systems. This section provides several insights about the behavior of users in U1.

6.1 Distinguishing Online from Active Users

Online and active users. We consider a user as *online* if his desktop client exhibits any form of interaction with the server. This includes automatic client requests involved in maintenance or notification tasks, for which the user is not responsible for. Moreover, we consider a user as *active* if he performs data management operations on his volumes, such as uploading a file or creating a new directory.

Fig. 6 offers a time-series view of the number of online and active users in the system per hour. Clearly, *online users are more numerous than active users*: The percentage of active users ranges from 3.49% to 16.25% at any moment in the trace. This observation reveals that the actual storage workload that U1 supports is light compared to the potential usage of its user population, and gives a sense on the scale and costs of these services with respect to their popularity.

Frequency of user operations. Here we examine how frequent the protocol operations are in order to identify the hottest ones. Fig. 7(a) depicts the absolute number of each operation type. As shown in this figure, the most frequent operations correspond to *data management operations*, and in particular, those operations that relate to the download, upload and deletion of files.

Given that active users are a minority, it proves that the U1 protocol does not imposes high overhead to the server-side, since the operations that users issue to manage their sessions and are typically part of the session start up (e.g., `ListVolumes`) are not dominant. And consequently, the major part of the processing burden comes from active users as desired. This is essentially explained by the fact that the U1 desktop client does not need to regularly poll the server during idle times, thereby limiting the number of requests not linked to data management.

As we will see in § 7, the frequency of API operations will have an immediate impact on the back-end performance.

Traffic distribution across users. Now, we turn our attention to the distribution of consumed traffic across users. In Fig. 7(b) we observe an interesting fact: in one month, only 14% of users downloaded data from U1, while uploads

[6] Our interviews with Canonical engineers confirmed that these activity spikes correspond to DDoS attacks, instead of a software release or any other legitimate event.

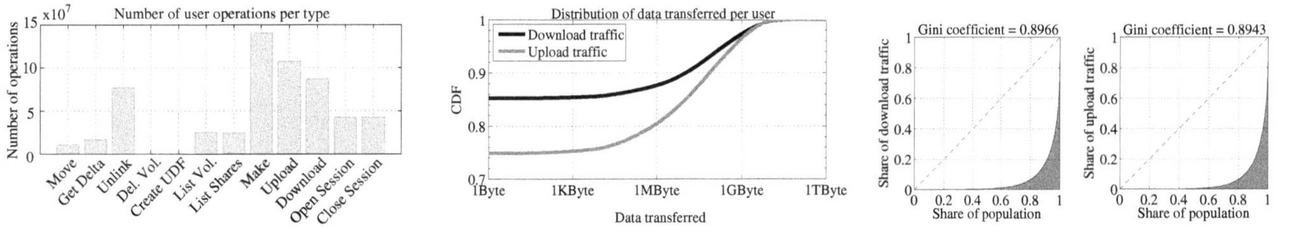

(a) Total number of requests per type. (b) CDF of traffic across users. (c) Lorenz curve of traffic vs active users.

Figure 7: User requests and consumed traffic in U1 for one month.

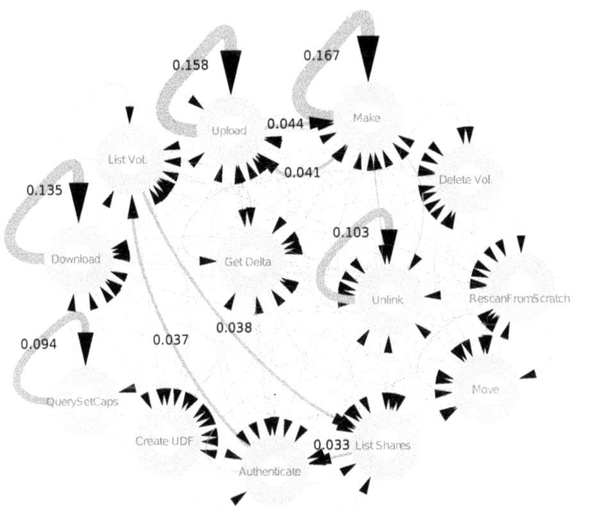

Figure 8: Desktop client transition graph through API operations. Global transition probabilities are provided for main edges.

represented 25%. This indicates that a minority of users are responsible for the storage workload of U1.

To better understand this, we measure how (un)equal the traffic distribution across active users is. To do so, we resort to the Lorenz curve and the Gini coefficient[7] as indicators of inequality. The Gini coefficient varies between 0, which reflects complete equality, and 1, which indicates complete inequality (i.e., only one user consumes all the traffic). The Lorenz curve plots the proportion of the total income of the population (y axis) that is cumulatively earned by the bottom x% of the population. The line at 45 degrees thus represents perfect equality of incomes.

Fig. 7(c) reports that the consumed traffic across active users is very unequal. That is, the Lorenz curve is very far from the diagonal line and the Gini coefficient is close to 1. The reason for this inequality is clear: 1% of active users account for the 65.6% of the total traffic (147.52TB). Providers may benefit from this fact by identifying and treating these users more efficiently.

Types of user activity. To study the activity of users, we used the same user classification than Drago et al. in [2]. So we distinguished among *occasional*, *download/upload only* and *heavy* users. A user is *occasional* if he transfers less than 10KB of data. Users that exhibit more than three orders of magnitude of difference between upload and download (e.g., 1GB versus 1MB) traffic are classified as either *download-only* or *upload-only*. The rest of users are in the *heavy* group.

Given that, we found that 85.82% of *all* users are occasional (mainly online users), 7.22% upload-only, 2.34% download-only and 4.62% are heavy users. Our results clearly differ from the ones reported in [2], where users are 30% occasional, 7% upload-only, 26% download-only and 37% heavy. This may be explained by two reasons: (i) the usage of Dropbox is more extensive than the usage of U1, and (ii) users in a university campus are more active and share more files than other user types captured in our trace.

[7]`http://en.wikipedia.org/wiki/Gini_coefficient`

6.2 Characterizing User Interactions

User-centric request graph. To analyze how users interact with U1, Fig. 8 shows the sequence of operations that desktop clients issue to the server in form of a graph. Nodes represent the different protocol operations executed. And edges describe the transitions from one operation to another. The width of edges denotes the global frequency of a given transition. Note that this graph is user-centric, as it aggregates the different sequence of commands that every user executes, not the sequence of operations as they arrive to the metadata service.

Interestingly, we found that the *repetition of certain operations* becomes really frequent across clients. For instance, it is highly probable that when a client transfers a file, the next operation that he will issue is also another transfer —either upload or download. This phenomenon can be partially explained by the fact that many times users synchronize data at *directory granularity*, which involves repeating several data management operations in cascade. File editing can be also a source of recurrent transfer operations. This behavior can be exploited by predictive data management techniques in the server side (e.g., download prefetching).

Other sequences of operations are also highlighted in the graph. For instance, once a user is authenticated, he usually performs a `ListVolumes` and `ListShares` operations. This is a regular initialization flow for desktop clients. We also observe that `Make` and `Upload` operations are quite mixed, evidencing that for uploading a file the client first needs to create the metadata entry for this file in U1.

Burstiness in user operations. Next, we analyze inter-arrival times between consecutive operations of the same user. We want to verify whether inter-operation times are Poisson or not, which may have important implications to the back-end performance. To this end, we followed the same methodology proposed in [21, 22], and obtained a time-series view of `Unlink` and `Upload` inter-operation times and their approximation to a power-law distribution in Fig. 9.

Fig. 9(a) exhibits large spikes for both `Unlink` and `Upload` operations, corresponding to *very long inter-operation times*. This is far from an exponential distribution, where long inter-operation times are negligible. This shows that the interactions of users with U1 are not Poisson [21].

Now, we study if the `Unlink` and `Upload` inter-operation times exhibit *high variance*, which indicates *burstiness*. In all cases, while not strictly linear, these distributions show a downward trend over almost six orders of magnitude. This

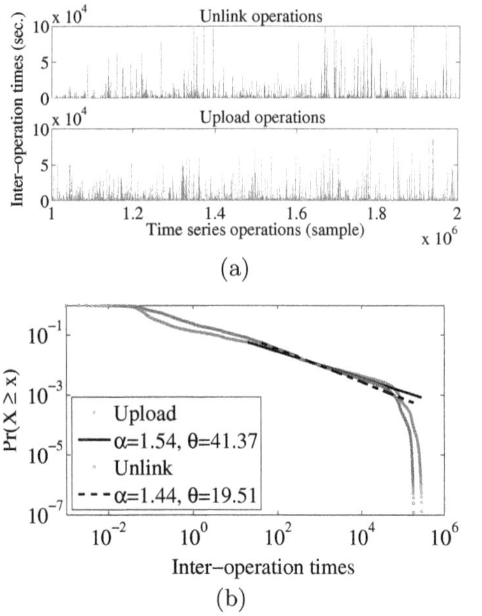

Figure 9: Time-series user operations inter-arrival times and their approximation to a power-law.

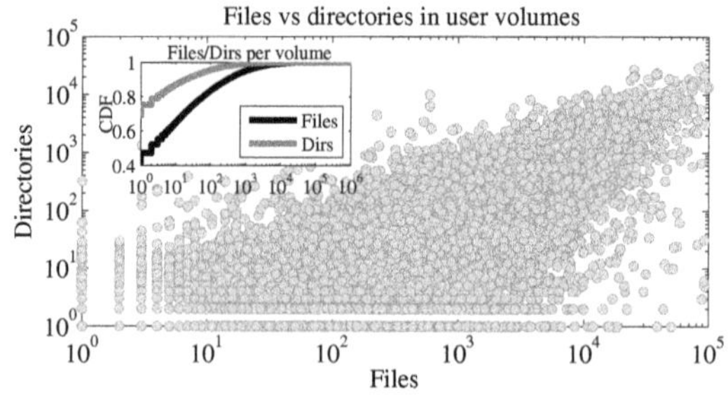

Figure 10: Files and directories per volume.

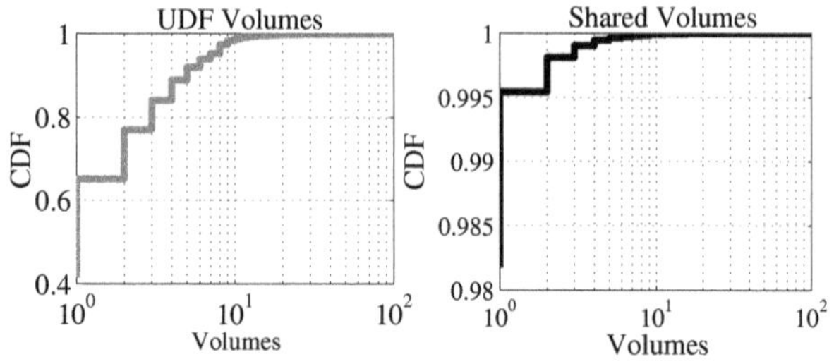

Figure 11: Distribution of shared/user-defined volumes across users.

suggests that high variance of user inter-arrival operations is present in time scales ranging from seconds to several hours. Hence, users issue requests in a *bursty non-Poisson way*: during a short period a user sends several operations in quick succession, followed by long periods of inactivity. A possible explanation to this is that users manage data at the *directory granularity*, thereby triggering multiples operations to keep the files inside each directory in sync.

Nevertheless, we cannot confirm the hypothesis that these distributions are heavy-tailed. Clearly, Fig. 9(b) visually confirms that the empirical distributions of user `Unlink` and `Upload` inter-arrivals can be only approximated with $P(x) \approx x^{-\alpha}, \forall x > \theta$, $1 < \alpha < 2$, for a central region of the domain.

We also found that metadata operations follow more closely a power-law distribution than data operations. The reason is that the behavior of metadata inter-operation times are not affected by the actual data transfers.

In conclusion, we can see that user operations are bursty, which has strong implications to the operation of the back-end servers (§ 7).

6.3 Inspecting User Volumes

Volume contents. Fig. 10 illustrates the relationship between files and directories within user volumes. As usual, files are much more numerous than directories. And we have that over 60% of volumes have been associated with at least one file. For directories, this percentage is only of 32%, but there is a strong correlation between the number of files and directories within a volume: Pearson correlation coefficient is 0.998. What is relevant is, however, that a small fraction of volumes is heavy loaded: 5% of user volumes contain more than 1,000 files.

Shared and user-defined volumes. At this point, we study the distribution of user-defined/shared volumes across users. As pointed out by Canonical engineers, sharing is not a popular feature of U1. Fig. 11 shows that only 1.8% of users exhibits at least one shared volume. On the contrary, we observe that user-defined volumes are much more popular; we detected user-defined volumes in 58% of users —the rest of users only use the root volume. This shows that the majority of users have some degree of expertise using U1.

Overall, these observations reveal that U1 was used more as a storage service rather than for collaborative work.

7. METADATA BACK-END ANALYSIS

In this section, we focus on the interactions of RPC servers against the metadata store. We also quantify the role of the Canonical authentication service in U1.

7.1 Performance of Metadata Operations

Here we analyze the performance of RPC operations that involve contacting the metadata store.

Fig. 12 illustrates the distribution of service times of the different RPC operations. As shown in the figure, all RPCs exhibit *long tails of service time distributions*: from 7% to 22% of RPC service times are very far from the median value. This issue can be caused by several factors, ranging from interference of background processes to CPU power saving mechanisms, as recently argued by Li et al. in [9].

Also useful is to understand the relationship between the service time and the frequency of each RPC operation. Fig. 13 presents a scatter plot relating RPC median service times with their frequency, depending upon whether RPCs are of type *read*, *write/update/delete* or *cascade*, i.e., whether other operations are involved. This figure confirms that the type of an RPC strongly determines its performance. First, *cascade* operations (`delete_volume` and `get_from_scratch`) are the slowest type of RPC —more than one order of magnitude slower compared to the fastest operation. Fortunately, they are relatively infrequent. Conversely, *read* RPCs, such as `list_volumes`, are the fastest ones. Basically, this is because *read* RPCs can exploit lockless and parallel access to the pairs of servers that form database shards.

Write/update/delete operations (e.g. `make_content`, or `make_file`) are slower than most *read* operations, but exhibiting comparable frequencies. This may represent a performance barrier for the metadata store in scenarios where users massively update metadata in their volumes or files.

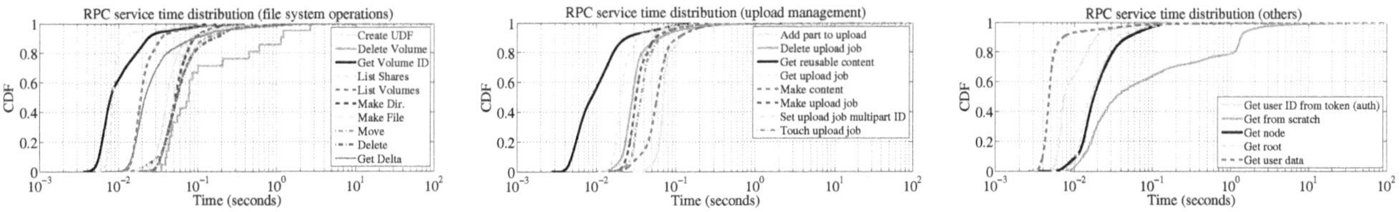

(a) File system management RPCs. (b) Upload management RPCs. (c) Other read-only RPCs.

Figure 12: Distribution of RPC service times accessing to the metadata store.

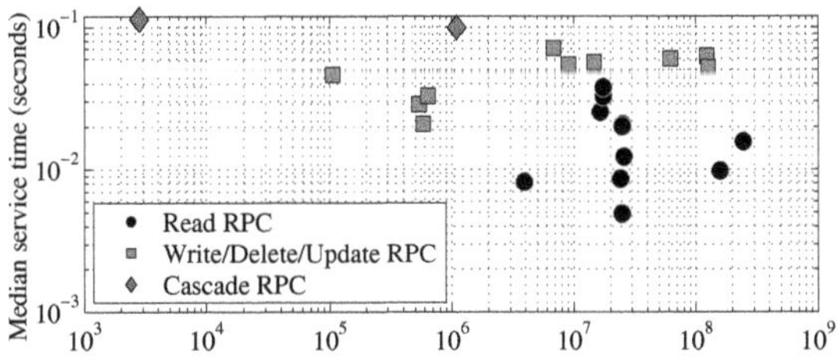

Figure 13: We classified all the U1 RPC calls into 3 categories, and every point in the plot represents a single RPC call. We show the median service time vs frequency of each RPC (1 month).

7.2 Load Balancing in U1 Back-end

We are interested in analyzing the internal load balancing of both API servers and shards in the metadata store. In the former case, we grouped the processed API operations by physical machine. In the latter, we distributed the RPC calls contacting the metadata store across 10 shards based on the user id, as U1 actually does. Results appear in Fig. 14, where bars are mean load values and error lines represent the standard deviation of load values across API servers and shards per hour and minute, respectively.

Fig. 14 shows that server load presents a *high variance across servers*, which is symptom of bad load balancing. This effect is present irrespective of the hour of the day and is more accentuated for the metadata store, for which the time granularity used is smaller. Thus, this phenomenon is visible in short or moderate periods of time. In the long term, the load balancing is adequate; the standard deviation across shards is only of 4.9% when the whole trace is taken.

Three particularities should be understood to explain the poor load balancing. First, user load is *uneven*, i.e., a small fraction of users is very active whereas most of them present low activity. Second, the cost of operations is *asymmetric*; for instance, there are metadata operations whose median service time is 10x higher than others. Third, users display a *bursty* behavior when interacting with the servers; for instance, they can synchronize an entire folder. So, operations arrive in a correlated manner.

We conclude that the load balancing in the U1 back-end can be significantly improved, which is object of future work.

7.3 Authentication Activity & User Sessions

Time-series analysis. Users accessing the U1 service should be authenticated prior to the establishment of a new session. To this end, U1 API servers communicate with a separate and shared authentication service of Canonical.

Fig. 15 depicts a time-series view of the session management load that API servers support to create and destroy sessions, along with the corresponding activity of the authentication subsystem. In this figure, we clearly observe that the authentication and session management activity is

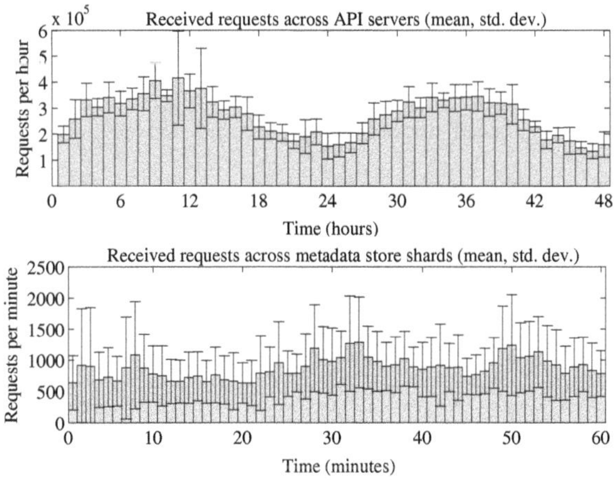

Figure 14: Load balancing of U1 API servers and metadata store shards.

closely related to the habits of users. In fact, daily patterns are evident. The authentication activity is 50% to 60% higher in the central hours of the day than during the night periods. This observation is also valid for week periods: on average, the maximum number of authentication requests is 15% higher on Mondays than on weekends. Moreover, we found that 2.76% of user authentication requests from API servers to the authentication service fail.

Session length. Upon a successful authentication process, a user's desktop client creates a new U1 session.

U1 sessions exhibit a similar behavior to Dropbox *home* users in [2] (Fig. 15). Concretely, 97% of sessions are shorter than 8 hours, which suggests a strong correlation with user working habits. Moreover, we also found that U1 exhibits a high fraction of very short-lived sessions (i.e. 32% shorter than 1s.). This is probably due to the operation of NAT and firewalls that normally mediate between clients and servers, which might be forcing the creation of new sessions by closing TCP connections unexpectedly [2, 23]. Overall, Fig. 15 suggests that *domestic users are more representative* than other specific profiles, such as university communities, for describing the connection habits of an entire Personal Cloud user population.

We are also interested in understanding the data management activity related to U1 sessions. To this end, we differentiate sessions that exhibited any type of data management operation (e.g., upload) during their lifetime (*active sessions*) from sessions that do not (*cold sessions*).

First, we observed that the majority of U1 sessions (and, therefore, TCP connections) do not involve any type of data management. That is, only 5.57% of connections in U1 are active (2.37M out of 42.5M), which, in turn, tend to be much longer than *cold* ones. From a back-end perspective, the unintended consequence is that a fraction of server resources is *wasted keeping alive TCP connections* of cold sessions.

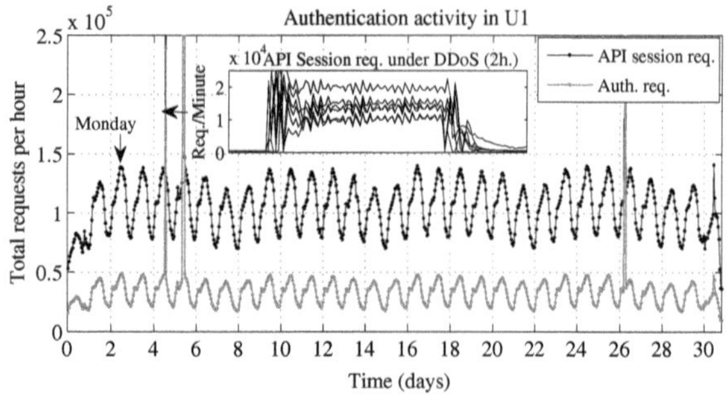

Figure 15: API session management operations and authentication service requests. The inner plot shows API session requests under a DDoS.

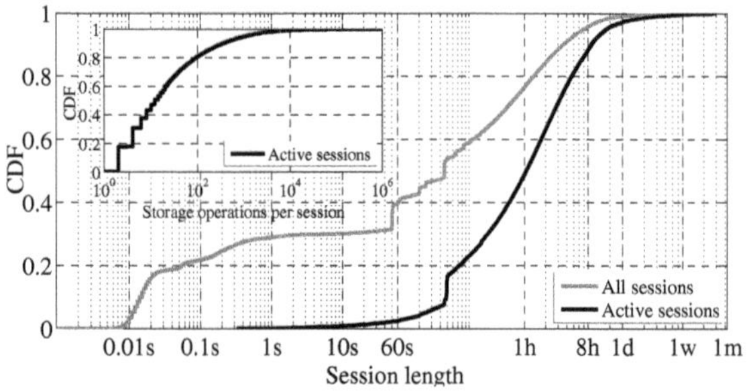

Figure 16: Distribution of session lengths and storage operations per session.

Moreover, similarly to the distribution of user activity, the inner plot of Fig. 15 shows that 80% of active sessions exhibited at most 92 storage operations, whereas the remaining 20% accounted for 96.7% of all data management operations. Therefore, the are sessions much more active than others.

A provider may benefit from these observations to optimize session management. That is, depending on a user's activity, the provider may wisely decide if a desktop client works in a *pull* (cold sessions) or *push* (active sessions) fashion to limit the number of open TCP connections [24].

8. RELATED WORK

The performance evaluation of cloud storage services is an interesting topic inspiring several recent papers. Hill et al. in [25] provide a quantitative analysis of the performance of the Windows Azure Platform, including storage. Palankar et al. in [26] perform an extensive measurement against Amazon S3 to elucidate whether cloud storage is suitable for scientific Grids. Similarly, [27] presents a performance analysis of the Amazon Web Services. Liu et. al. [18] inspected in depth the workload patterns of users in the context of a storage system within a university campus. This work concentrates on macroscopic storage workload metrics and type of requests, as well as the differences in access patterns of personal and shared folders. Unfortunately, these papers provide no insights into Personal Clouds.

Perhaps surprisingly, despite their commercial popularity, only few research works have turned attention to analyze the performance of Personal Cloud storage services [2, 3, 5, 6, 7, 12, 28, 29]. We classify them into two categories:

Active measurements. The first analysis of Personal Cloud storage services we are aware is due to Hu et al. [6] that compared Dropbox, Mozy, Carbonite and CrashPlan storage services. However, their analysis was rather incomplete; the metrics provided in [6] are only backup/restore times depending on several types of backup contents. They also discuss potential privacy and security issues comparing these vendors. The work of Hu et al. [6] was complemented by Gracia-Tinedo et al. [7] that extensively studied the REST interfaces provided by three big players in the Personal Cloud arena, analyzing important aspects of their QoS and potential exploitability [12].

Recently, Drago et al. [3] presented a complete framework to benchmark Personal Cloud desktop clients. One of their valuable contributions is to set a benchmarking framework addressed to compare the different data reduction techniques implemented in desktop clients (e.g, file bundling).

Passive measurements. Drago et al. [2] presented an external measurement of Dropbox in both a university campus and residential networks. They analyzed and characterized the traffic generated by users, as well as the workflow and architecture of the service. [29] extended that measurement by modeling the behavior of Dropbox users. Similarly, Mager et al. [28] uncovered the architecture and data management of Wuala, a peer-assisted Personal Cloud.

Unfortunately, these works do not provide insights on the provider's metadata back-end, since this is not possible from external vantage points. Moreover, [2, 29] study the storage workload and user behavior on specific communities (e.g., university campus) that may lead to false generalizations. In contrast, we analyze the entire population of U1.

Furthermore, Li et al. [5] analyzed a group of Personal Cloud users in both university and corporate environments. Combined with numerous experiments, they studied the efficiency of file sync protocols, as well as the interplay between data reduction techniques integrated in desktop clients and users' workload (update frequency, file compressibility).

Key differences with prior work. The main difference with previous works is that we study in details the *metadata back-end servers* of a Personal Cloud, instead of simply measuring it from outside. The unique aspect of our work is that most of our insights could have been obtained only by taking a perspective from within a data center; this goes, for example, for the internal infrastructure of the service, or the performance of the metadata store, to name a few.

Also, apart from guiding simulations and experiments, we believe that the present analysis will help researchers to optimize several aspects of these services, such as file synchronization [4, 10] and security [30], among others.

9. DISCUSSION AND CONCLUSIONS

In this paper, we focus on understanding the nature of Personal Cloud services by presenting the internal structure and measurement study of UbuntuOne (U1). The objectives of our work are threefold: (i) to unveil the internal operation and infrastructure of a real-world provider, (ii) to reconfirm, expand and contribute observations on these systems to generalize their characteristics, and (iii) to propose potential improvements for these systems.

This work unveils several aspects that U1 *shares* with other large-scale Personal Clouds. For instance, U1 presents clear similarities with Dropbox regarding the way of decoupling data and metadata of users, which seems to be a standard design for these systems [10]. Also, we found characteristics in the U1 workload that reconfirm observations of prior works [2, 5] regarding the *relevance of file updates*, the *effectiveness of deduplication* or the execution of user operations in *long sequences*, among other aspects. Therefore, our analysis and the resulting dataset will enable researchers to get closer to the nature of a real-world Personal Cloud.

Thanks to the scale and back-end perspective of our study, we expanded and contributed insights on these services. That is, we observed that the distribution of activity across users in U1 is even *more skewed* than in Dropbox [2] or that the behavior of domestic users dominate session lengths in U1 compared to other user types (e.g., university). Among the novelties of this work, we modeled the *burstiness of user operations*, we analyzed the *behavior of files* in U1, we provided evidences of *DDoS attacks* to this service, and we illustrated the performance of the U1 *metadata back-end.*

An orthogonal conclusion that we extract from our study is that understanding *the behavior of users is essential* to adapt the system to its actual demands and reduce costs. In the following, we relate some of our insights to the running costs of U1 as well as potential optimizations, which may be of independent interest for other large-scale systems:

Optimizing storage matters. A key problem to the survival of U1 was the growing costs of outsourcing data storage [31], which is directly related to the data management techniques integrated in the system. For instance, the fact that file updates were responsible for 18.5% of upload traffic in U1, mainly due to the lack of delta updates in the desktop client, gives an idea of the margin of improvement (§ 5.1). Actually, we confirmed that a simple optimization like file-based deduplication could readily save 17% of the storage costs. This calls to further research and the application of advanced data reduction techniques, both at the client and server sides.

Take care of user activity. This observation is actually very important, as we found that 1% of U1 users generated 65% of traffic (§ 6.1), showing a weak form of the Pareto Principle. That is, a very small fraction of the users represented most of the OPEX for U1. A natural response may be to limit the activity of free accounts, or at least to treat active users in a more cost effective way. For instance, distributed caching systems like Memcached, data prefetching techniques, and advanced sync deferment techniques [5] could easily cut the operational costs down. On the other hand, U1 may benefit from cold/warm storage services (e.g., Amazon Glacier, f4 [19]) to limit the costs related to most inactive users.

Security is a big concern. Another source of expense for a Personal Cloud is related to its exploitation by malicious parties. In fact, we found that DDoS attacks aimed at sharing illegal content via U1 are indeed frequent (§ 5.4).The risk that these attacks represent to U1 is in contrast to the limited automation of its countermeasures. We believe that further research is needed to integrate secure storage protocols and automated countermeasures for Personal Clouds. In fact, understanding the common behavior of users in a Personal Cloud (e.g., storage, content distribution) may provide clues to automatically detect anomalous activities.

Acknowledgment

This work has been funded by the Spanish Ministry of Science and Innovation through projects DELFIN (TIN-2010-20140-C03-03) and "Servicios Cloud y Redes Comunitarias" (TIN-2013-47245-C2-2-R) as well as by the European Union through projects FP7 CloudSpaces (FP7−317555) and H2020 IOStack (H2020-644182). We also thank Jordi Pujol-Ahulló for his feedback in the latest versions of this paper.

10. REFERENCES

[1] F. Research, "The personal cloud: Transforming personal computing, mobile, and web markets." http://www.forrester.com, 2011.

[2] I. Drago, M. Mellia, M. M Munafo, A. Sperotto, R. Sadre, and A. Pras, "Inside dropbox: understanding personal cloud storage services," in *ACM IMC'12*, 2012, pp. 481–494.

[3] I. Drago, E. Bocchi, M. Mellia, H. Slatman, and A. Pras, "Benchmarking personal cloud storage," in *ACM IMC'13*, 2013, pp. 205–212.

[4] Z. Li, C. Wilson, Z. Jiang, Y. Liu, B. Y. Zhao, C. Jin, Z.-L. Zhang, and Y. Dai, "Efficient batched synchronization in dropbox-like cloud storage services," in *ACM/IFIP/USENIX Middleware'13*, 2013, pp. 307–327.

[5] Z. Li, C. Jin, T. Xu, C. Wilson, Y. Liu, L. Cheng, Y. Liu, Y. Dai, and Z.-L. Zhang, "Towards network-level efficiency for cloud storage services," in *ACM IMC'14*, 2014.

[6] W. Hu, T. Yang, and J. Matthews, "The good, the bad and the ugly of consumer cloud storage," *ACM SIGOPS Operating Systems Review*, vol. 44, no. 3, pp. 110–115, 2010.

[7] R. Gracia-Tinedo, M. Sánchez-Artigas, A. Moreno-Martínez, C. Cotes, and P. García-López, "Actively measuring personal cloud storage," in *IEEE CLOUD'13*, 2013, pp. 301–308.

[8] R. Sears, C. Van Ingen, and J. Gray, "To blob or not to blob: Large object storage in a database or a filesystem?" Microsoft Research, Tech. Rep., 2007.

[9] J. Li, N. K. Sharma, D. R. Ports, and S. D. Gribble, "Tales of the tail: Hardware, os, and application-level sources of tail latency," in *ACM SoCC'14*, 2014.

[10] P. García-López, S. Toda-Flores, C. Cotes-González, M. Sánchez-Artigas, and J. Lenton, "Stacksync: Bringing elasticity to dropbox-like file synchronization," in *ACM/IFIP/USENIX Middleware'14*, 2014, pp. 49–60.

[11] "FP7 cloudspaces EU project," http://cloudspaces.eu.

[12] R. Gracia-Tinedo, M. Sánchez-Artigas, and P. García-López, "Cloud-as-a-gift: Effectively exploiting personal cloud free accounts via REST APIs," in *IEEE CLOUD'13*, 2013, pp. 621–628.

[13] E. Hammer-Lahav, "The OAuth 1.0 Protocol," http://tools.ietf.org/html/rfc5849, 2010.

[14] M. G. Baker, J. H. Hartman, M. D. Kupfer, K. W. Shirriff, and J. K. Ousterhout, "Measurements of a distributed file system," in *ACM SIGOPS Operating Systems Review*, vol. 25, no. 5, 1991, pp. 198–212.

[15] N. Agrawal, W. J. Bolosky, J. R. Douceur, and J. R. Lorch, "A five-year study of file-system metadata," *ACM Transactions on Storage*, vol. 3, no. 3, p. 9, 2007.

[16] A. W. Leung, S. Pasupathy, G. R. Goodson, and E. L. Miller, "Measurement and analysis of large-scale network file system workloads." in *USENIX ATC'08*, vol. 1, no. 2, 2008, pp. 5–2.

[17] W. Hsu and A. Smith, "Characteristics of i/o traffic in personal computer and server workloads," *IBM Systems Journal*, vol. 42, no. 2, pp. 347–372, 2003.

[18] S. Liu, X. Huang, H. Fu, and G. Yang, "Understanding data characteristics and access patterns in a cloud storage system," in *IEEE/ACM CCGrid'13*, 2013, pp. 327–334.

[19] S. Muralidhar, W. Lloyd, S. Roy, C. Hill, E. Lin, W. Liu, S. Pan, S. Shankar, V. Sivakumar, L. Tang, and S. Kumar, "f4: Facebook's warm blob storage system," in *USENIX OSDI'14*, 2014, pp. 383–398.

`dal.add_part_to_uploadjob`	Continues a multipart upload by adding a new chunk.
`dal.delete_uploadjob`	Garbage-collects the server-side state for a multipart upload, either because of commit or cancellation.
`dal.get_reusable_content`	Check whether the server already has the content that is being uploaded.
`dal.get_uploadjob`	Get the server-side state for a multipart upload.
`dal.make_content`	Make a file entry in the metadata store (the equivalent of an inode).
`dal.make_uploadjob`	Set up the server-side structure for multipart upload.
`dal.set_uploadjob_multipart_id`	Set the requested Amazon S3 multipart upload id to the `uploadjob`.
`dal.touch_uploadjob`	Check if the client has canceled the multipart upload (garbage collection after a week).

Table 4: Upload related RPC operations that interact with the metadata store.

[20] J. Mirkovic and P. Reiher, "A taxonomy of DDoS attack and DDoS defense mechanisms," *ACM SIGCOMM Computer Communication Review*, vol. 34, no. 2, pp. 39–53, 2004.

[21] A.-L. Barabasi, "The origin of bursts and heavy tails in human dynamics," *Nature*, vol. 435, no. 7039, pp. 207–211, 2005.

[22] M. E. Crovella and A. Bestavros, "Self-similarity in world wide web traffic: evidence and possible causes," *IEEE/ACM Transactions on Networking*, vol. 5, no. 6, pp. 835–846, 1997.

[23] S. Hätönen, A. Nyrhinen, L. Eggert, S. Strowes, P. Sarolahti, and M. Kojo, "An experimental study of home gateway characteristics," in *ACM IMC'10*, 2010, pp. 260–266.

[24] P. Deolasee, A. Katkar, A. Panchbudhe, K. Ramamritham, and P. Shenoy, "Adaptive push-pull: disseminating dynamic web data," in *ACM WWW'01*, 2001, pp. 265–274.

[25] Z. Hill, J. Li, M. Mao, A. Ruiz-Alvarez, and M. Humphrey, "Early observations on the performance of windows azure," in *ACM HPDC'10*, 2010, pp. 367–376.

[26] M. R. Palankar, A. Iamnitchi, M. Ripeanu, and S. Garfinkel, "Amazon S3 for science grids: a viable solution?" in *ACM DADC'08*, 2008, pp. 55–64.

[27] A. Bergen, Y. Coady, and R. McGeer, "Client bandwidth: The forgotten metric of online storage providers," in *IEEE Pacific Rim Conference on Communications, Computers and Signal Processing*, 2011, pp. 543–548.

[28] T. Mager, E. Biersack, and P. Michiardi, "A measurement study of the wuala on-line storage service," in *IEEE P2P'12*, 2012, pp. 237–248.

[29] G. Gonçalves, I. Drago, A. P. C. da Silva, A. B. Vieira, and J. M. Almeida, "Modeling the dropbox client behavior," in *IEEE ICC'14*, vol. 14, 2014.

[30] M. Mulazzani, S. Schrittwieser, M. Leithner, M. Huber, and E. Weippl, "Dark clouds on the horizon: Using cloud storage as attack vector and online slack space." in *USENIX Security*, 2011.

[31] J. Silber, "Shutting down Ubuntu One file services," http://blog.canonical.com/2014/04/02/shutting-down-ubuntu-one-file-services/, April 2014.

APPENDIX

A. UPLOAD MANAGEMENT IN U1

The management of file uploads is one of the most complex parts in the U1 architecture[8]. Specifically, U1 resorts to the multipart upload API offered by Amazon S3[9]. The lifecycle of an upload is closely related to this API, where several U1 RPC calls are involved (see Table 4).

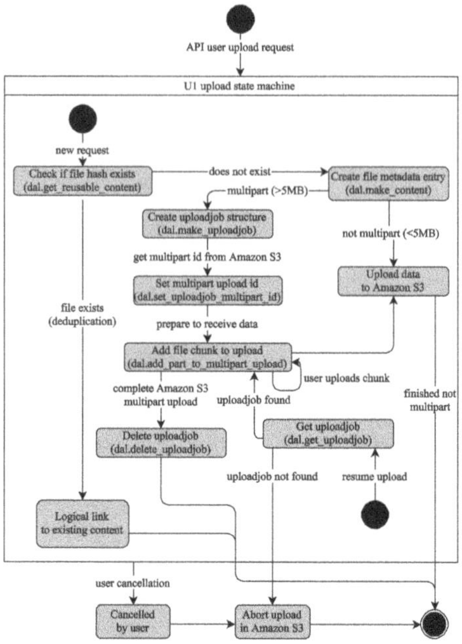

Figure 17: Upload state machine in U1.

Internally, U1 uses a persistent data structure called `uploadjob` that keeps the state of a multipart file transfer between the client and Amazon S3. The main objective of multipart uploads in U1 is to provide user with a way of interrupting/resuming large upload data transfers. `uploadjob` data structures are stored in the metadata store during their life-cycle. RPC operations during the multipart upload process guide the lifecycle of `uploadjobs` (see Fig. 17).

Upon the reception of an upload request, U1 first checks if the file content is already stored in the service, by means of a SHA-1 hash sent by the user. If deduplication is not applicable to the new file, a new upload begins. The API server that handles the upload sends an RPC to create an entry for the new file in the metadata store.

In the case of a multipart upload, the API server creates a new `uploadjob` data structure to track the process. Subsequently, the API process requests a multipart id to Amazon S3 that will identify the current upload until its termination. Once the id is assigned to the `uploadjob`, the API server uploads to Amazon S3 the chunks of the file transferred by the user (5MB), updating the state of the `uploadjob`.

When the upload finishes, the API server deletes the `uploadjob` data structure from the metadata store and notifies Amazon S3 about the completion of the transfer.

Finally, U1 also executes a periodic garbage-collection process on `uploadjob` data structures. U1 checks if an `uploadjob` is older than one week (`dal.touch_uploadjob`). In the affirmative case, U1 assumes that the user has canceled this multipart upload permanently and proceeds to delete the associated `uploadjob` from the metadata store.

[8]Downloads are simpler: API servers only perform a single request to Amazon S3 for forwarding the data to the client.

[9]`http://docs.aws.amazon.com/AmazonS3/latest/dev/UsingRESTAPImpUpload.html`

The Dark Menace: Characterizing Network-based Attacks in the Cloud

Rui Miao * Rahul Potharaju ‡ Minlan Yu* Navendu Jain†
* University of Southern California ‡ Microsoft † Microsoft Research

ABSTRACT

As the cloud computing market continues to grow, the cloud platform is becoming an attractive target for attackers to disrupt services and steal data, and to compromise resources to launch attacks. In this paper, using three months of NetFlow data in 2013 from a large cloud provider, we present the first large-scale characterization of *inbound* attacks towards the cloud and *outbound* attacks from the cloud. We investigate nine types of attacks ranging from network-level attacks such as DDoS to application-level attacks such as SQL injection and spam. Our analysis covers the complexity, intensity, duration, and distribution of these attacks, highlighting the key challenges in defending against attacks in the cloud. By characterizing the diversity of cloud attacks, we aim to motivate the research community towards developing future security solutions for cloud systems.

Categories and Subject Descriptors

C.2.0 [**Computer-Communication Networks**]: Security and protection; C.2.3 [**Network Operations**]: Network management

General Terms

Measurement, Security

Keywords

Attack Characterization; Network-based Attacks; DDoS

1. INTRODUCTION

The cloud computing market reached $40 billion in 2014 with a rapid growth of 23%-27% per year [1]. Hosting tens of thousands of online services, the cloud platform is increasingly becoming both the target and source of attacks. A recent survey of data center operators indicates that half of them experienced DDoS attacks, with 94% of those experiencing regular attacks [17]. Moreover, attackers can abuse hosted services or compromise VMs [30] in the cloud to target external sites via deploying botnets [29], sending spam [33, 44], selling VMs in the underground economy [23, 49], or launching DDoS attacks [21]. In April 2011, an attack on the Sony Playstation network compromising more than 100 million customer accounts was carried out by a malicious service hosted on Amazon EC2 [20]. While there have been some reports of individual attacks on enterprise and cloud networks [10, 29], to the best of our knowledge, there have not been any systematic measurement studies of attacks *on* and *off* the cloud which can guide the design of attack detection and mitigation systems. In fact, little has been published about the prevalence, diversity, and characteristics of these cloud-based attacks.

In this paper we investigate over 200 TB of NetFlow records collected from dozens of edge routers spread across multiple geographically distributed data centers of a major cloud provider. We group traffic based on public virtual IPs (VIPs) assigned to each cloud hosted service. We identify network-based attacks from the NetFlow data using four key features as also used in prior work [19, 32, 38, 48]: (1) significant traffic volume (e.g., packets per second), (2) abnormal fan-in or fan-out (e.g., number of unique clients or number of connections), (3) abnormal packet header signatures (e.g., TCP flags), and (4) communication with Internet malicious hosts [37]. Using these features, we identified nine types of attacks, ranging from various DDoS attacks to application-level attacks such as SQL injection and spam.

Due to sampling in the NetFlow data used in our study and the fact that NetFlow lacks application-level information, we do not aim at identifying *all* the attacks in the cloud. Instead, our goal is to understand the characteristics of attacks using low overhead network-level information typically collected in many data center networks. Thus, we take a conservative approach of setting the attack detection thresholds to ensure that most of the attacks we detect are real attacks.[1]

We validate the detected attacks against alerts from deployed security appliances and incident reports written by operators. Our detected attacks cover 78.5% of the inbound attack alerts from DDoS protection appliances and 83.7% of the incident reports on outbound attacks, due to the NetFlow sampling used in our study and our conservative approach. Note that the cloud provider we studied deploys a combination of software and hardware appliances to protect the infrastructure against such attacks.

Our broader goal is to (a) understand the key characteristics of these attacks to evaluate the effectiveness of existing DDoS mitigation approaches and (b) analyze their implications on building cloud-scale attack detection and mitigation solutions.

Although there have been many studies on Internet attacks, this paper presents one of the first analysis of the key characteristics of attacks to and from the cloud based on a three-month dataset.

[1]These attacks may also include some traffic anomalies caused by flash crowds or misconfigurations. We do not distinguish them because they all impact cloud services and it is an open problem to accurately distinguish them from benign traffic.

IMC'15, October 28–30, 2015, Tokyo, Japan.
© 2015 ACM. ISBN 978-1-4503-3848-6/15/10 ...$15.00.
DOI: http://dx.doi.org/10.1145/2815675.2815707.

We make the following main observations:

- We identify nine types of attacks and quantify their frequencies for inbound and outbound attacks (Section 3).
- We find that most VIPs experiencing attacks only incur one attack incident in a day. There is a very small fraction of VIPs that experience or generate many attacks (Section 4).
- We find multi-vector attacks and combinations of inbound and outbound attacks on the same VIP. While most attacks target only one VIP, there are a few cases of multiple attacks that target 20-60 VIPs simultaneously (Section 4).
- We observe high variations in attack throughput across time and VIPs, requiring cloud security solutions to have dynamic resource allocation over time and multiplexing of resources across VIPs. Attacks often have short duration (within 10 minutes), which require fast attack detection and mitigation (Section 5).
- We investigate the origins and targets of inbound and outbound attacks and identified the major types of Internet ASes that are involved in cloud-related attacks (Section 6).

Scope and Limitations. Our study analyzed traffic data from a single cloud provider and thus it may not generalize to other providers. However, the scale and diversity of our dataset, and our conversation with security operators (having a broader industry view and some having worked at other cloud networks) suggests that similar security challenges are likely faced by other providers. We collected NetFlow records from data center edge routers *before* they are filtered by the security appliances. Thus, the attacks we detected should not be interpreted as impacting the cloud infrastructure or services. Finally, since the traffic measurement is at one-minute granularity, it is likely to smooth the effect of short-lived attack spikes. Overall, our study highlights the need for developing programmable (to handle attack diversity), scalable (to handle varying intensity), and flexible approaches (for individual tenants) to protect against attacks.

2. DATASETS AND METHODOLOGY

We first present the basic setup in a major cloud provider we studied, and then describe the datasets we collected and the methodology for characterizing attacks.

2.1 Cloud provider overview

The cloud network we study comprises 10+ geographically distributed data centers across America, Europe, Asia, and Oceania, which are connected to each other and to the Internet via edge routers. Each data center hosts tens to hundreds of thousands of servers. The cloud provider hosts more than 10,000 services including web services, mobile application services, database and storage services, and data analytics. Each service is assigned a public virtual IP (VIP). The traffic to the VIP is load balanced across a group of virtual machines hosting the service; sometimes these VMs are located across multiple data centers.

Such scale of services makes the cloud an attractive target for *inbound* attacks. Incoming traffic to different services first traverses the edge routers and then the commercial security appliances (e.g., Arbor [17]). These security appliances, typically designed for enterprise-scale deployments, analyze inbound traffic to protect against a variety of well-known attacks such as TCP SYN flood, UDP flood, ICMP flood, and TCP NULL attacks; these appliances use NetFlow records for traffic monitoring. However, the detection logic is often limited to known high-volume attacks. Thus they risk missing other low-volume attack types which aim to probe vulnerabilities but that do not impact the cloud infrastructure such as stealth port scans and application-level attacks e.g., spam, SQL injection. To reduce false positives (noisy alerts), traffic thresholds for alerting can be set either on a per-tenant basis or across tenant groups on these devices.

Attackers can also abuse the cloud resources to launch *outbound* attacks. For instance, they can first launch brute-force attacks (e.g., password guessing) to compromise vulnerable VMs in the cloud. These compromised VMs may then be used for YouTube click fraud, BitTorrent hosting, Bitcoin mining, spamming, malware propagation, or launching DDoS attacks. To mitigate outbound attacks, the cloud provider we studied enforces several security mechanisms including limiting the outbound bandwidth per VM, preventing IP spoofing of egress traffic, shutting down the misbehaving VMs and isolating anomalous traffic. To our knowledge, no prior work has characterized the prevalence of outbound attacks from the cloud.

2.2 Dataset and attack detection methodology

We obtained more than 200TB NetFlow logs from a major cloud provider over three months (May, Nov, and Dec 2013). The NetFlow logs collected for our study had a 1 in 4096 packet sampling rate for both inbound and outbound traffic at the edge routers of the data centers, and aggregated over one-minute windows.[2] Since the edge routers (where we collect the logs) are located upstream of the security appliances, the attacks we detect are likely mitigated before they reach VMs hosting services in the cloud. We analyze the NetFlow data on Cosmos, a large scalable data storage system using SCOPE [26], a programming framework similar to Map-Reduce. Our SCOPE scripts use C# and SQL-like queries to perform the analysis described below.

We aggregate the NetFlow data by VIP in each one-minute window, and study the traffic to a VIP (inbound traffic) and from the same VIP (outbound traffic). For each VIP in each time window, we first filter the traffic based on the protocol number (e.g., UDP), TCP flags (e.g., TCP SYN), or port numbers (e.g., SQL traffic is filtered by TCP traffic with destination port 1433 or 3306). We then identify nine types of attacks listed in Table 1. Our attack detection is based on the following four network-level features:

Volume-based: Many volume-based attacks try to exhaust server or infrastructure resources (e.g., memory, bandwidth) by sending a large volume of traffic via a specific protocol such as TCP SYN and UDP floods, and DNS reflection attacks. We capture volume-based attacks by identifying traffic with large relative spikes. We use sequential change point detection [19, 32] by comparing the traffic volume at the current time window with the Exponentially Weighted Moving Average (EWMA) of the past 10 time windows. We then compare the difference with a change threshold of 100 packets per minute in NetFlow (1:4096 sampling rate), corresponding to an estimated value of about 7K pps in the original traffic. The threshold is suggested by the cloud security team based on the network capacity and prior attack incidents. As shown in Section 3.2, using such threshold settings, we can verify many of the attacks reported in the attack alerts and the incident reports.

Spread-based: For many services (e.g., mail, SQL, SSH), a single VIP typically connects to only a few Internet hosts in normal operation. Thus, if a VIP communicates with a large number of Internet hosts, it is likely an anomaly. To identify such anomalies, we use the NetFlow data to compute the spread of a VIP (i.e., the number of distinct Internet IPs communicating with a VIP during a time window) for inbound and outbound traffic. We then capture the relative spikes of the spread using sequential change point de-

[2] All the traffic volume numbers we show in the paper are estimated volumes calculated based on the number in the NetFlow data and the sampling rate.

Attacks	Description	Net/App	Target	Network features	Detection method	Inactive timeout
TCP SYN flood	Send many TCP SYN, UDP, ICMP packets to random or fixed ports on a server	Net	Server resources	#pkts/min	Volume-based	1 min
UDP flood		Net	Network bandwidth	#pkts/min	Volume-based	1 min
ICMP flood		Net	Server resources	#pkts/min	Volume-based	120 min
DNS reflection	A large number of DNS responses sent to a target from DNS servers (triggered by DNS requests sent by attackers with spoofed source addresses)	App	Network bandwidth	#pkts/min	Volume-based	60 min
Spam	Launch email spam to multiple SMTP servers	App	Users	fan-in/out ratio	Spread-based	60 min
Brute-force	Scan weak passwords or administrative control (using RDP, SSH, VNC)	App	Server vulnerability	fan-in/out ratio, #conn/min	Spread-based	60 min
SQL injection	Send different SQL queries to exploit software vulnerabilities	App	SQL server vulnerability	#conn/min	Spread-based	30 min
Port scan	Scan for open ports (using NULL, Xmas packets)	Net	Server vulnerability	#conn/min	Signature-based, Spread-based	60 min
Malicious web activity (TDS)	Communicate with hosts on malicious web infrastructure	App	Users	src IP/dst IP	Communication pattern-based	120 min

Table 1: Summary of the network-based attacks in the cloud we studied.

tection. Such spread-based detection of brute-force attacks has also been used in prior work [31]. We choose 10 and 20 Internet IPs as the threshold for brute-force and spam, respectively, and 30 connections for SQL in the sampled NetFlow, as recommended by the cloud security team.

Signature-based: Although packet payloads are not logged in our NetFlow data, we can still detect some attacks by examining the TCP flag signatures. Port scanning and stack fingerprinting tools use TCP flag settings that violate protocol specifications (and as such, they are not used by normal traffic) [6, 40]. For instance, the *TCP NULL port scan* sends TCP packets without any TCP flags, and the *TCP Xmas port scan* sends TCP packets with FIN, PSH, and URG flags (Table 1). If a VIP receives a packet with an illegal TCP flag setting during a time window, we mark the time window as under an attack. Since the NetFlow data is sampled, even a single logged packet may represent a significant number of packets with illegal TCP flag settings in the original traffic.

Communication pattern based: Previous security studies have identified blacklists of IPs in the Internet. We can identify attacks by filtering VIP traffic communicating with such blacklisted IPs. For example, the Traffic Distribution System (TDS) [37] includes a list of dedicated hosts that deliver malicious web content on the Internet. Since these hosts are hardly reachable via web links from legitimate sources, it is likely that cloud VIPs communicating with these hosts are involved in malicious web activities. In particular, these VIPs are either a victim of inbound attacks (e.g., spam, malicious advertising) or that they have been compromised to launch outbound attacks (e.g., drive-by downloads, scams, and phishing). Note that it is not always possible to infer the direction of an attack involving TDS nodes because some SYN packets may not get sampled in the NetFlow data. Thus, we distinguish the inbound from outbound communication pattern based attacks based on the destination IP in the flow records.

Counting the number of unique attacks. Given the attacks in each one minute time window, we identify the attack incidents that last multiple time windows for the same VIP. Due to NetFlow's low sampling rate, we may not be able to detect an attack over its entire duration. Therefore, similar to previous work [38, 40, 48], we *group* multiple attack windows as a single attack where the last attack interval is followed by T inactive windows (i.e., no attacks).

Instead of selecting a fixed T, we choose to select different T for different attacks based on analyzing the distributions of inactive times between two consecutive attack minutes of each type for both

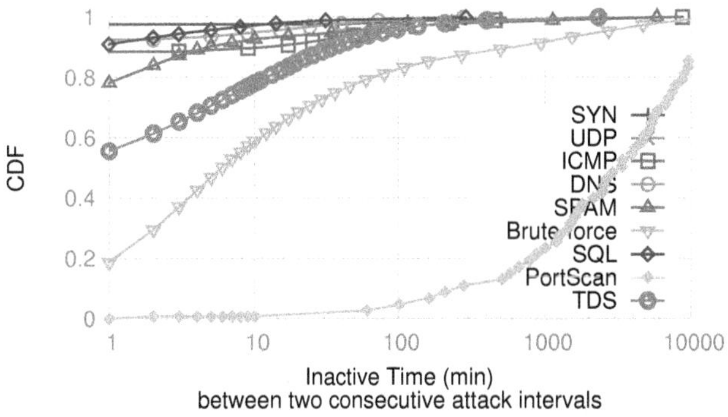

(a) Inbound

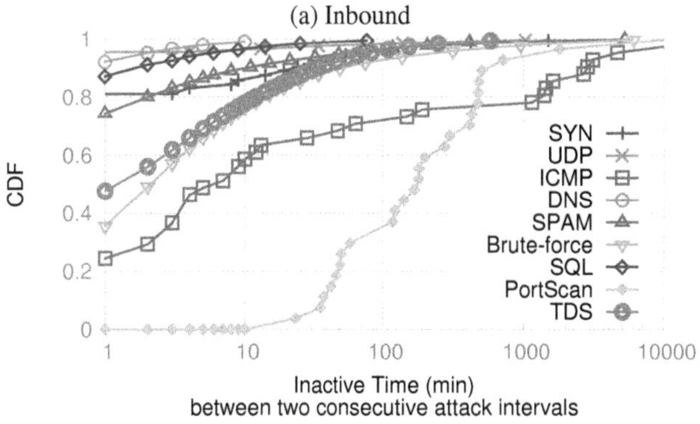

(b) Outbound

Figure 1: The distribution of inactive time for each attack type; the x-axis is on log-scale.

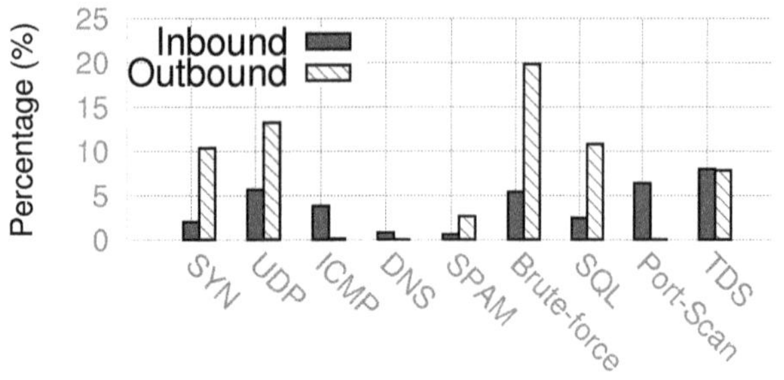

Figure 2: Percentage of total inbound and outbound attacks.

inbound and outbound attacks, as shown in Figure 1. We select the T value by generating a linear regression line between each point and the 99 percentile of each attack distribution curve and checking that the average R-squared [28] value for regression models of inbound and outbound curves is above 85%. We summarize the inactive timeout values we use for different attacks in Table 1.

3. ATTACK OVERVIEW AND VALIDATION

In this section we first give an overview of each type of inbound and outbound attack observed in our study. For validation, we compare these detected attacks using inbound attack alerts from DDoS security appliances and the attack incident reports.

3.1 Attack Overview

Figure 2 shows the distribution of inbound and outbound attacks; absolute counts omitted due to confidentiality and privacy concerns.

Flood attacks: Flood attacks (TCP, UDP, ICMP floods) in the Internet domain have been widely studied [39], and they can be launched in both inbound and outbound directions. Our analysis identified a significant increase of inbound flood attacks during Nov and Dec compared to May (breakdown by month not shown), possibly to disrupt the e-commerce sites hosted in the cloud during the busy holiday shopping season. UDP floods are often against media services hosted in the cloud and on HTTP ports. We also observe that there are about 5 times more outbound TCP SYN and about 2 times more UDP floods than inbound. This is likely because it is easier for attackers to leverage cloud resources to attack Internet users, while it is harder to attack the cloud where operators have high level of security expertise and many attacks floods can be filtered by commercial security appliances.

DNS reflection attacks: The DNS reflection attack is one of the most common amplification attacks in the Internet. It has received increasing attention from DDoS protection services [10, 17]. In DNS reflection attacks, attackers send DNS requests toward multiple open DNS servers with spoofed source address of the target, which results in a large number of DNS responses to the target from DNS servers. Since the cloud has its own DNS servers to answer DNS queries from hosted tenants, there should not be any DNS responses from the Internet to the cloud. Therefore, any activity of inbound DNS responses may signify a potential DNS reflection attack. Inbound DNS reflection attacks often come from up to 6K distinct sources (with 1500 byte full-size packets). We only observed outbound DNS responses from a single VIP hosting a DNS server at 5666 packets per second for a couple of days repeatedly.

Spam: Email services often communicate with a stable number of clients at any given time. If we see a large deviation in the number of email flows, they are likely to be spam. For instance, we observed an outbound spam eruption on a single day, which accounted for 40% of the total outbound spam instances in May. The spam traffic came from hundreds of VIPs towards thousands of external mail servers from email providers such as Yahoo and Lycos, enterprises like CenturyLink, and small clouds like SoftLayer. We observed prevalent on-off traffic pattern from the spamming VIPs. Specifically, each VIP generated slow rate spam traffic with a median of 2266 packets per second over a median of one hour period. It then subsided completely over a median of 5 hours, and launched new attacks again. We investigated these VIPs with the security team and found that most of these VIPs are free trial accounts which were quickly shut down. About 98% of these VIPs were new with no spam traffic recorded before, and the remaining ones were slow spammers lasting up to a month.

Brute-force attacks: Remote connection protocols like SSH, RDP (Remote Desktop Protocol), and VNC (Virtual Network Computing) often have just a few connections to a single VIP. If we observe many connections in the sampled NetFlow, they are likely caused by malicious behaviors such as password guessing (i.e., brute-force attacks). We observed that inbound brute-force attacks have a median of 24 distinct hosts communicating with a single VIP just in the sampled NetFlow data (i.e., there are likely other Internet hosts communicating with the VIP that are not in our sampled data). At the tail, a VIP can receive SSH traffic from up to 10K distinct hosts from the sampled NetFlow data. This can be caused by an attacker controlling multiple Internet hosts to try out different passwords in parallel. Outbound brute-force attacks have a median of 60 distinct hosts targeted by the same VIP in the sampled NetFlow data. This may be because the VIP is scanning a set of Internet servers with the same set of passwords. There are about 4 times more outbound brute-force attacks than inbound and more SSH-based brute-force attacks compared to the RDP ones, likely because the servers running in the cloud often use random ports (e.g., for RDP), and thus they are less likely to experience brute-force attacks compared to Internet hosts.

SQL injection attacks: Some attackers send a variety of malware SQL queries to exploit the vulnerability of SQL servers [16, 18]. Although these attacks are in the application layer, we can still observe such attacks in the network layer when there is a large number of connections issued towards SQL database servers. It is likely that they are exploiting all possible malformed user inputs to gain unauthorized access [16]. There are about 5 times more outbound SQL attacks compared to the inbound attacks.

Port scan: We observe many inbound port scan attacks such as TCP NULL and Xmas attacks. For example, we observed inbound traffic of 125k TCP NULL packets per second lasting for 4 minutes. Attackers usually leverage these packets to sneak through firewalls and packet filters that only handles normal TCP packets [6]. Moreover, there is a significant number of inbound TCP RST packets, which are likely caused by Internet hosts spoofing the IPs in the cloud, leading to TCP RST signals to be directed to VIPs inside the cloud. There are much fewer outbound port scans.

Malicious web activities (TDS): There are 0.039% of VIPs involved in communicating with TDS hosts in the Internet. These TDS hosts often use source ports uniformly distributed between 1024 and 5000. There is one attack incident with 89 unique Internet TDS IPs communicating with a single VIP with 31K packets per second lasting for 98 minutes.

Summary: There are more outbound attacks than inbound attacks (64.9% vs 35.1%). This implies that it is relatively easier for attackers to abuse cloud resources to launch outbound attacks than to attack the cloud-hosted tenants due to improved security over the years. At the same time, new security mechanisms need to

Attack	Inbound #detected/#alerts	Outbound #detected/#reports
TCP SYN flood	98/197	8/8
UDP flood	403/442	4/4
ICMP flood	0/0	0/0
DNS reflection	-	10/10
Spam	-	55/55
Brute-force	-	27/34
SQL injection	-	4/4
port scan	3/3	0/0
TDS	-	-
Others(Malware hosting/phishing)	-	0/14
Total	504/642=78.5%	108/129=83.7%

Table 2: Detected inbound alerts and outbound incident reports ("-" means that the alerts or reports do not support the attack type).

be developed to reduce the outbound attacks. The inbound attacks are dominated by flood attacks, brute-force attacks, port scan, and TDS attacks, while the outbound attacks are dominated by flood attacks, brute-force attacks, SQL attacks, and TDS attacks. While our study focuses on characterizing the diversity of cloud attacks, comparing across attack categories (e.g., by impact, traffic thresholds) may also reveal interesting insights. However, defining a universal metric to compare attack types is difficult because it requires normalizing the attack data across diverse metrics e.g., quantifying the impact of an attack in terms of the service downtime, privacy compromise, and the number of users impacted. Further, some of these measures may not be known till long after the attack happened. In Section 4, we study one aspect of how VIPs are affected by different attacks and leave the broader analysis to future work.

3.2 Validation

In a large heterogeneous network, it is difficult to verify whether all the detected attacks are real because it requires a snapshot of the actual traffic and the runtime application and system state before and during the attack. This problem becomes even harder given the coarsely sampled NetFlow data available for our analysis. We collect the security records including alerts from the DDoS protection hardware appliances for inbound attacks and the incident reports for outbound attacks. We compare our detected attacks with the alerts and incident reports to identify the attacks we miss. Note that the cloud provider deploys software and hardware security appliances to safeguard against these attacks so they should not be interpreted as impacting the infrastructure or tenants.

Inbound attacks: The cloud provider detects and mitigates inbound attacks using a combination of software and hardware DDoS protection appliances. These appliances generate alerts about TCP SYN floods, UDP floods, ICMP floods, and TCP NULL scan. Note that on hardware security appliances, the traffic thresholds are typically set to handle only the high-volume attacks (low-volume attacks don't cause any impact to the cloud infrastructure due to high network capacity) over a large time window, and these appliances aggregate multiple incidents together that occur close in time. Therefore, to do a side-by-side comparison with alerts from these devices, we also first group the attacks we detected based on the VIP, attack type and time window. We found that 73.2% of these attack instances were correlated. This is due to the fact that we set the traffic thresholds to (a) cover a broad range of inbound attacks, and (b) detect these attacks in their early stages. To check the latter hypothesis, we measured the detection latency of hardware security appliances by randomly sampling a few attack instances over a week and observed that these appliances detected them after an order of tens of seconds delays on average. In comparison, our detection approach (in offline mode) signaled the attack based on the NetFlow data for these instances within a minute.

Table 2 shows the number of alerts in each type and those alerts that we also detected. Overall, we successfully identified 78.5% of the alerts from hardware security appliances in our detected attacks. The remaining alerts are missed by our detection approach because of the low sampling in the NetFlow data and the false positives of these alerts. For other types of attacks, the cloud relies on individual tenants to detect and report them. However, we did not have the ground truth data to validate them.

Outbound attacks. The cloud security team detects every potential outbound attack, but they do not necessarily log all of them as incident reports to avoid false positives. Specifically, only the cases of anomalous activity reported by external sites are logged as incidents. Similar to inbound attacks, the cloud provider uses security appliances to mitigate the outbound attacks. The cloud security team may receive a complaint from an ISP when they notice malicious traffic originating from the cloud provider. Given such a complaint, the security team checks the logs of security appliances and investigates the corresponding tenant profile and payment information, and generates an incident report. Moreover, when the security team receives a complaint, the team may do traffic analysis for deeper investigation; they may also perform the VHD (Virtual Hard Disk) forensic analysis on behalf of the customer if the customer (who owns the VHD) requested it. Based on these investigations, the security team creates incident reports logging their findings such as the "attack" or "no attack found" label. We use NetSieve [45] to extract the attack information from these incident reports, and then compare it with our detected outbound attacks.

Since these incident reports come from Internet users' complaints, there is a large number of short-term transient attacks that are not covered by these reports. Therefore, we focus on the false negatives of those attacks that we missed in our approach when we compare with incident reports, rather than those attacks that we detect but are missed in these reports. For those attacks that are not covered by the incident reports, we randomly picked a few attacks for each type and investigated them. The attacks for which the packet traces got logged were verified as being mitigated by the security team.

Table 2 shows the number of incident reports (labeled as "attacks") and those that are also detected by our approach. We detect most of the attacks reported in the incident reports (83.7%). There are only two exceptions: (1) There are some incident reports about application-level attacks such as phishing and malware hosting that we cannot detect with network signatures. (2) We only investigate brute-force attacks on three remote communication protocols (SSH, RDP, VNC). Therefore we miss brute-force attacks on other protocols such as FTP.[3] There are four incident reports labeled as "no attacks" that are also covered by our detected attacks. We investigated these attacks manually and confirmed with the security team that they are real attacks (on TCP SYN floods, SSH and RDP brute-force attacks) but mislabeled. Our analysis has been leveraged by the cloud security team towards improving attack detection, reducing time to detect, and identifying correlations across attack types.

Limitations of NetFlow. Due to coarse-grained sampling in the NetFlow data collected for our study and the fact that NetFlow lacks application-level information, we do not aim at identifying all the attacks in the cloud. We may miss application-level attacks without network-level signatures and those attacks that do not appear

[3]Some incident reports do not describe the protocols that are involved in the brute-force attacks.

in sampled NetFlow (e.g., HTTP Slowloris [24]). Instead, our goal is to understand what we can learn about cloud attacks with low overhead network-level information.

Although we just detect a subset of attacks due to the conservative approach, it is still useful to understand the key characteristics of these attacks to shed light on the effectiveness of commercial attack-protection appliances, and the implications on designing future attack detection and protection solutions. Studies [12, 22, 34] have shown that sampled NetFlow does not affect the detection accuracy of flood attacks but it may underestimate the number of flows. Therefore, the number of flows we report should be viewed as a lower bound on the number in the original traffic.

4. ANALYSIS OF ATTACKS BY VIP

In our three-month trace data, there are on average 0.08% of VIPs per day under inbound attacks and 0.11% of VIPs per day generating outbound attacks. In this section we investigate these VIPs to understand the attack frequency per VIP, multi-vector attacks on the same VIP, inbound and outbound attacks on the same VIP, and attacks that involve multiple VIPs.

4.1 Attack frequency per VIP

Attack frequency per VIP: We count the number of attacks per VIP per day (Figure 3a). Most VIPs experiencing attacks only incur one attack incident during a day. Out of the 13K (VIP, day) pairs experiencing inbound attacks, 53% of pairs experience only one attack in a day. Out of 18K (VIP, day) pairs experiencing outbound attacks, 44% generate only one attack in a day because the misbehaving instances are aggressively shut down by the cloud security team.

At the tail, a VIP can get 39 inbound attacks in a day. This is a VIP hosting Media and HTTP services receiving frequent flood attacks (i.e., SYN, UDP, ICMP) with a median duration of 6 minutes and a median inter-arrival time of 64 minutes. For outbound attacks, there are 0.05% of outbound (VIP, day) pairs generating more than 100 attacks. We observed one VIP that generated more than 144 outbound TCP SYN flood attacks in a day to many web servers in the Internet with a median duration of 1 minute and a median inter-arrival time of 10 minutes. This VIP did not receive any inbound traffic during a whole month in the NetFlow data indicating that this VIP does not likely host any legitimate cloud service but it is only being used for malicious behavior.

VIPs with frequent and occasional attacks: We observed that there are only a few VIPs getting more than 10 attacks (2% of the inbound pairs and 5% of the outbound pairs). Therefore, we classify the VIPs into two classes: those VIPs with no more than 10 attacks per day and those with more than 10 attacks per day. Understanding the VIPs under frequent attacks is important for operators to extract the right attack signatures (e.g., popular attack sources) to protect these VIPs from future attacks.

Figure 3 shows that for inbound attacks, there are more TDS, port scan, and brute-force attacks for those VIPs with occasional attacks than those with frequent attacks (26.6% vs. 0% for TDS, 20.1% vs. 1.84% for port scan, and 15.7% vs. 0.359% for brute-force). It is natural for port scan and brute-force attacks to target VIPs with occasional attacks because these attacks search widely for vulnerabilities (e.g., open ports, weak passwords). TDS attacks also interact more with VIPs with occasional attacks, which makes TDS attacks harder to detect. Our further investigation shows that these occasional attacks mainly target applications running protocols like HTTP, HTTPS, DNS, SMTP, and SSH.

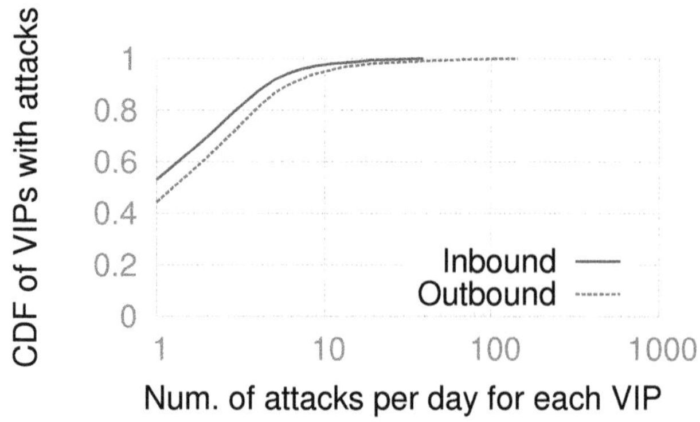

(a) Number of attacks per (VIP, day).

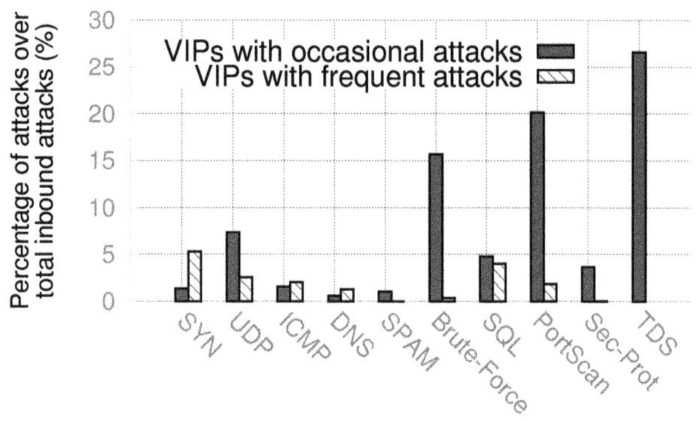

(b) Inbound attacks for VIPs with occasional/frequent attacks.

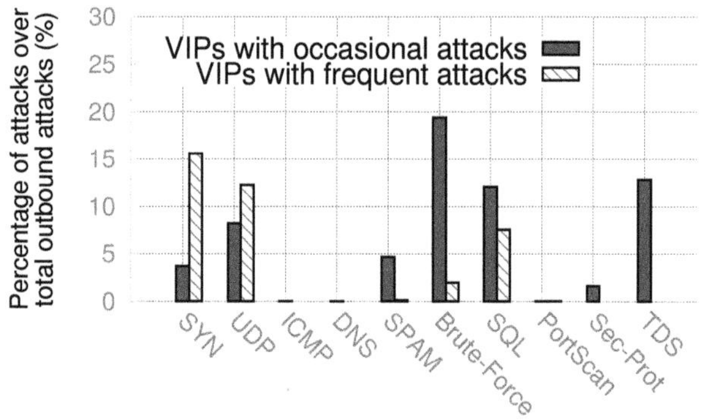

(c) Outbound attacks for VIPs with occasional/frequent attacks.

Figure 3: Attack characterization for VIPs with inbound and outbound attacks; the x-axis is on log-scale in the top figure.

VIPs under frequent attacks often experience relatively more TCP SYN flood attacks than those VIPs under occasional attacks (5.3% vs. 1.4%). Our investigation shows that these frequent flood attacks often target several popular cloud services on these VIPs including streaming applications, HTTP, HTTPS, and SSH.

Similarly, for outbound attacks, the VIPs with occasional attacks experience more brute-force, TDS, and spam attacks than the VIPs with frequent attacks (19.4% vs. 1.97% for brute-force, 12.8% vs. 0% for TDS, and 4.7% vs. 0.119% for spam). While attackers

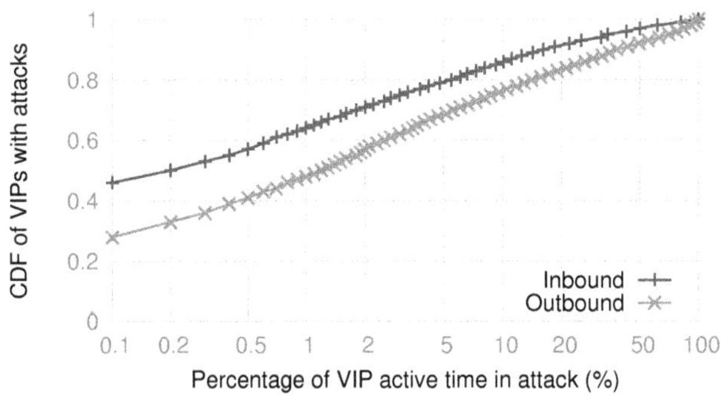

Figure 4: CDF of the percentage of VIP active time in attack.

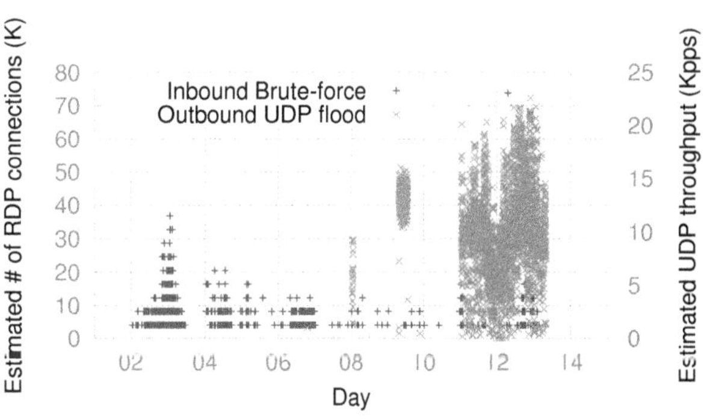

Figure 5: Inbound and outbound attacks on the same VIP. We estimate the UDP throughput and the upper bound of the number of RDP connections based on the 1 in 4096 sampling rate.

may try to use free-trials or create fake accounts to launch them, the attack activity is only short-lived because the anomalous VMs are aggressively shut down by the cloud operators. It is challenging to detect these attacks because they come from multiple VIPs in the case of occasional attacks (e.g., spam) and they typically last only a short time. In contrast, those VIPs with frequent attacks are often the sources for TCP SYN and UDP flood attacks. For a few cases, we manually verified that these VIPs have compromised VMs, which may be sold in the underground economy [23, 49].

Fraction of VIP's lifetime involved in inbound attacks: We investigated the fraction of the time a VIP is under inbound attacks or generating outbound attacks compared to its total active time (i.e., the time that the VIP has active traffic). Figure 4 shows that 50% of VIPs experience inbound attacks for 0.2% of their active times. These are occasional attacks that do not likely affect much of their service. However, 3% of the VIPs receive inbound attack more than 50% of their operating time. Further investigation reveals that these VIPs run media, web, mail, and database services. Cloud operators need to effectively block these attacks to eliminate their impact on cloud services.

Compromised VIPs vs. malicious VIPs for outbound attacks: We also study the fraction of time a VIP generates outbound attacks compared to its active time. Note that most of these compromised VMs had weak passwords highlighting the need to enforce security best practices such as configuring cryptographically strong passwords. Figure 4 shows that 50% of VIPs generate outbound attacks for 1.2% of their active times. These VIPs are likely legitimate tenants that may have been compromised by attackers to generate outbound attacks occasionally (see Section 4.2 for one such example). In contrast, 8% of attack VIPs generate outbound attack for more than 50% of their active times. These VIPs are likely to be recruited mainly for attacks e.g., attackers may buy compromised VMs in the cloud or leverage free trial accounts.

4.2 Attacks on the same VIP

Multi-vector attacks: We observe multiple types of attacks attacking the same VIP or coming from the same VIP at the same time. This is likely because a single malicious program tries to launch multiple types of attacks to exploit the vulnerabilities of targets or to exhaust target resources in different ways. We identify these attacks if their start times to/from the same VIP differ less than five minutes. We find that 106 VIPs experience more than one type of inbound attacks simultaneously, which accounts for 6.1% of the total inbound attacks. There are 74 VIPs that experience more than one type of outbound attacks simultaneously, which accounts for 0.83% of the total outbound attacks. Among these VIPs, 46 VIPs are targets of multi-vector volume-based attacks (i.e., TCP SYN, UDP, ICMP floods, and DNS reflection). There are 11 VIPs that launch multi-vector outbound volume-based attacks.

A new observation we make about outbound attacks is that there are 35 VIPs which launch brute-force attacks together with TCP SYN and ICMP flood attacks (which account for 22.3% of the outbound multi-vector attacks). This is likely a new attack pattern that attackers find effective in breaking Internet hosts.

Inbound and outbound attacks on the same VIP. There are also several cases of simultaneous inbound and outbound attacks. Figure 5 shows one such case. A VIP from a partner subscription was inactive (i.e., no traffic) for a long time. Starting the second day, the VIP started to receive inbound RDP brute-force attack for more than a week. These brute-force attacks originated from 85 Internet hosts, where 70.3% of attack packets are from three IP addresses within a single resident AS in Asia. These brute-force attack had a peak of estimated around 70 K flows per minute with a few packets sampled in each flow. On the eighth day, the VIP started to generate outbound UDP floods against 491 external sites. The outbound UDP attack had a peak volume at 23 Kpps, lasting for more than two days. Detecting such attacks requires first jointly analyzing the inbound and outbound traffic to identify the attack patterns of compromised VIPs, and then blocking their outbound traffic.

4.3 Attacks on multiple VIPs

If attacks of the same type start on multiple VIPs simultaneously, it is likely that these attacks are controlled by the same attacker. We identify attacks on multiple VIPs if the difference of their start times on different VIPs is less than five minutes.[4]

Figure 6 shows that most types of attacks are targeted by fewer than 10 VIPs in the 99th percentile. We also observe that most types of attacks are targeted at only one VIP in the median (not shown in the figure). Inbound brute-force attacks have simultaneous attacks on 53 VIPs in the 99th percentile and 66 VIPs in the peak. We investigated the attacks at the tail and find that there are two Internet hosts from small cloud providers that start attacking 66 VIPs at the same time, and move to other VIPs. During a single day, these two

[4]We choose five minutes because the ramp-up time is 1-3 minutes for flood attacks and the inactive time T_I (defined in Section 2) for other attacks is larger than 10 minutes.

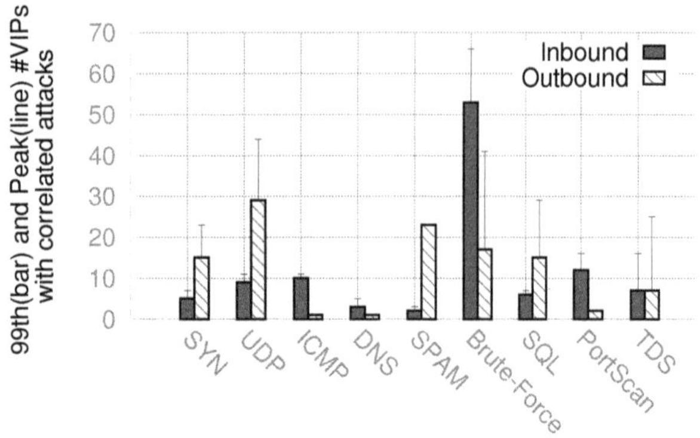

Figure 6: The 99th percentile and the peak number of VIPs simultaneously involved in the same type of attacks.

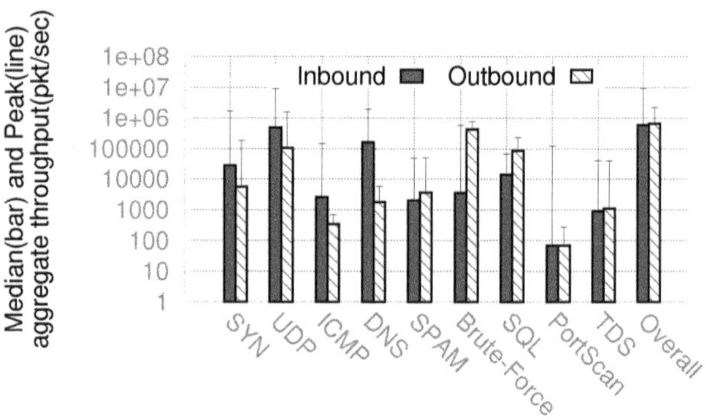

Figure 7: Median and maximum aggregate throughput by attack type; the y-axis is on log-scale.

Internet hosts attack more than 500 VIPs. These VIPs are located in five data centers in the cloud, and they belong to 8 IP subnets with different sizes (/17 to /21). The attacker scans through the entire IP subnet with up to 114.5 Kpps attack traffic per VIP. To prevent such attacks, we need to correlate the traffic to different VIPs and coordinate their attack detection and mitigation.

For outbound attacks, UDP flood, spam, brute-force, and SQL attacks involve around 20 VIPs simultaneously in the 99th percentile. In the peak, UDP flood and brute-force attacks involve more than 40 VIPs simultaneously.

4.4 Cloud services under inbound attack

We now investigate the major types of cloud services under inbound attacks. We capture the NetFlow records for VIPs receiving inbound attacks. We then filter all the attack traffic from the traffic on the VIPs, and the remaining traffic on the VIPs is mostly legitimate traffic. We use the destination port of inbound traffic to infer what type of applications and services are hosted on the VIPs. We count the application type if the traffic on the application port exceeds ten percent of its total traffic. Table 3 shows the percentage of VIPs with different types of cloud services that experience different types of inbound attacks.

Web services (HTTP/HTTPS) are major services in the cloud with 99% of the total traffic. VIPs hosting these web services receive a wide range of attacks such as SYN floods, ICMP floods, brute-force attacks, port scan, and TDS attacks. Web services receive the largest number of SYN attacks which aim to consume all the available connections of application servers. 1.2% of the SYN floods use source port 1024 and 3072, which are likely caused by a bug from an old SYN flood tool juno [9]. Blacklisting or rate-limiting these ports can help mitigate SYN floods.

We also observe other non-flood attacks targeting specific types of services. For instance, there are 35.06% VIPs hosting RDP servers with standard RDP port. The attackers often detect active RDP ports and then generate brute-force attacks against the server. TDS attacks mostly target VIPs running web services and mail services for spam, malware spreading, and malicious advertising. There are 6.94% of VIPs under attack running web services and 1.75% of VIPs running mail services.

5. ATTACK CHARACTERIZATION

We next investigate the characteristics of attacks to derive implications for the design of attack detection and prevention systems. First, to quantify the cloud bandwidth capacity needed to defend against attacks, we study the throughput of different types of attacks. Second, to understand how fast the attack detection system needs to react to attacks, we study the duration, ramp-up rate, and inter-arrival times of different types of attacks.

5.1 Attack throughput

Throughput by attack type: Figure 7 shows the median and peak aggregate throughput over the entire cloud for each type of attack and all the attacks overall. We measure the attack throughput using packets per second (pps) because the resources (CPU and memory) used to prevent these attacks are often correlated to the traffic rate. The overall inbound attack throughput has a median of 595 Kpps and a peak of 9.4 Mpps. The overall outbound attack throughput is lower with a median of 662 Kpps and a peak of 2.25 Mpps. Compared to the average throughput of legitimate traffic (54.3 Mpps for inbound and 49.7 Mpps for outbound), the median attack throughput is about 1% of the total traffic. These attacks can have a significant impact on both the cloud infrastructure (firewalls, load balancers) and services hosted in the cloud if we do not filter them at the network edge.

We now study the peak volumes of individual attacks to understand the resources we need to protect against them. TCP SYN floods have a peak throughput of 1.7 Mpps for inbound and 184 Kpps for outbound. It is important to prevent these attacks timely (e.g., using SYN cookies) before they exhaust many resources in the cloud infrastructure such as load balancers and firewalls.

The peak throughput for inbound UDP floods is 9.2 Mpps while that of outbound UDP floods is 1.6 Mpps. While these flood attacks aim to consume the cloud bandwidth or cause congestion to degrade service performance, the cloud networks are provisioned with a high network capacity to defend against them [7, 14]. Given that a software load balancer (SLB) can handle 300 Kpps per core [42] for simple Layer 4 packet processing, in the worst case handling inbound UDP floods may waste 31 extra cores in the data center infrastructure. If we fail to do in-network filtering of these UDP floods, they would cost even more resources per packet in the VMs which have more complex packet processing. However, detecting some application-level attacks (e.g., brute-force, spam), endpoint based approaches can leverage application semantics to better handle them compared to in-network defense approaches.

We also observe large variations in attack volumes over time. For inbound attacks, port scan has 1000x difference between the peak

Service(port)	Total	SYN	UDP	ICMP	DNS	SPAM	Brute-force	SQL	Portscan	TDS
RDP (3389)	35.06	0.11	0.21	0.54	0.11	0.07	33.88	0.11	0.32	0
HTTP (80,8080)	33.20	3.40	1.50	1.97	0.79	0.32	9.34	0.11	13.63	6.94
HTTPS (443)	13.27	1.22	0.29	1.40	0.21	0.07	4.44	0.04	8.05	0.14
SSH (22)	8.69	0	0.11	0	0.04	0	8.52	0	0.18	0
IP Encap (0)	6.55	0.54	1.57	0.79	1.07	0.04	0.29	0	0.39	0.04
SQL (1433, 3306)	3.11	0	0	0.07	0	0.04	1.29	1.79	0.11	0
SMTP (25)	2.75	0.04	0.04	0.04	0	0.86	0.04	0	0.04	1.75

Table 3: The percentage of total victim VIPs hosting different services involved with different inbound attacks; all numbers are in %.

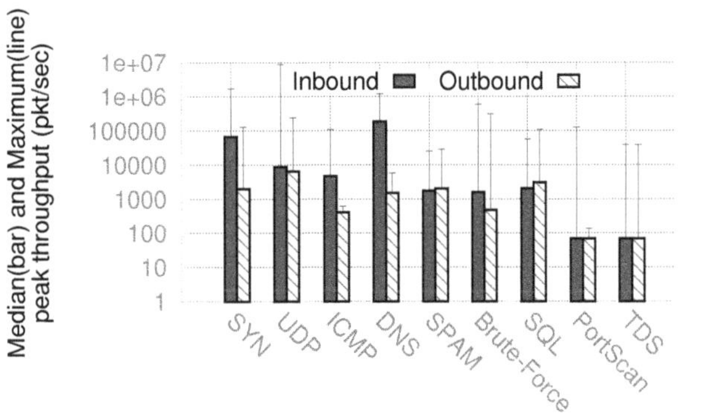

Figure 8: Median and maximum attack throughput across VIPs; the y-axis is on log-scale.

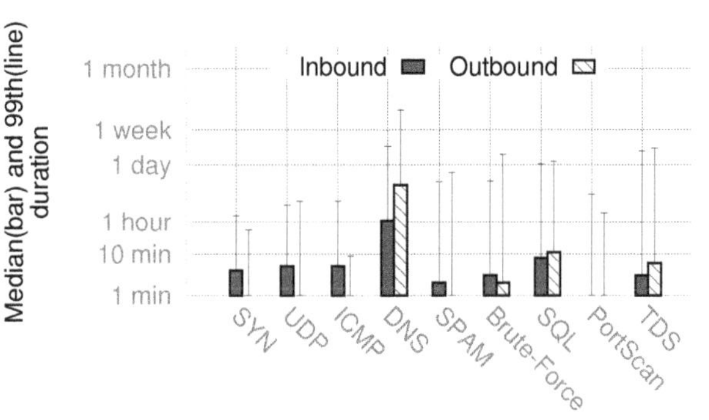

Figure 9: Median and 99th percentile of attack duration by attack type; the y-axis is on log-scale.

and median volumes. This implies that it would incur high costs and waste resources if we overprovision attack detection and mitigation solutions in hardware boxes. In comparison, elastic approaches that dynamically adjust resource usage over time may be a more cost-effective and efficient solution. The outbound attack throughput variations are relatively smaller, but for TCP SYN floods and TDS attacks, we still see a 20x-30x difference between the peak and median volumes.

Throughput per VIP: Today, cloud operators mostly focus on preventing large-volume attacks that may affect the cloud infrastructure, but they rely on tenants to secure their own services [47]. However, many of the attacks we investigated are smaller attacks targeting individual VIPs. Therefore, we study the peak attack throughput for individual VIPs and characterize the throughput differences across VIPs (Figure 8) to understand the resources individual VIPs need to defend against attacks.

We observe that some VIPs experience a high peak volume of attacks at a certain time (ranging from 100 pps to 8.7 Mpps). At times, the per-VIP peak volume is even higher than the median throughput for the entire cloud. For example, a single VIP can experience up to 8.7 Mpps inbound UDP floods. The per VIP inbound TCP SYN flood has a peak of 1.7 Mpps. We found one inbound TCP SYN flood that caused a CPU spike at the software load balancer (SLB) appliance and resulted in a restart of that appliance. However, the traffic from that device was quickly and automatically shifted to other SLBs.

There are large differences in the throughput volumes across VIPs. For example, for inbound brute-force attacks, the VIP having the peak throughput has 361 times larger volume than the VIP with the median value; for outbound brute-force attacks, this ratio is 75. Therefore, it may become too expensive to over-provision hardware security appliances for individual VIPs based on their maximum attack volumes. In comparison, resource management mechanisms that multiplex the attack protection resources across VIPs are likely to be more cost-effective.

Finally, we observe that for volume-based attacks (TCP SYN, UDP, ICMP, and DNS reflections), the peak volume of inbound attacks is 13 to 238 times higher than that of outbound. This is caused by the differences in attack resources and targets between the Internet and the cloud. For inbound attacks, there are more resources to leverage in the Internet (e.g., botnets, easily compromised personal machines) to launch high-volume attacks. These attacks also need to have high volumes to break the VIPs in the cloud, which have plenty of bandwidth and CPU resources. In contrast, outbound attacks can only leverage a few VMs in the cloud, because it is hard to compromise a large number of VMs or create multiple fake accounts to get many free VIPs.

5.2 Attack duration and inter-arrival time

Attack duration: Figure 9 shows that both inbound and outbound attacks have short duration with a median value within 10 minutes. This is consistent with other studies of Internet attacks [38, 40]. Interestingly, port scan attacks have a median duration within one minute for both inbound and outbound (but they can last for 100 minutes at the 99th percentile). There are several reasons that an attacker may launch short-duration attacks towards or from the cloud: (1) Shorter attacks are harder to be detected by cloud operators; (2) an attacker may attack one target for a short time and if not successful move quickly to another target. As a result, it is important to detect such short duration attacks in a timely fashion.

At the 99th percentile, most attacks have a duration longer than 80 minutes or even for days. For example, the TCP SYN flood attack lasts for 85 minutes at the 99th percentile. This is shorter than the previous study of Internet attacks [40], which observed

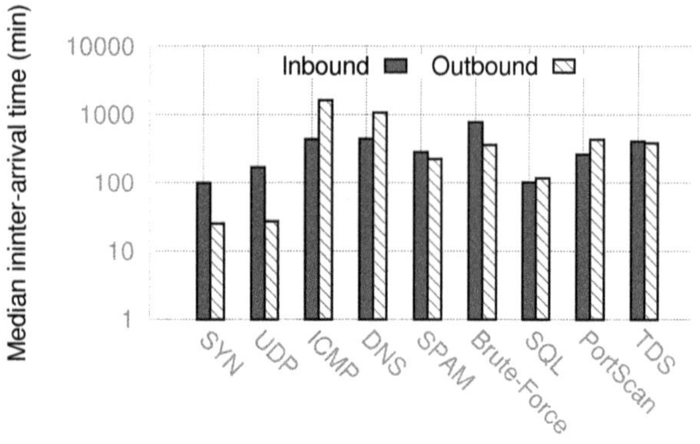

Figure 10: Median and 99th percentile of attack inter-arrival time by attack type; the y-axis is on log-scale.

that 2.4% of the attacks take more than five hours. This could be due to better security support in the cloud.

DNS reflection attacks last longer than others in both inbound and outbound directions. These attacks can sustain for a long time before being detected because they leverage many DNS resolvers simultaneously and each resolver receives relatively low query rate. Thus, it is hard to detect these attacks.

Ramp-up time: For volume-based attacks, we calculate the ramp-up time of an attack from its start time to the time when the packet rate grows to 90% of its peak. We observe a median ramp up time of 2-3 minutes for inbound attacks and 1 minute for outbound attacks. Today's flood detection solutions take about 5 minutes to detect the attacks [17, 48], and thus they are not fast enough to fully eliminate the flood attacks before they ramp up to affect the target with their peak strengths.

Inter-arrival time: We measure the inter-arrival time as the interval between the start times of two consecutive attacks to/from the same VIP. Figure 10 shows that most types of attacks have a median inter-arrival time of hundreds of minutes. The outbound TCP SYN and UDP flood attacks are shorter than inbound (about 25 minutes vs. 100 minutes). This indicates that malicious VIPs launch periodic attacks frequently. Attack protection systems can leverage such repeated attacks to identify and tune the right signatures for filtering attack traffic.

We identify two types of UDP flood attacks based on the correlations of inter-arrival time and peak attack size. 81% of the attacks have a median peak size with 8 Kpps but with large inter-arrival time (a median of 226 min). The rest 19% of the attacks have a median peak size with 457 Kpps, but with short inter-arrival time (a median of 95 min). The first type of small-scale, occasional attacks are relatively hard to distinguish from normal traffic and thus they are hard to mitigate without significant collateral damage. In contrast, the large-scale, frequent attacks require the cloud security operators to provision more resources to detect their traffic signatures and mitigate them.

6. INTERNET AS ANALYSIS

In this section we investigate the types of Internet ASes that are commonly involved in attacks to the cloud and that are under attacks from the cloud.

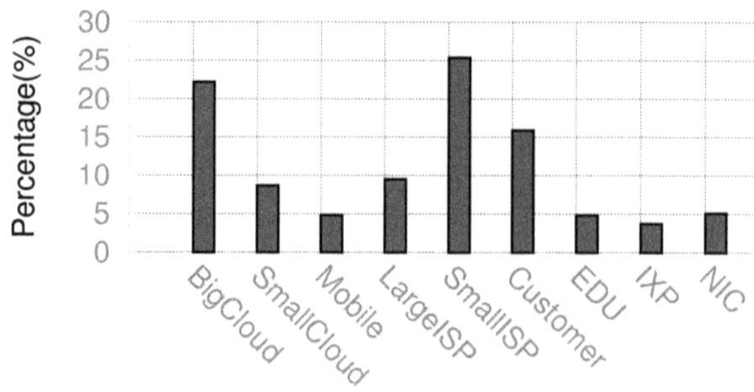

(a) Percentage of inbound attacks in each AS type.

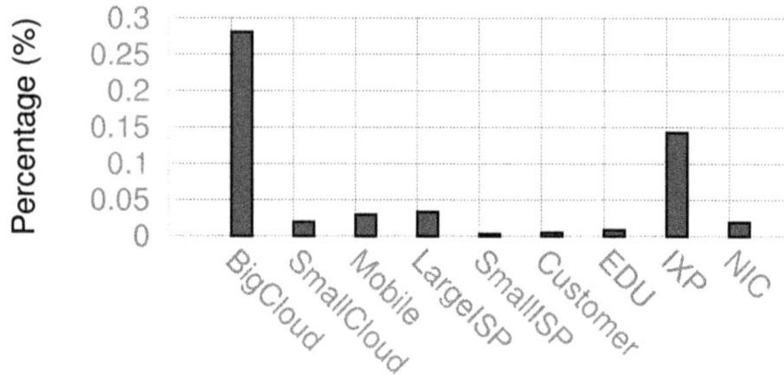

(b) Average of percentage of inbound attacks per AS in each AS type.

Figure 11: Different types of ASes generating inbound attacks.

6.1 Inbound attacks

Are source IPs spoofed? We investigate whether the Internet IPs of inbound attacks are spoofed to understand the effectiveness of blacklisting on preventing different inbound attacks. Similar to prior work [40], we leverage the Anderson-Darling test (A2) [43] to determine if the IP addresses of an attack are uniformly distributed (i.e., an attack has spoofed IPs if A2 value is above 0.05). We observe that 67.1% of the TCP SYN floods have spoofed IPs. This is contrary to the study in 2006 [38] which observed that most flood attacks are not spoofed.

AS classification: We first remove those spoofed IPs and then map the IP addresses of inbound attack sources and outbound attack targets to AS numbers using Quova [11]. We use AS taxonomy repository [27] to identify AS types, which include large ISPs, small ISPs, customer networks, universities (EDU), Internet exchange points (IXP), and network information centers (NIC). We further classify big cloud (i.e., Google, Microsoft, Amazon), small cloud (i.e., web hosting services), and mobile ASes based on the AS descriptions. We count the number of attack incidents of different types for each AS class if any of its IP is involved in the attack.

Figure 11a shows the distribution of attacks across different types of ISPs. We observe that small ISPs and customer networks generate 25.4% and 15.9% of the attacks, respectively. For instance, an ISP in Asia contributed to 3.53% of the total attack packets. This is probably because these local or regional ISPs have relatively less security expertise and weak defense systems, and thus they are more likely to be compromised and leveraged by attackers.

When we calculate the average of percentage of attacks per AS (Figure 11b), we observe that there are more attacks per AS from big cloud and IXP. Individual ASes in small ISPs and customer networks do not generate many attacks on average.

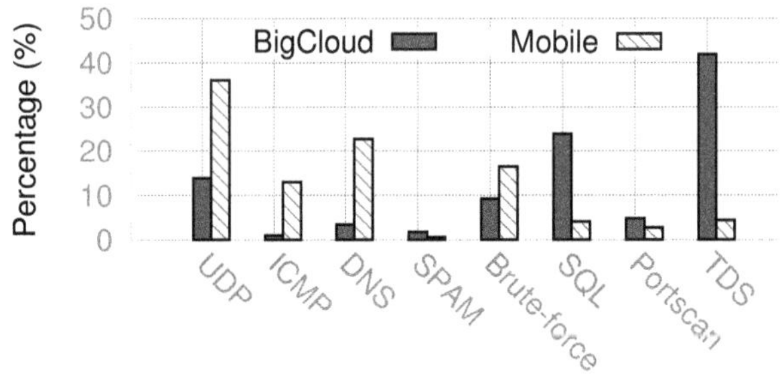

Figure 12: Percentage of inbound attacks from big clouds and mobile ASes in each attack type.

Attacks from big clouds: Figure 12 shows the distribution of attack types that originated from big clouds. UDP floods, SQL injections, and TDS attacks are the majority types. This is probably due to the availability of a large set of resources in big clouds to generate a high traffic volume and a large number of connections. In fact, big clouds contribute to 35% of TDS attacks with just 0.21% of TDS IPs.

Attacks from mobile and wireless ASes: With the growth of mobile devices, attackers can try to compromise and exploit their resources for malicious activities. Given the relatively weaker software model in mobile devices compared to desktop PCs and the wide deployment of third-party apps on them, they are more likely to be compromised by malware for launching attacks. Users may also jailbreak the security restrictions and install tools (e.g., AnDOSid or mobile LOIC) to participate in botnet activities [10]. In fact, there are 2.1% of the inbound attack traffic from mobile networks.

Figure 12 shows that mobile networks mainly generate UDP floods, DNS reflections, and brute-force attacks. These attacks are harder to mitigate because simple source-based blacklisting does not work well for mobile devices. This is because most mobile devices are often located behind a NAT. While NAT may become less common with IPv6 adoption, there would be more ephemeral addresses.

Origins of DNS attacks: Figure 13a shows that the cloud we studied received a similar number of DNS attacks from all types of ASes. Figure 13b shows that if we count per AS attacks, there are more DNS attacks from IXPs. Our further investigation shows that each DNS attack involved a median value of only 17 unique DNS resolvers in the NetFlow records.

Origins of spam: Figure 13a shows that spam attacks are mainly from large cloud, small ISPs, and customer networks. For example, 81.0% of the spam packets are from Amazon Web Services (AWS) [2] in Singapore.[5] However, each individual small ISP or customer network does not generate many attacks as indicated by the number of per AS attacks shown in Figure 13b. This indicates that it is easier for attackers to leverage the free trial accounts in large clouds, the end hosts in small ISPs, and customer networks to generate spams. Prior study of spams in the Internet [46] shows many spams come from network information centers (NIC), but we observed only a single attack from NICs in our data.

Geolocation distribution of inbound attacks: Figure 14a shows the geographical distribution of inbound attack sources. The inbound attack sources are spread mainly across places in Europe, Eastern Asia, and North America. Specifically, there is one AS in

[5]We did not validate these spam attacks with AWS.

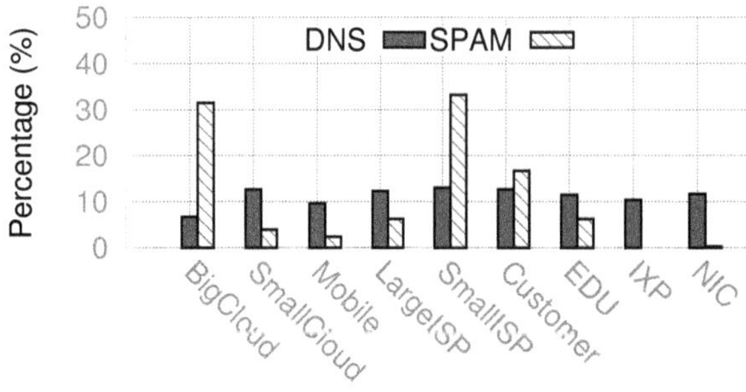

(a) Percentage of inbound DNS or spam attacks in each AS type.

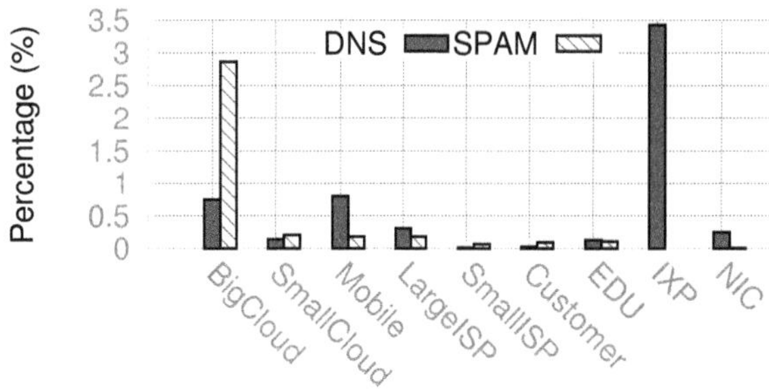

(b) Average percentage of inbound DNS or spam attacks per AS in each AS type.

Figure 13: Different types of ASes generating inbound DNS and SPAM attacks.

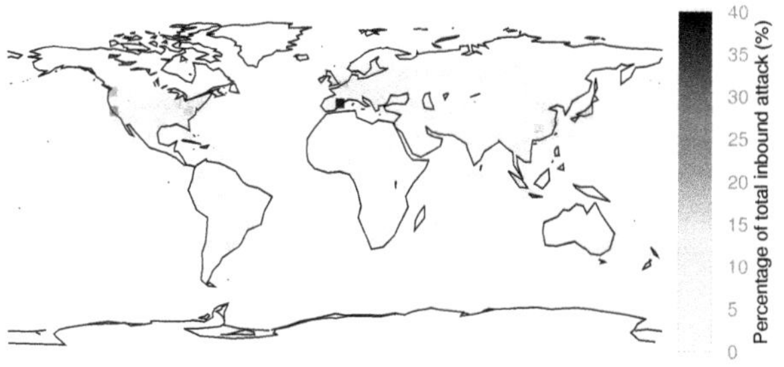

(a) Geolocation distribution of inbound attack sources.

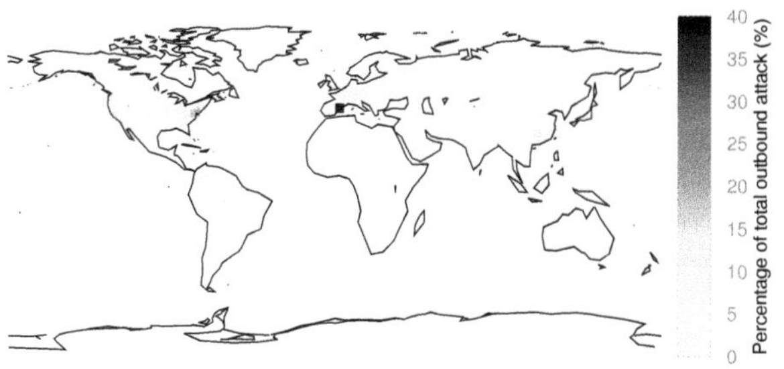

(b) Geolocation distribution of outbound attack targets.

Figure 14: Attack geolocation distribution.

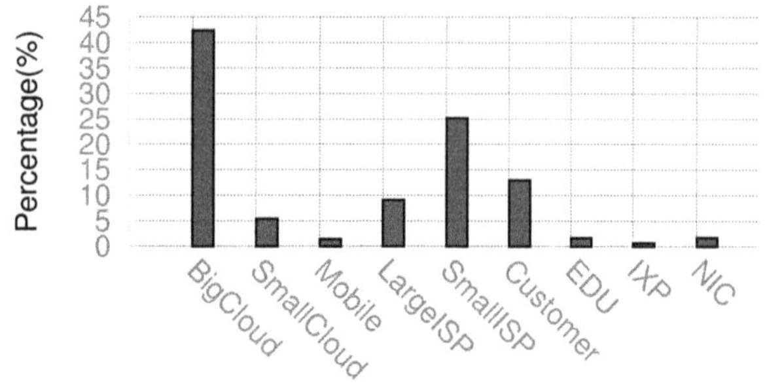

(a) Percentage of outbound attacks in each AS type.

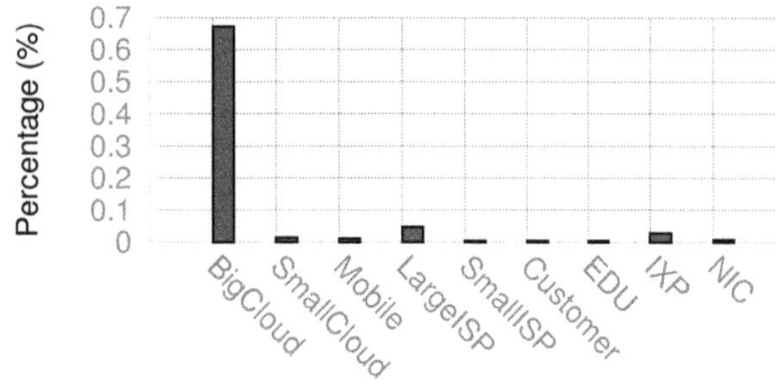

(b) Average percentage of outbound attacks per AS in each AS type.

Figure 15: Different types of ASes targeted by outbound attacks.

Spain involved with more than 35% of the total inbound attacks. It mainly generated UDP flood, TDS and SQL attacks. There are ASes from the west coast of North America that are involved with more than 20% of the total inbound attacks.

6.2 Outbound attacks

Are outbound attacks clustered? Unlike Internet floods which often target a single host [48], we observe outbound UDP flood target a median of 8 hosts, while TCP SYN floods often target a median of 25 Internet hosts just in our sampled NetFlow data. This means attackers often use cloud resources to attack a group of hosts instead of individual IPs. We count the number of unique victim IPs of outbound attacks in each AS to understand if the victims are clustered on particular ASes. We find that 80% of the attacks target hosts in a single AS.

While prior work has shown that a small number of ASes are involved in a significant fraction of attacks in ISP networks [38] and distributed intrusion detection system [50], we show that cloud-related attack incidents are widely spread across many ASes. Top 10 ASes are targets of 8.9% of the attacks; top 100 ASes are targets of 16.3% of the attacks. However, there is a small portion of attacks responsible for the major attack traffic. For instance, 40% of the outbound attack packets were directed from three VIPs towards a small cloud AS in Romania, which offers web hosting, online gaming, and VPN services.

AS classes of outbound attacks: Figure 15 shows that 42% of outbound attacks are against services in big clouds. Most of these attacks are SQL injection and TDS attacks. Small ISPs and customer networks face 25% and 13% of the outbound attacks (Figure 15a), but individual ASes do not generate many attacks (less than 0.01% of the total outbound attacks per AS) (Figure 15b). Small ISPs and customer networks are the major target for brute-force attacks and spam. This is probably because these networks often lack strong security support. For example, 23.6% of the outbound DNS reflection attack packets are sent to an ISP in France. It is therefore important to coordinate security measures across the cloud infrastructure and these networks to protect against these attacks.

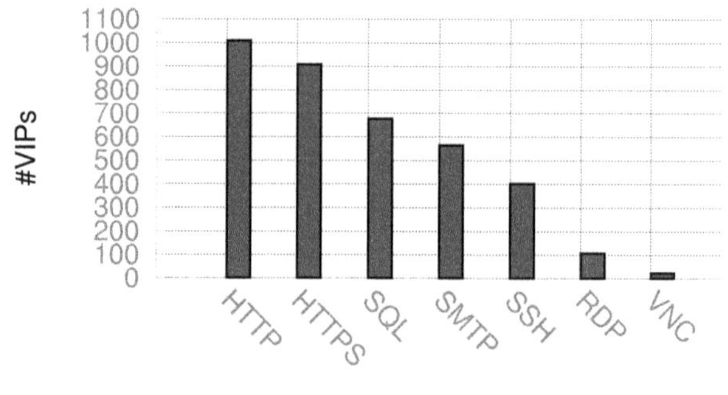

Figure 16: Top Internet applications under outbound attacks.

There are only a few brute-force attacks against mobile networks (1.4%). This may be because mobile devices are often behind a NAT preventing them from unsolicited connections, which makes it harder for attacks to get through.

Internet applications under attack: To understand the Internet applications under attacks, we investigate the destination port of outbound traffic coming from the VIPs generating outbound attacks (Figure 16). We find that most of the outbound attacks target web services (HTTP/HTTPS together form 64.5% of the attack VIPs involved with outbound attacks). For example, 69% of the outbound UDP floods use port 80 as the destination port targeting HTTP services. The other popular target services are SQL, SMTP, and SSH.

Geolocation distribution of outbound attacks: Outbound attack targets are mainly spread across places in Europe and North America (Figure 14b). There are less outbound attack targets than inbound attack sources in Eastern Asia. The same AS in Spain we discussed in inbound attacks also receives more than 35% of outbound attacks (mainly with brute-force, TDS, and SQL attacks).

7. EXISTING SECURITY PRACTICES

In this section we discuss how existing cloud security solutions handle the types of attacks observed in our study.

Inbound TCP SYN, UDP, ICMP floods, DNS reflection attacks: Cloud VMs are only accessible through virtual IPs (VIPs). Traffic towards VIPs is routed through a load-balancing infrastructure [42]. At the infrastructure, the cloud can monitor, detect and mitigate flood attacks (e.g., using SYN cookies, rate limiting, and connection limits) to help ensure that such attacks do not impact customer VM instances [7]. The tenants can also leverage scale-out (e.g., adding more VMs on demand) or scale-up (e.g., deploying resource-rich VMs) techniques to raise the bar for attacks [4].

There are multiple in-built mechanisms in cloud systems to safeguard tenants. For example, the hypervisor that hosts guest VMs in the cloud is neither directly addressable internally by other tenants nor it is externally addressable. Additional filters are put in place to block broadcast and multicast traffic, with the exception of what is needed to maintain DHCP leases. Inside the VMs, tenants can further enable web server add-ons that protect against certain DoS attacks [41]. For example, for TCP SYN flooding attacks, a security rule can be specified to track significant deviations from the norm in terms of the number of half-open TCP sessions, and then drop any further TCP SYN packets from specified sources [5].

Port scan: Unauthorized port scans are often viewed as a violation of cloud use policy and they are blocked by the cloud provider [3]. Port scans are likely to have limited effectiveness because, by default, all the inbound ports on VMs are closed except the ones opened by tenants; a tenant can author a service definition file that contains the internal endpoints that should be opened in service VMs and what roles can communicate with them [8]. Tenants can also use security groups or firewalls to further block unauthorized traffic [41].

Other inbound attacks: Some cloud providers choose not to actively block network traffic affecting individual tenants because the infrastructure does not interpret the expected behavior of customer applications. Instead, these cloud systems allow tenants to use firewall proxy devices such as Web Application Firewalls (WAFs) that terminate and forward traffic to endpoints running in a VM. Tenants can also use network ACLs or VLANs to prevent packets from certain IP addresses from reaching VMs [7].

Cloud providers can also leverage high-level signals emitted from workloads running on the cloud from customer accounts. One such signal is the number of open ports. Legitimate customers aim to minimize the susceptibility of their applications running in the cloud to any external attacks, and hence deploy services usually with a limited number of open ports (e.g., HTTP port 80). However, compromised accounts or VMs may perform a variety of anomalous activities such as running a Botnet controller or torrent services on multiple open ports. The cloud security team monitors such activities and aggressively shuts down any misbehaving tenant VMs.

Outbound attacks: To mitigate outbound attacks, the most important step is to identify fraudulent VMs when a tenant sets up a subscription. In the cloud, several anti-fraud techniques are used such as credit card validation, computing the estimated geographical distance from the IP address used for login to the billing address and ensuring it is within reasonable bounds, and determining whether the email address of the purchaser is from a free email provider.

Note that attackers can also exploit vulnerabilities in VMs of legitimate customers. If an attack is successful, the compromised VMs can then be used by attackers for malicious activity e.g., to send large amounts of unsolicited mail (spam). The cloud provider can enforce limits on how many emails a VM can send as well as prevent SMTP open relay, which can be used to spread spam [5].

8. RELATED WORK

This paper presented one of the first large-scale studies to investigate the prevalence of network-based attacks in the cloud. We compare our work with related work on detecting and understanding Internet-based attacks.

Attack detection methods: Previous works have used NetFlow logs to understand DDoS attacks and traffic anomalies [38, 22, 36, 35] in ISP networks. Our work takes a similar approach to understand a broader set of attacks in the cloud. Most previous studies on application-level attacks leverage analysis of the application content (e.g., spam [15, 25], SQL injection [18], SSH [32]). Our work shows that it is possible to detect some of these attacks by leveraging network-level signatures such as volumes, spread, TCP flags, and communication patterns. In fact, previous works have also shown that application-level attacks (e.g., spam) have strong network-level signatures [46]. We validate our network-based detection by comparing the detected attacks against the security appliance alerts and incident reports. Although network-based detection may not capture all types of application-level attacks (e.g., malware), they are more pragmatic to implement in today's cloud monitoring infrastructure.

Attack characterization: There is a large body of work on characterizing Internet-based attacks. Most prior efforts (e.g., [10, 13, 17, 40, 46, 51]) focus on one or a few types of attacks in the Internet. Given the importance of cloud services in today's Internet, understanding the attacks from/to the cloud is critical. Our study investigates a wide diversity of inbound and outbound attacks in the cloud. We differentiate DDoS attacks based on their protocols (TCP SYN, UDP, DNS reflection), and show that other types of attacks (e.g., brute-force, port scans, and TDS) also need cloud operator's attention. Moreover, we show the detailed characteristics of attacks in the cloud such as the cloud services affected by the attacks, the Internet origins and targets, and the intensity and frequency of these attacks. These results can provide guidelines for future design of attack detection and mitigation systems for the cloud.

9. CONCLUSION

We investigated the prevalence of network-based attacks both on and off the cloud. We performed the first measurement study of the characteristics of a wide range of cloud attacks that vary in complexity, intensity, duration and distribution. Our study shows a strong evidence of increasing scale, attack volume, and sophistication of these attacks. Our results have been leveraged by the cloud security team towards identifying correlations and improving mitigations for different attack types. We hope that this study motivates future research towards designing attack detection and mitigation systems for the cloud. In future work, we plan to extend our measurement study to analyze application level attacks, compare across attack categories and leverage packet traces for deeper analysis.

Acknowledgment

We thank Ramesh Govindan, Cormac Herley, Jelena Mirkovic, Vivek Narassaya, Jitu Padhye, Jay Stokes, Alec Wolman, and the anonymous reviewers for their insightful feedback and suggestions. This work is supported in part by the NSF grants CNS-1423505, CNS-1413972, and DHS-D15PC00184.

10. REFERENCES

[1] http://www.everestgrp.com/2015-04-40-billion-global-cloud-services-market-expected-to-grow-27-percent-per-annum-for-next-3-years-press-release-17218.html.

[2] Amazon web services. http://aws.amazon.com/.

[3] Amazon Web Services: Overview of Security Processes. https://d0.awsstatic.com/whitepapers/Security/AWS%20Security%20Whitepaper.pdf.

[4] AWS Best Practices for DDoS Resiliency. https://d0.awsstatic.com/whitepapers/DDoS_White_Paper_June2015.pdf.

[5] AWS Security Best Practices. https://d0.awsstatic.com/whitepapers/aws-security-best-practices.pdf.

[6] http://nmap.org/book/man-port-scanning-techniques.html.

[7] Microsoft Azure Network Security Whitepaper. http://blogs.msdn.com/b/azuresecurity/archive/2015/03/03/microsoft-azure-network-security-whitepaper-version-3-is-now-available.aspx.

[8] https://msdn.microsoft.com/en-us/library/azure/ee758711.aspx.

[9] juno.c. http://goo.gl/i1Qodc, 2013.

[10] Q4 2013 global ddos attack report. http://goo.gl/1IyRmK, 2013.

[11] Quova. http://www.quova.com, 2013.

[12] S. Ali, I. U. Haq, S. Rizvi, N. Rasheed, U. Sarfraz, S. A. Khayam, and F. Mirza. On Mitigating Sampling-induced Accuracy Loss in Traffic Anomaly Detection Systems. *ACM SIGCOMM Computer Communication Review 2010.*

[13] M. Allman, V. Paxson, and J. Terrell. A Brief History of Scanning. In *IMC*, 2007.

[14] Andrew Marshall, Michael Howard, Grant Bugher, Brian Harden. Security Best Practices For Developing Windows Azure Applications. http://download.microsoft.com/documents/uk/enterprise/88_security_best_practices_for_developing_windows_azure_applicat.pdf.

[15] I. Androutsopoulos, J. Koutsias, K. V. Chandrinos, G. Paliouras, and C. D. Spyropoulos. An Evaluation of Naive Bayesian Anti-Spam Filtering. *Proceedings of the workshop on Machine Learning in the New Information Age, 11th European Conference on Machine Learning*, 2000.

[16] C. Anley. Advanced SQL Injection in SQL Server Applications. In *Next Generation Security Software Ltd*, 2002.

[17] Arbor Networks. Insight into the global threat landscape. http://goo.gl/15oOx3, February 2013.

[18] S. Bandhakavi, P. Bisht, P. Madhusudan, and V. N. Venkatakrishnan. CANDID: Preventing SQL injection attacks using dynamic candidate evaluations. ACM CCS, 2007.

[19] M. Basseville and I. Nikiforov. Detection of Abrupt Changes: Theory and Application. Prentice Hall Englewood Cliffs, 1993.

[20] Bloomberg. Sony Network Breach Shows Amazon Clould's Appeal for Hackers. http://goo.gl/3WiAaj, 2011.

[21] G. Booth, A. Soknacki, and A. Somayaji. Cloud Security: Attacks and Current Defenses. In *ASIA*, 2013.

[22] D. Brauckhoff, B. Tellenbach, A. Wagner, M. May, and A. Lakhina. Impact of packet sampling on anomaly detection metrics. In *IMC*, 2006.

[23] J. Caballero, C. Grier, C. Kreibich, and V. Paxson. Measuring pay-per-install: The commoditization of malware distribution. In *USENIX Conference on Security*, 2011.

[24] E. Cambiaso, G. Papaleo, and M. Aiello. Taxonomy of Slow DoS Attacks to Web Applications. In *TCNDSS*. Springer, 2012.

[25] X. Carreras and L. Marquez. Boosting Trees for Anti-Spam Email Filtering. *Proceedings of RANLP*, 2001.

[26] R. Chaiken, B. Jenkins, P.-A. Larson, B. Ramsey, D. Shakib, S. Weaver, and J. Zhou. SCOPE: Easy and Efficient Parallel Processing of Massive Data Sets. *VLDB'08.*

[27] X. Dimitropoulos, D. Krioukov, G. Riley, and k. claffy. Revealing the Autonomous System Taxonomy: The Machine Learning Approach. In *Passive and Active Network Measurement Workshop (PAM)*, 2006.

[28] N. R. Draper, H. Smith, and E. Pownell. *Applied regression analysis*. Wiley New York, 1966.

[29] Google. Malware Distribution by Autonomous System. http://goo.gl/mZQeG4, 2013.

[30] C. Grier, L. Ballard, et al. Manufacturing Compromise: The Emergence of Exploit-As-A-Service. In *CCS*, 2012.

[31] L. Hellemons. Flow-based detection of ssh intrusion attempts. *Scanning*, 2012.

[32] M. Javed and V. Paxson. Detecting Stealthy, Distributed SSH Brute-forcing. CCS, 2013.

[33] C. Kanich, N. Weaver, D. McCoy, T. Halvorson, C. Kreibich, K. Levchenko, V. Paxson, G. M. Voelker, and S. Savage. Show Me the Money: Characterizing Spam-Advertised Revenue. In *USENIX SEC*, 2011.

[34] R. Kawahara, K. Ishibashi, T. Mori, N. Kamiyama, S. Harada, and S. Asano. Detection accuracy of network anomalies using sampled flow statistics. In *GLOBECOM '07. IEEE.*

[35] A. Lakhina, M. Crovella, and C. Diot. Diagnosing network-wide traffic anomalies. In *SIGCOMM*, 2004.

[36] A. Lakhina, M. Crovella, and C. Diot. Mining anomalies using traffic feature distributions. In *SIGCOMM*, 2005.

[37] Z. Li, S. Alrwais, Y. Xie, F. Yu, and X. Wang. Finding the Linchpins of the Dark Web: A Study on Topologically Dedicated Hosts on Malicious Web Infrastructures. In *Security and Privacy (SP), IEEE Symposium on*, 2013.

[38] Z. M. Mao, V. Sekar, O. Spatscheck, J. van der Merwe, and R. Vasudevan. Analyzing large DDoS attacks using multiple data sources. In *SIGCOMM Workshop on Large-scale Attack Defense*, 2006.

[39] J. Mirkovic and P. Reiher. A Taxonomy of DDoS Attack and DDoS Defense Mechanisms. *SIGCOMM CCR*, 2004.

[40] D. Moore, C. Shannon, D. J. Brown, G. M. Voelker, and S. Savage. Inferring Internet Denial-Of-Service Activity. *ACM Transactions on Computer Systems*, 2006.

[41] C. Nelson. Best practices to protect your azure deployment against "cloud drive-by" attacks. http://blogs.msdn.com/b/azuresecurity/archive/2015/07/05/best-practices-to-protect-your-azure-deployment-against-cloud-drive-by-attacks.aspx.

[42] P. Patel, D. Bansal, L. Yuan, A. Murthy, A. Greenberg, D. A. Maltz, R. Kern, H. Kumar, M. Zikos, H. Wu, et al. Ananta: Cloud Scale Load Balancing. In *ACM SIGCOMM*, 2013.

[43] V. Paxson, G. Almes, J. Mahdavi, and M. Mathis. Framework for IP performance metrics. In *RFC 2330*, 1998.

[44] A. Pitsillidis, C. Kanich, et al. Taster's Choice: A Comparative Analysis of Spam Feeds. In *IMC*, 2012.

[45] R. Potharaju, N. Jain, and C. Nita-Rotaru. Juggling the jigsaw: Towards automated problem inference from network trouble tickets. In *NSDI'13.*

[46] A. Ramachandran and N. Feamster. Understanding the network-level behavior of spammers. In *SIGCOMM*, 2006.

[47] B. Ridgway. Security best practices for windows azure solutions. *Azure Manual*, 2014.

[48] V. Sekar, N. G. Duffield, O. Spatscheck, J. E. van der Merwe, and H. Zhang. LADS: Large-scale automated DDoS detection system. In *USENIX ATC*, 2006.

[49] B. Stone-Gross, T. Holz, G. Stringhini, and G. Vigna. The underground economy of spam: A botmaster's perspective of coordinating large-scale spam campaigns. *USENIX Workshop on Large-Scale Exploits and Emergent Threats (LEET)*, 2011.

[50] V. Yegneswaran, P. Barford, and S. Jha. Global intrusion detection in the domino overlay system. In *NDSS*, 2004.

[51] V. Yegneswaran, P. Barford, and J. Ullrich. Internet intrusions: Global characteristics and prevalence. In *ACM SIGMETRICS 2003.*

An End-to-End Measurement of Certificate Revocation in the Web's PKI

Yabing Liu* Will Tome* Liang Zhang* David Choffnes* Dave Levin†
Bruce Maggs‡ Alan Mislove* Aaron Schulman§ Christo Wilson*

*Northeastern University †University of Maryland
‡Duke University and Akamai Technologies §Stanford University

ABSTRACT

Critical to the security of any public key infrastructure (PKI) is the ability to revoke previously issued certificates. While the overall SSL ecosystem is well-studied, the frequency with which certificates are revoked and the circumstances under which clients (e.g., browsers) check whether certificates are revoked are still not well-understood.

In this paper, we take a close look at certificate revocations in the Web's PKI. Using 74 full IPv4 HTTPS scans, we find that a surprisingly large fraction (8%) of the certificates served have been revoked, and that obtaining certificate revocation information can often be expensive in terms of latency and bandwidth for clients. We then study the revocation checking behavior of 30 different combinations of web browsers and operating systems; we find that browsers often do not bother to check whether certificates are revoked (including mobile browsers, which uniformly *never* check). We also examine the CRLSet infrastructure built into Google Chrome for disseminating revocations; we find that CRLSet only covers 0.35% of all revocations. Overall, our results paint a bleak picture of the ability to effectively revoke certificates today.

Categories and Subject Descriptors

C.2.3 [**Computer-Communication Networks**]: Network Operations; E.3 [**Data Encryption**]: Public Key Cryptosystems, Standards

Keywords

SSL; TLS; PKI; HTTPS; X.509; Certificates; Revocation; Extended validation, Web browsers, CRLSet

1. INTRODUCTION

The Secure Sockets Layer (SSL) and Transport Layer Security (TLS) protocols secure a significant fraction of Internet traffic today. Coupled with a Public Key Infrastructure (PKI), SSL[1] provides authentication via certificate chains and private communication via encryption.

Critical to the security of any PKI is the ability to *revoke* a previously-issued certificate, that is, to invalidate it before it expires. If the private key corresponding to a given certificate were compromised, the attacker could impersonate the certificate owner or eavesdrop on encrypted traffic sent to the certificate owner until the certificate's expiry date. Even more harrowing, if an *intermediate* certificate were compromised, an attacker could issue valid certificates for *any* domain (and, unfortunately, such attacks have occurred in the past [5,31,48]). The only recourse a certificate owner has is to request that their Certificate Authority (CA) create and disseminate revocations: signed attestations that the certificate should no longer be considered valid.

Successfully revoking a certificate requires action not only from website administrators and CAs; *clients*, especially web browsers, must request *and respect* revocations. If any of these principals fail to meet their responsibilities—if administrators fail to request revocations, CAs fail to distribute them, or browsers fail to fetch them—users risk being susceptible to impersonation attacks.

And yet, surprisingly, security practitioners have developed a strikingly negative view towards certificate revocation, even going so far as to doubt the fundamental usefulness of revocations [27,28,32,42,46]. These objections are largely rooted in the costs that the various parties incur in supporting revocations and the tradeoffs that clients (i.e., web browsers) face when they are unable to obtain the revocation status of certificates. While the incentives appear at odds with proper security, the extent to which they have led to inaction is largely unknown. This uncertainty leads to a chicken-and-egg problem: administrators argue that they need not revoke because clients rarely check, while clients argue they need not check because administrators rarely revoke. Without a concrete understanding of revocation in today's PKI, it is unclear how to break this logjam and improve the PKI's handling of certificate revocation.

In this paper, we empirically evaluate the extent to which all three parties involved—website administrators, CAs, and browsers—meet their revocation responsibilities. Our investigation extends prior work in the measurement of the SSL ecosystem; to date, most studies [7,14] have focused on live certificates (proper key lengths, trust aggregation among CAs, etc), and there have been few studies of the critical revocation mechanisms available today. In particular, we

[1] TLS is the successor of SSL, but both use the same certificates. We refer to "SSL certificates," but our findings apply equally to both.

IMC'15, October 28–30, 2015, Tokyo, Japan.

ACM 978-1-4503-3848-6/15/10 ...$15.00.
DOI: http://dx.doi.org/10.1145/2815675.2815685.

provide the first end-to-end evaluation of the Web's certificate revocation ecosystem, with the following contributions:

First, we study website administrators' revocation behavior using 74 separate, full IPv4 port 443 scans between October 2013 and March 2015, collected by Rapid7 [40]. We select all valid certificates from these scans, and then check their revocation status every day, starting in October 2014. Overall, we find that a surprisingly large fraction (> 8%) of these certificates are revoked, and that almost 1% of certificates that continue to be advertised are actually revoked. Additionally, we observe that OCSP Stapling, which addresses many of the difficulties of obtaining revocation information, is not widely deployed: only 3% of certificates are served by hosts supporting OCSP Stapling.

Second, we examine the CA's role in distributing certificate revocation information. We find that the most well-established distribution method, CRLs, can impose significant bandwidth and latency overhead on clients: the median certificate has a CRL of 51 KB, and some certificates have CRLs up to 76 MB in size. At the same time, we observe that checking certificate status via OCSP is significantly cheaper but still requires the client to delay accepting the connection until the OCSP responder can be contacted.

Third, we examine client-side revocation checking behavior, since clients are responsible for checking certificates' revocation status. We develop a test suite for web browsers that includes 244 distinct certificate configurations. We deploy this test suite to the most recent versions of all major browsers on both mobile and desktop devices. Overall, we find that the fraction of times that revocation information is actually checked is surprisingly low: Firefox *only* checks leaf and EV certificates for revocations, and *only* if the certificates have OCSP responders; all browsers except for Internet Explorer assume that a leaf certificate is valid if revocation information cannot be obtained; and not a single mobile browser checks revocation information for *any* certificates. In the process, we found three bugs in revocation checking behavior and filed bug reports with browser vendors.

Fourth, we examine the revocation checking policy for Chrome in more detail, as Chrome also uses a Google-curated subset of all CRLs called the *CRLSet*. Essentially, Google pre-selects a subset of all revoked certificates and pushes this information to Chrome browsers. Unfortunately, our analysis shows that the CRLSet contains only 0.35% of revoked certificates.

Taken together, our findings paint a bleak picture of certificate revocation on the Internet today. While a significant fraction of certificates *are* revoked, many clients will never receive these revocations and will obliviously accept the certificates as valid. Fortunately, our findings also point towards potential improvements that could be implemented in the very near term, including an improved CRLSet construction based on Bloom Filters (§7).

Our analysis relied on both public sources of data and those we collected ourselves. We make our data and our browser "test suite" available to the research community at

`http://www.sslresearch.org`

2. BACKGROUND

SSL and TLS provide confidentiality and integrity for the vast majority of secure online communication. When combined with a PKI, they also allow parties to authenticate the identity of the other communicating party. In this section, we provide a brief background of SSL/TLS and PKIs relevant to our study, and detail the protocols that exist to support certificate revocation. We refer the reader to the book by Gutmann [20] for a more in-depth treatment of these topics.

2.1 Certificates

A certificate is an attestation signed by an *issuer* that binds a *subject* to a *public key*. In the web's PKI, the issuers are Certificate Authorities (CAs) such as Verisign or GoDaddy, who possess their own certificates binding their identities to their public keys. These CA certificates are, in turn, signed by other CAs, and so on, terminating at a small set of self-signed *root certificates*. Clients are assumed to obtain these trusted root certificates out-of-band (e.g., most browsers and operating systems ship with a set of root certificates).

The PKI does not include a widely accepted mechanism for delegating partial authority to issue certificates to CAs.[2] As a result, *any* CA can issue a certificate for *any* domain.

To verify a *leaf certificate* (i.e., a certificate that is not permitted to sign other certificates, used by most websites), a client needs to obtain a logical *chain* of certificates, leading from a root certificate through zero or more *intermediate* (*CA*) certificates, to the leaf certificate.[3] The private keys for each certificate are used to sign the certificate at the next level, with the exception of the root (which is signed by its own private key). To verify the leaf's identity, the client thus needs to verify that each certificate along this chain has a correct signature, is still *fresh* (certificates have a well-defined period during which they can be accepted), and has not been revoked.

The most common format for certificates on the Internet today is X.509 [11], which contains an ASN.1 [34] encoding of the certificate along with its signature. The X.509 format allows for additional information to be supplied, including a certificate's serial number (unique for the issuer), the certificate's validity period, and where to check whether the certificate has been revoked.

Validating Identities. Ultimately, CAs exist to bind identities to public keys, and are therefore responsible for validating their customers' identities. Typically, a CA challenges an applicant to prove ownership of the domain for which they are applying, for instance by requiring the applicant to post CA-chosen data at a URL in that domain; this process is called *Domain Validation* (DV). To provide greater assurance to clients that certificates were issued properly, *Extended Validation* (EV) certificates are a mechanism for CAs to assert that the identity verification process has followed a set of established criteria.

EV certificates follow the same format as X.509 certificates, but simply contain an additional `Policy Identifier` that indicates that a more thorough verification was performed. Many browsers display EV certificates differently (typically with a green box in the address bar). As we will see later in the paper, browsers often also perform a different set of revocation checks on EV certificates.

[2] The X.509 specification includes the `Name Constraints` extension for exactly this, but it is rarely used and few clients support it.

[3] Certificates can also be cross-signed [22] by other issuers for redundancy, providing multiple valid chains for a given certificate.

2.2 Revocation

Most CAs allow entities who have been issued certificates to later request to have them *revoked*. Revocations are represented by attestations signed by the same CAs who issued the corresponding certificates. CAs are also responsible for disseminating the revocation status for all certificates they have issued.

When a client establishes an SSL connection, the server presents a chain of certificates as part of the SSL handshake. In addition to verifying the chain itself, the correct behavior of the client is to ensure that *all* certificates in the chain[4] have not been revoked before continuing with the connection. Each certificate typically includes information about how and where to check for revocation information (i.e., a protocol and a URL).

There are two predominant methods for disseminating revocations: Certificate Revocation Lists (CRLs) and the Online Certificate Status Protocol (OCSP):

CRLs. CRLs are the most well-established means of disseminating revocations. A CRL is simply an ASN.1-encoded file that contains a list of (serial number, revocation timestamp, revocation reason) tuples, all of which are collectively signed by the CA. Thus, checking the revocation status of a certificate using a CRL involves downloading the CRL file specified in the certificate and checking whether the certificate's serial number is listed in the CRL.

Similar to X.509 certificates, each CRL contains information specifying the range of time that it is good for; CAs are therefore required to re-issue CRLs periodically even if no additional certificates have been revoked. Clients can therefore cache CRLs, but must download an updated CRL once they expire.

CRLs have been criticized [15] for being an inefficient means of disseminating revocation information: clients must download information about *all* of the CA's revoked certificates even though they are typically only interested in the validity status of a single certificate. Thus, CRLs impose on CAs and clients a burden of excessive communication overhead.

OCSP. OCSP was designed to reduce the overhead of CRLs by allowing clients to query the CA for the revocation status of a *single* certificate. OCSP allows a client to generate an HTTP request for the status of a given certificate's serial number. The URL that clients should query is stated in the certificate. The CA returns a signed response that includes the certificate's current status (`good`, `revoked`, or `unknown`[5]), as well as a validity period, meaning clients can cache the response, typically on the order of days (longer than most CRLs).

OCSP addresses many of the inefficiencies of CRLs, but still requires request(s) to the CA(s) before a certificate can be trusted. Additionally, using OCSP reveals information about the users' browsing behavior to CAs, a potential privacy risk. Thus, checking the revocation status of certificates via OCSP still imposes a significant burden on clients.

[4]The client need not check the revocation status of the root certificate, as root certificates can only be "revoked" by removing them from the list of trusted certificates on clients.

[5]The OCSP specification [44] states that the `unknown` response "indicates that the status could not be determined by this responder". While the correct client behavior when receiving an `unknown` response is the subject of some debate, it is clear that the response does not indicate that certificate in question should be trusted.

OCSP Stapling. OCSP Stapling is an SSL/TLS extension that allows a server to cache OCSP responses and send them to clients as part of the SSL handshake. Thus, when communicating with a server that supports OCSP Stapling, a client receives *both* the server's certificate *and* an OCSP statement of the certificate's validity. The client can verify the OCSP statement and therefore be assured that the certificate is not revoked. OCSP Stapling removes most of the latency penalty associated with verifying a certificate's revocation status.

Unfortunately, OCSP Stapling does not entirely remove the latency penalty for clients, as OCSP Stapling only includes the OCSP response for the *leaf* certificate (the protocol does not allow the server to include cached OCSP responses for intermediate certificates). A recently proposed extension to OCSP Stapling [37] addresses this limitation by allowing the server to include stapled OCSP responses for intermediates and the leaf certificate, but has yet to see wide adoption.

2.3 Certificate Validation

Despite its critical importance for securing the integrity of the PKI, the X.509 specification [11] is somewhat vague when discussing revocation checking during certificate validation. While it is clear that a client should not trust a revoked certificate that appears in a CRL or OCSP response, there is an active discussion [20, 28] regarding what to do when a client is unable to access the revocation status of a certificate (e.g., if the browser cannot resolve the domain name of the CRL server, if the OCSP server is down, etc). The X.509 specification states that, in this case, the certificate should be given the status `undetermined` [11], but does not specify how this should be interpreted.

For maximum security, the client should not trust the certificate chain if any of its revocation information is unavailable; after all, the client cannot be certain that one of the certificates has not been revoked. But from a user's perspective, this would look like the browser's inability to load a page that an incorrect browser would successfully load. Thus, browser developers often *soft-fail* by deciding to trust certificates when revocation information is unavailable, so as not to rest their perceived reliability on the shoulders of a disparate set of third-party CAs.

Soft-failing when revocation information is unavailable may at first appear to be an innocuous trade-off for usability, but in practice it has surprisingly extensive implications on the security of the PKI. Any attacker who can block a victim's access to specific domains (e.g., an attacker on the same wireless network) could leverage soft-failures to effectively turn off the victim's revocation checking. As a result, some browser maintainers have concluded that requesting revocation information in direct response to visiting a website does not actually increase security [28], and have advocated instead for pushing incomplete subsets of revocation information to clients (§7).

To ensure user security, however, there is simply no replacement for maintaining as complete and up-to-date revocation information as possible. And when it is not possible, it is our opinion that hard-failing would better inform users of the potential security risks, and may apply useful customer pressure on CAs with unreliable services.[6] Thus, we

[6]Browser maintainers have also claimed that hard-failing browsers would also cause CRL servers and OCSP responders to become single

maintain that revocation is a critical component of a PKI, and in the remainder of this paper, we analyze to what extent it is supported by administrators, CAs, and clients.

3. DATA COLLECTION

In this section, we describe the data we use to understand certificate revocation behavior, and define several terms that we use in our analysis.

3.1 SSL Certificates

Obtaining representative statistics on certificates that are revoked is not entirely straightforward, as revoked certificates (by definition) should no longer be advertised. Thus, simply measuring the number of entries in CRLs is sufficient to count revocations, but does not reveal *which* certificates were revoked (CRLs only contain the certificates' serial numbers). As a result, it is necessary to collect data on advertised certificates over time, and then periodically check to see which of the certificates have been revoked. However, obtaining a representative sample of advertised certificates is also difficult; relying on data gathered from passive traces [16, 23] is likely to have good coverage of popular certificates but may miss unpopular ones.

We obtain our collection of SSL certificates from (roughly) weekly scans of port 443 over the entire IPv4 address space, made available by Rapid7 [40]. In this paper, we use 74 scans conducted between October 30, 2013 and March 30, 2015. Overall, we observe 38,514,130 unique SSL certificates.

Many of the certificates that we find in the scans are invalid (e.g., self-signed certificates on WiFi routers). Thus, we pre-process the dataset by verifying all observed certificates. We do so by first building the set of all *intermediate* certificates that can be verified relative to the roots.[7] This is an iterative process (as certain intermediates can only be verified once other intermediates are verified); in the end, we discover 1,946 intermediate certificates, which we refer to as the *Intermediate Set.*

We then proceed to verify all leaf certificates using this set of intermediate and root certificates. We configure OpenSSL to ignore certificate date errors (as our scans cover over 1.5 years), but to fail on any other error (except revocation, which we address later). This allows us to only keep certificates that were valid at some point in time. We find a total of 5,067,476 such leaf certificates; this *Leaf Set* is the set of certificates that we examine throughout the remainder of the paper. Of these, we observe that 2,291,511 (45.2%) were still being advertised in the latest port 443 scan.

3.2 Obtaining Revocation Information

We collect our data on certificate revocations using the revocation information present in the certificates. In the Leaf Set, we observe that 99.9% of the certificates list a potentially reachable[8] CRL distribution point, and 95.0% of certificates list a potentially reachable OCSP responder. Interestingly, we find 4,384 (0.09%) Leaf Set certificates that have *neither* a CRL distribution point nor an OCSP responder. These represent certificates that can *never* be revoked.

points of failure and attractive DDoS targets. However, CRLs and OCSP responses are cacheable, and existing techniques for distributing static content (e.g., CDNs) can be applied to them as well.

[7]We use the root store in OS X 10.9.2 [35] as our set of trusted roots; this includes 222 unique root certificates.

[8]We only consider `http[s]://` CRL URLs, and ignore distribution points in private networks such as `ldap://` and `file://` URLs.

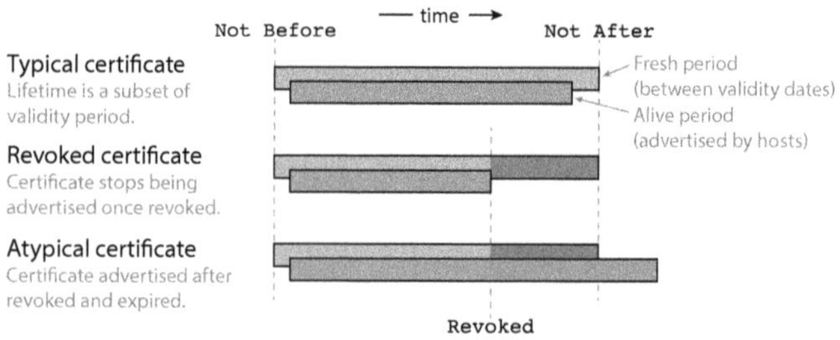

Figure 1: Diagram of events in a certificate's lifetime. Two different timelines exist for any certificate: when it is *fresh* (between validity dates) and when it is *alive* (advertised by servers). Certificates may also be revoked during the time they are fresh.

In the Intermediate Set, we observe that 98.9% of the certificates list a potentially reachable CRL distribution point, while 48.5% list a potentially reachable OCSP responder. Similar to the Leaf Set, we find 18 (0.92%) intermediate certificates that have no CRL distribution point or OCSP responder.[9] Being unable to revoke a CA certificate is particularly worrisome, as possessing a CA certificate's private key allows one to generate certificates for *any* Internet domain (and private keys for CA certificates have be inappropriately given out multiple times in the past [5, 31, 48]).

CRLs. For the certificates that include a CRL distribution point, we use this CRL to obtain revocation information for the certificate. We observe a total of 2,800 unique CRLs, and we configure a crawler to download each of these CRLs once per day between October 2, 2014 and March 31, 2015.

OCSP. We observe a total of 499 unique OCSP responders across all certificates. However, querying each of these responders to check the status of each certificate is prohibitively expensive, and also unnecessary in the case where a CRL distribution point is also provided. Thus, we only query the OCSP responders for the 642 certificates that *only* have an OCSP responder provided (i.e., no CRL distribution point). This data was collected on March 31, 2015.

3.3 Definitions

Throughout this study, we will consider a variety of events in the lifetime of an SSL certificate. For a given certificate, we are concerned with two interrelated timelines (Figure 1 demonstrates a few possible configurations of these timelines):

Fresh. We define a certificate's *fresh period* to be the time between its `Not Valid Before` date and its `Not Valid After` date. This is the period of time in which a client will potentially accept the certificate.

Lifetime. We consider a certificate to be *alive* during the time from when we first saw the certificate advertised (its birth) to when we last saw it advertised (its death). Typically, the lifetime is a strict subset of the certificate's fresh period, but we do observe many instances where expired certificates are still advertised.

Note that neither of these definitions account for revocations: we consider a certificate in its fresh period to still be

[9]This figure excludes root certificates, as these certificates have no CRL distribution points or OCSP responders by design.

fresh, and an advertised certificate to be alive, regardless of whether or not it has been revoked. We do so because clients that do not check revocation information will still accept revoked fresh certificates.

4. WEBSITE ADMIN BEHAVIOR

The revocation process begins with the website administrator making a request to its CA, and offering a reason for the revocation. We begin our analysis at the source by analyzing the frequency and reasons for revocations.

4.1 Frequency of Revocations

First, we examine the characteristics of individual certificates. Figure 2 shows the fraction of fresh and alive certificates that are revoked in our data set between January 2014 and March 2015. We first observe that a surprisingly large fraction of all fresh certificates are actually revoked: as of this writing, over 8% of them are revoked. The majority of these revocations are caused by the Heartbleed vulnerability [52]; this shows up in the graph as the "spike" starting in May 2014.[10] However, even before this vulnerability, over 1% of fresh certificates were revoked, indicating that a non-trivial fraction of SSL certificates are revoked even in steady-state.

Second, we observe that the fraction of alive certificates that are revoked is much smaller—less than 1% of all alive certificates—but still non-zero. Certificates in this category are surprising, as it suggests that the site administrator went to the effort to revoke the certificate, but failed to update (all of) their machines with the new certificate. Examples of such certificates include `https://west-secvpn.apple.com`, `https://vpn.trade.gov`, and `https://gamespace.adobe.com` (the last of which is both expired *and* revoked).

Third, when considering only EV certificates, we observe largely similar trends: Over 6% of fresh EV certificates are currently revoked, and over 0.5% of alive EV certificates are revoked. EV certificates have much stricter entity validation requirements by CAs, so it is surprising to see that a *higher* fraction of EV certificates are revoked but still advertised.

Compared to the revocation behavior shortly after Heartbleed [52], we find that certificate owners quickly returned to pre-Heartbleed behaviors, despite the fact that there were still many vulnerable certificates that needed to be revoked. Moreover, we find that revocation alone may not be enough, as there are many revoked certificates still being advertised. Whether they have any impact on client security depends on whether clients are downloading revocation information, which we study in §6.

4.2 Reasons for Revocation

We have observed that a significant fraction of all fresh certificates are revoked, but a key question remains: *Why* are these certificates revoked? Unfortunately, the reasons for revocation are typically difficult to measure; only the certificate owners (or, potentially, the CA) knows why a certificate is being revoked, and many administrators are likely to consider this information to be private or sensitive.

Zhang et al. [52] used CRL *reason codes*—which range from "Unspecified" to "Key Compromised" to "Privilege Withdrawn" [11]—to attempt to gain some insight, but found reason codes not to be particularly informative. We repeated their methodology with our dataset, extracting the reason code for all revocations. Even on our larger data set, we find a similar distribution of reason codes: in particular, the vast majority of revocations actually include no reason code. Thus, CRL reason codes provide some information (and as we will see in §7, they form the basis of Google's decision to include the revocation in CRLSets), but should likely be viewed with caution.

[10] Previous work demonstrated that, a full month after Heartbleed was announced, only about 13% of site owners that *should have* revoked did revoke [52]. Thus, an even larger fraction of fresh certificates *should be* revoked, but are not.

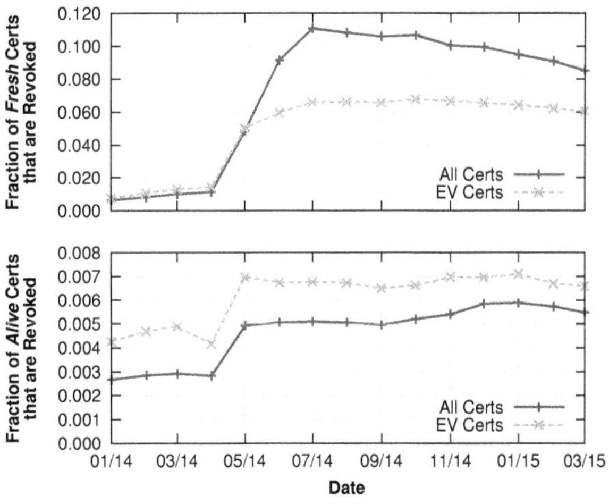

Figure 2: Fraction of fresh (top) and alive (bottom) certificates over time that are revoked (for all certificates and EV-only certificates). The large "spike" in April 2014 is due to certificate revocations caused by the Heartbleed vulnerability. We observe that today, over 8% of all fresh certificates are revoked, and more surprisingly, over 0.6% of *alive* certificates are revoked.

4.3 OCSP Stapling

Recall from §2.2 that OCSP Stapling was developed to address the limitations of CRLs and OCSP. One would thus expect that OCSP Stapling has been embraced at web servers. However, OCSP Stapling requires the website administrators to enable it on their web server (unlike CRLs and OCSP, which only involve the CA), so it is unclear how often website administrators do so.

To determine what fraction of certificates are hosted on servers that support OCSP Stapling, we use the IPv4 TLS Handshake scans conducted by the University of Michigan [49]. Each scan contains details about the port 443 SSL handshake with every IPv4 server, including the support for various TLS extensions. We examine the scan of March 28, 2015, and look for servers that were advertising certificates in the Leaf Set.

Some web servers that support OCSP Stapling (e.g., Nginx) may not include a staple in the response if they do not have a valid staple cached (in this case, they will then attempt to fetch a fresh staple). Thus, the scan data from above may underestimate the fraction of servers that actually support OCSP Stapling. To measure this effect, we chose 20,000 random servers and connected to them repeatedly (sleeping 3 seconds between connections) to see if we ever received a staple, and present the results in Figure 3. Overall, the results suggest that using only a single connection is likely to underestimate the true fraction of OCSP

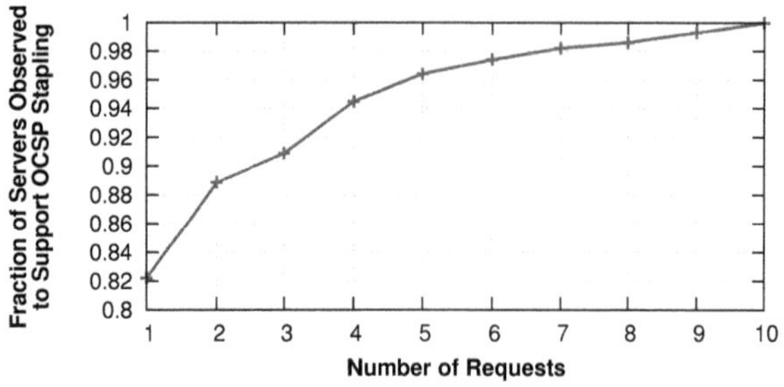

Figure 3: Fraction of servers observed to support OCSP Stapling as multiple requests are made; certain servers will only provide a staple if a fresh one is cached (note that the y-axis does not start at 0). Using only a single request is likely to underestimate the fraction of OCSP Stapling support by approximately 18%.

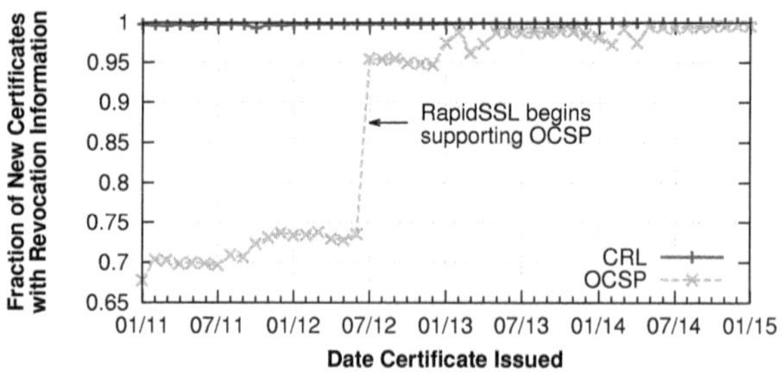

Figure 4: Fraction of new certificates that include CRL or OCSP revocation information over time (note that the y-axis does not start at 0). We observe that, today, almost all new certificates contain both types of revocation information.

Stapling support by about 18%; this effect should be taken into account when interpreting our results below.

Looking at the TLS Handshake scan data, we observe 12,978,883 servers advertising fresh Leaf Set certificates (this is larger than the number of Leaf Set certificates, as one certificate could be advertised by many servers), of which only 337,856 (2.60%) support OCSP stapling. However, this only tells us the fraction of servers that support OCSP Stapling, but not the fraction of *certificates* that we see it supported for. Of the 2,298,778 fresh certificates advertised in this scan, we observe that only 119,519 (5.19%) are served by at least one server that supports OCSP Stapling, and only 70,996 (3.09%) are served by servers that *all* do so.

If we narrow our focus to only EV certificates, we find that of the 83,974 fresh EV certificates advertised during the scan, only 2,644 (3.15%) are advertised by at least one server that supports OCSP Stapling, and only 1,640 (1.95%) are advertised by servers that *all* support OCSP Stapling. This is a smaller fraction than all certificates, and may be caused by many large hosting providers (commonly used by owners of EV certificates) not supporting OCSP Stapling.

Thus, while OCSP Stapling is supported by all major web server implementations, OCSP Stapling has still seen very little adoption. Even taking into account the underestimation of OCSP Stapling support from a single-connection scan, only about 6–7% of certificates are served by at least one server that supports OCSP Stapling. Our results stand in contrast to scans that focus only on popular web sites (e.g., Qualys' SSL Pulse [38] reports ~20% OCSP Stapling support), suggesting that less popular sites are significantly less likely to support OCSP Stapling.

4.4 Summary

Our results show that a considerable number of certificates are advertised even long after they are revoked. This should have no impact on security if clients are vigilant in downloading revocation information, but otherwise, could make impersonation attacks possible. Moreover, our results suggest that website administrators rarely enable OCSP Stapling, the most efficient and client-friendly protocol for distributing revocations. Next, we investigate the behavior of the distributors of revocation information: the CAs.

5. CA BEHAVIOR

Upon receiving a request to revoke a certificate, CAs are responsible for maintaining a highly available service for disseminating revocation information. In this section, we turn our study towards the CAs by investigating the characteristics of the distribution mechanisms they make available.

5.1 Availability of Revocation Information

We briefly explore how the inclusion of revocation information in certificates has evolved in Figure 4, where we plot the fraction of new certificates that contain potentially reachable CRL distribution points or OCSP responders each month. We observe that CRLs have been included in almost all certificates issued over the past four years, but that OCSP was slower to be adopted (unsurprisingly, as it was standardized much later than CRLs). Moreover, we observe a "spike" in the prevalence of OCSP information in July 2012, corresponding to the adoption of OCSP by RapidSSL (a low-cost CA owned by GeoTrust).

These encouraging results show that, today, both forms of revocation are included in nearly all certificates. Unfortunately, both of these schemes have their shortcomings: CRLs impose bandwidth burdens (which we investigate later in this section), and having to query an OCSP responder imposes slower page-load times for browsers. As a result, there has been push-back from both the CA and browser communities. Unfortunately, as we demonstrated in the previous section, OCSP Stapling is still only deployed on a small fraction of web servers.

5.2 Size of Revocation Information

One of the common criticisms of CRLs is the network traffic required to download them. We now examine the sizes of CRLs, and how this has evolved over time.

Recall that CRLs contain one entry for each certificate that is revoked. Thus, the size of the CRL (in bytes) is expected to correlate with the number of entries. We plot this correlation as a scatterplot in Figure 5, and observe a strong linear relationship (except for CRLs with just a few entries, which have some fixed overhead).[11] On average, each entry is 38 bytes.

Figure 5 suggests that most CRLs are small. We explore this trend further in Figure 6, which presents the CDF of CRL sizes as the *Raw* line. We immediately observe that half of all CRLs are under 900 B. However, this statistic is deceiving: if you select a certificate at random from the Leaf

[11] The variance between CRL sizes at the same number of entries is largely due to differences in serial number assignment policies for different CAs; some CAs use serial numbers of up to 49 decimal digits, which results in larger CRL file sizes.

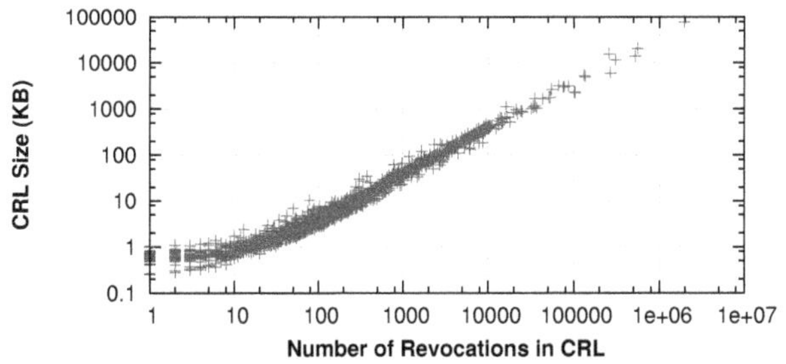

Figure 5: Scatterplot of the number of entries in CRLs versus CRL file size, for all 2,800 CRLs we crawled. As expected, a linear correlation is observed.

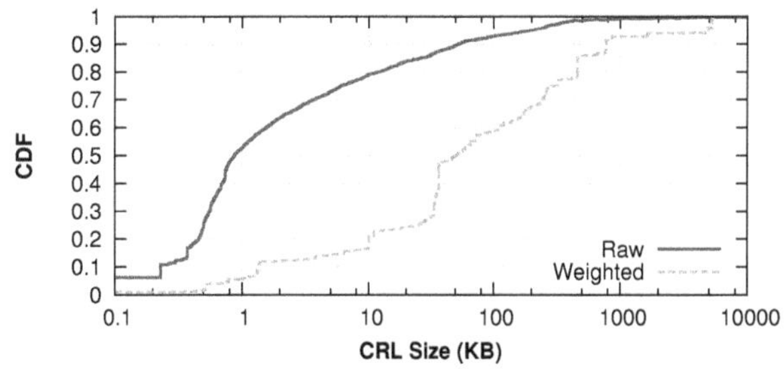

Figure 6: Cumulative distribution of the sizes of CRLs (shown under the *raw* line). Most CRLs are small (median size is less than 1 KB), but most CRLs cover few certificates. The *weighted* distribution shows the CRL size distribution across certificates; in this case, the mean certificate has a CRL size of 51 KB.

Set, it is unlikely to point to a tiny CRL, since the tiny CRLs cover very few certificates. To adjust for this issue, we plot the CRL size *per certificate* as the *Weighted* distribution in Figure 6.[12] The Weighted distribution tells a different story: the CRL size for the median certificate is 51 KB, and we observe CRLs ranging up to 76 MB.[13] Although one can argue that weighing CRLs is unfair (as clients can cache them), 95% of CRLs expire in less than 24 hours [52], reducing a client's ability to save bandwidth through caching.

One mechanism that CAs can use to reduce the size of CRLs is to maintain multiple CRLs [20], assigning only a subset of all issued certificates to each CRL. We explore the extent to which different CAs do this in Table 1, and observe that, in general, CAs use only a small number of CRLs. The CA that uses this technique to the largest extent is GoDaddy with 322 unique CRLs, but given the large number of GoDaddy revocations, their average certificate's CRL is still over 1MB in size. Moreover, the trend is not entirely consistent, as various CA policies will affect the resulting CRL size.[14]

Our findings confirm that fetching CRLs can be an expensive operation for clients, especially ones on bandwidth-constrained networks (e.g., mobile devices). Moreover, properly verifying a certificate requires the client to download the CRL before fully establishing the SSL connection; thus, for interactive applications like web browsers, downloading the CRL also comes with a latency penalty. The large size of CRLs is especially glaring when compared to the size of an OCSP query and response (which is typically less than 1 KB and often comes with a latency penalty under 250 ms [33]).

5.3 Summary

Overall, our results show that, while there are potentially high costs involved in disseminating revocation information, many CAs have not widely adopted smaller CRLs. Combined with the lack of wide OCSP Stapling adoption, we see that there are multiple opportunities to significantly lower the costs incurred by CAs and browsers when obtaining certificate revocation information.

[12]For certificates that have multiple CRLs, we pick the smallest.

[13]The 76 MB CRL is hosted by Apple at `http://crl.apple.com/wwdrca.crl` and contains over 2.6 million revoked certificates.

[14]One notable example in the table is StartCom, which has an outsized average CRL size relative to the number of revocations. This is due to a single CRL (`http://www.startssl.com/crt1-crl.crl`) that is over 22 MB and has over 290 K revocations. This CRL is for StartSSL "Free" certificates that, after a year of validity, *require* customers to revoke an expiring certificate (at a fee of $24.90) before a new certificate for the same domain will be reissued [45].

6. CLIENT BEHAVIOR

Recall that the burden of certificate validation is placed entirely on the client: it is up to the client to check the validity of the presented certificate chain and to obtain revocation information from CAs to make sure that none of the certificates have been revoked. We now explore the extent to which the most popular SSL clients—web browsers—do so. Because web browser developers care deeply about minimizing latency, and (as we observed above) checking certificate revocation information can take significant effort, web browser developers have a strong tension between minimizing latency and ensuring security.

6.1 Methodology

Our goal is to build a test harness that is able to determine whether a web browser chooses to check certificate revocation information for a variety of different kinds of certificates and chains. Ideally, we would like to use real certificates, but doing so would require obtaining access to a real intermediate certificate (an unlikely prospect). Instead, we generate our own root certificate and install it so that the web browser trusts it. This allows us to then generate and sign intermediate and leaf certificates as we wish.

We build a test suite that covers many combinations of chain length, protocols, etc. For each test, we generate a *unique* set of certificates (i.e., the intermediates and leaf certificates are not re-used across tests, in order to eliminate caching effects). Each intermediate contains a unique subject name, and each leaf contains a unique common name. Each test is served by a dedicated Nginx web server. When generating test cases, we consider four different dimensions:

CA	Unique CRLs	Certificates Total	Certificates Revoked	Avg. CRL size (KB)
GoDaddy	322	1,050,014	277,500	1,184.0
RapidSSL	5	626,774	2,153	34.5
Comodo	30	447,506	7,169	517.6
PositiveSSL	3	415,075	8,177	441.3
GeoTrust	27	335,380	3,081	12.9
Verisign	37	311,788	15,438	205.2
Thawte	32	278,563	4,446	25.4
GlobalSign	26	247,819	24,242	2,050.0
StartCom	17	236,776	1,752	240.5

Table 1: Number of CRLs, certificates (total and revoked), and the average CRL size per certificate for the largest CAs.

		Desktop Browsers										Mobile Browsers			
		Chrome 44			Firefox	Opera		Safari	IE			iOS	Andr. 4.1–5.1		IE
		OS X	Win.	Lin.	40	12.17	31.0	6–8	7–9	10	11	6–8	Stock	Chrome	8.0
CRL															
Int. 1	Revoked	EV	✓	EV	✗	✓	✓	✓	✓	✓	✓	✗	✗	✗	✗
	Unavailable	EV	✓	–	✗	✗	✓	✓	✓	✓	✓	✗	✗	✗	✗
Int. 2+	Revoked	EV	EV	EV	✗	✓	✓	✓	✓	✓	✓	✗	✗	✗	✗
	Unavailable	✗	✗	–	✗	✗	✗	✗	✗	✗	✗	✗	✗	✗	✗
Leaf	Revoked	EV	EV	EV	✗	✓	✓	✓	✓	✓	✓	✗	✗	✗	✗
	Unavailable	✗	✗	–	✗	✗	✗	✗	✗	A	✓	✗	✗	✗	✗
OCSP															
Int. 1	Revoked	EV	EV	EV	EV	✗	✓	✓	✓	✓	✓	✗	✗	✗	✗
	Unavailable	✗	✗	–	✗	✗	L/W	✗	✓	✓	✓	✗	✗	✗	✗
Int. 2+	Revoked	EV	EV	EV	EV	✗	✓	✓	✓	✓	✓	✗	✗	✗	✗
	Unavailable	✗	✗	–	✗	✗	✗	✗	✗	✗	✗	✗	✗	✗	✗
Leaf	Revoked	EV	EV	EV	✓	✓	✓	✓	✓	✓	✓	✗	✗	✗	✗
	Unavailable	✗	✗	–	✗	✗	✗	✗	✗	A	✓	✗	✗	✗	✗
Reject `unknown` status		✗	✗	–	✓	✓	✗	✗	✗	✗	✗	–	–	–	–
Try CRL on failure		EV	EV	–	✗	✗	L/W	✓	✓	✓	✓	–	–	–	–
OCSP Stapling															
Request OCSP staple		✓	✓	✓	✓	✓	✓	✗	✓	✓	✓	✗	I	I	✗
Respect `revoked` staple		✗	✓	–	✓	✓	L/W	–	✓	✓	✓	–	–	–	–

Table 2: Browser test results, when intermediate (Int.) and leaf certificates are either revoked or have revocation information unavailable. ✓ means browser passes test in all cases; ✗ means browser fails test in all cases. Other keys include EV (browser passes only for EV certificates), L/W (browser passes only on Linux and Windows), A (browser pops up an alert), and I (browser requests OCSP staple but ignores the response).

Chain Length. Recall that a certificate chain starts at a root certificate, has 0 or more intermediates, and finally contains a leaf certificate. As certificate chains get longer (i.e., more intermediates), revocation checking becomes more expensive for the client. We therefore generate tests that contain between 0 and 3 intermediate certificates (between 2 and 5 total certificates, including the root and leaf), with separate tests where each element of the chain is revoked.

Revocation Protocol. Browsers may treat different revocation protocols differently, so we generate some certificate chains that only contain CRL information and others that only contain OCSP information (i.e., for each chain, all certificates contain *either* CRL distribution points or OCSP responders), as well as some chains that contain both. We also implement tests where the server is configured to perform OCSP Stapling if the client requests it.[15,16]

Extended Validation. Browsers may have special rules for EV certificates, so we generate additional tests where the leaf certificate contains an object identifier (OID) indicating that it is an EV certificate.[17]

Unavailable Revocation Information. Finally, if the browser is unable to fetch certificate revocation information (e.g., the OCSP responder or CRL server is down), the browser must choose whether or not to accept the certificate or to try and obtain revocation information using a different protocol. We generate additional tests where the revocation information is unavailable due to four different failures: the domain name of the revocation server does not exist, the revocation server returns a HTTP 404 error code, the revocation server does not respond, or the OCSP responder generates a response with status `unknown`.

Considering all possible combinations, the result is a suite of 244 different tests. When running tests, we also capture network traces to examine the SSL handshake and communication with revocation servers.

6.2 Test Suite Implementation

We implement our test suite with a script that, for each test, (1) generates a unique DNS name, (2) uses OpenSSL to generate a certificate chain and CRLs, (3) configures OpenSSL OCSP responders[18] (if OCSP is used), and (4) generates an Nginx server configuration for the test. Thus, each test has a dedicated DNS name, Nginx instance to serve the certificate chain, and set of OCSP responders.

We create a web page containing JavaScript that iteratively tries to fetch a file from each test's domain using XHRs.[19] If the browser determines that one of the certificates has been revoked, the file fails to load and our script gets an error callback. Thus, we can programmatically determine the tests where the browser checks the revocation status of different certificates.

6.3 Desktop Browsers

We begin by examining the behavior of popular desktop web browsers. For each browser/OS combination, we create

[15] In this case, the OCSP responder is firewalled from the client, so the only way the client can access the revocation information is via the stapled OCSP response.

[16] By default, Nginx refuses to staple an OCSP response that contains the status `revoked` or `unknown`. We modified Nginx to disable this behavior.

[17] We use OID 2.16.840.1.113733.1.7.23.6, an OID used by Verisign to distinguish EV certificates.

[18] By default, the OpenSSL OCSP responder implementation only supports `POST` OCSP queries; we modified it to also support the more commonly used `GET` queries.

[19] Our Nginx instances were configured to enable CORS.

a distinct virtual machine (VM), configured with the default settings. Our only VM configuration was to install our root certificate.[20] Unless otherwise stated, all tests were done on Ubuntu 14.04, Windows 8.1, and OS X 10.10.2. Overall, we tested 30 different combinations of OS and browser; our results are summarized in Table 2.

Chrome. Chrome uses the Mozilla NSS library [1] for SSL connection establishment, but it uses platform-specific libraries for certificate validation [3]. Because Chrome aggressively auto-updates (i.e., it checks for new versions every few days), we only test with the latest version of Chrome (44.0).

On OS X, Chrome treats EV and non-EV certificates differently. For non-EV certificates, Chrome does not check any revocation information. For EV certificates, Chrome checks all elements of the chain (using either CRLs or OCSP responders). Chrome does request OCSP staples, but Chrome *does not* respect OCSP staples with the status of `revoked` (instead, it attempts to contact the OCSP responder), and it incorrectly treats OCSP responses with the `unknown` status as trusted. When certificate revocation information is unavailable, Chrome does try to fetch revocation information from the CRL if the OCSP responder is not available. If revocation information is still unavailable, Chrome only rejects the chain if the first intermediate's CRL is unavailable *and* the leaf is an EV certificate. Otherwise, Chrome silently accepts the certificate.

On Windows, Chrome also treats EV and non-EV certificates differently. For non-EV certificates, Chrome *only* checks the first intermediate in the chain, and *only* if it only has a CRL listed (Chrome does not check any non-EV OCSP responders). For EV certificates, Chrome checks the revocation status of all elements of the chain, both OCSP and CRLs. Additionally, Chrome requests OCSP staples on Windows for all certificates. Chrome's behavior when certificate revocation information is unavailable or when the revocation status is `unknown` is the same as above, except that it rejects the chain for non-EV certificates as well.

On Linux, we were able to import our root certificate, but we were unable to get Chrome to use our root certificate to verify CRL or OCSP signatures (i.e., we observed that Chrome would request the same certificate revocation information multiple times). As a result, we rely on packet traces to measure Chrome's behavior, and are unable to test Chrome with unavailable revocation information or different OCSP response statuses. Overall, we found that Chrome's behavior is largely consistent with the other platforms: it only checks CRLs and OCSP responders for EV certificates, and does request OCSP staples.

In addition to the distribution mechanisms analyzed in this section, Chrome also has a built-in list of revoked certificates called the CRLSet; we explore CRLSets in more detail in §7.

Firefox. Firefox uses Mozilla's NSS library [1]. We tested the most recent version of Firefox (40.0) and found it to have the same behavior on all platforms.[21] Firefox does not check *any* CRLs. For OCSP, Firefox treats EV and non-EV certificates differently: for Non-EV certificates, Firefox only queries the OCSP responder of the leaf certificate. For EV certificates, Firefox checks all OCSP responders. Firefox correctly rejects OCSP responses with the `unknown` status, but does not try to fetch the CRL if the OCSP responder is not available. Instead, if the revocation information is not available, Firefox accepts the certificate. Firefox does request OCSP staples.

Opera. In mid-2013, Opera re-architected its browser: up through version 12.17, Opera used its own rendering engine; for all versions afterwards, Opera uses a fork of the Chromium project. These two versions have different behavior, and we examine them separately.

On Opera 12.17, the behavior is consistent across all OSes. Opera checks the revocation information for all certificates in the chain if they have CRLs listed, but only the leaf certificate if the certificates have OCSP responders listed. If certificate revocation information is not available, Opera accepts the certificate. Opera correctly rejects OCSP responses with the `unknown` status, and requests OCSP staples on all platforms.

On Opera 31.0, the behavior is largely consistent across all OSes: Opera checks all certificates in the chain when certificates have CRLs or OCSP responders listed. If the revocation information is not available for the first intermediate certificate (or the leaf certificate if no intermediates exist), Opera rejects the certificate on all platforms (if using CRLs) and only on Linux and Windows (if using OCSP); in all other cases, Opera accepts the certificate. Opera incorrectly treats OCSP responses with the `unknown` status as trusted. Opera requests OCSP staples on all platforms; however, on OS X (similar to Chrome) Opera does not respect `revoked` staples and attempts to contact the OCSP responder directly.

Safari. We examined the three most recent major versions of Safari (6.0–8.0) and found them all to have the same behavior.[22] Safari checks all certificates in the chain using CRLs or OCSP. Safari incorrectly treats OCSP responses with the `unknown` status as trusted. Safari does attempt to fetch the CRL if the OCSP responder is unavailable. If the revocation information is not available for the first intermediate certificate (or the leaf certificate, if there are no intermediates) and the certificate has a CRL, Safari rejects the certificate; in all other cases, it accepts the certificate. Safari *does not* request OCSP staples.

OS X offers system-wide settings via Keychain Access that allow users to change certificate revocation checking behavior. The default behavior, which we used in our above analysis, is referred to as "Best attempt". If a user selects "Require if certificate indicates", Safari does indeed reject all chains where any of the revocation information is unavailable.

Internet Explorer. We tested every major version of Internet Explorer (IE) between 7.0 (on Vista) to 11.0 (on Windows 10, 8.1, and 7). We found that the behavior of IE changed between version 9.0 and 10.0, and again with IE 11.0; we therefore consider them separately.

[20]We must create separate VMs for each browser/OS, as some browsers use system-wide libraries and daemons for checking revocation information, which can lead to caching effects at the OS level.

[21]Firefox contains a hardcoded list of root certificates that are allowed to issue EV certificates. We recompiled Firefox 40.0 after adding our root certificate to Firefox's list.

[22]We observed strange behavior with the most recent Safari/OS X update (8.0.5/10.0.3). With this update, Safari does not check *any* CRLs and only checks OCSP responders for EV certificates. The release notes do not mention any SSL policy changes, so we believe this behavior to be a bug; we have filed a bug report with Apple.

On IE 7.0–9.0, IE checks all certificates in the chain for both CRLs and OCSP responders. If the OCSP responder is unavailable, IE does download the CRL. If the revocation information is not available for the first certificate in the chain, IE rejects the certificate; in all other cases, IE accepts the certificate. IE incorrectly treats OCSP responses with the `unknown` status as trusted. IE does request OCSP staples.

On IE 10.0, IE has the same behavior except that when revocation information is not available for the *leaf* certificate, IE pops up a warning to the user and asks them if they wish to proceed.

On IE 11.0, IE has the same behavior except that when revocation information is not available for the *leaf* certificate, IE correctly rejects the certificate without popping up a warning.

In summary, we observe that *no* browser in its default configuration correctly checks all revocations and rejects certificates if revocation information is unavailable (as described in §2.2). In fact, many browsers do not bother to check revocation information at all. Overall, Internet Explorer performs the most checks, followed closely by Safari and newer versions of Opera.

We also found that many browsers do not correctly interpret `unknown` OCSP responses, not all browsers support OCSP Stapling, and many do not understand `revoked` staples. This is surprising, as OCSP Stapling is the most efficient way of obtaining certificate revocation information, and it imposes almost no extra latency on clients.

6.4 Mobile Browsers

Next, we study the certificate revocation checking behavior of browsers on mobile devices. To make the tests easier to conduct, we use the device simulators provided by the OS vendors where possible, rather than physical devices. These simulators run a full version of the mobile OS, allowing us to easily test multiple versions.

iOS. We begin by checking the behavior of Mobile Safari on iOS. We used the Xcode-based iOS simulator to test iOS 7 and 8, and use a physical iPhone 3GS device for iOS 6.[23] We observe that Mobile Safari does not check *any* certificate revocation information, nor does it request OCSP staples.

Android. We test the certificate revocation checking behavior of Android by using the Android Emulator. We test the "stock" Browser app and Chrome on the three most recent versions of Android: Lollipop (5.1), KitKat (4.4), and Jelly Bean (4.3). Similar to iOS, we find that neither application checks *any* certificate revocation information. However, by examining the network traffic, we found that both applications *do* request OCSP staples, but *do not* use them in certificate validation. Even when served an OCSP staple with status `revoked`, both applications validate the certificate and continue with the connection.

We also attempted to test the Android port of the Firefox browser, but were unable to successfully import our root certificate into the application.

Windows Phone. Finally, we tested the mobile version of IE running on Windows Phone 8.0 using the Windows Phone Emulator. Mobile IE performs identically to all other tested browsers, not checking revocation information and not requesting OCSP staples.

[23]The iPhone simulator for iOS 6 does not provide an option for installing root certificates.

Overall, our results on mobile devices are disheartening. Despite the increasing fraction of web traffic that is generated by these devices, *none* of the major web browsers bother to check whether any certificates they are presented with are revoked. This design decision is likely driven by the higher cost (in terms of latency and power) of obtaining revocation information on a mobile device [20]. However, this decision does not excuse the universal lack of proper OCSP Stapling support, as requesting OCSP staples for the leaf certificate requires the client to create no additional connections.

6.5 Summary

If clients do not fetch *and respect* revocation information, the revocation efforts of website administrators and CAs are wasted. To analyze client behavior, this section presented our test suite, and the results from all major desktop and mobile browsers. While we see widely disparate behavior—often even among the same browser on different platforms—we find that *no browser* meets all necessary criteria for revocation checking. Moreover, we empirically demonstrate the extent to which EV certificates are validated differently. Perhaps most concerning is the fact that no mobile browsers check for revocations *at all.*

For desktop browsers, it is difficult to determine whether the absence of revocation checking is an explicit design decision or a set of common bugs. For mobile browsers, on the other hand, we believe the complete lack of revocation checking is an explicit decision to conserve users' bandwidth.

7. CRLSETS

In response to the cost of obtaining revocation information, Google adopted an additional approach in 2013 called *CRLSets* [26]. Chrome checks a small, pre-populated list of revoked certificates. This list is updated and sent to clients out-of-band, thus eliminating the cost of checking revocation information at page load time.

In this section, we characterize CRLSets and investigate their impact on security in the face of revocations. While CRLSets currently affect only users of the Chrome browser, this approach has recently been adopted by Firefox in the OneCRL [41] project[24], so understanding the implications of this approach can have a significant impact on a large number of web users.

7.1 Overview and Methodology

The high-level CRLSet approach is documented [2], but the process used for generating them is not public. Importantly, the developers state that: (1) the size of the CRLSet file is capped at 250 KB; (2) they populate it using an "internal list of crawled CRLs" (some of which are not public) fetched on the order of hours; (3) if a CRL has too many entries it will be dropped from the CRLSet; and (4) revocations are included only if they use one of a small number of reason codes[25] (we refer to these as *CRLSet reason codes*).

CRLSet files are published to a public URL and fetched periodically by Chrome. We fetched these files once per

[24]In contrast to CRLSets, OneCRL is for intermediate certificates. As of this writing, there are only 8 revoked certificates on the list.

[25]No reason code, Unspecified, KeyCompromise, CACompromise, or AACompromise

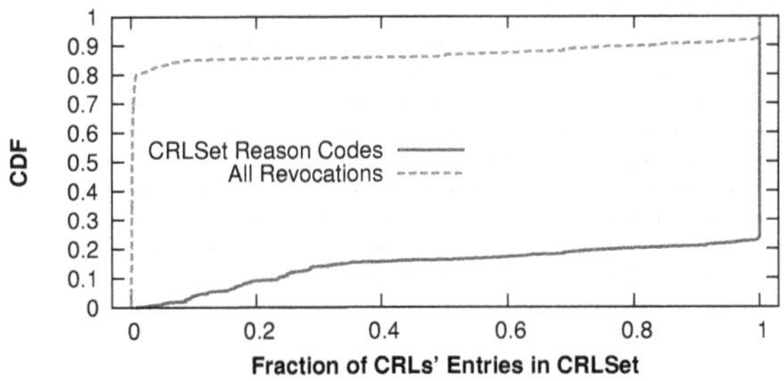

Figure 7: Cumulative distribution of the fraction of a CRL's entries that appear in CRLSets. Also shown are just those entries that have CRLSet reason codes. Most certificates with "valid" reasons are included the CRLSet, but most CRL entries overall are missing.

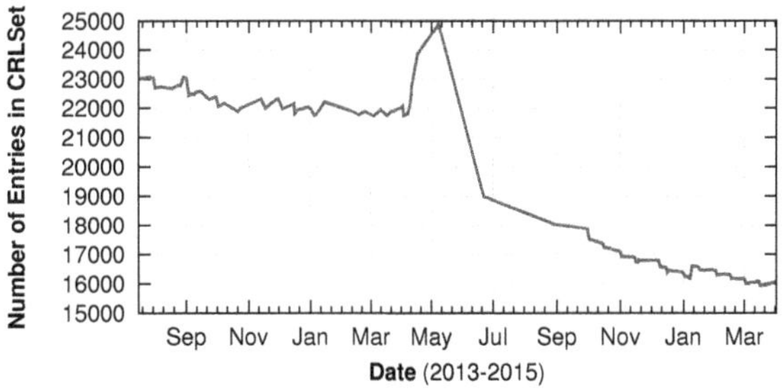

Figure 8: Number of entries in the CRLSet over time (note that the y-axis does not start at 0). The peak of nearly 25,000 entries is due to the Heartbleed vulnerability; since then the size of the CRLSet has decreased over time by more than a third.

day between September 23, 2014 and March 31, 2015, and crawled 110 historical CRLSets originally published between July 18th, 2013 and September 23, 2014; in total our dataset contains 300 unique CRLSets. CRLSets are internally organized as a list of key/value pairs, where the key is the SHA256 of the certificate issuer's public key (which we call the *parent*), and the values for that key are all the serial numbers of revoked certificates signed by that parent.[26]

Mapping a revoked certificate in a CRLSet to a CRL is nontrivial because CAs can have multiple signing certificates, public keys, and CRLs. When comparing CRLSet entries with CRLs (using the data described in §3.2), we compare the entries in the CRLSet for each parent with the entries in *all* CRLs for certificates signed by that parent.

7.2 CRLSet Coverage

We first determine the fraction of CAs covered by CRLSets. In our CRL dataset, we see 2,168 CA certificates (both intermediate and root) with 1,584 distinct public keys. In CRLSets, we observe 62 unique parents. Thus, CRLSets cover revocations for only 3.9% of CA certificates.[27] Of those 62, we can only map 52 to a CA certificate that we know of; the remainder are likely from non-public CA certificates.

Next, we investigate how entries in CRLSets compare with those in CRLs. Across all CRLs we crawled, we observe 11,461,935 revoked certificates; only 41,105 of these appear in CRLSets. Thus, only 0.35% of all revoked certificates ever appear in the CRLSet. Additionally, of the 2,800 total CRLs we observed, only 295 (10.5%) have ever had *any* entry appear in a CRLSet (this number is larger than the number of parents, as a given parent can sign multiple CRLs). We refer to these CRLs as *covered CRLs.*

Covered CRLs. For the covered CRLs, we examine the fraction of their entries that appear in the CRLSet. Figure 7 presents the cumulative distribution of CRLSet coverage across covered CRLs. Since the Chromium project states that only revocations with a certain reason codes will appear in the CRLSet, we also plot the cumulative distribution of coverage only for entries with CRLSet reason codes as well.

We find that for 75.6% of covered CRLs, *all* entries with CRLSet reason codes appear in the CRLSet. For the remaining CRLs, we find that the number of entries with CRLSet reason codes missing ranges from 1 to 5,826 (the latter comes from Verisign's "International EV" CRL, making it especially strange). Overall, we observe that for most covered CRLs, CRLSets provide perfect coverage; however, there are many CRLs for which CRLSets provide only partial coverage.

Un-covered Revocations. We now address the question of what certificates are *not* included in CRLSets. While there are millions of revoked certificates that do not appear in CRLSets, we focus on those that belong to popular websites, since they will impact the largest fraction of Internet traffic. Across all Alexa top one million domains, we see 42,225 revocations in CRLs, but only 1,644 (3.9%) in CRLSets. If we focus on the Alexa top 1,000 domains, we see 392 revoked certificates, but only 41 (10.4%) ever appear in CRLSets. Thus, unless these sites use EV certificates (which cause Chrome to perform the revocation checks described above), certificates presented by the many of the most popular domains are left unchecked by Chrome's CRLSets.

7.3 CRLSet Dynamics

We now examine CRLSet dynamics, and begin by investigating how the CRLSet size changes over time. Figure 8 shows that the number of entries in CRLSets ranges from 15,922 to 24,904, with the peak corresponding to the Heartbleed vulnerability, followed by a decrease over the following year. The significant decrease in May–June 2014 is largely explained by the removal of the "VeriSign Class 3 Extended Validation" parent (and its 5,774 entries) from the CRLSet, and general downward trend corresponds with the behavior of the underlying CRLs.

To better understand the dynamics of CRLSet entries, we zoom in on the number of entries added and removed from the CRLSet each day, and limit ourselves to the time period of October 1, 2014 to March 31, 2015 where we have daily scans of both CRLSet files and CRL entries. Figure 9 shows this, using a log scale on the y-axis. We observe that CRLs exhibit weekly patterns, with increased activity during the week and lulls during the weekend. We also observe that CRLSets are updated frequently, but there is a noticeable

[26]CRLSets also include a small set of leaf certificates that are explicitly blocked based on their public key; this list is called `BlockedSPKIs`. The list current contains 11 such certificates. Curiously, Chrome 44.0 declares these certificates as revoked in the URL Status Bar, but still completes the connection and renders the page. For an example, please see `https://revoked.grc.com/` and the corresponding discussion [8]. We have filed a bug with the Chrome developers regarding this behavior.

[27]We cannot say precisely what fraction of *CAs* are represented in CRLSets, as CAs often have many keys.

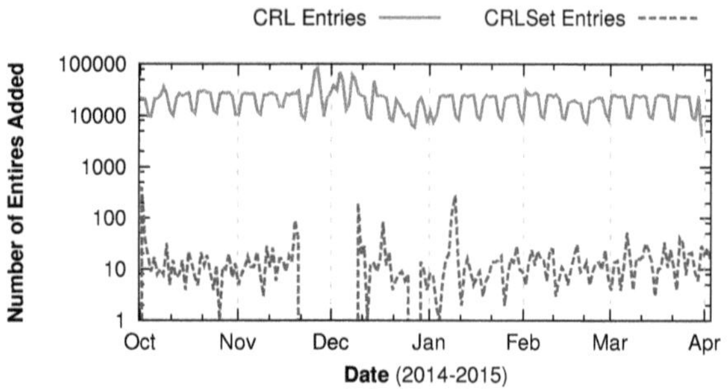

Figure 9: Number of daily new revocations appearing in CRLs (upper line) and CRLSets (lower line). CRL additions show weekly patterns and are much larger than CRLSet additions. For two weeks in late 2014, we observed no additions to CRLSets.

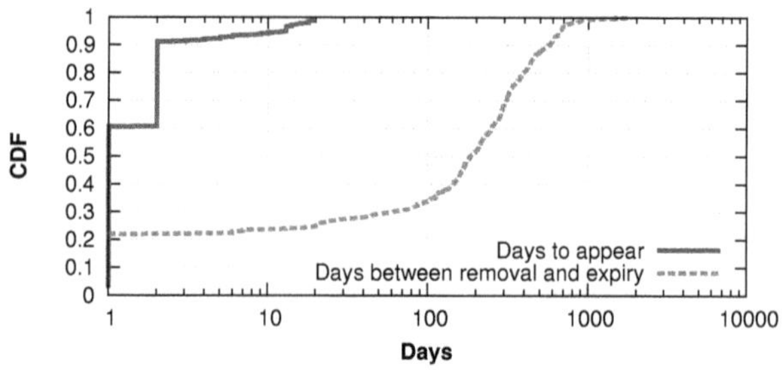

Figure 10: Number of days that clients are vulnerable to revoked certificates using CRLSets. Revoked certificates on covered CRLs are added quickly (within a day), but many revoked certificates are removed from the CRLSet well before they expire.

gap with no additions in November–December 2014. Otherwise we observe no direct correlation between peaks/troughs in CRL and CRLSet updates, consistent with the fact that CRLSets track only a small subset of the CRLs.

Lastly, we focus on the *security impact* of CRLSet dynamics, specifically for the set of revocations that appear in *both* CRLs and CRLSets. We focus on periods of time when a certificate appears in a CRL but not in the CRLSet (687 cases in our dataset), or was removed from a CRLSet before the revoked certificate expired (629 cases in our dataset). We refer to these as periods of *vulnerability*. Figure 10 shows this using the cumulative distribution of days of vulnerability over all certificates that appeared in CRLSets. We find that most revoked certificates appear in the CRLSets within one day (60%), and more than 90% appear within two days. This suggests that an automated process pulls CRL data into CRLSets, and thus there is a relatively small window of vulnerability after a revocation occurs.[28]

However, we observe that revoked certificates are sometimes removed from the CRLSet hundreds of days before they expire. This result is due to the significant decrease in CRLSet size seen in Figure 8. In one case, a revoked CA cert was removed from the CRLSet that is valid until the year 2020. In the median case, revocations are removed from CRLSets *187 days* before the certificate expires.

7.4 Improving CRLSets: Bloom Filters

As we have shown, Google's CRLSet implementation has very low coverage. An alternative data structure that could hold more revocations while also obeying Google's strict size constraints is a Bloom Filter [4]. A Bloom Filter has the advantage of no false negatives (if a certificate is revoked, it will be flagged as revoked by the filter); however, it will produce a tunable false positive rate (a non-revoked certificate may be flagged as revoked). Thus, when a certificate "hits" the filter, the client would need to check a CRL before flagging the connection as insecure. Although checking CRLs introduces lag, this lag would only impact performance for false positives (since true positives should be blocked anyway). Also note that the size of the Bloom Filter would depend on the number of revoked certificates (which is relatively easy to determine), not the number of fresh, issued certificates (which is unknown and much, much larger).

[28]Note that this does not take into account the time it takes to push updated CRLSets to clients, which may add to the window of vulnerability.

As a proof-of-concept, we briefly analyze the characteristics of a Bloom Filter-based revocation list. As shown in Figure 11, we examine the trade-offs between filter size m, the number of revoked certificates inserted into the filter n, and false positive rate p. The number of hash functions k is calculated using the optimal formula $k = \lceil \frac{m}{n} * \log 2 \rceil$.

Figure 11 highlights the advantages of our Bloom Filter-based implementation over CRLSet. The grey region shows the minimum and maximum revocations covered by CRLSets over time. For the same maximum file size (256 KB), our Bloom Filter can store an order of magnitude more revocations with only a 1% false positive rate (i.e., instances where the CRL would be checked to avoid actually blocking the connection). If we use a filter that is 2 MB in size, we can cover 1.7 million revocations at this false positive rate; this represents 15% of all revocations across all CRLs in our dataset.

The results of this analysis are similar to the examination of the suitability of Bloom Filters for distributing revocation information conducted by Langley [25]; Bloom Filters show significant promise as a mechanism for dramatically increasing the coverage of CRLSets at little cost to clients. In fact, Langley suggests that using a variant of Bloom Filters called Golomb Compressed Sets [17] may serve to reduce the space requirements even more.

7.5 Summary

To summarize, we find that CRLSets have limited coverage, their coverage of revoked certificates is diminishing over time, they are updated frequently but experience outages, and they leave browsers vulnerable to unexpired revoked certificates. While the CRLSet approach has a number of

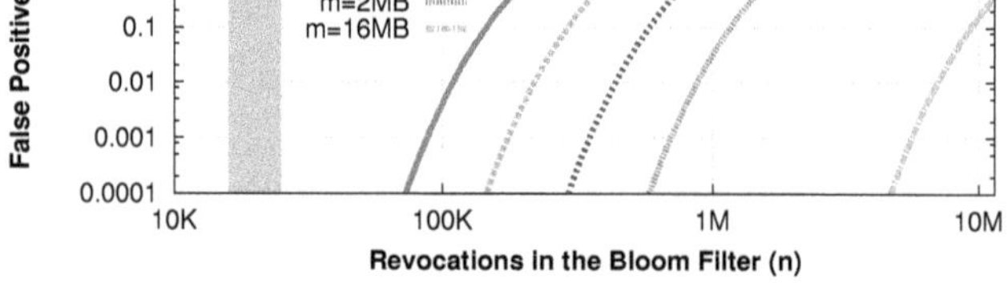

Figure 11: Number of revocations that would fit in Bloom Filters of various sizes, compared to CRLSets of today.

benefits to users, it is clear that the developers have chosen to provide security only for a small fraction of sites in order to decrease the amount of bandwidth required to disseminate revocation information; this leaves the vast majority of popular sites uncovered.

8. RELATED WORK

SSL Certificate Ecosystem. There has been a long thread of work that examines the SSL certificate ecosystem, ranging from the contents of different browser/OS root stores [36,50] to the trust relationships between CAs [14] and the patterns of certificates advertised by servers [22]. While Durumeric et al. [14] briefly examine certificate revocation in their study, our work builds on theirs by examining the dynamics of revocation behavior, different revocation protocols, and the cost of obtaining revocation information.

Researchers have proposed ideas to reduce the level of trust placed in CAs. Significant recent work has gone into increasing the transparency of the SSL ecosystem [24, 29, 30, 39, 43], ideally leading to better accountability. For example, the Certificate Transparency Project [29] introduces public logs to monitor all certificates issued by CAs. Others have proposed alternate architectures to the current CA-based system [9,12,47], often requiring modifications to both servers and clients. The DANE [47] proposal, for example, allows the owner of a DNS domain to distribute their public keys via DNS itself (thereby obviating the need for SSL certificates), while relying on DNSSEC to secure the binding.

Studying and Improving Revocations. There has been significant debate over the actual effectiveness of certificate revocation in practice [27, 28, 32], and researchers have attempted to improve the certificate revocation process and dissemination mechanisms. For example, there are proposals for very short certificate lifetimes [46], ideally making revoking a certificate as easy as not renewing it. Alternatively, Schulman et al. [42] proposed a broadcast system that disseminates revocation data over FM radio.

Two recent security incidents (a Debian vulnerability and the Heartbleed bug) provided opportunities to study whether site operators who should revoke their certificates actually do [13, 51, 52]. The results are disheartening, as only around 10% of vulnerable certificates were correctly revoked. Our work is complementary: we look at a larger set of certificates over a longer period of time, we investigate the burden that disseminating revocation information has on CAs, and explore when clients obtain this information.

Client-side Certificate Validation. Finally, much work has gone into understanding client-side behavior when creating SSL connections. Recent work has shown that many pieces of non-browser software do not correctly implement SSL checks, often due to mis-use of SSL APIs [18,19]. Others have shown that the SSL libraries themselves are buggy [10]. Because browsers often ask users whether or not to proceed when the SSL connection is suspicious, other work has focused on how browsers present warnings and how users react [6, 7]. Taken together, these results show that correctly implementing SSL validation is difficult to get right; our results show that this situation is further complicated by browsers that decline to check revocation information at all.

The GRC browser revocation test [21] is similar to our "test suite", but ours is much more comprehensive (the GRC test only contains a single certificate). As a result, our conclusions differ: while Firefox performed well on their test, we found that Firefox fails in other configurations of certificate chains/revocation protocols.

9. CONCLUDING DISCUSSION

Certificate revocation is a necessary component of any PKI, but it comes with costs, both real and perceived: CAs carry the cost of disseminating revocation information, while browsers risk the cost of increased web page load times. In the trade-off between low communication overheads and security, both ends of certificate revocation (those who issue and those who fetch) are naturally tempted towards the former. Indeed, the very utility of revocations has been debated and doubted [28] by the security community, but to date, these debates have had to largely depend on anecdotal CA and browser behavior.

We have presented in this paper an empirical measurement of the options at all parties' disposal—website administrators, CAs, and browsers—in terms of the communication overhead costs they impose and the extent to which they are currently being employed.

Overall, our results show that, in today's Web's PKI, there is extensive inaction with respect to certificate revocation. While many certificates are revoked (over 8% of fresh certificates and almost 1% of alive certificates), many web browsers either fail to check certificate revocation information or soft-fail by accepting a certificate if revocation information is unavailable.

On the positive side, our results also demonstrate that there are several clear paths to improvement. To reduce CRL sizes, CAs can simply maintain more, smaller CRLs (in the extreme, each certificate could be assigned a unique CRL, resulting in an approximation of OCSP)—surprisingly few CAs currently take such an approach (§5) and therefore incur greater bandwidth costs than strictly necessary. A promising improvement is OCSP Stapling, as it reduces CA bandwidth costs as well as web page load times—yet, not all browsers support it, and some that do simply ignore the responses. A more pervasive deployment of OCSP Stapling, at both websites and browsers, could lead to an immediate improvement in user security at little additional performance cost, particularly if the Multiple OCSP Staple Extension [37] were adopted to allow intermediate certificates to be stapled. Finally, we show that a straightforward modification to CRLSets could increase their coverage by several orders of magnitude.

From these results, we conclude that certificate revocation ought not be given up on—that indeed it serves a critical yet overlooked role that, with proper support from all parties, can be achieved at a cost far outweighed by the benefits. To realize this, we believe continued measurement and validation of future browsers will be of utmost importance, and to this end have made our data and our browser test suite publicly available at `http://www.sslresearch.org`

Acknowledgments

We thank the anonymous reviewers for their helpful comments. This research was supported by NSF grants CNS-1054233, CNS-1409191, CNS-1319019, CNS-1421444, and CNS-1345284, by USAF award FA8750-14-2-0150, and by the NSA as part of a Science of Security lablet.

10. REFERENCES

[1] Network Security Services. Mozilla Developer Network, 2014. http://mzl.la/1DRKqGZ.

[2] CRLSets. The Chromium Projects, 2015. http://bit.ly/1JPsUeC.

[3] Network Stack. The Chromium Projects, 2015. http://bit.ly/1GYuMhE.

[4] B. Andrei and M. Michael. Network applications of bloom filters: A survey. *Int. Math.*, 1(4), 2004.

[5] C. Arthur. DigiNotar SSL certificate hack amounts to cyberwar, says expert. *The Guardian*. http://www.theguardian.com/technology/2011/sep/05/diginotar-certificate-hack-cyberwar.

[6] D. Akhawe and A. P. Felt. Alice in Warningland: A Large-scale Field Study of Browser Security Warning Effectiveness. *USENIX Security*, 2013.

[7] D. Akhawe, B. Amann, M. Vallentin, and R. Sommer. Here's My Cert, So Trust Me, Maybe?: Understanding TLS Errors on the Web. *WWW*, 2013.

[8] An Evaluation of the Effectiveness of Chrome's CRLSets. Gibson Research Corporation. https://www.grc.com/revocation/crlsets.htm.

[9] A. Bates, J. Pletcher, T. Nichols, B. Hollembaek, and K. R.B. Butler. Forced Perspectives: Evaluating an SSL Trust Enhancement at Scale. *IMC*, 2014.

[10] C. Brubaker, S. Jana, B. Ray, S. Khurshid, and V. Shmatikov. Using Frankencerts for Automated Adversarial Testing of Certificate Validation in SSL/TLS Implementations. *IEEE S&P*, 2014.

[11] D. Cooper, S. Santesson, S. Farrell, S. Boeyen, R. Housley, and W. Polk. Internet X.509 Public Key Infrastructure Certificate and Certificate Revocation List (CRL) Profile. RFC 5280, IETF, 2008.

[12] Convergence. http://convergence.io.

[13] Z. Durumeric, J. Kasten, D. Adrian, J. A. Halderman, M. Bailey, F. Li, N. Weaver, J. Amann, J. Beekman, M. Payer, and V. Paxson. The Matter of Heartbleed. *IMC*, 2014.

[14] Z. Durumeric, J. Kasten, M. Bailey, and J. A. Halderman. Analysis of the HTTPS Certificate Ecosystem. *IMC*, 2013.

[15] C. Ellison and B. Schneier. Ten Risks of PKI: What You're not Being Told about Public Key Infrastructure. *Computer Security Journal*, 16(1), 2000.

[16] EFF SSL Observatory. https://www.eff.org/observatory.

[17] P. Felix, S. Peter, and S. Johannes. Cache-, hash- and space-efficient bloom filters. *Experimental Algorithms*, Springer, 2007.

[18] S. Fahl, M. Harbach, T. Muders, L. Baumgärtner, B. Freisleben, and M. Smith. Why Eve and Mallory Love Android: An Analysis of Android SSL (in)Security. *CCS*, 2012.

[19] M. Georgiev, S. Iyengar, S. Jana, R. Anubhai, D. Boneh, and V. Shmatikov. The Most Dangerous Code in the World: Validating SSL Certificates in Non-browser Software. *CCS*, 2012.

[20] P. Gutmann. Engineering Security. 2014. https://www.cs.auckland.ac.nz/~pgut001/pubs/book.pdf.

[21] S. Gibson. Security Certificate Revocation Awareness Test. 2014. https://www.grc.com/revocation.htm.

[22] R. Holz, L. Braun, N. Kammenhuber, and G. Carle. The SSL Landscape – A Thorough Analysis of the X.509 PKI Using Active and Passive Measurements. *IMC*, 2011.

[23] ICSI SSL Notary. http://notary.icsi.berkeley.edu.

[24] T. H.-J. Kim, L.-S. Huang, A. Perring, C. Jackson, and V. Gligor. Accountable Key Infrastructure (AKI): A Proposal for a Public-key Validation Infrastructure. *WWW*, 2013.

[25] A. Langley. Smaller than Bloom filters. 2011. https://www.imperialviolet.org/2011/04/29/filters.html.

[26] A. Langley. Revocation checking and Chrome's CRL. 2012. https://www.imperialviolet.org/2012/02/05/crlsets.html.

[27] A. Langley. Revocation still doesn't work. 2014. https://www.imperialviolet.org/2014/04/29/revocationagain.html.

[28] A. Langley. No, don't enable revocation checking. 2014. https://www.imperialviolet.org/2014/04/19/revchecking.html.

[29] B. Laurie, A. Langley, and E. Kasper. Certificate Transparency. 2013. https://tools.ietf.org/html/rfc6962.

[30] S. Matsumoto, P. Szalachowski, and A. Perrig. Deployment Challenges in Log-based PKI Enhancements. *EuroSec*, 2015.

[31] Mozilla piles on China's SSL cert overlord: We don't trust you either. http://bit.ly/1GBPwfG.

[32] NetCraft. How certificate revocation (doesn't) work in practice. 2013. http://news.netcraft.com/archives/2013/05/13/how-certificate-revocation-doesnt-work-in-practice.html.

[33] NetCraft. OCSP Server Performance in April 2013. 2013. http://news.netcraft.com/archives/2013/05/23/ocsp-server-performance-in-april-2013.html.

[34] D. Olivier. *ASN. 1 communication between heterogeneous systems*. Morgan Kaufmann, 2001.

[35] OS X Yosemite: List of available trusted root certificates. https://support.apple.com/en-us/HT202858.

[36] H. Perl, S. Fahl, and M. Smith. You Won't Be Needing These Any More: On Removing Unused Certificates from Trust Stores. *FC*, 2014.

[37] Y. Pettersen. The Transport Layer Security (TLS) Multiple Certificate Status Request Extension. RFC 6961 (Proposed Standard), IETF, 2013.

[38] Qualys SSL Pulse. https://www.trustworthyinternet.org/ssl-pulse/.

[39] M. D. Ryan. Enhanced Certificate Transparency and End-to-End Encrypted Mail. *NDSS*, 2014.

[40] Rapid7 SSL Certificate Scans. https://scans.io/study/sonar.ssl.

[41] Revoking Intermediate Certificates: Introducing OneCRL. *Mozilla Security Blog*. http://mzl.la/1zLFp7M.

[42] A. Schulman, D. Levin, and N. Spring. RevCast: Fast, Private Certificate Revocation over FM Radio. *CCS*, 2014.

[43] P. Szalachowski, S. Matsumoto, and A. Perrig. PoliCert: Secure and Flexible TLS Certificate Management. *CCS*, 2014.

[44] S. Santesson, M. Myers, R. Ankney, A. Malpani, S. Galperin, and C. Adams. X.509 Internet Public Key Infrastructure Online Certificate Status Protocol - OCSP. RFC 6960 (Proposed Standard), IETF, 2013.

[45] StartSSL: Frequently Asked Questions. https://www.startssl.com/?app=25.

[46] E. Topalovic, B. Saeta, L.-S. Huang, C. Jackson, and D. Boneh. Towards Short-Lived Certificates. *W2SP*, 2012.

[47] The DNS-Based Authentication of Named Entities (DANE) Transport Layer Security (TLS) Protocol: TLSA. 2012. https://tools.ietf.org/html/rfc6698.

[48] Trustwave to escape 'death penalty' for SSL skeleton key. http://bit.ly/1RbPlNe.

[49] University of Michigan Daily Full IPv4 HTTPS Handshakes. https://scans.io/series/https-full-ipv4.

[50] N. Vallina-Rodriguez, J. Amann, C. Kreibich, N. Weaver, and V. Paxson. A Tangled Mass: The Android Root Certificate Stores. *CoNEXT*, 2014.

[51] S. Yilek, E. Rescorla, H. Shacham, B. Enright, and S. Savage. When Private Keys Are Public: Results from the 2008 Debian OpenSSL Vulnerability. *IMC*, 2009.

[52] L. Zhang, D. Choffnes, T. Dumitras, D. Levin, A. Mislove, A. Schulman, and C. Wilson. Analysis of SSL certificate reissues and revocations in the wake of Heartbleed. *IMC*, 2014.

Detecting Malicious Activity with DNS Backscatter

Kensuke Fukuda
National Institute of Informatics/Sokendai
kensuke@nii.ac.jp

John Heidemann
University of Southern California
Information Sciences Institute
johnh@isi.edu

ABSTRACT

Network-wide activity is when one computer (the *originator*) touches many others (the *targets*). Motives for activity may be benign (mailing lists, CDNs, and research scanning), malicious (spammers and scanners for security vulnerabilities), or perhaps indeterminate (ad trackers). Knowledge of malicious activity may help anticipate attacks, and understanding benign activity may set a baseline or characterize growth. This paper identifies *DNS backscatter* as a new source of information about network-wide activity. Backscatter is the reverse DNS queries caused when targets or middleboxes automatically look up the domain name of the originator. Queries are visible to the authoritative DNS servers that handle reverse DNS. While the fraction of backscatter they see depends on the server's location in the DNS hierarchy, we show that activity that touches many targets appear even in sampled observations. We use information about the queriers to classify originator activity using machine-learning. Our algorithm has reasonable precision (70–80%) as shown by data from three different organizations operating DNS servers at the root or country-level. Using this technique we examine nine months of activity from one authority to identify trends in scanning, identifying bursts corresponding to Heartbleed and broad and continuous scanning of ssh.

Categories and Subject Descriptors

C.2.3 [**Computer-Communication Networks**]: Network Operations—*Network monitoring*

General Terms

Measurement

Keywords

Internet; Domain Name System; DNS; network activity; scanning

IMC'15, October 28–30, 2015, Tokyo, Japan.

ACM 978-1-4503-3848-6/15/10 ...$15.00.
DOI: http://dx.doi.org/10.1145/2815675.2815706.

1. INTRODUCTION

Network-wide activity is when one computer (the *originator*) touches many others (the *targets*). Malicious activity is a growing problem in the Internet. *Spammers* exploit compromised computers to send mail, one part of the gray-market ecosystem [30]. *Scanners* walk the IP address space, for research [25, 19], in academic [18] or commercial [35] vulnerability scanning, as cyber criminals searching for vulnerabilities [17] (or joyriding [6]), or as nation-states espionage [24, 28]. Knowledge of malicious activity may help anticipate attacks [12]. Non-malicious activity is of concern as well: ad trackers and content-delivery networks (CDNs) also interact with many computers. Studies of benign activity help set a baseline [54] or characterize growth (results like Calder et al. [10], but without active probing).

Unfortunately, it is difficult to understand the scope of these potential threats because of the Internet's decentralization. While firewalls observe activity directed at one network, and a few security providers aggregate data from a few hundreds [3], by design the Internet has no central vantage point to detect widespread activity. Prior work has used Domain Name System (DNS) traffic to assess misbehavior seen in specific networks or resolvers [56, 26, 40, 55, 2], but this work does not generalize to network-wide activity. Darknets [37, 34, 54, 13, 14, 17] and honeypots (for example, [41]) are effective at understanding network-wide activity, but they miss targeted scans (scanning only Alexa top websites [17]), and new large darknets are unlikely given IPv4 full allocation and the huge IPv6 space. Search engines gather information about activity that appears in the public web, but information is unstructured and may be delayed by indexing [48]. (§ 6 has detailed related work.)

This paper identifies a new source of information on network-wide activity: *DNS backscatter*, the reverse DNS queries triggered by such activity (Figure 1 as explained in § 2). Activities of interest are those that touch many Internet devices, including malicious or potentially malicious activity such as spamming and scanning, as well as widespread services such as CDNs, software updates, and web crawling. These activities trigger *reverse DNS queries* as firewalls, middleboxes, and servers (*queriers*) resolve map the IP address of the originator to DNS name in the process of logging or host-based authentication. Authoritative DNS servers provide a point of concentration of these queries that allows detection of large activities. Since backscatter occurs mostly as automated processes, and we consider only originators with many queriers, our approach avoids traffic from individuals and so has minimal privacy concerns. Since

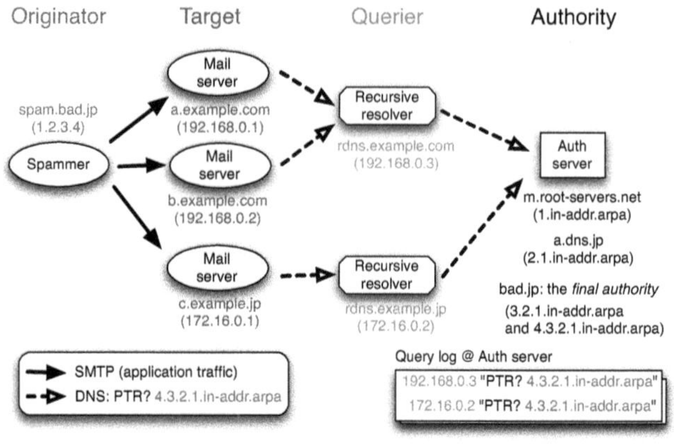

Figure 1: The process behind a DNS backscatter sensor: an originator sends mail to targets, causing queries that are observed at the authority.

backscatter is generated by the targets of network activity, not the originator, an adversarial originator cannot prevent its generation.

The contribution of this paper is to identify DNS backscatter as a new concentrator of information about network-wide activity (§ 2). We show that this source is noisy and attenuated by caching, but careful interpretation of aggregate queriers allows construction of a new type of sensor (§ 3) that detects large, automated activities that touch many targets. We use machine learning to classify the originators of each activity into broad groups (spammers, scanners, and several types of commercial activity) with reasonable precision (70–80%) and robustness (§ 4). Finally, we use backscatter and classification to examine world-wide scanning activity from three sources and up to nine months (§ 5). We characterize the "natural footprint" of different activities for two days at two sensors at the DNS root and one national-level server. We also examine nine months of data, showing that there is a continuous background of scanning, and identifying increased scanning following announcements of vulnerabilities such as Heartbleed [38]. Through this study, our work helps characterize scanning and other network-wide activity; our approach may also serve to support detection and response.

2. DNS BACKSCATTER'S POTENTIAL

DNS backscatter is the set of reverse DNS queries observed by a DNS *authority* as the result of a *network-wide activity*. In such activity, an *originator* interacts with many *targets*. Targets usually do not directly interact with the authority, but do so through a *querier* that acts on their behalf. Figure 1 shows these players. We use DNS backscatter observations to identify and classify the originators.

Origination of Network Activity: We look for network activity that affects many targets. An *originator* interacts with many *target* hosts, for purposes that are legitimate (large mailing lists and web crawlers), malicious (spam), or perhaps in between (scanning and peer-to-peer sharing). Our goal is to infer and classify the originator (§ 3) and to understand the size of its *footprint* (from [47])—how many targets it touches. In Figure 1, the originator is `spam.bad.jp` from IP address 1.2.3.4, and it sends spam emails to (`a.example.com` and its neighbors; our goal is to identify an otherwise unknown originator.

An originator is a single IP address that touches many targets. In the application classes we study, originators interact with their targets. In principle the originator could be the victim of spoofed traffic (such as a DNS server as part of an amplification attack); we have not identified such originators in our data. (For a few application classes, such as software update service, ad-trackers, and CDNs, the activity is initiated by the target and some other service co-located with the target does a reverse-DNS query.)

At the Target: The activity prompts the target's interest in discovering the originator's domain name from its IP address: a reverse DNS mapping that causes a *querier* to make a reverse query if the result is not already cached. This query may be for logging (as by firewalls), to perform domain-name based access control, or to characterize the originator (for example, mail servers that consider the sender's hostname as part of anti-spam measures). The querier is defined as the computer that does resolution of the reverse name. That the target and the querier may be the same computer, or the querier may be a dedicated recursive resolver shared by several targets.

A reverse DNS query will have the query name (QNAME `4.3.2.1.in-addr.arpa` in Figure 1) with the reversed IP address of the originator, and will ask for a reverse Internet name (QTYPE PTR, QCLASS IN). In this example, this query returns `spam.bad.jp`, but we do not use this response or even depend on the existence of a reverse name for the originator.

At the Authority: An authoritative DNS nameserver (the *authority*) will reply to this query. We analyze DNS traffic at the authority to infer information about the originator.

DNS is a hierarchical, distributed database with many authoritative servers that cover different levels and parts of the namespace. In addition, DNS uses aggressive caching at nearly all levels of the system. These factors mean that there are multiple authorities that will see different reverse-DNS traffic with different amounts of sampling due to caching and coverage.

The ideal place to observe reverse queries is the *final authority* directly responsible for the originator. In typically the originator's company or ISP (serving `3.2.1.in-addr.arpa` in our example), the final authority will see *all* queriers. However, authorities higher in the DNS hierarchy will see some attenuated fraction of queriers and can discover unknown originators. We consider several authorities: a national-level, top-level server (we examine Japan), and root nameservers (we consider B and M, two of the 14), as well as a final authority. Our national-level view sees traffic only for originators in address space delegated to that country (perhaps `2.1.in-addr.arpa` in our example). Roots potentially see all originators, but caching of the top of the tree (`in-addr.arpa` and `1.in-addr.arpa`) filters many queries, and visibility is affected by selection algorithms that favor nearby DNS servers. Some *recursive* servers, such as those run by large ISPs or large open DNS providers, will also have broad visibility.

Backscatter Evaluation: We observe reverse queries at the authority and use this backscatter to identify the originator's application. Queries directly provide the IP address of the originator, but we use that only to group queriers (we ignore the originator reverse DNS record, if any). Instead we use information about *queriers* to suggest the originator's application. Each individual query has little information, but the *collective behavior* of all queriers generating backscatter indicates the nature of an originator's activity. For example, spammers send mail to many mail servers, generating backscatter from these servers and anti-spam middleboxes. Similarly, large-scale network scanning causes firewalls at targets log the originator's domain name.

The number of reverse queriers also provides a rough idea of the size of the originator's activity. Unfortunately, the DNS's caching policies make it extremely difficult to quantify originator traffic rates—we caution that querier counts only *approximate* activity sizes.

An adversarial originator may seek to hide its activity. Spreading activity over many originators will reduce detection, but other aspects of our approach depend on targets and thus are outside the control of the originator.

Privacy: Analysis of DNS traffic raises potential privacy issues, since much DNS traffic originates from activity by individuals. Our approach minimizes these concerns for several reasons. First, the data sources we use intrinsically mask the visibility and identity of individuals. Caching heavily attenuates all queries seen by the authority, and a shared cache obscures the identity of any individual. We see network-wide activity only because of its many targets, while activity of any given individual is extremely unlikely to appear. Second, authorities have little or no direct contact with individuals due to indirection from recursive resolvers. Finally, while raw data at an authority is a mix of individual and automated traffic, the reverse queries we consider is nearly all automated. Humans typically use DNS to map names to addresses; almost all reverse queries are from automated sources. (As evidence, we examined ten minutes of B-Root queries in B-post-ditl. Using not-found replies [NXDomain] as evidence of typos, only 8 of 126,820 reverse queries against `in-addr.arpa` are not-found, while about half of the forward queries for IP addresses are not-found.)

Our analysis and its output also raise minimal concern. Our automated analysis effectively anonymizes its input through abstraction and aggregation, as input becomes feature vectors about collective queriers. It identifies and classifies originators in bulk, and we consider only originators in the top fraction of network-wide activity—a set that is necessarily automated to reach that scope. Finally, when examining specific originators to validate our results, we would anonymize any that present personally-identifiable information (PII). None so far show any PII.

Our work has been institutionally reviewed and approved as non-human-subjects research (USC IIR00001718). We see minimal privacy risk in this work, and substantial benefit in better understanding the scope of network-wide activity such as scanning.

3. METHODOLOGY: BACKSCATTER TO ACTIVITY SENSOR

We next summarize our approach to make DNS backscatter a sensor for network-wide activity: collecting DNS data at the authority, classifying data for each originator with features based on the queries and queriers, and then clustering originators into activities.

3.1 Data Collection: Queries at the Authority

We begin with data collection at the authority. We observe all DNS queries at arrival and retain only reverse DNS queries (PTR queries made against `in-addr.arpa`). Each query results in an (originator, querier, authority) tuple; we identify the originator from the QNAME, and the querier and authority are the source and destination of the DNS packet.

Queries may be obtained through packet capture on the network or through logging in DNS server itself. DNS packet capture techniques are widely used [51, 20]. DNS logging is supported in most servers, and tools such as dnstap define standard logging formats [50]. Centralized DNS information is available today through services such as SIE [45]. We describe the datasets used in this paper in § 3.6.

3.2 Interesting and Analyzable Originators

We want to focus our classification on only those originators that are *interesting*, carrying out activities that affect large parts of the network, and that are *analyzable*, providing enough information from queriers that we can reasonably classify them.

We identify these originators by analyzing data over time intervals that are long enough to include a significant number of analyzable originators, and then identifying the most interesting among them based on how many targets they touch.

We generate a *feature vector* v^o for each originator o over some time interval lasting d days. The time interval under consideration must be long enough that the originator touches enough targets to allow inference of the originator's application class. We consider 20 or more unique queriers per originator to be sufficient for analysis. We select the time interval for each dataset to meet this goal (details of the datasets are shown in § 3.6). DITL datasets [16] last 1–2 days, and for each we generate one feature vector for each originator across the whole dataset (d is the dataset duration, 36 or 50 hours). For the M-sampled dataset we use $d = 7$ days, thus generating an array of feature vectors v_i^o where $i \in [0, 35]$.

Originators that touch many targets have larger, more interesting activities. To identify the most prolific originators we record the number of unique (originator, querier) combinations in each time interval. We rank originators by number of unique queriers in the time interval and retain only the N originators with the most unique queriers. When we count originators (§ 5.3) we take all originators with more than 20 unique queriers.

3.3 Queries to Originator Features

We define static and dynamic features for each originator. *Static* features are derived from the domain names of the queriers, using differences in which targets different originators touchto infer the originator's intentions. *Dynamic* features use spatial and temporal patterns in queries.

Querier domain names provide these static features, often determined by specific keywords:

home computers with automatically assigned names like `home1-2-3-4.example.com`. The name includes digits of the IP address and a keyword: ap, cable, cpe, customer, dsl, dynamic, fiber, flets, home, host, ip, net, pool, pop, retail, user.

mail mail servers like `mail.example.com`. Keywords: mail, mx, smtp, post, correo, poczta, send*, lists, newsletter, zimbra, mta, pop, imap.

ns nameservers like `ns.example.com`. Keywords: cns, dns, ns, cache, resolv, name.

fw firewalls like `firewall.example.com`. Keywords: firewall, wall, fw.

antispam anti-spam services, like `spam.example.com`. Keywords: ironport, spam.

www web servers like `www.example.com`

ntp NTP servers like `ntp.example.com`

cdn CDN infrastructure, including suffix of Akamai, Edgecast, CDNetworks , LLNW.

aws Amazon AWS, including suffix of amazonaws.

ms Microsft Azure, checked with web page.

google IP addresses assigned to Google, as confirmed by SPF record in DNS.

other-unclassified a name not matching the categories above.

unreach cannot reach the authority servers.

nxdomain no reverse name exists.

Domain names may match multiple static features (for example, `mail.google.com` is both google and mail). We match by component, favoring matches by the left-most component, and taking first rule for components with multiple keywords. (Thus both `mail.ns.example.com` and `mail-ns.example.com` are *mail*).

The static portion of the feature vector for an originator is the fraction of queriers that match each of the features. For example, an originator where all queriers have "mail" in their domain names would have the mail feature as 1 and all others as zero. Another where a quarter have "mail" and the rest have "firewall" would have feature vector with (mail= 0.25, firewall= 0.75). We use the fraction of queriers rather than absolute counts so static features are independent of query rate.

We use these dynamic features to capture temporal and spatial aspects of the queries:

queries per querier (temporal) As a *rough* query rate we compute the mean number of queries per querier.Differences in caching and TTLs prevent generate an exact rate, but this metric is roughly proportional to query rate.

query persistence (temporal) To show how often an originator is active we count the number of 10-minute-long periods that include the originator.

local entropy (spatial) To see if an activity affects many people we compute the Shannon entropy of /24 prefixes of all queriers.

global entropy (spatial) We compute the Shannon entropy of the /8 prefix of all querier IP addresses. Since /8 prefix are assigned geographically, wide variation here shows global activity.

unique ASes (spatial) the number of ASes across all queriers normalized by the total number of ASes that appear in the time interval. (ASes are from IP addresses via whois.)

unique countries (spatial) the number of countries across all queriers, normalized by the total number of countries that appear in the time interval. We determine country from the IP using MaxMind GeoLiteCity database [32].

queriers per country (spatial) unique queriers per country.

queriers per AS (spatial) unique queriers per AS.

To avoid excessive skew of querier rate estimates due to queriers that do not follow DNS timeout rules [52, 11] we eliminate duplicate queries from the the same querier in a 30 s window. Some variation remains due to different caching times (TTLs) for different portions of the namespace. In some cases, such as fast flux domains, low TTLs will assist detection.

We selected the features and classes (in this section and the next) after iteration with our several datasets. Different features and classes will produce different results (for example, although we omit details due to space, we see higher accuracy with fewer application classes), but our results show the general approach is sound.

3.4 Originator Features to Application Classes

Finally we classify each originator based on its feature vector using machine learning. We use several standard machine-learning algorithms: a decision tree (Classification And Regression Tree; CART) [8], random forest (RF) [7], and kernel support vector machines (SVM) [43]. For non-deterministic algorithms (both RF and SVM use randomization), we run each 10 times and take the majority classification. These algorithms classify each originator into one of the following classes:

ad-tracker Servers implementing web-bugs (objects in embedded in web pages) to track user for advertising.

cdn Computers that are part of public content delivery networks (Akamai, CDNetworks, etc.)

cloud Front-end hosts of cloud service such as Google map, Goggle drive, and Dropbox.

crawler Web crawlers by Google, Bing, Baidu, etc.

dns Large DNS servers

mail Mail servers that send mail to large mailing lists and webmail service

ntp Large Network Time Protocol (NTP) servers

p2p End-user computers that participate in peer-to-peer file sharing. (We added this late in our work; our analysis of root servers does not include it.)

push Push-based messaging services for mobile phones (Android and iPhone); typically TCP port 5223.

scan Internet scanners using ICMP, TCP, or UDP.

spam Computers (end-user or mail servers) that send spam to many destinations.

update Servers for software update distribution run by OS, computer, and printer vendors

Data over time: For short datasets, each originator has one feature vector and one class. For longer datasets we see an array of feature vectors (v_i^o) and a time-specific class c_i^o. Because our observations are incomplete and classification is imperfect, an originator may change class over time, so our final step is to identify the originator as the most common class seen over all time (the statistical mode of c_i^o). We divide the M-sampled data into 35 week-long periods; all other datasets are analyzed as one period of 1–2 days. Longer observations for the M-sampled data partially compensate for attenuation in the data due to its 1:10 downsample (see also § 3.6).

Training: Classification requires training. We label a subset of each dataset as ground truth, manually identifying the application class of 200–300 originators in each dataset. Traffic seen by each authority is different for many reasons: placement in the DNS hierarchy, size, physical location, use of anycast, and possible use of sampling (for M-sampled). For this reason, we currently train for each dataset separately, although in some cases originators appear in multiple datasets and so we can reuse labeled ground-truth. (Studying of training portability and its effects on accuracy is ongoing.)

We do training by generating feature vectors as described above, then feed this input and known output into each ML algorithm.

3.5 Constraints in Backscatter as a Data Source

While DNS backscatter provides a new tool to identify network-wide activity, it is an incomplete source about originators and their activity.

First, querier domain-names only provide limited information about targets. Domain names may be overly general, unavailable, or never assigned. Currently we see 14–19% of queriers without reverse names, and the fraction serves as a classification feature, but if *all* queriers lacked reverse names our approach would not work. Other network services use reverse names, such as anti-spam and network reputation services, finding as we do that they are imperfect but still useful. Our results use only backscatter, but we show that applications will benefit from combining it with other sources of information (such as small darknets) to overcome the limitations of querier names alone.

Second, the signal provided in DNS backscatter is spread over many authorities by DNS anycast, attenuated by caching in recursive DNS resolvers, and complicated by caching durations (TTLs) that differ across the DNS hierarchy.These challenges prevent us from getting strong estimates on the rates of originator activity, but we show that they do not prevent their identification or classification.

Finally, an adversarial originator may try to defeat our analysis. As with spam, spreading traffic from an activity across many separate originating IP addresses or longer durations disperses the signal. We cannot prevent this countermeasure, but it greatly increases the effort required by an adversarial originator. Fortunately our classification depends on queriers (not originators), and they cannot be manipulated by the originator.

In this paper we show that querier provides reasonable classification accuracy and backscatter's signal identifies hundreds of originators. We are working to refine our estimates of accuracy and sensitivity, and of course additional data sources, larger labeled ground-truth, and more refined classes may improve on our work.

3.6 Datasets

This paper uses DNS datasets from three authorities: one national-level top-level domain, operators of two root servers as shown in Table 1.

JP-DNS operates the `.jp` country code domain for Japan; we have data from all seven of their anycast sites. We obtained data from two root server operators: B is a single site in the US west coast, and M operates 7 anycast sites in Asia, North America, and Europe. We use root datasets from the short-term, complete (unsampled) observations taken as part of the 2014 DITL collection [16] (for B-Root, shortly after 2014 DITL). We also use data for M-Root's 2015 DITL collection (§ 4.4). These root datasets are available to researchers through DNS-OARC.

For longitudinal analysis we draw on 9 months of data taken at the M-Root server. This dataset (M-sampled) is sampled with only 1 out of every 10 queries in deterministic manner; this sampling decreases our sensitivity but is part of their policy for long-term collection. We also use an 5-month unsampled dataset (B-long) taken from B-Root to evaluate for controlled experiments (§ 4.4).

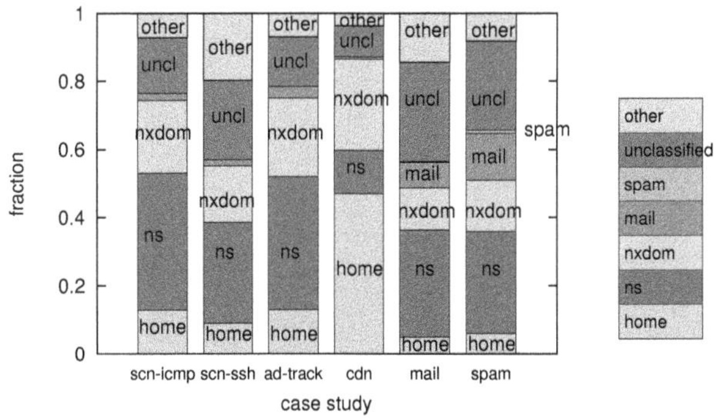

Figure 2: Static features for case studies, derived from querier domain names. (Dataset: JP-ditl.)

4. VALIDATION

Classification with machine learning requires appropriate features and accurate training data. Here we illustrate our features with several different type of originators, then identify external sources we use to label the ground truth for training and validation. Finally, we validate our approach by training on a random portion of the ground truth and testing the remainder.

4.1 Distinguishing Different Classes of Originators

We first illustrate how the DNS backscatter allows us to differentiate the activity of six different originators: scan-icmp, scan-ssh, ad-tracker, cdn, mail, and spam. Figure 2 and Table 2 show their static and dynamic features.

Static features: Static features (Figure 2) distinguish several cases. We examine two scanners: *scan-icmp* is the Japanese site for a research scanner doing outage detection [42], while *scan-ssh* is an unknown party probing ssh (TCP port 22) on all computers. Scanners trigger many queries from shared nameservers (NS), as well as nxdomain, home, and static addresses. We believe this mix results from scanners walking all IP addresses and triggering firewall and logging reverse queries; the large number of NS queriers suggest these services often use an ISP's shared resolver, but not always.

Ad-trackers are servers triggered by user's web behavior. While similar to scanners, this classes see more shared nameservers, perhaps because it is queried by end-users's web browsers.

Our *cdn* case is an Akamai server based in Japan. It shows a *much* higher fraction of home queriers than others. We believe this shift results from heavy CDN use at homes.

type	dataset	operator	start (UTC)	duration	sampling	queries ($\times 10^9$) (all)	queries ($\times 10^9$) (reverse)	qps ($\times 10^3$) (all)	qps ($\times 10^3$) (reverse)
ccTLD	JP-ditl	JP-DNS	2014-04-15 11:00	50 hours	no	4.0	0.3	22	1.8
root	B-post-ditl	B-Root	2014-04-28 19:56	36 hours	no	2.9	0.04	22	0.2
root	B-long	B-Root	2015-01-01	5 months	no	290*	5.14	22*	0.39
root	M-ditl	M-Root	2014-04-15 11:00	50 hours	no	8.3	0.06	46	0.3
root	M-ditl-2015	M-Root	2015-04-13 11:00	50 hours	no	9.9	0.07	55	0.4
root	M-sampled	M-Root	2014-02-16	9 months	1:10	36.2	1.5	1.6	0.07

Table 1: DNS datasets used in this paper.

case	queries/ querier	global entropy	local entropy	queriers/ country
scan-icmp	3.3	0.83	0.92	0.006
scan-ssh	4.7	0.84	0.96	0.006
ad-track	2.3	0.85	0.94	0.017
cdn	4.4	0.48	0.97	0.018
mail	1.7	0.71	0.94	0.009
spam	3.4	0.85	0.95	0.005

Table 2: Dynamic features for case studies.

Finally, *mail* and *spam* both show a much higher fraction of the mail feature, consistent with application. Although hard to see on the graph, spam shows more than twice the fraction of spam-related queriers (0.1% compared to 0.03%), indicating heavier involvement of spam-filtering and logging systems.

Dynamic features: Table 2 lists the distribution of some dynamic features for the six originators. As described in § 3.3, query counts only approximate true rates because of caching, but we believe relative comparisons are appropriate for classification.

We see that the queries:querier ratio helps distinguish mail from spam. Global entropy demonstrates geographic dispersion of the queriers. Low global entropy for *cdn* reflects CDN selection algorithms that associate our Japan-based CDN server with Asian clients. Similarly, the global entropy *mail* is lower because the language of this specific list is Japanese. Queries per country also reflects geographic coverage, with high values of *ad-tracker*, *cdn*, and *mail* suggesting geographically constrained targets.

The examples in § 3.3 illustrate how these features help identify our application classes, and their overlap suggests the potential for machine learning as a framework to interpret them optimally. We quantify our approach in § 4.3.

4.2 Confirming Labeled Ground-Truth

We require ground truth with originators labeled into our twelve application classes (§ 3.4) both to train our classifier and to evaluate its accuracy (§ 4.3).

In labeling ground truth we strive for *accuracy* over quantity because a mix of inaccurate originators will mis-train our classifier. We draw on multiple sources of external data (blacklists, darknets, and manual investigation) to get reasonable coverage of most application classes, with 180 to 700 samples depending on the dataset (Table 3).

We generate moderate to large lists of potential IP addresses in each application class from external sources (described below), then intersect it with the top-10000 originators in dataset by the number of queriers. We then verify the intersection manually. We determine the verifying application class of each originator manually using the methods described below. We added two categories (push and update) after examining all of the top 100 and 1000 largest originators, respectively.

Validation for each class is as follows:

ad-tracker We identify servers associated with advertising affiliation and tracking systems (such as `doubleclick.net` and `kauli.net`) by crawling around 20 blog pages. We also registered with ad affiliation programs for four services and added the servers they recommended.

cdn We identified content-distribution networks for several large providers (Akamai, Edgecast, CDNetworks, ChinaCache, and, CloudFlare) based on their reverse domain names and WHOIS on their IP addresses.

cloud We crawled IP addresses of front-end hosts for Google services such (map, drive, and news) and Dropbox from Japan and the US.

crawler We confirm web crawler IP addresses from UserAgent strings in web server logs of NII, originator reverse domain names, and `http://botvsbrowsers.com`.

dns We started with all root DNS servers, country-code TLD servers, then we added servers for large Japanese ISPs that had large originator footprints.

mail We confirm mail originators by examining over 100 Japanese mailing lists operated by mail ASPs and companies themselves. We see about 300 IP addresses over about three months in 2014. We also identify mail originators for cloud-based mail including Google, Microsoft, Apple, Facebook, Linkedin, and Amazon, as confirmed by domain names in e-mail message headers.

ntp We consider well-known Stratum 1 servers and crawled IP addresses of NTP servers in Open NTP project (at `*.pool.ntp.org`).

push We list IP addresses that send packets with TCP port 5223 (Lync mobile client push), as observed in sampled netflow traffic from the University of Tokyo.

p2p We identify IP addresses running DHT-based BitTorrent from `htindex.com` in fall 2014 (As of 2015, this service no longer operates).

scan We confirm scanners by looking at traffic in two darknets (one a /17 and the other a /18 prefix) located in Japan. A confirmed scanner sends TCP (SYN only, not SYN-ACK), UDP, or ICMP packets to more than 1024 addresses in at least one darknet, or is a known research scanner (such as Trinocular [42] and shadowserver [46]).

spam We confirm spammer IP addresses with data from DNS blacklists (DNSBL) run by 9 organization (badips, barracuda, dnsbl.sorbs, inps.de, junkemail, openbl, spamhaus, spamrats, spam.dnsbl.sorbs); we consider only the spam portion of blacklists that distinguish spam from others such as ssh-brute force.

dataset	ad-track	cdn	cloud	crawler	dns	mail	ntp	p2p	push	scan	spam	update	total
JP-ditl	15	8	-	-	26	44	10	37	-	25	64	6	**235**
B-post-ditl	13	29	16	17	16	46	5	-	12	29	35	-	**214**
M-ditl	13	36	16	16	17	50	8	-	12	33	43	-	**240**
M-sampled	54	81	82	35	52	111	-	-	73	124	136	-	**746**

Table 3: Number of examples of each application class in labeled ground-truth, per dataset.

dataset	algorithm	accuracy	precision	recall	F1-score
	CART	0.66 (0.05)	0.63 (0.08)	0.60 (0.06)	0.61 (0.06)
JP	**RF**	**0.78** (0.03)	**0.82** (0.05)	**0.76** (0.06)	**0.79** (0.05)
ditl	SVM	0.73 (0.04)	0.74 (0.05)	0.71 (0.06)	0.73 (0.05)
B	CART	0.48 (0.05)	0.48 (0.07)	0.45 (0.05)	0.46 (0.05)
post-	**RF**	**0.62** (0.05)	**0.66** (0.07)	**0.60** (0.07)	**0.63** (0.07)
ditl	SVM	0.38 (0.11)	0.50 (0.14)	0.32 (0.13)	0.39 (0.13)
	CART	0.53 (0.06)	0.52 (0.07)	0.49 (0.06)	0.51 (0.06)
M	**RF**	**0.68** (0.04)	**0.74** (0.06)	**0.63** (0.05)	**0.68** (0.05)
ditl	SVM	0.60 (0.08)	0.68 (0.10)	0.52 (0.08)	0.59 (0.09)
	CART	0.61 (0.03)	0.65 (0.04)	0.58 (0.04)	0.61 (0.04)
M	**RF**	**0.79** (0.02)	**0.82** (0.02)	**0.77** (0.03)	**0.79** (0.02)
sampled	SVM	0.72 (0.02)	0.76 (0.03)	0.70 (0.03)	0.73 (0.02)

Table 4: Validating classification against labeled ground-truth.

update We identified 5 large software update services hosted in Japan corresponding to computer and printer vendors such as Sony, Ricoh, and Epson.

We identified these classes after iteration and manual examination of data, traces, and applications. They share in common that a single originator touches many targets that make reverse DNS queries, but activity is sometimes initiated by the originator (spam, mail, and scan) and other times likely a side effect of activity at the target (such as update, ad-tracker, and cdn).

4.3 Classification Accuracy and Algorithm Choice

We next carry out cross-validation, using random subsets of labeled ground-truth to test the classification accuracy and to compare three classification algorithms: Classification And Regression Tree (CART), Random Forest (RF), and Kernel Support-Vector Machines (SVM).

Classification accuracy: To evaluate a particular machine-learning algorithm, for each dataset we pick a random 60% of the labeled ground-truth for training, then test on the remaining 40% of data. We repeat this process 50 times, testing each subset with all three algorithms. For each run we compute accuracy ($(tp+tn)/all$), precision ($tp/(tp+fp)$), recall ($tp/(tp+fn)$), and F1-score ($2tp/(2tp+fp+fn)$), where tp: true positive, tn: true negative, fp: false positive, fn: false negative. Table 4 shows the mean of each metric over the 50 iterations, with standard deviations in smaller type.

Overall, we find that RF outperforms SVM and CART in most metrics.The accuracy of the best algorithm over each dataset is 0.7 to 0.8, suggesting classification from our limited data is not easy, but fairly strong given 12 categories (thus an expected 0.08 accuracy for guessing). We see mislabeling of application classes where the training data is sparse: *ntp*, *update*, *ad-tracker*, and *cdn* for JP-ditl. In particular, the classification ratio of *update* events is very low. Reducing the number of classes would improve accuracy, at the cost of less useful results. Improving the accuracy of classification across multiple classes with unbalanced training data is an active area of research in machine learning. Our current results show promise and will improve as the field progresses.

	JP-ditl		M-ditl	
rank	feature	Gini	feature	Gini
1	mail(S)	8.4	mail(S)	12.5
2	home(S)	7.9	ns(S)	8.3
3	spam(S)	6.3	unreach(S)	7.0
4	nxdomain(S)	6.2	query rate(D)	6.2
5	unreach(S)	5.2	home(S)	6.0
6	global entropy(D)	5.0	nxdomain(S)	5.8

Table 5: Top discriminative features. Classifier: RF.

Similarly, for JP-ditl, *p2p* is sometimes misclassified as scan. Manual inspection shows that misclassified *p2p* actually sent traffic to dynamically-assigned ports in our darknets as well. We conclude that they are mis-behaving P2P-clients [31, 9] and these random probes are triggered by software bugs or by injection of random IP addresses by anti-P2P services.

Choice of authority: While accuracy is good, accuracy for B post-ditl and M-ditl are slightly poorer (60–75%) because roots are attenuated and these datasets are short. M-sampled does better because it uses longer observations (7 days, not 2). JP accuracy is highest because it is unsampled and lower in hierarchy. We conclude that approach can be strong, but one must be careful to match the quality of the signal and training data.

Feature choice: In evaluating classification, we naturally would like to know what features are most discriminative. Random Forest provides this information, and Table 5 lists the top discriminative features for two datasets, as determined by Gini coefficient [53]. Larger Gini values indicate features with greater discriminative power. We see that *mail*, *home*, *nxdomain*, and *unreach* are important static features in both datasets. *Query rate* and *global entropy* are important in different datasets, perhaps reflecting M-ditl's weaker global signal and JP-ditl's more regional signal. These results are consistent with intuitive case studies (§ 4.1).

Algorithm choice: Since Random Forest provides the best accuracy and is consistent (small standard deviations), we use that algorithm to characterize originators in the next section, after retraining with the full labeled ground-truth data.

4.4 Controlled Experiments to Evaluate DNS Caching

Attenuation from DNS caching makes interpreting backscatter challenging. Such caching is difficult to model: first, the DNS resolver infrastructure can be quite complex [44]. Second, DNS caches are kept for varying durations and caching

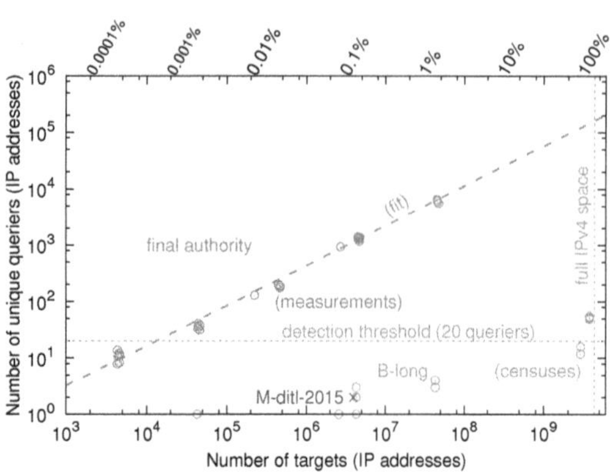

Figure 3: Size of footprint of random network scans at the final authority. (Datasets: B-long and M-ditl.)

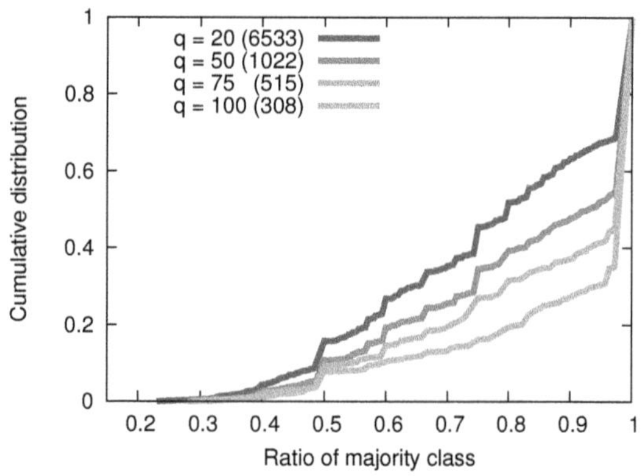

Figure 4: CDF of r, the fraction of the most common class over all weeks with q or more queriers per originator. (Dataset: M-sampled.)

of the resolution tree (`in-addr.apra`) will be caused by many competing users.

Attenuation: To estimate the number of queriers that respond to a large network event we conducted a controlled experiment where we probe a fraction of the IPv4 Internet from a host where we can monitor queries sent to the final reverse DNS server for the prober. We set the TTL of the reverse DNS record (PTR) to zero to disable or minimize caching (some resolvers force a short minimum caching period), thus we should observe all queriers triggered in response to our scan. We scan several protocols (ICMP, TCP port 22, 23, 80, and UDP port 53, 123) using ZMap [19], varying the fraction of the address space we scan from 0.0001% (4k addresses) to 0.1% (4M addresses) of the whole IPv4 space. The time required for the biggest scan (0.1%) was 13 hours. We run each scan up to 5 times. We also examine 8 full-internet scans (nearly 100% of unicast IP) taken with Trinocular [42], starting at two different months (January and April 2015) from four different sites [49].

Figure 3 shows the number of queries we see as we grow the size of the scan. Circles represent experimental trials measured at the final authority (slightly jittered). The diagonal line represents a best fit: roughly 1 querier per 1000 targets, but actually a power-law fit with power of 0.71. We also examine M-sampled and B-long, reporting what they see for 0.1% and 1% ZMap scans and the 100% Trinocular scans. This large reduction in responses at root servers is due to both DNS caching and because not all targets are actually interested in the scanner.

False negatives: Our controlled experiments can evaluate false negatives (missed network-wide events). The horizontal line at 20 queriers is our detection threshold, so we see that the final authority will detect all events scanning 0.001% of the Internet or more.

We expect greater caching at higher levels of the DNS hierarchy. To measure this, we examined M-ditl-2015 data for evidence of these trials. Only two trials overlap with this datasets: one for 0.01% and the other for 0.1%. Of these, we find two queriers for the 0.1% trial (the blue X) in Figure 3. Greater attenuation at higher levels of DNS means that it will detect only much larger (space) or longer (in time) activity. (We are currently extending this study to trials at larger percentages.)

This experiment shows that backscatter is highly attenuated due to disinterested targets and DNS caching, but responses follow the number of targets.

4.5 Sensitivity of Results

Finally, we use M-sampled to evaluate the sensitivity of our conclusions by looking at when or if classifications change over time. We current vote on classifications of each originator over all weeks. To estimate degree of consensus in a vote, we define r as the fraction of weeks when the preferred class (the most common response) occurred of all weeks that originator appeared. When r is near one, we see consistent activity, but when $r < 0.5$ it seems likely that either the originator is changing activity over time (perhaps different machines behind a NAT, or a botnet node being repurposed), or doing two things concurrently, or we classify variations in behavior differently, suggesting an incomplete training set or indistinguishable classes.

Figure 4 shows the cumulative distribution of the ratio r, looking at subsets of data with at least q queriers per originator. To avoid overly quantized distributions we show only originators that appear in four or more samples (weeks). Requiring more queriers per originator (larger q) reduces the number of eligible originators, but the number of samples (shown in parenthesis in the legend) are all large enough to be robust.

We see that more queriers (thus more data for classification) provide more consistent results, since with $q = 100$, about 60% of originators are strongly consistent. Even with a threshold of 20 querier per originator, 30% of originators are consistent. In addition, almost all originators (85–90%, depending on q) have a class that has strict majority ($r > 0.5$). Thus our approach almost always (85–90%) provides a consistent result.

For the few where the strongest class is only a plurality ($r \leq 0.5$), we wanted to see if there are two nearly equally strong classes. We examined the entropy for originators in this case: we find that usually there is a single dominant class and multiple others, not two nearly equally common classes.

These initial results suggest our approach is consistent for observers with at least 20 queriers, although noise grows as queriers approach that threshold.

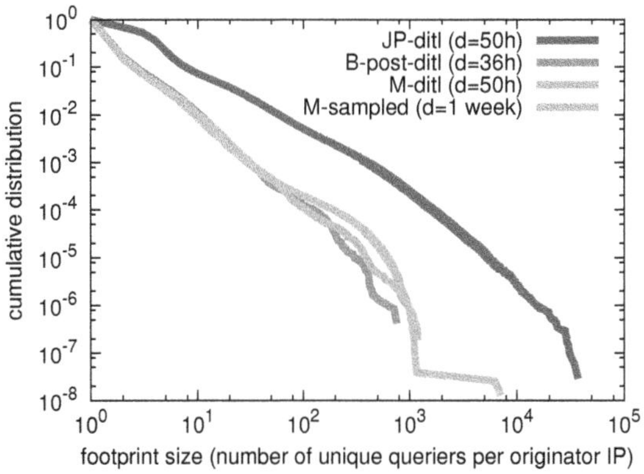

Figure 5: Distribution of originator footprint size.

5. RESULTS

We next study network-wide activities with our method, identifying large network events and trends in different applications and over time. Since our approach is based on feedback from targets, our results complement prior studies (such as darknets) and will observe targeted events will not appear in darknets.

5.1 Sizes of Originator Footprints

We estimate the footprint of each originator as the number of unique queriers per originator. Figure 5 shows the fraction of originators with each footprint size a log-log scale for each of our three datasets.

Our data suggests *there are hundreds of originators that touch large parts of the Internet.* Our controlled trials (§ 4.4) show high attenuation at root servers, yet hundreds of originators have footprints suggesting they scan most or all of the Internet (590 in M-ditl and 298 in B-post-ditl have footprints larger than 10^2).

The *distributions* of footprints is consistent across our datasets. (We cannot directly compare footprint sizes due to variation in duration and sampling.) As one would expect, they are a heavy-tailed, with some originators triggering queries from 10k queriers. We focus the remainder of our analysis of the originators with the largest footprints, typically the top-10000 (about 0.5% of each dataset), or the top-1000 or -100. Considering only large originators will miss those that are intentionally trying to be stealthy, but many scanners make no such attempt [17], and we expect commercial large services to also be open.

The largest footprints here are larger than those we observe in controlled trials at M-Root (Figure 3). Those scans were quite short (a few to a dozen hours), while here we aggregate data over one or two days. In addition, our trials used random targets, most of which are unoccupied (only 6–8% respond, as seen before [25]); many real-world scans are targeted, resulting in higher responses rates and thus greater backscatter.

5.2 Observability and Size of Application Classes

We next classify the top originators. Our goal is to understand what activity is taking place and approximately how aggressive they are. Our key observations are: there are *thousands* of originators causing network-wide activity, different *authorities see different applications*, and *we see evidence of team of coordinated scanners* even with *no direct information from originators.*

Size of application classes: There are *thousands* of unique originators that touch large parts of the Internet. Table 6 shows how many originators we see in each originator class for each dataset, with classes with counts within 10% of the largest count in bold. We use our preferred classifier (RF) with per-dataset training over the entire ground-truth. Classes that lack ground truth for some dataset have no matches (a "-").

Applications vary by authority: The classes of applications seen at *different authorities vary considerably.* For JP-ditl, *spam* is the most common class of originator. Although Japan hosts computers for most major CDNs, the size of the *cdn* class seen from backscatter is small because CDNs often use address space assigned by other registrars (we verify this statement for Akamai and Google with geolocation, whois and prior work [21]). The *update* class is exactly those in labeled ground-truth. We identified this class in examining the data (not from an external source), and lack of additional examples suggests either class has insufficient training data to avoid over-fitting, or update servers are rare.

Both unsampled root servers (B-post-ditl and M-ditl) show similar distributions of activity, with *mail* the most common and *spam* and *cdn* both close. The larger number of CDNs in at M-Root is due to 300 *cdn* originators located in two Chinese ISPs and interacting with queriers in China. Classification appears correct (they do not send traffic to darknets, nor appear in spam blacklists), but the originators lack domain names and we cannot identify them. Such originators appear only in M-ditl, suggesting that their queriers may be using DNS resolvers that prefer nearby authorities, since M-Root is well provisioned in Asia while B-Root is only based in North America.

Long-term, sampled root data (M-sampled) has some important differences from short term (M-ditl). Consider relative sizes of classes (since absolute counts vary due to dataset duration), we see many more scanner and spammers in long-term data. We believe the size of these categories reflect churn in the population carrying out the activity. We expect churn in spamming where computers known for spamming are less effective. We measure churn directly for scanners in § 5.3.

Big footprints can be unsavory: The mix of applications varies as we examine originators with smaller footprints, but we see that *big footprints are often unsavory activity.* Figure 6 shows how originator classes change as we look at more originators with smaller footprints (from Figure 6a to Figure 6c).

The largest footprints are often spammers (in JP-ditl) or scanners (for B and M). By contrast, we see that *mail* appears only in the top-1000 and top-10000, suggesting that legitimate mail servers may service large mailing lists (to many targets), but spammers touch many more targets. For B and M, more spammers rise in Figure 6c, suggesting spreading of traffic over many smaller originators to evade filtering.

By contrast, large but not top originators are often infrastructure: *cloud, mail, ad-tracker,* and *crawler.* In general, we find that application classes have a "natural" size, with some favoring origins with large footprints (prominent in

data	ad-track	cdn	cloud	crawl	dns	mail	ntp	p2p	push	scan	spam	update
JP-ditl	210	49	-	-	414	1412	237	2235	-	355	**5083**	6
B-post-ditl	72	1782	168	361	76	**3137**	8	-	318	1228	2849	-
M-ditl	76	**2692**	135	557	258	**2750**	67	-	119	983	2353	-
M-sampled	1329	17,708	2035	885	1202	14,752	-	-	3652	**47,201**	34,110	-

Table 6: Number of originators in each class for all datasets. (Classifier: RF.)

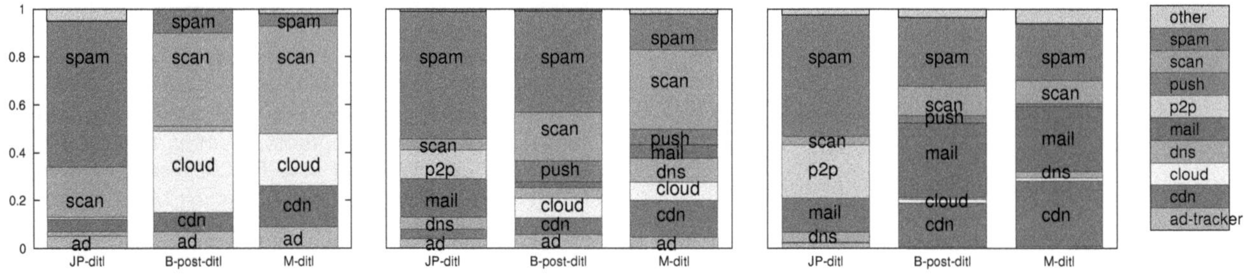

(a) Top 100 (b) Top 1000 (c) Top 10,000

Figure 6: Fraction of originator classes of top-N originators. (Dataset: JP-ditl, B-post-ditl, M-ditl; classifier: RF.)

Figure 6a), while others favor smaller footprints and so are more common in Figure 6c.

The *ad-tracker* class is most common in the prominent in top-most originators (a larger red *ad-tracker* fraction in Figure 6a compared to to Figure 6c). There are relatively a few originators (we see 5 companies as 22 unique originating addresses for top-100/JP-ditl). Unlike spam, they need not hide, and are likely prominent because tracking needs little traffic (a few originators can support a network-wide service), and because they use DNS records with short cache lifetimes (small TTLs). *Cloud* follows this pattern as well; 1 company across 21 distinct originating IPs for top-100 in M-ditl.

The *crawler* class shows the opposite behavior: most crawlers appear only in the top-10000, with few in top-1000 (554 vs. 3). This shift is consistent with web crawlers being data intensive, operating across many distributed IP addresses in parallel.

We also see that the physical location of the authority influences what they see. We earlier observed how differences in *cdn* for M-Root and B-Root are explained by their physical location to CDNs in China. B-Root's U.S.-only location may place it closer to more services in *cloud* (see Figure 6a) compared to M-Root's locations mainly in Asia and Europe.

New and old observations: A new observation in our data is *potential teams of scanners.* We have manually identified several /24 address blocks where many addresses are engaged in scanning, suggesting possible parallelized scanning. Without direct scan traffic, we cannot confirm coordination, but backscatter suggests networks for closer examination. To understand with scope of potential collaborative teams, we start with a a very simple model where a team is multiple originators in the same /24 IP address block. In M-sampled we see 5606 unique scan originators (by IP address), across 2227 unique originating /24 address blocks. Of these, 167 blocks have 4 or more originators, suggesting a potential team of collaborators. While 128 of these blocks have multiple application classes, suggesting against collaboration (or possibly mis-classification), we see 39 blocks with 4 or more originators all with the same application class. Such blocks warrant closer examination.

We also confirmed prior observations that clients linger on retired services. Originators we find include four retired root DNS servers (B, D, J, L), two prior cloud-based mail servers, and one prior NTP server. These cases show our methods can be used to systematically identify overly-sticky, outdated clients across many services, automating prior reports of clients that stick to retired servers in DNS [29] and NTP [39].

Classification on originator actions: An important benefit of our approach is that we classify on *indirect actions caused by the originator, with no direct information* from the originator. In fact, about a quarter of the originators in JP-ditl and half of those in the root datasets have no reverse domain names, but originator omissions have no affect on our approach because we do not observe *any* traffic or reverse names of originators. This separation makes it more difficult for adversarial originators to conceal their activities.

5.3 Trends in Network-Wide Activity

We next look for long-term trends in our data. We believe this is the first longitudinal study of network-wide activities such as scanning (prior work focused on specific events [17]). Our goal is to understand the ebb and flow of network-wide activity, so rather than examine the N largest originators, we count all originators with footprints of at least 20 queriers (see also Figure 5). While we see no growth in network-wide events, we see *peaks that respond to security events* and *a core of slow-and-steady scanners.*

Peaks in numbers of originators: The top *all* line in Figure 7 shows the absolute number of originators over time, each class (the lower, colored lines) and total (the top, black line). There are fairly large week-by-week changes, showing churn in the number of active originator activities,

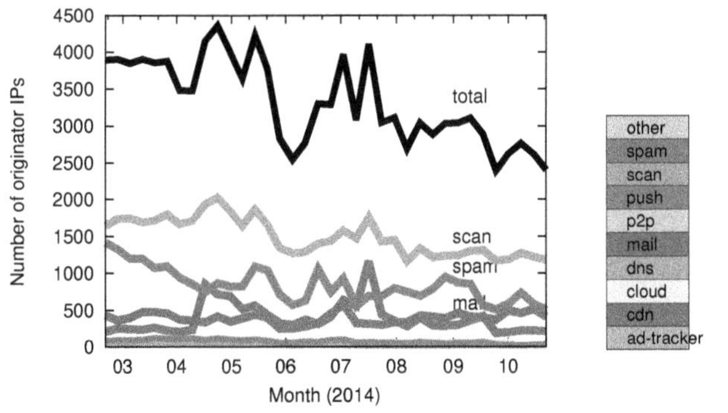

Figure 7: Number of originators over time. (Dataset: M-sampled; classifier: RF.)

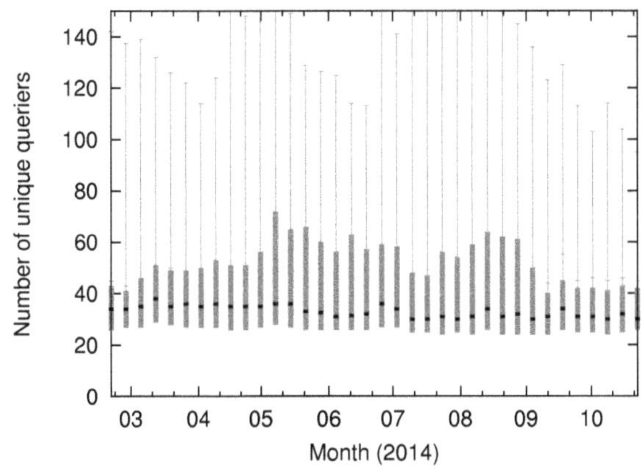

Figure 8: Box plot of originator footprint (queriers per scanner) over time; whiskers: 10%ile/90%ile. (Dataset: M-sampled.)

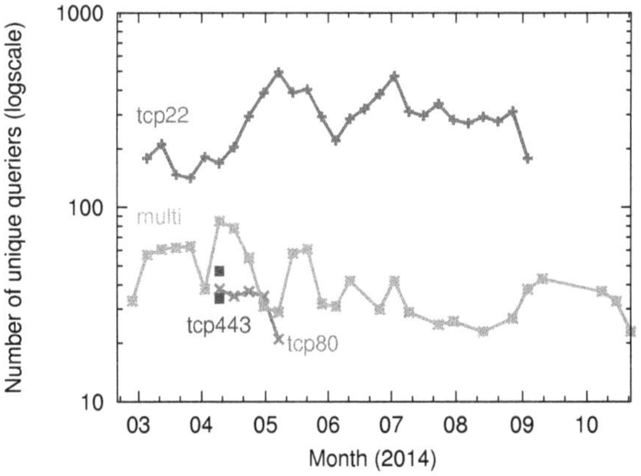

Figure 9: Three example originators with application class *scan*. (Dataset: M-sampled with darknet.)

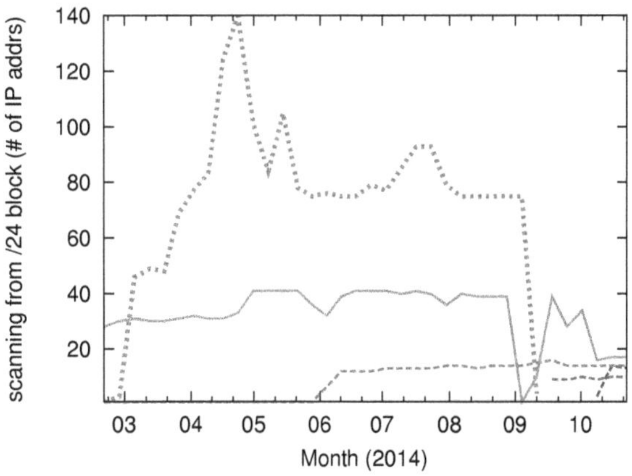

Figure 10: Five example blocks originating scanning activity. (Dataset: M-sampled.)

and peaks that can be explained by reactions to network security events.

To understand how network activity results from real-world events we next look the *scanner* application class. Our observation period includes public announcement of the Heartbleed vulnerability on 2014-04-07 [38], and we know that there were multiple research [1, 18], commercial, and presumably government scanning activities triggered by that announcement. The green scanner line in Figure 7 shows more than a 25% increase in scanning by mid-April, from 1400 originator IPs per week to 1800 at its peak. While this change is noticeable, it is smaller than we might expect. Instead, it shows that reaction to Heartbleed is small compared to *the large amount of scanning that happens at all times*—the 1200–1400 scanners we saw in March, and the 1000–1200 scanners that are present from June to October.

Churn: To understand long-term scanning, Figure 8 shows the distribution of footprint sizes over time for class *scan*. While the median and quartiles are both stable over these 36 weeks, but the 90th percentile varies considerably. This variation suggests a few very large scanners that come and go, while a core of slower scanners are always present.

We illustrate this observation with three different scanners that appear in both M-sampled and our darknet data (Figure 9). Two are long-lived (the top "tcp22" line scanning ssh, and the middle line scanning multiple ports), while the tcp80 scanner occurs in April and May. Furthermore, two tcp443 scans only appear in one week in April (shown as dark squares), suggesting they are Heartbleed-related. We also see that tcp22 has a bigger footprint than the others, and it looks a part of a big campaign whose 140 IP addresses belong to the same /24 block. Using our darknets, we confirm 164 scanners for TCP ports 22, 80, or 443, and while there is no "typical" scanner, these variations are common.

Our approach also *identifies networks supporting scanners*. For each /24 block, we count the number of IP addresses in class *scan* over time; Figure 10 shows five of these blocks. The top dotted line is a block with large scanning peaks corresponding with Heartbleed and Shellshock, ending in September. The solid line shows a block that scans continuously, while the three dotted lines are blocks that start scanning during our observation.

To understand if *who* scans changes over time, Figure 11 measures week-by-week change in scanner IP addresses. The bar above the origin shows the number of scanners each week, showing both new originators (top, dark) and con-

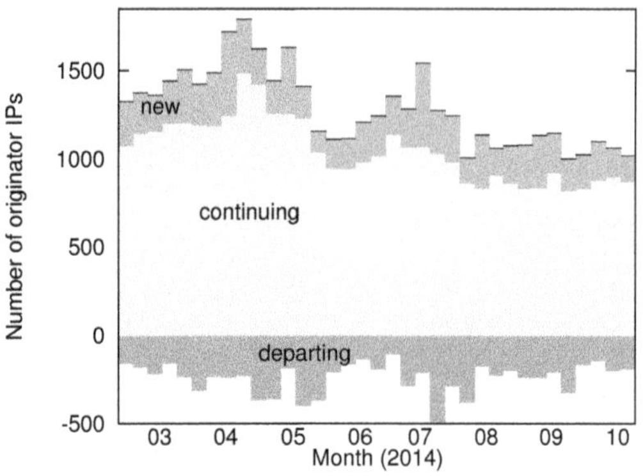

Figure 11: Week-by-week churn for originators of class *scan*. (Dataset: M-sampled.)

tinuing originators (middle, light) The red bar below the origin shows scanners that were lost from the prior week. While there are always scanners coming and going (about 20% turnover per week), this data confirms that there is a stable core of scanners that are consistently probing, week-after-week.

6. RELATED WORK

We next review prior work in both DNS- and non-DNS-based sensors and analysis. Overall, our contribution is to show that reverse DNS queries can identify network-wide behavior. Prior work instead considers forward DNS traffic and typically applies it to specific problems, or uses non-DNS sensors such as darknets and search engines.

DNS-specific sensors: Several groups use forward DNS queries to identify spam [56, 27], fast-flux [56, 26], automatically generated domain names [55], and cache poisoning [2]. Like our work, several of these approaches use machine learning to classify activity. However, this prior work focuses on *forward* DNS queries, while we consider *reverse* queries. Moreover, many use algorithms optimized to detect specific malicious activities, while we detect a range of network-wide behavior.

Recent work has used DNS to infer the structure of CDN networks [4] or internal to DNS resolvers [44]. They infer specific services from DNS traffic, we search for network-wide events from reverse queries.

An earlier work uses targeted scan and DNS backscatter for detecting Tor exit routers peeking POP3 authentication information [33], an earlier use of DNS backscatter de-anonymization; we generalize this use to detect scanners.

Plonka and Barford use machine-learning-based clustering and visualization to identify undesirable activity from local DNS traffic [40]. They use DNS traffic from an organization's recursive resolver to infer activity about that organization. Overall, our approach provides larger coverage, both by using data from authoritative DNS servers that aggregate queries from many organizations, unlike their single organization, and by examining trends in ten months of data, unlike their week-long analysis.

Antispam software has long used reverse DNS lookups to directly classify sources of mail. We use the domain names of queriers to indirectly classify originators.

Non-DNS Passive sensors: Darknets (or network telescopes) are a commonly used passive technique to characterize large-scale network activity [37, 34, 54, 13, 14, 17]. By monitoring a large, unoccupied blocks of addresses, darknets see active probes from viruses and scanners, queries from misconfiguration, and backscatter from spoofed traffic; traffic that can predict global malware, and its absence, network outages. Our analysis of DNS backscatter shares the goal of understanding network-wide activity from a simple, passive observer, but we observe at DNS authorities rather than large ranges of addresses. Like Durumeric et al. [17], we seek to enumerate scanners, but our use of DNS backscatter will see targeted scans that miss their darknet, and our study considers eight months of activity, not just one.

Some security services use middleboxes with deep-packet inspection to passively monitor large ISPs [3]. They observe all traffic from multiple points, while we monitor DNS backscatter from a single provider only.

Staniford monitored network traffic for scanners [47], and Gates emphasized rapid detection with scanner modeling [23]. Rather than protecting a single network, we look for network-wide activity with a simple observer.

Honeypots (for example, [41]) are a form of application-level darknet. By interacting with originators they see attacks darknets miss, but they miss attacks that probe specific targets (such as Alexa top sites). Interactivity also makes them fewer because of deployment expense. DNS backscatter uses information from existing servers.

Unconstrained endpoint profiling [48] uses search engines to gather information on addresses that leak into the public web, possibly complementing network flow data. We both seek to understand network-wide activity, but we use different data sources and methods. They use largely unstructured information from the web, while we infer features from semi-structured domain names and also traffic patterns. Their work depends on the speed of search engine indexing, while our work can provide rapid feedback given data from a DNS authority.

General DNS traffic analysis and privacy: Finally, a wide body of work has explored DNS traffic in general (examples include [15, 52, 11, 22]). Their work seeks to understand DNS, while we instead study what reverse DNS tells us about network-wide activities.

Work in DNS privacy focuses on client-to-recursive resolvers for end-users (examples include [36, 57], and proposals in the IETF DPRIVE working group). Our use of reverse queries from automated systems triggered by originators should see almost no human-triggered, end-user queries (§ 2). Use of query minimization [5] at the queriers will constrain the signal to only the local authority (that immediately serving the originator's reverse address).

7. CONCLUSION

We identified DNS backscatter as a new source of information about benign and malicious network-wide activity, including originators of mailings list traffic, CDN infrastructure, spammers and scanners. Their activity triggers reverse DNS queries by or near their targets, and we show that classification of these queriers allows us to identify classes of activity with reasonable precision. We use our approach to identify trends in scanning across nine months of data from one data source, and we characterize several kinds of activity for two days over three data sources. Our work provides a new approach to evaluate classes of network-wide activity.

Acknowledgments: We thank Yuri Pradkin for B-Root data collection, Akira Kato for M-Root data, and Yoshiro Yoneya and Takeshi Mitamura for JP data. We thank Xun Fan for input about Google and Akamai sites in Japan. We thank Terry Benzel, Kenjiro Cho, Ethan Katz-Bassett, Abdul Qadeer, and John Wroclawski comments on this paper.

Kensuke Fukuda's work in this paper is partially funded by Young Researcher Overseas Visit Program by Sokendai, JSPS KAKENHI Grant Number 15H02699, and the Strategic International Collaborative R&D Promotion Project of the Ministry of Internal Affairs and Communication in Japan (MIC) and by the European Union Seventh Framework Programme (FP7/2007- 2013) under grant agreement No. 608533 (NECOMA). The opinions expressed in this paper are those of the authors and do not necessarily reflect the views of the MIC or of the European Commission.

John Heidemann's work in this paper is partially sponsored by the Department of Homeland Security (DHS) Science and Technology Directorate, HSARPA, Cyber Security Division, via SPAWAR Systems Center Pacific under Contract No. N66001-13-C-3001, and via BAA 11-01-RIKA and Air Force Research Laboratory, Information Directorate under agreement number FA8750-12-2-0344. The U.S. Government is authorized to make reprints for Governmental purposes notwithstanding any copyright.The views contained herein are those of the authors and do not necessarily represent those of DHS or the U.S. Government.

8. REFERENCES

[1] Mustafa Al-Bassam. Top Alexa 10,000 Heartbleed scan. https://github.com/musalbas/heartbleed-masstest/blob/94cd9b6426311f0d20539e696496ed3d7bdd2a94/top1000.txt, April 14 2014.

[2] Manos Antonakakis, David Dagon, Xiapu Luo, Roberto Perdisci, and Wenke Lee. A centralized monitoring infrastructure for improving DNS security. In *Proc. of the 13th International Symposium on Recent Advances in Intrusion Detection*, pages 18–37, Ottawa, Ontario, Canada, September 2010. Springer.

[3] Arbor Networks. Worldwide infrastructure security report. Technical Report Volume IX, Arbor Networks, January 2014.

[4] Ignacio Bermudez, Marco Mellia, Maurizio M. Munafo, Ram Keralapura, and Antonio Nucci. DNS to the rescue: Discerning content and services in a tangled web. In *Proc. of the ACM Internet Measurement Conference*, pages 413–426, Boston, MA, November 2012.

[5] S. Bortzmeyer. DNS query name minimisation to improve privacy. Work in progress (Internet draft draft-bortzmeyer-dns-qname-minimisation-02), May 2014.

[6] Carna Botnet. Internet census 2012: Port scanning /0 using insecure embedded devices. web page http://census2012.sourceforge.net/paper.html, March 2013.

[7] Leo Breiman. Random forests. *Machine Learning*, 45:5–32, October 2001.

[8] Leo Breiman, Jerome Friedman, Richard Olshen, and Charles Stone. *Classification and Regression Trees.* Chapman and Hall, 1984.

[9] Nevil Brownlee. One-way traffic monitoring with iatmon. In *Proc. of the Passive and Active Measurement Workshop*, pages 179–188, Vienna, Austria, March 2012.

[10] Matt Calder, Xun Fan, Zi Hu, Ethan Katz-Bassett, John Heidemann, and Ramesh Govindan. Mapping the expansion of Google's serving infrastructure. In *Proc. of the ACM Internet Measurement Conference*, pages 313–326, Barcelona, Spain, October 2013. ACM.

[11] Sebastian Castro, Duane Wessles, Marina Fomenkov, and kc Claffy. A day at the root of the Internet. *ACM SIGCOMM Computer Communication Review*, 38(5):41–46, October 2008.

[12] Jakub Czyz, Michael Kallitsis, Manaf Gharaibeh, Christos Papadopoulos, Michael Bailey, and Manish Karir. Taming the 800 pound gorilla: The rise and decline of NTP DDoS attacks. In *Proc. of the ACM Internet Measurement Conference*, pages 435–448, Vancouver, BC, Canada, November 2014. ACM.

[13] Jakub Czyz, Kyle Lady, Sam G. Miller, Michael Bailey, Michael Kallitsis, and Manish Karir. Understanding IPv6 Internet background radiation. In *IMC'13*, pages 105–118, Barcelona, Spain, 2013.

[14] Alberto Dainotti, Claudio Squarcell, Emile Aben, Kimberly C. Claffy, Marco Chiesa, Michele Russo, and Antonio Pescape. Analysis of country-wide internet outages caused by censorship. In *Proc. of the ACM Internet Measurement Conference*, pages 1–18, Berlin, Germany, November 2011.

[15] Peter B. Danzig, Katia Obraczka, and Anant Kumar. An analysis of wide-area name server traffic: A study of the Domain Name System. In *Proc. of the ACM SIGCOMM Conference*, pages 281–292, January 1992.

[16] DNS-OARC. Day in the life of the internet (DITL) 2014. https://www.dns-oarc.net/oarc/data/ditl, April 2014.

[17] Zakir Durumeric, Michael Bailey, and J. Alex Halderman. An Internet-wide view of Internet-wide scanning. In *Proc. of the 23rd USENIX Security Symposium*, pages 65–78, San Diego, CA, August 2014. USENIX.

[18] Zakir Durumeric, Frank Li, James Kasten, Johanna Amann, Jethro Beekman, Mathias Payer, Nicolas Weaver, David Adrian, Vern Paxson, Michael Bailey, and J. Alex Halderman. The matter of Heartbleed. In *Proc. of the ACM Internet Measurement Conference*, pages 475–488, Vancouver, BC, Canada, November 2014. ACM.

[19] Zakir Durumeric, Eric Wustrow, and J. Alex Halderman. ZMap: Fast Internet-wide scanning and its security applications. In *Proc. of the USENIX Security Symposium*, pages 605–620, Washington, DC, USA, August 2013. USENIX.

[20] Robert Edmonds. ISC passive DNS architecture. Technical report, Internet Systems Consortium, Inc., March 2012.

[21] Xun Fan, Ethan Katz-Bassett, and John Heidemann. Assessing affinity between users and CDN sites. In *Proc. of the 7th Workshop on Traffic Monitoring and Analysis (TMA)*, pages 95–110, Barcelona, Spain, April 2015. Springer.

[22] Hongyu Gao, Vinod Yegneswaran, Yan Chen, Phillip Porras, Shalini Ghosh, and Jian Jiang Haixing Duan. An empirical reexamination of global DNS behavior. In *Proc. of the ACM SIGCOMM Conference*, pages 267–278, Hong Kong, China, 2013.

[23] Carrie Gates. Coordinated scan detection. In *Proc. of the ISOC Network and Distributed System Security Symposium*, San Diego, CA, February 2009. The Internet Society.

[24] Kenneth Geers, Darien Kindlund, Ned Moran, and Rob Rachwald. World War C: Understanding nation-state motives behind today's advanced cyber attacks. Technical report, FireEye, September 2014.

[25] John Heidemann, Yuri Pradkin, Ramesh Govindan, Christos Papadopoulos, Genevieve Bartlett, and Joseph Bannister. Census and survey of the visible Internet. In *Proc. of the ACM Internet Measurement Conference*, pages 169–182, Vouliagmeni, Greece, October 2008. ACM.

[26] Thorsten Holz, Christian Gorecki, Konrad Rieck, and Felix Freiling. Measuring and detecting fast-flux service networks. In *Proc. of the ISOC Network and Distributed System Security Symposium*, San Diego, CA, USA, February 2008. The Internet Society.

[27] Keisuke Ishibashi, Tsuyoshi Toyono, Katsuyasu Toyama, Masahiro Ishino, Haruhiko Ohshima, and Ichiro Mizukoshi. Detecting mass-mailing worm infected hosts by mining DNS traffic data. In *Proc. of the ACM SIGCOMM MineNet Workshop*, pages 159–164, Philadelphia, PA, August 2005.

[28] Julian Kirsch, Christian Grothoff, Monika Ermert, Jacob Appelbaum, Laura Poitras, and Henrik Moltke.

NSA/GCHQ: The HACIENDA program for internet colonization. *C'T Magazine*, Aug.15 2014.

[29] Matthew Lentz, Dave Levin, Jason Castonguay, Neil Spring, and Bobby Bhattacharjee. D-mystifying the D-root address change. In *Proc. of the ACM Internet Measurement Conference*, pages 57–62, Barcelona, Spain, October 2013. ACM.

[30] Kirill Levchenko, Andreas Pitsillidis, Neha Chachra, Brandon Enright, Márk Félegyházi, Chris Grier, Tristan Halvorson, Chris Kanich, Christian Kreibich, He Liu, Damon McCoy, Nicholas Weaver, Vern Paxson, Geoffrey M. Voelker, and Stefan Savage. Click trajectories: End-to-end analysis of the spam value chain. In *Proc. of the IEEE Symposium on Security and Privacy*, pages 431–446, Oakland, CA, USA, May 2011. IEEE.

[31] Zhichun Li, Anup Goyal, Yan Chen, and Aleksandar Kuzmanovic. Measurement and diagnosis of address misconfigured P2P traffic. In *INFOCOM'10*, pages 1–9, San Diego, CA, March 2010.

[32] MaxMind LLC. GeoIP. http://www.maxmind.com/geoip.

[33] Damon McCoy, Kevin Bauer, Dirk Grunwald, Tadayoshi Kohno, and Douglas Sicker. Shining light in dark places: Understanding the tor network. In *Proc. of the IEEE International Workshop on Performance Evaluation of Tracking and Surveillance (PETS)*, pages 63–76, Leuven, Belgium, July 2008.

[34] Jon Oberheide, Manish Karir, Z. Morley Mao, and Farnam Jahanian. Characterizing dark DNS behavior. In *Proc. of the 4th International Conference on Detection of Intrusions & Malware, and Vulnerability Assessment (DIMVA)*, pages 140–156, Lucerne, Switzerland, July 2007. Springer.

[35] Robert O'Harrow, Jr. Cyber search engine Shodan exposes industrial control systems to new risks. *The Washington Post*, June 3 2012.

[36] OpenDNS. DNSCrypt: Introducing DNSCrypt. web page http://www.opendns.com/about/innovations/dnscrypt/, January 2014.

[37] Ruoming Pang, Vinod Yegneswaran, Paul Barford, Vern Paxson, and Larry Peterson. Characteristics of Internet background radiation. In *Proc. of the ACM Internet Measurement Conference*, pages 27–40, Sicily, Italy, 2004.

[38] Nicole Perlroth. Thought safe, websites find the door ajar. *New York Times*, page A1, Apr. 9 2014.

[39] Dave Plonka. Flawed routers flood university of wisconsin internet time server. http://pages.cs.wisc.edu/~plonka/netgear-sntp, 2003.

[40] David Plonka and Paul Barford. Context-aware clustering of DNS query traffic. In *Proc. of the ACM Internet Measurement Conference*, pages 217–229, Vouliagmeni, Greece, October 2008.

[41] Niels Provos. A virutal honeypot framework. In *Usenix Security Symposium 2004*, pages 1–14, San Diego, CA, August 2004.

[42] Lin Quan, John Heidemann, and Yuri Pradkin. Trinocular: understanding Internet reliability through adaptive probing. In *Proc. of the ACM SIGCOMM Conference*, pages 255–266, Hong Kong, China, August 2013.

[43] Bernhard Scholkopf and Alexander J. Smola. *Learning with Kernels: Support Vector Machines, Regularization, Optimization, and Beyond*. MIT Press, 2001.

[44] Kyle Schomp, Tom Callahan, Michael Rabinovich, and Mark Allman. On measuring the client-side DNS infrastructure. In *Proc. of the ACM Internet Measurement Conference*, pages 77–90, Barcelona, Spain, October 2013.

[45] Farsight Security. SIE (Security Information Exchange). https://www.farsightsecurity.com/Services/SIE/, 2013.

[46] Shadow server foundation. http://www.shadowserver.org/.

[47] Stuart Staniford, James A. Hoagland, and Joseph M. McAlerney. Practical automated detection of stealthy portscans. *Journal of Comptuer Security*, 10(1):105–136, 2002.

[48] Ionut Trestian, Supranamaya Ranjan, Aleksandar Kuzmanovi, and Antonio Nucci. Unconstrained endpoint profiling (Googling the Internet). In *Proc. of the ACM SIGCOMM Conference*, pages 279–290, Seattle, WA, Aug 2008.

[49] USC/LANDER project. Internet address census, datasets internet_address_census it63w, it63c, it63j, it63g, it64w, it64c, it64j, it64g. web page http://www.isi.edu/ant/lander, January (it63) and April (it64) 2015.

[50] Paul Vixie. Passive DNS collection and analysis, the 'dnstap' approach. Keynote talk at FloCon, January 2014.

[51] Florian Weimer. Passive DNS replication. In *Proc. of the 17th Forum of Incident Response and Security Teams (FIRST)*, Singapore, April 2005.

[52] Duane Wessels and Marina Fomenkov. Wow, that's a lot of packets. In *Proc. of the Passive and Active Measurement Workshop*, La Jolla, CA, April 2003.

[53] Wikipedia. Gini coefficient. http://en.wikipedia.org/wiki/Gini_coefficient, 2015.

[54] Eric Wustrow, Manish Karir, Michael Bailey, Farnam Jahanian, and Geoff Houston. Internet background radiation revisited. In *Proc. of the 10th ACM Internet Measurement Conference*, pages 62–73, Melbourne, Australia, November 2010. ACM.

[55] Sandeep Yadav, Ashwath Kumar, Krishna Reddy, A.L. Narasimha Reddy, and Supranamaya Ranjan. Detecting algorithmically generated malicious domain names. In *Proc. of the ACM Internet Measurement Conference*, pages 48–61, Melbourne, Australia, November 2010.

[56] Bojan Zdrnja, Nevil Brownlee, and Duane Wessels. Passive monitoring of DNS anomalies. In *Proc. of the 4th International Conference on Detection of Intrusions & Malware, and Vulnerability Assessment (DIMVA)*, pages 129–139, Lucerne, Switzerland, 2007.

[57] Liang Zhu, Zi Hu, John Heidemann, Duane Wessels, Allison Mankin, and Nikita Somaiya. Connection-oriented DNS to improve privacy and security. In *Proc. of the 36th IEEE Symposium on Security and Privacy*, pages 171–186, San Jose, Californa, USA, May 2015. IEEE.

Opprentice: Towards Practical and Automatic Anomaly Detection Through Machine Learning

Dapeng Liu†, Youjian Zhao†, Haowen Xu†, Yongqian Sun†, Dan Pei†*, Jiao Luo‡, Xiaowei Jing§, Mei Feng§
†Tsinghua University, ‡Baidu, §PetroChina
{liudp10, xhw11, sunyq12}@mails.tsinghua.edu.cn, {zhaoyoujian, peidan}@tsinghua.edu.cn, luojiao01@baidu.com, {jxw, fm}@petrochina.com.cn

ABSTRACT

Closely monitoring service performance and detecting anomalies are critical for Internet-based services. However, even though dozens of anomaly detectors have been proposed over the years, deploying them to a given service remains a great challenge, requiring manually and iteratively tuning detector parameters and thresholds. This paper tackles this challenge through a novel approach based on supervised machine learning. With our proposed system, Opprentice (**Op**erators' ap**prentice**), operators' only manual work is to periodically label the anomalies in the performance data with a convenient tool. Multiple existing detectors are applied to the performance data in parallel to extract anomaly features. Then the features and the labels are used to train a random forest classifier to automatically select the appropriate detector-parameter combinations and the thresholds. For three different service KPIs in a top global search engine, Opprentice can *automatically* satisfy or approximate a reasonable accuracy preference (recall $\geq$ 0.66 and precision $\geq$ 0.66). More importantly, Opprentice allows operators to label data in only tens of minutes, while operators traditionally have to spend more than ten days selecting and tuning detectors, which may still turn out not to work in the end.

Categories and Subject Descriptors

C.2.3 [**Network Operations**]: Network monitoring

General Terms

Measurement; Design

Keywords

Anomaly Detection; Tuning Detectors; Machine Learning

*Dan Pei is the corresponding author.

IMC'15, October 28–30, 2015, Tokyo, Japan.

DOI: http://dx.doi.org/10.1145/2815675.2815679.

1. INTRODUCTION

Closely monitoring service quality and detecting performance anomalies are critical for Internet-based services, such as search engines, online shopping, and social networking. For example, a search engine can monitor its search response time (SRT) [1] by detecting anomalies in SRT time series in an online fashion. However, even though dozens of anomaly detectors [1–24] have been proposed over the years in the context of both Internet-based services and telecom services, deploying detectors to a given service remains a great challenge. This is, we argue, because there exists no convenient method to automatically match operators' practical detection requirements with the capabilities of different detectors. Currently, for a given service quality metric, selecting and applying detectors usually require manually and iteratively tuning the internal parameters of detectors and the detection thresholds, which operators are neither interested nor feel comfortable in doing. Instead, based on our experience of working with operators from a large search engine, a campus network, and an enterprise network, operators are used to specify simple requirements for detection accuracy and manually spot-check anomalies occasionally. As a result, services either settle with simple static thresholds (*e.g.*, Amazon Cloud Watch Alarms [24]), intuitive to operators although unsatisfying in detection performance, or, after time-consuming manual tuning by algorithm designers, end up with a detector specifically tailored for the given service, which might not be directly applicable to other services.

We elaborate on the challenges of anomaly detection by reviewing the current practice. The detectors proposed in the literature [1–24] typically work on (*time*, value) pair time series data,[1] which we call KPI (Key Performance Indicator) data hereinafter. Given a KPI, the first step for the anomaly detection practitioner is to collect the requirements from the service operators. This step encounters **Definition Challenges**: it is difficult to precisely define anomalies in reality [21, 25]. In particular, the operators often have trouble describing their domain knowledge completely when "put on the spot" [25]. In addition, it is often impossible for the operators to quantitatively define anomalies, let alone to translate the vague definition into specific parameters and thresholds of a detector [21] (*e.g.*, how many times of the standard deviation [1]) . On the contrary, according to our experience of building detection systems with operators, they prefer to describe the anomalies qualitatively, with anecdotal anomaly cases as examples.

[1] In this paper, we focus on the performance anomalies of time series (also known as volume-based anomalies) rather than other types of anomalies, *e.g.*, intrusion detection using the payload information of packets.

Detector Challenges: In order to provide a reasonable detection accuracy, selecting the most suitable detector requires both the algorithm expertise and the domain knowledge about the given service KPI. The best parameters and thresholds of a given detector often highly depend on the actual data in the studied service. As such, it is very time-consuming to tune the parameters and thresholds of the detector. Sometimes, it might even require a combination of multiple detectors [8, 21, 22] for a given KPI. As a result, many rounds of time-consuming iterations between anomaly detection practitioners and operators are needed to find appropriate detectors and tune their parameters and thresholds. In reality, we observe that it is not uncommon for operators to give up after a few rounds of iterations and settle with static threshold-based detection.

To address the definition challenge and the detector challenge, we advocate for using supervised machine learning techniques,[2] well known for being able to capture complex concepts based on the features and the labels from the data (*e.g.*, KPI data). Our approach relies on two key observations. First, it is straightforward for operators to visually inspect the time series data and label anomaly cases they identified [1, 4, 9, 12, 14, 17, 26]. Operators can periodically (*e.g.*, weekly) label the cases as new data arrive, the only manual work for operators. Because anomalies are typically infrequent [16], the time for labeling is quite reasonable with the help of a dedicated labeling tool, as shown in [27] and §4.2. The second key observation is that the anomaly severities measured by different detectors can naturally serve as the features in machine learning, so each detector can serve as a feature extractor (see §4.3). Opprentice then learns from the labeled data, automatically capturing the domain knowledge from the operators, just as a smart and diligent apprentice of the operators would do. Specifically, multiple detectors are applied to the KPI data in parallel to extract features. Then the features and the labels are used to train a machine learning model, *i.e.*, random forests [28], to automatically select the appropriate detector-parameter combinations and the thresholds. The training objective is to maximally satisfy the operators' accuracy preference.

The major contributions of the paper are summarized as follows. First, to the best of our knowledge, Opprentice is the first detection framework to apply machine learning to acquiring realistic anomaly definitions and automatically combining and tuning diverse detectors to satisfy operators' accuracy preference. Second, Opprentice addresses a few challenges in applying machine learning to such a problem: labeling overhead, infrequent anomalies, class imbalance, and irrelevant and redundant features, elaborated on in §3.2 and addressed in §4. Third, we build and evaluate Opprentice in a top global search engine (§5). 14 existing detectors have been implemented and plugged into Opprentice. For three different service KPIs, Opprentice can *automatically* satisfy or approximate a reasonable accuracy preference (recall ≥ 0.66 and precision ≥ 0.66). Furthermore, although the best performing detector-parameter combination changes with different KPIs, Opprentice consistently performs similarly or even better than them. More importantly, Opprentice takes operators only tens of minutes to label data. In comparison, operators traditionally have to spend days learning and selecting detectors, then another tens of days tuning them, which may still turn out not to work in the end. We believe this is the first anomaly detection framework that does not require manual detector selection, parameter configuration, or threshold tuning.

[2] In the rest of this paper, machine learning refers particularly to supervised machine learning.

2. BACKGROUND

In this section, we first introduce the background of KPI anomaly detection. Then we present the goals and the challenges of designing Opprentice.

2.1 KPIs and KPI Anomalies

KPIs: The KPI data, which Opprentice aims to work with, are the time series data with the format of (timestamp, value). These data can be collected from SNMP, syslogs, network traces, web access logs, and other data sources. In this paper, we choose three representative KPIs from a global top search engine as a case study. Table 1 describes their basic information, and Fig. 1 shows their 1-week examples. We hide the absolute values for confidentiality. Fig. 1(a) shows the search page view (PV), which is the number of successfully served queries. PV has a significant influence on the revenue of the search engine. Fig. 1(b) shows the number of slow responses of search data centers (#SR), which is an important performance metric of the data centers. Fig. 1(c) is the the 80th percentile of search response time (SRT). This KPI has a measurable impact on the users' search experience [29].

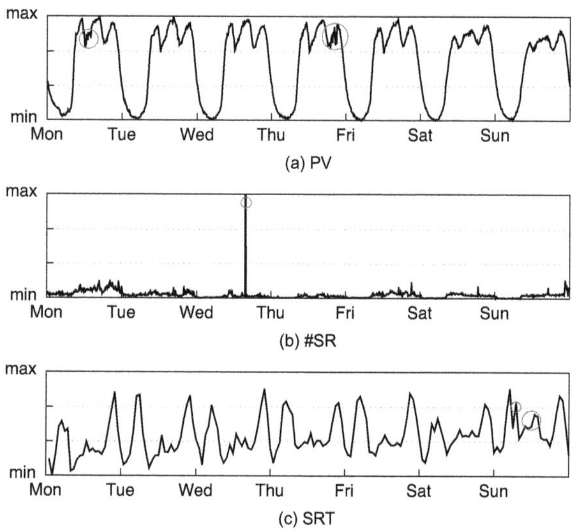

Figure 1: 1-week examples of three major KPIs of the search engine. The circles mark some obvious (not all) anomalies.

Beyond the physical meanings, the characteristics of these KPI data are also different. First, they have different levels of seasonality. For example, by visually inspecting, we see that the PV is much more regular than the other two KPIs and shows a strong seasonality. In addition, the dispersions of the KPIs are different too. Since we have to hide the absolute values, we use the coefficient of variation (C_v) to measure the dispersions. C_v equals the standard deviation divided by the mean. In Table 1, #SR has $C_v = 209\%$ and is spread out the most; SRT has $C_v = 7\%$ and concentrates the most to the mean.

Table 1: Three kinds of KPI data from the search engine.

	PV	#SR	SRT
Interval (minute)	1	1	60
Length (week)	25	19	16
Seasonality	Strong	Weak	Moderate
C_v	0.48	2.1	0.07

Anomalies: KPI time series data can also present several unexpected patterns (*e.g.*, jitters, slow ramp-ups, sudden spikes and dips) in different severity levels, such as a sudden drop by 20% or 50%. When identifying anomalies, operators care about certain patterns with different severities, which can vary among KPIs. Fig. 1 shows a few anomaly examples. However, this knowledge is difficult to be described accurately by some pre-defined rules [1,2]. This is because operators usually determine anomalies according to their own understandings of the KPIs and the real operational demands. Throughout this paper, we assume that operators have no concept drift [30] regarding anomalies. This is consistent with what we observed when the operators labeled months of data studied in this paper.

To identify anomalies automatically, researchers have proposed many detectors using a variety of techniques. We call them *basic detectors* in the rest of the paper. More details about detectors will be discussed in §4.3.

2.2 Problem and Goal

The KPI data labeled by operators are the so called "ground truth". The fundamental goal of anomaly detection is to be accurate, *e.g.*, identifying more anomalies in the ground truth, and avoiding false alarms. We use *recall* ($\frac{\text{\# of true anomalous points detected}}{\text{\# of true anomalous points}}$) and *precision* ($\frac{\text{\# of true anomalous points detected}}{\text{\# of anomalous points detected}}$) to measure the detection accuracy. Precision describes what matters to operators better than false positive rate (FPR), because anomalies are infrequent [31]. Precision is also equivalent to 1-FDR (false discovery rate: $\frac{\text{\# of false anomalous points detected}}{\text{\# of anomalous points detected}}$). Based on our experience, operators not only understand the concepts of recall and precision, but can also specify their accuracy preference using them in the format of "recall $\geq x$ and precision $\geq y$ ". For example, the operators we worked with specified "recall ≥ 0.66 and precision ≥ 0.66" as the accuracy preference, which is considered as the **quantitative goal** of Opprentice in this paper. These values come from the operators' experience of using other detectors and their accuracy before. As anomalies are relatively few in the data, it is difficult for those detectors to achieve both high recall and precision. In fact, precision and recall are often conflicting. The trade-off between them is often adjusted according to real demands. For example, busy operators are more sensitive to precision, as they do not want to be frequently disturbed by many false alarms. On the other hand, operators would care more about recall if a KPI, *e.g.*, revenue, is critical, even at the cost of a little lower precision. We also evaluate Opprentice under different accuracy preference in §5.

In addition to the above quantitative goal of accuracy, Opprentice has one **qualitative goal**: being automatic enough so that the operators would not be involved in selecting and combining suitable detectors, or tuning them.

In this paper, we focus on identifying anomalous behaviors in KPI time series. This is an important first step for monitoring the service performance. However, further investigation and troubleshooting of those anomalies are beyond the research scope of this paper.

3. OPPRENTICE OVERVIEW

3.1 Core Ideas

Opprentice approaches the above problem through supervised machine learning. Supervised machine learning can be used to automatically build a classification model from historical data, and then classify future data based on the model. Because of the data-driven property, supervised machine learning has become a popular solution where hand-crafted rules of classification are difficult to specify in advance, *e.g.*, computer vision and data mining. In anomaly detection, manually pre-defining anomalies is also challenging, which motivates us to tackle the problem through supervised machine learning.

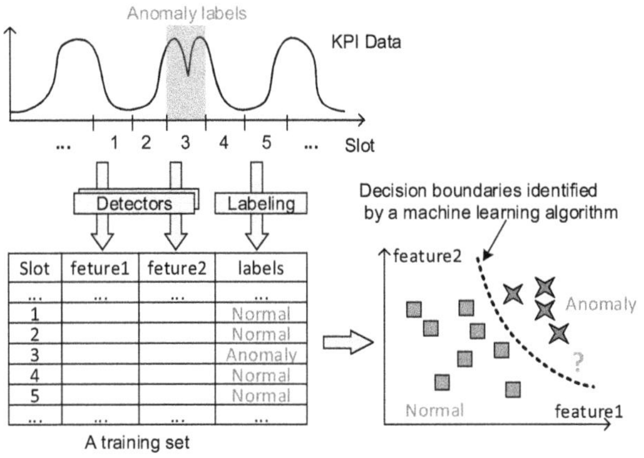

Figure 2: High level idea of applying machine learning in Opprentice.

Fig. 2 shows the high-level idea of how machine learning is applied in Opprentice. We generate a training set from historical KPI data, which is used by a machine learning algorithm to build a classification model. To this end, first, operators need to label the anomalies in the data. In the meanwhile, we use existing basic anomaly detectors to quantify anomalous level of the data from their own perspectives, respectively. The results of the detectors are used as the features of the data. The features and operators' labels together form the training set. Then a machine learning algorithm takes advantage of a certain technique to build a classification model. For example, given the decision boundaries in Fig. 2, the point represented by the question mark is classified as an anomaly.

In this way, operators' only job in building an anomaly detection system is to label anomaly cases, which is much easier (§4.2) and costs less time (§5.7). The rest would be handled by the machine learning based framework, including combining diverse detectors and adjusting their thresholds. Note that, although prior work has applied machine learning algorithms to anomaly detection [16,20,32], they only deem machine learning algorithms as *basic detectors*. To the best of our knowledge, Opprentice is the first framework that use machine learning to automatically *combine* and *tune* existing detectors to satisfy operators' detection requirements (anomaly definitions and the detection accuracy preference). Furthermore, to the best of our knowledge, this is the first time that different detectors are modeled as the feature extractors in machine learning (§4.3).

3.2 Addressing Challenges in Machine Learning

Although the above machine learning based idea seems promising, applying it in designing Opprentice poses a number of interesting and practical challenges.

- **Labeling overhead.** Labeling anomalies requires a lot of manual efforts. To help operators label effectively, we developed a dedicated labeling tool with a simple and convenient interaction interface. §5.7 shows that labeling time of our studied KPIs with our tool is less than 6 minutes for each month of data.

- **Incomplete anomaly cases.** The performance of machine learning algorithms can be affected by whether the training set contains enough anomaly cases. However, since anomalies occur less frequently in practice, an arbitrary training set is unlikely to cover enough anomalies [16]. For example, new types of anomalies might emerge in the future. To address this challenge, we incrementally retrain the classifier with newly labeled data. Through this way, Opprentice is able to catch and learn new types of anomalies that do not show up in the initial training set.

- **Class imbalance problem.** Another effect of infrequent anomalies is that the normal data always outnumber the anomalies in the training set. When learning from such "imbalanced data", the classifier is biased towards the large (normal) class and ignores the small (anomaly) class [31]. It results in low detection rate, which may not satisfy operators' accuracy preference. We solve this problem in §4.5 through adjusting the machine learning classification threshold (**cThld** henceforth).

- **Irrelevant and redundant features.** To save manual efforts, we neither select the most suitable detectors nor tune their internal parameters. Instead, many detectors with different parameters are used simultaneously to extract features (§4.3). In this case, some of the features would be either irrelevant to the anomalies or redundant with each other. Prior work has demonstrated that some learning algorithms would degrade in accuracy when handling such features. We solve this problem by using an ensemble learning algorithm, *i.e.*, random forests [28], which is relatively robust and works well for our problem (§5).

4. DESIGN

In this section we first present the architecture of Opprentice, and then describe the design details.

4.1 Architecture

Fig. 3 illustrates the architecture of Opprentice. From the operators' view, they interact with Opprentice in two ways (Fig. 3(a)). First, before the system starts up, operators specify an accuracy preference (recall $\geq x$ and precision $\geq y$), which we assume does not change in this paper. This preference is later used to guide the automatic adjustment of the cThld. Second, the operators use a convenient tool to label anomalies in the historical data at the beginning and label the incoming data periodically (*e.g.*, weekly). All the data are labeled only once.

From the Opprentice-side view, first in Fig. 3(a), an anomaly classifier is trained as follows. Numerous detectors function as feature extractors for the data. Based on the features together with the operators' labels, a machine learning algorithm (*e.g.*, random forests used in this paper) incrementally retrains the anomaly classifier with both the historical and the latest labeled data. After that, in Fig. 3(b), the same set of detectors extract the features of incoming data, and the classifier is used to detect/classify them. Note that, unlike the traditional way, the detectors here only extract features rather than reporting anomalies by themselves. Next, we introduce the design of each component in detail.

4.2 Labeling Tool

We developed a dedicated tool to help operators effectively label anomalies in historical data. The user interface of the tool is shown in the left part of Fig. 4, with a brief user manual on the right side. The tool works as follows. First, it loads KPI data, and displays them with a line graph in the top panel. To assist operators in identifying anomalies, the data of the last day and the last week are also shown in light colors. The operators can use the arrow keys on the keyboard to navigate (forward, backward, zoom in and zoom out) through the data. Once the operators have identified anomalies, they can left click and drag the mouse to label the window of anomalies, or right click and drag to (partially) cancel previously labeled window. Besides, they can adjust the Y axis scale via the slider on the right side. The data navigator in the bottom panel shows a zoom-out view of the data.

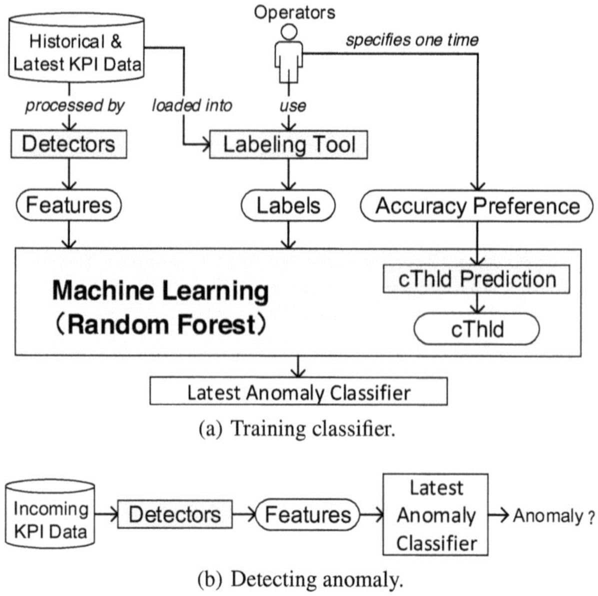

Figure 3: Opprentice architecture.

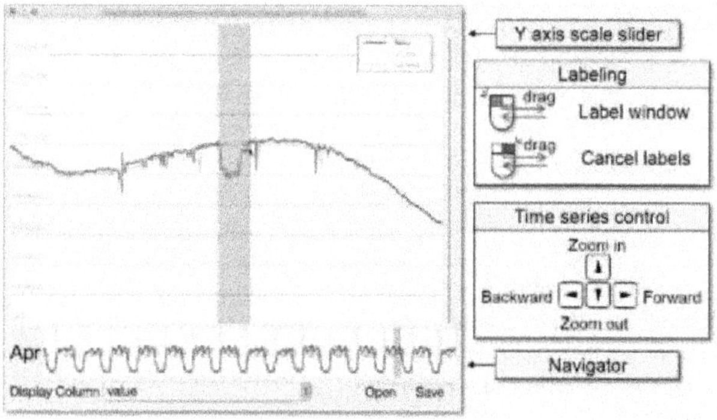

Figure 4: Labeling tool.

The labeling tool is effective because operators do not have to label each time bin one by one. They first see a relatively zoomed-out view of the KPI curve. In this view, we do not smooth the curve. Thus, even if one time bin is anomalous, it is visible to operators. Then, operators can zoom in to locate the specific anomalous time bin(s), and label them by a window. Labeling windows, as opposite to individual time bins, significantly reduces labeling overhead. §5.7 shows that it only takes operators a few minutes to label a month of data in our studied KPIs.

One issue of labeling is that errors can be introduced, especially that the boundaries of an anomalous window are often extended or narrowed when labeling. However, machine learning is well known for being robust to noises. Our evaluation in §5 also attests that the real labels of operators are viable for learning.

Our labeling tool in spirit is similar to WebClass [27], a labeling tool for NetFlow data. However, WebClass cannot be used directly in our problem because it only supports NetFlow data rather than general time series data. More importantly, it only allows operators to label the anomalies already identified by detectors as *false positives* or *unknown*. In contrast, our labeling tool enables operators to freely label all the data rather than labeling the detection results.

4.3 Detectors

We now describe how detectors function as extractors of anomaly features in Opprentice, and introduce the considerations when choosing detectors to work with Opprentice.

4.3.1 Detectors As Feature Extractors

Inspired by [21, 33], we represent different detectors with a unified model:

$$\text{data point} \xrightarrow{\text{a detector with parameters}} \text{severity} \xrightarrow{\text{sThld}} \{1, 0\}$$

First, when a detector receives an incoming data point, it internally produces a non-negative value, called *severity*, to measure how anomalous that point is. For example, Holt-Winters [6] uses the residual error (*i.e.*, the absolute difference between the actual value and the forecast value of each data point) to measure the severity; historical average [5] assumes the data follow Gaussian distribution, and uses how many times of standard deviation the point is away from the mean as the severity. Most detectors are parameterized and have a set of *internal parameters*. For example, Holt-Winters has three parameters $\{\alpha, \beta, \gamma\}$, and historical average has one parameter of window length. The severity of a given data point depends on both the detector and its internal parameters. Afterwards, a detector further needs a threshold to translate the severity into a binary output, *i.e.*, anomaly (1) or not (0). We call this threshold the severity threshold (**sThld** henceforth).

Since the severity describes the anomalous level of data, it is natural to deem the severity as the anomaly feature. To produce features, for each parameterized detector, we sample their parameters [34] so that we can obtain several fixed detectors. We call a detector with specific sampled parameters a (detector) *configuration*. Thus a configuration acts as a *feature extractor*:

$$\text{data point} \xrightarrow{\text{configuration (detector + sampled parameters)}} \text{feature}$$

The feature extraction, training, and classification (detection) in Opprentice are all designed to work with individual data points, not anomalous windows. This way, the machine learning algorithm can have enough training data, and the classifier can detect individual anomalous data point fast.

4.3.2 Choosing Detectors

When choosing detectors, we have two general requirements. First, the detectors should fit the above model, or they should be able to measure the severities of data. In fact, a lot of widely-used detectors all work in this way [1, 4–7, 10–12, 24]. Second, since anomalies should be detected timely, we require that the detectors can be implemented in an online fashion. This requires that once a data point arrives, its severity should be calculated by the detectors without waiting for any subsequent data. In addition, the calculation time should be less than the data interval, which is not difficult to fulfill. For example, the shortest data interval is one minute in our studied data. Besides, some detectors, such as those based on moving averages, need one window of data to warm up. We cope with such detectors by skipping the detection of the data in the warm-up window, which has no influence on the detection of future data.

Since we intend to free operators from carefully selecting detectors, the detectors meeting the above requirements are used to work with Opprentice without carefully evaluating their effectiveness. Although some detectors might be inaccurate in detecting certain KPIs (§5.3.1), Opprentice can find suitable ones from broadly selected detectors, and achieve a relatively high accuracy. In this paper, we implement 14 widely-used detectors (introduced later in §5.2) in Opprentice as a case study.

4.3.3 Sampling Parameters

We have two strategies to sample the parameters of detectors. The first one is to sweep the parameter space. We observe that the parameters of some detectors have intuitive meanings. For example, EWMA (Exponentially Weighted Moving Average) [11], a prediction based detector, has only one weight parameter $\alpha \in [0, 1]$. As α goes up, the prediction relies more upon the recent data than the historical data. Consequently, we can sample $\alpha \in \{0.1, 0.3, 0.5, 0.7, 0.9\}$ to obtain 5 typical features from EWMA. As for the detectors with multiple parameters and a large parameter space, we can reduce the sampling granularity. For example, Holt-Winters has three [0,1] valued parameters α, β, and γ. To limit the number of samples, we can choose $\{0.2, 0.4, 0.6, 0.8\}$ for α, β, and γ, leading to $4^3 = 64$ features. Other types of detectors may need window parameters, and we can adopt windows of several points, days, or weeks according to the characteristics of the detectors. For example, moving average based detectors with a short window aim at identifying local anomalies, while time series decomposition [1] usually uses a window of weeks to capture long-term violations. Although such sampling strategies do not guarantee that we can find the most suitable parameters (or features) due to the relatively coarse sampling granularity, we only need a set of good enough features, and Opprentice can achieve a promising accuracy by combining them (§5).

On the other hand, the parameters of some complex detectors, *e.g.*, ARIMA (Autoregressive Integrated Moving Average) [10], can be less intuitive. Worse, their parameter spaces can be too large even for sampling. To deal with such detectors, we estimate their "best" parameters from the data, and generate only one set of parameters, or one configuration for each detector. The estimation method is specifically designed for each such detector. For example, [35,36] provide the parameter estimation for ARIMA. Besides, since the data characteristics can change over time, it is also necessary to update the parameter estimates periodically.

4.4 Machine Learning Algorithm

4.4.1 Considerations and Choices

We need to be careful when choosing machine learning algorithms. This is because in our problem, there are redundant and irrelevant features, caused by using detectors without careful evaluation. Some learning algorithms such as naive Bayes, logistic regression, decision tree, and linear SVM, will perform badly when coping with such training data (§5.3.2). Additionally, a promising algorithm should be less-parametric and insensitive to its parameters, so that Opprentice can be easily applied to different data sets. In this paper, we choose random forests [28], which has been proved to be robust to noisy features and work well in practice [28, 37]. Furthermore, random forests have only two parameters and are not very sensitive to them [38]. Our evaluation results also show that the random forest algorithm perform better, and are more stable than other commonly-used algorithms.

Note that we do understand that *feature selection* [39, 40] is a commonly used solution to mitigate the influences of irrelevant and redundant features. However, we do not explore feature selection in this paper and consider it as future work, because it could introduce extra computation overhead, and the random forest works well by itself (§5.3.2).

4.4.2 *Random Forest*

In the interest of space, we only introduce some basic ideas of random forests. More details are in [28].

Preliminaries: decision trees. A decision tree [41] is a popular learning algorithm as it is simple to understand and interpret. It has been used widely to uncover the relationships between features and labels [42, 43]. At a high level, it provides a tree model with various if-then rules to classify data. Fig. 5 shows a compacted decision tree learned from our SRT data set. The tree contains three if-then rules on the features of three detectors, *i.e.*, time series decomposition, singular value decomposition, and diff (See §5.2 for the details of the detectors). The numbers on branches, *e.g.*, 3 for time series decomposition, are the feature split points. The tree is then used to classify incoming data. The tree is greedily built top-down. At each level, it determines the *best* feature and its split point to separate the data into distinct classes as much as possible, or produce the "purest" sub nodes. A goodness function, *e.g.*, information gain and gini index, is used for quantifying such an ability of each feature. The tree grows in this way until every leaf node is pure (fully grown). In the decision tree, a feature is more important for classification if it is closer to the root. For example, in Fig. 5, the feature of time series decomposition is most effective to distinguish different data.

There are two major problems of decision tree. One is that the greedy feature selection at each step may not lead to a good final classifier; the other is that the fully grown tree is very sensitive to noisy data and features, and would not be general enough to classify future data, which is called *overfitting*. Some pruning solutions have been proposed to solve overfitting. For example, stop growing the tree earlier after it exceeds a threshold of depth. However, it is still quite tricky to determine such a threshold.

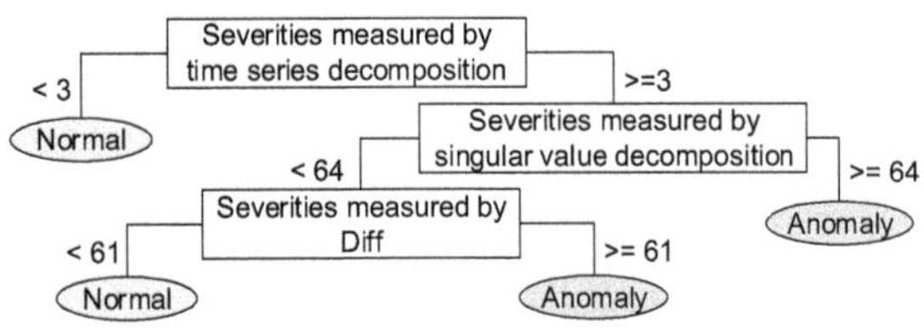

Figure 5: Decision tree example. The rectangles represent the features extracted by different detectors and the ellipses are the classification results.

A Random forest is an ensemble classifier using many decision trees. Its main principle is that a group of weak learners (*e.g.*, individual decision trees) can together form a strong learner [44]. To grow different trees, a random forest adds some elements or randomness. First, each tree is trained on subsets sampled from the original training set. Second, instead of evaluating all the features at each level, the trees only consider a random subset of the features each time. As a result, some trees may be not or less affected by the irrelevant and redundant features if these features are not used by the trees. All the trees are fully grown in this way without pruning. The random forest then combines those trees by majority vote. That is, given a new data point, each of the trees gives its own classification. For example, if 40 trees out of 100 classify the point into an anomaly, its anomaly probability is 40%. By default, the random forest uses 50% as the classification threshold (*i.e.*, cThld).

The above properties of randomness and ensemble make random forests more robust to noises and perform better when faced with irrelevant and redundant features than decision trees.

4.5 Configuring cThlds

4.5.1 *PC-Score: A Metric to Select Proper cThlds*

We need to configure cThlds rather than using the default one (*e.g.*, 0.5) for two reasons. First, when faced with imbalanced data (anomalous data points are much less frequent than normal ones in data sets), machine learning algorithms typically fail to identify the anomalies (low recall) if using the default cThlds [31]. Second, operators have their own preference regarding the precision and recall of anomaly detection. Configuring cThlds is a general method to trade off between precision and recall [31]. In consequence, we should configure the cThld of random forests properly to satisfy the operators' preference.

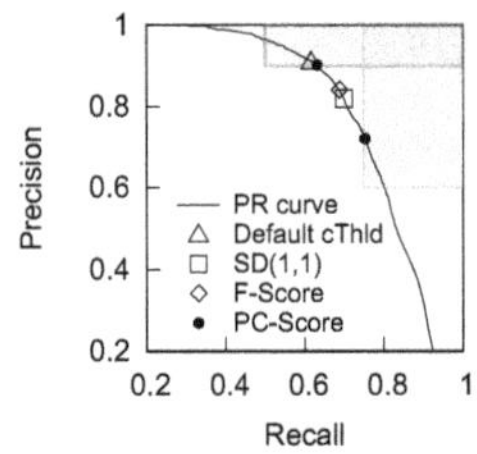

Figure 6: PR curve of a random forest trained and tested on the PV data. Different methods select different cThlds and result in different precision and recall. The two shaded rectangles represent two types of assumed operators' preferences.

Before describing how we configure the cThld, we first use Precision-Recall (PR) curves to provide some intuitions. PR curves is widely used to evaluate the accuracy of a binary classifier [45], especially when the data is imbalanced.[3] A PR curve plots precision against recall for every possible cThld of a machine learning algorithm (or for every sThld of a basic detector). Typically, there is a trade-off between precision and recall. Fig. 6 shows an exemplary PR curve derived from a random forest trained and tested on PV data. Two types of assumed operators' preferences (1) "recall $\geq$ 0.75 and precision $\geq$ 0.6" and (2) "recall $\geq$ 0.5 and precision $\geq$ 0.9" are represented by the shaded rectangles. Configuration of cThlds is to seek a proper point on the PR curve. In Fig. 6, the triangle symbol is selected by the default cThld 0.5. Besides, we also show the results of another two accurate metrics: a *F-Score* based method, which selects the point that maximizes F-Score $= \frac{2 \cdot precision \cdot recall}{precision + recall}$; *SD(1,1)*, a metric similar to that in [46], which selects the point with the shortest Euclidean distance to the upper right corner where the precision and the recall are both perfect. We see that in Fig. 6, the PR curve has points inside both the rectangles, however, the default threshold only satisfies the preference (2) but not (1); F-Score and SD(1,1) do not satisfy

[3] A similar method is Receiver Operator Characteristic (ROC) curves, which show the trade-off between the false positive rate (FPR) and the true positive rate (TPR). However, when dealing with highly imbalanced data sets, PR curves can provide a more informative representation of the performance [45].

either of the preferences. This is because these metrics select cThld without considering operators' preferences.

Motivated by the above fact, we develop a simple but effective accuracy metric based on F-Score, namely PC-Score (preference-centric score), to explicitly take operators' preference into account when deciding cThlds. First, for each point (r, p) on the PR curve, we calculate its PC-Score as follows:

$$\text{PC-Score}(r,p) = \begin{cases} \frac{2 \cdot r \cdot p}{r+p} + 1 & , r \geq R \text{ and } p \geq P \\ \frac{2 \cdot r \cdot p}{r+p} & , \text{otherwise} \end{cases}$$

where R and P are from the operators' preference "recall $\geq R$ and precision $\geq P$". Basically, the PC-Score measures the F-Score of (r, p). In order to identify the point satisfying operators' preference (if one exists), we add an incentive constant of 1 to F-score if $r \leq R$ and $p \leq P$. Since F-Score is no more than 1, this incentive constant ensures that the points satisfying the preference must have the PC-Score larger than others that do not. Hence, we choose the cThld corresponding to the point with the largest PC-Score. In Fig. 6, we see that the two points selected based on the PC-Score are inside the two shaded recectangles, respectively. Note that, in the case when a PR curve has no points inside the preference region, the PC-Score cannot find the desired points, but it can still choose approximate recall and precision.

4.5.2 EWMA Based cThld Prediction

The above describes how to configure cThlds based on the PC-Score in an offline or "oracle" mode. That is, we configure cThlds after the data to be detected (also called a test set) have already arrived. These cThlds are the best ones we can configure for detecting those data, and are called *best cThlds*. However, in online detection, we need to predict cThlds for detecting future data.

To this end, an alternative method is k-fold cross-validation [47]. First, a historical training set is divided into k subsets of the same length. In each test (k tests in total), a classifier is trained using $k-1$ of the subsets and tested on the rest one with a cThld candidate. The candidate that achieves the smallest average PC-Score across the k tests is used for future detection. In this paper we use $k = 5$, and sweep the space of cThld with a very fine granularity of 0.001, that is, we evaluate 1000 cThld candidates in a range of $[0, 1]$.

However, we found that this cross-validation method does not work quite well in our problem (§5.6). A potential explanation is that, as shown in Fig. 7, the best cThlds can differ greatly over weeks. As a result, in the cross-validation, the cThld that achieves the highest average performance over all the historical data might not be similar to the best cThld of the future week.

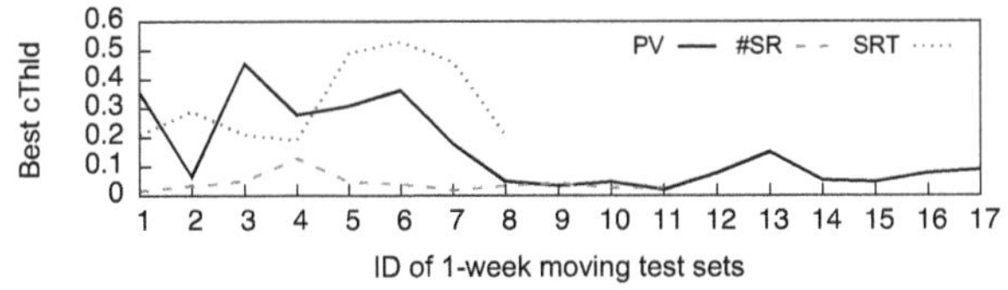

Figure 7: Best cThld of each week from the 9th week. The first 8-week data are used as the initial training set.

Our method is motivated by another observation in Fig. 7. That is, though the best cThlds changes over weeks, they can be more similar to the ones of the neighboring weeks. A possible explanation is that the underlying problems that cause KPI anomalies might last for some time before they are really fixed, so the neighboring weeks are more likely to have similar anomalies and require similar cThlds. Hence, we adopt EWMA [11] to predict the cThld of the ith week (or the ith test set) based on the historical *best cThlds*. Specifically, EWMA works as follows:

$$\text{cThld}_i^p = \begin{cases} \alpha \cdot \text{cThld}_{i-1}^b + (1-\alpha) \cdot \text{cThld}_{i-1}^p & , i > 1 \\ \text{5-fold prediction} & , i = 1 \end{cases}$$

cThld_{i-1}^b is the best cThld of the $(i-1)^{\text{th}}$ week. cThld_i^p is the predicted cThld of the ith week, and also the one used for detecting the ith-week data. $\alpha \in [0, 1]$ is the smoothing constant. For the first week, we use 5-fold cross-validation to initialize cThld_1^p. EWMA is simple but effective here as it does not require a lot of historical data to start. As α increases, EWMA gives the recent best cThlds more influences in the prediction. We use $\alpha = 0.8$ in this paper to quickly catch up with the cThld variation. Our results show that the EWMA based cThld prediction method gains a noticeable improvement when compared with the 5-fold cross-validation (§5.6).

5. EVALUATION

We implement Opprentice and 14 detectors with about 9500 lines of python, R, and C++ code. The machine learning block is based on the scikit-learn library [48]. In this section, we evaluate Opprentice using three kinds of KPI data from a top global search engine. These data are labeled by the operators using our labeling tool.

Fig. 8 shows the evaluation flow. In the first four steps, we compare the accuracy of each component of Opprentice with different approaches. The accuracy of Opprentice as a whole is shown in the §5.6. In addition to the accuracy, the qualitative goal of Opprentice, *i.e.*, being automatic, is also evaluated through directly applying Opprentice to three different KPIs without tuning. The only manual effort is to label the KPI data. We also interviewed the operators about their previous detector tuning time, and compare it with the labeling time (§5.7). Last, we evaluate the online detecting lag and the offline training time of Opprentice (§5.8). Next we first describe the data sets in §5.1 and the detectors we select in §5.2, then we show the evaluation results.

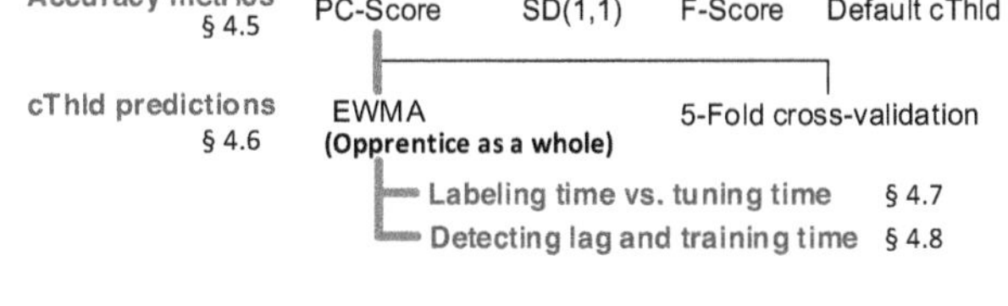

Figure 8: Evaluation flow.

5.1 Data sets

We collect three representative types of KPI data (*i.e.*, PV, #SR, and SRT) from a large search engine (§2.1). These data are labeled by the operators from the search engine using our labeling tool. There are 7.8%, 2.8%, and 7.4% data points are labeled as anomalies for PV, #SR, and SRT, respectively. Although the data we used are from the search engine, they are not special cases only for the search engine. For example, based on previous literature and our experience, the PV data we used are visually similar to other kinds of volume data. For example, the PV of other Web-based services [1, 49], the RTT (round trip time) [6] and the aggregated traffic volume [5] of an ISP, and online shopping revenue. So we believe that these three KPIs are sufficient to evaluate the idea of Opprentice, and we consider a more extensive evaluation with data from other domains beyond search as our future work. Table 2 shows several ways to generate training sets and test sets from the labeled data sets.

Table 2: Training sets and test sets. The test sets all start from the 9th week and move 1 week for each step. The training sets use different data before the test sets. I1 is the fashion of Opprentice (incremental retraining). Others are used for evaluating different strategies of training sets.

Training set	Test set	ID
All historical data	1-week moving window	I1
	4-week moving window	I4
Recent 8-week data	4-week moving window	R4
First 8-week data	4-week moving window	F4

5.2 Detector and Parameter Choices

According to the detector requirements (§4.3.2), in this proof of concept prototype, we evaluate Opprentice with 14 widely-used detectors (Table 3).

Table 3: Basic detectors and sampled parameters. Some abbreviations are MA (Moving Average), EWMA (Exponentially Weighted MA), TSD (Time Series Decomposition), SVD (Singular Value Decomposition), win(dow) and freq(uency).

Detector / # of configurations	Sampled parameters
Simple threshold [24] / 1	none
Diff / 3	last-slot, last-day, last-week
Simple MA [4] / 5	win = 10, 20, 30, 40, 50 points
Weighted MA [11] / 5	
MA of diff / 5	
EWMA [11] / 5	α = 0.1, 0.3, 0.5, 0.7, 0.9
TSD [1] / 5	win = 1, 2, 3, 4, 5 week(s)
TSD MAD / 5	
Historical average [5] / 5	
Historical MAD / 5	
Holt-Winters [6] / $4^3 = 64$	α, β, γ = 0.2, 0.4, 0.6, 0.8
SVD [7] / $5 \times 3 = 15$	row =10, 20, 30, 40, 50 points, column =3, 5, 7
Wavelet [12] / $3 \times 3 = 9$	win = 3, 5 ,7 days, freq = low, mid, high
ARIMA [10] / 1	Estimation from data
In total: 14 basic detectors / 133 configurations	

Two of the detectors were already used by the search engine we studied before this study. One is namely "Diff", which simply measures anomaly severities using the differences between the current point and the point of last slot, the point of last day, and the point of last week. The other one, namely "MA of diff", measures severities using the moving average of the difference between current point and the point of last slot. This detector is designed to discover continuous jitters. The other 12 detectors come from previous literatures. Among these detectors, there are two variants of detectors using MAD (Median Absolute Deviation) around the median, instead of the standard deviation around the mean, to measure anomaly severities. This patch can improve the robustness to missing data and outliers [3, 15]. In the interest of space, the details of these detectors and the ways they produce severities are not introduced further, but can be found in the references in Table 3. The sampled parameters of each detector are also shown in Table 3. Here, the parameter of ARIMA is estimated from the data. For other detectors, we sweep their parameter space.

In total, we have 14 detectors and 133 configurations, or 133 features for random forests. Note that, Opprentice is not limited to the detectors we used, and can incorporate emerging detectors, as long as they meet our detector requirements in §4.3.2.

5.3 Accuracy of Random Forests

Now we present the evaluation results. First, we compare the accuracy of random forests with other detection approaches in an offline mode. Since we are not aware of the thresholds of other approaches, we cannot compare specific recall and precision fairly. Alternatively, we use the area under the PR curve (AUCPR) [50] as the accuracy measure. The AUCPR is a single number summary of the detection performance over all the possible thresholds. The AUCPR ranges from 0 to 1. Intuitively, a detection approach with a large AUCPR is more likely to achieve high recall and precision.

5.3.1 Random Forests vs. Basic Detectors and Static Combinations of Basic Detectors

First, in Fig. 9, we would like to compare random forests with the 14 basic detectors with different parameter settings (133 configurations) in Table. 3. We also compare random forests with two static combination methods: the *normalization schema* [21] and the *majority-vote* [8]. These two methods are designed to combine different detectors, but they treat them equally no matter their accuracy. For comparison purposes, in this paper, we also use these two methods to combine the 133 configurations as random forests do. All the above approaches detect the data starting from the 9th week. The first 8 weeks are used as the initial training set for random forests.

Table 4: Maximum precision when recall $\geq$ 0.66. The precision greater than 0.66 is shown in bold. The top 3 basic detectors are different for each KPI (see Fig. 9 for their names).

Detection approach	Precision		
	PV	#SR	SRT
Random forest	**0.83**	**0.87**	**0.89**
Normalization scheme	0.11	0.30	0.21
Majority-vote	0.12	0.32	0.19
1st basic detector	**0.67**	**0.71**	**0.92**
2nd basic detector	0.39	**0.70**	0.61
3rd basic detector	0.37	**0.67**	0.24

Focusing on the left side of Fig. 9, we see that for the AUCPR, random forests rank the first in Fig. 9(a) and Fig. 9(b), and rank the second in Fig. 9(c), where the AUCPR of random forests is only 0.01 less than the highest one. On the other hand, the AUCPR of the two static combination methods is always ranked low. This is because most configurations are inaccurate (having very low AUCPR in Fig. 9), as we do not manually select proper detectors or tune their parameters. However, the two static combination methods treat all the configurations with the same priority (*e.g.*, equally weighted vote). Thus, they can be significantly impacted by inaccurate configurations.

The right side of Fig. 9 shows the PR curves of random forests, two combination methods, and the top 3 highest-AUCPR basic

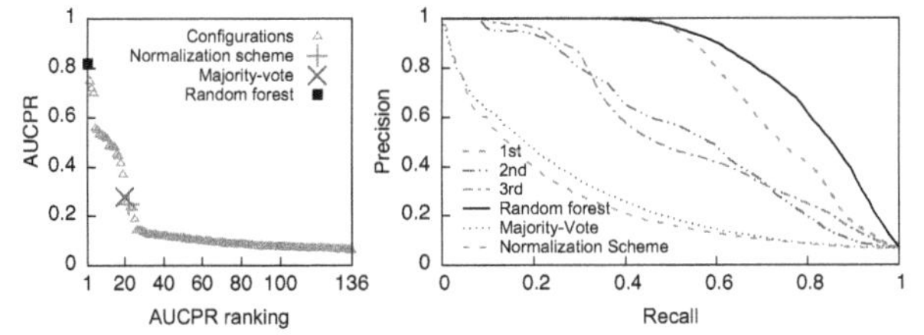

(a) KPI: PV. The basic detector ranking first in AUCPR is TSD MAD (win = 5 weeks), the 2nd one is historical MAD (win = 3 weeks), and the third one is TSD (win = 5 weeks).

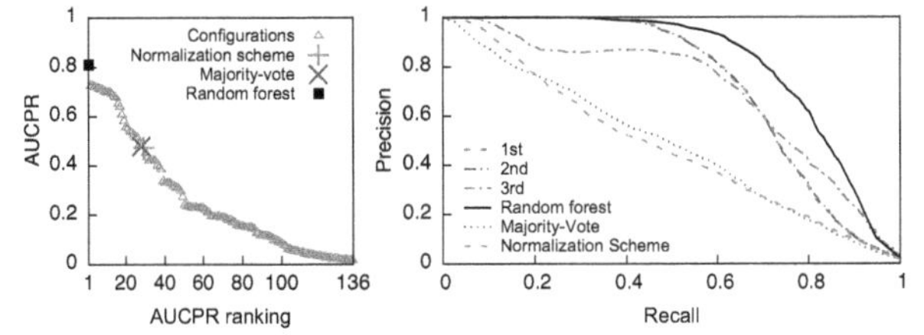

(b) KPI: #SR. The basic detector ranking first in AUCPR is simple threshold, the 2nd one is SVD (row = 50, column = 3), and the third one is wavelet (win=3, freq=low).

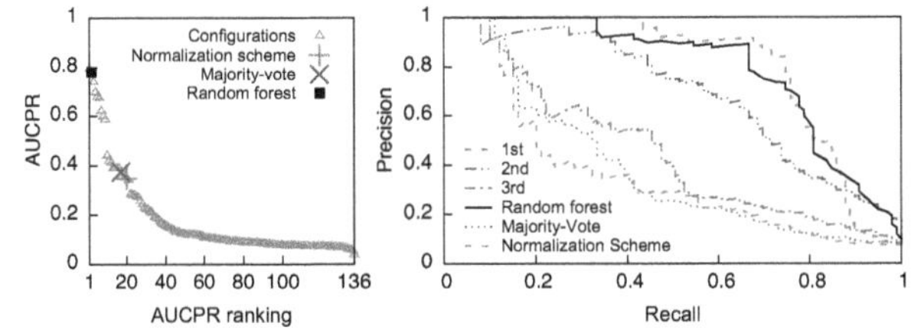

(c) KPI: SRT. The basic detector ranking first in AUCPR is SVD (row = 20, column = 7), the 2nd one is TSD MAD (win = 3 weeks), and the third one is TSD (win = 2 weeks).

Figure 9: The left side is the AUCPR rankings of different detection approaches. The right side is the PR curves. Only the top 3 highest AUCPR ranking configurations from instinct detectors are shown in PR curves.

detectors. We observe that the best basic detectors are different for each KPI, which indicates that the operators are interested in different kinds of anomalies for each KPI. Table 4 shows the maximum precision of these approaches when their recall satisfies the operators' preference (recall $\geq$ 0.66). We find that for all the KPIs, random forests achieve a high precision (greater than 0.8). The result shows that random forests significantly outperforms the two static combination methods, and perform similarly to or even better than the most accurate basic detector for each KPI.

5.3.2 Random Forests vs. Other Algorithms

We also compare random forests with several other machine learning algorithms: decision trees, logistic regression, linear support vector machines (SVMs), and naive Bayes. All these algorithms are trained and tested on I1 in Table 2. To illustrate the impact of irrelevant features (*e.g.*, the configurations with low AUCPR in Fig. 9) and redundant features (*e.g.*, a detector with similar parameter settings), we train these learning algorithms by using one feature for the first time, and adding one more feature each time. The features are added in the order of their mutual information [51], a common metric of feature selection. In Fig. 10, we observe that, while the AUCPR of other learning algorithms is unstable and decreased as more features are used, the AUCPR of random forests is still high even when all the 133 features are

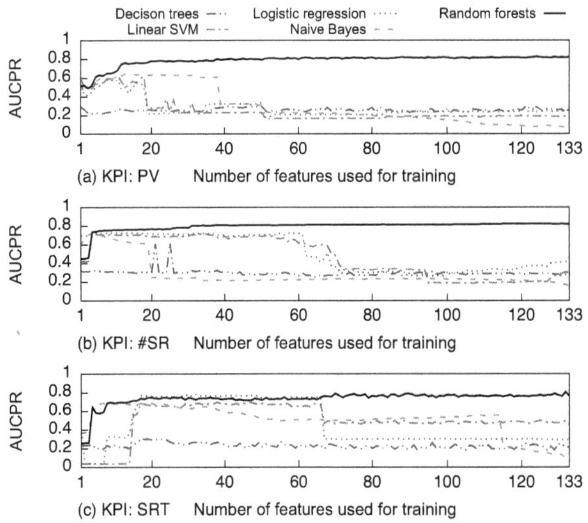

Figure 10: AUCPR of different machine learning algorithms as more features are used.

used. The result demonstrates that random forests are quite robust to irrelevant and redundant features in practice.

5.4 Incremental Retraining

After demonstrating the accuracy and stability of random forests, we want to show the effects of different training sets. We will focus only on random forests in this and the following evaluation steps. We compare three methods of generating training sets: I4, F4, and R4 in Table 2. Fig. 11 shows the AUCPR of random forests on different training sets. We see that I4 (also called incremental retraining) outperforms the other two training sets in most cases. This result is consistent with the challenge mentioned earlier that an arbitrary data set is unlikely to contain enough kinds of anomalies. In Fig. 11(b) we see that the three training sets result in similar AUCPR. This implies that the anomaly types of #SR are relatively simple and do not change much, so that they can be captured well by any of these training sets. Overall, since labeling anomalies does not cost much time (§5.7), we believe that incremental retraining is a more general and accurate method to generate training sets.

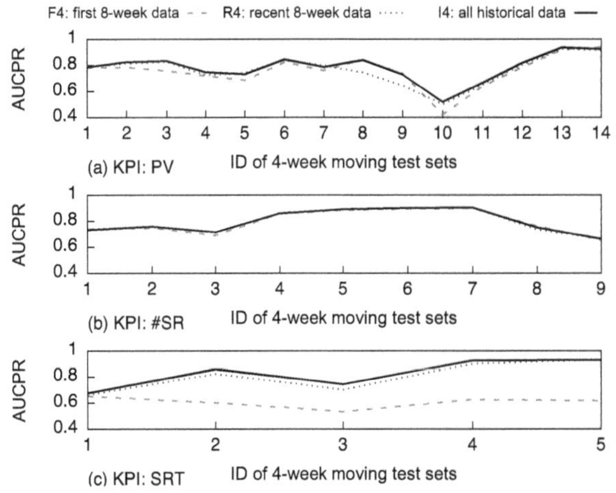

Figure 11: AUCPR of different training sets.

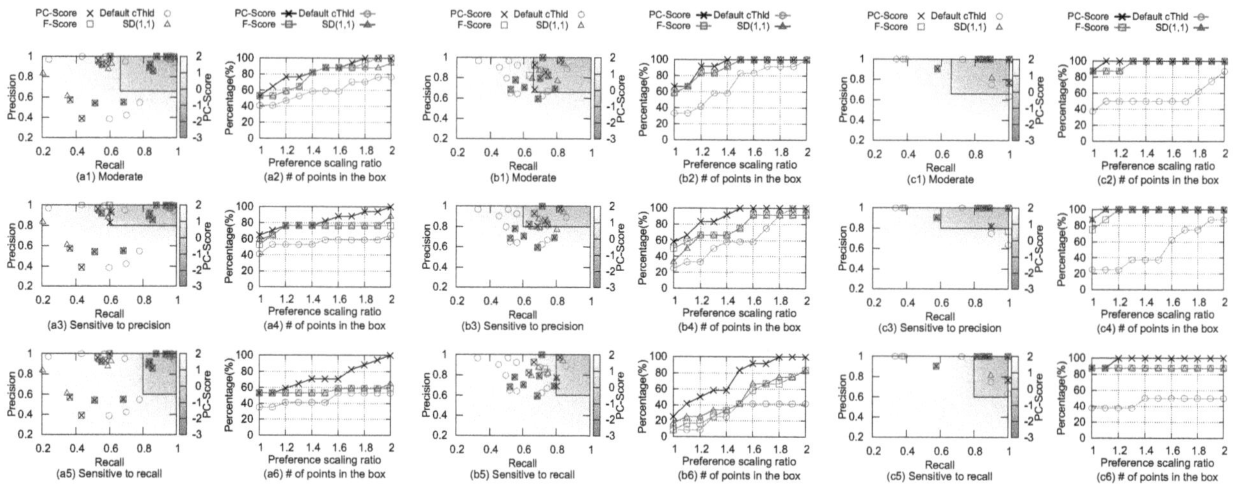

(a) KPI: PV (b) KPI: #SR (c) KPI: SRT

Figure 12: Offline-fashion evaluation for the four accuracy metrics. In each sub-figure, the left side heat maps show the points of (recall,precision) produced by the four accuracy metrics, respectively. Different rows show different kinds of operators' preferences, represented by the boxes at the top-right corner. The right side line charts depict the percentage of points inside the boxes as the boxes scale up (starting from the original preferences, *i.e.*, a scale ratio of 1).

5.5 PC-Score vs. Other Accuracy Metrics

So far, we have showed the offline AUCPR of random forests without a specific cThld. Next, we evaluate different accuracy metrics that are used to configure cThlds. We compare the PC-Score we proposed against the default cThld, the F-Score, and SD(1,1). Specifically, we train and test random forests on I1 in Table 2, and let those four metrics determine the cThlds for each one-week test set. Then, we measure their performance using recall and precision of each week. Notice that, this evaluation considers an offline or oracle setting where we assume we have the test set when configuring the cThld. We will show the cThld prediction for future test set (online detection) in §5.6.

Fig. 12 shows the results of the four metrics for three KPIs, respectively. In the left-side heat maps, each point represents the recall and the precision of one week. The first row shows the results under the preference (recall≥0.66 and precision≥0.66), called a *moderate* preference. We also evaluate another two preferences: *sensitive-to-precision* (recall≥0.6 and precision≥0.8) in the second row and *sensitive-to-recall* (recall≥0.8 and precision≥0.6) in the third row. The preferences are represented by the top-right boxes in the heat maps. The right-side line charts show the percentage of the points inside the boxes (satisfying the preferences) if we use the original or lowered preferences, *e.g.*, scaling the boxes up.

Focusing on the heat maps, we see that while the points obtained by the other three metrics remain unchanged for different preferences, the PC-Score has the ability of adjusting the recall and precision according to different preferences. Because of this advantage, we see in the line charts that PC-Score always achieve the most points inside the boxes for both the original preference and the scaled-up ones.

We also notice that it is not easy to satisfy the preference for all the weeks, because anomalies are very rare in some weeks. For example, we find that for the weeks where no point satisfies the moderate preference, anomalies are 73% and 78% fewer than other weeks for PV and #SR, respectively. Thus it is inevitable to generate more false positives in order to identify those few anomalies, leading to low precision. In addition, missing just a few anomalies can lead to an obvious degradation in recall. Fortunately, as the anomalies are few in those weeks, relatively low precision or recall would not cause a large *number* of false positives or false negatives. For example, if there are ten anomalous data points and we identify four of them (40% recall), we would miss only six anomalous data points; in such case, if we have 40% precision, we would just identify six false positives. The operators we work with suggest that they are actually OK with this small number of false positives or false negatives.

5.6 EWMA vs. 5-Fold for cThld Prediction

Previously, we show the offline evaluation of different metrics for cThld configuration, and find that PC-Score outperforms the other three. Now we evaluate the performance of online cThld prediction based on the PC-Score, which is also the detection accuracy of Opprentice as a whole. We compare the EWMA based method used by Opprentice with 5-fold cross-validation. The evaluation is similar to §5.5 except that the cThld prediction only uses the historical data (the training set) rather than the future data (the test set). As aforementioned, the result of each week can vary greatly because anomalies are quite rare in some weeks. To obtain a stable result, we calculate the average recall and precision of a 4-week moving window. The window moves one day for each step so that we can obtain a more fine-grained result. Here, we show the result under the operators' actual preference (recall≥0.66 and precision≥0.66). The recall and precision of each window are shown in Fig. 13. The offline result (called the best case here) is also shown as a baseline.

The result shows that, for PV, #SR, and SRT, the EWMA achieves 40%, 23%, and 110% more points inside the shaded regions, respectively, when compared with the 5-fold cross validation. In total, 8403 (7.3%), 2544 (2.1%), and 86 (6.4%) data points are identified as anomalies by Opprentice in the test sets (after the 9th week) for the three KPIs, respectively (not shown). We notice that there are some points falling outside of the shaded regions, such as the window between 58 and 70 in Fig. 13(a). It is mainly because the anomalies during those weeks are quite rare.

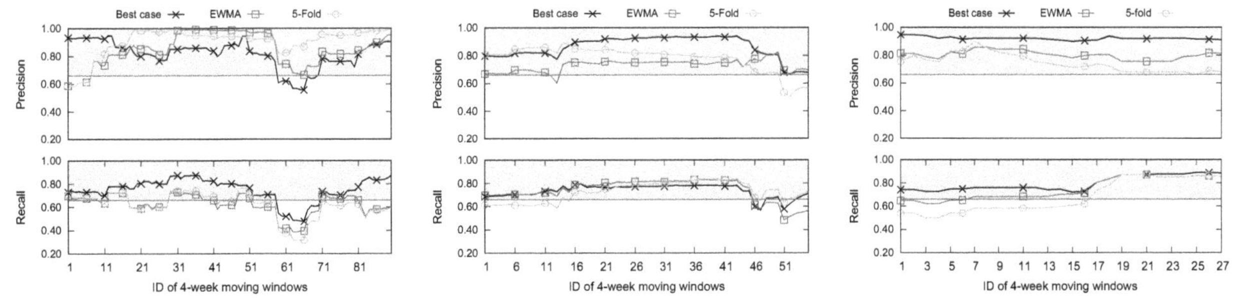

(a) KPI: PV (b) KPI: #SR (c) KPI: SRT

Figure 13: Online detection accuracy of Opprentice as a whole. The best case is obtained from offline mode. The shaded regions represent to the operators' accuracy preference (recall ≥ 0.66 and precision ≥0.66).

For example, there are only on average 4% anomalous points in the ground truth of PV data for the window between 58 and 70. However, as mentioned earlier in §5.5, in such case, a little low precision or recall would not generate many false positives or false negatives for operators. In summary, Opprentice can automatically satisfy or approximate the operators' accuracy preference.

5.7 Labeling Time vs. Tuning Time

Next, we show the time cost of labeling, the only manual job required for operators when they use Opprentice. Fig. 14 shows the operators' labeling time when they label the three types of KPI data using our tool (§4.2). The result shows that the labeling time of one-month data basically increases as the number of anomalous windows in that month. An anomalous window refers to a window of continuous anomalies derived from one label action. Among the three KPIs, SRT requires less labeling time for each month of data because it has less data points in a month as its data interval is 60 minutes. Overall, the labeling time of one-month data is less than 6 minutes. The total labeling time for PV, #SR, and SRT is 16, 17, and 6 minutes, respectively. One intuitive reason for the low labeling overhead is that the operators each time label a window of anomalies rather than labeling individual anomalous data points one by one. The anomalous windows can be much fewer (Fig. 14) than the anomalous points in the data.

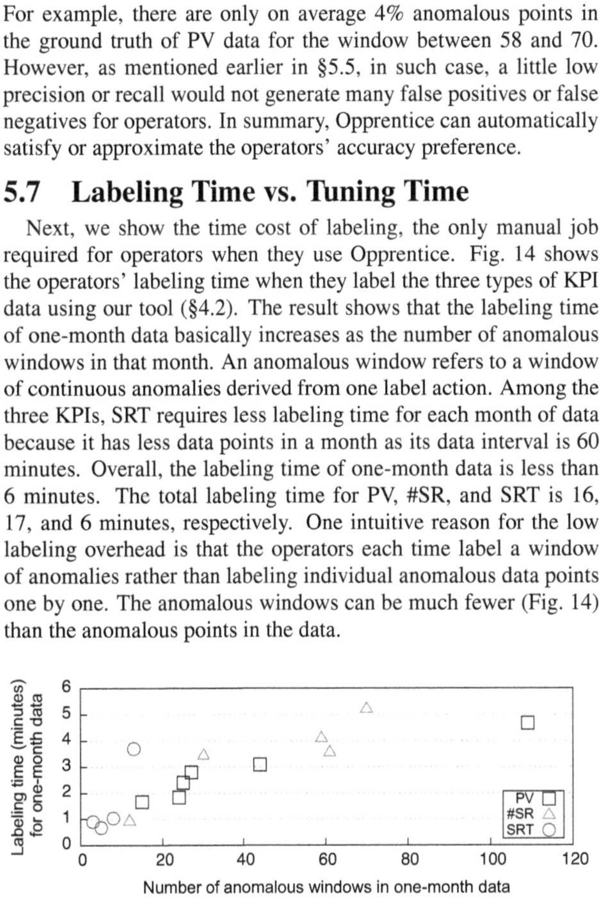

Figure 14: Operators' labeling time vs. the number of anomalous windows for every month of data.

To show the value of how Opprentice help reduce operators' manual efforts, we also present some anecdotal examples of operators' tuning time of detectors, including the time they learn the detectors and understand their parameters. We interviewed three operators from the search engine, who have experienced tuning detectors before. The first operator uses SVD, and he said it took him about 8 days to tune the detector; the second operator uses Holt-winters and historical average, and he spent about 12 days tuning these two detectors; the third operator applies time series decomposition, and he said that after the detector was implemented, it further cost him about 10 days to test and tune the detector. In the above cases, after days of tuning, only the first operator' detector works relatively well; yet, the other two operators are still not satisfied with the accuracy of their detectors, and finally abandon them. We have compared the accuracy of Opprentice with these basic detectors in §5.3.1.

Although the time reported above is not the exactly time used for tuning, it provides a basic idea of the overhead and the difficulty of manually tuning detectors. The operators we interviewed confirmed that detector tuning is very time-consuming, and they are neither interested nor feel comfortable in doing so. In summary, Opprentice can help replace the time-consuming and boring detector tuning with fast and convenient anomaly labeling.

5.8 Detection Lag and Training Time

The detection lag, in principle, consists of the feature extraction time and the classification time. We run Opprentice on the Dell PowerEdge R420 server with the Intel Xeon E5-2420 CPU and 24GB memory. The total time of extracting 133 features is on average 0.15 second for each data point. The classification takes trivial time, which is on average less than 0.0001 second per data point. Besides, the offline training time is less than 5 minutes each round. Since all the detectors can run in parallel, and training of random forests is also able to be parallelized, we believe that one can get a better performance by taking advantage of multi-threaded techniques and distributed computing on server clusters.

6. DISCUSSION

Anomaly detection is complex in practice. In this section, we discuss some issues regarding anomaly detection and clarify the scope of Opprentice.

Anomaly detection, not troubleshooting. Sometimes, although the operators admit the anomalies in the KPI curve, they tend to ignore them as they know that the anomalies are caused by some normal activities as expected, such as service upgrades and predictable social events. However, since our study focuses on identifying abnormal behaviors of the KPI data (called anomaly detection in this paper), we ask the operators to label anomalies based on the data curve itself without considering the reasons behind. Anomaly detection is a first important step of monitoring service performance. We believe that the detection results should be reported to operators and let operators decide how to deal with them, or more ideally, input into a troubleshooting system for analyzing the root causes and generating more actionable suggestions. For example, the troubleshooting system may find that the anomalies are due to normal system upgrades and suggest operators to ignore them. However, troubleshooting anomalies itself is outside our research scope.

Anomaly duration. The duration of continuous anomalies could be another important consideration of raising alarms. In this paper, we do deliberately omit this factor. One reason is that it will make our model too complex to show the core idea. Another one is that it is relative easy to implement a duration filter based upon the point-level anomalies we detected. For example, if operators are only interested in continuous anomalies that last for more than 5 minutes, one can solve it through a simple threshold filter.

Detection across the same types of KPIs. Some KPIs are of the same type and operators often care about similar types of anomalies for them [5]. For example, the PV originated from different ISPs. When applying Opprentice to such case, operators only have to label one or just a few KPIs. Then the classifier trained upon those labeled data can be used to detect across the same type of KPIs. Note that, in order to reuse the classifier for the data of different scales, the anomaly features extracted by basic detectors should be normalized. We plan to explore this direction in future work.

Dirty data. A well known problem is that detectors are often affected by "dirty data". Dirty data refer to anomalies or missing points in data, and they can contaminate detectors and cause errors of detectors. We address this problem in three ways. (a) Some of our detectors, *e.g.*, weighted MA and SVD, can generate anomaly features only using recent data. Thus, they can quickly get rid of the contamination of dirty data. (b) We take advantage of MAD [3,15] to make some detectors, such as TSD, more robust to dirty data; (c) Since Opprentice uses many detectors simultaneously, even if a few detectors are contaminated, Opprentice could still automatically select and work with the remaining detectors.

Learning limitations. A supervised learning based approach requires labeled data for initialization. This is an additional overhead when compared with applying basic detectors directly. Fortunately, the KPI data, nowadays, are easy to obtain [1,4,9,12,14,17,26]. Meanwhile, labeling can also be effective and cost less time as we demonstrated earlier with out labeling tool. Another issue is that a learning based approach is limited by the anomalies within a training set. For example, anomalies can be rare, and new types of anomalies might appear in the future [16]. We solve this problem by incrementally retraining the classifier to gather more anomaly cases and learn emerging types of anomalies.

Detection accuracy. Because of the many practical challenges mentioned above, anomaly detection is a complex and challenging task. It is intractable to achieve high precision and recall all the time. We also cannot guarantee Opprentice to be able to always satisfy the operators' accuracy preference. But our evaluation shows that the accuracy of Opprentice is still promising, especially for the operators' preference in the studied service.

7. RELATED WORK

Many efforts have been put into the field of anomaly detection. Researchers have developed numerous detectors using different techniques [1–24]. In addition, researchers try to address several challenges of applying detectors in practice. (a) For auto-tuning the internal parameters of detectors, Krishnamurthy *et al.* [11] proposes a multi-pass grid search to find appropriate parameters from data. Himura *et al.* [23] searches for the parameters to maximize the ratio of detected events. In comparison, beyond detector internal parameters, we also consider automatically selecting detectors and their thresholds. (b) Some work uses ROC curves to evaluate the performance of different detectors regardless of their thresholds [9, 14, 26]. This technique is also used in our work. (c) MAD is used to improve the robustness of detectors to dirty data [3, 15]. We also implement two detectors with MAD. (d) Some solutions attempt to statically combine different detectors together [8, 21]. We compared Opprentice with them. (e) Machine learning has also been applied in anomaly detection [16, 20, 32], but it serves as basic detectors. On the contrary, we use machine learning to combine different existing detectors.

Another important challenge of anomaly detection is to obtain the ground truth to evaluate detectors. Three commonly-used solutions are: (a) using the real anomalies identified or confirmed by domain operators [1,4,9,12,14,17,26]; (b) generating synthetic anomalies by injecting real or pre-defined anomalies into the background data [9, 14, 18, 19]; (c) pair-wise comparisons, which treat the anomalies reported by other detectors as the ground truth [1, 8, 10, 17, 18]. Because our fundamental goal is to satisfy operators' demands, we believe that solution (a) makes more sense in this paper.

8. CONCLUSION

Applying anomaly detection to an Internet-based service has been challenging in practice. This is because the anomalies are difficult to quantitatively define, and existing detectors have parameters and thresholds to tune before they can be deployed. Our proposed framework, Opprentice, tackles the above challenges through a novel machine learning based approach. The unclear anomaly concepts are captured by machine learning from real data and operators' labels, while numerous existing detectors can be automatically combined by machine learning to train a classifier to identify the anomalies. Our evaluation on real-world search KPIs show that Opprentice consistently performs similarly or even better than the best performing basic detectors which can change for different data sets.

To the best of our knowledge, Opprentice is the first detection framework to apply machine learning to acquiring practical anomaly concepts and automatically combining and tuning diverse known detectors to satisfy operators' accuracy preference. Emerging detectors, instead of going through time-consuming and often frustrating parameter tuning, can be easily plugged into Opprentice, making the former be deployed more easily and the latter more accurate. In addition, although machine learning is a promising solution, applying it in designing a practical system needs to be careful as it presents several interesting challenges, such as imbalance class and irrelevant and redundant features. We explore and solve some of them in this paper. We believe that Opprentice provides a new schema to bridge the gap between practical operational demands and the state-of-art anomaly detectors. In our future work, we plan to work on the several issues mentioned in §6, and apply the idea of Opprentice to other network operation tasks such as automating intrusion detection and network troubleshooting.

Acknowledgement

We thank our shepherd, Renata Teixeira and the anonymous reviewers for their thorough comments and valuable feedback. We also thank Jun Zhu for his knowledge of machine learning, and Kaixin Sui for her suggestion on the detection framework. At last, we thank Juexing Liao, Guo Chen, and Xiaohui Nie for proofreading this paper.

This work was supported by the National Natural Science Foundation of China (NSFC) under Grant No. 61472214, the National Key Basic Research Program of China (973 program) under Grant No. 2013CB329105, the State Key Program of National Science of China under Grant No. 61233007, the National Natural Science Foundation of China (NSFC) under Grant No.

61472210, the National High Technology Development Program of China (863 program) under Grant No. 2013AA013302.

9. REFERENCES

[1] Yingying Chen, Ratul Mahajan, Baskar Sridharan, and Zhi-Li Zhang. A provider-side view of web search response time. In *Proceedings of the ACM SIGCOMM 2013 conference on SIGCOMM*, pages 243–254. ACM, 2013.

[2] Ajay Anil Mahimkar, Han Hee Song, Zihui Ge, Aman Shaikh, Jia Wang, Jennifer Yates, Yin Zhang, and Joanne Emmons. Detecting the performance impact of upgrades in large operational networks. In *Proceedings of the ACM SIGCOMM 2010 Conference*, SIGCOMM '10, pages 303–314. ACM, 2010.

[3] Ajay Mahimkar, Zihui Ge, Jia Wang, Jennifer Yates, Yin Zhang, Joanne Emmons, Brian Huntley, and Mark Stockert. Rapid detection of maintenance induced changes in service performance. In *Co-NEXT*, page 13. ACM, 2011.

[4] David R. Choffnes, Fabián E. Bustamante, and Zihui Ge. Crowdsourcing service-level network event monitoring. In *Proceedings of the ACM SIGCOMM 2010 Conference*, SIGCOMM '10, pages 387–398. ACM, 2010.

[5] Suk-Bok Lee, Dan Pei, M Hajiaghayi, Ioannis Pefkianakis, Songwu Lu, He Yan, Zihui Ge, Jennifer Yates, and Mario Kosseifi. Threshold compression for 3g scalable monitoring. In *INFOCOM, 2012 Proceedings IEEE*, pages 1350–1358. IEEE, 2012.

[6] He Yan, Ashley Flavel, Zihui Ge, Alexandre Gerber, Daniel Massey, Christos Papadopoulos, Hiren Shah, and Jennifer Yates. Argus: End-to-end service anomaly detection and localization from an isp's point of view. In *INFOCOM, 2012 Proceedings IEEE*, pages 2756–2760. IEEE, 2012.

[7] Ajay Mahimkar, Zihui Ge, Jia Wang, Jennifer Yates, Yin Zhang, Joanne Emmons, Brian Huntley, and Mark Stockert. Rapid detection of maintenance induced changes in service performance. In *Proceedings of the Seventh COnference on Emerging Networking EXperiments and Technologies*, CoNEXT '11, pages 13:1–13:12, New York, NY, USA, 2011. ACM.

[8] Romain Fontugne, Pierre Borgnat, Patrice Abry, and Kensuke Fukuda. Mawilab: Combining diverse anomaly detectors for automated anomaly labeling and performance benchmarking. In *Proceedings of the 6th International COnference*, Co-NEXT '10, pages 8:1–8:12. ACM, 2010.

[9] Augustin Soule, Kavé Salamatian, and Nina Taft. Combining filtering and statistical methods for anomaly detection. In *Proceedings of the 5th ACM SIGCOMM conference on Internet Measurement*, pages 31–31. USENIX Association, 2005.

[10] Yin Zhang, Zihui Ge, Albert Greenberg, and Matthew Roughan. Network anomography. In *Proceedings of the 5th ACM SIGCOMM Conference on Internet Measurement*, IMC '05, pages 30–30, Berkeley, CA, USA, 2005. USENIX Association.

[11] Balachander Krishnamurthy, Subhabrata Sen, Yin Zhang, and Yan Chen. Sketch-based change detection: methods, evaluation, and applications. In *Proceedings of the 3rd ACM SIGCOMM conference on Internet measurement*, pages 234–247. ACM, 2003.

[12] Paul Barford, Jeffery Kline, David Plonka, and Amos Ron. A signal analysis of network traffic anomalies. In *Proceedings of the 2nd ACM SIGCOMM Workshop on Internet measurment*, pages 71–82. ACM, 2002.

[13] Jake D Brutlag. Aberrant behavior detection in time series for network monitoring. In *LISA*, pages 139–146, 2000.

[14] Fernando Silveira, Christophe Diot, Nina Taft, and Ramesh Govindan. Astute: Detecting a different class of traffic anomalies. In *Proceedings of the ACM SIGCOMM 2010 Conference*, SIGCOMM '10, pages 267–278. ACM, 2010.

[15] Benjamin I.P. Rubinstein, Blaine Nelson, Ling Huang, Anthony D. Joseph, Shing-hon Lau, Satish Rao, Nina Taft, and J. D. Tygar. Antidote: Understanding and defending against poisoning of anomaly detectors. In *Proceedings of the 9th ACM SIGCOMM Conference on Internet Measurement Conference*, IMC '09, pages 1–14, New York, NY, USA, 2009. ACM.

[16] Varun Chandola, Arindam Banerjee, and Vipin Kumar. Anomaly detection: A survey. *ACM Comput. Surv.*, 41(3):15:1–15:58, July 2009.

[17] Xin Li, Fang Bian, Mark Crovella, Christophe Diot, Ramesh Govindan, Gianluca Iannaccone, and Anukool Lakhina. Detection and identification of network anomalies using sketch subspaces. In *Proceedings of the 6th ACM SIGCOMM Conference on Internet Measurement*, IMC '06, pages 147–152, New York, NY, USA, 2006. ACM.

[18] Anukool Lakhina, Mark Crovella, and Christophe Diot. Diagnosing network-wide traffic anomalies. In *Proceedings of the 2004 Conference on Applications, Technologies, Architectures, and Protocols for Computer Communications*, SIGCOMM '04, pages 219–230. ACM, 2004.

[19] Anukool Lakhina, Mark Crovella, and Christophe Diot. Mining anomalies using traffic feature distributions. In *Proceedings of the 2005 Conference on Applications, Technologies, Architectures, and Protocols for Computer Communications*, SIGCOMM '05, pages 217–228. ACM, 2005.

[20] Makoto Yamada, Akisato Kimura, Futoshi Naya, and Hiroshi Sawada. Change-point detection with feature selection in high-dimensional time-series data. In *Proceedings of the Twenty-Third International Joint Conference on Artificial Intelligence*, IJCAI '13, pages 1827–1833. AAAI Press, 2013.

[21] Shashank Shanbhag and Tilman Wolf. Accurate anomaly detection through parallelism. *Network, IEEE*, 23(1):22–28, 2009.

[22] Ayesha Binte Ashfaq, Mobin Javed, Syed Ali Khayam, and Hayder Radha. An information-theoretic combining method for multi-classifier anomaly detection systems. In *Communications (ICC), 2010 IEEE international conference on*, pages 1–5. IEEE, 2010.

[23] Y. Himura, K. Fukuda, K. Cho, and H. Esaki. An automatic and dynamic parameter tuning of a statistics-based anomaly detection algorithm. In *Communications, 2009. ICC '09. IEEE International Conference on*, pages 1–6, June 2009.

[24] Amazon cloudwatch alarm. http://docs.aws.amazon.com/AmazonCloudWatch/latest/DeveloperGuide/ConsoleAlarms.html.

[25] He Yan, Lee Breslau, Zihui Ge, Dan Massey, Dan Pei, and Jennifer Yates. G-rca: A generic root cause analysis platform for service quality management in large ip networks. In *Proceedings of the 6th International COnference*, Co-NEXT '10, pages 5:1–5:12, New York, NY, USA, 2010. ACM.

[26] Daniela Brauckhoff, Xenofontas Dimitropoulos, Arno Wagner, and Kavè Salamatian. Anomaly extraction in backbone networks using association rules. In *Proceedings of the 9th ACM SIGCOMM Conference on Internet Measurement Conference*, IMC '09, pages 28–34. ACM, 2009.

[27] Haakon Ringberg, Augustin Soule, and Jennifer Rexford. Webclass: Adding rigor to manual labeling of traffic anomalies. *SIGCOMM Comput. Commun. Rev.*, 38(1):35–38, January 2008.

[28] Leo Breiman. Random Forests. *Machine Learning*, 45(1):5–32, 2001.

[29] Ioannis Arapakis, Xiao Bai, and B. Barla Cambazoglu. Impact of response latency on user behavior in web search. In *Proceedings of the 37th International ACM SIGIR Conference on Research & Development in Information Retrieval*, SIGIR '14, pages 103–112, New York, NY, USA, 2014. ACM.

[30] Alexey Tsymbal. The problem of concept drift: definitions and related work. *Computer Science Department, Trinity College Dublin*, 2004.

[31] Haibo He, Edwardo Garcia, et al. Learning from imbalanced data. *Knowledge and Data Engineering, IEEE Transactions on*, 21(9):1263–1284, 2009.

[32] Taeshik Shon and Jongsub Moon. A hybrid machine learning approach to network anomaly detection. *Information Sciences*, 177(18):3799 - 3821, 2007.

[33] F. Silveira and C. Diot. Urca: Pulling out anomalies by their root causes. In *INFOCOM, 2010 Proceedings IEEE*, pages 1–9, March 2010.

[34] Øivind Due Trier, Anil K Jain, and Torfinn Taxt. Feature extraction methods for character recognition-a survey. *Pattern recognition*, 29(4):641–662, 1996.

[35] George EP Box, Gwilym M Jenkins, and Gregory C Reinsel. *Time series analysis: forecasting and control*. John Wiley & Sons, 2013.

[36] Auto arima. http://www.inside-r.org/packages/cran/forecast/docs/auto.arima.

[37] Ramón Díaz-Uriarte and Sara Alvarez De Andres. Gene selection and classification of microarray data using random forest. *BMC bioinformatics*, 7(1):3, 2006.

[38] Andy Liaw and Matthew Wiener. Classification and regression by randomforest. *R news*, 2(3):18–22, 2002.

[39] Isabelle Guyon and André Elisseeff. An introduction to variable and feature selection. *J. Mach. Learn. Res.*, 3:1157–1182, March 2003.

[40] Ron Kohavi and George H. John. Wrappers for feature subset selection. *Artificial Intelligence*, 97(1ÂÍC2):273 – 324, 1997. Relevance.

[41] Leo Breiman, Jerome Friedman, Charles J Stone, and Richard A Olshen. *Classification and regression trees*. CRC press, 1984.

[42] Athula Balachandran, Vyas Sekar, Aditya Akella, Srinivasan Seshan, Ion Stoica, and Hui Zhang. Developing a predictive model of quality of experience for internet video. In *Proceedings of the ACM SIGCOMM 2013 conference on SIGCOMM*, pages 339–350. ACM, 2013.

[43] Athula Balachandran, Vaneet Aggarwal, Emir Halepovic, Jeffrey Pang, Srinivasan Seshan, Shobha Venkataraman, and He Yan. Modeling web quality-of-experience on cellular networks. In *Proceedings of the 20th Annual International Conference on Mobile Computing and Networking*, MobiCom '14, pages 213–224, New York, NY, USA, 2014. ACM.

[44] Yoav Freund, Robert Schapire, and N Abe. A short introduction to boosting. *Journal-Japanese Society For Artificial Intelligence*, 14(771-780):1612, 1999.

[45] Jesse Davis and Mark Goadrich. The relationship between precision-recall and roc curves. In *Proceedings of the 23rd international conference on Machine learning*, pages 233–240. ACM, 2006.

[46] Neil J Perkins and Enrique F Schisterman. The inconsistency of "optimal" cutpoints obtained using two criteria based on the receiver operating characteristic curve. *American journal of epidemiology*, 163(7):670–675, 2006.

[47] Ron Kohavi et al. A study of cross-validation and bootstrap for accuracy estimation and model selection. In *IJCAI*, volume 14, pages 1137–1145, 1995.

[48] F. Pedregosa, G. Varoquaux, A. Gramfort, V. Michel, B. Thirion, O. Grisel, M. Blondel, P. Prettenhofer, R. Weiss, V. Dubourg, J. Vanderplas, A. Passos, D. Cournapeau, M. Brucher, M. Perrot, and E. Duchesnay. Scikit-learn: Machine learning in Python. *Journal of Machine Learning Research*, 12:2825–2830, 2011.

[49] Adam Lazur. Building a billion user load balancer. In *Velocity Web Perfomance and Operations Conference*. O'REILLY, 2013.

[50] Kendrick Boyd, Kevin H Eng, and C David Page. Area under the precision-recall curve: Point estimates and confidence intervals. In *Machine learning and knowledge discovery in databases*, pages 451–466. Springer, 2013.

[51] Hanchuan Peng, Fuhui Long, and Chris H Q Ding. Feature Selection Based on Mutual Information: Criteria of Max-Dependency, Max-Relevance, and Min-Redundancy. *IEEE Trans. Pattern Anal. Mach. Intell. ()*, 27(8):1226–1238, 2005.

Understanding Mobile Traffic Patterns of Large Scale Cellular Towers in Urban Environment

Huandong Wang[1], Fengli Xu[1], Yong Li[1], Pengyu Zhang[2], Depeng Jin[1]
[1]Tsinghua National Laboratory for Information Science and Technology
Department of Electronic Engineering, Tsinghua University, Beijing 100084, China
[2]University of Massachusetts Amherst
{liyong07, jindp}@tsinghua.edu.cn, pyzhang@cs.umass.edu

ABSTRACT

Understanding mobile traffic patterns of large scale cellular towers in urban environment is extremely valuable for Internet service providers, mobile users, and government managers of modern metropolis. This paper aims at extracting and modeling the traffic patterns of large scale towers deployed in a metropolitan city. To achieve this goal, we need to address several challenges, including lack of appropriate tools for processing large scale traffic measurement data, unknown traffic patterns, as well as handling complicated factors of urban ecology and human behaviors that affect traffic patterns. Our core contribution is a powerful model which combines three dimensional information (time, locations of towers, and traffic frequency spectrum) to extract and model the traffic patterns of thousands of cellular towers. Our empirical analysis reveals the following important observations. First, only five basic time-domain traffic patterns exist among the 9,600 cellular towers. Second, each of the extracted traffic pattern maps to one type of geographical locations related to urban ecology, including residential area, business district, transport, entertainment, and comprehensive area. Third, our frequency-domain traffic spectrum analysis suggests that the traffic of any tower among the 9,600 can be constructed using a linear combination of four primary components corresponding to human activity behaviors. We believe that the proposed traffic patterns extraction and modeling methodology, combined with the empirical analysis on the mobile traffic, pave the way toward a deep understanding of the traffic patterns of large scale cellular towers in modern metropolis.

Categories and Subject Descriptors

C.2.0 [**Computer Communication Networks**]: General–Data communications; C.4 [**Performance of Systems**]: Modeling techniques

IMC'15, October 28–30, 2015, Tokyo, Japan.

ACM 978-1-4503-3848-6/15/10 ...$15.00
DOI: http://dx.doi.org/10.1145/2815675.2815680

General Terms

Measurement, Traffic

Keywords

Mobile data traffic; Measurement study; Traffic patterns; Geographical location

1. INTRODUCTION

The past few years have seen a dramatic growth in cellular network traffic, contributed by billions of mobile devices as the first-class citizens of the Internet. The global cellular network traffic from mobile devices is expected to surpass 24 exabytes (10^{18}) per month by 2019 [1], 9× larger than the traffic served by existing cellular network. While we are embracing a world with ambient cellular connectivity, however, we are facing a critical and challenging problem — we have limited understanding about the patterns of traffic experienced by cellular towers deployed in urban areas, especially when 3G and LTE networks are widely available in current modern metropolis[1, 2, 5]. We do not completely understand how urban functional regions and ecologies, such as business district, affect the mobile traffic of cellular towers[2]. In addition, the dominant factors that affect their traffic variations are still unknown. Such limited knowledge significantly increases the cost of operating thousands of cellular towers in big cities.

Despite of the aforementioned lack of knowledge, understanding the traffic patterns of cellular towers in the large scale urban environment is extremely valuable for Internet service providers (ISP), mobile users, and government managers of modern cites[6, 16, 21]. If we can *identify and model* the patterns of cellular towers, instead of using the same strategy to provide services, such as using the same load balancing and data pricing algorithms on each tower, an ISP can exploit the modeled traffic patterns and customize the strategies for individual cellular towers. For example, an ISP can potentially have different pricing on individual cellular tower based on the traffic it experiences. In addition, mobile users will benefit from the traffic modeling as well because they can choose towers with predicted lower traffic and enjoy better services. Surprisingly, management departments of government will benefit from the traffic modeling as well because they may infer the land usage and human economy activities by looking at the patterns of cellular traffic[14].

On the other hand, understanding the traffic patterns of cellular towers is challenging for three reasons. First, the traffic experienced by thousands of cellular towers deployed in large scale modern cities is complicated and hard to analyze. For example, our dataset includes 9,600 cellular towers and 150,000 subscribers, where lots of redundant and conflict logs are observed. To identify traffic patterns embedded in the thousands of towers, we need to design a system that is able to clean and handle the data of large scale cellular traffic. Second, we do not have the priori about the existence of patterns that can be used for representing the behavior of thousands of cellular towers. To make matters worse, even if such patterns exist, we do not know their profiles. Without these profiles, it is challenging to group thousands of cellular towers into a small number of patterns. Third, the traffic of a cellular tower is affected by many factors, such as time and locations, etc. These factors, sometimes, compound with each other and further complicate our analysis. For example, significant traffic variation is observed at both fine-grained (hours) and coarse-grained (days) time scale, and across towers deployed in different locations[25, 16]. By addressing these challenges, in this paper, we investigate how to extract and model the mobile traffic patterns of thousands of cellular towers in a large scale urban environment via credible dataset collected by one of the largest commercial mobile operators.

Our core contribution is a powerful model which combines three dimensional information, including time, locations of towers, and traffic frequency spectrum, for extracting and modeling the traffic patterns of thousands of cellular towers. A breakdown of the core contribution comprises three parts. First, we design a system which leverages machine learning to identify and extract five patterns from the traffic of thousands of cellular towers. Our system is built with processing large scale data in mind and is able to process the traffic of thousands of towers with granularity of 10 minutes. Second, we identify the geographical context of traffic experienced by cellular towers by investigating the correlation between time-domain traffic characteristics and geographical locations of towers. Therefore, by looking at the traffic pattern of a tower, we can infer the type of location where it is deployed and the type of users it serves. Third, our frequency-domain traffic spectrum analysis reveals that any traffic of the 9,600 cellular towers can be constructed using a linear combination of four primary components corresponding to human activity behaviors. This observation provides an unique angle (frequency) for analyzing cellular traffic and significantly simplifies the process of analysis by a linear model.

Through investigating the traffic of 9,600 cellular towers, we find following interesting observations. First, the 9,600 cellular towers can be classified into five groups using features extracted from time-domain traffic. This experimental result confirms our motivation that a small number of patterns do exist among thousands of cellular towers. Second, each of the traffic pattern maps to one type of geographical locations, including resident, office, transport, entertainment, and comprehensive area. Therefore, the traffic pattern of a cellular tower does suggest the urban ecology and geographical location context where it is deployed as well as the type of users it serves. Third, our frequency-domain analysis reveals that the transition between the five traffic patterns encodes the mobility of human. For example, when the phase of residential pattern moves toward the phase of transport pattern, people start their commute from home to work. In summary, we believe that the proposed traffic patterns extraction and modeling, combined with the empirical study on large scale cellular towers, pave the way toward a deep understanding of the traffic patterns of large scale cellular towers.

This paper is structured as follows. In Section 2, we provide details about the utilized dataset, and present some basic observations of traffic spatio-temporal distributions. In Section 3, we design our traffic processing system and identify the key traffic patterns of the large scale cellular towers. Based on the discovered five traffic patterns, in Section 4 and 5, we conduct a deep analysis and reveal the correlation among data traffic, urban ecology and human behaviors in the time and frequency domain respectively. After discussing related work in Section 6, we summarize our discoveries and discuss potential investigations in Section 7.

2. DATASET AND VISUALIZATION

In this section, we provide details about the dataset we investigate as well as the needed preprocessing. In addition, we visualize the spatial-temporal distribution of cellular traffic.

2.1 Dataset Description

The dataset is an anonymized cellular trace collected by an ISP from Shanghai, a big city in China, between Aug 1st and Aug 31st 2014. Each entry of the trace contains detailed mobile data usage of 150,000 users, including the ID of devices (anonymized), start-end time of data connection, base station ID, address of base station, and the amount of 3G or LTE data used in each connection. The trace logs 1.96 billion tuples of the described information, contributed by approximately 9,600 base stations all over Shanghai. The trace contains 2.4 petabytes (10^{15}) logs, 77 terabytes (10^{12}) per day and 8 gigabytes (10^{9}) per base station on average. This large scale and fine-grained dataset guarantees the credibility of our traffic pattern analysis and modeling.

2.2 Preprocessing

The trace collected by the ISP needs to be preprocessed because of the existence of redundant and conflict traffic logs as well as the incomplete information of base stations' locations. The preprocessing includes three steps. First, we eliminate the redundant and conflict logs, such as the identical traffic logs, introduced by technical issues. Second, to solve the problem of incomplete information, we convert the addresses of base stations to their geographical longitudes and latitudes through APIs provided by Baidu Map, the most popular online map service provider in China. This conversion gives us the precise geographical location of a base station, which is important for analyzing the ground truth of urban functional regions. The last step of preprocessing is computing the traffic density (byte/km^2) across the city. The obtained traffic density allows us to understand the spatial distribution of cellular traffic.

2.3 Data Visualization

Before diving into a deep analysis of mobile data traffic, we first visualize the spatial-temporal traffic distribution of the 9,600 base stations, where we find two interesting observations.

First, the data embeds fundamental temporal patterns of mobile data traffic. Figure 1 shows the aggregated traffic of the 9,600 towers at different time scales. Figure 1(a)

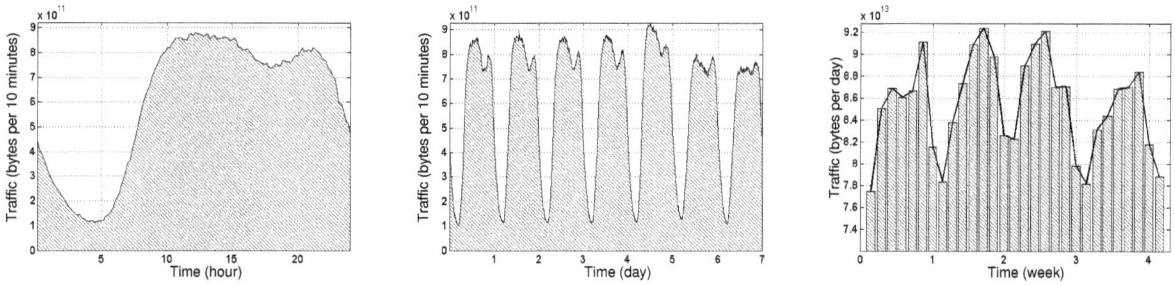

(a) Hourly (b) Daily (c) Weekly

Figure 1: The temporal distribution of cellular traffic at different time scales.

shows the traffic distribution of a day (Aug 7th 2014, Thursday) where we observe that the aggregated network traffic is tightly coupled with the sleep pattern of humans. High cellular traffic is observed during the day and low traffic is experienced during midnight. There are two traffic peaks in each day: one around 12PM and the other around 10PM. Similar patterns are observed in Figure 1(b). The timing of the two peaks suggests that most people tend to consume data traffic heavily after lunch and before sleep. Figure 1(b) shows the traffic distribution of a week (from Aug 4 to Aug 10 2014) and Figure 1(c) shows the traffic distribution of a month (from Aug 3 to Aug 31 2014). Both figures show that the traffic exhibits a periodical pattern on the scale of a week, where weekend's traffic is less than weekday's traffic. Such traffic variation comes from people's weekly work schedule.

On the other hand, our trace also records the spatial distribution of mobile data traffic. Surprisingly, we find that the spatial and temporal characteristics of traffic are correlated. Figure 2 shows the geographical traffic density (bytes transmitted per hour per km^2) at 4AM, 10AM, 4PM and 10PM. As shown in the color bar, the red one indicates higher traffic and the blue one stands for lower traffic. We find the following observations. First, towers deployed at the center of the city experience high traffic despite of the time of a day. Second, at 4AM, most areas of the city are covered by dark color, which suggests that traffic demand is small because of human sleep. In contrast, at 10AM, most areas of the city are covered by light color, suggesting that traffic demand becomes high because people start working. Therefore, the areas of peak traffic map to areas occupied by human, such as residential housing or central business district (CBD).

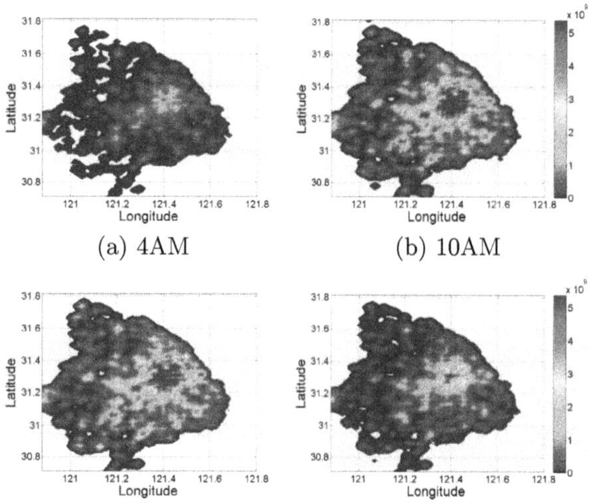

(a) 4AM (b) 10AM (c) 4PM (d) 10PM

Figure 2: The spatial distribution of cellular traffic at different time.

3. IDENTIFYING TRAFFIC PATTERNS OF CELLULAR TOWERS

Now, we investigate the data traffic of the thousands of 3G/LTE cellular towers and design a system that is able to identify key traffic patterns of large scale cellular towers. We start from understanding the traffic patterns of a few cellular towers to motivate our study.

3.1 Motivation and Problem Statement

Our cellular network traffic measurement and analysis are motivated by a key observation — the traffic pattern of one cellular tower is vastly different from another. Through online map service, we randomly select four towers from the positions of residential areas and four towers from business districts, and plot their normalized traffic profile in the left and right column of Figure 3, respectively. We can clearly observe the difference of traffic between these two types of cellular towers, where the traffic profiles of residential towers have two peaks within a day and remain high across night, while the traffic profiles of towers in business district experience only one peak within a day and get close to zero across night. This comparison clearly reveals the difference of traffic patterns between the two specific types of cellular towers. However, from the perspective of an ISP, which manages thousands of cellular towers, is the traffic pattern of one cellular tower vastly different from another? To understand this problem, we conduct a large scale measurement and investigate the recorded 9600 cellular towers in our dataset of Shanghai.

Figure 4 shows the normalized traffic variations within one day with 40 randomly selected cellular towers for each 0.01 degree latitudes or longitudes respectively. The x-axis shows the time in hours and y-axis shows the logical positions of the selected cellular towers in terms of latitude (a) or longitude (b). For example, the first row of pixels in Figure 4(a) represent the traffic variations of one cellular towers, of which the latitude is around 121.60 and the longitude is randomly selected. Traffic measured on each cellular

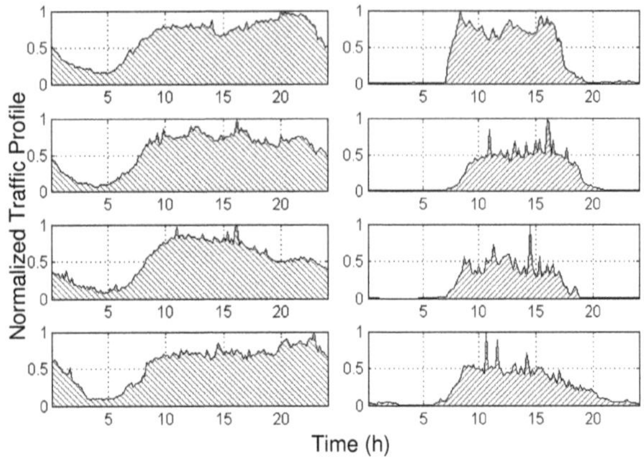

Figure 3: Cellular traffic experienced by base stations deployed in the residential area and business district.

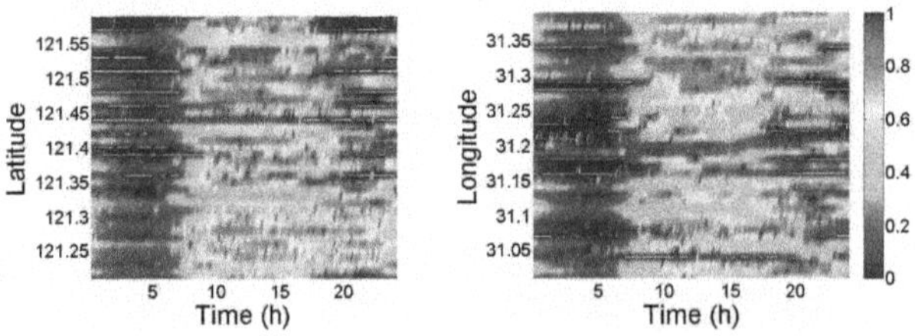

(a) Latitudes (b) Longitudes

Figure 4: Cellular traffic experienced by base station randomly selected from different latitudes and longitudes. Large traffic variations are observed.

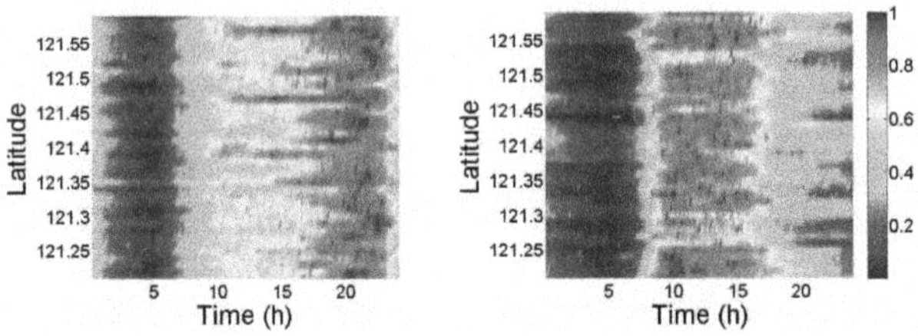

(a) Residential Area base stations (b) Business District base stations

Figure 5: Cellular traffic experienced by base stations selected from residential and business district.

tower is normalized by its maximum, and the color presents the normalized value where red color indicates higher traffic and blue color stands for lower traffic as shown in the color bar. In these measurements, we find two observations. First, the peak hour of one cellular tower, which is marked as red, is vastly different from another during the day time when serving mobile users. In fact, the variance of the peak among the selected towers is about 10 hours. Second, while most of towers experience low traffic in early morning, the first several towers in Figure 4(a), of which the latitude is around 121.60, also have low traffic during evening. Therefore, significant differences of data traffic are observed across cellular towers. Such differences cause troubles for an ISP to manage its cellular network. For example, because of the unique pattern of individual traffic, an ISP cannot obtain the optimal performance by using the same load balancing strategy, which is built on top of traffic patterns, on different towers. Therefore, a natural question to ask is that is it possible to model the traffic pattern of thousands of cellular towers? More specifically, can we utilize a few simple patterns to present the traffic of thousands of cellular towers? Identifying these patterns of cellular towers would give an ISP significant benefits on network management, including load balancing, pricing, etc.

Our investigation suggests that at least two, maybe more, traffic patterns exist among thousands of cellular towers. Figure 5 shows the normalized traffic profile of 40 selected cellular towers deployed in residential area and in business district for each 0.01 degree latitudes. Compared with the disorder in both temporal and spatial dimension exhibited in Figure 4, traffic variations for cellular towers in a single kind of regions are more regular and similar to each other. In addition, we find other two observations in this investigation. First, in terms of the traffic of residential area, all residential towers experience similar traffic patterns where the peak traffic is present around 9PM. In addition, only a small amount of traffic is observed between 8AM and 4PM because most users leave home for work. Similar conclusion can be drawn for towers deployed in business district. Second, the traffic pattern of residential towers is different from towers deployed in business district where peak hour appears around 1PM. Inspired by these two observations, we conclude that traffic patterns do exist among thousands of cellular towers. One key question addressed by this paper is finding out how many traffic patterns exist among thousands of cellular towers and how to identify them.

3.2 Identifying Traffic Patterns of Cell-towers

Investigating traffic patterns among thousands of cellular towers is extremely challenging for three reasons. First, we have little prior knowledge about the data traffic, and do not know which cell towers may share the same traffic pattern and how the pattern may look like. Second, the measured cellular traffic data is huge in terms of tracing 9,600 cellular towers for a month. To make matters worse, the measured data is not clean in terms of unstructured logs. Last but not least, the measured cellular traffic data is noisy where large variation of traffic is observed because the absolute traffic depends on the number of mobile users served. All these factors make the analysis of cellular traffic patterns extremely challenging. To tackle these challenges, we design, implement, and evaluate a system which is able to identify the key traffic patterns of such large scale cellular towers. Our system is composed by three key elements: traffic vectorizer, pattern identifier and metric tuner.

Traffic vectorizer: We implement a traffic vectorizer on Hadoop platform to convert the large scale unstructured traffic logs into traffic usage vectors. The key of designing the traffic vectorizer is a parallel transformer, which takes the time-domain traffic logs of thousands of cellular towers as its input and converts each cell tower's logs into a time-domain traffic vector. The vector is constructed in two phases — aggregation and normalization. In the first phase, each cellular tower's traffic logs are segmented into thousands of chunks, with each chunk contains 10-minutes traffic logs. Then we aggregate the traffic logs in each chunk and generate a traffic usage vector. In the second phase, we perform zero-score normalization on each vector to eliminate their differences in amplitude, in order to find out the similar traffic patterns without the interference of different amplitude. We define the traffic vector of cellular tower j as $X_j = (x_j[1], ..., x_j[N])^T$, with $x_j[i]$ stands for the normalized traffic amount in the i_{th} 10-minute time slot. We remove 3 days from the month to make the duration consist of four entire weeks. Thus, N is number of 28 days' 10-minutes segmentation, i.e., 4032 in our analysis.

Pattern identifier: Pattern identifier takes the vectorized data from the vectorizer and runs an unsupervised machine learning algorithm for identifying the key patterns of cellular tower traffic. The pattern identifier addresses one key challenge of the mining process — unknown patterns, by exploiting hierarchical clustering[4]. The basic idea of hierarchical clustering is iteratively merging the nearest two clusters. It first considers each input point as a cluster and then bottom-up iteratively merges the nearest two clusters until the stop condition is met. In the clustering, we use the euclidean distance as the distance metric and define the distance between clusters as average-linkage distance. In addition, we set a threshold value as stop condition, which stops the clustering when the distance between two clusters is above the threshold value.

Metric tuner: As the number of traffic patterns is unknown, a key question is when the identifier should stop its clustering. In our system, we use Davies-Bouldin index [18] to explicitly inform the identifier that the optimum number of patterns have been identified. Davies-Bouldin index is utilized because it measures both the separation of clusters and cohesion within clusters, which mathematically guarantees good clustering result. The mathematic formulation of Davies-Bouldin index is as follows,

$$\text{minimize} \quad \frac{1}{R}\sum_{i=1}^{R} \max_{j=1, j\neq i}^{R} \frac{S_i + S_j}{M_{i,j}},$$

$$\text{subject to} \quad M_{i,j} = ||A_i - A_j||_2,$$

$$S_i = \frac{1}{T_i}\sum_{k=1}^{T_i} ||X_k - A_i||_2,$$

where the objective function is the Davies-Bouldin index, X_i is the vectorized data of cellular tower i, A_i is the centroid of each cluster, R is the number of clusters and T_i is the numbers of towers within the i_{th} cluster. We minimize the Davies-Bouldin index by considering two factors — the distance between clusters $M_{i,j}$ and S_i, which are the average distance from points to their cluster's centroid. When the minimum Davies-Bouldin index is obtained, the optimum number of patterns is identified. The variation of DBI is shown in Figure 6(a), according to which we set the stop condition—threshold value at 16.33 to achieve optimal clustering result.

Figure 6 shows the five time-domain patterns identified by our system from the 9,600 cellular towers((c) to (g)) and each cluster's CDF of points' distance to its centroid(b). The five clusters differ in terms of the time where peak traffic appears as well as the amount of traffic experienced during weekday and weekends. Figure 6(b) shows that the distance CDF curves of clusters are similar and all of them increase rapidly as distance increases. 80% of points' distance to their clusters' centroid are less than 10, which implicates the clustering result is good. The percentage of each cluster's cell towers is shown in Table 1, which indicates the third cluster has most cell towers and second cluster the least.

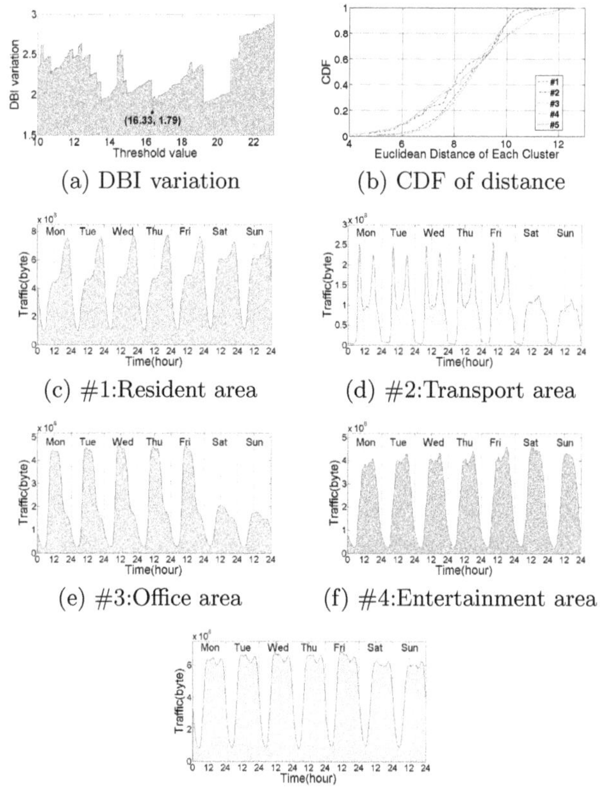

(a) DBI variation (b) CDF of distance

(c) #1:Resident area (d) #2:Transport area

(e) #3:Office area (f) #4:Entertainment area

(g) #5:Comprehensive area

Figure 6: Patterns of the five identified clusters and CDF of clustering distance.

In conclusion, we implement a system that is able to identify the key traffic patterns among thousands of cellular towers in this subsection. Since the five clusters are given by the hierarchical classifier, an interesting question to ask is what are the geographical locations where these five types of towers are deployed?

3.3 Geographical Context of Traffic Patterns

To understand the geographical locations of cell towers of the five clusters, we first manually label typical towers in the five patterns with urban functional regions and then validate the labels of all towers in each pattern with ground truth.

Cluster Index	Functional Regions	Percentage
1	Resident	17.55%
2	Transport	2.58%
3	Office	45.72%
4	Entertainment	9.35%
5	Comprehensive	24.81%

Table 1: Percentage of cell towers classified in each cluster.

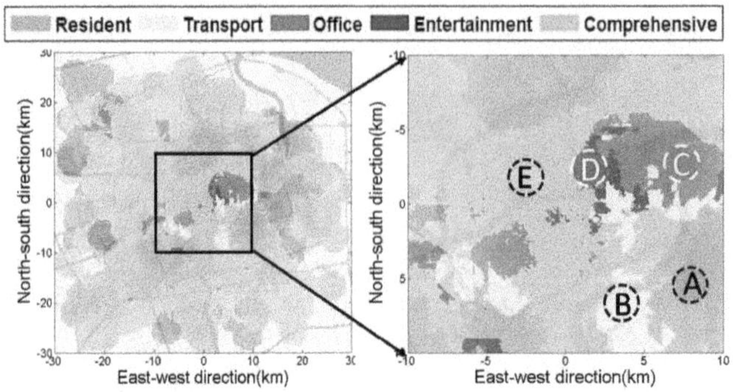

Figure 7: Geographical distribution of base stations from the five identified patterns.

3.3.1 *Label Patterns with Urban Functional Regions*

To understand the geographical context of traffic patterns, we label the five traffic patterns using urban functional regions. This process is nontrivial because given thousands of cellular towers, labelling cannot be done one by one manually. To address this challenge, we use a few human-labeled areas and combine with points of interests (POI) distribution to achieve accurate labelling. POI is a specific point location of a certain function such as restaurant and shopping mall. An area's POI distribution reflects its function. Therefore, studying POI distribution of one location can help us to accurately identify patterns' labels. The POI data we study is collected via APIs provided by Baidu Map introduced before. For calculating the POI distribution, we measure the number of four main types of POI, which are resident, transport, office and entertainment, within 200m of each cell towers. Figure 7 shows the geographical density map of towers in each cluster where deep color stands for higher density. Zooming in the urban area, for each cluster we pick the point with the highest tower density and calculate their POI distribution as summarized in Table 2. Then, we infer the urban function region of each cluster by checking the geographical location information in Figure 7 and POI distribution in Table 2. We obtain the following geographical labels for the five clusters.

Resident area: Figure 7 shows that the towers in this cluster (green color) are mainly distributed on the surrounding areas of the city. In addition, the highest density point, ***A***, is located in a large resident neighborhood. Table 2 also shows that the number of residential points in ***A*** is more than others. Therefore,we label the area covered by this cluster's cell towers as residential area.

Transport area: In Figure 7, the second cluster's highest density point ***B*** is close to an area with three subway stations and one overpass. In addition, Table 2 shows that around location ***B*** the number of transport POI is higher than the rest even though its absolute number is small. Therefore, we label this cluster as transport area.

Office area: Figure 7 shows that the highest density point ***C*** is a well-known business district in Shanghai. This location mark is also verified by the third row of Table 2 where the number of office POI is dominant for the area 200m from ***C***. As a result, we label this cluster as office area.

Table 2: Distribution of POI at Chosen Point.

Point	Points of Interest			
	Resident	Transport	Office	Entertain
A	195	0	19	51
B	68	2	56	36
C	151	1	1016	157
D	16	0	108	2165
E	59	0	179	26

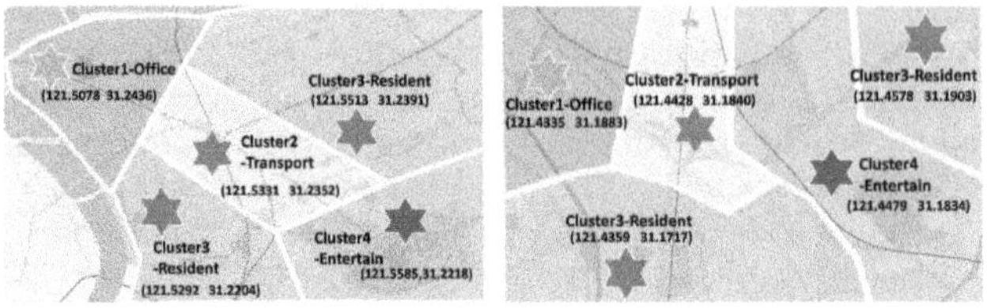

(a) Area A (b) Area B

Figure 8: Two case studies for validating the geographical context of the five identified patterns.

Entertainment area: The highest density point ***D*** in Figure 7 is a large shopping mall and entertainment park in Shanghai. Table 2 also shows that its number of entertainment POI is more than the rest. Therefore, we label this cluster as entertainment area.

Comprehensive area: Figure 7 shows the tower density map of the last cluster, where we observe uniform distribution of towers across the city. In addition, the highest density point, ***E***, is a comprehensive area, which includes all kinds of urban functions, including residential area, offices, etc. The POI distribution of point E does not suggest obvious land mark either. Therefore, it is labeled as comprehensive area.

3.3.2 *Validate the Labels*

In this section, we validate the labels of the five patterns in both micro and macro scale. Our labels are obtained by checking the geographical locations of a few towers in each cluster and verifying with the corresponding POI distribution. However, the correctness of labelling across all 9,600 cellular towers remains unknown. Therefore, we perform further analysis to validate our labels with POI data from micro and macro two perspectives.

Validate with case study: To validate our labels in micro scale, we randomly choose two areas shown in Figure 8. According to the POI data, we first color different functional regions in the area with different colors. Green represents residential area, yellow represents transport area, red represents office area, and blue represents entertainment area. After that, we investigate the labels of cell towers locating in the area. Observing both Figure 8(a) and (b), we find that the labels attached to the cell towers exactly match with the functional regions, which justifies our labels' correctness.

Validate with 9,600 towers' POI: To validate our labels in macro scale, we perform further analysis on all 9,600 towers' POI. However, different types POI vary in magnitude significantly because of their different nature. To eliminate this interference, we first perform min-max normalization on each type's POI and then average them by clusters,

Table 3: **Averaged normalized points of interest of five clusters.**

Cluster	Points of Interest			
	Resident	Transport	Office	Entertain
#1	0.0528	0.0285	0.0232	0.0269
#2	0.0473	0.2000	0.1012	0.1020
#3	0.0439	0.0813	0.1034	0.0515
#4	0.0474	0.1201	0.0976	0.1674
#5	0.0508	0.0373	0.0453	0.0403

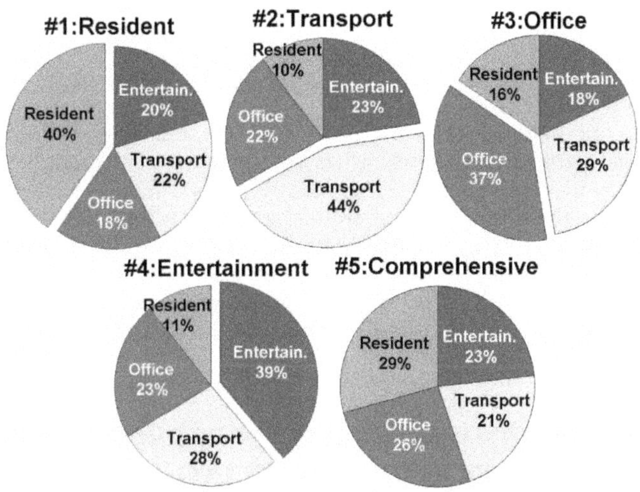

Figure 9: Pie chart of averaged normalized points of interest of five clusters.

which is summarized in Table 3. The maximum of each row and column is marked with color, which shows the dominant urban function in each cluster. Figure 9 explicitly shows each POI's percentage in five clusters. According to Table 3 and Figure 9, transport type POI dominates the region labeled as transport area, with 44% of this area's POI, while entertainment area is dominated by entertainment type POI for 39%. These measurements validate the labels obtained from the sampled towers of each cluster.

To conclude, in this subsection we verify our identified key traffic patterns as well as establish their relationships with urban functional regions.

4. UNDERSTANDING MODELED TRAFFIC PATTERNS: TIME DOMAIN ASPECT

Understanding the hidden physical meanings of traffic patterns is important for exploiting them to solve practical problems, such as traffic load balancing or land usage identification. Although we have identified key traffic patterns and linked them to corresponding urban functional regions, we still have little knowledge of the hidden physical meaning of these patterns. In this section, we conduct an analysis to reveal the time and geographical characteristics of modeled traffic patterns.

We start from quantifying the distinct time-domain characteristics of each pattern and find out the interrelationships between these patterns. These time-domain characteristics

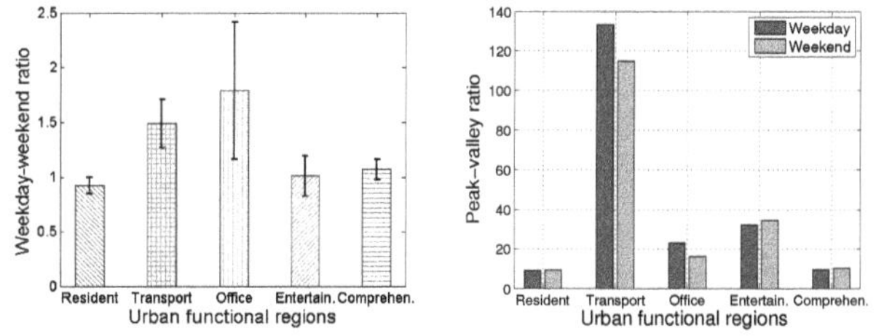

(a) Weekday-weekend traffic amount ratio. (b) Weekday and weekend's peak-valley ratio

Figure 10: Time-domain characteristics of the five identified patterns.

have not been quantified and the interrelationships between these traffic patterns remain unknown, which are two obstacles preventing us from further understanding these traffic patterns. Therefore, in order to understand the hidden meaning of modeled patterns, we conduct the following studies.

4.1 Quantify Time-Domain Characteristics

It is obvious that traffic patterns of different urban functional regions possess different characteristics in time-domain. In this subsection, we dedicate to quantify these characteristics and provide insights of traffic behaviours in different urban functional regions.

Weekday-Weekend traffic amount ratio: Observing Figure 6, traffic amount during weekday is significantly different from weekend in transport area and office area. We quantify this characteristic by computing the ratio between weekday's traffic amount and weekend's, which is presented in Figure 10(a). According to Figure 10(a), one day's traffic amount in resident area, entertainment area and comprehensive area is almost identical between weekday and weekend. However, weekday-weekend traffic amount ratio in transport area is 1.49 and the ratio in office area is 1.79, which suggests weekday's traffic amount of those two regions is much more than weekend. This phenomenon makes sense because people typically go to work in weekday while they do not in weekend.

Peak-valley features: Observing Figure 6, all traffic patterns experience periodic peaks and valleys. However, the traffic patterns are significantly different in peak value, valley value and peak-valley ratio. We quantify these characteristics and summarize them in Table 4. According to Table 4, in transport area and office area weekend's maximum traffic and minimum traffic is much less than weekday, which is consistent with last paragraph's finding. What's more, the transport's peak-valley ratio is much higher than other regions, which is explicitly presented in Figure 10(b). However, transport area's maximum traffic is less than other regions both in weekday and weekend. It suggests that transport area has the least traffic amount and the largest peak-valley traffic difference, while resident area and comprehensive area are the opposite.

Time of traffic peak and valley: Different urban functional regions' traffic patterns differ not only in peak volume, but also in peak time. We quantify this characteristic and present it in Table 5. We leave the blank unfilled, if there is not a periodic peak or valley. Observing Table 5, we find

Regions / Features	resident area		transport area		office area		entertainment area		comprehensive area	
	weekday	weekend	weekday	weekend	weekday	weekend	weekday	weekend	weekday	weekend
maximum traffic	7.77×10^8	7.99×10^8	2.76×10^8	1.55×10^8	4.69×10^8	2.78×10^8	4.55×10^8	4.90×10^8	7.36×10^8	7.38×10^8
minimum traffic	8.70×10^7	8.71×10^7	2.07×10^6	1.35×10^6	2.04×10^7	1.74×10^7	1.41×10^7	1.42×10^7	7.77×10^7	7.29×10^7
peak-valley ratio	8.93	9.17	133.33	114.81	22.99	15.98	32.27	34.51	9.47	10.12

Table 4: Peak-valley features

Regions / Features	resident area		transport area		office area		entertainment area		comprehensive area	
	weekday	weekend	weekday	weekend	weekday	weekend	weekday	weekend	weekday	weekend
time of peak	21:30	21:30	8:00 18:00		10:30	12:00	18:00	12:30		
time of valley	5:00	5:00	4:00	4:30	5:00	5:00	5:00	5:0	5:00	5:00

Table 5: Time of traffic peak and valley

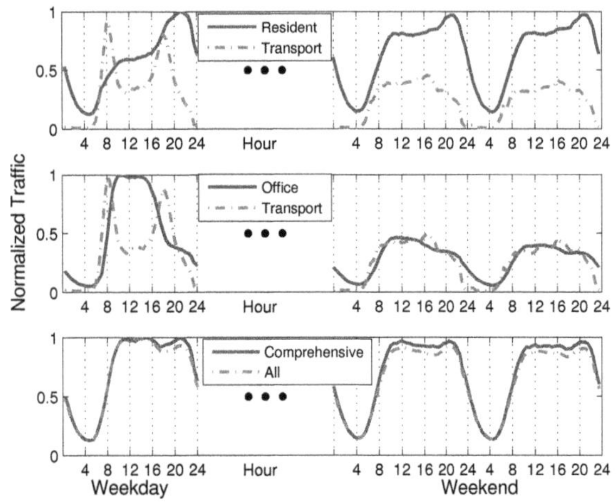

Figure 11: Understanding the interrelationships between traffic patterns.

that traffic valley always takes place in 4:00~5:00. In weekday, transport area has two peaks in 8:00 and 18:00, which are probably caused by rush hour. In entertainment area, weekday's traffic peak time is 18:00 while weekend's traffic peak time is 12:30. It suggests that people go for entertainment later in weekday because of work.

To conclude, we quantify the time-domain characteristics of each identified traffic pattern, which paves the way towards a deep understanding of cellular traffic patterns.

4.2 Interrelationships Between Traffic Patterns

We compare the interrelationships between normalized modeled traffic patterns in Figure 11. The first row of Figure 11 compares the modeled traffic patterns of residential areas and transport hot spots. The peak of residential area is about 3 hours later than the second peak of transport, and the slope of these two peaks is almost identical. In addition, when we compare traffic patterns of transport hot spots and business district shown in Figure 11, we find that the peak in business district takes place in the time period between the two peaks of transport hot spots. Both observations suggest that the traffic patterns in these three areas are related. These three traffic patterns probably depict the daily routine of working populations, for them rush through heavy traffic area to work in morning and rush back home in evening.

In the third row of Figure 11, blue line stands for the traffic pattern in comprehensive area, and red line stands for the average traffic pattern of all cell towers. In fact, we find that these two patterns are of great similarity, which suggests that comprehensive area really is a mixture of other four kinds of functional areas. In conclusion, we analyze the interrelationships between the traffic patterns of different urban functional regions, which provides insightful understanding.

5. FREQUENCY-DOMAIN REPRESENTATION FOR TRAFFIC MODELING

In this section, we conduct frequency-domain analysis. Such frequency-domain analysis is motivated by observing the inherent time-domain periodicity of traffic and the disadvantages of pure time-domain traffic analysis, where time-domain traffic identification is not easy, especially when cellular towers are deployed in the comprehensive areas with couples of behaviors. For example, we know that traffic of cellular tower in the office area reaches the valley in weekends, and traffic of cellular tower in transport area has two peaks in one day, but for an arbitrary cellular tower which has both characteristics, we do not know which of the two will predominate. On the other hand, in frequency domain, we can quantify these characteristics by using the amplitude and phase of frequency corresponding to one day and one week. Thus, we can grasp the key points and compare the strength of different characteristics of traffic for one cellular tower, which is not intuitive in time domain. Here, a natural question to ask is what are the most discriminating and essential features to present traffic patterns of cellular towers. Motivated by answering this question, we conduct frequency domain analysis on the five extracted patterns and reveal several important discoveries.

5.1 Frequency Transform

In order to analyze the strong periodicity existing in time domain, we first carry out discrete fourier transform (DFT) on the time-domain traffic vector $X = (x[1], ..., x[N])^T$. X can be either the time-domain traffic vector of one cellular tower, *i.e.*, X_j for cellular tower j, or the aggregate traffic vector of a cluster, *i.e.*, $\sum_{j \in C} X_j$ for the cluster C. The process can be formulated as the following:

$$\hat{X}[k] = \sum_{n=1}^{N} x[n] e^{-2\pi i k n / N},$$

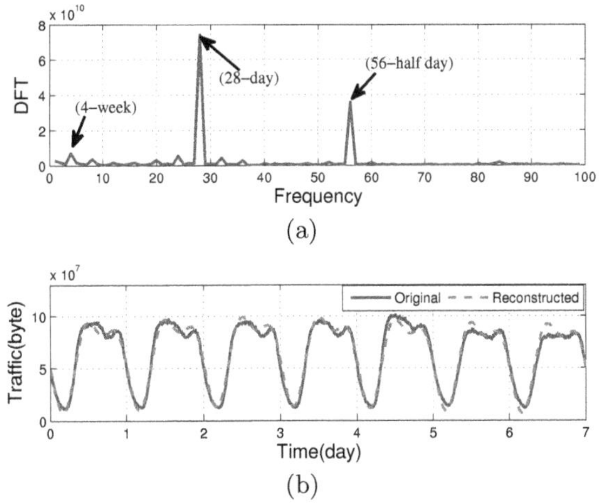

Figure 12: Time-domain traffic reconstructed by the three principal frequency-domain components (k=4, 28, 56).

where N is the number of traffic samples, that is 28 days' 10-minutes segmentation, *i.e.*, 4032 as discussed before in our analysis. $\hat{X}[k]$ is the frequency spectrum of time-domain traffic X. Figure 12(a) shows the DFT of the aggregate traffic of all cellular towers, where three peaks are observed, *i.e.* k =4, 28, 56. Since the duration of our series is 4 weeks, the $4th$ point is corresponding to time-domain periodic patterns of one week. Similarly, the $28th$ and $56th$ points stand for the time-domain periodic patterns of one day and half a day, respectively. The absolute values of the three components are much higher than the rest of points, which suggests that most information of the time-domain traffic could be retained by the three components. Motivated by this hint, we use the three components for presenting the time-domain traffic. To evaluate the information loss of ignoring the rest of frequency components, we reconstruct the time-domain traffic using the three main frequency components, which is expressed as follows:

$$\begin{cases} \hat{X}^r[k] = \begin{cases} \hat{X}[k], & \text{if } k = 0,\ 4,\ 28,\ 56,\ N\text{-}4,\ N\text{-}28,\ N\text{-}56, \\ 0, & \text{otherwise,} \end{cases} \\ \\ x^r[n] = \frac{1}{N}\sum_{k=0}^{N-1}\hat{X}^r[k]e^{2\pi ikn/N}, \end{cases}$$

where $x^r[n]$ is the reconstructed time-domain traffic. The reconstructed time-domain traffic of the aggregate traffic of all cellular towers is also shown in Figure 12(b). From the result, we can observe that the reconstructed curve is very close to the original curve. Specifically, the lost energy, $\sum_{n=1}^{N} x^r[n]^2 - \sum_{n=1}^{N} x[n]^2$, is less than 6% relative to the total energy of the original traffic $\sum_{n=1}^{N} x[n]^2$, which suggests the negligible energy contributed by frequency components beyond the three main components.

To further understand the capability of signal reconstruction using the three points, we analyze the variance of amplitude of DFT at each frequency component for different cellular tower, and the result is shown in Figure 13. We can observe that the DFT variances of the three frequency components are larger compared to the rest. In addition, we use the DFT to analyse the aggregate traffic for cellular towers

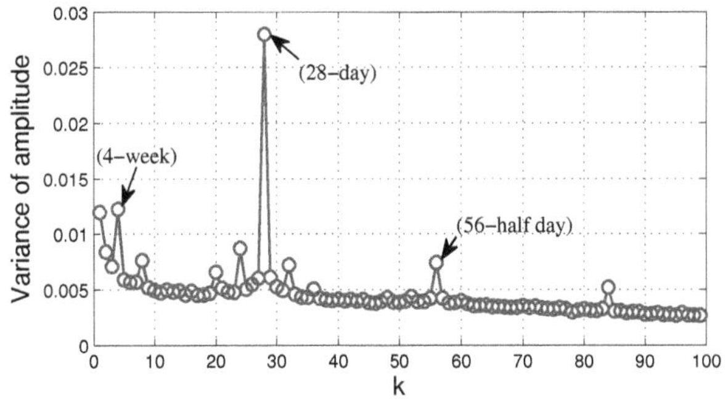

Figure 13: Variance of the frequency components across the five identified patterns.

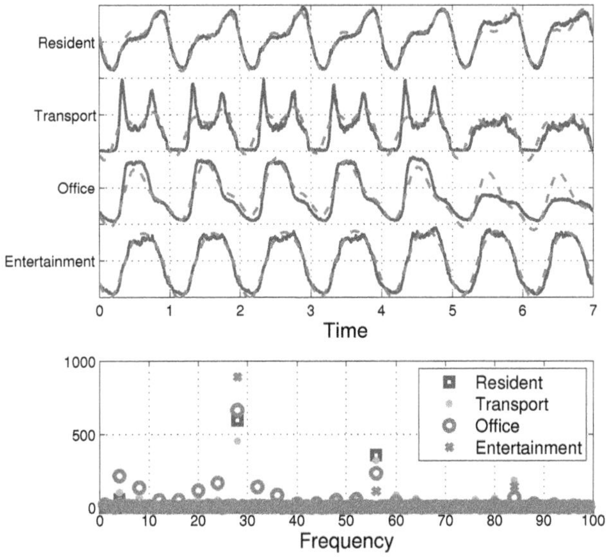

Figure 14: Reconstructed time-domain traffic of the five patterns using the three principal frequency domain components.

of the four primary traffic patterns in Figure 14. We can find that the reconstructed curves are also very close to the original curves, and their DFT spectrum varies most significantly at the three frequency components, which suggests that these three frequencies are the most important components in distinguishing towers of different traffic patterns as well as constructing a time-domain traffic.

5.2 Visualized Analysis in Frequency Domain

In order to better understand the five traffic patterns of towers in frequency domain, we now provide visualized frequency analysis of them. In addition, based on our earlier observation in Section 5.1, we only analyze the three frequencies corresponding to one week, one day, and half a day. Since each DFT point is a complex number, we analyze the distribution of its amplitude and phase extracted

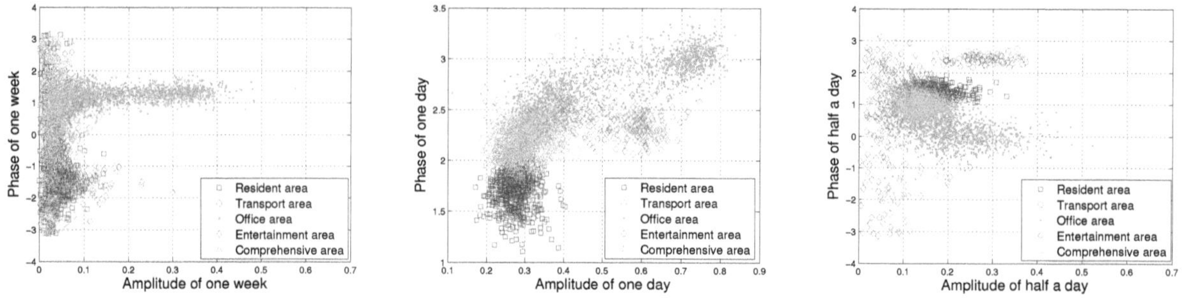

(a) k=4 (b) k=28 (c) k=56

Figure 15: Phase and amplitude distribution of the three principal frequency components in the frequency domain.

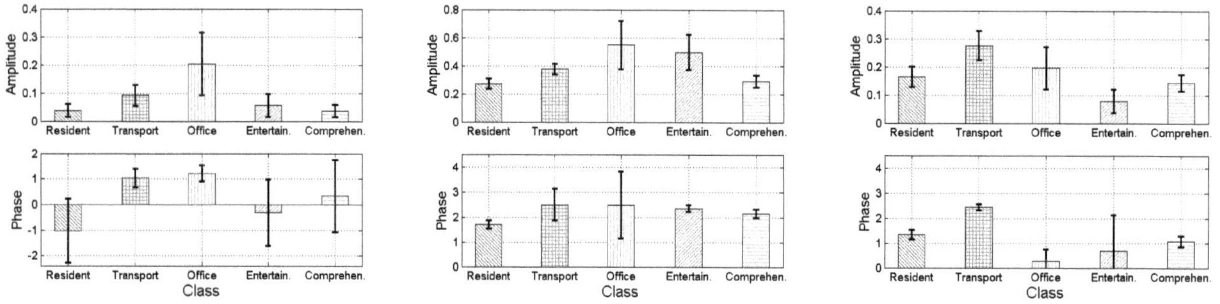

(a) Week (b) One day (c) Half a day

Figure 16: Means and standard deviations of amplitude and phase for cellular towers from the five identified patterns.

by the following expressions:

$$\begin{cases} A_k^m = ||X^m[k]||, \\ P_k^m = arg\ X^m[k], \end{cases}$$

where A_k^m and P_k^m are the amplitude and phase of DFT for tower m at the k_{th} frequency component. The larger amplitude reflects the stronger periodicity at corresponding frequency, while different phases of DFT indicate different peak time or valley time. Intuitively, for example, larger A_{28}^m indicates the cellular tower m is located at the area that is significantly influenced by the holiday at the weekend, such as office and entertainment area. On the other hand, since the traffic peak at office area tends to be reached at weekdays, while it at entertainment area tends to be reached at weekends, their P_{28}^m will have much difference. Thus, by frequency analysis, we can quantify the inherent time-domain periodicity of traffic, which is difficult to achieve by the time domain analysis.

Figure 15 shows the distribution of the amplitude and phase of towers deployed in the comprehensive, residential, office, transport, and entertainment areas. Meanwhile, means and standard deviations of the amplitude and phase for towers at the three frequency components of towers in the 4 types of areas are presented in Figure 16.

From Figure 15(a) and Figure 16(a), we can observe that towers in office area have the strongest periodicity of one week. Their phases mainly concentrate around 1.35, while the phase of towers in residential and entertainment area centers around -1.65, about π away from 1.35. This π separation suggests that towers in residential and entertainment area have reverse traffic characteristics as that in the office area in the scale of one week.

As we can observe in Figure 15(b), the distribution of towers is continuous with respect to the phase of one day. Moreover, it shows a smooth traffic transition from residential area to comprehensive and transport area, and finally to office area. On the other hand, according to our priori knowledge, the human migration flow usually leads to the peaks of traffic of areas appear sequentially with the same order that the flow passes through, which coincides with our observed phenomenon. Thus, such transition suggests the human migration flow from home to office via transport during rush hours. In Figure 16(b), we can also observe that the means of their phase are incremental with the same order.

Figure 15(c) and Figure 16(c) show characteristics of the amplitude and phase of the frequency component which stands for half a day. The amplitude of this frequency component indicates the strength of double-hump characteristic. In Figure 16(c), we can observe that the amplitude of towers in transport area is the largest, indicating their strongest double-hump characteristic. This result coincides with our priori knowledge that there are two rush hours of transport area in the morning and evening, respectively. In Figure 15(c), we find that traffic of residential and office area are not separated by traffic of transport area. This observation is not contradictory to our pervious analysis because the directions of people commute in the morning and afternoon are reversed.

Overall, the amplitude and phase of the three frequency components show a strong capability of differentiating towers with different traffic patterns. Based on the observations, we make the following statements. First, the most representative tower in each cluster is not the centroid. In fact, it is the farthest non-noise point from the hyperplanes, which separate clusters. To understand this problem, let us think about the points around a hyperplane, where we observe similar traffic patterns of points even though they belong to different clusters. In geographical context, these towers are deployed in areas of mixed urban functions. In contrast, the points far from the separating hyperplane are located at areas of a single urban function. Although perhaps not the most representative points, cluster centroids can well characterize the traffic patterns since they are distant from others clusters.

Second, the frequency-domain features of towers are distributed in a polygon. Such polygon is formed because the profile of each cluster in Figure 15 has a cigar shape. Thus, different features of towers can be regarded as being linear relevant or piecewise linear relevant approximately, which overlayed with a Gaussian noise can form the cluster with the cigar shape. As a result, a point in the frequency domain can be seen as a linear combination of the four vertex of the polygon, *i.e.*, the four most representative points, which we call as the four primary components.

To illustrate these two statements, we plot the distribution of towers and corresponding polygon in Figure 17. For better understanding, we only show three features, including amplitude and phase of one day, and amplitude of half day. According to our first statement, the most representative tower in each cluster is the furthest one from the hyperplane. Specifically, we do not calculate the hyperplanes, and only search for points with largest distance from points of other clusters. In addition, we use the density of the towers, i.e., the number of towers within a fixed distance away from it in the feature space, as a decision function to ensure that the tower is not a noise point. Figure 17 shows that all the towers are distributed in or along the edge and plane of the polygon, as we discussed above.

5.3 Component Analysis of Cellular Towers in Comprehensive Area

Based on the statements above, we may use a linear combination of the four most representative cellular towers to present each point in the polygon. By looking at the coefficient of each primary component, we can obtain the percentage of corresponding urban function of the area where an arbitrary cellular tower is deployed. We formulate the process of obtaining the coefficients as a quadratic programming problem, which is shown below:

$$\text{minimize} \quad ||F - F^r||^2$$
$$\text{subject to} \quad \begin{cases} \sum_{i=1}^{4} F_i^0 x_i = F^r, \\ \sum_{i=1}^{4} x_i = 1, \\ x_i \geq 0, \quad i = 1, ..., 4, \end{cases}$$

where $||\cdot||$ is the 2-norm of a vector, F is the feature of the target tower, F_i^0 is the feature of the most representative tower for cluster i in the frequency domain, and x_i is the obtained coefficient for cluster i. In this example, the feature of tower m, F^m, is $(A_{28}^m, P_{28}^m, A_{56}^m)$, where A_{28}^m ,P_{28}^m, A_{56}^m are the amplitude of one day, phase of one day, and amplitude of half a day for tower m, respectively. We use the quadratic programming to solve the problem because the traffic of an actual tower is usually overlayed with various noises, such that these points close to the plane of the the polygon may be driven out of the polygon. By solving this quadratic programming, for points inside the polygon, we can find their exact convex combinations, while for some point outside the polygon, we can find the point in the polygon with the smallest distance to the target point, which is a good approximation.

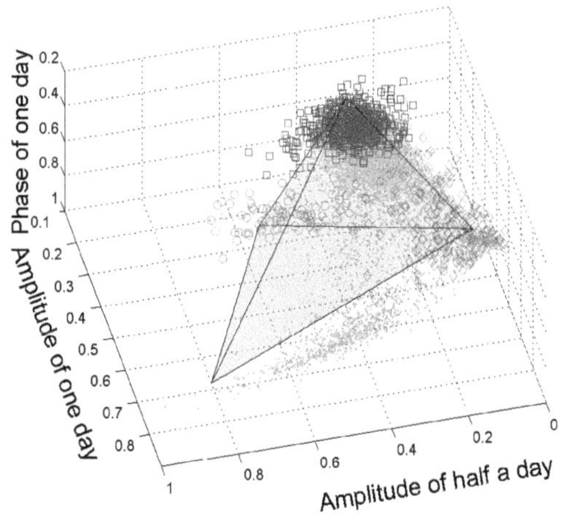

Figure 17: Three-dimensional view of the distribution of cellular towers in the frequency domain.

We dedicatedly select a list of towers in the comprehensive area. Then, we use the method presented above to solve the convex combinatorial coefficients of them. We compare these coefficients with a transform of the previously introduced POI, *i.e.*, the term frequency-inverse document frequency (TF-IDF) of the corresponding types and locations. TF-IDF is a numerical statistic that is intended to reflect how important a word is to a document. Similarly, it is used to reflect how important the POI of a specific type is in our analysis, which has been proposed in existing works, i.e., Yuan *et al.* [27] provided a TF-IDF-based method to cluster regions of different functions, which solely uses the POI data. Specifically, TF-IDF can be calculated as the following:

$$\begin{cases} \text{IDF}_i = \log(M/M_i), \\ \text{TF-IDF}_i^m = \text{IDF}_i \cdot \log(1 + \text{POI}_i^m), \end{cases}$$

where M is the total number of towers, and M_i is the number of towers of which the POI of type i appears within a specific distance, and POI_i^m is the times that the POI of type i appears within a fixed distance of tower m. To be better compared with, we normalize the TF-IDF of each tower by the sum of TF-IDF of all the four types for this tower, which is called as the normalized TF-IDF (NTF-IDF). This process can be formulated as the following:

$$\text{NTF-IDF}_i^m = \text{TF-IDF}_i^m / \sum_{j=1}^{4} \text{TF-IDF}_j^m.$$

Table 6: Convex combination coefficients and NTF-IDF.

	Coefficient				NTF-IDF			
	1	2	3	4	1	2	3	4
F1	1.00	0.00	0.00	0.00	1	0	0	0
F2	0.00	1.00	0.00	0.00	0.00	0.81	0.05	0.14
F3	0.00	0.00	1.00	0.00	0.00	0.00	1.00	0.00
F4	0.00	0.00	0.00	1.00	0.00	0.00	0.28	0.72
P1	0.79	0.13	0.08	0.00	0.44	0.36	0.04	0.16
P2	0.09	0.07	0.00	0.84	0.36	0.39	0.03	0.22
P3	0.23	0.00	0.15	0.62	0.68	0.00	0.07	0.25
P4	0.00	0.29	0.42	0.29	0.00	0.68	0.07	0.24
P5	0.35	0.18	0.22	0.25	0.12	0.55	0.05	0.28

The obtained NTF-IDF is proportional to the POI for each type, which roughly represents the density of the corresponding function in the corresponding area. Specifically, NTF-IDF close to 0 indicates this area do not have the corresponding function. However, the largest NTF-IDF do not completely indicate the corresponding function is dominant in the area, since it is also influenced by the size of related points and corresponding distance. For example, a large and close subway station has more influence than a small and far residential building on a cellular tower.

Then, the result is shown in Table 6. Expect for the towers in the comprehensive area, the NTF-IDF of the four most representative towers is also provided in the table. We can observe that their NTF-IDF of corresponding types is much larger than others, which is very close to 1, indicating the areas where they are located have a single type of function. As for towers in the comprehensive area, There are multiple relative large NTF-IDF for a cellular tower. As discussed earlier, this may lead to inaccuracy since the influence of the size of related points and corresponding distance. Thus, we only consider the consistency of the small NTF-IDF and combination coefficients. We can observe that the majority of the smallest NTF-IDF$_i^m$ in all m for some fix i corresponds to the smallest coefficient in all m for the same i, respectively. For example, NTF-IDF$_2^{P3}$ and NTF-IDF$_1^{P4}$ are 0, and their corresponding coefficients are also 0. Thus, the obtained convex combination coefficients coincide with the POI distribution, indicating the correctness of our theory.

To further illustrate the convex combination, we take the tower P5 in Table 6 as an example, and show its combination of frequency and time domain, respectively in Figure 18 and Figure 19. For a point inside the polygon, we can find its exact convex combination, that is:

$$F = F^r = \sum_{i=1}^{4} F_i^0 x_i = F_3^0 + \sum_{i=1, i \neq 3}^{4} x_i(F_i^0 - F_3^0).$$

As shown in Figure 18, in the feature space, the vector $(0, Fr)$ can be divided to the vector $(0, F3)$ and the weighted sum of the vector $(F3, F1), (F3, F2), (F3, F4)$. For P5, the weights are 0.35, 0.18 and 0.25, respectively, which is just as coefficients of cluster 1, 2, 4 in Table 6 of P5.

On the other hand, in Figure 19, we show the components of traffic corresponding to four primary clusters for the comprehensive tower P5. Areas of different colors in the left figure represent components of different primary traffic patterns. To be better distinguished, each component is added with a static bias. In addition, we plot each component individually in the right figure. The result indicates that traffic patterns of an arbitrarily cellular tower can be approximated by a convex combination of four primary traffic patterns. The size of each component is highly related to density of corresponding function around the tower. It further demonstrates the correctness and usefulness of our frequency analysis method.

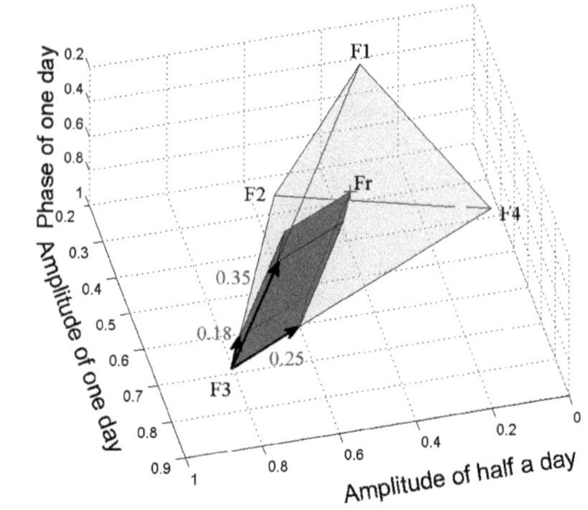

Figure 18: Convex combination for P5 in Table 6 in frequency domain.

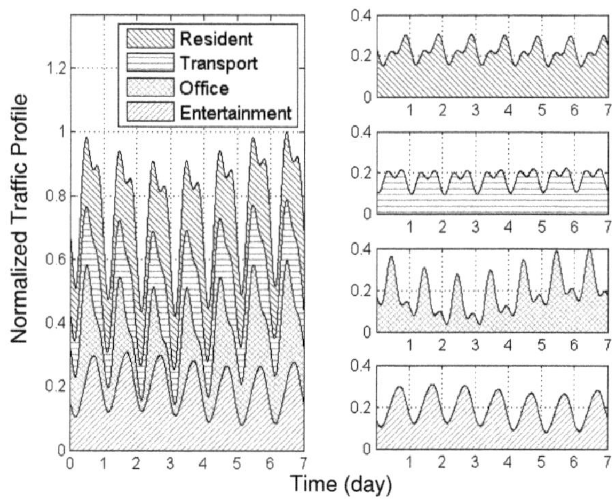

Figure 19: Convex combination for P5 in time domain.

6. RELATED WORK

The digital footprints of human activities and network behaviors contributed by mobile devices have led to a plethora of investigations on the intersection between human and network dynamics[14, 15]. This section summarizes relevant research from three perspectives — data sources, types of collected data and targeted applications.

Dataset collected from mobile devices for investigating human behaviors and network performance can be divided into two broad categories: (1) data collected from mobile devices and (2) traces collected by mobile operators [2]. For the first categories, users or experimenters report their semantically annotated data about the locations, phone usages and network performance by installing some Apps in their devices[19, 10]. The limitation of this approach comes from the limited number of users sampled, which cannot stand for the global characteristics of a large scale cellular network. On the other hand, in the dataset collected by cellular operators, users are passively monitored and the operators decide which information to collect[9, 24]. As a result, the collected data is continuous as long as devices are connected, and includes detailed information of users behaviors, such as duration of each Internet connection. As a result, data collected via the second approach enables the study of overall network behaviors, such as large scale of human mobility and call activities analysis. In this paper, we use the data collected by an ISP for investigating the traffic patterns of large scale cellular towers.

Extensive studies have used various types of cellular data for understanding the characteristics of large scale cellular towers. For example, cell phone activities, commonly know as Call Description Records (CDR), are used for capturing human communication activities[3]. In addition, it is also used for recovering the human mobility trajectory[9], inferring demographics[6], and uncovering urban ecology[2]. Another type of data is the device-level metric obtained from mobile devices, such as device and application usage[8, 21], network access bandwidth[10], energy computation[11], personal GPS locations[28], etc. With the popularity of 3G and LTE access, mobile and application data traces become available as well. Cici et al. [2] characterizes the relationship between people's application interests and mobility patterns based on a population of over 280, 000 users of a 3G mobile network. Lee et al. [16] demonstrated that the spatial distribution of the traffic density can be approximated by the log-normal or Weibull distribution. However, mobile data traffic across a city-wide range with different time scale and variations contains complicated interaction between the space and time, which requires a deep and comprehensive understanding. The analysis and models in this work provide such insights.

Cellular network traces have been used for enabling a set of applications. The footprint of mobile devices and cellular network has been used to model human mobility and trajectories [9, 7, 24, 5]. Barabasi et al. [9, 23, 22] studied the mobility behaviors of 100k mobile users by analyzing the CDR data, and found that the trajectories of human is not as random as previously proposed levy flight or random walk models. Instead, it presents a high confidence of predictability[23], and temporal and spatial regularity[9]. The cellular network traces have also been used for characterizing and modelling the cellular data traffic patterns. Shafiq et al. [17] modelled the internet traffic dynamics of cellular devices. Jin et al. [12] characterized data usage patterns in large cellular network. And Zhang et al. [26] tried to understand the characteristics of cellular data traffic by comparing it to wireline data traffic. Other studies combine the CDR, GPS locations, and application traces to investigate the land usage[24, 20], social interactions[7], location-based patterns[5], and web and data access patterns[13, 12]. In this paper, we focus on investigating the mobile data traffic patterns from different domains, including time, location and frequency, which provides a comprehensive understanding of the traffic patterns of large scale cellular towers with a simple but deep model that is able to characterize the city geographical features and human communication regularity.

In conclusion, we study a large scale urban mobile data access traces collected by the commercial mobile operators involving over 9600 towers and 150,000 subscribers. We first design an analysis framework for processing large scale cellular traffic data. Then, we reveals the basic but fundamental patterns embedded in thousands of cellular towers, which paves a way toward a comprehensive understanding of the connection among mobile data traffic, urban ecology and human behaviors.

7. CONCLUSIONS

In this paper, we carry out, to the best of our knowledge, the first study of traffic patterns embedded in large scale 3G and LTE towers deployed in the urban environment. We propose a powerful model which combines time, location and frequency information for analyzing the traffic patterns of thousands of cellular towers. Our analysis reveals that the dynamic urban mobile traffic usage exhibits only five basic time domain patterns. In addition, the traffic of any tower can be reconstructed accurately using a linear combination of four primary components corresponding to human activity behaviors. Our analysis provides a systematic and comprehensive understanding of dynamic and complicated mobile traffic, and opens a set of new research directions.

Acknowledgment

This work is supported by National Basic Research Program of China (973 Program) (No. 2013CB329105) and National Nature Science Foundation of China (No. 61301080, No. 91338203, No. 91338102, and No. 61321061).

8. REFERENCES

[1] Cisco visual networking index: Global mobile data traffic forecast. 2014.

[2] B. Cici, M. Gjoka, A. Markopoulou, and C. T. Butts. On the decomposition of cell phone activity patterns and their connection with urban ecology. In *Proc. of ACM MobiHoc*, pages 317–326, 2015.

[3] B. Cici, A. Markopoulou, E. Frías-Martínez, and N. Laoutaris. Quantifying the potential of ride-sharing using call description records. In *Proc. of ACM HotMobile*, page 17, 2013.

[4] F. Corpet. Multiple sequence alignment with hierarchical clustering. *Nucleic acids research*, 16(22):10881–10890, 1988.

[5] A. K. Das, P. H. Pathak, C.-N. Chuah, and P. Mohapatra. Contextual localization through network traffic analysis. In *Proc. of IEEE INFOCOM*, pages 925–933, 2014.

[6] Y. Dong, Y. Yang, J. Tang, Y. Yang, and N. V. Chawla. Inferring user demographics and social strategies in mobile social networks. In *Proc. of ACM SIGKDD*, pages 15–24, 2014.

[7] N. Eagle, A. S. Pentland, and D. Lazer. Inferring friendship network structure by using mobile phone data. *Proc. of the National Academy of Sciences*, 106(36):15274–15278, 2009.

[8] H. Falaki, D. Lymberopoulos, R. Mahajan, S. Kandula, and D. Estrin. A first look at traffic on

smartphones. In *Proc. of ACM IMC*, pages 281–287, 2010.

[9] M. C. Gonzalez, C. A. Hidalgo, and A.-L. Barabasi. Understanding individual human mobility patterns. *Nature*, 453(7196):779–782, 2008.

[10] W. Hu and G. Cao. Quality-aware traffic offloading in wireless networks. In *Proc. of ACM MobiHoc*, pages 277–286, 2014.

[11] W. Hu and G. Cao. Energy-aware video streaming on smartphones. In *Proc. of IEEE INFOCOM*, 2015.

[12] Y. Jin, N. Duffield, A. Gerber, P. Haffner, W.-L. Hsu, G. Jacobson, S. Sen, S. Venkataraman, and Z.-L. Zhang. Characterizing data usage patterns in a large cellular network. In *ACM CellNet Workshop*, pages 7–12, 2012.

[13] R. Keralapura, A. Nucci, Z.-L. Zhang, and L. Gao. Profiling users in a 3g network using hourglass co-clustering. In *Proc. of ACM MobiCom*, pages 341–352, 2010.

[14] M. Kosinski, D. Stillwell, and T. Graepel. Private traits and attributes are predictable from digital records of human behavior. *Proc. of the National Academy of Sciences*, 110(15):5802–5805, 2013.

[15] J. K. Laurila, D. Gatica-Perez, I. Aad, O. Bornet, T.-M.-T. Do, O. Dousse, J. Eberle, M. Miettinen, et al. The mobile data challenge: Big data for mobile computing research. In *Pervasive Computing*, number EPFL-CONF-192489, 2012.

[16] D. Lee, S. Zhou, X. Zhong, Z. Niu, X. Zhou, and H. Zhang. Spatial modeling of the traffic density in cellular networks. *Wireless Communications, IEEE*, 21(1):80–88, 2014.

[17] J. A. X. L. J. W. M. Zubair, Shafiq Lusheng. Characterizing and modeling internet traffic dynamics of cellular devices. *Performance evaluation review*, 39(1):305–316, 2011.

[18] U. Maulik and S. Bandyopadhyay. Performance evaluation of some clustering algorithms and validity indices. *Pattern Analysis and Machine Intelligence, IEEE Transactions on*, 24(12):1650–1654, 2002.

[19] A. Noulas and C. Mascolo. Exploiting foursquare and cellular data to infer user activity in urban environments. In *Proc. of IEEE MDM*, volume 1, pages 167–176, 2013.

[20] T. Pei, S. Sobolevsky, C. Ratti, S.-L. Shaw, T. Li, and C. Zhou. A new insight into land use classification based on aggregated mobile phone data. *International Journal of Geographical Information Science*, 28(9):1988–2007, 2014.

[21] M. Z. Shafiq, L. Ji, A. X. Liu, J. Pang, and J. Wang. Characterizing geospatial dynamics of application usage in a 3g cellular data network. In *Proc. of IEEE INFOCOM*, pages 1341–1349, 2012.

[22] C. Song, T. Koren, P. Wang, and A.-L. Barabási. Modelling the scaling properties of human mobility. *Nature Physics*, 6(10):818–823, 2010.

[23] C. Song, Z. Qu, N. Blumm, and A.-L. Barabási. Limits of predictability in human mobility. *Science*, 327(5968):1018–1021, 2010.

[24] J. L. Toole, M. Ulm, M. C. González, and D. Bauer. Inferring land use from mobile phone activity. In *Proc. of ACM SIGKDD*, pages 1–8, 2012.

[25] H. Wang, J. Ding, Y. Li, P. Hui, J. Yuan, and D. Jin. Characterizing the spatio-temporal inhomogeneity of mobile traffic in large-scale cellular data networks. In *Proc. of ACM HOTPOST*, pp. 19-24, 2015.

[26] k. A. Ying Zhang. Understanding the characteristics of cellular data traffic. In *ACM SIGCOMM CellNet Workshop*, 42(4):13–18, 2012.

[27] J. Yuan, Y. Zheng, and X. Xie. Discovering regions of different functions in a city using human mobility and pois. In *Proc. ACM SIGKDD*, pages 186–194, 2012.

[28] Y. Zheng, Q. Li, Y. Chen, X. Xie, and W.-Y. Ma. Understanding mobility based on gps data. In *Proc. of ACM UbiComp*, pages 312–321, 2008.

Identifying Traffic Differentiation in Mobile Networks

Arash Molavi Kakhki
Northeastern University
arash@ccs.neu.edu

Abbas Razaghpanah
Stony Brook University
arazaghpanah@cs.stonybrook.edu

Anke Li
Stony Brook University
ankeli@cs.stonybrook.edu

Hyungjoon Koo
Stony Brook University
hykoo@cs.stonybrook.edu

Rajesh Golani
Stony Brook University
rgolani@cs.stonybrook.edu

David Choffnes
Northeastern University
choffnes@ccs.neu.edu

Phillipa Gill
Stony Brook University
phillipa@cs.stonybrook.edu

Alan Mislove
Northeastern University
amislove@ccs.neu.edu

Abstract

Traffic differentiation—giving better (or worse) performance to certain classes of Internet traffic—is a well-known but poorly understood traffic management policy. There is active discussion on whether and how ISPs should be allowed to differentiate Internet traffic [8, 21], but little data about current practices to inform this discussion. Previous work attempted to address this problem for fixed line networks; however, there is currently no solution that works in the more challenging mobile environment.

In this paper, we present the design, implementation, and evaluation of the first system and mobile app for identifying traffic differentiation for arbitrary applications in the mobile environment (*i.e.,* wireless networks such as cellular and WiFi, used by smartphones and tablets). The key idea is to use a VPN proxy to record and replay the network traffic generated by arbitrary applications, and compare it with the network behavior when replaying this traffic outside of an encrypted tunnel. We perform the first known testbed experiments with actual commercial shaping devices to validate our system design and demonstrate how it outperforms previous work for detecting differentiation. We released our app and collected differentiation results from 12 ISPs in 5 countries. We find that differentiation tends to affect TCP traffic (reducing rates by up to 60%) and that interference from middleboxes (including video-transcoding devices) is pervasive. By exposing such behavior, we hope to improve transparency for users and help inform future policies.

Categories and Subject Descriptors

C.2.2 [**Computer-Communication Networks**]: Network Protocols

IMC'15, October 28–30, 2015, Tokyo, Japan.

DOI: http://dx.doi.org/10.1145/2815675.2815691.

Keywords

Traffic differentiation; mobile networks; network neutrality

1. INTRODUCTION

The rise in popularity of bandwidth-hungry applications (*e.g.,* Netflix) coupled with resource-constrained networks (*e.g.,* mobile providers) has reignited discussions about how the different applications' network traffic is treated (or mistreated) by ISPs. One commonly discussed approach to managing scarce network resources is *traffic differentiation*—giving better (or worse) performance to certain classes of network traffic—using devices that selectively act on network traffic (*e.g.,* Sandvine [25], Cisco, and others). Differentiation can enforce policies ranging from protecting the network from bandwidth-hungry applications, to limiting services that compete with those offered by the network provider (*e.g.,* providers that sell voice/video services in addition to IP connectivity).

Recent events have raised the profile of traffic differentiation and network neutrality issues in the wired setting, with Comcast and Netflix engaged in public disputes over congestion on network interconnects [11, 15, 18]. The situation is more extreme in the mobile setting, where historically regulatory agencies imposed few restrictions on how a mobile provider manages its network, with subscribers and regulators generally having a limited (or no) ability to understand and hold providers accountable for management polices.[1]

Despite the importance of this issue, the impacts of traffic differentiation on specific applications—and the Internet as a whole—are poorly understood. Previous efforts attempt to detect traffic differentiation (*e.g.,* [6, 30, 36, 37]), but are limited to specific types of application traffic (*e.g.,* peer-to-peer traffic [6]), or focus on shaping behaviors on general classes of traffic as opposed to specific applications [13, 30, 37]. Addressing these limitations is challenging, due to the wide variety of applications (often closed-source) that users may wish to test for differentiation, coupled with the closed nature of traffic shapers. As a result, external observers struggle to detect if such shapers exist in networks,

[1] As we discuss throughout this paper, FCC rules that took effect in June 2015 [9] now prohibit many forms of traffic differentiation in the US.

what exactly these devices do, and what is their impact on traffic. What little we do know is concerning. Glasnost [6] and others [26, 30, 36] found ISPs throttling specific types of Internet traffic, Cogent admitted to differentiating Netflix traffic [23], and recent work by Google and T-Mobile [12] indicated that unintentional interactions between traffic shaping devices has been known to degrade performance.

This paper tackles three key challenges that have held back prior work on measuring traffic differentiation: (1) the inability to test arbitrary classes of applications, (2) a lack of understanding of how traffic shaping devices work in practice, and (3) the limited ability to measure mobile networks (*e.g.,* cellular and WiFi) from end-user devices such as smartphones and tablets. Designing methods that can measure traffic differentiation in mobile networks (in addition to well-studied wired networks) presents unique challenges, as the approaches must work with highly variable underlying network performance and within the constraints of mobile operating systems. By addressing these challenges, we can provide tools that empower average users to identify differentiation in mobile networks, and use data gathered from these tools to understand differentiation in practice.

This paper makes the following key contributions:

- **The design and implementation of a system for detecting traffic differentiation in mobile networks (Sec. 3).** We design an application-layer trace record-and-replay system that enables testing of arbitrary network applications, and works even if these applications are closed source. Our solution does not require special privileges on client devices, making it readily deployable on a global scale. The key idea is to use a VPN proxy to record arbitrary application traffic, and later replay that traffic both with and without the VPN to identify differentiation. We implement this both as an Android and desktop application.
- **Validation of our approach using commercial shaping devices (Sec. 4).** To the best of our knowledge, we are the first study to validate that our detection system correctly triggers differentiation on commercial shaping devices. Using a testbed consisting of two such devices, we establish a ground truth to evaluate the accuracy of our approach and identify several pitfalls of previous approaches.
- **Evaluating statistical techniques for identifying differentiation (Sec. 5).** Previous work uses a variety of statistical techniques to determine when differentiation occurs. We use our testbed with commercial shaping products (with configurable shaping rates), a controlled network with no differentiation, and controlled loss with Linux Traffic Control (`tc`) to systematically evaluate the accuracy of different statistical techniques for identifying differentiation.
- **An Android app that conducts our differentiation tests and a measurement study of differentiation in mobile networks (Sec. 6).** We develop an Android app that conducts our differentiation tests on unmodified Android OSes, as part of an IRB-approved study of differentiation in mobile networks worldwide. We deploy our software in the US and four other countries, and find several instances of shaping, in addition to pervasive interference from middleboxes.

  In addition to being the first approach to reliably detect differentiation from mobile devices without special privileges, our study also identifies several instances of middleboxes violating end-to-end principles for a variety of popular apps. In particular, we find evidence of video transcoding, HTTP header manipulation in requests and responses, and proxies that modify TCP behavior. While previous work identified such behavior for Web traffic, we are the first to do so for arbitrary app traffic.

The following section discusses related work and defines differentiation that we detect. After detailing our key contributions listed above, we discuss issues with differentiation and its detection that are beyond the scope of this work (Sec. 7), and we conclude in Sec. 8.

2. BACKGROUND

There is an ongoing debate about whether the network should be neutral with respect to the packets it carries [4]; *i.e.,* not discriminate against or otherwise alter traffic except for lawful purposes (*e.g.,* blocking illegal content). Proponents such as President Obama argue for an open Internet [21] as essential to its continued success, while some ISPs argue for shaping to manage network resources [6, 26].

The regulatory framework surrounding traffic differentiation is rapidly changing; between submission and publication of this manuscript, the FCC transitioned from imposing few restrictions on how mobile providers manage their network, to new rules that prohibit many forms of differentiation [9]. In this environment, it is important to monitor traffic differentiation in practice, both to inform regulators and enforce policies.

In the remainder of this section, we overview related work on measuring traffic differentiation and network neutrality and then define the types of traffic differentiation our system aims to detect.

2.1 Related Work

Comcast's blocking of BitTorrent [28] in the mid 2000s spurred research efforts to study traffic differentiation. This led to several studies that focus on applications or flows known to be subject to classification, and design tests to detect differentiation on those flows. For example, Glasnost focuses on BitTorrent [6] and NetPolice [36] tests five applications (HTTP, BitTorrent, SMTP, PPLive and VoIP). Bonafide [3] takes a similar approach to Glasnost in the mobile environment, including tests for HTTP, FlashVideo (YouTube), SIP, RTSP, BitTorrent, and VoIP H323. These approaches focus on *protocols* rather than *specific application implementations.* A key limitation is that the shaping devices we observed support application/provider granularity, *e.g.,* shape RTSP traffic for one content provider, but not other RTSP applications (see Sec. 4). Such application-based differentiation may not be detected by these systems. They also require manually implementing protocol details and thus have limited extensibility. We address these limitations in this work.

Furthermore, these projects treat traffic differentiation as a "black box" which they aim to detect by sending traffic and observing network performance metrics. Notably, these prior studies lack ground-truth information about how differentiation is implemented, and whether or not their detection mechanisms would trigger traffic shaping in practice (an issue we address in this work).

Another approach avoids testing specific applications and focuses on detecting differentiation for arbitrary traffic. NANO [30] uses Bayesian analysis to detect differentiation, while Zhang et al. [37] focus on identifying when it is feasible to detect and isolate differentiation. Other related projects focus on performance issues in ISPs [7,16,18,19] and shaping of all of a subscriber's traffic [13], but do not detect differentiation itself.

Other related studies detect proxies on network paths, and conduct tests to identify a wide range of application-specific proxy behaviors [2,14,29,32,33]. A recent paper [31] specifically focuses on proxies and other middleboxes in mobile networks, and discusses how these devices vary according to mobile virtual network operator (MVNO). Zarinni et al. use Bonafide [3] to test for differentiation of BitTorrent, VoIP-H323 and RTSP [35] in MVNOs. The authors did not observe differentiation of this limited set of applications; in contrast, our approach identified differentiation in three of the networks they tested.

2.2 Differentiation considered in our work

In this work, we consider the problem of detecting differentiation caused by traffic-shaping middleboxes (rather than interconnection provisioning [11,15,18]). We focus on the mobile environment, in large part due to minimal regulation and scarce network resources in mobile data networks. However, our techniques also work in the fixed-line environment.

We focus on differentiation affecting network performance *as perceived by applications*. In our experiments, we observe that even high-bandwidth mobile applications such as video streaming do not necessarily exhaust the bandwidth available, possibly to avoid wasting data transfer in case of viewer abandonment. This is in contrast to protocols that previous approaches focused on (e.g., BitTorrent), which aim to saturate the link bandwidth. For applications that do not exhaust the available resources, we do *not* consider traffic shaping where the shaping rate is higher than the bandwidth demands to be differentiation. For example, if a shaper limited a given application to 200 KB/s, but the application never sent faster than 150 KB/s, we would not consider this differentiation (as the application would never be affected by it). This more conservative approach gives us a clearer picture of shaping that actually impinges on the network resource demands of applications.

We make the assumption that traffic differentiation is likely triggered by at least one of the following factors: IP addresses, port numbers, payload signatures, number of connections, total bandwidth, and time-of-day.

We confirmed these assumptions are consistent with features listed in online manuals of deep packet inspection (DPI) devices and traffic shapers. We also run experiments with two commercial packet shapers and show that our assumptions hold for these devices (Sec. 4.2).

Nongoals. In this work, there are certain types of traffic management policies that we are not able to detect. First, we do not focus on detecting congestion at peering points, a tactic used by certain ISPs to extract payment from large bandwidth consumers [11]. Second, we do not focus on blocking (*e.g.,* censorship) or content modification (*e.g.,* transcoding) by middleboxes. While our methodology is able detect these types (and we found cases of both), they are orthogonal to the issue of shaping. Third, we currently do not support detecting differentiation based on the destination IP address contacted by clients. Our analysis of commercially deployed traffic shapers indicates that IP addresses are not commonly used to identify applications, since none of our observed configurations use them for shaping. We speculate this is due to the fact that many applications contact servers with IPs shared by many services (*e.g.,* EC2, or Google frontends that serve both search and YouTube traffic), and the IPs used by any service may change over time. Thus, IP addresses are a poor classifier for shaping a specific application. Regardless, we are investigating how to use limited forms of IP spoofing to address this limitation.

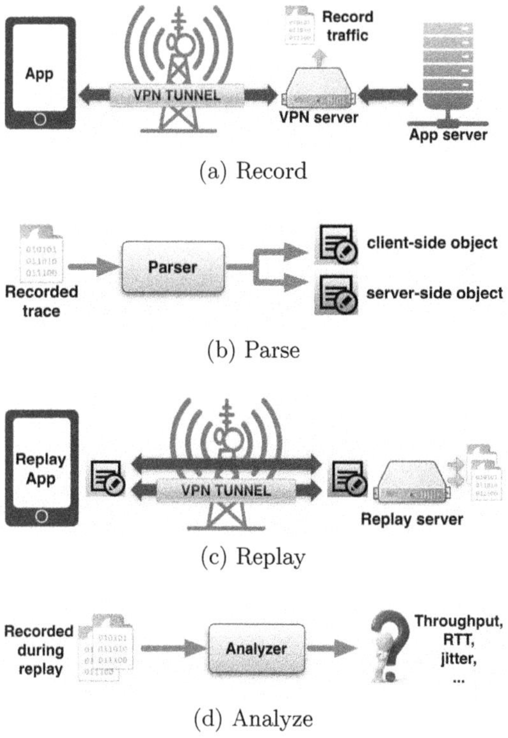

Figure 1: System overview: (a) Client connects to VPN, that records traffic between the client and app server(s). (b) Parser produces transcripts for replaying. (c) Client and replay server use transcripts to replay the trace, once in plaintext and once through a VPN tunnel. Replay server records packet traces for each replay. (d) Analyzer uses the traces to detect differentiation.

3. METHODOLOGY

We use a trace record-replay methodology to reliably detect traffic differentiation for arbitrary applications in the mobile environment. We provide an overview in Figure 1. We record a packet trace from a target application (Fig. 1(a)), extract bidirectional application-layer payloads, and use this to generate a transcript of messages for the client and server to replay (Fig. 1(b)). To test for differentiation, the client and server coordinate to replay these transcripts, both in plaintext and through an encrypted channel (using a VPN tunnel) where payloads are hidden from any shapers on the path (Fig. 1(c)). Finally, we use validated statistical tests to identify whether the application traffic being tested was subject to differentiation (Fig. 1(d)). We discuss each of these steps below.

3.1 Recording the trace

Our method requires a packet trace to replay. While it is straightforward to gather one on desktop operating systems, recording packet traces on today's mobile operating systems requires "rooting" and/or "jailbreaking" the phone (potentially voiding the phone's warranty). This is not a problem for small-scale testbed experiments, but traffic differentiation—and the applications it affects—is a moving target that requires running experiments for a variety of applications on a large set of devices in different networks worldwide. Thus, we need a way to enable end users to capture traces of mobile application traffic without requiring modifications to the OS.

To address this challenge, we leverage the fact that all major mobile operating systems natively support VPN connections, and use the Meddle VPN [22] to facilitate trace recording. Figure 1(a) illustrates how a client connects to the Meddle VPN, which relays traffic between the client and destination server(s). In addition, the Meddle VPN collects packet traces that we use to generate replay transcripts. When possible, we record traffic using the same network being tested for differentiation because applications may behave differently based on the network type, *e.g.,* a streaming video app may select a higher bitrate on WiFi.

Our methodology is extensible to arbitrary applications—even closed source and proprietary ones—to ensure it works even as the landscape of popular applications, the network protocols they use, and their impact on mobile network resources changes over time. Prior work focused on specific applications (e.g., BitTorrent [6]) and manually emulated application flows. This approach, however, does not scale to large numbers of applications and may even be infeasible when the target application uses proprietary, or otherwise closed, protocols.[2]

3.2 Creating the replay script

After recording a packet trace, our system processes it to extract the application-layer payloads as client-to-server and server-to-client byte streams. We then create a replay transcript that captures the behavior of the application's traffic, including port numbers, dependencies between application-layer messages (if they exist) and any timing properties of the application (*e.g.,* fixed-rate multimedia).[3] Finally, we use each endpoint's TCP or UDP stack to replay the traffic as specified in the transcript. Figure 1(b) shows how we create two objects with the necessary information for the client and server to replay the traffic from the recorded trace.

Logical dependencies. For TCP traffic, we preserve application-layer dependencies using the implicit *happens-before* relationship exposed by application-layer communication in TCP. More specifically, we extract two unidirectional byte streams s_{AB} and s_{BA} for each pair of communicating hosts A and B in the recorded trace. For each sequence of bytes in s_{AB}, we identify the bytes in s_{BA} that preceded them in the trace. When replaying, host A sends bytes in s_{AB} to host B only after it has received the preceding bytes in s_{BA} from host B. We enforce analogous constraints from B to A. For UDP traffic, we do not enforce logical dependencies because the transport layer does explicitly not impose them.

Timing dependencies. A second challenge is ensuring the replayed traffic maintains the inter-message timing features of the initial trace. For example, streaming video apps commonly download and buffer video content in chunks instead of buffering the entire video, typically to reduce data-consumption for viewer abandonment and to save energy by allowing the radio to sleep between bursts. Other content servers use packet pacing to minimize packet loss and thus improve flow completion times.

Our system preserves the timings between packets for both TCP and UDP traffic to capture such behavior when replaying (this feature can be disabled when timing is not intrinsic to the application). Preserving timing is a key feature of our approach, that can have a significant impact on detecting differentiation, as discussed in Section 2.2. In short, it prevents us from detecting shaping that does not impact application-perceived performance.

Specifically, for each stream of bytes (UDP or TCP) sent by a host, A, we annotate each byte with *time offset* from the first byte in the stream in the recorded trace. If the ith byte of A was sent at t ms from the start of the trace, we ensure that byte i is *not sent before* t ms have elapsed in the replay. For TCP, this constraint is enforced after enforcing the happens-before relationship.

In the case of UDP, we do not retransmit lost packets. This closely matches the behavior of real-time applications such as VoIP and live-streaming video (which often tolerate packet losses), but does not work well for more complicated protocols such as BitTorrent's µTP [20] or Google's QUIC [1]. We will investigate how to incorporate this behavior in future work.

3.3 Replaying the trace

After steps 1 and 2, we replay the recorded traffic on a target network to test our null hypothesis that there is no differentiation in the network. This test requires two samples of network performance: one that *exposes* the replay to differentiation (if any), and a *control* that is not exposed to differentiation.

A key challenge is how to conduct the control trial. Initially, we followed prior work [6] and randomized the port numbers and payload, while maintaining all other features of the replayed traffic. However, using our testbed containing commercial traffic shapers (Section 4.2), we found that some shapers will by default label "random" traffic with high port numbers as peer-to-peer traffic, a common target of differentiation. Thus, this approach is unreliable to generate control trials because one can reasonably expect it to be shaped.

Instead, we re-use the Meddle VPN tunnel to conduct control trials. By sending all recorded traffic over an encrypted IPSec tunnel, we preserve all application behavior while simultaneously preventing any DPI-based shaper from differentiating based on payload. Thus, each replay test consists of replaying the trace twice, once in plaintext (exposed trial), and once over the VPN (control trial), depicted in Figure 1(c). To detect differentiation in noisy environments, we run multiple back-to-back tests (both control and exposed). Note that we compare exposed and control trials with each other and not the original recorded

[2]The Glasnost paper describes an (unevaluated) tool to support replaying of arbitrary applications but we were unsuccessful in using it, even with the help of a Glasnost coauthor.

[3]This approach is similar to Cui et al.'s [5]; however, our approach perfectly preserves application payloads (to ensure traffic is classified by shapers) and timing (to prevent false positives when detecting shaping).

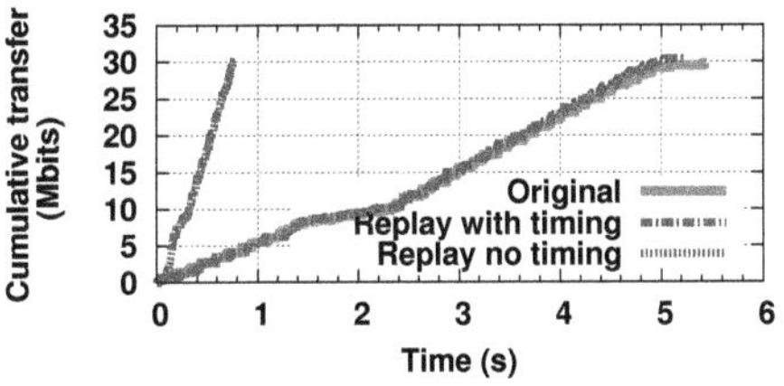

(a) YouTube

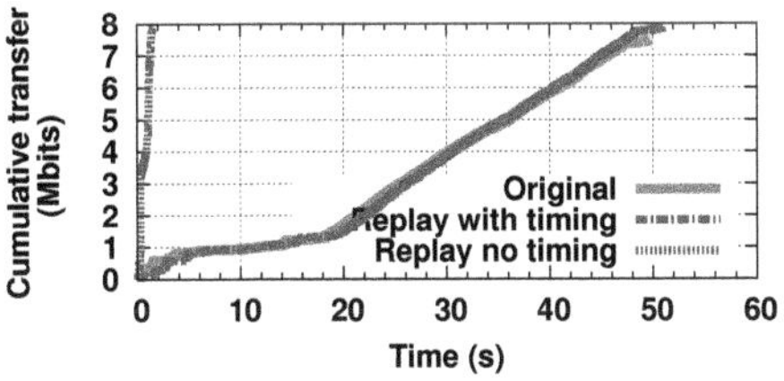

(b) Skype

Figure 2: Plots showing bytes transferred over time, with and without preserving packet timings for TCP (YouTube) and UDP (Skype) applications. By preserving inter-packet timings, our replay closely resembles the original traffic generated by each app.

trace. We explore potential issues of using a VPN as a control in Sections 4.3 and 7.

3.4 Detecting differentiation

After running the exposed and control trials, we compare performance metrics (throughput, loss, and delay) to detect differentiation (Fig. 1(d)). We focus on these metrics because traffic shaping policies typically involve bandwidth rate-limiting (reflected in throughput differences), and may have impacts on delay and loss depending on the queuing/shaping discipline. We base our analysis on server-side packet captures to compute throughput and RTT values for TCP, because we cannot rely on collecting network-level traces on mobile clients. For UDP applications, we use jitter as a delay metric and measure it at the client at the application layer (observing inter-packet timings).

A key challenge is how to automatically detect when differences between two traces are caused by differentiation, instead of signal strength, congestion, or other confounding factors. In Section 5, we find that previous techniques to identify differentiation are inaccurate when tested against commercial packet shaping devices with varying packet loss in our testbed. We describe a novel area test approach to compare traces that has perfect accuracy with no loss, and greater than 70% accuracy under high loss (Fig. 9).

4. VALIDATION

We validate our methodology using our replay system and a testbed comprised of two commercial shaping devices. First, we verify that our approach captures salient features of the recorded traffic. Next, we validate that our replays trigger differentiation and identify the relevant features used for classification. To the best of our knowledge, this is first study to use commercial shapers to validate differentiation detection. Finally, we discuss potential overheads of using a VPN connection as a control and how we mitigate them.

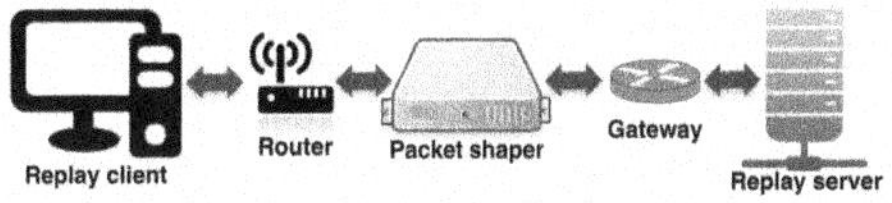

Figure 3: Our testbed for testing our differentiation detector.

4.1 Record/Replay similarity

Our replay script replicates the original trace, including payloads, port numbers, and inter-packet timing. We now show that the replay traffic characteristics are essentially identical to the recorded traffic. Figure 2 shows the results for a TCP application (YouTube (a)) and a UDP application (Skype (b)). As discussed above, preserving inter-packet timings is important to produce a replay that closely resembles the original trace (otherwise, we may claim that differentiation exists when the application would never experience it).

Figure 2(a) shows that our replay captures the behavior of the application, presenting the cumulative transfer over time for a YouTube trace collected and replayed over the Verizon mobile network. The figure shows the behavior for the original trace and two replays, one which preserves the inter-packet timing (overlaps with original) and one which transfers as fast as possible while preserving application-layer dependencies. Preserving inter-packet timings results in a replay that closely follows the recorded application behavior. Figure 2(b) shows similar results for Skype traffic.

4.2 Traffic shapers detect replayed traffic

We now validate that our replay traffic is properly classified for differentiation using commercial shaping products. We acquired traffic shaping products from two different vendors and integrated them into a testbed for validating whether replays trigger differentiation (Fig. 3). The testbed consists of a client connected to a router that sits behind a traffic shaper, which exchanges traffic with a gateway server that we control. The gateway presents the illusion (to the packet shaper) that it routes traffic to and from the public Internet. We configure the replay server to listen on arbitrary IP addresses on the gateway, giving us the ability to preserve original server IP addresses in replays (by spoofing them inside our testbed). We describe below some of our key findings from this testbed.

Differentiation testing must be extensible. One device lists more than 700 applications that it uniquely identifies, the other lists approximately 2,000 application filters. Further, both devices routinely update their classification rules, on timescales of months (if not shorter). Thus, testing only a small number of applications is insufficient. By allowing users to create their own traces to conduct differentiation tests, our approach is extensible to evolving differentiation targets.

Our replays trigger traffic shaping. For replays to be effective, they need to "look" like legitimate application traffic from the perspective of the traffic shaper, *i.e.*, replay traffic should be classified as the application that was recorded. We validate this for a variety of popular mobile applications: YouTube, Netflix, Skype, Spotify, and Google Hangouts. Figure 4 shows the YouTube and P2P policies on the shaper applied to our replay as we vary the application payload.

Row	Changes in traffic	Detection result using: Original ports	Different ports
1	No changes	YouTube	YouTube
2	Added a packet with 1 byte of data to the beginning of traffic	HTTP	P2P
3	Added one byte of random data to the beginning of first packet	HTTP	P2P
4	Replaced "GET" with a random string (same size)	HTTP	P2P
5	Replaced "youtube" string with a random one (first packet only)	HTTP	P2P
6	Replaced "youtube" string with a random one (first packet, HOST header only)	YouTube	YouTube
7	Added one byte of random data to the end of first packet	YouTube	YouTube
8	Added "GET " to beginning of first packet	YouTube	YouTube

Table 1: Effect of different parameters on YouTube traffic detection for a popular commercial shaping device. IP addresses do not affect traffic classification, but ports and payloads have effects that vary.

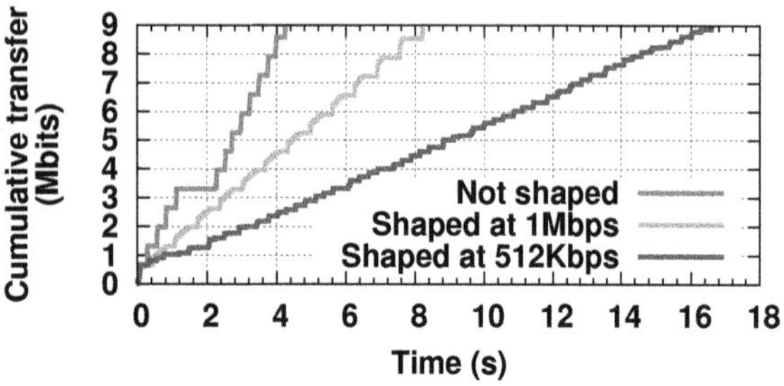

Figure 4: The shaper has rules to rate limit YouTube and P2P at 1Mbps and 512Kbps, respectively. *Shaped at 1Mbps* line is the YouTube replay in plaintext where shaper correctly detects as YouTube and shapes at 1Mbps. *Shaped at 512Kbps* is YouTube replay with randomized payload and ports, where shaper detects as P2P and limits at 512Kbps. The *Not shaped* line is YouTube replay with string "youtube" being replaced by a random string, which the shaper detects as "HTTP" and does not limit (since there are no rules for generic HTTP traffic).

Reverse-engineering classification. We use our testbed to understand which features of the traffic were used to trigger shaping, and should be preserved in replays. We replay a recorded trace in our testbed multiple times, each time modifying a different feature of the traffic (destination IP, ports, and packet payloads) and observe its effect on classification.

Table 1 summarizes the results for running tests using YouTube. We find that regular expressions on packet payload are the primary signature, with YouTube being correctly identified when payloads were unmodified, despite changes to the server IP and ports (row 1). We modify three different aspects of the packet payload: the first payload byte, application-layer protocol details in the first packet, and arbitrary bytes after the first packet. The second row of the table shows that adding a one-byte packet caused the shaper to classify the replay as HTTP (when using port 80) or P2P (when using high, random ports). This behavior is identical if replacing the first byte, the "GET" command, or removing the string "youtube" from the payload of the first packet (rows 3-8). However, if the GET command was unmodified and at least one "youtube" string appeared in the first packet, the flow was classified as YouTube. This indicates that this shaping device is using regular expressions and falling back to port-based classification when regular expressions do not match. Interestingly, modifying any subsequent packets or payload after the GET command has no impact on classification.

We now summarize other key findings:

- **Server IP addresses do not affect classification.** While our shapers support IP-based policies, we found no evidence of IP-based classification rules.
- **Non-standard ports may still be subject to differentiation.** An important outcome of our testing is that traffic with random high port numbers may be classified as P2P. Glasnost's [6] detection approach (among others) assumes that traffic sent on random ports will not be subject to differentiation, but traffic sent on standard ports will. However, our shaping device classifies traffic on random ports as P2P, which itself is often subject to differentiation.
- **Traffic shaping decisions are made early.** For HTTP requests, the first packet with payload, *i.e.*, request packet from client, is enough for classification. For UDP flows, *e.g.*, Skype, the shaper requires more packets for classification (*e.g.*, ~10). This means that traffic differentiation tests can trigger differentiation using a small amount of data and only need to run long enough to observe steady state performance. This observation is particularly salient for mobile users who may be subject to data caps.
- **HTTPS does not preclude classification.** We expected that the shaper would not identify applications using HTTPS as their transport. However, we found that in practice the devices do detect applications, specifically via the SNI (Server Name Indication) field in the TLS handshake. Modifying this field results in detection as HTTPS (instead of the specific application).

A key question is whether our replay approach is effective for *all* shapers, not just those in our lab. While we can evaluate only the shapers we possessed, our replay approach successfully detects differentiation in operational networks (Section 6), indicating that our effectiveness is not limited only to the lab environment. It remains an open question whether there are other shaper models that are not accounted for in our design.

4.3 VPN overhead

Our control trials use a VPN tunnel, due to potential issues that arise when randomized ports and payloads are classified as P2P, or otherwise shaped. We now investigate the overhead of this approach.

VPN overheads can stem from (1) IPSec encapsulation and (2) latency added by going through the VPN (*e.g.*, if the VPN induces a circuitous route to the replay server). The overhead for IPsec encapsulation varies depending on the size of the payload, with smaller packets incurring higher overheads. The impact on throughput is relatively small, as shown in Table 2. For most applications, the difference in

App	Avg packet size (bytes)	Avg throughput diff (%)
Youtube	705	1.13
Netflix	679	0.42
Hangout	435	2.06
Skype	234	15.64

Table 2: Minimal effect of VPN on our measurements. Skype packets are small, leading to larger throughput overhead compared to other apps.

throughput with the VPN is 2% or less. However, for Skype, which has an average packet size of less than 300 bytes the throughput overhead is higher (15%). Note that we both record and replay traffic using an MTU that is small enough to prevent fragmentation in the VPN tunnel.

To minimize the impact of latency, we run the replay and VPN server on the same machine (currently running on Amazon EC2), which adds less than 2ms of latency compared to contacting the replay server directly (without a VPN tunnel). We argue these overheads are acceptably low, and represent a reasonable lower bound on the amount of differentiation we can detect.

5. DETECTING DIFFERENTIATION

In this section, we present the first study that uses ground-truth information to compare the effectiveness of various techniques for detecting differentiation, and propose a new test to address limitations of prior work. We find that previous approaches for detecting differentiation are inaccurate when tested against ground-truth data, and characterize under what circumstances these approaches yield correct information about traffic shaping as perceived by applications.

When determining the accuracy of detection, we separately consider three scenarios regarding the shaping rate and a given trace (shown in Figure 5):

- **Region 1.** If the *shaping rate is less than the average throughput* of the recorded traffic, a traffic differentiation detector should always identify differentiation because the shaper is guaranteed to affect the time it takes to transfer data in the trace.
- **Region 3.** If the *shaping rate is greater than the peak throughput* of the recorded trace, a differentiation detector should never identify differentiation because the shaper will not impact the application's throughput (as discussed in Section 2.2 we focus on shaping that will actually impact the application).
- **Region 2.** Finally, if the *shaping rate is between the average and peak throughput* of the recorded trace, the application may achieve the same average throughput but a lower peak throughput. In this case, it is possible to detect differentiation, but *the impact of this differentiation will depend on the application.* For example, a non-interactive download (*e.g.,* file transfers for app updates) may be sensitive only to changes in average throughput (but not peak transfer rates), while a real-time app such as video-conferencing may experience lower QoE for lower peak rates. Given these cases, there is no single definition of accuracy that covers all applications in region 2. Instead, we show that we can configure detection techniques to consistently detect differentiation or consistently *not* detect differentiation in this region, depending on the application.

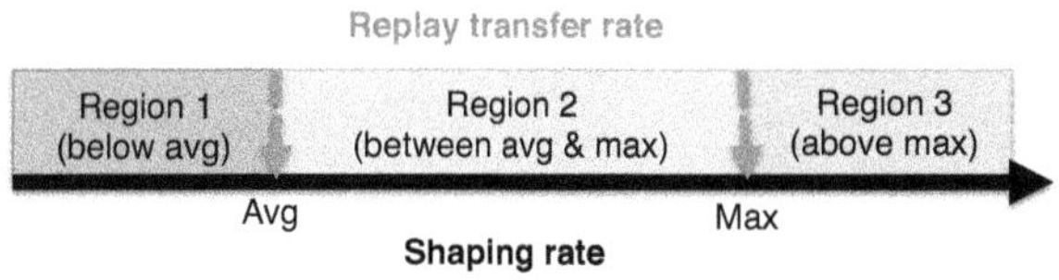

Figure 5: Regions considered for determining detection accuracy. If the shaping rate is less than the application's average throughput (left), we should always detect differentiation. Likewise, if the shaping rate is greater than peak throughput (right), we should never detect differentiation. In the middle region, it is possible to detect differentiation, but the performance impact depends on the application.

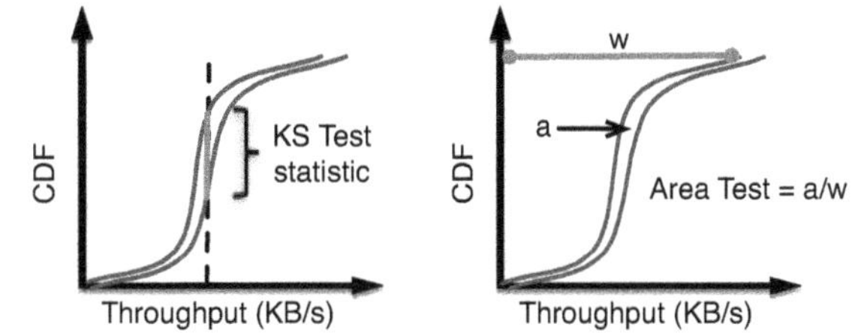

Figure 6: KS Test statistic (left) and Area Test statistic (right). In the former case, the difference between the distributions is small in terms of throughput, but the KS Test statistic is large. In the Area Test statistic, we find the area between the distributions and normalize it by the smaller of the peak throughputs for each distribution.

In the remainder of this section, we use this region-based classification to evaluate three techniques for detecting differentiation. We describe them in the next section, explain how we calibrate their respective thresholds and parameters, then discuss how resilient these approaches are to noise (*e.g.,* packet loss), and how efficient they are in terms of data consumption.

5.1 Statistical tests

We explore approaches used in Glasnost [6] and NetPolice [36], and propose a new technique that has high accuracy in regions 1 and 3, and reliably does not detect differentiation in region 2.

Glasnost: Maximum throughput test. Glasnost [6] does not preserve the inter-packet timing when replaying traffic, and identifies differentiation if the maximum throughput for control and exposed flows differ by more than a threshold. We expect this will always detect differentiation in region 1, but might generate false positives in regions 2 and 3 (because Glasnost may send traffic at a higher rate than the recorded trace).

NetPolice: Two-sample KS Test. As discussed in NetPolice [36], looking at a single summary statistic (*e.g.,* maximum) to detect differentiation can be misleading. The issue is that two distributions of a metric (*e.g.,* throughput) may have the same mean, median, or maximum, but vastly different *distributions.* A differentiation detection approach should be robust to this.

To address this, NetPolice uses the two-sample Kolmogorov–Smirnov (KS) test, which compares two empirical distribution functions (*i.e.,* empirical CDFs) using the maximum distance between two empirical CDF sample sets

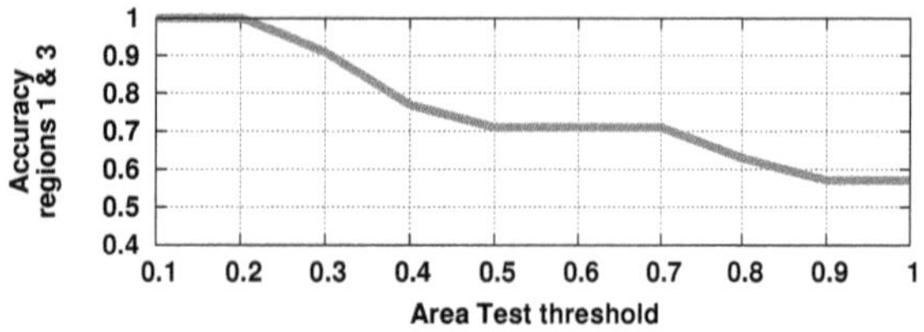

Figure 7: Calibrating Area Test for Youtube. We pick 0.2 as the threshold.

for a confidence interval α. To validate the KS Test result, NetPolice uses a resampling method as follows: randomly select half of the samples from each of the two original input distributions and apply the KS Test on the two sample subsets, and repeat this r times. If the results of more than β% of the r tests agree with the original test, they conclude that the original KS Test statistic is valid.

Our approach: Area Test. The KS Test only considers the difference between distributions along the y-axis (as shown in Figure 6, left) even if the difference in the x-axis (in this case, throughput) is small. In our experiments, we found this makes the test very sensitive to small changes in performance not due to differentiation, which can lead to inaccurate results or labeling valid tests as invalid.

To address this, we propose an *Area Test* that accounts for the degree of differentiation detected: we find the area, a, between the two CDF curves (as shown in Fig. 6, right) and normalize it by the minimum of peak throughputs for each distribution, w. This test concludes there is differentiation if the KS Test detects differentiation *and* the normalized area between the curves is greater than a threshold t. We discuss how we select thresholds in Sec. 5.4.

5.2 Testbed environment

Our testbed consists of a commercial traffic shaper, a replay client, and a replay server (Figure 3). We vary the shaping rate using the commercial device to shape each application to throughput values in regions 1-3. Depending on the average and maximum throughputs for each trace, we vary the shaping rate from 0.1 Mbps to 30 Mbps (9% to 300% of peak throughput).

We emulate noisy packet loss in our tests using the Linux Traffic Control (`tc`) and Network Emulation (`netem`) tools to add bursty packet loss according to Gilbert-Elliott (GE) model [10]. We perform all our evaluations and calibrations under three conditions: 1) low loss (no added loss), 2) moderate loss (1.08%), and 3) high loss (1.45%). We found that correlated losses higher than 1.5% had disastrous effects on TCP performance and all detection techniques were inaccurate.

Evaluation method. We explore the parameter space by varying the application, loss rate, shaping rate, and number of replay repetitions for each statistical test. We present results for a few popular TCP-based applications (YouTube and Netflix) and UDP-based applications (Skype and Hangout); we also performed tests on a number of other applications (omitted for space). We repeat each test 10 times, where a test is a replay performed with a given set of parameters, with and without shaping. We present results that aggregate these tests to produce statistically significant results.

5.3 Evaluation criteria

We now describe the criteria under which we evaluate the three differentiation tests.

Overall accuracy: Using the taxonomy in Figure 5, a statistical test should always detect differentiation in region 1, and never detect differentiation in region 3. We define accuracy as the fraction of samples for which the test correctly identifies the presence or absence of differentiation in these regions.

Resilience to noise: Differences between two empirical CDFs could be explained by a variety of reasons, including random noise [30]. We need a test that retains high accuracy in the face of large latencies and packet loss that occur in the mobile environment. When evaluating and calibrating our statistical tests, we take this into account by simulating packet loss.

Data consumption: To account for network variations over time, we run multiple iterations of control and exposed trials back to back. We merge all control trials into a single distribution, and similarly merge all exposed trials. As we show below, this can improve accuracy compared to running a single trial, but at the cost of longer/more expensive tests. When picking a statistical test, we want the one that yields the highest accuracy with the smallest data consumption.

5.4 Calibration

We identify the most accurate settings of threshold values.

Glasnost: We used the threshold suggested by Glasnost, $\delta = 0.2$. This yields perfect accuracy in region 1, but generates 100% false positives in region 3 (as expected). Glasnost always detects differentiation in region 2. For applications that are sensitive to changes in peak throughput, this test will yield the correct result.

KS Test: We use thresholds suggested by NetPolice, *i.e.*, $\alpha = 0.95$ and $\beta = 0.95$. This yields good accuracy in regions 1 and 3, but inconsistent behavior in region 2. In other words, this test will sometimes detect differentiation in region 2, and sometimes not — making it difficult to use for detection in this region. We also observed that even for tests with no added loss in our testbed over well-provisioned wired network, up to 8% of tests were considered invalid by KS Test due to the issue shown in Fig. 6, while the Area Test can correctly detect for differentiation (or no differentiation) in those cases.

Area Test: We find that $t = 0.1$ or $t = 0.2$ yield the best accuracy, depending on the application (Fig. 7). This yields good accuracy in regions 1 and 3, and consistent decisions of no differentiation for region 2. For apps that are insensitive to changes only to peak throughput (average throughput stays the same), this will yield the correct result.

5.5 Evaluation results

Summary results for low noise. We first consider the accuracy of detecting differentiation under low loss scenarios. Table 3 presents the accuracy results for four popular apps in regions 1 and 3. We find that the KS Test and Area Test have similarly high accuracy in both regions 1 and 3, but Glasnost performs poorly in region 3 because it will detect differentiation, even if the shaping rate is above the maximum. We explore region 2 behavior later in this section; until then we focus on accuracy results for regions

App	KS Test		Area Test		Glasnost	
	R1	R3	R1	R3	R1	R3
Netflix	100	100	100	100	100	0
YouTube	100	100	100	100	100	0
Hangout	100	100	100	100	100	0
Skype	100	100	100	100	90	0

Table 3: Shaping detection accuracy for different apps, in regions 1 and 3 (denoted by R1 and R3). We find that the KS Test (NetPolice) and Area Test have similarly high accuracy in both regions (1 and 3), but Glasnost performs poorly in region 3.

App	Region 2		
	KS Test	Area Test	Glasnost
Netflix	65	28	100
YouTube	67	0	100
Hangout	40	0	100
Skype	55	10	92

Table 4: Percent of tests identified as differentiation in region 2 for the three detection methods. Glasnost consistently identifies region 2 as differentiation, whereas the Area Test is more likely to not detect differentiation.

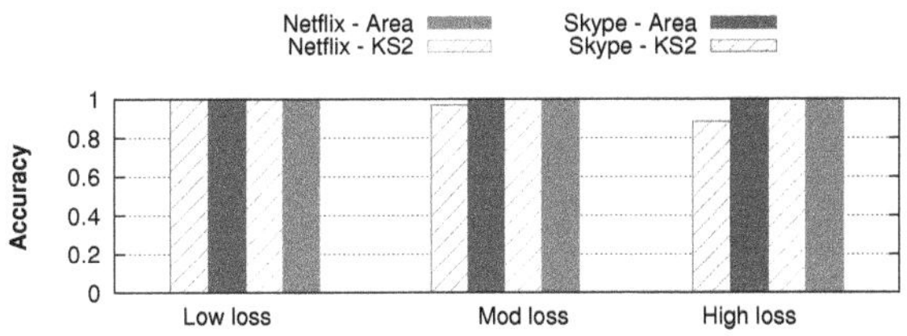

Figure 8: Accuracy against loss.

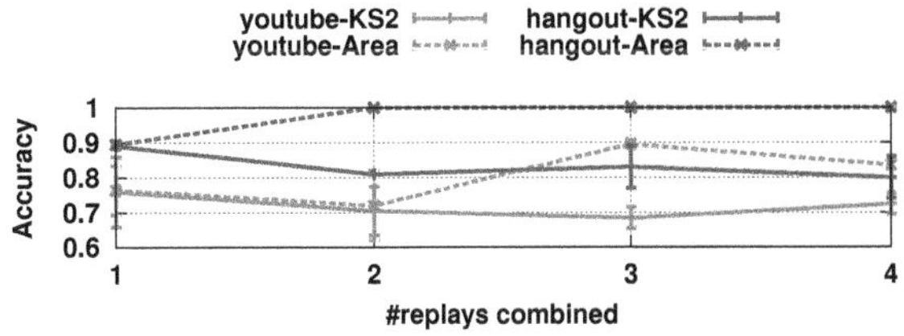

Figure 9: Effect of combining replays on accuracy in **high loss**.

1 and 3 and the two KS Tests (as they do not identify differentiation in region 3)

Impact of noise. Properties of the network unrelated to shaping (*e.g.*, congested-induced packet loss) may impact performance and cause false positives for differentiation detectors. In Fig. 8 we examine the impact of loss on accuracy for one TCP application (Netflix) and one UDP application (Skype). We find that both variants of the KS Test have high accuracy in the face of congestion, but the Area Test is more resilient to moderate and high loss for Skype.

Impact of number of replays. One way to account for noise is to use additional replays to average out any variations from transient noise in a single replay. To evaluate the impact of additional replays, we varied the number of replays combined to detect differentiation under *high loss* and plotted the detection accuracy in Fig. 9.[4] In the case of moderate or high loss, increasing the number of replays improves accuracy, particularly for a short YouTube trace. In all cases, the Area Test is more accurate than (or equal to) the KS Test. Importantly, the accuracy does not significantly improve past 2 or 3 replays. In our deployment, we use 2 tests (to minimize data consumption).

Region 2 detection results. Recall that our goal is to identify shaping that impinges on the network resources required by an application. However, in region 2, shaping may or may not impact the application's performance, which makes identifying shaping with actual application impact challenging. We report detection results for the three tests in region 2 in Table 4. We find that Glasnost consistently identifies differentiation, the Area Test consistently does *not* detect differentiation, and the KS Test is inconsistent. When testing an application that is sensitive to shaping of its peak throughput, the Glasnost method may be preferable, whereas the Area Test is preferred when testing applications that can tolerate shaping above their average throughput.

When detecting differentiation, we conservatively avoid the potential for false positives and thus do not report differentiation for region 2. Thus, we use the Area Test in our implementation because it will more reliably achieve this result (Table 4). Determining which apps are affected by region 2 differentiation is a topic of future work.

[4]Additional replays did not help when there is low loss.

6. MEASUREMENT STUDY

We now use our calibrated detection approach to identify cases of differentiation using measurement study of production networks. For each network, we focus on detection for a set of popular apps that we expect might be subject to differentiation: streaming audio and video (high bandwidth) and voice/video calling (competes with carrier's line of business). The data from these experiments was initially collected between January and May 2015. We then repeated the experiments in August 2015, after the new FCC rules prohibiting differentiation took effect.

6.1 System implementation

We now describe the implementation of our client and server software. To promote transparency and guide policy for traffic differentiation, our source code and analysis results will be made continuously available at `http://dd.meddle.mobi`.

Client. We implement our replay client in an Android app called *Differentiation Detector*. It does not require any root privileges, and is available for download in the Google Play store.[5] The app consists of 14,000 lines of source code (LOC), which includes the Strongswan VPN implementation [27] (4,600 LOC). The app conducts differentiation tests and reports results to our replay servers as part of an IRB-approved study. Users undergo informed consent when the app first runs, and cannot run any tests unless they consent to participate in our study. An iOS implementation is under development.

The app (Fig. 10) is pre-loaded with replay transcripts for Viber, Netflix, Spotify, Skype, YouTube, and Google Hangouts, so that users can test for differentiation of these apps

[5]`https://play.google.com/store/apps/details?id=com.stonybrook.replay`

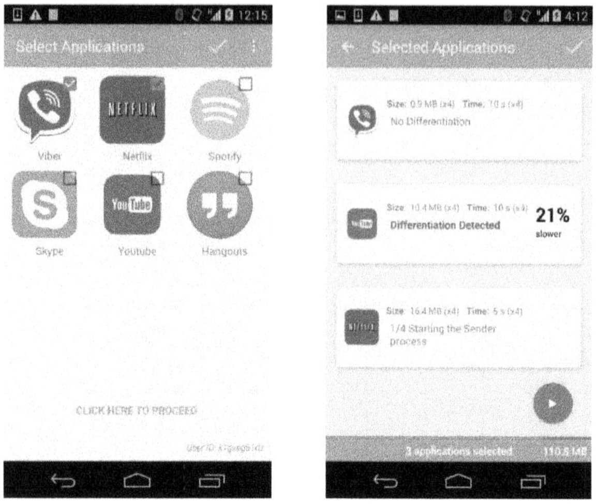

Figure 10: Screenshot of our Android Differentiation Detector app.

without recording traffic.[6] For each trace, the app follows the replay procedure described in Section 3 and repeats the replay tests twice[7] back to back.

At the end of each replay, metadata such as carrier name, OS information, network type, and signal strength, is collected and sent to the server for analysis. To account for the case where background traffic might affect our detection results, future version of the app will measure data consumption during replays and discard results where we detect interference from other traffic. Users can also access their historical results through the app.

Server and analysis code The server coordinates with the client to replay traces, and records packet traces for analysis. This interaction is managed by side-channel connections that identify which trace is being replayed and what ports will be opened in the case of NAT traversal. For networks that allow it (*e.g.,* in our testbed), we support IP spoofing so our replay server can send packets using the IP addresses in arbitrary recorded traces. The server logic is 1,850 lines of code (Python).

Our analysis code implements tests for throughput, RTT, jitter, and loss differentiation. We implement KS Test and Area Test, and use simple scalar metrics (average, max) for loss. Our parsing script supports TCP and streaming UDP applications. It uses `tshark` to extract conversations. Together, these artifacts consist of 1,170 lines of code.

6.2 Challenges in operational networks

In this section we discuss several challenges that we encountered when attempting to identify differentiation in mobile networks. To the best of our knowledge, we are the first to identify these issues for detecting differentiation and discuss workarounds that address them.

[6]While we currently only support Android, the approach should also work on any mobile OS that supports VPN connectivity, including iOS. We are currently developing support for users to record their own traces from mobile devices.

[7]Users can increase the number of back-to-back replays for more accuracy.

Per-client management. To replay traffic for multiple simultaneous users, our replay server needs to be able to map each received packet to exactly one app replay. A simple solution is to put this information in the first few bytes of each flow between client and server. Unfortunately, as shown in Section 4.2, this can disrupt classification and lead to false negatives. Instead, we use side-channel connections out of band from the replay to supply information regarding each replay run.

NAT behavior. We also use the side-channel to identify which clients will connect from which IPs and ports. For networks without NAT devices, this works well. However, many mobile networks use NAT, meaning we can't use the side-channel to identify the IP and port that a replay connection will use (because they may be modified by the NAT). For such networks, each replay server can reliably support only one active client per ISP and application. While this has not been an issue in our initial app release, we are investigating other work-arounds. Moreover, to scale the system, we can use multiple replay servers and a load balancer. The load balancer can be configured to assign clients with the same IP address to different servers.

"Translucent" HTTP proxies. It is well known that ISPs use transparent proxies on Web traffic [34]. Our system works as intended if a proxy simply relays exactly the same traffic sent by a replay client. In practice, we found examples of "translucent" proxies that issue the same HTTP requests as the client but change connection keep-alive behavior; *e.g.,* the client uses a persistent connection in the recorded trace and the proxy does not. To handle this behavior, our system must be able to map HTTP requests from unexpected connections to the same replay.

Another challenge with HTTP proxies is that the proxy may have a different public IP address from other non-HTTP traffic (including the side-channel), which means the server will not be able to map the HTTP connections to the client based on IP address. In these cases the server replies to the HTTP request with a special message. When the client receives this message, it restarts the replay. This time the client adds a custom header (X-) to HTTP requests with client's ID, so the server can match HTTP connections with different IP addresses to the corresponding clients. The server then ignores this extra header for the remainder of the replay. We have also observed that some mobile providers exhibit such behavior for other TCP and UDP ports, meaning we cannot rely on an X- header to convey side-channel information. In these cases we can identify users based on ISP's IP subnet, which means we can only support one active client per replay server and ISP, regardless of the application they are replaying.

Content-modifying proxies and transcoders. Recent reports and previous work highlight cases of devices in ISPs that modify customer traffic for reasons such as tracking [17], caching [34], security [24], and reducing bandwidth [32]. We also saw several cases of content-modifying proxies. For example, we saw Sprint modifying HTTP headers, Verizon inserting global tracking cookies, and Boost transcoding YouTube videos.

In our replay methodology, we assumed that packets exchanged between the client and server would not be not modified in flight, and trivially detect modification because packet payloads do not match recorded traces. In the case of header manipulation, we use an edit-distance based approach to match modified content to the recorded content it corresponds to. While our system can tolerate moderate amounts of modification (*e.g.,* HTTP header manipulation/substitution), if the content is modified drastically, *e.g.,* transcoding an image to reduce its size, it is difficult to detect shaping because the data from our control and exposed trials do not match. In our current system, we simply notify the user that there is content modification but do not attempt to identify shaping. We leave a more detailed analysis of this behavior to future work.

Caching. Our replay system assumes content is served from the replay server and not an ISP's cache. We detect the latter case by identifying cases where the client receives data that was not sent by the server. In the few cases where we observed this behavior, the ISPs were caching small static objects (*e.g.,* thumbnail images) which were not the dominant portion of the replay traffic (*e.g.,* when streaming audio) and had negligible effect on our statistical analysis.[8] Going forward, we expect this behavior to be less prominent due to the increased use of encrypted protocols, *e.g.,* HTTP/2 and QUIC. In such cases, an ISP may detect and shape application traffic using SNI for classification, but they cannot modify or cache content.

6.3 Differentiation results

In this section, we present results from running our *Differentiation Detector* Android app on popular mobile networks. This dataset consists of 4,786 replay tests, covering traces from six popular apps. We collected test results from most major cellular providers and MVNOs in the US; further, we gathered measurements from four international networks.

Our app supports both VPN traffic and random payloads (but not random ports) as control traffic. We use the latter only if a device does not support VPN connectivity or the cellular provider blocks or differentiates against VPN traffic. After collecting data, we run our analysis to detect differentiation; the results for US carriers are presented in Table 5. In other networks such as Idea (India), JazzTel (Spain), Three (UK), and T-Mobile (Netherlands), our results based on a subset of the traces (the traces that users selected) indicated no differentiation.

Our key finding is that our approach successfully detect differentiation in three mobile networks (BlackWireless, H2O, and SimpleMobile), with the impact of shaping resulting in up to 65% difference in average throughput. These shaping policies all apply to YouTube (not surprising given its impact on networks), but not always to Netflix and Spotify. We did not identify differentiation for UDP traffic in any of the carriers. Interestingly, H2O consistently gives *better* performance to port 80 traffic with random payloads, indicating a policy that gives relatively worse performance to VPN traffic and streaming audio/video. We tested these networks again in August 2015 and did not observe such differentiation. We speculate that these networks ceased their shaping practices in part due to new FCC rules barring this behavior, effective in June 2015.

We contacted these ISPs we tested for comment on the behavior we observed in their networks. At the time of publication, only one ISP had responded (Sprint) and did not wish to comment.

[8]Boost was one exception, which we discuss later.

ISP	YT	NF	SF	SK	VB	HO
Verizon	M	M	M	-	-	-
T-Mobile	-	-	-	-	-	-
AT&T	F	F	F	-	-	-
Sprint	M/P	M/P	M/P	-	-	-
Boost	M	M	M	-	-	-
BlackWireless	60%	-	-	-	-	-
H2O	37%*	45%*	65%*	-	-	-
SimpleMobile	36%	-	-	-	-	-
NET10	P	P	P	-	-	-

Table 5: Shaping detection results per ISP in our dataset, for six popular apps: YouTube (YT), Netflix (NF), Spotify (SF), Skype (SK), Viber (VB), and Google Hangout (HO). When shaping occurs, the table shows the difference between average throughput (%) we detected. A dash (-) indicates no differentiation, (F) means IP addresses changed for each connection, (P) means a "translucent" proxy changed connection behavior from the original app behavior, and (M) indicates that a middlebox modified content in flight between client and server. *For the H2O network, replays with random payload have better performance than VPN and exposed replays, indicating a policy that favors non-video HTTP over VPN and streaming video.

While attempting to detect differentiation, we identified other interesting behavior that prevented us from identifying shaping. For example, Boost transcodes YouTube video to a fraction of the original quality, and then caches the result for future requests. Other networks use proxies to change TCP behavior. We found such devices to be pervasive in mobile networks.

7. DISCUSSION

This paper focuses on detecting differentiation that impacts application performance. While investigating shaping, our technique revealed a number of other issues that are beyond the scope of this paper.

Assigning blame. When differentiation is detected, we generally assign blame to the network from where the test is launched, *i.e.,* the access network. While in theory it might be caused by any network along the path between the access network and our replay server, we expect that transit networks will not have incentive to differentiate and we ensure that our replay hosting sites also do not differentiate traffic. As part of future work, we will investigate how to combine differentiation results from multiple vantage points (*e.g.,* using tomography) to identify cases when differentiation is not caused by the access network, but rather an intermediate network.

Differentiation against VPN traffic. A subtle challenge arises when recording traces of app-generated network traffic over a production network: what happens when recorded traffic is subject to differentiation (*e.g.,* shaping)? If the recorded and replayed traffic are both shaped, a naïve detector will indicate that the network has no differentiation. One simple solution is to allow users to run traces captured from a network of the same type (*e.g.,* WiFi, 3G, LTE) where we know the recorded traces were not subject to differentiation (our current version of the app ships with traces from different applications recorded over a well-provisioned network that does not shape traffic).

While this solves the problem, it does not tell us when there is a problem in the first place. For this, we need to detect that the VPN traffic itself is subject to differentia-

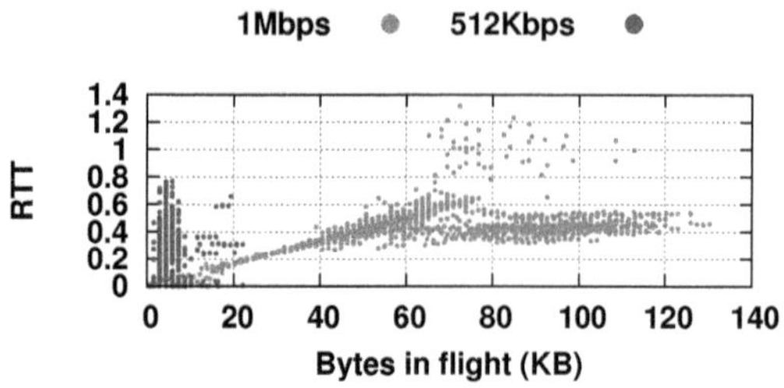

Figure 11: Effect of shaping on latency for a TCP stream. Shaping at 1 Mbps exhibits expected queuing delays that identify the size of the buffer (x=75 KB); however, shaping at a lower rate (512 kbps) leads to bimodal RTTs largely due to TCP never exiting slow start.

tion. If there exists at least one class of traffic that is *not* shaped in our tests, then it will get higher performance outside the VPN tunnel compared to inside the tunnel. In this case, there will be at least one case where tunneled performance will be different from non-tunneled. As a result, we can reliably conclude that there is some kind of differentiation[9]; however, we cannot yet directly attribute it to shaping against a VPN.

One potential way to address this is to exploit the observation that popular shaping devices use token-bucket queues to enforce fixed-rate shaping. As shown in Fig. 11 (1 Mbps) shaping devices exhibit a characteristic queueing delay evident when plotting bytes in flight vs. RTT. If a traffic class is subject to differentiation, we will observe increased delays compared to a case that is not managed via a queue.

If indeed the control traffic is shaped, it limits our ability to test other types of traffic for differentiation—this is true of *any* differentiation detection approach. However, *detection of this behavior itself is important information*; for example, in the US even this behavior should be in violation of FCC rules effective June 12, 2015 [9].

Shaping configurations can have unintended consequences for TCP. In one sample configuration already used by an ISP (Fig. 11, 512 Kbps), we found that the shaping rate was so low that it prevented TCP from ever exiting slow start. Importantly, TCP increased its congestion window exponentially in time while the shaper's queue drained linearly in time, leading to substantial queuing and packet loss.

This is problematic for two reasons. First, this policy leads to wasted bandwidth at the network edge, which will cost the ISP running the shaper. Second, it is unclear how the user is being charged for this lost traffic. If users are billed based on bytes entering the network before hitting the shaper, the ISP will over charge the user for packets that were never delivered. Such policies, and their implications, merit further investigation as part of a future study.

Evasion. One of our goals is to improve transparency for network management practices in cellular data networks. ISPs wishing to avoid characterization may attempt to do so by blocking VPN traffic or selectively changing policies for our replay traffic. If ISPs choose to block our traffic, we can easily detect it and report this result to users and policy makers. For cases where the traffic is selectively given different treatment, we can attempt to disguise replay traffic, using different servers, ports and control traffic techniques (*e.g.,* different payload/port randomization scheme).

Data caps. Some providers have "unlimited" data plans with lower data rates after usage exceeds a certain cap. We do not expect to detect this from a single user, but may be able to identify it by combining results from multiple users or by monitoring data usage via Android APIs.

[9] More generally, we can draw the same conclusion if at least one class of traffic is shaped *differently* from VPN traffic.

8. CONCLUSION

We presented and evaluated a new tool for accurately detecting differentiation using a VPN to record and replay traffic generated by apps to improve transparency in mobile networks. We found extensive use of middleboxes that break end-to-end principles in mobile networks, and identified their impact on applications.

From a network neutrality perspective, our findings are concerning in part due to observed shaping policies and third-party modification of traffic, both of which are pervasive. There is little research into the impact of such devices, and currently policymakers have essentially no guidance as to how to regulate this behavior. As part of our ongoing work, we are using a Web site to make our results public — both to improve transparency for users and to guide future policies. In addition, we are investigating how to fingerprint middleboxes in mobile networks and developing techniques to understand their impacts on a wide range of applications.

Acknowledgements

We thank the anonymous reviewers for their helpful comments. This research was partially supported in part by NSF grants CNS-1054233, CNS-1318396, and CNS-1319019, CNS-1350720, and a Google Faculty Research Award.

9. REFERENCES

[1] Experimenting with QUIC. `http://blog.chromium.org/2013/06/experimenting-with-quic.html`.

[2] Neubot – the network neutrality bot. `http://www.neubot.org`.

[3] V. Bashko, N. Melnikov, A. Sehgal, and J. Schonwalder. Bonafide: A traffic shaping detection tool for mobile networks. In *IFIP/IEEE International Symposium on Integrated Network Management (IM2013)*, 2013.

[4] D. Clark. Network neutrality: Words of power and 800-pound gorillas. *International Journal of Communication*, 2007.

[5] W. Cui, V. Paxson, N. Weaver, and R. H. Katz. Protocol-independent adaptive replay of application dialog. In *Proc. of NDSS*, 2006.

[6] M. Dischinger, M. Marcon, S. Guha, K. P. Gummadi, R. Mahajan, and S. Saroiu. Glasnost: Enabling end users to detect traffic differentiation. In *Proc. of USENIX NSDI*, 2010.

[7] FCC announces "Measuring Mobile America" program. `http://www.fcc.gov/document/fcc-announces-measuring-mobile-america-program`.

[8] FCC. Order 10-201: Preserving the open internet. `https://apps.fcc.gov/edocs_public/attachmatch/FCC-10-201A1_Rcd.pdf`, December 2010.

[9] FCC. Protecting and promoting the open internet. https://www.federalregister.gov/articles/2015/04/13/2015-07841/protecting-and-promoting-the-open-internet, April 2015.

[10] G. Hasslinger and O. Hohlfeld. The Gilbert-Elliott model for packet loss in real time services on the Internet, 2008.

[11] S. Higginbotham. The Netflix–Comcast agreement isn't a network neutrality violation, but it is a problem. http://gigaom.com/2014/02/23/the-netflix-comcast-agreement-isnt-a-network-neutrality-violation-but-it-is-a-problem/, February 2014.

[12] J. Hui, K. Lau, A. Jain, A. Terzis, and J. Smith. How YouTube performance is improved in T-Mobile network. http://velocityconf.com/velocity2014/public/schedule/detail/35350.

[13] P. Kanuparthy and C. Dovrolis. ShaperProbe: end-to-end detection of ISP traffic shaping using active methods. In *Proc. of IMC*, 2011.

[14] C. Kreibich, N. Weaver, B. Nechaev, and V. Paxson. Netalyzr: Illuminating the edge network. In *Proc. of IMC*, 2010.

[15] M. Luckie, A. Dhamdhere, D. Clark, B. Huffaker, and k. claffy. Challenges in inferring internet interdomain congestion. In *Proc. of IMC*, 2014.

[16] R. Mahajan, M. Zhang, L. Poole, and V. Pai. Uncovering performance differences among backbone ISPs with Netdiff. In *Proc. of USENIX NSDI*, 2008.

[17] J. Mayer. How verizon's advertising header works. http://webpolicy.org/2014/10/24/how-verizons-advertising-header-works/.

[18] Measurement Lab Consortium. Isp interconnection and its impact on consumer internet performance. http://www.measurementlab.net/blog/2014_interconnection_report, October 2014.

[19] A. Nikravesh, H. Yao, S. Xu, D. R. Choffnes, and Z. M. Mao. Mobilyzer: An open platform for controllable mobile network measurements. In *Proc. of MobiSys*, 2015.

[20] A. Norberg. uTorrent transport protocol. http://www.bittorrent.org/beps/bep_0029.html.

[21] B. Obama. Net neutrality: President Obama's plan for a free and open internet. http://www.whitehouse.gov/net-neutrality#section-read-the-presidents-statement.

[22] A. Rao, J. Sherry, A. Legout, W. Dabbout, A. Krishnamurthy, and D. Choffnes. Meddle: Middleboxes for increased transparency and control of mobile traffic. In *Proc. of CoNEXT 2012 Student Workshop*, 2012.

[23] D. Rayburn. Cogent now admits they slowed down netflix's traffic, creating a fast lane & slow lane. http://blog.streamingmedia.com/2014/11/cogent-now-admits-slowed-netflixs-traffic-creating-fast-lane-slow-lane.html, November 2014.

[24] C. Reis, S. D. Gribble, T. Kohno, and N. C. Weaver. Detecting In-Flight Page Changes with Web Tripwires. In *Proc. of USENIX NSDI*, 2008.

[25] Sandvine - intelligent broadband networks. http://www.sandvine.com.

[26] F. Sarkar. Prevention of bandwidth abuse of a communications system, Jan. 9 2014. US Patent App. 14/025,213.

[27] Strongswan. www.strongswan.org.

[28] P. Svensson. Comcast blocks some internet traffic. http://www.washingtonpost.com/wp-dyn/content/article/2007/10/19/AR2007101900842.html, October 2007.

[29] Switzerland network testing tool. https://www.eff.org/pages/switzerland-network-testing-tool.

[30] M. B. Tariq, M. Motiwala, N. Feamster, and M. Ammar. Detecting network neutrality violations with causal inference. In *CoNEXT*, 2009.

[31] N. Vallina-Rodriguez, S. Sundaresan, C. Kreibich, N. Weaver, and V. Paxson. Beyond the radio: Illuminating the higher layers of mobile networks. In *Proc. of MobiSys*, 2015.

[32] N. Weaver, C. Kreibich, M. Dam, and V. Paxson. Here Be Web Proxies. In *Proc. PAM*, 2014.

[33] N. Weaver, R. Sommer, and V. Paxson. Detecting forged TCP reset packets. In *Proc. of NDSS*, 2009.

[34] X. Xu, Y. Jiang, T. Flach, E. Katz-Bassett, D. Choffnes, and R. Govindan. Investigating transparent web proxies in cellular networks. In *Proc. PAM*, 2015.

[35] F. Zarinni, A. Chakraborty, V. Sekar, S. Das, and P. Gill. A first look at performance in mobile virtual network operators. In *Proc. of IMC*, 2014.

[36] Y. Zhang, Z. M. Mao, and M. Zhang. Detecting Traffic Differentiation in Backbone ISPs with NetPolice. In *Proc. of IMC*, 2009.

[37] Z. Zhang, O. Mara, and K. Argyraki. Network neutrality inference. In *Proc. of ACM SIGCOMM*, 2014.

Tracking the Evolution and Diversity in Network Usage of Smartphones

Kensuke Fukuda
National Institute of Informatics / Sokendai
kensuke@nii.ac.jp

Hirochika Asai
University of Tokyo
panda@hongo.wide.ad.jp

Kenichi Nagami
Intec
nagami@inetcore.com

ABSTRACT

We analyze the evolution of smartphone usage from a dataset obtained from three, 15-day-long, user-side, measurements with over 1500 recruited smartphone users in the Greater Tokyo area from 2013 to 2015. This dataset shows users across a diverse range of networks; cellular access (3G to LTE), WiFi access (2.4 to 5GHz), deployment of more public WiFi access points (APs), as they use diverse applications such as video, file synchronization, and major software updates.

Our analysis shows that smartphone users select appropriate network interfaces taking into account the deployment of emerging technologies, their bandwidth demand, and their economic constraints. Thus, users show diversity in both how *much* traffic they send, as well as on what networks they send it. We show that users are gradually but steadily adopting WiFi at home, in offices, and public spaces over these three years. The majority of light users have been shifting their traffic to WiFi. Heavy hitters acquire more bandwidth via WiFi, especially at home. The percentage of users explicitly turning off their WiFi interface during the day decreases from 50% to 40%. Our results highlight that the offloading environment has been improved during the three years, with more than 40% of WiFi users connecting to multiple WiFi APs in one day. WiFi offload at offices is still limited in our dataset due to a few accessible APs, but WiFi APs in public spaces have been an alternative to cellular access for users who request not only simple connectivity but also bandwidth-consuming applications such as video streaming and software updates.

Categories and Subject Descriptors

C.2.3 [**Computer-Communication Networks**]: Network Operations—*Network monitoring*

General Terms

Measurement

IMC'15, October 28–30, 2015, Tokyo, Japan.

ACM 978-1-4503-3848-6/15/10 ...$15.00.
DOI: http://dx.doi.org/10.1145/2815675.2815697.

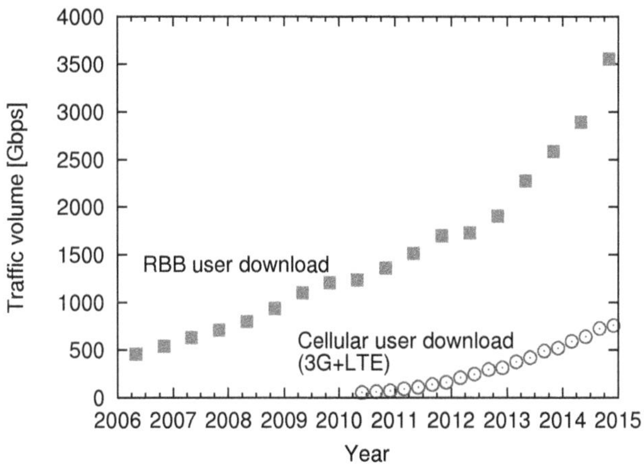

Figure 1: Growth in residential broadband and cellular traffic in Japan [34].

Keywords

Smartphone traffic; LTE; WiFi; WiFi offload

1. INTRODUCTION

In recent years the deployment of high-speed Internet at home and bandwidth-consuming applications have been driving the growth of residential broadband traffic. Following this growth, smartphone traffic has had a large impact on cellular providers. Figure 1 illustrates the growth in the total residential broadband and cellular (3G+LTE) download traffic volumes in Japan [34]. The total residential broadband traffic was estimated from the traffic volume measured at the customer edges of six Japanese commercial Internet service providers (ISPs). The total cellular traffic was measured in the backbones of four Japanese cellular providers covering most cellular users in Japan. The cellular traffic volume from smartphones accounted for 20% of the residential broadband traffic volume at the end of 2014. One reason for this trend is the rapid deployment of smartphones with rich applications. Most Japanese smartphone users are charged a flat rate with a soft bandwidth cap where user's maximum bandwidth is limited (e.g., 128kbps) during peak hours for a few days if the previous three days download volume surpasses a threshold (e.g., 1GB); thus, most light users are not concerned about saving their cellular traffic volume.

A crucial issue for cellular providers is the limited resource of channels in cellular networks. Cellular providers employ several methods to minimize quality of service/quality of experience (QoS/QoE) degradation. One commonly used technique to mitigate this issue is to apply a bandwidth cap to heavy hitters. Second, providers are deploying new capacity such as the new 4G LTE network reaching full coverage in Japanese cities. Finally, they are currently encouraging their customers to offload cellular traffic to WiFi networks (WiFi offloading). To enable WiFi offloading, cellular providers are deploying new free WiFi access points (APs) for their customers in public places (e.g., cafes, metro stations, streets, and airports). Furthermore, they have begun to give customers free home WiFi routers with the expectation that these will increase offloading at home to residential broadband. The Japanese government also plans to promote the deployment of more free APs in public spaces towards the 2020 Olympic Games in Tokyo [35]. This promotion is expected with the goal of supporting Internet access for foreign visitors. Rapid deployment of better WiFi coverage enables cellular providers to offload 3G/LTE traffic to WiFi networks in many places if they appropriately manage to lead their users to these networks.

The success of these WiFi deployment hinges on this key question: *how do smartphone users select a network from the alternatives available to them?* Prior work has not supported a straightforward answer to this question due to the difficulty in tracking all traffic flows upstream.

To answer this question, we characterize smartphone traffic behavior from measurements at the user-side. We previously gave preliminary analysis of a two-days-long Android smartphone measurement in [18]. Here we go further, presenting analysis of three measurements, each 15 days long, covering over 1500 Android and iPhone users in the Greater Tokyo area from 2013 to 2015. We characterize the evolution of smartphone usage in terms of cellular access, WiFi access, geolocation, application, device OS, and bandwidth cap.

The main findings of the paper are as follows. (1) Smartphone traffic is becoming the main player in home networks (§ 3.1, § 3.2, and § 4). We estimate that the daily offloaded traffic volume for light users accounts for 12% of residential broadband light user traffic volume. Also, the estimated total offloaded traffic volume accounts for 28% of the total broadband traffic volume. (2) WiFi traffic volume has increased more than cellular traffic volume due to the large contribution of heavy hitters. Even for light users (i.e., median), the WiFi traffic is higher than that of cellular traffic as of 2015 (§ 3.2, and § 4). (3) Users properly select network interfaces; the number of users explicitly turning off WiFi has decreased by 10% in three years (§ 3.3). Also, the number of associated WiFi networks per user has increased. As of 2015, 40% of WiFi users are associated with at least two APs in one day (§ 3.4). The traffic volume to public and office WiFi APs, however, only accounts for 2% of the total WiFi traffic volume. (4) The signal strength of the associated WiFi network is generally high; however, 12% of the public WiFi networks exhibit subpar quality (§ 3.4, and § 3.5). We further confirm the rapid deployment of 5GHz APs in public WiFi networks though dominant APs at home and office are still 2.4GHz APs. (5) Bandwidth-consuming applications (e.g., video, online storage) have become more popular (§ 3.6) in WiFi networks. We see indications that users use such bandwidth-consuming applications on public WiFi networks (§ 3.7). Also, software updates require WiFi networks by default, thus the timing of software update can be delayed for users without home APs. For security-critical updates, this delay may leave users vulnerable longer.

year	duration	#And	#iOS	#total	%LTE
2013	07 Mar - 22 Mar	948	807	1755	25%
2014	28 Feb - 22 Mar	887	789	1676	70%
2015	25 Feb - 25 Mar	835	781	1616	80%

Table 1: Overview of datasets.

Overall, we characterize the diverse network usage of smartphones under certain demands (e.g., rich applications) and constraints (e.g., bandwidth cap and network availability). Our results show *slow but clear growth of WiFi traffic offloading during these three years.* In particular, the deployment of public WiFi networks provides users both simple network connectivity and also more bandwidth for bandwidth-intensive applications such as video streaming and software updates. However, we find that WiFi offloading at offices is still limited.

2. METHODOLOGY AND DATASET

We developed measurement software for Android[1] and iPhone[2]. The software supports iPhone 4-6 series for iOS, and Android devices with OS version > 2.1. It runs in the background and records several pieces of device information such as byte and packet counts per network interface, application information, battery status, geolocation information, network information (e.g, BSSID, ESSID for WiFi), and a unique random device ID. While most information is similar across both OSes, there are some differences due to what information is available. Android OS reports application categories and their total traffic volume, but iOS has no interface to obtain the traffic volume per application. Similarly, Android OS reports non-associated WiFi AP information as well as associated WiFi APs if the WiFi interface is turned on, whereas iOS only reports the associated AP information. In concern for energy use and privacy, we report only coarse geolocation (5km precision) and do not report throughput. The software collects statistics every 10 minutes and uploads this data to a central server. If the upload fails the software caches the data and sends it later.

We conducted three measurement campaigns in March of 2013, 2014, and 2015 (Table 1)[3]. Each campaign used an independently recruited group of subjects from the greater Tokyo area, with more than 800 Android and 700 iPhone users. Each recruiting and selection process was done by a marketing research company in consideration of the market share of major Japanese cellular providers. During the campaigns, a wide variety of users were selected as listed in Table 2, and they were requested to use their smartphones as usual. The male-female ratio of the users was about 50:50. We also conducted a user survey at the end of the measurements in order to better understand user's behavior that

[1]https://play.google.com/store/apps/details?id=com.inetcore.linkspeed

[2]https://itunes.apple.com/jp/app/li-yong-shi-tai-diao-zha/id597320740?l=en&mt=8

[3]Our work has been institutionally reviewed and approved as human-subjects research (NII260128, NII270129).

Occupation	Percentage		
	2013	2014	2015
government worker	2.1	3.4	2.4
office worker	20.0	20.1	23.6
engineer	16.7	14.7	16.6
worker (other)	12.8	13.7	13.2
professional	2.4	2.0	2.8
self-owned business	6.1	6.7	5.6
part timer	9.0	10.1	10.6
housewife	15.0	14.2	13.3
student	9.6	8.3	2.7
other	6.3	6.8	7.1

Table 2: User survey: user demographics.

cannot be seen in the network data (see details in § 4.2). The number of analyzed unique device IDs was about 1600-1700 over three years. This number includes non-recruited users who installed the measurement software from respective app stores.

We intend to characterize users behaviors depending on their exchanged traffic volume. Throughout the paper, we refer to light users as those whose daily download traffic ranges from the 40th to 60th percentiles, and heavy hitters as users whose daily download traffic is ranked in the top 5%. Note that as daily user traffic volume is highly variable, one user may be a light user one day and heavy hitter on another.

To focus on typical use, we cleaned our data to avoid distortion due to two atypical events. First, we removed tethering traffic data from the datasets since such data have different traffic characteristics.

Second, we removed traffic relating to the iOS update in 2015 from our main analysis. Apple updated iOS(to iOS 8.2) during our measurement in 2015. We identified each devices update (around March 10th, 2015) and ignored all user traffic data in the day and the next day of the update for our main analysis due to its huge data size (over 500MB). We discuss traffic from this update specifically in § 3.7.

Possible measurement biases: An online market research company selected these participants from pooled users, so they are likely more advanced users than the average smartphone user. The availability of public WiFi networks in metro stations, cafes, shops, and on the streets is higher in Tokyo than in different areas. Most commuters in this area use public transportation (e.g., trains, subways, and buses) rather than personal cars. Thus, the probability to encounter public WiFi networks is likely high, and resulting WiFi traffic volume in public spaces is also high.

3. ANALYSIS OF SMARTPHONE TRAFFIC

3.1 Aggregated traffic behavior

We first examine the aggregated traffic behavior of cellular (3G and LTE) and WiFi networks in our datasets. Figure 2 indicates the weekly variations in the aggregated traffic volume in March 2015. The notations TX and RX in the figure are traffic volumes from and to smartphones, respectively. As expected, the WiFi volume exceeds the cellular volume. Thus the traditional measurements of cellular traffic such as Figure 1 *underrepresent* all smartphone activity due to WiFi offload. The ratio of WiFi traffic to the total traffic increases over time from 59% in 2013 to 67% in 2015. Also, the cellular traffic is mainly composed of LTE traffic accounting for 32% in 2013 but 80% in 2015 (see also Table 1).

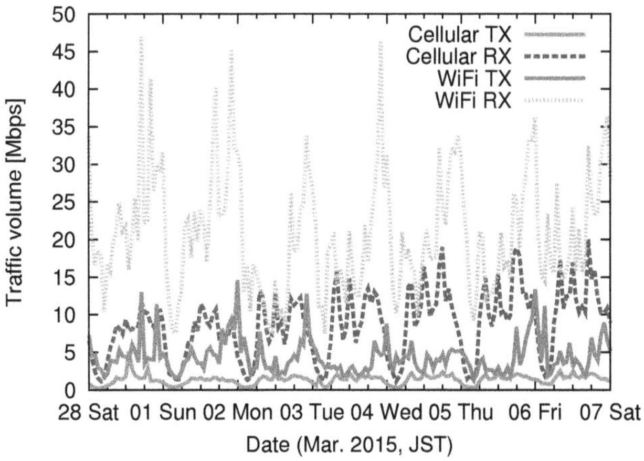

Figure 2: Aggregated traffic volume.

We see that network selection depends strongly on the time of day, with cellular traffic peaks corresponding to commute times and WiFi peaks to evening times at home. Three traffic peaks in cellular RX are affected by human activities in the morning (8am), noon (12am), and evening (7-9pm). Morning and evening peaks corresponded to the peak time of commuting mainly by public transportation in the Greater Tokyo area. In contrast, major peaks of the WiFi RX (11pm-1am) are right after the evening peak of cellular RX (9pm), though we also confirm peaks for morning and noon in WiFi RX. Cellular traffic on weekends is smaller than that on weekdays, while WiFi traffic is the opposite. Thus, these observations clearly present different temporal usage of WiFi and cellular networks.

3.2 Daily user traffic volume

We next focus on the daily traffic usage pattern per user. Our goal is to understand the impact of light users and heavy hitters by characterizing traffic distribution for each user as it changes over three years.

Daily total traffic: We first show that daily traffic increases each year, and users show a large variation in how much they send. Figure 3 shows the CDF of the daily traffic volume starting from midnight per user per day in a semi-log plot. Note that a single user appears one time for each day in the trace. We omitted users that downloaded less than 0.1MB. The shape of the curves is close to a unimodal distribution. The traffic volumes obviously increase over time, and the RX traffic volumes are about five times larger than the TX traffic volumes. While these two observations have been reported in residential broadband traffic [10], the results clearly show the client-server type user behavior.

Daily cellular and WiFi traffic: Next, we present that daily WiFi and cellular traffic volumes per user are largely distributed. Figure 4 presents the CDFs of the daily user traffic volume for cellular and WiFi network interfaces in 2015. As expected, the download and upload traffic volumes are highly skewed. On one hand, 8% of cellular interfaces and 20% of WiFi interfaces do not send and receive any data. On the other hand, the data shows that nearly all users respect traffic caps, with only 1.4% of users exceeding

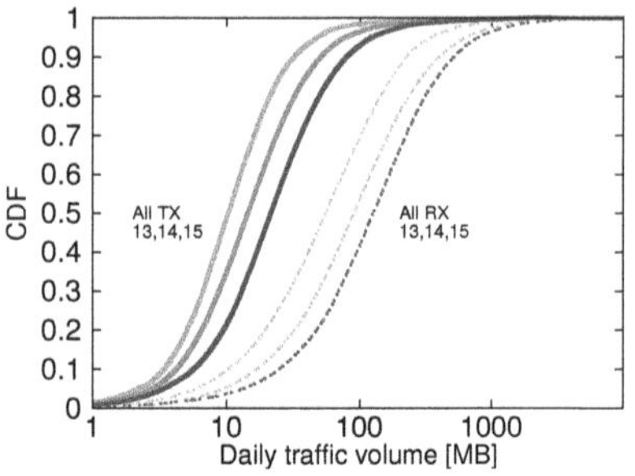

Figure 3: CDFs of daily total traffic volume per user.

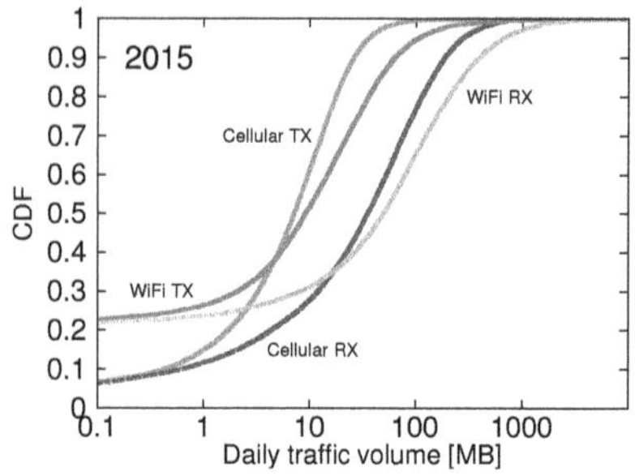

Figure 4: CDFs of daily traffic volume per type.

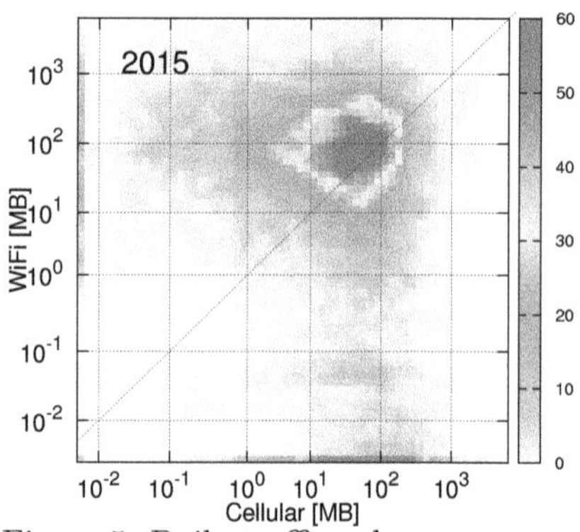

Figure 5: Daily traffic volume per user.

median	2013	2014	2015	AGR
All	57.9	90.3	126.5	48%
Cell	19.5	27.6	35.6	35%
WiFi	9.2	24.3	50.7	134%
mean	**2013**	**2014**	**2015**	**AGR**
All	102.9	179.9	239.5	53%
Cell	42.2	58.5	71.5	30%
WiFi	60.7	121.5	168.1	66%

Table 3: Daily download traffic volume per user (MB/day) and annual growth rate.

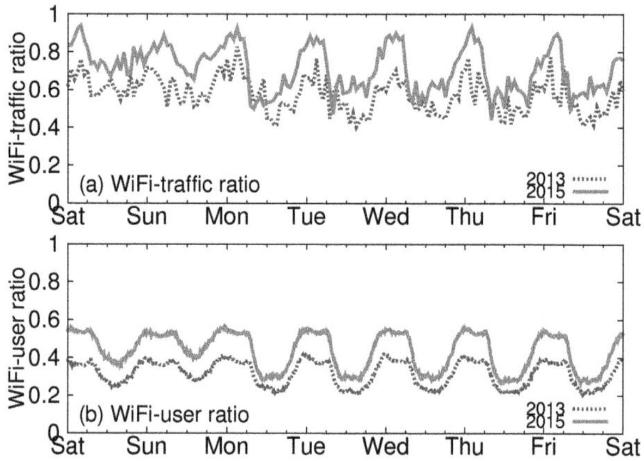

Figure 6: (a) WiFi-traffic ratio and (b) WiFi-user ratio.

the 1GB per 3-day soft bandwidth cap. We examine the details of the bandwidth cap in § 3.8. When unconstrained by limits, we see a much longer tail of heavy users—the top heavy hitter downloaded 11GB in one day.

Traffic growth: We emphasize the difference of growth in median and mean daily user traffic volume; they reflect traffic behavior of light users and heavy hitters, respectively. To investigate traffic growth, we list the median and mean daily user download traffic volumes in Table 3. The median traffic indicates the typical light user's traffic volume, and the mean traffic reflects traffic from all users, but is biased by heavy hitters. The annual growth rates (AGRs) are obtained by linear fit.

We see that users download more traffic via WiFi in late years. In fact, the traffic growth of median WiFi RX is significant while the median cellular RX is higher than the median WiFi RX in 2013. Thus, light users overlook the importance of WiFi offloading in 2013, but they change their behavior depending on the increase in traffic volume. Similarly, the growth of the mean WiFi traffic volume is high. Heavy hitters are also heavier in WiFi than cellular in mean traffic volume.

3.3 WiFi vs. Cellular

To assess the impact of traffic offloading we next examine of how users select between WiFi and cellular network interfaces.

3.3.1 Aggregated view

WiFi-intensive and cellular-intensive users: We introduce three types of users (cellular-intensive, WiFi-intensive, and mixed user) from the usage of network interfaces. Figure 5 shows a heat map of traffic volumes (log-log scale), for each user and each day by network (cellular and WiFi). The color bar indicates the number of users per day for a specific traffic ratio. The diagonal line indicates reference users who downloaded equal amounts of data from both cellular and WiFi networks.

We find the existence of three typical user types; *Cellular-intensive* users do not use their WiFi interfaces due to no available WiFi APs or no WiFi configuration. *WiFi-intensive* users only rely on their WiFi interfaces to avoid their cellular traffic fees. *Mixed* users select both cellular and WiFi network interfaces. The figure indicates that 22% of users are cellular-intensive and 8% are WiFi-intensive users. We see a decrease in cellular-intensive users: from 35% in 2013 to 22% in 2015, while the fraction of WiFi-intensive users is stable during the three years. Interestingly, both WiFi-intensive and cellular-intensive users show a wide spread in traffic volume; thus either can be heavy hitters.

User-level WiFi offloading: This data shows that mixed-network users often offload traffic to WiFi networks. Users above the diagonal are evidence of offloading, since their WiFi traffic exceeds their cellular traffic. The concentration of users above the diagonal shows WiFi offloading is common. Although 55% of mixed users are above the diagonal, a large number of users remain below it, suggesting WiFi usage can be further improved, especially for high cellular traffic volume users.

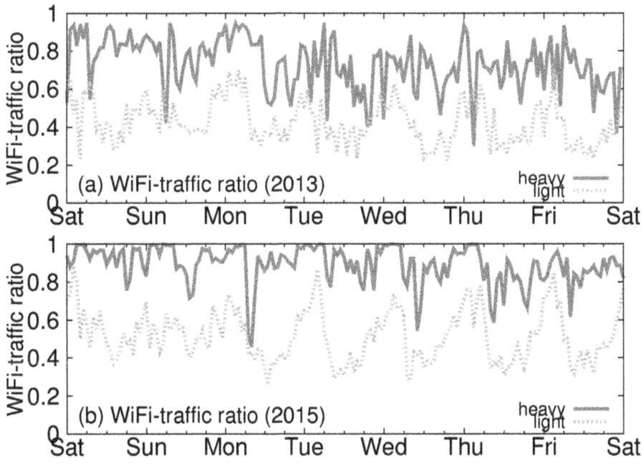

Figure 7: WiFi-traffic ratio (2013 and 2015).

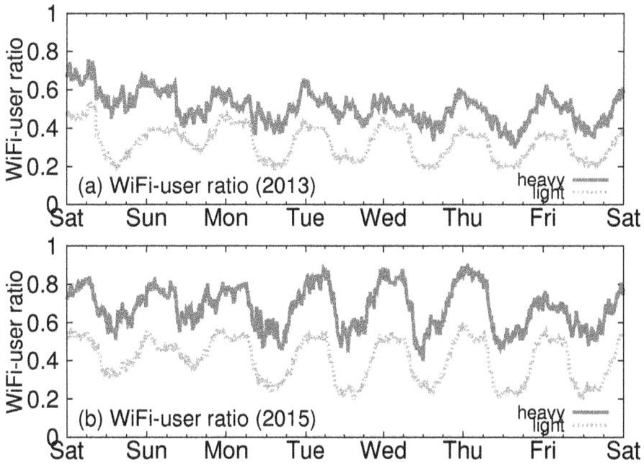

Figure 8: WiFi-user ratio (2013 and 2015).

3.3.2 *WiFi-traffic ratio and WiFi-user ratio*

We introduce two metrics to highlight the benefit of using WiFi networks: The *WiFi-traffic ratio* is defined as the WiFi download traffic volume divided by the total download traffic volume in one-hour time bins. A ratio close to 1.0 indicates that most traffic volume is downloaded via WiFi. The second metric is the *WiFi-user ratio*, defined as the ratio of the number of users associating to WiFi networks in each time bin. A ratio close to 1.0 means that, at that time, most users are using WiFi.

We see that the WiFi-traffic ratio increases showing increasing use of WiFi offloading. Figure 6(a) compares the WiFi-traffic ratio over each day of the week in 2013 with 2015. We observe that the WiFi-traffic ratio varies between 0.4 and 0.9 with clear diurnal trend. WiFi traffic is the highest from 11pm to 2am and the lowest in weekday afternoons. This temporal pattern differs from the simple WiFi traffic volume (Figure 2). Traffic penetration via WiFi is common at night though cellular traffic is still dominant in some time periods during the daytime. This data also confirms that WiFi offload is increasing, with the mean WiFi-traffic ratio growing to 0.71 in 2015 from 0.58 in 2013.

WiFi-user ratio shows that more users connect to WiFi networks in later years, however *only 50% of users connect to WiFi during peak hours.* We examine the temporal variation in the WiFi-user ratio in Figure 6(b). The number of users peaks from 9pm to 2am, while 10am to 6pm is the off-peak. The mean WiFi-user ratio also increases from 32% in 2013 to 48% in 2015. Thus, not only heavy hitters but also light users recognize the benefit of connecting to WiFi. However, only 50% of devices use WiFi even in the peak time.

3.3.3 *Difference in users*

We now highlight the difference in the WiFi-traffic ratio and WiFi-user ratio between light users and heavy hitters. We emphasize that in 2015, heavy hitters offload most of their traffic volume to WiFi, and that the ratio of offload traffic for light users also increases over the years. Figure 7 represents changes in WiFi-traffic ratio from 2013 to 2015. Heavy hitters already offload most of their traffic to WiFi and this trend shows no obvious diurnal pattern in 2013 (mean: 73%) and 2015 (mean: 89%). For light users, the ratio increased over the three years (from 42% to 52% in mean), particularly its diurnal pattern is much clearer in 2015, characterized by stable activity on weekends and typical daily trend on weekdays.

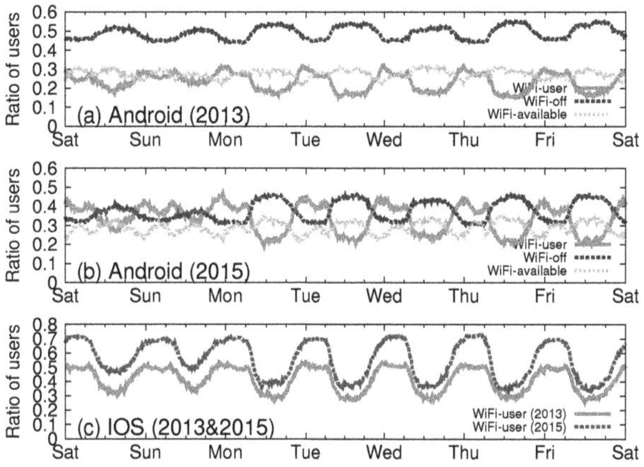

Figure 9: Ratio of users: (a) Android 2013, (b) Android 2015, and (c) iOS 2013 & 2015.

We see a large increase of WiFi-user ratio especially for heavy-hitters during the three years. Figure 8 illustrates the increase of the WiFi-user ratio. The difference between heavy hitters and light users is dispersed over the three years. In 2013, about 60% of heavy hitters connect to WiFi during their peak traffic time (mean: 51%). In 2015, more than 80% of heavy hitters use WiFi during their peak time (mean: 68%). These results suggest that some heavy hitters in 2013 are mainly connected to cellular networks, but this trend weakens as traffic volume increases over time.

3.3.4 *Difference in device OS*

We show that there are differences in offloading patterns correlated with device OS. We first define more detailed cellular and WiFi usage to quantify the potential opportunity of WiFi offloading. For Android devices, we categorize users into three groups, as shown in Figure 9(a). The first category is users connecting their device to WiFi networks (*WiFi-user*; pink curve). The second category consists of *WiFi-off users* whose WiFi interfaces are off (blue curve). The third consists of *WiFi-available users* who use cellular interfaces as the primary link but still turn on their WiFi interface (green curve). Note that the WiFi-off users explicitly turn off the WiFi interface and the WiFi-available users do not connect to any WiFi AP.

We confirm that *40% of Android devices explicitly turn off their WiFi interface, but this ratio decreases during the three years.* The ratio of the WiFi-available users is stable at around 0.25 in both 2013 and 2015, meaning that a quarter of the users could offload their traffic to WiFi if any appropriate APs are discovered. We discuss these users later in § 3.5. In comparison, the variation in the ratio of WiFi-off users is opposite of that of WiFi users; the peak time is business hours (10am-6pm). Our results show that nearly 50% of Android users *explicitly* turn off their WiFi devices during the day in 2013 (blue curve). However, the situation of the low WiFi usage improves in 2015, demonstrating that the ratio of WiFi-off users drops from 50% to 40% (Figure 9(b)).

WiFi connectivity of iOS is higher than that of Android. For iOS devices, the software does not report detailed information about the WiFi interface. However, we conclude that iOS devices connect to WiFi 30% more than do Android devices, as shown in Figure 9(c). We also confirm that there is no difference in the WiFi-user ratios among three cellular carriers providing iPhones. Thus, WiFi-user ratio differs between the two device OSes rather than cellular carriers.

3.4 Usage of WiFi networks

Next we illustrate the results of user adoption of available WiFi networks at home, in offices, and in public places.

3.4.1 Home, public, and other WiFi networks

We first define the locations of WiFi APs users connected to. We identify each WiFi AP users associate with by its (BSSID, ESSID) pair (the MAC address of AP and its network name). We then categorize WiFi networks into these three types:

Home: We identify home locations as the most common (BSSID, ESSID) pair to which each device connects during at least 70% of the time between 10pm and 6am in one day. Note that users do not always have at least one home network. In fact, the percentage of users with estimated home AP increases over time; 66% in 2013, 73% in 2014 and 79% in 2015. These numbers are roughly consistent with the result of our user survey in Table 8. Table 4 lists the numbers of detected APs.

Public: We identify public networks based on well known ESSID names (e.g., 0000docomo, 0001softbank, eduroam). These services are often deployed by Japanese cellular providers for their customers (§ 1), or by free/commercial WiFi providers (e.g., 7Spot and Metro_Free_Wi-Fi). We categorize FON APs that use a public ESSID at home as a home network because we find that some users connected to the public ESSID over 24 hours instead of using the default private ESSID by FON. The number of detected public APs doubles in three years as shown in the table.

Other: Other associated pairs are mainly located at offices or mobile WiFi APs. It also includes some open APs provided by shops and hotels. We further estimate APs at offices when they (1) mainly connect between 11am and 5pm on weekdays and (2) are not otherwise classified as home, public or mobile APs. The number of estimated office APs is stable over the years.

This classification shows a wide deployment of APs especially in public spaces. Figure 10 visualizes the locations

type	2013	2014	2015
home	1139	1223	1289
public	5041	9302	10481
other	545	673	664
(office)	166	168	166
total	6725	11198	12434

Table 4: Number of estimated APs.

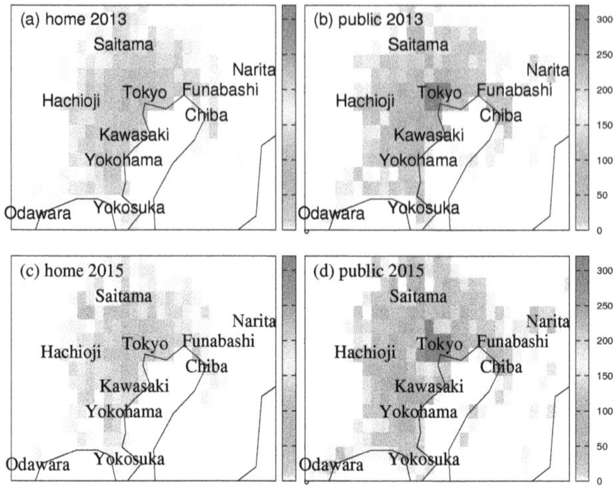

Figure 10: Number of associated unique APs per 5km cell: (a) home in 2013, (b) public in 2013, (c) home in 2015, and (d) public in 2015.

and densities of associated APs in the Greater Tokyo area. Each cell is a 5km square, with color showing identified AP density. The four quadrants of the figure show home and public distribution in 2013 and 2015. Home networks are widely dispersed, reflecting many residential areas. There are only minor differences between the two datasets.

This data suggests that *coverage of public WiFi networks is broad in the Greater Tokyo.* The maps of public networks highlight strong densities in the downtown Tokyo area. The number of associated public networks is over 300 in the highest density areas (Shinjuku and Shibuya areas). We also confirm the wide coverage of public APs even far from the downtown area. By comparing the two datasets, furthermore, high-density areas are more dispersed in 2015. For example, the number of cells with at least one AP increases from 229 to 265, and that of cells with larger than 100 APs increases from 10 to 23. This result suggests that users can potentially connect to widely deployed public WiFi APs if devices are appropriately configured.

However, *the contribution of public and office APs is still small when measured by traffic volume.* Figure 11 represents the weekly traffic variations for home, public, and office in 2013 and 2015. The major contribution of WiFi traffic volume is home networks (95% of the total volume). The public and office WiFi traffic volumes are much smaller (4% of the total volume), though those volumes double during this period. The diurnal patterns of public and office WiFi are in opposition to that of home WiFi. These clear patterns in 2015 emphasize the increase of users associated to these WiFi networks.

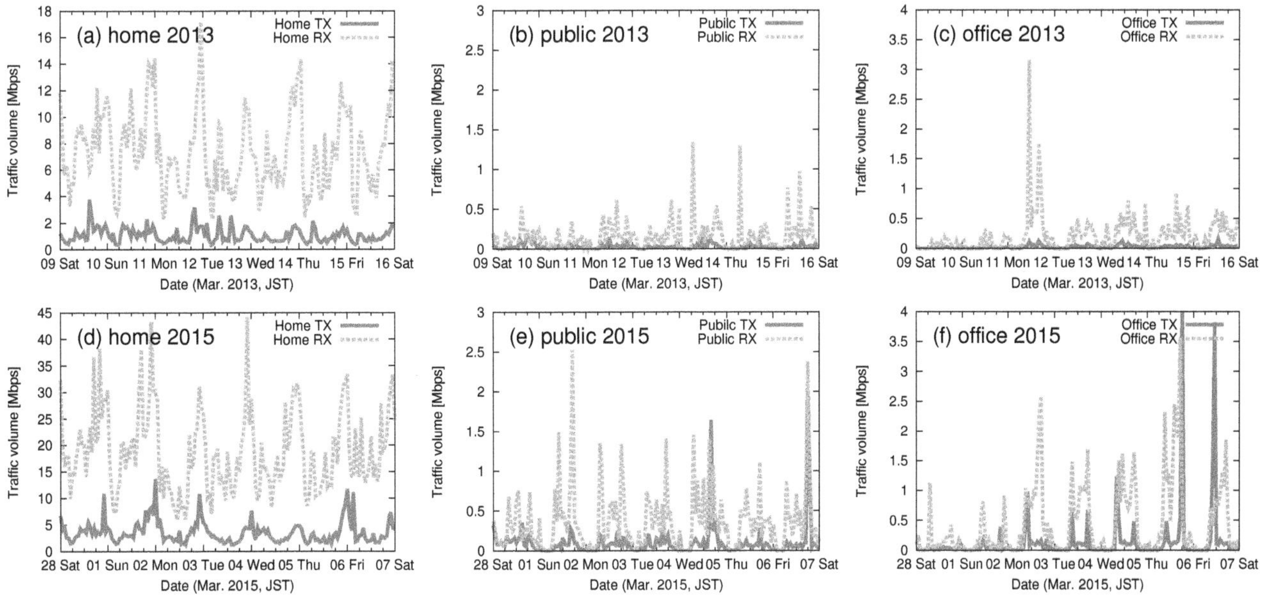

Figure 11: WiFi traffic volume: (a) home in 2013, (b) public in 2013, (c) office in 2013, (d) home in 2015, (e) public in 2015, and (f) office in 2015.

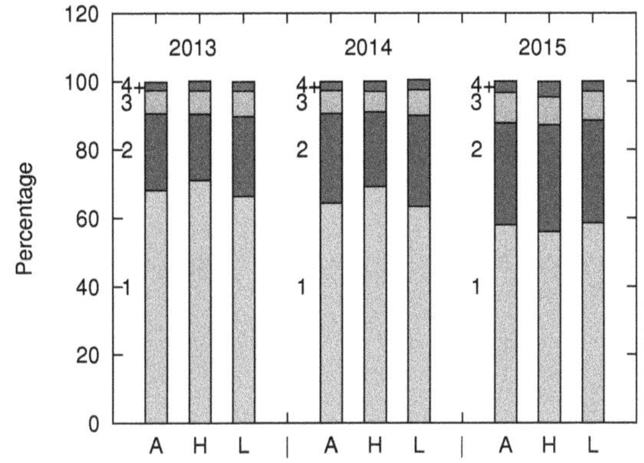

Figure 12: Percentage of the number of associated APs per day per user: All users (A), heavy hitters (H), and light users (L).

3.4.2 *Access patterns of WiFi networks: location*

We first show the number of associated APs increases over time, and that daily traffic volume per user does not correlate to mobility pattern. Figure 12 illustrates the number of associated APs per user per day for all users (A), heavy hitters (H), and light users (L). We find evidence that *users connect to multiple WiFi APs in late years.* In 2013, 70% of users only connect to one AP per day, but it decreases 10% in three years. Moreover, we do not see a significant difference between heavy hitters and light users. Thus, user traffic volume does not correlate to the mobility patterns.

Next we detail that the main usage patterns of WiFi networks are still only at home, and that the use of multiple APs has been more common. Table 5 lists the breakdown of the number of associated ESSIDs per device in one day for all users. The HPO column indicates the possible combinations of WiFi network types; home (H), public (P), and other (O) networks. For example, HPO = 120 represents the number of devices that connect to one home network, two public networks, and no other network in one day. For users using one AP, the percentage of using home WiFi decreases from 55% to 46%, though it is still dominant. About 10% of the users do not have any home WiFi network but connect to other WiFi networks. They have no broadband wired links at home for WiFi offloading; however, they are aware of WiFi traffic offloading. For users using two APs, the top connection pattern is one home and one other network. However, our manual inspection reveals that iOS devices connect more to public networks than to other networks whereas Android devices connect oppositely. We also confirm low percentages (2.2-3.4%) of users who connect to more than three networks in one day. The maximum number of associated ESSIDs per user per day is eight in our datasets: one home, four public, and three other networks.

We further show that the distribution of user connection durations to one WiFi network do not change over time. Figure 13 shows the complementary cumulative distribution of the consecutive time with the same AP in a log-log plot. All plots are characterized by long tails with a cutoff. Ninety percent of the users connect for less than 12 hours for home networks, 8 hours for office networks, and 1 hour for public networks. The results of home and office are consistent with typical user activity by definition. No clear difference is observed between the three datasets, meaning that *the usage patterns in connection duration do not change for any WiFi network type from 2013 to 2015.*

3.4.3 *Access patterns of WiFi networks: 2.4 and 5GHz*

Recent WiFi APs operate in two frequency bands: 2.4 and 5GHz. We find that *deployment of 5GHz APs has been rapid for public networks, but most home and office networks are at 2.4GHz.* Deployment of 2.4GHz APs is wider than 5GHz because of their earlier availability on the market. However,

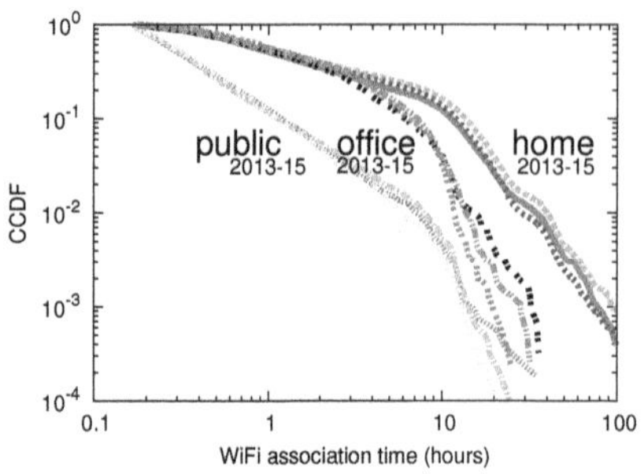

Figure 13: CCDFs of WiFi connection duration.

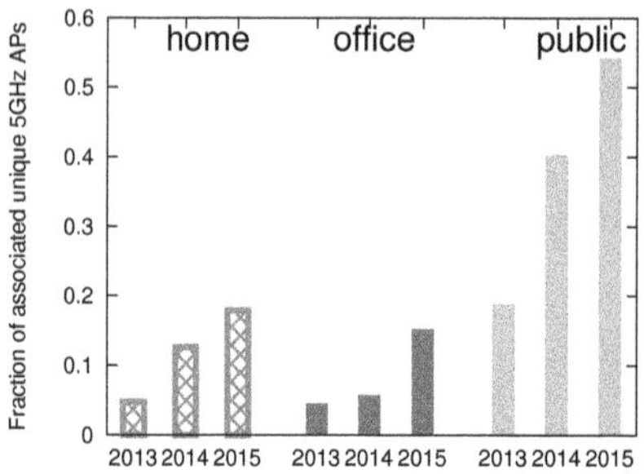

Figure 14: Fractions of associated unique 5GHz APs.

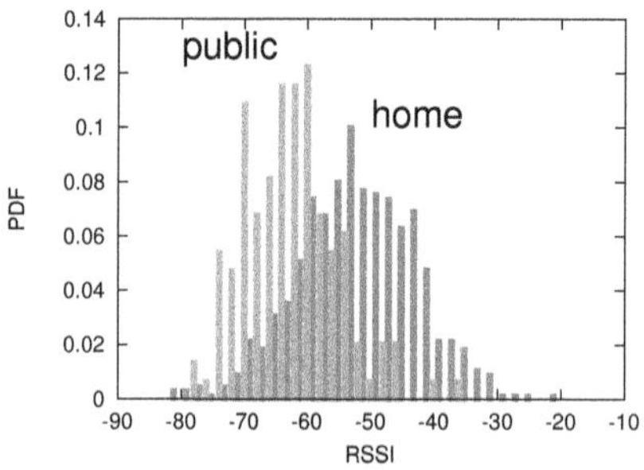

Figure 15: PDFs of WiFi RSSI for associated APs (2015).

ESSIDs per day	**HPO**	**2013**	**2014**	**2015**
	100	54.7%	52.6%	46.4%
1	010	3.0%	2.4%	2.4%
	001	10.5%	9.4%	9.2%
	110	8.2%	10.0%	9.0%
	101	10.7%	12.9%	16.5%
2	011	1.4%	1.3%	1.7%
	020	0.6%	0.3%	0.3%
	002	1.5%	1.8%	2.4%
	102	1.8%	2.0%	2.7%
	120	1.9%	1.4%	1.4%
3	111	2.2%	2.3%	3.4%
	012	0.3%	0.4%	0.6%
	021	0.4%	0.2%	0.3%
	003	0.3%	0.4%	0.5%
4+	—	2.3%	2.5%	3.2%

Table 5: Breakdown of number of associated APs (user·day): home (H), public (P), and other (O) networks.

the 2.4GHz spectrum is less robust against noise. We investigate the deployment status of 5GHz APs at home, in offices, and in public spaces. Figure 14 shows the fraction of unique associated 5GHz APs to the total unique associated APs for the three years. The fraction of 5GHz APs varies across homes, offices, and public spaces. Still less than 20% at home and office APs are 5GHz, i.e., most WiFi APs mainly operate in 2.4GHz. For public WiFi, we see that more than half are 5GHz APs in 2015. We believe that wide use of 5GHz in public location is due to recent aggressive rollout of WiFi, while long device lifecycle means that home and office have not yet needed to upgrade.

3.4.4 Quality of WiFi networks: signal strength

There are several factors that affect the QoS/QoE of smartphones, in which the received signal strength indication (RSSI) is a common metric for quantifying the strength of the receiver-side signal in wireless communication. A larger RSSI represents a stronger signal, and an RSSI larger than -70dBm is generally better for WiFi connectivity. For example, it has been reported that the retransmission probability of a TCP session is $\approx 10\%$ for RSSI $= -70$dBm and rapidly increases for RSSI < -70dBm in a dataset measured at a conference WiFi network [41].

The signal strength at home is generally sufficient for network connectivity. We calculate the maximum RSSI of each associated AP in 2.4GHz, and plot the probability density of RSSIs of associated home and public networks in Figure 15. Home networks are characterized by a bell shape with a mean of -54dBm, consistent with those in French home networks [13, 14]. Three percent of the home networks report a weaker RSSI than -70dBm. We also confirm that the shape of the plots of office networks is similar to that of home networks.

On the other hand, *a small percentage of associated public APs indicate subpar quality.* The plot of public WiFi networks clearly shifts to smaller RSSIs around -60dBm. For narrowing the cell size in public WiFi, the mean signal strength can be weaker than that of home WiFi networks. As the result, we confirm that 12% of associated public WiFi networks indicate weaker signal strength (< -70dBm), likely causing poor QoS/QoE to the users. This low-quality connectivity is a reason to deploy more 5GHz APs in public WiFi networks.

3.4.5 Quality of WiFi networks: channel usage

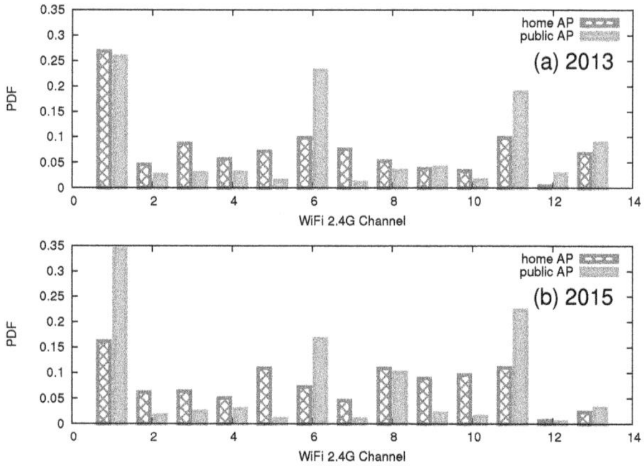

Figure 16: Associated 2.4GHz channels (2013 and 2015).

Finally, we investigate the efficacy of channel selection of APs. In addition to the RSSI, channel selection of WiFi networks is an important factor that affects the performance of the WiFi networks. In an IEEE 802.11b/g/n network, 13 channels are available in the 2.4GHz band, and two BSSIDs using neighboring channels may interfere with each other due to the overlap of channel bandwidth (i.e., cross channel interference). It is known that at least a five-channel interval is necessary to avoid cross channel interference between two channels. Some recent home-use APs have a function for detecting and avoiding channel interference. In addition, public WiFi providers design and deploy their APs to avoid cross channel interference between their APs; however, they can still interfere with other public APs.

We confirm that *deployment of public APs is generally well designed, and the concentration on the default channel has been relaxed in home APs.* Figure 16 shows the probability density of the associated channels in the 2.4GHz band for Android devices. Devices connected mainly to Ch1, Ch6, and Ch11 in public WiFi APs, indicating that devices are set up to minimize interference. Such observation is also recently reported in [38, 6]. In 2013, the numerous connections to Ch1 at home are, however, potentially causing more channel interference. This poor setting is likely due to the lack of intelligent channel selection mechanisms at the APs. However, we observe improvement in avoiding possible interference in later years; WiFi channels at home are more dispersed and have less concentration on Ch1 in 2015.

3.5 Availability of public WiFi APs

To understand how much cellular traffic *WiFi-available* users can offload to *public* WiFi networks, we next look at WiFi coverage, signal strength, and how much traffic they can offload.

We first suggest a wide coverage of potentially available public WiFi APs. We sum up all detected public networks (all) and detected public networks with a signal strength strong enough to be associated with (i.e., RSSI $\geq$ -70dBm) (strong), in a 5km cell. We confirm that 2.4GHz public WiFi networks are widely deployed in the Greater Tokyo area in our data, though the coverage of our data is imperfect due to the limited number of recruited users. In the downtown area (Shinjuku, Shibuya area), for example, the number of public WiFi networks with strong signal is over 10000 in one cell, while the number of detected networks is about 45000 in one cell. Comparing the two datasets (2013 and 2015), the number of cells with more than 100 strong 2.4GHz APs increases from 102 to 139, and that with more than 100 strong 5GHz APs is from 10 to 84. This observation indicates that deployment of 5GHz APs in public networks has largely improved.

Next, we identify that WiFi-available users (§ 3.3.4) encounter a few strong and available public WiFi APs, and that the number of such APs increases. Figure 17 represents the complementary cumulative distribution of the number of detected public APs per WiFi-available device per 10 minutes in 2015. The plot labeled as "strong" represents the number of detected networks with strong maximum signal strength, and "all" represents the number of all detected networks. Both plots represent that a few users see many APs but most see only a few. We observe that most users (90%) see fewer than 10 2.4GHz APs. As expected, the number of strong WiFi networks is much smaller than all detected WiFi networks. The data shows that 5GHz deployment is still early, since only a few users (10%) could find strong 5GHz APs, and only slightly more (30%) can find any 5GHz. However, this deployment is better than that in 2013; 10% for all APs and 3% for strong APs. Tail behavior of strong 2.4GHz and strong 5GHz APs resembles each other, suggesting WiFi APs operating in both bands.

Finally, we infer that *WiFi offloading to available public WiFi networks can reduce 15-20% of daily cellular traffic for WiFi-available users.* As described in § 1, cellular providers deploy free public WiFi service to their customers. Devices whose WiFi interfaces are enabled but not associated with any WiFi networks (i.e., WiFi-available user) can offload their cellular traffic to the public WiFi networks of their providers. Examining of such available WiFi networks for WiFi-available users, we confirm that 60% of WiFi-available users have opportunities to connect to stable public WiFi networks. We sum up cellular download traffic volume during these periods as possible offloading traffic, then conclude that 15-20% of daily cellular traffic volume for such WiFi-available users can be transferred to public WiFi networks.

	Cell home		**Cell other**		**WiFi home**		**WiFi public**	
	type	%	type	%	type	%	type	%
2013	brows.	38.0	brows.	38.5	brows.	28.0	brows.	44.1
	social	7.3	comm.	7.7	social	6.8	social	4.0
	comm.	6.2	social	7.6	comm.	4.3	life	3.3
	video	5.7	news	2.6	video	4.0	comm.	3.0
	news	2.0	video	2.1	news	3.5	news	2.9
2014	brows.	36.4	brows.	31.4	video	30.4	dload	22.5
	video	7.4	comm.	9.9	brows.	20.7	brows.	21.9
	comm.	7.4	video	8.0	comm.	6.5	video	13.8
	social	6.3	news	6.6	news	6.0	life	4.9
	news	6.2	game	6.3	dload	4.7	health	3.2
2015	brows.	28.3	brows.	28.3	video	25.4	brows.	24.0
	video	11.0	comm.	12.7	brows.	20.0	video	19.6
	comm.	9.5	video	12.0	dload	11.1	dload	9.9
	social	7.9	news	7.6	comm	7.4	life	4.1
	news	5.8	social	6.9	social	4.7	comm	3.6

Table 6: Top application categories, as ranked by RX traffic volume.

3.6 Application breakdown

WiFi offloading often requires application support, so we now examine applications, their traffic volumes, and their support for offload.

We first group popular applications into 26 categories in Google Play. Major application categories are: browser, social networking (e.g., Facebook, Twitter), video and media (e.g., Youtube, Nicovideo), communication (e.g., Line, email clients), news, gaming, music, travel, shopping, downloading, entertainment (e.g., lottery, survey), tools (e.g., printer, speed test), productivity (e.g., online file storage service), and lifestyle (e.g., restaurant info, cooking). Note that the browser category includes web use; some web use may overlap with other categories (such as videos and social networks that are accessed from the browser instead of an application).

We distinguish application usage at home or other places with WiFi and cellular network interfaces. Table 6 and Table 7 show the percentage of the traffic volume (sum of RX and TX) generated from the five largest Android application categories in each year, broken out by network type and location. We infer home locations of cellular networks with the same classification technique described in § 3.4.1.

First of all, *users are more likely to use high-bitrate applications like video when they are on free networks like WiFi.* The ratio of video traffic increases especially in WiFi networks over the years, while we see that most common application categories in all scenarios are: browser, social networking, video, and communications. Thus, watching video with a smartphone has been a casual usage, though the users understand that a rich and low-cost network environment is

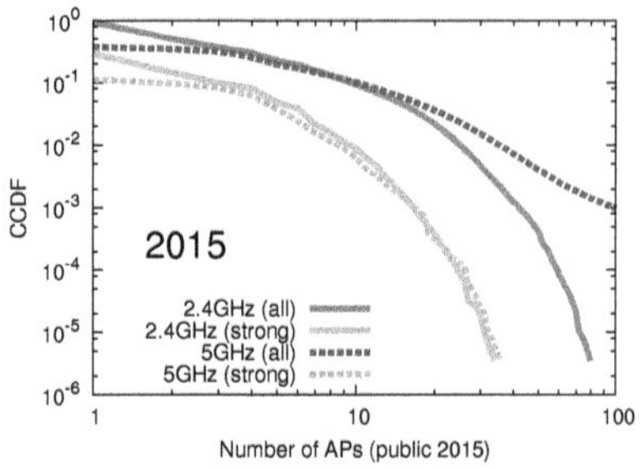

Figure 17: CCDFs of the number of detected public WiFi networks per device per 10 min.

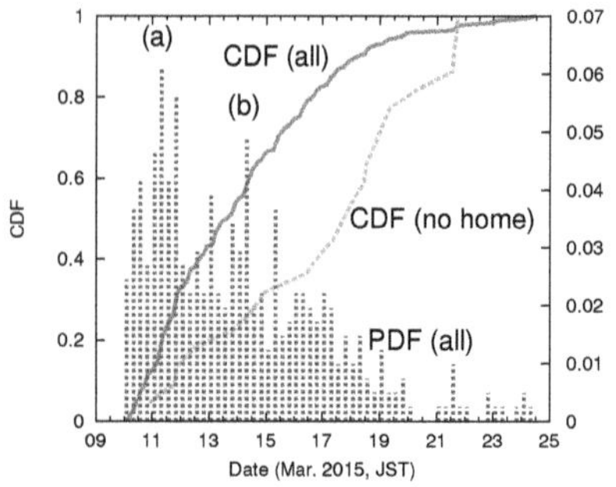

Figure 18: Software update timing.

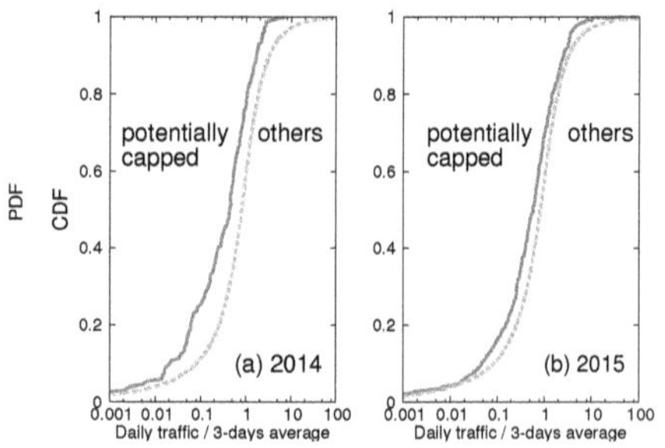

Figure 19: Effect of soft bandwidth cap.

	Cell home type	Cell home %	Cell other type	Cell other %	WiFi home type	WiFi home %	WiFi public type	WiFi public %
2013	brows.	23.0	brows.	24.5	social	24.8	brows.	33.8
	video	16.1	social	15.1	brows.	18.4	social	9.1
	social	14.2	video	10.6	video	14.7	comm.	4.2
	comm.	10.8	comm.	6.6	prod.	13.8	prod.	3.5
	prod.	2.1	prod.	3.0	comm	5.2	video	2.1
2014	brows.	31.0	brows.	28.5	prod.	39.5	brows.	41.8
	social	9.5	social	15.8	video	18.7	prod.	15.2
	prod.	9.0	comm.	11.5	brows.	15.7	life	6.9
	video	9.0	video	7.5	social	6.9	comm.	5.0
	comm.	8.5	game	3.8	comm.	5.8	news	4.6
2015	brows.	33.7	brows.	29.7	brows	19.9	video	35.6
	comm	11.2	comm	14.5	prod	15.7	brows.	25.8
	social	11.0	social	11.3	video	12.7	prod	5.2
	game	9.9	life	5.9	social	10.5	comm.	5.0
	news	3.7	game	5.1	comm.	8.0	busi	4.6

Table 7: Top application categories, as ranked by TX traffic volume.

preferable for this purpose. Furthermore, we observed an increase in video traffic in public WiFi networks. Thus, *users demand for public WiFi networks is changing from simple connectivity-sensitive to more bandwidth-consuming applications.* Instead, most traffic of video and media category in cellular at home is due to cellular-intensive users (without APs at home).

We also confirmed *some applications force users to use WiFi networks to reduce traffic volume in cellular networks.* The percentage of the productivity category increases in upload volume. In particular, in WiFi networks at home, this category accounts for a high percentage of traffic volume due to online storage software that uploads/downloads large files only if a WiFi interface is available. Thus, applications seem to play a major role in promoting WiFi offloading.

Finally, for light users, the contribution of video applications to download traffic becomes small. We investigate the application usage of light users in 2015 (data omitted due to space). The results are almost consistent with those for all users. A notable difference is a low contribution of video traffic; it is not ranked in the top five categories in both cellular and WiFi networks.

3.7 Software update

While § 3.6 looked at typical application use, in 2015 we captured an unusual event where many iOS devices carried out software upgrades. Apple only allows iOS upgrades on WiFi, not cellular, by default. Thus, this event provides a case study of application-forced WiFi offloading.

The impact of the update on traffic volume is high; the size of the update is 565MB which is more than ten times larger than the daily median download traffic volume (50.7MB), and it is more than half of the soft bandwidth cap limit.

Timing of software updates follows a typical flash crowd, with a large burst and a long tail. Figure 18 shows the time-of-day of updates in CDF and PDF since we first see an iOS update on March 10th, 2015 (JST). In two weeks, 58% of all iPhone devices are updated to iOS 8.2. Half users updated in the first four days, with 10% of on the first day (cf. CDF (all)). We also confirm two broad peaks; one is the first and second days (label (a) in the figure), and the other is the first weekend (label (b)). Considering the percentage of the un-updated devices, the time for migrating to the new version would have a longer tail.

We find that *availability of WiFi is important to timely deploy updates; lack of WiFi can delay OS upgrades.* In fact, only 14% of users without inferred home APs updated their device OS. Moreover, the CDF of updates without home APs demonstrates that the updates of such users are delayed. The median update delay of users with home WiFi and without is 3.5 days. For security-critical updates, this delay may leave users vulnerable longer.

Furthermore, we observed that some users without home WiFi seem to go out-of-their way to access public WiFi to obtain the update. We inspect 19 updated devices that have no inferred home APs. *Eleven users without home AP update their devices via public WiFi*, and two via office APs. This observation is unexpected but reasonable behavior that reduces update costs.

3.8 Effect of soft bandwidth cap

Japanese cellular providers commonly limit heavy hitter's maximum bandwidth especially in peak hours. A typical bandwidth cap begins after 1GB is received over the previous three days. The download speed of users over the cap will be limited (e.g., 128kbps) during peak hours for the next few days. However, two cellular providers relaxed this policy in February 2015, so we expect less impact from bandwidth caps in 2015 compared to prior years.

We detect potentially capped users from their current and past traffic volumes, and find that the ratio of such users is small. The number of potentially capped users grows each year, from 0.5% in 2013, 0.8% in 2014, to 1.4% in 2015.

We can also see the effects of bandwidth limitation after exceeding the cap. To observe this effect, we plot the ratios of the daily traffic volume per user to the mean daily traffic volumes for the previous three days in 2014 and 2015 in Figure 19, where "potentially capped" represents users whose traffic volume in the previous three days exceeds the threshold (= 1GB). The gap between potentially capped users and others indicates the effect of the soft bandwidth cap. The download traffic volume of capped users decreases due to the cap in 2014. Typically, 45% of capped users download less than half the mean of three-day traffic volume. On the other hand, only 30% of other users download the same percentage of traffic volume. Further manual inspection clarified that 65% of capped users have no inferred home APs.

However, some users that exceed the threshold for bandwidth capping but appear to not be penalized with slower bit rates. A reason of this large traffic volume is likely download traffic in off-peak hours.

By comparing the two figures, we confirm that *the gap between the capped users and others is small in 2015, showing the change of the policy.* The figure shows that the gap is 0.15 in 2015 at the median while 0.29 in 2014. This change also supports the reason of traffic increase of bandwidth-consuming applications in cellular networks from 2014 to 2015 (Table 6).

4. IMPLICATIONS

Next, we provide implications on the contribution of smartphone traffic on residential broadband traffic, connectivity and quality of WiFi networks, and bandwidth-consuming applications.

4.1 Large impact of home WiFi offload

We start by examining the impact of offloaded traffic volume on the total volume of residential broadband traffic. As shown in Figure 1, the nationwide cellular traffic volume (3G+LTE) corresponds to 20% of the estimated nationwide residential wired broadband traffic volume [34], so a large amount of smartphone traffic offloading will suggest an increase in broadband traffic. In our measurements, the median cellular download traffic volume is 36MB/day and the median WiFi download traffic is 51MB/day in 2015 (§ 3.2). Thus, 58% of smartphone traffic is WiFi; a 1.4:1 ratio of WiFi-to-cellular traffic. This ratio is higher than that in Cicso's report (45% in 2014) [11]. As a result, we roughly estimate 28% (= 20%*1.4) of the total residential broadband traffic volume as WiFi traffic by smartphones because 95% of WiFi traffic is at home (§ 3.4.1).

We also compare smartphone traffic volume with broadband traffic volume per user. A different source of residential broadband traffic data reported that the median download traffic volume of a residential customer per day in a Japanese ISP is 436MB/day as of 2015 [9]. We again infer with this volume that traffic share of one smartphone in a home network is 12% (= 51MB / 436MB).

Thus, *the growth in offloaded WiFi traffic even for light users has had a large impact on legacy broadband ISPs, where it is hidden in the traffic volume of heavy hitters.*

4.2 Connectivity of WiFi networks

To understand the behavior of user that cannot be seen in the network data, we had all our users fill out a questionnaire. In the post questionnaire, we asked two questions about WiFi APs to users. The first question is "where did you connect to WiFi APs in three locations (home, office, and public)?" (Table 8), to compare with the results of our location-based analysis (§ 3.4.2). The second one is "why did you not connect to WiFi APs in these three locations?" (Table 9), to understand possible causes of unavailability of WiFi networks.

WiFi	home			office			public		
AP	13	14	15	13	14	15	13	14	15
yes	70.4	72.9	78.2	31.6	25.6	28.0	44.9	47.9	53.6
no	25.9	22.8	18.6	63.2	69.0	67.4	48.9	44.9	40.9
NA	3.7	4.3	3.2	5.1	5.4	4.6	6.1	7.2	5.5

Table 8: User survey: associated WiFi APs during the measurements (%: 2013/2014/2015).

The answer to the first question shows that the percentage of associated APs at home and in public increased while that for office network is low and stable. The percentages of home WiFi APs are consistent with our estimation (Table 5), but, high percentages of public WiFi differ from our estimation. This gap represents the difference between user's recognition and actual connectivity; users think they have more connectivity than they really do in public WiFi networks. However, the results of the associated WiFi networks demonstrate that *the percentage of users with multiple APs has been increasing, and it is more than 40% in 2015* (§ 3.4).

From the measurement results and the answer to the second question (Table 9), we summarize the plausible reasons for the low availability of WiFi networks during daytime as follows. (1) Users report that connecting private smartphones to WiFi networks at offices (Bring your own device; BYOD) is still not common in Japan. It is supported by high percentages of the answer "there is no deployment of APs" in Table 9. In addition, a major reason of "Other" for office WiFi networks is due to the security policy that does not allow employees to connect their personal smartphone to the office WiFi networks. Our traffic data showed a significant increase in office WiFi traffic volume (Figure 11) though the number of inferred office APs (Table 4) remains stable during the three years.

(2) Configuring WiFi APs is difficult. Configuration problems decrease in public WiFi networks over time in the survey. Users report in our questionnaire that entering WiFi passwords into their mobile devices is often complicated. To reduce complexity, since 2013 WiFi APs from cellular providers use SIM-based authentication [25] without user and password information. As a result, smartphone customers can use WiFi APs from their provider with no manual actions. Coupled with the deployment of more access points (Figure 10), we believe this simplification in their use helps increase the degree of WiFi offload.

(3) Many users have no incentive to use public WiFi networks because the current quality of cellular networks is enough and are charged a flat fee per month. High percentage of the answer "communication speed in LTE is enough" in Table 9 supports this claim. Nonetheless, we estimated that 15-20% of the traffic data can be offloaded if users appropriately configure the settings for public WiFi networks (§ 3.5).

(4) Finally, we found that security with public WiFi was a significant concern, and that battery life was not.

Reason	home			office			public		
	13	14	15	13	14	15	13	14	15
No available APs	33	34	40	46	49	52	25	24	23
Difficult to set up	32	27	21	16	15	11	31	31	25
No configuration	48	35	32	33	25	22	43	31	29
Battery drain	18	14	15	16	9	7	25	18	13
Failed	5	6	8	7	7	7	9	8	11
Security issue	NA	6	14	NA	9	14	NA	15	35
LTE is enough	NA	25	21	NA	12	10	NA	22	23
Other	6	5	5	12	10	10	9	5	4

Table 9: User survey: reasons for unavailability of WiFi APs (%). Multiple answers were allowed.

4.3 Quality of public WiFi networks

We discuss how public WiFi networks can improve their quality. The quality and accessibility of WiFi networks have been improved over the years. However, 12% of associated public WiFi networks using 2.4GHz are characterized by a low RSSI (§ 3.4.4). Such low-quality network environments are likely a reason for users hesitating to use the public WiFi network, though over half of the associated public networks have sufficient quality. To cope with this problem, device OSes should implement tests for the quality of a WiFi network before starting to offload to prevent the degradation of user QoE.

The coordinated deployment of public APs is a difficult problem in reality because they use unlicensed bands. To mitigate performance degradation due to channel interference among different public WiFi networks, deployment of APs that support multiple providers by announcing multiple ESSIDs from a single AP should be promoted, especially in downtown areas. In fact, we confirmed this type of APs in our dataset, by checking similar BSSIDs assigned to different providers. It will be also cost-effective to use these APs for providing free WiFi APs to foreign visitors instead of deploying new APs, towards the 2020 Olympic Games. Extended usage of such APs has already been discussed in the context of providing free WiFi in disaster areas after the Tohoku earthquake.

We also observed a significant deployment of 5GHz APs in public spaces (§ 3.4.3). 5GHz APs are more robust against noise and helpful in improving the quality of WiFi network [40, 46]. This migration also contributes to increases in availability, use, and traffic in public WiFi networks. Furthermore, the limited spatial and more reliable nature of 5GHz APs may allow new types of applications to emerge, such as fine-grained targeting advertisement.

4.4 Bandwidth-consuming applications

We observed a large growth of bandwidth-consuming application traffic (§ 3.6). Users with WiFi access download more video (Table 7), suggesting that users understand that rich-bandwidth and low-cost WiFi networks are available, and changing their usage accordingly. Similarly, other bandwidth-consuming applications contribute to WiFi offloading. For example, iOS shows a pop-up message to users to promote the use of WiFi for software updates. We see a similar change in upload use when WiFi is available. For example, WiFi has been largely used for the productivity category, which includes online file storage (Table 6).

This intelligent network connectivity management by software has two different perspectives. On one hand, it will be more common and necessary to cope with bandwidth-consuming applications in the future, particularly to avoid bandwidth caps. On the other hand, *it causes another adaptive behavior of users.* Some users rely on public WiFi networks for their software updates (§ 3.7). Furthermore, we observed an increase in video traffic even in public WiFi networks. User demand is towards casual use of bandwidth-consumption applications in public WiFi networks. This trend may introduce a change of the economic cost and the QoS model (i.e., traffic engineering) of public and free WiFi networks, because low-cost connectivity is the main advantage with current WiFi networks.

5. RELATED WORK

Cellular smartphone usage: Quantifying the diverse usage of smartphones has been one of the hot topics in traffic measurement and analysis. Some studies have pointed out that the flow-level performance of the 3G/LTE cellular network is affected by many aspects such as the differences in the cellular providers, types of devices, transport protocols, and mobility [32, 28, 29, 27, 37, 19, 42, 17]. The application usage and resulting performance in cellular networks also indicate large diversity [47, 16, 28, 51, 44, 27]. In particular, the usage pattern of applications in smartphones depends on the mobility and geographical region of users [47, 51, 52]. Recent studies addressed the impact of user measurement environment on network performance [21, 43]. There are several approaches to characterize this diversity such as application identification [50, 36], app store usage [49], and geolocation mapping [3, 48]. Another direction of current research is to quantify and model energy consumption of smartphones [27, 15, 7]. Regarding bandwidth caps, a recent experiment concerning cellular service pricing shows that time-dependent pricing helps reduce peak traffic volume in cellular networks [30].

WiFi smartphone usage: Some studies focused on WiFi smartphone usage in campus networks [26, 22, 8], city-level networks [1], or networks in public transportations [24]. They argued that typical applications of such WiFi networks were HTTP, more specifically video, social networking, and software updates. In addition, the deployment of WiFi APs and their interference are discussed [2].

Throughput/delay performance of WiFi and 3G/LTE networks: Several performance metrics have been compared using vehicle-based [4, 20, 12] and speedtest-based [45] measurements. They showed that the throughput and delay performance of WiFi networks are basically better than those of cellular networks, and they are also highly variable depending on the environment, different from broadband wired access. Furthermore, in the context of traffic offloading, some studies evaluated the performance gain of WiFi offloading on the basis of WiFi APs discovered using vehicle based measurements [31, 23].

WiFi networks: Home WiFi usage has been analyzed in detail [33, 39, 13, 14]. An earlier report pointed out a low percentage of traffic volume from mobile devices at home in 2009 [33]. Also, the performance [40, 46], the traffic ratio [33], and the availability [13, 14] of home WiFi networks have been intensively studied. A large analysis of ESSIDs focused on the social relationships of users [5]. A recent large-scale survey of WiFi networks revealed application usage and channel interference in the wild [6].

The main difference between our work and others is to provide a comprehensive view of smartphone usage in cellular and WiFi networks from measurements with over 1500 users, for better understanding the adoption of smartphone users to avaialble WiFi networks. We previously explained the preliminary results of WiFi traffic offloading performance based on a two-day measurement with 450 Android users [18]. However, the measurement period was short and the available information was limited mainly to traffic volume without application and geographical information. For the current study, we analyzed three 15-day-long detailed datasets and provided more comprehensive results including the differences regarding device OS, location, and applications.

6. CONCLUDING REMARKS

We measured WiFi and 3G/LTE smartphone usage from more than 1500 Android/iOS smartphone users in the Greater Tokyo area for two weeks each in 2013, 2014, and 2015. Our results showed that smartphone users select WiFi and cellular networks based on several tradeoffs. In particular, we highlighted slow but clear adoption of available WiFi environment at home, in offices, and in public spaces. Light users have been offloading their traffic to WiFi networks, while heavy hitters totally rely on WiFi networks for their traffic offload. Moreover, we confirmed that wide deployment of WiFi APs enables users to obtain more opportunities to offload their traffic to WiFi networks. Users who have access to public WiFi send more traffic, and WiFi-availability results in heavier use of video and is required for large software updates. This adoption indicates that users recognize public WiFi networks as a part of the common network infrastructure.

Acknowledgments

We thank our shepherd Dina Papagiannaki, the IMC reviewers, Kenjiro Cho, Romain Fontugne, John Heidemann, Johan Mazel, and João Taveira Araújo for their valuable comments, and the Ministry of Internal Affairs and Communications, Japan for its support.

7. REFERENCES

[1] M. Afanasyev, T. Chen, G. M. Voelker, and A. C. Snoeren. Analysis of a mixed-use urban WiFi network: When metropolitan becomes neapolitan. In *IMC'08*, pages 85–98, Vouliagmeni, Greece, Oct 2008.

[2] A. Akella, G. Judd, S. Seshan, and P. Steenkiste. Self-management in chaotic wireless deployments. In *MobiCom'05*, pages 185–199, Cologne, Germany, Aug 2005.

[3] M. Balakrishnan, I. Mohomed, and V. Ramasubramanian. Where's that phone?: Geolocating IP addresses on 3G networks. In *IMC'09*, pages 294–300, Chicago, IL, Nov 2009.

[4] A. Balasubramanian, R. Mahajan, and A. Venkataramani. Augmenting mobile 3G using WiFi. In *MobiSys'10*, pages 209–222, San Francisco, CA, Jun 2010.

[5] M. V. Barbera, A. Epasto, A. Mei, V. C. Perta, and J. Stefa. Signals from the crowd: Uncovering social relationships through smartphone probes. In *IMC'13*, pages 265–276, Barcelona, Spain, Oct 2013.

[6] S. Biswas, J. Bicket, E. Wong, R. Musaloiu-E, A. Bhartia, and D. Aguayo. Large-scale measurements of wireless network behavior. In *SIGCOMM'15*, pages 153–165, London, UK, Aug 2015.

[7] X. Chen, N. Ding, A. Jindal, Y. Hu, M. Gupta, and R. Vannithamby. Smartphone energy drain in the wild: Analysis and implications. In *SIGMETRICS'15*, pages 151–164, Portland, OR, Jun 2015.

[8] X. Chen, R. Jin, K. Suh, B. Wang, and W. Wei. Network performance of smart mobile handhelds in a university campus WiFi network. In *IMC'12*, pages 315–328, Boston, MA, 2013.

[9] K. Cho. Broadband traffic report. In *Internet Infrastructure Review*, volume 28, pages 28–33. Internet Initiative Japan, Aug 2015.

[10] K. Cho, K. Fukuda, H. Esaki, and A. Kato. Observing slow crustal movement in residential user traffic. In *CoNEXT'08*, page p.12, Madrid, Spain, Dec 2008.

[11] Cisco. Cisco visual networking index. http://www.cisco.com/c/en/us/solutions/collateral/service-provider/visual-networking-index-vni/white_paper_c11-520862.html.

[12] P. Deshpande, X. Hou, and S. R. Das. Performance comparison of 3G and metro-scale WiFi for vehicular network access. In *IMC'10*, pages 301–307, Melbourne, Australia, Nov 2010.

[13] L. DiCioccio, R. Teixeira, and C. Rosenberg. Characterizing home networks with homenet profiler. Technical report, Technicolor Technical Report CR-PRL-2011-09-0001, 2011.

[14] L. DiCioccio, R. Teixeira, and C. Rosenberg. Measuring home networks with homenet profiler. In *PAM'13*, pages 176–186, Hong Kong, China, Mar 2013.

[15] N. Ding, D. Wagner, X. Chen, A. Pathak, Y. Hu, and A. Rice. Characterizing and modeling the impact of wireless signal strength on smartphone battery drain. In *SIGMETRICS'13*, pages 29–40, Pittsburgh, PA, Jun 2013.

[16] H. Falaki, R. Mahajan, S. Kandula, D. Lymberopoulos, R. Govindan, and D. Estrin. Diversity in smartphone usage. In *MobiSys'10*, pages 179–194, San Francisco, CA, Jun 2010.

[17] P. Fiadino, M. Schiavone, and P. Casas. Vivisecting whatsapp in cellular netoworks: Servers, flows, and quality of experience. In *TMA'15*, pages 49–63, Barcelona, Spain, Apr 2015.

[18] K. Fukuda and K. Nagami. A measurement of mobile traffic offloading. In *PAM'13*, pages 73–82, Hong Kong, China, Mar 2013.

[19] Z. Gao, A. Venkataramani, J. F. Kurose, and S. Heimlicher. Towards a quantitative comparison of location-independent network architectures. In *SIGCOMM'14*, pages 259–270, Chicago, IL, Aug 2014.

[20] R. Gass and C. Diot. An experimental performance comparison of 3G and Wi-Fi. In *PAM'10*, pages 71–80, Zurich, Switzerland, Apr 2010.

[21] A. Gember, A. Akella, J. Pang, A. Varshavsky, and R. Caceres. Obtaining in-context measurements of cellular network performance. In *IMC'12*, pages 287–317, Boston, MA, Nov 2013.

[22] A. Gember, A. Anand, and A. Akella. A comparative study of handheld and non-handheld traffic in campus Wi-Fi networks. In *PAM'11*, pages 173–183, Mar 2011.

[23] B. Han, P. Hui, V. A. Kumar, M. V. Marathe, G. Pei, and A. Srinivasan. Cellular traffic offloading through opportunistic communications: A case study. In *CHANTS'10*, pages 31–38, Chicago IL, Sep 2010.

[24] J. Hare, L. Hartung, and S. Banerjee. Beyond deployments and testbeds: Experiences with public usage on vehicular WiFi hotspots. In *MobiSys'12*, pages 393–405, Low Wood Bay, UK, Jun 2012.

[25] H. Haverinen and J. Salowey. EAP-SIM Authentication. RFC4186, Jan 2006.

[26] T. Henderson, D. Kotz, and I. Abyzov. The changing usage of a mature campus-wide wireless network. In *MobiCom'04*, pages 187–201, Philadelphia, PA, 2004.

[27] J. Huang, F. Qian, Y. Guo, Y. Zhou, Q. Xu, Z. M. Mao, S. Sen, and O. Spatscheck. An In-depth study of LTE: Effect of network protocol and application behavior on performance. In *SIGCOMM'13*, pages 363–374, Hong Kong, China, Aug 2013.

[28] J. Huang, Q. Xu, B. Tiwana, Z. M. Mao, M. Zhang, and P. Bahl. Anatomizing application performance differences on smartphones. In *MobiSys'10*, pages 165–178, San Francisco, CA, Jun 2010.

[29] K. Jang, M. Han, S. Cho, H.-K. Ryu, J. Lee, Y. Lee, and S. Moon. 3G and 3.5G wireless network performance measured from moving cars and high-speed trains. In *MICNET'09*, pages 19–24, Beijing, China, Oct 2009.

[30] C. Joe-Wong, S. Ha, S. Sen, and M. Chiang. Do mobile data plans affect usage? results from a pricing trial with isp customers. In *PAM'15*, pages 96–108, New York, NY, Mar 2015.

[31] K. Lee, I. Rhee, J. Lee, S. Chong, and Y. Yi. Mobile data offloading: How much can WiFi deliver? In *CoNEXT'10*, page 12, Philadelphia, PA, Dec 2010.

[32] X. Liu, A. Sridharan, S. Machiraju, M. Seshadri, and H. Zang. Experiences in a 3G network: interplay between the wireless channel and applications. In *MobiCom'08*, pages 211–222, San Francisco, CA, Sep 2008.

[33] G. Maier, F. Schneider, and A. Feldmann. A first look at mobile hand-held device traffic. In *PAM'10*, pages 161–170, Zurich, Switzerland, Apr 2010.

[34] Ministry of Internal Affairs and Communications. Information and communications statistics database. http://www.soumu.go.jp/johotsusintokei/field/tsuushin06.html.

[35] Ministry of Internal Affiars and Communications. SAQ^2 Japan Project: Action Plan for Establishing ICT Use Environment for Foreign Tourists. http://www.soumu.go.jp/main_content/000306547.pdf, 2014.

[36] S. Miskovic, G. M. Lee, Y. Liao, and M. Baldi. AppPrint: automatic fingerprinting of mobile applications in network traffic. In *PAM'15*, pages 57–69, New York, NY, Mar 2015.

[37] A. Nikravesh, D. R. Choffnes, E. Katz-Bassett, Z. M. Mao, and M. Welsh. Mobile network performance from user devices: A longitudinal, multidimensional analysis. In *PAM'14*, pages 12–22, Mar 2014.

[38] Ofcom. Study on the use of Wi-Fi for metropolitan area applications. http://stakeholders.ofcom.org.uk/market-data-research/other/technology-research/2013/wifi-met-area/, 2013.

[39] K. Papagiannaki, M. Yarvis, and W. S. Conner. Experimental characterization of home wireless networks and design implications. In *INFOCOM'06*, page 13, Barcelona, Spain, Apr 2006.

[40] A. Patro, S. Govindan, and S. Banerjee. Observing home wireless experience through wifi aps. In *MobiCom'13*, pages 339–350, Miami, FL, Sep 2013.

[41] M. Rodrig, C. Reis, R. Mahajan, D. Wetherall, and J. Zahorjan. Measurement-based characterization of 802.11 in a hotspot setting. In *E-WIND'05*, pages 5–10, Philadelphia, PA, Aug 2005.

[42] P. Romirer-Maierhofer, M. Schiavone, and A. D'Alconzo. Device-specific traffic characterization for root cause analysis in cellular networks. In *TMA'15*, pages 49–63, Barcelona, Spain, Apr 2015.

[43] M. Z. Shafiq, L. Ji, A. X. Liu, J. Pang, S. Venkataraman, and J. Wang. A first look at cellular network performance during crowded events. In *SIGMETRICS'13*, pages 17–28, Pittsuburgh, PA, Jun 2013.

[44] M. Z. Shafiq, L. Ji, A. X. Liu, and J. Wang. Characterizing and modeling internet traffic dynamics of cellular devices. In *SIGMETRICS'11*, pages 305–316, San Jose, CA, Jun 2011.

[45] J. Sommers and P. Barford. Cell vs. WiFi: On the performance of metro area mobile connections. In *IMC'12*, pages 301–314, Boston, MA, Nov 2012.

[46] S. Sundaresan, N. Feamster, and R. Teixeira. Measuring the performance of user traffic in home wireless networks. In *PAM'15*, pages 305–317, New York, NY, Mar 2015.

[47] I. Trestian, S. Ranjan, A. Kuzmanovic, and A. Nucci. Measuring serendipity: Connecting people, locations and interests in a mobile 3G network. In *IMC'09*, pages 267–279, Chicago, IL, Nov 2009.

[48] S. Triukose, S. Ardon, A. Mahanti, and A. Seth. Geolocating IP addresses in cellular data networks. In *PAM'12*, pages 158–167, Vienna, Austria, 2012.

[49] N. Viennot, E. Garcia, and J. Nieh. A measurement study of google play. In *SIGMETRICS'14*, pages 221–233, Austin, TX, Jun 2014.

[50] X. Wei, L. Gomez, L. Neamtiu, and M. Faloutsos. Profiledroid: Multi-layer profiling of android applications. In *MobciCom'12*, page 12, Istanbul, Turkey, Aug 2012.

[51] Q. Xu, J. Erman, A. Gerber, Z. Mao, J. Pang, and S. Venkataraman. Identifying diverse usage behaviors of smartphone apps. In *IMC'11*, pages 329–344, Berlin, Germany, Nov 2011.

[52] Z. Zhu, G. Cao, R. Keralapura, and A. Nucci. Characterizing data services in a 3G network: Usage, mobility and access issues. In *ICC'11*, page 6, Kyoto, 2011.

Opportunities and Challenges in Crowdsourced Wardriving

Piotr Sapiezynski
Technical University of Denmark

Radu Gatej
University of Copenhagen

Alan Mislove
Northeastern University

Sune Lehmann
Technical University of Denmark

ABSTRACT

Knowing the physical location of a mobile device is crucial for a number of context-aware applications. This information is usually obtained using the Global Positioning System (GPS), or by calculating the position based on proximity of WiFi access points with known location (where the position of the access points is stored in a database at a central server). To date, most of the research regarding the creation of such a database has investigated datasets collected both artificially and over short periods of time (e.g., during a one-day drive around a city). In contrast, most in-use databases are collected by mobile devices automatically, and are maintained by large mobile OS providers.

As a result, the research community has a poor understanding of the challenges in creating and using large-scale WiFi localization databases. We address this situation using the deployment of over 800 mobile devices to real users over a 1.5 year period. Each device periodically records WiFi scans and its GPS coordinates, reporting the collected data to us. We identify a number of challenges in using such data to build a WiFi localization database (e.g., mobility of access points), and introduce techniques to mitigate them. We also explore the level of coverage needed to accurately estimate a user's location, showing that only a small subset of the database is needed to achieve high accuracy.

Categories and Subject Descriptors

H.4 [**Information Systems Applications**]: Miscellaneous

Keywords

wifi; wardriving; mobility; location

1. INTRODUCTION

Localization is an increasingly important trend on mobile devices today. Mobile applications use localization to provide users with accurate driving directions, recommendations for local points of interest (e.g., restaurants), and even as a form of authentication [10]. Determining a mobile device's location is typically accomplished in one of two ways: First, mobile devices can use various satellite-based systems (GPS, Galileo, or GLONASS). While most mobile devices today ship with dedicated GPS hardware, relying on GPS alone for determining location has a number of downsides: obtaining an initial GPS fix introduces non-negligible delay, and causes significant power consumption.

Second, mobile devices can use *WiFi localization*. In brief, WiFi localization works by having the mobile device listen for advertised WiFi networks (each WiFi access point periodically announces its unique identifier or *BSSID*, as well as the name of the network, referred to as *SSID*), and report that list to a central server. The server then computes the most likely location of the mobile device and returns the result. Thus, for WiFi localization to be effective, the server must have a pre-computed database of WiFi access points (APs) and their locations. Unfortunately, building such a database is time-consuming and expensive: the database must be comprehensive (covering many locations) and up-to-date (as new APs are deployed and existing ones move).

Originally, the aim of such databases was to enable indoor positioning through finger-printing [3, 9, 20] and later through RF-modeling [15, 5]. Most recent work on indoor localization achieves sub-meter accuracy by rotating the sensing device to simulate directional antennas [14]. As the APs became more wide spread it became possible to use them for outdoor localization as well. The databases were then created by manually going to different locations and recording the observed APs (often termed *wardriving*) [4, 18, 7, 11]. Today, however, these databases are often built by having dedicated software on the mobile devices collect and report data back both in indoor [21, 27] and outdoor [2, 19, 26] contexts. Therefore, creating such a database at scale is typically only the domain of mobile OS providers (e.g., Apple, Google) or dedicated companies (e.g., Skyhook Wireless).

As a result, the research community currently has a relatively poor understanding of large-scale WiFi localization databases. In this paper, we address this situation by providing insights into the challenges underlying the creation of such a database, and the trade-offs in using them. We first collect a data set based on a deployment of over 800 mobile phones to students at a university in Copenhagen, Denmark for over 1.5 years. These phones run a stock Android OS with custom collection software instrumented to gather GPS location and overheard WiFi APs.

Overall, we collect over 1.8M simultaneous measurements of WiFi APs and GPS location, and observe more than 1.3M

IMC'15, October 28–30, 2015, Tokyo, Japan.

ACM 978-1-4503-3848-6/15/10 ...$15.00.
DOI: http://dx.doi.org/10.1145/2815675.2815711.

unique WiFi APs. Many of the APs are only seen a small number of times, so we focus on the 376K APs that we observe at least five times. To the best of our knowledge, this represents the most comprehensive data set of this kind that has been examined in the research literature. Using this data set, we build a WiFi localization database for Copenhagen. We discuss and identify a number of key challenges and issues in doing so:

The scale of the dataset. Most existing studies were performed either in controlled environments or over a short time. Here, we show that the WiFi landscape is constantly changing, new access points are added and old ones are moved to new locations or retired.

Mobility. With increasing trend of mobile WiFi APs, such as MiFi devices, routers on buses and trains, and mobile phones which also serve as hotspots, we observe that discovering and filtering mobile APs presents a significant challenge. Failing to properly filter these can lead to gross errors when estimating a device's location.

Noisy data. Unsurprisingly, relying on commodity hardware introduces noise into the measurements of location, signal strength, and detectability of APs, which must be handled when inferring the location and mobility of APs.

We also explore using the database we build to estimate the locations of devices given a set of overheard APs. Specifically, we examine the trade off between the number of APs in the database and the estimation accuracy. We show that knowing the location of only a small fraction of all the APs (3.7%) is actually needed to locate users to within 15 meters 75% of time.

2. METHODS

We now describe the data we use to build our WiFi localization database.

Phone deployment. We use data collected by the Copenhagen Networks Study experiment [23]. In this experiment, students opt-in to receive a smartphone in exchange for agreeing to let us use to collect data (e.g., Bluetooth and WiFi scan results, location estimations, call and SMS metadata, etc). The students agree to use the device as their primary phone. The experiment has been reviewed and approved by the Danish Data Protection Agency, and participants are provided with a web interface where they can access and remove any of their collected data.

The data analyzed in this work covers a period from September 2013 through March 2015 and involves more than 800 students, with 300–600 participants active on any given day. Because of software failures and physical destruction some phones had to be replaced, and thus 1,000 devices were used in total. The primary focus of the Copenhagen Networks Study experiment is the study of human interactions, hence the setup was not explicitly optimized towards discovering the locations of APs. Nevertheless, we show in this paper that the WiFi scans and GPS data allow us to do so.

Data collection app. On the phones, we install an app based on the Funf framework [1]. It starts automatically when the phones boot, so the users do not need to take action to begin collecting and uploading data.

The app collects data both actively (it requests location and WiFi updates every 5 minutes) and opportunistically (whenever another app requests updates). In order to save the battery, most of the location data is obtained using the network and/or fused provider (i.e., an existing WiFi localization database). Since we intend to use the GPS measurements as ground truth, we focus only on the 10.5% of location readings that are provided by the GPS hardware.

As a consequence, while the median sampling period between GPS readings is 1 second, only 29% of per-user hourly bins have at least one GPS sample (i.e., we only know the GPS location of users in 29% of the hours, on average). This distribution is a consequence of apps like Google Maps that either use GPS data constantly or not at all.

Since we are studying WiFi localization databases, in the remainder of the paper we focus on the 1,794,473 GPS samples which happened within the same second[1] as a WiFi access point scan. According to our measurements, a single WiFi scan lasts approximately 500 ms and this time does not depend on the number of saved networks.

It is important to note that the securing the wireless network does not make it impossible to scan it: regardless of the encryption, each router broadcasts its unique identifier and the name of the network in clear text.[2]

Filtering data. In the 567 days of observations, our participants observed 7,203,471 unique APs, out of which 1,320,838 (18.3%) were scanned at least once in the same second as a GPS estimation. However, the majority of these APs were observed with a GPS estimation a very small number of times: 944,904 (71.5%) have less than five observations. Thus, in the remainder of the paper, we focus only on the 375,934 APs that were observed at least five times *together with* a GPS estimate in the same second to build our WiFi localization database.

3. BUILDING THE DATABASE

We now examine the collected data, with the goal of building a WiFi localization database.

3.1 Estimating the locations of APs

The primary challenge we face is estimating the positions of the APs, given our WiFi scan data. Intuitively, this seems straightforward, but AP mobility presents a number of challenges. In general, we expect APs to fall into one of three categories:

- **Static.** We expect that many APs are static and have a fixed location that does not change over the course of the experiment.
- **Moved.** Given that our data covers 1.5 years, some APs may remain static for long periods of time, but may be moved a small number times. For example, businesses may redeploy APs, and residents of Copenhagen may change apartments, taking their APs with them.

[1] Allowing for even a short time difference would introduce noise into the measurements. For example, a car driving within city speed limits moves at 14 m/s. Because of uneven and sparse sampling, it is not feasible to calculate the speed of the measuring device and discard the scans that were performed by phones in motion.

[2] We note that is possible to *hide* a network by disabling the access point's SSID broadcasts (though this provides little actual security [17]). Routers configured this way still broadcast their BSSID and are present in our dataset.

- **Mobile.** We also expect to see some APs that show no static behavior; these could include APs located on buses and trains, as well as MiFi devices and mobile phone hotspots.

We categorize APs into these three classes by *clustering* the observed WiFi scan data. Specifically, every time a GPS estimation happens in the same second as a WiFi scan, we add the latitude/longitude to the list of observations of each AP visible in the scan. We then categorize the APs as follows:

Static access points. We first compute the geometric median [16] of all locations associated with each AP; if "most" of the observations are "close" together, we then declare the AP to be static, and declare the geometric median to be the AP's location.[3]

However, selecting the right thresholds for "most" and "close" to use is more complex than it may seem, as it is difficult to determine the operating range of an AP. First, devices compliant with popular standards can be expected to have a range from 20 meters indoors (the 802.11 standard) to 250 meters outdoors (802.11n) [25]. We therefore set the radius for a static AP to be no more than 300 meters. Second, due to the complex nature of signal propagation, the range can be shortened or enlarged due to characteristics of the local environment (e.g. buildings, narrow corridors). Third, GPS devices are known to sometimes return erroneous readings [6]; to deal with these, we allow for up to 5% of locations associated with an AP to be in a bigger distance than 300 meters from the median position.

We classify the APs that satisfy this condition (95% of readings within 300 meters) as **static**, and find that 263,281 (70%) of the APs fall into this category.

Moved and mobile access points. We assume that the rest of the APs are either moved or mobile. To disambiguate the two cases, we repeat the clustering above but allow for *multiple* such clusters.

Specifically, we group any two locations within 600 meters (twice the radius) into the same cluster, and discard any clusters that have fewer than 5 measurements. If at least 95% of the points can be associated with one of the clusters, and the clusters can be cleanly separated in time, we categorize the AP is **moved**. We observe that 1,087 (0.3%) APs fall into this category. Otherwise, we categorize the AP as **mobile**. We observe that 111,566 (29.7%) APs fall into this category.

3.2 Classification evaluation

We now briefly evaluate our classification. As a sanity check, in Figure 1 we show the locations of all APs with the SSID of `dtu`, which is the SSID of APs installed at our university. The left panel shows the APs on a metro area scale; each group of APs is correctly placed at one of the university campuses and out-of-campus buildings. The right panel shows the APs around the main campus of the university. While this is not a definite confirmation of the accuracy of our approach, this example of 1,100 APs shows that we should not expect too many gross errors.

We evaluate our method of identifying the mobile APs by verifying the classification of APs that are nearly certainly

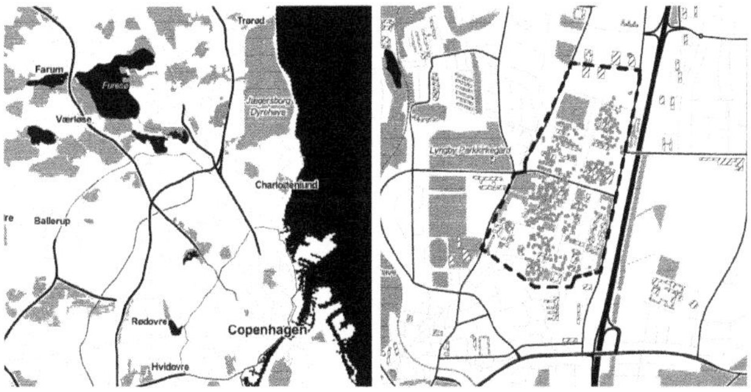

Figure 1: Sanity check of the method: estimated locations of APs belonging to Technical University of Denmark On the metro area scale (left panel), different campuses and out-of-campus buildings are visible, while none of the APs is estimated to be at a location not associated with the university. A detailed view of the main campus (right panel) reveals that the APs are grouped within perimeter.

static and those that are nearly certainly mobile. First, we choose APs with `eduroam` SSID as examples of APs which we expect to be stationary, since these are the names of APs at universities. Out of 3,654 such APs with at least 5 observations, 3,117 (85.3%) were identified as static and 9 (0.2%) as moved. Universities are known to relocate APs, which may partially explain why our accuracy is not 100%. Next, we choose APs with `Bedrebustur` or `Commutenet` SSIDs as examples of APs we expect to be mobile, since these are the official names of networks on buses and trains in Copenhagen. Out of 650 such APs with at least 5 observations, 642 (98.8%) were identified as mobile, and 8 (1.2%) as static.

It is important to note that access points with more observations are less likely to be classified as mobile (e.g., 29.7% of access points seen at least 5 times are classified as mobile, while only 10.0% of access points seen at least 200 times are classified as mobile). This effect is likely due to the the biased sampling of access points by users (i.e., static access points are more likely to be sampled many times, due to their static nature).

Overall, our results suggest that our AP classification methodology is likely to have high accuracy.

3.3 Accuracy of database

Next, we explore two aspects of the accuracy of the WiFi localization database: (1) how the number of measurements of a given AP affect our estimate of its location, and (2) how the number of measurements of a given AP affects our ability to classify it as mobile or fixed location.

Number of measurements needed. While we cannot measure the error of location estimation without knowing the ground truth location, we can analyze how the location estimation changes with the number of observations. We select 46,000 APs classified as static and with more than 50 measurements. For each of these APs we select N random observations, calculate the distance between the location of the AP estimated from all the observations and the estimation based on N random observations. We vary N from 1 to 50 and repeat the process 10 times.

In Figure 2 we show that even in case of APs with fixed location, using too few measurements leads to significant deviations in the estimated position. For example, calculating the position of the AP based on only two observations leads

[3]Following the definition of accuracy from the Android Location API, we calculate the radius around the median within which 68% of points are enclosed [8].

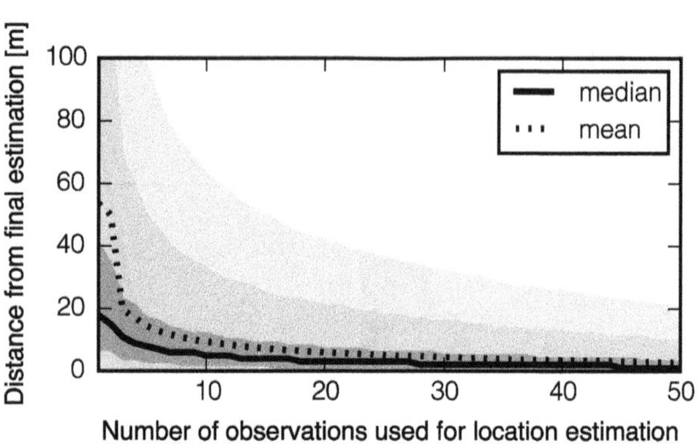

Figure 2: Too few observations lead to estimation errors. We randomly subsample the measurements of 40,000 static APs to measure the error caused by fewer measurements. The shaded bands represent percentiles 1-99, 5-95, and 25-75. To ensure estimation error below 50 meters in 99% cases, 15 observations are necessary. Five observations, which we use as minimal threshold, are enough to estimate the location of an AP with error not higher than 50 meters in 95% of cases.

to a 50 meter error, on average. 15 observations are necessary to ensure that the error is not larger than 50 meters in 99% of cases.

Mobility and sample size. Because of the prevalence of APs that are mobile, too few observations might lead to their incorrect classification as stationary. To evaluate this, we select 20,000 APs classified as mobile and more than 50 observations. For each of them we select N random observations and re-run our classification procedure. We vary N from 2 to 50 and repeat the process 10 times.

Because we only allow 5% of observations to be outside of the 300 meter radius around the median, with too few observations we might classify a fixed AP as mobile. We repeat the described experiment but with fixed APs and calculate the fraction of misclassified fixed location APs as a function of N.

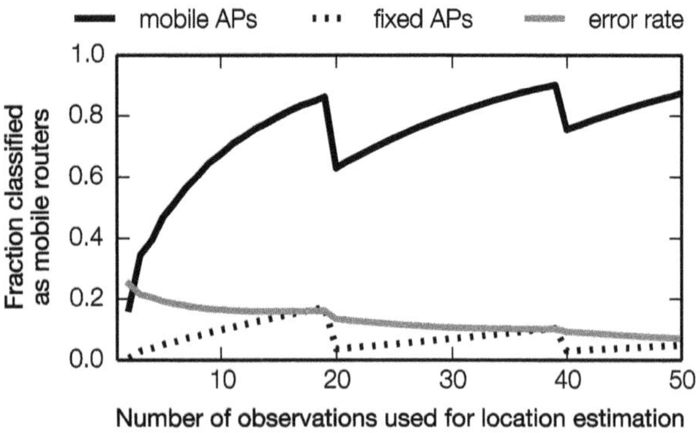

Figure 3: Too few observations lead to misclassifications between mobile and static APs. We randomly subsample the observations of 46,000 static APs and 20,000 mobile APs to measure the classification error caused by too few observations. With just 5 observations, 46% of mobile APs are classified as static and of 5% of static APs are misclassified as mobile. Given the class imbalance, that results in 18% misclassification rate.

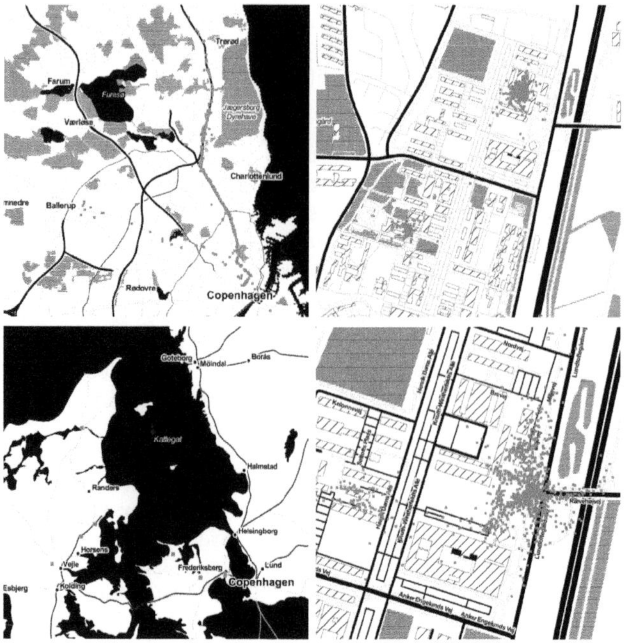

Figure 4: Longitudinal observations reveals mobile and moved APs. Shown are the observed locations of a mobile AP installed on a bus (top left), an moved AP (top right), an AP moved 6 times (bottom left), and an AP with ambiguous behavior (bottom right).

As we show in Figure 3, the more observations we base our estimations on, the more accurate the results are. The "spikes" at 20 and 40 APs are caused by the fact that the 5% noise threshold translates to 0 noisy samples with less than 20 observations, 1 noisy sample with 20-39 observations, etc.

Taken together, these results suggest that building an accurate WiFi localization database requires large amounts of data collected continuously over time. To better visualize the importance of longitudinal observation, we provide several examples of APs with different patterns of observation. The top left panel of Figure 4 shows a clear example of a mobile AP; in this case, it is installed in a bus. In such cases, a few observations should be sufficient to correctly classify the AP as mobile. In other cases however—as shown in top right and bottom left panels of Figure 4—a long observation period is beneficial. While in the top right example not knowing the new location of the AP would lead to errors at the range of hundreds of meters, the bottom left example shows an AP whose location changes hundreds of kilometers during the observation period. Still in some cases, even a long observation period might not be enough to determine the nature of the AP, as shown in the bottom right panel: the AP seems to have two major placements, but they overlap in time, so we classify this AP as mobile.

4. USING THE DATABASE

With our WiFi localization AP database built, we now turn to using the database to estimate the location of a user. In brief, when a user requests their location to be calculated, they present the database with (a) a list of the AP SSIDs and BSSIDs that it current observes, and (b) the received signal strength (RSSI) of each of these APs. We first explore

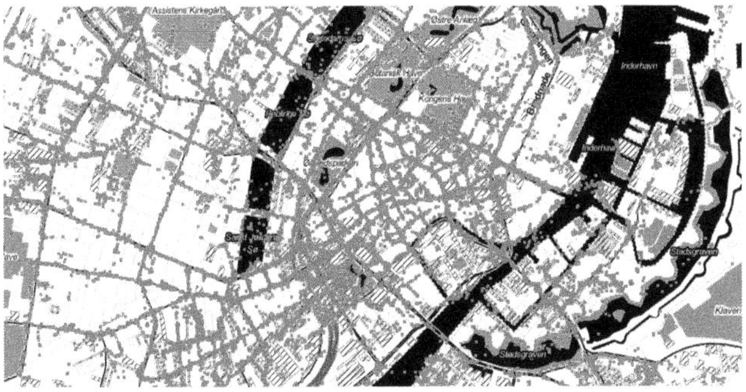

Figure 5: Using a population of students from one university results in uneven sampling. Each red point on the maps represents a single AP. The inferred locations of APs in the city center indicate that sampling is not uniform across space: the routers seem to be located along the streets, not inside the buildings.

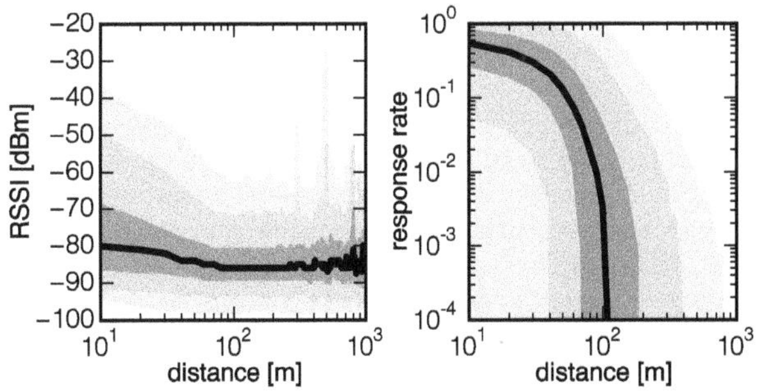

Figure 6: RSSI (left) and response rate (right) as functions of distance from the AP. The shaded bands represent percentiles 1-99, 5-95, and 25-75, the bold line represents the median value. There is a weak correlation between RSSI and distance with Spearman's correlation of $\rho = -0.23$ for distances from 0 to 100 meters, and no correlation for larger distances. There is a strong correlation between response rate and distance ($\rho = -0.64$) for distances from 0 to 100 meters, and a weaker ($\rho = -0.30$) correlation for larger distances. Using non-specialized hardware raises a number of challenges, including noisy measurements of RSSI and location. As a result, RSSI is not a reliable proxy for distance.

how the signal strength relates to the distance to AP before examining our ability to estimate the user's location.

4.1 Estimating distance from APs

RSSI. As radio waves propagate through space they become attenuated; the amount of attenuation can be used to calculate the distance d. There are a number of models describing the attenuation of WiFi signals and one of the simplest is the log-distance path loss (LDPL) model [12], from which the distance can be calculated using Equation 1:

$$d_{ij} = 10^{(\frac{P_i - p_{ij}}{10\gamma_i})} \quad (1)$$

In Equation 1 mobile user j is at distance d_{ij} (m) from access point i and sees the signal strength of p_{ij} (dBm). P_i is the power transmitted by the AP. The path loss exponent γ_i captures the rate of fall of RSSI around the AP i which depends on the environment the router is in [13]. If the transmitted power and path loss exponent are known, three non-collinear measurements of the AP should theoretically be enough to determine its position using trilateration.

However, accurately estimating the distance given RSSI has been shown to be a challenging problem. First, because the transmitted power and the propagation loss exponent are different for every router and need to be calculated, two more measurements are necessary to solve the system of LDPL equations. Second, since the receiver characteristics vary greatly even among devices of the same make and model [24, 9, 5], more measurements are necessary to compensate for individual characteristics [5]. Third, due to the inherent noise in the measurements and a dynamically changing environment (e.g., people walking by) the RSSI reading can be very noisy in practice. For example, our previous work observed that the RSSI reading can deviate as much as 10 dB from the mean even when the source and destination are static [22]. We note that while there are methods that take advantage of the variable attenuation introduced by a human body [28], they require accelerometer data to be collected as well (which we were unable to collect in our experiment).

Nevertheless, RSSI has been reported in other studies of war-driving as a useful, if somewhat noisy, proxy for distance [4]. To verify this finding, we randomly select 5.6M observations of 30,000 APs classified as static and present RSSI as function of distance from the inferred location in the left panel of Figure 6. There is only a weak correlation between the measured signal strength ($\rho = -0.23$) and the inferred location, and that correlation disappears for distances larger than 100 meters. The figure also reveals that a strong RSSI can be used as an indicator of close distance, but a weak RSSI does not indicate that the APs is far away. We use Spearman's rank correlation coefficient, instead of Pearson's product-moment correlation because we cannot expect a linear relationships between RSSI and distance. Pearson's ρ values are lower in the analyzed relationships.

The low correlation could still be caused by the differences between routers (the emitted power and the influence of obstacles). We therefore calculate the correlation between distance and RSSI for each router separately. We find that about 35% of the routers with at least 50 observations have statistically significant, negative relation between distance and RSSI with mean $\rho = -0.36$. On the other hand, 16% of such routers have a positive relation between the RSSI and distance, with mean $\rho = 0.32$. All reported correlations are statistically significant with $p_{val} < 0.01$.

Response rate. Here, we reevaluate the response rate as a proxy of distance from the AP, first suggested in [4]. Response rate at distance d is defined as the fraction of WiFi scans at distance d from the position of the AP which report finding the AP. We select a random subsample of 11,700 static APs with at least 50 observations. Then, for each AP, we find all scans recorded at distance d from its inferred location, varying the d from 0 to 1,000 meters. We define the response rate of a AP at distance d as a fraction of scans in which the AP was found. In the right panel of Figure 6 we show the correlation of distance and response rate. As expected, the response rate drops as the distance from the inferred location increases, with a much stronger correlation than RSSI ($\rho = -0.55$ for distances up to 100 meters). However, to measure the response rate, one must perform multiple scans at the same distance from the router.

4.2 Estimating the location of users

We now turn to estimating the locations of users using our database of the location of APs. Unfortunately, while response rate provides a much better correlation with AP distance, it is not ideal for estimating users locations: when estimating locations, doing so quickly is of paramount importance, and estimating response rate requires a number of scans. Thus, in the approach below, we simply use RSSI, and leave leveraging response rates to future work.

Knowing the list of APs recently observed, along with their RSSI, we explore estimating the user's location using four different approaches:

Mean coordinates. We ignore the RSSI and calculate the mean latitude and mean longitude among all the APs for which we know the location.

Geometric median. We ignore the RSSI and calculate the geometric median of the APs for which we know the location.

Mean weighted by RSSI. Each AP is assigned a weight based on the RSSI, with the weight defined by RSSI+100.[4]

We examine instances where different numbers of APs are observed in the scans, selecting 100 random instances between 0 and 30 observed APs. In the left panel of Figure 7, we show the cumulative error distributions for estimating the user's location using these three methods. The approach with geometric median location works best, followed closely by mean weighted by RSSI. While there are some differences in the performance of the three selected methods, they are negligible: all methods locate more than 50% of scans within 13 meters from the ground truth, 90% of scans within 70 meters, and 95% of scans within 120 meters.

In the right panel of Figure 7 we compare our best method (based on the geometric median) to the estimations which we acquired from the Google Geolocation API. We show the median error as a function of the number of APs used for the estimation. While our approach performs slightly better than Google's location API, the performance is similar. Google's crowd sourced data is collected using a wide variety of uncalibrated hardware (all of our phones are exactly the same model), which might lead to more measurement noise for Google's database. Since the number of APs in each scan is highly correlated with the population density [22], and the estimation errors are lower with more routers available, we expect that the location estimations will be best in densly populated areas.

4.3 Applicability of the localization database

In total, we identified 263,281 APs as static, constituting only 3.7% of the total of 7.2M unique APs observed. We revisit the original dataset with all the scans collected to verify whether this small set of APs can be used for localization in the broader context. We randomly select 51M of those scans and find that at least two of our static APs are visible in 73% of all scans, meaning we would provide an average error of 15 meters for 73% of all WiFi scans we observed.

The median error of 15 meters means that certain problems—such as car navigation—cannot be solved using WiFi signals alone. There are, however, a number of applications where the advantages outweigh the problems related to a relatively high positioning error. First, using geo-localized WiFi routers enables tracking the location of mobile devices with sub-minute time resolution at low costs in terms of battery or data consumption. As a consequence, it becomes possible to accurately measure for example time spent at each location, or detect whether the user changed their location in between two location scans pointing to the same place. Second, we show it is feasible to store a lookup database on the mobile devices themselves, thus enabling positioning without access to the Internet. Our database for the Greater Copenhagen area is only 9 MB, it could be a part of a mobile application targeted at tourists.

[4]The range of RSSI given by Android is -99dBm to 0dBm.

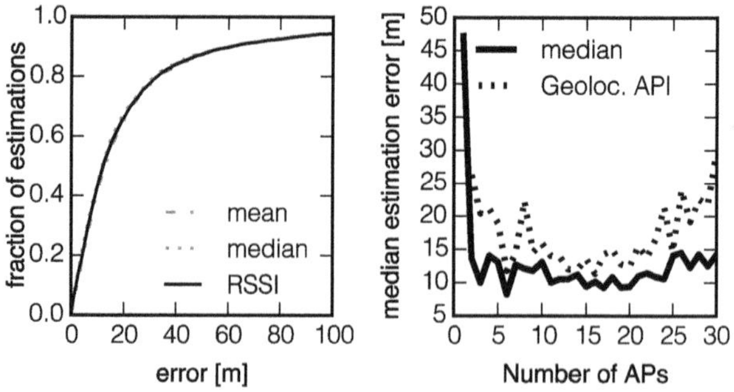

Figure 7: Location estimation accuracy does not strongly depend on the method. All methods perform similarly, and are able to locate 50% of scans with error no larger than 13 meters. Additionally, we compare our estimates to the results from the Google Geolocation API in the right panel; while our approach performs better, the differences are small.

5. SUMMARY

Being able to quickly and efficiently determine the location of a mobile device is becoming increasingly important. While mobile devices often contain dedicated GPS hardware to do so, they often opt to instead rely on WiFi localization databases as they are much quicker and more power-efficient. However, building such a database requires access to large-scale WiFi scan data over time, and is typically only available to the large mobile OS vendors.

In this work, we explored the opportunities and challenges in building such a database using a deployment of over 800 mobile devices. We found that mobility of *access points* was a key challenge in ensuring that the database is accurate; a significant fraction (30%) of APs are actually non-static. However, we found that using just the APs that we are confident are static, we can provide a location estimate for 73% of *all* scans with a median accuracy of 15 meters. Overall, our results provide the largest-scale look at WiFi localization databases that we know of in the research community.

Acknowledgements

We thank the anonymous reviewers for their helpful comments. This research was supported in part by NSF grants CNS-1054233, CNS-1319019, and CNS-1421444. All map tiles used in the article are by Stamen under CC BY 3.0. Map data by OpenStreetMap under CC BY SA.

6. REFERENCES

[1] N. Aharony, W. Pan, C. Ip, I. Khayal, and A. Pentland. Social fMRI: Investigating and shaping social mechanisms in the real world. *Pervasive and Mobile Computing*, 7(6):643–659, Dec. 2011.

[2] Apple. Apple Q&A on Location Data. http://goo.gl/dkPCAZ.

[3] P. Bahl and V. N. Padmanabhan. RADAR: An in-building RF-based user location and tracking system. In *INFOCOM 2000. Nineteenth Annual Joint Conference of the IEEE Computer and Communications Societies. Proceedings. IEEE*, volume 2, pages 775–784. Ieee, 2000.

[4] Y.-C. Cheng, Y. Chawathe, A. LaMarca, and J. Krumm. Accuracy Characterization for Metropolitan-scale Wi-Fi Localization. In *Proceedings of the 3rd International Conference on Mobile Systems, Applications, and Services*, MobiSys '05, pages 233–245, New York, NY, USA, 2005. ACM.

[5] K. Chintalapudi, A. Padmanabha Iyer, and V. N. Padmanabhan. Indoor localization without the pain. In *Proceedings of the sixteenth annual international conference on Mobile computing and networking*, pages 173–184. ACM, 2010.

[6] S. Duncan, T. I. Stewart, M. Oliver, S. Mavoa, D. MacRae, H. M. Badland, and M. J. Duncan. Portable global positioning system receivers: static validity and environmental conditions. *American journal of preventive medicine*, 44(2):e19–e29, 2013.

[7] A. Eustace. WiFi data collection: An update. http://goo.gl/VFJ9mM.

[8] Google. Android Developer Reference: Location. http://goo.gl/21VB7P.

[9] A. Haeberlen, E. Flannery, A. M. Ladd, A. Rudys, D. S. Wallach, and L. E. Kavraki. Practical robust localization over large-scale 802.11 wireless networks. In *Proceedings of the 10th Annual International Conference on Mobile Computing and Networking*, MobiCom '04, pages 70–84, New York, NY, USA, 2004. ACM.

[10] A. Hammad and P. Faith. Location based authentication, Oct. 24 2008. US Patent App. 12/258,322.

[11] D. Han, D. G. Andersen, M. Kaminsky, K. Papagiannaki, and S. Seshan. Access point localization using local signal strength gradient. In *Passive and Active Network Measurement*, pages 99–108. Springer, 2009.

[12] M. Hata. Empirical formula for propagation loss in land mobile radio services. *Vehicular Technology, IEEE Transactions on*, 29(3):317–325, 1980.

[13] M. Hidayab, A. H. Ali, and K. B. A. Azmi. Wifi signal propagation at 2.4 GHz. In *Microwave Conference, 2009. APMC 2009. Asia Pacific*, pages 528–531. IEEE, 2009.

[14] S. Kumar, S. Gil, D. Katabi, and D. Rus. Accurate indoor localization with zero start-up cost. In *Proceedings of the 20th annual international conference on Mobile computing and networking*, pages 483–494. ACM, 2014.

[15] H. Lim, L.-C. Kung, J. C. Hou, and H. Luo. Zero-configuration, robust indoor localization: Theory and experimentation. In *Proceedings of the 25th IEEE International Conference on Computer Communications (INFOCOM'06)*, 2006.

[16] J.-H. Lin and J. S. Vitter. Approximation algorithms for geometric median problems. *Information Processing Letters*, 44(5):245–249, 1992.

[17] J. Lindqvist, T. Aura, G. Danezis, T. Koponen, A. Myllyniemi, J. Mäki, and M. Roe. Privacy-preserving 802.11 access-point discovery. In *Proceedings of the second ACM conference on Wireless Network Security (WiSec'09)*, 2009.

[18] B. Meyerson. Aol introduces location plug-in for instant messaging so users can see where buddies are. http://goo.gl/2W1uYh.

[19] Microsoft. Location and my privacy faq. http://goo.gl/vvaZwZ.

[20] N. B. Priyantha, A. Chakraborty, and H. Balakrishnan. The cricket location-support system. In *Proceedings of the 6th annual international conference on Mobile computing and networking*, pages 32–43. ACM, 2000.

[21] A. Rai, K. K. Chintalapudi, V. N. Padmanabhan, and R. Sen. Zee: Zero-effort crowdsourcing for indoor localization. In *Proceedings of the 18th annual international conference on Mobile computing and networking*, pages 293–304. ACM, 2012.

[22] P. Sapiezynski, A. Stopczynski, R. Gatej, and S. Lehmann. Tracking Human Mobility Using WiFi Signals. *PLoS ONE*, 10(7), 07 2015.

[23] A. Stopczynski, V. Sekara, P. Sapiezynski, A. Cuttone, M. M. Madsen, J. E. Larsen, and S. Lehmann. Measuring large-scale social networks with high resolution. *PLoS ONE*, 9(4), 04 2014.

[24] P. Tao, A. Rudys, A. M. Ladd, and D. S. Wallach. Wireless LAN Location-sensing for Security Applications. In *Proceedings of the 2nd ACM Workshop on Wireless Security*, WiSe '03, pages 11–20, New York, NY, USA, 2003. ACM.

[25] Wikipedia. Ieee 802.11. http://goo.gl/molLPd.

[26] D. Wu, Q. Liu, Y. Zhang, J. McCann, A. Regan, and N. Venkatasubramanian. CrowdWiFi: efficient crowdsensing of roadside WiFi networks. In *Proceedings of the 15th International Middleware Conference*, pages 229–240. ACM, 2014.

[27] S. Yang, P. Dessai, M. Verma, and M. Gerla. Freeloc: Calibration-free crowdsourced indoor localization. In *INFOCOM, 2013 Proceedings IEEE*, pages 2481–2489. IEEE, 2013.

[28] Z. Zhang, X. Zhou, W. Zhang, Y. Zhang, G. Wang, B. Y. Zhao, and H. Zheng. I am the antenna: Accurate outdoor AP location using smartphones. In *Proceedings of the 17th annual international conference on Mobile computing and networking*, pages 109–120. ACM, 2011.

MoonGen: A Scriptable High-Speed Packet Generator

Paul Emmerich, Sebastian Gallenmüller, Daniel Raumer, Florian Wohlfart, and Georg Carle
Technische Universität München
Department of Computer Science
Chair for Network Architectures and Services
{emmericp|gallenmu|raumer|wohlfart|carle}@net.in.tum.de

ABSTRACT

We present MoonGen, a flexible high-speed packet generator. It can saturate 10 GbE links with minimum-sized packets while using only a single CPU core by running on top of the packet processing framework DPDK. Linear multi-core scaling allows for even higher rates: We have tested MoonGen with up to 178.5 Mpps at 120 Gbit/s. Moving the whole packet generation logic into user-controlled Lua scripts allows us to achieve the highest possible flexibility. In addition, we utilize hardware features of commodity NICs that have not been used for packet generators previously. A key feature is the measurement of latency with sub-microsecond precision and accuracy by using hardware timestamping capabilities of modern commodity NICs. We address timing issues with software-based packet generators and apply methods to mitigate them with both hardware support and with a novel method to control the inter-packet gap in software. Features that were previously only possible with hardware-based solutions are now provided by MoonGen on commodity hardware. MoonGen is available as free software under the MIT license in our git repository at `https://github.com/emmericp/MoonGen`.

Categories and Subject Descriptors

C.4 [**Performance of Systems**]: Measurement techniques

Keywords

Packet generation; User space networking; Lua; DPDK

1. INTRODUCTION

Tools for traffic generation are essential to quantitative evaluations of network performance. Hardware-based solutions for packet generation are expensive and in many cases inflexible. Existing software solutions often lack performance or flexibility and come with precision problems [2].

The state of the art in packet generation, discussed further in Section 2, motivated us to design MoonGen. Our novel software packet generator is flexible, fast, and precise without relying on special-purpose hardware. Moving the packet generation logic into user-controlled Lua scripts ensures flexibility. We build on the JIT compiler LuaJIT [20] and the packet processing framework DPDK [14]. Our architecture and its implementation are described in detail in Section 3. This combination allows us to send 14.88 Mpps, line rate at 10 GbE with minimum-sized packets, from a single CPU core while executing script code for each packet. Explicit support for multi-core architectures allows us to load multiple 10 GbE interfaces simultaneously: We have tested MoonGen with 178.5 Mpps, line rate at 120 Gbit/s using twelve 2 GHz CPU cores.

MoonGen is controlled through its API instead of configuration files. We explain the interface in Section 4 by presenting code examples for typical use cases. The API allows for applications beyond packet generation as it makes DPDK packet processing facilities available to Lua scripts. Section 5 evaluates the performance of our approach. We show that running Lua code for each packet is feasible and can even be faster than an implementation written in C.

Our packet generator can also receive packets and measure round-trip latencies with sub-microsecond precision and accuracy. We achieve this by using hardware features of Intel commodity NICs that are intended for clock synchronization across networks. Section 6 features a detailed evaluation.

Section 7 investigates different methods for rate limiting on NICs. It focuses on established methods for traffic rate limiting by controlling the inter-departure times of packets based on either software mechanisms or explicit hardware features on modern NICs. Aiming for a more generic and more powerful approach to traffic limiting, Section 8 proposes a new mechanism introduced by MoonGen. This solution allows generating complex traffic patterns without additional hardware support.

MoonGen is available as free software under the MIT license [5]. Section 9 describes how to use the published code to reproduce all experiments in this paper.

IMC'15, October 28–30, 2015, Tokyo, Japan.

DOI: http://dx.doi.org/10.1145/2815675.2815692.

2. STATE OF THE ART

Packet generators face a tradeoff between complexity and performance. This is reflected in the available packet generators: Barebone high-speed packet generators with limited capabilities on the one hand and feature-rich packet generators that do not scale to high data rates on the other hand. While high-speed packet generators often only send out pre-crafted Ethernet frames (e.g., pcap files), more advanced packet generators are able to transmit complex load patterns by implementing and responding to higher-layer protocols (e.g., web server load tester). Consequently, there is a lack of fast *and* flexible packet generators. Besides mere traffic generation, many packet generators also offer the possibility to capture incoming traffic and relate the generated to the received traffic.

The traditional approach to measure the performance of network devices uses hardware solutions to achieve high packet rates and high accuracy [2]. Especially their ability to accurately control the sending rate and precise timestamping are important in these scenarios. Common hardware packet generators manufactured by IXIA, Spirent, or XENA are tailored to special use cases such as performing RFC 2544 compliant device tests [3]. They send predefined traces of higher-layer protocols, but avoid complex hardware implementations of protocols. Therefore, these hardware appliances are on the fast-but-simple end of the spectrum of packet generators. They are focused on well-defined and reproducible performance tests for comparison of networking devices via synthetic traffic. However, the high costs severely limit their usage [2].

NetFPGA is an open source FPGA-based NIC that can be used as a packet generator [17]. Although costs are still beyond commodity hardware costs, it is used more often in academic publications. For example, in 2009, Covington et al. [4] described an open-source traffic generator based on NetFPGA with highly accurate inter-packet delays. The OFLOPS framework by Rotsos et al. [24] is able to measure latencies with nanosecond accuracy via a NetFPGA.

Software packet generators running on commodity hardware are widespread for different use cases. Especially traffic generators that emulate realistic traffic, e.g., Harpoon [26], suffer from poor performance on modern 10 GbE links. We focus on high-speed traffic generators that are able to saturate 10 GbE links with minimum-sized packets, i.e., achieve a rate of 14.88 Mpps. Bonelli et al. [1] implement a software traffic generator, which is able to send 12 Mpps by using multiple CPU cores. Software packet generators often rely on frameworks for efficient packet transmission [18, 23, 14] to increase the performance further to the line rate limit. Less complex packet generators can be found as example applications for high-speed packet IO frameworks: zsend for PF_RING ZC [18] and pktgen for netmap [23]. Wind River Systems provides Pktgen-DPDK [27] for DPDK [14]. Pktgen-DPDK features a Lua scripting API that can be used to control the parameters of the generator, but the scripts cannot modify the packets themselves. Further, existing tools for packet generation like Ostinato have been ported to DPDK to improve their performance [19]. Previous studies showed that software solutions are not able to precisely control the inter-packet delays [2, 4]. This leads to micro-bursts and jitter, a fact that impacts the reproducibility and validity of tests that rely on a precise definition of the generated traffic.

Ostinato is the most flexible software packet solution of the investigated options as it features configuration through Python scripts while using DPDK for high-speed packet IO. However, its scripting API is limited to the configuration of predefined settings, the scripts cannot be executed for each packet. Precise timestamping and rate control are also not supported. [19]

One has to make a choice between flexibility (software packet generators) and precision (hardware packet generators) with the available options. Today different measurement setups therefore require different packet generators. For example, precise latency measurements currently require hardware solutions. Complex packet generation (e.g., testing advanced features of network middleboxes like firewalls) requires flexible software solutions. We present a hybrid solution with the goal to be usable in all scenarios.

3. IMPLEMENTATION

We identified the following requirements based on our goal to close the gap between software and hardware solutions by combining the advantages of both. MoonGen must...

(R1) ...be implemented in software and run on commodity hardware.

(R2) ...be able to saturate multiple 10 GbE links with minimum-sized packets.

(R3) ...be as flexible as possible.

(R4) ...offer precise and accurate timestamping and rate control.

The following building blocks were chosen based on these requirements.

3.1 Packet Processing with DPDK

Network stacks of operating systems come with a high overhead [23]. We found the performance too low to fulfill requirement (R2). Packet IO frameworks like DPDK [14], PF_RING ZC [18], and netmap [23] circumvent the network stack and provide user space applications exclusive direct access to the DMA buffers to speed up packet processing. All of them have been used to implement packet generators that fulfill requirement (R2) [18, 23, 27]. We have investigated the performance of these frameworks in previous work [6] and found that DPDK and PF_RING ZC are slightly faster than netmap.

We chose DPDK for MoonGen as it supports a wide range of NICs by multiple vendors (Intel, Emulex, Mellanox, and Cisco), is well-documented, fast, and available under the BSD license [14]. PF_RING ZC was not considered further as some parts of this framework, which are needed for high-speed operation, require purchasing a license. In netmap, user space applications do not have access to the NIC's registers. This is a safety precaution as a misconfigured NIC can crash the whole system by corrupting memory [23]. This restriction in netmap is critical as it is designed to be part of an operating system: netmap is already in the FreeBSD kernel [22]. However, MoonGen needs to access NIC registers directly to implement requirement (R4).

3.2 Scripting with LuaJIT

MoonGen must be as flexible as possible (R3). Therefore, we move the whole packet generation logic into user-defined scripts as this ensures the maximum possible flexibility. LuaJIT was selected because related work shows that it is suitable for high-speed packet processing tasks [7] at high packet rates (R2). Its fast and simple foreign function interface allows for an easy integration of C libraries like DPDK [20].

LuaJIT may introduce unpredictable pause times due to garbage collection and compilation of code during run time.

This can lead to exhausted receive queues or starving transmission queues. Pause times introduced by the JIT compiler are in the range of "a couple of microseconds" [21]. The garbage collector (GC) works in incremental steps, the pause times depend on the usage. All packet buffers are handled by DPDK and are invisible to the GC. A typical transmit loop does not allocate new objects in Lua, so the GC can even be disabled for most experiments.

Pause times are handled by the NIC buffers: The currently supported NICs feature buffer sizes in the order of hundreds of kilobytes [11, 12, 13]. For example, the smallest buffer on the X540 chip is the 160 kB transmit buffer, which can store 128 μs of data at 10 GbE. This effectively conceals short pause times. These buffer sizes were sufficient for all of our test cases.

3.3 Hardware Architecture

Understanding how the underlying hardware works is important for the design of a high-speed packet generator. The typical operating system socket API hides important aspects of networking hardware that are crucial for the design of low-level packet processing tools.

A central feature of modern commodity NICs is support for multi-core CPUs. Each NIC supported by DPDK features multiple receive and transmit queues per network interface. This is not visible from the socket API of the operating system as it is handled by the driver [10]. For example, both the X540 and 82599 10 GbE NICs support 128 receive and transmit queues. Such a queue is essentially a virtual interface and they can be used independently from each other. [12, 13]

Multiple transmit queues allow for perfect multi-core scaling of packet generation. Each configured queue can be assigned to a single CPU core in a multi-core packet generator. Receive queues are also statically assigned to threads and the incoming traffic is distributed via configurable filters (e.g., Intel Flow Director) or hashing on protocol headers (e.g., Receive Side Scaling). [12, 13] Commodity NICs also often support timestamping and rate control in hardware. This allows us to fulfill (R1) without violating (R4).

MoonGen does not run on arbitrary commodity hardware, we are restricted to hardware that is supported by DPDK [14] and that offers support for these features. We currently support hardware features on Intel 82599, X540, and 82580 chips. Other NICs that are supported by DPDK but not yet explicitly by MoonGen can also be used, but without hardware timestamping and rate control.

3.4 Software Architecture

MoonGen's core is a Lua wrapper for DPDK that provides utility functions required by a packet generator. The MoonGen API comes with functions that configure the underlying hardware features like timestamping and rate control. About 80% of the current code base is written in Lua, the remainder in C and C++. Although our current focus is on packet generation, MoonGen can also be used for arbitrary packet processing tasks.

Figure 1 shows the architecture of MoonGen. It runs a user-provided script, the *userscript*, on start-up. This script contains the main loop and the packet generation logic.

The userscript will be executed in the *master task* initially by calling the *master* function provided by the script. This master function must initialize the used NICs, i.e., configure the number of hardware queues, buffer sizes and filters for received traffic. It can then spawn new instances of itself running in *slave tasks* and pass arguments to them. A slave task runs a specified *slave* function. It usually receives a hardware queue as an argument and then transmits or receives packets via this queue. Starting a new slave task spawns a completely new and independent LuaJIT VM that is pinned to a CPU core. Tasks only share state through the underlying MoonGen library which offers inter-task communication facilities such as pipes. All functions related to packet transmission and reception in MoonGen and DPDK are lock-free to allow for multi-core scaling.

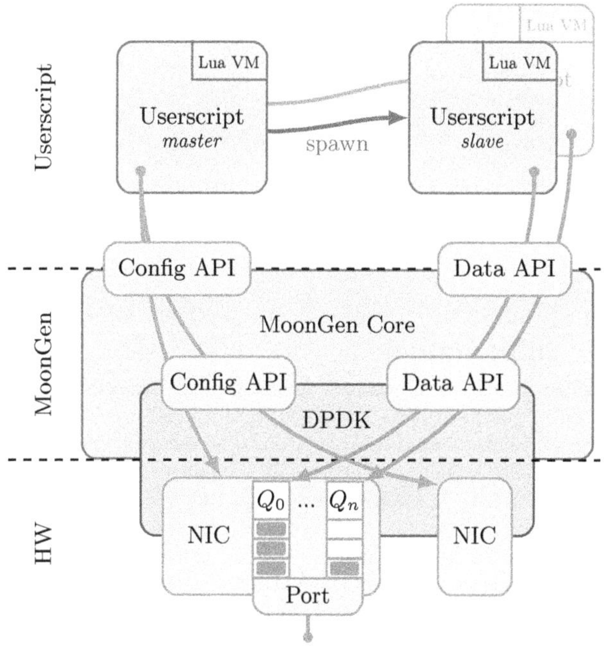

Figure 1: MoonGen's architecture

MoonGen comes with example scripts for generating load with IPv4, IPv6, IPsec, ICMP, UDP, and TCP packets, measuring latencies, measuring inter-arrival times, and generating different inter-departure times like a Poisson process and bursty traffic.

4. SCRIPTING API

Our example scripts in the git repository are designed to be self-explanatory exhaustive examples for the MoonGen API [5]. The listings in this section show excerpts from the `quality-of-service-test.lua` example script. This script uses two transmission tasks to generate two types of UDP flows and measures their throughput and latencies. It can be used as a starting point for a test setup to benchmark a forwarding device or middlebox that prioritizes real-time traffic over background traffic.

The example code in this section is slightly different from the example code in the repository: it has been edited for brevity. Error handling code like validation of command-line arguments is omitted here. The timestamping task has been removed as this example focuses on the basic packet generation and configuration API. Most comments have been removed and some variables renamed. The interested reader is referred to our repository [5] for the full example code including timestamping.

```
1  function master(txPort, rxPort, fgRate, bgRate)
2      local tDev = device.config(txPort, 1, 2)
3      local rDev = device.config(rxPort)
4      device.waitForLinks()
5      tDev:getTxQueue(0):setRate(bgRate)
6      tDev:getTxQueue(1):setRate(fgRate)
7      mg.launchLua("loadSlave", tDev:getTxQueue(0), 42)
8      mg.launchLua("loadSlave", tDev:getTxQueue(1), 43)
9      mg.launchLua("counterSlave", rDev:getRxQueue(0))
10     mg.waitForSlaves()
11 end
```

Listing 1: Initialization and device configuration

4.1 Initialization

Listing 1 shows the `master` function. This function is executed in the master task on startup and receives command line arguments passed to MoonGen: The devices and transmission rates to use in this case. It configures one transmit device with two transmit queues and one receiving device with the default settings. The call in line 4 waits until the links on all configured devices are established. It then configures hardware rate control features on the transmission queues and starts three slave threads, the first two generate traffic, the last counts the received traffic on the given device. The arguments passed to `mg.launchLua` are passed to the respective functions in the new task. The `loadSlave` function takes the transmission queue to operate on and a port to distinguish background from prioritized traffic.

4.2 Packet Generation Loop

Listing 2 shows the `loadSlave` function that is started twice and does the actual packet generation. It first allocates a memory pool, a DPDK data structure in which packet buffers are allocated. The MoonGen wrapper for memory pools expects a callback function that is called to initialize each packet. This allows a script to fill all packets with default values (lines 5 to 10) before the packets are used in the transmit loop (lines 17 to 24). The transmit loop only needs to modify a single field in each transmitted packet (line 20) to generate packets from randomized IP addresses.

Line 13 initializes a packet counter that keeps track of transmission statistics and prints them in regular intervals. MoonGen offers several types of such counters with different methods to acquire statistics, e.g., by reading the NICs statistics registers. This example uses the simplest type, one that must be manually updated.

Line 15 allocates a `bufArray`, a thin wrapper around a C array containing packet buffers. This is used instead of a normal Lua array for performance reasons. It contains a number of packets in order to process packets in batches instead of passing them one-by-one to the DPDK API. Batch processing is an important technique for high-speed packet processing [6, 23].

The main loop starts in line 17 with allocating packets of a specified size from the memory pool and storing them in the packet array. It loops over the newly allocated buffers (line 18) and randomizes the source IP (line 20). Finally, checksum offloading is enabled (line 22) and the packets are transmitted (line 23).

Note that the main loop differs from a packet generator relying on a classic API. MoonGen, or any other packet generator based on a similar framework, cannot simply re-use buffers because the transmit function is asynchronous. Passing packets to the transmit function merely places pointers

```
1  local PKT_SIZE = 124
2  function loadSlave(queue, port)
3      local mem = memory.createMemPool(function(buf)
4          buf:getUdpPacket():fill{
5              pktLength = PKT_SIZE,
6              ethSrc = queue, -- get MAC from device
7              ethDst = "10:11:12:13:14:15",
8              ipDst = "192.168.1.1",
9              udpSrc = 1234,
10             udpDst = port,
11         }
12     end)
13     local txCtr = stats:newManualTxCounter(port, "plain")
14     local baseIP = parseIPAddress("10.0.0.1")
15     local bufs = mem:bufArray()
16     while dpdk.running() do
17         bufs:alloc(PKT_SIZE)
18         for _, buf in ipairs(bufs) do
19             local pkt = buf:getUdpPacket()
20             pkt.ip.src:set(baseIP + math.random(255) - 1)
21         end
22         bufs:offloadUdpChecksums()
23         local sent = queue:send(bufs)
24         txCtr:updateWithSize(sent, PKT_SIZE)
25     end
26     txCtr:finalize()
27 end
```

Listing 2: Transmission slave task

to them into a memory queue, which is accessed by the NIC later [14]. A buffer must not be modified after passing it to DPDK. Otherwise, the transmitted packet data may be altered if the packet was not yet fetched by the NIC.

Therefore, we have to allocate new packet buffers from the memory pool in each iteration. Pre-filling the buffers at the beginning allows us to only touch fields that change per packet in the transmit loop. Packet buffers are recycled by DPDK in the transmit function, which collects packets that were sent by the NIC earlier [14]. This does not erase the packets' contents.

4.3 Packet Counter

Listing 3 shows how to use MoonGen's packet reception API to measure the throughput of the different flows by counting the incoming packets.

The task receives packets from the provided queue in the `bufArray bufs` in line 5. It then extracts the UDP destination port from the packet (line 8) and uses counters to track statistics per port. The final statistics are printed by calling the counters' finalize methods in line 19. Printed statistics

```
1  function counterSlave(queue)
2      local bufs = memory.bufArray()
3      local counters = {}
4      while dpdk.running() do
5          local rx = queue:recv(bufs)
6          for i = 1, rx do
7              local buf = bufs[i]
8              local port = buf:getUdpPacket().udp:getDstPort()
9              local ctr = counters[port]
10             if not ctr then
11                 ctr = stats:newPktRxCounter(port, "plain")
12                 counters[port] = ctr
13             end
14             ctr:countPacket(buf)
15         end
16         bufs:freeAll()
17     end
18     for _, ctr in pairs(counters) do
19         ctr:finalize()
20     end
21 end
```

Listing 3: Packet counter slave task

include the average packet and byte rates as well as their standard deviations.

The format to print in is specified in the counter constructor in line 11. All example scripts use the `plain` formatter, the default value is `CSV` for easy post-processing. The output can also be diverted to a file. Details are in the documentation of `stats.lua`.

This script can be used for another similar test setup by adapting the code to the test setup by changing hardcoded constants like the used addresses and ports. The full script in the repository [5] includes a separate timestamping task to acquire and print latency statistics for the two flows.

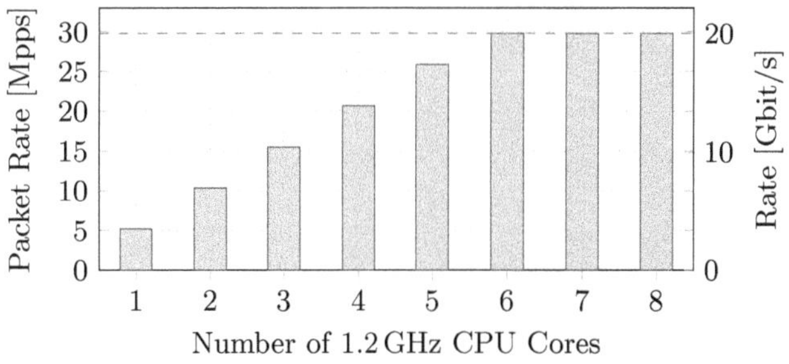

Figure 2: Multi-core scaling under high load

5. PERFORMANCE

Writing the whole generation logic in a scripting language raises concerns about the performance. One important feature of LuaJIT is that it allows for easy integration with existing C libraries and structs: it can directly operate on C structs and arrays without incurring overhead for bound checks or validating pointers [20]. Thus, crafting packets is very efficient in MoonGen.

The obvious disadvantage is that unchecked memory accesses can lead to memory corruption, a problem that is usually absent from scripting languages. However, most critical low-level parts like the implementation of the NIC driver are handled by DPDK. The MoonGen core then wraps potentially unsafe parts for the userscript if possible. There are only two operations in a typical userscript that can lead to memory corruption: writing beyond packet buffer boundaries and trying to operate on buffers that are null pointers. This is an intentional design decision to aid the performance by avoiding unnecessary checks.

5.1 Test Methodology

Measuring the CPU load caused by a DPDK-based application is difficult because DPDK recommends a busy-wait loop [14], i.e., the CPU load is always 100% for a typical application. MoonGen and other DPDK-based generators like Pktgen-DPDK [27] are no exceptions to this. The bottleneck for packet transmission is usually not the CPU but the line rate of the network, so just measuring the achieved rate provides no insight. We therefore decrease the clock frequency of our CPU such that the processing power becomes the bottleneck. The performance can then be quantified as CPU cycles per packet. The same approach was used by Rizzo to evaluate the performance of netmap [23].

The tests in this section were executed on an Intel Xeon E5-2620 v3 CPU with a frequency of 2.4 GHz that can be clocked down to 1.2 GHz in 100 MHz steps. To ensure consistent and reproducible measurement results, we disabled Hyper-Threading, which may influence results if the load of two virtual cores is scheduled to the same physical core. TurboBoost and SpeedStep were also disabled because they adjust the clock speed according to the current CPU load and interfere with our manual adjustment of the frequency.

5.2 Comparison with Pktgen-DPDK

Our scripting approach can even increase the performance compared to a static packet generator slightly. We show this by comparing MoonGen to Pktgen-DPDK 2.5.1 [27], a packet generator for DPDK written in C.

We configured both packet generators to craft minimum-sized UDP packets with 256 varying source IP addresses on a single CPU core. We then gradually increased the CPU's frequency until the software achieved line rate. Pktgen-DPDK required 1.7 GHz to hit the 10 GbE line rate of 14.88 Mpps, MoonGen only 1.5 GHz. Pktgen-DPDK achieved 14.12 Mpps at 1.5 GHz. This means MoonGen is more efficient in this specific scenario.

This increased performance is an inherent advantage of MoonGen's architecture: Pktgen-DPDK needs a complex main loop that covers all possible configurations even though we are only interested in changing IP addresses in this test scenario. MoonGen, on the other hand, can use a script that consists of a tight inner loop that exclusively executes the required tasks: allocating pre-filled packet buffers, modifying the IP address, and sending the packets with checksum offloading. You only pay for the features you actually use with MoonGen.

5.3 Multi-core Scaling

The achieved performance depends on the script; the previous example was a light workload for the comparison to Pktgen-DPDK, which is limited to such simple patterns. Therefore, we test a more involved script to stress MoonGen to show the scaling with multiple cores sending to the same NIC via multiple transmission queues.

Figure 2 shows the performance under heavy load and the scaling with the number of CPU cores. MoonGen was configured to generate minimum-sized packets with random payload as well as random source and destination addresses and ports. The code generates 8 random numbers per packet to achieve this. Each core generated and sent packets on two different 10 GbE interfaces simultaneously. Linear scaling can be observed up to the line rate limit (dashed line).

The code was written in idiomatic Lua without specific optimizations for this use case: LuaJIT's standard random number generator, a Tausworthe generator [20], was used. Since a high quality random number generator is not required here, a simple linear congruential generator would be faster. The code also generates a random number per header field instead of combining multiple fields (e.g., source and destination port can be randomized by a single 32-bit random number).

Despite the lack of optimizations, the code was initially found to be too fast for meaningful scalability measurements (10.3 Mpps on a single core). We therefore reduced the CPU's clock speed to 1.2 GHz and increased the number of NICs to 2 for this test. This test shows that sending to a single NIC port via multiple queues scales linearly, an important assumption made for our architecture (cf. Section 3.3).

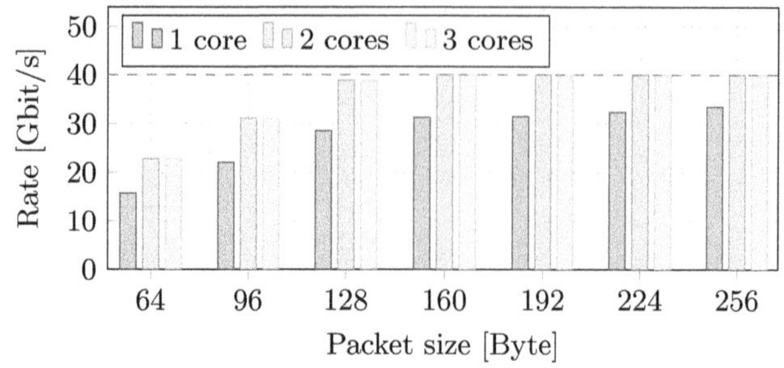

Figure 3: Throughput with an XL710 40 GbE NIC

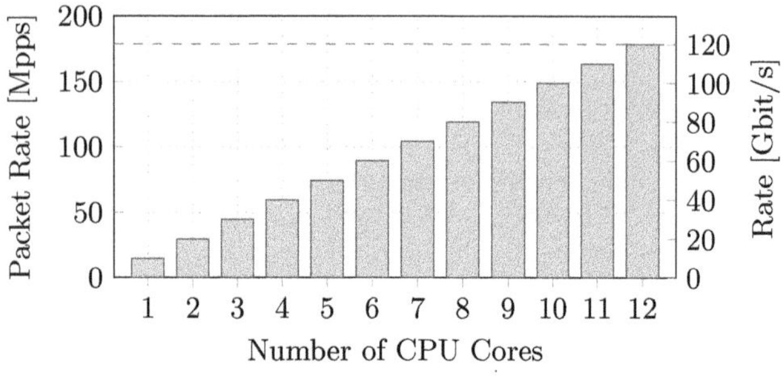

Figure 4: Multi-core scaling (multiple 10 GbE NICs)

5.4 Scaling to 40 Gigabit Ethernet

40 GbE NICs like the dual port Intel XL710 [15] are currently being introduced to the market. However, these first generation NICs come with bandwidth limitations that do not exist on the 10 GbE NICs discussed previously: they cannot saturate a link with minimum-sized packets [16] and they cannot saturate both ports simultaneously regardless of the packet size [15]. This may limit their use in some scenarios where a large number of small packets is required, e.g., stress-testing a router.

We are currently adding support for these NICs in MoonGen and present preliminary results here. Figure 3 shows the achieved throughput with various packet sizes and number of 2.4 GHz CPU cores used to generate the traffic. Packet sizes of 128 bytes or less cannot be generated in line rate. Using more than two CPU cores does not improve the speed, so this is a hardware bottleneck as described by Intel [16].

The second bandwidth restriction of this NIC is the aggregate bandwidth of the two ports. One obvious restriction is the 63 Gbit/s bandwidth of the PCIe 3.0 x8 link that connects the NIC to the CPU. However, the main bottleneck is the media access control layer in the XL710 chip: it is limited to a maximum aggregate bandwidth of 40 Gbit/s (cf. Section 3.2.1 of the XL710 datasheet [15]). We could achieve a maximum bandwidth of 50 Gbit/s with large packets on both ports simultaneously and a maximum packet rate of 42 Mpps (28 Gbit/s with 64 byte frames).

5.5 Scaling to 100 Gigabit Ethernet

100 GbE is currently restricted to hardware appliances like switches and routers and not yet available on commodity server hardware. We can emulate higher speeds by using multiple NICs.

We equipped one of our test servers with six dual-port 10 GbE Intel X540-T2 NICs to investigate the performance at high rates. Figure 4 shows the achieved packet rate when generating UDP packets from varying IP addresses. We used two Intel Xeon E5-2640 v2 CPUs with a nominal clock rate of 2 GHz for this test, but the clock rate can even be reduced to 1.5 GHz for this packet generation task (cf. Section 5.2).

Note that sending to multiple NICs simultaneously is architecturally the same as sending to multiple queues on a single NIC as different queues on a single NIC are independent from each other (cf. Section 5.3) in an ideal well-behaved NIC like the current generation of 10 GbE NICs. We do not expect significant challenges when moving to 100 GbE due to this architecture and promising tests with multiple 10 GbE ports. However, the first generation of 100 GbE NICs will likely have similar hardware restrictions as the 40 GbE NICs discussed in Section 5.4 which need to be taken into account.

Operation	Cycles/Pkt
Packet transmission	76.0 ± 0.8
Packet modification	9.1 ± 1.2
Packet modification (two cachelines)	15.0 ± 1.3
IP checksum offloading	15.2 ± 1.2
UDP checksum offloading	33.1 ± 3.5
TCP checksum offloading	34.0 ± 3.3

Table 1: Per-packet costs of basic operations

5.6 Per-Packet Costs

MoonGen's dynamic approach to packet generation in userscripts does not allow for a performance analysis in a general configuration as there is no typical scenario. Nevertheless, the cost of sending a packet can be decomposed into three main components: packet IO, memory accesses, and packet modification logic. We devised a synthetic benchmark that measures the average number of CPU cycles required for various operations that are commonly found in packet generator scripts. These measurements can be used to estimate the hardware requirements of arbitrary packet generator scripts. We repeated all measurements ten times; the uncertainties given in this section are the standard deviations.

5.6.1 Basic Operations

Table 1 shows the average per-packet costs of basic operations for IO and memory accesses. The baseline for packet IO consists of allocating a batch of packets and sending them without touching their contents in the main loop. This shows that there is a considerable per-packet cost for the IO operation caused by the underlying DPDK framework.

Modification operations write constants into the packets, forcing the CPU to load them into the layer 1 cache. Additional accesses within the same cache line (64 bytes) add no measurable additional cost. Accessing another cache line in a larger packet is noticeable.

Offloading checksums is not free (but still cheaper than calculating them in software) because the driver needs to set several bitfields in the DMA descriptor. For UDP and TCP offloading, MoonGen also needs to calculate the IP pseudo header checksum as this is not supported by the X540 NIC used here [13].

5.6.2 Randomizing Packets

Sending varying packets is important to generate different flows. There are two ways to achieve this: one can either

Fields	Cycles/Pkt (Rand)	Cycles/Pkt (Counter)
1	32.3 ± 0.5	27.1 ± 1.4
2	39.8 ± 1.0	33.1 ± 1.3
4	66.0 ± 0.9	38.1 ± 2.0
8	133.5 ± 0.7	41.7 ± 1.2

Table 2: Per-packet costs of modifications

generate a random number per packet or use a counter with wrapping arithmetic that is incremented for each packet. The resulting value is then written into a header field. Table 2 shows the cost for the two approaches, the baseline is the cost of writing a constant to a packet and sending it (85.1 cycles/pkt).

There is a fixed cost for calculating the values while the marginal cost is relatively low: 17 cycles/pkt per random field and 1 cycle/pkt for wrapping counters. These results show that wrapping counters instead of actual random number generation should be preferred if possible for the desired traffic scenario.

5.6.3 *Cost Estimation Example*

We can use these values to predict the performance of the scripts used for the performance evaluation in Section 5.3. The example generated 8 random numbers for fields with a userscript that is completely different from the benchmarking script: it writes the values into the appropriate header fields and the payloads, the benchmarking script just fills the raw packet from the start. The script also combines offloading and modification; the benchmark tests them in separate test runs.

The expected cost consists of: packet IO, packet modification, random number generation, and IP checksum offloading, i.e., 229.2 ± 3.9 cycles/pkt. This translates to a predicted throughput of 10.47 ± 0.18 Mpps on a single 2.4 GHz CPU core. The measured throughput of 10.3 Mpps is within that range. This shows that our synthetic benchmark can be used to estimate hardware requirements.

5.7 Effects of Packet Sizes

All tests performed in the previous sections use minimum-sized packets. The reason for this choice is that the per-packet costs dominate over costs incurred by large packets. Allocating and sending larger packets without modifications add no additional cost in MoonGen on 1 and 10 GbE NICs. Only modifying the content on a per-packet basis adds a performance penalty, which is comparatively low compared to the fixed cost of sending a packet. Using larger packets also means that fewer packets have to be sent at line rate, so the overall fixed costs for packet IO are reduced: minimum-sized packets are usually the worst-case.

Nevertheless, there are certain packet sizes that are of interest: those that are just slightly larger than a single cache line. We benchmarked all packet sizes between 64 and 128 bytes and found no difference in the CPU cycles required for sending a packet. Since MoonGen also features packet reception, we also tried to receive packets with these sizes and found no measurable impact of the packet size.[1]

Rizzo notes that such packet sizes have a measurable impact on packet reception, but not transmission, in his evaluation of netmap [23]. He attributes this to hardware bottlenecks as it was independent from the CPU speed. We could not reproduce this with MoonGen. The likely explanation is that we are using current (2014) server hardware, while the evaluation of netmap was done in 2012 on an older system with a CPU launched in 2009 [23].

[1]Note that this is not true for XL710 40 GbE NICs which can run into hardware bottlenecks with some packet sizes.

6. HARDWARE TIMESTAMPING

Another important performance characteristic beside the throughput is the latency of a system. Modern NICs offer hardware support for the IEEE 1588 Precision Time Protocol (PTP) for clock synchronization across networks. PTP can be used either directly on top of Ethernet as a layer 3 protocol with EtherType 0x88F7 or as an application-layer protocol on top of UDP [8].

We examined the PTP capabilities of the Intel 82580 GbE and the 82599 and X540 10 GbE chips. They support timestamping of PTP Ethernet and UDP packets, the UDP port is configurable on the 10 GbE NICs. They can be configured to timestamp only certain types of PTP packets, identified by the first byte of their payload. The second byte must be set to the PTP version number. All other PTP fields in the packet are not required to enable timestamps and may contain arbitrary values. [11, 12, 13] This allows us to measure latencies of almost any type of packet.

Most Intel NICs, including all 10 GbE chips, save the timestamps for received and transmitted packets in a register on the NIC. This register must be read back before a new packet can be timestamped [12, 13], limiting the throughput of timestamped packets. Some Intel GbE chips like the 82580 support timestamping all received packets by prepending the timestamp to the packet buffer [11].

6.1 Precision and Accuracy

Timestamping mechanisms of the Intel 82599 and Intel X540 10 GbE chips operate at 156.25 MHz when running at 10 GbE speeds [12, 13]. This frequency is reduced to 15.625 MHz when a 1 GbE link is used, resulting in a precision of 6.4 ns for 10 GbE and 64 ns for 1 GbE. The datasheet of the Intel 82580 GbE [11] controller lacks information about the clock frequency. Testing shows that the acquired timestamps are always of the form $t = n{\cdot}64\,ns{+}k{\cdot}8\,ns$ where k is a constant that varies between resets, so the precision is 64 ns.

All of these NICs timestamp packets late in the transmit path and early in the receive path to be as accurate as possible [11, 12, 13]. We tested the timestamping functionality by using loop-back multimode OM3 fiber cables on an 82599-based NIC with a 10GBASE-SR SFP+ module and Cat 5e cable between the two ports of a dual-port X540-based NIC. Table 3 on the next page shows measured latencies t_x for different cable lengths x for each NIC as well as the (de-)modulation time k and propagation speed v_p, which can be calculated from these data points with the equation $t = k + l/v_p$. k is higher on the copper-based NIC, this is likely due to the more complex line code required for 10GBASE-T [9]. This calculation does not take any errors in the cable length into account; we rely on the vendor's specification[2]. The actual propagation speed and encoding times may therefore be outside the interval given in Table 3.

[2]We believe that the 50 m cable is actually slightly shorter.

NIC	t_{2m} [ns]	$t_{8.5m}$ [ns]	t_{10m} [ns]	t_{20m} [ns]	t_{50m} [ns]	k [ns]	v_p
82599 (fiber)	320	352	-	403.2	-	310.7 ± 3.9	$0.72c \pm 0.056c$
X540 (copper)	2156.8	-	2195.2	-	2387.2	2147.2 ± 4.8	$0.69c \pm 0.019c$

Table 3: Timestamping accuracy measurements

We repeated each measurement at least 500 000 times. All measurements for the fiber connection on the 82599 NIC yielded the same result except for the 8.5 m cable. This cable caused a latency of 345.6 ns in 50.2% of the measurements and 358.4 ns in the other 49.8% (Table 3 shows the average). This variance is due to the fact that the timer that is saved when the timestamp is taken is incremented only every two clock cycles on the 82599 chip [12], i.e., the granularity of the timer is 12.8 ns but the timestamping operates at 6.4 ns.

The timestamp timer on the X540 is incremented every 6.4 ns so it does not have this problem. However, it faces a different challenge: the 10GBASE-T standard uses a block code on layer 1 [9] which introduces variance. Table 3 shows the median latency. More than 99.5% of the measured values were within $\pm$ 6.4 ns of the median. The difference between the minimum and maximum latencies was 64 ns. These variations were independent of the cable length.

The absence of a variance on the 82599 chip demonstrates a high precision, the plausible results for the modulation time [28] and the linear behavior of the propagation latency show a high accuracy.

6.2 Clock Synchronization

Test setups can involve multiple network ports that may even be on different NICs. For example, measuring the forwarding latency of a switch requires timestamping a packet on two different ports. MoonGen therefore needs to be able to synchronize the clocks between two network ports. This is even necessary between two ports of a dual-port NIC, which are completely independent from the user's point of view.

MoonGen synchronizes the clocks of two ports by reading the current time from both clocks and calculating the difference. The clocks are then read again in the opposite order. The resulting differences are the same if and only if the clocks are currently synchronous (assuming that the time required for the PCIe access is constant). We observed randomly distributed outliers in about 5% of the reads. We therefore repeat the measurement 7 times to have a probability of $> 99.999\%$ of at least 3 correct measurements. The median of the measured differences is then used to adjust one of the clocks to synchronize them. This adjustment must be done with an atomic read-modify-write operation. The NICs support this as it is also required for PTP.

Tests show that this technique synchronizes the clocks with an error of ± 1 cycle. Therefore, the maximum accuracy for tests involving multiple network interfaces is 19.2 ns for the 10 GbE chips.

6.3 Clock Drift

Using two different clocks also entails the risk of clock drifts. Drift on X540-based NICs depends on the physical wiring as the timestamping clock is synchronized to the physical layer. Two ports on different X540-based NICs that are directly connected do not exhibit any clock drift while the link is established. However, the clocks of two ports on the same X540 NIC will drift if they are connected to two different NICs. We measured the drift between different X540 and 82599 NICs. The worst-case observed drift was 35 μs per second between a NIC on the mainboard and a discrete NIC.

MoonGen handles clock drift by resynchronizing the clocks before a timestamped packet is sent, so this drift translates to a relative error of only 0.0035%. This is not significant for latency measurements. Since the measurements show a constant clock drift, it would also be possible to subtract the accumulated drift from the acquired timestamps to avoid resynchronization.

6.4 Limitations

Our approach for latency measurements comes with limitations. The latency measurements are restricted to Ethernet frames with the PTP EtherType and UDP packets. MoonGen cannot measure latencies of other protocols.

The naïve handling of clock drift by resynchronizing the clocks for each packet allows for only a single timestamped packet in flight, limiting the throughput to $1\,Pkt/RTT$. MoonGen scripts therefore use two transmission queues, one that sends timestamped packets and one that sends regular packets. The regular packets can be crafted such that the device under test cannot distinguish them from the timestamped packets, e.g., by setting the PTP type in the payload to a value that is not timestamped by the NIC. So MoonGen effectively samples random packets in the data stream and timestamps them. Note that the benchmarking standard RFC 2544 calls for only one timestamped packet in a 120 second interval [3]. MoonGen can timestamp several thousands of packets per second to calculate average latencies and histograms.

The investigated NICs refuse to timestamp UDP PTP packets that are smaller than the expected packet size of 80 bytes. Larger packets are timestamped properly. This restriction does not apply to packets with the PTP EtherType as the minimum PTP packet size is below 64 bytes in this configuration. Measurements of inter-arrival times are restricted to GbE networks due to lack of hardware support for timestamping in line rate on 10 GbE NICs.

Based on the discussed measurement results and despite these limitations, we argue that special-purpose hardware is not necessary to conduct highly precise and accurate latency and inter-arrival time measurements.

7. RATE CONTROL

An important feature of a packet generator is controlling the packet rate and generating specific timing patterns to simulate real-world scenarios. MoonGen utilizes hardware rate control features of Intel NICs to generate constant bit rate and bursty traffic. We also implement a novel software-based rate control for realistic traffic patterns, e.g., based on a Poisson process. That is discussed further in Section 8, this section focuses on software rate control in other packet generators and hardware rate control.

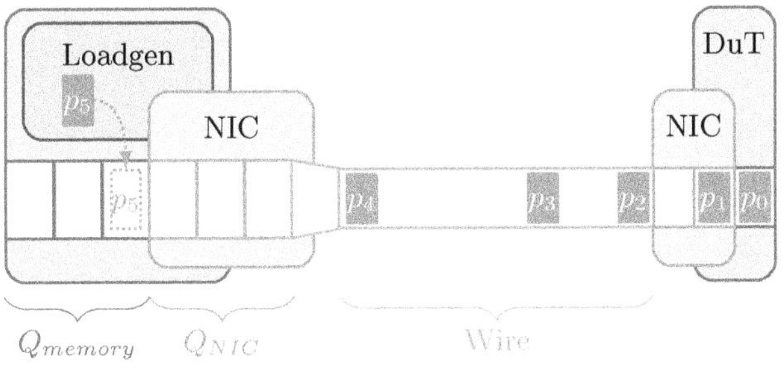

Figure 5: Software-based rate control

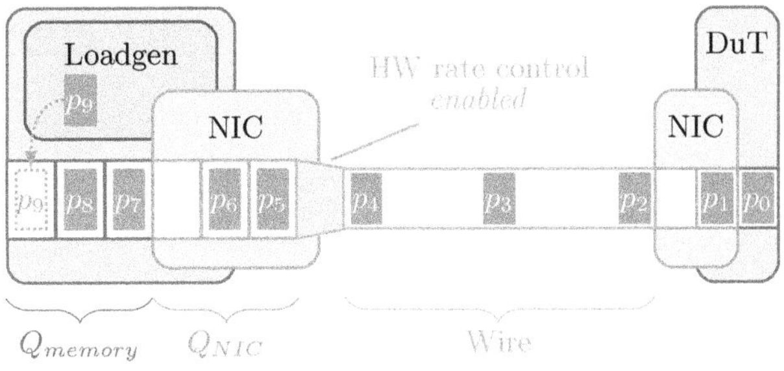

Figure 6: Hardware-based rate control

7.1 Software Rate Control in Existing Packet Generators

Trying to control the timing between packets in software is known to be error-prone [2, 4]. The main problem with software-based rate control is that the software needs to push individual packets to the NIC and then has to wait for the NIC to transmit it before pushing the next packet.

However, modern NICs do not work that way: they rely on an asynchronous push-pull model and not on a pure push model. The software writes the packets into a queue that resides in the main memory and informs the NIC that new packets are available. It is up to the NIC to fetch the packets asynchronously via DMA and store them in the internal transmit queue on the NIC before transmitting them. A good explanation of this packet flow can be found in the datasheet of the X540 chip [13] (Section 1.7), other NICs follow a similar process.

Figure 5 visualizes this packet flow. Only a single packet at a time is allowed in the queues (Q_{memory} & Q_{NIC}) to generate packets that are not back-to-back on the wire.

This hardware architecture causes two problems: the exact timing when a packet is retrieved from memory cannot be controlled by the software and queues cannot be used (unless bursts are desired). The former results in a low precision, as the exact time when the packet is transferred cannot be determined. The latter impacts the performance at high packet rates as high-speed packet processing relies on batch processing [6, 23].

7.2 Hardware Rate Control

Intel 10 GbE NICs feature hardware rate control: all transmit queues can be configured to a specified rate. The NIC then generates constant bit-rate (CBR) traffic. This solves the two problems identified in the previous section. The software can keep all available queues completely filled and the generated timing is up to the NIC. Figure 6 shows this architecture. The disadvantage is that this approach is limited to CBR traffic and bursty traffic (by changing the rate parameter periodically).

7.3 Evaluation

We compare our hardware-assisted solution to the software-based rate control found in zsend 6.0.2 (an example application of the PF_RING ZC framework [18]), and Pktgen-DPDK 2.5.1 [27] to quantify the adverse effects of software-based rate control. We use an Intel 82580 GbE controller, which is able to timestamp arbitrary received packets in line rate (cf. Section 6) to measure inter-arrival times.

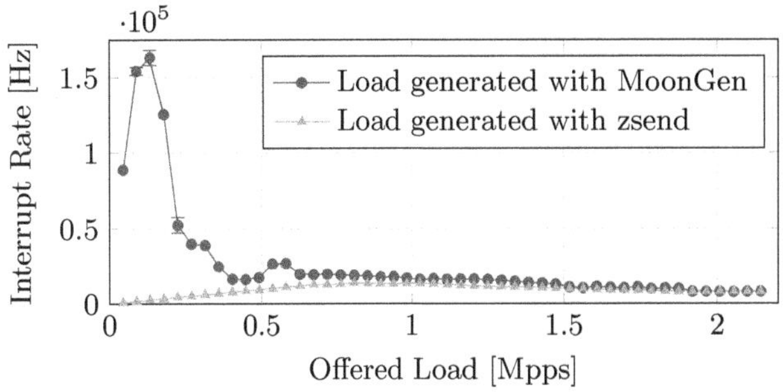

Figure 7: Interrupt rate with micro-bursts

Figure 8 on the next page compares the inter-arrival times generated by different packet generators. The generators use an X540 NIC, which also supports 1 Gbit/s. The histograms have a bin size of 64 ns (precision of the 82580 chip) and were generated by observing at least 1 000 000 packets.

Traffic from the hardware rate-controlled NIC oscillates around the targeted inter-arrival time by up to 256 ns and it avoids generating bursts almost completely (inter-arrival time of 672 ns, marked with a black arrow in Figure 8). Table 4 summarizes the results. The best result in each column is highlighted.

We discussed these findings with the authors of zsend as we configured it explicitly to avoid bursts. We then tested several suggested configurations and versions. We concluded that these observations indicate a bug in the PF_RING ZC framework that is being investigated.

It stands to reason that the precision problems as well as the micro-bursts intensify further at rates beyond 1 Gbit/s with software-based rate control. Measuring inter-arrival times on 10 GbE is a challenging task: Reliable measurements require special-purpose hardware. We do not yet have such hardware. We predict that the precision of our hardware-assisted approach will improve at 10 GbE speeds: The frequency of the internal clock on the NIC that controls the inter-departure times is scaled up by a factor of 10 when operating at 10 GbE compared to GbE [13].

7.4 Effects of Micro-Bursts on Linux Systems

Figure 7 visualizes the interrupt rate on a Linux packet forwarder running Open vSwitch under increasing load generated by MoonGen and zsend. Open vSwitch was configured with a static OpenFlow rule to forward between two ports. The micro-bursts generate a low interrupt rate. The likely explanation for this is that the bursts trigger the interrupt rate moderation feature of the driver earlier than expected. This shows that bad rate control can have a measurable impact on the behavior of the tested system.

Rate	Packet Generator	Micro-Bursts	±64 ns	±128 ns	±256 ns	±512 ns
500 kpps	MoonGen	0.02%	**49.9%**	**74.9%**	**99.8%**	**99.8%**
	Pktgen-DPDK	**0.01%**	37.7%	72.3%	92%	94.5%
	zsend	28.6%	3.9%	5.4%	6.4%	13.8%
1000 kpps	MoonGen	**1.2%**	**50.5%**	52%	**97%**	**100%**
	Pktgen-DPDK	14.2%	36.7%	**58%**	70.6%	95.9%
	zsend	52%	4.6%	7.9%	24.2%	88.1%

Table 4: Rate control measurements

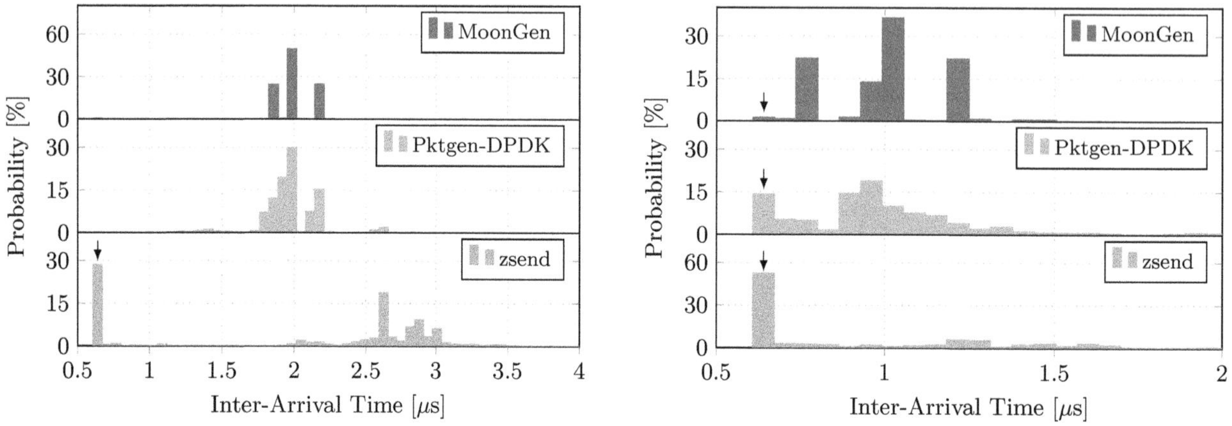

(a) 500 kpps (b) 1000 kpps

Figure 8: Histograms of inter-arrival times

7.5 Limitations of Hardware Rate Control

In our tests we encountered unpredictable non-linear behavior with packet rates above ~9 Mpps (~6 Gbit/s wire-rate with 64 byte packets) on Intel X520 and X540 NICs. A work-around is configuring two transmission queues and sending a CBR stream from both of them. Note that this is not equivalent to a single transmission queue with proper rate control as both queues control their transmission rate independently from each other.

Hardware rate control of the investigated NICs is also restricted to CBR traffic, so MoonGen still needs an implementation of software-based rate control for other traffic patterns.

8. CONTROLLING INTER-PACKET GAPS IN SOFTWARE

To overcome this restriction to constant bit rate or bursty traffic, MoonGen implements a novel mechanism for software-based rate control. This allows MoonGen to create arbitrary traffic patterns.

8.1 Sending Gaps on the Wire

We were not satisfied with the precision of existing software rate control mechanisms (cf. Section 7.3 and [2, 4]) so we present a new method here. All existing packet generators try to delay sending packets by not sending packets for a specified time, leading to the previously mentioned problems. MoonGen fills the gaps between packets with invalid packets instead. Varying the length of the invalid packet precisely determines the time between any two packets and subsequently allows the creation of arbitrary complex traffic

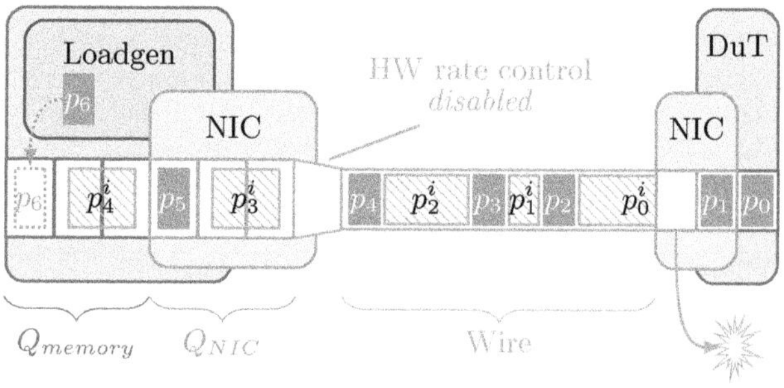

Figure 9: Precise generation of arbitrary traffic patterns in MoonGen

patterns. With this technique, we can still make use of the NIC's queues and do not have to rely on any timing related to DMA accesses by the NIC.

This approach requires support by the device under test (DuT): it needs to detect and ignore invalid packets in hardware without affecting the packet processing logic. MoonGen uses packets with an incorrect CRC checksum and, if necessary, an illegal length for short gaps. All investigated NICs in our testbed drop such packets early in the receive flow: they are dropped even before they are assigned to a receive queue, the NIC only increments an error counter [11, 12, 13]. Subsequently, the packet processing logic is not affected by this software rate control mechanism.

Figure 9 illustrates this concept. Shaded packets p_j^i are sent with an incorrect CRC checksum, all other packets p_k with a correct one. Note that the wire and all transmission queues are completely filled, i.e., the generated rate has to be the line rate.

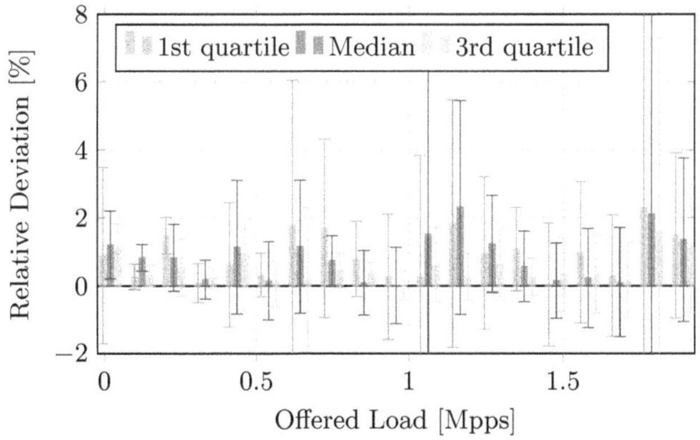

Figure 10: Differences in forwarding latencies of Open vSwitch with CBR traffic generated by hardware and our software approach

In theory, arbitrary inter-packet gaps should be possible. The NICs we tested refused to send out frames with a wire-length (including Ethernet preamble, start-of-frame delimiter, and inter-frame gap) of less than 33 bytes, so gaps between 1 and 32 bytes (0.8 ns to 25.6 ns) cannot be generated. Generating small frames also puts the NIC under an unusually high load for which it was not designed. We found that the maximum achievable packet rate with short frames is 15.6 Mpps on Intel X540 and 82599 chips, only 5% above the line rate for packets with the regular minimal size. MoonGen therefore enforces a minimum wire-length of 76 bytes (8 bytes less than the regular minimum) by default for invalid packets. As a result, gaps between 0.8 ns and 60.8 ns cannot be represented.

8.2 Evaluation

We generate CBR traffic with our approach and compare it to CBR traffic generated by the hardware facilities of our NIC by comparing the response of a DuT.

We use Intel's hardware implementation as reference generator. The same measurement with other software-based packet generators is not possible as they don't support accurate timestamping. However, the results from Section 7.4 indicate that the latency would be affected at low rates due to the measurably different interrupt rate (cf. Figure 7).

Figure 10 shows the difference of the 25th, 50th, and 75th percentiles of the forwarding latency on a server running Open vSwitch. The test is restricted to the range 0.1 Mpps to 1.9 Mpps as the DuT becomes overloaded at higher rates and the latency is a function of the buffer size of the DuT after this point. We repeated the whole test 10 times, the error bars in the figure show the resulting standard deviations. The relative deviation is within 1.2σ of 0% for almost all measurement points, only the 1st quartile at 0.23 Mpps deviates by $1.5\%\pm0.5\%$. Minor activity on the DuT, e.g., an active SSH session, shows a significantly larger ($\geq 10\%$) effect on the latency with both rate control methods. This shows that loading the DuT with a large number of invalid packets does not cause system activity; the DuT does not notice the invalid packets.

8.3 Example: Poisson Traffic

CBR traffic is often an unrealistic test scenario for measurements of latency. Bursts or a Poisson process allow for more sophisticated tests that also stress buffers as the DuT becomes temporarily overloaded.

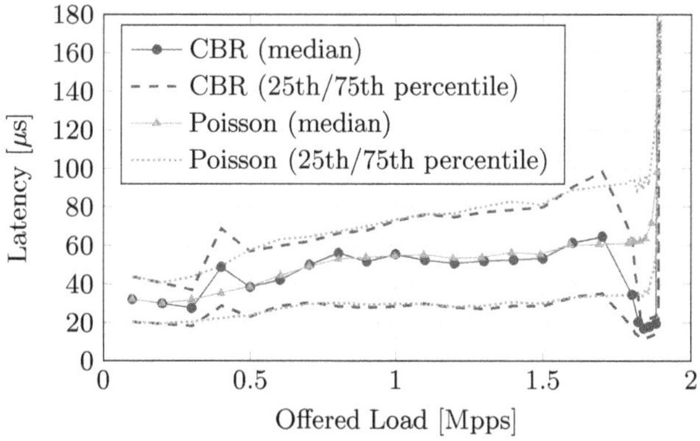

Figure 11: Forwarding latency of Open vSwitch with CBR and Poisson traffic patterns

Figure 11 shows measured latencies of Open vSwitch configured to forward packets between two ports. We generate packets with CBR (hardware rate control) and Poisson (CRC-based software rate control) traffic patterns and compare their latencies. The outlier at 0.4 Mpps for CBR traffic was reproducible across multiple re-measurements on different servers. The sudden drop in latency before the system becomes overloaded was also reproducible. Both are likely artifacts of the interaction between the interrupt throttle algorithm found in the Intel driver [10] and the dynamic interrupt adaption of Linux [25] on the DuT. The artifacts are present regardless of how the CBR traffic is generated (cf. Figure 10), so this is not caused by MoonGen but an effect of the traffic pattern on DuT.

The system becomes overloaded at about 1.9 Mpps, resulting in packet drops and a very large latency (about 2 ms in this test setup) as all buffers are filled. The overall achieved throughput is the same regardless of the traffic pattern and method to generate it. This result shows that the traffic pattern can affect the DuT in an experiment measurably, underlining the importance of a reliable precise packet generator.

8.4 Limitations of our Approach

A shorter per-byte transmission time improves both the granularity and the minimum length that can be generated. This means our solution works best on 10 GbE where the granularity is 0.8 ns.

Due to the artificially enforced minimum size of 76 bytes, gaps between 1 and 75 bytes (0.8 ns to 60 ns) cannot be precisely represented (cf. Section 8.1). It is possible to reduce this range for tests with larger packets or lower rates. We approximate gaps that cannot be generated by occasionally skipping an invalid packet and increasing the length of other gaps. The overall rate still reaches the expected average with this technique, i.e., the accuracy is high but the precision is relatively low[3] for these delays.

A possible work-around for gaps with a length between 1 and 75 bytes is using multiple NICs to generate traffic that is sent to a switch. The switch then drops the invalid frames and multiplexes the different streams before forward-

[3]Note that $\pm30\,ns$ is still better than hardware rate control and other software solutions (cf. Section 7.3).

ing them to the DuT. This only works if the generated pattern can be split into multiple streams, e.g., by overlaying several Poisson processes.

However, short delays are often not meaningful in modern networks. For example, the 10GBASE-T transmission standard used by most experiments for this paper operates on frames with a payload size of 3200 bits on the physical layer as defined in IEEE 802.3 Section 4 55.1.3.1 [9]. This means that any layers above the physical layer will receive multiple packets encoded in the same frame as a burst. So two back-to-back packets cannot be distinguished from two packets with a gap of 232 bytes (185.6 ns) in the worst case and failure to represent gaps between 1 and 75 bytes should not be noticeable. Note that this limit on the physical layer only applies to relatively short inter-arrival times, bad rate control generating bursts is still inferior to our approach (cf. Figure 7 in Section 7.3).

Another limitation is that our approach is optimized for experiments in which the DuT (or the first hop in a system under test) is a software-based packet processing system and not a hardware appliance. Hardware might be affected by an invalid packet. In such a scenario, we suggest to route the test traffic through a store-and-forward switch that drops packets with invalid CRC checksums. This effectively replaces the invalid packets with real gaps on the wire. Note that the effects of the switch on the inter-arrival times need to be carefully evaluated first.

9. REPRODUCIBLE RESEARCH

We encourage you to install MoonGen and reproduce the results from this paper to verify our work. All experiments presented here can be reproduced with the included example scripts and NICs based on Intel 82599, X540, 82580, and XL710 chips.

The performance evaluation in Section 5 is based on the scripts found in `examples/benchmarks`, an Intel Xeon E5-2620 v3 CPU, and Intel X540 NICs. The timestamping accuracy in Section 6 was measured with the script `timestamps.lua`, the clock drift measurements with `drift.lua`. Inter-arrival times in Section 7 were measured with `inter-arrival-times.lua`. The script `l2-load-latency.lua` with the timestamping task disabled was used to generate the analyzed traffic. The suggested work-around for the hardware rate control limitations at high rates is also implemented in `l2-load-latency.lua`. Sending bursty traffic is implemented in `l2-bursts.lua`. The example measurement of the interrupt rate in Section 7.4 was conducted with `l2-load-latency.lua` and zsend 6.0.2.

`compare-rate-control-mechanisms.lua` was used for the evaluation in Section 8.2. The latency measurements with Poisson and CBR traffic in Section 8.3 are based on `l2-load-latency.lua` and `l2-poisson-load-latency.lua`. The DuT for these tests was Open vSwitch 2.0.0 on Debian Linux 3.7 with ixgbe 3.14.5 running on a server with a 3.3 GHz Intel Xeon E3-1230 v2 CPU. Only a single CPU core was used by configuring the NIC with only one queue. Each test was run for at least 30 seconds with at least 30 000 timestamped packets.

All measurements were conducted on Intel X540 NICs except for the inter-arrival times (Intel 82580), fiber loopback measurements (Intel 82599), and 40 GbE tests (Intel XL710). We used different development versions of MoonGen for the experiments described throughout this paper. The performance evaluation with 10 GbE in Section 5 was done with commit `492c0e4`, and on 40 GbE with commit `a70ca21`. We confirmed that all described experiments still work with the example scripts from commit `a70ca21` in our git repository [5].

10. CONCLUSIONS AND FUTURE WORK

We have presented a general-purpose packet generator that uses hardware features of commodity NICs to implement functionality that was previously only available on expensive special-purpose hardware. MoonGen represents a hybrid between a pure software-based solution and one based on hardware. It combines the advantages of both approaches while mitigating shortcomings by using both hardware-specific features and novel software approaches.

MoonGen measures latencies with sub-microsecond accuracy and precision. The desired packet rate can be controlled precisely through both hardware-support and our rate control algorithm based on filling gaps with invalid packets.

We have shown that it is feasible to use modern implementations of scripting languages to craft packets without sacrificing speed. This makes MoonGen flexible and extensible. The flexibility goes beyond the capabilities provided by hardware load generators as each packet can be crafted in real-time by a script. Tests that respond to incoming traffic in real-time are possible as MoonGen also features packet reception and analysis.

In the future, we will add additional example scripts and support for hardware features of more NICs. MoonGen currently comes with example scripts to handle IPv4, IPv6, UDP, TCP, ICMP, IPsec, and ARP traffic.

MoonGen's flexible architecture allows for further applications like analyzing traffic in line rate on 10 GbE networks or doing Internet-wide scans from 10 GbE uplinks. MoonGen is under active development, the latest version is available in our public git repository [5].

Acknowledgments

This research was supported by the DFG MEMPHIS project (CA 595/5-2), the KIC EIT ICT Labs on SDN, and the EUREKA-Project SASER (01BP12300A).

We would like to thank the anonymous reviewers and our colleagues Dominik Scholz, Johannes Reifferscheid, Rainer Schönberger, Patrick Werneck, Lukas Märdian, Lukas Erlacher, and Stephan M. Günther for valuable contributions to MoonGen and this paper.

11. REFERENCES

[1] Nicola Bonelli, Andrea Di Pietro, Stefano Giordano, and Gregorio Procissi. Flexible High Performance Traffic Generation on Commodity Multi–Core Platforms. In *Proceedings of the 4th International Conference on Traffic Monitoring and Analysis*, pages 157–170. Springer, 2012.

[2] Alessio Botta, Alberto Dainotti, and Antonio Pescapé. Do You Trust Your Software-Based Traffic Generator? *IEEE Communications Magazine*, 48(9):158–165, 2010.

[3] Scott Bradner and Jim McQuaid. Benchmarking Methodology for Network Interconnect Devices. RFC 2544 (Informational), March 1999.

[4] G. Adam Covington, Glen Gibb, John W. Lockwood, and Nick Mckeown. A Packet Generator on the NetFPGA Platform. In *17th IEEE Symposium on Field Programmable Custom Computing Machines*, pages 235–238, 2009.

[5] Paul Emmerich. MoonGen. `https://github.com/emmericp/MoonGen`.

[6] Sebastian Gallenmüller, Paul Emmerich, Florian Wohlfart, Daniel Raumer, and Georg Carle. Comparison of Frameworks for High-Performance Packet IO. In *ACM/IEEE Symposium on Architectures for Networking and Communications Systems (ANCS 2015)*, May 2015.

[7] Luke Gorrie. Snabb Switch. `https://github.com/SnabbCo/snabbswitch/`.

[8] IEEE Standard for a Precision Clock Synchronization Protocol for Networked Measurement and Control Systems. *IEEE 1588-2008*, July 2008.

[9] IEEE. IEEE 802.3-2012 IEEE Standard for Ethernet Section Four, 2012.

[10] Intel. Intel Server Adapters - Linux ixgbe Base Driver. `http://www.intel.com/support/network/adapter/pro100/sb/CS-032530.htm`. Last visited 2015-08-24.

[11] Intel 82580EB Gigabit Ethernet Controller Datasheet Rev. 2.6. Intel, 2014.

[12] Intel 82599 10 GbE Controller Datasheet Rev. 2.76. Intel, 2012.

[13] Intel Ethernet Controller X540 Datasheet Rev. 2.7. Intel, 2014.

[14] Data Plane Development Kit. `http://dpdk.org/`. Last visited 2015-08-24.

[15] Intel Ethernet Controller XL710 Datasheet Rev. 2.1. Intel, December 2014.

[16] Product Brief - Intel Ethernet Controller XL710 10/40 GbE. Intel, 2014.

[17] NetFPGA. `http://netfpga.org/`. Last visited 2015-08-24.

[18] Ntop. PF_RING ZC (Zero Copy). `http://www.ntop.org/products/pf_ring/pf_ring-zc-zero-copy/`. Last visited 2015-04-28.

[19] Srivats P. ostinato. `http://ostinato.org/`. Last visited 2015-08-24.

[20] Mike Pall. LuaJIT. `http://luajit.org/`. Last visited 2015-08-24.

[21] Mike Pall. LuaJIT in realtime applications. `http://www.freelists.org/post/luajit/LuaJIT-in-realtime-applications,3`, July 2012. Mailing list post.

[22] Luigi Rizzo. The netmap project. `http://info.iet.unipi.it/~luigi/netmap/`. Last visited 2015-08-24.

[23] Luigi Rizzo. netmap: A Novel Framework for Fast Packet I/O. In *USENIX Annual Technical Conference*, pages 101–112, 2012.

[24] Charalampos Rotsos, Nadi Sarrar, Steve Uhlig, Rob Sherwood, and Andrew W Moore. Oflops: An Open Framework for OpenFlow Switch Evaluation. In *Passive and Active Measurement*, pages 85–95. Springer, 2012.

[25] Jamal Hadi Salim, Robert Olsson, and Alexey Kuznetsov. Beyond Softnet. In *Proceedings of the 5th Annual Linux Showcase & Conference*, volume 5, pages 18–18, 2001.

[26] Joel Sommers and Paul Barford. Self-Configuring Network Traffic Generation. In *Proceedings of the 4th ACM SIGCOMM Conference on Internet Measurement*, IMC '04, pages 68–81, New York, NY, USA, 2004. ACM.

[27] Keith Wiles. Pktgen-DPDK. `http://github.com/Pktgen/Pktgen-DPDK/`.

[28] Yinglin Yang, Sudeep Goswami, and Carl G. Hansen. 10GBASE-T Ecosystem is Ready for Broad Adoption, 2012. White paper.

Ting: Measuring and Exploiting Latencies Between All Tor Nodes

Frank Cangialosi
University of Maryland
frank@cs.umd.edu

Dave Levin
University of Maryland
dml@cs.umd.edu

Neil Spring
University of Maryland
nspring@cs.umd.edu

ABSTRACT

Tor is a peer-to-peer overlay routing network that achieves unlinkable communication between source and destination. Unlike traditional mix-nets, Tor seeks to balance anonymity and performance, particularly with respect to providing low-latency communication. As a result, understanding the latencies between peers in the Tor network could be an extremely powerful tool in understanding and improving Tor's performance and anonymity properties. Unfortunately, there are no practical techniques for inferring accurate latencies between two arbitrary hosts on the Internet, and Tor clients are not instrumented to collect and report on these measurements.

In this paper, we present Ting, a technique for measuring latencies between arbitrary Tor nodes from a single vantage point. Through a ground-truth validation, we show that Ting is accurate, even with few samples, and does not require modifications to existing clients. We also apply Ting to the live Tor network, and show that its measurements are stable over time. We demonstrate that the all-pairs latency datasets that Ting permits can be applied in disparate ways, including faster methods of deanonymizing Tor circuits and efficiently finding long circuits with low end-to-end latency.

Categories and Subject Descriptors

C.4 [**Performance of Systems**]: Measurement Techniques; C.2.2 [**Computer-Communication Networks**]: Network Protocols; C.2.0 [**Computer-Communication Networks**]: Security and Protection

Keywords

Latency measurement; Tor; Deanonymization

IMC'15, October 28–30, 2015, Tokyo, Japan.

ACM 978-1-4503-3848-6/15/10 ...$15.00.
DOI: http://dx.doi.org/10.1145/2815675.2815701.

1. INTRODUCTION

Tor [7] is a popular peer-to-peer service for providing unlinkable communication and anonymous services. It operates by allowing a source node to create a *circuit* through multiple Tor *relays*, each of whom learns only about the node preceding and the node following it in the circuit. To keep the nodes on the path from linking the source and destination, Tor circuit creation mandates at least two relays.

Arguably, the primary feature of Tor that has led to its widespread success is Tor's balance between anonymity and good end-to-end performance, particularly with respect to network latency. One consequence of this trade-off is that Tor defaults to circuits of length three: an entry node, a middle node, and an exit node. Another consequence of this design choice is that Tor relays do not arbitrarily introduce delays or "mixing" like in other anonymity systems [22, 4, 29], and instead forward as quickly as is possible (and fair).

Tor's performance and anonymity are therefore highly dependent on the round-trip time latencies between the nodes within the Tor network. For example, there have been many proposals for improving how Tor selects its circuits [2, 28, 20, 8] that benefit from understanding the inter-Tor-node latencies, and as we demonstrate in Section 5.1, latency knowledge can speed up existing deanonymization techniques [16, 9, 12, 10].

However, to date, there are no techniques available within Tor or through other Internet measurement to accurately measure the round-trip times between two arbitrary Tor nodes. Researchers and practitioners have thus had to rely on approximations such as geographic distances, which simply cannot model network phenomena such as triangle inequality violations (TIVs) in Internet routing [15].

In this paper, we present *Ting*, a technique for accurately measuring the round-trip times between *any arbitrary pair of Tor nodes.* Ting operates strictly at Tor's "data plane": it carefully constructs circuits and directly measures latencies to and through Tor relays. Critically, Ting works without requiring any modifications to the Tor protocol, to Tor clients, or special permission from Tor users. Through a ground-truth validation on PlanetLab [21], we show that Ting is extremely accurate, imposes little communication or computational overhead on the Tor network, and can be run from a single host.

We also show three applications of such an unprecedentedly accurate and thorough latency dataset. Among these, we show for the first time the presence of TIVs in the Tor network, and the extent to which Ting's measurements can be used to improve end-to-end paths.

Ting fills a gap that has formed in network measurement tools: the ability to directly measure the latencies between two hosts, neither of which are under the control of the experimenter. The King technique [11], introduced in 2002, indirectly measured latency between two arbitrary hosts by cleverly constructing queries to publicly available recursive DNS servers. Unfortunately, since then, most publicly available DNS servers have disallowed recursive queries due to security concerns, rendering King narrowly applicable. Conversely, we show that Ting can be used to infer with *direct measurements* the end-to-end latencies among *any* pair of active Tor nodes. In other words, as Tor's user base increases, so too does Ting's applicability. We show that Tor's current user base span a diverse set of networks (including, in particular, residential hosts) from among ~6000 unique /24 networks, making Ting a viable tool for wide-scale network measurement.[1]

This paper makes the following contributions:

- We present the design, implementation, and validation of Ting, a technique for measuring round-trip times between any arbitrary pair of Tor relays. Ting does not require modifications to or special participation from Tor clients. To the best of our knowledge, *Ting is the only practical tool today for measuring pairwise RTTs in the Tor network.*
- We thoroughly validate Ting's accuracy (80% of the time, its estimates are within 10% of ground-truth), stability (over a week, Ting's estimates vary by less than 5ms), and trade-offs between speed and accuracy.
- We present algorithms that use all-pairs latency measurements to drastically improve the time (a median 1.5× speedup) to deanonymize Tor circuits.
- Finally, we show that Ting's measurements can be used to improve path selection: We find an abundance of so-called triangle inequality violations in inter-Tor-node latencies, and show that circuits *longer* than three hops can be used to achieve *lower* end-to-end latencies.

The rest of this paper is structured as follows. In Section 2, we present related work on ascertaining and applying round-trip time estimations among arbitrary hosts. We present the design of Ting in Section 3, and an extensive validation of Ting in Section 4. In Section 5, we show several ways to apply Ting's measurements, including circuit deanonymization and improved path selection. We conclude in Section 6.

The Ting code and the latency datasets it generated are publicly available at

`https://www.cs.umd.edu/projects/ting`

2. BACKGROUND AND RELATED WORK

Our motivation derives from two sources: the desire to directly perform latency measurements between two hosts not under our control, and the desire to improve the performance or anonymity of Tor circuits by performance-informed path selection. With measured latencies between Tor nodes, we can determine whether the Internet paths follow geographic shortest paths, whether Tor performance is intentionally degraded, and whether there are opportunities for performance optimization. We can evaluate how often Tor's default random relay selection produces high latency paths and whether different path selection approaches might be more difficult to deanonymize. By taking advantage of Tor as a system that is representative of volunteer-administered overlay, we can also learn about the networks that host relay nodes (§5.3).

Prior work has observed that latency information would be beneficial, but have avoided attempting to incorporate it explicitly into the Tor protocol [20, 28]. Our approach is to use, rather than redesign, the protocol in order to measure inter-relay latency information. This permits immediate, incremental deployment of Ting-capable clients, since they can use existing Tor relays.

There are few workable alternatives for estimating the latency between Tor nodes. To make broad, immediate deployment possible, we cannot modify the Tor protocol, e.g., to ask relays to ping one another. There are large scale network measurement services that use hardware at clients to ping often: RIPE Atlas pings root DNS servers from specialized "probe" devices [24]. Such special purpose hardware [31, 25] could be applied to measure and construct a database of inter-node latencies, but they require users to deploy hardware in their networks. Conversely, Ting operates completely within the Tor peer-to-peer network, and does not require any additional user deployment. There has also been considerable work towards estimating inter-node latencies through the use of relatively few landmarks deployed throughout the network [6, 18, 33]. Such estimation systems offer considerably greater coverage than Ting—they can be applied to virtually any pair of nodes—but suffer from the fact that Internet latencies are inherently difficult to estimate accurately, e.g., due to triangle inequality violations [26, 15] (§5.2.1). Ting, on the other hand, achieves greater accuracy by performing *direct measurements.*

An approach that inspires us is that of Gummadi et al. [11], who aimed to estimate the latency between clients and servers by clever use of recursive DNS queries. Their "King" tool sent a recursive DNS request to a name server associated with the first host that could only be answered by a name server associated with the second. Although King required only that one of the two name servers support recursive queries, in recent years, DNS servers have stopped responding to recursive queries for concern over amplification. This means that using King directly is no longer practical.

Instead, in this paper, we attempt to apply the idea of King to Tor.

3. TING TECHNIQUE

In this section, we describe the design of *Ting*, our technique for determining the round-trip time (RTT) between two arbitrary Tor relays. We show that Ting is able to obtain theoretically accurate RTT measurements without requiring any modifications to Tor, without any explicit participation from other users, and while introducing only tiny amounts of work for other Tor nodes. Ting is able to do so by leveraging the fact that Tor allows users to select their own (almost arbitrary) end-to-end circuits. In Section 4, we show that these theoretical properties are upheld in practice.

[1] Ting's applicability is limited to where Tor can be deployed, and unfortunately, some countries censor Tor traffic to or from their residents [23].

3.1 Building Blocks

Ting has two major components. The first is the ability to construct nearly arbitrary end-to-end circuits. Fortunately, this can be done without requiring modifications to any Tor clients. In particular, we make use of Stem [30], a Tor controller that provides a clean programmatic interface for both constructing Tor circuits and attaching TCP connections to them. Even with this control, we are constrained to several natural policies that our local, unmodified Tor client enforces: (1) one-hop circuits are disallowed[2], and (2) a node cannot appear on a given circuit more than once. Both of these are logical policies for ensuring a user's anonymity, but we emphasize that we need not worry about anonymity with Ting—it performs its measurements explicitly, and does not, for instance, piggyback measurements on real user data. Nonetheless, we seek to be able to work within these constraints, so that we can operate without having to modify future versions of Tor and without requiring participation from other users.

Ting's second component is an end-to-end echo client and server to allow us to collect RTT measurements through Tor circuits. While similar in spirit to `ping`—which uses ICMP messages to estimate RTTs—the key difference is that our application operates over TCP, and can thus be used over Tor. As we will see, we do not also require `ping` itself: all of our measurements occur strictly over Tor circuits.

Both of these components are easily attainable and available online, but we make our code and data public for the community.

3.2 Strawman Approach

Consider the task of determining $R(x, y)$: the RTT between two Tor nodes x and y. Suppose further that we have our echo client running at a source node s and echo server at destination node d, both under our control.

An initially tempting approach is to use a method similar in spirit to the technique used by King [11], as shown in Figure 1:

1. Create a circuit C through nodes x and y, attach a TCP connection from s to d to this circuit, and measure the end-to-end RTT $R_C(s,d) = R(s,x)+R(x,y)+R(y,d)$.

2. Ping x from s to obtain an estimate of the RTT between s and x: $\widetilde{R}(s,x)$, and similarly obtain an estimate of the RTT between y and d: $\widetilde{R}(y,d)$.

3. Subtract the values from (2):
$R(x,y) \stackrel{?}{=} R_C(s,d) - \widetilde{R}(s,x) - \widetilde{R}(y,d)$.

Unfortunately, we have identified two sources of error that make this approach untenable. First, note that it relies heavily on `ping` traffic taking a sub-path of that taken by the Tor traffic. However, not all packets are treated equally; we have observed that some networks treat ICMP and TCP traffic differently, exhibiting significantly different latencies for each, and in ways that we did not find easy to predict. Moreover, we found that some networks exhibited differential treatment for Tor traffic in particular. We find this unsurprising; given the perceived sensitive nature of Tor traffic, we expected network operators to, e.g., apply additional firewall or monitoring rules. But again, we were unable to predictably determine how this special treatment affected latencies: sometimes we saw higher `ping` times than Tor, and vice versa. In summary, we find that any technique that mixes Tor and non-Tor traffic is subject to uncertainty in path differences, and thus that *only traffic over Tor should be used.*

[2]In particular, by default, Tor relays refuse to be both the entry and exit node for a circuit.

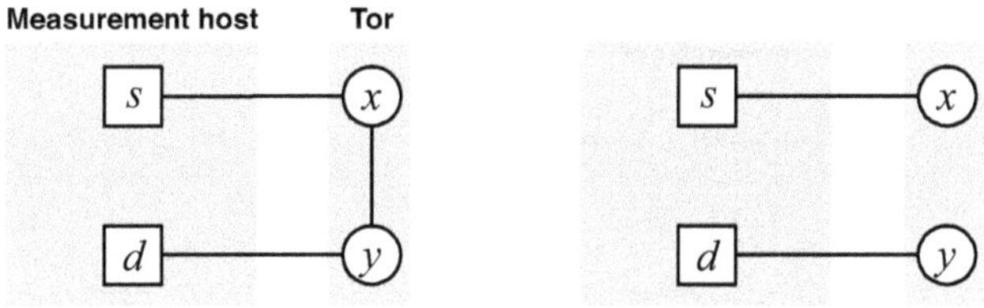

Figure 1: A strawman approach consisting of an end-to-end circuit (left) and direct RTT measurements (right). Unfortunately, because Tor does not permit one-hop circuits, direct RTT measurements would need to be performed using `ping`; because `ping` can experience noticeably different latencies, the estimate of $R(x, y)$ is likely to be inaccurate.

The second threat to validity with the above strawman is that it ignores the fact that, while processing Tor packets, each relay imposes a *forwarding delay*, which comprises (at least) the time to swap to and from user-space, the time the packet spends enqueued, and the time to decrypt and encrypt packets. Each of these time sinks is low in expectation, but because they can introduce additive errors, *forwarding delays must at be at least partially accounted for.* (We empirically evaluate Tor forwarding delays in Section 4.3.)

Guided by these two observations, we next present the design of Ting.

3.3 Ting Design

Ting determines the round-trip time between an arbitrary pair of Tor relays (x, y). It extends the above strawman to operate strictly over Tor (instead of using incompatible `ping`s), and to account for Tor nodes' forwarding delays. With Ting, we run an echo client and server (s and d), but run them on the same machine (or at least within the same subnet); the key distinction being that the RTT from s to an arbitrary host is equal to d's RTT to the same host.

As described in Section 3.2, we must avoid mixing Tor and `ping` measurements, but we also need the ability to isolate the RTT between the nodes we control and those we do not (x and y). Ideally, we could create a one-hop circuit through x or y, but recall that Tor disallows this. To this end, we locally run two Tor peers, w and z, both also hosted within the same network as s and d.

While this may seem like an extensive measurement infrastructure, in practice, we simply run all four processes on the same host h: the echo client and server (s and d) and both of our Tor nodes (w and z). However, our design extends to other configurations, as well.

Ting begins its measurement of $R(x, y)$ by first constructing a full circuit $C_{x,y} = (w, x, y, z)$, as in Figure 2(a). Ting then attaches to $C_{x,y}$ a TCP connection between s and d, and measures the end-to-end RTT over this circuit. Let F_i denote Tor node i's forwarding delay. Then, because s, w, z, and d are all running on the same host h, the overall RTT can be expressed as:

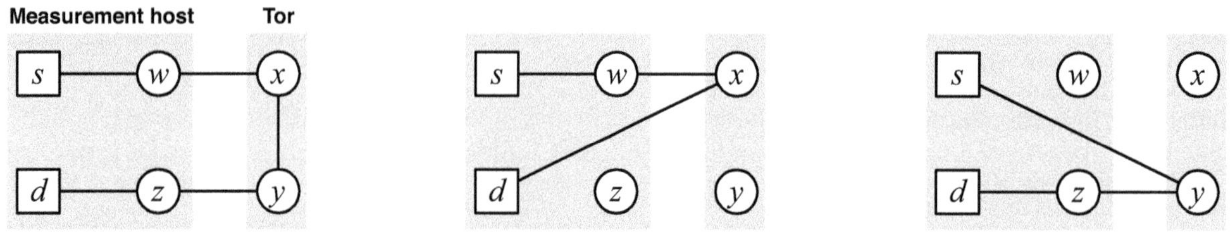

(a) The RTT across the full circuit. (b) Isolating the RTT to x. (c) Isolating the RTT to y.

Figure 2: An overview of Ting's algorithm, capturing the steps necessary to isolate $R(x, y)$ by building multiple circuits through x and y. Circles represent Tor clients, while squares represent our echo client and server.

$$\begin{aligned} R_{C_{x,y}}(s,d) &= R(h,h) + 2F_h + R(h,x) \\ &\quad + 2F_x + R(x,y) + 2F_y \\ &\quad + R(h,y) + 2F_h + R(h,h) \end{aligned} \tag{1}$$

Each line of this equation represents a different part of the end-to-end path: the first line represents the RTT from s to w to x; the second line represents the RTT between x and y; and the third line represents the RTT from y to z back to our server d.

The above equation contains our target measurement, $R(x, y)$, but it also contains additional latency measurements; in particular, we must subtract the RTT over Tor from h to x and from h to y. To measure the RTT to x, Ting creates the circuit $C_x = (w, x)$, as depicted in Figure 2(b), and likewise for y, as in Figure 2(c). Attaching new TCP connections to them and measuring the end-to-end RTTs gives us:

$$R_{C_x}(s,d) = 2R(h,h) + 4F_h + 2R(h,x) + 2F_x \tag{2}$$
$$R_{C_y}(s,d) = 2R(h,h) + 4F_h + 2R(h,y) + 2F_y \tag{3}$$

Observe that all three equations account for two forwarding delays at their respective x and y nodes: this reflects the fact that there is both a ping and a pong message sent in opposite directions on the circuit.

All that remains is to calculate:

$$\begin{aligned} R_{C_{x,y}}(s,d) - \frac{1}{2}R_{C_x}(s,d) - \frac{1}{2}R_{C_y}(s,d) \\ = R(x,y) + F_x + F_y \end{aligned} \tag{4}$$

We arrive at an estimate of the RTT between x and y with an expected error equal to the sum of the forwarding delays of the two nodes. The predominant factor in a node's forwarding delay is the number of other circuits and overall load at that node. For instance, if our measurement packet arrives at a node when our circuit is not first in the schedule, it will have to wait to be dequeued. To account for this, every time we measure an RTT, we do not limit it to a single sample; rather, we take multiple samples, and use the minimum value. We describe in Section 4 that, in practice, this results in minimum forwarding delays typically in the range of 0–3ms; for most pairs of x and y, this is a negligible error within the typical variation of latencies.

3.4 Properties

Ting has several features that make it a feasible and effective measurement tool. Primarily, it operates strictly within Tor, meaning that we can be relatively certain that all measurement traffic will be treated equally: all packets will traverse the same paths, and through the same software stacks. As a result, the theoretical accuracy is high; although our final estimation (Eq. (4)) does not entirely eliminate forwarding delays, it accounts for them explicitly, and measures in such a way as to minimize their impact.

Additionally, Ting is trivial to deploy: it does not require any modifications to the Tor protocol, to existing nodes, or even to a local Tor client. Moreover, it can be run on a single host, as described above.

Finally, Ting can be applied to any pair of Tor nodes, regardless of whether they are exit nodes. In all of Ting's circuits, we use a node we control (z) as the circuit's exit node.

In sum, Ting is a novel, easy to use tool that provides unprecedented insight into the RTTs within the Tor network. In the next section, we validate Ting empirically and demonstrate that it can determine the latency of a pair of Tor nodes in less than 15 seconds with high accuracy.

4. TING VALIDATION

In this section, we validate Ting along several dimensions. First, using a set of globally distributed PlanetLab [21] nodes as ground-truth, we measure Ting's accuracy and evaluate how many samples are necessary to minimize errors caused by forwarding delays. Then, we turn to measuring Ting on the *real Tor network* and demonstrate that it achieves measurements that are consistent over time.

4.1 Ground-truth Testbed

In order to prove that Ting measurements are representative of the actual latency between two Tor servers, we require a ground-truth to compare to. To this end, we ran Tor relays on 31 PlanetLab [21] hosts. Further, to ensure that these hosts realistically reflect the geographically diverse Tor network, we guided our selection of random hosts such that:

- They covered a wide geographic area: 6 countries throughout Europe, 9 states throughout the U.S., and at least one relay in each of the following regions were represented: Asia, South America, Australia, and the Middle East.

- Their geographic distribution resembled that of the current Tor network, which contains a concentration

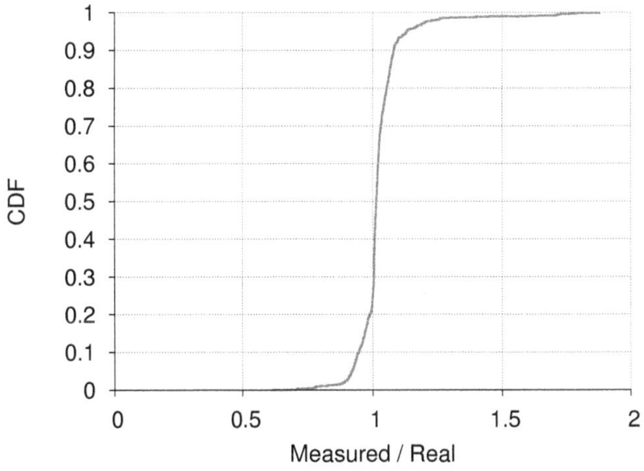

Figure 3: CDF of Ting's estimation for a given pair on PlanetLab relative to "real" latency values reported by `ping`.

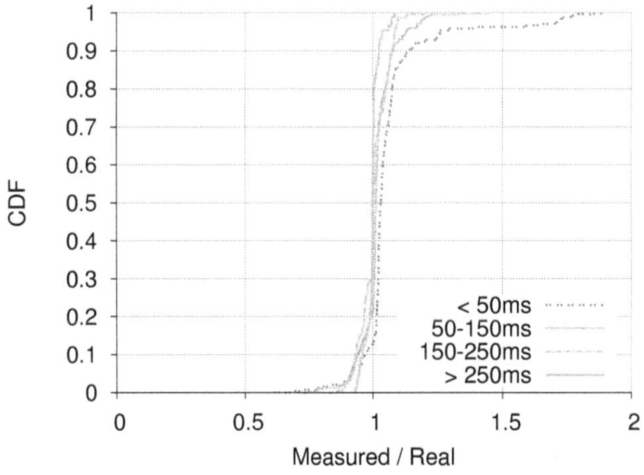

Figure 4: CDF of Ting performance separated into different intervals based on real latency.

of relays in the U.S. and Europe, and only a few nodes sparsely distributed throughout other countries.

- The latencies between all the pairs were unique and ranged from very close (~0ms) to nearly antipodal (~500ms).

We ran an unmodified version of Tor-0.2.4.22, with a restrictive exit policy that only allowed exiting to two specific IP addresses under our control (to avoid take-down notices to or from the institutions hosting the PlanetLab nodes). In addition, we maintained the relays for over a month before conducting our measurements in order to ensure that they would be receiving standard usage and traffic patterns in addition to our probe traffic, which we assume will be the situation for any arbitrary relays we attempt to measure.

For all of our experiments, we performed our measurements using two machines. The first machine ran both our client and server (s and d from Section 3). The client program was written in Python and controlled a Tor onion proxy (running a patched version of Tor-0.2.3.25) using the Stem controller library [30]. The server program, also written in Python, was an extremely minimal TCP-based echo server.

The second machine ran two instances of an unmodified version of Tor-0.2.4.22 to act as our relays w and z. To demonstrate that Ting operates with minimal setup or modification, we allowed these two nodes to publish their descriptors to the Tor directory authorities, but this is not necessary; one can prevent Tor from publishing the descriptors (by supplying "`PublishDescriptors 0`" in the torrc configuration file) and simply hard-code the descriptors (mainly, the public keys) into the client's descriptor list.

4.2 Ting Accuracy

To begin our validation of Ting, we measure the RTT between all 930 pairs of nodes from our 31-node testbed, and compare these against direct, all-pairs `ping` measurements. We probe each pair in a randomized order, taking 1000 Ting samples[3] followed immediately by 100 `ping`s. As described in Section 3, we use the minimum sample from both techniques as their final estimate of the pairs' RTTs.

Figure 3 shows the distribution of the ratio between Ting's estimate and the ground-truth RTT measurement. In this plot, an x-value of 1 represents perfect accuracy. For 91% of the pairs, Ting's estimates are within 10% of the true value.[4] Fewer than 2% of all estimates had an error greater than 30%. The lack of an obvious skew to either side of $x = 1$ indicates that Ting is effective at ruling out the vast majority of errors caused by forwarding delays.

Ting is able to obtain such high rates of accuracy in large part because it is able to perform its measurements *directly* through the nodes whose RTTs it seeks to ascertain. In comparison, King [11] used DNS resolvers near the nodes it sought to measure, but could not completely account for the latencies between resolvers and their respective clients; as a result, King exhibits a distribution skewed to the left of $x = 1$ [11, Fig. 5].

To understand if Ting's accuracy is dependent on how large the true end-to-end RTT is, we break up the accuracy data into four latency regimes in Figure 4, based on the ground-truth RTTs. These results show that Ting is more accurate for pairs with greater end-to-end latency, as the CDF for each successive range becomes increasingly vertical and centered around $x = 1$, with the final range of 250–500ms having a nearly vertical curve at $x = 1$. We can also observe that a majority of outliers (identified as tails on the curve) come from pairs measured in the "< 50ms" group, indicating that what appears to be a large relative error is in fact attributable to a small absolute error.

For some applications, it suffices to know only the rank order of latencies [11]. The Spearman's rank-order correlation between Ting's estimates and our ground-truth data is 0.997 (a value of 1.0 denotes perfect agreement in rank order).

We find these results extremely encouraging, particularly given that they were collected on PlanetLab nodes, which

[3]We show in Section 4.4 that Ting can achieve comparable accuracy with far fewer samples.

[4]For the remaining pairs, we observed errors distributed mostly uniformly across the hosts we measured (as opposed to a few nodes being highly erroneous).

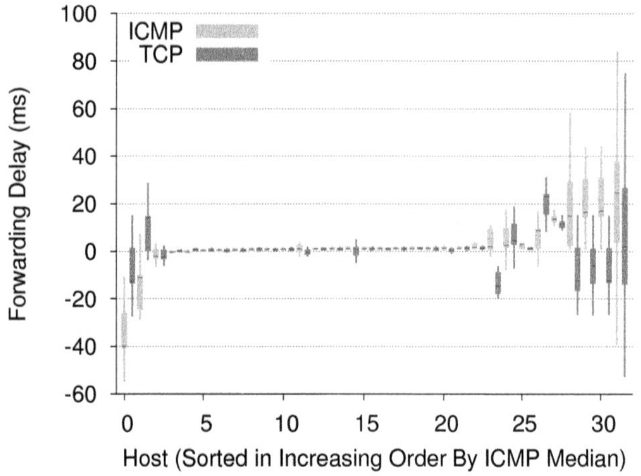

Figure 5: Forwarding delays measured across 31 Tor relays. Abnormal values indicate networks that treat ICMP, TCP, and Tor traffic differently. For all other networks, Ting can consistently find low forwarding delays.

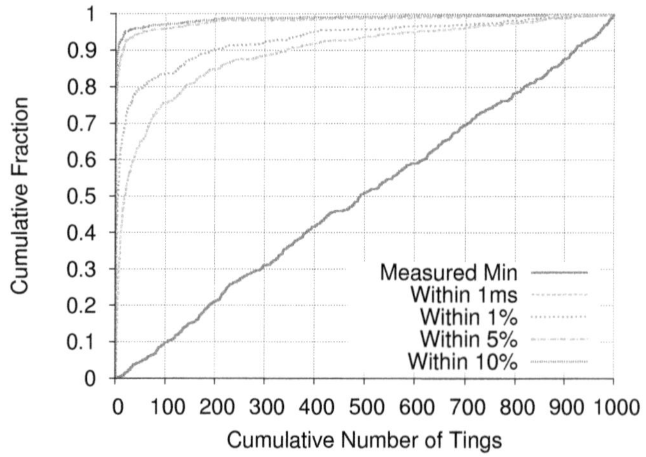

Figure 6: Number of samples required to reach different approximations of the minimum of 1000 samples.

are known to exhibit high variance in their computation and communication speeds.

To summarize, these ground-truth results show that Ting provides an accurate method of estimating the round-trip times between hosts on the Tor network without requiring modifications to Tor or explicit participation from other Tor users. Moreover, our experimental setup included nodes that were geographically distributed and not dedicated to our use—PlanetLab is a shared infrastructure. Thus, these experiments additionally show that Ting's accuracy is not highly dependent on factors about the host which are out of our control. This is an important implication moving forward in assuming that Ting can be used to measure all relays on the network.

4.3 Forwarding Delays

In Section 3.2, we made two claims about forwarding delays that we now seek to validate: (1) that forwarding delays are typically negligible, but (2) that they must be at least partially accounted for in order to minimize the error introduced in the event that they are non-negligible.

In order to measure the forwarding delay for a given node x, we apply the following approach, which resembles our method of measuring latency:

1. Set up an echo client s and echo server d on one host, and two instances of Tor, w and z, on a second host.
2. Create a circuit $C_1 = (w, z)$ from s and probe d to measure end-to-end RTT $R_{C_1}(s,d) = R(s,w) + F_w + R(w,z) + F_z + R(z,d)$.
3. Use `ping` or `tcptraceroute` from s to w to obtain $\widetilde{R}(s,w)$ and $\widetilde{R}(z,d)$, the *estimated* RTTs between the hosts, which should be equivalent as w and z are running on the same host.
4. Subtract these latencies to calculate the forwarding delay of w and z, $F_w = F_z = \frac{R_{C_1}(s,d) - \widetilde{R}(s,w) - \widetilde{R}(z,d)}{2}$ (here we leverage the fact that $\widetilde{R}(w,z) \approx 0$).
5. Create a circuit $C_2 = (w, x, z)$ from s and probe d to measure the end-to-end RTT $R_{C_2}(s,d) = R(s,w) + F_w + R(w,x) + F_x + R(x,z) + F_z + R(z,d)$.
6. Use `ping` or `tcptraceroute` from s to w and from w to x to obtain $\widetilde{R}(s,w) = \widetilde{R}(z,d)$ and $\widetilde{R}(w,x) = \widetilde{R}(x,z)$, estimates of the respective RTTs.
7. Subtract the values from (4) and (6): $F_x = R_{C_2} - F_w - F_z - 2\widetilde{R}(w,x) - 2\widetilde{R}(s,w)$

We use both `ping` (which uses ICMP) and `tcptraceroute` (which uses TCP) to investigate whether it is necessary or sufficient to measure RTTs using the same transport layer protocol as Tor's.

We applied this technique to compute the forwarding delay for our set of 31 Tor relays running on PlanetLab once an hour over a 48-hour period. Figure 5 shows the distributions of our measurements over time, with individual nodes sorted by median `ping`-measured forwarding delay. The box-plots capture the median, interquartile ranges, and minimum and maximum values within the interquartiles. Nearly 65% of all nodes exhibit a distribution tightly closed around the range of 0–2ms with very little variance. These nodes match our expectations of a low minimum forwarding delay: if a packet arrives at a Tor relay very shortly before when it would be scheduled to be dequeued, then the forwarding delay should consist only of the time to process the packet, which mostly consists of symmetric key cryptography, and is thus fast.

However, the remaining 35% of nodes show extremely odd behavior, with forwarding delays often *negative*. These abnormalities are due to our observation from Section 3 that not all packets are treated equal: negative forwarding delays indicate that it took less time to communicate with a node over Tor than to directly ping that node, sometimes on the order of tens of milliseconds. This is simply not possible unless packets follow different paths. Using both ICMP- and TCP-based measurements makes this even more stark; we see for these outliers consistent disparity between how ICMP and TCP packets are treated. We therefore place very little confidence in forwarding delays measured from networks that exhibit such disparate behavior; of all remaining networks, we see only near-zero estimates of forwarding delay.

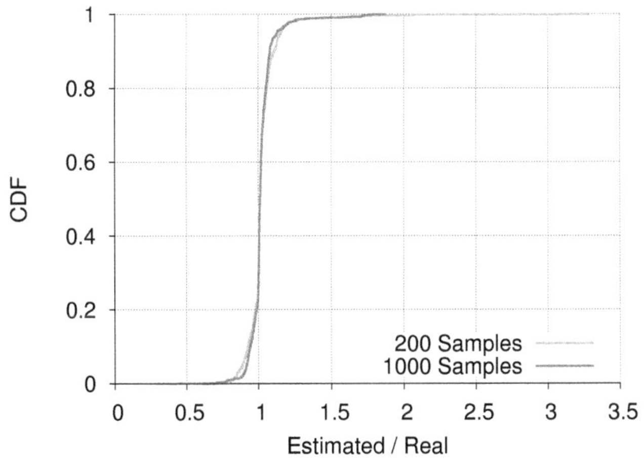

Figure 7: Comparison of taking 200 samples for each pair vs. 1000 samples for each pair.

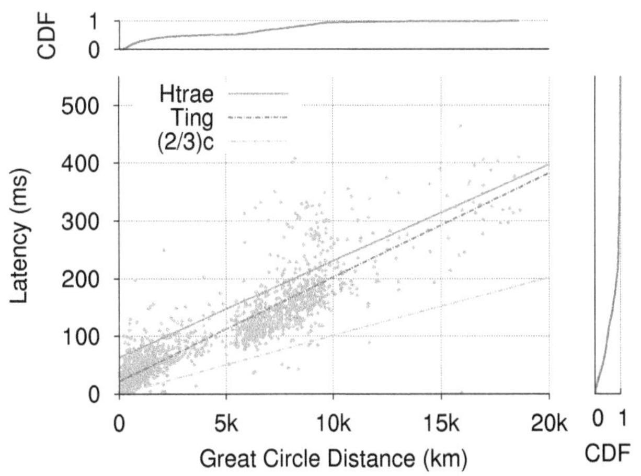

Figure 8: Relationship between geographic distance and RTTs measured by Ting, using GPS coordinates from Neustar IP Geolocation [17].

We draw two important conclusions from this experiment. First, for networks that do not appear to differentiate how they treat packets of different protocols, Ting observes forwarding delays to be relatively negligible, at ~2ms. This explains why our theoretical estimate in Eq. (4) is able to perform so well in practice. Second, this experiment concretely demonstrates the importance of avoiding using `ping` or even TCP-based RTT estimation techniques in combination with Tor-based measurements. Collectively, these results validate Ting's approach and accuracy.

4.4 Sample Sizes

The Ting algorithm takes as a parameter the number of times to sample each circuit, which allows one to adjust the balance between speed of measurement and accuracy. Since we only end up using the minimum value of all RTTs measured for each circuit, the question is: how many samples does it take to reach a true minimum, or at least how many does it take to reach within an acceptable interval of this minimum?

Jansen et al. [13] observed that it can sometimes take an incredible number of latency samples through Tor before obtaining a true minimum. We recreated this experiment by using Ting to measure 100 random pairs of *live* Tor nodes, taking 1000 samples from each circuit. In Figure 6, we present how many iterations were necessary across all pairs to obtain the minimum estimate, and approximations thereof. This confirms the prior result of Jansen et al.: it does indeed take a considerable number of iterations to reach the actual minimum. However, we also present the number of iterations necessary to get *close to* the minimum. Even modest departures from minimum can be found far more quickly; for instance, to get within 1ms of the minimum requires roughly 25× fewer probes at the median.

To further solidify this fact, we re-measured the latency between the 930 pairs of Planet Lab nodes from our experiment in 4.2, this time taking 200 samples rather than 1000. In Figure 7, we plot the CDF of the ratio between measured and real values (again using `ping` as a ground-truth for RTTs) and compare this to the CDF of taking the minimum of 1000 samples. The fact that the CDFs are almost identical reinforces our claim that there is very little benefit to taking a large number of samples.

Because the number of samples is a tunable parameter, one can turn it down even further to measure more quickly. For instance, in our experiments, Ting took an average of 2.5 minutes to measure a pair using 200 samples in order to ensure very high accuracy. However, if one were willing to accept 5% error, then Ting could measure a pair in less than 15 seconds on average. For the remainder of the experiments in this paper, we continue using 200 samples.

4.5 Ting on the Live Tor Network

We now investigate Ting's effectiveness in measuring pairs in the wild, outside of our controlled environment, and without the limitations imposed by PlanetLab. We used Ting to measure 10,000 pairs of Tor relays, chosen uniformly at random from the pool of all currently running relays. Since we cannot directly compare the accuracy of specific measurements in this scenario, we now look at general trends.

Figure 8 shows the relationship between the Ting-measured RTTs and the geographic distance for each of the 10,000 pairs of Tor nodes. We used the Neustar IP Geolocation service [17] to obtain an estimate of the GPS coordinates for each of the relays, and calculated the great circle distance between each pair. Additionally, in the margins, we plot CDFs of the two axes to show the relative distribution of latencies and distances covered. We annotate the plot with three lines. One line represents the generally accepted *maximum speed* that packets can traverse a given distance in the Internet: 2/3 the speed of light. This serves as a sanity check; indeed, we see only a handful of points below this line. Manually inspecting these nodes, we see that they are almost all likely errors in the underlying geolocation database.

The other two lines represent fits to more accurate latency datasets. At the top is the estimate derived from a large study of latencies among Halo gamers as part of the Htrae system [1], and below that is our linear fit to our own data. The gap between these two lines is due to the fact that Htrae measured *median* latencies, while we seek to detect the minimum latency between a pair of nodes. Their

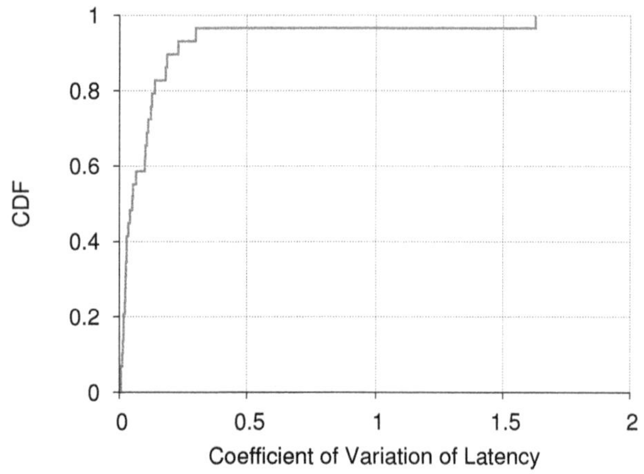

Figure 9: Measuring the latency between a pair of relays using Ting produces relatively consistent results over time.

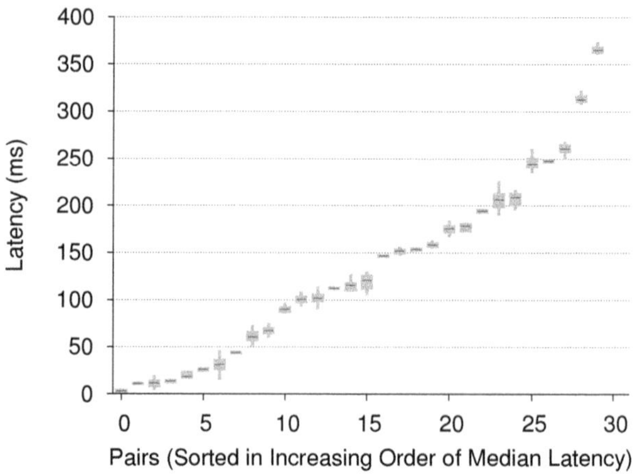

Figure 10: Larger relative variance is revealed as small absolute errors when the mean is low.

similar values are encouraging validation. However, one interesting feature of our linear fit is that it has a greater slope. We believe this is due to the surge of latencies between 5000 and 10,000 km: these are likely international links that are traversing at least one country's border. Note, for instance, that the CDF at the top of the plot does not have the same shape as the one on the right; if the relationship was strictly linear, they should have the same shape. We speculate that this is evidence that, at least for international circuits, Tor traffic is being treated differently than more traditional traffic, such as gaming. More investigation into these differences is an interesting area of future work.

4.6 Stability of Ting Measurements over Time

In the following section, we demonstrate the impact that an all-pairs RTT matrix can have on various applications. However, an all-pairs matrix can be time-consuming to calculate. Here, we measure whether Ting captures snapshots that are representative over time—that is, how *stable* are Ting's measurements?

In order to evaluate the stability of Ting measurements over time, we picked a set of 30 pairs of Tor relays and measured the RTT between them once an hour over the course of a week. The pairs were chosen such that: (1) Both relays were running for over a month, in order to mitigate the chance that they would go down over the course of the experiment, (2) The distribution of the RTTs of the pairs would match the distribution shown in Figure 8, which displays a relatively uniform distribution from low to high latencies, in order to observe the effects of RTT on variance.

In Figure 9 we plot the CDF of the coefficient of variance c_v (the standard deviation normalized to the mean) which can be used to compare the degree of variation between a series of data sets with different means. 96.7% of all pairs (all but one pair) have $c_v < 0.5$, indicating high stability; further, over 50% of pairs have $c_v \approx 0$.

Although the c_v measures variance well in a majority of cases, it is very sensitive to changes when the mean is low. Figure 10 provides another view of the data, displaying Ting's distribution of measurements for each pair. Again, these boxes show the median, interquartiles, and the maximum and minimum within the interquartile ranges. The outlier in Figure 9 corresponds to the first pair in Figure 10, indicating that the high c_v was in fact biased towards having a low mean (~3ms). 67% of the pairs do not show a single outlier, and have third and first quartiles that differ by less than 5ms. Even in the remaining cases where the latencies span a wider range, such as pair 15, it is worth noting that the outliers are still relatively close to the mean, and do not represent a very large error. This suggests that taking measurements with Ting infrequently and caching them is sufficient, and thus permits obtaining a large dataset of RTTs between Tor nodes.

Summary

This section has shown that Ting is incredibly accurate because it can measure nodes *directly* rather than through a nearby proxy, as with prior approaches [11]. Moreover, we demonstrated that Ting's measurements are resilient over time, and do not require many samples to obtain reasonable accuracy. Ting can thus be used to generate all-pairs RTT measurements of the Tor network. In the next section, we show how we can leverage such an all-pairs matrix to benefit various applications.

5. APPLICATIONS

In this section, we discuss three disparate applications that benefit from the highly accurate RTT measurements Ting provides. We provide what we believe to be the first deanonymization technique that precludes certain circuits through application of latency measurements. We also show how Ting can be used to find longer circuits that results in *lower* end-to-end latency. Finally, we show Ting's value as a network measurement platform by evaluating the diversity of Tor relays.

5.1 Deanonymization of Tor

Tor seeks to balance anonymity with low-latency communication, and as a result, various techniques have been introduced to *deanonymize* users by introducing small but noticeable fluctuations in their latencies [16, 9, 12, 10].

A common form of deanonymization assumes that the attacker is somewhere on the path, from source to destination: either the attacker is on the three-node Tor circuit (consisting of an entry node, a middle node, and an exit node), or it is the destination itself (e.g., in the case of a malicious server). The attacker's goal is to determine all of the nodes on the circuit, as this has been shown to assist in determining the source and destination [12].

Active probing attacks have been shown to make deanonymization with an on-path attacker possible. The attacker can determine if Tor relay t is on the victim source-destination path by (1) creating many circuits through t and sending traffic through them, and (2) seeing if this induces extra delay on the victim's packet inter-arrival times. This is a somewhat heavy-handed approach to deanonymization—it is expensive for an attacker to launch, as it requires creating multiple circuits simply to rule out a single Tor relay. For such attacks to be feasible in practice, it is important that the number of active probes performed remain small.

5.1.1 *Speeding up deanonymization with Ting*

Here, we consider how knowledge of RTTs between all pairs of Tor nodes can speed up existing deanonymization algorithms. The specific setting we consider is when the attacker is the destination: he already knows the exit node, and wishes to determine the entry and middle nodes. Our insight is, broadly speaking, that because the attacker knows the end-to-end RTT R_{e2e}, then we can rule out any circuit whose hops' RTTs add up to greater than R_{e2e}.

More concretely, consider the standard, RTT-unaware deanonymization process. Initially, the attacker knows: its RTT r to the exit node, the exit node x itself, and the end-to-end RTT R_{e2e}. Suppose during the deanonymization algorithm, the attacker learns that Tor node c is on the circuit. Let $R(a, b)$ denote the RTT between Tor nodes a and b. Then the attacker learns the following by "ignoring too-large RTTs":

- If there exists no potential entry node e such that $R(e, c) + R(c, x) + r \leq R_{e2e}$, then c cannot be the middle node in the circuit, and therefore must be the entry node.
- Alternatively, if there exists no potential middle node m such that $R(c, m) + R(m, x) + r \leq R_{e2e}$, then c cannot be the entry node, and must be the middle node.
- If c has been identified as the entry node, then any node m for which $R(c, m) + R(m, x) + r > R_{e2e}$ cannot be in the circuit, and therefore m need not be tested.
- Similarly, if c has been identified as the middle node, then any node e for which $R(e, c) + R(c, x) + r > R_{e2e}$ cannot be in the circuit and need not be tested.

Each of these rules is somewhat conservative; the inequalities do not take the RTT between the source and the entry node into account, and thus the above criteria will likely remove only extreme outliers. The RTT information that Ting provides can further speed up deanonymization by preferentially testing nodes who are more likely to be on the circuit. Our insight is as follows: Nodes choose circuits at random, and therefore, if for node i to be on the path, the source would have to be improbably close to or far from an entry node, then i is probably not on the path. Of course, the source being very close to or far from i is not definitive proof that i is not in the circuit, so we do not rule i out. Instead, we assign a "score" to each node, and preferentially

Algorithm 1 Informed target selection for fast deanonymization.

1. For each node i who has not yet been ruled out:
   (a) Enumerate all possible circuits C involving i, after applying the above criteria for ignoring too-large RTTs.
   (b) Let $R(c)$ denote the sum of RTTs of circuit c, and let μ denote the average RTT among all pairs of Tor nodes; then i's score is $\min_{c \in C}\{|R_{e2e} - (R(c) + r + \mu)|\}$.
2. Probe the node with the lowest score, and then apply the criteria for ignoring too-large RTTs.

test nodes with the lowest score. More concretely, we apply Algorithm 1 at every iteration of the deanonymization process.

This algorithm uses μ—the average RTT across the entire all-pairs data supplied by Ting—to approximate the expected (average) RTT between the source and its entry node. Thus, this algorithm chooses the node whose expected end-to-end latency, $R(c) + r + \mu$, most closely approaches the measured end-to-end latency R_{e2e}.

Weighted Node Selection. As stated, our informed target selection algorithm (Alg. 1) assumes that each node in a Tor circuit is chosen uniformly at random from the set of all active nodes. In practice, Tor no longer operates this way, but rather assigns a *weight* to each node, reflecting how its measured bandwidth compares to the overall population's. The benefit of preferentially choosing higher-capacity nodes is that it increases the throughput of the overall circuit, but the downside is the circuits become more predictable. These weights can be incorporated into our algorithm by simply dividing each node's score by the node's weight. However, in the remainder of this section, we evaluate Ting in its worst case scenario—when all weights are equal (traditional Tor).

5.1.2 *Evaluation*

To evaluate how well RTT values can speed up deanonymization efforts, we used Ting to generate an all-pairs RTT dataset among a set of 50 randomly chosen Tor nodes. We present the distribution of RTTs in Figure 11, and note that the shape of the distribution is consistent with that from Figure 8. Using this all-pairs dataset, we simulate three deanonymization techniques, each of which assumes the existence of a technique such as that described by Murdoch and Danzeis [16] to brute-force probe whether a given Tor node is on a circuit. For all of our results, we use 1000 runs from our simulator, with the source chosen uniformly at random from the set of Tor nodes. In addition to the two techniques described above (that which ignores too-large RTTs, and our informed target selection), we also include as a baseline an RTT-unaware technique that simply brute-force tests nodes until it has discovered the entire circuit.

The critical evaluation metric is how many probes it takes to deanonymize a circuit. Recall that, because such brute-force probes are more bandwidth-intensive and time-consuming in practice, techniques which require fewer probes will finish more quickly and with less impact on the network as a whole.

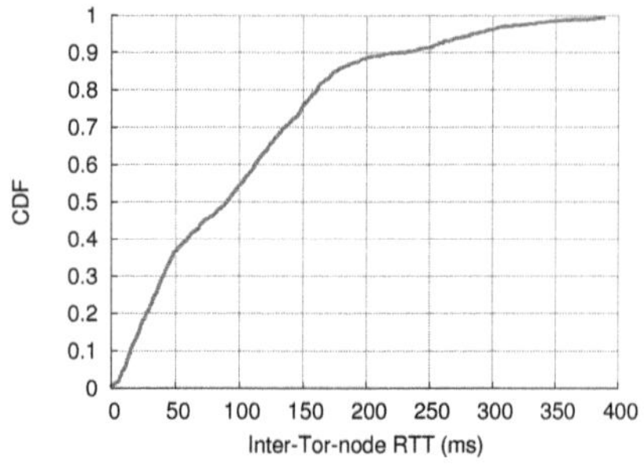

Figure 11: Distribution of RTTs from running Ting on all pairs of a random 50-node set of Tor nodes.

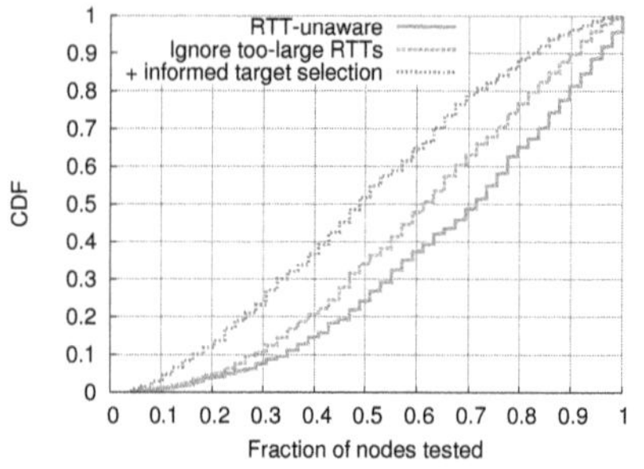

Figure 12: Knowledge of RTT between all Tor nodes speeds up deanonymization.

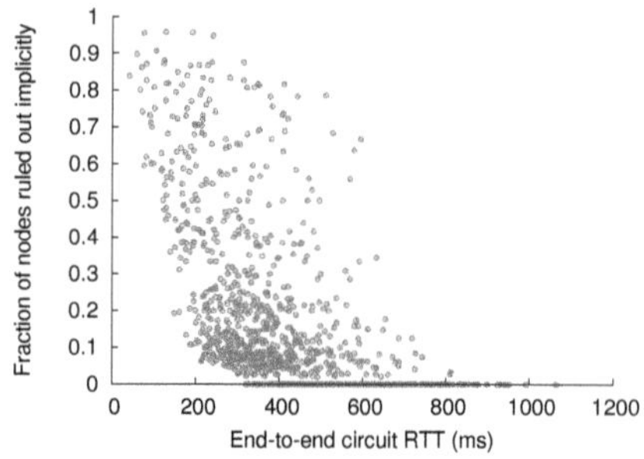

Figure 13: RTT knowledge is particularly useful when deanonymizing circuits with lower end-to-end RTT.

Figure 12 shows the distribution of the fraction of nodes each technique needed to probe in order to deanonymize the circuit. Without any RTT knowledge, determining the entry and middle nodes of the circuit requires probing a median of 72% of the network. Simply ignoring too-large RTT values improves this noticeably, requiring probes to a median of 62% of the network. Incorporating the more intelligent target node selection described in Algorithm 1, we see an even more drastic decline, requiring probes to a median of 48% of the network. In other words, through the application of Ting's RTT information, deanonymization efforts can experience a 1.5× speedup.[5]

Next, we seek to better understand for what circuits Ting's information helps deanonymize. Intuitively, our deanonymization algorithms are best suited for circuits with low end-to-end RTTs. As a simple example: if the end-to-end RTT were 50ms, then any node with an RTT greater than 50ms to the exit node could not be the middle node in the circuit. On the other hand, if the end-to-end RTT were over one second (larger than any single RTT we measured), then any node could ostensibly be in the circuit.

Using the same 1000 runs from our simulator, we plot in Figure 13 the fraction of nodes that we could ignore due to too-large RTTs, and compare that to the end-to-end RTT—from the source, through the circuit, to the destination. This shows a strong correlation: the lower the end-to-end RTT, the more nodes Ting helps us to rule out, while for the absolute highest RTTs, Ting's information was not helpful. However, interestingly, Ting successfully speeds up deanonymization efforts of circuits with moderate to high RTTs. We conclude that, along with the algorithms from this section, Ting can considerably speed up the deanonymization for most circuits.

5.1.3 *Defenses*

Unfortunately, defending against this kind of attack is difficult; as long as there is a pair of nodes that provide lower latency than other pairs, this deanonymization attack could apply. One countermeasure would be to artificially inflate latencies within a circuit, but the Tor designers do not appear willing to accept this cost [7]. Another approach that would slow down, but not completely eliminate, this deanonymization attack would be to randomize the *length* of circuits. The primary concern with this approach is that longer circuits typically result in greater latencies, but as we will show in Section 5.2.2, latency measurements from Ting can guide the creation of longer circuits without higher latency.

In summary, Ting's ability to measure all-pairs RTT among Tor nodes can considerably speed up existing deanonymization techniques, particularly (though not exclusively) with smaller end-to-end RTTs. We believe that these techniques can be improved further, and that it is an interesting area of future work.

5.2 Improving Path Selection in Tor

Recall that a typical Tor circuit consists of three relays: one guard, one middle, and one exit. By default, a Tor client selects these relays at random according to the bandwidth capacity of each router, as reported by the set of trusted Tor bandwidth authorities.[6] The rationale behind using three hops is that it is the minimum required to provide unlinkability between source and destination, and has thus been expected to avoid extra end-to-end latency.

There have been considerable efforts toward reducing end-to-end RTTs [2, 28, 20, 8], but lacking the ability to efficiently predict a circuit's RTT complicates these efforts. For instance, LASTor [2] relies on geographic distances as a proxy for latencies; while we have shown a strong correlation between distance and RTT (Section 4), we demonstrate here that there are many instances where latency can be reduced in ways that geographic distance *cannot* predict.

Here, we investigate whether explicit measurements can guide path selection toward paths that have lower latency or longer length at modest performance cost.

5.2.1 *Triangle Inequality Violations*

A *triangle inequality violation* (TIV) in routing occurs when the lowest-latency path between two nodes s and d is not the direct path between them ($s \leftrightarrow d$), but rather through an intermediate ($s \leftrightarrow r \leftrightarrow d$). In other words, when there is a TIV, the shortest distance between two points is not a straight line, and a relay can provide access to this shorter path [26, 15].

[5]We have also evaluated the weighted version of our deanonymization algorithms, and find that, compared to a scheme that tests nodes in decreasing order of weight, the Ting-based approach speeds up deanonymization by a median of 2×; an even greater improvement than with unweighted node selection.

[6]Tor applies several other filters, such as requiring that relays come from distinct /16s; our results extend to such criteria, but we do not enumerate them here for ease of presentation.

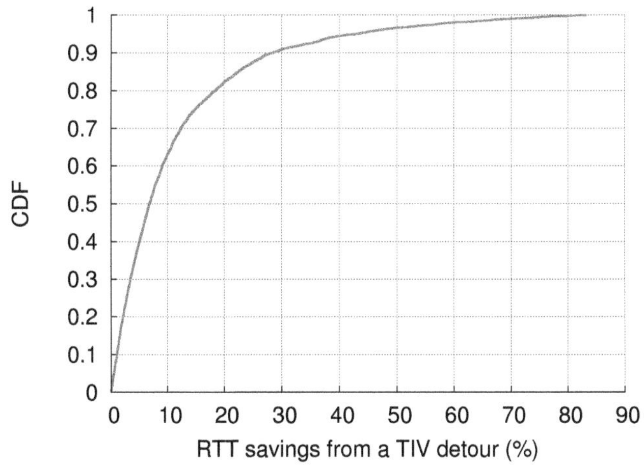

Figure 14: Savings from using a TIV relay instead of direct paths between two Tor nodes.

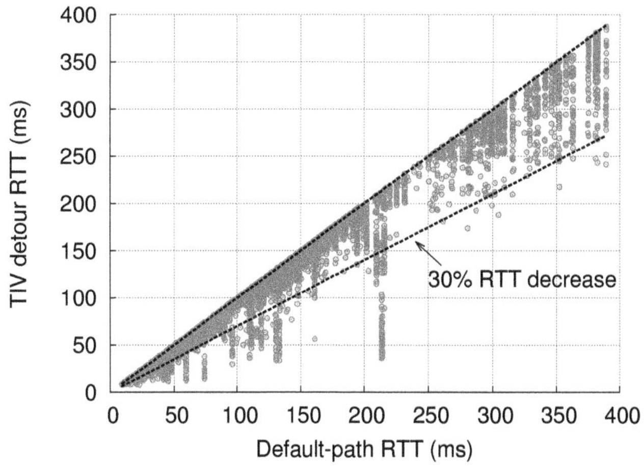

Figure 15: TIV-capable pairs are not relegated to any particular range of RTTs.

Here, we investigate to what extent TIVs exist in Tor, and whether they permit lower-latency paths to a wide range of circuits. To investigate this question, we make use of our 50-node all-pairs Ting dataset, and simply identify all pairs of nodes (s, d) such that there exists a node r for which $R(s, d) > R(s, r) + R(r, d)$. Surprisingly, we find that, for 69% of all pairs of Tor nodes in our data, there exists at least one circuit that results in a TIV.[7]

Figure 14 shows the distribution of the percentage improvement in RTT from using a TIV relay. Here, the x-axis reflects the ratio between $R(s,r) + R(r,d)$ to $R(s,d)$. The median decrease in latency is 7.5%; this is somewhat modest, but an all-pairs RTT dataset allows us to choose relays that offer greater RTT savings: 10% of TIVs reduce RTTs by 28% or more.

To show that TIVs in Tor are not specific to high or low latency paths, we plot in Figure 15, for every TIV we find, the correlation between the default-path RTT and that through the TIV relay. The number of available TIVs and overall savings are mostly consistent, regardless of the default path's RTT. Substantial drops below $x = y$ typically indicate performance-insensitive Internet routing; smaller drops may indicate congestion. Greater detail about such paths is provided by Detour [26] or PeerWise [15].

Using Ting, we are able to demonstrate the prevalence of TIVs in the Tor network. This has two important ramifications: First, *geographic distance is an imperfect proxy for RTTs in Tor.* Distances do not violate the triangle inequality, while Tor often does. Direct measurements of node-to-node latencies are necessary to find these paths. Second, the traditional assumption that longer circuits yield greater end-to-end latency is not necessarily true: *longer circuits can reduce latencies*, if chosen in a way that favors TIVs. Encouraged by this result, we now investigate: do circuits that are long but quick compromise user anonymity?

[7]Since Ting estimates *minimum* RTTs, this indicates that 69% of pairs may exhibit at least one TIV, but does not directly allow us to reason about the average reduction in latency.

5.2.2 Longer Circuits

Tor's default of three-hop circuits balances between anonymity and end-to-end latencies, but are there longer circuits that actually *reduce* latencies? Longer circuits may increase anonymity by frustrating tracing, but of course increases the resource use at relays. To answer this question, we again make use of the 50-node, all-pairs RTT dataset provided by Ting, and calculate circuits with lengths from 3 to 10. We sample 10,000 random circuits for each length ℓ and scale our results to the maximum number of circuits: $\binom{50}{\ell}$.

Round-Trip Times. Figure 16 shows, for varying circuit lengths, how many circuits are available for a given RTT. Clearly, circuits with more hops are able to obtain higher maximum RTTs: for instance, we identified no 3-hop circuits in our dataset with RTT over 1 second, but we identified over 1M 10-hop circuits with RTT over 2 seconds. More interestingly, observe the range of 200–300ms; in our dataset, we find roughly 10,000 3-hop circuits able to achieve RTTs in this range. But we are able to find an order of magnitude more 4-hop circuits able to achieve the same RTTs—for 10-hop circuits, there are *four orders of magnitude* more circuits capable of achieving the same RTT. This scales up so drastically because of how quickly $\binom{50}{\ell}$ grows: though the probability of any given ℓ-hop circuit having a given RTT is low, there are many circuits for even moderate sizes of ℓ.

These results show that, if chosen with knowledge of inter-Tor-node RTTs, *longer paths can be used in lieu of default 3-hop paths without imposing greater RTTs.*

Circuit Diversity. One potential concern, however, is that these long circuits with low latency reduce anonymity by relying on a few well-connected nodes. To evaluate this concern, we plot in Figure 17, for each circuit length, the median probability of a node being on a path with RTT = x. Intuitively, this metric captures how "entropic" the set of circuits are for a given RTT and path length. For instance, in our dataset, the set of 10-hop circuits capable of achieving an RTT of 1.9 seconds is very small: this is reflected by the small value at x =1.9. Figure 17 shows that, for many values of circuit length, low-latency circuits do not rely on a small

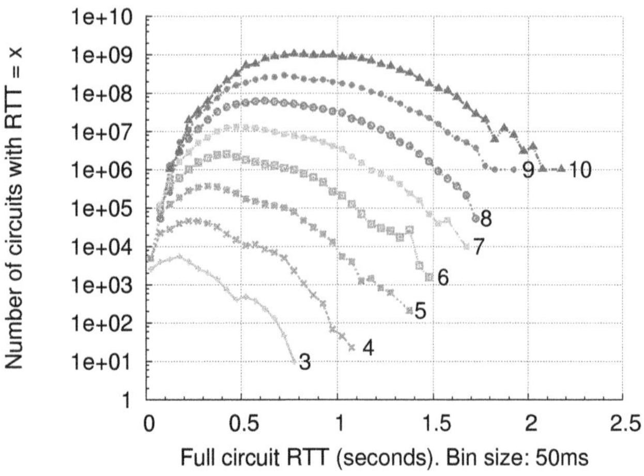

Figure 16: Longer Tor circuits have more options for lower-latency paths, as well as higher-latency paths. Each line is annotated with its corresponding circuit lengths.

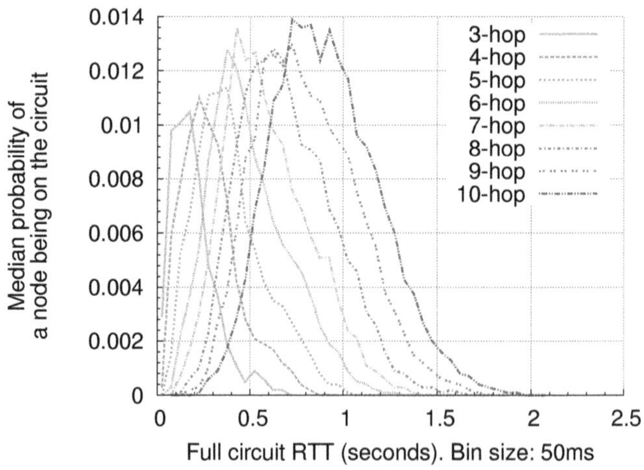

Figure 17: Choosing shorter or longer paths induces skew in the probability of a given node being selected to be on a circuit.

fraction of peers; it is only 10-hop circuits which significantly sacrifice entropy for RTTs less than 500ms.

Using measurements like those in Figure 17, if an attacker knows a victim's circuit length and end-to-end RTT, then he may be able to quickly pare down the set of potential circuits in use. The most entropic region for any given circuit length is naturally in the intermediate RTT values; choosing circuits in this range of RTT values thwarts such attacks.

A user can increase the number of potential circuits for a given RTT by consulting these data that Ting provides. For instance, suppose the user seeks a circuit in the range of 200–300 ms. Within this range of RTTs, there are many 3-hop, 4-hop, and 5-hop circuits. As a result, were an attacker to learn the end-to-end RTT (e.g., if the attacker were running a web server and sought to identify which users were connecting via Tor), there would be over two orders of magnitude more circuits that the user could have constructed than if he had restricted himself only to 3-hop nodes.

Ramifications of Longer Circuits. The use of longer circuits represents a tragedy of the commons: the end-users may benefit, but longer circuits consume more resources from the Tor network as a whole. However, because circuits are determined strictly by the source, there is little the system can do to prevent a selfish but rational user from adopting longer circuits. We believe that approaches to provide incentive-compatibility in Tor [19, 3, 5] are of increasing importance as longer circuits become feasible.

Although longer circuits can help defend against attackers external to Tor, it is less clear how they fare in the presence of active adversaries within the Tor network. Assuming a fixed fraction of active, bad Tor nodes, as circuits grow longer, the probability increases that an adversary is one of the chosen hops—this, too, makes deanonymization by traffic analysis possible [14]. Whether this increased probability outweighs the obfuscation of longer circuits merits future study.

The results in this section suggest that there is potential for a larger design space than Tor's three-hop default: longer hops need not induce greater latency. How this should be leveraged to achieve different balances between security and performance is an interesting area of future work.

5.3 Ting as a Measurement Platform

The final application we consider is arguably Ting's most natural: as a platform for directly measuring latencies between hosts that researchers may not otherwise have access to.

King [11] measured the latency between DNS servers thought to be near clients or servers in the Internet to estimate the latency between those hosts. In 2002, Gummadi et al. found that 72–79% of authoritative name servers supported remote recursive queries to support King; we find that only 3% continue to today, presumably due to concerns over amplification attacks. This change inspired us to apply Ting to the same problem: to estimate latency between hosts thought to be near Tor relays. Relative to King, Ting has an advantage in accuracy in that the Tor node representing a prefix is a member of that prefix, rather than an authoritative name server that may be much better connected or remote. However, Ting has the disadvantage in that not every residential subnet has a Tor node. In this section, we evaluate this coverage and show that Tor nodes are spread between residential networks and data centers.

Coverage. We can evaluate Ting's coverage in three dimensions: geography, network, and host type. The geographical coverage of Tor is well-known: On one hand, many countries are represented: Tor Metrics [32] reported 77 countries with relays in November 2014. On the other hand, there are exceptional countries in which Tor is blocked.

In terms of network diversity, we show the number of unique /24 IP address prefixes and the total number of relays in the Tor network from February 28, 2015 to April 28, 2015 in Figure 18. We consider /24 prefixes because they represent a network allocation likely to be geographically clustered. At any point in this two-month window, we observed between 5426 and 6044 unique /24s. Compared with past data collected by Tor Metrics [32], the total number of relays has grown by roughly 30% since one year prior. If the

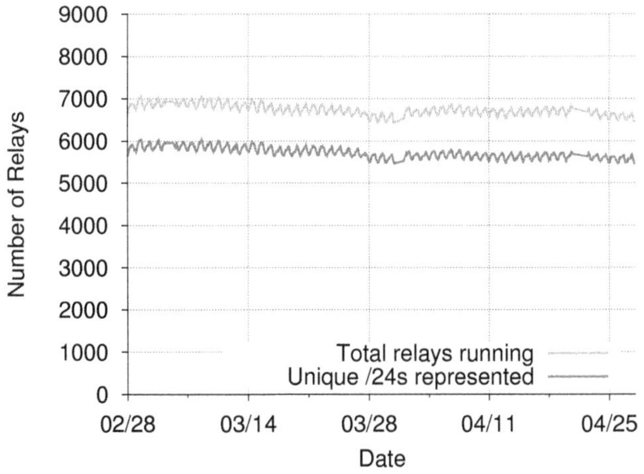

Figure 18: Number of /24s represented in the Tor network from February to April 2015.

Tor network continues to grow, it will become increasingly useful for medium-scale measurement across the network.

Finally, host types are diverse. The pool of relays is predominantly volunteer-run, and thus many relays are run from within homes. To quantify the number of residential hosts, we extended the residential detection technique described by Schulman et al. [27], which involves classifying hosts based on their reverse DNS name, including suffix and presence of numbers—the original technique is only intended for hosts within the U.S., while our extension also considers hosts in Europe. Using this technique, we found that, of the 5484 currently running Tor relays with a reverse DNS name, at least 3355, or roughly 61%, are residential. This underestimates the fraction of residential hosts both because there are a number of Tor relays outside of the U.S. and Europe which are not accounted for, and because the remaining 1150 of the 6634 currently running relay addresses have no reverse DNS name. Data centers are also represented: 361 are at hosting sites identified by reverse DNS name (`linode.com`, `amazonaws.com`, `ovh.com`, `cloudatcost.com`, `your-server.de`, and `leaseweb.com`), and another 345 are within Digital Ocean's IP address range.

Summary

This section demonstrated a wide swath of applications that benefit from Ting's accurate RTT measurements. We believe the set of applications to which Ting is beneficial is both broader and deeper than what is covered here. But even with these few examples, we can conclude that Ting's accurate, all-pairs RTT estimation can be an extremely powerful tool in securing and improving Tor.

6. CONCLUSION

In this paper, we presented Ting, a novel and practical technique for measuring round-trip times between any arbitrary pair of Tor relays with accuracy and at scale. Ting sets itself apart from previous attempts to compute latency information in that: (1) it does not require any modification of the Tor client or protocol, (2) it does not require any additional infrastructure deployment, and (3) it calculates latencies by sending packets along the entire network path and software stack, ensuring an accurate reflection of Tor relays' view of the network. By conducting experiments on both our own controlled relays on PlanetLab and live relays on the Tor network, we validated Ting's ability to estimate true latencies.

We suggest and evaluate three applications wherein data acquired by Ting could be used to improve Tor performance. On the other hand, we provide evidence that it could also be used to improve the latency of Tor while maintaining, and even improving, the level of anonymity it provides, by greatly increasing the set of acceptable circuits for a given RTT, though we leave specific algorithms to future work. Finally, Tor's geographic diversity, both in terms of countries and number of /24s covered, makes it a viable platform for measuring a wide swath of the Internet. We believe that Ting provides unique insight into measurements within residential networks, and hope that it will complement existing techniques. Furthermore, given the current rate of growth of the Tor network, we suspect that Ting's usefulness will scale with Tor's increased adoption. We believe these applications to be representative of a much larger set of improvements to the Tor network that explicit RTT measurements could permit.

Acknowledgments

We thank our shepherd, Phillipa Gill, and the anonymous IMC reviewers for their helpful comments. This research was supported in part by NSF grant CNS-1409191, the National Security Agency as part of a Science of Security lablet, and an Amazon Web Services in Education grant.

7. REFERENCES

[1] S. Agarwal and J. R. Lorch. Matchmaking for online games and other latency-sensitive P2P systems. In *ACM SIGCOMM*, 2009.

[2] M. Akhoondi, C. Yu, and H. V. Madhyastha. LASTor: A low-latency AS-aware Tor client. In *IEEE Symposium on Security and Privacy*, 2013.

[3] E. Androulaki, M. Raykova, S. Srivatsan, A. Stavrou, and S. M. Bellovin. PAR: Payment for anonymous routing. In *Symposium on Privacy Enhancing Technologies (PETS)*, 2008.

[4] D. Chaum. Untraceable electronic mail, return addresses, and digital pseudonyms. *Communications of the ACM*, 24(2):84–88, Nov. 1981.

[5] Y. Chen, R. Sion, and B. Carbunar. XPay: Practical anonymous payments for Tor routing and other networked services. In *Workshop on Privacy in the Electronic Society (WPES)*, 2009.

[6] R. Cox, F. Dabek, F. Kaashoek, J. Li, and R. Morris. Practical, distributed network coordinates. In *Workshop on Hot Topics in Networks (HotNets)*, 2003.

[7] R. Dingledine, N. Mathewson, and P. Syverson. Tor: The second-generation onion router. In *USENIX Security Symposium*, 2004.

[8] R. Dingledine and S. J. Murdoch. Performance improvements on Tor or, why Tor is slow and what we're going to do about it. Online: `https://www.torproject.org/press/presskit/2009-03-11-performance.pdf`, 2009.

[9] N. S. Evans, R. Dingledine, and C. Grothoff. A practical congestion attack on Tor using long paths. In *USENIX Security Symposium*, 2009.

[10] Y. Gilad and A. Herzberg. Spying in the dark: TCP and Tor traffic analysis. In *Privacy Enhancing Technologies*, pages 100–119. Springer, 2012.

[11] K. P. Gummadi, S. Saroiu, and S. D. Gribble. King: Estimating latency between arbitrary Internet end hosts. In *ACM Internet Measurement Workshop (IMW)*, 2002.

[12] N. Hopper, E. Y. Vasserman, and E. Chan-Tin. How much anonymity does network latency leak? *ACM Transactions on Information and System Security (TISSEC)*, 13(2):13, 2010.

[13] R. Jansen, J. Geddes, C. Wacek, M. Sherr, and P. Syverson. Never been KIST: Tor's congestion management blossoms with kernel-informed socket transport. In *USENIX Security Symposium*, 2014.

[14] A. Johnson, C. Wacek, R. Jansen, M. Sherr, and P. Syverson. Users get routed: Traffic correlation on Tor by realistic adversaries. 2013.

[15] C. Lumezanu, R. Baden, D. Levin, N. Spring, and B. Bhattacharjee. Symbiotic relationships in Internet routing overlays. In *Symposium on Networked Systems Design and Implementation (NSDI)*, 2009.

[16] S. J. Murdoch and G. Danezis. Low-cost traffic analysis of Tor. In *USENIX Security Symposium*, 2005.

[17] Neustar IP Geolocation. `https://www.neustar.biz/services/ip-intelligence`.

[18] T. E. Ng and H. Zhang. Towards global network positioning. In *ACM Internet Measurement Workshop (IMW)*, 2001.

[19] T.-W. Ngan, R. Dingledine, and D. S. Wallach. Building incentives into Tor. In *Financial Cryptography (FC)*, 2010.

[20] A. Panchenko and J. Renner. Path selection metrics for performance-improved onion routing. In *Symposium on Applications and the Internet (SAINT)*, 2009.

[21] L. Peterson, T. Anderson, D. Culler, and T. Roscoe. A blueprint for introducing disruptive technology into the Internet. In *Workshop on Hot Topics in Networks (HotNets)*, 2002.

[22] M. K. Reiter and A. D. Rubin. Crowds: Anonymity for web transactions. *ACM TISSEC*, 1(1):66–92, Nov. 1998.

[23] Reporters Without Borders. Enemies of the Internet 2013 Report. `https://surveillance.rsf.org/en/wp-content/uploads/sites/2/2013/03/enemies-of-the-internet_2013.pdf`, Mar. 2013.

[24] RIPE NCC. RIPE Atlas. `https://atlas.ripe.net`.

[25] SamKnows. `https://www.samknows.com`.

[26] S. Savage, A. Collins, E. Hoffman, J. Snell, and T. Anderson. The end-to-end effects of Internet path selection. In *ACM SIGCOMM*, 1999.

[27] A. Schulman and N. Spring. Pingin' in the rain. In *ACM Internet Measurement Conference (IMC)*, 2011.

[28] M. Sherr, M. Blaze, and B. T. Loo. Scalable link-based relay selection for anonymous routing. In *Privacy Enhancing Technologies Symposium (PETS)*, 2009.

[29] R. Sherwood, B. Bhattacharjee, and A. Srinivasan. $\mathcal{P}5$: A protocol for scalable anonymous communication. *Journal of Computer Security*, 13(6):839–876, 2005.

[30] Stem Controller Library. `https://stem.torproject.org`.

[31] S. Sundaresan, S. Burnett, N. Feamster, and W. De Donato. BISmark: A testbed for deploying measurements and applications in broadband access networks. In *USENIX Annual Technical Conference*, 2014.

[32] Tor Metrics. `https://metrics.torproject.org`.

[33] B. Wong, I. Stoyanov, and E. G. Sirer. Octant: A comprehensive framework for the geolocalization of Internet hosts. In *Symposium on Networked Systems Design and Implementation (NSDI)*, 2007.

Timeouts: Beware Surprisingly High Delay

Ramakrishna Padmanabhan
University of Maryland
ramapad@cs.umd.edu

Patrick Owen
University of Maryland
powen@cs.umd.edu

Aaron Schulman
Stanford University
aschulm@stanford.edu

Neil Spring
University of Maryland
nspring@cs.umd.edu

ABSTRACT

Active probing techniques, such as ping, have been used to detect outages. When a previously responsive end host fails to respond to a probe, studies sometimes attempt to confirm the outage by retrying the ping or attempt to identify the location of the outage by using other tools such as traceroute. The latent problem, however, is, how long should one wait for a response to the ping? Too short a timeout risks confusing congestion or other delay with an outage. Too long a timeout may slow the process and prevent observing and diagnosing short-duration events, depending on the experiment's design.

We believe that conventional timeouts for active probes are underestimates, and analyze data collected by Heidemann et al. in 2006–2015. We find that 5% of pings from 5% of addresses take more than 5 seconds. Put another way, for 5% of the responsive IP addresses probed by Heidemann, a false 5% loss rate would be inferred if using a timeout of 5 seconds. To arrive at this observation, we filtered artifacts of the data that could occur with too-long a timeout, including responses to probes sent to broadcast addresses. We also analyze ICMP data collected by Zmap in 2015 to find that around 5% of all responsive addresses observe a greater than one second round-trip time consistently. Further, the prevalence of high round trip time has been increasing and it is often associated with the first ping, perhaps due to negotiating a wireless connection. In addition, we find that the Autonomous Systems with the most high-latency addresses are typically cellular. This paper describes our analysis process and results that should encourage researchers to set longer timeouts when needed and report on timeout settings in the description of future measurements.

Categories and Subject Descriptors

C.2.5 [**Computer-Communication Networks**]: Local and WideArea Networks—Internet

IMC'15, October 28–30, 2015, Tokyo, Japan.

ACM 978-1-4503-3848-6/15/10 ...$15.00.
DOI: http://dx.doi.org/10.1145/2815675.2815704.

Keywords

Timeouts; ICMP Echo; Ping; Outages; Reachability; Outage Detection; Maximum Segment Lifetime

1. INTRODUCTION

Active probes, such as the echo requests sent by ping, can be used to study network reliability [10,14,18,21,23]. A path to a destination is working if the ping is successful: an echo request solicits an echo response. An outage is detected if a previously responsive destination stops responding to successive probes, using multiple probes because infrequent loss is expected in the Internet [17]. Each study then applies a different approach to confirm or diagnose the outage.

Unfortunately, the time one should wait for a response is not well understood. Protocols like TCP and DNS use timeouts near three seconds, and various tools use comparable thresholds: iPlane [14] uses 2 seconds with one retry, Trinocular [18] uses 3 seconds, and Scriptroute [22] defaults to 3 second timeouts. However, TCP and DNS are both able to tolerate longer delays because the timeout is merely a trigger for retransmission: both give up on the connection much later. In contrast, network measurements that timeout quickly have the advantage of being responsive—they may send follow up probes to explore a potential outage—but a disadvantage in that these detected losses, and ultimately outages, may not be real.

In this paper, we try to find a good timeout for active probing. We begin by studying ping latencies from Internet-wide surveys [7] conducted by ISI, including 9.64 billion ICMP Echo Responses from 4 million different IP addresses in 2015. The probing scheme for this survey sets a timeout threshold of 3 seconds [7], although this timeout appears to vary in practice, and only matches responses that arrive before this timer fires: we call these responses *survey-detected responses*. Survey-detected responses include a microsecond-precise round-trip time. When an echo request does not receive a response before the timeout, it is recorded in the data with a timestamp in seconds. When an echo response is received that does not match an echo request that has not yet timed out, that response is also recorded in the data with a timestamp in seconds. Thus it is possible to re-process the data to identify echo responses that took longer than the timeout to arrive. We term such responses *unmatched responses*, and can determine a round trip time precise only to seconds.

We classify unmatched responses into three categories: (a) *delayed responses* potentially caused by congestion, (b) responses that were triggered by later requests sent to broadcast addresses (*broadcast responses*), and (c) *duplicate responses*, some of which appear consistent with denial of service attacks. Since broadcast responses and duplicate responses do not contribute to the latency analysis, we term them *unexpected responses* and remove them with filters. We then *verify* the high latencies by repeating measurements using other probing techniques, comparing the statistics of various surveys, and investigating high-latency behavior of ICMP compared to UDP and TCP. Finally, we explain these distributions by isolating satellite links, considering sequences of latencies at a higher sampling rate, and classifying a complete sample of the Internet address space through a modified Zmap client. The classification process reveals that the Autonomous Systems with the most high latency addresses are cellular.

This paper is organized as follows. We discuss related work, primarily as a means of motivating our study by describing prior timeouts, in Section 2. We describe the ISI survey dataset and our methods of extracting high latency despite a short timeout in Section 3. Section 4 provides the key results: how long a timeout must be to capture a high percentage of responses from a high percentage of hosts. Section 5 addresses doubts about whether these latencies are real, and Section 6 focuses on identifying the networks and behaviors responsible for high latencies. We conclude in Section 7 with our recommendations.

2. IMPORTANCE OF PROBE TIMEOUTS

In this section, we describe why it is important to choose an appropriate timeout for active probes, especially when used for outage detection. We also describe measurement studies with particular attention to what timeouts were used and how those timeouts were chosen.

2.1 Selecting a timeout

Conventional wisdom suggests that active probes on the Internet should timeout after a few seconds. The belief is that after a few seconds there is a very small chance that a probe and response will still exist in the network.

When a probe experiences a timeout, it is generally assumed that either the probe is lost or the end-host is no longer reachable. For most active probing systems, any timed out active probes are followed up with retransmissions to increase the confidence that a lack of response is due to a lack of reachability and not loss. These followup probes will also have a timeout that is generally the same as the first attempt.

Studies on Internet outages and connectivity problems rely on these probe timeouts to indicate that hosts are no longer reachable. However, non-responses to active probes within a timeout can occur for other reasons than the host being offline. Selecting a timeout value that is too-low will ignore delayed responses and might add to congestion by performing retransmissions to an already congested host. Timeout values that are too high will delay retransmissions that can confirm an outage. In addition, too-high timeouts increase the amount of state that needs to be maintained at a prober, since every probe will need to be stored until either the probe times out, or the response arrives.

Even for studies that don't focus upon outages, selecting a good timeout is important. For instance, in the ISI surveys we study, most probes solicit no responses. To the best of our knowledge, this is the first paper that investigates this broad lack of responses to see if researchers are simply using timeouts that are too short.

2.2 Timeouts used in outage and connectivity studies

Outage detection systems such as Trinocular [18] and Thunderping [21] tend to use a 3 second timeout for active probes because it is the default TCP SYN/ACK timeout [3]. Trinocular probes all /24s on the Internet [18]. It does so by sending ICMP echo requests to a few addresses in all /24 address blocks and analyzes responses to detect outages on the block level. Trinocular performs adaptive retransmission and sends up to 15 additional probes to an address block before declaring an outage for that block. Thunderping [21] sends ICMP echo requests to IP addresses that are likely to be subject to severe weather from multiple vantage points periodically and detects outages when all vantage points fail to receive a response. It executes its probing with Scriptroute [22], where each probe has a 3 second timeout. Thunderping retransmits probes ten times before declaring a host is unresponsive.

Internet performance monitoring systems use a wide range of probe timeouts. On the shorter side, iPlane [14] and Hubble [10] send ICMP echo requests with a 2 second timeout. iPlane declares a host unresponsive after one failed retransmission. Hubble waits two minutes after a failed probe then retransmits probes six times and finally declares reachability with traceroutes. On the longer side, Feamster et al. [6] used a one hour timeout after each probe. However, they chose a long timeout to avoid errors due to clock drift between their probing and probed hosts; they did not do so to account for links that have excessive delays. PlanetSeer [23] assumed that four consecutive TCP timeouts (3.2-16 seconds) indicates a path anomaly.

It is especially important for connectivity measurements from probing hardware placed inside networks to have timeouts because of the limited memory in the probing hardware. The RIPE Atlas [19] probing hardware sends continuous pings to various hosts on the Internet to observe connectivity. The timeout for their ICMP echo requests is 1 second [8]. The SamKnows probing hardware uses a 3 second timeout for ICMP echo requests sent during loaded intervals [20].

We started this study with the expectation that these timeout values might need minor adjustment to account for large buffers in times of congestion; what we found was quite different.

3. PRIMARY DATASET OVERVIEW

In this section, we describe the ISI survey dataset we use for our analysis of ping latency. We perform a preliminary analysis of ping latency and find that the dataset contains different types of responses that should (or should not) be matched to identify high-latency responses. Finally, we describe techniques to remove responses that could induce errors in the latency analysis.

3.1 Raw ISI survey data

ISI has conducted Internet wide surveys [7] since 2006. Precise details can be found in Heidemann et al. [7], and technical details of the data format online [9], but we present a brief overview here.

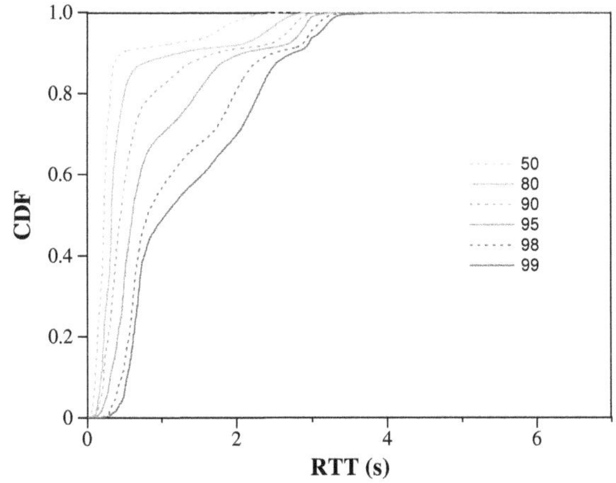

Figure 1: CDF of percentile latency of survey-detected responses per IP address: Each point represents an IP address and each curve represents the percentile from that IP address's response latencies. The slope of the latency percentiles increases around the 3 second mark, suggesting that ISI's prober timed out responses that arrived after 3 seconds.

Each survey includes pings sent to approximately 24,000 /24 address blocks, meant to represent 1% of all allocated IPv4 address space. Once an address block is included, ICMP echo request probes are sent to all 256 addresses in the selected /24 address blocks once every 11 minutes, typically for two weeks. The blocks included in each survey consist of four classes, including blocks that were chosen in 2006 and probed ever since, as well as samples of blocks that were responsive in the last census—another ISI project that probes the entire address space, but less frequently. However, we treat the union of these classes together.

We use data from 103 surveys taken between April 2006 and February 2015, and performed initial studies based on 2011–2013 data, but focus on the most recent of them, in January and February of 2015 for data quality and timeliness. The dataset consists of all echo requests that were sent as part of the surveys in this period, as well as all echo responses that were received. Of particular importance is that echo responses received within, typically, three seconds of an echo request to the same address are matched into a single record and given a round-trip measurement precise to microseconds. Should an echo response take four seconds to arrive, a "timeout" record is recorded associated with the probe, and an "unmatched" record is recorded associated with the response. These two packets have timestamps precise only to seconds. The dataset also includes ICMP error responses (e.g., "host unreachable"); we ignore all probes associated with such responses since the latency of ICMP error responses is not relevant.

In later sections, we will complement this dataset with results from Zmap [5] and additional experiments including more frequent probing with Scamper [13] and Scriptroute [22].

3.2 Matched response latencies are capped at the timeout

In this section, we present the latencies we would observe when considering only those responses that were matched to requests because they arrived within the timeout. We call these responses *survey-detected responses.*

We aggregate round trip time measurements in terms of the distribution of latency values per IP address, focusing on characteristic values on the median, 80th, 90th, 95th, 98th and 99th percentile latencies. That is, we attempt to treat each IP address equally, rather than treat each ping measurement equally. This aggregation ensures that well-connected hosts that reply reliably are not over-represented relative to hosts that reply infrequently.

Taking ISI survey datasets from 2011–2013 together, we show a CDF of these percentile values considering only survey-detected responses in Figure 1. Taken literally, 95% of echo replies from 95% of addresses will arrive in less than 2.85 seconds. However, it is apparent that the distribution is clipped at the 3 second mark, although a few responses were matched even after 7 seconds.

We observe three broad phases in this graph: (1) the lower 40% of addresses show a reasonably tight distribution in which the 99th percentile stays close to the 98th; (2) the next 50% in which the median remains low but the higher percentiles increase; and (3) the top 10% where the median rises above 0.5 seconds.

3.3 Unmatched responses

If a probe takes more than three seconds to solicit a response, it appears as if the probe timed-out and the response was unsolicited or *unmatched.* Since it appears from Figure 1 that three seconds is short enough that it is altering the distribution of round trip times, we are interested in matching these echo responses to construct the complete distribution of round trip times.

Matching these responses to find *delayed responses* is not a simple matter, however. In particular, we find two causes of *unexpected responses* that should not yield samples of round trip times: unmatched responses solicited by echo requests sent to broadcast addresses and apparent denial of service responses.

We match a delayed response with its corresponding request as follows: Given an unmatched response having a source IP address, we look for the last request sent to that IP address. If the last request timed out and has not been matched, the latency is then the difference between the timestamp of the response and the timestamp of the request. ISI recorded the timestamp of unmatched responses to a 1 second precision, thus the latencies of inferred delayed responses are precise only to a second.

The presence of unexpected responses can lead to the inference of incorrect latencies for delayed responses using this technique: not all unexpected responses should be matched by source address. We thus develop filters to remove unexpected responses from the set of unmatched responses.

We note that it is possible to match responses to requests explicitly using the id and sequence numbers associated with ICMP echo requests, and even perhaps using the payload. These attributes were not recorded in the ISI dataset, which motivates us to develop the source address based scheme. We use these fields when running Zmap or other tools to confirm high latencies in Section 5 below.

3.3.1 Broadcast responses

The dataset contains several instances where a ping to a destination times out, but is closely followed by an un-

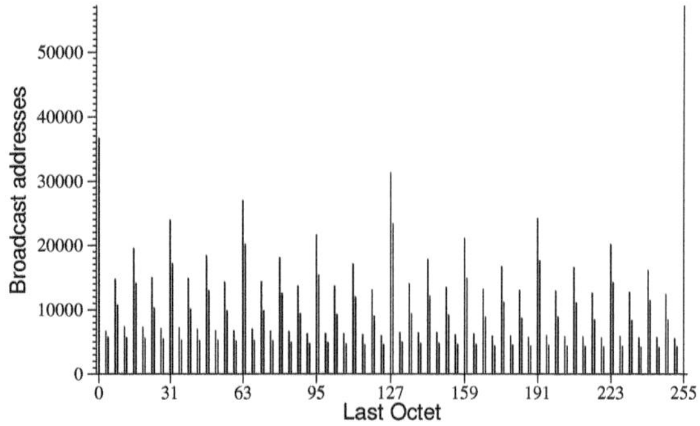

Figure 2: Broadcast addresses that solicit responses in Zmap: Broadcast addresses usually have last octets whose last N bits are either 1 or 0 (where N > 1).

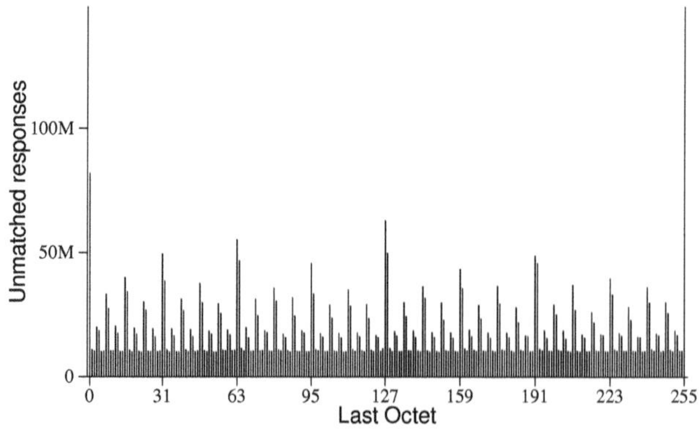

Figure 3: Number of unmatched responses that followed a probe sent to address with last octet X. Last octets with last N bits ending in 0s and 1s (where N > 1) observe spikes, likely caused by broadcast responses. Not all unmatched responses are caused by broadcast responses, however, since there exist roughly 10M unmatched responses distributed evenly across all last octets.

matched response from a source address that is within the same /24 address block, but different from the destination. In each round of probing, this behavior repeats. Here, we analyze these unmatched responses, find that they are likely caused by probing broadcast addresses, and filter them.

Network prefixes often include a broadcast address, where one address within a subnet represents all devices connected to that prefix [16]. The broadcast address in a network should be an address that is unlikely to be assigned to a real host [16], such as the address whose host-part bits are all 1s or 0s, allowing us to characterize broadcast addresses. Devices that receive an echo request sent to the broadcast address may, depending on configuration, send a response [3], and if sending a response, will use a source address that is their own. We call these responses *broadcast responses.* No device should send an echo response with the source address that is the broadcast destination of the echo request.

We hypothesize that pings that trigger responses from different addresses within the same /24 address block result when the ping destination is a broadcast address. We examine ping destinations that solicit a response from a different address in the same /24 address block, and check if they appear to be broadcast addresses.

We extended the ICMP probing module in the Zmap scanner [5] to embed the destination into the echo request, then to extract the destination from the echo response. Doing so allows us to infer the destination address to which the probe was originally sent. Zmap collected the data and made it available for download at scans.io.

We choose the Zmap scan conducted closest in time to the last ISI survey we studied, on April 17 2015, to investigate the host-part bits of destination addresses that triggered responses from a different address from the same /24 address block. We plot the distribution of the last octets of these addresses in Figure 2. Last octets with the last N bits ending in 1 or 0, where N is greater than 1, such as 255, 0, 127, 128 etc., have spikes. These addresses are likely broadcast addresses. On the other hand, last octets that end in binary '01' or '10' have very few addresses.

Broadcast responses exist in the dataset

We examine if unmatched responses in the ISI dataset are caused by pings sent to broadcast addresses. Since broadcast responses are likely to be seen after an Echo Request sent to a broadcast address, we find the most recently probed address within the same /24 prefix for each unmatched response. We then extract the last octet of the most recently probed address. Figure 3 shows the distribution of unmatched responses across these last octets. We find that around 10M unmatched responses are distributed evenly across all last octets: these are unmatched responses that don't seem to be broadcast responses. However, last octets that have their last N bits as 1s and 0s ,when N is greater than 1, observe spikes similar to those in Figure 2.

If left in the data, broadcast responses could yield substantial latency overestimates in the following, common, scenario, which we illustrate in Figure 4. Assume that the echo request sent to an address 211.4.10.254 is lost and that the device is configured to respond to broadcast pings. The echo request sent to 211.4.10.254 could then be matched to the response to the request sent to 211.4.10.255, the broadcast address of the enclosing prefix. This would lead to a latency based on the interval between probing 211.4.10.254 and 211.4.10.255, as shown in the figure.

Filtering broadcast responses

We develop a method which uses ISI's non-random probing scheme to detect addresses that source broadcast responses. We call such addresses *broadcast responders,* and seek to filter all their responses. We believe that delayed responses are likely to exhibit high variance in their response latencies, since congestion varies over time. On the other hand, a broadcast response is likely to have relatively stable latency.

ISI's probing scheme sends probes to each address in a /24 address block in a nonrandom sequence, allowing us to develop a filter that checks if a source address responds to a broadcast address each round. Addresses are probed such that last octets that are off by one, such as 254 and 255, receive pings spaced 330 seconds apart (half the probing interval of 11 minutes) as shown in Figure 4. For every unmatched response with a latency of at least 10 seconds, the filter checks if the same source address had sent an unmatched response with a similar latency in the previous round. We take an exponentially weighted moving average of the number of times this occurs for a given source address

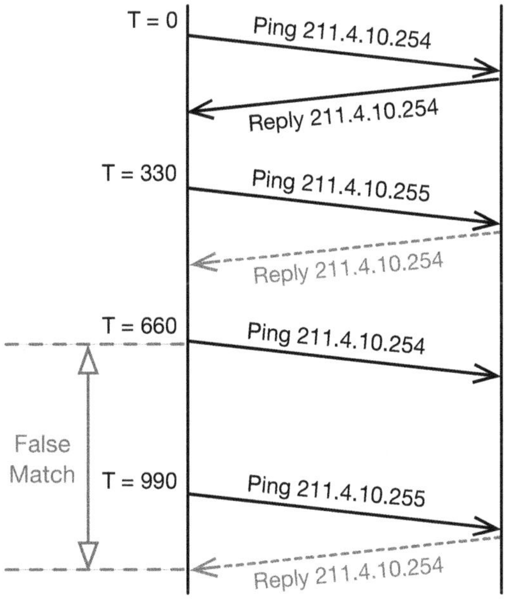

Figure 4: We filter broadcast responses since they can lead to the inference of false latencies. This figure illustrates a potential incorrect match caused by a broadcast response. Echo requests sent to the broadcast address 211.4.10.255 at T = 330 and T = 990 seconds solicit responses from 211.4.10.254. When a timeout occurs for a request sent directly to 211.4.10.254 at T = 660 seconds, we would falsely connect that request to the response at T = 990 seconds.

with $\alpha = 0.01$. Most broadcast responders have the maximum of this moving average > 0.9, but since probe-loss can potentially decrease this value, we mark IP addresses with values > 0.2 and filter all their responses.

We confirm that we find broadcast responders correctly in the ISI surveys by comparing the ones we found in the ISI 2015 surveys with broadcast responders from the Zmap dataset. Zmap detected 939,559 broadcast responders in the April 17 2015 scan, of which 7212 had been addresses that provided Echo Responses in ISI's IT63w (20150117) and IT63c (20150206) datasets. The filter detected 7044 (97.7%) of these as broadcast responders. We inspected the 168 remaining addresses and found that 154 addresses have 99th percentile latencies below 2.5 seconds. Since ISI probes a /24 prefix only once every 2.5 seconds, these addresses cannot be broadcast responders. Another 5 addresses have 99th percentiles latencies below 5 seconds; these are unlikely to be broadcast responders as well.

The remaining 9 addresses had 99th percentile latencies in excess of 300s and seem to be broadcast responders. Upon closer inspection, we found that these addresses only occasionally sent an unmatched response: around once every 50 rounds. The α parameter of the filter can tolerate some rounds with missing responses, but these addresses respond in so few rounds that they pass undetected. If these 9 are indeed broadcast responders as suggested by high 99th percentile latencies, this yields a false negative rate of our filter of 0.13%.

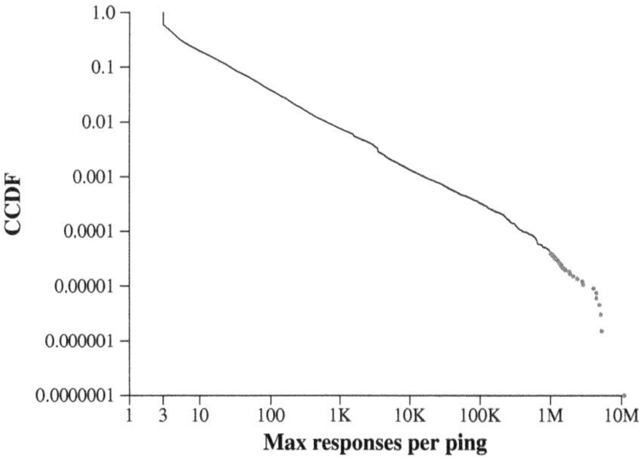

Figure 5: Maximum number of responses received for a single echo request, for IP addresses that sent more than 2 responses to an echo request. The red dots indicate instances where addresses responded to a single echo request with more than 1M echo responses. We believe that these are caused by DoS attacks.

3.3.2 *Duplicate responses*

Packets can be duplicated. A duplicated packet will not affect inferred latencies as long as the original response to the original probe packet reaches the prober, since our scheme ignores subsequent duplicate responses. However, we find that some IP addresses respond many times to a single probe. In this case, the incoming packets aren't responses to probes, but are either caused by incorrect configurations or malicious behavior.

Figure 5 shows the distribution of the maximum number of echo responses observed in response to a single echo request. Since broadcast responses can also be interpreted as duplicate responses, we look only at IP addresses that sent more than 2 echo responses for an echo request. Of 658,841 such addresses, we find that 4,985 (0.7%) sent at least 1,000 echo responses. The red dots in the figure show 26 addresses that sent more than one million echo responses, with one address sending nearly 11 million responses in 11 minutes.

Zmap authors reported that they observed retaliatory DoS attacks in response to their Internet-wide probes [5]. We believe that some of the responses in the ISI dataset are also caused by DoS attacks.

We filter duplicate responses by ignoring IP addresses that ever responded more than 4 times to a single echo request, based on observing the distribution of duplicates shown in Figure 5. Packets can sometimes get duplicated on the Internet, and we want to be selective in our filtering to remove as little as necessary. Even if a response from the probed IP address is duplicated and a broadcast response is also duplicated, there should be only 4 echo responses in the dataset. We believe that IP addresses observing more than 4 echo responses to a single echo request are either misconfigured or are participating in a DoS attack. In either case, the latencies are not trustworthy.

4. RECOMMENDED TIMEOUT VALUES

In this section, we analyze the ping latencies of all pings obtained from ISI's Internet survey datasets from 2015 to find reasonable timeout values. We demonstrate the effectiveness of our matching scheme for recovering delayed

	Packets	Addresses
Survey-detected	9,644,670,150	4,008,703
Naive matching	9,768,703,324	4,008,830
Broadcast responses	33,775,148	9,942
Duplicate responses	67,183,853	20,736
Survey + Delayed	9,667,744,323	3,978,152

Table 1: Adding unmatched responses to survey-detected responses

	% of pings						
% of addresses	**1%**	**50%**	**80%**	**90%**	**95%**	**98%**	**99%**
1%	0.01	0.03	0.04	0.07	0.10	0.13	0.18
50%	0.16	0.19	0.21	0.26	0.42	0.53	0.64
80%	0.19	0.26	0.33	0.43	0.54	0.74	1.21
90%	0.22	0.31	0.42	0.57	0.84	1.61	3
95%	0.25	1.42	2.38	3	5	9	15
98%	0.30	1.94	4	6	12	41	78
99%	0.33	2.31	4	8	22	76	145

Table 2: Minimum timeout in seconds that would have captured c% of pings from r% of IP addresses in the IT63w (20150117) and IT63c (20150206) datasets (where r is the row number and c is the column number).

responses from the dataset. We then group the survey-detected responses and delayed responses together to determine what timeout values would be necessary to recover various percentiles of responses. Some IP addresses observe very high latencies in the ISI dataset; we verify that these are real in Section 5 and examine causes in Section 6.

4.1 Incorporating unmatched responses

ISI detected 9.64 Billion echo responses from 4 Million IP addresses in 2015 in the IT63w (20150117) and IT63c (20150206) datasets, as shown in the first row of Table 1. The next row shows the number of responses we would have obtained if we had used a naive matching scheme where we simply matched each unmatched response for an IP address with the last echo request for that IP address, without filtering unexpected responses. The number of responses increases by 1.3% to 9.77 Billion; however, this includes responses from addresses that received broadcast responses and duplicate responses. After filtering unexpected responses, the number of IP addresses reduces to 99.23% of the original addresses. Of 30,678 discarded IP addresses, 9,942 (32.4%) addresses were discarded because they also received broadcast responses. The majority of discarded IP addresses, 20,736 (67.6%) were addresses that sent more than 4 echo responses in response to a single echo request.

Though the number of discarded IP addresses is relatively small, removing them eliminates responses that cluster around 330, 165, and 495 seconds. Figure 6 shows the distribution of percentile latency per IP address before and after filtering unexpected responses. Comparing these two graphs shows that the "bumps" in the CDF are removed by the filtering.

After discarding addresses, our matching technique yields 23,074,173 additional responses for the remaining addresses, giving us a total of 9.67 Billion Echo Responses from 3.98 Million IP addresses. We perform our latency analysis on this combined dataset.

4.2 Recommended Timeout Values

We now find retransmission thresholds which recover various percentiles of responses for the IP addresses from the combined dataset. For each IP address, we find the 1st, 50th, 80th, 90th, 95th, 98th and 99th percentile latencies. We then find the 1st, 50th, 80th, 90th, 95th, 98th and 99th percentiles of all the 1st percentile latencies. We repeat this for each percentile and show the results in Table 2.

The 1st percentile of an address's latency will be close to the ideal latency that its link can provide. We find that the 1st percentile latency is below 330ms for 99% of IP addresses: most addresses are capable of responding with low latency. Further, 50% of pings from 50% of the addresses have latencies below 190ms, showing that latencies tend to be low in general.

However, we see that a substantial fraction of IP addresses also have surprisingly high latencies. For instance, to capture 95% of pings from 95% addresses requires waiting 5 seconds. Restated, at least 5% of pings from 5% of addresses have latencies higher than 5 seconds. Thus, even setting a timeout as high as 5 seconds will infer a false loss rate of 5% for these addresses.

Note that retrying lost pings cannot be used as a substitute for setting a longer timeout since a retried ping is not an independent sample of latency. Whatever caused the first one to be delayed is likely to cause the followup pings to be delayed as well, as we show in Section 6.

At the extreme, we see 1% of pings from 1% of addresses having latency above 145 seconds! These latencies are so high that we investigate these addresses further. *We now consider 60 seconds to be a reasonable timeout to balance progress with response rate, at least when studying outages and latencies, although an ideal timeout may vary for different settings.* A timeout of 60 seconds easily covers 98% of pings to 98% of addresses, yet does not seem long enough to slow measurements unnecessarily.

5. VERIFICATION OF LONG PING TIMES

In this section, we address doubts that long observed ping times are real: that they are a product of ISI's probing scheme, that they might be caused by errors in a particular data set, or that they might derive from discrimination against ICMP.

5.1 Are high latencies observed by other probing schemes?

Some of the latencies in Table 2 are so high that we considered if they could be artifacts of ISI's probing scheme. We investigate latencies obtained using two other probing techniques, Zmap and scamper, and check if the high latencies observed in the ISI datasets are reproducible.

Does Zmap observe high latencies?

We check for high latencies using the Zmap scanner [5]. As part of our extension of the ICMP probing module in the Zmap scanner, we also embed the probe send time into the echo request, and extract it from the echo response, allowing us to estimate the RTT, albeit without the precision of kernel send timestamps.

Zmap has performed these scans since April 2015. Scans have been conducted over a range of different times, different days of the week and across four months in 2015 (as of Sep 5, 2015), as shown in Table 3. Typically, scans were per-

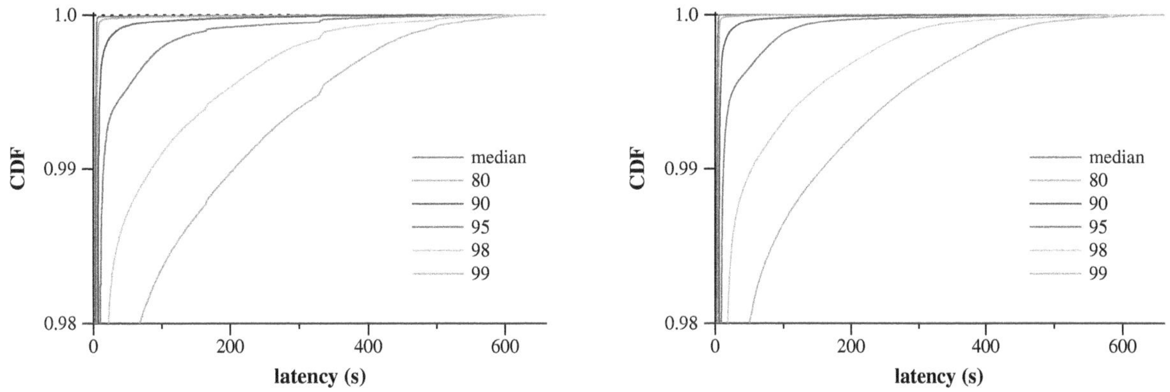

(a) Before filtering

(b) After filtering

Figure 6: CDF of Percentile latency per IP address before and after filtering unexpected responses. Each point represents an IP address and each color represents the percentile from that IP address's response latencies. Before filtering unexpected responses, there are bumps caused by broadcast responses at 330s, 165s and 495s, fractions of the 11 minute (660s) probing interval.

Scan Date	Day	Begin Time	Echo Responses
Apr 17, 2015	Fri	02:44	339M
Apr 19, 2015	Sun	12:07	340M
Apr 23, 2015	Thu	12:07	343M
Apr 26, 2015	Sun	12:07	343M
Apr 30, 2015	Thu	12:08	344M
May 3, 2015	Sun	12:08	344M
May 17, 2015	Sun	12:09	347M
May 22, 2015	Fri	00:57	371M
May 24, 2015	Sun	12:09	369M
May 31, 2015	Sun	12:09	362M
Jun 4, 2015	Thu	12:10	368M
Jun 15, 2015	Mon	13:53	357M
Jun 21, 2015	Sun	12:11	368M
Jul 2, 2015	Thu	12:00	369M
Jul 5, 2015	Sun	12:00	368M
Jul 9, 2015	Thu	12:00	369M
Jul 12, 2015	Sun	12:00	367M

Table 3: Zmap scan details: For each Zmap scan in Figure 7, the table shows the date, day of the week, the time at which the scan began (in UTC time), and the number of destinations that responded with Echo Responses.

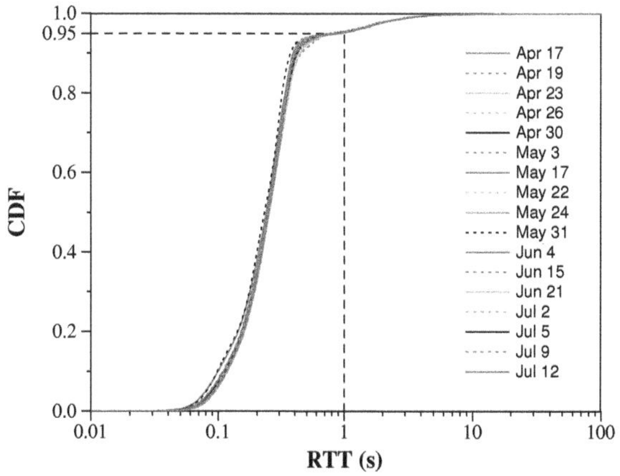

Figure 7: Distribution of RTTs for all Zmap scans performed in 2015. Around 5% of addresses have latencies greater than 1s in each scan, and 0.1% of addresses observed latencies in excess of 75s.

formed on Sundays or Thursdays, beginning at noon UTC time. However, the scans on April 17, May 22, and June 15 were conducted on other days and at other times, increasing diversity. Each Zmap scan takes 10 and a half hours to complete and recovers Echo Responses from around 350M addresses.

We choose all available scans and analyze the distribution of RTTs for the Echo Responses in Figure 7. Most responses arrive with low latency, having a median latency lower than 250ms for each scan. However, 5% of addresses responded with RTTs greater than 1 second in each scan. Further, 0.1% of addresses responded with latencies exceeding 75 seconds in each scan although the 99.9th percentile latency exhibited some variation: the May 22 scan had the lowest 99.9th percentile latency (77 seconds) whereas the July 9 scan had the highest (102 seconds). We infer from these nearly identical latency distributions that high latencies are persistent for a consistent fraction of addresses.

Does scamper also observe high latencies?

Both ISI and Zmap probe millions of addresses, and we investigate whether latencies are affected by these probing schemes triggering rate-limits or firewalls. We select a small sample of addresses that are likely to have high latencies from the ISI dataset, probe them using scamper [13], and check for unusually high latencies.

In the 2011 - 2013 ISI dataset, 20,095 IP addresses had at least 5% of their pings with latencies 100 seconds and above. We chose 2000 random IP addresses from this subset and sent 1000 pings to them, once every 10 seconds using scamper [13] and analyzed the responses. In this analysis, we used scamper's default packet response matching mechanism: so long as scamper continues to run, received responses will be matched with sent packets. Because we used scamper's defaults, scamper ceased to run 2 seconds after the last packet was sent, so we missed responses to the last few pings that arrived after scamper ceased running. Although scamper can be configured to wait longer for responses, in

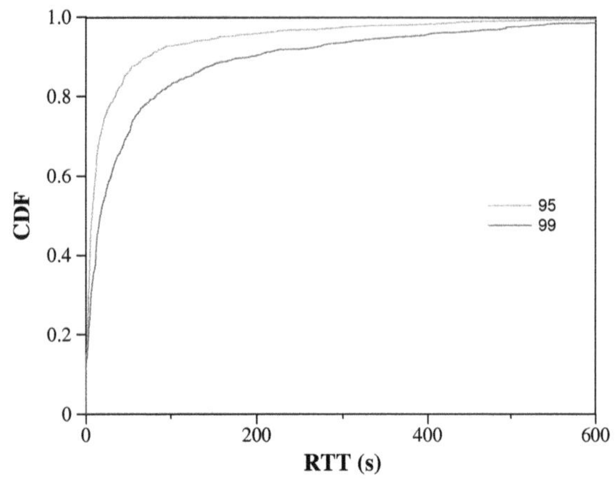

Figure 8: Confirmation of high latency: Percentile latency per IP address for 2000 randomly chosen IP addresses from ISI's 2011 - 2013 surveys that had > 5% of pings with latencies 100s and above. Each point represents an IP address and the lines represent the percentile latency from that IP address. 17% of them continue to observe 1% of their pings with latencies > 100s.

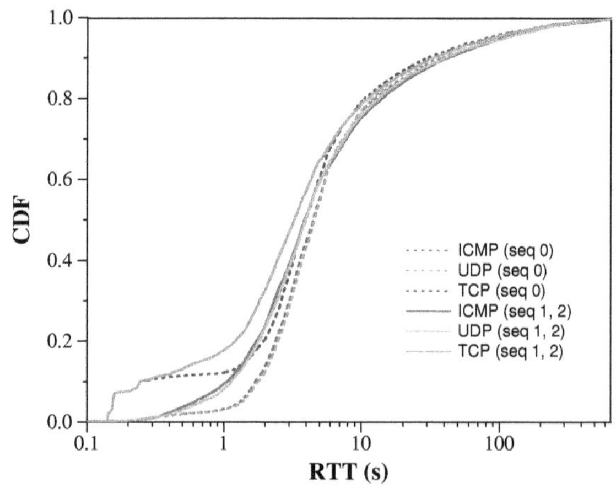

Figure 10: 98th percentile RTTs associated with high-latency IP addresses using different probe protocols. The first probe of a triplet (seq 0) often has a higher latency than the rest; TCP probes appear to have a similar distribution except for firewall-sourced responses.

later analyses, we ran tcpdump simultaneously and matched responses to sent packets separately.

Of the 2000 addresses, 1244 responded to our probes. Figure 8 shows the percentile latency per IP address. The 95th percentile latency for 50% of the addresses is now considerably lower, at 7.3s. This suggests that addresses prone to extremely high latencies vary with time: we investigate addresses with this behavior further in Section 6.

Nevertheless, Figure 8 shows that scamper also observes some instances of very high latencies. 17% of addresses observe latencies greater than 100 seconds for 1% of their pings. We therefore rule out the possibility that the high latencies are a product of the probing scheme.

5.2 Is it a particular survey or vantage point?

ISI survey data are collected from four vantage points at different times. Vantage points are identified by initial letter, and are in Marina del Rey, California, "w"; Ft. Collins, Colorado, "c"; Fujisawa-shi, Kanagawa, Japan, "j"; and Athens, Greece, "g".

In this section, we look at summary metrics of each of the surveys. In Figure 9, our intent was to ensure that the results were consistent from one survey to the next, but we found a surprising result as well. The consistency of values is apparent: the median ping from the median address remains near 200ms for the duration. However, there are exceptions in the following data sets: IT59j (20140515), IT60j (20140723), IT61j (20141002), IT62g (20141210). These higher sampled latencies are coincident with a substantial reduction in the fraction of responses that are matched: in typical ISI surveys, 20% of pings receive a response; in these, between 0.02% and 0.2% see a response. It appears that these data sets should not be considered further. Additionally, it54c (20130524) it54j (20130618) and it54w (20130430) were flagged by ISI as having high latency variation due to a software error [11].

Ignoring the outliers, trends are apparent. The timeout necessary to capture 95% of responses from 95% of addresses increased from near two seconds in 2007 to near five seconds in 2011. (We note that the apparent stability of this line may be misleading; since the y-axis is a log scale and our latency estimates are only precise to integer seconds when greater than 3, small variations will be lost.) The 98th percentile latency from the 98th percentile address has increased steadily since 2011, and the 99th increased from a modest 20 seconds in 2011 to a surprising 140 in 2013. These latency observations are not isolated to individual traces.

In sum, high latency is increasing, and although some surveys show atypical statistics, early 2015 datasets that we focus on appear typical of expected performance.

5.3 Is it ICMP?

One might expect that high latencies could be a result of preferential treatment against ICMP. RFC 1812 allows routers responding to ICMP to rate-limit replies [1,12], however, this limitation of ICMP should not substantially affect the results since each address is meant to receive a ping from ISI once every eleven minutes. Nevertheless, one can imagine firewalls or similar devices that would interfere specifically with ICMP.

To evaluate this possibility, we selected high-latency addresses from the IT63c (20150206) survey. To these addresses we sent a probe stream consisting of three ICMP echo requests separated by one second, then 20 minutes later, three UDP messages separated by one second, then again 20 minutes later, three TCP ACK probes separated by one second. We avoided TCP SYNs because they may appear to be associated with security vulnerability scanning. We then consider the characteristics of these hosts in terms of the difference between ICMP delay and TCP or UDP delay.

"High-latency" addresses to sample

We choose the top 5% of addresses when sorting by each of the median, 80th, 90th and 95th percentile latencies. Many of these sets of addresses overlap: those who have among the highest medians are also likely to be among the highest 80th percentiles. However, we considered these different sets

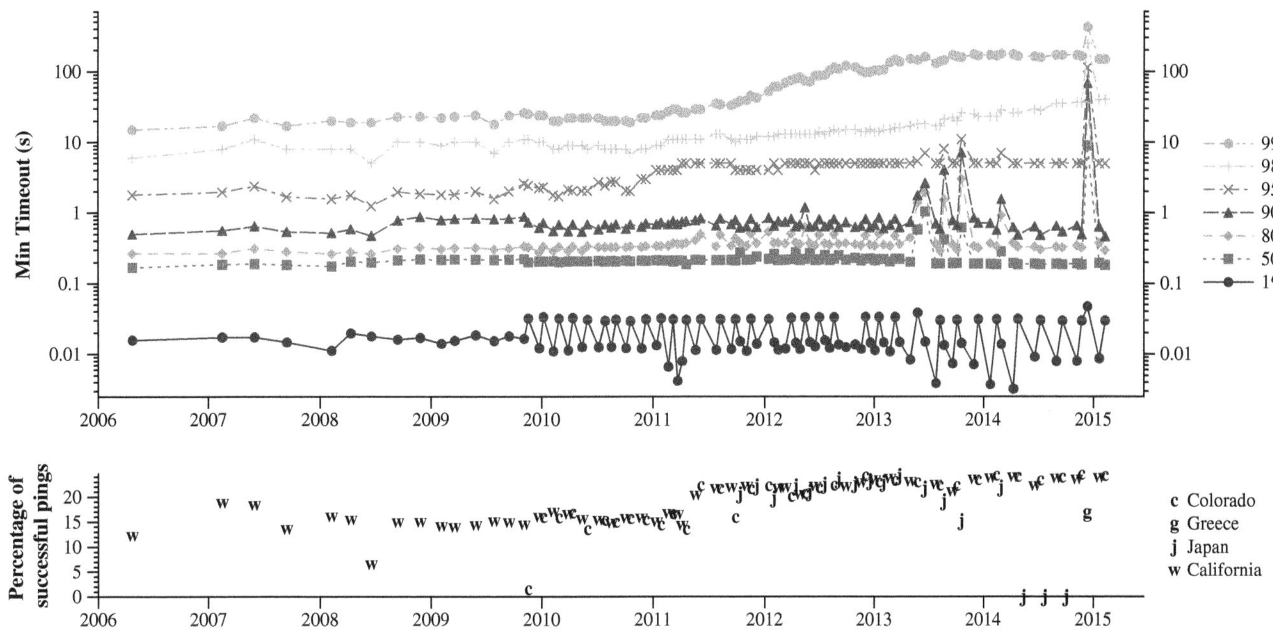

Figure 9: Top: Minimum timeout required to capture the cth percentile latency sample from the cth percentile address in each survey, organized by time. Each point represents the timeout required to capture, e.g., 95% of the responses from 95% of the addresses. The 1% line is indicative of the minimum. Bottom: Response rate for each survey; symbols represent which vantage point was used. Surveys from Japan with very few successes are not plotted on the top graph.

to be important so that the comparison would include both hosts with high persistent latency and those with high occasional latency. After sampling 15,000 addresses from each of these four sets, then removing duplicates, we obtain 53,875 addresses to probe.

From these addresses, we found that only 5,219 responded to all probes from all protocols on April 29, 2015. This is somewhat expected: Only 27,579 responded to any probe from any protocol.

To complete the probing, we use Scamper [13] to send the probe stream to each of the candidate addresses. Note that scamper uses a 2s timeout by default although the timeout can be configured. Instead of setting an alternate timeout in Scamper, we run tcpdump to collect all received packets, effectively creating an "indefinite" timeout. This allows us to observe packets that arrive arbitrarily late since we continue to run tcpdump days after the Scamper code finished.

All protocols are treated the same (mostly)

For each protocol, we select the 98th percentile RTT per address and plot the distribution in Figure 10. We noticed two obvious features of the data: that the first packet of the triplet often had a noticeably different distribution of round trip times, and that the TCP responses often had a mode around 200ms. We will investigate the "first ping" problem in Section 6.3.

The TCP responses appear to be generated by firewalls that recognize that the acknowledgment is not part of a connection and sent a RST without notifying the actual destination: this cluster of responses all had the same TTL and applied to all probes to entire /24 blocks. That is, for each address that had such a response, all other addresses in that /24 had the same.

Ignoring the quick TCP responses apparently from a firewall, it does not appear that any protocol has significant preferential treatment among the high-latency hosts. Of course, this observation does not show that prioritization does not occur along any of these paths; our assertion is only that such prioritization, if it exists, is not a source of the substantial latencies we observe.

5.4 Summary

In this section, we confirmed that extremely high latencies are also observed by techniques besides ISI's. We find that the high latencies are not a result of a few individual ISI datasets, even though some did appear atypical. Further, high latencies affect all protocols the same.

We also found that the prevalence of high latencies has been increasing since 2011. In 2015, a consistent 5% of addresses have latencies greater than a second.

6. WHY DO PINGS TAKE SO LONG?

In this section, we aim to determine what causes high RTTs. We investigate the RTTs of satellite links and find that they account for a small fraction of high RTT addresses. We follow up with an analysis of Autonomous Systems and geographic locations that are most prone to two potentially different types of high RTTs: RTTs greater than 1s and RTTs greater than 100s. We then investigate addresses that exhibit each type of RTT and find potential explanations.

6.1 Are satellites involved?

A reasonable hypothesis is that satellite links, widely known for their necessarily high minimum latency, would also be responsible for very high maximum latencies. Transmissions via geosynchronous satellite must transit 35,786km to

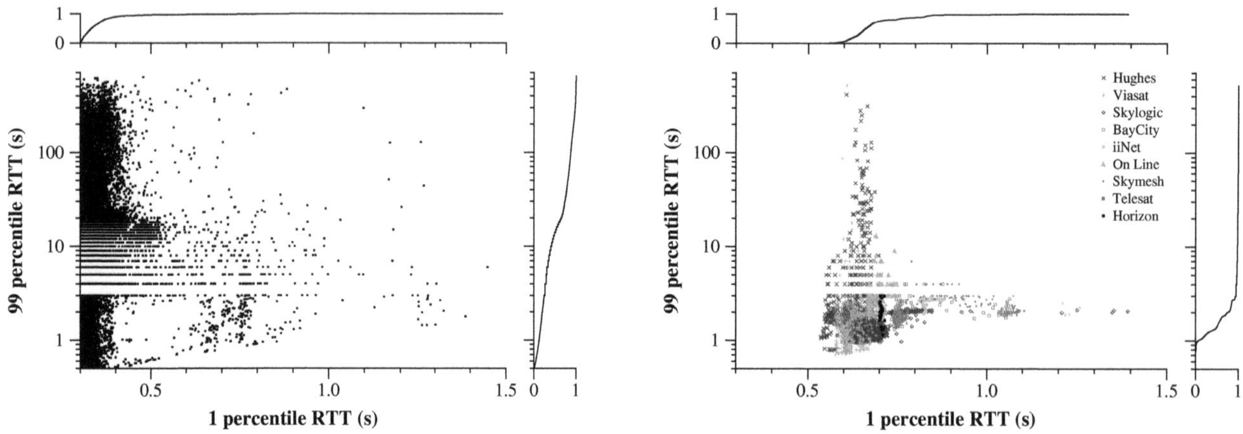

Figure 11: Scatterplot of 1st and 99th percentile latencies for addresses with high values of both in survey IT63c; Left omits satellite-only ISPs; Right includes only satellite-only ISPs.

a satellite and back, leading to about 125 ms of one way delay [2, 15]. Another 125 ms for the return trip yields a theoretical minimum of 250ms.

We expect satellite ISPs to have high 1st percentile latencies, but we consider whether they have high 99th percentile latencies as well. We use data from ISI survey IT63c (20150206) for this analysis because it provides hundreds of ping samples per IP address, and we wish to study relatively few addresses in some detail. Figure 11 shows the plot of 1st percentile latencies vs. the 99th percentile latencies for addresses in this survey. We separate addresses that the Maxmind database maps to known satellite providers, including Hughes and ViaSat. At left, we show the overall distribution without addresses from known satellite ISPs; at right, we show only satellite ISPs. (Recall that the precision of values just above the ISI timeout of three seconds is limited to integers; this creates the horizontal bands.) The satellite-only ISPs plot shows that the 1st percentile RTT for these addresses exceeds 500ms in all cases, showing that the RTTs are almost double the theoretical minimum. There are some points in the left plot that remain within the satellite-like cluster; at least some of these are from rural broadband providers that provide both satellite and other connectivity, such as xplorenet in Canada, which had at least one IP address report with a below 0.5s first percentile.

Each satellite provider has a distinct cluster in this scatter plot, and two smaller providers, Horizon and iiNet, have clusters of reports that produce near-horizontal lines in the graph, with varying 1st percentile but fairly consistent 99th percentile, as if queuing for these addresses is capped but the base distance to the satellite varies by geography.

Although some satellite hosts do have remarkably high RTT values—up to 517s—their 99th percentile values are predominantly below 3s. They do not have such high 99th percentile values as the rest of the hosts with over 0.3s first percentiles (those shown on the left graph). Thus, satellite ASes accounted for very few of the high latency addresses.

6.2 Autonomous Systems with the most high latency addresses

Next, we investigate the ASes and geographic locations with the most high latency addresses to identify relationships. For this analysis, we use Zmap scans from 2015 to identify high latency addresses. Zmap pings every IPv4 address, thereby covering addresses from all ASes. We chose the May 22, Jun 21 and Jul 9 Zmap scans to study. These scans were conducted at different times of the day, on different days of the week and in different months, as shown in Table 3. For each of these Zmap scans, we use Maxmind to find the ASN and geographic location for every address that responded.

ASes most prone to RTTs greater than 1 second

Figure 7 showed that the percentage of addresses that sent high latency Echo Responses remained stable over time. In particular, around 5% of addresses observed RTTs greater than a second in each scan. We refer to these addresses as *turtles* and investigate their distribution across Autonomous Systems to identify relationships.

For each Zmap scan, we found the turtles and identified their AS, and ranked ASes by the number of contributed turtles. Finally, we summed the turtles from each AS across the three scans and sort ASes accordingly and show the top ten in Table 4. For example, AS26615 had the second-largest sum of turtles across the three Zmap scans, but was ranked third within the May 2015 scan.

Inspecting the owners of each of these Autonomous Systems reveals that a majority of them are cellular. AS26599 (TELEFONICA BRASIL), a cellular AS in Brazil, has the most turtles, more than double that of the next largest AS in each of the scans. The next two ASes, AS45609 (Bharti Airtel Ltd.), and AS26615 (Tim Celular), are also cellular, and so are 5 of the remaining 7 ASes in the top 10.

Also notable is the percentage of responding addresses that are turtles for these ASes. Most of the cellular ASes have around 70% of all probed addresses being turtles. AS9829, one of the two ASes with turtles accounting for lower than 50% of probed addresses, is known to offer other services in addition to cellular. AS4134, with only 1% of its probed addresses being turtles, is also known to offer other services. We believe that the cellular addresses observe high RTTs while others do not, explaining the low ratio of probed addresses with RTTs greater than 1 second.

Finally, nine ASes were observed in the top ten in every scan. AS4134 was the only exception, but it ranked 11th

ASN	Owner	May 2015 >1s	%	Rank	June 2015 >1s	%	Rank	July 2015 >1s	%	Rank
26599	TELEFONICA BRASIL	3.56M	80.4	1	3.87M	77.5	1	4.20M	77.0	1
26615	Tim Celular S.A.	1.35M	74.5	3	1.42M	71.5	2	1.72M	71.6	2
45609	Bharti Airtel Ltd.	1.46M	76.6	2	1.21M	81.0	3	1.03M	79.2	3
22394	Cellco Partnership	0.55M	73.4	8	0.58M	73.5	4	0.63M	72.7	4
1257	TELE2	0.67M	69.5	5	0.42M	65.5	9	0.58M	67.4	5
27831	Colombia Movil	0.53M	68.8	9	0.54M	64.3	5	0.53M	62.8	6
6306	VENEZOLAN	0.69M	77.3	4	0.41M	76.4	10	0.40M	75.7	10
9829	National Internet Backbone	0.57M	27.6	7	0.43M	30.9	7	0.43M	29.5	9
4134	Chinanet	0.60M	1.5	6	0.38M	0.9	11	0.34M	0.9	11
35819	Etihad Etisalat (Mobily)	0.42M	54.0	10	0.43M	54.5	6	0.45M	55.8	8

Table 4: Autonomous Systems sorted by the addresses summed across three Zmap scans for addresses that observed RTTs greater than 1s. The table shows for each AS: the number and percentage of addresses with RTT greater than 1s and the rank in that scan.

Continent	May 2015 >1s	%	June 2015 >1s	%	July 2015 >1s	%
South America	7.27M	26.7	7.41M	25.8	8.05M	26.9
Asia	5.56M	3.8	4.73M	3.4	4.56M	3.2
Europe	2.56M	2.7	2.09M	2.2	2.32M	2.4
Africa	1.12M	29.4	1.20M	30.3	1.30M	31.7
North America	0.93M	1.0	1.04M	1.1	1.14M	1.2
Oceania	0.08M	3.9	0.08M	3.7	0.08M	3.7

Table 5: Continents sorted by the addresses summed across three Zmap scans for addresses that observed RTTs greater than 1s. The table shows for each AS: the number and percentage of addresses with RTT greater than 1s in that scan.

ASN	Owner	May 2015 >100s	%	Rank	June 2015 >100s	%	Rank	July 2015 >100s	%	Rank
26599	TELEFONICA BRASIL	51.9K	1.2	1	63.5K	1.3	1	77.6K	1.4	1
12430	VODAFONE ESPANA S.A.U.	12.8K	4.4	2	11.6K	4.1	2	14.6K	5.2	3
26615	Tim Celular S.A.	6.2K	0.3	7	9.4K	0.5	3	14.7K	0.6	2
3352	TELEFONICA DE ESPANA	8.5K	0.2	3	7.3K	0.1	5	7.5K	0.2	4
6306	VENEZOLAN	7.5K	0.8	5	8.4K	1.5	4	6.6K	1.2	6
22394	Cellco Partnership	6.9K	0.9	6	6.6K	0.8	6	7.5K	0.9	5
27831	Colombia Movil	3.2K	0.4	10	5.0K	0.6	7	5.2K	0.6	7
45609	Bharti Airtel Ltd.	7.8K	0.4	4	2.6K	0.2	9	2.9K	0.2	9
35819	Etihad Etisalat (Mobily)	3.8K	0.5	9	3.9K	0.5	8	4.0K	0.5	8
1257	TELE2	6.2K	0.4	8	1.7K	0.3	14	2.4K	0.3	12

Table 6: Autonomous Systems sorted by the addresses summed across three Zmap scans for addresses that observed RTTs greater than 100s. The table shows for each AS: the number and percentage of addresses with RTT greater than 100s and the rank in that scan.

in the June and July scans. Thus, the Autonomous Sytems with the most turtles also remain consistent over time.

Table 5 shows the continents with the most turtles. South America and Asia alone account for around 75% of all turtles. Further, around a quarter of all addresses in South America and a third of the addresses in Africa experienced RTTs greater than 1s in each scan. On the other hand, only 1% of North America's addresses are turtles (of which more than half come from a single ASN: AS22394).

ASes most prone to RTTs greater than 100 seconds

Next, we investigate the Autonomous Systems of addresses with RTTs greater than 100 seconds in the three Zmap scans: we refer to these addresses as sleepy-turtles. We consider whether these addresses are different from turtles to identify whether there is a different underlying cause. Following the same process in identifying ASes and sorting them as in Table 4, Table 6 shows Autonomous Systems that are most prone to RTTs greater than 100 seconds.

We find that sleepy-turtles exhibit similarities to turtles. Every Autonomous System in Table 6 is cellular. Further, the ranks of the Autonomous Systems remain stable over time across the scans. However, there is more variation across the scans for the percentage of sleepy-turtles among all probed addresses for an AS. This suggests that the fraction of addresses experiencing RTTs greater than 100 seconds is less stable over time.

6.3 Is it the first ping?

RTTs that are consistently greater than a second are sufficiently high that interactive application traffic would seem impractical with these delays. We suspected that the latencies measured by ISI and Zmap might not be typical of application traffic.

We considered two broad explanations—extraordinary persistent latency due to oversized queues associated with low-bandwidth links, or extraordinary temporary, initial latency due to MAC-layer time slot negotiation or device wake-up.

In this section, we find that the latter appears to be a more likely explanation, qualitatively consistent with prior investigations of GPRS performance characteristics [4], but showing quantitatively more significant delay.

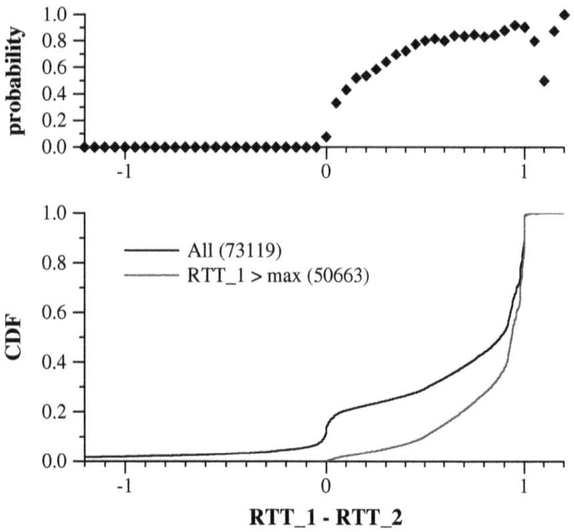

Figure 12: Bottom: Difference between initial latency and second probe latency; values around 1 indicate that both responses arrive at about the same time, values near zero indicate that the RTTs were about the same. The second line includes only those where $RTT_1 > max(RTT_2 \ldots RTT_n)$. Top: The probability that, given $RTT_1 - RTT_2$ on the x-axis, that $RTT_1 > max(RTT_2 \ldots RTT_n)$.

We extracted 236,937 IP addresses from the 20150206 ISI dataset (February 2015), including all addresses with a median RTT of at least one second. To select only responsive addresses that still had high latency, for each of these IP addresses, we sent two pings, separated by five seconds, with a timeout of 60 seconds. We omit 151,769 addresses that did not respond to either probe and 1,994 addresses that responded, on average, within 200ms.

Of the 83,174 addresses that remain, we wait approximately 80 seconds before sending ten pings, once per second with the same 60-second timeout. We next classify how the round trip time of the first ping, RTT_1, differs from those of the rest of the responded pings, $RTT_2 \ldots RTT_n$, where n may be smaller than 10 if responses are missing. For most of these addresses, 51,646, the first response took longer than the *maximum* of the rest. This suggests that roughly 2/3 of high latency observations are a result of negotiation or wake-up rather than random latency variation or persistent congestion. For 11,874, $median(RTT_2 \ldots RTT_n) < RTT_1 < max(RTT_2 \ldots RTT_n)$, i.e., the first response took longer than the *median*, but not the maximum, of the rest. The first response was smaller than the median of the rest for a comparable 10,910. That the first is above or below the median in roughly equal measure suggests that for these addresses there is little observed penalty to the first ping. Finally, we omit analysis of 8,329 addresses because we did not receive a response to, at least, the first probe, even though they did respond to the initial pair of probes, and we omit an additional 415 addresses that did respond to the first probe, but not to at least four probes overall (i.e., we require $n \geq 4$ before computing the median or maximum for comparison).

Can the overestimate be detected?

We show in Figure 12 the differences between the first and second round trip times for all those that had a first and second response. (1,311 addresses responded to the first but not the second). Rarely, latency increases from first to the second (yielding a negative difference) or decreases sufficient to indicate reordering (yielding a difference greater than one second). Typical among these addresses is for the second ping to be one second less than the first, that is, for both responses to arrive at about the same time.

We infer that a measurement approach that sent a second probe after one second could detect this behavior. The top graph of Figure 12 shows the probability that the maximum will be less than the first based on the difference between the first two latencies. (When the RTT difference exceeds 1 at the right edge of the upper graph, there are very few samples in an environment of substantial reordering.) Any significant drop from RTT_1 to RTT_2 is indicative of an overestimate with high probability.

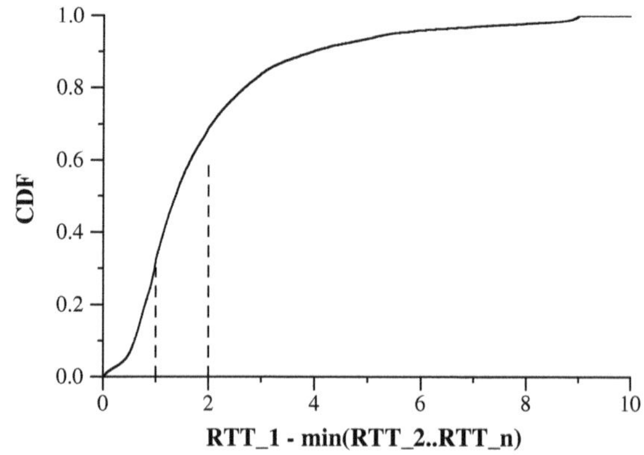

Figure 13: Difference between initial latency and observed minimum. The typical setup time is below four seconds.

How long does the negotiation or wake-up process take, and how large is the overestimate?

We observe that this can be estimated by comparing the first round trip time to the lowest seen among the ten probes. Of course, if the negotiation takes 15 seconds, the first probe rtt will take at most 9 seconds longer than the last, so this data set will treat all instances of a setup time between 10 and 60 seconds as taking 9. We show in Figure 13 the differences between RTT_1 and $min(RTT_2 \ldots RTT_n)$ for those 51,646 addresses that had a higher first rtt than the maximum of the rest. The median is 1.37 seconds, and 90% of the differences are below 4 seconds. Only 2% of the samples are above 8.5 seconds, suggesting that we do not underestimate this time substantially, and thus conclude that the wake-up or negotiation process generally takes from one-half to four seconds.

Are the addresses that show a high initial ping scattered across the IP address space or clustered into /24s?

The 236,937 IP addresses that we decided to probe initially are from only 1,887 "/24" prefixes. This is somewhat fewer prefixes than would be expected, given that there are 3.6M addresses in 34K prefixes in the overall 20150206 dataset. That is, as one might expect, greater than one second latencies do seem to be a property of the networks associated with selected prefixes. The 83,174 addresses that responded are from only 1,230 prefixes. We show the percentage of re-

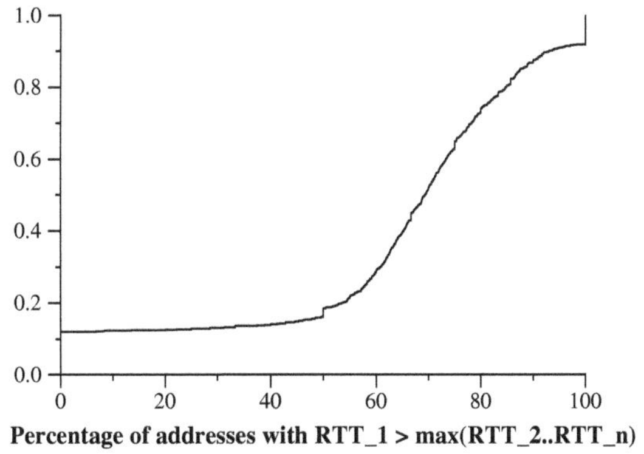

Figure 14: Percentage of addresses in a /24 prefix showing a drop from the initial to the maximum.

sponsive addresses within each prefix that dropped from the initial ping to the maximum of the rest in Figure 14. Several prefixes did not have an initial latency greater than the maximum; these typically had very few responsive addresses. In other prefixes, most addresses showed a reduction. Finally, the 51,646 that showed a reduction from the initial ping are from only 1,083 prefixes. Of the 161 prefixes that had only one address with above one-second median latency, only 39 showed a reduced from the initial RTT to the maximum of the rest. Taken together, we believe this distribution of addresses across relatively few prefixes indicates that the wake-up behavior is associated with some providers but not restricted to them.

6.4 Patterns associated with RTTs greater than 100 seconds

Finally, we look at addresses with extraordinarily high latencies (greater than 100 seconds); in particular, we want to understand whether these high latencies are an instance of a first-ping-like behavior, where wireless negotiation or buffering during intermittent connectivity creates the high value, or, on the other hand, are instances of extreme congestion. To separate the two types of events, we consider a sequence of probes, looking for whether or not the latency diminishes after a ping beyond 100 seconds.

We sample 3,000 of 38,794 addresses whose 99th percentile latency was greater than 100 seconds in the IT63c (20150206) dataset. Of this sample, 1,400 responded. We sent each address 2000 ICMP Echo Request packets using Scamper, spaced by 1 second. To collect responses with very high delays without altering the Scamper timeout, we simultaneously run tcpdump to capture packets.

Ping samples that saw a round trip time above 100 seconds exist in the context of a few very distinct patterns. Often, a series of successive ping responses would be delivered together almost simultaeously, leading to a steady decay in their round trip times. For example, after 136 seconds of no response from IP address 191.225.110.96, we received all 136 responses over a one second interval: every subsequent response's round-trip latency was 1 second lower than the previous. This pattern is sometimes preceded by a relatively low latency ping (< 10 seconds) and at other times, follows a few lost pings: we distinguish between these two cases and call the former *Low latency, then decay* and the latter *Loss, then decay*. It is possible that these are both observing the same underlying action on the network, but we leave them separate since there are substantially many of each.

Pattern	Pings	Events	Addrs
Low latency, then decay	615	13	10
Loss, then decay	1528	81	33
Sustained high latency and loss	2994	21	14
High latency between loss	12	12	12

Table 7: We observed distinct patterns of latency and loss near high latency responses, classifying all 5149 pings above 100 seconds from the sample.

Another characteristic pattern is that a high round trip time is followed by several responses of even greater latency, possibly with intermittent losses. This behavior is usually sustained for several minutes with latencies remaining higher than normal (>10 seconds) throughout the duration: we call this behavior *Sustained high latency and loss.* Finally, there are some cases where a single ping has a latency > 100 seconds and is preceded and followed by loss. We call these cases *High latency between loss.*

We count the number of occurrences of each pattern in Table 7. For each pattern, we show the number of pings greater than 100 seconds that were part of that pattern, the number of instances of that pattern occurring, and the number of unique addresses for which it occurred. We observe that the majority of events and addresses are *Loss, then decay*, yet almost twice as many pings are part of *Sustained high latency and loss.*

6.5 Summary

High latencies appear to be a property mainly of cellular Autonomous Systems, though a few also appear on satellite links. Latencies in the ISI data that are regularly above one second seem to be caused by the first-ping behavior associated with several addresses, where the first ping in a stream of pings has higher latency than the rest. Egregiously high latencies, i.e., latencies greater than a hundred seconds, occur in two broad patterns. In the first, latencies steadily decay with each probe, as if clearing a backlog. In the second, latencies are continuously high and are accompanied by loss, as if the network link is oversubscribed.

7. CONCLUSIONS AND DISCUSSION

Researchers use tools like ping to detect network outages, but generally guessed at the timeout after which a ping should be declared "failed" and an outage suspected. The choice of timeout can affect the accuracy and timeliness of outage detection: if too small, the outage detector may falsely assert an outage in the presence of congestion; if too large, the outage detector may not pass the outage along quickly for confirmation or diagnosis.

We investigated the latencies of responses in the ISI survey dataset to determine a good timeout, considering the distributions of latencies on a per-destination basis. Foremost, latencies are higher than we expected, based on conventional wisdom, and appear to have been increasing. We show that these high latencies are not an artifact of measurement choices such as using ICMP or the particular vantage points or probing schemes used, although different data sets vary somewhat. We show that high latencies are not caused by links with a substantial base timeout, such as satellite links. Finally, we showed that in many instances, the initial communication to cellular wireless devices is largely to blame for high latency measures. Similar spikes that may be consistent with handoff also dissipate over time, to more conventional latencies that support application traffic. With this data, researchers should be able to reason about what to expect in terms of false outage detection for a given timeout and how to design probing methods to account for these behaviors.

Our initial hypothesis was that it would be a simple matter to confirm that widely used timeout values would be adequate for studying outages, or failing that, that one or two additional seconds would be enough. However, as memory capacity and performance becomes less of a limiting factor, we believe that the lesson of this work is to design network measurement software to approach outage detection using a method comparable to that of TCP: send another probe after 3 seconds, but continue listening for a response to earlier probes, at least for a duration based, at least in part, on the error rates implied by Table 2. We plan to use 60 seconds when we need a timeout, and avoid timeouts otherwise.

Acknowledgments

We would like to express our sincere appreciation to the authors of the ISI Internet survey for both publishing their data and designing their data collection method to collect the unmatched responses that enabled this analysis.

We also would like to thank Zakir Durumeric for incorporating our changes into https://github.com/zmap/zmap/blob/master/src/probe_modules/module_icmp_echo_time.c in order to support explicit matching of responses and calculating round trip times in the stateless Zmap.

This research was supported in part by ONR grant N00173-13-1-G001.

8. REFERENCES

[1] Fred Baker. Requirements for IP version 4 routers. IETF RFC-1812, June 1995.

[2] Chadi Barakat, Nesrine Chaher, Walid Dabbous, and Eitan Altman. Improving TCP/IP over geostationary satellite links. In *Global Telecommunications Conference, 1999. GLOBECOM'99*, volume 1, pages 781–785, 1999.

[3] R. Braden, Editor. Requirements for internet hosts – communication layers. IETF RFC-1122, October 1989.

[4] Rajiv Chakravorty, Andrew Clark, and Ian Pratt. GPRSWeb: Optimizing the web for GPRS links. In *MOBISYS*, May 2003.

[5] Zakir Durumeric, Eric Wustrow, and J Alex Halderman. ZMap: Fast Internet-wide Scanning and Its Security Applications. In *USENIX Security*, pages 605–620, 2013.

[6] Nick Feamster, David G. Andersen, Hari Balakrishnan, and M. Frans Kaashoek. Measuring the effects of Internet path faults on reactive routing. In *ACM SIGMETRICS*, 2003.

[7] John Heidemann, Yuri Pradkin, Ramesh Govindan, Christos Papadopoulos, Genevieve Bartlett, and Joseph Bannister. Census and Survey of the Visible Internet. In *IMC*, 2008.

[8] Philip Homburg. [atlas] timeout on ping measurements. http://www.ripe.net/ripe/mail/archives/ripe-atlas/2013-July/000891.html, July 2013. Posting to the ripe-atlas mailing list.

[9] ISI ANT Lab. Internet address survey binary format description. http://www.isi.edu/ant/traces/topology/address_surveys/binformat_description.html.

[10] Ethan Katz-Basset, Harsha V. Madhyastha, John P. John, Arvind Krishnamurthy, David Wetherall, and Thomas Anderson. Studying black holes in the internet with Hubble. In *NSDI*, 2008.

[11] Landernotes. https://wiki.isi.edu/predict/index.php/LANDER:internet_address_survey_reprobing_it54c-20130524.

[12] Mathew J. Luckie, Anthony J. McGregor, and Hans-Werner Braun. Towards improving packet probing techniques. In *IMW*, pages 145–150, San Francisco, CA, November 2001.

[13] Matthew Luckie. Scamper: A Scalable and Extensible Packet Prober for Active Measurement of the Internet. In *IMC*, pages 239–245, 2010.

[14] Harsha V. Madhyastha, Tomas Isdal, Michael Piatek, Colin Dixon, Thomas Anderson, Aravind Krishnamurthy, and Arun Venkataramani. iPlane: An information plane for distributed services. In *OSDI*, Seattle, WA, November 2006.

[15] Ina Minei and Reuven Cohen. High-speed internet access through unidirectional geostationary satellite channels. In *IEEE Journal on Selected Areas in Communications*, 1999.

[16] Jeffrey Mogul. Broadcasting Internet datagrams. IETF RFC-919, October 1984.

[17] Vern Paxson. End-to-end routing behavior in the Internet. In *ACM SIGCOMM*, pages 25–38, Palo Alto, CA, August 1996.

[18] Lin Quan, John Heidemann, and Yuri Pradkin. Trinocular: Understanding Internet Reliability Through Adaptive Probing. In *ACM SIGCOMM*, pages 255–266, 2013.

[19] RIPE NCC. Atlas. http://atlas.ripe.net.

[20] SamKnows. Test methodology white paper, 2011.

[21] Aaron Schulman and Neil Spring. Pingin' in the rain. In *IMC*, Berlin, November 2011.

[22] Neil Spring, David Wetherall, and Thomas Anderson. Scriptroute: A public Internet measurement facility. In *USITS*, pages 225–238, Seattle, WA, March 2003.

[23] Ming Zhang, Chi Zhang, Vivek Pai, Larry Peterson, and Randy Wang. PlanetSeer: Internet path failure monitoring and characterization in wide-area services. In *OSDI*, San Francisco, CA, December 2004.

Is There WiFi Yet? How Aggressive Probe Requests Deteriorate Energy and Throughput

Xueheng Hu, Lixing Song, Dirk Van Bruggen, Aaron Striegel
University of Notre Dame
Notre Dame, Indiana 46556
xhu2@nd.edu, lsong2@nd.edu, dvanbrug@alumni.nd.edu, striegel@nd.edu

ABSTRACT

WiFi offloading has emerged as a key component of cellular operator strategy to meet the rich data needs of modern mobile devices. Hence, mobile devices tend to aggressively seek out WiFi in order to provide improved user Quality of Experience (QoE) and cellular capacity relief. For home and work environments, aggressive WiFi scans can significantly improve the speed at which mobile nodes join the WiFi network. Unfortunately, the same aggressive behavior that excels in the home environment incurs considerable side effects in crowded wireless environments. In this paper, we analyze empirical data collected from large (stadium) and medium (classroom) venues, and show through controlled experiments (laboratory) how aggressive WiFi scans can have significant implications for energy and throughput for mobile nodes. We close with several thoughts on the disjoint incentives for properly balancing WiFi discovery speed and crowded network interactions.

Categories and Subject Descriptors

C.2 [**Computer-Communication Networks**]: Miscellaneous

Keywords

WiFi; Probe Request; Energy; Performance

1. INTRODUCTION

The past several years have seen a veritable explosion of data consumption on mobile devices. Smartphones, tablets, and more recently the Internet of Things (IoT) have created a nearly insatiable demand for ubiquitous wireless connectivity. While the peak speeds for cellular (LTE) have risen impressively, dense and indoor environments remain challenging scenarios. Although LTE-Advanced (LTE-A) will offer relief with the introduction of small cell support, questions remain with regards to small cell economic viability and management complexity [1].

IMC'15, October 28-30, 2015, Tokyo, Japan.
© 2015 ACM. ISBN 978-1-4503-3848-6/15/10 ...$15.00.
DOI: http://dx.doi.org/10.1145/2815675.2815709.

For dense or crowded environments, WiFi offloading has emerged as a cornerstone of wireless network operator strategy. Despite the unlicensed nature of WiFi and potential issues with unpredictable Quality of Experience (QoE), the peak speeds of WiFi and more importantly the offloading of demand from the cellular network remain irresistible. Hence, nearly all mobile devices aggressively push the user onto WiFi networks. Whether the mobile device is configured to prompt the user anytime WiFi is available or certain services are restricted to WiFi only, the desire to offload is quite clear. Further efforts by standards bodies on protocols such as ANDSF (Access Network Discovery and Service Function) [2], Hotspot 2.0 [3], ANQP (Access Network Query Protocol), and 802.11ax (successor to 802.11hew) only reinforce that notion.

However, unlike cellular service, WiFi is neither pervasive nor contiguous. Although ANDSF can effectively steer the user to WiFi and Hotspot 2.0 can streamline the user joining WiFi, the mobile node must still find the channel in the WiFi spectrum where the intended WiFi service is located. The root of this discovery process can be found in the 802.11 Probe Request (PR) whereby a mobile node will actively scan across the WiFi space (2.4, 5 GHz) for viable 802.11 access points (APs). Access points, if inclined, can respond with Beacon Responses. The entire process allows the mobile device to quickly locate and join the WiFi network rather than passively waiting to discover an AP. Through the aggressive employment of active scans, mobile nodes can be rapidly directed to WiFi, satisfying both user QoE and decreasing cellular network load. For the ideal case of the home and work environment where the density of mobile devices is relatively manageable and the SSIDs are well known, such a setup tends to work fairly well.

Unfortunately, the tuning that is wonderful for the home and workplace tends to fare quite badly in the crowded or ultra-dense environment, namely venues such as sports arenas [4], large conferences [5, 6], or large classrooms where there is a significant density of individuals. Moreover, the ultra-dense environment is where WiFi offloading is needed most. In our paper, we show that not only do most mobile nodes excessively waste energy trying to find WiFi, we also show that aggressive scans have significant secondary effects on the legitimate users of any established WiFi networks. In short, the purpose of our paper is to argue that aggressive Probe Requests in the ultra-dense cases (hundreds or thousands of nodes) are the wireless equivalent of *'Are we there yet?'*, just as annoying, wasteful, and infuriating but with significant implications for overall network health and performance. While most practitioners in the wireless field would surmise such excessive Probe Requests to be a problem [7, 8], the degree to which such Probe Requests clutter the network in today's wireless devices is simply stunning. To that end, the contributions of this paper are three-fold:

- *Ultra-dense probe request dynamics:* We capture and analyze the dynamics of PRs via packet sniffers at four home football games, measuring PR prevalence both at the exterior (gates) and interior (bowl) in various manners across those four games. We demonstrate that most mobile devices continue to unashamedly probe despite never finding WiFi. We show that the PR rate in the stadium approaches nearly an order of magnitude more prevalence than even reasonably dense classroom settings (2,500 per minute in 2.4 GHz, 900 per minute in 5 GHz vs. 350 / 100 in the classroom). We further characterize the scanning patterns of various devices observed in such ultra-dense environments.
- *Energy impact of probe requests:* While the bulk of our paper focuses on Probe Request dynamics, we characterize the energy cost of active WiFi scanning, exploring the energy cost of a complete WiFi scan (Probe Request across all channels with appropriate Preferred Network Lists (PNLs)). We show that aggressive scanning can burn up to 44% more energy with little to no adaptation in response to the success or failure of WiFi scans to find available WiFi.
- *Throughput impact of probe requests:* Finally, we isolate the negative effects of aggressive WiFi scanning across the 2.4 and the 5 GHz bands on network throughput. We demonstrate that even only a relatively few UEs (user equipments) under default settings can significantly reduce network throughput.

2. RELATED WORK

WiFi has received incredible attention from the research community. For the purposes of this paper though, we are chiefly concerned with works focusing on increased discovery speed [9] and most notably, improved efficiency or accuracy for WiFi scanning [5–8, 10–12]. Our work is unique in that we highlight the prevalence of Probe Requests in the ultra-dense venue (affirmed by [4]) as well as exploring the patterns of the various devices observed in said venues.

The ability to efficiently and quickly scan is a fundamental requirement for fast, seamless handoffs in WiFi. Teng. et. al in [9] proposed D-Scan, specifically targeted at improving scan efficiency in dense environments. Monitoring also plays a key role in distinguishing performance issues with Yeo in [10] and more contemporary work by Rayanchu et. al in [11] trying to pin down interference issues related to WiFi. In their work, Gupta and Mohapatra [12] focused specifically on the power consumption of WiFi on phones while the work by Raghavendra et. al in [5] and Gupta et. al in [6] looked at larger scale venues (i.e., conferences) and overall performance. The issue of ultra-dense venues and WiFi performance was recently discussed in a Cisco slide deck for the 802.11ax working group meeting in Athens in late 2014 [4].

Although the notion of needless Probe Requests is not a new or necessarily a misunderstood topic, the challenge of how to reduce such spurious PRs has seen some research attention. Wu et. al proposed the concept of Footprint [8] while Ananthanarayanan and Stoica proposed Blue-Fi [7] for the express purpose of using cellular (Footprint) or Bluetooth (Blue-Fi) to efficiently guide WiFi scans. Unfortunately, while admirable with regards to the focus of the respective solutions, deployment and in particular the construction of security relationships make such solutions exceptionally difficult to realize in practice. Industry standardization efforts such as Hotspot 2.0, ANDSF, and efforts by the 802.11ax (previously 802.11hew) working groups are making some progress but are still must also be deployed.

3. ULTRA-DENSE DATASET

In this section, we summarize the data collected from four football games and two large class periods at the University of Notre Dame. We begin with a general description of how the data was gathered and continue with in-depth analyses of the data.

3.1 Data Summary

The football data was gathered near gate entrances (during normal queuing prior to ticketed entry) and in the bowl of the stadium. Multiple Linux laptops (Ubuntu 14.04) were used with extended wireless adapters (TP-Link TL-WN722N, Airpcap NX-900) placed into monitor mode and running *tcpdump*. Notably, the stadium does not have publicly accessible WiFi. Several small WiFi APs line the edge of the stadium as used for the ticketing system but that WiFi is not publicly accessible. The stadium itself seats roughly 80,000 with five separate entrance gates (A-E). Crowds of up to 150,000 gather around the stadium and tailgate, resulting in an exceptionally overwhelmed cellular network where cellular network coverage is provided via the campus DAS (Distributed Antenna System) for each of the three major campus carriers (AT&T, Verizon, Sprint). For the Michigan, Stanford, and North Carolina games, data gathering commenced roughly one hour before the start of the game to coincide when most ticket holders began to arrive at the stadium. For the Northwestern game, data was collected inside the stadium bowl in the student section during game time. Two of the games (Stanford, Northwestern) had notable weather impacts with the Stanford game having the most significant impact due to consistent rain and abnormally cold temperatures. Furthermore, fan interest had waned over the course of the season following a mid-season defeat to Florida State (mid-October) and various subsequent losses.

For the classroom venue, data was gathered at various points in the largest classroom on campus (DeBartolo 101) across multiple class periods. DeBartolo 101 can hold up to 450 individuals though attendance at each of the observed periods ranged in multiple hundreds. Each classroom observation began prior to the start of the class and ran through the end of the class session which lasted roughly 75 minutes. The classroom venue offers an alternative view whereby most UEs should have already established WiFi connectivity with the well-established WiFi infrastructure. In contrast to the stadium venue where UEs were especially keen to search for WiFi due to the overloaded cellular network, the classroom venue should demonstrate considerably less scans once a mobile device is settled and joined to the network.

Table 1: Probe Request Data Summary

Venue		Michigan		Stanford		North Carolina		Northwestern		Class 1		Class 2	
Date		2014/09/06		2014/10/04		2014/10/11		2014/11/15		2015/04/20		2015/04/22	
Time Duration		27 min		42 min		60 min		35 min		72 min		76 min	
Weather		Warm		Rainy,Cold		Good		Cold		N/A		N/A	
Location		Stadium Gate		Stadium Gate		Stadium Gate		Stadium Bowl		DB 101		DB 101	
Band		2.4G	5G	2.4G	5G	2.4G	5G	2.4G	5G	2.4G	5G	2.4G	5G
# of PRs		75,791	7,977	86,195	4,335	82,174	21,244	87,322	32,897	28,010	8,676	27,867	6,839
# of Source MACs		4,785	1,458	6,813	805	7,144	3,191	12,802	3,853	1,087	522	1,051	443
PRs / Min	Mean	2,778	294	2,098	103	1,362	353	2,568	967	379	118	366	90
	Max	3,721	596	3,029	223	1,855	603	3,505	1,344	673	227	722	249
	Median	2,690	295	2,168	97	1,330	349	2,612	1,005	346	105	334	78
	Stdev	460	119	663	56	202	79	584	266	115	42	107	45

In each of the data gathering scenarios, multiple laptops were used as noted earlier with each laptop possessing multiple external wireless adapters. Individual laptops were configured to monitor multiple channels both within a band and between bands, i.e., either monitor multiple 2.4 GHz channels (Channel 1, Channel 11) or across multiple bands (2.4 GHz Channel 1, 5 GHz Channel 153). The intuition behind the setup was to capture both the scan width (how long does it take for a device to complete a scan across the 2.4 GHz band) as well as dual-band capabilities (2.4 vs. 5 GHz). Notably, 5 GHz adoption rose significantly even over the course of this study making our dataset likely to underestimate the net PRs / minute with the most recent slate of mobile devices. Data was processed through a combination of *tshark* and Python with PR information stored in a MySQL database. Following processing, data files are discarded and only anonymized header information is preserved for the purpose of analysis.

Table 1 shows the key characteristics observed across each of the respective venues. The data is broken for each band and represents the impact on only one particular channel (Channel 1 for 2.4 GHz, Channel 153 for 5 GHz). Taking the Michigan game as an example, for the 2.4 GHz band, the average density of PRs comes in at 2,778 per minute, just over 46 PRs per second. The 5 GHz channel sees remarkably fewer PRs (294 per minute) but it is also notable that many devices were still not fully 5 GHz capable at the time of our experiment as noted earlier. While we had expected to see a bump in 5 GHz PRs at the Stanford game due to the recent release of iPhone 6, the inclement weather had clear impacts in terms of attendance for the game (upper 30°F, rainy). Even with the reduced fan turnout, the number of PRs for the Stanford game still averaged 2098 per minute in Channel 1 (nearly 35 PRs per second).

The introduction of the iPhone 6, iOS 8, and newer versions of Android also added peculiarities to the experiment as the source MAC on WiFi scans could no longer safely be viewed as an indicator of the device density [13]. Android also introduced similar functionality. Hence, while the number of PRs is accurate, the number of unique source MACs from the Stanford game onwards is reasonably suspect.

Regardless of the issues with device counts via unique source MACs, PRs can serve as an alternative indicator of device density as PRs are a function of existing WiFi connectivity, device type / configuration (ex. Android, iOS), and device usage (screen on, WiFi scanning screen). In contrast to the stadium, each of the class periods exhibits dramatically different prevalences with regards to PRs. As would be expected with an established WiFi infrastructure, most UEs are likely to have been associated and hence do not nearly as aggressively probe the WiFi spectrum. Most importantly as noted earlier in the contributions, the prevalence of PRs in the reasonably populated large classroom (several hundred individuals) is dwarfed by nearly an order of magnitude versus the stadium environment. Critically, while a legitimate WiFi deployment in the stadium would be likely to reduce the prevalence of PRs, there still would likely be a non-trivial number of unaffiliated UEs who will continue to aggressively probe in such venues.

Circling back around, from an overhead perspective for nearly all cases aside from initial entry to the venue, each Probe Request can be viewed as wasteful as either no public WiFi exists (stadium) or the infrastructure is unlikely to change (classroom). The waste manifests itself from a foundational perspective by virtue of time consumed on the primary channel as well as secondary consumption on interfering channels. Hence, a simplistic way to evaluate the waste of PR is to explore the time consumption for each request. From a distributional analysis, the most common rate setting (92%) for PRs in the 2.4 GHz spectrum was 1.0 Mb/s with speeds observed for PRs up to 11.0 Mb/s. PRs in the 5 GHz spectrum were universally set to 6.0 Mb/s. If we assume a rough PR size of 100 bytes, a perfect PR (ignoring CIFS, DIFS, 802.11 headers, DCF effects) would be 800 microseconds. The reality though is that the PR consumes an impact of much more than the 800 microseconds of air time due to, for example, the exponential back-off introduced by DCF.

First, frequent PRs are highly likely to impact the DCF of any mobile nodes affiliated with WiFi. While the stadium does not offer WiFi, we could view the mobile nodes as captured as being indicative of nodes without ANDSF policies / uncooperative mobile nodes, the extent of which would require careful observation that is beyond the scope of this paper. Second, for the 2.4 GHz channels, the lack of channel orthogonality means that as a mobile node iterates through an active scan, it may cause issues as it traverses nearby channels (ex. Channel 2, Channel 3, Channel 4, Channel 5 on Channel 1). If we are lucky, the overlapping channels have a minimal impact. Otherwise, the air time consumed on the overlapping channels may create significant bit errors for the primary users. Third, while PRs are relatively short, the low data rates of the PRs means that the actively scanning nodes tend to clutter / slow down the higher speed / affiliated nodes (ex. 1 Mb/s vs. 54 Mb/s). This disparity of speed is only amplified in the 5 GHz bands with higher

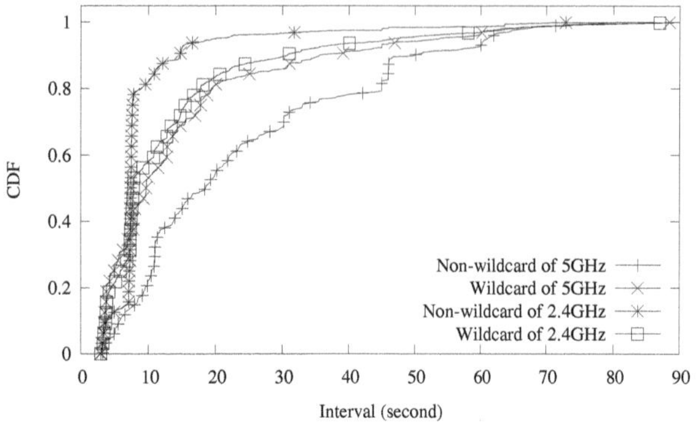

(a) Michigan

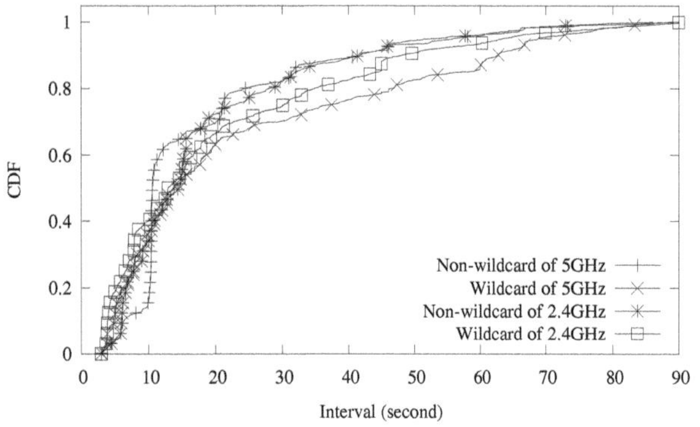

(b) Northwestern

Figure 1: CDF of Scan Interval

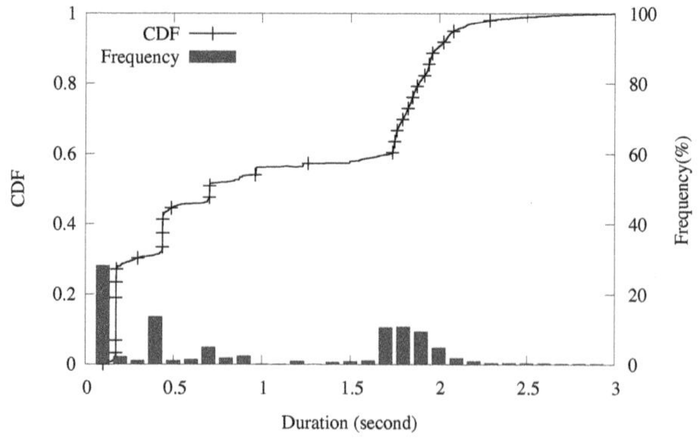

Figure 2: Distribution of Scan Duration

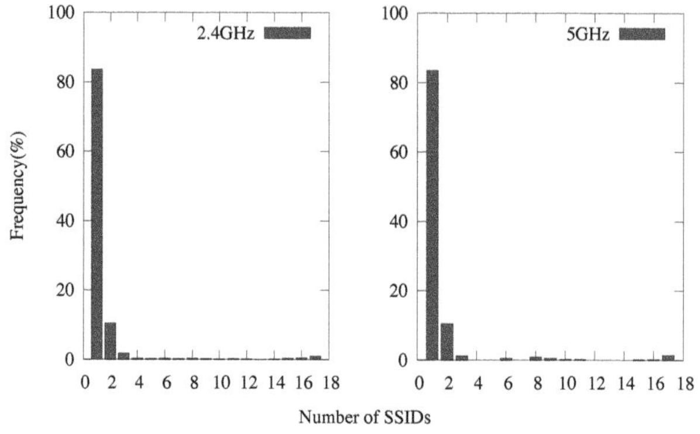

Figure 3: Number of SSIDs per Active Scan

potential peak speeds afforded by 802.11n (270 Mb/s) and 802.11ac (1.3 Gb/s). Later in this paper, we explore the impacts on 802.11n via small scale experiments. Fourth, as indicated by the observations from the classroom, mobile nodes may continue to scan even once affiliated with an AP if AP performance is insufficient or simply if the mobile nodes hopes for observing 'better' WiFi.

3.2 Scanning Behavior Analysis

To explore the data further, we dive into the data as observed from the games of Northwestern and Michigan. The reason for exploring the Northwestern game is that observations from the bowl allowed us to experience a much more representative sample of the ultra-dense environment at scale. In contrast to the gate-based observations for the prior three games with somewhat transient behavior (queuing at the gates), the Northwestern game presented observations from a fixed vantage point. We also include the Michigan game (before iOS 8) for the purpose of investigating how iOS 8 MAC randomization could potentially impact our measurements on WiFi scanning behaviors, particularly, the scan interval [13].

Figure 1 plots CDFs of the inter-scan interval that represents the average wait time between successive scans initiated by mobile nodes across both the 2.4 and 5 GHz bands. Each CDF is also broken out by the requests for empty SSIDs (interval between unknown SSIDs) and known SSIDs via the PNL. A low-pass filter is applied with a floor of three seconds as observed by the data distributions which means the interval is only counted if the node has at least three seconds of idle time between requests from the same MAC with the same SSID. SSIDs from the PNL may only be counted once for a given MAC (ex. BestBuy matching with BestBuy counts and then precludes any subsequent matches in the same scan for that UE). The interesting result is that at the 2.4 GHz spectrum many nodes (60% for Michigan and 40% for Northwestern) scanned quite frequently at intervals around or smaller than 10 seconds. The frequent scan may in part be driven by the cellular network on campus being overwhelmed on game day (nearly 150k individuals can be on campus) as well as individuals turning on their phone trying to find WiFi while waiting in line to enter the stadium.

Next, Figure 2 measures the average time duration for a particular active scan. The duration is recorded by measuring the occurrence of the first PR for a UE in Channel 1 followed by the appearance of the last PR for that same UE in Channel 11. Time synchronization is provided by running each of the monitors on the same laptop in monitor mode. The data for Figure 2 was focused only on the 2.4 GHz band. Both the CDF and the Frequency (PDF) are plotted in the figure. Interestingly, there are two clusters that can largely be attributed to differences between the respective mobile operating systems. On the left side, Android devices tend to frequently try to cap the maximum scan width ranging typically less than 800 milliseconds. Alternatively, iOS devices tend to fan out over a wider period of time by scanning for up to 2 seconds at a time. Critically, Android devices tend to squeeze as many PRs as possible into a shorter pe-

Table 2: WiFi Scan Interval

	In WiFi Settings Screen	
Device Type	**Yes**	**No**
iPod touch	3 s, 8 s, 10 s	15 s → 480 s
Dell Venue 7	10 s	43 s
Nexus 10	10 s	10 s
Galaxy S4	10 s	60 s

riod of time while iOS devices tend to spread out the PRs over time.

In addition, we have investigated the varying numbers of SSIDs contained within a PNL of individual PRs. WiFi scans are divided into sweeps representing a complete active scans with the number of unique SSIDs requested being mapped to each individual source MAC within that time frame. As demonstrated by Figure 3, most nodes (80%) do not make requests for SSIDs from their PNL but rather only make requests for the the empty (unknown) SSID. We comment a bit later on scan mechanisms and how the length of the PNL has only a minimal impact on the actual number of resulting scans (ex. some mobile nodes tend to scan for a timed duration rather than simple PNL coverage). Recent trends with regards to privacy indicate that the scan for only a single empty SSID is more likely to be the norm than scans with long and varied PNLs.

4. PERFORMANCE DETERIORATION

We now explore the energy and throughput costs of aggressive WiFi scanning in a controlled laboratory setting. Although it would be ideal to instrument the entirety of the stadium and to provide pervasive instrumentation, the laboratory experiments can shed some light on what might occur in the larger scale scenarios. To that end, we conducted a group of small-scale, controlled experiments with four types of handsets: the iPod touch (iOS 8.4), the Dell Venue 7 (Android 4.4), the Nexus 10 (Android 5.1), and the Samsung Galaxy S4 smartphone (Android 4.2). We are particularly interested in measuring the power cost of an active WiFi scan as well as the throughput impacts associated with WiFi scans. Moreover, the lab setting provides ideal cases for attempting to replicate the various intra-scan behavior observed in the stadium and the respective energy implications.

For our experiments, we investigated WiFi scanning behaviors for the aforementioned devices by configuring the devices with two different settings while at the same time running *tcpdump* in monitor mode for capturing PRs. The laptops utilized for packet capture were identical to the setups used for packet capture in the stadium environment. Scanning behaviors of the devices are summarized in Table 2. The distinguishing factor between the two columns refers to whether or not the WiFi settings screen was open (which implies a much more aggressive approach to scan). We observed for each active scan, all four types of devices typically sweep the PNL on one specific channel and then hop to the next channel.

As indicated by Table 2, for all four types of devices (WiFi enabled), if the listing of current WiFi is open, the intervals between two consecutive WiFi scans are roughly 10 seconds (3 s and 8 s were also observed for iOS device). If WiFi is still on but the user is not in the WiFi settings screen (and not connected to WiFi), the scan interval for different devices varies from 10 seconds to up to 8 minutes. Interestingly, iOS 8 tends to exponentially increase the scanning interval from 15 s to 480 s (i.e., 15 s, 30 s, 60 s, ... 480 s) when not in the WiFi settings panel. For all other experiments presented in this section, we forced the handset to stay in WiFi settings screen as this configuration allows us to better mimic denser environmental scenarios. We surmise though more difficult to measure, that the lack of cellular connectivity may also have caused more rapid scanning as the cellular network tended to be quite overwhelmed with the nearly 150k users in the local area (good perceived downlink signal but impossible to actually send data on the uplink).

Table 3: Energy Cost: Baseline vs. Scanning

	Power Consumption (uAh)	
Settings	**Average**	**Std Dev**
Baseline	12,333.42	7.18
Scanning	17,801.18	60.08

4.1 Energy Impact

For the purpose of evaluating energy cost per WiFi scan, we use the Monsoon power monitor and its PowerTool software [14]. We instrument the Galaxy S4 smartphone as it is the only device possessing a removable battery. Power for the phone is supplied by the Monsoon power monitor with the energy consumption recorded at a sampling rate of 5 KHz. The phone is evaluated in two different settings, *Baseline* where WiFi is off but the screen remains on and *Scanning* where the phone stays in the WiFi settings screen but remains unaffiliated with regards to WiFi. Power monitoring was run for an extended period of time (5 minutes). The average and standard deviation of power consumption with each setting are given in Table 3.

After recording the average power consumption for both the Baseline and the Scanning settings, the energy cost of an active WiFi scan can be approximated by calculating the delta between the consumption values of these two settings over the entirety of the monitoring period, yielding 5467.76 uAh for the 5-minute time window. Notably, this represents a 44.3% increase over the Baseline consumption despite the fact that the screen is on for both cases. We can further infer the power cost per scan since Table 2 has indicated WiFi scan is invoked every 10 seconds if WiFi settings screen is active. While somewhat crude in its approximation, each WiFi scan in an ideal scenario (no background traffic, no DCF issues) consumes roughly 182.26 uAh. An individual waiting in line for 10 minutes without WiFi while aggressively scanning could end up consuming nearly 10936 uAh extra energy, effectively 0.4% of a fully charged battery (2600 mAh).

4.2 Throughput Loss

While the energy losses may be tolerable (though still wasteful), aggressive WiFi scanning also has impacts on performance by introducing overhead to the wireless channels. For the purpose of measuring the potential network performance degradation, we designed a small-scale experiment using *iperf2* configured for UDP throughput. The components of this experiment are described follows:

iperf client and server: We instrumented a Dell EliteBook 8560 with a 802.11n dual-band network interface as the *iperf* client and a HP 3450 laptop with Ubuntu Linux installed as the *iperf* server.

Handsets: We used one iPod Touch, one Dell Venue 7 tablet, and thirteen Android smartphones as our handsets. All devices are dual-band capable. For each device, we de-associated the device from any known WiFi and created a PNL consisting of two hidden SSIDs. Screens were kept on and the devices were kept in the WiFi scan screen.

Wireless router: A Netgear AC1900 router (dual-band, 802.11ac capable) was used to set up the WLAN. The router provided up to 600 Mbps and 1300 Mbps WiFi down-link speeds on the 2.4 and 5 GHz bands respectively. The client was the only node associated with the AP and the server was directly connected to the router via GigE. A full 40 MHz of spectrum (full 802.11n speeds) was selected for the router with validation. Experiments were conducted in a basement with minimal interference from other devices. The distance between the client and the server was roughly three meters and all handsets were positioned between the client and the server.

The client was tuned in order to determine the maximum lossless send rate between the client and the server. Communications were unidirectional going only from the client to the server. On the 5GHz band, client performance topped out at roughly 180 Mb/s without any background traffic (see Figure 4). Each experiment setting was repeated multiple times with a typical test duration of five minutes. Once the baseline was established, the experiments were conducted by gradually increasing the number of UEs actively scanning. Notably, WiFi performance decreased by 16.7% once all fifteen devices were introduced, i.e., from the peak of 180.0 Mb/s down to 149.8 Mb/s. While degradation of performance is not entirely unexpected with WiFi, the fact that this performance decrease comes by virtue of 'useless' PRs is problematic. As noted earlier, stadium environments may have nodes both associated and un-associated with the WiFi infrastructure with the unaffiliated mobile nodes still chirping for WiFi. Furthermore, our limited lab experiments were actually quite benign entailing only roughly 360 PRs per min (observed via tcpdump). In the stadium case, such as the Northwestern game where 967 PRs were generated every minute, unaffiliated nodes could have significant performance issues even in the 'better' 5 GHz bands. As noted in Figure 4, the 2.4 GHz performance has a similar degradation pattern except with an obviously lower baseline and would potentially be much worse for the stadium case with dramatically higher numbers of PRs (360 PRs per minute versus 2568 PRs per minute).

5. DISCUSSIONS AND FUTURE WORK

The issue of how to solve the dilemma of aggressive WiFi speaks to the complexities of the wireless industry. On one hand, the solution would appear to be fairly trivial: slow down the WiFi scanning rate and scan only on a screen activation. The reality though is decidedly more complicated as applications largely do not wait to send data until there is WiFi available and the delay before locating WiFi at home could be considerable. Critically, the vast majority of a user experience tends to be dominated by the simple cases, ex. only a few devices and well-known SSIDs. In those cases, the first scan when in range tends to be successful and faster scanning means faster hopping onto WiFi.

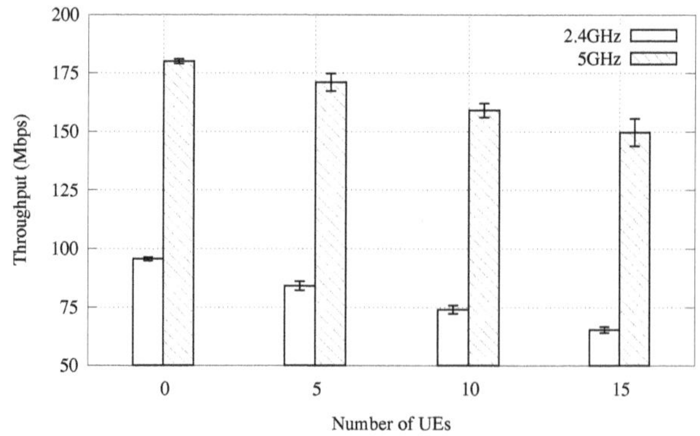

Figure 4: Throughput Reduction

Furthermore, the vendors at first glance most impacted by aggressive Probe Requests tend to be the WiFi infrastructure vendors who have little to no control over the mobile devices. After all, WiFi exists in the unlicensed bands which means that for all practical purposes, the equipment infrastructure vendors must simply endure. Recent discussions with the 802.11ax standard have noted that indeed, aggressive Probe Requests do create sizable issues in ultra-dense venues [4]. Handset and OS vendors are only marginally motivated by claims of reduced throughput as the vast majority of throughput scenarios are OK (the typical cases). However, we would argue that the energy cost of being aggressive is non-trivial and moreover, that energy cost burns worst when most users tend to be suffering energy issues (ex. the ultra-dense venue).

In conclusion, we believe that aggressive WiFi scanning has significant side effects on normal wireless network users, both with respect to energy and throughput. Moreover, we believe that our stadium analyses show that not only are aggressive Probe Requests wasteful in the ultra-dense case, the degree to which such wasteful Probe Requests occur far outstrips what is perceived in the literature. Moreover, despite research efforts to tamp down the impacts of Probe Requests, the perceived benefits with regards to WiFi joining speed seem to largely outweigh occasional problems in dense venues. Future work is needed to explore how one can bridge the conflicting goals of rapid WiFi detection with the cost of wasted WiFi scans in a deployable manner, likely with the assistance of handset or cellular carriers, a considerable challenge. For encouraging such efforts, the full anonymized stadium and classroom datasets are made publicly available.

6. ACKNOWLEDGMENTS

This material is based upon work supported by the National Science Foundation under Grant No. IIS-0968529. Further support was provided through the University of Notre Dame and Sprint.

7. REFERENCES

[1] J. Andrews, S. Buzzi, W. Choi, S. Hanly, A. Lozano, A. Soong, and J. Zhang, "What Will 5G Be?" *IEEE Journal on Selected Areas in Communications*, vol. 32, no. 6, pp. 1065–1082, June 2014.

[2] "Cellular-Wi-Fi Integration," InterDigital, Tech. Rep., 2012.

[3] "The Future of Hotspots: Making Wi-Fi as Secure and Easy to Use as Cellular," Cisco, Tech. Rep., 2012.

[4] B. Hart, M. Swartz, J. Suhr, and M. Silverman, "Stadium Measurements," 802.11ax Working Group (Doc 1223), September 2014.

[5] R. Raghavendra, E. Belding, K. Papagiannaki, and K. Almeroth, "Unwanted Link Layer Traffic in Large IEEE 802.11 Wireless Networks," *IEEE Transactions on Mobile Computing*, vol. 9, no. 9, pp. 1212–1225, September 2010.

[6] A. Gupta, J. Min, and I. Rhee, "WiFox: Scaling WiFi Performance for Large Audience Environments," in *CoNEXT 2012, ACM*, 2012, pp. 217–228.

[7] G. Ananthanarayanan and I. Stoica, "Blue-Fi: Enhancing Wi-Fi Performance Using Bluetooth Signals," in *MobiSys 2009, ACM*, 2009, pp. 249–262.

[8] H. Wu, K. Tan, J. Liu, and Y. Zhang, "Footprint: Cellular Assisted Wi-Fi AP Discovery on Mobile Phones for Energy Saving," in *WINTECH 2009, ACM*, 2009, pp. 67–76.

[9] J. Teng, C. Xu, W. Jia, and D. Xuan, "D-Scan: Enabling Fast and Smooth Handoffs in AP-Dense 802.11 Wireless Networks," in *INFOCOM 2009, IEEE*, April 2009, pp. 2616–2620.

[10] J. Yeo, M. Youssef, and A. Agrawala, "A Framework for Wireless LAN Monitoring and Its Applications," in *WiSe 2004, ACM*, 2004, pp. 70–79.

[11] S. Rayanchu, A. Patro, and S. Banerjee, "Catching Whales and Minnows Using WiFiNet: Deconstructing non-WiFi Interference Using WiFi Hardware," in *NSDI 2012, USENIX*, 2012, pp. 57–70.

[12] A. Gupta and P. Mohapatra, "Energy Consumption and Conservation in WiFi Based Phones: A Measurement-Based Study," in *SECON 2007, IEEE*, June 2007, pp. 122–131.

[13] B. Misra, "iOS8 MAC Randomization," accessed: 2015-05-05. [Online]. Available: http://blog.airtightnetworks.com/ios8-mac-randomization-analyzed/

[14] "Monsoon Power Monitor." [Online]. Available: https://www.msoon.com/LabEquipment/PowerMonitor/

Electri-Fi Your Data: Measuring and Combining Power-Line Communications with WiFi

Christina Vlachou, Sébastien Henri, Patrick Thiran
EPFL, Switzerland
firstname.lastname@epfl.ch

ABSTRACT

Power-line communication (PLC) is widely used as it offers high data-rates and forms a network over electrical wiring, an existing and ubiquitous infrastructure. PLC is increasingly being deployed in hybrid networks that combine multiple technologies, the most popular among which is WiFi. However, so far, it is not clear to which extent PLC can boost network performance or how hybrid implementations can exploit to the fullest this technology. We compare the spatial and temporal variations of WiFi and PLC.

Despite the potential of PLC and its vast deployment in commercial products, little is known about its performance. To route or load balance traffic in hybrid networks, a solid understanding of PLC and its link metrics is required. We conduct experiments in a testbed of more than 140 links. We introduce link metrics that are crucial for studying PLC and that are required for quality-aware algorithms by recent standardizations of hybrid networks. We explore the spatial and temporal variation of PLC channels, showing that they are highly asymmetric and that link quality and link-metric temporal variability are strongly correlated. Based on our variation study, we propose and validate a capacity estimation technique via a metric that only uses the frame header. We also focus on retransmissions due to channel errors or to contention, a metric related to delay, and examine the sensitivity of metrics to background traffic. Our performance evaluation provides insight into the implementation of hybrid networks; we ease the intricacies of understanding the performance characteristics of the PHY and MAC layers.

Categories and Subject Descriptors

C.2 [**Computer-Communication Networks**]: Network Architecture and Design, Local and Wide-Area Networks; C.4 [**Performance of Systems**]: Measurement techniques

Keywords

Power-line communications; HomePlug AV; IEEE 1901; IEEE 1905; Hybrid networks; Capacity estimation; Link metrics.

IMC'15, October 28–30, 2015, Tokyo, Japan.

DOI: http://dx.doi.org/10.1145/2815675.2815689.

1. INTRODUCTION

Wireless technology is dominant in local networks; it offers mobility and attractive data-rates. Nevertheless, it often leaves "blind spots" in coverage, and the network becomes saturated because of the increasing demand for higher rates and of the explosion of network applications. Today's networks call for additional, simple technologies that can boost network performance, extend coverage, and improve quality of service. Several candidates, among which power-line and coaxial communications, are on the market. As the demand for combining diverse technologies increases, new specifications for hybrid networks are developed, such as the IEEE 1905 standard [2] which specifies abstraction layers for topology, link metrics, and forwarding rules.

Due to the growing demand of reliability in home networks, wireless and power-line communications (PLC) are combined by several vendors to deliver high rates and broad coverage without blind spots. PLC is at the forefront of home networking, as it provides easy and high data-rate connectivity. Its main advantage is coverage wider than WiFi and data-rates up to 1Gbps without requiring the wiring of a new network. It is obvious that PLC can be a lucrative backbone for WiFi. However, in the quest to provide *reliable* performance, some questions arise: Where and when does PLC perform better than WiFi? How fast does PLC channel quality change? What are the differences between the two technologies and which medium(s) should an application use? Such questions remain unanswered as of today and a goal of this work is to address them.

Despite its wide adoption, PLC has received far too little attention from the research community. Moreover, IEEE 1905 is technology agnostic and it does not provide any forwarding nor metric-estimation methods. To fully exploit the potential of each medium, hybrid networks require routing and load-balancing algorithms. In turn, these algorithms require accurate capacity estimation methods, and a solid understanding of the underlying layers of each network technology. To the best of our knowledge, there has not been any study on PLC; so far a very large body of work has only introduced theoretical channel models. In this work, we investigate PLC from an end-user perspective, and we explore link metrics and their variations with respect to space, time, and background traffic; this is our main contribution. We focus on two metrics required by IEEE 1905 [2]: the *PHY rate* (capacity) and the *packet errors* (loss rate).

The most popular specification for high data-rate PLC, employed by 95% of PLC devices [1], is HomePlug AV[1]. This specification was adopted by the IEEE 1901 standard [6]. In this work, we dig deeply into the 1901 performance and provide link-quality estimation techniques. We first present the key elements of the PHY and MAC layers in Section 2, and we detail on our measurement methodology for PLC in Section 3. In Section 4, we explore experimentally the gains of incorporating PLC in a WiFi network and explain why temporal variation studies are crucial for a reliable performance. We focus on WiFi blind spots and bad links and discuss how PLC can mitigate high-traffic scenarios.

We delve into both the PHY and MAC layers of PLC via a testbed of more than 140 links. In Section 5, we investigate the spatial variation of PLC and find that PLC links are highly asymmetric. This has two consequences: (*i*) Link metrics should be carefully estimated in both directions; (*ii*) Predicting which PLC links will be good is challenging. We study the temporal variation of the PLC channel in Section 6, and distinguish three different timescales for the link quality. Exploring temporal variation is important for exploiting to its fullest extent each medium and for efficiently updating link metrics (e.g., high-frequency probing yields accurate estimations but high overhead). In Section 7, we explore the accuracy of a capacity-estimation technique by designing a load-balancing algorithm and by employing our temporal-variation study. To explore the 1905 metric related to packet losses, we examine the retransmission procedure and how link metrics are affected by contention in Section 8. By employing our temporal variation study and our two link metrics, PLC performance can be fully characterized and simulated, thus reducing the overhead complexity of the exact representation of the channel model and the PHY layer mechanisms. We summarize our guidelines for link-metrics estimation in Section 9. We verify our findings by using devices from two vendors and HomePlug technologies. Our key findings and contributions are outlined in Table 1.

WiFi vs PLC	Section
In short distances, WiFi yields higher throughput, but with much higher variability, compared to PLC.	4.1
PLC usually offers high gains in quality of service enhancements, coverage extension and link aggregation.	4.1, 7.4
Capacity estimation methods and temporal variation studies are needed to fully exploit the mediums.	7.4
Channel Quality and Variation	**Section**
PLC links can exhibit severe asymmetry and spatial variation is difficult to predict.	5
Temporal variation of the PLC channel occurs over three different time-scales.	6
Variation on the short-term depends on the noise produced by electrical appliances.	6.2
Variation on the long-term depends on the appliances and their power consumption.	6.3
Link quality and link metric variation are strongly correlated and good links can be probed much less often than bad ones.	6.2, 8.1
Introduction of metrics and guidelines for accurate capacity estimation, which is required by IEEE 1905 [2].	7
Retransmissions Due to Errors or Contention	**Section**
Discussion on metrics that use broadcast probing.	8.1
Expected transmission count (ETX) in PLC.	8.1
Sensitivity of link metrics to background traffic.	8.2

Table 1: Main findings and contributions

2. BACKGROUND ON PLC

We now recall the main features of the PHY and MAC layers for the most popular PLC specification, which is HomePlug AV (HPAV) equivalently, IEEE 1901 [6].

2.1 PHY Layer

The physical layer of HPAV is based on an OFDM scheme with 917 carriers in the 1.8-30 MHz frequency band. Each OFDM carrier can employ a different modulation scheme among BPSK, QPSK, 8/16/64/256/1024-QAM. In contrast, in WiFi technologies, such as 802.11n, all carriers employ the same scheme and the *modulation and coding scheme* (MCS) index is used for decoding the frame [3]. Because each carrier employs different modulation schemes, PLC stations exchange messages with the modulation per carrier, the forward error correction code (FEC) rate, and other PHY layer parameters [6]. The entity that defines these PHY options is called the *tone map*, and it is estimated during the channel estimation process. To do so, the source initially sends *sound* frames to the destination by using a default, robust modulation scheme that employs QPSK for all carriers. This scheme is used for the initial channel estimation and communication between two stations, but also for broadcast and multicast transmissions. The destination estimates the channel quality using the sound frames, then it determines and sends the tone map with a unique identification – which is analogous to MCS for 802.11n – back to the source. The destination can choose up to 7 tone maps: 6 tone maps for different sub-intervals of the AC line cycle called *slots*, and one default tone map. PLC uses multiple tone maps for the different sub-intervals of the AC line cycle, because the noise and impulse response of the channel are varying along the AC line cycle. Tone maps are updated dynamically, either when they expire (after 30 s) or when the error rate exceeds a threshold [6].

2.2 MAC Layer

We now review the MAC layer and describe its most important sub-functions.

Physical Blocks (PB): The MAC layer employs two-level frame aggregation. First, the data are organized in *physical blocks* (PB) of 512 bytes, then the PBs are merged into PLC frames. A selective acknowledgment (SACK) of the PLC frame acknowledges each PB, so that only the corrupted PBs are retransmitted.

Access Methods: The MAC layer of IEEE 1901 includes both TDMA and CSMA/CA protocols [6]. However, to the best of our knowledge, all current commercial devices implement only CSMA/CA. The CSMA/CA protocol is similar to 802.11 for wireless communications, but with important differences that are summarized in [19]. The main difference is that, contrary to WiFi, PLC stations increase their contention windows (CW) not only after a collision, but also after sensing the medium busy. This is regulated by an additional counter, called the deferral counter. One of the main consequences is short-term unfairness that might yield high jitter [19], [21].

[1]HomePlug alliance is the leader in PLC standardization [1]. In addition to high data-rate PLC, there are low-rate specifications for home automation, such as HomePlug GreenPhy.

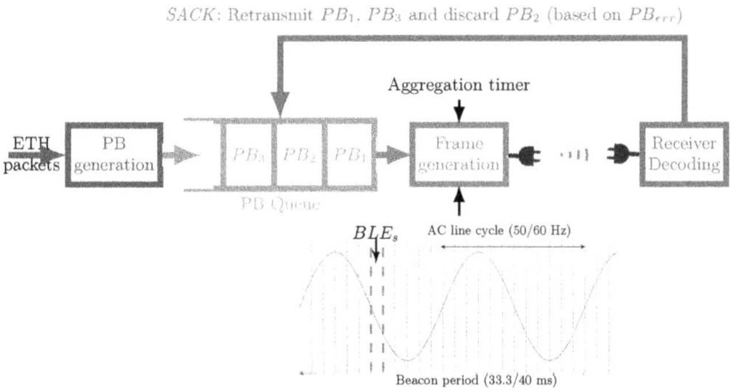

Figure 1: The PLC MAC layer

Management Messages (MMs): Management messages are a key feature of PLC. They are used for network management, tone-map establishment and updating. Stations must exchange MMs each time the tone map is updated, because the source has to be notified for the modulation scheme of each carrier.

Vendor-Specific Mechanisms: IEEE 1901 leaves the implementation of some mechanisms, such as the channel estimation procedure described in Section 2.1, unspecified. Therefore, they are vendor-specific and so far, vendors have not released any detailed specification for their devices.

In addition to MMs specified by the standard [6], there are vendor-specific MMs. Vendor-specific MMs are employed to configure the devices, modify the firmware, or measure statistics. We use vendor-specific MMs to measure statistics or configure the devices, as described in the next section.

Start-of-Frame Delimiter (SoF): The frame control, or the start-of-frame (SoF) delimiter, of PLC contains information for both PHY and MAC layers. The bit loading estimate (BLE) is retrieved from the SoF delimiter and is an estimation for the capacity, as we observe in Section 7. The BLE is an estimation of the number of bits that can be carried on the channel per μs.

DEFINITION 1. *[6] Let T_{sym} be the OFDM symbol length in μs (including the guard interval), R be the FEC code rate, and PB_{err} be the PB error rate (chosen based on the expected PB error rate on the link when a new tone map is generated. It remains fixed until the tone map becomes invalidated by a newer tone map). Let also B represent the sum of number of bits per symbol over all carriers. Then, BLE is given by*

$$BLE = \frac{B \times R \times (1 - PB_{err})}{T_{sym}}. \quad (1)$$

We now describe the MAC layer processes that aggregate the Ethernet packets into PLC frames. Figure 1 sketches the IEEE 1901 MAC layer. The Ethernet packets are organized in PBs. Then, the PBs are forwarded to a queue, and based on the BLE of the current tone-map slot s BLE_s, they are aggregated into a PLC frame. The frame duration is determined by BLE_s, the maximum frame duration (specified by [6]), and an aggregation timer that fires every few hundreds of ms after the arrival of the first PB, as concluded from our measurements[2]. The PLC frame is transmitted by a CSMA/CA protocol explained in [19]. The receiver decodes the frame and transmits a SACK that informs the transmitter of which PBs were received with errors. We observe that the full retransmission and aggregation process, and, as a result, the MAC and PHY layers, can be modeled using only two metrics: PB_{err} and BLE_s.

[2]Note that the frame duration is a multiple of the symbol duration, and that padding is used to fill these symbols.

Today's home networks, running 802.11n and/or 1901, contain fields in the frame header that help the receiver decode the frame and that accurately estimate capacity. We successfully employ these fields to aggregate bandwidth between the two mediums in Section 7. In the following, our PLC link metrics will be BLE and PB_{err}.

3. EXPERIMENTAL FRAMEWORK

We describe the experimental settings used to produce the measurements of this work. We provide guidelines for configuring and for obtaining various metrics from PLC devices.

3.1 Testbed and Setup

Our main testbed consists of 19 Alix 2D2 boards running the Openwrt Linux distribution [4]. The boards are equipped with a HomePlug AV miniPCI card (Intellon INT6300 chip), which interacts with the kernel through a Realtek Ethernet driver and with an Atheros AR9220 wireless interface. All our stations are placed on the same floor of a university building with offices. Figure 2 represents a map of the testbed along with the electrical map of the floor.

We next explain the PLC network structure. PLC uses a centralized authority called the central coordinator (CCo) to manage the network. To operate, each station must join a network with a CCo. Usually, the CCo is the first station plugged and it can change dynamically if another station has better channel capabilities than it does. Our floor has two distribution boards that are connected with each other at the basement of the building. This means that the cable distance between the two boards (more than 200m) makes the PLC communication between two stations at different boards challenging. Due to the two distribution boards, none of the stations can communicate with all stations and be the CCo. Hence, we create two different networks, shown with different colors in Figure 2. To avoid modifications in the network structure, we set the CCo statically in our testbed using [5], a tool described in the next subsection. These networks have different encryption keys (there is encryption on the MAC layer) and thus, only stations belonging to the same network can communicate with each other. In total, 144 links are formed.

In addition to using our main testbed, we experiment and validate our findings with HPAV500 devices, the Netgear XAVB5101 (Atheros QCA7400 chip)[3]. Due to space constraints, results are presented for our main testbed, unless otherwise stated.

3.2 Measurement and Traffic Tools

To retrieve the metrics for the PHY and MAC performance evaluation, we use a tool that interacts with the HomePlug AV chips, i.e., the Atheros Open Powerline Toolkit [5][4]. The tool uses vendor-specific management messages (MMs), as described in Section 2.2, to interact with, and to configure the devices. It also enables a sniffer mode with which we can

[3]Note that, compared to HPAV described in Section 2.1, HPAV500 extends the bandwidth to 1.8-68 MHz.

[4]We have been equipped with devices from 6 vendors and have been able to retrieve statistics from all devices using [5].

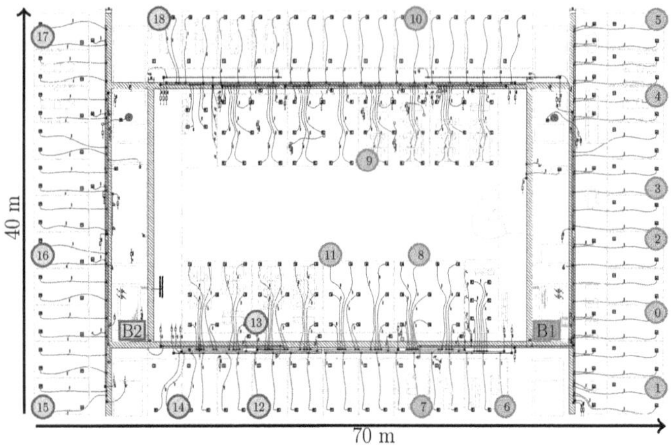

Figure 2: The electrical plan and the stations (0-18) of our testbed. There are two different PLC networks with CCo's at stations 11 and 15. Stations marked with the same color belong to the same network and are connected to the same distribution board (either B1 or B2).

capture the SoF delimiters of all received PLC frames. To generate traffic, we use **iperf**. For all the experiments, links are saturated with UDP traffic (unless otherwise stated), i.e., stations transmit at maximum available rates, so that we can measure metrics such as capacity. All the experiments of this work have been repeated multiple times over a period of one year to make sure that similar results are reproduced. Table 2 outlines the metrics used throughout this work, as well as the methods used to measure them.

Metric	Notation	Measured with
Arrival timestamp	t	SoF delimiter
Bit loading estimate	BLE	SoF delimiter
PB error probability	PB_{err}	MM (`ampstat` [5])
Average BLE	BLE	MM (`int6krate` [5])
Throughput	T	`iperf` or `ifstat`
MCS index (WiFi)	MCS	WiFi frame control

Table 2: Metrics and measurement methods

We are now ready to present our study on PLC.

4. WIFI VS PLC AND CHALLENGES

We first study the spatiotemporal variation of WiFi vs PLC in order to explore the possibilities of combining the two mediums towards quality of service improvement, coverage extension and bandwidth aggregation. We then discuss the challenges of hybrid implementations.

4.1 Spatial Variation: WiFi vs PLC

We first compare the spatial variation of Wifi and PLC in our testbed, with WiFi and PLC interfaces having similar nominal capacities[5]. This study quantifies the gains that PLC can yield in situations with wireless "blind spots" or bad links and also examines which medium an application should use. We conduct the following experiment: For each pair of stations, we measure the available throughput of both mediums back-to-back for 5 minutes, at 100ms intervals. These experiments are carried out during working hours to emulate a realistic residential/enterprise environment. We show the average and standard deviation of these measurements (for links with a non-zero throughput for at least one medium).

Let T_W and σ_W be, respectively, the average value and standard deviation of throughput for WiFi (T_P and σ_P, respectively, for PLC). Figure 3 illustrates the results of our experiment. Our key findings are as follows.

Connectivity: PLC yields a better connectivity than WiFi. 100% of station pairs that are connected with WiFi are also connected with PLC. In contrast, 81% of station pairs that are connected by PLC links, are also connected by WiFi links. At long distance (more than 35m), there is no wireless connectivity whereas PLC offers up to 41 Mbps. Thus, PLC can eliminate, to a large extent, blind spots.

Average performance: 52% of the station pairs exhibit throughput higher with PLC than with WiFi. PLC can achieve throughput up to 18 times higher than WiFi (40.1 vs 2.2Mbps). The maximum gain of WiFi vs PLC was similar, i.e., 12 times (46.3 vs 3.8Mbps).

Variability: At short distances (less than 15m), WiFi usually yields higher throughput, but PLC offers significantly lower variance. WiFi has higher variability with the maximum standard deviation of throughput being $\sigma_W = 19.2$ Mbps vs $\sigma_P = 3.8$ Mbps for PLC. The vast majority of PLC links yield a σ_P smaller than 4 Mbps.

Conclusion: At long distances, PLC eliminates wireless blind spots or bad links, yielding notable gains. At short distances, although WiFi provides higher throughput, PLC provides significantly lower variance, which can be beneficial for TCP or applications with demanding, constant-rate requirements, such as high-definition streaming. We explain this difference by the ability of PLC to adapt each carrier to a different modulation scheme, contrary to WiFi (see Section 2.1). PLC reacts more efficiently to bursty errors than WiFi, which has to lower the rate at all carriers.

The spatial variation of WiFi has been extensively studied (e.g., [14]). However, very few works exist on PLC; [11] focuses on a much older technology, and, due to the insufficient literature on specifications, [13] treats PLC as a black-box and focuses on average performance and not on variability. We next discuss the temporal variation of the two mediums.

4.2 Temporal Variation: WiFi vs PLC

We now look at the concurrent temporal variation of WiFi and PLC during working hours for a much longer duration than before. We are interested in exploring the timescales at which the two mediums vary. Figure 4 shows the capacity for concurrent tests on WiFi and PLC, estimated by using MCS and BLE respectively, and averaged over 50 packets. We observe that link 3-8, which is a good link, exhibits a variation much higher with WiFi than with PLC. Although we would expect channel changes due to switching electrical appliances in the building, the PLC link is almost not affected by people leaving the premises (around 6pm). The average link 3-0 varies more for both mediums.

These preliminary results imply that PLC has low variability for good links and high for bad links. To the best of our

[5]We use 802.11n, with 2 spatial streams, 20MHz bandwidth and 400 ns guard interval, yielding a maximum PHY rate of 130 Mbps. We selected a frequency that does not interfere with other wireless networks in our building. The highest PLC data-rate is 150 Mbps hence, both interfaces have similar nominal capacities. This is confirmed by the maximum throughputs exhibited by both mediums, shown in Figure 3.

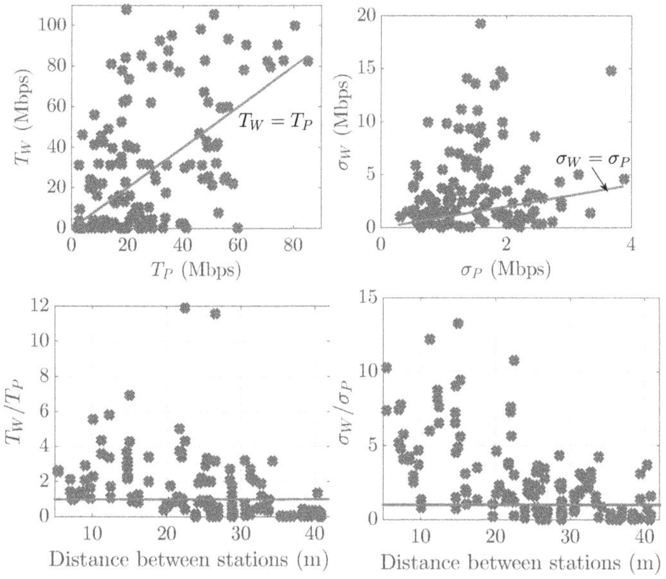

Figure 3: WiFi vs PLC performance for all links (top). Spatial variation of the performance ratio between WiFi and PLC (bottom).

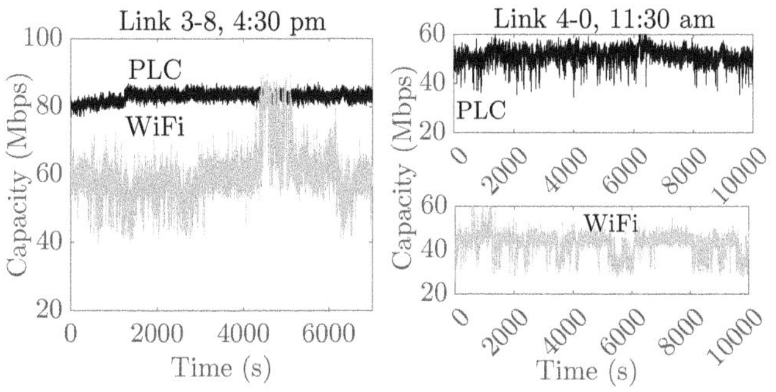

Figure 4: Temporal variation of capacity for PLC and WiFi for two links during working hours (started time written).

knowledge, there are not any temporal-variation studies of the end-to-end performance of PLC. In contrast, many studies have focused on WiFi temporal variation. In Section 6, we study the PLC temporal variation and we observe that the variability is high in timescales of hours, because of the variations of the electrical load. We notice however, that this variation is not significant, compared to the one of Wifi, and that it is high only for bad links.

4.3 Challenges in Hybrid Networks

As we observe in Section 4.1, although PLC boosts network performance, there are still a few links that perform poorly with both WiFi and PLC. As a result, mesh configurations, hence routing and load balancing algorithms, are needed for seamless connectivity in home or office environments. A challenge for these algorithms is that they have to deal with two different interference graphs with diverse spatio-temporal variation, and that, to fully exploit all mediums, they require accurate metrics for capacity and loss rates. To this end, unicast probes must be exchanged among the stations[6]. In a network of n stations, probing introduces an $\mathcal{O}(n^2)$ overhead that can be significantly reduced by employing temporal variation studies of each medium.

A significant challenge, highlighted by recent studies in 802.11n networks [16], is the accuracy of established quality metrics, such as the expected transmission count (ETX) or time (ETT) [8], in modern networks, i.e., 802.11n/ac. The authors in [16] show that due to the MAC/PHY enhancements introduced in 802.11n, these metrics perform poorly and that they should be revised, given that they have been evaluated only under 802.11a/b/g.

The above arguments raise a few questions: How often should the PLC link metrics, such as capacity, be updated in load-balancing or routing algorithms in order to achieve both small overhead and accurate estimation? How would ETX perform in PLC? We will answer these questions in Sections 5–8. In the rest of this work, we design link metrics for PLC and explore their variation with respect not only to time, but also to space and to background traffic.

5. SPATIAL VARIATION OF PLC

We explore the spatial variation of PLC, as it is important for predicting coverage and good locations for PLC stations, and for implementing link metrics. We find that PLC is highly asymmetric, and this should be considered when estimating link metrics.

We first explain the main properties of the channel that affect both spatial and temporal variations. The two main components of PLC channel modeling are attenuation and noise. Consider an example of a simple electrical network with a transmitter (TX) and receiver (RX), as given in Figure 5. The main sources of attenuation and noise are the electrical appliances plugged in between. Modeled with dashed boxes in Figure 5, each connected appliance has an impedance and produces some noise that is non-Gaussian and that depends on the device type, as shown in [9]. The authors in [9] summarize the different types of noise existing in the PLC channel.

The spatial variation of PLC is mainly affected by the position, the impedance, and the number of appliances connected to the network. When it comes to PLC, the electrical cable becomes a transmission line, with a characteristic impedance. The connection of appliances creates impedance mismatches to this transmission line, causing the transmitted signal to be reflected multiple times. For example, in Figure 5, at point M, we have an impedance mismatch and any signal s arriving at M is partly reflected (signal r) and partly propagates (signal t) towards the same direction as the original signal s. Reflections of signals at various impedance-mismatched points result in multiple versions of the initially transmitted signal arriving at different times at the receiver, thus establishing a multi-path channel for PLC. We will see in the next section that temporal variation is affected by multi-path effects, i.e., the appliances' impedance, in long-term timescales, whereas it is affected only by noise at short-term timescales.

A very important characteristic of power-line channels is that they exhibit performance asymmetry, i.e., capacity can differ significantly between the two directions of the link. In all the experiments we run (both with AV and AV500),

[6]Broadcast packets cannot be used to estimate capacity. See for example [7], [8].

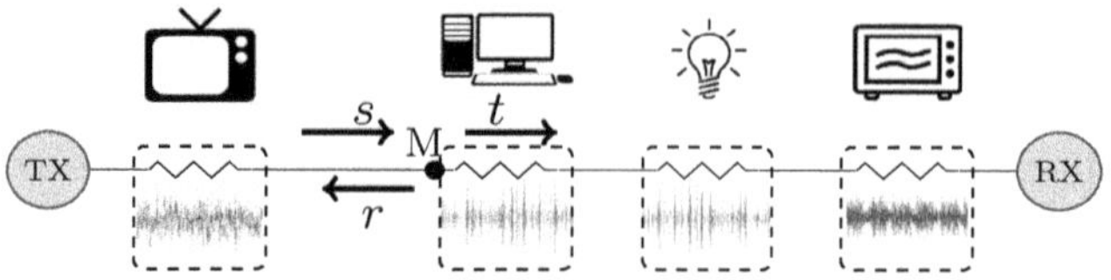

Figure 5: Multi-path and noise in PLC channels

we observe a performance asymmetry of more than 1.5x in approximately 30% of stations pairs in our testbed. Figure 6 presents typical examples of these links, for which the throughput in one direction is less than 60% of the throughput in the opposite direction. By re-conducting the experiments with AV500 devices, we verify that the asymmetry is not due to the hardware. Link asymmetry in PLC has been also observed in [13]. We attribute this asymmetry to a high electrical-load (for instance, one or more appliances with much higher impedance than cable's impedance) existing close to one of the two stations. In this case, the channel cannot be considered as symmetric and the two transmission directions in the link experience different attenuations.

In our tests with WiFi, presented in Section 4, we also observe that wireless channels can also exhibit asymmetry. However, compared to PLC, this occurs on a much smaller subset of links, and is much less severe (for instance, the WiFi asymmetry was up to 1.5x for good links and up to 3.5x for bad links). An asymmetry of loss rates has been found experimentally for residential WiFi networks in [14].

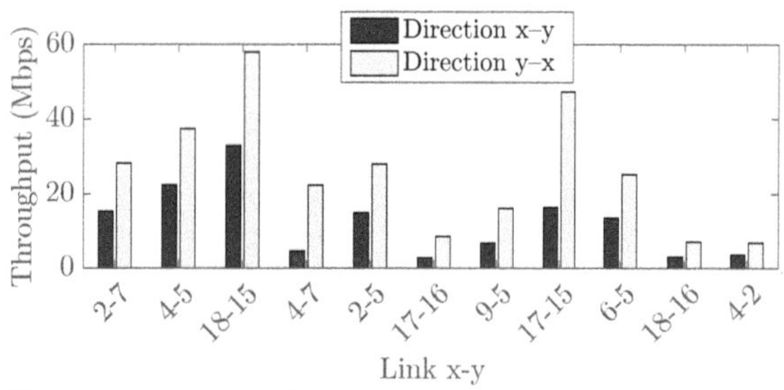

Figure 6: Throughput asymmetry in PLC links.

We now turn to our spatial variation study, where we use both AV and AV500. Figure 7 provides the available UDP throughput of *single* links as a function of the *cable* distance between the source and the destination of the traffic from a single experiment. There is a clear degradation of throughput as distance increases. However, because of the diversity in positions and types of connected appliances, there is a large range of possible throughputs at any specific distance. We observe that small distances (<30m) guarantee good links, but that large distances (30-100m) can yield either good or bad links. By comparing AV and AV500, we observe that AV500 enables some links with no AV connectivity to still enjoy a non-zero throughput, but with severe asymmetries (e.g., link 10-2 with 10x asymmetry).

To further explore the causes that affect the attenuation, we run some experiments with two stations connected by a long electrical cable and without any devices attached. We notice that the attenuation in an up to 70 m cable causes a throughput drop of at most 2 Mbps. The attenuation is therefore caused by the multi-path nature of the PLC channel. By plugging electrical appliances in this isolated

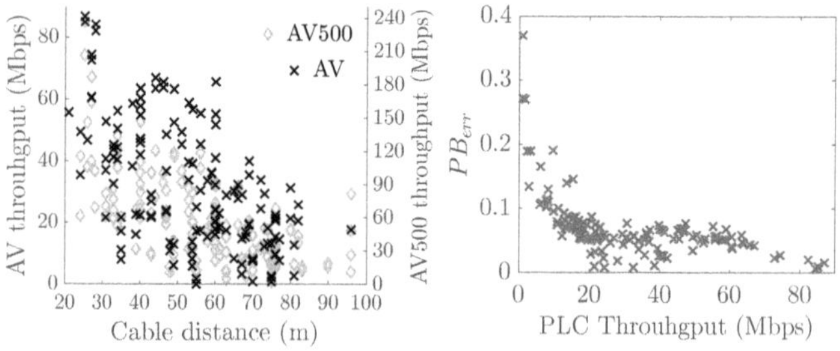

Figure 7: Throughput vs cable distance between source and destination for all links of the test-bed (left). PB_{err} vs throughput for AV (right).

experiment, we observe that asymmetry was introduced, as also found in [13].

Conclusion: The spatial variation of the PLC channel depends on two factors: (*i*) the structure of the electrical networks, i.e., the appliances attached and their position on the grid, (*ii*) the distance between the stations. PLC channels are very asymmetric and this is a key feature for their spatial variability.

To optimize performance not only in terms of throughput but also delay, hybrid networks need some estimation of the retransmissions a frame suffers due to channel errors. We also evaluate the relationship of the metric PB_{err} with the available throughput. Figure 7 illustrates PB_{err} vs the available throughput for all the links of our testbed. It shows that PB_{err} decreases as throughput increases, as expected. However, because the tone maps are updated based on this metric, some average links might have lower PB_{err} than the best links of the testbed. We further study the PB_{err} metric in Section 8, by delving into packet retransmissions. We show that PB_{err} can be used to predict the expected number of retransmissions due to errors.

6. TEMPORAL VARIATION OF PLC

Little is known about PLC temporal variation, and we observe in Section 4 that a temporal-variation study could improve the quality of service in hybrid networks and the accuracy of link metrics estimation. We now investigate the temporal variation of the PLC channel.

We examine separately the two main components of channel modeling, i.e., the variation of noise generated by the attached electrical appliances, and the variation of channel transfer function (or attenuation). We employ *BLE* to investigate the main properties of PLC channels by using existing commercial devices. We show that *BLE* reflects the channel quality and the fundamental features of PLC channel modeling explained in Section 5.

We now discuss the timescales within which the channel varies. These timescales have been introduced for channel modeling and simulation in [15] (from which we borrow the terminology to name these timescales). We first focus on noise generated by electrical appliances. It has been shown by measurements, e.g., in [9], that the noise level varies across subintervals of the mains cycle[7] which yields the first scale governing PLC temporal variation (scale (*i*)). Due to the periodic nature of the mains, this noise also varies in a

[7]The term mains cycle refers to the alternating electrical current.

scale of multiples of the mains cycle, which results in another timescale for the temporal variation (scale (*ii*)).

We next focus on attenuation. As discussed in Section 5, attenuation is introduced due mainly to impedance mismatches in the transmission line (electrical cable) that are created by connected appliances. As expected, this attenuation changes when the structure of the electrical network changes hence, in scales of minutes or hours (scale (*iii*)). This variability strongly depends on appliances usage and on switching the appliances, as this creates impulsive noise in the channel.

As hinted above, our study adopts an analysis of three timescales that is validated by our measurements in the following subsections. Our work differs from [15] in that we examine the channel quality from an end-user and practical perspective, exploring metrics affecting the end-to-end performance. The three timescales are as follows.

(*i*) **Invariance Scale:** subintervals of the mains cycle, such as the 6 tone-map slots of HPAV;

(*ii*) **Cycle Scale:** multiples of the mains cycles – depends on the noise produced by appliances;

(*iii*) **Random Scale:** minutes or hours – related to connection or switching of electrical appliances and depends on human activity.

We now introduce our variables, starting with some notations. For the invariance scale, we use the term tone-map slots for the subintervals of the mains cycle, as we can measure the channel quality with respect to tone-map slots by using PLC devices. Let L be the total number of tone-map slots of the mains cycle, with each slot s having a duration T_s, so that the total slots duration $\sum_{s=1}^{L} T_s$ is equal to half mains period (as specified in [6]). Let BLE_s, $1 \leq s \leq L$, denote the BLE of tone-map slot s. In order to study the channel with respect to the three scales defined above, we assume that time is discrete, with one time unit having real-time duration equal to the mains cycle. Let $\mu_s \in \mathbb{R}^+$ and $\sigma_s \in \mathbb{R}^+$, $1 \leq s \leq L$, represent the expected value and the standard deviation of BLE_s, and let ν_{σ_s} be a continuous random variable with 0 mean and variance equal to σ_s^2. In the cycle scale, the mean and variance of BLE_s, μ_s and σ_s, respectively, are considered to be constant, and the variation of BLE_s around its mean is described by ν_{σ_s}. In the random scale, μ_s and σ_s vary with time due to electrical load variability. Given the above, at any time step t, the channel quality is described as

$$BLE_s(t) = \mu_s(t) + \nu_{\sigma_s(t)}(t), 1 \leq s \leq L. \quad (2)$$

The process ν_{σ_s} is different for each link and its distribution can be time-varying over the random scale for a specific link, due to the different types of operating appliances and to different channel transfer-functions. The exact characterization of ν_{σ_s} is out of the scope of this work. In our study for cycle-scale variation, we study how often the value of ν_{σ_s} changes and how σ_s behaves with respect to the link quality. Figure 8 illustrates the three timescales and the factors causing variability. We next examine each timescale.

6.1 Invariance Scale

The invariance scale of BLE is affected by the noise levels that appliances produce at different subintervals of the mains cycle, and it has direct consequences on estimating link metrics. All our tests showed that noise has varying

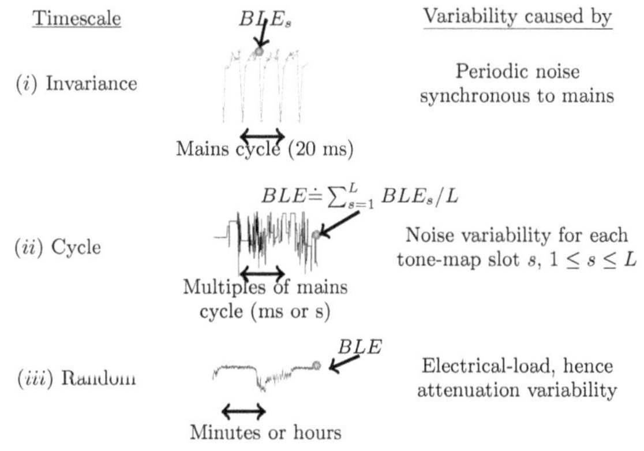

Figure 8: BLE temporal variation.

levels over different tone-map slots. Figure 9 shows the instantaneous BLE_s from captured frames in typical examples of good and average links. We observe that in HPAV, the total duration of the 6 tone-map slots is equal to half of the mains cycle, thus BLE_s changes periodically, with a period of 10 ms. Each PLC frame uses a different BLE_s, depending on which tone-map slot s its transmission takes place.

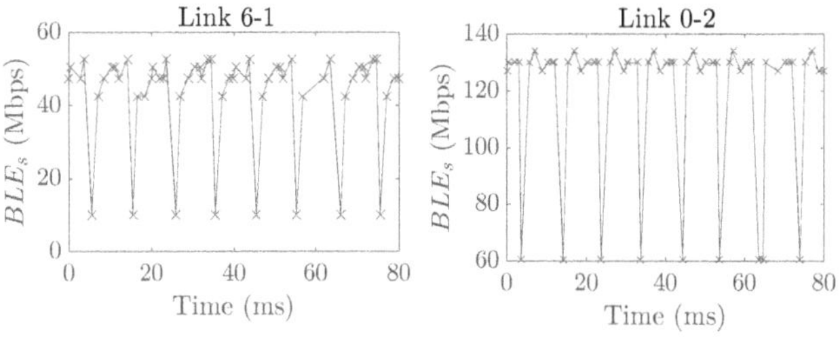

Figure 9: Invariance-scale variation of BLE from captured PLC frames of saturated traffic.

We highlight that this timescale is crucial for capacity estimation in PLC. With the examples of Figure 9, we observe that there might be significant variation along the mains cycle, even for good and average links. Thus, link metrics have to be estimated or averaged over all $L = 6$ tone-map slots. We next study the average BLE of all 6 slots to examine the variability of the average link-quality at longer time-scales, i.e., (*ii*), and (*iii*).

6.2 Cycle Scale

We now examine the average time during which the quality of the links is preserved in the cycle scale. This sheds light on the average length of probing intervals for link metrics, as there exists a tradeoff in probing: too large intervals might yield a non-accurate estimation, whereas too small intervals can generate high overhead.

We conduct experiments that last 4 minutes, over all links of the testbed. During each experiment, we request BLE_s, $1 \leq s \leq L$, every 50 ms, as this is the fastest rate at which we can currently send MMs to the PLC chip. As we need to avoid random changes in the channel due to switching electrical appliances, all the experiments of this subsection are conducted during nights or weekends (given the office environment). For the cycle scale variation of the channel, we assume that the electrical network structure is fixed.

Here, we evaluate the cycle-scale variation by using $BLE \doteq \sum_{s=1}^{6} BLE_s/6$, that is the average BLE over all tone-map slots. We compare the performance between good and bad links[8]. Figure 10 presents the variation for typical good and bad links of our testbed. Observe that depending on their quality, links exhibit different behaviors. Our findings, validated not only by the representative examples shown here, but also by experiments over one year period in all the links of our testbed, are as follows.

Bad Links: Bad links, e.g., 11-4 and 6-5, tend to modify the tone maps much more often than good links do. Moreover, they yield a significantly higher standard deviation of BLE than good links.

Average Links: Average links, e.g., 18-15 and 1-2, vary less than bad links, and might preserve their tone maps for a few seconds. During periods when average links vary often, the standard deviation of BLE can be high, depending on the channel conditions.

Good Links: The tone maps of good links can be valid for several seconds, e.g., link 15-18. Good links that update often the tone maps, such as link 3-1, have insignificant increments or decrements, e.g., of up to 1%, or have impulsive drops of BLE, e.g., of up to 5%, with the channel estimation algorithm needing a few time-steps to converge back to the average BLE value.

Asymmetry in Temporal Variability: By observing links 15-18 and 18-15, we find that the asymmetry discussed in Section 5 translates not only in an average performance asymmetry, but also in a temporal-variation asymmetry.

Channel Estimation Algorithms: Temporal variation of link 15-18 is the same with HPAV and with HPAV500. By noticing the impulsive BLE drops in link 18-15 and by comparing HPAV with HPAV500, we detect a feature of the channel estimation algorithm that might be vendor-specific: The HPAV500 performance oscillation shows that the estimation algorithm returns very low BLE values when bursty errors occur. This uncovers that temporal variation in PLC link quality also depends on the channel estimation algorithm and future work should focus on comparing link-metric estimations for different vendors and technologies.

We next corroborate the above findings over all links of our testbed. Let α be the inter-arrival time of two consecutive BLE updates. Figure 11 shows the results of the average α values and the standard deviation of BLE for all links sorted by increasing BLE order, i.e., link quality. We observe that good links tend to update less often their tone maps, and also that BLE variability is smaller compared to bad links. Although some good links might update BLE at a similar frequency as bad links ($\sim$ 100 ms), as we discussed above, these links tend to have small increments and decrements of BLE, yielding a stable average performance over minutes and a low BLE standard deviation.

Conclusion: In cycle scales, that is seconds or minutes, good links should be probed less often than bad links to reduce overhead. The cycle-scale variation unveils how link metrics should be updated depending on their quality.

6.3 Random Scale

In Sections 4.2 and 6.2, we observe that during timescales of minutes, PLC does not vary much, with a standard deviation of throughput up to 4 Mbps. We now look at longer timescales, i.e., in terms of minutes and hours, with two goals: (*i*) to examine whether some links could be probed at a slow rate, thus reducing overhead; (*ii*) to characterize the variability of PLC performance in presence of high and low electrical loads. To study the channel quality variation over the random scale, we run tests over long periods, i.e., two days and two weeks, for various links. During these tests we measure the throughput, BLE, and PB_{error} every second. We now denote by μ the mean of $BLE = \sum_{s=1}^{6} BLE_s/6$, and by σ its standard deviation.

[8]The classification of the links based on their capacity depends on the PLC technology thus, we do not introduce strict thresholds for this characterization.

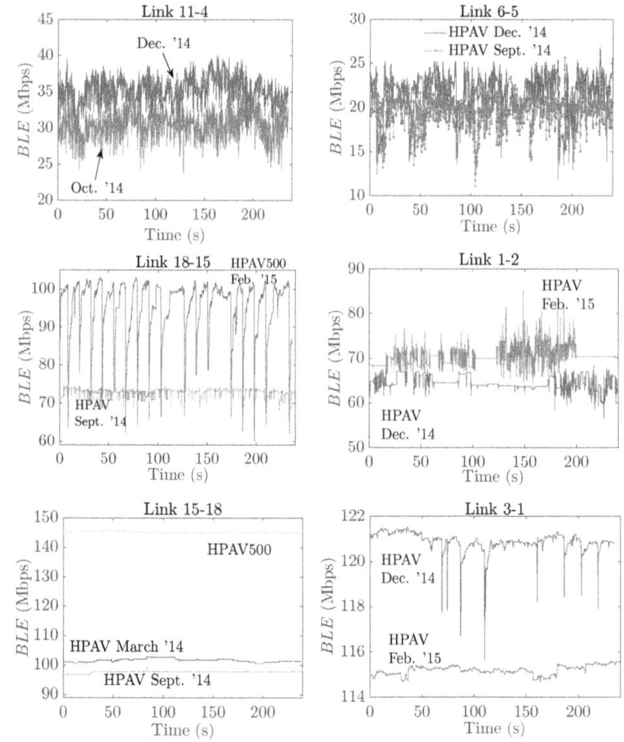

Figure 10: Examples of cycle-scale variation of BLE for links of various qualities

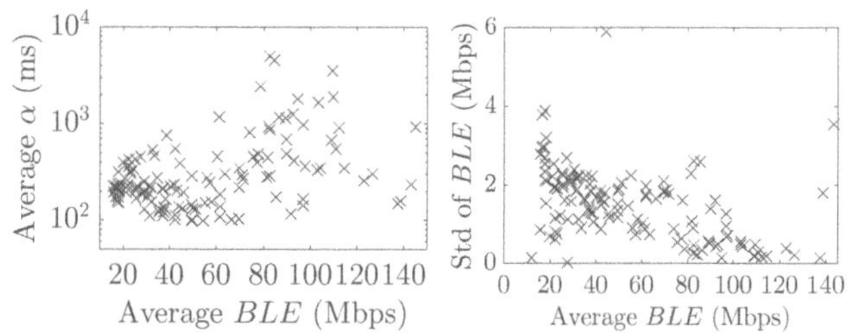

Figure 11: Cycle-scale variation of BLE with respect to the link quality (links are sorted with increasing average BLE order).

Figures 12-14 show the results of our measurements. Our observations are as follows.

Link Quality vs Time: The variation of μ is governed by the electrical load. The larger the number of switched-on devices is (e.g., at working hours) the larger the attenuation is, and the lower μ is, as we have discussed in Section 5.

Link Quality vs Variability: Observe the differences in the y-axis scales in Figures 13 and 14 that represent a good

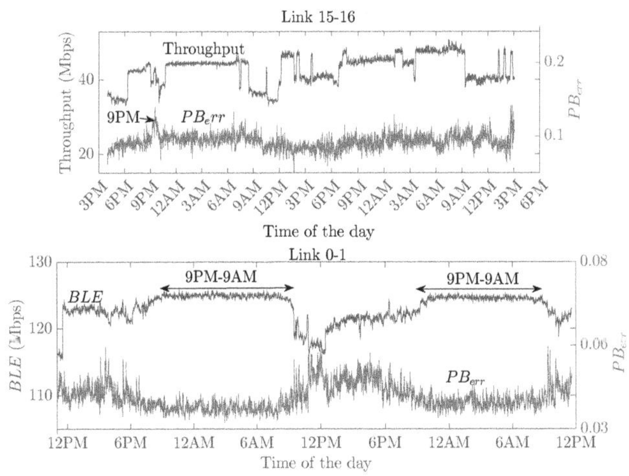

Figure 12: Random-scale variation of PLC over a total duration of 2 days. Metrics are averaged over 1 minute intervals. Every day at 9pm, all lights are turned off in our building, leading to a channel change for PLC.

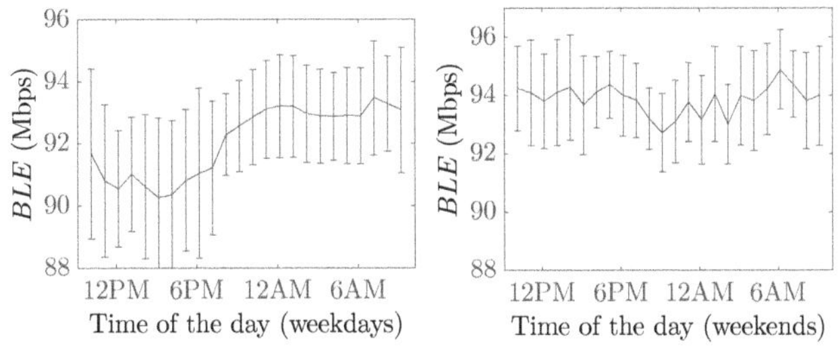

Figure 13: Random-scale variation of BLE for link 1-8 over 2 consecutive weeks. Lines represent the BLE averaged over the same hour of the day and error bars show standard deviation.

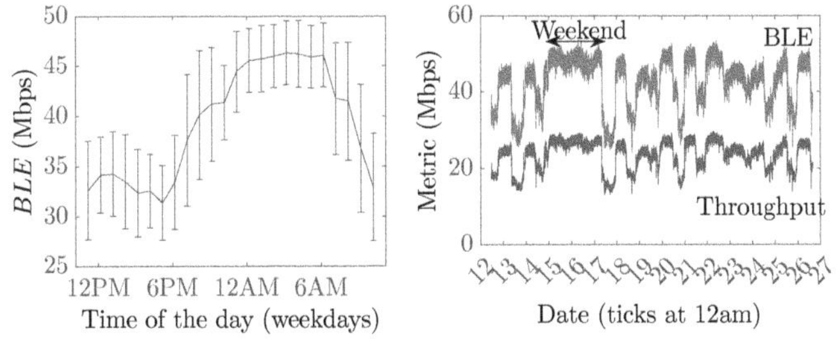

Figure 14: Random-scale variation of BLE for link 2-11 over 2 consecutive weeks in Nov. 2014.

and a bad link, respectively. For a given link, the random-scale variation of σ strongly depends on the noise of the electrical devices attached, and it is higher when μ is lower, as this implies that more devices are switched on and therefore, more noise is produced, or that devices are switched on/off more often, creating impulsive noise phenomena. σ is very small for good links; it increases as the link quality, i.e., μ, decreases.

Link Probing: Good links exhibit a negligible standard deviation, which implies that they can be probed every minute or hour, depending on the time of the day.

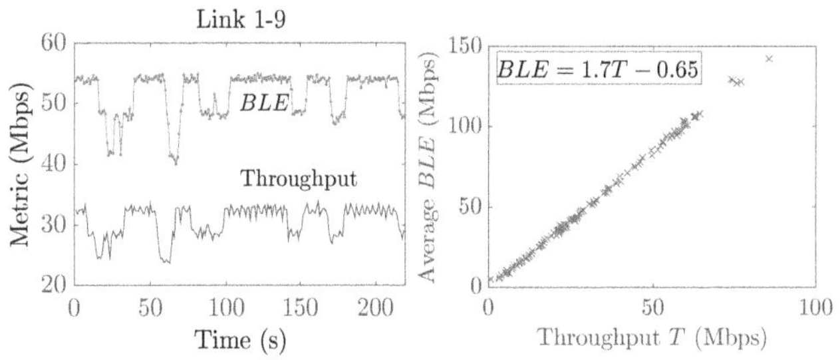

Figure 15: BLE and throughput averaged every 1 s, vs time, for link 1-9 (left). Average BLE vs throughput for all the links (right).

7. CAPACITY ESTIMATION PROCESS

We now explore a capacity estimation process for PLC. As mentioned in Section 2.1, stations estimate a tone map if and only if they have data to send. Thus, to estimate link metrics, a few unicast probe packets have to be sent. In Section 6, we discuss how fast the capacity changes given the link quality by sending saturated traffic. Here, we examine how capacity can be estimated with a few probe packets and we explore the size and the frequency of these packets.

7.1 BLE as a Capacity Estimator

First, we show that BLE, which is included in the header of every PLC frame, accurately estimates the capacity of any PLC link. We repeat saturated tests for our 144 links and with a duration of 4 min. Figure 15 presents the measured throughput and BLE. We observe that BLE is an exact estimation of the actual throughput received by the application. Let T be the average throughput. Fitting a line to the data points, we get $BLE = 1.7T - 0.65$. We verified that the residuals are normally distributed.

We next discuss a capacity estimation technique that uses BLE and probe packets. To conduct a capacity estimation using BLE, a few packets per mains cycle and estimation interval should be captured, given our temporal variation study in Section 6.1. Here, we investigate an alternative technique that uses MMs to request the instantaneous BLE. The PLC devices provide statistics of the average BLE used over all 6 tone map slots. Probe packets need not to be sent at all sub-intervals of the mains cycle, because according to 1901 [6], the channel estimation process yields a BLE for all slots when at least 1 packet is sent.

We explore whether the number of the probes affects the estimation. To this end, we reset the devices before every run. We perform experiments to estimate the capacity, by sending only a limited number of packets of size 1300B per second (1- 200 packets per second)[9]. Figure 16 shows that the estimated capacity converges to a value that does not depend on the number of packets sent; however, the number of packets sent per second affects the convergence time to the real estimation. We observe that the channel-estimation algorithm can have a large convergence time to the optimal allocation of bits per symbol for all the carriers, because it needs many samples from many PBs to estimate the error for every frequency, i.e., carrier. This convergence time depends on the (vendor-specific) channel-estimation algorithm and on the initial estimation (which was reset by us).

[9]Note that the probe packets can be of any size. PLC always transmits at least a PB (500B), using padding.

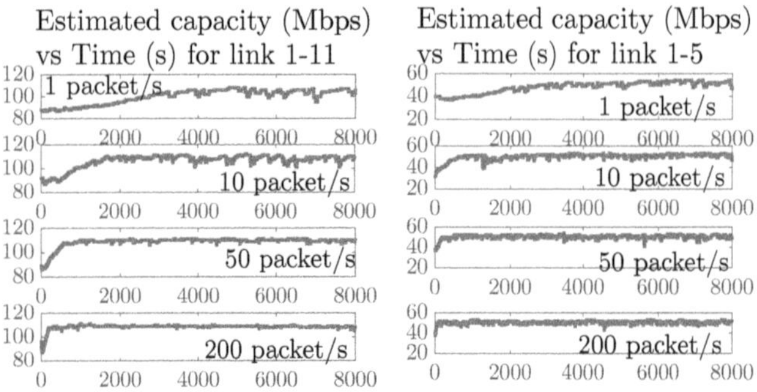

Figure 16: Estimated capacity for two links and different number of packet-probes per second.

To evaluate the convergence time in realistic scenarios, we now perform a test in which we reset the devices at the beginning, but after 2300 s we pause the probing for approximately 7 minutes. Figure 17 shows the results of the experiments for various links. It turns out that the devices maintain the channel-estimation statistics, as the estimated capacity resumes from the previous value before stopping the probing process. Thus, the convergence time of the capacity estimation does not apply in realistic probing conditions.

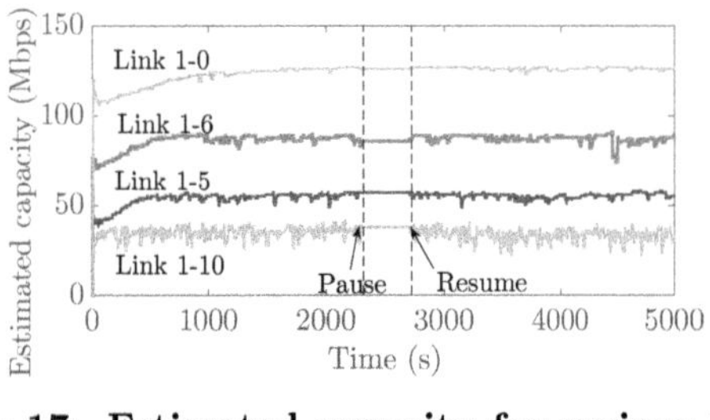

Figure 17: Estimated capacity for various links by probing with 20 packets per second. After 2300s, we pause the probing for 7 minutes and we observe that this does not affect the estimation.

Conclusion: Capacity should be estimated by sending probe packets and measuring BLE in PLC networks. To estimate capacity, given our study in Section 6.1, we have to take into account the invariance scale and to either compute the average $BLE = \sum_{s=1}^{6} BLE_s/6$, by capturing PLC frames or request it using MMs. One of the remaining challenges in link-metric estimation is to take into account the technology-specific MAC mechanisms, such as frame aggregation. This remains a challenge also for the latest WiFi technologies, as highlighted in [16].

7.2 Size of Probe Packets

We now investigate the size of probe packets. We observe that for the special case of sending 1 probe-packet with size less than one PB per second, the estimation might converge to a smaller value than the true one for HPAV and remain constant with time, independently of the channel conditions.

A representative example of this behavior is shown in Figure 18, where HPAV capacity converges to approximately 89 Mbps when sending only 1 packet per second with size less than one physical block (520B including 8B PB header). After this convergence, the estimated capacity remains constant. A simple computation shows that the rate required to transmit one PB in one OFDM symbol is $R_{1sym} = (520 \times 8)/T_{sym} \approx 89.4$Mbps with HPAV, given the symbol duration $T_{sym} = 40.96\mu s$. When sending packets smaller than one PB, the rate converges to R_{1sym} for all 6 slots of the mains cycle, because increasing the rate does not reduce the transmission time (it is not possible to transmit less than 1 OFDM symbol) while decreasing the probability of error (higher rates yield less robust modulation schemes). Hence, we unveil that to estimate the capacity of a link by sending only one probe packet per second, it is crucial to send packets larger than 1 PB or 1 OFDM symbol.

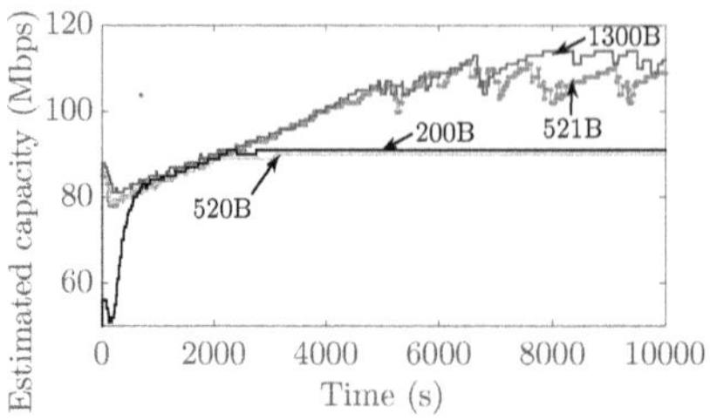

Figure 18: Estimated capacity with 1 probe packet per sec and various sizes for link 11-6.

We next provide an example of how our temporal variation study can be used to adjust the frequency of the probe packets such that the overhead is reduced, while maintaining a good level of accuracy.

7.3 Frequency of Probe Packets

We explore the tradeoff of accuracy vs overhead in probing for capacity estimation. To this end, we run a simple example that uses the measurements of Section 6.2. We assume that any link is probed at a specific interval which is 1) the same for all links; 2) depends on link quality. We employ the BLE measured at these intervals as an *estimation* of the capacity and we consider as *exact capacity* the average values of BLE until the next probe. Let t be an *estimation* instant and i the probing interval in multiples of 50ms (period of measurements). The estimation is BLE_t, and the *exact capacity* is $BLE_{e(t)} = \sum_{l=t}^{t+i-1} BLE_l/i$. Then, the *estimation error* is computed as the absolute value of the difference between the estimation and the exact capacity, i.e., $|BLE_t - BLE_{e(t)}|$.

Our network consists of at least 10 stations, thus, to achieve low overhead, we assume that stations send at most 1 probe packet per 5 seconds (which yields a 240Kbps probing overhead if 1500B probes are used), and we adopt this interval as a baseline. We also explore probing at lower frequencies, such as once per 80 seconds. The method that uses our temporal variation study, probes bad links once per 5 seconds, average links 8 times slower, and good links 16 times slower (once per 80 seconds)[10]. To classify the quality of the links, we use heuristics based on our study in Section 6.2: bad links have a BLE below 60Mbps, good links have a BLE above 100 Mbps, and average links have a BLE in between. Figure 19 presents the CDF of the estimation error for all links and all intervals. With our method, we manage to reduce the probing overhead by 32% compared to probing all links once per 5 seconds, while maintaining very good accuracy.

[10]The exact frequency of probes should be adjusted to the network size and the PLC technology.

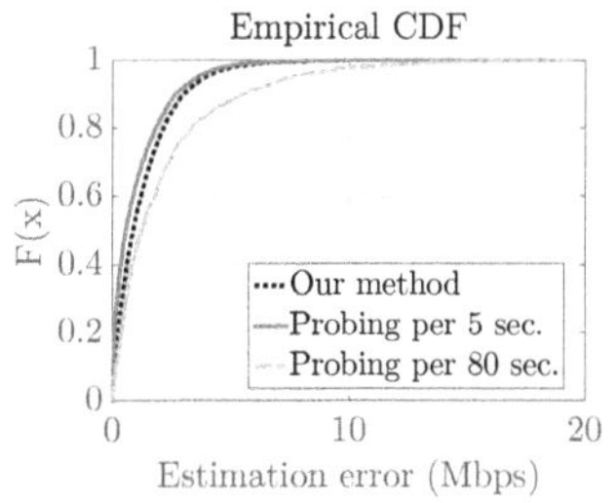

Figure 19: Comparison of estimation error for different probing frequencies. By adjusting the probing frequency to the link quality (*our method*), we achieve very good accuracy with 32% overhead reduction compared to probing once per 5 seconds.

These results suggest that by studying the PLC network and its temporal variation, probing can be optimized to achieve a good tradeoff between overhead and accuracy. To estimate an appropriate probing interval based on the network size and the aggregate link quality, the CCo of the network can employ the information on the quality of all the links and update the interval value by broadcasting to all stations. We next validate our capacity estimation and temporal variation studies by a load-balancing algorithm.

7.4 Bandwidth Aggregation Using Capacity

To further validate our capacity estimation method, we employ a simple load-balancing algorithm that aggregates bandwidth between WiFi and PLC and operates between the IP and MAC layers. To implement our algorithm, we use the *Click Modular Router* [10]. We forward each IP packet to one of the mediums with a probability proportional to the capacity of the medium. At the destination, we reorder the packets according to a simple algorithm that checks the identification sequence of the IP header. We measure the jitter and compare it with the jitter when using only one interface, making sure that it does not worsen. The details of our implementations are given in [20].

To estimate the capacities, we probe links with 1 packet per second and request BLE and MCS from the interfaces. The capacity for PLC is estimated using BLE, i.e., averaged over the 6 tone-map slots of the invariance scale, whereas for WiFi MCS capacity is averaged over the transmissions (data and probes) during every second, because, as we observe in Section 4.2, WiFi varies more than PLC within a second. Our load-balancing algorithm takes into account our temporal variation study on PLC: In Section 6.1, we uncover that the PLC channel quality is periodic, with every packet using a different BLE. Because an accurate synchronization at this time-scale is challenging for algorithms operating above the MAC layer (such as in IEEE 1905 standard), the capacity of PLC in hybrid networks has to be estimated by averaging over the invariance scale.

In Figure 20, we first present the throughput of experiments on one link. We run four experiments back-to-back, using only one of the interfaces (WiFi, PLC) in two, using both interfaces and our load-balancing algorithm (Hybrid) in one, and using both interfaces and a round-robin scheduler for the packets (Round-robin) in the last one. We observe that by using simple load-balancing and reordering algorithms, and our capacity-estimation technique, we can achieve a throughput that is very close to the sum of the capacities of both mediums. In contrast, the throughput of a round-robin scheduler, which has no information on capacity, is limited to twice the minimum capacity of the two mediums (i.e., WiFi in this example), because it assigns the same number of packets to each medium and the slowest medium becomes a bottleneck. To evaluate our algorithm across our testbed, we also compare the completion times of a 600Mbyte file download using (*i*) only WiFi, and (*ii*) both mediums[11], observing in the same figure, a drastic decrease in completion times when using both mediums.

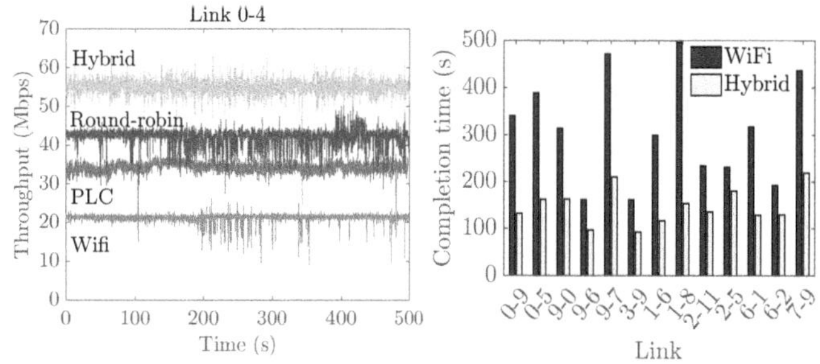

Figure 20: Performance boost by using hybrid Wifi/PLC, and our load-balancing and capacity-estimation techniques.

Our tests validate our capacity estimation methods. They also show that, to exploit each medium to the fullest extent, accurate link-quality metrics are required. However, an open question to be answered is: How should the link metrics be updated to take into account delay or contention? In the next section we investigate another link metric, i.e., the expected number of retransmissions, and the performance of link metrics with respect to background traffic.

8. RETRANSMITTING IN PLC CHANNELS

Capacity is a good metric for link quality. However, it does not take into account interference, which is very important for selecting links with high available bandwidth. Moreover, another metric could be useful for delay sensitive applications that do not saturate the medium but have low delay requirements. Delay is affected by retransmissions either due to bursty errors or to contention, and metrics, such as PB_{err} introduced in Section 5 (or *packet errors* [2]), are related to retransmissions. We explore the mechanism of retransmissions in PLC networks. We first study another link metric, which is the expected transmission count (ETX). Numerous works, e.g., [7], [8], study this metric (or its variations) in WiFi networks by sending broadcast probes. We examine how ETX performs in PLC and the relationship between broadcast and unicast probing.

After studying retransmissions due to errors, we evaluate the sensitivity of link metrics to background traffic. Link metrics in hybrid networks should estimate the amount of background traffic, or be insensitive to background traffic [7]. Thus, a critical challenge for hybrid networks is to design link metrics achieving one of the aforementioned properties.

[11]Contrary to WiFi, PLC uses queues that are non-blocking: the transport layer is not stopped from sending packets when the MAC queues are full. For these experiments, we omit PLC tests as dropped packets yield an unfair comparison.

8.1 Retransmission Due to Errors

We first explore how ETX would perform in PLC by sending broadcast packets. Because broadcast packets in PLC are transmitted with the most robust modulation and are acknowledged by some proxy station [6], we expect that this method yields very low loss rates.

For the purpose of this study, we set each station in turn to broadcast 1500B probe-packets (1 every 100ms) for 500 sec. The rest of the stations count the missed packets by using an identification in our packet header. We repeat the test for all stations of the testbed during night and working hours (day). Figure 21 shows the loss rate from these tests for all station pairs, as a function of throughput and PB_{err}. Each pair is represented with its link throughput (respectively, PB_{err}) during the night experiment.

Conclusion: Loss rate of broadcast packets in PLC is a very noisy metric for the following reasons:

(*i*) A wide range of links with diverse qualities have very low loss rates ($\sim 10^{-4}$), and some links even have 0 loss rates. By observing high loss rates, e.g., larger than 10^{-1}, ETX can classify bad links in PLC, but nothing can be conjectured for link quality from low loss rates.

(*ii*) There is no obvious difference between experiments during the day, when the channel is worse, and night. A few bad links have worse loss rates during the day, but at the same time, a few average links yield much lower loss rates.

(*iii*) As PLC adapts the modulation scheme to channel conditions when data is transmitted, broadcast packets – sent at most robust modulation scheme – cannot reflect the real link quality. Moreover, given the low loss rates of a wide range of links, ETX appears to be 0 at short-time scales, which provides no or misleading information on link quality.

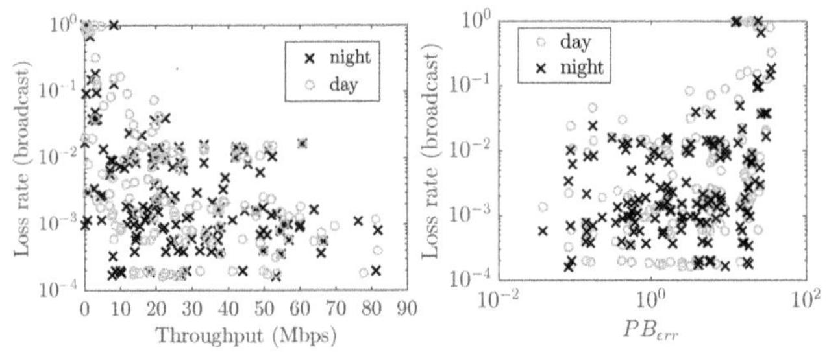

Figure 21: Loss rate for broadcast packets vs link throughput and PB_{err} for all station pairs.

Due to the above observations, we further explore the mechanism of retransmissions with respect to link quality with unicast traffic. We now delve into the retransmissions of PBs by sending unicast, low data-rate traffic, i.e., 150Kbps, and by capturing the PLC frame headers. Under this scenario, an Ethernet packet of 1500 bytes is sent approximately every 75ms. The test has a duration of 5 min per link. As we have discussed above, broadcast packets might be missed by some stations when channel conditions are bad, because they are not retransmitted as soon as a proxy station acknowledges them. In contrast, unicast packets are being retransmitted until the receiver acknowledges them, hence are always received. For this reason, we look at the frame header SoF to study retransmissions. Because there is no indication on whether the frame is retransmitted in the PLC SoF, we employ the arrival time-stamp of the frame to characterize it as a retransmission or new transmission (if the frame arrives within an interval of less than 10ms compared to the previous frame, then it is a retransmission). We also measure PB_{err} every 500 ms.

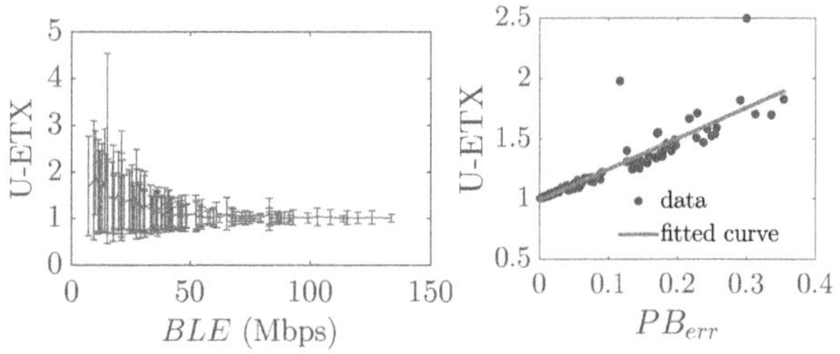

Figure 22: U-ETX vs BLE and U-ETX vs PB_{err}.

We conduct the experiment described above for all the links of our testbed. We compute the unicast ETX (U-ETX) for all the links of the testbed. We count the total number of retransmissions for a packet of 1500 bytes, which produces 3 PBs. A retransmission occurs if at least one of these PBs is received with errors. Figure 22 presents U-ETX as a function of average BLE (with links sorted in increasing BLE order) and PB_{err}. U-ETX is measured by averaging the number of PLC retransmissions for all packets transmitted during the experiment. We also plot error-bars with the standard deviation of the transmission count. It turns out that link quality is negatively correlated with link variability, a conclusion made also when exploring BLE in Section 6.2. The higher the U-ETX is, the higher the standard deviation of transmission count is. Links with high BLE are very likely to guarantee low delays, as U-ETX does not vary a lot. U-ETX and the averaged PB_{err} are highly correlated, with almost a linear relationship.

8.2 Retransmission Due to Contention

To explore the sensitivity of link metrics to background traffic and to examine how interference can be considered in link metrics, we now experiment with two contending flows. We set a link to send unicast traffic at 150Kbps as in the previous subsection, emulating probe packets. After 200 seconds, we activate a second link sending "background" traffic at various rates. We measure both BLE and PB_{err}. In these experiments, we observe that BLE is insensitive to low data-rate background traffic for all pairs of links. However, BLE appears to be affected by high data-rate background traffic on a few pair of links. So far, we have not found any correlation between these pairs of links. We explain this phenomenon with the "capture effect", where the best link decodes a few PBs even during a collision due to very good channel conditions, yielding high PB_{err}. In this case, the channel-estimation algorithm cannot distinguish between errors due to PHY layer and errors due to collisions, hence it decreases BLE. Figure 23 presents two representative examples of link pairs for which BLE is sensitive and nonsensitive to high data-rate background traffic. Observe that PB_{err} explodes in link 6-11, which is sensitive to background traffic.

To tackle the sensitivity of BLE to high data-rate background traffic, we take advantage of the frame aggregation procedure of the MAC layer, described in Section 2.2. We observe that transmitting a few PBs per 75ms (150Kbps rate) yields a sensitivity of metrics to background traffic.

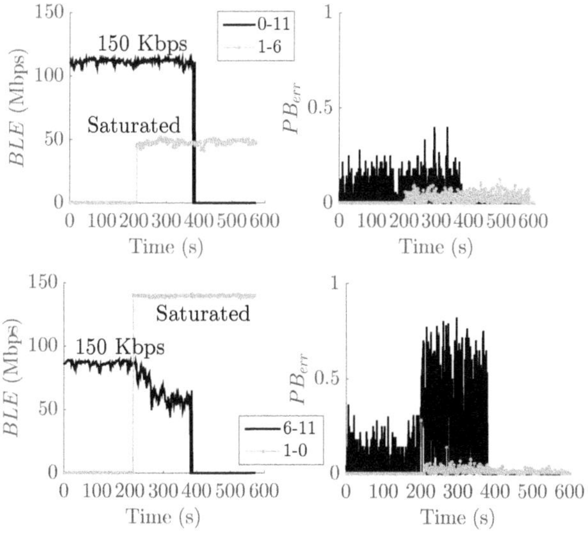

Figure 23: Link metrics of 2 sets of contending links with low data-rate and saturated traffic.

However, when two saturated flows are activated, we never notice an effect on BLE (see [20] for more details). Due to frame aggregation, packets from different saturated flows have approximately the same frame length (i.e., maximum) and when they collide, the channel estimation algorithm works more efficiently than when short probe-packets collide with long ones. To emulate the long frame lengths of saturated traffic, we send bursts of 20 packets such that the traffic rate per second (i.e., the overhead) is kept the same (150Kbps). In Figure 24, we show another link for which BLE is sensitive to background traffic, and the results of our solution. By sending bursts of probe packets, BLE is no more affected by background traffic. This shows that by exploiting the frame aggregation process[12], we can tackle the sensitivity of link metrics to background traffic.

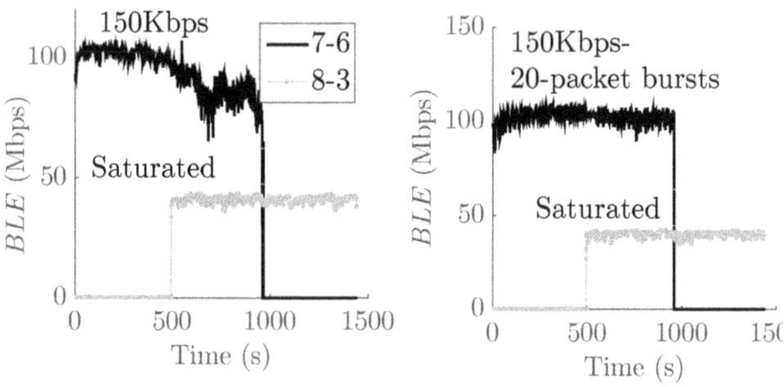

Figure 24: Tackling the link-metric sensitivity to background traffic by sending bursts of probes.

Conclusion: We have studied the mechanism of retransmissions in PLC. Although broadcast probe-packets yield significantly less overhead in link-quality estimation, they do not provide accurate estimations. In contrast, unicast probe-packets reflect the real link quality, but by producing more overhead. We observe that PB_{err} can be used to estimate U-ETX and to indicate interference in PLC. However, estimating the amount of interference is challenging and should be further investigated. We leave this extension for future work. We introduce techniques to tackle the potential sensitivity of link metric to background traffic.

[12]Depending on the PLC technology, these bursts can be transmitted such that only one PLC frame is generated hence, without large MAC overhead. A measurement study of the maximum frame duration of HPAV is given in [20].

9. LINK-METRIC GUIDELINES

We now summarize our guidelines for efficient link-metrics estimation with PLC, given our experimental study in the previous sections.

Policy	Guideline/Explanation	Section
Metrics	BLE and PB_{err}, defined by IEEE 1901.	7, 8.1
Unicast probing only	Broadcast probing cannot be used, as it does not give any information on link quality.	8.1
Shortest time-scale	BLE should be averaged over the mains cycle.	6.1
Size of probes	Larger than one PB (or one OFDM symbol) to avoid inaccurate convergence of rate adaptation algorithm.	7.2
Frequency of probes	Should be adapted to link quality for lower overhead.	6.2, 6.3, 7.3
Burstiness of probes	Can tackle a potential inaccurate convergence of the channel estimation algorithm or the sensitivity of link metrics to background traffic.	7.2, 8.2
Asymmetry in probing	There is both spatial and temporal variation asymmetry in PLC links. This could affect bidirectional traffic, such as TCP, that requires routing in both directions.	5, 6.2

Table 3: Guidelines for PLC link-metric estimation

10. RELATED WORK

A large body of work (e.g., [9], [15]) focuses on channel modeling and noise analysis, and very little work, such as [13], investigates the PLC performance from an end-user perspective. The authors in [13] explore the performance of HomePlug AV when household devices operate in the network. They observe that switching the appliances affects significantly the performance and introduces asymmetry, and that different appliances create diverse noise levels. Liu et al. [12] employ a testbed to investigate the interoperability and coexistence of different HomePlug AV networks and propose a scheme that can be employed to ameliorate the performance of multiple contending AV networks.

Many previous experimental works focus on the PLC MAC layer under single contention domain scenarios and ideal channel conditions in order to model and evaluate MAC characteristics. To achieve these conditions, the stations are plugged to the same power-strip and are isolated from the power-grid. Zarikoff and Malone [22] give the guidelines for a PLC testbed construction and perform measurements with both UDP and TCP traffic, and multiple contending flows. We [21] study the fairness of the CSMA/CA protocol both analytically and experimentally. We show that when 2 saturated stations are contending, the 1901 MAC is unfair and might yield high jitter. We also use a testbed setup of 7 stations to evaluate and enhance the performance of the HomePlug AV CSMA/CA process in [19], [18].

A few works focus on comparing the wireless and PLC performance [11, 17]. [11] investigates older specifications of PLC and WiFi, i.e., HomePlug 1.0 and 802.11 a/b, respectively. The authors provide testbed measurements from 20 houses for metrics such as coverage, throughput, and connectivity. [17] introduces a comparison between hybrid PLC/WiFi networks and single-technology networks. The authors find that hybrid networks contribute to increase coverage in home networks; they also argue that using alternating technologies for multi-hop routes yields good performance. However, they do not study link metrics that can be used to optimize routing in such networks.

11. CONCLUSION

We have shown that PLC can yield significant performance gains when combined with WiFi networks. Yet, there were open questions on how to exploit to the fullest the two mediums and PLC has received far too little attention from the research community; we introduce an experimental framework and investigate the performance of PLC. To this end, we explore its spatial and temporal variation, delving into the diverse time-scales of PLC channel variability.

We have studied PLC link metrics and their variation with respect to space, time, and background traffic. Similar metrics have been long pursued by the research community for WiFi and have been required by recent standardization of hybrid networks. We have given guidelines on efficient metric-estimation in hybrid implementations. We have observed that there is a high correlation between link quality and its variability, which has a direct impact on probing overhead and accurate estimations.

Acknowledgment

This work is financially supported by a grant of the Smart-World project of the Hasler Foundation, Bern, Switzerland.

12. REFERENCES

[1] HomePlug Alliance. `http://www.homeplug.org/`.

[2] IEEE 1905.1-2013 Std for a Convergent Digital Home Network for Heterogeneous Technologies.

[3] IEEE 802.11n-2009-Amendment 5: Enhancements for Higher Throughput.

[4] OpenWrt. `http://https://openwrt.org/`.

[5] Qualcomm Atheros Open Powerline Toolkit. `https://github.com/qca/open-plc-utils`.

[6] IEEE Standard for Broadband over Power Line Networks: Medium Access Control and Physical Layer Specifications. *IEEE Std 1901-2010*, 2010.

[7] S. M. Das, H. Pucha, K. Papagiannaki, and Y. C. Hu. Studying wireless routing link metric dynamics. In *Proc. of the 7th ACM Conf. on Internet measurement*, pages 327–332, 2007.

[8] R. Draves, J. Padhye, and B. Zill. Routing in multi-radio, multi-hop wireless mesh networks. In *Proc. of ACM MobiCom, 2004*, pages 114–128.

[9] S. Guzelgoz, H. B. Celebi, T. Guzel, H. Arslan, and M. K. Mıhçak. Time frequency analysis of noise generated by electrical loads in PLC. In *17th International Conf. on Telecommunications (ICT)*, pages 864–871. IEEE, 2010.

[10] E. Kohler, R. Morris, B. Chen, J. Jannotti, and M. F. Kaashoek. The Click modular router. *ACM TOCS*, 18(3):263–297, 2000.

[11] Y.-J. Lin, H. A. Latchman, R. E. Newman, and S. Katar. A comparative performance study of wireless and power line networks. *Communications Magazine, IEEE*, 41(4):54–63, 2003.

[12] Z. Liu, A. El Fawal, and J.-Y. Le Boudec. Coexistence of multiple homeplug av logical networks: A measurement based study. In *IEEE Global Telecommunications Conf. (GLOBECOM), 2011*, pages 1–5.

[13] R. Murty, J. Padhye, R. Chandra, A. R. Chowdhury, and M. Welsh. Characterizing the end-to-end performance of indoor powerline networks. Technical report, Harvard University Microsoft Research Technical Report, 2008.

[14] K. Papagiannaki, M. D. Yarvis, and W. S. Conner. Experimental characterization of home wireless networks and design implications. In *IEEE INFOCOM 2006*.

[15] S. Sancha, F. Canete, L. Diez, and J. Entrambasaguas. A channel simulator for indoor power-line communications. In *IEEE International Symposium on Power Line Communications and Its Applications (ISPLC)*, pages 104–109, 2007.

[16] R. K. Sheshadri and D. Koutsonikolas. Comparison of routing metrics in 802.11n wireless mesh networks. In *IEEE INFOCOM 2013*, pages 1869–1877.

[17] P. Tinnakornsrisuphap, P. Purkayastha, and B. Mohanty. Coverage and capacity analysis of hybrid home networks. In *IEEE International Conf. on Computing, Networking and Communications (ICNC), 2014*, pages 117–123.

[18] C. Vlachou, A. Banchs, J. Herzen, and P. Thiran. Analyzing and boosting the performance of power-line communication networks. In *Proceedings of the 10th ACM International on Conference on emerging Networking Experiments and Technologies*, pages 1–12. ACM, 2014.

[19] C. Vlachou, A. Banchs, J. Herzen, and P. Thiran. On the MAC for Power-Line Communications: Modeling Assumptions and Performance Tradeoffs. In *IEEE International Conf. on Network Protocols (ICNP)*, 2014.

[20] C. Vlachou, S. Henri, and P. Thiran. Electri-Fi Your Data: Measuring and Combining Power-Line Communications with WiFi (Technical Report 210617). Infoscience EPFL 2015.

[21] C. Vlachou, J. Herzen, and P. Thiran. Fairness of MAC protocols: IEEE 1901 vs. 802.11. In *Proc. of IEEE ISPLC 2013*.

[22] B. Zarikoff and D. Malone. Construction of a PLC testbed for network and transport layer experiments. In *Proc. of IEEE ISPLC 2011*, pages 135–140.

Revisiting Network Energy Efficiency of Mobile Apps: Performance in the Wild

Sanae Rosen, Ashkan Nikravesh, Yihua Guo, Z. Morley Mao, Feng Qian†, Subhabrata Sen*
University of Michigan, †Indiana University, *AT&T Labs – Research
{sanae,ashnik,yhguo,zmao}@umich.edu,
fengqian@indiana.edu, sen@research.att.com

ABSTRACT

Energy consumption due to network traffic on mobile devices continues to be a significant concern. We examine a range of excessive energy consumption problems caused by background network traffic through a two-year user study, and also validate these findings through in-lab testing of the most recent versions of major mobile apps. We discover a new energy consumption problem where foreground network traffic persists after switching from the foreground to the background, leading to unnecessary energy and data drain. Furthermore, while we find some apps have taken steps to improve the energy impact of periodic background traffic, energy consumption differences of up to an order of magnitude exist between apps with near-identical functionality. Finally, by examining how apps are used in the wild, we find that some apps continue to generate unneeded traffic for days when the app is not being used, and in some cases this wasted traffic is responsible for a majority of the app's network energy overhead. We propose that these persistent, widespread and varied sources of excessive energy consumption in popular apps should be addressed through new app management tools that tailor network activity to user interaction patterns.

Categories and Subject Descriptors

C.2.1 [**Network Architecture and Design**]: wireless communication; C.4 [**Performance of Systems**]: measurement techniques, performance attributes

Keywords

4G LTE; smartphones; cellular network performance; mobile energy consumption

1. INTRODUCTION

Fueled by powerful mobile devices and ubiquitous cellular data network access, smartphone applications (*apps*) have become an indispensable part of modern life. There have been more than 100 billion mobile app downloads from the Apple App Store as of June 2015 [2]. However, battery life remains a scarce resource. Over the past 15 years, CPU performance has improved 250x while Li-Ion battery capacity has only doubled [11]. It is known that inefficient app design can lead to excessive battery drain. In particular, certain app traffic patterns, like periodic requests, interact poorly with the power-hungry cellular interface [22, 8, 21]. Despite these known problems, however, apps continue to drain user batteries.

In this paper, we measure the prevalence of excessive mobile app network energy consumption by analyzing data collected from 20 real smartphone users and 342 unique apps over a period of 22 months. This unique long-term dataset allows us to examine the smartphone and app ecosystem in the wild. We focus on the impact of background traffic — traffic sent when the app has no UI element visible — which makes up 84% of the total network energy consumed across all users. Periodic background traffic is often power-hungry [21], but apps have flexibility in scheduling background traffic due to the absence of real-time user interaction, and can use strategies such as bundling traffic or reducing update frequencies to reduce energy consumption. We examine global trends across all apps and determine that energy overconsumption remains a pervasive problem, despite many apps taking steps to reduce their energy overhead. Furthermore, some of this traffic is likely unintentional and not useful to the end user.

Our key findings are as follows:

- We identify a significant new source of excessive background energy consumption (§4.1), where network traffic persists after an app transitions from the foreground to the background, sometimes for as long as a day. 30% of background traffic from one major browser is caused by this phenomenon. Over 80% of apps transmit more than 80% of their background data in the first minute after the app is sent to a background state, in total across all user devices in our study.
- We show that there is high variation in the energy overhead of apps that rely on frequent background traffic, even between apps with similar background functionality (§4.2). By examining case studies of apps that require background updates, we find that the energy consumed by similar apps can vary by up to an order of magnitude. Furthermore, we find that apps studied in previous work have often improved their energy overheads but that other new apps continue to make the same mistakes. There is substantial room for improvement by adopting energy-efficient design approaches, such as batching background updates.
- By examining apps as they are used in the wild, we find that many apps are frequently not used for days, including apps with substantial background traffic. We demonstrate that the network energy overhead of these apps can be reduced by up to a half in some cases if the OS were to proactively terminate long-running apps after three days of inactivity (§5). More generally, we emphasize the need for apps to be aware of their foreground/background

IMC'15, October 28–30, 2015, Tokyo, Japan.
© 2015 ACM. ISBN 978-1-4503-3848-6/15/10 ...$15.00.
DOI: http://dx.doi.org/10.1145/2815675.2815713.

state when scheduling network requests, and our findings suggest that new suggestions for managing background traffic are likely to be highly valuable.

2. RELATED WORK

Mobile network and app performance is an area that has received a great deal of interest, and prior work has examined many aspects of this problem, including papers on TCP-cellular interactions [17], accurate active performance measurements [14], app usage [27], wireless data drain [23], comparing cellular and Wi-Fi performance [25], application performance [19], energy efficiency when downloading and rendering web content in the foreground [26], and the impact of user behavior [13]. We focus on background network energy consumption specifically, specifically where it occurs in the wild.

Prior work has also examined various aspects of background network activity as well, which or work builds upon. Aucinas *et al.* examined smartphone energy efficiency through in-lab experiments with a number of major apps which maintain a continuous online presence [8]. Work by Huang *et al.* [18] examined traffic sent when the screen is off (note that background traffic can also occur when the screen is on, including from minimized apps). Other work has examined periodic transfers [21], and the disproportionate impact of small background requests [12, 9]. Tamer [20] demonstrates it is possible to modify the energy impact of app wakeups by interposing on wakeup events to better manage them. Our work is complementary, examining a broad set of apps and focusing on their behavior in the wild over a long time period, which enabled us to uncover new energy drain problems as well as understand how old problems have evolved.

There has also been a great deal of interest in the impact of background traffic in work developed concurrently with this paper. In particular, Google announced Android M after the submission of this paper, which introduces Doze and App Standby, which should decrease the energy impact of the excessive background traffic we uncovered in this paper [15, 5]. Other concurrent work includes ZapDroid [24], which automatically isolates or disables infrequently-used apps, a solution which our findings suggest would be highly valuable. Work by Chen et al [10] presents a large-scale user study of how users use their phones and how that interacts with app battery consumption. Their study is complementary, covering all sources of energy consumption and trends across categories of devices, whereas we focus on examining the role of background network transfers specifically in depth and exploring the root causes of this excessive background consumption.

3. DATA COLLECTION AND OVERVIEW

We first summarize our measurement dataset. We recruited 20 students[1] at the University of Michigan and provided each of them with a Samsung Galaxy S III smartphone with an unlimited LTE data plan. We pre-installed custom data collection software on each phone that transparently collects complete network traces. These traces include packet payloads (note we are unable to decrypt SSL traffic), user input events, and packet-process mappings. All collected data was kept strictly confidential. The data was collected over a period of 623 days (December 2012 to November 2014) with an overall raw data size of 125 GB, including cellular and WiFi packet traces and user input and context data. We focus primarily on cellular traffic in this study as it consumes far more energy than WiFi. Processes are labeled with names derived from the app package name, allowing us to straightforwardly map packets to the originating apps. In a few cases, requests are delegated to some system services such as the Media Server. We label this traffic according to the service from which it originated rather than the app which triggered it, as mapping back to the originating app in this specific case cannot always be done with high accuracy.

[1]This user trial was approved by University of Michigan IRB-HSBS #HUM00044666.

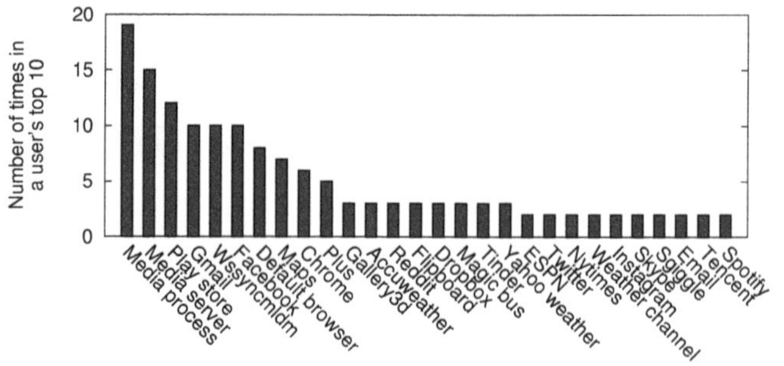

Figure 1: Number of times each app appears in a user's top 10 apps, ranked by total data consumption.

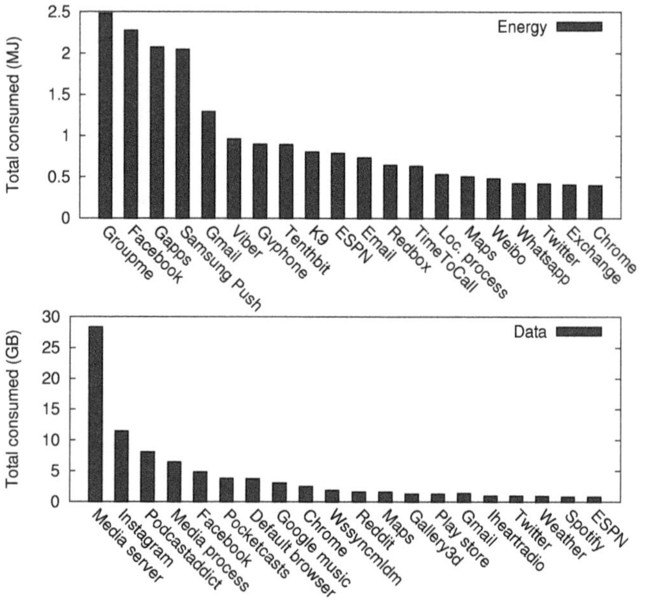

Figure 2: Highest cellular data and network energy usage by app across all users.

3.1 Measurement Data Overview

We next give an overview of this 22 month dataset before focusing on specific apps.

App Popularity and Diversity. Users differ greatly in the apps they use. Figure 1 shows apps that appear in at least two users' top-10 lists (by total data consumption). While a handful of apps are popular among all users (*e.g.*, the built-in media player, Facebook, and Google Play), users' top-ten lists otherwise exhibit significant diversity. Similar diversity of app usage was observed in previous work [13, 27].

Data- and Energy-Hungry apps. First, we examine trends in applications that consume a large amount of energy or data. We use a standard power model for LTE [16, 22] supported by measure-

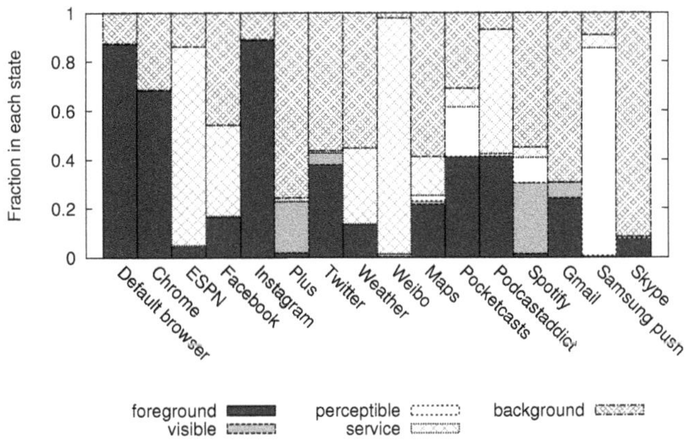

Figure 3: Fraction of energy in each foreground/background state, based on process codes assigned by the Android operating system.

ments gathered with a Monsoon power monitor to compute radio energy consumption[2].

We summarize the top energy and data consumers in Figure 2. Note the top energy consumers and the top data consumers are not necessarily the same. For example, the default email app consumes network energy disproportionate to its data usage, whereas the built-in media server consumes significantly less energy per byte. In cellular networks, the radio remains active for several seconds after a data transmission, consuming additional energy called *tail energy* [9]. Since tail energy consumption is dependent on the number of traffic bursts and the time between them rather than the amount of data sent, apps sending data intermittently incur a disproportionate amount of energy.

As we evaluate the impact of each app in the wild, rather than the impact of apps in isolation, we assign any tail energy to the last packet sent during the tail period to avoid double-counting energy when there are multiple concurrent flows. In this way, the total cellular network energy consumed by each device is the sum of the energy assigned to each app.

Longitudinal Trends. We examined trends in network usage and energy consumption over time. However, the diversity of apps, the smaller user set, users' propensity to change the apps they use over time, and changes in user behavior, obscured the overall impact of app design changes over time or any trends towards more energy efficiency. Background energy fluctuated by up to 60% from week to week throughout the study. Examining specific apps, we did determine that some apps have become more energy-efficient due to adjusting the inter-packet intervals of background traffic, which we discuss in more detail in §4.2.

4. BACKGROUND ENERGY CONSUMPTION

Energy consumption in the background makes up 84% of the total network energy, and is thus the focus of this study. An app running in the background may run until either the user kills it manually or Android does (such as when more memory is needed). Many apps sync with a server, receive push notifications, or run updates in the background. Since no user interaction is present, these processes have much more freedom to determine when they transmit data than when running in the foreground, where they may be subject to time constraints to meet user expectations. Furthermore, there is often a tradeoff between ensuring updates are timely and avoiding wasted background updates the user never looks at. For this reason, apps vary greatly in the amount of energy that they consume in the background, even when providing similar functionality. In this section, we analyze the resource efficiency of app background network activities through detailed case studies, identifying large disparities between apps due to diverse design approaches. We also identify several cases where large numbers of network requests are sent unnecessarily, verified through in-lab testing.

Our definition of "background" traffic is based on five main process states defined by Android [6]: *foreground*, where the process is responsible for the main UI; *visible*, where the process is responsible for a secondary UI element; *perceptible*, where a process not visible to the user may still affect the user experience (e.g. playing music); *service*, where a background process should not be terminated if possible; and *background*, where the OS will kill the app if system memory is low. We summarize the cellular energy in each of these five states for twelve data- or energy-hungry apps in Figure 3. We refer to the first two categories as "foreground" processes and the last three as "background" processes for the remainder of the paper. Note that for all but three of these apps, background energy of some sort contributes more than half of the overall network energy consumed by the app. Across all apps, 84% of cellular network energy is consumed in a background state. This included only 8% of energy consumed by "perceptible traffic", as only a few users used streaming services and it is apparent from Figure 3 that not all apps made use of this feature when expected. 32% was consumed by "service" traffic.

We focus on two main categories of background transfers. In §4.1, we examine background traffic that occurs when an app switches from the foreground to the background. In §4.2 we investigate traffic initiated automatically in the background, such as that for periodic updates, push notifications, or music streaming. We supplement our longitudinal traces with in-lab measurements to validate our findings and determine the context and purpose of the traffic in our traces.

4.1 Foreground Traffic not Terminated

While it is expected that some apps will transmit data in the background, such as when checking email, updating a social networking app or streaming music, other apps such as browsers are expected to mainly transmit data when the app is in the foreground. However, we find some such apps appear to inadvertently transmit data in the background. As shown in Figure 3, about 30% of the Chrome browser's network energy is consumed while the app is running in the background. To understand why, we examine a representative trace from the user study dataset in Figure 4. We have highlighted the time period after Chrome switches to the background in grey. During this time packets continue to be sent for several minutes: note that some websites also generate periodic background requests.

To validate our hypothesis that Chrome allows web pages to continue sending periodic traffic after the app is minimized, we first created a custom web page that only sends XMLHttpRequest asynchronously to a server every second. We found that the Chrome app allows this web page to transfer data when tabs are not selected and thus invisible to the user; when the screen is off; and even when the app has been sent to the background. To further confirm this problem exists in the wild, we also opened several web pages, minimized Chrome, and recorded the resulting network traces. In general, any web page which automatically refreshes content has this problem, including some ad and analytics content. In one partic-

[2]In the rest of the paper, "energy" refers to the network energy unless otherwise noted.

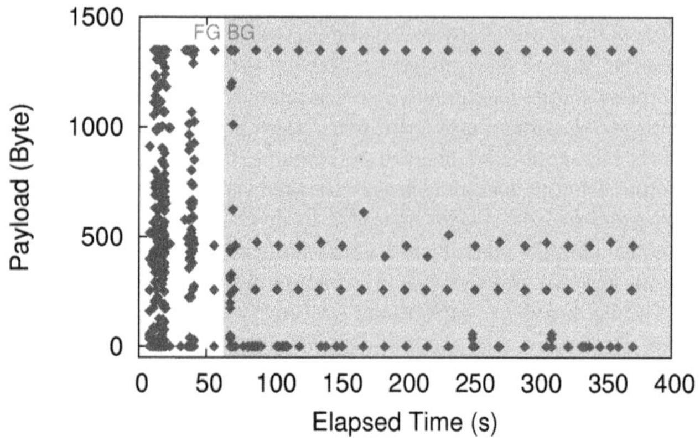

Figure 4: Chrome allows webpages to continue sending and receiving data in the background.

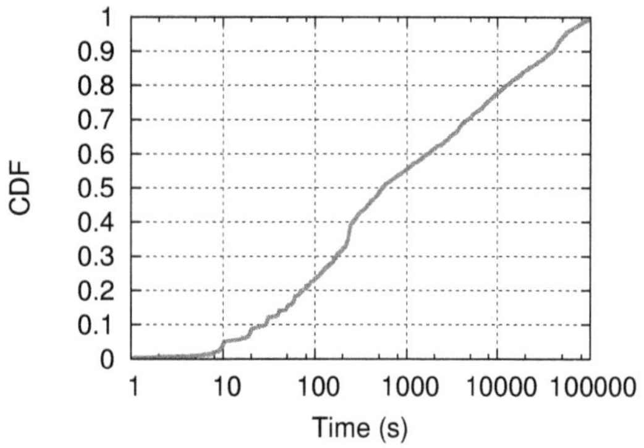

Figure 5: Duration for which traffic continues to be sent/received after the app is sent to the background. Each data point represents one transition to the background.

ularly egregious case, a popular local transit information webpage sends background requests roughly every 2 seconds, indefinitely, keeping the cellular radio alive and draining the battery until the app is killed or the tab is closed.

To quantify the severity of the problem on a larger scale, we plot the distribution of the length of time during which Chrome continues to transmit data after being sent to the background in Figure 5. This includes flows that were started when Chrome was in the foreground but persist after Chrome is sent to the background. Each data point represents one instance of the app being minimized. In some cases background traffic flows persist for more than a day! While updating pages in the background may have some benefit to users who then revisit that page, in most cases continuing to send data for so long is likely not intended or useful behavior. Note that our data points do not include cases where the app remains in the foreground but a tab other than the one being viewed is sending data, and so the scope of the problem is likely even bigger.

We compared this behavior against that exhibited by Firefox and the default Android browser. Neither allow data to be sent when the app is in the background or the screen is off, and Firefox blocks data from being sent by inactive tabs. To estimate the prevalence of this problem among other apps, we examine the data sent by apps in the background as a function of the time since the app was last in the foreground. As we show in Figure 6, the more recently the app was

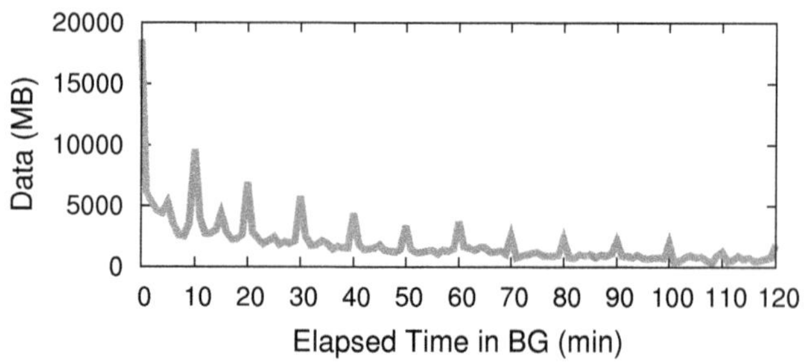

Figure 6: Total background data sent by all apps, as a function of the time since switching from a foreground state. Note the periodic spikes at 5 and 10 minute intervals, the large amount of traffic in the first minute, and the long tail of persisting, continuous flows.

sent to the background, the more traffic is sent, with substantially more traffic being sent in the first few minutes than any other time. Some of this traffic is periodic: there are peaks at 10 minute and 5 minute intervals, which are common time intervals for intentional periodic background traffic. However, there is also a non-periodic pattern, where the overall volume of background traffic falls off rapidly in the first few minutes. To estimate the prevalence of this problem, we look for apps where 80% of the background traffic is sent within 60 seconds of the app going to the background than any other time. 84% of apps meet this criteria.

There are some apps, like Dropbox, which may have valid reasons to upload content immediately after the app is closed, but in many other cases transmitting a large amount of traffic after the app is closed is undesirable. Developers of apps which send a large amount of data immediately after sending the app to the background should determine if this is expected or necessary behavior.

4.2 Transfers Initiated in the Background

We next evaluate data transfers that intentionally occur in the background. Even though these transfers may be beneficial to the user, depending on the frequency of user interaction with the app, the overhead of these transfers can be disproportionate. We examine a number of energy-hungry apps in depth, as well as some energy-conserving apps with similar functionality. Finally, we study a number of apps examined in previous work to evaluate how background update energy efficiency has improved over time. The energy efficiency of background transfers are primarily determined by their frequency, with small updates incurring a disproportionate amount of tail energy. Large transfers are known to be more efficient, as they make better use of available bandwidth [17]. As a result, apps with similar functionality can have very different overheads depending on the traffic pattern used.

We summarize key findings in Table 4.2, focusing on five classes of apps that are responsible for a substantial fraction of background updates in the user study: social media apps, widgets, music streaming, podcasts and services that provide background updates. We break down the energy overhead into average per-day energy consumption and average per-flow energy consumption. Note that it is not always the case that there is only one flow per periodic update, nor that for periodic updates that the updates necessarily continue for the entire day, as background applications may be forced to close for a variety of reasons.

First, we examine social media apps. These apps generally ask for updates from a central server periodically, regardless of user activity, and can thus potentially consume a large amount of energy.

	MJ/ day	MJ/ flow	MB/ flow	Avg. J/B	Update frequency	Notes
Social media						
Weibo	3500	57	0.3	190	5-10 min	Frequent, nearly-empty requests
Twitter	220	11	17	0.65	1h	
Facebook	930	14	7.7	1.8	5 min ⇒ 1 h	Previously every 20-60s [21] in 2012
Plus	180	11	8.9	1.2	1h	Rarely actively used but installed by default
Periodic update services						
Samsung Push	1500	140	2.2	64	15 min to 15h	
Urbanairship	2000	310	1.9	163	5-30 min	Library; period varies by app
Maps	190	21	55	0.38	20-30 min	Decreased to a few hours near the end
Gmail	410	20	10	2	30 min ⇒ varying	30 min in 2012 [21]; updates appear to become discontinuous.
Widgets						
Go Weather widget	300	12	1.6	7.5	5 min	
Go Weather	220	2.8	5.6	0.5	5 min ⇒ 40 min	Switched push notification approaches
Accuweather	1500	51	3.2	16	7 min but high variation	
Accuweather widget	33	1.7	18	0.094	~3h	More efficient than the app
Streaming						
Spotify	310	50	220	0.23	5 min ⇒ 40 min	
Pandora	35	3.9	45	0.087	1 min ⇒ 2h	Previously every 1 min [21] in 2012
Podcasts						
Pocketcasts	36	4.3	2200	0.002	~2h average	0.4 mJ per minute running.
Podcastaddict	92	2.9	750	0.004	12 min average	3.7 mJ per minute running.

Table 1: Case studies. Energy per flow and per day are averages over time, and one flow may not correspond to one periodic update. These can vary as apps change over time or as background apps are forced to close, and energy consumption values vary by device and carrier.

Apps with small, periodic background traffic (such as Weibo) have very high energy overhead and send little data, whereas apps with similar functionality (such as Twitter) have a much smaller footprint. Facebook, which had previously been identified as a heavy energy user, improved its energy efficiency over the course of our study by decreasing its background update frequency from 5 minutes to 1 hour, which is much longer than the 1-minute periodicity measured in 2012 [21].

Applications oriented towards providing periodic background updates, such as certain push notification services, may consume a lot of energy compared to the amount of data they send. In an in-lab experiment, one third-party library transmitted nearly empty HTTP requests every five minutes for hours, but only provided one user-visible notification during this time. Another example is Google Maps, which by default provides a background location service which continuously collects anonymous location data. This service consumed up to 90% of the app's total energy usage at the beginning of the study, but the frequency decreased to once every few hours by the end. GMail also leverages periodic updates using push notifications: it has actually increased its inter-update intervals, but updates appear to no longer be periodic, arriving only on demand, leading to an overall low degree of energy consumption.

Widgets are a class of apps that appear on the home screen and have little or no direct user interaction. In many cases their functionality revolves around periodic background updates (such as to keep the user updated on the latest weather). There is a tradeoff between timeliness of information and energy consumption. However, even just examining weather widgets, the difference in update frequency between two apps (and the resulting energy overhead) varies by an order of magnitude. Note also that the Accuweather app is far less efficient than the corresponding widget, as the widget updates itself less frequently. Widgets and apps made by the same developers may have very different behavior.

We also examined several multimedia streaming apps. Music streaming apps were not as popular in our dataset as in prior work, but their update frequency was generally much lower than before [21], having apparently moved away from a continuous streaming model to larger batch downloads, although particularly long update frequencies may reflect users who only intermittently use these apps. Podcasts were far more popular, and we compare two popular apps. Podcastaddict consumed more energy overall, as Pocketcasts downloads an entire podcast in one chunk whereas Podcastaddict downloads smaller chunks as needed. While the latter approach may reduce data consumption if users don't finish listening to a podcast, it consumes more energy.

5. WHAT-IF ANALYSIS: PREEMPTIVELY KILLING IDLE BACKGROUND APPS

In §4 we determined that background traffic has a substantial impact on energy consumption, and in some cases much of this traffic is from apps users are not frequently using. We propose having the OS kill background apps that have remained in the background for several days. A new permission or whitelist could address corner cases where apps (such as widgets) have a legitimate need to run in the background for an extended period of time, and OS feedback on background energy consumption could disincentivize unnecessary use of this functionality. In fact, the preview of Doze in Android M, a project announced after our submission, appears to add such functionality [15, 5]. We have identified a number of apps where this type of functionality has the potential to greatly reduce background traffic, although we do not evaluate Doze itself in this paper.

To evaluate the effectiveness of this approach, we simulate restricting background traffic after three days, and highlight six apps

	Plus	Weibo	Maps	ESPN	Accuweather	Skype
A: % days with only background traffic	42	83	70	13	43	62
B: Max consecutive background days	40	24	84	10	18	49
C: Disable after 3 days: avg.% energy reduction	14	54	39	6.2	22	45

Table 2: Example trends in background traffic when apps are infrequently used, and simulated energy savings from suppressing this traffic.

in Table 5. In row A we show the fraction of days where we see only background traffic from the app, and in row B we show the maximum number of such days that we see occurring consecutively, considering only time periods where there is foreground traffic at the beginning and end of the time period. These apps are rarely used by certain users, creating energy savings opportunities if the apps were to be preemptively killed. Row C summarizes the average savings per user of killing the app after three consecutive days. Note in particular that Weibo, which we showed was very energy-hungry, can have its network energy consumption more than halved this way.

Due to the large number of apps users in our study had installed on their phone, the impact of each app individually on a user's total network consumption was small. Thus, this would have resulted in total network energy savings of less than 1% on average overall. However, we found that for the users running Weibo, disabling Weibo alone after just three days of inactivity could have reduced their total network energy consumption by 16% on those days. Overall, how much users benefit from this functionality depends greatly on the set of apps involved and on user behavior, so it is hard to draw definite conclusions on the average benefits of our proposed system for or other systems such as Doze, but such an approach seems especially promising in protecting users from poorly optimized or buggy apps, and reducing the worst-case energy consumption generally.

6. CONCLUDING REMARKS AND RECOMMENDATIONS

Excessive energy consumption by mobile apps has long been known to be a significant problem, and background traffic continues to be a major battery drain. We have examined a significant but previously unstudied phenomenon where network traffic initiated in the foreground persists unnecessarily when the app is sent to the background. Furthermore, we have shown that improvements for known inefficiencies have not been universal, even for professionally developed apps with a large user base. While we recommend that app developers continue to carefully consider the cost of the traffic they send, more is needed to improve the situation, especially for background traffic.

We make several recommendations. First, apps should be designed to explicitly account for their foreground/ background state and adjust network transfers accordingly. Most crucially, apps should ensure network transfers are terminated when the app is minimized where possible. In §5 we demonstrate that more aggressively killing apps that run in the background for days could greatly reduce the energy impact of infrequently used apps. Since submitting this paper, Google announced Android M, where all background activity is disabled when the device is idle, and users are able to manually specify exemptions for specific apps. Our findings suggest this is likely a very positive step towards improving battery life. Similar tools to manage other aspects of network content overconsumption would also be valuable, such as to terminate flows meant to only occur in the foreground.

Finally, the impact of periodic background transfers can also be reduced in many cases. We have seen that some of the improvements described in prior work, such as batching requests, have been implemented with positive effect [18, 21], but background data continues to have a large relative overhead. As proposed in prior work, app developers should continue to batch traffic to minimize the frequency of background updates, as well as tailor updates to reflect the frequency with which useful, new data is provided. Our findings also emphasize the importance of previously proposed approaches to reducing the energy consumption of background traffic at the OS level, such as by providing explicit OS support for periodic updates or by using radio-layer energy saving features such as fast dormancy [7]. Even if some apps improve energy consumption, new apps will likely emerge that make the same mistakes.

In this paper, we have focused on background energy issues on Android. Other systems take different approaches: IOS, for instance, has the OS manage background tasks for applications, restricting the potential impact of suboptimal app designs [1]. Although we have not evaluated these systems, we can speculate as to how our findings might apply to these systems. OS management allows transfers to be batched, providing opportunities for energy consumption optimization. However, some of their design approaches and guidelines may suggest scheduling approaches inconsistent with our findings. For instance, prioritizing apps who download a small amount of data in the background quickly may incentivize the wrong behavior. Windows Phones also put restrictions on background apps [3], restricting resource-intensive tasks to WiFi and limiting the frequency with which background apps can run, but there have still been consumer reports of specific apps draining the battery when running in the background [4]. Overall, there is a tradeoff between developer flexibility and the potential for excessive energy consumption; we leave examining the energy impact of these alternate approaches to future work.

7. ACKNOWLEDGEMENTS

We would like to thank our anonymous reviewers as well as Erich Nahum, our shepherd, for their valuable comments. This research was supported in part by NSF under CNS-1059372 and CNS-1345226, as well as by an NSERC Canada PGS D scholarship.

8. REFERENCES

[1] App Programming Guide for iOS — Background Execution. https://developer.apple.com/library/prerelease/ios/documentation/iPhone/Conceptual/iPhoneOSProgrammingGuide/BackgroundExecution/BackgroundExecution.html.

[2] Apple's app store has passed 100 billion app downloads. http://www.theverge.com/2015/6/8/8739611/apple-wwdc-2015-stats-update.

[3] Background agents for Windows Phone 8. https://msdn.microsoft.com/en-us/library/windows/apps/Hh202942(v=VS.105).aspx.

[4] Conserve windows phone battery life by managing background apps. http://www.windowscentral.com/conserve-windows-phone-battery-life-managing-background-apps.

[5] Developer preview - power-saving optimizations. https://developer.android.com/preview/features/power-mgmt.html.

[6] ActivityManager.RunningAppProcessInfo documentation. https://developer.android.com/reference/android/app/ActivityManager.RunningAppProcessInfo.html.

[7] P. K. Athivarapu, R. Bhagwan, S. Guha, V. Navda, R. Ramjee, D. Arora, V. N. Padmanabhan, and G. Varghese. RadioJockey: Mining Program Execution to Optimize Cellular Radio Usage. In *Proc. ACM MobiCom*, 2012.

[8] A. Aucinas, N. Vallina-Rodriguez, Y. Grunenberger, V. Erramilli, K. Papagiannaki, J. Crowcroft, and D. Wetherall. Staying Online while Mobile: The Hidden Costs. In *CoNEXT*, 2013.

[9] N. Balasubramanian, A. Balasubramanian, and A. Venkataramani. Energy Consumption in Mobile Phones: A Measurement Study and Implications for Network Applications. In *Proc. ACM IMC*, 2009.

[10] X. Chen, N. Ding, A. Jindal, Y. C. Hu, M. Gupta, and R. Vannithamby. Smartphone energy drain in the wild: Analysis and implications. In *Proc. Sigmetrics*, 2015.

[11] E. Cuervo, A. Balasubramanian, D. ki Cho, A. Wolman, S. Saroiu, R. Chandra, and P. Bahl. MAUI: Making Smartphones Last Longer with Code Offload. In *Proc. ACM MobiSys*, 2010.

[12] H. Falaki, D. Lymberopoulos, R. Mahajan, S. Kandula, and D. Estrin. A First Look at Traffic on Smartphones. In *Proc. ACM IMC*, 2010.

[13] H. Falaki, R. Mahajan, S. Kandula, D. Lymberopoulos, R. Govindan, and D. Estrin. Diversity in Smartphone Usage. In *Proc. ACM MobiSys*, 2010.

[14] A. Gember, A. Akella, J. Pang, A. Varshavsky, and R. Caceres. Obtaining In-Context Measurements of Cellular Network Performance. In *Proc. ACM IMC*, 2012.

[15] R. Holly. Checking out Doze and App standby on the Android M Developer Preview. http://www.androidcentral.com/checking-out-doze-android-m-developer-preview.

[16] J. Huang, F. Qian, A. Gerber, Z. M. Mao, S. Sen, and O. Spatscheck. A Close Examination of Performance and Power Characteristics of 4G LTE Networks. In *Proc. ACM MobiSys*, 2012.

[17] J. Huang, F. Qian, Y. Guo, Y. Zhou, Q. Xu, Z. M. Mao, S. Sen, and O. Spatscheck. An In-Depth Study of LTE: Effect of Network Protocol and Application Behavior on Performance. In *ACM SIGCOMM Computer Communication Review*, volume 43, 2013.

[18] J. Huang, F. Qian, Z. M. Mao, S. Sen, and O. Spatscheck. Screen-off Traffic Characterization and Optimization in 3G/4G Networks. In *Proc. ACM IMC*, 2012.

[19] J. Huang, Q. Xu, B. Tiwana, Z. M. Mao, M. Zhang, and P. Bahl. Anatomizing Application Performance Differences on Smartphones. In *Proc. ACM MobiSys*, 2010.

[20] M. Martins, J. Cappos, and R. Fonseca. Selectively Taming Background Android Apps to Improve Battery Lifetime. In *Proc. Usenix ATC*, 2015.

[21] F. Qian, Z. Wang, Y. Gao, J. Huang, A. Gerber, Z. Mao, S. Sen, and O. Spatscheck. Periodic Transfers in Mobile Applications: Network-wide Origin, Impact, and Optimization. In *Proceedings of the 21st international conference on World Wide Web*, pages 51–60, 2012.

[22] F. Qian, Z. Wang, A. Gerber, Z. M. Mao, S. Sen, and O. Spatscheck. Profiling Resource Usage for Mobile Applications: a Cross-layer Approach. In *Proc. ACM MobiSys*, 2011.

[23] A. A. Sani, Z. Tan, P. Washington, M. Chen, S. Agarwal, L. Zhong, and M. Zhang. The Wireless Data Drain of Users, Apps, & Platforms. *ACM SIGMOBILE Mobile Computing and Communications Review*, 17(4), 2013.

[24] I. Singh, S. V. Krishnamurthy, H. V. Madhyastha, and I. Neamtiu. ZapDroid: Managing Infrequently Used Applications on Smartphones. In *Proc. UbiComp*, 2015.

[25] J. Sommers and P. Barford. Cell vs. WiFi: On the Performance of Metro Area Mobile Connections. In *Proc. ACM IMC*, 2012.

[26] N. Thiagarajan, G. Aggarwal, A. Nicoara, D. Boneh, and J. P. Singh. Who Killed my Battery?: Analyzing Mobile Browser Energy Consumption. In *Proceedings of the 21st international conference on World Wide Web*, 2012.

[27] Q. Xu, J. Erman, A. Gerber, Z. Mao, J. Pang, and S. Venkataraman. Identifying Diverse Usage Behaviors of Smartphone Apps. In *Proc. ACM IMC*, 2011.

StreetSense: Effect of Bus Wi-Fi APs on Pedestrian Smartphone

Sehyun Bae
Seoul National University[1]
kbird@popeye.snu.ac.kr

Daehyun Ban
Samsung Electronics
daehyun.ban@samsung.com

Dahyeon Han
Seoul National University
hann862@popeye.snu.ac.kr

Jiyoung Kim
Seoul National University
beyondj@popeye.snu.ac.kr

Kyu-haeng Lee
Seoul National University
khlee@popeye.snu.ac.kr

Sangsoon Lim
Samsung Electronics
ssoon.lim@samsung.com

Woojin Park
Samsung Electronics
woojin1.park@samsung.com

Chong-kwon Kim
Seoul National University[2]
ckim@snu.ac.kr

ABSTRACT

Recently, we have received a growing number of reports that complain about poor and unstable internet connections at bus stops in metro Seoul. Careful analyses led us to conclude that Wi-Fi APs equipped on buses instigate the trouble. According to the ambitious free Wi-Fi expansion plan by the city of Seoul, public buses started to equip Wi-Fi APs. As buses with APs stop and go, they actualize intermittent connection opportunities to riders waiting at the bus stops. However, the connection durations are too short such that bus APs are a nuisance rather than a convenience. We collected the basic statistics such as AP inter-arrival and sojourn times and measured link level performance metrics. We observed the effect of frequent frame losses on the TCP congestion control and eventually on the TCP throughput. We also measured the performance of applications such as PLT (Page Load Time). The measurement results showed that passing APs are useful only for some applications in very limited situations while they are virtually useless and just irritations in many cases. We also discovered that poor Wi-Fi connections pervert MPTCP; MPTCP performs worse than the generic single path TCP over the LTE network. We expect that our results will be used as the reference data in redesigning Wi-Fi offloading mechanisms as well as in planning and deploying urban Wi-Fi networks.

[1]This work has been done while the author was taking academic course in Seoul National University under support by Samsung Electronics.

[2]This work has been done while the author was with Samsung Electronics.

IMC'15, October 28-30, 2015, Tokyo, Japan

DOI : http://dx.doi.org/10.1145/2815675.2815715

Categories and Subject Descriptors

C.4 [**Performance of Systems**]: Reliability, availability, and serviceability; Performance attributes; C2.3 [**Computer-Communication Networks**]: Network Operations-Public networks

Keywords

AP, WiFi, LTE, MPTCP, Smartphone, Bus

1. INTRODUCTION

Aided by rapid technology advancements, nomadic convenience, and repeated cost reductions, we have observed widespread diffusion of Wi-Fi networks as one of most popular Internet access techniques. At the time of writing, more than 180 Million Wi-Fi APs are deployed worldwide [1]. Started as an indoor novelty that replaces unwieldy cables, Wi-Fi has expanded its horizon as outdoor amenities that transform urban landscape. Numerous grassroots movements to offer private Wi-Fi APs to the public as well as citywide or even nationwide campaigns to install free Wi-Fi hotspots have been reported. For example, Google funded the municipal Wi-Fi network in Mountain View, CA [2] and NY City announced an ambitious plan to construct free Wi-Fi cities [3].

In addition to open and free Internet access, Wi-Fi networks have been used by cellular network companies as a traffic offloading system. The demands for mobile data traffic have increased explosively and this tendency is expected to continue in the future [4]. Even though cellular operators keep expanding the network infrastructure, the capacity increments failed to overtake the demands that are estimated to explode at a 69% annual growth rate. Because Wi-Fi network construction is much more economical than cellular network and Wi-Fi can be easily set up without careful planning, operators multiply Wi-Fi hotspots to alleviate the data overloading conditions on the cellular infrastructure. Many operators designate Wi-Fi as the default connection; when both cellular and Wi-Fi are available, smartphones prefer to connect to Wi-Fi. Aggregated with the pricing strategy that Wi-Fi is complimentary while cellular is still prohibitively expensive, default use of Wi-Fi appeases subscribers also. In addition, the operators installed Wi-Fi hotspots at locations such as cafés, libraries, subway stations and other gatherings where relative location of APs and subscribers are static. In static environments, Wi-Fi hotspots of constrained coverage render satisfactory performances.

Wi-Fi hotspots are now being deployed to moving mass transportation including subway trains and public buses. For example, the city of Seoul recently announced a plan that they will install Wi-Fi APs to every bus in Seoul such that passengers can access the Internet while on board [5]. Even before the ambitious plan rolled out, several metro Seoul buses have already started to be geared with APs. While APs on bus provide convenience to passengers, they inflict unforeseen side effects to riders and pedestrians at bus stops. As buses with APs make stops for a short duration to let passengers to get on/off, prioritized Wi-Fi provokes smartphones to switch connections from cellular networks to the APs. However the connection durations generally are less than 30 seconds which is too short for finishing transactions. The passengers started to report poor Internet connections in 2014 when buses started to equip APs and the number of complaints to Samsung Electronics, a major smartphone supplier, has increased as the number of AP installed buses increase. Our quality assurance team investigated the problem and discovered that the APs on passing buses are the root of the problem.

Like many large cities in Asia, public transportation is the most popular means of mobility in Seoul. More than 5.8 million citizens ride buses daily and busy bus stops serve tens of scheduled regular bus routes. Some busy bus stops have fixed Wi-Fi APs but usually bus stops do not have fixed APs. While waiting for their buses, many riders (See Figure 1 that shows riders at a busy bus stop in Gangnam) use their smartphones surfing the Web, watching streaming videos, etc. At a busy bus stop, several buses arrive every minute and it is not unusual to observe more than ten buses are queued for getting passengers on/off board. Normally, buses stay at a bus stop for 30~90 seconds and this triggers a connection switch to the APs on passing buses. After a few, and sometimes no frame transmissions, currently available APs disappear and new APs turn up. This pattern repeats and causes serious irritations to riders some of who are running time-critical jobs such as searching restaurants or reading electronic maps.

This paper presents the measurement results that we have collected for three weeks in April 2015 at bus stops in Seoul. Busy bus stops serve more than 20 bus routes each of which has inter-service time between 5 to 10 minutes during rush hour. We measured basic statistics such as AP (= bus) inter-arrival time, sojourn time, signal strength changes in the time domain. We also measured TCP and UDP throughputs and analyzed how intermittent connections affect the rate adaptation at the MAC layer and congestion control at the TCP layer. Because user perceived QoEs (Quality of Experience) such as PLT (Page Load Time) and buffering rate might be more important performance metric than network level metrics, we thoroughly investigate QoE metrics also. Finally, we investigated the performance of MPTCP that use both cellular network and intermittent Wi-Fi connections.

Our measurement results illuminated the adverse effects of poor and intermittent Wi-Fi connections. In most cases, the connection duration over bus Wi-Fi is less than 30 seconds. Only a handful of packets can be transferred during the short connection interval. Because TCP congestion control prevents the use of available bandwidth instantly, the effect of the short connection time amplifies at the TCP layer. Poor TCP performance is again directly translated to poor QoE (Quality of Experience) at the application domain. The PLT and download speed are two or three times worse than the LTE connections. The performance of MPTCP that spans over both LTE and Wi-Fi is particularly discouraging; its performance is about three times worse than the generic single path TCP over LTE networks.

2. RELATED WORK

Wi-Fi networks have been widely deployed as the tether-less last mile as well as supplementary networks offloading cellular data traffic. Several cities and municipals provided free Wi-Fi access in their communities [2, 3, 6]. [11] observed the Wi-Fi usage patterns in the Google's Mountain View community network and identified three usage patterns according to device types [11]. The usage pattern of smartphones is characterized by the shortest session length and the least bandwidth use. However, as smartphones are rapidly replacing PCs[7], the usage pattern of smartphones may change also.

[24, 19] examined the feasibility of accessing Wi-Fi APs from moving vehicles. These early studies – even though performed in synthetic environments with only one or a few APs – confirmed the possibility of dynamic connections to Wi-Fi APs from moving vehicles and triggered numerous further investigations. Early research efforts focused on measuring the performance of Wi-Fi connections from moving vehicles in real-world environments. Later the research is extended to Wi-Fi offloading. Particularly, an early study [13], which measured the performance of Wi-Fi connections from moving vehicles in a metropolitan area, revealed both the feasibility and the limitation of Wi-Fi accesses from moving vehicles: the average connection time is 13 seconds and the bandwidth is 30 KB/s.

The explosive growth of mobile data demands superimposed with the confined radio spectrum and the high CAPEX of cellular infrastructure prompted cellular companies to employ Wi-Fi networks as a mobile traffic offloading system. The 3GPP standard includes architectures I-WLAN [8] and IFOM [9] that integrate cellular networks and Wi-Fi networks seamlessly. Wi-Fi offloading has been one of the most intensively studied topics handling both non-vehicle environments [20, 21] and vehicle moving cases[12]. Usually Wi-Fi offloading attains less performance gains in vehicular mobility scenarios than in stationary or slow moving scenarios due to more dynamic changes in channel states and shorter connection durations. [15, 25] provided technical overview and challenges of vehicular Wi-Fi offloading.

[20] dealt with stationary and walking mobility scenarios with 100 smartphone users in metropolitan areas. They showed that data offloading yields greater performance enhancement in static environments than vehicle moving cases. However, another study[21] with 200 students in a University campus well equipped with Wi-Fi hotspots showed the limited applicability of Wi-Fi offloading due to the fact that Wi-Fi hotspots are optimized for laptops rather than smartphones.

[12] conducted an extensive performance study of Wi-Fi offloading in three cities in the USA. Their results showed the poor performance of Wi-Fi networks mainly due to limited availability. [17] performed a direct head-to-head comparison between a 3G network and Wi-Fi network in a vehicular communication scenario in Long Island, NY. They discovered that 3G and Wi-Fi networks present different and complementary characteristics; Cellular networks provide wide and stable coverage while Wi-Fi networks furnish intermittent but higher bandwidth. However, the improved

cellular network infrastructure and the introduction of new techniques such as LTE and LTE-A might change the technical landscape. Several studies indicate that cellular networks offer throughput comparable to or even larger than Wi-Fi while Wi-Fi still maintains the shorter latency [15, 16].

Many researchers proposed mechanisms to enhance the performance of Wi-Fi offloading for fast moving vehicles. [12] devised a fast switching mechanism called Wiffler that enables significant performance gains for delay tolerant traffic. [26] proposed a mechanism that predicts the mobility of vehicles and performs data prefetching to projected hotspots to maximize Wi-Fi traffic offloading for both delay sensitive and delay tolerant applications. ATOM [22] selects Wi-Fi or cellular interfaces intelligently to optimize user QoE. Cedos [23] is another mechanism that maximizes Wi-Fi use for delay tolerant traffic.

Generalization and proliferation of Wi-Fi networks naturally triggered the adoption of MPTCP [18] in recent smartphones such as the Samsung Galaxy S6 [10]. [14] explored the performance of MPTCP with smartphones focusing on the impact of several factors such as flow size, rate/route control algorithms and path characteristics on the performance. Their results showed that MPTCP generally improved the application level performance. Recently, extensive experiments [16] carried out in 167 countries over a 6-month period showed that MPTCP is good for elephants but not very effective for short flows necessitating clever mechanisms that adaptively select the best interface and optimal application of MPTCP.

Unlike the previous studies that handled scenarios where vehicles move around stationary Wi-Fi APs, we study the performance of Wi-Fi offloading in an environment where stationary subscriber accesses moving APs mounted on buses. Initially, we thought that these two environments are similar and expected similar results. However, further investigations showed that there are significant differences. Passengers in moving vehicles can use relatively long and stable Wi-Fi connections when the vehicles stop at traffic signals. On the other hand, subscribers waiting at bus stops are encountered with APs that dynamically appear and are available only for short durations that are too short for performing meaningful transactions.

3. EXPERIMENT ENVIRONMENT

Figure 1 shows passengers waiting at a busy bus stop in Gangnam, Seoul. Because the BIS (Bus Information System) informs the expected bus arrival times, riders know their waiting times and many run various smart phone applications such as web browsing, mobile massaging, video streaming and etc. Several large bus stops have fixed APs but many more do not have fixed APs. Even at bus stops with fixed APs, riders far from the fixed AP may find the APs on the bus near them provide stronger signals and they connect to a passing bus APs dynamically.

Figure 2 shows a typical network model employed by cellular operators. Cellular networks are carefully planned and deployed such that most subscribers at any locations receive adequate performance. Operators also deployed expansive networks of fixed Wi-Fi hotspots, but this paper concentrates on Wi-Fi APs on moving buses. KT (Korea Telecom), a major cellular operator in Korea, connects bus Wi-Fi APs to a P-GW via an LTE connection to provision large bandwidth and quick handovers between heterogeneous networks.

As mentioned earlier, we are focusing on how the Wi-Fi on moving buses affects the performance of riders waiting for buses. To do this, we have conducted extensive measurements at tens of different bus stops located in Seoul such as Gangnam, Yangjae, and Banpo for three weeks. We use Samsung Galaxy Note 3 smartphones and laptops to capture the traffic. Note that Samsung Galaxy Note 3 has an 802.11n Wi-Fi interface. We collect BSSIDs of connected APs, RSSI, data rate, and throughput with measured time from both smartphone and laptop while downloading files. We use the Wireshark packet analyzer on laptop computers for a detailed inspection of packet contents. In addition to basic performance metrics such as L2 level transmission rates, frame loss probabilities and L4 level throughput, we measure page loading time of some popular web sites with chrome browser on the smartphones to examine the QoE(Quality of Experience).

Figure 1. Passengers at a bus stop in Gangnam, Seoul

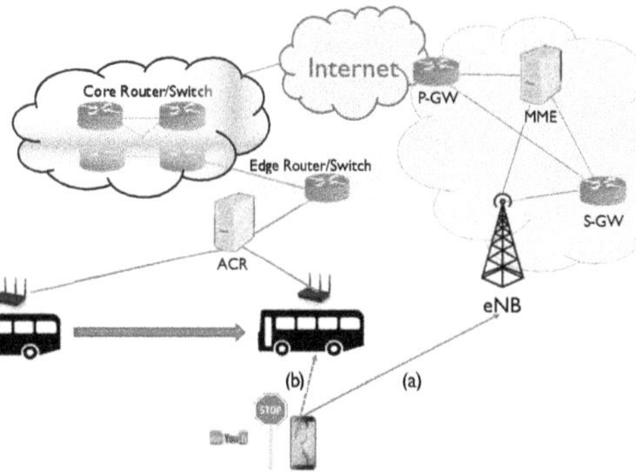

Figure 2. A simplified model of the network. Users can access the Internet via both LTE (connection (a)) and Wi-Fi LTE (connection (b)). Wi-Fi is the default network and subscribers prefer to connect to Wi-Fi if possible.

4. MEASUREMENT RESULTS

Before delving into performance measurements, we first display some basic statistics to illustrate the dynamicity of bus arrivals and departures at bus stops in Seoul. We then examine the performance measures at various protocol layers. Particularly, we analyzed the effect of unstable Wi-Fi connections on the performance of rate adaptation at the MAC layer and congestion control at the TCP layer.

4.1 Basic Statistics

The important factors that affect the performance of waiting passengers include the arrival frequency of APs, their signal strength, sojourn time, and the number of simultaneous users. Among these statistics, the inter-arrival time and sojourn time determine the dynamicity of Wi-Fi AP connection opportunities. Figure 3 illustrates the inter-arrival time and sojourn time at a bus stop in Gangnam. We only show the result measured at one stop because inter-arrival times can be different depending on the number of bus routes at the stop. The arrival time of an AP is the time when we first receive a beacon from the AP and sojourn time is the time between the first beacon and the last beacon. Note that buses frequently queued up for a long line (frequently over 50 meters) and some buses passed the observation point without stopping. In this case, we may fail to detect the APs. We identify APs by their MAC addresses.

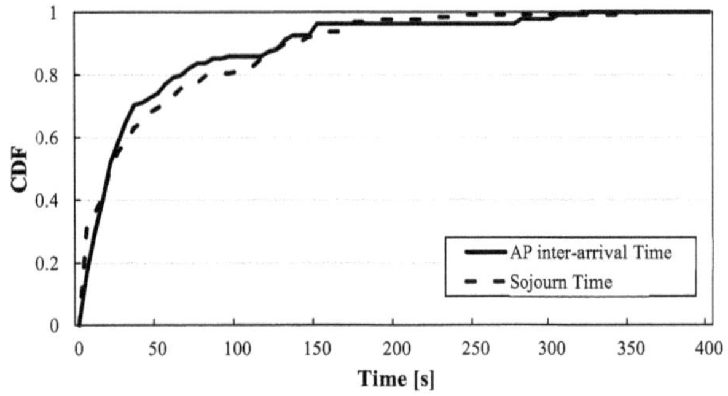

Figure 3. Inter-arrival time and sojourn time of APs on buses at a bus stop.

We can observe from the figure that the AP(=bus) inter-arrival time and the sojourn time are quite short: mean inter-arrival time and sojourn time are 22 seconds and 23 seconds, respectively.

Figure 4 shows one exemplary measurement result displaying the RSSI of signals from bus APs. Signals from different APs are shown in different colors. Short inter-arrival time and sojourn time define the high dynamicity of Wi-Fi AP availability. First, short inter-arrival and sojourn times force frequent switches between APs as well as between AP and LTE. Frequent switching incurs the switching overhead on mobile devices and also increases latency and energy consumption. The short sojourn times can inflict significant adverse effects also; TCP connections are set up and disconnected frequently, and short-lived TCP connections fail to fully utilize the available bandwidth due to the slow start characteristics of the TCP congestion control mechanism.

We argue that the Wi-Fi availability pattern at a bus stop is different from what we observed from moving vehicles. Moving vehicles usually pass APs on the streets unnoticed and access Wi-Fi APs mostly when they stopped for a traffic signal or at bus stations. Therefore, moving vehicles can realize the better utilization of Wi-Fi networks than riders at bus stops.

4.2 Link Layer and TCP Performance

Figure 5 shows the changes in transmission rates at the data link layer (Figure 5.(a) and (b)) and the TCP goodput (Figure 5.(c)) during an interval of (50, 230) of Figure 4. We use the same colors in Figures 4 and 5 to identify APs. During this period, the smartphone made connections to four different APs. The connection times are 77, 20, 22, and 25 seconds, respectively. Many smartphones use the de factor standard rate adaptation scheme called ARF (Automatic Rate Fallback) or its variations. Except short durations in (80, 100), transmission rates change very dynamically. Note that ARF was not optimized for dynamic signal changes and short ephemeral connections that are the norm at bus stops. We believe this is not a problem particular to ARF; most of current rate adaptation schemes may not perform well in the bus stop environment.

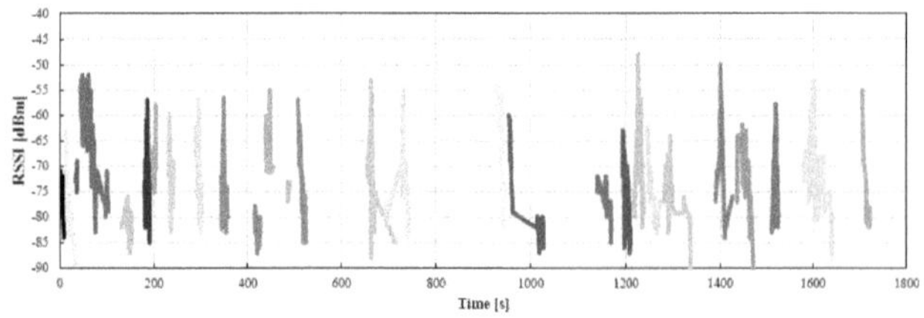

Figure 4. RSSI of signals from bus APs. We can observe that 28 buses with AP arrived at the bus stop during the 30 minutes-long observation period. Typically, a bus stops for less than 30 seconds. Occasionally, when stuck by a traffic stop, a bus stays at more than 60 seconds (Observed at time points of 40 second, 700 second, 1300 second and 1600 second).

Figure 5 (c) and (d) show the throughput and congestion window size of a TCP connection. To measure TCP performance, we let the smartphone to download a movie file from our server. The average RTT of the connection is 564 msec. The first connection during (55, 80) achieves the most TCP throughput while the last connection contributes virtually none. Let us examine the TCP throughput in an interval (50, 100). Most TCP throughput is achieved before the 80 second mark. During this period, congestion window size increases intermittently but steadily from the minimum to 250 KB. Even though the link layer tries to transmit frames after the 80 second mark, most of them fail with virtually no TCP throughput. Note the stable uplink transmission rate in the (80, 100) interval does not guarantee good TCP performance. We scrutinized the packets captured by the Wireshark during the observation period. The associated Wi-Fi connection is disconnected at 80 second due to the bad channel quality and TCP finishes its session via RST after the timeout at 224 second.

Two short connections at 150 second and 180 second are the examples that manifest the importance of connection length on TCP performance. Due to the short connection times, congestion window size, even though it increases up to 50KB from the minimum, it fails to reach the maximum and bandwidth available for short durations is wasted. We also investigated the connection at the 200 second mark. Over this connection, TCP tries to continue the previous session with a new AP via TCP keep-alive, but the new connection is too unstable to re-initiate the TCP connection.

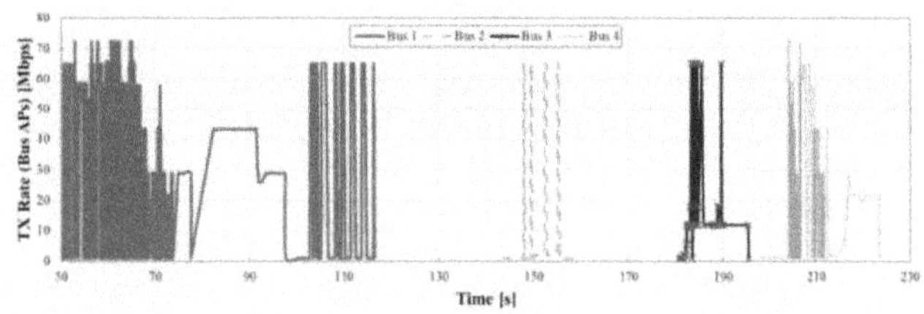

(a) TX Rate (Uplink)

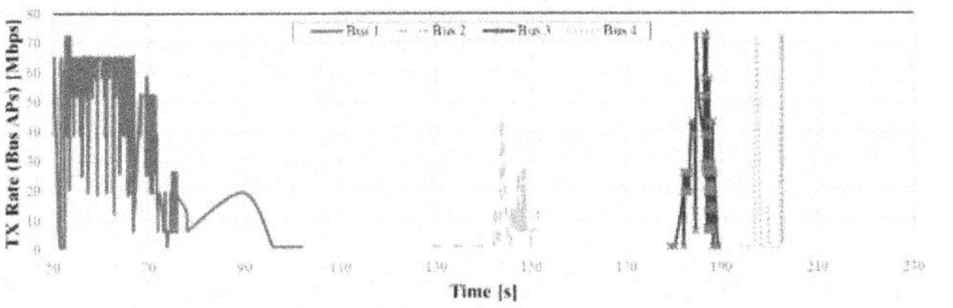

(b) TX Rate (Downlink)

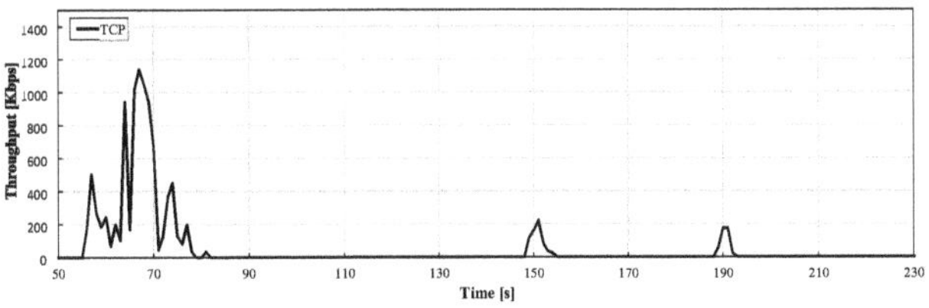

(c) TCP Throughput

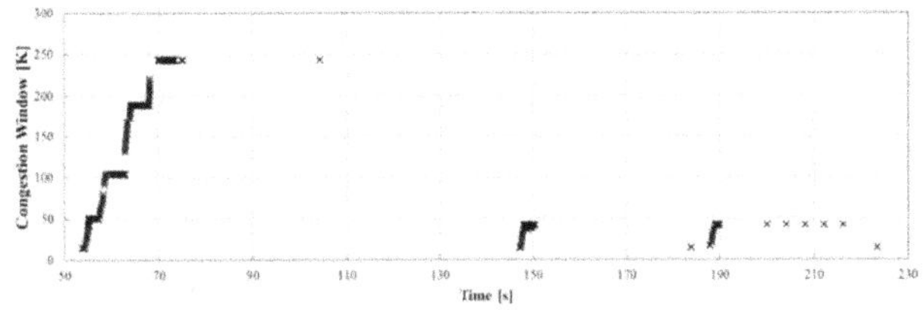

(d) Congestion Window Size

Figure 5. One snapshot of wireless traces

4.3 Comparison of TCP and UDP Performance

In this section, we compare the throughputs of UDP and TCP. Since the IP addresses of the mobile devices and laptops change as their Wi-Fi connections are switched, it is very hard to measure the UDP throughput on a downlink; the server cannot comprehend the client's address. For this reason, we measured the uplink throughput of UDP and compare it with that of TCP. Unlike the previous set of measurements, we used Iperf to generate uplink traffic for both UDP and TCP. In particular, we mimicked CBR-like traffic that transmits 1470 byte long packets to the server every 0.5s and measured throughput at the server every one minute.

Figure 6 shows the throughputs of UDP and TCP. We repeated the same experiment of uploading for 100 times. The throughput of UDP, as expected, is greater than that of TCP; 1.7Mbps for UDP, 1.0Mbps for TCP on average. However, both TCP and UDP fail to utilize the Wi-Fi bandwidth fully. The maximum throughputs are only about 7Mbps and 5Mbps for UDP and TCP, respectively.

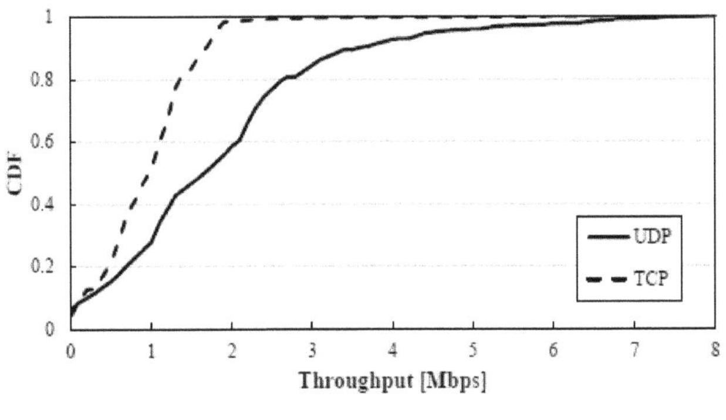

Figure 6. Throughputs of UDP and TCP

4.4 Application Layer Performance

User perceived performance called QoE(Quality of Experience) may be the more important performance measure than network level performance. Important application level quality metrics include PLT (Page Load Time), page loading failure rate and latencies.

We measured the time taken to load the YouTube home page (https://www.youtube.com/). The PLT is defined to be the time difference from when the request is submitted to finish time. Figure 7 (a) compares the PLTs of two connections; one over the LTE network and another over the Wi-Fi network. Over the LTE connection, web pages are loaded in less than 4 seconds in all trials and the variation is very small. However, over the Wi-Fi network, 4 seconds of PLT is achieved only by 8% of trials. Because some trials require unusually long time, we define a trial as a failure if the web page loading does not finish in 75 seconds. The failure rate is 25%, and the median time of a successful page load is about 15 seconds.

Figure 7 (b) illustrates the page loading failure rates when Wi-Fi connections are used to download homepages of YouTube, Yahoo and Facebook, respectively. Again, we define a trial as a failure if it waits more than 75 seconds to load the homepage. The failure rates over the LTE networks are all zero. The YouTube homepage whose size is largest among the three experienced the largest failure rate.

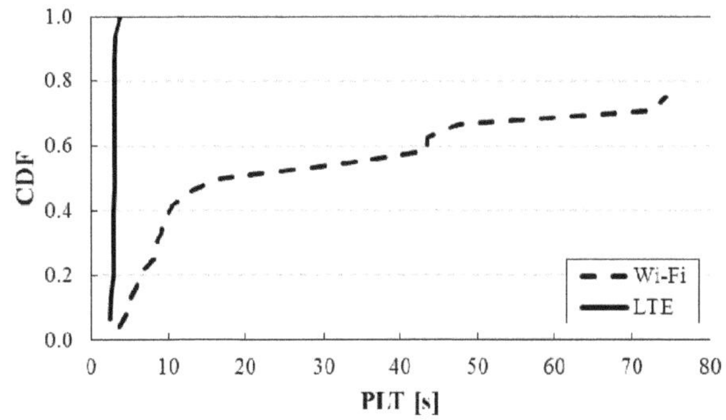

(a) PLT

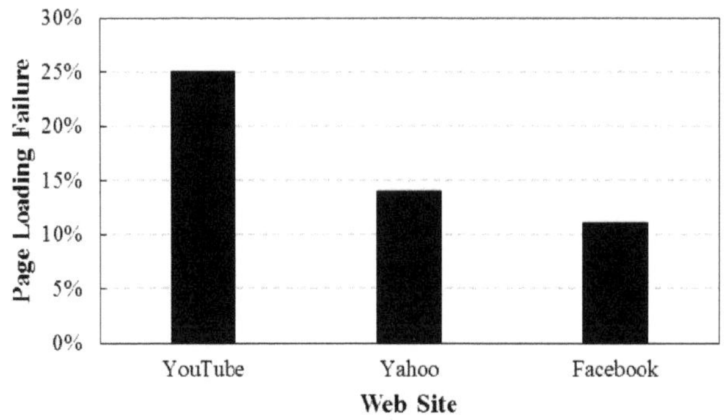

(b) Page Loading failure Rate

Figure 7. Application layer performance (a) PLTs of the YouTube.com homepage over LTE and Wi-Fi connections, (b) Page loading failure rate

4.5 MPTCP Performance

MPTCP has been recently introduced to expedite TCP throughput using multiple connections. Ubiquitous availability of both the cellular network and Wi-Fi network triggered the adoption of MPTCP in recent smartphones. Prior performance studies of MPTCP over LTE and Wi-Fi networks confirmed that MPTCP improved TCP throughput, especially for large files. The prior work dealt with stable Wi-Fi networks. We posit that poor quality Wi-Fi, the norm at Seoul bus stops, may assert negative effects on MPTCP unless intelligent load balance mechanisms are accompanied.

Figure 8 shows that the apprehension might indeed be true. We compared the times to finish downloading a file of size 37.8MB in three different scenarios; a) a generic single path TCP over the LTE network, b) MPTCP over both LTE and Wi-Fi APs on buses, and c) MPTCP over LTE and stable Wi-Fi networks. We included the third case to highlight the effect of poor Wi-Fi connection quality on the performance of MPTCP. The download time of MPTCP over stable APs is shortest, re-confirming the prior work that MPTCP is effective for long files over stable networks. However, the advantage of MPTCP over the generic TCP is not as great as the previous studies. Note that Korean cellular network operator have invested heavily on LTE and LTE-A network constructions and their bandwidth is two or three times larger than that of stable Wi-Fi networks. This large performance discrepancy might be the reason why the advantage of MPTCP over generic TCP is reduced.

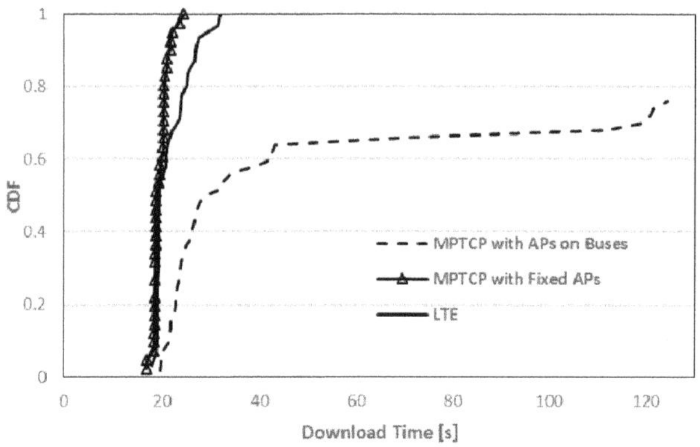

Figure 8. The comparison of time to take download 37.8 MB file through LTE, MPTCP with Aps on buses, and MPTCP with fixed APs

Poor Wi-Fi connections exert a significant negative effect on MPTCP. We define a trial as a failure if it takes more than 130 seconds to finish. The failure rate is 24%; this is particularly unacceptable considering that the failure rate of generic TCP is zero. Also, the mean download time of successful trials is around two times larger than that of generic TCP.

5. CONCLUSION and FUTURE WORK

While APs installed on buses provide convenient Internet accesses to the passengers on board, they can be a nuisance to riders and pedestrians at bus stops. The impact of this side effect has not been measured before and as far as we know this study is the first attempt for thorough investigation of the problem.

Our measurement study carried out at bus stops in Seoul showed that the side effect of bus Wi-Fi APs is quite critical. APs on buses not only fail to provide convenience but also deteriorate the performance of waiting riders significantly. The performance degradation seems to be amplified at upper layers such as TCP and application layers.

The results may indicate the necessity to re-address the prior principle of mobile data offloading; use Wi-Fi as the default network. Instead of connecting to Wi-Fi networks blindly, a careful survey of the quality of the Wi-Fi connection should be performed. Also, to guarantee the proper performance of MPTCP, intelligent and dynamic load balancing to sub-flows might be required.

6. ACKNOWLEDGEMETNS

We are grateful to the anonymous reviewers for their valuable comments and feedback, which greatly improved the quality of the paper.

This work was supported by the National Research Foundation of Korea(NRF) grant funded by the Korea government(MSIP) (No. NRF-2015R1A2A1A01007400) and by Institute for Information & communications Technology Promotion(IITP) grant funded by the Korea government(MSIP) (No.B0190-15-2017, Resilient/Fault-Tolerant Autonomic Networking Based on Physicality, Relationship and Service Semantic of IoT Devices)

7. REFERENCES

[1] WiGLE: Wireless Network Mapping. Available: https://wigle.net/.

[2] Google Wi-Fi: Available: http://wifi.google.com/

[3] ABC News. New York City Pay Phone Booths Noew Free WiFi Hotspots, 2012. http://abcnews.go.com/Technology/yorkcity-pay-phone-booths-now-freewifi/story?id=16756016.

[4] Cisco Annual Reports. Available: http://www.cisco.com/

[5] Money Today Korea. Available: http://news.mt.co.kr/.

[6] Tim Carmody, Wi-Not? South Korea's Seoul To Blanket The City With Free Wi-Fi, Fastcompany. Available: http://www.fastcompany.com/1760834/wi-not-south-koreas-seoul-blanket-city-free-wi-fi.

[7] A Future Fueled by Phablets – Worldwide Phablet Shipments to Surpass Portable PCs in 2014 and Tablets by 2015, According to IDC, Sep 2014, http://www.idc.com/getdoc.jsp?containerId=prUS25077914

[8] Mobility between 3GPP Wireless Local Area Network (WLAN) interworking (I-WLAN) and 3GPP systems, 3GPP TS 24.327.

Available: http://www.3gpp.org/dynareport/24327.htm

[9] IP flow mobility and seamless Wireless Local Area Network (WLAN) offload, 3GPP TS 23.261. Available: http://www.3gpp.org/dynareport/23261.htm

[10] Samsung Galaxy S6. Available: http://www.samsung.com/us/explore/galaxy-s-6-features-and-specs/.

[11] M. Afanasyev, T. Chen, G. M. Voelker, and A. C. Snoeren. Usage patterns in an urban wifi network. *IEEE/ACM Trans. Netw.*, 18(5):1359–1372, Oct. 2010.

[12] A. Balasubramanian, R. Mahajan, and A. Venkataramani. Augmenting mobile 3g using wifi. In *Proceedings of the 8th International Conference on Mobile Systems, Applications, and Services*, MobiSys '10, pages 209–222, New York, NY, USA, 2010. ACM.

[13] V. Bychkovsky, B. Hull, A. Miu, H. Balakrishnan, and S. Madden. A measurement study of vehicular internet access using in situ wi-fi networks. In *Proceedings of the 12th Annual International Conference on Mobile Computing and Networking*, MobiCom '06, pages 50–61, New York, NY, USA, 2006. ACM.

[14] Y.-C. Chen, Y.-s. Lim, R. J. Gibbens, E. M. Nahum, R. Khalili, and D. Towsley. A measurement-based study of multipath tcp performance over wireless networks. In *Proceedings of the 2013 Conference on Internet Measurement Conference*, IMC '13, pages 455-468, New York, NY, USA, 2013. ACM.

[15] N. Cheng, N. Lu, N. Zhang, X. S. Shen, and J. W. Mark. Vehicular wifi offloading: Challenges and solutions. Vehicular Communications, 1(1):13-21, 2014.

[16] S. Deng, R. Netravali, A. Sivaraman, and H. Balakrishnan. Wifi, lte, or both?: Measuring multi-homed wireless internet performance. In Proceedings of the 2014 Conference on Internet Measurement Conference, IMC '14, pages 181-194, New York, NY, USA, 2014. ACM.

[17] P. Deshpande, X. Hou, and S. R. Das. Performance comparison of 3g and metro-scale wifi for vehicular network access. In *Proceedings of the 10th ACM SIGCOMM Conference on Internet Measurement*, IMC '10, pages 301–307, New York, NY, USA, 2010. ACM.

[18] A. Ford, C. Raiciu, M. Handley, S. Barre, J. Iyengar, et al. Architectural guidelines for multipath tcp development. IETF, Informational RFC, 6182:2070{1721, 2011.

[19] P. Hui, A. Chaintreau, J. Scott, R. Gass, J. Crowcroft, and C. Diot. Pocket switched networks and human mobility in conference environments. In *Proceedings of the 2005 ACM SIGCOMM Workshop on Delay-tolerant Networking*, WDTN '05, pages 244–251, New York, NY, USA, 2005. ACM.

[20] K. Lee, J. Lee, Y. Yi, I. Rhee, and S. Chong. Mobile data offloading: How much can wifi deliver? In *Proceedings of the 6th International COnference*, Co-NEXT '10, pages 26:1–26:12, New York, NY, USA, 2010. ACM.

[21] S. Liu and A. Striegel. Casting doubts on the viability of wifi offloading. In *Proceedings of the 2012 ACM SIGCOMM Workshop on Cellular Networks: Operations, Challenges, and Future Design*, CellNet '12, pages 25–30, New York, NY, USA, 2012. ACM.

[22] R. Mahindra, H. Viswanathan, K. Sundaresan, M. Y. Arslan, and S. Rangarajan. A practical traffic management system for integrated lte-wifi networks. In *Proceedings of the 20th Annual International Conference on Mobile Computing and Networking*, MobiCom '14, pages 189–200, New York, NY, USA, 2014. ACM.

[23] Y. Moon, D. Kim, Y. Go, Y. Kim, Y. Yi, S. Chong, and K. Park. Practicalizing delay-tolerant mobile apps with cedos. In MobiSys. ACM, 2015

[24] J. Ott and D. Kutscher. Drive-thru internet: IEEE 802.11b for "automobile" users. In *INFOCOM 2004. Twenty-third AnnualJoint Conference of the IEEE Computer and Communications Societies*, volume 1, pages –373, March 2004.

[25] A. Sathiaseelan and J. Crowcroft. Internet on the move: Challenges and solutions. *SIGCOMM Comput. Commun. Rev.*, 43(1):51–55, Jan. 2012.

[26] V. A. Siris and D. Kalyvas. Enhancing mobile data offloading with mobility prediction and prefetching. In *Proceedings of the Seventh ACM International Workshop on Mobility in the Evolving Internet Architecture*, MobiArch '12, pages 17–22, New York, NY, USA, 2012. ACM.

Going Wild: Large-Scale Classification of Open DNS Resolvers

Marc Kührer
Ruhr-University Bochum
marc.kuehrer@rub.de

Thomas Hupperich
Ruhr-University Bochum
thomas.hupperich@rub.de

Jonas Bushart
Saarland University
s9jobush@stud.uni-saarland.de

Christian Rossow
Saarland University
crossow@mmci.uni-saarland.de

Thorsten Holz
Ruhr-University Bochum
thorsten.holz@rub.de

ABSTRACT

Since several years, millions of recursive DNS resolvers are—deliberately or not—open to the public. This, however, is counter-intuitive, since the operation of such openly accessible DNS resolvers is necessary in rare cases only. Furthermore, open resolvers enable both amplification DDoS and cache snooping attacks, and can be abused by attackers in multiple other ways. We thus find open recursive DNS resolvers to remain one critical phenomenon on the Internet.

In this paper, we illuminate this phenomenon by analyzing it from two different angles. On the one hand, we study the landscape of DNS resolvers based on empirical data we collected for over a year. We analyze the changes over time and classify the resolvers according to device type and software version. On the other hand, we take the viewpoint of a client and measure the response authenticity of these resolvers. Besides legitimate redirections (e.g., to captive portals or router login pages), we find millions of resolvers to deliberately manipulate DNS resolutions (i.e., return bogus IP address information). To understand this threat in more detail, we systematically analyze non-legitimate DNS responses and reveal open DNS resolvers that manipulate DNS resolutions to censor communication channels, inject advertisements, serve malicious files, perform phishing, or redirect to other kinds of suspicious or malicious activities.

Categories and Subject Descriptors

C.2.3 [**Network Operations**]: Network monitoring

Keywords

Domain Name System; DNS Resolution Paths; Content Delivery Network; Agglomerative Hierarchical Clustering

IMC'15, October 28–30, 2015, Tokyo, Japan.

ACM 978-1-4503-3848-6/15/10 ...$15.00.
DOI: http://dx.doi.org/10.1145/2815675.2815683 .

1. INTRODUCTION

The *Domain Name System* (DNS) is a hierarchical, distributed naming system and one of the core elements of the Internet. Its most common task is to provide a mapping between domain names and the associated IP addresses. As DNS is an open system, anyone is allowed to operate a publicly accessible resolver. Prior empirical studies identified millions of such resolvers that are available on the Internet [17,27]. This, however, is counter-intuitive since the operation of publicly accessible DNS resolvers is only mandatory in rare cases only (e.g., for public DNS services such as Google DNS or OpenDNS). Furthermore, DNS resolvers are an attractive target, e.g., for cache snooping attacks [14] or as participants of amplification DDoS attacks [17,24,29,37].

In 2008, an interesting attack was revealed by Dagon et al. [10], who were one of the first that documented the creation of malicious DNS resolution paths by attackers. The authors found attackers to force victims to use rogue DNS servers for all resolutions, thus being able to redirect arbitrary network connections by providing incorrect DNS replies. To understand such attacks in more detail, they performed an empirical analysis of this phenomenon: they analyzed 600,000 open DNS resolvers on the Internet and performed DNS lookup requests of 84 distinct domain names to identify unexpected, suspicious, and malicious responses.

Seven years later, this threat of open DNS resolvers continues to pose a serious problem, especially since the footprint left by attackers is small (i.e., only the clients' DNS resolution is changed). Furthermore, it is unclear how the threat landscape evolved in the last seven years. Weaver et al. provided a glimpse into this problem based on DNS traffic aggregated from Netalyzr sessions [40,41]. Netalyzr is a Java-based applet running on end hosts of volunteers and analyzes multiple properties of the clients' Internet connections such as the reliability of the utilized DNS resolvers. In their measurement study, the authors mainly focused on DNS error monetization, a technique to redirect clients to specific advertisement websites upon requests for non-existent (`NX`) domain names. Furthermore, they also observed sessions in which DNS resolvers redirected end hosts to systems of malicious character. Yet, the number of analyzed DNS resolvers was rather low, thus it remains unclear whether the observed results generalize to all DNS servers world-wide. Several other studies analyzed DNS resolvers [1,4,25,33,34], yet these studies were mainly conducted on a small subset of all resolvers in the IPv4 address space. As such, open DNS resolvers and the potential of malicious DNS resolution paths remain an underexplored phenomenon on the Internet.

In this paper, we illuminate this phenomenon and present the results of a long-term, large-scale empirical study of DNS resolvers on the Internet. In a first step, we monitor the landscape of devices that listen to DNS requests and reply with valid DNS responses. Based on the data collected via weekly Internet-wide scanning activities for more than one year, we provide a comprehensive overview of the resolvers' landscape. During our 13-month-long study, the number of DNS resolvers dropped from 26.8 to 17.8 million servers. To get a better understanding of these hosts, we analyze their properties in terms of geographical and network-based distribution, operated DNS server software, and underlying hardware. We find 76.4% of the resolvers in the Top 25 networks (that operate most servers) to be associated with various broadband telecommunication providers world-wide.

In the second phase of our study, we take the viewpoint of a client system to analyze the *integrity* of the DNS resolutions provided by open recursive DNS resolvers. That is, we aim to understand whether the resolvers actually return legitimate answers or perform bogus resolutions to provide clients with false IP address information. To this extent, we manually selected a set of 155 domains from 13 different website categories (i.e., banking pages, ad providers, adult sites, etc.) that an attacker potentially wants to tamper with. We then perform DNS lookup requests for all domain names on each identified open DNS resolver in the IPv4 address space. By prefiltering "correct" pairs of resolvers and the IP addresses they returned, we sort out all previously seen legitimate answers to significantly reduce the data set. The remaining answers are potentially incorrect, hence we aim to understand them in more detail. We thus request HTTP content for each non-legitimate DNS response and cluster the responses by leveraging agglomerative hierarchical clustering. In the final step, a manual labeling of these clusters enables us to understand the nature of bogus resolutions. Besides legitimate redirects (e.g., captive portals), we find many cases of censorship, ad redirections, and suspicious activities. More specifically, more than 3 million resolvers redirect requests of specific domain names to a small set of IP addresses that host landing pages for censorship of 34 countries. Our in-depth analysis of the HTTP content also enables us to reveal other kinds of abuses. We find 281 resolvers to redirect ad traffic of two large ad providers, while 228 DNS resolvers redirect client systems to malicious content. Further 10,179 resolvers returned a set of IP addresses that act as HTTP proxies for all requested domains. As such, clients might risk to disclose sensible login information when relying on these open recursive DNS resolvers.

To summarize, our contributions are as follows:

- We perform a long-term, large-scale empirical monitoring of DNS resolvers on the Internet, study the changes over time, and classify the resolvers based on characteristics such as device type and software version.
- We systematically evaluate the authenticity of DNS responses when querying open recursive DNS resolvers. That is, we study whether DNS resolvers return incorrect responses upon requesting a set of 155 domain names from 13 different categories, whereas one main focus of our analyses is DNS-based censorship.
- We study in detail the content returned by manipulated DNS responses from open DNS resolvers and uncover different cases of fraudulent manipulation, respectively, phishing of web content and email traffic.

Domains and Datasets. The complete list of scanned domains can be found at `http://syssec.rub.de/research/dns`. Upon request, we further provide access to all datasets that we addressed throughout our analyses in this paper.

2. DNS RESOLVERS IN THE WILD

We begin with a general overview of DNS resolvers in the IPv4 address space. That is, we provide information regarding the magnitude of systems responding to DNS requests and aim to shed light onto the deployed software versions and hardware devices of these hosts. We then discuss our findings in terms of IP address churn and analyze the utilization of the identified DNS resolvers in more detail.

2.1 Terminology

Before going into our analyses, we briefly introduce the DNS-specific terminology that we use throughout this paper. We distinguish between *recursive resolvers* (or "resolvers") and *authoritative name servers* (or "AuthNS"). When requesting the resolution of a domain, a resolver follows the domain name hierarchy and iteratively contacts the AuthNSes of the domain to look up a DNS request. In contrast, an AuthNS is responsible for answering lookup requests for its *zone*, i.e., a subset of the DNS hierarchy (e.g., a domain). An AuthNS does not need to process lookup requests for domains other than in its zone, hence we strictly separate AuthNSes from resolvers (although we may find hosts that serve both roles). For resolvers, we further distinguish between *open* resolvers, which accept and process DNS queries from any external location, and *closed* DNS resolvers, which allow queries from a trusted subset of IP addresses only.

2.2 Resolver Magnitude

First, we monitor the landscape of devices that listen to DNS requests and reply with valid DNS responses. That is, we perform weekly Internet-wide scans in IPv4 for more than one year and enumerate the responsive DNS resolvers.

Scanning Setup. To perform Internet-wide scans in the IPv4 address space, we implemented an efficient scanning software. We adopted multiple scanning practices suggested by Durumeric et al. [12] to abide reasonable scanning behavior. For example, our scanner applies a linear feedback shift register (LFSR) of order $2^{32} - 1$ to distribute the sequence of target IP addresses. As such, scanned networks receive a limited number of DNS requests within a short time frame.

In an IPv4 scan, we send a single DNS `A` lookup request for a specific domain to each IP address in IPv4, excluding well-known private and unallocated network ranges. Each request is specifically crafted and includes a random domain prefix (to avoid caching) and the hex-formatted IP address of the target host in the form `prefix.hex-ip.domain.edu`. This allows us to obtain the IP address of the target host to which the request was sent by inspecting the DNS response.

To offer networks to opt-out from our scanning activities, we defined a reverse DNS (rDNS) record for the scanning system and set up a web server with project details. In total, we added 208 network ranges and 50 individual IP addresses to our blacklist upon request of a network administrator,

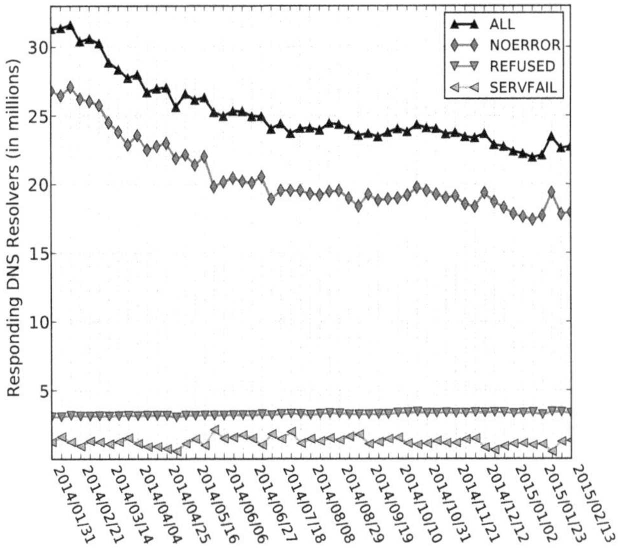

Figure 1: DNS resolvers identified in our weekly scans

resulting in 20,834,166 blacklisted IP addresses. To allow comparisons between the individual weekly scans, we ignore blacklisted IP addresses in all of our scanning results.

Results. We initiated the first DNS scan on Jan 31, 2014 and performed weekly scans for more than one year. Figure 1 outlines the total number of unique IP addresses responding to our requests and illustrates the number of systems that replied with the most common DNS status codes (`NOERROR`, `REFUSED`, and `SERVFAIL`). Note that `NOERROR` includes all hosts that sent a DNS response with this status flag set—regardless of the actual content of the DNS answer section. That is, we consider resolvers that returned legitimate IP addresses for the requested domain as well as hosts that specified empty answer sections or bogus `A` records.

At the beginning of our scanning activities, we find more than 26.8 million systems to respond with `NOERROR`. The number of resolvers drops to 17.8 million IP addresses over time, a phenomenon we address later on. Resolvers specifying the `REFUSED` error flag remain stable during our monitoring, whereas the number of systems returning `SERVFAIL` fluctuates between 633,393 on Dec 19, 2014 and 2,141,539 on May 30, 2014. For the remaining error codes (e.g., `NXDOMAIN`), we find a negligible number of DNS servers only.

When comparing the source IP addresses in the UDP packets with the target addresses that were encoded in the requested domain names, we observe 630,000 to 750,000 resolvers per week to respond to DNS requests that were sent to different target hosts. Prior work has shown that these resolvers are either multi-homed systems or DNS proxies that forward DNS requests to different recursive resolvers [17].

Scan Verification. We further estimate the effect of networks blocking our periodic DNS requests. We thus performed an Internet-wide DNS scan from a secondary host in a different /8 network and compared the number of responsive systems. We find 692,283 DNS resolvers to respond to our verification scan but not to the corresponding weekly scan. 482,158 of these hosts (69.6%) returned `SERVFAIL`, while 64,821 systems (9.4%) refused our DNS request. Accordingly, we missed 145,304 resolvers replying with `NOERROR` in our weekly scan, which is < 1% of all identified resolvers.

Table 1: Resolver fluctuation per country

	Resolvers (in #)		Fluctuation	
Country	Jan 31, 2014	Feb 06, 2015	(in #)	(in %)
US	2,958,640	2,537,269	-421,371	-14.2
CN	2,418,949	2,104,663	-314,286	-13.0
TR	1,439,736	976,226	-463,509	-32.2
VN	1,393,618	1,039,075	-354,543	-25.4
MX	1,372,934	1,175,343	-197,591	-14.4
IN	1,269,714	1,431,522	+161,808	+12.7
TH	1,214,042	564,482	-649,560	-53.5
IT	1,172,001	722,756	-449,245	-38.3
CO	1,062,080	677,572	-384,508	-36.2
TW	1,061,218	453,016	-608,202	-57.3

Table 2: Resolver fluctuation per *Regional Internet Registry*

	Resolvers (in #)		Fluctuation	
RIR	Jan 31, 2014	Feb 06, 2015	(in #)	(in %)
RIPE	11,193,636	7,475,795	-3,717,841	-33.2
APNIC	10,431,352	7,878,208	-2,553,144	-24.5
LACNIC	5,136,320	3,335,895	-1,800,425	-35.1
ARIN	3,143,388	2,761,875	-381,513	-12.1
AFRINIC	1,305,747	1,193,178	-112,569	-8.6

We also compared our numbers of active resolvers to those provided by the *Open Resolver Project* [27] and find the numbers for each scan to match within a 2% error margin.

2.3 Geographical Distribution

After observing the resolvers' landscape, we shed light onto the geographical and network-based distribution.

GeoIP-based Statistics. We first determine the geographical distribution of the resolvers using the MaxMind GeoIP database [26]. That is, we enumerate the number of DNS resolvers per country at the beginning and the end of our scans and determine the fluctuation of resolvers. Table 1 outlines the Top 10 countries hosting 49.1% of all DNS resolvers on Jan 31, 2014 and their fluctuation within one year. During our measurement study, the number of resolvers decreased for most countries. The highest decrease is found for Argentina with -75.0%, while the numbers also dropped significantly for Great Britain (-63.6%) as well as Taiwan (-57.3%). We further identify six countries in which all DNS resolvers (up to 63 hosts per country) vanished.

While the number of resolvers declined for many countries, we also observe opposite behavior. Besides India with an increase of +12.7%, also Malaysia and Lebanon had significantly more resolvers (+59.7% and +76.7%, respectively).

Table 2 outlines the resolver distribution per *Regional Internet Registry*. The decrease in resolvers is not seen for a single registry only, yet can be observed best for RIPE, APNIC, and LACNIC, which (roughly) represent the regions Latin America and Caribbean, Europe, and Asia-Pacific.

AS-based Statistics. We now analyze the Autonomous Systems (AS) distribution of the DNS resolvers to get a more detailed understanding what might have caused the drop in resolvers during our scanning activities. We find the highest decrease of 720,843 resolvers (-97.8%) in the network of an Argentinean telecommunication provider, primarily causing the high decrease of DNS resolvers in Argentina. While this network operated 737,424 resolvers in Jan 2014, we find less than 17,000 systems in 2015. We observe similar results for a South Korean Internet service provider (ISP): 434,567 resolvers replied to our initial scan in Jan 2014, whereas we find only 22 DNS resolvers in the last weekly IPv4 scan.

In total, 28 networks operated more than 1,000 DNS resolvers in Jan 2014 (76,973 hosts in total, i.e., 0.2% of all identified resolvers in Jan 2014), however, not a single active resolver at the end of our measurement study. There are three possible explanations: (i) our requests were blocked at the network level during the measurement period, (ii) DNS egress or ingress filtering was added to the network, or (iii) all actively operated DNS resolvers have been shut down.

Explanation (i) holds for 21 networks, as we still observe active DNS resolvers in our verification scan. To distinguish between the other two explanations, we monitor the fluctuation of resolvers for each weekly scan. If a network operates $\geq$ 100 resolvers and we cannot find a single active resolver in the subsequent week, we assume this network to apply DNS filtering. For networks that have less than 100 DNS resolvers, we assume explanation (iii) to hold. For the remaining seven networks, five networks perform DNS filtering, while two seem to have shut down all servers. Note that we chose these thresholds to allow comparisons with the decrease in NTP amplifiers addressed by Kührer et al. [17].

For the Top 25 networks that include most of the DNS resolvers in Feb 2015, at least 20 networks offer end user services such as telecommunication and Internet via broadband. While this does not necessarily imply that all DNS resolvers in these networks are running on consumer devices such as modems and routers, it is a first indication that at least a set of DNS servers might be running on devices of broadband customers—potentially unsupervised or operating unknowingly by the end users. We thus assume that a certain number of vanishing DNS resolvers is caused either (i) by ISPs when introducing egress or ingress filtering of DNS traffic for their customer IP spaces or (ii) by software updates (such as on home routing equipment via TR-069 [8]) that—among other bug fixes—also restricted the accessibility of the DNS stub resolvers from outside the local network.

2.4 Resolver Classification

Next, we classify the resolvers according to the operated server software and the underlying hardware specifications.

Fingerprinting DNS Server Software. On Dec 17, 2014, we initiated an IPv4 scan using CHAOS [13] `version.bind` and `version.server` requests to identify the DNS server software and obtained responses from 19,925,818 open resolvers, of which 42.7% replied with error codes (`REFUSED` or `SERVFAIL`) for both version requests. Further 4.6% replied with `NOERROR`, however, did not specify any version in both responses. Additional 18.8% of the responding systems returned arbitrary version strings that were specified by administrators to hide software information. As such, two thirds of the DNS resolvers did not leak software details.

For the remaining 33.9% of open resolvers (i.e., 6,753,748 systems), we could obtain software and version information. Table 3 illustrates the Top 10 used server software among the responses that include version details. The majority of these resolvers (60.2%) operate *BIND* (i.e., at least 20.4% of all identified DNS resolvers). Alarmingly, not all operate the newest *BIND* versions, though. For example, about 20% of the resolvers run *BIND* 9.8.2, which is known to be vulnerable to memory-exhaustion attacks. Furthermore, two versions of *BIND* (23.7%) are prone to IP range bypassing, enabling remote attackers to circumvent IP address restrictions and perform requests at closed DNS resolvers. In addition, all Top 10 software versions are susceptible to DoS attacks that can crash the operated DNS server software.

Table 3: Results for the CHAOS version requests based on the 6,753,748 DNS resolvers returning version information

Software	Resolvers	Released	Deprecated	CVE
BIND 9.8.2	19.8 %	Apr 2012	May 2012	IP Bypass, DoS Mem. Corr./Leak.
BIND 9.3.6	8.9 %	Nov 2008	Jan 2009	DoS
BIND 9.7.3	5.7 %	Feb 2012	Nov 2012	Mem. Overfl., DoS
BIND 9.9.5	5.2 %	Feb 2014	Sep 2014	DoS
Unbound 1.4.22	4.8 %	Mar 2014	Nov 2014	Mem. Overfl., DoS
Dnsmasq 2.40	4.6 %	Aug 2007	Feb 2008	RCE, DoS
BIND 9.8.4	3.9 %	Oct 2012	May 2013	IP Bypass, DoS Mem. Overfl.
PowerDNS 3.5.3	3.2 %	Sep 2013	Jun 2014	DoS
Dnsmasq 2.52	2.9 %	Jan 2010	Jun 2010	DoS
MS DNS 6.1.7601	2.5 %	Jun 2011	Aug 2011	DoS

Fingerprinting Hardware Devices. Our next goal was to obtain more detailed system information about the individual resolvers such as the OS and the hardware specifications of the underlying device. The DNS protocol itself does not provide any of this information. As such, we rely on system information provided by other services that might be running on a resolver. That is, we initiate FTP, HTTP, HTTPS, SSH, and Telnet connections and analyze potentially returned banner information and text fragments to fingerprint the device [17]. Upon our connection attempts, we obtained payload data for at least one TCP protocol for 26.3% of the responsive DNS resolvers (i.e., 5,459,524 systems). The remaining resolvers (15,307,037 servers in total) did not offer any public TCP services for the scanned protocols that we could leverage for the device fingerprinting.

To generate fine-granular fingerprints, we manually compiled more than 2,245 regular expressions by closely analyzing the aggregated responses for tokens such as device identifiers. We then aimed to find more specific information about each device type and leveraged manuals and online specifications to attribute details for fingerprinting. The token "dm500plus login", for example, is associated with a DVR running a Linux-based OS on a PowerPC architecture.

Table 4 illustrates the device fingerprinting results. We group routers, modems, and gateways in one category, as these devices often provide overlapping functionality. Category *Embedded* includes devices which we find to run embedded OSes or applications (e.g., the web servers *GoAhead-Webs* and *RomPager*) but lack information to fingerprint the hardware more precisely. This category further includes devices such as *Serial to LAN* converters or micro controller boards such as *Arduino* and *Raspberry Pi*. We find 34.1% of the DNS resolvers responding to our TCP requests to be business and consumer routing devices. In particular, we find three major manufacturers of consumer broadband devices to be prevalent. For example, *ZyNOS*, an OS deployed on devices of manufacturer *ZyXEL*, runs on 16.6% of the DNS resolvers. Besides the large group of routing equipment, we find smaller clusters such as IP-based cameras and DVRs as well as 10,962 NAS devices and 5,061 DSLAMs, operated by ISPs to provide DSL support to their customers.

2.5 IP Address Churn of Resolvers

Seeing a vast number of DNS resolvers to run on routing equipment, we next evaluate the churn of IP addresses of these systems. That is, we estimate the interval between

Table 4: Device fingerprinting results of the 5,459,524 DNS resolvers responding to our TCP-based requests

	Hardware (in %)							Operating System (in %)								
	Router	Embedded	Firewall	Camera	DVR	Others	Unknown	Linux	Unix	ZyNOS	Windows	SmartWare	RouterOS	CentOS	Others	Unknown
DNS	34.1	30.6	1.9	1.8	1.2	1.1	29.3	23.2	21.3	16.6	5.0	3.6	2.6	1.7	2.1	23.9

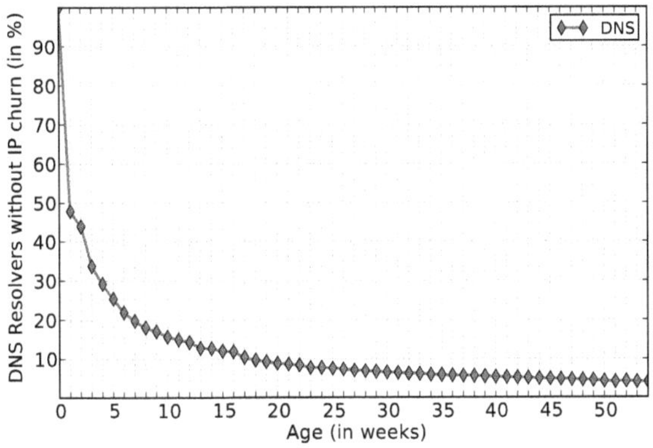

Figure 2: IP address churn of DNS resolvers for 55 weeks

observing a DNS resolver in our Internet-wide scans and the resolver changing its IP address. To this end, we enumerate the DNS resolvers that we identified in our first scan on Jan 31, 2014 based on the observed IP addresses. In the subsequent weeks, we probe these 26,820,486 servers to check if they continuously provide DNS resolutions over time.

Figure 2 outlines the ratio of DNS resolvers that remain stable in terms of their IP addresses during our scanning activities. The initial IP address churn is quite high—52.2% of the DNS servers disappear within a single week. After one year, 1,073,211 systems (i.e., 4.0% of the initially discovered DNS resolvers) still offer DNS resolutions. A fifth (19.7%) of these systems is operated in networks of a Colombian (9.5%), respectively, Turkish (5.3%) telecommunication provider and a US hosting company (4.9%), while the remaining resolvers are widely distributed in terms of ASes.

Observing the high IP address churn within the first week, we measure when exactly the resolvers changed their IP addresses. In fact, more than 40% disappear within the first day—an indicator for DNS resolvers running on devices with low IP lease times such as consumer routing devices. To verify our assumption, we aggregate rDNS records for all resolvers that disappeared after one day and match the records against tokens indicating dynamic IP address assignment (e.g., `broadband`, `dialup`, and `dynamic`). Indeed, at least 67.4% of the 1,989,502 IP addresses we find to provide rDNS records are assigned to dynamic broadband Internet links.

2.6 Resolver Utilization

Faced with the high number of DNS resolvers we wondered if these resolvers are in use at all, hence providing DNS services to actual clients. We therefore analyzed the resolvers' caches using DNS cache snooping [14]. That is, we requested name server (`NS`) records for 15 Top Level Domains (TLDs) (i.e., *br*, *cn*, *co.uk*, *com*, *de*, *fr*, *in*, *info*, *it*, *jp*, *net*, *nl*, *org*, *pl*, and *ru*) every 60 minutes for 36 hours to monitor the associated Time To Live (TTL) values. We then checked if these TLDs were re-added to the resolvers' caches after their expiration. This indicates that a client performed DNS requests for domains associated with these TLDs, causing a resolver to request information from the corresponding AuthNSes. We do not expect to aggregate results from each DNS resolver for the whole time due to IP address churn. Yet, caching values for a few hours might already reveal the desired details about a resolver's usage.

On Nov 30, 2014, we initiated an Internet-wide scan to identify the active resolvers and successively performed the monitoring of the resolvers' caches. Of the identified resolvers, 83.2% (i.e., 13,214,020 systems) respond to at least one of our DNS cache snooping requests, while we suspect the remaining hosts to become unreachable due to IP churn in the mean-time. We find 7.3% of all resolvers to reply with empty DNS responses instead of `NS` records. Additional 3.3% of the hosts send a single response for each TLD before stopping to reply—presumably due to IP churn. For 4.0% of the DNS resolvers we obtain either a static TTL value for each `NS` request or the TTL was set to value 0.

For the remaining resolvers, we flag a resolver as *in use* when we indeed observe TLDs getting re-added to the cache after their expiration. To verify that our results are not biased due to Internet-wide scans performed by other organizations or research projects, we monitored incoming DNS requests to our network and identified a small set of hosts that performed DNS scanning activities. That is, we observe a single daily DNS request initiated by the *Shadowserver Foundation* and single DNS requests from *Team Cymru* and the *Open Resolver Project* within our monitoring period of 10 days. These scans performed `A` lookup requests for three domains assigned to two distinct TLDs. To ensure that at least one TLD cache refresh was initiated by a real client, we require at least three TLDs to be re-added to a resolver's cache during our monitoring to flag a resolver as *in use*. In total, we find 61.6% of all resolvers (i.e., 9,788,740 hosts) to be actively used, i.e., we find at least three TLDs that are refreshed during our monitoring. 6,142,328 systems (i.e., 38.7% of identified DNS resolvers) seem to be used frequently by clients, as we find at least one TLD to be re-added to the resolvers' cache within 5 seconds after expiration. For 4.0% of all DNS resolvers, we monitor a decreasing TTL value for each `NS` request, yet did not obtain sufficient responses to observe the caching entries to expire. Another 19.6% kept resetting the TTL values way ahead before expiration. We assume that many of these resolvers either (i) reset TTL values proactively before expiration or (ii) are associated with groups, connected via load balancers. Depending on which DNS resolver handles the hourly request, we obtain caching values from different DNS server caches.

As a follow-up of our work, one can use a more fine-grained DNS cache snooping technique to evaluate the time gap be-

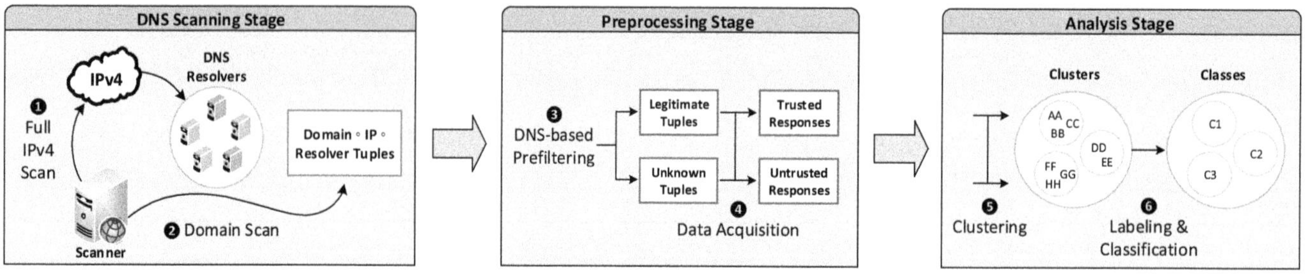

Figure 3: Processing chain to identify manipulated DNS resolutions

tween recaching entries, aiming to approximate the *popularity* of open resolvers, as suggested by Rajab et al. [28].

3. MANIPULATED DNS RESOLUTIONS

So far, we found millions of DNS resolvers that pose a potential security threat. Not only that many of these systems are potentially susceptible to exploitation due to outdated DNS server software, but DNS servers are also known to significantly contribute to large-scale amplification DDoS attacks [17, 24, 29, 37], such as the 300 Gbps attack against Spamhaus in 2013 [23]. However, the vast number of open resolvers also allows us to dig closer into the behavior of DNS resolutions world-wide. In particular, we are interested to understand the *integrity* of the DNS resolutions. We thus ask the following research question: do the open resolvers actually operate *correctly*, i.e., do they strictly follow the clearly-defined hierarchy in the Domain Name System?

We use the processing chain illustrated in Figure 3 to answer this question. First, we identify open DNS resolvers in an Internet-wide scan (step 1) and query them for a manually-chosen list of domain names of various categories (step 2). Afterwards, we perform a prefiltering process to sort out the vast majority of "correct" DNS responses, i.e., we filter ($domain \circ ip \circ resolver$) tuples for all DNS resolver and domain combinations for which we find the resolver to return legitimate IP addresses (step 3). Accordingly, all non-filtered (i.e., unexpected) responses are considered as suspicious and grouped as "unknown". For further analyses and classification—particularly of the unexpected DNS responses—we request HTTP(S) content (and for particular domain names IMAP, POP3, and SMTP banner information) for all legitimate and unknown ($domain \circ ip \circ resolver$) tuples in step 4. In step 5, we cluster the unexpected responses, while we manually label the resulting groups in step 6 to classify virtually all received responses. The following subsections describe these processing steps in more detail.

Note that the DNS protocol offers various features and record types, yet in this section we focus on name resolutions in the IPv4 address space (i.e., `A` records that return IP address information upon requesting a domain name).

3.1 Threat Model

Our threat model affects clients that use and blindly trust DNS resolvers, which may or may not return "correct" recursive DNS resolutions. With "correct" we refer to DNS lookups that strictly follow the hierarchy, i.e., starting at the root (`.`), resolving the TLD (e.g., `.com.`), and then iteratively querying the AuthNSes of a domain name to resolve the fully-qualified domain (e.g., `example.com.`). In principle, we suspect the majority of actively operated recursive DNS resolvers to follow this general resolution procedure, yet prior work [10, 40, 41] already revealed that adversaries tend to deploy bogus resolvers to return non-legitimate responses. This is a severe attack, as bogus resolvers have almost complete control over the network traffic of their clients, thus can redirect the end hosts to arbitrary IP addresses for the requested domains. In our threat model, we thus focus on resolvers that do *not* follow the general DNS hierarchy but respond with forged DNS resolutions. So far, it is unclear to which extent these fraudulent DNS resolvers are actively operated in the entire IPv4 address space.

Note that the threat of incorrect DNS resolutions is not specific to *open* DNS resolvers only and may similarly affect correctly-protected resolvers (i.e., DNS resolvers that only respond to lookup requests of particular IP addresses). In this paper, however, we focus on open resolvers, as they are reachable to the public, and thus allow us to perform large-scale measurements of the DNS resolutions world-wide.

Furthermore, any client system that utilizes open DNS resolvers is potentially threatened by bogus DNS resolutions. This does not only affect the presumably few people who deliberately choose these servers as their personal DNS resolvers. In fact, as we have seen, many resolvers operate on networking equipment, indicating that these systems—by default—have end users who use the provided DNS services.

In our threat model, we do not make any assumption on specific threats that clients may face when relying on incorrect DNS responses. Instead, we systematically analyze the responses and categorize the monitored threats. In general, we can only speculate on the reasons why DNS resolvers turn wild and return unexpected responses. For example, DNS servers might simply be incorrectly configured or return IP addresses of captive portals to redirect client systems to the login page of a (e.g., wireless) network. Furthermore, resolvers can redirect users to search websites for misspelled or non-existing domain names. However, there are also more severe reasons for abnormal DNS responses, e.g., censorship to restrict the access to certain web pages (such as adult content or social networks). Likewise, attackers might aim to sniff on the clients' Internet traffic by transparently proxying the communication to the original websites. Similarly, we imagine attackers that slightly manipulate the web content, e.g., in order to inject advertisements or malicious code.

3.2 Datasets

For our analysis, we determine the response behavior for various types of domain names and check whether we find incorrect DNS responses. Assuming a malicious DNS resolver, it is unclear for which particular domain names it manipulates the answers. Clearly, in order to scale, we cannot exhaustively query thousands of domains at millions of resolvers. We therefore choose a reasonable domain set by selecting a few domain names from different categories. Based on our threat model, we select domain names for various categories that could be relevant for DNS response forgery. For example, we selected banking domains that were targeted by banking trojans via web injects in our dynamic malware analysis platform SANDNET [30]. Furthermore, we include DNS protection services such as operated by antivirus companies, which alter DNS responses for domains associated with prevalent malware families, while the chosen dating and gambling domains are censored in various countries. In total, our domain set consists of 155 domain names, grouped in the following 13 website categories:

- *Ads*: 9 domains associated with ad providers.
- *Adult*: 4 domains taken from the *Alexa Traffic Ranking* [2] that provide adult content.
- *Alexa*: Top 20 ranked domains taken from Alexa.
- *Antivirus*: 15 domains of web pages and update servers of AV and malware protection companies.
- *Banking*: 20 domain names of banking and credit card websites. This includes popular online payment websites such as Alipay, Ebay, and PayPal.
- *Dating*: 3 domains of dating sites, e.g., `match.com`.
- *Filesharing*: 5 domain names of file sharing websites, e.g., `kickass.to` and `thepiratebay.se`.
- *Gambling*: 4 domains associated with online betting and gambling such as `bet-at-home.com`.
- *Malware*: 13 domains associated with malicious activities that are knowingly listed by many common malware blacklists [18], e.g., `irc.zief.pl`.
- *MX*: 13 hostnames of IMAP, POP3, and SMTP servers of 6 organizations offering mail services (Aim, Gmail, Mail.me, Outlook, Yahoo, Yandex).
- *NX*: 8 domain names that are non-existent, 5 NX subdomains of popular domains such as `rswkllf.twitter.com`, and 8 NX domains that include spelling mistakes or missing/additional letters or permutations such as `amason`, `ghoogle`, and `wikipeida`.
- *Tracking*: 5 domains of user tracking libraries such as operated by BlueCava and ThreatMetrix.
- *Miscellaneous*: 6 domains of update servers (e.g., Adobe and Windows), 3 domains of intelligence agencies (NSA, GCHQ, and Mossad), 3 domains of OAuth services (Amazon, Google, and Twitter), and 10 individual domains such as `rotten.com` and `wikileaks.org`.

Finally, we resolve a domain name, for which we operate the AuthNSes. This domain serves as ground truth (GT) to identify DNS servers that return legitimate IP addresses for the GT domain but bogus or empty DNS responses for the remaining domains in the above-mentioned domain sets.

3.3 Domain Scanning Setup

For each of the domain categories, we perform an individual scanning process to obtain DNS responses from all open resolvers. The scanning setup resembles the setup that we discussed in Section 2. Yet, instead of probing all IPv4 addresses, we send DNS `A` lookup requests for all domains in a particular domain set (plus the GT domain) to only those open resolvers that we identified as such by an Internet-wide scan right before initiating the domain scan. We again employ an LFSR and highly reduce the scanning speed in order to distribute and limit the load both on the individual DNS resolvers and on the AuthNSes of the scanned domains.

We again encode the IP address of each target host (i.e., resolver) in the DNS request to differentiate between DNS responses that specify the same source IP address in the UDP packet, although the actual request was sent to a different target host. However, we cannot specify the target IP directly in the queried domain name as conducted in Section 2, as the set of domains is fixed. Instead, we assign each previously identified open resolver a unique identifier. As we find up to 20 million open resolvers in the weekly IPv4 scans in 2015, we have to store $\lceil log_2(20,000,000) \rceil = 25$ bits of information in each request, reducing the number of required bits to encode an IP address from 2^{32} to 2^{25}. We encode 16 bits of information in the DNS transaction ID of the request, while the remaining 9 bits are encoded in the UDP source port (i.e., we send packets using 2^9 different ports). To render redundancy—some resolvers change the destination port of the DNS response for some reason—we encode the 9 bits also in the domain name using `0x20` encoding [9] (i.e., setting specific characters to upper and lower case).

3.4 DNS-based Prefiltering

When initiating DNS `A` lookup requests for 155 domains at 20 million resolvers, we are consequently flooded with billions of DNS responses. As we do not expect the majority of DNS servers to provide forged responses, we aim to filter the vast majority of legitimate answers. As such, we apply a heuristic to determine the legitimacy of each IP address in every DNS response. Note that at this stage we do not want to risk filtering bogus responses but can tolerate to not filter legitimate responses, which we can filter in a later step.

As long as domains are assigned to a fixed set of IP addresses, identifying valid DNS responses is quite easy. However, load balancing and *Content Delivery Networks* (CDNs) may lead to the effect that domains point to thousands of distinct IP addresses and answers may vary on the resolvers' geographical location. To complicate filtering further, IP addresses assigned to a domain name may span multiple ASes. As we request domain information from DNS resolvers located at various places world-wide, we thus likely obtain large sets of IP addresses for particular domain names.

To filter legitimate DNS responses and reduce the initial set of replies to a reasonable size, we apply multiple filtering methods. For *non-existing* domains, we filter responses that either return `NXDOMAIN` or return `NOERROR` without specifying any IP addresses in the answer section. DNS responses for *existing* domain names are filtered when we find each returned IP address to match one of the two following criteria:

(i) We perform a DNS `A` lookup at (trusted) recursive resolvers and find the IP in question to be located in the same ASes as the IP addresses we resolved ourself.

(ii) A rDNS record is assigned to the IP address. If the domain part of the record resembles the requested domain, we filter the IP address. However, as rDNS records can be set to arbitrary domains even without owning the domain, we further require that an `A` lookup request of the rDNS record returns the IP in question, as only the domain owner can set up the `A` record.

Using these filtering rules, we identify legitimate IP addresses for domains that are located in one or a few networks only. Yet, we miss IP addresses of CDN providers that are not located in the providers' primary networks but distributed in various networks world-wide. For example, Akamai is directly associated with at least 8 ASes, yet also distributes their content in several other ASes. In order to find IP addresses that belong to CDN providers, we request HTTPS certificate information at all previously-unfiltered IP addresses using the domains for which these IP addresses were returned. More specifically, we perform two HTTPS requests for each ($domain \circ ip$) pair we find in ($domain \circ ip \circ resolver$) tuples—the first with the TLS *Server Name Indication* (SNI) extension enabled, while we disable SNI in the second request to also obtain the default certificate delivered by a web server. We only consider an IP to be legitimate, if a valid and known certificate was returned for the requested domain name. For the largest CDN providers, we further consider an IP address to be valid, if the non-SNI certificate is legitimate and includes a particular common name.

Note that we might not identify each legitimate DNS response for every queried domain name, as some IP addresses could still be valid, even though none of our filtering rules applied. Furthermore, we do not want to risk filtering bogus DNS responses but can tolerate to not filter legitimate responses. As such, the resulting dataset of "unknown" DNS responses might also include legitimate IPs, yet these can be filtered in a later step (i.e., by analyzing the served content).

3.5 Data Acquisition

Prefiltering supports us in eliminating the vast majority of legitimate responses. For all remaining (i.e., mostly unexpected) responses, we mimic a client system that utilizes the "abnormal" resolvers to aggregate data for further analyses.

To aggregate HTTP data, we use the IPs returned by the resolvers upon resolving the domains and request HTTP information as if they belong to the original website that we tried to contact. That is, we request HTTP and HTTPS content by impersonating a client using the Mozilla Firefox web browser (version 28.0) for all ($domain \circ ip \circ resolver$) tuples we could not classify as legitimate during our prefiltering phase. If HTTP content includes redirections or frames (i.e., an `<iframe>`), we follow these redirections two times at most. If content redirects to further (sub-)domains, we resolve these new domain names at the DNS resolver that returned the initial ($domain \circ ip \circ resolver$) tuple. Note that our succeeding analyses are performed on the plain HTTP(S) payload data, i.e., we do not execute JavaScript.

For the *MX* domain set (cf. Section 3.2), we further initiate IMAP, POP3, and SMTP connections to the respective IP addresses to aggregate banner information for analysis.

We furthermore obtain a list of ($domain \circ ip \circ resolver$) tuples from our own (trusted) DNS resolvers for all domain names in the scanned domain set. Similar to the previous steps, we aggregate HTTP(S) (and IMAP, POP3, and SMTP) content for this legitimate dataset. The resulting payload data serves as ground truth to allow comparisons with potentially-malicious and benign responses.

3.6 HTTP Data Analysis

The HTTP data acquisition leaves us with huge datasets for further analysis. We aim to analyze the aggregated payload data as exhaustively as possible, however, given millions of HTTP responses, this is not feasible using a purely-manual process. We therefore use unsupervised learning to group similar responses. Later on, we manually analyze the resulting groups and augment them with descriptive labels. In the following, we describe this procedure in more detail.

Coarse-Grained Clustering: Grouping Similar HTTP Responses. In a first step, we aim to shrink the scale of the HTTP payload data that we need to manually inspect. We decided to use agglomerative hierarchical clustering, an unsupervised machine learning technique, which helps us to group similar responses into *clusters*. Hierarchical clustering is known to be helpful for inspecting the clustering results (e.g., using the dendrograms) and enables the analyst to understand the clustering steps (e.g., via the distance matrix).

In addition, hierarchical clustering allows us to define a custom distance function to measure the similarity of two individual HTTP responses. We deploy seven normalized features of equal weight as part of our distance function:

- Length difference of the HTTP response body as a first coarse-grained comparison feature.
- Jaccard distance (i.e., $\frac{A \cap B}{A \cup B}$) for multisets with the set of HTML tags in the HTTP payload.
- Edit distance between the sequence of opening HTML tags, whereas we convert each HTML tag to a 2-byte-long identifier to normalize all tags. In contrast to the previous tag multiset comparison, this feature also considers the order of the elements. It reflects the structural similarity between two web pages
- Edit distance on the `<title>` value. We focus on the title only for content comparison as it is rather constant. We do not consider any other texts, as these could highly differ for dynamic web pages.
- Edit distance of all JavaScript code. The motivation here is that many websites largely rely on JavaScript (e.g., AJAX) to control the content of the page.
- Lastly, each individual feature focuses on (i) embedded resources and (ii) outgoing links, respectively. Resources and links can be used to attack or track visitors. We compute the Jaccard distance for all embedded resources (i.e., the values of `src=""` attributes), and for outgoing links (i.e., the values of `href=""` attributes), respectively.

Clustering assists us in grouping similar representations of certain web pages, deliberately ignoring most of the (possibly dynamic) HTML content. In addition, clustering is tolerant to slight changes in the page structure. Similar instances are grouped using average linkage. This way, we can label all instances in a cluster once the cluster has been identified, largely reducing the manual inspection effort.

Fine-Grained Clustering: Finding Page Modifications. While our coarse-grained clustering step is helpful to group similar websites, it also abstracts from slight modifications in the HTML structure. This can be problematic, as we are interested in cases where a potential adversary uses a known representation of a website and modifies it. Therefore, we also use clustering to analyze the difference of websites compared to the respective legitimate representations (i.e., comparisons to the *ground truth*). The key idea is to find small, possibly malicious modifications (e.g., JavaScript injections) that were done to the original representation.

To this end, we first use the `diff` utility to find the exact differences between an unknown response and the legitimate representation(s) of a website. If we have multiple legitimate representations, we select the ground truth with the highest similarity for further processing. From the exact difference, we then extract which HTML tags were added and removed—the smaller these sets, the fewer modifications were done to the website. Again, we aim to group responses, but this time we are interested in similar *modifications*. We thus use hierarchical clustering based on the Jaccard distance for multisets for the tag differences between the unknown response and the (most similar) GT response.

4. EVALUATION ON BOGUS RESOLVERS

In the following, we present the findings of our analyses on open DNS resolvers. Our data is based on domain name scans and data aggregation between Jan 15 and Feb 10, 2015.

4.1 DNS-based Prefiltering

In the prefiltering process, we identified 85.8% (*MX* domain set) to 93.2% (*AV* set) of the aggregated DNS responses for the scanned domain sets (cf. Section 3.2) to be legitimate, considerably reducing the number of DNS responses we need to further analyze. Furthermore, 4.9–8.4% of the responses did not specify any IP addresses in the answer section. The highest value was observed for the *Malware* set, partially caused by DNS resolvers that aim to protect clients from accessing malicious domains. The number of *unexpected* ($domain \circ ip \circ resolver$) tuples ranges between 0.6% of all responses for the *MX* dataset and 4.4% for the *Malware* dataset, with a single exception for *NX* with 13.7% of unexpected responses. In total, we obtained 86,655,560 unexpected DNS responses (this does not include the empty DNS replies) from 19,180,169 distinct resolvers. Note that the high number of resolvers is caused by IP churn in combination with distributing our scanning activities over several days, as we often observed suspicious resolvers to switch to different IP addresses in the same ISPs' address spaces.

Up to 15.1% of the suspicious DNS resolvers for a particular domain set return their own IP for at least a single domain name. Moreover, 8,194 resolvers return their IP address for each requested domain in at least 75% of our domain sets. 5,404 of these IP addresses (65.9%) redirected to login web pages of routing equipment, distributed by two major manufacturers, while further 574 IPs (7.0%) are assigned to a specific brand of IP-based cameras. 50.4% of all suspicious DNS resolvers (i.e., 9,659,437 hosts) return the same set of IP addresses for more than one domain. In the extreme, 4.4% of all suspicious resolvers return even a single static IP address regardless of the domain name we queried. Further 2.0% return only `NS` records for the requested domain names, i.e., effectively denying recursive lookups.

4.2 HTTP Response Classification

When aggregating HTTP content for all unexpected DNS responses, we could obtain HTTP payload data for 88.9% of the ($domain \circ ip \circ resolver$) tuples. For the remaining 11.1% of tuples, we observe up to 65.1% of the suspicious DNS servers to return LAN IP addresses, while up to 32.2% replied with IP addresses located in the same AS or /24 network as the resolver. By taking a closer look at the rDNS records associated with these IP addresses we suspect some of the systems to belong to captive portals, which serve the actual login page to clients in specific IP ranges only. We verified other IP addresses to be associated with particular CDN providers (i.e., by checking AS and rDNS information). We assume these content servers to be disabled and not distributing actual HTTP(S) payload data, at least at the time of requesting content for our analysis. As such, certain resolvers might have delivered outdated IP address information for domain names associated with CDN providers.

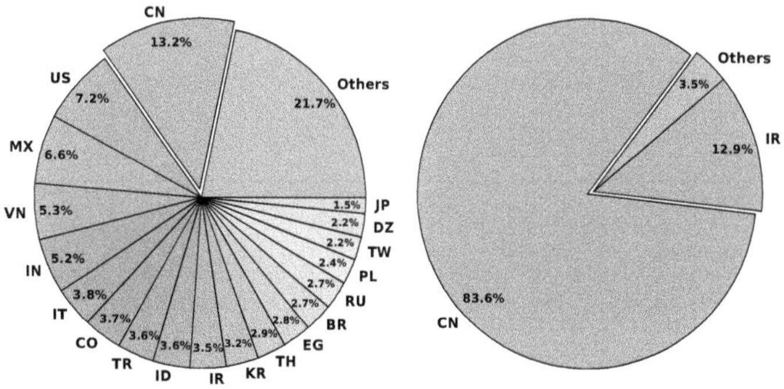

(a) All responses (b) Unexpected responses

Figure 4: Resolver distribution per country for the domain names of Facebook, Twitter, and YouTube for (a) all DNS responses and (b) unexpected responses only

For non-legitimate tuples which provided HTTP data, we were able to classify 97.6–99.9% of the HTTP content. In fact, we classified over 99% of the responses for all but one domain category, indicating a close-to-exhaustive coverage of our analysis. Our clustering mechanism helped to group similar HTTP responses and served as data exploration step to further categorize the results. That is, we assigned labels to each individual cluster and mapped these labels to website categories that classify the type of served HTTP content. Table 5 summarizes these classification results. We mapped the response labels according to the following six categories:

Blocking. This category consists of websites to which a client system is redirected when the requested domain name has been blocked. This includes landing pages of multiple providers (e.g., parental control, ISPs or security organizations) when accessing forbidden or malicious content. We observe this type of data particularly for malware domains (e.g., 12,543 systems, i.e., 21.4% of the suspicious resolvers for the Virut domain `irc.zief.pl`, redirected to IP addresses to block the respective requests) and dating domains (e.g., 6,961 resolvers blocked the dating page `okcupid.com`, i.e., 10.9% of the suspicious DNS resolvers for this domain).

Censorship. We observe hundreds of thousands of suspicious resolvers to respond to requests of specific domains with a small set of IP addresses which we identified as landing pages for censorship. To distinguish between ordinary blocking and censorship, we closely analyzed the HTTP content and the behavior of the resolvers. If we find HTML content to specify text fragments such as `blocked by the order of [...] court/authority`, we flag the IP to be associated with censorship. We manually verified that the 299 IPs of landing pages are related to 34 different countries.

Next to the landing pages, we identified another type of censorship. When analyzing the legitimate and unexpected responses for particular domain names, we observe a conspicuous distribution of countries for the corresponding DNS resolvers. Figure 4-a illustrates that DNS resolvers are widely distributed in terms of geographical location for the combined set of DNS responses for Facebook, Twitter, and YouTube. When isolating the unexpected DNS responses, we find the majority of DNS servers to be located in China.

Table 5: Clustering and labeling results of the HTTP payload data for unexpected (*domain* ∘ *ip* ∘ *resolver*) tuples

	Average number of resolvers in % / (Highest number of resolvers seen for a domain in the particular dataset in %)													
Label	*Ads*	*Adult*	*Alexa*	*Antivirus*	*Banking*	*Dating*	*Filesharing*	*Gambling*	*GroundTr.*	*Malware*	*Misc.*	*MX*	*NX*	*Tracking*
Blocking	0.3	2.2	0.7	0.3	0.4	6.2	3.1	3.7	0.2	9.0	0.9	0.9	1.9	0.6
	(0.5)	(3.3)	(2.5)	(0.4)	(1.0)	(10.9)	(6.5)	(6.4)	(0.2)	(21.4)	(4.8)	(1.9)	(16.2)	(2.2)
Censorship	10.8	88.6	19.1	0.1	0.1	31.8	36.5	75.9	0.1	0.8	8.4	0.1	3.2	0.1
	(96.2)	(91.3)	(97.1)	(0.1)	(0.1)	(87.3)	(91.3)	(90.4)	(0.1)	(8.1)	(92.5)	(0.2)	(37.1)	(0.1)
HTTP Error	48.1	5.2	45.8	57.0	55.4	34.8	32.6	15.8	55.0	29.8	50.8	57.0	24.7	57.0
	(70.4)	(6.9)	(63.9)	(75.0)	(63.5)	(50.1)	(52.0)	(49.8)	(56.0)	(53.7)	(71.1)	(65.9)	(55.8)	(69.4)
Login	12.2	1.2	12.8	15.5	16.8	10.2	9.5	1.9	16.1	9.5	14.3	17.0	2.8	12.5
	(16.8)	(1.6)	(19.1)	(17.4)	(19.6)	(15.4)	(15.1)	(3.9)	(17.2)	(17.2)	(18.5)	(19.8)	(9.4)	(16.2)
Misc.	11.5	0.9	5.3	5.9	5.0	3.2	4.9	0.7	5.1	3.3	5.1	5.0	8.5	11.2
	(56.4)	(1.6)	(21.6)	(16.2)	(10.5)	(4.8)	(12.5)	(1.4)	(5.8)	(5.6)	(9.7)	(5.8)	(19.7)	(5.5)
Parking	17.1	1.8	16.1	21.2	22.2	13.8	13.4	2.0	23.4	26.2	20.5	20.0	23.2	18.6
	(23.9)	(2.4)	(24.0)	(25.0)	(24.3)	(21.5)	(22.4)	(2.4)	(23.9)	(92.1)	(83.6)	(23.4)	(42.4)	(24.0)
Search	0.0	0.1	0.2	0.0	0.1	0.0	0.0	0.0	0.1	21.4	0.0	0.0	35.7	0.0
	(0.1)	(0.1)	(2.7)	(0.1)	(0.1)	(0.1)	(0.0)	(0.0)	(0.6)	(69.3)	(0.5)	(0.1)	(65.1)	(0.0)

Interestingly, 2.4% of the Chinese resolvers (125,660 hosts) returned multiple DNS responses for particular domains: the first response specified a forged IP, while the second includes the legitimate IP address(es) for the requested domain, yet arriving a few milliseconds after receiving the bogus response. This effect is caused by the *Great Firewall of China* [3, 22, 42], which injects forged DNS responses upon monitoring DNS requests in the network traffic. Succeeding experiments underpin this assumption, as we obtain arbitrary IPs for specific domains when sending requests to randomly chosen IP ranges in Chinese networks, while requesting other domains does not trigger any response. We thus assume the *Great Firewall of China* to not modify responses of DNS resolvers but inject forged replies that (likely) arrive before the legitimate DNS responses at the client-side.

Figure 4-b outlines that 83.6% of the suspicious resolvers found for the domains Facebook, Twitter, and YouTube (i.e., 5,235,827 systems in total) are located in China, apparently returning randomly-chosen IP addresses. Further 805,559 systems (i.e., 12.9% of the suspicious resolvers for the three domains) are associated with Iranian censorship.

Besides China and Iran, we find more than 3 million resolvers that support censorship in other countries. Moreover, 491,032 resolvers (i.e., 74.2% of the hosts returning unexpected IP addresses for `adultfinder.com`) are associated with Indonesian censorship. Further 90.6% of the suspicious resolvers for domain *youporn.com* (696,777 systems in total) redirected to hosts that belong to Turkish (52.9%), Indonesian (29.3%), and Malaysian (8.4%) censorship. Yet, we also find Italian and Russian resolvers to be prevalent for *Filesharing* and *Gambling* domains. 92.1% of the suspicious resolvers for `rotten.com` (813,183 resolvers in total) are associated equally to Indonesian and Turkish censorship. For the domain `blogspot.com`, 396,681 resolvers (i.e., 88.5% of all suspicious DNS resolvers found for this domain name) redirected to IP addresses linked to Indonesian censorship.

Observing the prevalence of censorship in various countries, we wondered whether we observe all DNS resolvers located in a particular country to comply with censorship, indicating a strict policy or a government-controlled censorship system. We thus enumerated all resolvers that returned legitimate and unexpected responses by their geographical location and checked whether we find any DNS resolvers in a country to return legitimate responses, while others redirected to IP addresses assigned to censorship mechanisms.

For China, we indeed observe a high coverage: 99.7% of the Chinese resolvers returned bogus responses for Facebook, Twitter, and YouTube. For all other censoring countries, including Asia and Europe, we observe a lower coverage of blocking resolvers. 78.9% of the Mongolian resolvers blocked each of the four adult domains. For Indonesia, we observe varying numbers of resolvers blocking individual domains: a single adult domain is blocked by 91.6% of the Indonesian resolvers, while only 28.7% of the resolvers block another gambling and adult domain. In Europe, 83.9% of the Greek and 78.6% of the Belgian DNS resolvers restricted access to two gambling domains. Similarly, 69.3% of the Italian resolvers comply with censorship by blocking multiple online betting domains. Finally, 10.0% of the Turkish DNS resolvers did *not* censor otherwise-blocked domain names.

HTTP Error. This category includes web servers that either return HTTP error codes (`4xx`, `5xx`), respectively, error pages indicating invalid requests. Except for the domain sets *Adult* and *Gambling*—for which we find the majority of resolvers to return IP addresses assigned to censorship—an average of 40.6% of the suspicious resolvers per domain set directed to systems that serve various types of error pages, indicating that the requested content could not be found.

Login. About 10.9% of the suspicious DNS resolvers per domain set direct users to login websites, ranging from captive portals of ISPs, hotels, and educational institutions to router login pages and web mail logins. We observe 91.7% of the suspicious resolvers assigned to this category to forward client systems to login pages of routing equipment, manufactured by two large distributors of networking devices.

Parking. This category includes landing pages of parking providers, domain resellers, and hosting companies offering similar services. Parking can be observed most for the *Malware* domain set. 92.1% of the suspicious DNS resolvers for two of three Chinese domains in the *Malware* set (i.e., 1,371,67 systems) returned IP addresses that are linked to parking. It is known that domain resellers and parking providers tend to re-register malicious domain names to monetize the traffic [18, 20]. Yet, 261,116 systems (83.6% of the suspicious DNS resolvers for `torproject.org`) also redirect to parked content upon requesting this domain.

Search. The *Search* category groups all redirections to legitimate or mimicries of search pages. Responses like this are common for *NX* domain names—we find 35.7% of the suspicious DNS resolvers to redirect to search websites. Similar results were also observed for six out of 13 malware domains—even though these domains were existing when performing our scans. Similarly to parked domains, search websites might embed ad banners to monetize the traffic.

4.3 Miscellaneous Case Studies

Most of the HTTP content that was delivered by IP addresses in the non-legitimate DNS responses could be assigned to one of the categories outlined in Table 5. Yet, our in-depth analyses of HTTP(S), IMAP, POP3, and SMTP payload data also enabled us to classify content that was returned by a low number of suspicious resolvers. For reasons of brevity, we highlight the most interesting cases only.

Ad Redirects / Injections. We observe 281 suspicious DNS resolvers to return four IP addresses that redirected, respectively, replaced ad traffic of two large advertisement providers. Two of these hosts inject ad banners directly into the HTML content, while the other two IP addresses serve suspicious JavaScript code. We identify seven IP addresses from 14 suspicious resolvers that block ad traffic on purpose by replacing the ad banners with empty placeholders. Furthermore, two IP addresses were returned by seven DNS resolvers that serve content similar to the Google search web page, yet embedding ad banners underneath the search bar.

Transparent Proxies. We identify 20 IP addresses to act as proxies for all domain names, providing the same content as obtained from the original websites. We distinguish between proxies that support TLS encryption and provide the original certificate, and proxies that do not offer HTTPS. For proxies that forward valid certificate information for the requested domain names, we observe 99 DNS resolvers to return the associated 10 IP addresses. TLS prevents a potential eavesdropper from reading the actual content, yet traffic analysis may reveal insights to an adversary [11, 35]. In contrast, HTTP-only proxies might immediately eavesdrop on the communication channel, e.g., to sniff for credentials of login pages. We find 10,179 suspicious resolvers to return 10 IP addresses that proxy the original content, without accepting HTTPS requests. While we do not suspect all of these hosts to be malicious, users risk disclosing sensible login credentials when relying on these servers.

Phishing. Next to the proxies that serve original content for all requested domains, we also observe 39 hosts returned by 1,360 resolvers that provide content for particular domains only—potentially phishing for credentials. For PayPal, 176 resolvers served 16 IPs that provide content similar to the PayPal website. Yet, when investigating the HTML structure, we could reveal a phishing attempt: the body consists of 46 `<img>` tags reproducing the PayPal website and an HTML form that attempts to forward the entered login credentials to a `php` file via HTTP `POST`. Three of these servers accept HTTPS connections with self-signed certificates. Moreover, two suspicious phishing servers mimic an Italian banking domain. The first server is returned by 285 DNS resolvers and located in a Brazilian network. The second host is returned by 46 DNS resolvers and located in Russia. While the legitimate banking domain solely accepts HTTPS requests, none of the suspicious IP addresses does.

Mail Servers. We observe 64.7% of the suspicious DNS resolvers for the *MX* domain set to redirect to 1,135 IP addresses that listen to mail communication via IMAP, POP3, or SMTP. While we do not find any evidence of mail servers actively harvesting for login credentials (i.e., by attempting to log in with fake credentials and sending emails), attackers could secretly sniff on traffic. For Gmail and Yandex, we observe eight resolvers to point to IPs that provide similar or exactly the same banner information for SMTP as monitored for the legitimate SMTP servers. However, these bogus IPs are located in different networks (e.g., a Chinese research network), indicating that these might be suspicious.

Malware. Finally, 228 DNS resolvers redirect client systems to 30 distinct IP addresses that provide content similar to Adobe Flash and Java update pages, convincing the user to install potential software updates. We found these executables to be linked to malicious software. That is, we analyzed the samples dynamically and observed them to attempt downloading further (potentially malicious) executables. In line with our observations, the majority of anti-virus vendors classified these samples as malware downloaders.

5. DISCUSSION

We now discuss limitations of our methodology and conducted analyses, respectively, the DNS protocol in general.

Completeness. Performing Internet-wide DNS analyses implies several limitations on the significance of the obtained network data. First, DNS is a UDP-based protocol. As such, we might not obtain a response for each of our DNS requests due to packet loss. Second, a DNS packet might be corrupted, i.e., the checksum of the underlying UDP packet is invalid. As we do not know which part of the packet is bogus, we ignore invalid packets in all of our analyses. Also, our analyses are limited to *open* resolvers, while there is no reason to assume that closed resolvers do not likewise manipulate resolutions. Analyzing such resolvers, however, requires in-network measurement points such as Netalyzr [16].

Another concern regarding completeness is IP churn. DNS resolvers associated with dynamic broadband Internet links might be enumerated multiple times when they occasionally switch to IP addresses that are scanned in the later course of a DNS scan. Further, we might miss (parts of) the DNS responses in our domain scans when DNS resolvers become unavailable. Determining the error rate, however, is unfeasible as resolvers might simply ignore particular requests, as observed for censorship or badly configured resolvers. Hence, we cannot distinguish between requests that are unanswered on purpose or due to the above-mentioned limitations. Furthermore, the number of identified resolvers fluctuates per day and time we perform our scans. As such, when initiating multiple IPv4 scans on the same day, the number of active resolvers might differ due to the various geographical locations and time zones. To cope with these limitations, we adjusted the rate of outgoing DNS requests to achieve a low packet loss and started our weekly scans at the same time (on Friday evenings CET). To reduce the impact of IP churn, we scanned the domains in a timely manner, i.e., the delay between an Internet-wide scan and the aggregation of HTTP data (and potentially requesting further domains at these resolvers upon redirections) was at most 8 hours.

In order to scale, our domain set is limited to 155 domain names of 13 different categories that could be relevant for DNS response forgery. As such, our dataset is far from complete and we consequently miss suspicious activities for domains that are not covered by the set. Performing analyses on dozens or hundreds of additional domains, however, would significantly increase the impact on the individual resolvers as well as the amount of data that needs to be processed in a timely manner. Furthermore, the dataset would still remain incomplete, as attackers may choose arbitrary domain names to perform suspicious or malicious activities.

Our evaluation results are constrained to suspicious DNS activities performed in the period from Jan 15 to Feb 10, 2015, thus rather represent a snapshot of the DNS threat landscape. Repeated analyses could have been performed, however, we refrained from doing so for multiple reasons. First, as we aimed to obtain a detailed understanding of all suspicious DNS resolvers in IPv4 at once, we performed one large evaluation instead of conducting (repeated) smaller analyses on subsets of open resolvers, which would increase the impact on these servers. Second, we assume that repeated analyses will only provide minor changes in the DNS threat landscape, thus do not justify repeated scanning.

Finally, we used heuristics and clustering to group DNS and HTTP responses. This way, we could label about 99% of the responses, leaving a minor percentage unclassified. We argue that the remaining responses represent rather uninteresting behavior, as attackers typically strive for larger coverage (thus would have been identified in our analyses). We still manually investigated a random sample set of the unclassified HTTP responses and found them to be associated with personal, shopping, or similar categories of websites.

Illegitimacy. Multiple IP addresses acted as an HTTP(S) proxy between a client system and a web server of the requested domain name. As such, we obtained similar or the same HTML content as provided by the legitimate IP address(es). By analyzing the HTTP payload of websites only, we are limited to identifying IP addresses that could potentially be performing malicious activities. That is, we have no evidence of eavesdropping activities, yet attackers could trivially sniff on traffic (especially for HTTP-only proxies).

We queried dozens of domain names at millions of open DNS resolvers, causing network traffic which might unintentionally harm a remote network. Within our long-term empirical measurement study of DNS resolvers, however, we have not received a single abuse complaint that our Internet-wide scanning activities caused a congestion of either an open resolver or an AuthNS of a scanned domain. As such, we assume the combination of rate-limiting the outgoing DNS requests and distributing the sequence of target IP addresses over time using an LFSR to be reasonable in practice.

In addition, one has to be careful judging certain politically-driven actions (such as censorship) as "malicious". Tolerating the constitutions and cultures of other countries, we merely provide our rational insights and technical inputs.

DNS Authenticity. The DNS protocol—in general—does not deploy any security measures to validate the data authenticity of DNS responses, hence security extensions such as DNSSEC [5] have been proposed and implemented. It yet has to be evaluated whether the DNS extensions also protect against strong "adversaries" such as the Chinese firewall, which inject forged DNS responses that arrive way ahead of the legitimate replies at the requesting clients. As a resolver typically utilizes the first response that matches an open transaction (and ignores succeeding responses), DNSSEC does not effectively protect against this kind of attack unless the client *waits* for a correctly signed DNS response and drops all previously incoming unsigned and incorrectly signed replies [5, 6, 43]. Yet, this strategy can be deployed only when either (i) all domains globally deploy DNSSEC, or (ii) the client gained previous knowledge that the particular domain indeed supports DNSSEC, thus only a signed DNS response is acceptable at all. As of May 2015, the global coverage of DNSSEC was rather low [21, 37, 38], e.g., less than 0.6% of the domains associated with the `.net` TLD operated DNSSEC. Further, there is no reliable way for a client to determine the state of the DNSSEC deployment for specific domains (except by performing DNS requests and check the replies—yet these could also be forged). As such, the DNS protocol and its security extensions may require improvements to cope with attacks or censorship measures such as packet injections conducted by the *Great Firewall of China*.

6. RELATED WORK

This work is inspired by the analysis of corrupted DNS resolution paths by Dagon et al. [10] in 2008. The authors analyzed DNS resolutions of 600,000 open resolvers for 84 domain names to identify suspicious responses. Similar to our work, they requested `A` records for various banking, antivirus, and search engine websites. The aggregated responses, however, were analyzed and presented rather coarse-grained, i.e., the authors performed a manual analysis on 250 randomly sampled web pages only and did not provide detailed statistics about their findings—except illustrating a limited number of categories such as Chinese splash pages. Furthermore, it remains rather unclear how the authors identified the legitimate IP addresses of each domain, particularly important when filtering IP addresses of CDNs that may span hundreds of ASes. In our work, we outline our prefiltering and identification of legitimate IP addresses in detail and perform a more fine-granular and thorough analysis of the unexpected DNS responses to cluster and classify non-legitimate DNS responses accordingly, resulting in a more comprehensive overview of the DNS resolver behavior. As such, we are the first to perform an in-depth analysis of incorrect DNS resolutions provided by all open DNS resolvers operated in the entire IPv4 address space. That is, we were capable of labeling about 99% of the obtained DNS and HTTP responses, achieving fine-granular classification results on the DNS resolution paths of open DNS resolvers.

Prior work by Weaver et al. [40, 41] analyzed DNS traffic aggregated from Netalyzr sessions, a Java-based applet running on individual client systems of volunteers. The authors mostly focused on DNS error monetization—a technique to redirect clients to ad websites upon requests for non-existent domains. Yet, the authors also observed sessions, in which DNS resolvers redirect clients to websites of malicious character or deliberately disabled the resolution of the Windows update website to prevent system updates. Unfortunately, it remains unclear how the authors identified the corresponding DNS servers to block the update page on purpose and not due to erroneous configurations. The results further provide rather little insight, as the analyses were conducted on limited DNS traffic, and as such the number of analyzed DNS resolvers was low. Contrary, we perform a large-scale analysis on all resolvers in the entire IPv4, achieving a more detailed insight to the resolvers' landscape. Still, a benefit of the approach proposed by Weaver et al. is the detection of suspicious and malicious DNS resolutions caused by closed DNS resolvers, while we have to stick to the analysis of open DNS resolvers only. Combining both approaches thus presumably increases the detection of forged DNS resolutions.

We group further related works by their topic.

Measurements on the DNS Protocol. A large body of work exists on analyzing DNS resolvers [1, 4, 25, 33]. Most of these analyses are conducted on a small subset of all resolvers. As such, it is unclear if the observed results generalize to all resolvers world-wide. Sisson [34] analyzes open resolvers based on sampled scans that repeatedly query the same set of resolvers, thus covering only a small fraction of all open resolvers. We omit a detailed comparison, as Sisson scans only known AuthNS and resolvers contacting their AuthNS, therefore relying on a non-random sample. Overall, their measurements cover less than 0.2% of the resolvers in our dataset. Jiang et al. [15] analyzed the caching behavior of resolvers. The authors identified an attack vector in DNS software that allows to extend the caching of domains even after they have been removed from the upper DNS hierarchy. Schomp et al. [31] randomly probed the IPv4 address space to enumerate DNS resolvers and distinguish between recursive DNS resolvers and DNS proxies. Furthermore, the authors closely analyzed the caching behavior of resolvers in more detail. Similar to our work, the authors performed device fingerprinting of the identified DNS resolvers, yet without providing an overview of the results. The authors further focused on device information provided by the HTTP header only, thus missing various device categories, e.g., provided by the HTTP body, respectively, other protocols such as FTP and Telnet. Takano et al. [36] performed measurements based on responses for Internet-wide CHAOS `version.bind` requests. The authors primarily focused on DNS server software and their distribution in each *Regional Internet Registry*. Contrary to our work, no device fingerprinting was conducted. Concurrent to our work, Scott et al. [32] probed the IPv4 address space for open resolvers to analyze DNS resolutions. Instead of focusing on suspicious DNS resolution paths, the authors queried the Top 10,000 Alexa domain names at the identified resolvers to analyze the infrastructure of *Content Delivery Networks*. By deploying automated clustering mechanisms, they were capable of accurately detecting CDN deployments in their scanning results. Contrary, we performed the identification of CDNs by leveraging AS, rDNS, and HTTPS certificate information in our prefiltering step. Combining both techniques could improve the detection capabilities of CDNs and thus the effectiveness of our prefiltering, reducing the amount of unfiltered but legitimate DNS responses that needs to be processed in the latter processing steps.

Censorship. Bailey and Labovitz [7] provided an overview of various countries restricting access to certain websites. Verkamp and Gupta [39] focused on how censorship is technically implemented. By using PlanetLab nodes and personal contacts in various countries, the authors identified all eleven examined countries to perform censorship, either by filtering at the DNS-level or directly on URLs and keywords. In contrast, we obtained responses directly from arbitrary DNS resolvers world-wide. As such, our results are not derived from a limited number of hosts per country. Levis [19] focused on censorship conducted by injecting forged DNS packets into network traffic, e.g., performed by the *Great Firewall of China* [3, 22, 42]. The author claims that Chinese censorship may not only affect clients in China but also systems in other countries when their DNS traffic is routed through China via transit—an observation we can confirm for our datasets. Apart from China, similar behavior is also observed for other countries, e.g., 56.9% of the Estonian DNS resolvers respond with IP addresses for gambling domains that we assigned to Russian censorship.

Internet-wide Scanning. Durumeric et al. [12] proposed ZMap, a high-speed application to run Internet-wide scans. While we do not leverage ZMap for our scans, we apply many of the guidelines and techniques. Rossow [29] and Kührer et al. [17] performed Internet-wide scans for multiple UDP- and TCP-based protocols to identify and monitor systems that are prone to abuse for amplification DDoS attacks.

7. CONCLUSION

In this paper, we studied the landscape of DNS resolvers on long term, i.e., we analyzed empirical data of Internet-wide DNS scans we performed for more than one year. More precisely, we analyzed the fluctuation of DNS resolvers over time and classified the resolvers according to the operated DNS server software, underlying hardware specifications, and their utilization by actual client systems. To analyze further attack vectors in the *Domain Name System*, we took the viewpoint of a client system and determined the response authenticity and integrity of all open DNS resolvers in the entire IPv4 address space. By performing billions of DNS lookup requests for 155 domains at millions of open resolvers, we identified millions of resolvers that deliberately manipulated DNS resolutions and returned unexpected IP address information. Besides legitimate redirections (e.g., to captive portals such as router login pages), our analyses revealed thousands of resolvers that manipulated DNS resolutions to censor communication channels, inject advertisements, serve malicious files, or perform phishing. As such, the DNS protocol does not only have flaws at the network-level in terms of traffic amplification vulnerabilities [17, 24, 29] but also lack verification mechanisms at the application-level to sufficiently protect end hosts from malicious resolvers that redirect clients to suspicious content.

Acknowledgment

This work was supported by the German Federal Ministry of Education and Research (BMBF Grant 01IS14009B BDSec). We would like to thank our shepherd Georgios Smaragdakis for his support in finalizing this paper and the anonymous reviewers for their constructive and valuable comments.

8. REFERENCES

[1] AGER, B., MÜHLBAUER, W., SMARAGDAKIS, G., AND UHLIG, S. Comparing DNS Resolvers in the Wild. In *Internet Measurement Conference* (2010).

[2] ALEXA INTERNET, INC. Top 1 Million Traffic Ranking. `http://www.alexa.com/topsites/`.

[3] ANONYMOUS. Towards a Comprehensive Picture of the Great Firewall's DNS Censorship. In *USENIX Workshop on Free and Open Communications on the Internet* (2014).

[4] ANTONAKAKIS, M., DAGON, D., LUO, X., PERDISCI, R., LEE, W., AND BELLMOR, J. A Centralized Monitoring Infrastructure for Improving DNS Security. In *Symposium on Recent Advances in Intrusion Detection* (2010).

[5] Arends, R., Austein, R., Larson, M., Massey, D., and Rose, S. RFC 4033: DNS Security Introduction and Requirements, 2005.

[6] Atkins, D., and Austein, R. RFC 3833: Threat Analysis of the Domain Name System (DNS), 2004.

[7] Bailey, M., and Labovitz, C. Censorship and Co-option of the Internet Infrastructure. *Ann Arbor 1001* (2011).

[8] Blackford, J., and Digdon, M. TR-069, CPE WAN Management Protocol, CWMP Version: 1.4. `http://www.broadband-forum.org/technical/download/TR-069_Amendment-5.pdf`, 2013.

[9] Dagon, D., Antonakakis, M., Vixie, P., Jinmei, T., and Lee, W. Increased DNS Forgery Resistance Through 0x20-Bit Encoding: SecURItY viA LeET QueRieS. In *ACM Conference on Computer and Communications Security* (2008).

[10] Dagon, D., Provos, N., Lee, C. P., and Lee, W. Corrupted DNS Resolution Paths: The Rise of a Malicious Resolution Authority. In *Symposium on Network and Distributed System Security* (2008).

[11] Danezis, G. Traffic Analysis of the HTTP Protocol over TLS. `http://www0.cs.ucl.ac.uk/staff/G.Danezis/papers/TLSanon.pdf`, 2009.

[12] Durumeric, Z., Wustrow, E., and Halderman, J. A. ZMap: Fast Internet-Wide Scanning and its Security Applications. In *USENIX Security Symposium* (2013).

[13] Eastlake, D. RFC 5395: Domain Name System (DNS) IANA Considerations, 2008.

[14] Grangeia, L. DNS Cache Snooping. Tech. rep., Securi Team-Beyond Security, 2004.

[15] Jiang, J., Liang, J., Li, K., Li, J., Duan, H., and Wu, J. Ghost Domain Names Revoked Yet Still Resolvable. In *Symposium on Network and Distributed System Security* (2012).

[16] Kreibich, C., Weaver, N., Nechaev, B., and Paxson, V. Netalyzr: Illuminating The Edge Network. In *Internet Measurement Conference* (2010).

[17] Kührer, M., Hupperich, T., Rossow, C., and Holz, T. Exit from Hell? Reducing the Impact of Amplification DDoS Attacks. In *USENIX Security Symposium* (2014).

[18] Kührer, M., Rossow, C., and Holz, T. Paint It Black: Evaluating the Effectiveness of Malware Blacklists. In *Symposium on Recent Advances in Intrusion Detection* (2014).

[19] Levis, P. The Collateral Damage of Internet Censorship by DNS Injection. *ACM SIGCOMM CCR 42*, 3 (2012).

[20] Li, Z., Alrwais, S., Xie, Y., Yu, F., and Wang, X. Finding the Linchpins of the Dark Web: A Study on Topologically Dedicated Hosts on Malicious Web Infrastructures. In *IEEE Symposium on Security and Privacy* (2013).

[21] Lian, W., Rescorla, E., Shacham, H., and Savage, S. Measuring the Practical Impact of DNSSEC Deployment. In *USENIX Security Symposium* (2013).

[22] Lowe, G., Winters, P., and Marcus, M. L. The Great DNS Wall of China. *MS, New York University 21* (2007).

[23] M. Prince; CloudFlare, Inc. `http://blog.cloudflare.com/the-ddos-that-almost-broke-the-internet`, March 2013.

[24] MacFarland, D. C., Shue, C. A., and Kalafut, A. J. Characterizing Optimal DNS Amplification Attacks and Effective Mitigation. In *Passive and Active Measurement Conference* (2015).

[25] Mao, Z. M., Cranor, C. D., Douglis, F., Rabinovich, M., Spatscheck, O., and Wang, J. A Precise and Efficient Evaluation of the Proximity Between Web Clients and Their Local DNS Servers. In *USENIX Annual Technical Conference* (2002).

[26] MaxMind GeoIP Database. `http://www.maxmind.com/en/ip-location`.

[27] Open Resolver Project. `http://openresolverproject.org/`.

[28] Rajab, M. A., Monrose, F., Terzis, A., and Provos, N. Peeking Through the Cloud: DNS-Based Estimation and Its Applications. In *Applied Cryptography and Network Security* (2008).

[29] Rossow, C. Amplification Hell: Revisiting Network Protocols for DDoS Abuse. In *Symposium on Network and Distributed System Security* (2014).

[30] Rossow, C., Dietrich, C. J., Bos, H., Cavallaro, L., van Steen, M., Freiling, F. C., and Pohlmann, N. Sandnet: Network Traffic Analysis of Malicious Software. In *Workshop on Building Analysis Datasets and Gathering Experience Returns for Security* (2011).

[31] Schomp, K., Callahan, T., Rabinovich, M., and Allman, M. On Measuring the Client-Side DNS Infrastructure. In *Internet Measurement Conference* (2013).

[32] Scott, W., Berg, S., and Krishnamurth, A. Satellite: Observations of the Internet's Star. Tech. rep., University of Washington, 2015.

[33] Shue, C. A., and Kalafut, A. J. Resolvers Revealed: Characterizing DNS Resolvers and their Clients. *ACM Transactions on Internet Technology 12*, 4 (2013), 14.

[34] Sisson, G. DNS Survey: October 2010. Tech. rep., The Measurement Factory, 2010.

[35] Sun, Q., Simon, D. R., Wang, Y.-M., Russell, W., Padmanabhan, V. N., and Qiu, L. Statistical Identification of Encrypted Web Browsing Traffic. In *IEEE Symposium on Security and Privacy* (2002).

[36] Takano, Y., Ando, R., Takahashi, T., Uda, S., and Inoue, T. A Measurement Study of Open Resolvers and DNS Server Version. In *Internet Conference (IEICE)* (2013).

[37] van Rijswijk-Deij, R., Sperotto, A., and Pras, A. DNSSEC and Its Potential for DDoS Attacks: A Comprehensive Measurement Study. In *Internet Measurement Conference* (2014).

[38] VeriSign, Inc. DNSSEC Scoreboard. `http://scoreboard.verisignlabs.com/`.

[39] Verkamp, J.-P., and Gupta, M. Inferring Mechanics of Web Censorship Around the World. *Free and Open Communications on the Internet* (2012).

[40] Weaver, N., Kreibich, C., Nechaev, B., and Paxson, V. Implications of Netalyzr's DNS Measurements. In *Workshop on Securing and Trusting Internet Names* (2011).

[41] Weaver, N., Kreibich, C., and Paxson, V. Redirecting DNS for Ads and Profit. In *USENIX Workshop on Free and Open Communications on the Internet* (2011).

[42] Xu, X., Mao, Z. M., and Halderman, J. A. Internet Censorship in China: Where Does the Filtering Occur? In *Passive and Active Measurement Conference* (2011).

[43] Zmijewski, E. DNS: When Governments Lie. `http://research.dyn.com/2010/12/dns-when-governments-lie-2/`, December 2010.

Who is .com? Learning to Parse WHOIS Records

Suqi Liu
suqi@cs.ucsd.edu

Ian Foster
idfoster@cs.ucsd.edu

Stefan Savage
savage@cs.ucsd.edu

Geoffrey M. Voelker
voelker@cs.ucsd.edu

Lawrence K. Saul
saul@cs.ucsd.edu

Department of Computer Science and Engineering
University of California, San Diego

ABSTRACT

WHOIS is a long-established protocol for querying information about the 280M+ registered domain names on the Internet. Unfortunately, while such records are accessible in a "human-readable" format, they do not follow any consistent schema and thus are challenging to analyze at scale. Existing approaches, which rely on manual crafting of parsing rules and per-registrar templates, are inherently limited in coverage and fragile to ongoing changes in data representations. In this paper, we develop a statistical model for parsing WHOIS records that learns from labeled examples. Our model is a conditional random field (CRF) with a small number of hidden states, a large number of domain-specific features, and parameters that are estimated by efficient dynamic-programming procedures for probabilistic inference. We show that this approach can achieve extremely high accuracy (well over 99%) using modest amounts of labeled training data, that it is robust to minor changes in schema, and that it can adapt to new schema variants by incorporating just a handful of additional examples. Finally, using our parser, we conduct an exhaustive survey of the registration patterns found in 102M `com` domains.

Categories and Subject Descriptors

I.5.4 [**Pattern Recognition**]: Applications—*Text processing*; C.2.3 [**Computer-Communication Networks**]: Network Operations—*Public networks*; K.4.1 [**Computer and Society**]: Public Policy Issues

General Terms

Measurement

Keywords

WHOIS; Named Entity Recognition; Machine Learning; Information Extraction

IMC'15, October 28–30, 2015, Tokyo, Japan.
 ISBN 978-1-4503-3848-6/15/10 ...$15.00.
DOI: http://dx.doi.org/10.1145/2815675.2815693.

1. INTRODUCTION

Most common Internet protocols today offer standardized syntax and schemas. Indeed, it is the ability to easily parse and normalize protocol fields that directly enables a broad array of network measurement research (e.g., comparing and correlating from disparate data sources including BGP route tables, TCP flow data and DNS measurements). By contrast, the WHOIS protocol—the sole source of information mapping domain names to their rich ownership and administrative context—is standard only in its transport mechanism, while the format and contents of the registration data returned varies tremendously among providers. This situation significantly hampers large-scale analyses using WHOIS data, and even those researchers who do use it commonly document the complexities and limitations in doing so [1, 7, 8, 17, 24, 25, 26]. While there are a number of open source and commercial WHOIS parsers available, the lack of an underlying data schema requires them to constantly update hand-written parsing rules or templates, both limiting coverage and increasing fragility to format changes. For example, in one recent study of domain name registration, Janos reports that the tool used (*PHPWhois*) was only able to parse registrant information for 65% of their data [25]. Overall, the situation is well summarized in a recent statement by the Coalition Against Unsolicited Commercial Email (CAUCE):

> Currently whois is offered on something of a "hobbyist" basis, particularly in TLDs that use the "thin" whois model. At one provider it will use one format, while at other times and at other providers, it will use another. This lack of consistent formatting, along with restrictive access policies, makes whois access something that's only suitable for small scale interactive "craft" access rather than being a production-ready and robust service that's appropriate for the volume of domains and other resources involved in today's domain name ecosystem [2].

In this paper, we offer a statistical, data-driven approach to tackling the WHOIS parsing problem. Since such data is designed to be "human-readable" [4], we hypothesize that modest amounts of labeled data could be sufficient to train a more general model. To this end, we show that conditional random fields (CRFs) [15]—a popular class of models for problems in statistical language processing—are particularly well-suited to the problem of parsing WHOIS records. Using a highly customized CRF, we show that 100 random training examples are sufficient to obtain over 98% parsing accuracy on com WHOIS records and 1000 such examples brings accuracy to well over 99%. Historically, com is operated using a "thin" registry model that places no limits on format diversity and is, by far, the hardest top-level domain (TLD) to parse—yet, com accounts for 45% of all registered domains in the Internet. Moreover, we demonstrate that this model generalizes well to other TLDs and is robust in the sense that deviations or evolutions in data format are incorporated into the model with a handful of additional labeled examples. Finally, using our trained statistical parser, we systematically crawl and parse the com WHOIS registration data. Using this data set, our final contribution is to provide an initial characterization of com registration data.

2. BACKGROUND

The WHOIS protocol was introduced in the early 1980s to provide directory information for domains, people and resources (e.g., the IP address space). Over time it has become the principal mechanism by which outside stakeholders associate registered domain names with corresponding metadata such as the identity of the registrar, the registrant and contact information for administrative and technical issues. Among these uses, ICANN identifies the following: *allowing network administrators to find and fix system problems, determining domain name availability, combating inappropriate uses such as spam or fraud, facilitating the identification of trademark infringement and enhancing domain registrant accountability* [14]. Unfortunately, for a variety of reasons, WHOIS data is stored in a wide assortment of unstructured text formats and thus, while it is easily human readable, bulk systematic parsing of WHOIS data is challenging in practice. Indeed, when the National Opinion Research Center (NORC) was contracted to study WHOIS data accuracy for ICANN, they only examined 2,400 domains in com and net and admitted that "many domains need[ed] to be parsed by hand" [13].

In the remainder of this section, we briefly outline the evolution of WHOIS operations, explain how this evolution has produced the data parsing challenges faced today, and review the limitations of current approaches for addressing this problem.

2.1 History

First standardized in 1982, WHOIS was closely derived from the contemporary FINGER protocol, and defined a simple text-based request response protocol (via TCP port 43) with no formal requirements on data content or format [12].[1] At the time, all such requests were handled by a single server (src-nic.arpa), operating on behalf of a single U.S. government organization (the Defense Communications Agency) and thus there was little need for a formal data schema standard. However, with the commercial and international federation of the Internet, this model came under significant pressure. By the late 1990s, commercial domain registration had become a big business and a source of considerable conflict.[2] Ultimately, it was decided to open domain registration to competition and move overall governance to a non-governmental body, the Internet Corporation for Assigned Names and Numbers (ICANN).

[1]The second iteration of the WHOIS specification, RFC954, requests that each individual on the ARPANET or MILNET register with their full name, U.S. mailing address, ZIP code, telephone number and e-mail address. These requirements were removed in the subsequent version, RFC 3912, reflecting the Internet's increasingly international nature.

[2]This conflict reaches its apex with an anti-trust lawsuit filed against Network Solutions, who then operated all commercial registration under contract to the U.S. Department of Commerce.

2.2 Through Thick and Thin

At the core of this transition, domain registration was split into two independent functions: registries, who managed the zone files for their own top-level domains (TLDs), and registrars, who contracted with registries for the right to sell domains in their TLDs to consumers. Thus, today Verisign operates the registry for com, while GoDaddy is a registrar who sells com domains (among others) to consumers. One of the complexities of this split was how to handle WHOIS data and two distinct proposals were introduced: "thick" registries and "thin" registries. Thick registries would centrally manage all registration data and thus a WHOIS query could return all available information. By contrast, thin registries would only maintain a subset of this information (particularly the identity of the registrar, dates and status of registration, and the address of the responsible name servers). All other information, notably regarding the identity and nature of the registrant, would be maintained by the individual registrar who had been contracted for that domain. Thus, in thin registries, to obtain the full registration record is a two step process: first querying the registry for the thin record, extracting the designated registrar, and then sending an additional WHOIS query to that registrar. At the time of this change, Network Solutions opted to create a thin registry for the TLDs it managed: com, net and org.[3]

This operational distinction, thick vs. thin, indirectly impacted the diversity of schemes used for WHOIS data. Thick registries typically created a single schema (driven by the operational needs of domain provisioning), and thus each such TLD exported a single schema for all of its domains (and many such TLDs share schemas due to the use of common software). By contrast, since thin registries did not store or manage this data, their registrars could format it as they saw fit. With many more registrars than registries (there are over 1400 accredited registrars for com alone[4] and an unknown number of unaccredited resellers), this delineation of responsibilities implicitly encouraged diversity of WHOIS schemas.

With the benefit of hindsight, there is widespread sentiment that the "thick" registry model is preferable—particularly due to the key need to normalize the representation of and oversight over WHOIS data. Today all new generic TLDs (gTLDs) are required to implement the thick model, 99% of existing gTLDs registries do also, and many of the 250+ Country Code TLDs (ccTLDs) do as well.[5] Unfortunately, the few gTLDs whose registries still implement the thin model include com and net, which together comprise 45% of all registered domains (and a large majority of domains in DNS and Web searches). While there have been attempts to pressure Verisign (the registry operator for com and net) to change, and well-received proposals to completely scrap the WHOIS system altogether for a protocol with a well-defined structured data schema [20], neither have happened yet. Indeed, since Verisign's contract to manage com and net will not come up for renewal again until 2018, it seems likely that users of WHOIS data will need to accommodate this status quo for some time yet. Thus, today there are two sources of format diversity in WHOIS data: between-registry diversity for thick registries and between-registrar diversity for thin registries. In this paper, we touch on both but focus primarily on com which contains the greatest range of schema diversity due to its size and age.

[3]In 2003, the Internet Society's Public Interest Registry won the contract to manage org and switched it to a thick registry model.

[4]https://www.icann.org/registrar-reports/accredited-list.html

[5]There are few studies on ccTLD operations, but one recent study of 22 ccTLDs found that only four use the thin model [22] suggesting that this community has migrated to the thick model as well.

2.3 Parsing WHOIS

The existing approaches to WHOIS parsing are template-based and rule-based.

Template-based

Most existing parsers, including the popular `deft-whois` written in Perl, `Ruby whois` and `WhoisParser` for PHP, are template-based. These parsers first classify each domain based on their TLD and provide a per-registry parser (in many cases such parsers can be shared among registries that use a common schema). If a record calls into a thin registry such as `com`, template-based parsers will extract the designated registrar's WHOIS server address from the thin record and then parse the associated thick record using a per-registrar template. This approach is very straightforward and highly effective when a good template is available. However, they do not generalize and if a template for a particular registrar or registry is not available then they will fail completely. Moreover, they are highly fragile to variation even within the templates they parse; changing a single word in the schema or reordering field elements can easily lead to parsing failure.[6] Thus, this approach is sensitive to the number and currency of the templates available—an ongoing manual task.

To make these issues concrete, we consider one of the best such template-based parsers: Clayton's deft-whois (used in his 2014 study of WHOIS abuse [3]). The version we have, $alpha - 0.0.3$, has 6 generic templates and 575 specific templates, 403 of which were written to manage registrar-based diversity in `com`. Using $97,917$ randomly selected `com` WHOIS records, we find that 94% of our test data comes from registrars or registries that are represented by these templates.[7] However, minor changes in formats since the templates were written cause the parser to fail on the vast majority of these examples, thus reinforcing our observation that this approach is fragile in the face of change.

Rule-based

The other parsing approach, exemplified by `pythonwhois`, is to craft a more general series of rules in the form of regular expressions that are designed to match a variety of common WHOIS structures (e.g., name:value formats). If carefully constructed, such rules can still achieve high coverage with less fragility to minor changes (rules will still need to be updated for more significant changes in format structure). However, unlike template-based parsers, rule-based systems do not have a crisp failure signal (i.e., the lack of a template) and thus are more challenging to evaluate. Thus, we filtered our test data to only include those entries with a *registrant* field ($93,711$ records). When running `pythonwhois` against this corpus it correctly identifies the registrant only 59% of the time.

Summary

In general, both template and rule based parsing suffer from incompleteness and fragility. Moreover, keeping them up to date requires an ongoing investment in skilled labor. There are a number of companies that provide such services (e.g., domaintools) but even they fail to parse some domains (e.g., domaintools does not report a registrant for `albygg.com`, likely due to its unusual format).

To address these challenges, this paper introduces a statistical, data-driven approach to WHOIS parsing which at once provides greater accuracy than existing methods, less fragility to variation, and lower overhead to update (typically just one labeled example of each new format).

[6]Indeed, we see such changes in practice—with one large registrar modifying their schema significantly during the four months of WHOIS measurements we took for this paper.

[7]Using the same metric, the more popular "Ruby whois" has templates only for 63% of the test data.

3. STATISTICAL PARSING

In this section we describe our statistical model for parsing thick WHOIS records. As input to the model, we divide (or chunk) each WHOIS record into its individual lines of text. Given input of this form, the goal of parsing is to label each line of text by the type of information it provides about the registered domain (e.g., name of registrant, country of origin). The statistical model we use is known as a conditional random field (CRF), and we estimate its parameters from labeled examples of parsed records; these are records in which every line of text has been tagged (manually or otherwise) by its correct label. Once a CRF is trained from examples of this form, it can be used to parse WHOIS records that have not been previously labeled. Section 3.1 reviews the basics of CRFs, and Sections 3.2–3.3 describe specifically how we apply them to the problem of parsing WHOIS records.

3.1 Conditional random fields

A conditional random field (CRF) is a probabilistic model for mapping sequences of discrete inputs (or *tokens*) into sequences of discrete outputs (or *labels*) that have the same length. We denote a token sequence by $\mathbf{x} = (x_1, x_2, \ldots, x_T)$, where each token x_t is drawn from some (possibly infinite) alphabet, and we denote a label sequence by $\mathbf{y} = (y_1, \ldots, y_T)$, where each label y_t is drawn from some finite state space. CRFs define a powerful but tractable family of probabilistic models for the posterior distribution $\Pr(\mathbf{y}|\mathbf{x})$.

There have been many successful applications of CRFs to problems in text and natural language processing [4, 16, 23]. In this paper, we use CRFs to parse WHOIS records. Thus for our application the token x_t denotes the text on the tth (non-empty) line of the WHOIS record, and the label y_t represents the type of information on this line. We assume that line breaks are used to separate different fields of information in the WHOIS record, so that each line x_t has a unique correct label y_t. Also we do not attach labels to lines that are empty or that do not contain any alphanumeric characters.

CRFs are based on a special assumption of conditional independence. In particular, they exhibit the Markov property

$$\Pr(y_t|y_{t-1}, y_{t+1}, x_t) = \Pr(y_t|y_1, \ldots, y_T, x_1, \ldots, x_T);$$

in other words, they assume that the label y_t is conditionally independent of other inputs and labels given the input x_t and the adjacent labels $y_{t\pm1}$. This is a common assumption for text processing of human-readable documents, and it is an especially natural one for the parsing of WHOIS records. Recall that in our application, the label y_t indicates the type of information provided by the line of the WHOIS record containing the text x_t. Essentially, we are assuming that this label is strongly predicted by the text x_t and the labels of adjacent lines, and that distant lines of the WHOIS record do not provide additional information for this prediction. While CRFs are able to model the strong dependence of labels on local context, the assumption of conditional independence gives rise to extremely efficient algorithms (based on dynamic programming) for inference and parameter estimation.

The Markov property in CRFs dictates the form of the posterior distribution $\Pr(\mathbf{y}|\mathbf{x})$. Of special importance is how CRFs model the strong local dependence between labels and text. At a high level, CRFs use a large number of binary-valued "features" to indicate when certain labels and text co-occur. We use

$$f_k(y_{t-1}, y_t, x_t) \in \{0, 1\} \quad (1)$$

to denote the kth such feature, which takes as its arguments one line of text x_t, its corresponding label y_t, and in some (though not necessarily all) cases, the preceding label y_{t-1}. Each of the CRF's features is designed to test a particular property of its arguments—for example, whether the text x_t is preceded by a new line and the labels y_{t-1} and y_t are not equal (which might be likely, say, if empty lines in the WHOIS record are used to separate different blocks of information). Section 3.3 describes the features of our CRF in much greater detail. In terms of these features, the posterior distribution of the CRF is given by:

$$\Pr_{\boldsymbol{\theta}}(\mathbf{y}|\mathbf{x}) = \frac{1}{Z_{\boldsymbol{\theta}}(\mathbf{x})} \exp\left[\sum_t \sum_k \theta_k f_k(y_{t-1}, y_t, x_t)\right], \quad (2)$$

where the parameters θ_k (one for each feature) model the dependence[8] between labels and text, and where the denominator

$$Z_{\boldsymbol{\theta}}(\mathbf{x}) = \sum_{\mathbf{y}} \exp\left[\sum_t \sum_k \theta_k f_k(y_{t-1}, y_t, x_t)\right] \quad (3)$$

normalizes the distribution so that $\sum_{\mathbf{y}} \Pr(\mathbf{y}|\mathbf{x}) = 1$. To compute the normalization factor in eq. (3), we must sum over all possible sequences of labels, the number of which is exponential in the sequence length. However, we can perform this sum efficiently by dynamic programming; the details of this calculation can be found in the appendix.

The parameters $\boldsymbol{\theta}$ of the model can be estimated from a labeled set of parsed WHOIS records. This *training data* takes the form of R labeled WHOIS records $\{(\mathbf{x}^r, \mathbf{y}^r)\}_{r=1}^R$, consisting of one token sequence and one label sequence for each record. To estimate the parameters $\boldsymbol{\theta}$, we maximize the log-likelihood of the training data,

$$\mathcal{L}(\boldsymbol{\theta}) = \sum_{r=1}^{R} \ln \Pr_{\boldsymbol{\theta}}(\mathbf{y}^r|\mathbf{x}^r), \quad (4)$$

which measures how well the CRF predicts the correct label sequence for each WHOIS record. It can be shown that this log-likelihood is a convex function of the parameters $\boldsymbol{\theta}$. Thus we can find the optimal parameters using iterative, gradient-based methods such as L-BFGS [21].

After estimating the parameters $\boldsymbol{\theta}$, we can use the CRF to parse new WHOIS records that have not been previously labeled. Let $\mathbf{x}$ denote the non-empty lines of text in a new WHOIS record. Then using the CRF, we predict the label sequence with highest posterior probability:

$$\mathbf{y}^* = \arg\max_{\mathbf{y}} \Pr_{\boldsymbol{\theta}}(\mathbf{y}|\mathbf{x}). \quad (5)$$

This computation is an instance of Viterbi decoding; again details are given in the appendix.

3.2 States

The labels in our CRFs belong to a discrete state space: each of them identifies a particular type of information provided by the WHOIS record. It is typical for the fields of information in WHOIS records to appear in blocks, and for the lines within these blocks to contain details that can be viewed as more specialized subfields. Accordingly, we pursue a two-level strategy for parsing WHOIS records. First we train a CRF to parse the records into coarse, high-level blocks of information. Then for blocks that are of special interest, we train another CRF to parse the sub-fields of information within these blocks.

Our first-level CRF is designed to parse WHOIS records into the following six blocks of information:

registrar	information about the registrar, such as its name, URL, and ID.
domain	information such as domain name, name server, and domain status.
date	dates when the domain was created, when it expired, when it was last updated, etc.
registrant	name, address, phone, email, and other information about the registrant
other	administrative, billing, and technical contacts, which may or may not be identical to the registrant
null	boilerplate text and legalese, often describing claim, use, and notice

Accordingly, the discrete labels *registrar*, *domain*, *date*, *registrant*, *other*, and *null* form the state space of our first-level CRF, and the model associates each non-empty line of text x_t in the WHOIS record to a label y_t from this list. We note that thin WHOIS records provide some of this information (e.g., *registrar*, *domain*, *date*), at least for the top-level domains where such records exist. On the other hand, only thick WHOIS records provide *registrant* information, as well as listing additional contacts (*other*) that may serve as a reasonable proxy when the registrant information is missing or incomplete. We use the *null* state to label large blocks of boilerplate and otherwise uninformative text in WHOIS records.

The *registrant* information in thick WHOIS records is of special interest precisely because it is not available anywhere else. Thus we use our second-level CRF to further analyze the blocks of *registrant* information identified by the first-level CRF. Specifically, for each registrant we attempt to extract the following (self-explanatory) subfields of text:

name	*id*	*org*
street	*city*	*state*
postcode	*country*	*phone*
fax	*email*	*other*

These twelve labels form the state space of our second-level CRF: in particular, each token x_t of *registrant* information in thick WHOIS records is mapped to a more specialized label y_t from this list.

3.3 Features

The effectiveness of CRFs depends on the design of features $f_k(y_{t-1}, y_t, x_t)$ that capture the distinctive properties of different states. For the parsing of thick WHOIS records, we design these features to account for the appearance of certain words, empty spaces, and punctuation markers in each line of text. These features are based on recurring patterns of text that we describe here.

Many lines of text in thick WHOIS records contain well-defined *separators*, such as colons, tabs, or ellipses. Typically the separator is used to distinguish the *titles* of fields in the WHOIS record (e.g., `Registrant Name`) from the *values* of these fields (e.g., `John Smith`). This is also a useful distinction for our CRFs to preserve when they are parsing WHOIS records. In each line of text, we

[8] To simplify the expressions in eqs. (2–3), we have adopted a slight abuse of notation: it should be understood here, and in what follows, that the sums over k at time $t = 1$ range only over those features f_k that do not depend on the argument y_{t-1} (which does not exist at the first time step).

therefore append all words to the left of the first-appearing separator with the characters @T (for title); likewise, we append all words to the right of the separator with the characters @V (for value). If a line does not contain a separator, then we append all of its words with @V.

We do not attach labels to empty lines of text in WHOIS records. But we know that these empty lines, when they occur, often signal that the next block of text describes a new field of the WHOIS record. To preserve this signal, we mark whenever a non-empty line of text is preceded by one or more line breaks; we do this by prepending NL (for new line) to the line's observed token x_t. We use similar methods to mark other revealing forms of leading white spaces or tabs (e.g., shifts) and instances of non-alphanumeric characters (e.g., punctuation, special symbols).

With the above in mind, we can now describe in general terms the features that appear in our CRFs. To generate these features, we first compile a list of all the words (ignoring capitalization) that appear in the training set of WHOIS records. We trim words that appear very infrequently from this list, but otherwise our dictionary is quite extensive, with tens of thousands of entries. Most of the features in our CRFs simply test for the appearance of a word in a line of a text x_t with a particular label y_t. For example, here is a particular feature from our first-level CRF:

$$f_1(y_t, x_t) = \begin{cases} 1 & \text{if } x_t \text{ contains the word} \\ & \texttt{organization@T} \text{ and} \\ & y_t = \mathit{registrant} \\ 0 & \text{otherwise} \end{cases} \quad (6)$$

We obtain several hundred thousand features of this general form simply by composing all the words in our dictionary with the different states of the CRF. We also generate features that test for the appearance of more general classes of words. For example, here is a particular feature from our second-level CRF:

$$f_2(y_t, x_t) = \begin{cases} 1 & \text{if } x_t \text{ contains a five-digit} \\ & \text{number and } y_t = \mathit{zipcode} \\ 0 & \text{otherwise} \end{cases} \quad (7)$$

Note that the features in eqs. (6–7) only examine the label y_t for the current line of text x_t, but not the label y_{t-1} for the preceding one. However we also construct features that examine both labels. For example, here is another feature from our first-level CRF:

$$f_3(y_{t-1}, y_t, x_t) = \begin{cases} 1 & \text{if } x_t \text{ contains the word} \\ & \texttt{owner@T} \text{ and} \\ & y_{t-1} = \mathit{domain} \text{ and} \\ & y_t = \mathit{registrant} \\ 0 & \text{otherwise} \end{cases} \quad (8)$$

It is relatively simple, in this way, to generate many binary-valued features that test for distinctive patterns of text in the different fields of WHOIS records. In total, our first-level CRF for parsing WHOIS records has nearly 1M features, and our second-level CRF for parsing more detailed *registrant* information has nearly 400K features.

The goal of learning in CRFs is to determine which of these features have predictive power—namely, to estimate, for each feature $f_k(y_{t-1}, y_t, x_t)$, the weight θ_k that appears in the posterior distribution, eq. (2). There are several well-known packages (e.g., MALLET, crfsgd, CRF++) for feature generation and learning in CRFs. For the application, we implemented our own model, with a specialized feature extraction pipeline and optimization routines such as stochastic gradient descent. We also modified a well-known implementation of the limited-memory BFGS algorithm to run in parallel for our experiments.

Label	Words
registrant	registrant@T, organization@T
registrar	registrar@T, reseller@T, www@V, SEP, NL, by@T, server@T, url@T, registered@T, whois@V, provided@T, http@V, service@T
domain	dnssec@T, status@T, domain@T, com@V, server@T, nameserver@T, unsigned@V, punycode@T, SEP, org@V, clienttransferprohibited@V, 1@V, information@T, no@V
date	date@T, updated@T, created@T, 2015@V, on@V, 2014@V, expiration@T,
other	tech@T, billing@T, administrative@T, admin@T, contact@T
null	service@T, SYM, registration@T, by@T, http@T, provided@T, for@V, of@T, for@T, the@T, more@T, cn@V, contacts@T, learn@T, here@T, is@V, whois@V, information@V, server@V

Table 1: Heavily weighted features, of the form in eq. (6), for the first-level CRF that parses WHOIS records into differently labeled blocks of information.

3.4 Model parameters

Once a CRF has been estimated from data, it can be instructive to examine the features with the highest statistical weights; roughly speaking, these are the features that the model finds most useful for prediction. We do so here for the first-level CRF described in Section 3.2. The parameters of these CRFs were learned from the labeled data set described in Section 4.

First we examine the model parameters for the simplest features, of the form in eq. (6). For each label in the CRF's state space, Table 1 lists the features with the model's highest weights. Recall that words to the left of a separator are indicated by the suffix @T, while other words are indicated by the suffix @V. On one hand, many of the results are highly intuitive: for example, the word organization to the left of a separator suggests that the current line of text contains information about the domain's *registrant*. On the other hand, there are associations discovered by the model that could not have been guessed beforehand. This is the power of a data-driven approach.

Next we examine the model parameters for the CRF's transition-detecting features, of the form in eq. (8). Figure 1 visualizes these features as a graph: the nodes in this graph represent the labels in the CRF's state space, and the edges are annotated by the top features that the CRF uses to detect the end of one block of information and the beginning of another. Many of these features are highly intuitive; for example, the word "created" often signifies the beginning of *date* information. (There are also features, not shown in the graph, that the CRFs uses to detect self-transitions—that is, when a block of information extends across multiple lines of the WHOIS record.)

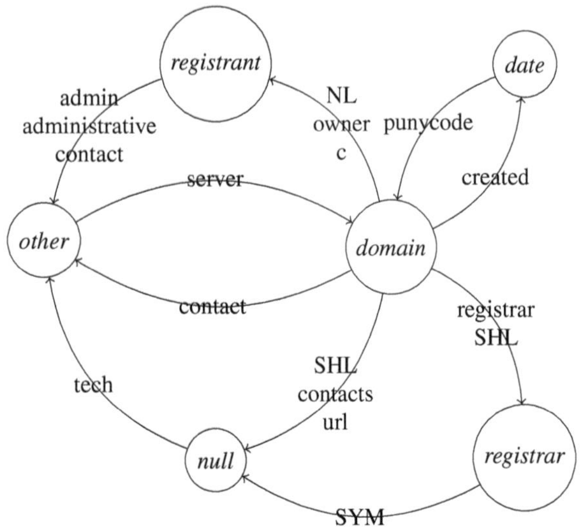

Figure 1: Visualization of predictive features for detecting adjacent blocks of information in WHOIS records. The edges of the graph show words (lower-case) and punctuation markers (upper-case) that are highly correlated with transition between differently labeled blocks. Punctuation key: NL = new line; SHL = shift left; SYM = line starts with symbols such as # or %.

4. DATA COLLECTION AND LABELING

Our dataset consists of 102M WHOIS records in the com domain (over 90% of the domains registered under the TLD), as well as some comparative samples of data from new gTLDs. We have matching thin and thick records for over 92M of these domains, but only thin records for the other cases (e.g., when a registrar server returned "no match," when our crawler was blocked, etc). In this section, we describe how the data was obtained and how we labeled a subset of it (86K randomly selected domains with thick records from com) to establish a baseline ground truth for evaluating our statistical parser.

4.1 WHOIS Crawling

Our primary dataset was obtained via long-term crawling the list of domains found in the com zone file in February of 2015. We performed an initial crawl from February to May 2015, and a second crawl from July to August 2015. As discussed earlier com is managed by Verisign under a thin registry model and thus, for each domain, there are at least two queries needed: one to Verisign to obtain the thin record and then, extracting the address of the registrar's WHOIS server from the thin record, a second query to obtain its thick record on some registrar-specific format.

The key challenge in completing this crawl is per-IP rate limiting, which we observed both at Verisign and individual registrars. Typically, once a given source IP has issued more queries to a given WHOIS server in a period than its limit, the server will stop responding, return an empty record or return an error. Queries can then resume after a penalty period is over. Unfortunately, the implementation of this rate limiting, its thresholds and triggers are rarely published publicly. This is a common problem for most research efforts that perform comprehensive online data gathering (e.g., [5, 9, 10, 18, 19]) and our solutions are not unique.

In particular, we use a simple dynamic inference technique to avoid hitting rate limits whereby we track our query rate for each WHOIS server. When a given server stops responding with valid data, we infer that our query rate was the culprit and we record this limit, subsequently querying well under this limit for that server. We use multiple servers to provide for parallel access to WHOIS servers, and we retry each query after a failure at three different servers before we mark the request as a failure.[9] We obtained 102M WHOIS records from this crawl (a bit over 90% of the com TLD). Some domains in the February 2015 zone file snapshot were expired by the time we crawled them; also, in some cases we failed for other reasons to obtain a WHOIS record (e.g., we exceeded a registrar's rate limit).

4.2 Rule-based WHOIS labeling

As we will show, our statistical parser requires only a modest amount of supervision and thus human experts are more than sufficient to source training data. However, to *evaluate* our technique requires a much larger set of ground truth data which we can compare our results to. To this end, we have manually built a rule-based parser *specifically developed* to accurately parse the thick WHOIS records of 86K com domains randomly selected from our larger corpus. As with all such systems, the resulting rule-based parser is fragile and is unlikely to generalize well outside the data it was developed for, but its purpose is to efficiently establish a large set of known results against which our own work can be benchmarked. For completeness, we describe its design here.

As with our statistical parser, our rule-based parser divides each record into line-granularity tokens. The underlying assumption, validated by our experience, is that each line encodes at most one "kind" of information. We then identify common separators (i.e., colons, spaces, tabs, etc.) that might separate any given line into "title: value" pairs (e.g., a line starting with "`Registrant Name:`" indicates that the text immediately following the colon is the name of the registrant). As well, we capture the common case where this relation is contextual and a field title appears alone with the following block representing the associated value (e.g., a line starting with "`Registrant`" might then be followed by a name, address, e-mail address and phone number). Upon this framework, we have added a large number of special case rules, iterating repeatedly until our rule-based parser was able to completely label the entries in our test corpus.

5. EVALUATION

In this section we evaluate the accuracy of the model described in Section 3. We also compare the performance of rule-based and statistical parsers that have been constructed from the same (possibly limited) set of manually labeled WHOIS records within the com domain. It is important to realize that these parsers can correctly label all the records that were used to construct them. Thus we must devise more careful ways to compare them.

We use both types of parsers to label the fields of WHOIS records as *registrar*, *domain*, *date*, *registrant*, *other*, or *null*. Then, we seek to answer three questions. First, which type of parser—rule-based or statistical—generalizes better to new WHOIS records in the same TLD? Second, how well do these parsers generalize (if at all) to WHOIS records in different TLDs? Third, when these parsers fail—presumably because they encounter WHOIS records with unfamiliar templates—how much effort is required to correct these failures? We explore each question in turn.

[9] Roughly 7.5% of domains we queries resulted in a failure after all 3 attempts.

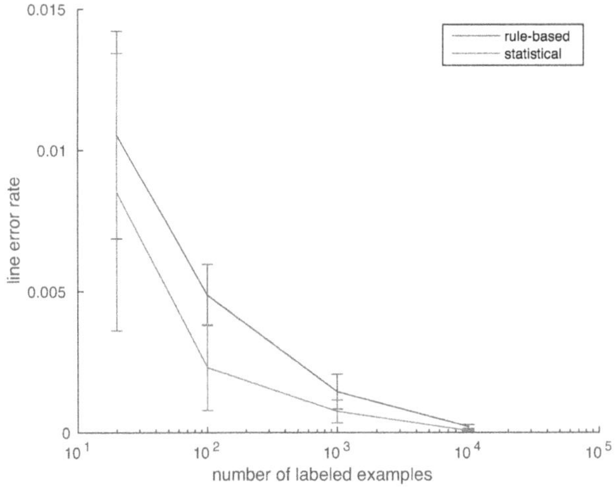

Figure 2: Line error rate versus number of labeled examples in the training set. Each point shows the average error rate from five-fold cross-validation, and each error bar shows the standard deviation across folds.

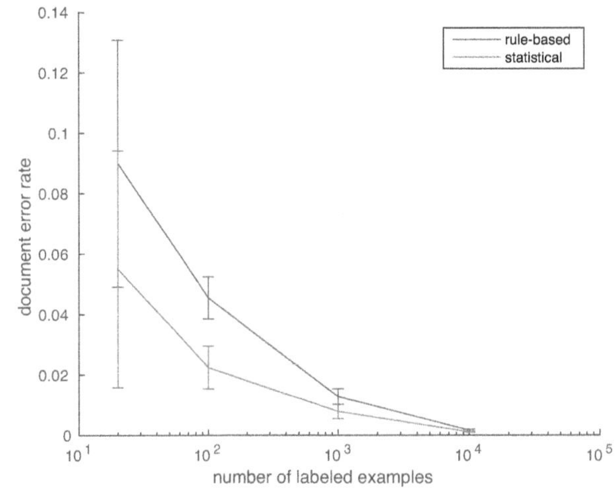

Figure 3: Document error rate versus number of labeled examples in the training set. Each point shows the average error rate from five-fold cross-validation, and each error bar shows the standard deviation across folds.

5.1 Comparison on .com

We investigate the first question, using five-fold cross-validation, on our data set of 86K labeled WHOIS records from the com domain. We randomly split this data set into five folds of roughly 17K records each. Within each fold we further subsample the records to obtain smaller training sets of 20, 100, 1000, and 10000 WHOIS records. Finally, we use these training sets to construct rule-based and statistical parsers, then evaluate these (purposely handicapped) parsers on the test set of the remaining WHOIS records (roughly 68K) in other folds. Thus for each training set size, we obtain five estimates of the test error, and we measure the mean and standard deviation of these estimates.

The goal of these experiments is to understand which type of parser generalizes better to new WHOIS records. To construct the statistical parsers in these experiments, we merely limit the WHOIS records that are used to estimate their model parameters. Likewise, to construct the rule-based parsers, we simply "roll back" our best rule-based parser, retaining only those rules that are necessary to label the WHOIS records in these smaller subsets. Note, however, that some pattern-matching rules cannot be rolled back, so the rule-based parser that we derive in this way is always stronger than one derived from "scratch" on the smaller subsets of WHOIS records.

Domain (Example)	*Rule-based*	*Statistical*
aero (bluemed.aero)	4/99	2/99
asia (islameyat.asia)	20/114	3/114
biz (aktivjob.biz)	36/82	0/82
coop (emheartcu.coop)	91/127	16/127
info (travelmarche.info)	0/79	0/79
mobi (amxich.mobi)	2/69	0/69
name (emrich.name)	1/28	0/28
org (fekrtna.org)	0/64	0/64
pro (olbrich.pro)	2/97	1/97
travel (tabacon.travel)	34/80	0/80
us (vc4.us)	38/88	0/88
xxx (celly.xxx)	1/66	0/66

Table 2: Comparison of parser performance in new TLDs. The columns show the fraction of mislabeled lines for a sample WHOIS record from each TLD (# error/total).

Figures 2 and 3 compare the performances of the rule-based and statistical parsers in these experiments. We measure the performance by two types of error rates on the test set: the *line* error rate, equal to the fraction of lines across all WHOIS records that are mislabeled, and the *document* error rate, equal to the fraction of records that are not perfectly labeled (i.e., in which there is at least one incorrectly labeled line). The figures show, not surprisingly, that both types of parsers improve with broader exposure to WHOIS records in com. However, comparing the rule-based and statistical parsers, we see that the latter dominate the former, especially when limited numbers of WHOIS records are available as labeled examples. These results suggest that the statistical parsers are learning to detect patterns of text in WHOIS records that are of broader applicability than those manually identified by the rule-based parsers. Indeed, with only 100 labeled records the statistical parser reaches an accuracy of over 97%, and with 1000 it reaches over 99%.

5.2 Comparison on new TLDs

We also compare the rule-based and statistical parsers on WHOIS records from new, unseen TLDs outside of com. It turns out that each of these new TLDs is owned by a single registrar, and that the WHOIS records within each TLD follow a consistent template. However, these templates are not necessarily ones that have been observed in the training set of WHOIS records from the com domain.

Table 2 compares the number of lines mislabeled by each type of parser on these new TLDs. In these comparisons, it is enough to sample one WHOIS record from each TLD because the formatting within each TLD is identical. There is no case in which the rule-based parser performs better than the statistical one, and there are many cases (**asia**, **biz**, coop, **travel**, **us**) in which it performs far worse. Again these results suggest that the statistical parser has discovered patterns of wider applicability than the rule-based one.

5.3 Comparison of maintainability

Finally we consider which type of parser is easier to maintain in an actual deployment. There are two issues here: first, how many errors are encountered when the parser is exposed to WHOIS records in different formats than it has already experienced; second, how much effort is required to fix these errors going forward?

Registrants across all time				Registrants in 2014	
Country	*Number*	*(% All)*	*(% All)*	*Number*	*Country*
United States	34,236,575	(47.6)	(41.1)	6,952,306	United States
China	6,908,865	(9.6)	(18.2)	3,072,575	China
United Kingdom	3,398,561	(4.7)	(3.5)	597,212	United Kingdom
Germany	2,518,551	(3.5)	(2.9)	482,313	France
France	2,404,450	(3.3)	(2.5)	428,306	Canada
Canada	2,152,208	(3.0)	(2.5)	426,755	India
Spain	1,480,000	(2.1)	(2.1)	356,479	Japan
Australia	1,311,191	(1.8)	(1.9)	321,504	Germany
Japan	1,242,697	(1.7)	(1.7)	293,041	Spain
India	1,143,422	(1.6)	(1.7)	293,064	Turkey
(Other)	12,609,909	(17.5)	(18.9)	3,197,172	(Other)
(Unknown)	2,458,888	(3.4)	(2.9)	482,818	(Unknown)
Total	71,865,317	(100.0)	(100.0)	16,903,545	Total

Table 3: Top 10 countries of domain registrants across all time (left) and just in 2014 (right).

Company	*Domains*
Amazon	20,596
AOL	17,136
Microsoft	16,694
21st Century Fox	14,249
Warner Bros.	13,674
Yahoo	10,502
Disney	10,342
Google	6,612
AT&T	3,931
eBay	2,570
Nike	2,566

Table 4: Well-known brand companies with the most com domains.

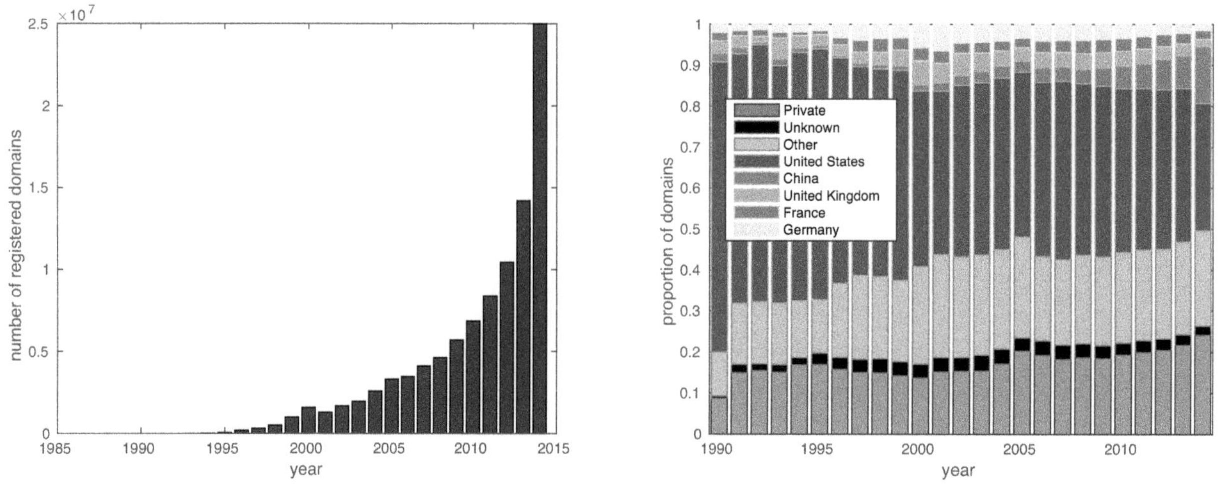

(a) Creation Date

(b) Country Proportions

Figure 4: Histogram of domain creation dates, and country and privacy protect breakdowns.

The results of the previous sections provide some guidance. We have already seen that the statistical parser generalizes better across familiar and unfamiliar TLDs, so that fewer errors will be encountered. Of the errors that are encountered, we can then compare the amount of effort required to fix them. For the rule-based parser, the errors can only be fixed by a human expert who is willing (on an ongoing basis) to revise the parser's existing rules or to craft altogether new ones. For the statistical parser, this manual exercise is not required: once the errors are identified, the correctly labeled WHOIS record can be added to the existing training set, and the model can be enlarged and retrained to work as desired. We emphasize here that the procedures for feature generation and parameter estimation in these models are easily automated.

We can make this comparison even more concrete for the results in Table 2. Note that the rule-based parser made errors in 10 out of the 12 new TLDs; the statistical parser made errors in just 4 of them. To fix the errors in the rule-based parser, it would be necessary for a human expert to alter the parser's rule base, one time after another, for each of these 10 TLDs. On the other hand, after retraining the model with just four additional labeled examples the resulting statistical parser has no errors.

6. SURVEYING .COM

With our parser in hand, we applied it to our crawl of the WHOIS records of com domains and constructed a database of the fields extracted by the parser. The information in the database provides a convenient global view of domain registrations in the largest TLD, and in this section we use this global perspective to look at registrations through the lenses of registrants, registrars, and the use of privacy protection. Since domain information is often used when examining Internet abuse, we also briefly look at WHOIS features of com domains found on the DBL blacklist. For the results in this section, we use 102,077,202 com domains that were created through the end of 2014.

6.1 Registrants

Where are registrants located? Table 3 shows the top 10 countries of all domain registrants, with the remaining countries combined in the "Other" row. The left half of the table shows the breakdown for all com domains, and the right half shows the breakdown for domains created in 2014. Because we have a recent snapshot of WHOIS records, we will not see domains that were registered in com

Registrations across all time			Registrations in 2014		
Registrar	*Number*	*(% All)*	*(% All)*	*Number*	*Registrar*
GoDaddy	34,932,668	(34.2)	(34.4)	8,904,002	GoDaddy
eNom	8,841,158	(8.7)	(7.7)	1,984,900	eNom
Network Solutions	5,094,458	(5.0)	(4.3)	1,111,857	Network Solutions
1&1 Internet	3,111,934	(3.0)	(3.7)	952,430	HiChina
Wild West Domains	2,636,577	(2.6)	(3.3)	846,137	Xinnet
HiChina	2,101,937	(2.1)	(3.2)	815,095	Public Domain Reg.
Public Domain Reg.	2,100,018	(2.1)	(3.0)	782,496	GMO Internet
Register.com	2,076,612	(2.0)	(2.4)	620,131	Wild West Domains
FastDomain	1,896,785	(1.9)	(2.1)	556,102	Register.com
GMO Internet	1,878,897	(1.8)	(2.1)	531,578	1&1 Internet
(Other)	37,406,158	(36.6)	(33.9)	7,714,351	(Other)
Total (All Years)	102,077,202	(100.0)	(100.0)	25,875,686	Total (2014)

Table 5: Top 10 registrars of com domains registered across all time (left) and just in 2014 (right).

Registrations using privacy protection		
Registrar	*Number*	*(% All)*
GoDaddy	6,405,390	(33.1)
eNom	2,444,342	(12.6)
GMO Internet	1,118,634	(5.8)
HiChina	764,177	(4.0)
Public Domain Reg.	644,720	(3.3)
Register.com	632,179	(3.3)
FastDomain	630,905	(3.3)
Wild West Domains	581,873	(3.0)
DreamHost	545,147	(2.8)
1&1 Internet	536,671	(2.8)
(Other)	5,021,446	(26.0)
Total	19,325,484	(100.0)

Table 6: Top 10 registrars used by privacy protected domains.

years ago and that have expired before our crawl. By also looking at just the domains registered in the last year, though, we can capture both recent registration behavior as well as a nearly complete set of domain registrations for that period (since domains typically are registered for a minimum of one year). For these results, we have also removed the 20% of all domains that use a privacy protection service since the country of the registrant cannot be inferred (we explore domains using the protection services in more detail below). For WHOIS records that do not have country information for the registrant, we list these as "Unknown".

For the WHOIS records with country information, they support the general reputation of the US dominating registrations in the com TLD: 47% of all com domains are from US registrants. Many European countries also have significant numbers of registrants, but those in China are the second most numerous. Indeed, the number of com registrants in China was nearly half those of the US in 2014, and far more than any remaining country.

Looking at these temporal trends more broadly, Figure 4a shows a histogram of the number of domains created in com over time at the granularity of a year. Figure 4b shows the same data, but normalizes it and breaks down the domains by the five largest countries of registrants as well as those using privacy protection services and registrants with missing country information.

Some general trends emerge. Registrations in com continue to grow dramatically, and the rate is increasing over time. The fraction of domains registered with privacy protection is also increasing over time, passing 20% in 2014. While US registrants dominate the total set of registered com domains, the trends are changing (at least for domains that report registrant country in their WHOIS records). The fraction of new domains from US registrants is decreasing over time, while Chinese registrants are the growth market.

Which organizations have many com domains? For the records that report organizational information, the types of organizations that stand out with the most domains are domain sellers (BuyDomains.com, HugeDomains.com, Domain Asset Holdings, etc.), online marketers (Dex Media, Yodle), and Internet hosting companies in Japan (Sakura Internet, Xserver). Beyond these, Table 4 lists well-known brand companies that have registered the most com domains. Not surprisingly, they fall into large retail, service, and media companies.[10]

[10]Note that similar company searches using services like DomainTools often return larger counts; such searches match text on the entire WHOIS record, not just particular com domains as we do.

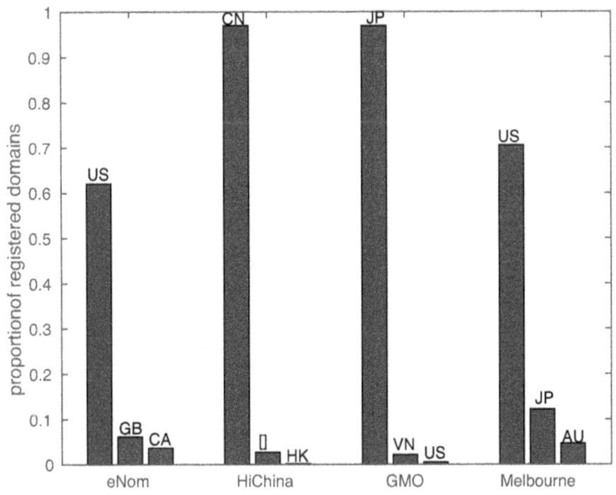

Figure 5: Top 3 registrant countries for selected registrars.

6.2 Registrars

Table 5 shows the top 10 registrars by number of com domains registered overall, and for domains created in 2014. GoDaddy is well known to be a dominant registrar, and indeed we find that it has registered over one-third of com domains. Overall registration market share is heavily skewed: the top three registrars account for nearly half of com domains, and the top 10 account for 73%. Reflecting the temporal trends in Figure 4b, we see the rise of Chinese registrars HiChina and Xin Net in the 2014 list corresponding to the rise in demand from Chinese registrants.

The registrar names evoke their countries of origin. To examine how registrants are distributed across registrars in more detail, Figure 5 shows the top three countries of registrants for four of the top registrars. For the most part, the countries of registrants reflect their registrars: eNom has US, UK, and Canadian registrants, HiChina has Chinese registrants (the "[]" corresponds to records lacking country information), and GMO Internet primarily has Japanese registrants. Interestingly, although Melbourne IT does have Australian registrants, US customers dominate its business followed by Japanese customers.

Protection Service	*Number (% All)*
Domains By Proxy	6,901,026 (35.7)
WhoisGuard	1,336,312 (6.9)
Whois Privacy Protect	1,312,559 (6.8)
FBO REGISTRANT	945,924 (4.9)
PrivacyProtect.org	813,836 (4.2)
Aliyun	763,101 (3.9)
Perfect Privacy	651,785 (3.4)
Happy DreamHost	547,338 (2.8)
MuuMuuDomain	417,705 (2.2)
1&1 Internet	380,223 (2.0)
(Other)	5255675 (27.2)
Total	19,325,484 (100.0)

Table 7: Top 10 privacy protection services used for com domains.

Country	*Number (% All)*
United States	32,513 (43.8)
Japan	18,630 (25.1)
China	11,882 (16.0)
Vietnam	965 (1.3)
Canada	893 (1.2)
France	860 (1.2)
India	696 (0.9)
United Kingdom	693 (0.9)
Turkey	546 (0.7)
Russia	402 (0.5)
(Other)	4,390 (5.9)
(Unknown)	1,831 (2.5)
Total	74,301 (100.0)

Table 8: Top 10 countries of registrants of com domains on the DBL in 2014.

Registrar	*Number (% All)*
eNom	21,844 (25.1)
GoDaddy	18,085 (20.8)
GMO Internet	17,866 (20.5)
Register.com	3,880 (4.5)
Moniker	3,298 (3.8)
Network Solutions	3,164 (3.6)
Public Domain Registry	2,189 (2.5)
Xinnet	2,383 (2.7)
Name.com	2,381 (2.2)
Bizcn.com	1,991 (2.3)
(Other)	12,399 (14.2)
Total	87,099 (100.0)

Table 9: Top 10 registrars of domains on the DBL in 2014.

6.3 Privacy Protection

From Section 6.1, we saw that the use of privacy protection services is increasing over time and, overall, we found that 20% of all com domains use a privacy protection service. Table 7 shows the top 10 services as reported in the WHOIS records, both in terms of the number of com domains registered through their service and as the percentage of all domains using privacy protection. We identify privacy protection services using a small set of keywords to match against registrant name and/or organization fields in the WHOIS records, which we crafted by looking through lists of records sorted by registrants and organizations (they stand out because they by definition have many domains associated with them).

The most prominent privacy protection service is Domains By Proxy, which is owned by the founder of the GoDaddy registrar and accounts for 36% of protected com domains. Although there is a long tail of service names, the top 10 account for 73% of protected domains. However, the names used in the WHOIS records for protected domains do not always correspond to organizations that we could identify (Private Registration, Hidden by Whois Privacy Protection Service). This behavior suggests that exploring the use, identity, and operation of protection services in further detail, in addition to the registrants of those services [3], could be an interesting open topic.

From a different perspective, Table 6 shows the top 10 registrars through which privacy protection domains have been registered. The registrars used largely track the list of all com domains in Table 5.[11]

6.4 Blacklisted Domains

Domain blacklists are a common source of identifying abusive domains. As a final survey, we look at the WHOIS records for com domains that appear on the Domain Block List (DBL).[12] Note that the DBL blacklist is populated from domains that appear in spam. Because domains in other TLDs are often cheaper than com, com domains only represents a portion (46%) of all domains in the DBL. But doing the analysis provides some insight into trends revealed from looking at WHOIS features. Also, we focus on just those domains created in 2014 to minimize domain expiration; 58.8% of com domains on the DBL were created in 2014, so this set represents the bulk of com domains on the DBL.

Table 8 shows the top 10 registrant countries for com domains on the DBL. Comparing with the countries for all domains in Table 3, both the percentages and rank orderings have notable differences for domains on the blacklist: in particular, registrants from Japan, China, and Vietnam are much more pronounced.

From another perspective, Table 9 shows the top 10 registrars through which com domains on the DBL are registered. Similarly comparing with the registrars for all domains in Table 5, the results have some interesting differences. Registrars that have been implicated in abuse (eNom, Xin Net) are more prominent, and new registrars appear on the top list (Moniker, evoPlus, Bizcn.com, etc.).

These results suggest that, in addition to registrar, country information would likely be a useful feature, e.g., for predicting domains used in abuse [6, 11].

[11]Note that our crawler exceeded the rate limit for Network Solutions domains, so we only have their thin records and cannot report the prevalence of privacy protection in Network Solutions.

[12]https://www.spamhaus.org/dbl

7. CONCLUSION

In this paper we have developed a statistical parser for WHOIS records that learns a general model from labeled examples, is easy to maintain and achieves extremely high accuracy in practice. We demonstrate its utility by providing an initial survey of registration patterns in the com TLD. Finally, code and data from our study is available at: `http://www.sysnet.ucsd.edu/projects/whois`.

Acknowledgments

We would like to thank our shepherd Walter Willinger for his valuable guidance, and the anonymous reviewers for their helpful suggestions. We are also very grateful to Neha Chachra and Chris Grier for their assistance with the proxy network, and we are particularly indebted to Paul Pearce for going above, beyond and beyond again in our time of need. We would also like to thank Cindy Moore for managing the software and systems used for this project. This work was supported by National Science Foundation grant NSF-1237264 and by generous research, operational and/or in-kind support from Google, Microsoft, Yahoo, and the UCSD Center for Networked Systems (CNS).

8. REFERENCES

[1] X. Cai, J. Heidemann, B. Krishnamurthy, and W. Willinger. Towards an AS-to-Organization Map. In *Proceedings of the 10th ACM/USENIX Internet Measurement Conference (IMC)*, Nov. 2010.

[2] CAUCE. Submission to ICANN WHOIS Team review. `http://www.cauce.org/2011/04/submission-to-icann-whois-team-review.html`, Apr. 2011.

[3] R. Clayton and T. Mansfield. A Study of Whois Privacy and Proxy Service Abuse. In *Proceedings of the 13th Workshop on Economics of Information Security (WEIS)*, June 2014.

[4] L. Daigle. RFC 3912: WHOIS Protocol Specification. *IETF*, Sept. 2004.

[5] Z. Durumeric, E. Wustrow, and J. A. Halderman. ZMap: Fast Internet-Wide Scanning and its Security Applications. In *Proceedings of the 22nd USENIX Security Symposium*, Aug. 2013.

[6] M. Felegyhazi, C. Kreibich, and V. Paxson. On the Potential of Proactive Domain Blacklisting. In *Proceedings of the USENIX Workshop on Large-scale Exploits and Emergent Threats (LEET)*, San Jose, CA, Apr. 2010.

[7] I. Fette, N. Sadeh, and A. Tomasic. Learning to Detect Phishing Emails. In *Proceedings of the International World Wide Web Conference*, May 2007.

[8] T. Frosch. Mining DNS-related Data for Suspicious Features. Master's thesis, Ruhr Universitat Bochum, 2012.

[9] M. Gabielkov and A. Legout. The Complete Picture of the Twitter Social Graph. In *ACM CoNEXT 2012 Student Workshop*, Dec. 2012.

[10] H. Gao, J. Hu, C. Wilson, Z. Li, Y. Chen, and B. Y. Zhao. Detecting and Characterizing Social Spam Campaigns. In *Proceedings of the 10th ACM SIGCOMM Conference on Internet Measurement (IMC)*, 2010.

[11] S. Hao, M. Thomas, V. Paxson, N. Feamster, C. Kreibich, C. Grier, and S. Hollenbeck. Understanding the Domain Registration Behavior of Spammers. In *Proceedings of the 13th ACM/USENIX Conference on Internet Measurement (IMC)*, 2013.

[12] K. Harrenstien, M. Stahl, and E. Feinler. RFC 812: NICNAME/WHOIS. *IETF*, Mar. 1982.

[13] ICANN. Draft Report for the Study of the Accuracy of WHOIS Registrant Contact Information. `https://www.icann.org/en/system/files/newsletters/whois-accuracy-study-17jan10-en.pdf`, Jan. 2010.

[14] ICANN. Policy Issue Brief — gTLD WHOIS. `https://www.icann.org/resources/pages/whois-2012-06-14-en`, June 2012.

[15] J. D. Lafferty, A. McCallum, and F. C. N. Pereira. Conditional Random Fields: Probabilistic Models for Segmenting and Labeling Sequence Data. In *Proceedings of the Eighteenth International Conference on Machine Learning (ICML)*, 2001.

[16] A. McCallum and W. Li. Early Results for Named Entity Recognition with Conditional Random Fields, Feature Induction and Web-enhanced Lexicons. In *Proceedings of the Seventh Conference on Natural Language Learning (CONLL)*, 2003.

[17] D. K. McGratn and M. Gupta. Behind Phishing: An Examination of Phisher Modi Operandi. In *Proceedings of the USENIX Workshop on Large-scale Exploits and Emergent Threats (LEET)*, Apr. 2008.

[18] A. Mislove, H. S. Koppula, K. P. Gummadi, P. Druschel, and B. Bhattacharjee. Growth of the Flickr Social Network. In *Proceedings of the 1st ACM SIGCOMM Workshop on Social Networks (WOSN)*, Aug. 2008.

[19] A. Mislove, M. Marcon, K. P. Gummadi, P. Druschel, and B. Bhattacharjee. Measurement and Analysis of Online Social Networks. In *Proceedings of the 5th ACM/USENIX Internet Measurement Conference (IMC)*, Oct. 2007.

[20] A. Newton and S. Hollenbeck. Registration Data Access Protocol Query Format: Draft Standard. `https://tools.ietf.org/html/draft-ietf-weirds-rdap-query-18`, Dec. 2014.

[21] J. Nocedal and S. J. Wright. *Numerical Optimization*. Springer, New York, 2nd edition, 2006.

[22] Nominet. Contact Data Disclosure in the .uk WHOIS: Appendix I. `http://www.nominet.org.uk/sites/default/files/Appendix-I-Comparative-registry-and-WHOIS-data-publication-review.pdf`, 2015.

[23] F. Sha and F. Pereira. Shallow Parsing with Conditional Random Fields. In *Proceedings of the Conference of the North American Chapter of the Association for Computational Linguistics on Human Language Technology (NAACL)*, 2003.

[24] T. Stallings, B. Wardman, G. Warner, and S. Thapaliya. "WHOIS" Selling All The Pills. *International Journal of Forensic Science*, 7(2):46–63, 2012.

[25] J. Szurdi. Understanding the Purpose of Domain Registrations. Master's thesis, Budapest University of Technology and Economics, 2012.

[26] T. Vissers, W. Joosen, and N. Nikiforakis. Parking Sensors: Analyzing and Detecting Parking Domains. In *Proceedings of the Network and Distributed System Security Symposum (NDSS)*, Feb. 2015.

APPENDIX

A. PROBABILISTIC INFERENCE

In this appendix we describe the essential computations for probabilistic inference in CRFs. By exploiting the Markov property in CRFs, we can efficiently compute both the log-likelihood in eq. (4) and the most likely label sequence in eq. (5).

First, we consider the normalization factor in eq. (3), whose computation requires summing over the exponentially many label sequences of length T. Let n denote the number of states in the CRF. As a useful shorthand, we define an $n \times n$ matrix $\mathbf{M_t}$ at each time step t, whose elements are given by:

$$[\mathbf{M_t}]_{ij} = \exp\left[\sum_k \theta_k f_k(y_{t-1}{=}i, y_t{=}j, x_t)\right]. \quad (9)$$

As previously noted, it is to be understood in eq. (9) that the sum over k at time $t{=}1$ only ranges over those features that do not have any dependence on the argument y_{t-1}. It is then a straightforward exercise to show that the normalization factor in eq. (3) is given by:

$$Z_\theta(\mathbf{x}) = \sum_{ij} [\mathbf{M_1 M_2} \ldots \mathbf{M_T}]_{ij}. \quad (10)$$

This computation, which involves T matrix-vector products, can be performed in $O(n^2T)$ operations.

Once the normalization factor in eq. (10) is computed, the log-likelihood in eq. (4) follows immediately. In particular, substituting eq. (2) into eq. (4), we obtain:

$$\mathcal{L}(\theta) = \sum_{r=1}^{R}\left[\sum_{t,k} \theta_k f_k(y^r_{t-1}, y^r_t, x^r_t) - \log Z_\theta(\mathbf{x}^r)\right]. \quad (11)$$

Eq. (11) gives the log-likelihood $\mathcal{L}(\theta)$ explicitly as a function of the model parameters θ. In order to optimize these parameters, it is of course necessary to compute the gradient $\frac{\partial \mathcal{L}}{\partial \theta}$. This can be done using the forward-backard algorithm for CRFs, which involves just a simple extension of the procedure for computing the normalization factor $Z_\theta(\mathbf{x})$. In particular, the elements of the gradient are closely related to the marginal probabilities of the distribution in eq. (2). But these, for example, are given simply by:

$$\begin{aligned}&\Pr_\theta(y_{t-1}{=}\ell, y_t{=}m|\mathbf{x}) \\ &= \frac{1}{Z_\theta(\mathbf{x})}\sum_{ij} [\mathbf{M_1} \ldots \mathbf{M_{t-1}}]_{i\ell}\, [\mathbf{M_t} \ldots \mathbf{M_T}]_{mj}. \quad (12)\end{aligned}$$

We refer the reader to the classic treatment [15] of CRFs for more details.

Finally we show how to compute the most likely sequence of labels in eq. (5). The computation is simplified by working in the log-domain and noting that the normalization factor $Z_\theta(\mathbf{x})$ is independent of $\mathbf{y}$. From these considerations we obtain the simpler expression:

$$\mathbf{y}^* = \arg\max_{\mathbf{y}}\left[\sum_{t,k} \theta_k f_k(y_{t-1}, y_t, x_t)\right]. \quad (13)$$

The computation in eq. (13) is a straightforward exercise in dynamic programming. We introduce an $n \times T$ matrix $\mathbf{V}$ and define its first column by:

$$V_{i1} = \sum_k \theta_k f_k(y_1{=}i, x_1). \quad (14)$$

Then we fill in the matrix elements recursively, one column at a time, as follows:

$$V_{jt} = \max_i \left[V_{i,t-1} + \sum_k \theta_k f_k(i,j,x_t)\right]. \quad (15)$$

In terms of this matrix, the most likely label at time T is simply by $y^*_T = \arg\max_i V_{iT}$. To derive the most likely labels at earlier times, we only need to record the index used at each step of the recursion in eq. (15). In particular, let

$$\text{INDEX}_t(j) = \arg\max_i \left[V_{i,t-1} + \sum_k \theta_k f_k(i,j,x_t)\right]. \quad (16)$$

Then in terms of these indices, the most likely labels at all earlier times are derived from the backtracking procedure:

$$y^*_t = \text{INDEX}_{t+1}(y^*_{t+1}). \quad (17)$$

Finally we note that this computation for the most likely labels y^*_t can also be performed in $O(n^2T)$ operations.

From .academy to .zone: An Analysis of the New TLD Land Rush

Tristan Halvorson
trhalvorson@cs.ucsd.edu

Matthew F. Der
mfder@cs.ucsd.edu

Ian Foster
idfoster@cs.ucsd.edu

Stefan Savage
savage@cs.ucsd.edu

Lawrence K. Saul
saul@cs.ucsd.edu

Geoffrey M. Voelker
voelker@cs.ucsd.edu

Department of Computer Science and Engineering
University of California, San Diego

ABSTRACT

The `com`, `net`, and `org` TLDs contain roughly 150 million registered domains, and domain registrants often have a difficult time finding a desirable and available name. In 2013, ICANN began delegation of a new wave of TLDs into the Domain Name System with the goal of improving meaningful name choice for registrants. The new rollout resulted in over 500 new TLDs in the first 18 months, nearly tripling the number of TLDs. Previous rollouts of small numbers of new TLDs have resulted in a burst of defensive registrations as companies aggressively defend their trademarks to avoid consumer confusion. This paper analyzes the types of domain registrations in the new TLDs to determine registrant behavior in the brave new world of naming abundance. We also examine the cost structures and monetization models for the new TLDs to identify which registries are profitable. We gather DNS, Web, and WHOIS data for each new domain, and combine this with cost structure data from ICANN, the registries, and domain registrars to estimate the total cost of the new TLD program. We find that only 15% of domains in the new TLDs show characteristics consistent with primary registrations, while the rest are promotional, speculative, or defensive in nature; indeed, 16% of domains with NS records do not even resolve yet, and 32% are parked. Our financial analysis suggests only half of the registries have earned enough to cover their application fees, and 10% of current registries likely never will solely from registration revenue.

Categories and Subject Descriptors

C.2.m [**Computer Communication Networks**]: Miscellaneous; K.4.1 [**Computers and Society**]: Public Policy Issues

Keywords

Domain Name System; Top-Level Domains; Registration Intent; Internet Economics

IMC'15, October 28–30, 2015, Tokyo, Japan.
© 2015 ACM. ISBN 978-1-4503-3848-6/15/10 ...$15.00.
http://dx.doi.org/10.1145/2815675.2815696.

1. INTRODUCTION

Nearly any successful company today needs a good Internet presence, and most see a memorable domain name as a key part of that presence. Though a nearly infinite set of possible domain names exist, any given name is unique, and memorable names often change hands for thousands or even millions of dollars. The Domain Name System (DNS) originally included only a small handful of top-level domains (TLDs), and ICANN has kept that number low until recent times. The benefits of a new TLD seem obvious at first glance: simple and memorable strings, long since taken in the older TLDs, become available again under a new namespace. However, many registrations in new TLDs go towards defensive registrations, brand or trademark owners trying to protect their names.

Starting in 2013, delegation began of a whole new wave of TLDs. Whereas ICANN debated the inclusion of previous TLDs independently and over the course of multiple ICANN board meetings, TLDs in the new program go through a standard application process which does not include ICANN-wide attention. The new expansion has resulted in a swift expansion of the TLD namespace: on October 1, 2013, shortly before the beginning of the program, the root zone contained 318 TLDs, mostly country code TLDs (ccTLDs). As of April 15, 2015, the root zone contained 897 TLDs, an expansion of 579 TLDs in less than two years.

This paper identifies the impact of the New gTLD Program on the domain name ecosystem. Previous TLD additions, such as `biz` [12] and `xxx` [11], caused widespread speculation and defensive registrations, but this larger expansion could discourage both. With hundreds of new TLDs, we expect many smaller companies to find it infeasible to defend their name in each. Additionally, such a sharp increase in simple-word second-level domains could make it difficult for speculators to resell even desirable names. The program's success also depends on how Internet users view the new domains. Do consumers see TLDs as interchangeable, or will new TLDs discourage users from visiting the associated domain? To answer these questions, we make the following contributions:

- We **classify registration intent** with a methodology derived from our work on `xxx` [11]. The application of the methodology to the New gTLD Program presented additional scaling difficulties, most notably requiring further automation of domain analysis. Our main contribution is the timely result of this methodology applied to the TLD landscape during its current period of swift expansion.

- We determine the program's **impact on the old TLDs**, both on registration rates and on the types of registrations.
- We examine **registry profitability** to learn where the registration money goes and what kinds of TLDs get the most registrations.

Taken together, our findings suggest that the new gTLDs have yet to provide value to the Internet community in the same way as legacy TLDs. Although the new TLDs greatly expand the domain name space, overall we find that speculative and defensive registrations dominate the growth of registrations in new TLDs. For domains that resolve with some kind of content, over 45% are speculative in nature, nearly 40% are defensive, and less than 15% host primary Web content. Users also visit new domains in the new TLDs less frequently than in the old, and new TLD domains are more than twice as likely to appear on a blacklist within the first month of registration. Finally, we also find that the new TLDs have yet to have significant impact on the old TLDs. Registrations in the new TLDs generally increase the number of total registrations, and `com` continues to dominate Internet domain name registration activity overall.

2. BACKGROUND

The Domain Name System (DNS) is the Internet service that maps human-readable names to machine addresses. In the Internet today, the DNS is overseen by the Internet Corporation for Assigned Names and Numbers (ICANN), which holds the authority for establishing new top-level domains (TLDs). After a number of minor TLD additions in the decade previous (e.g., `biz`, `info`, `mobi`, `xxx`), ICANN initiated a new process in 2008 to normalize the policies for creating new gTLDs. In late 2013, the first new gTLD was delegated. The length of this process reflects the significant complexity involved, the range of stakeholders and the significant potential for conflict. In this section, we provide background on how the domain name ecosystem works, how companies apply for a TLD in the new program, and who the significant players are.

There are three key actors in the DNS ecosystem:

Registries operate TLDs and have a contract with ICANN for each one.

Registrars sell domain names, typically in many different TLDs, and also have an ICANN accreditation.

Registrants are entities that buy domain names.

and our goal in this paper is to explore how these actors have reacted to the rapid expansion of the DNS name space.

2.1 The Delegation Process

In preparation for the expansion, ICANN formalized a detailed application process for those seeking to sponsor new TLDs (well over 300 pages in English) [19]. Each applicant prepared an extensive submission covering business, technical and operational issues and paid a USD 185,000 evaluation fee for the initial evaluation. These applications in turn were open to public comment and for review by government interests and interested stakeholders. In such cases, the TLD might undergo extended evaluation, dispute resolution, or a contention period when multiple applications pursue the same TLD (and in such cases the fees could increase considerably). With the addition of legal fees, drafting fees, data escrow fees, auctions for contested names and operational costs, applications for a new gTLD require significant capital and thus favor those large organizations (e.g., Google, Amazon, Donuts) who would amortize these expenses across many such applications.

Those applicants whose submission survived evaluation transitioned to a phase called "delegation" (when the TLD is entered into the zones of the root DNS servers) subject to a series of contractual obligations (e.g., a registry agreement with ICANN covering dispute resolution, fees, technical standards, etc.) and technical tests. Delegation marks the time when end users can first resolve domains under the new TLD and is thus a major milestone for any registry. Due to capacity constraints inside ICANN and changes in applicant business goals, there can be considerable delay between evaluation and delegation.

2.2 TLD Rollout

After delegation, the TLD life cycle depends on the registry. TLDs intended for public use have a sunrise phase, a period of time during which only trademark holders may register. This phase gives brand holders a first chance to defend their names. Most TLDs follow with a "land rush" phase where registrants can get an earlier chance at any domain name for a price premium, usually on the order of a few hundred dollars. Finally, public TLDs will have a general availability phase, where registrations become first-come first-served, and registrants just pay the standard yearly registration rate for most names. Though ICANN has some minimum length standards for the sunrise phase, the registry chooses the exact length of sunrise, domain pricing and promotions, and all of the details about the other introductory phases.

A subset of TLDs are never made available for public registration. For these private TLDs, the only intended registrant is the registry itself, frequently to protect a brand mark. For example, the TLD `aramco` is closed to the public and only Saudi Aramco and its affiliates can operate domains under this TLD.

2.3 Examples

The data for this paper comes from hundreds of new TLDs, many of them managed by unique registries. We cannot describe all actors due to space limitations, but this section describes some of the larger registries and their TLDs.

2.3.1 Donuts

Though most registries run one or a small handful of new TLDs, Donuts Inc. is the largest and manages hundreds. Their TLDs largely consist of topical English words, such as "singles", "digital", and "coffee". The company's founders each have years of experience in the domain name industry, and the company secured over USD 100 million in venture capital [9]. Another large registry, Rightside, runs the technical infrastructure for Donuts TLDs. In return, Donuts gives some of its TLDs to Rightside after they reach delegation.

2.3.2 The `xyz` TLD

The `xyz` TLD is a generic alternative to `com` and is the largest in the new program. In the middle of 2014, Network Solutions, a large registrar, began offering `xyz` domains for free to some of their customers on an opt-out basis (e.g., the owner of `example.com` would find the domain `example.xyz` had appeared in their account). While registrants received these domains for free, Network Solutions still paid the registry full price for each domain [16, 26], although documents released as part of a lawsuit by Verisign suggest Network Solutions may have paid for these domains with advertising credit [8].

Due to this promotion, the number of registered domains in `xyz` rose by thousands per day in its earliest days until early August, when the number of registrations slowed to around 428,806 domains. Since then, `xyz` registrations appear at a much lower rate:

the number of domains finally doubled on April 13, 2015, taking over eight months to register a number of domains that originally took only two.

Registrants, however, appear to have only limited interest in these free domains. In our data set, 351,457 `xyz` domains (46% of `xyz`) remain unused and display a standard Network Solutions registration page when visited in a Web browser. Upon further analysis, we find that 351,440 of these domains appeared in the zone file in its first two months and still showed the unused Network Solutions template six months later. In fact, 82% of the 428,806 `xyz` domains in the August 2, 2014 zone file originated from this promotion and remained unclaimed as of early February 3, 2015. According to the monthly reports, Network Solutions had acted as registrar for only 360,683 `xyz` domains at the end of July, 2015, so registrants from this promotion claimed fewer than 10,000 free domains in the first six months.

2.3.3 *The* `science` *TLD*

The `science` TLD allows generic registrations, but targets the scientific community. Starting with general availability on February 24, 2015, the AlpNames registrar offered `science` TLDs for free. Similar to `xyz`, this promotion appears to have significantly impacted the number of `science` registrations: within only a few days, the TLD boasted 36,952 unique domains. The promotion has since ended, but the AlpNames registrar still sells `science` domains for $0.50, making it one of the cheapest TLDs. Two months after the start of general availability it had 174,403 registrations. Even though general availability started after our cutoff date, `science` is already the third largest TLD.

2.3.4 *The* `realtor` *TLD*

The National Association of Realtors owns the `realtor` TLD and targets accredited realtors, but also requires all registrants to prove that they are members of their association [22]. The registry provides the first year of registration for free to anyone that provides their NAR membership information. The promotion only applies to a single domain per NAR membership number. 46,920 `realtor` domains (51%) still show the default Web template provided by the registrar.

3. DATA AND INFRASTRUCTURE

We use data from many sources in our analysis, including zone files and several reports from ICANN. We actively crawl Web and DNS for each domain, and compare our findings with Alexa rankings and various blacklists. In this section we describe our data sources and data collection infrastructure.

3.1 Zone Files

When a registrant purchases a new domain from a registrar, the registrar sends a request to the registry with the domain and name server information. Once the domain goes live, it will appear in that TLD's *zone file*. At a high level, a zone file reflects a snapshot of a DNS server's anticipated answers to DNS queries. For a domain to resolve, it must have name server information in the zone file.

ICANN requires most registries to provide zone file access for a variety of purposes, including research. Some registries, such as most ccTLDs, do not need to provide access. For zones delegated prior to 2013, we gained access to their zone files by signing and faxing a paper contract to the TLD's registry, each of which gave us FTP credentials. We originally used this method to gain access to `aero`, `biz`, `com`, `info`, `name`, `net`, `org`, `us`, and `xxx`.

In anticipation for the rapid TLD expansion, ICANN developed a more scalable solution to zone file access requests, known as the Centralized Zone Data Service (CZDS). Registries and interested third parties can all apply for accounts on the service. After filling out their online profile with contact information and project details, requesting access to multiple zone files becomes straightforward. Registries still see multiple requests and can approve or deny them individually, but the process is much simpler. Once the registry provides access, the user can download the zone file through a simple API call up to once per day. Older TLDs can migrate to the new system for zone access, but progress has been slow; so far, only `museum`, `coop`, and `xxx` have migrated.

We have an account on CZDS, and manually refresh all new or expired approval requests almost once per day.[1] We have access to the zone files for hundreds of domains, most using the new CZDS system. We download a new snapshot of each daily, totaling 3.8 GB of gzipped text, more than half from `com`. For the analysis in this paper we simplify the zones and store all NS, A, and AAAA records on our HDFS cluster, and then store the raw zones on our archive server for future use.

3.2 ICANN Public Data

ICANN also requires each registry to provide a handful of summary reports. We have used most of them at some point in our methodology. The monthly transaction reports are particularly useful for our study. ICANN requires each registry to publish monthly summary statistics about the number of domains registered, transferred, expired, and renewed for each accredited registrar. We use the monthly summary reports to identify the number of registered domains that do not have any name server information and therefore do not appear in the zone file. We also use their breakdown of domains per registrar when estimating registration costs.

We also relied upon ICANN's New gTLD Current Application Status listing [20]. We used the data provided to determine TLD status and registry information as the new TLDs worked through the application system.

3.3 Our TLD Set

We include results for new TLDs that started general availability by the date of publication of ICANN's latest monthly registry reports on January 31, 2015, which altogether totals 502 new TLDs. Table 1 breaks down these new TLDs into various high-level categories, together with the total number of new domains registered in them at the time we crawled them.

We have focused our analysis on why registrants spend money on domains in the new TLD program. Some companies defensively register private TLDs, while others simply want a shorter domain name for their services. However, some companies in the latter category have not established their presence in their new TLDs yet, so we do not have a methodology to differentiate between these cases. Thus, we are more interested in public TLDs, where we can establish the registrant intent of individual domain names.

We differentiate public and private TLDs by checking public information about the start of general availability, as provided by several large domain registrars and nTLDStats [21], a Web site that tracks information on the new TLD program and is well-regarded in the domain community. Registries include their TLDs in these listings when they want public registrations, since the registrar collects this list in anticipation of selling domains in the TLD. This classification technique held up to the 15 randomly sampled private domains we verified manually. With this classification, 128 of the 502 new TLDs are private.

---

[1]We considered scripting our requests, but CZDS blocked obvious scripting attempts, so we did not pursue this further.

	TLDs	Registered Domains
Private	128	—
IDN	44	533,249
Public, Pre-GA	40	—
Public, Post-GA	290	3,657,848
Generic	259	3,061,416
Geographic	27	494,824
Community	4	101,608
Total	502	4,191,097

Table 1: The number of new TLDs in each category on February 3, 2015, and their sizes. For the three TLDs for which we had pending access requests, we used the size of the closest zone file.

GTLD	Domains	Availability
xyz	768,911	2014-06-02
club	166,072	2014-05-07
berlin	154,988	2014-03-18
wang	119,193	2014-06-29
realtor	91,372	2014-10-23
guru	79,892	2014-02-05
nyc	68,840	2014-10-08
ovh	57,349	2014-10-02
link	57,090	2014-04-15
london	54,144	2014-09-09

Table 2: The ten largest TLDs in our public set with their general availability dates.

In addition to the above, we found it difficult to learn substantial information about the new internationalized TLDs. In many cases, registrants can only purchase domains for them from international registrars. They tend to have rules for sunrise and general availability that we found unclear even with the help of a native speaker. As a result, we also do not include these 44 new TLDs in our analysis. Additionally, we focus on domains that reached general availability (GA) before our February 3, 2015 Web crawl so the set of registrants can include all prospective domain owners.

After removing private and internationalized TLDs from those that had already began general availability, we end with a set of 290 new public TLDs. The total set of TLDs includes generic words like `bike` and `academy` and geographical regions like `berlin` and `london`, both represented in Table 1. Additionally, four TLDs gate registrations to members of a particular community, such as the `realtor` TLD for accredited realtors. To give a sense of how many common word TLDs exist, our data set contains four synonyms for "picture": `photo` (12,933 domains), `photos` (17,500 domains), `pics` (6,506 domains), and `pictures` (4,633 domains). Table 2 gives an overview of the largest TLDs in our set, with some of the geographic TLDs featuring prominently. In the rest of this paper, we restrict our analyses to these 290 TLDs.

3.4 Active Web

For each domain in the zone file of a new gTLD, we visit the Web page hosted on port 80 of the domain with a crawler based on Firefox, an improved version of the crawler used in our previous study of `xxx` [11]. Our browser-based Web crawler executes JavaScript, loads Flash, and in general renders the page as close as possible to what an actual user would see. We also follow redirects of all kinds. After the browser loads all resources sent by the remote server, we capture the DOM and any JavaScript transformations it has made. We also fetch page headers, the response code, and the redirect chain.

Our primary data set for this paper is our Web crawl of all domains in the new TLDs on February 3, 2015. We chose this date due to its proximity to the timing of the latest ICANN reports, which reflect the number of registered domains in each TLD as of the end of January 2015.

3.5 Active DNS

Every time we Web crawl a domain, we also perform a DNS query using a DNS crawler developed for [15]. We follow CNAME and NS records and continue to query until we find an A or AAAA record, or determine that no such record exists. We save every record we find along the chain. We use DNS data to detect invalid NS records and to annotate each Web crawl with its CNAME chain.

3.6 Active WHOIS

Registry operators for most TLDs must publicly provide accurate domain ownership data using the WHOIS protocol. ICANN intends the use of WHOIS for "any lawful purpose except to enable marketing or spam, or to enable high volume, automated processes to query a registrar or registry's systems" [14]. In particular, ICANN encourages its use by consumers, registrars, and law enforcement, and discourages its use by spammers [29].

WHOIS server operators have leeway in how they achieve these goals. They typically rate limit requests, and responses do not need to conform to any standard format, which causes parsing difficulty even once records are properly fetched. We only query WHOIS for a small percentage of domains in the new gTLD program as an investigative step towards understanding ownership and intent.

3.7 Pricing Data

One dimension of our analysis focuses on the economic impact of the new TLD program, a task that requires domain pricing information. Unfortunately for our data collection purposes, registries do not sell domain names directly, but instead sell them through ICANN-accredited registrars. A registry can sell their domain names through any registrars they choose, but each must get similar wholesale prices and promotions [5].

We gathered pricing data for domains in the new gTLDs from a wide range of registrars. First, we collected data from the most common registrars for as many TLDs as possible. In some cases the registrar included a pricing table with information for many TLDs and we were able to automate the data collection process. Other registrars only showed pricing information after querying a domain name's availability, which required many separate queries. We made these queries manually. Some registrars made us solve a single captcha after five to ten requests.

Obtaining pricing information for the most common registrars simplifies the process and allows us to obtain a large number of (registrar, TLD) pairs in a short amount of time. However, we ultimately want to estimate pricing per TLD, so we would like to have registrar pricing data for many domain registrations in each TLD. Some TLDs do not sell well or are not available at the most common registrars (e.g., geographical TLDs for non-Western regions). We use the monthly registry reports to learn how many domains each registrar manages in each TLD, and we collect pricing information for the top five in each. Where possible, we also removed registry-owned domains from our analysis, since they did not cost anything. When registrars reported prices for non-standard time intervals or in foreign currencies, we used the current exchange rate to convert all prices to US dollars per year.

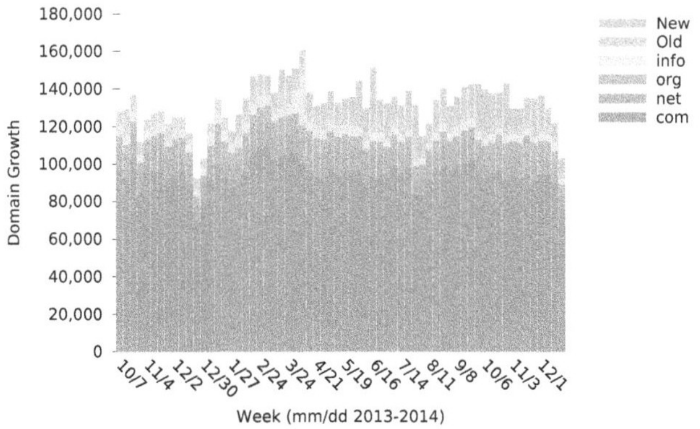

Figure 1: Number of new domains per day. Bars indicate the average rate for each week.

Registries reserve a set of strings which they sell for increased prices, known as *premium domain names*. For instance, GoDaddy sells normal `club` domains for $10 USD, but `universities.club` costs $5,000 USD, and this increase in price represents revenue to both the registry and registrar. These domains number in the thousands for any given TLD, and prices can vary per string. Our methodology treats premium domains as normal domains, thus underestimating registry and registrar revenue. Premium domain sales do not always correlate with wholesale revenue, and we do not see a scalable method to address this problem.

3.8 Alexa

We use the Alexa top million domains list to make an estimate of how often users visit domains in the new TLDs [1]. Alexa collects their data by allowing browser extensions to include their measurement code in exchange for providing domain analytics, and by allowing Web page operators to do the same. We use a domain's presence in the list as an indication that users visit it, but do not place any emphasis on domain rankings.

3.9 Blacklists

We also compare new domain registrations with URIBL, a publicly available domain blacklist, to see how the blacklist rate compares between old and new TLDs [27]. We use their high-volume rsync instance to download a new copy of the blacklist every hour. Though they provide many types of blacklists, we only use the standard and highest-volume blacklist, labeled "black", as the rest tend to be lower volume. This list represents the domains most likely to be malicious, while the other lists include domains detected through more experimental methodologies.

4. REGISTRATION VOLUME

We first look at the impact of the new TLDs on overall registration volume. The new TLDs represent new opportunities for registering domains. As registrants create new domains, one possibility is that they decide to create them in the new TLDs rather than the old, thereby displacing registration activity in the old TLDs (e.g., because names taken in `com` are available in the new TLDs). Another possibility is that the new opportunities motivate even more registrations, thereby growing total registration activity overall.

Figure 1 shows the number of new domain registrations per week broken down into various categories. Days for which we did not have access to the zone files resulted in slight drops in the graph.

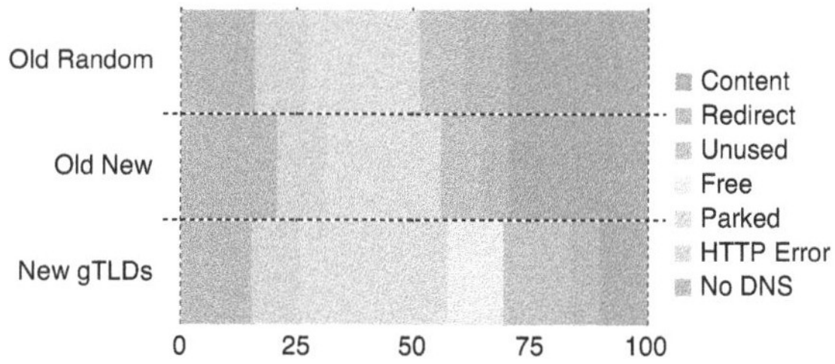

Figure 2: Classifications for all domains in the new TLDs, a random sample of the old TLDs, and a month of new domain registrations in the old TLDs.

We show the most active old TLDs individually, the remaining old TLDs grouped into "Old", and the new TLDs in "New".

Overall, the introduction of the new TLDs had only minimal impact in the rate of registration of the old TLDs. The new TLDs generally increase the total number of registrations rather than shift focus from old to new TLDs. However, the new TLDs see far fewer registrations than the old TLDs, largely because `com` continues to dominate.

5. CONTENT CATEGORIES

As a first step towards learning the intent of each domain's registrant, we classify the technical data each domain returns when queried by our DNS or HTTP infrastructure. We perform this classification with features of both crawls, including DNS CNAME records, Web headers, Web contents, and the NS records in the zone files.

Domains with invalid DNS or HTTP errors are straightforward to identify, but in many instances, we need to classify the domains based on the textual content they return to HTTP queries. We use a combination of automated machine learning techniques and manual inspection of Web pages hosted at these domains.

We assign each domain to one of the following seven categories:

No DNS domains do not successfully resolve DNS queries.

HTTP Error domains have valid DNS, but do not return an HTTP 200 when queried.

Parked domains are owned by an ad network or are for sale by their owners and typically return Web pages dominated by ads.

Unused domains return HTTP content that is not consumer-ready, including empty pages, default Web server templates, or PHP errors.

Free domains include domains given out as part of a promotion that still have the original template, as well as domains with registry-owned Web templates.

Defensive Redirect domains redirect through one of several technical mechanisms to a different domain name.

Content domains host valid Web content for users to visit.

We start by presenting high-level content categorizations, including domains in the older TLDs as a reference point. Then Section 5.2 provides more detail about our clustering methodology, and Section 5.3 describes the seven categories in more detail.

5.1 Content Summary

To place the new TLD results in context, we present domain classifications for three data sets. The first includes all domains in the new TLDs as of February 3, 2015. The second includes 3 mil-

Content Category	*Results*	
No DNS	567,390	15.6%
HTTP Error	362,727	10.0%
Parked	1,161,892	31.9%
Unused	504,928	13.9%
Free	432,323	11.9%
Defensive Redirect	236,380	6.5%
Content	372,569	10.2%
Total	3,638,209	100.0%

Table 3: Overall content classifications for all domains in the zone file for the new public TLDs.

lion domains from the old TLDs defined in Section 3.1 chosen uniformly at random. The third includes all domains in the same set of old TLDs that were newly registered during December 2014. (Delays in our `com` processing pipeline prevented us from using a more recent data set.) Figure 2 summarizes all three data sets. This paper focuses on the new TLDs, so we focus on those domains. Table 3 shows exact values for the 290 public English TLDs described in Section 3.3, minus `quebec`, `scot`, and `gal`, the TLDs for which we did not have zone file access at the time.

For most categories the classification breakdown is comparable among the three data sets: erroneous domains (No DNS and HTTP Error) account for about a quarter of all domains, another quarter utilizes domain parking, and roughly 20% of domains are either unused or redirect elsewhere. The old and new TLDs differ greatly in content and promotional domains: the new TLDs show a dearth of content, but make up for it with a high volume of free domains, which domain owners do not actively use yet.

Figure 3 shows our content classification for the 20 largest TLDs that allow public registrations. Most TLDs show a typical split between the major content categories, but other TLDs show very different registration types, especially those with free domains.

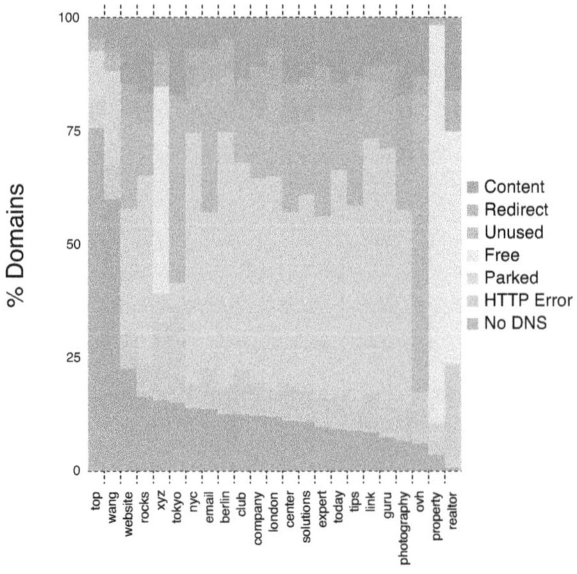

Figure 3: Domain classifications in individual TLDs for the 20 most common. We have sorted TLDs by fraction of "No DNS" to better highlight the category breakdowns of successful content.

5.2 Content Clustering

Our goal is to cluster Web pages hosted at domains into one of the content categories. Two key challenges to classifying content are the sheer size of the data (millions of domains), and the lack of labeled data for training a classifier. With so many unlabeled Web pages, we must learn from scratch to classify the domains.

Our first step is to cluster Web pages with highly similar content. This procedure groups together duplicate and near-duplicate Web pages, which commonly arise when HTML is automatically generated using a fixed template. Prevalent examples include parked pages, and default placeholder pages served by a registrar before the registrant publishes any content.

To map Web pages to inputs for a clustering algorithm, we follow a conventional "bag-of-words" approach which extracts HTML features from the Web pages. In particular, we compose a dictionary of all terms that appear in the HTML source code, and for each Web page, we count the number of times that each term appears. In this way, each Web page is represented as a sparse, high-dimensional vector of feature counts. We implemented a custom bag-of-words feature extractor which forms tag-attribute-value triplets from HTML tags, as described in [7].

For reasons of computability and conciseness of results, we begin by clustering roughly one tenth of the crawled Web pages. We used the k-means clustering algorithm with $k = 400$ to organize these Web pages into groups of high similarity (based on the Euclidean distance between their feature vectors). We set k to be intentionally large because we wished to discover especially cohesive clusters of replicated Web pages.

Next we manually inspected the resulting clusters using a custom visualization tool. The tool displays screenshots of how the Web pages rendered in our crawler and provides a link to the HTML source next to each screenshot. To facilitate efficient manual review, the tool presents a condensed view of the clusters by showing only a sample of Web pages in each one. Specifically, it sorts the Web pages in each cluster by their distance to the cluster centroid, then displays the top and bottom-ranked pages as well as a random sample of pages in between. If all Web pages in this sample are visually nearly identical, we can conclude with confidence that the entirety of Web pages in the cluster have been appropriately grouped. Furthermore, we can classify Web pages in these perfectly homogenous clusters all together.

By examining the clusters, we placed domains into three broad categories according to their content: parked, content-free, and meaningful content. Our clustering approach was particularly effective at identifying large numbers of parked domains and content-free (or unused) domains that host a default registration page. The class of Web pages with meaningful content exhibits the most variety: Web content is highly diverse and unlikely to have the same degree of replication as the other two classes. Thus at this stage, we focused only on bulk labeling of clusters that clearly contained parked or content-free Web pages. If it was not visually obvious how to label a cluster in bulk, then its pages remained unclassified at this point. (In practice, though, we found that Web pages with content often were grouped together in clusters with wide diameters.)

After this phase of clustering, manual inspection, and labeling, we then aimed to classify domains that were not included in the initial subset. Now equipped with a large number of labeled examples, we used nearest neighbor classification to discover many more candidate Web pages which are likely parked or content-free. First, we extracted HTML features from the remaining Web pages, then mapped the pages into the same feature space as the original subset.

Then for each unlabeled Web page, we found its nearest neighbor by Euclidean distance in the labeled set and, if the distance was less than a strict threshold, we marked the page as a candidate for its neighbor's class. This thresholding minimizes false positives. This step continues to focus only on parked and content-free pages; no content pages were classified in this way. We modified our visualization tool to display candidates next to their nearest neighbor; if the Web pages were visually nearly the same, then we were confident in assigning the appropriate label to the candidates.

In one round of this nearest neighbor method, we were able to label many of the remaining (non-content) Web pages in our data set with high confidence. However, since we only clustered about one tenth of the Web pages at the outset, we likely missed different templates that did not appear in the initial subset. Thus, we iterated this approach to achieve greater coverage. That is, we clustered the remaining unlabeled Web pages, manually inspected and labeled homogenous clusters, and performed thresholded nearest neighbor classification—now with a larger set of labeled examples. We iterated this process until there were no more obviously cohesive clusters. Finally, after identifying all parked and content-free domains, we manually inspected a random sample of the remaining unlabeled Web pages. The results gave us confidence to conclude that the remaining Web pages contain legitimate content.

5.3 Content Categories

We use this content clustering methodology to create a cluster label for each domain. Then, we took any page metadata (e.g., DNS errors, HTTP status code, the redirect chain, etc.) and combined these features together to make a final classification.

The rest of this subsection describes how we combined those features to determine a final content category. For domains that might fall into multiple categories, we prioritize categories in the order listed in Table 3. For example, for parked domains that redirect to a different domain, usually as part of the parking program, we only classify as "Parked" and not "Defensive Redirect".

5.3.1 No DNS

Registrants purchase domain names from a registrar and pay a yearly fee to keep them, yet a large fraction of domains in the new gTLDs do not even resolve. Some of these registrants associate name server information with their domains, but these servers do not respond to DNS queries, or only respond with the DNS `REFUSED` error code. For instance, `adsense.xyz` has an NS record for `ns1.google.com`, but its name server returns `REFUSED` for all queries (which recursive resolvers usually report as `SERVFAIL` to the end user). Out of 3,638,209 domains in the new TLDs, we had 567,390 DNS failures with an associated NS record, or 15.6%.

Other registrants buy domains and then do not associate name server information with them. Since the zone files only contain associations between domain names and name servers, they contain no entries for this set of domains. We do not have a list of these domain names and do not have a clear mechanism to find them.

While we cannot enumerate these domains, we can infer their presence through the ICANN monthly reports. The monthly reports provide a summary of domain activity and transactions for all registered domains (i.e., domains with a yearly fee). We can use the difference between the number of domains in the ICANN reports and the number of domains in the zone file as an estimate for the number of domains with no name server information.

Our analysis shows that out of 3,754,141 total domains in the reports, 207,184 domains (5.5%) do not appear in their respective zone files. Registrants pay for these domains like any other, but they do not resolve.

Error Type	*Result*	
Connection Error	110,144	30.4%
HTTP 4xx	82,298	22.7%
HTTP 5xx	138,471	38.2%
Other	31,814	8.8%
Total	362,727	100.0%

Table 4: Breakdown of HTTP errors encountered when visiting Web pages.

5.3.2 HTTP Error

We next classify domains that resolve to an IP address, but return no result or an HTTP error code when queried on port 80. We suspect some of these error conditions are temporary. Others are likely longer-term misconfigurations by owners who do not care about the content hosted on the domains, making them likely brand defenders. Alternatively, these domains might serve a legitimate purpose that is motivated by content other than Web. Because we use the status code from the final landing page, even HTTP 3xx status codes indicate errors, typically a redirect loop.

We received 362,727 responses to that we classified as HTTP errors. Table 4 provides a breakdown. Notably, most domains in this category exhibit connection issues such as timeouts or return HTTP 5xx return codes, meant for internal server issues. The variety of errors is multifarious: overall we received responses with 43 unique HTTP status codes.[2]

5.3.3 Parked

Many domain registrants do not have a plan to monetize the content of their domain names. Most of them are speculating on the name itself, intending to sell it later for a profit. Some may have a plan to develop the site later in its lifetime, but have not put up any content yet. Still other owners initially created Web properties that turned out to be unsuccessful, and later parked them while waiting for expiration. Whatever the reason, domain parking is common in all TLDs. We discovered 1,161,892 parked domains in our data set, or 31.9% of all domains in the zone files.

Potential domain speculators have the choice of a large number of parking services. Some parking services also act as domain registrars (e.g., GoDaddy and Sedo), while others focus solely on parking. Registrants use their services by setting their name server (NS) record to the parking service's DNS servers, redirecting their Web traffic to the parking service, or setting a CNAME. Parking services that also act as registrars may or may not use different name servers for parked domains compared to normal registrations.

Parked domains come in two main varieties [3]. Most domain parking monetization is through pay per click (PPC) advertising. These parked pages look much like search result pages with links pertaining to words in the domain name. Each link on this page is an advertisement. Other parked domains use pay per redirect (PPR). When the target domain's owner purchases "direct navigation traffic" from an ad network used by the parking program, the parking service will redirect the user to a page run by an ad purchaser. Decisions to serve PPC or PPR to any particular visitor happen in real time based on characteristics provided by the traffic purchaser, including domain keywords or traffic from limited geographic regions.

[2]Six domains responded with the HTTP response code 418, an error code added as part of the Hyper Text Coffee Pot Control Protocol in a satirical RFC [13]. The return code means "I'm a teapot".

Feature	Domains	Coverage	Unique
Content Cluster	1,080,283	92.3%	277,754
Parking Redirect	638,757	55.0%	81,468
Parking NS	279,903	24.1%	124
Total	1,161,892	—	

Table 5: Our capture methods for parking and how many domains each catches. We identify most parking domains with more than one classifier; column 2 shows how many domains each classifier identifies, while the last column shows how many are unique to that classifier.

As a starting point, two previous studies also needed to classify parked domains as part of their work. Alrwais et al. focus on how parking programs operate, and use domains from known parking name servers as their source [3]. Vissers et al. focus on classifying parked domains, but use parking pages from known parking name servers as their inputs [28]. However, our problem is slightly different since we want to identify random pages from the Internet as parked or not. Some parking programs host both legitimate and parked pages using the same name servers, including one of the largest parking services, GoDaddy. We need a different approach to identifying parking than either of these papers suggest.

We identify parked domains with three mechanisms. First, we use our k-means content classifier to identify PPC parking services. Often there are many of these pages for each parking service, with variations only in the displayed links; all layout and remote resources remain constant for any given parking service. As such, they tend to cluster well and are easy to identify with this method.

Second, we use the visit's full redirect chain, acquired with the methodology described in Section 5.3.6, to identify PPR parking. These domains usually redirect through an ad network before landing at their final destination for accounting purposes. We manually inspected redirect chains for visits to known parking name servers to compile a set of URL features that indicate parking. For instance, if any URL contains "zeroredirect1.com" or both "domain" and "sale", we classify the domain as parked.

Finally, we use known parking name servers, such as those for `sedoparking.com`. We use this method only for servers we are confident host solely parked domains. We start by taking the intersection of the different sets used by Alrwais et al. [3] and Vissers et al. [28]; the intersection includes all but one of the name servers from the latter set. For each name server in the set intersection, we use our k-means classifier to determine if domains using that name server are parked or not. For those we did not identify as parking (a very small set), we manually inspect a random selection of screenshots and their redirect chains. If we believe them all to be parking traffic missed by our classifier, then we assume all domains using the name server are parked. With this additional verification step, we concluded with high confidence that all 14 name servers in our set are used strictly for domain parking. Finally, we added one additional name server (`parklogic.com`) to our set, which we found to be dedicated to parking services through our classification experiments.

Table 5 shows how many parked domains we identify with each method. We identify most parking domains with more than one of our three methods. In particular, we identify all but 124 of nearly 280,000 domains on our set of parking name servers with another approach. This high detection accuracy provides validation of our other parking classifiers, and further increases our confidence that we have identified the prevalent parking behaviors.

Mechanism	Domains	Coverage	Unique
CNAME	2,020	0.9%	729
Browser	211,065	89.3%	203,941
Frame	30,437	12.9%	24,571
Total	236,380	—	

Table 6: The mechanisms domain owners use to redirect to a different domain. Most domain owners use only browser-level redirects, but frames are still very common. Very few content domains use multiple redirect methods.

5.3.4 Unused

In our analysis, we find many Web pages that fit in none of the above categories, but also do not provide meaningful content. Most of these are placeholder pages served by a large registry with instructions for the owner on how to develop their domain. Others are empty Web pages, or the default template provided by a software package. Whatever the reason, these pages do not provide meaningful content to end users and we refer to them as "Unused".

Unused pages often appear in bulk, so we identify them using our k-means classifier. With this technique, we find 504,928 content-free domains in our data set, or 13.9% of domains in the new TLDs.

5.3.5 Free

Domains we identify as part of a promotion, such as those described in Section 2.3, get their own content classification. Most of these domains fall into the "Unused" category through a strict categorization, but the registrant plays a different role for these (which will be relevant when determining intent in Section 6).

Though not part of a promotion, the `property` TLD largely contains domains owned by Uniregistry, its registry. The TLD showed slow growth in all other time periods, but on February 1, 2015 it grew from 2,472 to 38,464 domains in a single day. Uniregistry owns all of these domains and hosts a standard sale page with the text "Make this name yours." We place these registry-owned content placeholders into the "Free" category as well.[3] In total, we find 432,323 free domains in the new TLD program (11.9%).

5.3.6 Defensive Redirects

Many domains in the new gTLDs have at least one redirect, and most of these point to a different domain. The role of the redirect depends on the type of content. Some parking programs redirect from the initial domain to a standard parking page, using the URL parameters to pass a domain identifier for revenue sharing purposes. Defensive registrations often redirect to the owner's other domain names, typically in an older TLD. We check for three kinds of redirects: CNAMEs, browser-level redirects, and single large frames. Table 6 shows how many domains redirect with each mechanism.

A CNAME is a DNS record type that acts like a symbolic link between two domains. Any DNS query that results in a CNAME causes the resolver to perform the same query on the target. Sometimes the result is another CNAME, which our DNS crawler must follow before finally resulting in an answer to the original query. Most domains with a CNAME only have a single CNAME, but chains of up to four are not uncommon in CDNs. For example, in our February 3 data set, the domain `tangyao.xyz` has a CNAME to `scwcty.gotoip2.com`. This domain has its own CNAME to `hkvhost660.800cdn.com`.

[3] We do not classify them as "Parking" because they do not show ads and they are owned by the registry.

Redirect To	*Number*
Defensive	236,380
Same TLD	7,135
Different New TLD	5,843
Different Old TLD	98,923
com	124,479
Structural	75,073
Same Domain	74,379
To IP	694
Total	311,453

Table 7: Which locations our visits were ultimately redirected towards.

Browser-level redirects happen when DNS resolves to a host running an HTTP server, but a query to that server returns a redirect which our browser will follow automatically. For example, an HTTP request to `tucsonphotobooth.com` returns an HTTP 302 redirect to `bumblebeephotobooth.com`, which modern browsers obey without user interaction. A domain owner can do this in a very large number of ways, such as with a 300–399 status code, an HTTP header, an HTML `meta` tag, or using JavaScript to set window.location. We find and store these redirects at crawl time, so we are robust to these and less common methods.

In practice, we find many pages that return valid HTML, do not redirect, and present only a single large frame to the end user, such that all visual content comes through the frame. Although it does not use an explicit redirection mechanism, this technique provides the same effect: a user visits one domain on their browser, and sees content from another. Since these frames serve the same purpose as a CNAME or an HTTP redirect, we consider these to be redirects as well.

To determine if a page contains only a single large frame, we first check how many frames the page contains. We do this in JavaScript in the browser, so we do not need to use textual analysis to find them. The remaining challenge is to differentiate between pages with a single large frame, and pages with real content that have a smaller frame, such as for page navigation or tracking purposes.

We differentiate between these classes using the DOM. First, we remove non-visible components from the page, as well as anything having to do with the frame itself: the `head` tag, `frameset` and `iframe` tags, and long URLs. These modifications are safe because we operate on the DOM, not the original HTML, so non-visible components that transform visual components (such as JavaScript) have already run. By examining the string length of the resulting DOM, the pages we crawl fall cleanly into two classes. Altogether, 49% of the filtered DOMs have a string length of less than 55 characters, but show variable behavior based on the few remaining tags. The remaining pages distribute mostly evenly with a few spikes corresponding to common page templates. A visual examination of the pages in these clusters shows that the short pages do show only a single large frame, while most of the large pages have other visual content.

The most important two pieces of the overall redirect chain are the starting domain and the final page that serves content. To determine the last, we check for a single large frame first, then a browser-level redirect, and finally a CNAME. A domain with all three behaviors serves its real content through the frame; the CNAME and browser-level redirects only point to the next resource. We classify redirects by the domain they point to: same-domain, same-TLD, "com", new-TLD, old-TLD, or IP.

Table 7 shows which of these six location types domains in the new TLDs tend to point towards. Though each of these domains has some form of redirect when fetching Web content, redirects to a page under the same domain name are less interesting because they reflect aspects of the structure of the Web page itself. Similarly, we cannot make any strong claims about redirects to a hard-coded IP address.

Instead, we only consider redirects to a different domain to fall into our redirect category. We do include redirects to other domains within the same TLD because in this case, the registrant is only using the destination domain for primary purposes. We find 236,380 off-domain redirects in our data set, or 6.5% of all domains in the new TLD zone files. 94.5% of defensive redirects point to domains in the old TLDs, with over half of those to `com`. In short, defensive redirects are only a small fraction of the overall registration behavior in the new TLDs.

5.3.7 *Content*

We classify domains under "Content" when they do not fit into another of our content classifications. The other aspects of our categorization pull out common errors, interesting features like redirects, and Web responses that appear frequently. Domains that do not fit into any of those categories resolve in the DNS, return HTTP 200 status codes, and provide vaguely unique responses to Web queries. Only 372,569 domains (10.2%) fall into this category. By comparing this category with the previous, we find that 38.8% of the 608,949 domains with real content redirect to a different domain to serve it.

6. REGISTRATION INTENT

In the previous section, we focused on understanding the types of content that domains in the new gTLDs host. In this section we explore the high-level intent of the domain's registrant. For each domain, we infer what motivated its registrant to spend money on the name. We classify registration intent into one of three broad categories:

Defensive registrants purchased a new domain to defend an existing Web presence.

Primary registrants own domains with the intent to establish a Web presence.

Speculative registrants intend to profit off of the name itself and never plan to develop a meaningful Web presence.

Before classifying domains by registration intent into one of the above categories, we must remove some types of domains. We ignore domains in the "Unused" and "HTTP Error" categories. We could guess that these domains tend to include more defensive than primary motivations since they are not user-ready and therefore the use of the name is the only relevant effect on the Internet. However, registrants likely buy domains they intend to develop all the time, and these domain names may transition to other categorizations given time or result in expirations.

We also ignore domains in the "Free" content category before deciding registration intent. In a typical domain registration scenario, we know registrants have expressed genuine interest in the domains they own because they paid money for them. Without ignoring the "Free" content category, we could not use the results of our registrant intent classifications to make any claims about why registrants purchase domain names.

Table 8 summarizes our results. In the following sections, we describe each registration intent category in more detail. We discuss what types of registrants we expect each category to cover and how we map content categories to registration intents for each domain.

Intent	*Results*	
Primary	372,569	14.6%
Defensive	1,010,954	39.7%
Speculative	1,161,892	45.6%
Total	2,545,415	100.0%

Table 8: Registration intent categorizations for the new public TLDs.

6.1 Defensive

Our defensive registration intent set begins with domains that redirect to a different domain name. Some off-domain redirects could reflect primary registrations: registrants could use their old name for technical or historical reasons but primarily use and market the new domain name. However, we find in practice that most are defensive, and many lead to sites whose branding and headers clearly advertise the landing domain.[4]

Additionally, we include domains that return invalid DNS results in this set. Owners of non-resolving domains could only use their names for private purposes, since traffic routed through the public Internet cannot correctly address a remote server. A more likely explanation is that the registrant only cares about the name. We include domains with invalid NS records as well as those that do not appear in the zone file (both described in Section 5.3.1), for a total of 774,574 non-resolving domains. Combined with the 236,380 defensive redirects, we find defensive registrations of 1,010,954 domains in the new TLDs.

6.2 Primary

Primary domains include all those purchased by a registrant with the intent to use that specific domain. Most primary registrants purchased their domain to establish a Web presence, but there are other kinds of primary registrants as well. We only classify domains in our "Content" category as primary registrations. Each of these domains resolves and could conceivably host content intended for end users. Our clustering technique did not find similar Web content for these domains, so registrants of those domains at a minimum host sufficiently unique content.

6.3 Speculative

Many registrants purchase domains to speculate on the domain itself with no intent to develop content. Most make use of the first-come first-served nature of domain registrations to grab domains they believe others will find desirable in the hope of selling them later for a profit. Others host parking-based advertising and pay-per-redirect services with the goal of monetizing through ad revenue, but still with no intent to develop unique content. In practice, most speculators in the first case also host parked content because it is essentially free (and often bundled with domain registration fees), and also serves as a signal to prospective buyers that the name is available.

From a content standpoint, the difference between a defensive and speculative registration is relatively narrow. Defensive registrants purchase domains to defend the string but with no intent to develop content, while speculative registrants purchase domains to resell later with no intent to develop content. However, speculative registrants are monetarily motivated on a per-domain margin, while defensive registrants have revenues outside the domain business. A speculator must monetize the name, but a defender does not. Therefore, we classify parked domains as speculative and non-resolving domains as defensive based on this distinction.

[4]Trademark holders make defensive registrations on their own brands. The same registration made by a different actor with malicious intent would instead qualify as cybersquatting.

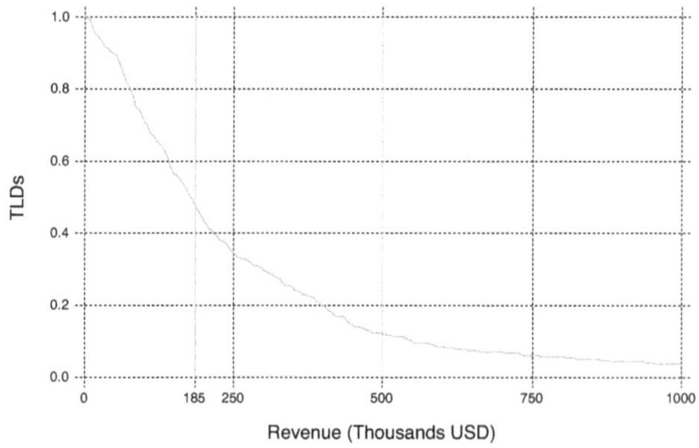

Figure 4: New gTLD program revenue as a CCDF across all TLDs. The vertical line at $185,000 USD corresponds to the minimum ICANN application fee, and the line at $500,000 USD corresponds to a more realistic estimate of the cost of establishing a new TLD.

7. REGISTRATION COSTS

Previously, we focused on the new TLD system from a registrant-centric perspective. In this section we look at the new TLD rollout from the point of view of the registries. We examine how registries make money and how they interact with registrars in practice.

7.1 Registry Financials

Using the methodology described in Section 3.7, we obtained pricing information for 2,006 (TLD, registrar) pairs, which account for 73.8% of all domain registrations. In only four TLDs do we record prices from fewer than three registrars; in each case, however, the one or two registrars we do record account for at least 97.5% of all domains. In the remaining 26.2% of domain registrations for which we do not have matching data, we use the median price for the TLD.

Figure 4 shows a complementary cumulative distribution function of the cost to registrants per TLD. A point on the line shows the ratio of new TLDs that have made at least the corresponding amount in registration costs. We included a vertical line at $185,000 USD, the standard application fee for a new TLD [19]. At this cost, roughly half of all TLDs made this money back. We estimate the total cost to registrants for domains in the new TLDs at $89 million USD through March 2015.

The application fee, however, only represents a lower bound on the amount each registry spent on their TLD. Additional costs to ICANN include a quarterly $6,250 fee [5], a per-domain transaction fee for registries with more than 50,000 transactions per year (a threshold only 18 TLDs have met), and additional application fees for TLDs that must enter the contention process. While registries do not have many other explicit costs, the TLD application process ran for years before the first delegation; presumably registries built up legal or personnel costs in the meantime. Registries also need to connect with registrars, market and brand their TLDs, build a Web presence, and run or outsource technical operations.

As a result, we also include 500,000 USD as a more realistic estimate for the cost of establishing a new TLD. While it is conjecture, some TLDs have already gone up for auction, like `reise` [23] and

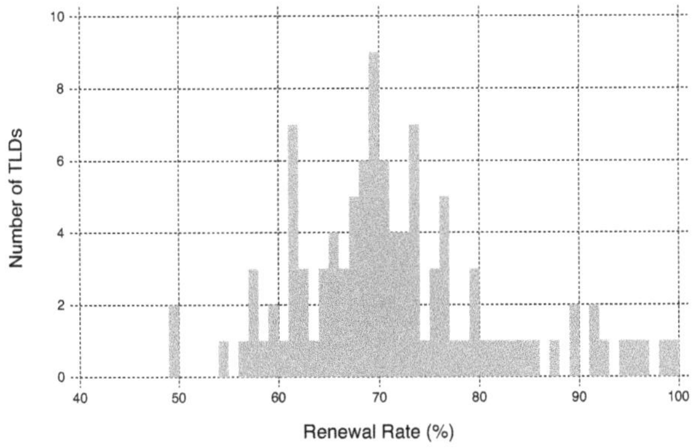

Figure 5: A histogram of renewal rates per TLD.

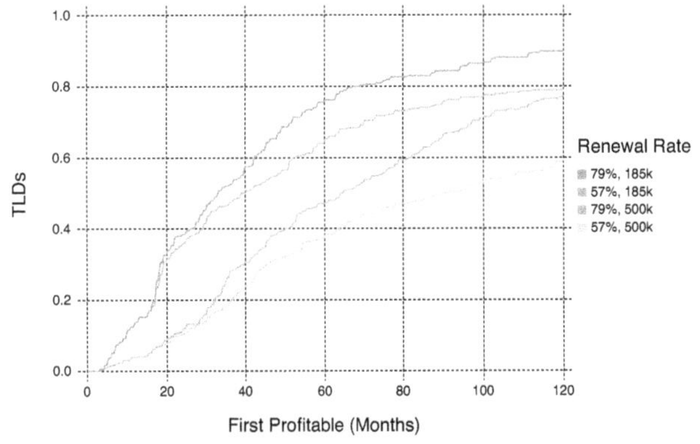

Figure 6: Registry profitability over time under different revenue models. A point on a line indicates the fraction of TLDs that were profitable within the given time since general availability.

versicherung [4], which set reserve prices of 400,000 USD and 750,000 USD, respectively. Given the small number of registrations each had at the time, these TLDs were valuable because they had completed the delegation process, suggesting the sale price roughly reflects the cost of delegation. With these reserve prices, we chose 500,000 USD as a rounded estimate in this range. At this estimate, only about 10% of TLDs are profitable.

Revenue from domain registrations does not all go to the registry. Instead, registries and registrars split revenue based on a previously agreed upon model. For instance, Verisign makes $7.85 USD per com registration [6] and $6.79 per net registration [18]. During our pricing data collection, we found registration prices for both com and net names ranging from $8 to $13 USD, or markups ranging from $0.15 to $6.[5]

Unfortunately, the new registry agreements do not specify maximum wholesale prices, only fees the registry must pay to ICANN. For calibration, we can get a handful of prices through registry-reported earning data. Rightside, one of the largest back-end registry providers, is funded through private investors and has released some revenue statistics online in a presentation meant for investors and analysts [25]. They provide end-of-November wholesale and total revenue numbers for five TLDs, two of them aggregated. Our estimate is too low for reviews,[6] but our other estimates over-estimate the wholesale price by close to a factor of 1.4. Our model does not factor in premium domain name sales, a non-trivial revenue source that does not correlate well with wholesale price. As a result, Figure 4 represents a low estimate of domain name costs, and we discuss the limitations of our model further in Section 7.4.

7.2 Renewal Rates

All registries in the new gTLD program anticipated the one year and 45 day mark since the introduction of the earliest TLDs [2].[7] This milestone provides the first chance for registrants in the new TLDs to renew their domain names, and hence reflects ongoing demand for domains in the new TLDs after one year's actual, rather than anticipated, experience with the domains. Donuts, the largest registry with over a hundred new TLDs, published statistics on renewal rates for their earliest TLDs [10, 24], likely in an attempt to attract registrars and investors [30]. However, Donuts limited their analysis to their own TLDs, and also did not provide numbers past 26 days.

Figure 5 shows a histogram of renewal rates by TLD. We only performed our analysis on TLDs where at least a hundred domains completed a full year of registrations plus the 45-day Auto-Renew Grace Period. The Donuts TLDs in our data set show renewal rates within a few percentage points of the numbers Donuts reported in April. We calculate an overall renewal rate of 71%.

7.3 Future Profit Modeling

In this section, we take a look at registry profitability using a variety of parameters. In face of the limitations of our profit modeling discussed in Section 7.4, we acknowledge that drawing higher-order conclusions from such limited data could lead to models that are incorrect in unpredictable ways. However, we would still like to attempt to classify "successful" TLDs, and profitability is a strong indicator of the success of any company.

We start by graphing TLD profitability over time under four different models in Figure 6. A point on a line indicates the fraction of TLDs that were profitable within the given time since general availability. We show four curves that reflect different values for two parameters. Two of the models assume an initial cost to the registry of only 185,000 USD, or the amount of the ICANN application fee. This is the minimum amount we know all registries must pay. The other models assume an initial cost of 500,000 USD, which better reflects our understanding of the cost of creating a registry. The second parameter is renewal rates. We show models with renewal rates of 57% and 79%, which reflect lower and higher than average rates and show the sensitivity of the model to renewals.

For each TLD, we collect registration volume data from the reports provided via ICANN. We consider TLDs for which we have three monthly reports after general availability. The first month typically contains a burst of registrations, and then the second and third provide two data points at a more typical registration rate. We model future months based on new registrations at this rate, and renewals of domains registered or renewed 12 months prior at the indicated renewal rate. We estimate the wholesale price as 70% of the total price at the cheapest registrar.

[5]Registries can offer "bulk discounts and marketing support and incentive programs" but must offer similar terms to all registrars [6].

[6]The price we found for reviews domains through two registrars owned by the same company as Rightside is less than its wholesale price. We found pricing for November through archive.org [17] and found that the price to registrants of a review domain has halved. We do not know if this reflects a reduction in its wholesale price or a promotion.

[7]The extra 45 days is for the Auto-Renew Grace Period, which allows registrars to keep the registrations for free. Usually the registrar uses this time to offer the registrant one last chance for renewal, in case they let it expire accidentally.

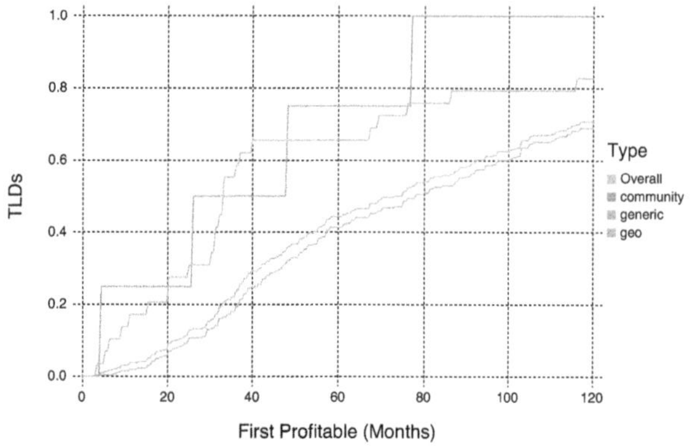

Figure 7: Modeling profitability by type of TLD. The gray line represents the aggregate, and the colored lines represent the set of TLDs of the indicated type.

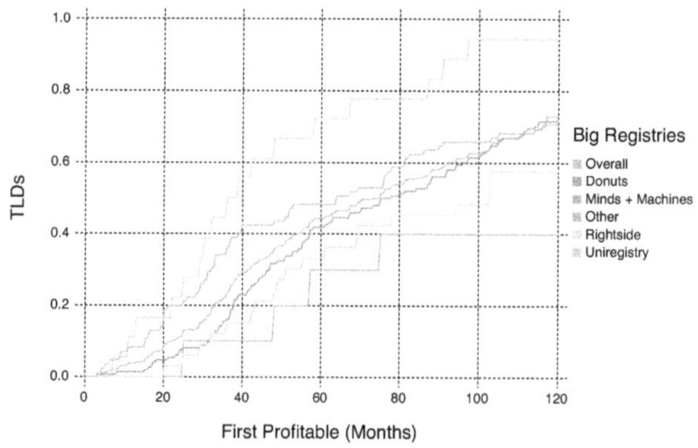

Figure 8: Modeling profitability by registry for the registries with the most TLDs. The gray line represents the aggregate, with colored lines representing individual registries.

Figure 6 shows that the initial cost plays a much larger role than the renewal rate in the short term, but that both parameters are important in the long term. We find that even under the most permissive model, with high renewal rates and no fees beyond those imposed by ICANN, 10% of TLDs still do not become profitable within the first 10 years.

Since there are a wide variety of registries operating new TLDs, and there is a wide variety of domain registration activity across the TLDs, we were interested to see if there were features that might separate profitable and unprofitable TLDs. To that end, we compared profitability based on four metrics:

- lexical string length;
- the registry for TLDs belonging to the top four registries, otherwise "Other";
- the type of registry ("generic", "community", or "geographic"); and
- whether or not the most common registrars all sell domains in the TLD.

In practice, we only found minor variations in profitability based on these metrics. We present results for the most significant differentiators, type and registry, below.

Figure 7 shows variations in profitability by type of TLD. The gray line represents the overall profitability CDF. It is equivalent to the profitability CDFs in Figure 6 with an initial cost of 500,000 USD and an overall renewal rate of 71%. The remaining lines represent non-overlapping TLD subsets which combine to the same overall set. Though community and geographical TLDs become profitable much sooner than generic TLDs, there are so few of them in comparison that the profitability of generic TLDs still closely tracks the overall rate.

Similarly, Figure 8 shows variations in profitability by registry. Of the large registries, only Uniregistry TLDs become profitable sooner than the average. Instead, our data suggests owners of multiple TLDs mainly benefit by spreading the risk. Many registries only manage between one and three TLDs, and those strings tend to become profitable sooner than most of the large registries.

7.4 Limitations

We see profitability as an important metric with which to compare registries, but our methodology has some limitations. In this section, we describe the known limitations and their expected impact on the results.

First, our pricing model does not include premium domain name sales, as described in Section 3.7. For the few TLDs for which we have seen premium domain revenue reports, these sales vary considerably. For different TLDs, we have seen the total revenue from premium domain sales range from $0 to the same amount as the total revenue of wholesale domains. It is also plausible that some TLDs could get more total revenue from premium domain names than from standard registrations. As a result, this category represents the largest unknown in our model. Premium domain names renew for the normal registration cost, so this unknown only affects the initial upfront purchase of the name and not ongoing renewal revenue.

Second, for any given TLD/registrar pair, we only record a single price, when domain name prices could change over time. To date we find that, after the beginning of general availability, domain prices do not change very frequently. Future studies could address this assumption by periodically regathering pricing data. For practical reasons, doing so would require deploying a more automated method of gathering prices than we used in this paper.

Finally, we estimate wholesale prices as 70% of the lowest price for domains in the TLD. We leave a better estimation of this price to future work.

8. VISITS

As an alternative to our registrant-focused analysis, we also analyze the new TLD program from an end user perspective. In particular, we want to know whether actual users visit domains in the new TLDs, and how that compares to similar domains in the old TLDs. We use a domain's presence or absence in the Alexa top million domains as a metric for whether or not users visit it. We do not consider the ranking order as we only care whether or not the domain gets traffic at all.

We begin by splitting new domain registrations from December 2014 into two sets, one for domains in the new TLDs and one for domains in the old TLDs. We find 326,974 registrations in December 2014 in the new TLDs, and 3,461,322 in the old TLDs. We compare these sets with the Alexa top million from April 13, 2014. We use a newer Alexa list to allow the new domain registrations time to develop their Web presence. Due to the order of magnitude size difference between our new registration sets, we report results per hundred thousand new registrations.

	New Per 100,000	*Old* Per 100,000
Alexa 1M	88.1	243
Alexa 10K	0.3	1.1
URIBL	703	331

Table 9: The rate at which new domains in the old and new TLDs appear in blacklists and Alexa. This table only includes domains registered within the same one-month time window to compare old and young TLDs on equal terms.

Table 9 summarizes our results. New domain registrations in the old TLDs are nearly three times more likely to appear in the Alexa top million when compared to registrations in the new TLDs. This ratio is also consistent with appearances on the Alexa top ten thousand. While this is a notable difference, it is also consistent with the proportion of primary registrations described in Section 5.1.

We use a similar method with the URIBL blacklist as an indicator of abusive behavior. We use the same sets of newly registered domains. We use a blacklist contemporaneous with our registration data because blacklist operators add abusive domains as soon as possible. Table 9 summarizes our results.

We find that domains in new TLDs are twice as likely to appear on the URIBL blacklist within the first month. Our data does not reveal why spammers find the new TLDs attractive. However, we can guess based on the registrar pricing data we collected as described in Section 3.7. Domains in new TLDs tended to cost more on average, but individual registrars sometimes sold them for significantly reduced prices. In the extreme we found `xyz` domains for less than $1 USD per year at some registrars.

Table 10 shows the ten TLDs for which a new registration is most likely to appear on a blacklist. Domains registered in December 2014 in most TLDs had less than a 1% chance of appearing on a blacklist in the same month, but the `link`, `red`, and `rocks` TLDs showed significantly higher rates of blacklisting. We found `link` domains for as cheap as $1.50 USD, but `rocks` domains cost at least $7.99 USD. The characteristics of these domains that consistently contribute towards higher rates of abusive behavior remains an open question.

9. CONCLUSION

ICANN greatly expanded the TLD name space to increase consumer choice and to allow more domain registrants to get short and memorable domain names. As we have found in previous TLD expansions [11, 12], new TLDs can increase primary domain registrations but can also lead to speculation and defensive registrations. ICANN's new rapid expansion of the available TLDs gives primary registrants a lot more choice, but also increases the demands on defensive registrants seeking to protect their marks.

We take a comprehensive approach to understanding how registrants use domain names in ICANN's new TLD program. We used data from many sources, including zone file data available to researchers, extensive crawls of Web and DNS information, and public data from ICANN, registries and registrars. We determined that only 15% of domains purchased by a registrant show behavior consistent with primary registrations and that domain parking drives over 30% of registrations in the new gTLD zone files. We use domain pricing information to estimate that only half of all registries have recouped their application fee in wholesale revenue. Similarly, we conservatively estimate that registrants have spent roughly $89 million USD on domain registrations in the new TLDs. Finally, we validate the expectation that users visit fewer new domains in new gTLDs than those in old, and that new domains are more than twice as likely to appear on a commonly available blacklist within the first month of registration. Taken together, our findings suggest that new gTLDs, while accruing significant revenue for registrars, have yet to provide value to the Internet community in the same way as legacy TLDs.

TLD	New Domains	Blacklisted	Percent
link	4,087	917	22.4%
red	7,599	614	8.1%
rocks	7,191	360	5.0%
tokyo	3,252	40	1.2%
black	919	10	1.1%
club	16,490	173	1.0%
blue	4,971	41	0.8%
support	435	3	0.7%
website	7,876	49	0.6%
country	1,154	7	0.6%

Table 10: The ten most commonly blacklisted TLDs.

Acknowledgments

We would like to thank He Liu for providing the use of his active DNS crawler, and Brian Kantor and Cindy Moore for managing our hardware. Thank you as well to our reviewers for their feedback. This work was supported by National Science Foundation grant NSF-1237264 and by generous research, operational and/or in-kind support from Google, Microsoft, Yahoo, and the UCSD Center for Networked Systems (CNS).

10. REFERENCES

[1] Alexa. `http://www.alexa.com`.

[2] All eyes on Donuts as first new gTLD renewal figures roll in. `http://domainincite.com/18209-all-eyes-on-donuts-as-first-new-gtld-renewal-figures-roll-in`.

[3] S. Alrwais, K. Yuan, E. Alowaisheq, Z. Li, and X. Wang. Understanding the Dark Side of Domain Parking. In *Proceedings of the USENIX Security Symposium*, San Diego, CA, Aug. 2014.

[4] Another new gTLD up for sale with $750,000 reserve. `http://domainincite.com/19021-another-new-gtld-up-for-sale-with-750000-reserve`.

[5] Base Registry Agreement. `https://www.icann.org/resources/pages/registries/registries-agreements-en`.

[6] .com Registry Agreement. `https://www.icann.org/resources/pages/agreement-2012-12-05-en`.

[7] M. Der, L. K. Saul, S. Savage, and G. M. Voelker. Knock It Off: Profiling the Online Storefronts of Counterfeit Merchandise. In *20th ACM SIGKDD Conference on Knowledge Discovery and Data Mining*, New York, NY, USA, Aug. 2014.

[8] Did XYZ.com pay NetSol $3m to bloat .xyz? `http://domainincite.com/19139-did-xyz-com-pay-netsol-3m-to-bloat-xyz`.

[9] Donuts Launches Domain Namespace Expansion with 307 gTLD Applications. `http://www.donuts.domains/donuts-media/press-`

releases/donuts-launches-domain-namespace-expansion-with-307-gtld-applications.
[10] Donuts Renewal Trends: First Definitive Report. http://www.donuts.domains/donuts-media/blog/donuts-renewal-trends-first-definitive-report.
[11] T. Halvorson, K. Levchenko, S. Savage, and G. M. Voelker. XXXtortion? Inferring Registration Intent in the .XXX TLD. In *Proceedings of the International World Wide Web Conference (WWW)*, Seoul, Korea, Apr. 2014.
[12] T. Halvorson, J. Szurdi, G. Maier, M. Felegyhazi, C. Kreibich, N. Weaver, K. Levchenko, and V. Paxson. The BIZ Top-Level Domain: Ten Years Later. In *Proceedings of the Passive and Active Measurement Conference*, Vienna, Austria, Mar. 2012.
[13] Hyper Text Coffee Pot Control Protocol (HTCPCP/1.0). http://tools.ietf.org/html/rfc2324.
[14] ICANN Whois: Purpose. https://whois.icann.org/en/purpose.
[15] K. Levchenko, A. Pitsillidis, N. Chachra, B. Enright, M. Félegyházi, C. Grier, T. Halvorson, C. Kanich, C. Kreibich, H. Liu, D. McCoy, N. Weaver, V. Paxson, G. M. Voelker, and S. Savage. Click Trajectories: End-to-End Analysis of the Spam Value Chain. In *Proceedings of the IEEE Symposium and Security and Privacy*, pages 431–446, Oakland, CA, May 2011.
[16] My Interview with Daniel Negari Addressing Reported Inflated .xyz Registrations. http://www.ricksblog.com/2014/06/interview-daniel-negari-addressing-inflated-xyz-registrations/.
[17] name.com Pricing for Common TLDs. https://web.archive.org/web/20141128024531/http://www.name.com/pricing.
[18] .net Fees. https://www.icann.org/sites/default/files/tlds/net/net-fees-01feb15-en.pdf.
[19] New gTLD Applicant Guidebook. https://newgtlds.icann.org/en/APPLICANTS/AGB.
[20] New gTLD Current Application Status. https://gtldresult.icann.org/application-result/applicationstatus.
[21] new gTLDs Launches. https://ntldstats.com/launch.
[22] .realtor Fact Sheet. http://www.realtor.org/sites/default/files/handouts-and-brochures/2014/DotREALTOR-Launch-Factsheet.pdf.
[23] .reise to start at $400k in no-reserve auction. http://domainincite.com/17988-reise-to-start-at-400k-in-no-reserve-auction.
[24] Renewal Trends: Day 26. http://www.donuts.domains/donuts-media/blog/renewal-trends-day-26.
[25] Rightside Analyst and Investor Day 2014, slide 104. http://edge.media-server.com/m/p/f9o6abq7.
[26] The Rest of the Story, 2014 Edition. http://www.npr.org/blogs/money/2014/12/31/374225531/episode-595-the-rest-of-the-story-2014-edition.
[27] URIBL. http://uribl.com/about.shtml.
[28] T. Vissers, W. Joosen, and N. Nikiforakis. Parking Sensors: Analyzing and Detecing Parked Domains. In *Proceedings of the Network and Distributed System Security Symposium (NDSS)*, San Diego, CA, Feb. 2015.
[29] Whois Policy Review Team Final Report. https://www.icann.org/en/system/files/files/final-report-11may12-en.pdf.
[30] Why Donuts is revealing domain name renewal rates. http://domainnamewire.com/2015/03/31/why-donuts-is-revealing-domain-name-renewal-rates/.

Management Plane Analytics

*Aaron Gember-Jacobson, *Wenfei Wu, *Xiujun Li, *Aditya Akella, †Ratul Mahajan

*University of Wisconsin-Madison, †Microsoft Research

ABSTRACT

While it is generally held that network management is tedious and error-prone, it is not well understood which specific management practices increase the risk of failures. Indeed, our survey of 51 network operators reveals a significant diversity of opinions, and our characterization of the management practices in the 850+ networks of a large online service provider shows significant diversity in prevalent practices. Motivated by these observations, we develop a management plane analytics (MPA) framework that an organization can use to: (i) infer which management practices impact network health, and (ii) develop a predictive model of health, based on observed practices, to improve network management. We overcome the challenges of sparse and skewed data by aggregating data from many networks, reducing data dimensionality, and oversampling minority cases. Our learned models predict network health with an accuracy of 76-89%, and our causal analysis uncovers some high impact practices that operators thought had a low impact on network health. Our tool is publicly available, so organizations can analyze their own management practices.

Categories and Subject Descriptors

C.2.3 [**Computer-Communication Networks**]: Network Operations—*Network management*

Keywords

Network management practices; network health; quasi-experimental design; decision trees

1. INTRODUCTION

Computer networks are logically composed of three planes: data, control, and management (Figure 1). The data plane forwards packets. The control plane generates forwarding tables and filters for the data plane using configuration files and routing protocols (e.g., OSPF and BGP)—or control programs in the case of software defined networking (SDN). The management plane is a collection of practices that define the network's physical composition, control plane configuration, and monitoring schemes based on an organization's policies and objectives.

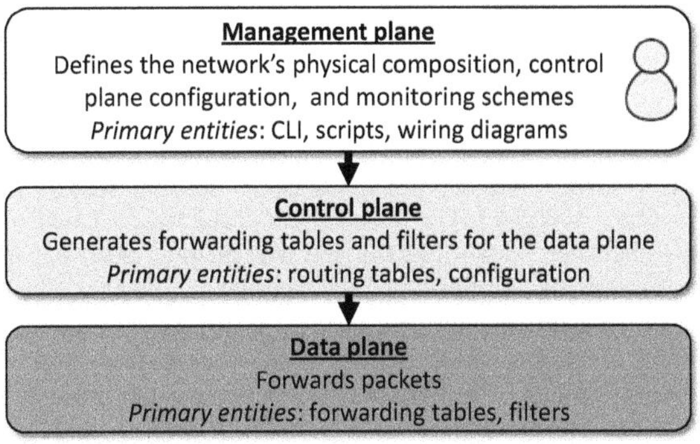

Figure 1: The three network planes

The networking community has a strong track record of developing innovative tools and techniques to discover how control and data planes function, even when the network does not directly reveal that information. Examples include techniques to infer the paths taken by packets [35], link characteristics [10], available bandwidth along a path [16], loss rate and re-ordering [24], network topology [31], and so on.

However, little work has gone into characterizing the management plane, despite its importance to well-functioning networks. As a result, we lack a systematic understanding of what *management practices* are common today—i.e., how do operators design and (re)configure the physical and logical structure of their networks? Even simple practices such as how heterogeneous are a network's devices, and how often and why are networks changed, are poorly understood in the research community. Furthermore, while it is generally held that network management is tedious and error-prone, researchers and operators alike don't have a principled understanding of which management practices pose a higher risk of performance and availability problems. Indeed, our survey of 51 network operators (Figure 2) reveals a significant diversity of opinions regarding this issue.

This paper makes two contributions. First, we present a systematic characterization of the management practices employed in over 850 networks managed by a large online service provider. Our characterization offers the first in-depth look into the management practices used in modern networks. Second, we propose a *management plane analytics* (MPA) framework that uncovers the relationship between network health (e.g., the frequency of performance and availability problems) and management practices. An organization can apply MPA to its networks to: (i) determine which practices *cause* a decline, or improvement, in network health; and

IMC'15, October 28–30, 2015, Tokyo, Japan.
© 2015 ACM. ISBN 978-1-4503-3848-6/15/10 ...$15.00.
DOI: http://dx.doi.org/10.1145/2815675.2815684.

(ii) develop a predictive model of health, based on management practices, to help shape future practices and aid what-if analysis.

In our work we face three main challenges. First, management practices and their impact are rarely directly logged. We show how management practices and network health can be *inferred* from other data, including inventory records, snapshots of device configurations, and trouble ticket logs. This data is indirect and noisy, but useful information can be extracted from it.

The second challenge is dealing with a limited amount of data. For any given network in an organization (e.g., a data center network hosting a certain Web service) the number of available snapshots of its design and operation may be limited, and some snapshots may be missing due to incomplete or inconsistent logging. Our key insight is to identify causal relationships and build predictive models by aggregating data from many networks and many months. This aggregation eliminates noise from individual networks and provides a broader picture of an organizations' practices.

Finally, we show that skew in network operations data makes it challenging to identify causal relationships and build accurate predictive models. Common approaches for decomposing dependencies (e.g., ANOVA [3] or ICA [9]) are unsuitable, because relationships between network health and management practices may be non-monotonic. Similarly, quasi-experimental designs (QEDs) that rely on exact matching to eliminate the effects of confounding practices [21] do not work, because many management practices are strongly related. Furthermore, predictive models constructed using standard learning algorithms (e.g., decisions trees built using C4.5 [27]) inaccurately predict situations that lead to poor network health due to the presence of substantially more "healthy network" cases in the data.

We use three main techniques to overcome this skew. First, we use *mutual information* to uncover statistical dependencies between network health and management practices. Mutual information quantifies the extent to which knowing a management practice reduces uncertainty about network health. Second, we use QEDs based on *propensity score matching* [33] to discover causal relationships between management practices and network health. Propensity scores systematically account for the bias in treatment selection caused by confounding practices. Finally, when learning predictive models, we use oversampling and boosting [12] to improve accuracy for the minority (i.e., "unhealthy network") cases.

Key findings from applying our methods to several hundred networks of a large online service provider (OSP) are:

- There is significant variation in management practices across the networks, even though they are all managed based on the same set of recommended guidelines. For instance, we find networks differ substantially with respect to hardware and firmware heterogeneity, the extent of automation used, and the way changes are made to them.
- By applying MPA to the OSP's data, we determine that number of devices, number of change events, and number of change types have a strong statistical dependence and causal relationship with network health (quantified using number of tickets). While in some cases our causal analysis agrees with operator feedback (e.g., number of change events has high impact), in other cases it contradicts them (e.g., the fraction of changes where an ACL is modified has moderately high impact, despite a majority opinion that its impact is low).
- Decision trees for predicting two coarse-grained health classes have 91% (cross-validation) accuracy, whereas those for five fine-grained classes have 81% accuracy. While our enhancements improve multi-class accuracy significantly, fine-grained predictions are still suboptimal due to a lack of sufficient data. When applied in an online fashion, our 2-class (5-class) model can predict network health with 89% (76%) accuracy.

Our work is a step toward designing a better management plane that reduces the burden on operators and reduces the frequency of failures. Although the observations we make for the OSP's networks may not apply to all networks—due to differences between organizations and types of networks (e.g., data centers vs. wide area networks)—our publicly available MPA framework [2] can be applied to any set of networks to identify the extent to which particular management practices impact the health of those networks. Now is a particularly relevant time for this undertaking because, in the form of SDN, the community is engaged in re-architecting networks. By providing operators a detailed understanding of the strengths and weaknesses of their current management plane, our work can help inform the design of the next generation management plane.

2. INFERRING MANAGEMENT PRACTICES

Our goal is to design a framework that an organization that operates a collection of networks (e.g., a university campus, or an online service provider) can use to understand and improve its management plane. Organizations that manage a large number of devices typically do not view all devices as belonging to one network, but instead view the devices as partitioned across multiple networks. A *network* in this context is a collection of devices that either connects compute equipment that hosts specific workloads or connects other networks to each other or the external world. A *workload* is a service (e.g., a file system, or an application) or a group of users (e.g., students using PCs in a department).

A challenge in designing our desired framework is that management practices are not explicitly logged. While the control and data planes can be queried to quantify their behavior [10, 16, 24, 31, 35], no such capability exists for the management plane. This gap stems from humans being the primary actors in the management plane. Operators translate high-level intents into a suitable setup of devices, protocols, and configurations to create a functional, healthy network. Even when recommended procedures are documented, there is no guarantee that operators adhere to these practices.

Fortunately, we are able to infer management practices from other readily available data sources. In this section, we describe these sources and the management practice *metrics* we can infer.

2.1 Data Sources

We can infer management practices and network health from three data sources that are commonly available. Such data sources have already been used in prior work, albeit to study a limited set of management practices [6, 20, 26, 34]. We build upon these efforts to provide a more thorough view of management practices and their relationship to network health. The data sources are:

1) Inventory records. Most organizations directly track the set of networks they manage, and the role the networks play. They also record the vendor, model, location, and role (switch, router, load balancer, etc.) of every device in their deployment, and the network it belongs to. This data can be used to infer a network's basic composition and purpose.

2) Device configuration snapshots. Network management systems (NMS) track changes in device configurations to aid network operators in a variety tasks, such as debugging configuration errors or rolling back changes when problems emerge. NMSes such as RANCID [28] and HPNA [36] subscribe to syslog feeds from network devices and snapshot a device's configuration whenever the

Design practices
$D1$. Number of services, users, or networks connected
$D2$. Number of devices, vendors, models, roles (e.g., switch, router, firewall), and firmware versions
$D3$. Hardware and firmware heterogeneity
$D4$. Number of data plane constructs used (e.g., VLAN spanning tree, link aggregation), and instance counts
$D5$. Number and size of BGP & OSPF routing instances
$D6$. Intra- and inter-device config reference counts
Operational practices
$O1$. Number of config changes and devices changed
$O2$. Number of automated changes
$O3$. Number and modality of changes of specific types (e.g., interface, ACL, router, VLAN)
$O4$. Number of devices changed together

Table 1: Management practice metrics

device generates a syslog alert that its configuration has changed. Each snapshot includes the configuration text, as well as metadata about the change, e.g., when it occurred and the login information of the entity (i.e., user or script) that made the change. The snapshots are archived in a database or version control system.

3) Trouble ticket logs. When users report network problems, or monitoring systems raise alarms, a trouble ticket is created in an incident management system. The ticket is used to track the duration, symptoms, and diagnosis of the problem. Each ticket has a mix of structured and unstructured information. The former includes the time the problem was discovered and resolved, the name(s) of device(s) causing or effected by the problem, and symptoms or resolutions selected from pre-defined lists; the latter includes syslog details and communication (e.g., emails and IMs) between operators that occurred to diagnose the issue.

2.2 Metrics

Using these data sources, we can infer management practices and network health, and model them using *metrics*. We broadly classify management practices into two classes (Table 1): *design practices* are long-term decisions concerning the network's structure and provisioning (e.g., selecting how many switches and from which vendors); *operational practices* are day-to-day activities that change the network in response to emerging needs (e.g., adding subnets).

Design Practices. Design practices influence four sets of network artifacts: the network's purpose, its physical composition, and the logical structure and composition of its data and control planes. The metrics we use to quantitatively describe a network's purpose and its physical composition are rather straightforward to compute, and are listed in lines $D1$ and $D2$ in Table 1. We synthesize these metrics to measure a network's *hardware heterogeneity* using a normalized entropy metric (line $D3$): $\frac{-\sum_{i,j} p_{ij} log_2 p_{ij}}{log_2 N}$, where p_{ij} is the fraction of devices of model i that play role j (e.g., switch, router, firewall, load balancer) in the network, and N is the size of the network. This metric captures the extent to which the same hardware model is used in multiple roles, or multiple models are used in the same role; a value close to 1 indicates significant heterogeneity. We compute a similar firmware heterogeneity metric.

Computing metrics that capture the logical composition and structure of the data and control planes is more intricate as it involves parsing configuration files. To conduct our study, we extended Batfish [11] to parse the configuration languages of various device vendors (e.g., Cisco IoS). Given parsed configurations, we determine the logical composition of the data plane by enumerating the number of logical data plane constructs used (e.g., spanning tree, VLAN, link aggregation), as well as the number of instances of each (e.g., number of VLANs configured); Table 1, line $D4$.

To model control plane structure, we leverage prior work on configuration models [5]. In particular, we extract routing instances from device configurations, where each instance is a collection of routing processes of the same type (e.g., OSPF processes) on different devices that are in the transitive closure of the "adjacent-to" relationship. A network's routing instances collectively implement its control plane. We enumerate the number of such instances, as well as the average size of each instance (Table 1, line $D5$) using the same methodology as Benson et al. [5].

Finally, we enumerate the average number of inter- and intra-device configuration references in a network [5]. These metrics (Table 1, line $D6$) capture the configuration complexity imposed in aggregate by all aspects of a network's design, as well as the impact of specific configuration practices followed by operators.

Operational Practices. We infer operational practices by comparing two successive configuration snapshots from the same device. If at least one stanza differs, we count this as a configuration change.

We compute basic statistics about the configuration changes observed over a certain time window (Table 1, line $O1$). In addition, we study the modality of changes (line $O2$). We infer modality (automated vs. manual) using the login metadata stored with configuration snapshots: we mark a change as *automated* if the login is classified as a special account in the organization's user management system. Otherwise we assume the change was *manual*. This conservative approach will misclassify changes made by scripts executing under a regular user account, thereby under-estimating the extent of automated changes.

To model change type, we leverage the fact that configuration information is arranged as *stanzas*, each containing a set of options and values pertaining to a particular construct—e.g., a specific interface, VLAN, routing instance, or ACL. A stanza is identified by a type (e.g., interface) and a name (e.g., TenGigabit0/1). When part (or all) of a stanza is added, removed, or updated, we say a change of type T occurred, where T is the stanza type. We count the number of changes of each type over a certain time window (Table 1, line $O3$).

There are a few challenges and limitations with this approach. First, type names differ between vendors: e.g., an ACL is defined in Cisco IoS using an `ip access-list` stanza, while a `firewall filter` stanza is used in Juniper JunOS. We address this by manually identifying stanza types on different vendors that serve the same purpose, and we convert these to a vendor-agnostic type identifier. Second, even after generalizing types, a change with the same effect may be typified differently on different vendors: e.g., an interface is assigned to a VLAN in Cisco IoS using the `switchport access vlan` option within an `interface` stanza, while in Juniper JunOS the `interface` option is used within a `vlan` stanza; even though the effect of the change is the same, it will be typified as an interface change on a Cisco device and a VLAN change on a Juniper device. Operators using MPA should be aware of this limitation and interpret prediction results according to the mix of vendors in their networks.

In addition to computing change metrics over changes on individual devices, we compute change metrics over *change events* (Table 1, line $O4$). Change events account for the fact that multiple devices' configurations may need to be changed to realize a desired outcome. For example, establishing a new layer-2 network segment (e.g., a VLAN) requires configuration changes to all devices participating in the segment.

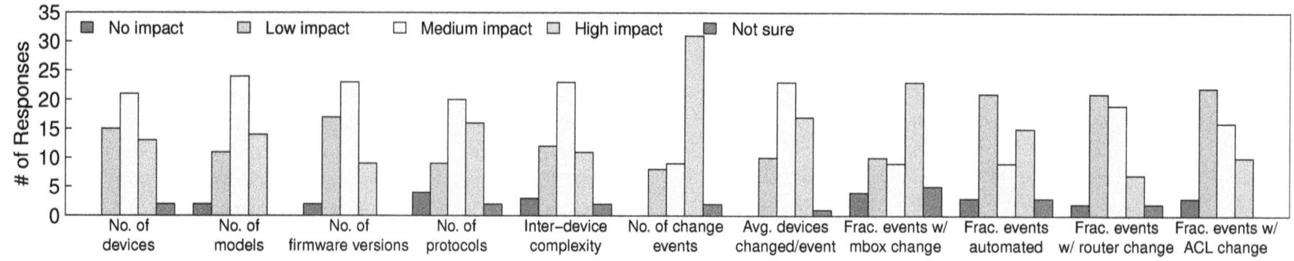

Figure 2: Results of operator survey

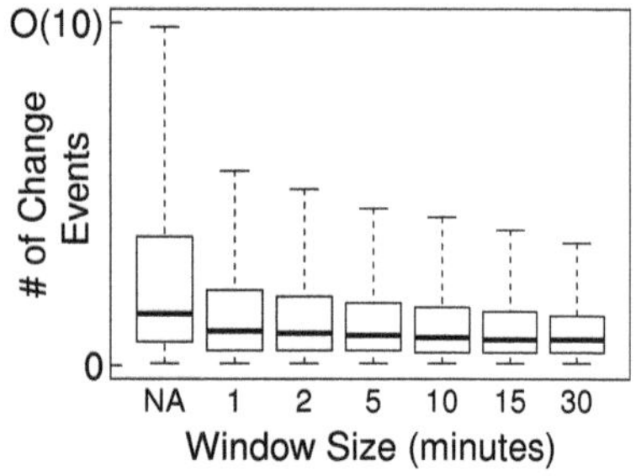

Figure 3: Impact of change grouping threshold (δ) on the number of change events; each box shows the 25th, 50th, and 75th percentile number of change events per-network per-month using various values of δ; whiskers indicate the most extreme datapoints within twice the interquartile range

To identify change events, we group changes using a simple heuristic: if a configuration change on a device occurs within δ time units of a change on another device in the same network, then we assume the changes on both devices are part of the same change event. Figure 3 shows how different values of δ influence the number of change events. The rest of our analysis uses $\delta = 5$ minutes, because operators indicated they complete most related changes within such a time window. In the future, we plan to also consider the change type and affected entities (e.g., VLAN or subnet) to more finely group related changes.

Network Health. The health of a network can be analyzed from many perspectives, including performance (e.g., latency or throughput), quality of experience (e.g., application responsiveness), and failure rate (e.g., packet loss or link/device downtime). Networks are often equipped with monitoring systems that track these metrics and raise alarms when critical thresholds are crossed. In the networks we study, trouble tickets are automatically created when such alarms are raised. Tickets are also created when users report problems or operators conduct planned maintenance. We exclude the latter from our analysis, because maintenance tickets are unlikely to be triggered by performance or availability problems.

Given that ticket logs capture a wide-range of network issues, operators view tickets as a valuable measure of network health. In particular, operators from the OSP indicated that number of tickets is a useful metric. Other metrics computed from network tickets (e.g., number of high impact problems, mean time to resolution, etc.) are less useful because of inconsistencies in ticketing practices: e.g., impact levels are often subjective, and tickets are sometimes not marked as resolved until well after the problem has been fixed. As future work, we plan to explore how to accurately obtain more fine-grained health measures using tools like NetSieve [26].

Property	Value
Months	17, Aug 2013 – Dec 2014
Networks	850+
Services	O(100)
Devices	O(10K)
Config snapshots	O(100K), ≈450GB
Tickets	O(10K), ≈80MB

Table 2: Size of datasets

3. MANAGEMENT PRACTICES TODAY

Today, there is little consensus in the community on the impact of different management practices on networks' health. We conducted two studies that demonstrate this lack of consensus. One study is qualitative in which we surveyed network operators regarding which practices mattered for network health. The other is quantitative in which we systematically characterized management practices in use at a large OSP. The diversity in opinions and actual practices uncovered by these studies motivate the need for MPA. We describe these studies below.

3.1 Operators' Perspectives

Our operator survey covered 51 network operators, whom we recruited through the NANOG mailing list (45 operators), from our campus network (4), and from the large OSP (2). For ten of the practices in Table 1, we asked operators how much they thought each practice would matter to their networks' health. Results of our survey are summarized in Figure 2. We see clear consensus in just one case—number of change events. Otherwise, we note a general diversity of opinion: for several practices—e.g., network size, number of models used, and inter-device configuration complexity—the fractions of operators who said the practice has low vs. high impact are roughly the same. We observed similar diversity even among operators of the OSP and those of the campus network. A handful of operators indicated that they are unsure of the impact of certain management practices.

We also asked operators to "write-in" other practices they believe to have a high impact on network health. The responses included: number of operators, skill levels of operators, documentation and training provided, extent of auditing tools, and extent of pre-change analysis. Unfortunately, these metrics are difficult to quantify, because they relate to the operators (e.g., skill level) rather than the networks. We leave the integration of such metrics into MPA as future work.

3.2 Management Practices in a Large OSP

The diversity in opinions uncovered by the survey could be due to the fact that the operators manage different networks. It is possible that operators know which practices impact their own network, and it is just that this set of practices differs across organizations but is internally consistent. However, our characterization of management practices inside an OSP suggests this is not the case; we find significant heterogeneity in the practices inside the OSP. While detailed characterization is presented in Appendix A, we summarize example findings here.

The OSP owns 850+ networks that are managed based on documented "best practices." Each network hosts one or more Web services or interconnects other networks. Our datasets cover a 17 month period from August 2013 through December 2014. Table 2 shows its key aspects. For confidentiality, we do not list exact numbers for several measures.

Design Practices. We find the control and data planes of networks to be quite heterogeneous in their physical and logical structure. For instance, while the median network's hardware and firmware heterogeneity is low (entropy metric < 0.3), there are several networks ($\approx 10\%$) that are highly heterogeneous on both fronts (metric > 0.67) (Figure 11(a)). Likewise, the number of data and control plane protocols configured across networks is distributed almost uniformly between 1 and 8 (Figure 11(b)). Perhaps most interestingly the overall configuration complexity metrics (intra- and inter-device references) vary by 1-2 orders of magnitude across networks (Figure 11(d)). Per the operator survey (Figure 2), many of these metrics may have a modest impact on health.

Operational Practices. We similarly find significant diversity in what and how networks are changed. For instance, changes to router stanzas are not as common for the median network (where 5% of changes are to router stanzas), but such changes are quite prevalent (>0.5 of all changes) in about 5% of the networks (Figure 12(c)). Likewise, number of change events and changes involving middleboxes—both of which were considered impactful by operators (Figure 2)—show significant diversity: e.g., change event count in the 10th vs 90th percentile network is 3 vs 34 (Figure 12(e)). The modality of changes is also diverse: in 40% of the networks at least half the changes are automated, but in 10% of the networks only 15% of changes are automated (Figure 12(d)).

This level of diversity within the networks of the same organization suggests that operators have little agreement on which practices are good. This lack of agreement is confirmed by our conversation with the operators of the OSP. These conversations also confirm that the operators do not have a way to map adjustments in management practices to shifts in network health. Helping such operators is the goal of MPA.

4. MPA OVERVIEW

Given the diversity and complexity of management practices, we need a systematic framework to understand their impact on network health, and in turn improve management practices. MPA is one such framework.

MPA has two goals. The first is to help operators derive the top k management practices that impact the health (e.g., problem incidence) of their networks. Armed with this information, operators can develop suitable best practices to improve organization-wide design and operational procedures. The main challenges here are that: (i) management practices can differ significantly in the nature of their relationship with network health; and (ii) many practices are often related, impacting both one another and network health. Thus, systematically distilling the "heavy hitters" is not easy. In Section 5, we show how to overcome these challenges by using mutual information to uncover statistical dependencies, and nearest neighbor matching of propensity scores, in the context of quasi-experimental designs (QEDs), to identify causal relationships.

The second goal of MPA is to help operators predict, in an ongoing fashion, what impact the current set of management practices have on the health of *individual* networks. This goes beyond focusing on the top practices; it incorporates the effects of one-off deviations from established procedures, as well as the effects of management practices whose impact on network health manifests only in a narrow set of situations. Armed with such metrics, operators can closely monitor networks that are predicted to have more problems and be better prepared to deal with failures. The main challenge is drawing meaningful conclusions despite limited data for individual networks, especially data for "unhealthy" networks which is often the minority. In Section 6, we show how to overcome this challenge, and build models that accurately predict the health of individual networks, using boosting and oversampling of unhealthy network data.

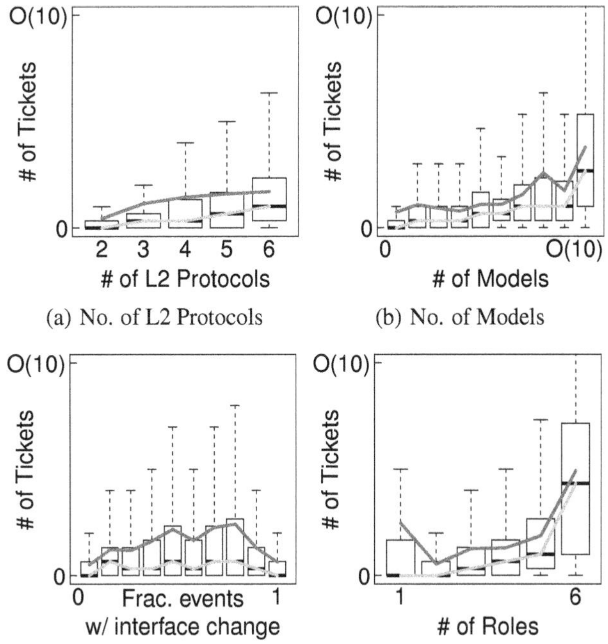

(a) No. of L2 Protocols (b) No. of Models

(c) Frac. of events with interface change (d) No. of Roles

Figure 4: Tickets based on management practices; boxes show 25th & 75th %tile, while whiskers show 2x the interquartile range; red (dark) line shows the average number of tickets, while orange (light) line shows the median

5. MANAGEMENT PRACTICES THAT IMPACT NETWORK HEALTH

Identifying management practices that impact network health is valuable to operators, yet non-trivial to accomplish. The nature of management practices is such that we face at least two challenges. First, practices may not have a linear, or even monotonic, relationship with network health; this makes it difficult to clearly identify *statistical dependencies*. For example, Figure 4 shows three different management practices—*number of L2 protocols*, *number of models*, and *fraction of events with an interface change*—that have a linear, monotonic, and non-monotonic relationship, respectively, with number of tickets. Second, management practices are often related, such that a change in one practice impacts another practice, as well as network health. For example, Figures 4 and 5 show that *number of models* and *number of roles* are related to network health, and each other. This makes it challenging to identify *causal relationships*.

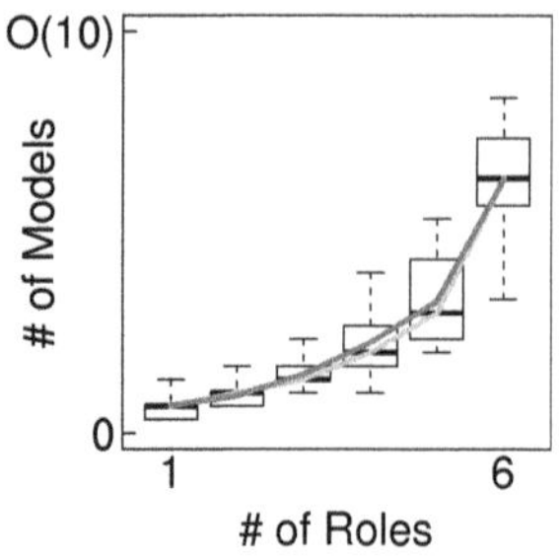

Figure 5: Relationship between *number of models* and *number of roles*

In this section, we present the techniques we use to overcome these challenges. We illustrate how they work using our data from the OSP.

5.1 Dependence Analysis

Common approaches for decomposing the impact of different factors include analysis of variance (ANOVA) [3] and principal/independent component analyses (PCA/ICA) [9]. However, these techniques make key assumptions about underlying dependencies that make them inapplicable to MPA. ANOVA assumes linear relations, which may not always hold, as illustrated earlier in Figure 4. ICA attempts to express the outcome (health metric) as a linear or non-linear combination of independent components; applying PCA first helps identify the components to feed to ICA. The main issue is that the components output by PCA are linear combinations of a subset of management practices. Thus, this approach also makes the implicit assumption that linear combinations of practice metrics can explain network health. Furthermore, the outcome of ICA may be hard to interpret (especially if it relies on a non-linear model).

Instead, we identify statistical dependencies using a more general approach: *mutual information* (MI). When computed between a management practice metric and network health, MI measures how much knowing the practice reduces uncertainty about health. Crucially, MI does not make assumptions about the nature of the relationship.

5.1.1 Mutual Information

The MI between variables X and Y (a management practice and network health) is defined as the difference between the entropy of Y, $H(Y)$, and the conditional entropy of Y given X, $H(Y|X)$. Entropy is defined as $H(Y) = -\sum_i P(y_i) log P(y_i)$, where $P(y_i)$ is the probability that $Y = y_i$. Conditional entropy is defined as $H(Y|X) = \sum_{i,j} P(y_i, x_j) log \frac{P(x_j)}{P(y_i, x_j)}$, where $P(y_i, x_j)$ is the probability that $Y = y_i$ and $X = x_j$. MI is symmetric.

We also examine statistical dependencies between management practices using *conditional mutual information* (CMI). The CMI between a pair of management practices and network health measures the expected value of the practices' MI, given health.[1] The CMI for two variables X_1 and X_2 relative to variable Y is defined as $H(X_1|Y) - H(X_1|X_2, Y)$. Like MI, CMI is also symmetric (with respect to X_1 and X_2).

Binning. Prior to computing MI or CMI, we compute the mean value of each management practice and health metric on a monthly basis for each network, giving us $\approx$11K data points. We bin the data for each metric using 10-equal width bins, with the 5th percentile value as the lower bound for the first bin, and the 95th percentile value as the upper bound for the last bin. Networks whose metric value is below the 5th (above the 95th) percentile are put in the first (last) bin.

[1] In a sense, the pair's joint probability distribution.

Management Practices	Avg. Monthly MI
No. of devices (D)	0.388
No. of change events (O)	0.353
Intra-device complexity (D)	0.329
No. of change types (O)	0.328
No. of VLANs (D)	0.313
No. of models (D)	0.273
No. of roles (D)	0.221
Avg. devices changed per event (O)	0.215
Frac. events w/ interface change (O)	0.201
Frac. events w/ ACL change (O)	0.198

Table 3: Top 10 management practices related to network health according to average monthly MI; parenthetical annotation indicates practice category (D=design, O=operational)

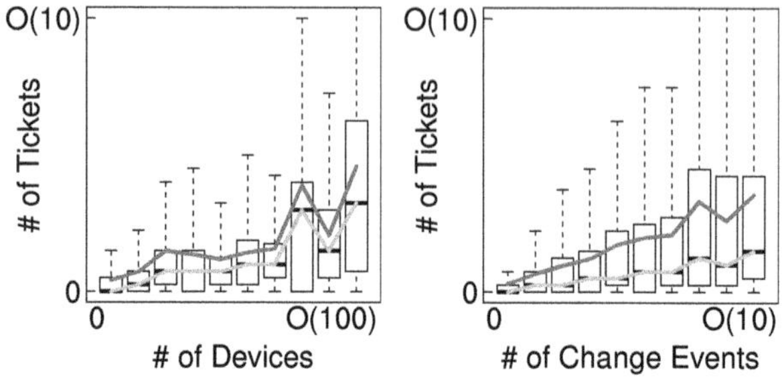

(a) No. of Devices (b) No. of Change Events

Figure 6: Tickets based on management practices

Our motivation for this binning strategy is twofold. First, in our characterization of management practices (Appendix A), we observe that many management practices have a long tail: e.g., number of VLANs (Figure 11(c)). Using the 5th and 95th percentile bounds for the first and last bins significantly reduces the range of values covered by each bin, thereby reducing the likelihood that the majority of networks will fall into just one or two bins. Second, minor deviations in a management practice or health metric—e.g., one more device or one more ticket—are unlikely to be significant. Our binning helps reduce noise from such minor variations

5.1.2 Results for the OSP

We now present statistical dependence results for the OSP. Table 3 shows the 10 management practices that have the strongest statistical dependence with network health. It includes five *design practices* and five *operational practices*, thus highlighting the potential importance of both types of practices to a healthy network.

We visually confirmed the assessment that the practices in Table 3 have a statistical dependence with network health. For example, Figure 6 illustrates the strong statistical dependence with network health for the top two practices. Likewise, Figure 4, which we described earlier, illustrates the relationships for *number of models*, *number of roles*, and *fraction of change events with an interface change* (ranked 6th, 7th, and 9th, respectively, in Table 3).

Interestingly, one of the practices which has high impact according to the survey (Figure 2)—*fraction of events with a middlebox change*—does not appear in the top 10 practices (Table 3); this practice is ranked 23 out of 28. This may be due to the fact that the majority of changes to the OSP's middleboxes are simple adjustments to the server pools configured on load balancers.

Table 4 shows the 10 management practices that have the strongest statistical dependence with *each other*. We observe that six of the top 10 practices related to network health (Table 4) are statistically dependent with other practices; this includes all five of the top

Management Practice Pair		CMI
Frac. events w/ pool change (O)	Frac. events w/ mbox change (O)	1.107
Firmware entropy (D)	Hardware entropy (D)	0.978
No. of OSPF instances (D)	No. of L3 protocols (D)	0.923
No. of models (D)	No. of change types (O)	0.735
No. of BGP instances (D)	Inter-device complexity (D)	0.732
No. of roles (D)	No. of models (D)	0.713
No. of BGP instances (D)	No. of L2 protocols (D)	0.601
Avg. size of an OSPF instance (D)	No. of change types (O)	0.576
Intra-device complexity (D)	Inter-device complexity (D)	0.574
No. of devices (D)	No. of VLANs (D)	0.569

Table 4: Top 10 pairs of statistically dependent management practices according to CMI; highlighted practices are in the top 10 according to MI; parenthetical annotation indicates practice category (D=design, O=operational)

design practices and one operational practice. In general, more design practices (as opposed to operational practices) are statistically dependent with each other. This trend stems from the natural connections between many design decisions: e.g., configuring more BGP instances results in more references between devices and increases inter-device complexity.

We also observe from Table 4 that several practices are dependent with multiple other practices: e.g., *number of models* is dependent with *number of roles* and *number of change types*, and *number of change types* is also dependent with *average size of an OSPF instance*. Thus, evaluating the impact of a management practice on network health requires accounting for many other practices; we next discuss how we achieve this.

5.2 Causal Analysis

Although we can select the k practices with the highest MI as the top k management practices associated with network health, there is no guarantee these practices actually impact health. To establish a *causal relationship* between a management practice and network health, we must eliminate the effects of *confounding factors* (i.e., other practices) that impact this practice and network health [18]. Figures 4 and 5, discussed earlier, illustrate such an effect.

Ideally, we would eliminate confounding factors and establish causality using a *true randomized experiment*. In particular, we would ask operators to employ a specific practice (e.g., decrease the number of device models) in a randomly selected subset of networks; we would then compare the network health (outcome) across the selected (treated) and remaining (untreated) networks. Unfortunately, conducting such experiments takes time (on the order of months), and requires operator compliance to obtain meaningful results. Moreover, true experiments ignore already available historical network data.

To overcome these issues, we use *quasi-experimental design* (QED) [30]. QED uses existing network data to affirm that an independent (or treatment) variable X has a causal impact on a dependent (or outcome) variable Y.

5.2.1 Matched Design

We use a specific type of QED called the *matched design* [33]. The basic idea is to pair cases—each case represents a network in a specific month—that have equal (or similar) values for all confounding variables $Z_1 ... Z_n$, but different values for the treatment variable X. Keeping the confounding variables equal negates the effects of other practices on the outcome (network health), and increases our confidence that any difference in outcomes between the paired cases must be due to the treatment (practice under study).

Using a matched design to identify a causal relationship between a management practice and network health entails four key steps: (1) determine the practice metric values that represent treated and untreated; (2) match pairs of treated and untreated cases based on a set of confounding factors, a distance measure, and a pairing method; (3) verify the quality of the matches to ensure the effect of confounding practices is adequately accounted for; and (4) analyze the statistical significance of differences in outcomes between the treated and untreated cases to determine if there is enough support for a causal relationship.

A key challenge we face in using a matched design is obtaining a sufficient number of quality matches to provide an adequate foundation for comparing the outcomes between treated and untreated cases. As shown in Appendix A, practices tend to vary significantly across networks. Furthermore, many management practices are statistically dependent with network health and each other (Section 5.1). We use nearest neighbor matching based on propensity scores [33] to partially addresses this challenge, but there are also fundamental limitations imposed by the size of our datasets.

We now describe the analysis steps in more detail, using *number of change events* as an example management practice for which we want to establish a causal relationship with network health. At the end of the section, we present results for the 10 management practices that have the highest statistical dependence with network health for the OSP (Table 3).

5.2.2 Determining the Treatment

While most other studies that use QEDs (e.g., those in the medical and social sciences) have a clear definition of what constitutes "treatment," there is no obvious, definitive choice for most management practices. The majority of our management practice metrics have an (unbounded) range of values, with no standard for what constitutes a "normal range": e.g., for the OSP's networks, the average number of change events per month ranges from 0 to hundreds (Figure 12(e)). Hence, we must decide what value(s) constitute *treated* and *untreated*.

One option is to define untreated as the practice metric value that represents the absence of operational actions (e.g., no change events), or the minimum possible number of entities (e.g., one device model or one VLAN). However, we find it is often the case that: (i) several confounding practices will also have the value 0 or 1 (or be undefined) when the treatment practice has the value 0 or 1—e.g., when *number of change events* is 0, *number of change types*, *average devices changed per event*, and *fraction of events with a change of type T* are undefined; and (ii) several confounding practices will be non-zero (or >1) when the treatment practice is non-zero. This observation makes sense, given that our CMI results showed a strong statistical dependence between many management practices (Table 4). Unfortunately, it makes it difficult to find treated cases with similar confounding practices that can be paired with the untreated cases.

Comp. Point	Untreated Cases	Treated Cases	Pairs	Untreated Matched	Abs. Std. Diff. of Means	Ratio of Var.
1:2	8259	1745	1742	1109	0.0000	1.0091
2:3	1745	616	614	431	-0.0002	1.0314
3:4	626	296	295	200	0.0052	1.0744
4:5	296	783	673	174	-0.0002	1.0411

Table 5: Matching based on propensity scores

Given the absence of a "normal range," and the strong statistical dependence between practices, we choose to use multiple definitions of treated and untreated and conduct multiple causal analyses. In particular, we use the same binning strategy discussed in Section 5.1 to divide cases into 5 bins based on the value of the treatment practice. Then we select one bin (b) to represent untreated, and a neighboring bin ($b + 1$) to represent treated. This gives us four points of comparison: bin 1 (untreated) vs. bin 2 (treated), 2 vs. 3, 3 vs. 4, and 4 vs. 5; we denote these experimental setups as *1:2*, *2:3*, *3:4*, and *4:5*, respectively. More (or fewer) bins can be used if we have an (in)sufficient number of cases in each bin. In Section 5.2.4, we discuss how to evaluate the quality of matches, which can help determine whether more (fewer) bins can be used.

5.2.3 Matching Pairs of Cases

Matching each treated case with an untreated case is the next step in the causal analysis process. For our causal conclusions to be valid, we must carefully select the confounding factors, distance measure, and pairing method used in the matching process.

During the matching process, it is important to consider all practices (except the treatment practice) that may be related to the treatment or outcome. Excluding a potentially important confounding practice can significantly compromise the validity of the causal conclusion, while including practices that are actually unassociated with the outcome imposes no harm—assuming a sufficiently large sample size and/or a suitable measure of closeness [32]. Therefore, we include all 28 of the practice metrics we infer, minus the treatment practice, as confounding factors.

One caveat of including many confounding practices is that it becomes difficult to obtain many *exact matches*—pairs of cases where both cases have the exact same values for all confounding practices. For example, exact matching produces at most 17 pairs (out of ≈11K cases) when *number of change events* is the treatment practice. The same issue exists when matching based on Mahalanobis distance [29].

We overcome this challenge using *propensity scores*. A propensity score measures the probability of a case receiving treatment (e.g., having a specific *number of models*) given the observed confounding practices (e.g., *number of roles*) for that case [33]. By comparing cases that have the same propensity scores—i.e., an equally likely probability of being treated based on the observed confounding practices—we can be confident that the actual presence or absence of treatment is not determined by the confounding practices. In other words, a treated case and an untreated case with the same propensity score have the same probability of having a given value for a confounding practice (e.g., *number of roles*); thus propensity score matching mimics a randomized experiment.

Given propensity scores for all treated and untreated cases, we use the most common, and simplest, pairing method: *k=1 nearest neighbor* [32]. Each treated case is paired with an untreated case that results in the smallest absolute difference in their propensity scores. To obtain the best possible pairings, we match *with replacement*—i.e., allow multiple treated cases to be paired with the same untreated case. We also follow the common practice of discarding treated (untreated) cases whose propensity score falls outside the range of propensity scores for untreated (treated) cases.

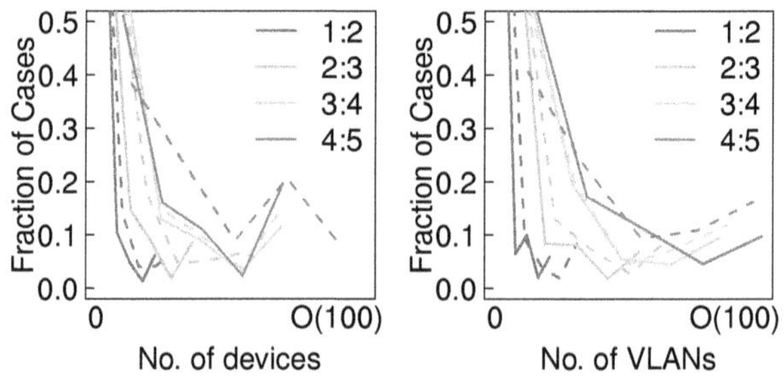

Figure 7: Visual equivalence of confounding practice distributions; lines of the same color are for the same comparison point; solid lines are for matched untreated cases and dashed lines are for matched untreated cases

Table 5 shows the matching results for each of the four comparison points for *number of change events*. There are significantly more matched pairs using propensity scores: up to 99.8% of treated cases are matched, versus <1% with exact matching. Furthermore, the number of untreated cases that are matched with treated cases is less than the number of matched pairs, implying that matching with replacement is beneficial.

5.2.4 Verifying the Quality of Matches

When matching based on propensity scores, rather than the raw values of confounding practices, it is important to verify that the distribution of values for each confounding practice is similar for both the matched treated cases and the matched untreated cases. Otherwise, the effects of confounding practices have not been successfully mitigated, and any causal conclusions drawn from the matched pairs may not be valid.

Figure 7 visually confirms the distribution equivalence for two of the confounding practices. However, to facilitate bulk comparison, we use two common numeric measures of balance: standardized difference of means and ratio of variances [32]. The former is computed as $\frac{\bar{Z}_T - \bar{Z}_U}{\sigma_T}$, where $\bar{Z}_T$ and $\bar{Z}_U$ are the means of a confounding practice Z for the matched treated and matched untreated cases, respectively, and σ_T and σ_U are the standard deviations. The ratio of variances is computed as σ_T^2/σ_U^2. For each confounding practice, the absolute standardized difference of means should be less than 0.25 and the variance ratio should be between 0.5 and 2 [32]. These equations and thresholds also apply to the propensity scores for the matched cases.

As shown in Table 5, the absolute standard difference of means and the ratio of variances of the propensity scores satisfy the quality thresholds for all comparison points. The same also holds for all confounding factors (not shown).

Although we consider a large set of management practices in our causal analysis, it is possible that other practices or factors also contribute to the observed outcomes. We can easily incorporate new practices into our propensity scores as we learn about them. Additionally, our matching based on propensity scores introduces some randomness that can help mitigate the effects of any unaccounted for factors. However, we can never definitely prove causality with QEDs [21]; any causal relationships identified by MPA should thus be viewed as "highly-likely" rather than "guaranteed".

5.2.5 Analyze the Statistical Significance

The final step is to analyze the statistical significance of the difference in outcomes between the matched treated and untreated cases. For each matched pair, we compute the difference in outcome (*number of tickets*) between the treated and untreated case: $y_t - y_u$. If the result is positive (negative), then the treatment prac-

Comparison Point	Fewer Tickets	No Effect	More Tickets	p-value
1:2	562	350	830	6.80×10^{-13}
2:3	251	61	302	3.34×10^{-2}
3:4	110	25	160	2.80×10^{-3}
4:5	282	38	343	1.63×10^{-2}

Table 6: Statistical significance of outcomes; causality is deemed to exist for higlighted comparison points

tice has led to worse (better) network health; if the result is zero, then the practice has not impacted health. We use the outcome calculations from all pairs to produce a binomial distribution of outcomes: more tickets (+1) or fewer tickets (-1). Table 6 shows the distribution for the matched pairs at each comparison point.

If the treatment practice impacts network health, we expect the median of the distribution to be non-zero. Thus, to establish a causal relationship, we must reject the null hypothesis H_0 that the median outcome is zero. We use the *sign test* to compute a *p-value*—the probability that H_0 is consistent with the observed results. Crucially, the sign test makes few assumptions about the nature of the distribution, and it has been shown to be well-suited for evaluating matched design experiments [15]. We choose a moderately conservative threshold of 0.001 for rejecting H_0.

Table 6 shows the p-value produced by the sign test for each of the comparison points for *number of change events*. We observe that the p-value is less than our threshold for the *1:2* comparison point. Hence, the difference in the *number of change events* between bins 1 and 2 is statistically significant, and a causal impact on network health exists at these values. In contrast, the results for the other comparison points (*2:3*, *3:4*, and *4:5*) are not statistically significant. This is due to either the absence of a causal relationship—i.e., increasing the *number of change events* beyond a certain level does not cause an increase in the *number of tickets*—or an insufficient number of samples. We believe the latter applies for our data, because there is at least some evidence of a non-zero median: the number of cases with more tickets is at least 20% higher than the number of cases with fewer tickets for the *2:3*, *3:4*, and *4:5* comparison points.

5.2.6 Results for the OSP

We now conduct a causal analysis for the 10 management practices with the highest statistical dependence with network health (Table 3). Due to skew in our data, we can only draw meaningful conclusions for low values of our practice metrics (bins 1 and 2).

Table 7 shows the p-value for the comparison between the first and second bin for each practice. We observe that 8 of the 10 practices have a causal relationship according to our p-value threshold. In fact, the p-values for these practices are well below our chosen threshold (0.001). Furthermore, several of the practices with a causal relationship, including *number of devices* and *average devices changed per event*, are practices for which operators had mixed opinions regarding their impact (Figure 2). Our analysis also matches the prevailing opinion that *number of change events* has a high impact on health, and, to some extent, discredits the belief that the *fraction of events with ACL changes* has low impact.

For the remaining two metrics, *intra-device complexity* and *fraction of events with an interface change*, there is not enough evidence to support a causal relationship. The high statistical dependence but lack of a causal relationship is likely due to these practices being affected by other practices which do have a causal relationship with network health. For example, *number of VLANs* has a causal relationship with network health and may influence *intra-device complexity*. Hence, a change in *number of VLANs* may change both network health and *intra-device complexity* in a way that makes *intra-device complexity* statistically similar to health.

Treatment Practice	p-value for 1:2
No. of devices	1.92×10^{-8}
No. of change events	1.05×10^{-12}
Intra-device complexity	1.53×10^{-2}
No. of change types	5.75×10^{-12}
No. of VLANs	6.46×10^{-6}
No. of models	1.31×10^{-7}
No. of roles	2.99×10^{-10}
Avg. devices changed per event	3.56×10^{-8}
Frac. events w/ interface change	5.27×10^{-3}
Frac. events w/ ACL change	9.10×10^{-9}

Table 7: Causal analysis results for the first and second bin for the top 10 statistically dependent management practices; highlighted p-values satisfy our significance threshold

Treatment Practice	Comparison Point 2:3	3:4	4:5
No. of devices	Imbal.	Imbal.	Imbal.
No. of change events	3.34×10^{-2}	2.80×10^{-3}	1.63×10^{-2}
Intra-device complexity	Imbal.	1.71×10^{-1}	1.47×10^{-1}
No. of change types	9.02×10^{-1}	1.42×10^{-5}	Imbal.
No. of VLANs	Imbal.	1.94×10^{-3}	Imbal.
No. of models	Imbal.	Imbal.	Imbal.
No. of roles	Imbal.	6.63×10^{-1}	Imbal.
Avg. devices changed per event	4.53×10^{-3}	2.25×10^{-1}	Imbal.
Frac. events w/ interface change	4.51×10^{-2}	4.58×10^{-1}	2.89×10^{-12}
Frac. events w/ ACL change	4.88×10^{-2}	2.78×10^{-1}	6.48×10^{-2}

Table 8: Causal analysis results for upper bins for the top 10 statistically dependent management practices; highlighted p-values satisfy our significance threshold

Table 8 shows the p-value for the comparison between the upper bins for the same 10 practices. We observe that over one-third of the matchings have poor quality (i.e., strong imbalance), and most of the others have large p-values. This primarily stems from management practice metrics following a heavy-tailed distribution. For example, when the treatment practice is *number of devices*, 81% of cases fall into the first bin and 8% fall into the second bin; this means there are few cases from which to select matched pairs for the *2:3*, *3:4*, and *4:5* comparison points. The only way to address this issue is to obtain (more diverse) data from more networks.

Acting on the Results. The ability to change practices that cause poor network health varies based on the class of practice and the needs of the organization. Changing design practices (e.g., number of models or roles) requires deploying new networks, or significantly overhauling existing networks. In contrast, operational practices can be adjusted more easily: e.g., changes can be aggregated or reduced by more carefully planning network reconfigurations. Some practices may be difficult to change due to workload demands (e.g., number of devices), but operators can still benefit from understanding these relationships to aid in setting service level objectives (SLOs) or making staffing decisions.

6. PREDICTING NETWORK HEALTH

We now move on to the second goal of MPA: building models that take a network's current management practices as input and predict the network's health. Such models are useful for network operators to explore how adjustments in management practices will likely impact network health: e.g., will combining configuration changes into fewer, larger changes improve network health?

We find that basic learning algorithms (e.g., C4.5 [27]) produce mediocre models because of the skewed nature of management practices and health outcomes. In particular, they over-fit for the majority healthy network case. Thus, we develop schemes to learn more robust models despite this limitation. We show that we can predict network health at coarse granularity (i.e., healthy vs. unhealthy) with 91% accuracy; finer-grained predictions (i.e., a scale of 1 to 5) are less accurate due to a lack of sufficient samples.

6.1 Building an Organization's Model

We start with the following question: given all data from an organization, what is the best model we can construct?

An intuitive place to start is support vector machines (SVMs). SVMs construct a set of hyperplanes in high-dimensional space, similar to using logistic regression to construct propensity score formulas during causal analysis. However, we found the SVMs performed worse than a simple majority classifier. This is due to unhealthy cases being concentrated in a small part of the management practice space.

To better learn these unhealthy cases, we turn to decision tree classifiers (the C4.5 algorithm [27]). Decision trees are better equipped to capture the limited set of unhealthy cases, because they can model arbitrary boundaries between cases. Furthermore, they are intuitive for operators to understand.

Methodology. Prior to learning, we bin data as described in Section 5.1.1. However, we use only 5 bins for each management practice (instead of 10), because the amount of data we have is insufficient to accurately learn fine-grained models. For network health, we use either 2 bins or 5 bins; two bins (classes) enables us to differentiate coarsely between *healthy* ($\leq$1 tickets) and *unhealthy* networks, while five bins captures more fine-grained classes of health—excellent, good, moderate, poor, and very poor ($\leq$2, 3–5, 6–8, 9–11, and $\geq$12 tickets, respectively). As is standard practice, we prune a decision tree to avoid over-fitting: each branch where the number of data points reaching this branch is below a threshold α is replaced with a leaf whose label is the majority class among the data points reaching that leaf. We set α=1% of all data.

Model Validation. We measure the accuracy, precision, and recall of the decision trees using 5-fold cross validation. *Accuracy* is the mean fraction of test examples whose class is predicted correctly. For a given class C, *precision* measures what fraction of the data points that were predicted as class C actually belong to class C, while *recall* measures what fraction of the data points that belong to class C are correctly predicted as class C.

We find that a 2-class model performs very well. Accuracy of the pruned decision tree—i.e., the mean fraction of test examples whose class is predicted correctly—is 91.6%. In comparison, a majority class predictor has a significantly worse accuracy: 64.8%. Furthermore, the decision tree has very high precision and recall for the healthy class (0.92 and 0.98, respectively), and moderate precision and recall for the unhealthy class (0.62 and 0.31, respectively). A majority class predictor has only moderate precision (0.64) for the healthy class and no precision or recall for the unhealthy class.

The accuracy for a 5-class model is 81.1%, but the precision and recall for the intermediate classes (good, moderate, and poor) are very low (DT bars in Figure 8). The root cause here is skew in the data: as shown in Figure 9(b), a majority of the samples represent the "excellent health" case (73%), with far fewer samples in other health classes (e.g., the poor class has just 2.3% of the samples). Our 5-class decision tree ends up overfitting for the majority class.

Addressing Skew. Because networks are generally healthy, such skew in data is a fundamental challenge that predictive models in MPA need to address, especially when attempting to predict fine-grained health classes. To address skew and improve the accuracy of our models for minority classes, we borrow two techniques

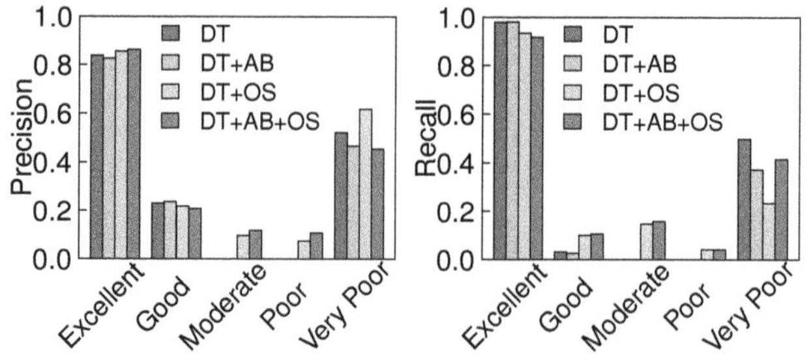

(a) Precision (b) Recall

Figure 8: Accuracy of 5 class models (DT=standard decision tree learning algorithm, AB=AdaBoost, OS=oversampling)

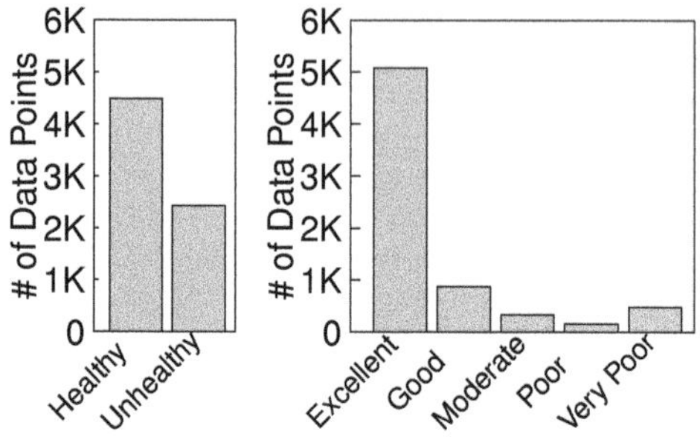

(a) 2 classes (b) 5 classes

Figure 9: Health class distribution

from the machine learning community: boosting (specifically, AdaBoost [12]) and oversampling.[2]

AdaBoost helps improve the accuracy of "weak" learners. Over many iterations (we use 15) AdaBoost increases (decreases) the weight of examples that were classified incorrectly (correctly) by the learner; the final learner (i.e., decision tree) is built from the last iteration's weighted examples. Oversampling directly addresses skew as it repeats the minority class examples during training. When building a 2-class model we replicate samples from the unhealthy class twice, and when building a 5-class model we replicate samples from the poor class twice and the moderate and good classes thrice.

The results from applying these enhancements are shown in Figure 8. We observe that AdaBoost results in minor improvement for all classes. In contrast, using oversampling significantly improves the precision and recall for the three intermediate health classes, and causes a slight drop in the recall for the two extreme classes (excellent and very poor). Using oversampling and AdaBoost in combination offers the best overall performance across all classes.

The final 5-class model is substantially better than using a traditional decision tree. However, it is still sub-optimal due to the significant skew in the underlying dataset. Separating apart a pair of nearby classes whose class boundaries are very close—e.g., excellent and good—requires many more *real* data points from either class; oversampling can only help so much. Thus, lack of data may pose a key barrier to MPA's ability to model network health at *fine granularity*. Nonetheless, we have shown that *good models can be constructed for coarse grained prediction.*

[2]We also experimented with random forests [8, 19]; neither balanced [8] nor weighted random forests [19] improve the accuracy for the minority classes beyond the improvements we are already able to achieve with boosting and oversampling.

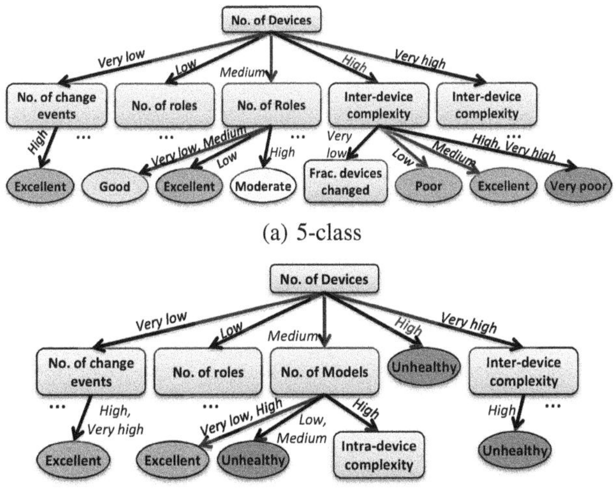

(a) 5-class

(b) 2-class

Figure 10: Decision trees (only a portion is shown)

6.2 Using an Organization's Model

Operators can use an organization's model to determine which combinations of management practices lead to an (un)healthy network, and to evaluate how healthy a network will be in the future when a specific set of management practices are applied.

Tree Structure. Figure 10(a) shows a portion of the best 5-class tree. Since decision trees are built by recursively selecting the node with the highest mutual information, the management practice with the strongest statistical dependence (identified in Section 5.1)—*number of devices*—is the root of the tree. In the second level, however, two of the three practices are not present in our list of the 10 most statistically dependent practices (Table 3). This shows that the importance of some management practices depends on the nature of other practices: e.g., when the *number of devices* is medium or low, the *number of roles* is a stronger determinant of health than the *number of change events*. Thus, examining the paths from the decision tree's root to its leaves provides valuable insights into which combinations of management practices lead to an (un)healthy network.

The same observations apply to the 2-class tree (Figure 10(b)).

Predicting Future Health. We now show that an organization's model can accurately predict the future health of an organization's networks. In particular, we build decision trees using data points from M months ($t - M$ to $t - 1$). Then, we use management practice metrics from month t to predict the health of each network in month t. The accuracy for month t is the fraction of networks whose health was correctly predicted.

Table 9 shows the average accuracy for M=1, 3, 6, and 9 for values of t between February and October 2014. We observe that *a 2-class model has consistently high prediction accuracy of 89%* irrespective of the amount of prior data used to train the model. This trend primarily stems from having less severe skew between the majority and minority classes when using two classes (Figure 9(a)).

The prediction accuracy of a 5-class model reaches 78% for $M = 9$. Also, accuracy improves with a longer history of training data: using 9 months, rather than 1 month, of training data results in a 5% increase in accuracy. However, as the amount of training data increases (i.e., increasing M) the relative improvement in accuracy diminishes. Thus, a reasonably accurate prediction of network health can be made with less than a year's worth of data.

M (months)	5 classes	2 classes
1	0.734	0.881
3	0.756	0.893
6	0.779	0.901
9	0.779	0.903

Table 9: Accuracy of future health predictions

7. DISCUSSION

Generality. While the observations we make for the OSP's networks provide a valuable perspective on the relationship between management practices and network health, the statistical dependencies and causal relationships we uncover may not apply to all organizations. Differences in network types (e.g., data center vs. wide area networks), workloads, and other organization-specific factors may affect these relationships. Nonetheless, our techniques are likely generally applicable, and any organization can run our tool [2] to discover these relationships for its networks.

Intent of Management Practices. The metrics we infer (Section 2.2) quantify management practices in terms of their direct influence on the data and control planes: e.g., how heterogeneous is network hardware, and which configuration stanzas are changed. However, we could also quantify management actions in terms of their *intent*, or the goal an operator is trying to achieve: e.g., an operator may want to reduce firmware licensing costs, so they design a network to use RIP rather than OSPF [5]. By analyzing the relationships between intent and network health, we can gain a richer understanding of what practices are the most problematic. Unfortunately, intent is much more difficult to infer from network data sources (Section 2.1), and doing so is part of our ongoing work.

8. RELATED WORK

An earlier version of this work [4] introduced the idea of management plane analytics and provided visual evidence of correlations between a few management practices and network health. This paper considers many more practices, conducts causal analyses, and shows how to build accurate predictive models.

Establishing, following, and refining management practices is an important part of information technology (IT) service management. ITIL [1] provides guidance on: service design, which focuses on health-related concerns such as availability and service levels; service transition, which focuses on change, configuration, and deployment management; and continual service improvement. Some of the general metrics used in ITIL to asses the health of an IT organization (e.g., *number of changes*) are also used in MPA, but MPA also considers may networking-specific metrics. This makes MPA a valuable tool for continual service improvement. The major steps in MPA—defining metrics, characterizing practices, and uncovering relationships between practices and health—are similar to the steps employed in security management [17], but MPA's analyses are focused more on causality and relationship modeling.

A few prior studies have examined network management practices. Kim et al. study several design and operational issues in two campus network: e.g., how network-wide configuration size grows over time, what causes this growth, how configurations of different device types (e.g., router, firewall, etc.) change and why, and the qualitative differences among the campuses in these aspects [20]. Others have looked at more narrow aspects of design and operations: e.g., Benson et al. examine configuration complexity in 7 enterprise networks [5] and study design and change patterns of various network-based services of a large ISP [6]; Garimella et al. and Krothapalli et al. study VLAN usage in a single campus network [13, 23]. In contrast to these prior works, we examine a much more comprehensive set of design and operational practices. Also, by virtue of studying many networks of a large OSP, we are able to provide a unique view into the *variation* in management practices. Finally, none of the prior studies tie their the observations to health.

Prior work has also examined network health in great detail. For example, Turner et al. use device logs, network probes and incident reports to understand causes and frequency of failures and their impact [37]. Failure in data center networks, and of middleboxes in data centers have been studied by Gill et al. [14] and Navendu et al. [25], respectively. Turner et al. examine how to combine various data sources to obtain a better view of failures and their root causes [38, 39]. However, these studies don't link network issues back to design and operational practices. That said, some of the data sources and techniques considered in these approaches could be valuable to deriving better network health metrics that could then improve MPA.

QEDs have been widely studied. Stuart [32] provides a comprehensive survey of the various techniques employed in matched design experiments. Our use of QEDs is inspired by recent network measurement studies focused on video streaming quality [21] and video ad placement [22]. While these works use exact matching in their QEDs, we use nearest neighbor matching of propensity scores, because exact matching cannot accommodate the large number of confounding factors in the management plane (Section 5.2).

MPA is inspired by how research into software engineering practices, also called "empirical software engineering," has helped improve the quality of software and reduced the number of bugs [7]. We expect similar positive impact from MPA.

9. CONCLUSION

We presented a *management plane analytics* framework for analyzing and improving network management practices. We showed that a systematic analysis of the management plane is: (*i*) *necessary*—given the diversity in prevalent management practices and in opinions among operators regarding what matters versus not; and (*ii*) *feasible*—by analyzing data from many networks using carefully selected techniques. We found that the nature of network management data necessitates the use of propensity scores to reduce data dimensionality and facilitate matched design quasi-experiments that identify causal relationships between practices and network health. Additionally, we showed that oversampling and boosting are necessary for building good predictive models in the face of heavily skewed data. Our application of MPA to networks of a large OSP revealed intriguing insights: e.g., the fraction of changes where an ACL is modified has a moderately high impact on network health despite a majority opinion that the impact is low, and the fraction of change events affecting a middlebox has low impact on health despite the belief that the impact is high.

However, we have just scratched the surface of such analysis. There are many issues left open by our work, including: studying other health metrics using MPA, determining how to extend MPA to apply across organizations, and developing tools for inferring management practices from outside a network (akin to probing tools such as trace-route) as opposed to analyzing internally-collected data. We believe this is a rich avenue for future research.

10. ACKNOWLEDGMENTS

We thank the operators of the online service provider for their suggestions and feedback, as well as the operators who took the time to answer our survey. We also thank our shepherd Anja Feldmann and the anonymous reviewers for their insightful comments. This work is supported by the Wisconsin Institute on Software-defined Datacenters of Madison and National Science Foundation grants CNS-1302041, CNS-1330308, and CNS-1345249. Aaron Gember-Jacobson is supported by an IBM PhD Fellowship.

11. REFERENCES

[1] ITIL – IT service management. `http://www.axelos.com/best-practice-solutions/itil`.

[2] Management plane analytics tool. `http://cs.wisc.edu/~agember/go/mpa`.

[3] NIST/SEMATECH e-handbook of statistical methods. `http://itl.nist.gov/div898/handbook`.

[4] A. Akella and R. Mahajan. A call to arms for management plane analytics. In *IMC*, 2014.

[5] T. Benson, A. Akella, and D. Maltz. Unraveling complexity in network management. In *NSDI*, 2009.

[6] T. Benson, A. Akella, and A. Shaikh. Demystifying configuration challenges and trade-offs in network-based ISP services. In *SIGCOMM*, 2011.

[7] C. Bird, B. Murphy, N. Nagappan, and T. Zimmermann. Empirical software engineering at Microsoft Research. In *Computer Supported Cooperative Work (CSCW)*, 2011.

[8] L. Breiman. Random forests. *Machine learning*, 45(1):5–32, 2001.

[9] P. Comon. Independent component analysis, a new concept? *Signal Processing*, 36(3):287–314, Apr. 1994.

[10] A. B. Downey. Using pathchar to estimate internet link characteristics. In *SIGCOMM*, 1999.

[11] A. Fogel, S. Fung, L. Pedrosa, M. Walraed-Sullivan, R. Govindan, R. Mahajan, and T. Millstein. A general approach to network configuration analysis. In *NSDI*, 2015.

[12] Y. Freund and R. E. Schapire. A decision-theoretic generalization of on-line learning and an application to boosting. *J. Computer and System Sciences*, 55(1):119–139, Aug. 1997.

[13] P. Garimella, Y. Sung, N. Zhang, and S. Rao. Characterizing VLAN usage in an Operational Network. In *SIGCOMM Workshop on Internet Network Management*, pages 305–306, 2007.

[14] P. Gill, N. Jain, and N. Nagappan. Understanding network failures in data centers: Measurement, analysis, and implications. In *SIGCOMM*, 2011.

[15] M. Hollander and D. Wolfe. *Nonparametric statistical methods*. Wiley, 1973.

[16] M. Jain and C. Dovrolis. End-to-end available bandwidth: Measurement methodology, dynamics, and relation with TCP throughput. In *SIGCOMM*, 2002.

[17] A. Jaquith. *Security Metrics: Replacing Fear, Uncertainty, and Doubt*. Addison-Wesley, 2007.

[18] D. D. Jensen, A. S. Fast, B. J. Taylor, and M. E. Maier. Automatic identification of quasi-experimental designs for discovering causal knowledge. In *KDD*, 2008.

[19] T. M. Khoshgoftaar, M. Golawala, and J. Van Hulse. An empirical study of learning from imbalanced data using random forest. In *International Conference on Tools with Artificial Intelligence (ICTAI)*, 2007.

[20] H. Kim, T. Benson, A. Akella, and N. Feamster. The evolution of network configuration: A tale of two campuses. In *IMC*, 2011.

[21] S. S. Krishnan and R. K. Sitaraman. Video stream quality impacts viewer behavior: Inferring causality using quasi-experimental designs. In *IMC*, 2012.

[22] S. S. Krishnan and R. K. Sitaraman. Understanding the effectiveness of video ads: A measurement study. In *IMC*, 2013.

[23] S. D. Krothapalli, X. Sun, Y.-W. E. Sung, S. A. Yeo, and S. G. Rao. A toolkit for automating and visualizing VLAN configuration. In *SafeConfig*, 2009.

[24] R. Mahajan, N. Spring, D. Wetherall, and T. Anderson. User-level Internet path diagnosis. In *SOSP*, 2003.

[25] R. Potharaju and N. Jain. Demystifying the dark side of the middle: A field study of middlebox failures in datacenters. In *IMC*, 2013.

[26] R. Potharaju, N. Jain, and C. Nita-Rotaru. Juggling the jigsaw: Towards automated problem inference from network trouble tickets. In *NSDI*, 2013.

[27] J. R. Quinlan. *C4.5: Programs for Machine Learning*. Morgan Kaufmann Publishers Inc., San Francisco, CA, USA, 1993.

[28] Really Awesome New Cisco Conflg Differ (RANCID). http://shrubbery.net/rancid.

[29] D. B. Rubin. Using multivariate matched sampling and regression adjustment to control bias in observational studies. *Journal of the American Statistical Association*, 74:318–328, 1979.

[30] W. Shadish, T. Cook, , and D. Campbell. *Experimental and Quasi-Experimental Designs for Generalized Causal Inference*. Houghton Mifflin, 2002.

[31] N. Spring, R. Mahajan, D. Wetherall, and T. Anderson. Measuring ISP topologies with Rocketfuel. *IEEE/ACM Transactions on Networking (ToN)*, 2004.

[32] E. A. Stuart. Matching methods for causal inference: A review and a look forward. *Statistical Science*, 25, 2010.

[33] E. A. Stuart and D. B. Rubin. Best practices in quasi-experimental designs: Matching methods for causal inference. In *Best Practices in Quantitative Methods*, pages 155–176. Sage, 2008.

[34] Y. Sung, S. Rao, S. Sen, and S. Leggett. Extracting network-wide correlated changes from longitudinal configuration data. In *PAM*, 2009.

[35] Traceroute.org. http://www.traceroute.org.

[36] HP OpenView TrueControl Software. http://support.openview.hp.com.

[37] D. Turner, K. Levchenko, J. C. Mogul, S. Savage, and A. C. Snoeren. On failure in managed enterprise networks. Technical Report HPL-2012-101, HP.

[38] D. Turner, K. Levchenko, S. Savage, and A. C. Snoeren. A comparison of syslog and is-is for network failure analysis. In *IMC*, 2013.

[39] D. Turner, K. Levchenko, A. C. Snoeren, and S. Savage. California fault lines: Understanding the causes and impact of network failures. In *SIGCOMM*, 2010.

APPENDIX

A. CHARACTERIZATION OF MANAGEMENT PRACTICES

We provide a detailed characterization of the management practices used at a large online service provider (OSP). This offers a unique and rich view into the practices used in a modern, professionally-managed infrastructure. We are not claiming that this view is representative. For brevity, we quantify a subset of the practice metrics in Table 1. We find significant diversity in the design and operational practices employed across the OSP's networks.

A.1 Design Practices

We start by examining the OSP's networks in terms of their network composition, structure, and purpose.

The majority (81%) of networks host *only one workload*—networks are quite homogeneous in this respect. A handful of networks do not host any workloads; they only connect networks to each other or the external world.

The networks contain a mix of device roles, including routers, switches, firewalls, application delivery controllers (ADCs)[3], and load balancers. Most networks (86%) have devices in multiple roles—although no single device has more than one role—and 71% of networks contain at least one middlebox (firewall, ADC, or load balancer). We also find that over 81% of networks contain devices from more than one vendor, with a maximum of 6, and over 96% of networks contain more than one device model, with a maximum of 25. Thus, some networks must use more than one device model for the same role. Indeed, a closer look at the hardware entropy of the networks (solid line in Figure 11(a)) shows that only 4% of networks have just one model and one role; *the remaining (96% of) networks have varying degrees of heterogeneity*, up to a maximum entropy metric value of 0.82. The extent of firmware heterogeneity is similar (dashed line in Figure 11(a)).

Next, we look at the logical composition and structure of the data and control planes. As shown in Figure 11(b), all networks use at least two layer-2 protocols (VLAN, spanning tree, link aggregation, unidirectional link detection (UDLD), DHCP relay, etc.), and 89% of networks use at least one routing protocol (BGP and/or OSPF). Furthermore, 10% of networks use 8 different protocols. Overall *there is significant diversity in the combination of protocols used.*

We find the same diversity in the number of instances of each protocol. Less than 5 VLANs are configured in 5% of networks, but over 100 VLANs are configured in 9% of networks (Figure 11(c)). Similarly, 86% of networks use BGP for layer-3 routing, with just one BGP instance in 39% of networks and more than 20 instances in 8% of networks (Figure 11(e)). In contrast, only 31% of networks use OSPF for layer-3 routing, with just one or two OSPF instances used in these networks.

Finally, to characterize configuration complexity, Figure 11(d) shows a CDF of intra- and inter-device referential complexity. We find that some networks' configuration is extremely complex (based on Benson et al.'s metrics [5]): in 20% of networks, the mean intra- and inter-device reference counts are higher than 100. However, it is worth noting that: (i) *the range in complexity is rather large*, and (ii) most networks have significantly lower configuration complexity metrics than the worst 10%.

A.2 Operational Practices

We now characterize the frequency, type, and modality of configuration changes, as well as those of change events.

In general, the average number of configuration changes per month is correlated with network size (Figure 12(a); Pearson correlation coefficient of 0.64). However, *several large networks have relatively fewer changes per month*: e.g., one network has over 300 devices but fewer than 150 changes per month. Likewise, *there are several small networks with a disproportionately high change rate.* Furthermore, not every device is changed every month—in 77% of networks less than half of a network's devices are changed in a given month—but most devices are changed at least once per year—in 80% of networks more than three-quarters of the devices are changed in a year (Figure 12(b)). Thus, *changes occur frequently, and to different sets of devices in different months.*

We now analyze different types of changes. Across our entire dataset there are ≈480 different types of changes. Figure 12(c) shows CDFs of the fraction of changes in which at least one stanza of a given type is changed. On a per-network basis, interface changes are the most common, followed by pool (used on load balancers), ACL, user, and router. [4]

Among the above most-frequently changed types, pool changes are also the most frequently automated—more than half of all pool changes are automated in 77% of networks—followed by ACL and interface changes. We also look at the extent of automation over *all* types of changes. As shown in Figure 12(d), more than half (quarter) of the changes each month are automated in 41% (81%) of networks. In general, *we note a significant diversity in the extent of automation*: it ranges between 10% and 70%. Equally interestingly, the fraction of automated changes is not strongly correlated with the number changes (Pearson correlation coefficient is 0.23). Furthermore, the types of changes that are automated most frequently—sflow and QoS—are not the most frequent types of changes.

[3] ADCs perform TCP and SSL offload, HTTP compression and caching, content-aware load balancing, etc.

[4] There are no pool changes in 63% of networks because these networks do not contain load balancers.

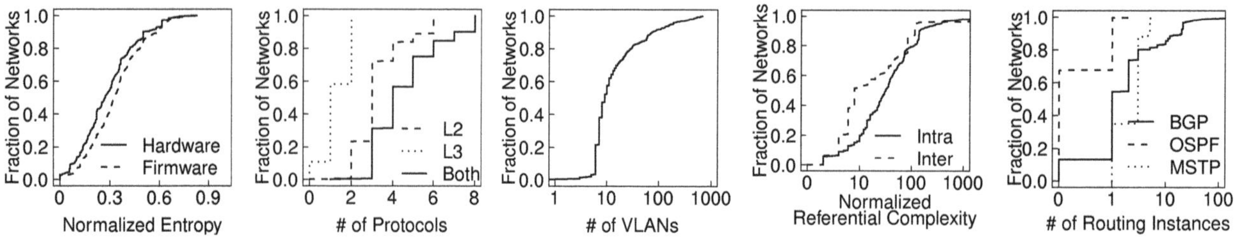

(a) Device heterogeneity (b) Protocol usage (c) No. of VLANs (d) Referential complexity (e) No. of routing Instances

Figure 11: Characterization of design practices

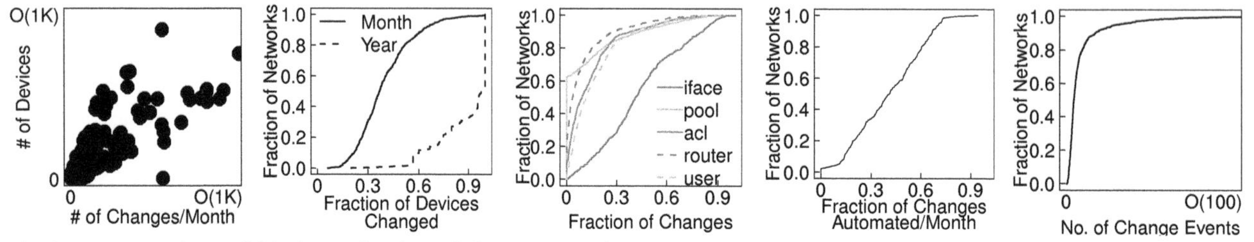

(a) Avg. number of changes per month (b) Avg. fraction of devices changed (c) Most frequent config changes (d) Frac. of changes automated (e) Avg. number of change events per month

Figure 12: Characterization of configuration changes

Lastly, we look at change events, both in terms of how many there are in a network as well as the composition of an event (in terms of number of devices changed). Figure 12(e) shows a distribution of the number of change events. They are few in number ($\mathcal{O}(10)$) in most networks (80%); however about 5% of the networks experience tens if not hundreds of change events in a month. We see a similar *diversity in the number of change events* involving middleboxes (Figure 13(b)). Both prevalence of change events, as well as events involving middleboxes, were flagged by the operators we surveyed as being impactful (Figure 2).

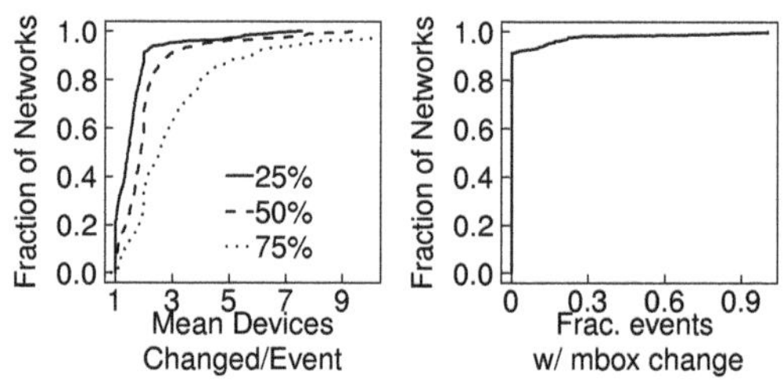

(a) Avg. devices changed per event (b) Frac. of events that change a middlebox

Figure 13: Characterization of configuration change events

Figure 13(a) shows a CDF of the average number of devices changed per change event. Most change events we see across networks are small: in about half of the networks, a change event affects only one or two devices (on average). Further, in almost all networks, the average change event affects only one device role and one device model. Limiting changes to just a few, similar devices is intuitively a good practice to simplify debugging and rollback.

PerfSight: Performance Diagnosis for Software Dataplanes

Wenfei Wu, Keqiang He, Aditya Akella
University of Wisconsin-Madison

ABSTRACT

The advent of network functions virtualization (NFV) means that data planes are no longer simply composed of routers and switches. Instead they are very complex and involve a variety of sophisticated packet processing elements that reside on the OSes and software running on compute servers where network functions (NFs) are hosted. In this paper, we argue that these new "software data planes" are susceptible to at least three new classes of performance problems. To diagnose such problems, we design, implement and evaluate, PerfSight, a ground-up system that works by extracting comprehensive low-level information regarding packet processing and I/O performance of the various elements in the software data plane. PerfSight then analyzes the information gathered in various dimensions (e.g., across all VMs on a machine, or all VMs deployed by a tenant). By looking across aggregates, we show that it becomes possible to detect and diagnose key performance problems. Experimental results show that our framework can result in accurate detection of the root causes of key performance problems in software data planes, and it imposes very little overhead.

Categories and Subject Descriptors

C.2 COMPUTER-COMMUNICATION NETWORKS [**C.2.3 Network Operations**]: Network management

Keywords

data center networks; software data plane; performance; diagnosis

1. INTRODUCTION

Data plane diagnosis tools are invaluable toward managing and troubleshooting networks. Tools such as ping and traceroute, and frameworks such as NetFlow [4] and sFlow [8], are routinely used by network operators both to understand whether the network is functioning as expected, and, if not, understand what may be causing the underlying problem.

However, in recent years, network data planes have changed in fundamental ways. In addition to simple L2 and L3 devices, they are increasingly composed of a wide range of network functions, or middleboxes, that perform custom packet processing to aid in satisfying various network-wide objectives pertaining to performance, security, and compliance; examples include firewalls, load balancers, application gateways, accelerators, etc. With the advent of software switching, and more importantly, network functions virtualization (NFV), traditional hardware switching elements and middleboxes are being realized using software running on generic compute platforms (e.g., a virtual machine, or VM).

Thus, the "data plane" that packets traverse on end-to-end paths now includes—in addition to hardware L2/L3 devices and links—a variety of software components that reside within compute servers' virtualization stacks and within the VMs running various middlebox software. Examples include physical and virtual NICs and their drivers, various packet processing routines in hypervisors and within middlebox logic, virtual switches, hypervisor I/O handlers, host and guest network stacks, etc. We refer to this new portion of the data plane as the *software data plane*.

Our community has developed a variety of innovative tools and frameworks for diagnosing problems in hardware dataplanes. Examples include traceroute, path MTU discovery [5], available capacity detection [34], tomography [13], etc. Unfortunately, we don't have similar tools for software data planes.

In fact, software data planes present new challenges to diagnosis. Because they span a variety of software components running on shared compute resources, where each component can perform fairly sophisticated actions, software data planes are much more susceptible to a range of *subtle performance problems*. We argue that there are at least three classes of performance problems—those arising due to mis-allocation of resources to software data plane elements, contention amongst elements for shared resources, and buggy design/implementation. Such problems either don't arise frequently in traditional hardware data planes (e.g., implementations with performance bugs are rare), or they are simpler to diagnose because only a handful of resources are allocated (e.g., bandwidth and router buffering, vs. CPU, disk, memory, network etc. in software data planes) and contention observed manifests at a small number of locations (e.g., buffers building up or link utilization growing vs. drops/buffering at a multitude of possible locations in the virtualization stack—See Section 2.1). Furthermore, because of stateful packet processing, problems arising in one middlebox may quickly propagate up- or down-stream to other middleboxes on an end-to-end path, which complicates accurate diagnosis of root causes (See Section 2.2).

We design a general system, called PerfSight, for accurate and quick diagnosis of a broad variety of performance problems that may arise in current and future software data planes. Our approach is rooted in viewing the software data plane as a *pipeline of ele-*

IMC'15, October 28–30, 2015, Tokyo, Japan.

ACM 978-1-4503-3848-6/15/10 ...$15.00.
DOI: http://dx.doi.org/10.1145/2815675.2815698.

ments, where an element is a logical unit that reads traffic from or writes traffic to another by buffers or function calls. This abstraction captures a variety of entities on the software data path, including middlebox logic, routines in the hypervisor, and routines in a VM's network stack. We decouple the problem of statistics collection from diagnosis. We identify elements and their input/output methods, and statically analyze their code paths to determine where packets can be buffered or dropped; we then instrument all such locations to collect a suite of statistics in a light-weight fashion. When queried by a controller at run-time, these statistics are returned in a generic format, and then consumed by diagnostic applications to perform interesting analytics.

We develop two novel applications that aid in diagnosing key software data plane problems, and we believe our approach covers a large variety of potential problems that may arise. At a high level, these diagnostic applications analyze the gathered element statistics in different "dimensions": e.g., across all VMs on a single physical machine, or across a collection of middlebox VMs that are chained together. We show that by identifying the exact locations in the software data plane where the performance problems are arising—i.e., which particular buffer or element in a VM, hypervisor or the kernel is facing a problem—we can detect contention across VMs vs. problems arising due to resource limitations within a single VM. Similarly, by studying the nature of the performance problem faced by a middlebox—e.g., whether it is stalled for read vs. writes—and in what status its neighboring middleboxes are (i.e., whether they are also stalled or not), we can quickly narrow down the root cause middlebox(es) whose performance problems have propagated throughout a chain.

We have built a prototype of PerfSight in an environment running a Linux 3.2 kernel, Open vSwitch [7], and QEMU /KVM [12]. We conduct several experiments with this prototype on a small scale experimental testbed, using topologies representing chains of middleboxes, and a variety of workloads. We study the effectiveness of PerfSight and find that in all cases PerfSight's low level instrumentation provides accurate information about the exact location in the software data plane of an observed performance problem. We also find that PerfSight can identify contention for a variety of different shared resources (e.g., memory or network bandwidth, CPU, or NIC capacity), it can accurately detect bottleneck middleboxes irrespective of the specific resource that was under-provisioned, and it can accurately pin-point the root cause of problems in complex multi-chain settings where problems can arbitrarily propagate. We also illustrate how an operator can use PerfSight to implement cross-tenant workload management and elastic scaling in a multi-tenant set-up. Finally, we show that PerfSight's instrumentation imposes an insignificant overhead ($< 1\%$).

The remainder of this paper is organized as follows. In Section 2, we describe the performance problems of software dataplanes and motivate the need for a better diagnosis framework. In Section 3, we sketch the high level architecture of PerfSight. Then, in Section 4 and Section 5, we present the design of PerfSight's two major tasks— statistics gathering and diagnostic applications. Section 6 describes the implementation details. We present experimental results showing the accuracy and overhead of PerfSight in Section 7. We present related work in Section 8 and conclude the paper in Section 9.

2. BACKGROUND AND MOTIVATION

In this section, we first present software dataplane definition and the performance problems associated with it. Then we talk about the challenges in accurate software dataplane diagnosis and the need for a better diagnosis approach.

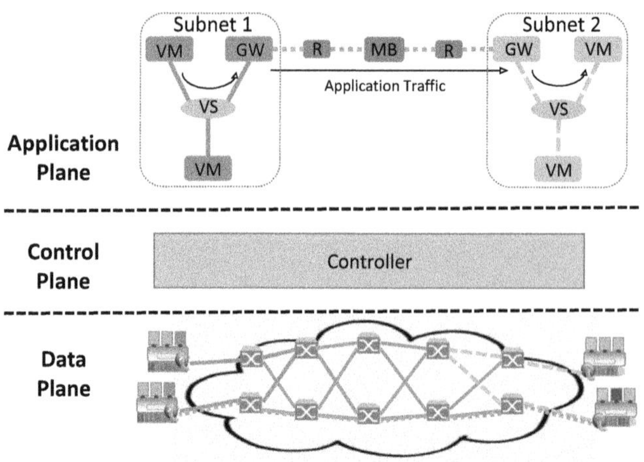

Figure 1: 3 Planes in the Cloud Architecture

2.1 Software Dataplane

While our work applies to general networking settings, for the purposes of this paper, we focus on multi-tenant cloud data centers. In this setting, tenants deploy *virtual private clusters* composed of application end-points (this could be service software in the case of private data centers, or VMs in the case of public clouds), network function services (or middeboxes), and logical links between subsets of them. Network functions improve network performance or security, and tenants increasingly desire to deploy sophisticated sets of middlebox functionality within their clusters [30].

This setting can be viewed logically as being composed of three planes (Figure 1): *control plane*, *application plane* and *data plane*. Tenants interact with the application plane, requesting (re)deployment of virtual private clusters. The control plane, which the cloud operator runs, responds to such requests by computing suitable deployment policies, e.g., determining where VMs and middleboxes ought to be placed, instantiating virtual links between VMs and middleboxes (using tunneling schemes or encapsulation policies [30]), and computing the forwarding state configuration to determine how traffic traverses VMs/middleboxes and virtual links. The dataplane for the tenant's virtual cluster, where fast path actions are performed on the tenant's traffic, then follows the configurations provided by the control plane to deliver network traffic between the appropriate end-points in each virtual cluster.

In this paper, we focus on middleboxes that are implemented as software and deployed in VMs attached to virtual switches, an increasingly popular trend also known as *network functions virtualization (NFV)* [15]. In NFV, the middlebox VMs, similar to application VMs, are allocated fixed resources (e.g. CPU, memory, network bandwidth); the controller deploys all VMs to physical machines that have sufficient resources.

Figure 2(a) shows a tenant with a simple virtual cluster, consisting of an application VM and a firewall; furthermore, the tenant requires all Internet traffic to traverse through the firewall. While this is a simple example, virtual clusters can have much more complex sequences of middleboxes, where a given sequence may only apply to a specific traffic substream. The physical deployment computed by the controller is shown in Figure 2(b). Consider the path that Internet-originated traffic would traverse to arrive at the tenant VM (and vice versa for the outgoing traffic). Each such packet is forwarded by the cloud gateway to the physical NIC (pNIC) of a physical server hosting the middlebox VM first; then it traverses

(a) A virtual Network Example

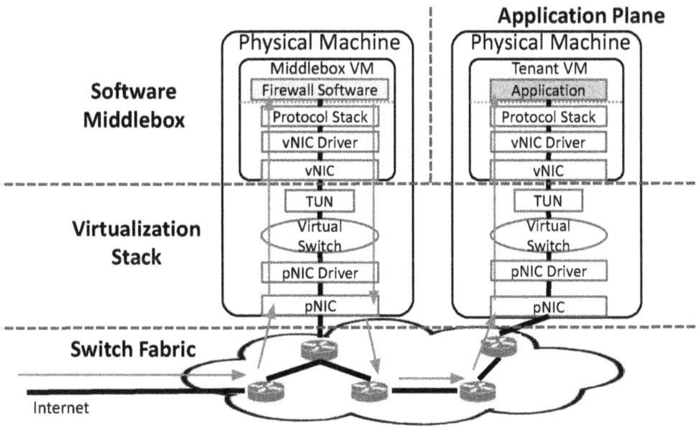

(b) Deployment in Dataplane

Figure 2: Data Plane Organization

the pNIC driver, the virtual switch, the hypervisor I/O handler, the virtual NIC (vNIC), the vNIC driver and the VM guest OS network stack, and finally arrives at the software firewall. After being processed by the software firewall, the packet traverses all the layers back down to the pNIC. Then it is delivered by the physical network to the next hop in the virtual network (tenant VM or another middlebox).

Whereas traditional dataplanes consisted just of hardware switching elements and network links connecting network end points, the advent of NFV means that we need to rethink what constitutes the data plane. In particular, it now also includes the software components shown above that are traversed within middlebox VMs. We refer to this portion of the data plane as the *software data plane*.

The software data plane is composed of a variety of *elements*, each of which performs a certain logical function. In Figure 2, each blue rectangle or oval is an element. The software dataplane can thus be viewed as a pipeline of elements with data traversing from one to the next. The output of one element is the input to its successor. Neighboring elements exchange messages via buffers or function calls.

Elements can be further divided into two categories: (a) Those belonging to the *virtualization stack*: such elements are *shared* by multiple VMs, and examples include the pNIC driver, the packet processing routine, virtual switches and the hypervisor I/O handler; (b) those belonging to the *software middlebox*: such elements are confined to one middlebox VM, and examples include the vNIC, vNIC driver, VM guest OS network stack and middlebox software.

In a multi-tenant setting, software data planes belonging to different tenants may "overlap" on one or more physical machines.

2.2 Performance Problems

In what follows, we argue that software data plane performance problems can arise due to at least three underlying reasons. Furthermore, addressing the problem requires a different approach in each case. A diagnostic approach therefore needs to carefully delineate and accurately identify the root cause.

When the offered load on a middlebox exceeds the capacity allocated to it (along some resource dimensions), the traversing flows' throughput/latency will be **bottlenecked**. Because most middleboxes perform complex actions, such bottlenecks may arise not just due to increased traffic volume but also due to sudden, unexpected changes in the traffic profile. Addressing bottlenecks is up to the tenant (e.g., the tenant can redeploy the middlebox in a "larger" VM).

If multiple elements contend for a shared resource, and their requirements exceed the available resource capacity, all involved elements cannot achieve their expected performance. Such **contention** usually happens in the virtualization stack, because all tenant VMs and middlebox VMs in one physical machine share the same datapath in the virtualization stack. What make things worse is that the shared resource may not be explicitly allocated. For example, it is hard to allocate memory bandwidth to individual VMs; shared buffers in the virtualization stack are similarly not allocated either. To address this, impacted middlebox VMs may have to be migrated to locations with less contention. Often, this requires the cloud operator's involvement.

Design and implementation defects that lead to inefficient computation widely exist in software, and thus software dataplanes are naturally impacted by such **performance bugs**. Indeed, it has been shown previously [33] that middlebox software bugs can result in "soft failures" (e.g., a significant drop in throughput when middlebox software is "upgraded"). To address such performance bugs, a tenant must reload their VMs with a suitable version of software.

2.3 Accurate Diagnosis is Challenging

After a tenant experiences performance problems and submits trouble tickets, we assume that she submits a ticket to her data center operator. Because there are many different kinds of middleboxes and a multitude of elements in software data planes, multiple middleboxes in a virtual cluster can often be operated in a sequence (or "chained"), and multiple tenants' clusters can overlap at arbitrary physical machines; accurately diagnosing data plane performance problems and identifying root causes is not easy for the operator.

A common approach to detect bottlenecks is to monitor the resource utilization on VMs [3]. While this may work in some cases, there are a variety of middleboxes for which resource utilization does not reflect workload intensity. For example, a video stream transcoder [19] may employ non-blocking I/O instead of blocking I/O to avoid context switching. For this middlebox, CPU utilization is always 100%, but we lack a way of distinguishing the portion of CPU cycles spent on processing vs. busy waiting. Another alternative—monitoring traffic volume changes—is also insufficient as bottlenecks may arise due to changes in traffic profiles (e.g., when a middlebox encounters a traffic profile that is different from the one it was optimized for).

Contention is similarly hard to diagnose. Some OS statistics such as packet drops at the pNIC can determine certain forms of contention (e.g., for network bandwidth), but such statistics are not always available today for other key resources. For instance, when multiple VMs on a machine are performing heavy memory copies, they contend with each other over the shared memory bus, which is hard to diagnose due to lack of suitable statistics. Another reason why contention is hard to diagnose is that its effects may only be indirectly felt. For instance, a VM trying to saturate a certain amount of network capacity may be unable to do so in the presence of competing memory intensive workloads, because the two sets of workloads contend for the memory bus (an empirical example is shown in Figure 3). Simply monitoring memory utilization or network packet drops does not reveal the root cause of contention.

The final factor that complicates diagnosis is that performance problems in a middlebox—arising due to, e.g., bugs—may *propagate* across a virtual cluster due to the chaining of middleboxes. The upshot is that the wrong middlebox may be identified as being the root cause of poor performance in a chain or cluster, and incor-

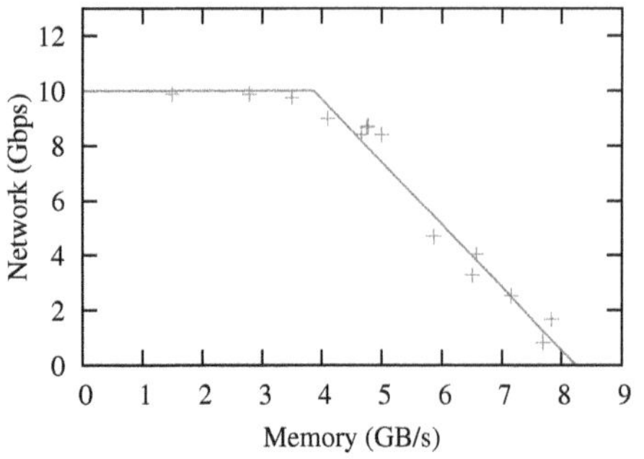

Figure 3: There are 8 VMs in a 8-core hypervisor with a 10Gbps NIC. Some of the VMs perform intensive memory copy operations, and the others send traffic to another machine by best effort. We vary the memory copy workload and measure the total throughput of the memory and the network respectively in each case. When memory throughput is low, the NIC capacity is fully saturated (10Gbps). However, when the memory throughput exceeds a threshold, every 1 GB/s increase of memory throughput causes 439 Mbps decrease of network throughput.

rect/inefficient counter-measures may be adopted. In Section 7 we will show such an example—a load balancer, a content filter and an HTTP server form a chain and the content filter writes logs to a shared NFS server (see Figure 12(d)). When the NFS server has a bug, performance degrades in the whole chain. In this case, it is challenging to find out the root cause middlebox.

2.4 Need for a New Approach

Existing troubleshooting techniques such as Anteater, HSA, NICE, Libra, etc. [31, 24, 14, 37] focus on the correctness of the network; thus, they cannot be used to detect performance problems. Tools such as ping and traceroute provide end-to-end tenant-level information which cannot pin-point root causes (e.g., those due to contention) accurately. Other diagnostic frameworks, such as NDB and VND [20, 35], collect traces on the datapath, either at network switches (NDB), or at vNICs or pNICs (VND). This can impact performance (of multiple tenants' virtual clusters) significantly. But, more importantly, such traces don't provide enough information to perform accurate root cause diagnosis; e.g., they cannot determine that packets were dropped due to memory contention.

Thus, we argue for a ground-up comprehensive framework for software dataplane diagnosis. We posit that given the complexity of the software data plane, a framework that performs *low-level, broad instrumentation* of various elements in the software dataplane, coupled with *suitable analytics*, can provide accurate and useful diagnoses.

3. PERFSIGHT OVERVIEW

We design and implement a system for software data plane diagnosis called PerfSight. Figure 4 shows the architecture of PerfSight. It has 3 high level components: an agent running on each physical server, a central controller, and a set of diagnostic applications atop the controller.

Diagnostic applications are developed using the controller-operator interfaces. These applications query the software data plane for various statistics; the controller then translates these to queries issued to agents running on the corresponding physical servers. The

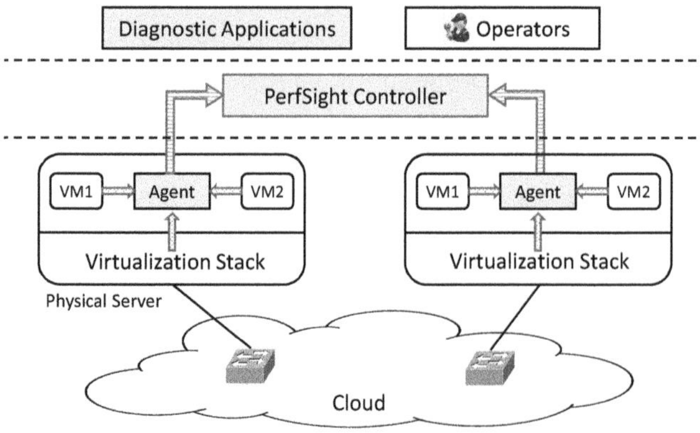

Figure 4: PerfSight Architecture

agents interrogate the relevant elements for statistics, and report the gathered statistics back to the application.

PerfSight uses a simple unified low-level interface for recording/retrieving statistics of the software data plane elements. This abstracts the complexity arising from the diversity of the data plane elements, and simplifies the task of designing analytics engines. The interface can be extended so that operators can easily enrich the set of statistics gathered.

PerfSight decouples data collection from analytics so that each can be improved or replaced by more advanced techniques. PerfSight's analytics applications work by performing *aggregate* diagnostics on the gathered statistics; more specifically, these applications jointly analyze data gathered across multiple instances of a middlebox, multiple middlebox VMs deployed on a single server, or multiple middleboxes deployed in one or more virtual clusters, to accurately pin-point the root cause of the observed performance problem.

In what follows, we first describe what statistics we collect and how they are collected. Then, we describe how these statistics are analyzed to obtain insights into software data plane performance problems.

4. STATISTICS GATHERING

The key insight we leverage to perform software dataplane diagnosis is to view the dataplane as a pipeline of low-level *elements*. By instrumenting at the element-level, we can obtain fine-grained statistics at key points in the software data plane. These then form the basis for interesting and accurate diagnostic applications. In what follows, we describe how we obtain element-level statistics on throughput, packet drops, and packet size. The key challenge lies in understanding where and how to instrument elements such that the data collection overhead is minimal.

4.1 Element Abstraction and Statistics

Figure 5 shows the elements and buffers in a virtualization environment that uses a Linux kernel, QEMU/KVM, and Open vSwitch (OVS). Each element receives packets from its predecessor, processes them based on internal logic, and delivers them to its successor. The exchange of packets between elements is often implemented by a buffer between them or by function calls. For example, in Figure 5, the pNIC driver and the packet processing routine (e.g., the NAPI routine in Linux) use the physical CPU (pCPU) backlog (a buffer) to exchange messages, whereas the NAPI routine and virtual switch use function calls.

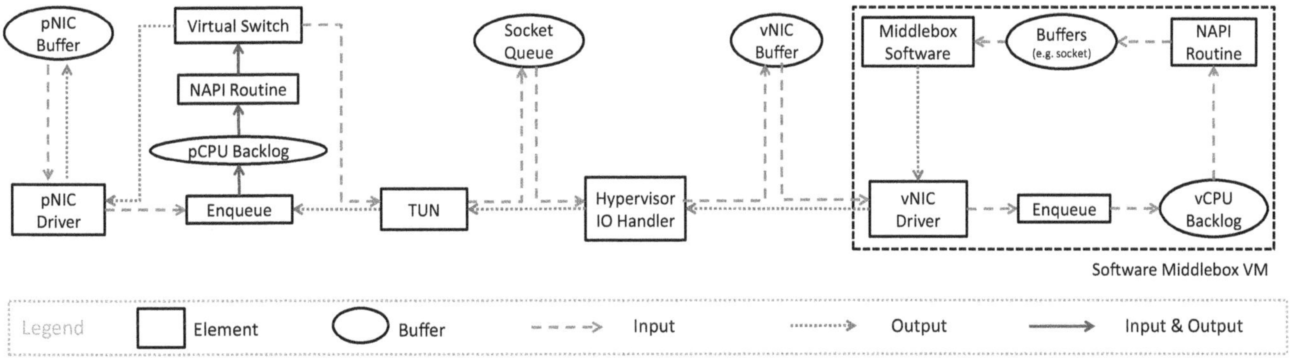

Figure 5: Elements in a Software Dataplane (QEMU/KVM, Open vSwitch, Linux)

Each element has *input methods* and *output methods*. For example, in the pNIC driver, the interrupt handler reads from the pNIC (or DMA mapped memory) and enqueues packets to the CPU backlog queue; the NAPI routine dequeues packets from the CPU backlog and calls the virtual switch frame handling function; the virtual switch frame handling function writes packets to a TAP's socket which is associated with a VM; and, the hypervisor I/O handler reads packets from the TAP and writes packets to the associated vNIC.

In each element, by analyzing its code, we can determine the code path that a packet traverses from input to output and possible code branches that might drop it. Statistics—e.g., how many bytes/packets were received/sent/dropped—of the traffic on the datapath between an element's input and output methods can be then recorded by instrumenting the code path and relevant branches. Another key statistic we gather is I/O time. This records the time spent on an I/O method (read and write). This can also be obtained in an easy and light-weight fashion by comparing the timestamps before and after the read/write function in an element. I/O time can reveal whether an element is facing starvation, and it plays a particularly crucial role in the diagnosis of propagation issues, as we show in Section 5.

In our current implementation, we perform the instrumentation task manually and exhaustively, but we believe it can be automated using program analysis. Interestingly, we find that many useful statistics actually don't require special instrumentation as they can be readily gathered, and hence statistics gathering imposes low overhead in this case. This is particularly true for elements residing in the host OS kernel. For example, packet count and byte count are basic statistics that already exist in most kernel elements. For other elements, e.g., those in the hypervisor and those inside middlebox software, we perform the instrumentation as indicated above; our extensive evaluation (Section 7) shows that the overhead is very low.

Our current prototype of PerfSight extracts/implements the 3 types of counters in each element: a packet counter, a byte counter, and an I/O time counter. The packet and byte counters are used by all types of elements while I/O time counter is only used for elements that interact with buffers. The counters accumulate as packets are processed.

Aggregate statistics such the instantaneous/average packet drop rates, throughput, and packet size can then be easily derived per element from these statistics. Operators can implement more complicated statistics at an element such as packet size distribution tracking if they can accept the resulting performance impact.

Our manual inspection of the code of many middleboxes, virtual switch implementations, and hypervisors has shown that several key entities in software data planes map to this abstraction. Thus, this abstraction is reasonable, and Section 5 shows that it is useful for diagnosis purpose. We show that our proposed statistics suffice to successfully diagnose the performance problems we discuss. In general, though, the set of statistics collected may fall short. That said, PerfSight itself is a framework, and, if necessary, the operator can add more statistics to suit her diagnostic needs.

4.2 Agent

An agent in each physical server gathers element statistics. To reduce overhead, the agent pulls counter values from elements only when required. Due to the diversity of elements, especially across the kernel, hypervisor and the middlebox software, the element/agent interfaces are tailor-designed for each type of element. In particular, we use custom APIs for elements in the kernel: e.g., in the NIC driver and the TAP, the counters are in net_device, and they can be accessed by reading the corresponding device file in the file system. When the NAPI routine processes packets in CPU backlogs, statistics are stored in the data structure softnet_data, and they can be accessed via /proc in the file system. In virtual switches, each switch rule has its own statistics and can be fetched by virtual switch control channels. For elements in the hypervisor and middleboxes, we design a common generic element-agent API.

After fetching statistics from elements, the agent provides statistics to the controller in a simple, unified format, which is as follows:

```
<TimeStamp, Element, (attr1, value1),
(attr2, value2), (attr2, value3)...>
```

That is, the response of a query to an element returns the timestamp, element ID, and a list of <attribute, value> pairs, where each pair describes a counter and its value at that timestamp. For example, a NIC driver's statistics can be described as

```
<t1, eth0, ("Rx bytes", v1),
("Tx bytes", v2), ... >
```

This interface is generic and simple for infrastructure operators to extend the statistics. When an operator needs to add a customized counter, she would need to add the counter into related elements, add logic in the agent to fetch this counter and add the result to the message that is returned to the controller.

4.3 Controller

The PerfSight controller delivers statistics requests and responses between operators and agents. When the operator requests a virtual cluster's information, the PerfSight controller obtains the physical location of the related virtual elements and sends requests to the agents of those elements.

```
function GETATTR(tenantID,elementID,attributes)
    return vNet[tenantID].elem[elementID].attr[attributes]

function GETTHROUGHPUT(tid, eid)
    attr ← ["time", "bytes"]
    <t1, b1> ← GETATTR(tid, eid, attr)
    sleep(T)
    <t2, b2> ← GETATTR(tid, eid, attr)
    return (b2 − b1) / (t2 − t1)

function GETPKTLOSS(tid, eid)
    attr ← ["inPkts", "outPkts"]
    < b1_i, b1_o > ←GETATTR(tid, eid, attr)
    sleep(T)
    < b2_i, b2_o > ←GETATTR(tid, eid, attr)
    return (b2_i − b2_o) − (b1_i − b1_o)

function GETAVGPKTSIZE(tid, eid)
    attr ← ["bytes", "pktCount"]
    <b1, c1> ← GETATTR(tid, eid, attr)
    sleep(T)
    <b2, c2> ← GETATTR(tid, eid, attr)
    return (b2 − b1) / (c2 − c1)
```

Figure 6: Basic Utility Routines

Through controller/operator interfaces, the operator can query the attributes of each element. To retrieve the attribute of an element in a virtual cluster, the PerfSight controller first finds the physical location of the element, i.e., vNet[tenantID].elem[elementID], and then sends a request for attributes to the element's agent, and finally receives the requested attributes' values.

This interface can be used by an operator to perform basic monitoring of the performance of specific portions of her infrastructure. Figure 6 provides examples of basic utility routines for monitoring element states. As we argue next, interesting diagnostic applications can be built on these statistics.

5. DIAGNOSIS

The most interesting aspect of PerfSight is the set of diagnostic applications it enables. In what follows, we show how the statistics gathered in the aforementioned fashion can be used to develop algorithms that help resolve the performance problems central to software dataplanes that we mentioned in Section 2.

5.1 Detecting Contention and Bottleneck Middleboxes

Before we describe our algorithms, we give a few comments on how contention and bottlenecks manifest, and what makes detection hard.

Contention: VMs on the same physical server can contend for hardware or software resources in the virtualization stack. Returning to the example situation outlined in Sections 2.2 and 2.3, memory bandwidth was the shared hardware resource in contention; in yet other situations, hardware resources such as CPU and the NIC may be in contention. Likewise, in Figure 5, the shared datapath of input traffic and output traffic (purple/solid arrows) can be the software resource in contention; similar contention can arise for other software resources such as shared buffers/queues.

Algorithm 1 Detect Contention and Bottleneck

```
function FINDCONTENTIONANDMIDDLEBOX()
    elements ← { e | e ∈ virtualization stack }
    elemLoss← ∅
    for e ∈ elements do
        loss = GETPACKETLOSS(e)
        elemLoss.add(<e, loss>)
    return SORTBYLOSS(elemLoss)
```

However, not all contentions display explicit symptoms. Among hardware resources, high CPU, memory and network utilization are explicit symptoms of contention, but memory bandwidth contention does not have an explicit manifestation. Whether symptoms of contention for software resources can be observed depends on the software implementation. For example, OVS provides QoS and statistics by which contention can be directly identified, but not all elements in the virtualization stack have appropriate instrumentation to enable such direct identification. Thus, on the whole, resource contention in the virtualization stack is difficult to detect.

Bottleneck Middlebox: A bottleneck middlebox is constrained by the amount of resources allocated to it, but, as discussed in Sections 2.2 and 2.3, whether a middlebox is a bottleneck cannot be judged solely based on its resource utilization.

Accurate Detection: The main idea underlying our diagnostic application here is as follows: Elements in the virtualization stack deliver packets to each other via intermediate buffers or function calls, and they typically use *nonblocking I/O* in doing so. That is, if an element cannot write to its successor, or its target buffer is full, packets get dropped. Thus, we obtain the *packet loss of each element* in the software data plane, and use it to locate where VMs are contending for resources or whether a VM is under-provisioned along some resource.

The application is designed as shown in Algorithm 1. For each element in the virtualization stack, we use the utility routing GetPktLoss() to obtain its packet loss; we sort all elements by their packet loss. Finally, the element with most packet loss is returned. This application monitors all related elements in the virtual network, so its cost is proportional to the size of the virtual network.

Crucially, the location of packet loss reveals the possible resources that VMs are contending for or are in shortage of. To aid in this, we build a simple offline *rule book* that maps packet loss locations to specific resources that may be running low or facing contention.

We construct the rule book as follows: we set up a variety of experiments where VMs contend for different resources, and we exhaustively track possible packet loss locations (details are in Section 7.1). The result is summarized in Table 1. Some symptoms reveal the resource in contention directly; for example, if incoming traffic exceeds pNIC capacity, packets are dropped at the pNIC.

In some cases, different kinds of contentions can have the same symptoms making detection hard: e.g., contention on CPU and memory bandwidth both lead to VMs being unable to fetch packets from TUN to vNIC, causing TUNs to drop packets which is the only externally visible symptom. In such cases, the operator can combine this with other symptoms such as CPU utilization and NIC throughput to distinguish the specific root cause.

Bottleneck middlebox detection is similar: when a tenant's deployment is facing end-to-end performance problems (and the tenant complains about it), the operator first selects middleboxes with

Table 1: Resource in Shortage and Symptom Rule Book

Resource in Shortage	Packet Drop Location
CPU	TUN (aggregated)
Memory Space	pNIC Driver
Memory Bandwidth	TUN (aggregated)
Incoming Bandwidth	pNIC
Outgoing Bandwidth	Backlog Enqueue
pCPU Backlog	Backlog Enqueue
VM Bottleneck (CPU or Bandwidth)	TUN (individual)

high resource utilization and includes them in a "suspicious" set; in the degenerate case (e.g., when no high utilization is apparent) all of the tenants middleboxes could be included in this set. Then, we use our light-weight statistics to distinguish those middleboxes that are facing legitimate issues, such as packet drops, against those whose resources naturally run at a high utilization but are otherwise not bottlenecks (e.g., a video encoder). Thus, we can more accurately pin-point bottleneck middleboxes.

Contention and bottleneck can be distinguished based on whether loss is spread across multiple VMs (contention) or confined to on VM's software data path (bottleneck).

5.2 Combating Propagation

Performance problems, e.g., due to implementation bugs, in one middlebox in a chain may propagate to others, causing them to appear to perform poorly as well. In particular, as we show below, the other middleboxes may appear to have stalled reading/writing from/to the network or I/O devices. Given this, however, determining the root cause middlebox can be challenging.

In what follows, we show how the statistics gathered by PerfSight can be used to infer the specific *states* that different middleboxes are operating under—e.g., under/over-loaded and read/write-blocked—which can then be used to identify the root cause.

Analysis and key insights Before describing our algorithm for identifying the root cause middlebox, we first present the underlying insights in identifying the states of different middleboxes in a chain.

In virtual settings, middlebox software exchanges data with the guest OS. Consider some time interval t_{total}; from the middlebox's perspective, this time interval can be split across the middlebox performing input, processing, and output. Thus, we have

$$t_{total} = t_{input} + t_{process} + t_{output}.$$

The input/output time is constituted by block time, t_{block}, and memory copy time, t_{memcpy}; i.e.:

$$t_{input/output} = t_{block} + t_{memcpy}.$$

Input block time is the time spent waiting for new data, and output block time is spent waiting for buffers in kernel to be ready (e.g., waiting for TCP sending window to open up). Memory copy time is the time spent on copying data between user space and kernel space. When the middlebox software is blocked or processing, the kernel is waiting for packet arrival or transmiting data from/to vNIC.

The input function of middlebox software (e.g., recv() in TCP, FromDevice() in Click [27]) fetches data from kernel space to user space. If the buffer in kernel is ready with data, the input function is not blocked ($t_{block} = 0$), so the input method is as fast as a memory copy (which is at least 2 orders of magnitude faster

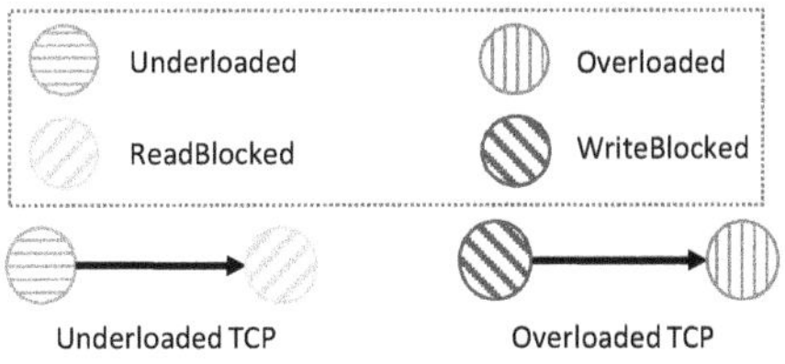

(a) Middlebox and TCP States

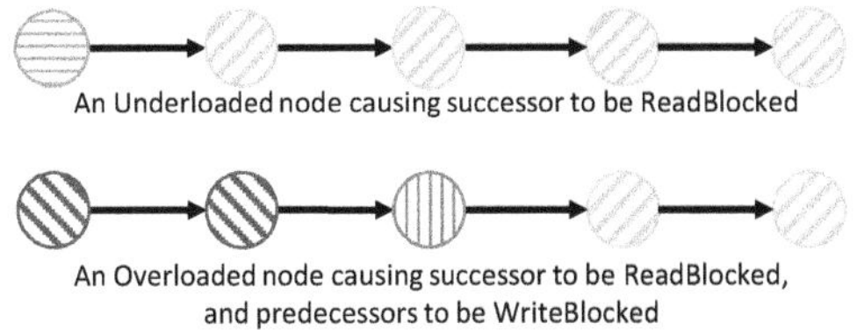

(b) State Propagation in a Chain

Figure 7: Middlebox States and Propagation

than network transmission). Assume that during the input function reading b bytes data from the kernel, the vNIC capacity is C and the memory copy speed is C_{mem}; in general, we have $C_{mem} \gg C$.

Thus, when there is no input blocking, we have:

$$t_{input} = t_{memcpy} = \frac{b}{C_{mem}} \ll \frac{b}{C}.$$

Thus, we can define a middlebox is *ReadBlocked* if it satisfies

$$\frac{b_{input}}{t_{input}} < C,$$

where b_{input} is the bytes read by the input function.

Similarly, when the output function (e.g., send() in TCP, ToDevice() in Click) sends data, the data (b bytes) would be copied from the user space to kernel space. As before, if the output function is not blocked,

$$t_{output} \ll \frac{b}{C}.$$

Thus, we can define a middlebox is *WriteBlocked* if it satisfies

$$\frac{b_{output}}{t_{output}} < C,$$

where b_{output} is the bytes written by the output function.

If two neighboring (in virtual topology) middleboxes use non-blocking I/O methods (e.g., packet-level processing) to exchange messages, their states do not impact each other. If they use TCP, TCP's congestion control makes the middlebox states influence each other, causing propagation. In particular, there are two possibilities: (1) the TCP sender does not send fast enough, causing the receiver to be ReadBlocked, (2) the receiver cannot receive or process data quick enough, causing the sender to be WriteBlocked. We define the sender in (1) as *Underloaded* and the receiver in (2) as *Overloaded* (Figure 7(a)). In a chain of TCP connections, an Underloaded source causes all its successors to be ReadBlocked, and an Overloaded middlebox causes all its predecessors to be WriteBlocked and successors to be ReadBlocked (Figure 7(b)).

Accurate Detection Of Root Cause(s) Based on the above analysis and insights, we develop the following algorithm (see Algorithm 2) underlying diagnostic application for determining the root cause middlebox(es): each middlebox's statistics are fetched (including input/output bytes/time and the middlebox vNIC capacity) (line 7). Then their respective states—under/overloaded, and

Algorithm 2 Locate Root Cause Middlebox

```
1: function GETSTAT(tid, mb)
2:     attr←["inBytes","inTime","outBytes","outTime"]
3:     return GETATTR(tid, mb, attr)
4: function GETROOTCAUSE(tid)
5:     midboxes←{mb|GetAttr(tid,mb,"type")="middlebox"}
6:     cand ← midboxes
7:     for mb ∈ midboxes do
8:         C ← GETATTR(tid, mb, "Capacity")
9:         < b1_i, t1_i, b1_o, t1_o > ← GETSTAT(tid, mb)
10:        sleep(T)
11:        < b2_i, t2_i, b2_o, t2_o > ← GETSTAT(tid, mb)
12:        if (t2_i − t1_i > (b2_i − b1_i)/C) then
13:            mb.state = ReadBlocked
14:            cand←cand−GETSUCCESSOR(mb)−mb
15:        else if (t2_o − t1_o > (b2_o − b1_o)/C) then
16:            mb.state = WriteBlocked
17:            cand←cand−GETPREDECESS(mb) −mb
18:    return cand
```

read/write blocked—are computed based on the statistics (line 12-15). If a middlebox is ReadBlocked, all its successors are waiting for its data and are also ReadBlocked; we filter out the entire such chain of ReadBlocked middleboxes from the suspicious candidates (line 14). Similarly, a WriteBlocked middlebox and all of its predecessors can be filtered out (line 17). The remaining middleboxes in the candidate set are returned (line 18) as the plausible root cause middleboxes. In Figure 7(b), this algorithm would identify the green middlebox in the first chain and the red middlebox in the second chain as the root cause. This application monitors all middleboxes in a virtual network, so its cost is linear to the size of the virtual network.

6. IMPLEMENTATION

Most elements (e.g., NIC driver and virtual switch) already have their own counters and logs implemented—in these cases, PerfSight simply makes use of the existing ones; if some counters are missing in an element, we instrument the elements and add augmented counters. The communication channel between an element and the corresponding agent on the physical server is implemented specifically according to the element. In the following paragraphs, we will describe the implementation details at each key element that a packet goes through on the software dataplane. The environment we use to simulate the cloud is Linux kernel v3.20, Open vSwitch and QEMU [1].

For the *physical NIC*, the Linux kernel maintains a data structure called net_device which records received/sent bytes/packets. net_device can be accessed via the file system interface from userspace (e.g., ifconfig). The PerfSight agent uses this. In the *NAPI routine* which processes packets in CPU backlog queues, a data structure called softnet_data is maintained for each queue. softnet_data records packets dropped between the CPU backlog queue and the target callback function (i.e., virtual switch packet handler). This record is accessable from the /proc file system. In *virtual switches*, each rule has statistics for packets processed and dropped. The statistics are accessable via the OpenFlow control channel. A *TAP*'s transmit function enqueues a packet into a socket queue. The TAP has a net_device record to keep track of Rx/Tx byte/packet counts, which are accessible via file system. QEMU, which delivers packets from TAP socket to a vNIC data structure, does not have intrinsic statistics. Thus, we instrument it to obtain statistics in QEMU. We write these counters into logs and PerfSight fetches the counters' values from the logs. Inside the *middlebox VM* (in the guest OS kernel), the difference from the virtualization stack is that the NAPI routine delivers a packet from vCPU backlog queues to another buffer in the kernel (e.g., socket). The statistics records are then similar to the virtualization stack. Middlebox software reads packets/messages from the kernel via system calls. After a middlebox performs its own processing, it sends packets/messages out to the guest OS kernel via system calls. We instrument middlebox software to record Rx/Tx byte/packet counts and the time spent on reading from/writing to the kernel. In PerfSight, we use sockets between middlebox software and the agent corresponding to the physical server on which the middlebox is located to fetch these counters.

When a middlebox sends a packet out, the packet is delivered across several elements and finally put into the pCPU backlog. The write function to the kernel calls the vNIC transmit function, which causes an interrupt in QEMU. The interrupt handler in QEMU calls the transmit function in the TAP. The TAP transmit function enqueues the packets into the pCPU backlog queue. When dequeued, the packet is processed by the virtual switch and sent to another device's (another TAP or pNIC according to the packet's destination) transmit function. In each layer that the packet goes through, the instrumentation and communication with the agent is similar to the packet receiving datapath.

Discussion. We assume that the cloud provider offers the virtual network services and the NFV service, so they have the source code. PerfSight is a framework, and it defines interfaces between components. Even if some services (e.g. middlebox) are provided by third party, they can use the interface to provide statistics so that PerfSight can perform diagnosis.

[1]Currently our solution is limited to this platform, but we believe PerfSight is a general solution to all platforms.

7. EVALUATION

To evaluate PerfSight, we set up a cluster with Dell T5500 servers, each of which has 8 cores, 16GB memory and a 10Gbps NIC. Each server runs Ubuntu with Linux kernel 3.2. We use Open vSwitch, QEMU to set up the virtualization stack. We install middlebox software in VMs and route tenant traffic to traverse the VM to simulate NFV-like settings.

In what follows, we first validate the basic functionalities of PerfSight, and then show the effectiveness of using PerfSight by illustrating how it can diagnose performance problems, reflecting the examples outlined in Section 2. Finally we show that it imposes negligible overhead.

7.1 Functional Validation

In what follows, we experimentally illustrate that PerfSight works as expected, using the example of the packet loss function (Section 4.3).

In this experiment, we start 8 VMs on a physical machine. Two of these VMs function as middleboxes and the rest as tenant VMs. The middlebox software we use is that of a load balancer [1]. We start a handful of long-lived TCP flows that traverse the middlebox VMs, and we monitor their throughput. Over time, we inject various performance problems. All the while, we run PerfSight's packet loss function at various software data plane elements in the 8 VMs to identify if, when and where packet loss happens.

The results are shown in Figure 8. We plot the average throughput of the middlebox flows on the left y axis, and the packet drop counts on the right y axis. During the interval 10-20 seconds, we flood a large amount of packets into the physical machine (these are

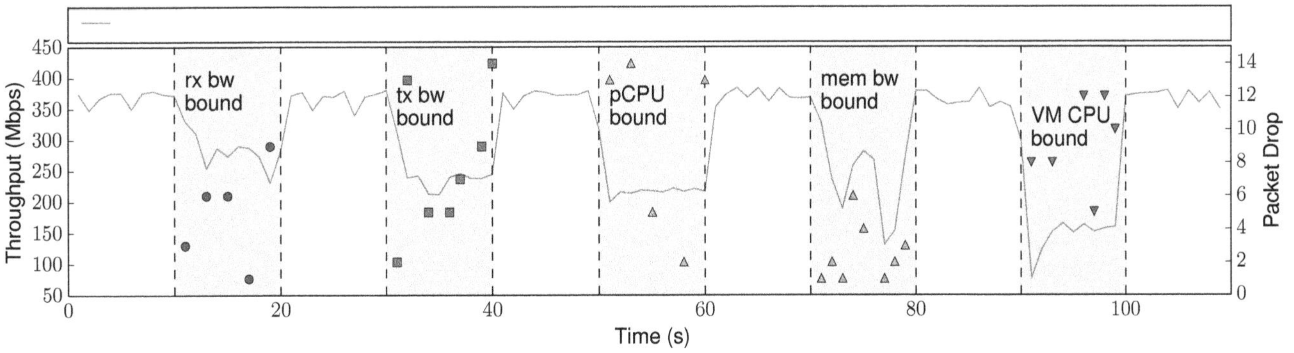

Figure 8: Throughput and Packet Drop in Virtualization Stack During Performance Problems

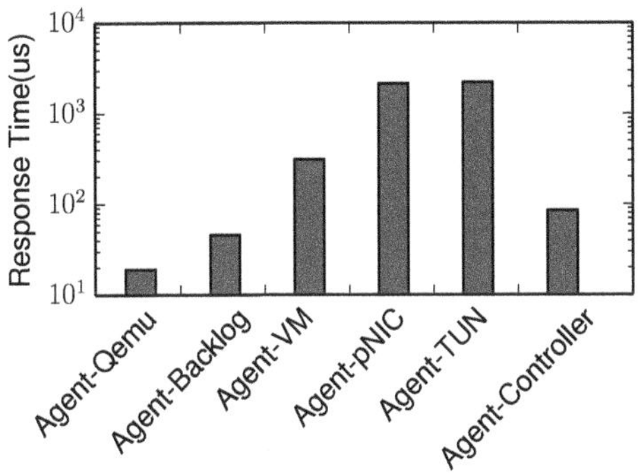

Figure 9: Response Time between Agent and other components

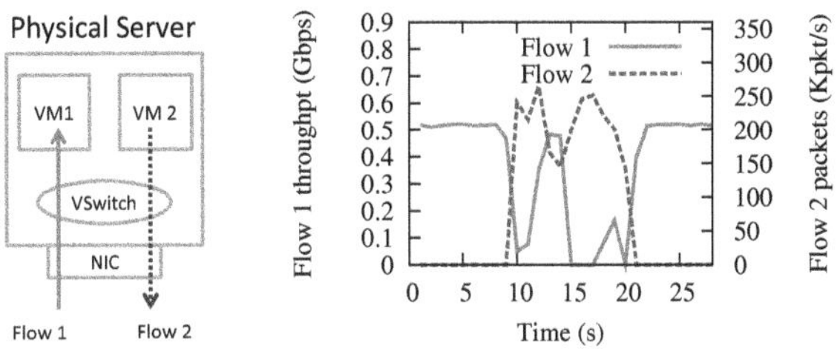

(a) 2 VMs (b) VM Traffic

Figure 10: CPU Backlog Queue Contention Detection Example

received by the non middlebox VMs). As such, the virtualization stack cannot clear the pNIC DMA buffer quickly enough, leading to lower TCP throughput for the middlebox VMs. What we noticed from PerfSight was that packets were dropped in the pNIC, which is as we expected (Table 1). During 30-40 seconds, the tenant VMs (non middlebox) flood a large amount of outgoing packets impacting middlebox traffic throughput. The flooded packets quickly fill up the CPU backlog first, leading to drops there for middlebox traffic, which is again as expected (Table 1). During 50-60 and 70-80 seconds, we make tenant VMs perform CPU intensive and memory access intensive workloads. As a result, the middlebox VMs do not acquire enough resources to process packets. This causes their packets to be accumulated and dropped at the TUN's socket buffer (which is the last buffer before entering VMs). When VMs are contending for resources, all VM's performance are impacted, so all VMs are dropping packets. While the above showed various forms of contention and interference, we now illustrate a single VM becoming a bottleneck. During 90-100 seconds, we start a CPU intensive workload inside one middlebox VM. From PerfSight, we note that only that VM drops packets at its associated TUN.

Response Time. The agent on each physical machine is the pivot of data collection and delivery. We measure how quickly the agent can exchange data with other components. As is shown in Figure 9, fetching statistics from network devices (e.g. TUN, pNIC) costs about 2ms, and all other components' statistics collection can be completed in 500us. This time granularity is fine enough to closely monitor the network states.

7.2 Diagnosis Accuracy

We now establish PerfSight's accuracy. We first conduct two experiments for detecting contention.

Detecting contention in virtualization stack (case 1). In Figure 5, we can observe that the pCPU backlog queue is exercised by multiple datapaths, which leads to the risk of it becoming a location where significant contention arises.

We set up two VMs - VM1 and VM2 - in a physical machine, and then make VM1 receive network traffic with a rate limit of 500Mbps. Roughly 10s into the measurement, we make VM2 send small packets as fast as it can. At this time, VM2's throughput decreases and oscillates; see Figure 10.

To diagnose this contention problem, PerfSight first checks if the VMs are overwhelming the NIC. VM2's peak sending rate (obtained using the GetThroughput() routine) is 250K packets per second (80Mbps); thus, the sum of the sending and receiving rates is well below the NIC capacity (1Gbps). PerfSight then checks packet drop counters at various elements in the virtualization stack. We found that the enqueue element in the virtualization stack (Figure 5) saw significant drops, and because outgoing bandwidth is not the problem (Table 1), the resource under contention ought to be the pCPU backlog queues (Table 1).

In a virtualized setup, both the incoming and outgoing packets are put into pCPU backlog queues first, and then forwarded during backlog processing. However, each CPU core's backlog queue length is limited to 300 packets. In our example, VM2 overwhelms the pCPU backlogs by flooding a large amount of small packets, and only a handful of VM1's packets can ever be enqueued into the backlog queue. This manifests as many more packets of VM1 arriving into the enqueue element and far fewer making it out.

Without PerfSight helping us identify where exactly packets are getting dropped and tying that back to the resource under con-

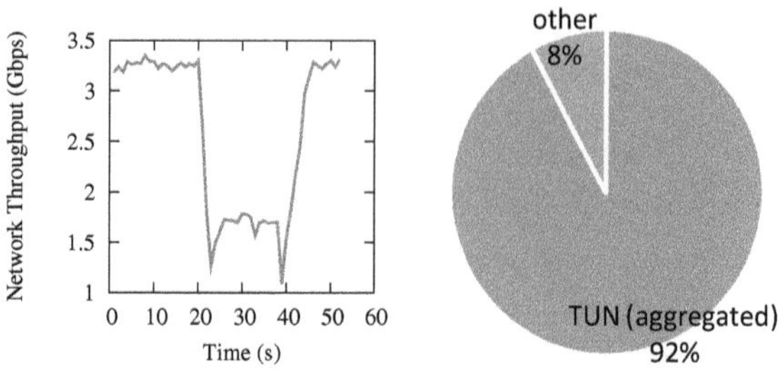

(a) Network Throughput (b) Packet Drop

Figure 11: Memory Bandwidth Contention Detection Example

tention (Table 1), it is difficult to determine the reason for VM1 and VM2 interfering with each other's performance.

Detecting contention in virtualization stack (case 2). Along the lines of the example Section 2, we simulated a machine with significant oversubscription in the virtualization stack. We start by running on a machine some number of VMs performing network transfers initially; their total network throughput is about 3.25Gbps as shown in Figure 11(a). At time 20s, another set of VMs start to access memory intensively. The total network throughput decreases to 1.7Gbps, because the two sets of VMs are contending for the memory bandwidth. We assume that the tenant running the former set of VMs wishes to diagnose this problem.

We observe that the physical machine is dropping packets at the network-intensive VMs' TUNs (Figure 11(b)). Thus, we infer that the machine's memory or outgoing bandwidth are overloaded (based on Table 1); at this time, we cannot distinguish which specific resource is experiencing contention. In response, wearing the operator's hat, we migrate some of the network-intensive VMs, and the network throughput recovers to the original 3.2Gbps.

Combating propagation. We validate our approach for identifying poorly-performing middleboxes in the face of propagation of problems where root cause cannot be obviously identified. The scenario we use is a multi-chain setting shown Figure 12(a): we deploy a load balancer (Balance [1]) and two content filter proxies (CherryProxy [2]) between clients and HTTP servers. We make the two content filter proxies output logs to a shared file system (NFS). All VMs' vNIC capacity are set to be 100Mbps.

In this virtual network, we simulate different cases and perform diagnosis; we find that our application always determines the root cause accurately. We conducted a variety of experiments where different points in this multi-chain are problematic and the issues can propagate arbitrarily through the chains, but for simplicity we focus on those exercising the VMs shown within the box shown by the dashed red line. For each experiment (figures b, c, and d) we show the performance metrics we derived for each middlebox (e.g., b/t_{in}, b/t_{out}), and the corresponding state we inferred for the middlebox.

In our first experiment, we make the client perform HTTP POSTs as fast as possible (with the idea of creating a bottleneck at the server within the dashed red box); we observe the state of middleboxes and determine that the load balancer and the content filter are WriteBlocked and the NFS server is Readblocked (Figure 12(b)). From this, our algorithm infers that server 1 is overloaded, identifying the true bottleneck.

In a second run, we have the client make HTTP POST requests at a slow rate. We monitor middlebox states and determine that other middleboxes are ReadBlocked, leading our algorithm to conclude that the client is Underloaded, which is indeed the case (Figure 12(c)).

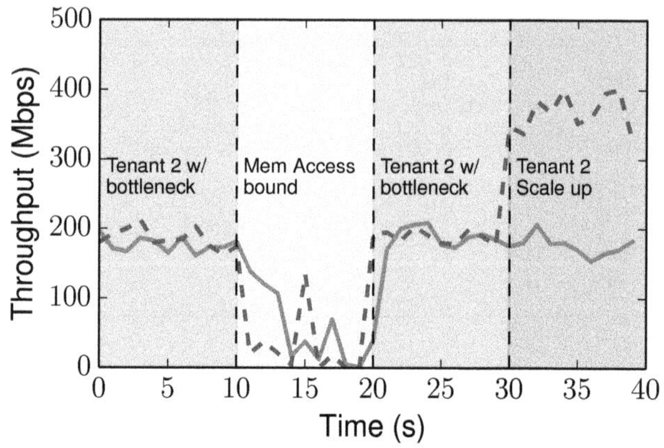

Figure 13: Throughput in Multi-tenant Experiment

As a final experiment, we inject an internal error (memory leak) into the NFS server,[2] causing it to become overloaded. The problem propagates through the chain middleboxes within the dashed red box, causing the load balancer and the content filter to be WriteBlocked. Using our algorithm, we exclude the ReadBlocked and WriteBlocked middleboxes and correctly determine that the NFS server is the bottleneck (Figure 12(d)).

7.3 Using PerfSight

We now consider a richer setting where we illustrate how we envision an operator using PerfSight. We show how an operator can detect and respond to contention and bottlenecks. We then describe propagation.

We use a setup with two tenants each with their own virtual network. Each network has a server, a load balancer proxy and a client with the client sending traffic to the server (Figure 14). We assume that the operator places the two load balancers in the same physical machine. We measure both tenants' throughput and show it in Figure 13.

Initially (0-10s), tenant 1 sends traffic at 180Mbps, while tenant 2 intends to send two flows at 360Mbps in total. However, tenant 2's load balancer can only process 200Mbps traffic, so tenant 2's total throughput is constrained by its load balancer. At this point, using PerfSight the operator identifies that the TUN of load balancer 2 is dropping packets and it is in an Overloaded state. Thus, the operator has identified tenant 2's bottleneck. Between 10 and 20s, the operator introduces a management task that happens to be memory access intensive into the physical machine. The operator finds that both tenants' load balancer VMs are impacted, they're dropping packets at their TUNs, and they're in ReadBlocked state. The operator identifies memory bandwidth over-subscription and responds by migrating the memory intensive task elsewhere. Thus, we see that the throughput immediately reverts to the original value (20-30s). However, this still does not address the bottleneck that tenant 2 is facing at its load balancer. After determining that tenant 2 is bottlenecked at its load balancer, the operator scales it out and reroutes half of tenant 2's traffic to the new instance. The total throughput increases to 360Mbps and no packets are dropped at the load balancers.

[2]CentOS bug track 7267.

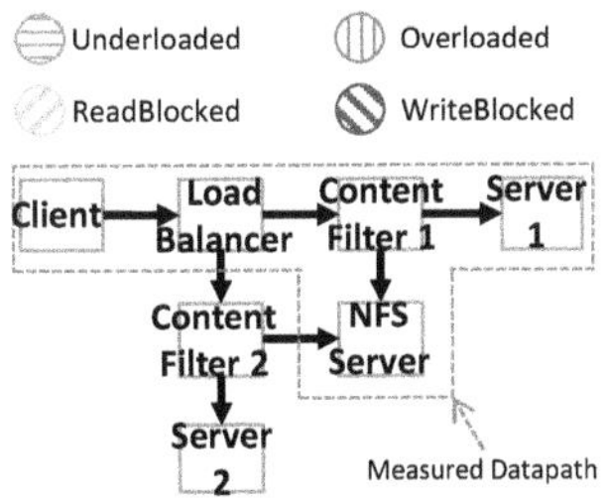

(a) Legend and Topology

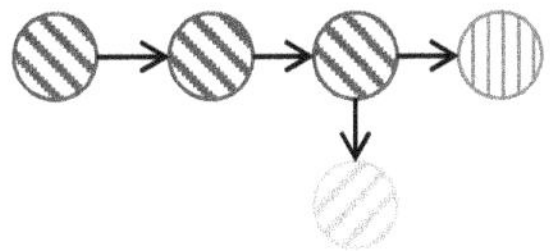

	LB	CF	NFS	Server
b/t_i	323	362	3.2	316
b/t_o	32	36	N/A	N/A

(b) Overloaded Server

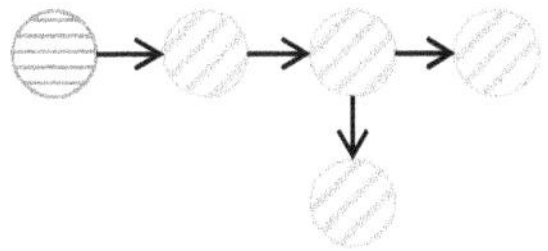

	LB	CF	NFS	Server
b/t_i	16.2	15.6	1.7	17
b/t_o	248	160	N/A	N/A

(c) Underloaded Client

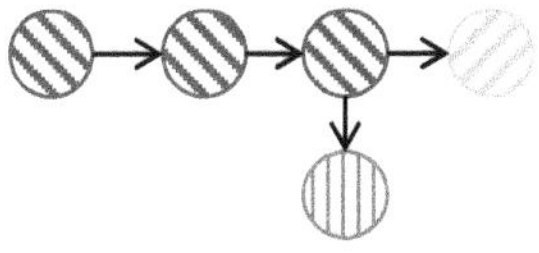

	LB	CF	NFS	Server
b/t_i	138	154	126	10
b/t_o	35	11.5	N/A	N/A

(d) Problematic NFS

Figure 12: Root cause detection in the face of propagation (Unit: Mbps, b: bytes, t_i: t_{input}, t_o: t_{output})

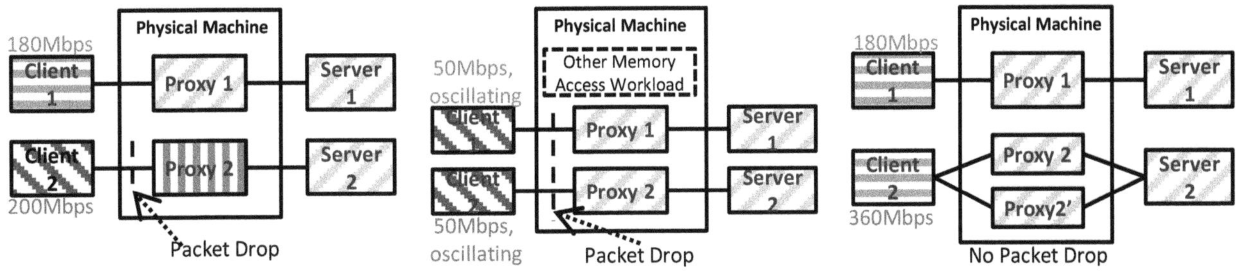

(a) Bottleneck (b) Memory Access Bound (c) Scale Up

Figure 14: A multi-tenant experiment illustrating how an operator can use PerfSight to aid her tenants

Table 2: Throughput with/without Time Counters
1: Blocked, without Counters, 2: Blocked, with Counters
3: Overloaded, without Counter, 4: Overloaded, with Counters.
Each experiment is repeated for 100 times

Experiment	1	2	3	4
Mean μ (Mbps)	42.02	41.79	499	490.2
Variance σ^2	4.57	4.92	1554	1281

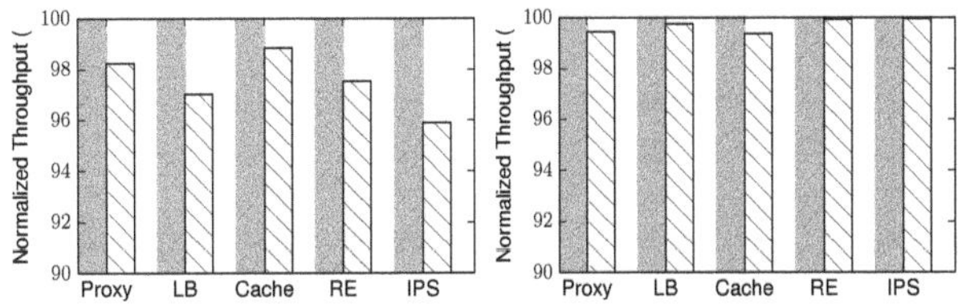

Figure 15: Time Counter Overhead within Middleboxes

7.4 Overhead and Scalability

Overhead. Among the counters we implemented, packet counts/bytes are simple/low overhead because each time they are incremented by a value; time counters are a bit more complex because they need to get time twice, and accumulate the difference. We first measure the time spent to update a counter. We find that simple counters consume 3ns per update, while a timer counter consumes 0.29us per update in our testbed. Even with the maximum throughput of 10Gbps and 1500 bytes MTU, each packet takes 1.2us to traverse an element. Thus, the simple counters impose 10^{-3} smaller overhead, which is negligible.

However, the time counters do have an impact on performance. If an element is overloaded and CPU bound, time counters would cost extra CPU cycles, which degrades the element's performance. To delve into this, we build a virtual network with an HTTP server, an HTTP client and a proxy. The client uploads data to the server via the proxy. In this setting, if we limit the client's sending rate (on its vNIC), the proxy will be ReadBlocked; if not, TCP would saturate the virtual link and cause the proxy to become Overloaded. We compare the throughput between the cases where the proxy is/not instrumented with time counters. The result is shown in Table 2. We can conclude that the impact of the time counters is very small (under 2% in terms of throughput; we also found the average latency impact to be under 1.5% (not shown for brevity)).

We repeat the similar experiments on different kinds of middleboxes [10, 1, 6], and show the results in Figure 15. In all kinds of middleboxes, the impact is less than 5%.

Another source of overhead is from polling these counters. The overhead is shown in Figure 16, and it still very small. Even if we poll them every 100ms (which is generally sufficient for the kind of diagnostics we wish to run), the CPU utilization is less than 0.5%, which is negligible.

Scalability. Our experimental set up is indeed small, but we believe that our system's response time and overhead will stay small even at larger set ups due to the following reasons: (1) The statistics gathering is distributed in each element, so it's not likely to become a bottleneck. (2) The diagnostic applications' complexity is O(n) where n is the number of involved elements. (3) Cloud operators can aggregate tenants' tickets to diagnose if they have elements overlapping with each other.

8. RELATED WORK

The systems and networking communities have developed a variety of diagnostic tools and frameworks. In this section, we place PerfSight in the context of these prior frameworks.

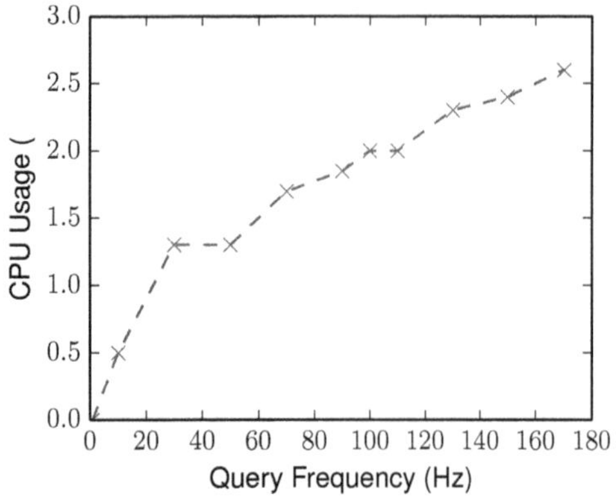

Figure 16: Query Frequency and CPU Usage

sFlow, NetFlow, ndb, tcpdump, X-Trace and SNAP [20, 9, 17, 36] provide various ways to collect key information from the network (and from network attached systems). Unfortunately, these techniques don't provide fine-grained information about which specific parts of the software data plane are facing/imposing problems. As a result, they are far less useful in diagnosing and fixing subtle software data plane issues. For example, compared with SNMP which only defines the format of management messages, PerfSight has statistics gathering, framework (interfaces) and diagnostics applications, so PerfSight is a complete diagnostic solution. Furthermore, some of these techniques (tcpdump and SNAP) can impose a high overhead.

Recent solutions such as header space analysis (HSA), NICE, Libra, Anteater, NetPlumber, VeriFlow [25, 24, 14, 37, 31, 23] are also useful for diagnosing virtual networks. However, they are not very useful toward diagnosing performance problems. In contrast with general network reachability issues that the above tools are very capable at helping with, performance problems are much more tricky: they are often ephemeral; they can manifest unexpectedly, e.g., under specific corner-case workloads; and, they can arise due to a wide variety of different issues (mainly because of the complexity of the software data plane), as a result of which doing root cause detection, and fixing the observed problems can both be very difficult.

For traditional networks, NeST [32] was proposed as a mechanism for instrumenting the network stack toward diagnosis. NeST uses a dependency graph to find stalled components. However, the virtualized network is more complex than the traditional network. Not only does it have more components, but also its components are much more heterogeneous (i.e., blocking/nonblocking middleboxes). Simple dependency analysis also does not suffice for some key performance problems (e.g., it does not aid in bottleneck middlebox detection).

There are some other works in the general distributed systems world that try to correlate symptoms of performance problems and their root causes. Some of them use end-to-end information to infer the internal components' states (i.e., Sherlock, netMedic, netDiagnoser [11, 22, 16, 18]). Unfortunately, these techniques are not as accurate as our direct instrumentation-based approach.

Some of the aforementioned prior systems (SCORE, MaxCoverage, shrink and codebook [28, 29, 21, 26]) are based on bipartite graph models (with symptoms on one side and possible causes on the other, and weight assignment used to determine the most likely root causes of problems observed). However, such models cannot be used when the problem propagates or in situations where components interfere with each other, both of which can arise very frequently in the context of software data planes.

On the whole, we believe that PerfSight is a novel, first-of-a-kind and important contribution to the space of diagnosis frameworks. Its particular focus on software data planes makes it invaluable for future network function virtualization set ups.

9. CONCLUSION

With the advent of NFV, data planes are becoming increasingly complex, involving a variety of software packet processing elements. In this paper, we argued that these new "software data planes" are susceptible to subtle performance problems that don't occur (or are infrequent) in traditional hardware-based data planes. We argued that diagnosing these problems is difficult because no existing tool or system provides the right level of information to tease apart various potential causes of the observed degradation. To this end, we present a system, PerfSight, a ground-up approach for extracting comprehensive low-level information regarding packet processing performance of the various elements in the data plane and for conducting rich analysis on the information gathered. Through careful experiments, we show that our framework can result in accurate detection of the root causes of performance problems in software data planes, and it imposes very little overhead.

Acknowledgement

We would like to thank Anja Feldmann (our shepherd) and the anonymous reviewers for their valuable feedback. We also thank Vyas Sekar for his comments in the early stage of this project. This work is supported in part by National Science Foundation (grants CNS-1345249, CNS-1302041 and CNS-1330308) and the Wisconsin Institute on Software-Defined Datacenters of Madison.

10. REFERENCES

[1] Balance: the open source load-balancer and tcp proxy. `http://www.inlab.de/balance.html`.

[2] Cherryproxy: a filtering http proxy extensible in python. `http://www.decalage.info/python/cherryproxy`.

[3] http://rightscale.com.

[4] http://tools.ietf.org/html/rfc3954.html.

[5] Path mtu discovery. `http://tools.ietf.org/html/rfc1191`.

[6] Snort: Open source network intrusion prevention. `http://www.snort.org`.

[7] www.openvswitch.org.

[8] www.sflow.org.

[9] www.tcpdump.org.

[10] A. Anand, V. Sekar, and A. Akella. Smartre: an architecture for coordinated network-wide redundancy elimination. In *ACM SIGCOMM Computer Communication Review*, volume 39, pages 87–98. ACM, 2009.

[11] P. Bahl, R. Chandra, A. Greenberg, and S. Kandula. Towards highly reliable enterprise network services via interence of multi-level dependencies. In *SIGCOMM*, 2007.

[12] F. Bellard. Qemu, a fast and portable dynamic translator. In *USENIX Annual Technical Conference, FREENIX Track*, pages 41–46, 2005.

[13] T. Bu, N. Duffield, F. L. Presti, and D. Towsley. Network tomography on general topologies. In *Proceedings of the 2002 ACM SIGMETRICS International Conference on Measurement and Modeling of Computer Systems*,

SIGMETRICS '02, pages 21–30, New York, NY, USA, 2002. ACM.

[14] M. Canini, D. Venzano, P. Peresini, D. Kostic, and J. Rexford. A nice way to test openflow applications. In *NSDI*, 2012.

[15] M. Chiosi, D. Clarke, P. Willis, A. Reid, J. Feger, M. Bugenhagen, W. Khan, M. Fargano, C. Cui, H. Deng, et al. Network functions virtualisation–introductory white paper. In *SDN and OpenFlow World Congress*, 2012.

[16] A. Dhamdhere, R. Teixeira, C. Dovrolis, and C. Diot. Netdiagnoser: Troubleshooting network unreachabilities using end-to-end probes and routing data. In *CoNEXT*, 2007.

[17] R. Fonseca, G. Porter, R. H. Katz, S. Shenker, and I. Stocia. X-trace: A pervasive network tracing framework. In *NSDI*, 2007.

[18] A. Gember, A. Akella, T. Benson, and R. Grandl. Stratos: Virtual middleboxes as first-class entities. In *UW-Madison, Technical Report*, 2012.

[19] A. Goel, C. Krasic, K. Li, and J. Walpole. Supporting low latency tcp-based media streams. In *Quality of Service, 2002. Tenth IEEE International Workshop on*, pages 193–203. IEEE, 2002.

[20] N. Handigol, B. Heller, V. Jeyakumar, D. Mazieres, and N. McKeown. I know what your packet did last hop: Using packet histories to troubleshoot networks. In *NSDI*, 2014.

[21] S. Kandula, D. Katabi, and J.-P. Vasseur. Shrink: A tool for failure diagnosis in ip networks. In *MineNet workshop*, 2005.

[22] S. Kandula, R. Mahajan, P. Verkaik, S. Agarwal, J. Padhye, and P. Bahl. Detailed diagnosis in enterprise networks. In *SIGCOMM*, 2009.

[23] P. Kazemian, M. Chang, H. Zeng, G. Varghese, N. McKeown, and S. Whyte. Real time network policy checking using header space analysis. In *NSDI*, 2014.

[24] P. Kazemian, G. Varghese, and N. McKeown. Header space analysis: Static checking for networks. In *NSDI*, 2012.

[25] A. Khurshid, W. Zhou, M. Caesar, and P. B. Godfrey. Veriflow: Verifying network-wide invariants in real time. In *HotSDN*, 2012.

[26] S. Kliger, S. Yemini, Y. Yemini, D. Ohsie, and S. Stolfo. A coding approach to event correlation. In *IM*, 1995.

[27] E. Kohler, R. Morris, B. Chen, J. Jannotti, and M. F. Kaashoek. The click modular router. *ACM Transactions on Computer Systems (TOCS)*, 2000.

[28] R. R. Kompella, J. Yates, A. Greenberg, and A. C. Snoeren. Ip fault localization via risk modeling. In *NSDI*, 2005.

[29] R. R. Kompella, J. Yates, A. Greenberg, and A. C. Snoeren. Detection and localization of network black holes. In *INFOCOM*, 2007.

[30] T. Koponen, K. Amidon, P. Balland, M. Casado, A. Chanda, B. Fulton, I. Ganichev, J. Gross, N. Gude, P. Ingram, et al. Network virtualization in multi-tenant datacenters. In *NSDI*, 2014.

[31] H. Mai, A. Khurshid, R. Agarwal, M. Caesar, P. B. Godfrey, and S. T. King. Debugging the data plane with anteater. In *SIGCOMM*, 2011.

[32] J. N. McCann. Automating performance diagnosis in networked systems. In *PHD thesis*, 2012.

[33] R. Potharaju and N. Jain. Demystifying the dark side of the middle: A field study of middlebox failures in datacenters. In *IMC*, 2013.

[34] C. D. P. Ramanathan and D. Moore. Packet dispersion techniques and capacity estimation.

[35] W. Wu, G. Wang, A. Akella, and A. Shaikh. Virtual network diagnosis as a service. In *SoCC*, 2013.

[36] M. Yu, A. Greenberg, D. Maltz, J. Rexford, and L. Yuan. Profiling network performance for multi-tier data center applications. In *NSDI*, 2011.

[37] H. Zeng, S. Zhang, F. Ye, V. Jeyakumar, M. Ju, J. Liu, N. McKeown, and A. Vahdat. Libra: Divide and conquer to verify forwarding tables in huge networks. In *NSDI*, 2014.

Leveraging Internet Background Radiation for Opportunistic Network Analysis

Karyn Benson[*†], Alberto Dainotti[†], kc claffy[†], Alex C. Snoeren[*], Michael Kallitsis[‡]
[*]Computer Science and Engineering, UC San Diego [†]CAIDA, UC San Diego [‡]Merit Network, Inc.
{karyn, alberto, kc}@caida.org, snoeren@cs.ucsd.edu, mgkallit@umich.edu

ABSTRACT

For more than a decade, unsolicited traffic sent to unused regions of the address space has provided valuable insight into malicious Internet activities. In this paper, we explore the utility of this traffic, known as Internet Background Radiation (IBR), for a different purpose: as a data source of Internet-wide measurements. We collect and analyze IBR from two large darknets, carefully deconstructing its various components and characterizing them along dimensions applicable to Internet-wide measurements. Intuitively, IBR can provide insight into network properties when traffic from that network contains relevant information and is of sufficient volume. We turn this intuition into a scientific investigation, examining which networks send IBR, identifying components of IBR that enable opportunistic network inferences, and characterizing the frequency and granularity of traffic sources. We also consider the influences of time of collection and position in the address space on our results. We leverage IBR properties in three case studies to show that IBR can supplement existing techniques by improving coverage and/or diversity of analyzable networks while reducing measurement overhead. Our main contribution is a new framework for understanding the circumstances and properties for which unsolicited traffic is an appropriate data source for inference of macroscopic Internet properties, which can help other researchers assess its utility for a given study.

Categories and Subject Descriptors

C.2.5 [**Local and Wide-Area Networks**]: Internet

Keywords

Internet background radiation; Network telescope; Opportunistic network analysis

1. INTRODUCTION

Obtaining data from a diverse set of hosts and networks is a major challenge in Internet measurement research. We explore the potential for an unconventional data source, unsolicited traffic sent to unused regions of the address space, known as Internet Background Radiation (IBR), to address this challenge.

Monitoring unused portions of the IPv4 address space reveals that IBR is of considerable volume, incessant, and originates from a variety of services [41, 48]. This unsolicited traffic is caused by scanning (e.g., searching for hosts running a vulnerable service), misconfigurations (e.g., a typo in the IP address for a mail server), backscatter (responses to packets with forged source IP addresses, including spoofed DoS attack), bugs, etc. Historically, researchers have used this traffic to study worms, DoS attacks, and scanning.

More recently, instead of studying malicious activities, researchers have leveraged IBR to learn about hosts and networks generating unsolicited traffic [12,15,20,22,24,32,44]. The pervasively sourced components of IBR make a darknet—a region of the address space exclusively dedicated to collecting IBR—the potential recipient of traffic from all networks connected to the global Internet: botnets employ machines worldwide to perform scans; misconfigurations can occur in any network; and many networks host services that are potential victims of DoS attacks (causing backscatter). Casado *et al.* [15] first proposed using IBR (and other types of "spurious" network traffic, such as SPAM emails) to illuminate regions of the address space where traditional techniques fail to provide visibility (e.g., in the presence of NAT). Recent studies of censorship events, IPv4 address space utilization, and filtering policies have verified this benefit [22, 24, 44].

However, these studies focused on isolated events or specific components of IBR. It is unclear if the same analysis techniques work on similar events or with different collections of IBR (e.g., using different times or IBR vantage points). More broadly, these studies do not provide insight into which properties are amenable to analysis using IBR and whether the networks themselves must have certain characteristics to allow IBR-based inferences.

To evaluate IBR's utility as an Internet-wide data source, we begin by evaluating properties that support opportunistically measuring many networks. In Section 4, we quantify the large number and diversity of sources, which facilitate insight into many networks. In Section 5, we analyze the components of IBR, through which we can glean considerable information from packet-level data (e.g., the operating system from TCP options). In Section 6, we evaluate IBR's persistent nature, which permits repeated observations and often predictable temporal behavior.

In the context of inferring global properties of Internet networks, IBR also has fundamental limitations and challenges. Although IBR originates from many sources, we lack control over who sends it and when. In particular, the mix of popular applications changes regularly [41], which reduces the predictability of IBR. Additionally, IBR is unidirectional; since a darknet does not respond to unsolicited traffic we cannot infer flow-level information. Moreover,

IMC'15, October 28–30, 2015, Tokyo, Japan.

ACM 978-1-4503-3848-6/15/10 ...$15.00.
DOI: http://dx.doi.org/10.1145/2815675.2815702 .

packets with spoofed source addresses will lead to inaccurate inferences; as a result, IBR needs to be sanitized. Section 3 provides a summary of our sanitization technique, which we previously verified [22].

The case studies we present in Section 8 highlight the strengths and weaknesses of using IBR as a data source for Internet-wide measurement. Our experience suggests that IBR is useful: (1) When the presence of a source in darknet traffic provides additional context. For example, although we find fewer open resolvers than active probing, we know that attackers are actively using the ones found in IBR. (2) To obtain a large sample. We could easily calculate uptime for over half-a-million sources, to determine that a common technique for inferring uptime is invalid for certain operating systems. (3) For hosts unreachable through active probing. We can determine the uptime for NATed clients, which are unlikely to respond to external probes. (4) To reduce measurement overhead. We can identify flapping and non-flapping routes without sending packets. Such an analysis could focus active probing on routes that have recently changed.

2. RELATED WORK

We are far from the first to analyize Internet Background Radiation. Pang *et al.* performed the first major characterization of IBR [41], with the aim of identifying and filtering out malicious traffic. Brownlee detected new activities in IBR based on interarrival time [14], while Wustrow *et al.* examined IBR from multiple darknets over several years to discover which destination addresses received a disproportionate amount of IBR, which is useful before assigning IP addresses [48]. We have different goals than these prior characterizations of IBR, however, leading us to consider different aspects: we ask "who sends IBR?" and "how often do we receive IBR?" instead of "why do we receive IBR?" or "where is IBR destined?" In particular, we focus on the *quantity and frequency of sources* sending IBR instead of the *volume of packets or bytes*. For this reason, another difference from previous IBR characterization studies is that we remove spoofed packets from IBR before performing our analyses (spoofed source IP addresses represent fake sources).

There have been a number papers that use IBR to provide proof-of-concept of a measurement technique [12,20–22,24], or examine the applicability of a certain type of traffic to Internet-wide measurement [32,44]. The primary goal of our three case studies is not to lengthen this list, but to demonstrate the effects of IBR's nature on our ability to extract Internet-wide properties. Casado *et al.* considered (but did not quantify) the nature of unsolicited traffic in their proposal for its utilization in opportunistic measurement [15]. However, this paper provides a more comprehensive view of IBR as a measurement data source. We put other related work into this framework in Table 4.

3. DATASETS

Our primary datasets are collections of IBR. To assist in analyzing IBR, we also use a mapping of IP addresses to prefixes, ASes and geographic locations, and a classification of the types of Autonomous Systems (ASes).

IBR Traffic. A darknet or network telescope is a collection of routed but unused IP addresses, i.e., all traffic these addresses receive is unsolicited. Darknets capture—but do not respond to—IBR. Both UC San Diego and Merit Network operate large darknets, which we call UCSD-NT and MERIT-NT respectively. UCSD-NT observes traffic destined to more than 99% of IP addresses in a contiguous /8 block. MERIT-NT covers about 67% of a different /8 block.

We study packet traces captured from July 31 to September 2, 2012 and July 23, 2013 to August 25, 2013. We choose these time periods because they align with the ICMP-ping based census conduced by ISI [29]. We refer to these 34-day periods as the *2012 census* and *2013 census*, respectively. We label our datasets based on the collection site and the year: `UCSD-12`, `UCSD-13`, and `MERIT-13` (which are 5.1, 4.0 and 1.5 TB of compressed data, respectively). To perform a longitudinal analysis spanning several years, in Section 7.1 we also use flow-level datasets—a summary of pcap data (i.e., protocol, source IP, destination IP, source port, destination port, flags, TTL, and number of packets)—collected by UCSD-NT from April 2008 to January 2015.

We use two darknets to study how position within the address space influences our results. Comparing UCSD-NT and MERIT-NT is not straightforward since the darknets are different sizes. For a fair comparison, we construct the dataset `partial-UCSD-13`, which is the traffic to a subset of IP addresses in UCSD's darknet. Specifically, we include traffic to an IP address UCSD.B.C.D if the IP address MERIT.B.C.D is part of MERIT-NT. As a result, approximately the same number[1] of destination IP addresses contributes to `partial-UCSD-13` and `MERIT-13`. We explore differences between `UCSD-12` and `UCSD-13` to study how the time of collection influences our results.

Including spoofed IBR traffic, i.e., traffic with a forged source IP, in our analyses would likely lead to incorrect inferences. We apply previously published techniques [22] to obtain a list of unrouted networks and remove spoofed traffic from the pcap datasets. The primary technique identifies spikes in unrouted addresses observed per hour. From these spikes we develop heuristics to exclude spoofed traffic. The heuristics also remove almost all traffic with source IP addresses in known dark blocks, providing validation (the validation results of "de-spoofing" in `UCSD-12` and `UCSD-13` are available elsewhere [21,22]). As a result, we reduce the number of /24 blocks that appear to send us traffic from $\approx$10M to $\approx$3M. As a final step, we exclude all traffic from unrouted IP addresses, which may exist due to failed egress filtering by remote networks or spoofed sources missed by our heuristics. We apply similar techniques to the flow-level data spanning several years.

Prefixes. To analyze networks at the prefix level, we map source IP addresses to BGP announced prefixes. We consider a prefix announced if, on the first day of the dataset, it is visible by 95% of the ASes peering—and providing a full routing table—with Routeviews and RIPE RIS collectors, based on RIB data.[2] For each IP address we use the most-specific prefix.

Autonomous Systems. We use CAIDA's Prefix-to-AS mapping dataset (pfx2as) to map IPv4 addresses to AS numbers [10]. CAIDA extracts this dataset from BGP announcements captured by Routeviews. Specifically, we use the mapping produced on the first day of the IBR datasets. To label ASes as transit/access providers, content providers, or enterprise networks, we use a dataset provided by CAIDA developed using a scheme similar to that proposed by Dhamdhere and Dovrolis [25].

Geolocation. We use historical MaxMind country-level databases to geolocate the .0 address of each /24 block in our IBR datasets. Since MaxMind updates the database regularly (to reflect changes in the address space), we use the databases produced on August 1, 2012 and August 16, 2013 for the *2012 census* and *2013 census* periods, respectively.

[1] A handful of IP addresses in UCSD-NT's /8 matching the MERIT.B.C.D criterion are not darknet addresses.

[2] We choose the same threshold as previous work [36].

	Announced 2012	Announced 2013	UCSD-12	UCSD-13	UCSD-13 Partial	MERIT-13
IP addresses	2.61B	2.66B	148M (5.7%)	133M (5.0%)	109M (4.1%)	111M (4.2%)
/24 blocks	10.2M	10.4M	3.13M (31%)	3.15M (30%)	2.65M (26%)	2.76M (27%)
Prefixes	410k	452k	198k (48%)	205k (45%)	170k (38%)	175k (39%)
ASes	44k	46k	24.3k (55%)	24.2k (54%)	19.3k (44%)	19.8k (45%)
Countries	245	236	234 (96%)	233 (99%)	231 (98%)	232 (98%)

Table 1: The number (and percentage of announced resources) of IP addresses, /24 blocks, prefixes, ASes, and countries observed in each dataset is consistent across sites (UCSD-NT vs. MERIT-NT) and years (2012 vs. 2013).

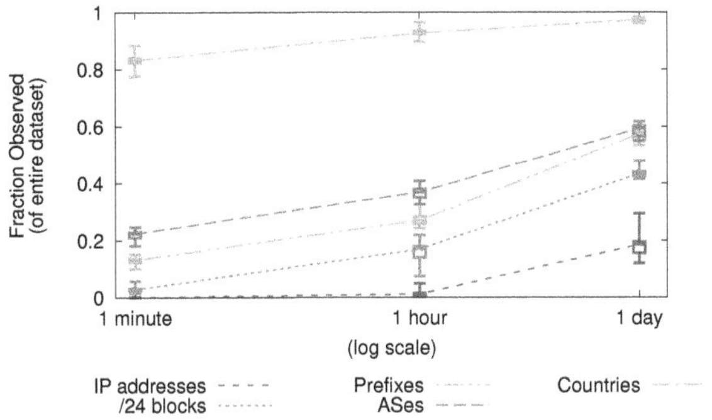

Figure 1: **Fraction of Sources Observed Per Minute, Hour and Day** (`UCSD-13`). The longer one observes, the more sources one can observe, especially at the IP address granularity.

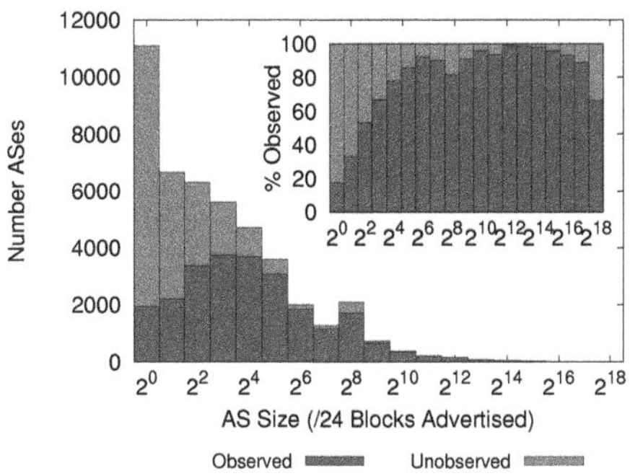

Figure 2: **Number and percentage of observed ASes by the number of /24 blocks announced.** Although we observe only half of announced ASes in `UCSD-13`, most missed ASes announce few /24 blocks.

4. WHO SENDS IBR?

We investigate how many and what type of networks send IBR. In all our datasets we observe traffic from a non-trivial number of IP addresses (> 100M), /24 blocks (> 2.6M) and prefixes (> 170k), and traffic from almost all countries and most large networks (including non-enterprise ASes). As a result, we can potentially use IBR to characterize many hosts and /24 blocks, and provide Internet-wide analysis at the AS or country-code level.

4.1 How many sources are observed?

Table 1 reports the absolute number of sources (IP addresses, /24 blocks, prefixes, ASes and countries) observed through our datasets. Compared to the total address space announced in BGP, we observe a few IP addresses, more than a quarter of /24 blocks, close to half of all prefixes and ASes, and almost all country codes. However, a large fraction of address space announced in BGP may not actually be "used", which we define as generating traffic on the global Internet [21, 50]. Based on previous literature, we observe about half of the inferred used /24 blocks: using seven different data sources, Dainotti *et al.* found 5.3M actually used /24 blocks in 2013 [21], while Zander *et al.* estimated that a total of 6.2M to 6.3M /24 blocks were used in June 2014 [50].

While the numbers in Table 1 are consistent across all four datasets, we find considerably fewer sources (except at country-level granularity) with shorter measurement intervals. Figure 1 shows statistics on the fraction of sources observed in a minute, hour, or day for `UCSD-13` (the other datasets show similar values for all source and time granularities). As expected, by lengthening the observation period, we capture additional sources. However, due to repeated contact, the growth in number of sources observed is less than linear.

At the time granularities depicted in Figure 1, the number of observed sources is highly variable. Diurnal patterns in IBR [48] are one cause of variability, especially for small source granularity (i.e., IP addresses and /24 blocks). The changing composition of IBR (Section 5) contributes to the variance on longer time scales. Section 7.1 describes this aspect, based on variations observed over years.

4.2 What types of networks are observed?

We observe traffic from diverse locations. In the `UCSD-13` dataset, we miss only three countries that announce /24 blocks. All three countries are small islands or collections of islands, each with a population of under 4,000 people [18].

Many ASes do not send IBR to our darknets: we observe about half of ASes announced in BGP. However, most missed ASes are small. Figure 2 shows, for `UCSD-13`, the distribution of observed ASes in terms of /24 blocks announced. Of the 20.6k unobserved ASes in `UCSD-13`, almost half announce a single /24 block, and 90% announce the equivalent of 8 or fewer /24 blocks. Conversely, we observe 86% of ASes that advertise the equivalent of at least a /16 block – we call these ASes large. ASes belonging to the US Department of Defense account for a fifth of unobserved large ASes, which appears to have many routed but "unused" /24 blocks [21]. In terms of AS type, we miss 26% of large ASes classified as enterprise, and about 4% of the large ASes classified as transit/access or content. The comprehensiveness of IBR's coverage of large ASes implies that it originates from diverse set of networks. In Section 6, we analyze how often the same ASes are observed over time.

4.3 Lessons learned

The number of sources captured by a network telescope is dependent on the duration of observation, the time of day, and the size of the network. Across our datasets, we consistently observe a significant fraction of the observably "used" IPv4 address space, and in particular nearly all large transit/access and content ASes. As a result, IBR has the potential to provide an Internet-wide view.

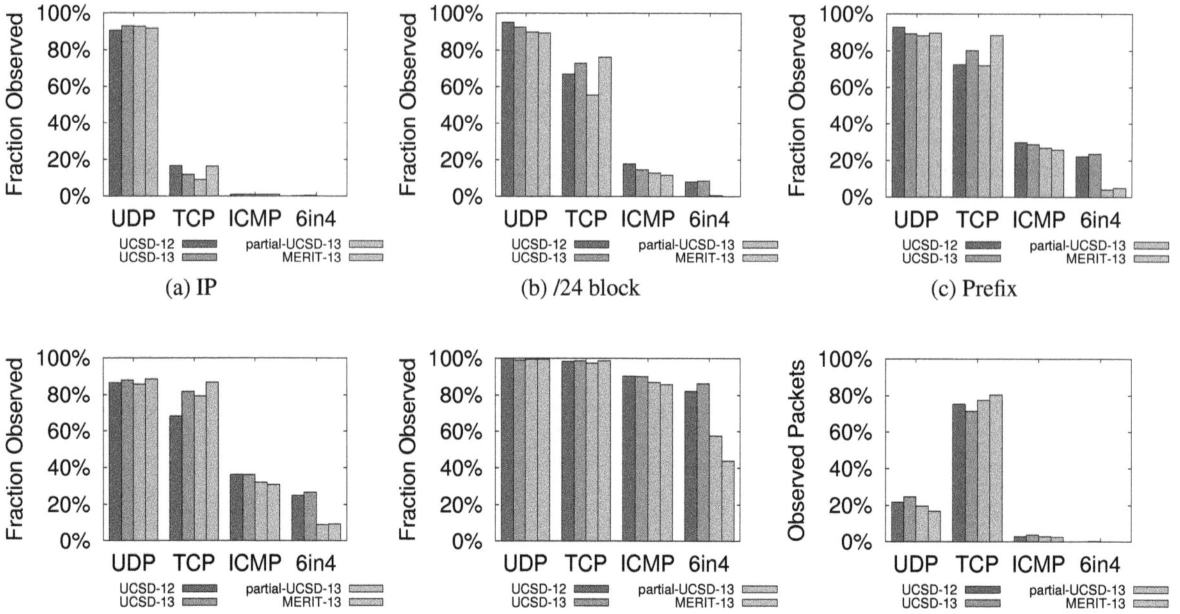

(a) IP (b) /24 block (c) Prefix

(d) AS (e) Country (f) Packets

Figure 3: **Top protocols.** Most IP addresses send UDP traffic. At the /24 block, prefix, AS and country levels we observe a similar percentage of sources sending TCP and UDP. TCP accounts for most packets.

5. WHAT IS IBR MADE OF?

Most often, only a certain type of traffic is helpful in inferring a property of a network. For example, the authors of a previous study [12] use the retransmission behavior of TCP to infer packet-loss. It is thus important to understand the composition of IBR with respect to its potential information content. Enumerating all types of IBR-derivable information is a daunting, and probably impossible task. Instead, we characterize IBR along two basic dimensions: transport layer protocol and application, since the information encoded in IBR is a function of them.

5.1 How many sources use TCP vs. UDP?

Figure 3 reports the fraction (out of the total observed in the respective dataset) of IP addresses, /24 blocks, prefixes, ASes, and country codes observed through the most popular transport layer protocols. We observe most IP addresses via UDP traffic. Both TCP and UDP packets provide high visibility into /24 blocks and ASes, although neither provides complete coverage. All transport layer protocols provide excellent coverage of countries.

Wustrow *et al.* [48] characterize IBR based on the volume of *packets*, and not the number of *sources*. They find that from 2006–2010 TCP was the dominant protocol (above 75% of packets) for all years except 2008. Although our datasets are not directly comparable (they do not remove spoofed packets), we also find that TCP is the dominant protocol by number of packets (Figure 3f). Since UDP is the dominant protocol in terms of source IP addresses and TCP is the dominant protocol in terms of packets, the protocols may have different strengths when inferring network properties: UDP is more likely to provide wide coverage, while TCP is more likely to support analyses requiring repeated contact (Section 6).

5.2 Which applications contribute the most?

Here we classify IBR in terms of the process that generates the traffic. Port-based analysis, used in previous characterizations of IBR [48], is insufficient to analyze application-layer data [23]. For example, Qihoo 360 Safe traffic is the dominant application for all top-10 UDP destination ports.

Unlike Pang *et al.* who responded to unsolicited traffic [41], we passively collect IBR. With limited information, we perform a best-effort classification of IBR into components (that is, classes of phenomena responsible for different traffic) based on observations of initial communication attempts. For well-studied phenomena, we leverage known properties (e.g., the ranges of addresses of Conficker targets and the decryption algorithm for Sality's command-and-control packets [17,27]). The "Bro Scanner" category is based on Bro's definition of a scanner: contacting at least 25 unique destinations on the same port within 5 minutes [46]. We assign to the "Encrypted" category traffic with packets where $\text{entropy}(\text{payload}) \approx \log_2(\text{len}(\text{payload}))$. We then manually look for abnormalities in the number of observed source /24 blocks and derive a packet or flow-level filter matching the responsible traffic. We investigate and identify new phenomena based on TCP/UDP ports, UDP payloads, packet lengths, TCP flags, and number of packets. We complete the analysis in time (e.g., why a certain hour captures many /24 blocks) and space (e.g., why a darknet /16 block receives many /24 blocks). We perform this analysis iteratively: once we identify a component, we remove it from our data and find additional components causing abnormalities.

Table 2 reports the components that contribute a significant number of source /24 blocks. We aggregate some small components and all unclassified components into the "Other" category. We group the components based on the reason they appear in IBR: accidentally (i.e., due to bugs or misconfigurations), as part of a scan, as a by-product of spoofed traffic, such as DoS attacks, received by a network (which sends backscatter to the darknet), and for unknown reasons. Our classification process discovers some interesting large Internet phenomena. For example, most BitTorrent traffic appears to be the result of index-poisoning attacks that pollute the DHT

Component	UCSD-12		UCSD-13			MERIT-13		
					Partial			
	Total	Unique	Total	Unique	Total	Total	Unique	∩ UCSD-13
Bugs & Misconfigurations								
File Sharing (BitTorrent, eMule, QQLive) [34, 35, 40]	2,640k	284k	2,490k	344k	1,910k	2,090k	377k	1,980k
Qihoo 360 Safe Bug [1]	1,450k	98.5k	1,340k	117k	1,110k	1,110k	138k	1,050k
Encapsulated IPv6 (6in4, Teredo) [5]	1,080k	9.48k	744k	11.5k	392k	368k	5.94k	312k
Gaming (Xbox, Steam) [3, 4]	503k	4.50k	490k	14.3k	258k	185k	11.9k	131k
Botnet C&C (ZeroAccess, Sality) [27, 38]	551k	17.3k	184k	4.97k	51.7k	51.6k	2.37k	25.7k
Scanning								
Conficker [17]	642k	24.4k	579k	58.1k	573k	568k	96.9k	563k
Bro Scanner [46]	597k	8.48k	197k	4.57k	104k	99.1k	4.06k	91.8k
Backscatter								
Backscatter [39]	394k	45.3k	392k	51.6k	247k	246k	21.3k	219k
Unclassified								
Encrypted [28]	1,450k	98.5k	1,340k	117k	819k	755k	29.8k	667k
Other	1,980k	73.8k	1,910k	127k	1,440k	1,70k	135k	1,410k
All Components	3,130k		3,150k		2,650k	2,760k		2,670k

Table 2: **/24 blocks observed by IBR component.** IBR is composed of many different types of traffic. File-sharing traffic contributes the highest number of /24 blocks in all datasets, but there are variations based on time (`UCSD-13` vs `UCSD-12`) and position (`partial-UCSD-13` vs `MERIT-13`). We observe most /24 blocks through multiple IBR components, implying that insight into a network is not dependent on a single type of traffic.

with bogus IP addresses. We determine a UDP payload was sent from Qihoo 360 Safe by investigating some live hosts at UC San Diego responsible for it. A byte-order bug, triggered when a host receives updates via a P2P network, causes this traffic. In Section 7, we link trends of the individual components to changes in IBR properties over time.

When studying 2010-era IBR reaching four /8 networks, Wustrow *et al.* find that scanning accounts for the majority of packets in all but 1.0.0.0/8 [48]. In our datasets, many well-studied, malicious IBR phenomena—scanning (including Conficker), backscatter—also account for most of the packets (collectively contributing about 83% of all packets in `UCSD-13`). But, surprisingly, malicious traffic is not the largest component of IBR in terms of sources. Packets with a P2P file-sharing payload contribute over 1.9M /24 blocks in all datasets, accounting for over two-thirds of all /24 blocks observed; Qihoo 360 Safe traffic alone contributes about 100M IP addresses.

We observe most /24 blocks through multiple IBR components, implying that many types of IBR can provide insight into the same networks. In particular, even without the top IBR components, the "Other" component alone, contributes with 1.4M /24 blocks. The "Unique" column of Table 2 reports the number of /24 blocks observed through a single IBR component. For each component, the number of unique /24 blocks is at least an order of magnitude smaller than the total number of /24 blocks observed through that component. As a result, if the composition of IBR changes slightly we would still observe many of the same networks.

5.3 Lessons learned

Some IBR-based inferences require a certain type of traffic; other network properties can be inferred regardless of the underlying application, but their success is dependent on the composition of IBR. Fortunately, IBR is made up of many components, each of which contributes relatively few unique /24 blocks (implying some analyses may be robust to fluctuations in IBR composition). While most packets are TCP (due to scanning and backscatter), we observe more IP addresses from UDP traffic (due to P2P and bugs). IBR is commonly known as malicious traffic. However, we find that the phenomena that contribute the highest number of sources (over 1M /24 blocks) appear to be of benign nature.

6. HOW OFTEN DO WE RECEIVE IBR?

In this section, we consider inferences that require multiple observations of a given host/network. For example, Benson *et al.* [12] determine that the path from hosts in an AS to a darknet changed by observing the behavior of the TTL field. In addition to looking for changes in given fields, we can leverage the timing between packets (e.g., to infer uptime [32]) and the predictability of repeated contacts (e.g., to infer outages [24]).

To study repeated contact from IBR sources, we report (1) how often a host/network is observed, (2) the length of time between the first and last observation of a source, and (3) the timing between contacts. Our approach is to partition our dataset into 1-minute, 1-hour, and 1-day time bins and record the sources sending IBR in each bin. In mathematical notation, let S and T be the set of all sources and time bins at given granularities, and $I_s(t)$ be an indicator function for a source s for a time bin t that is 1 if the source is observed, and 0 otherwise. For property (1) we compute, for each $s \in S$:

$$\sum_{\{t \in T\}} I_s(t);$$

for property (2) we determine, for each $s \in S$:

$$\max_t \{t \in T | I_s(t) = 1\} - \min_{t'} \{t' \in T | I_s(t') = 1\};$$

and property (3) can be expressed as a multiset, where we include for each $s \in S$ and $\{t \in T | I_s(t) = 1\}$ the value (if it exists)

$$t - \max_{t'} \{t' \in T | I_s(t') = 1 \wedge t' < t\}.$$

Communication attempts may span multiple time bins, which could lead to inadvertently skewing properties (1), (2) and (3). In Table 3, we report statistics on communication attempts (packets with the same {source ip, destination ip, protocol, source port, destination port} observed in one hour of data) by IBR component from `UCSD-13`. The number of communication attempts varies depending on the IBR component, as does the behavior of the hosts sending each type of traffic (as evidenced by the median number of attempts per source IP address). However, for all components, the average number of packets per communication attempt is small. Manual investigation reveals that the timing between packets is also

Component	Communication Attempts	Avg. Pkts per Attempt	Median Attempts per Source IP
File Sharing	1,120M	6.13	2
360 Safe	1,520M	1.62	11
Encap. IPv6	108M	4.49	2
Gaming	95.4M	1.04	1
Botnet C&C	13.3M	2.95	3
Conficker	13,800M	1.98	109
Bro Scanner	27,400M	1.10	684
Backscatter	20,700M	1.23	6
Encrypted	137M	2.33	1
Other	1,740M	3.33	3
Total	66,700M	1.50	11

Table 3: **Communication attempts by IBR component for** UCSD-13. IBR components vary in the number of communication attempts made, and the median attempts made per source IP addresses. But, all components have a low number of packets per attempt, which suggests binning the data will not result in significant double counting.

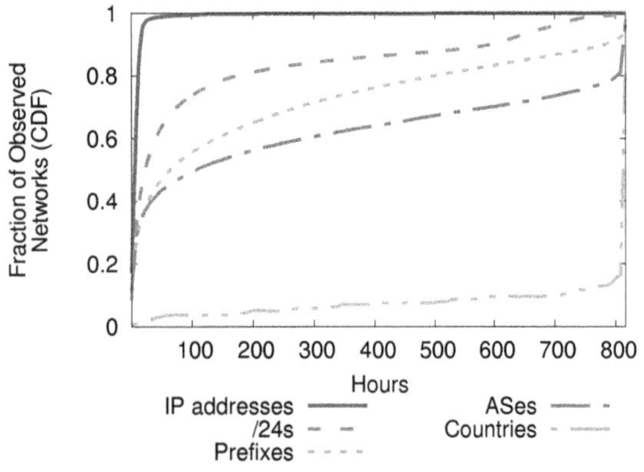

Figure 4: **CDF of fraction of sources observed using 1-hour time bins(UCSD-13).** We observe most countries and some ASes in nearly every time bin, which means we should be able to make repeated inferences at these source granularities.

small (e.g., 3 seconds between retransmission of Conficker packets). As a result, our partitioning approach confines most attempts to a single time bin, implying that binning does not significantly skew our calculations in the following sections.

6.1 How often do sources send IBR?

The frequency with which we can infer properties of a remote network depends on how often we receive traffic from that network. Figure 4 shows the cumulative distribution function of sources observed using 1-hour time bins in UCSD-13. The other datasets exhibit similar distributions. We observe frequent contact at coarse source granularities, i.e., countries and some ASes. The values on the far right of Figure 4 indicate the number of networks that we observed in every hour UCSD-13, which suggest that inferences requiring near-constant traffic samples are only possible for ≈80% of countries and ≈20% of ASes. We also explore (not shown here) the distribution of number of contacts with time bins of 1-minute and 1-day. As expected, the CDF curves shift towards more frequent contact as we move to larger time bins.

Approximately 12% of IP addresses are unsuited for repeated measurements because we observe them in only one 1-minute time bin, and we observe most IP addresses in less than 11 1-minute time bins. But as the size of the time bin increases to hours or days, the

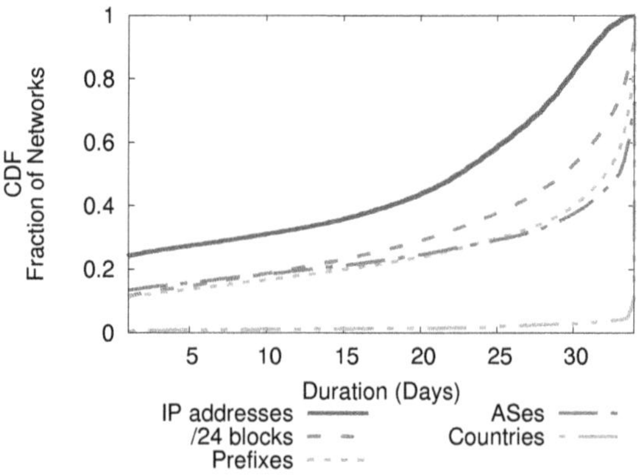

Figure 5: **CDF of contact duration (UCSD-13).** At all source granularities the contact duration is long, which is desirable for analysis throughout the datasets.

number of contacts per source increases. For example, we observe traffic from over 75% of IP addresses, /24 blocks, prefixes ASes and countries in multiple days.

6.2 What is the total duration of contact?

To conclude if our observations are the result of a single bursty event, or if sources are visible throughout the *2012* or *2013 census* periods, we investigate the range of times that we observe a source. We calculate each source's duration of contact (time of last contact minus time of first contact). Figure 5 shows the CDF of this distribution. The total duration of contact is long (over 29 days out of 34) for most /24 blocks, prefixes, ASes, and countries. Despite observing most IP addresses in only a few 1-minute or 1-hour time bins, the duration of contact is also long for IP addresses (50% IP addresses had a duration of contact longer than 22.5 days), implying that there is a long time between consecutive observations of a source (Section 6.3).

We attribute the long duration of contact at the IP level to Qihoo 360 Safe traffic, which has a diurnal cycle. Since about 70% of IP addresses send Qihoo 360 Safe traffic in UCSD-13, it strongly influences the overall duration at the IP address granularity. Without Qihoo 360 Safe traffic, 80% of IP addresses have a contact duration of less than one day. However, there is only a small influence on the duration of contact at the /24 block, prefix, AS, and country granularities. The signal for these aggregated granularities is comprised of a mix of traffic components and is not dependent on Qihoo 360 Safe.

This analysis shows the potential to make IBR-based inferences at the /24 blocks, prefixes, ASes and countries granularities for the duration of the datasets. At the IP-address granularity, we observe the sources throughout the datasets, but this is mostly due to Qihoo 360 Safe traffic.

6.3 Frequency of communication attempts?

To evaluate our ability to perform fine-grained analysis with IBR, we study the time between observations of traffic from a source. Figure 6a shows the median time between all sources that we observe in at least two 1-minute time bins. We observe most countries all the time: the median time between observations is 1 minute for 92% of countries. At the /24 block and AS levels, the time between observations is often longer, although the time between contacts at these granularities is often within 10 minutes. There is a longer period of time between observations of an IP address: half of IP

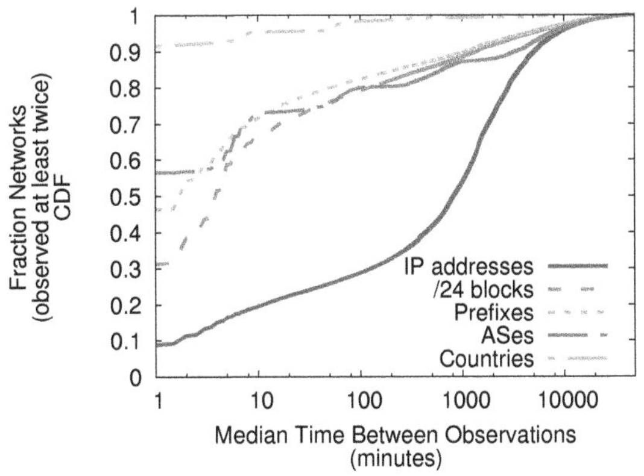

(a) All traffic.

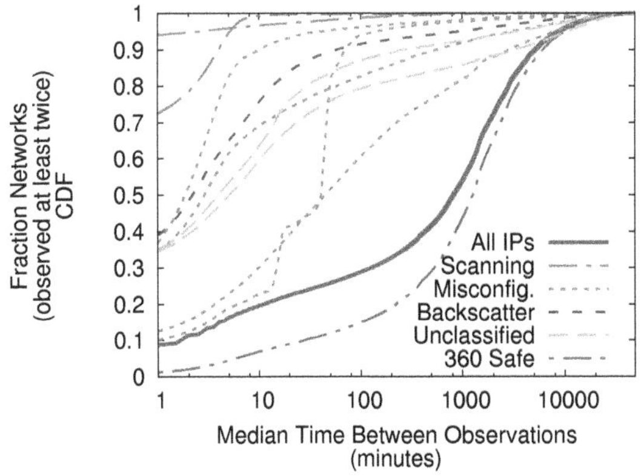

(b) By IBR component (IP addresses).

Figure 6: **Median time between observations (`UCSD-13`).** Most /24 blocks, prefixes, ASes, and countries observed multiple times have a short time between observations (less than 10 minutes), which is desirable for fine-grained analysis. By component, scanning traffic has the shortest median time between observations.

addresses have a median inter-observation time of more than 13.7 hours. However, for some IP addresses the inter-observation time is still short (27% of IP addresses have a median inter-observation time of less then 1 hour).

Figure 6b shows the breakdown of median time between observations for IP addresses by IBR component. 360 Safe traffic heavily influences the overall behavior of IP addresses: 50% of IP addresses associated with 360 Safe have a median time between observations of greater than 21.2 hours (presumably because they receive updates about once per day). The median time between observations is substantially shorter for the other IBR components. As a result, our ability to conduct fine-grained analysis comes from IBR components other than Qihoo 360 Safe. Scanning traffic has the shortest time between observations: for over 90% of IP addresses the median time between observations is less than 4 minutes. One type of misconfiguration causes hosts infected by a botnet to send C&C traffic to the UCSD darknet and wait either 15 minutes or 1 hour between communication attempts. 360 Safe traffic does not heavily influence the time between observations at the /24 block, AS or country levels.

6.4 Lessons learned

We find that many sources repeatedly contact our darknets. We almost always observe traffic from most countries and many ASes, e.g., we observe them in nearly all time bins, throughout the entire observation period, and with a short time between observations. We continually, but not constantly, observe most /24 blocks and prefixes, e.g., they have a long contact duration but the median time between observations is often over an hour. At the IP level, a diurnal bug in Qihoo 360 Safe generates traffic that heavily influences the contact duration and time between intervals. When we exclude the Qihoo 360 Safe traffic, three-quarters of IP addresses have a contact duration of less than one day (i.e., we observe the source in a single day of our 34-day observation period). As a result, IBR is not well suited for long-term inferences at the IP address granularity.

7. SENSITIVITY ANALYSIS

In this section, we examine the dependence of IBR on the time and site of data collection. We discover a number of differences, which can be attributed to the properties of influential IBR components. These results (1) confirm that the findings presented in the previous sections are representative in terms of number of IBR sources, the mix of components and visibility, (2) identify aspects of IBR that limit its ability to make inferences about remote networks, and (3) set expectations for the performance of other darknets.

7.1 Dependence on time of collection

Over time, IBR evolves. Not just in terms of its constituent packets and bytes, as studied by Wustrow *et al.* [48], but also in terms of the number of sources sending IBR. To identify times when significant changes occurred, we consider: (1) the number of IP addresses observed per hour for most of 2008–2015 (Figure 7a); (2) the per-day contribution of the major components[3] over the 28-month period from January 2012 to April 2014 (Figure 7b); and (3) the total number of /24 blocks per component during the *2012* and *2013 census* (Table 2). Our ability to make network inferences is influenced by both the trends and erratic nature of IBR, including the following events:

- *November 2008*: Conficker worm outbreak
- *March 2010*: Significant BitTorrent traffic observed
- *October 2010*: Start of traffic from 360 Safe bug
- *March 2013*: A spike in Backscatter traffic as the result of a DoS on Spamhaus
- *February 2014*: Increase in backscatter containing responses to DNS queries
- *2012 census vs 2013 census*: Due to activity by the Carna Botnet in 2012, the number of /24 blocks labeled as Bro Scanners in `UCSD-12` is three times the amount in `UCSD-13`

[3] We extract some IBR components with a pcap signature. When operating on flow-level data, we use heuristics instead. E.g., for BitTorrent traffic we use popular message lengths (with low false positive rate) instead of examining the payload.

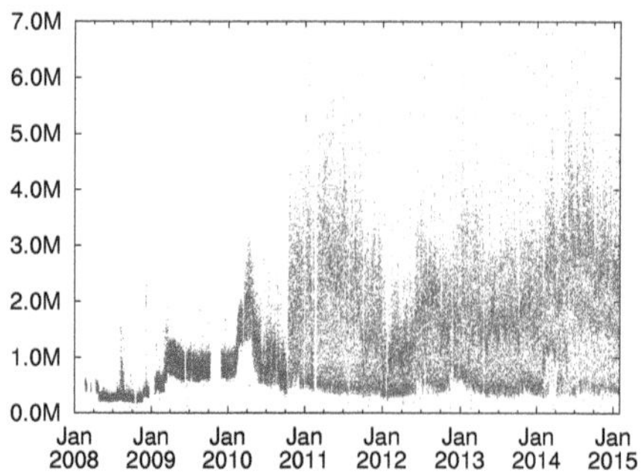

(a) **IP addresses observed per hour over a 7-year period (UCSD-NT).**

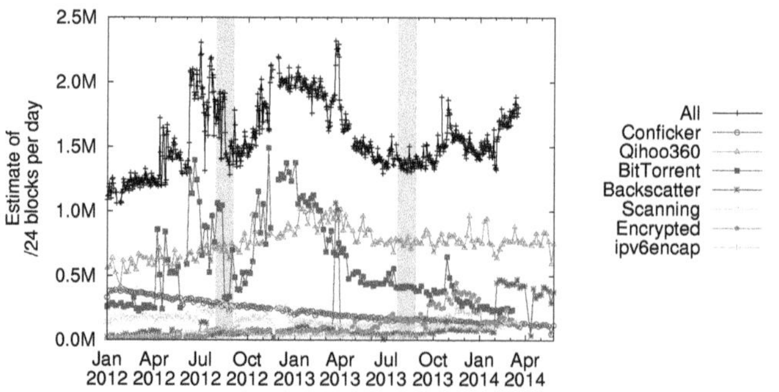

(b) **/24 blocks observed every 6th day at UCSD-NT by IBR component**. The shaded portions indicate the *2012* and *2013 census*.

Figure 7: Section 7 reviews interesting events represented in these plots.

In particular, we can attribute the increased number of sources in recent years to bugs and misconfigurations in P2P networks (Qihoo 360 Safe and BitTorrent). However, sources sending P2P traffic generally produce few connection attempts at irregular intervals. Combined with the decrease in Conficker traffic, this means that fine-grained analysis (repeated analysis on a short time scale, e.g., minutes) is becoming more difficult. To extract a predictable signal, we may need to analyze only specific components of IBR [12, 32]. On the other hand, erratic events may serve as an opportunity to increase visibility. For example, using IBR to assess IPv4 utilization during the Spamhaus event yielded more used /24 blocks [21]; locating open resolvers is possible with IBR as the result of an increase in DNS traffic. We group the events above into scanning activities (Conficker and Carna), P2P misconfigurations or bugs (BitTorrent and Qihoo 360 Safe), and backscatter (DNS responses and Spamhaus) and discuss each below.

Scanning activities. Both Conficker and Carna increased the number of sources scanning the darknet. Hosts participating in scans send many packets to the darknet—which we can leverage for repeated measurements. However, the Carna scans were a temporary phenomenon and Conficker is slowly declining. This decrease, combined with the emergence of BitTorrent and 360 Safe traffic (generated by sources which make relatively few connection attempts) results in fewer packets observed per IBR-visible host.

P2P misconfigurations/bugs. As a result of misconfigurations or bugs in P2P networks, we observe many sources, though these sources generally send few packets. We do not receive BitTorrent traffic consistently, and BitTorrent's erratic nature correlates with the total number of /24 blocks observed per day. In aggregate, 360 Safe traffic is diurnal: in `UCSD-13`, the average number of source IP addresses sending this traffic per hour varies between 165k at 20:00 UTC to 2.31M at 0:00 UTC. However, we do not observe clients using the software at predictable intervals. Thus P2P misconfigurations and bugs provide excellent coverage, but only when we do not need many packets per source or high predictability.

Backscatter. Normally, we think of backscatter from spoofed DoS attacks as coming from a small number of attacked machines or networks. Both the Spamhaus attack and the increase in DNS traffic show that the number of sources sending backscatter can actually be large. The Spamhaus attack [43] targeted Spamhaus' network, the networks carrying Spamhaus' traffic and strategically selected Internet exchange points. The increase in DNS traffic is caused by responses to spoofed queries — from many open resolvers simultaneously.

Backscatter events provide a period of increased visibility of remote networks, and it may be advantageous to infer network properties during these events. This window of opportunity may vary: the Spamhaus attack lasted a couple days, while DNS backscatter is an on-going phenomenon.

7.2 Dependence on position in IPv4 space

Wustrow *et al.* [48] find significant non-uniformity in the number of bytes and packets received by four /8 darknets in March 2010. However, we find more uniformity when considering the number of sources sending non-spoofed traffic to our /8 darknets. Intuitively, filtering out spoofed traffic removes some irregularities, and many IBR components target UCSD-NT and MERIT-NT with equal probability (e.g., scanning, backscatter, P2P misconfigurations).

In particular, we observe a similar number of /24 blocks through `partial-UCSD-13` and `MERIT-13` (2.65M and 2.76M respectively). Table 2 shows that `partial-UCSD-13` and `MERIT-13` also have a similar traffic composition. All components, except Gaming and Other, contribute approximately the same number of /24 blocks to each dataset. The Gaming difference can be explained by a misconfiguration: a single UCSD-NT IP observes 115k /24 blocks sending Steam traffic. In the Other category, 10 times as many /24 networks send TCP traffic destined to IP addresses matching {A.B.C.D | A=MERIT & C=13} than {A.B.C.D | A=UCSD & C=13}.

Additionally, many source /24 blocks send traffic to both UCSD-NT and MERIT-NT. The ∩UCSD-13 column of Table 2 shows the overlap—the number of /24 blocks observed in both `MERIT-13` and `UCSD-13` accounts for more than 84% of /24 blocks. We also observe an overlap of at least 49% in individual IBR components (Conficker produces the highest overlap, 99%) which implies that sources sending IBR likely target multiple /8 networks. Thus, it is likely that other portions of the address space receive packets from these sources.

However, we cannot examine all /8 darknets to understand the full effect of position. The non-uniform nature of IBR may cause variance when examining other darknets. Wustrow *et al.* find that many misconfigurations affect only the 1.0.0.0/8 block (e.g., traffic to 1.2.3.4) [48]; these misconfigurations may also influence the number of sources sending traffic to 1.0.0.0/8, in addition to bytes and packets. Additionally, we show in the next section that sources often do not target all subnets within a /8 darknet.

7.3 Dependence on darknet size

With smaller darknets, we expect to observe fewer sources and observe those sources less frequently. To study the effect of using a smaller darknet, we vary darknet size, from a /16 to a /8, by considering contiguous subnets of UCSD-NT as their own mini-darknet. Figure 8a reports for each darknet size, the range of source /24 blocks captured by these contiguous subnets in `UCSD-13`. We find, due to the non-uniform nature of IBR, significant differences in the number of sources captured by subnets of the same size.

Figure 8b shows for each /16 within UCSD-NT the number of /24 blocks captured during *2013 census*. In UCSD-NT, most variations can be attributed to: (1) the bug in Conficker's PRNG, (2) BitTorrent's RPC mechanism, KRPC, and (3) Encapsulated IPv6 traffic. Individual IP hotspots are observed as little spikes in Figure 8b, but create small discrepancies compared to the differences caused by the Conficker, BitTorrent and IPv6 components (for /16 or larger darknets).

Despite these discrepancies, based on median observations, the marginal utility of a single darknet IP address decreases as the size of the darknet increases (e.g., doubling the size of the darknet results in fewer than a 2x increase in the number of /24 blocks observed). In the /8 to /16 range, we observe a power-law relationship between the median number of /24 blocks observed and the number of darknet IP addresses monitored. Specifically, in the /8 to /16 range of UCSD-NT, reducing darknet size by a factor of two should yield about 89% of the original /24 blocks. As a result, we expect small darknets to also observe many /24 blocks. But this power-law relationship does not hold for all darknet sizes: the median number of /24 blocks observed by an IP in `UCSD-13` is an order of magnitude less than the number implied by the power law relationship.

8. CASE STUDIES

The previous sections identify and characterize aspects of IBR relevant to conducting opportunistic network analysis. In this section, we examine how these aspects influence network inferences with IBR. Table 4 shows 13 types of IBR-based inferences, which vary along the dimensions of packet-level information (Section 5) and number of required observations of the source (Section 6). Not all sources with the specified dimensions of (packet-level, number of observations) will be analyzable. For example, to calculate uptime with two TCP packets, the source needs to send packets with TCP timestamps from an operating system where the technique is valid.

The inferences in Table 4 include previous studies where the authors applied their method Internet-wide, previous studies where a technique used on a small scale may be usable for Internet-wide analysis, techniques used with measurement data other than IBR that may be applicable to IBR, and novel uses of IBR. While not exhaustive, Table 4 suggests that IBR is versatile in terms of the number and range of inferences it may be able to support, including existence (or active use) of a network resource, host attributes, and network behavior.

We consider three case studies in detail: locating open resolvers (Section 8.1), determining uptime (Section 8.2), and identifying path changes (Section 8.3). The goal of these case studies is to highlight some strengths and weaknesses of using IBR. The open resolver case study uses erratic but information-rich traffic; the uptime case study applies a common technique to a diverse set of hosts, but we need to take steps to ensure its accuracy; the path change case study takes advantage of repeated contact at the AS-level, but is not as accurate as the standard active technique (traceroute). Through these case studies we extend our knowledge of the state of the Internet and we identify some situations where IBR can assist in Internet-wide measurement: (1) when the presence of a source in IBR provides additional context; (2) to obtain a large sample; (3) for hosts unreachable through active probing; and (4) to reduce measurement overhead.

	`UCSD-12`	`UCSD-13`	`MERIT-13`	`UCSD-14-DNS`	Open Resolver Project [9]
Unique IPs	49,111	3,401	835	1,561,324	37,607,402
Recursion-Avail.	42,312	2,298	835	1,518,360	32,917,724
OK	48,746	2,991	329	1,437,310	32,595,867
FORMERR	43	7	7	1,422	841
SERVFAIL	317	148	43	1,445,276	919,899
NAMEFAIL	215	200	518	1,349,092	153,466
NOTIMP	7	8	7	64	166
REFUSED	173	241	35	136,328	4,433,126

Table 5: **Recursive DNS resolvers.** DNS responses reaching the darknet with the Recursion-Available bit set indicate an open resolver. The number of open resolvers sending IBR increased in 2014 (thirty-fold over `UCSD-12`), allowing us to infer their existence and provide insight into traffic reaching authoritative name servers.

8.1 Locating open DNS resolvers

In a reflective amplification attack, the attacker sends a small, spoofed packet to a node that responds with a much larger packet to the spoofed source IP address. These attacks often use DNS recursive queries. As a security mechanism, many DNS servers only answer recursive queries within their administrative domain. DNS servers not implementing this security mechanism are known as "open resolvers." Locating open resolvers is a first step in improving DNS security.

Our objectives with this case study are: (1) to show that the changing composition of IBR can provide an opportunity to learn about the Internet; (2) to show that IBR can supplement active probing techniques by providing additional information; (3) to expose limitations in IBR's ability to determine the existence of network components.

Method. If a darknet receives a DNS response, the most likely scenario is that a DNS server is responding to a spoofed query. In this section, we consider all UDP source port 53 traffic. We label an IP address as an open resolver if the Recursion-Available flag is set, as it indicates the willingness to resolve recursive queries. This way, we actually locate either a machine that accepts recursive queries from any IP address or that recursively resolves domains on behalf of a forwarding open DNS server [45]. We do not check the correctness or consistency of responses reaching the darknet, but we include response codes in our analysis.

Results. Table 5 shows that we observe few open resolvers in `UCSD-12,13` and `MERIT-13`. However, starting around February 2014, we observe a sustained increase in DNS responses (also visible as an increase in backscatter in Figure 7b). Van Nice reports that this type of attack is responsible for 3% of global ISP DNS traffic, which may result in DoS to (a) the resolvers, (b) authoritative name servers, and (c) web sites hosted by the authoritative servers [47]. To show the magnitude of open resolvers during this time period, we create a dataset, `UCSD-14-DNS`, between January 20, 2014 and March 1, 2014.

The Open Resolver Project (ORP) sends DNS queries to the entire IPv4 address space over a period of 6.5 hours, once per

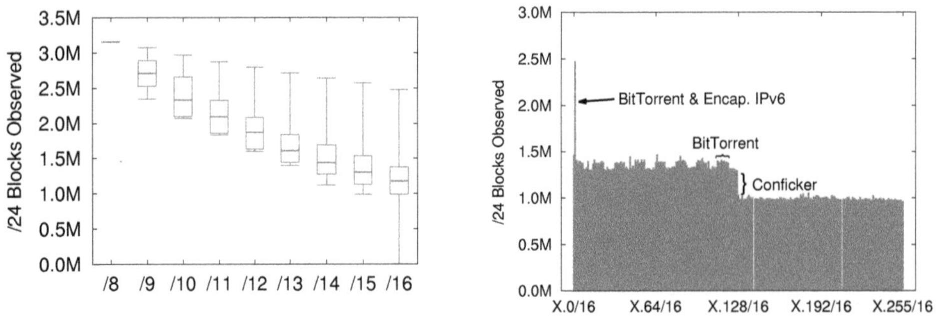

(a) Contiguous blocks of the darknet and how many blocks are observed.

(b) How many /24 blocks are observed by each /16 in UCSD-NT.

Figure 8: **Effect of size and position on number of /24 blocks observed**. There is a power-law relationship between number of /24 blocks observed and size of the darknet (Figure 8a), but significant variance based on position in the darknet (Figure 8b).

Number of Observations (Section 6)	**Packet Layer** (Section 5) **Internet (IP)**	**Transport (TCP/UDP)**	**Application**	
One	Ascertaining IPv4 Utilization † (through source IP) see: [21, 22]	Discovering Services † (through TCP flags) similar to: [39]	Locating Open Resolvers † (through DNS responses)	Determining Filtering Policy † (through Conficker) see: [44]
Two	Identifying Path Changes ◊ (through TTL) extend: [12]	Determining Uptime □ (through TCP timestamp) apply: [37]; other: [32]	Evaluating Security Improvements ◊ (through Conficker traffic reduction)	
Many	Deducing Packet Sending Rate □ (through IPID) apply: [16, 33]; other: [26, 32]	Detecting NAT Usage □ (through TCP options and TTL) apply: [49]; other: [11, 13]	Assessing BitTorrent Client Popularity □ (through uTP handshake messages)	
Predictable	Detecting Outages ◊ (through number sources) extend: [20, 24]	Recognizing Packet-loss ◊ (through pkts/connection attempt) extend: [12]	Determining Number of Disks □ (through re-seeding of Witty's PRNG) see: [32]	

† = Existence of Resource □ = Attributes of End Hosts ◊ = Network Changes

Table 4: **Example inferences.** Inferences made through IBR require various numbers of packets and types of packet-level information.

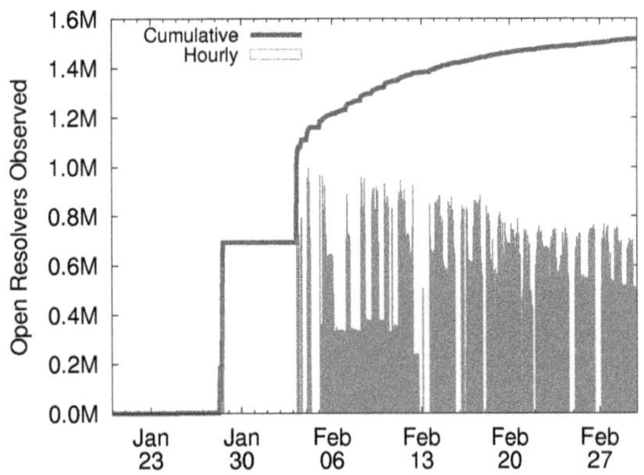

Figure 9: **Open resolvers in `UCSD-14-DNS`**

week [9]. For comparison, we consider all open resolvers[4] in ORP data in the same time period of `UCSD-14-DNS`. Table 5 shows that the 1.5M open resolvers found in `UCSD-14-DNS` are about 4% of the total found by ORP.

Figure 9 shows the number of open resolvers observed each hour, as well as the cumulative number, observed in `UCSD-14-DNS`. After an initial spike, the cumulative number of open resolvers grows slowly, despite observing over 200k open resolvers in many hour bins. Since we observe only a fraction of the known lower bound for open resolvers [9], this behavior indicates reuse, i.e., the phenomenon generating the DNS responses is repeatedly sending spoofed packets to the same set of open resolvers. Due to this repetition, smaller subnets of UCSD-NT capture a similar number of open resolvers (at least 89% of all open resolvers in `UCSD-14-DNS` with /16 subnets).

Validation. We verify that the open resolvers we include in `UCSD-14-DNS` are actually open resolvers by examining overlap with the ORP data in the same time period. Almost all (84%) of IP addresses observed in `UCSD-14-DNS` also appear as open resolvers in the ORP dataset. The remaining 16% are likely due to hosts intermittently online or were affected by Internet middleware (e.g., firewalls may drop packets from the ORP scan).

Comparison to other data sources. Although ORP has better coverage, active probing cannot reveal which open resolvers are actually used in attacks. The open resolvers ORP missed may include DNS servers that respond to packets from any source IP address, but only on certain interfaces (e.g., behind a firewall).

Through IBR, we can add to the knowledge of the phenomenon starting around February 2014. Specifically, we considered the "attack" traffic from the 462 second-level domains in `UCSD-14-DNS` that resulted in over 50k open resolvers sending traffic to UCSD-NT.

- baidu.com was the first second-level domain used in the attack – six days prior the second domain reaching our "attack" threshold. This was likely a testing phase.

[4] Specifically, the IP address of the responding DNS server, which is not necessarily the queried IP address.

- The attacks reused name servers (e.g., 36 domains had a nameserver matching *.dnspod.net), suggesting victims are repeatedly targeted.
- UCSD-14-DNS observes more sources with errors (e.g., SERVFAIL or NAMEFAIL) than ORP. Many of the open resolvers discovered in UCSD-14-DNS responded with non-errors and errors for queries for the same second-level domain, implying that the attack successfully inundated authoritative name servers with queries.

Discussion. IBR can supplement other measurement techniques, Dainotti *et al.* leveraged IBR to discover hosts that are intermittently used or behind firewalls in a study of IPv4 address space utilization [21, 22]. For similar reasons, we find additional open resolvers through IBR. Additionally, the observation in IBR or the differences between datasets may reveal additional information about our inferences, e.g., that an open resolver is being used maliciously, or that port filtering is used [44].

We observe more open resolvers due to a change in the composition of IBR. It is possible that this phenomenon could halt, in which case our coverage of open resolvers would decrease significantly. This variability is, in part, due to our dependence on a specific application. When many types of traffic contribute to a signal, we expect our ability to make inferences to improve. For example, in IPv4 address space utilization, any type of traffic can imply usage [21].

8.2 Determining uptime

We explore inferring end host uptime. Studying uptime can help understand human behavior, identify machines that have not applied security updates, and select resources with better availability.

Our objectives in this case study are: (1) to explore an inference requiring repeated contact; (2) to highlight the benefit of relying on information from the transport layer over upper-layer information from a specific application; (3) to show how IBR can provide unique insights, unavailable through other data sources.

Method. We use TCP timestamps to calculate uptime [37], a technique already implemented in Nmap [2] and p0f [49]. RFC 1323 specifies that TCP timestamps should be obtained from a clock that is approximately proportional to the real time [30]. Under the assumptions that (1) the OS zeros the counter at boot time, (2) the timestamp has not wrapped, and (3) network speeds are about constant, we can compute the frequency of the timestamp increments and total uptime. Specifically, for two packets j and k received at times r_j and r_k respectively with TCP timestamps t_j and t_k, the frequency of the timestamp increments is $f = \frac{t_k - t_j}{r_k - r_j}$, and the uptime (when packet k is sent) is $\frac{t_k}{f}$.

For each hour of data, we calculate frequency and uptime for each source IP sending TCP timestamps, and use p0f to determine the operating system that sent the packets. We then aggregate over all hours of data, excluding sources when either p0f reports conflicting OSes, or we determine that the OS violates assumption (1), or we receive packets that reveal conflicting uptimes (e.g., from two hosts behind a NAT). Additionally, we verify that the uptime is less than a year and that the frequency is close to a typically used value (e.g., one-third of IP addresses have a clock rate of 1000Hz) before including an IP address in our analysis.

Validation. To validate this technique, we analyze the accuracy of assumptions (1) and (2). Table 6 summarizes our findings in ensuring that the TCP timestamp is set to zero at boot time. First, we verify the accuracy of TCP timestamps on our own machines using p0f. We found inconsistencies for iOS and Mac OS, and exclude IP addresses with these OSes from analysis. Additionally,

OS (from p0f)	# Srcs	Verified	Distribution	Include?
Linux 2.4.x	217,989		Wraps @27 hours	no
Windows 7 or 8	102,097	✓	70% up for less than 1 day	yes
Linux 3.x	52,200	✓	Longer uptimes less likely	yes
iOS iPhone/iPad	48,360	×	Most uptimes 3 to 13 days	no
Mac OS X 10.x	32,721	×	Most uptimes 3 to 13 days	no
Linux 2.2.x-3.x	28,034		Wraps @27 hours	no
FreeBSD	21,717	✓	Reboots for patch [8]	yes
Linux 2.6.x	17,290		Longer uptimes less likely	yes
Linux 2.4.x-2.6.x	14,800		Longer uptimes less likely	yes

Table 6: We verify that the uptime inferred by TCP timestamp method matches the actual uptime of a machine, and by examining the distribution of suspected uptimes observed in UCSD-13.

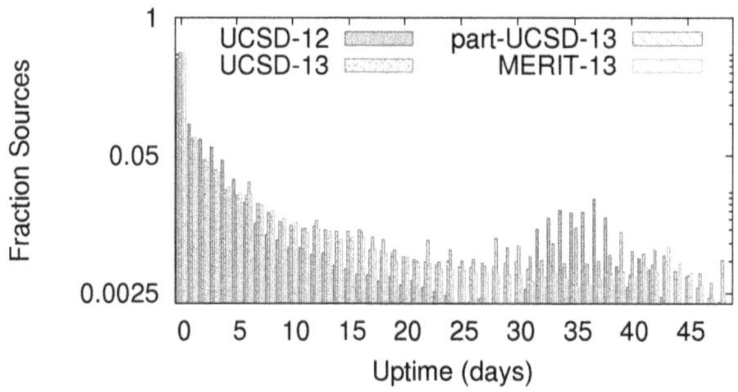

Figure 10: Distribution of uptime in days for IP addresses with TCP timestamps.

we examine the distribution of uptimes in UCSD-13 for each OS individually. We exclude two OSes, Linux 2.4.x and Linux 2.2.x-3.x, because the TCP timestamps appear to reset when the counter reaches 100M (at approximately 27 hours). We include Windows 7/8, which has a similar distribution from hour 0 to 24; but there is no evidence of a reset, implying that Windows 7/8 users generally turn off their machines every day.

Another concern is that the TCP timestamp will wrap once it meets its maximal value. The fastest timestamps we observe show clocks with frequencies on the order of 1000Hz, which will wrap about every 49 days. In Figure 10, about 0.1% percent of hosts have an uptime of 49 days, which suggest the impact of a wrapping timestamp is minimal.

Results. In UCSD-12, UCSD-13, partial-UCSD-13, and MERIT-13, we were able to infer uptimes associated with 290,697, 208,104, 57,990, and 47,122 IP addresses respectively. Both partial-UCSD-13 and MERIT-13 reveal significantly fewer uptimes than UCSD-12 and UCSD-13, showing the influence of darknet size and temporal fluctuations (Section 7). Despite the differences in coverage, the data sets provide a consistent picture of uptime. Figure 10 shows that most hosts have short uptimes in all datasets, and a significant fraction have an uptime of less than 1 day. For the next three weeks, the fraction of up hosts decays exponentially, consistent with a constant probability of being turned off/rebooted. In UCSD-12, we observe many hosts with an uptime of about 35 days, many of which run Linux. The boot times of these machines are consistent with applying a newly released kernel security fix [7]. Similarly, in 2013, FreeBSD required a reboot after an update to BIND [8], but the influence on our aggregated data is smaller.

Discussion. The main benefit of using IBR to infer uptime is the diversity in end hosts analyzed. To the best of our knowledge, this is the first study to provide an Internet-wide analysis of uptime. Nmap and p0f both use the TCP timestamp technique, but measurements from a single vantage point (and not based on IBR) are limited in the sources they can evaluate. Active probing will not reach end hosts behind a firewall or NAT, whereas passive observation will be biased based on the population observed. Our study used over a half a million sources to validate the approach; but we could only determine uptime for 40k to 200k hosts (our analysis could improve, if instead of discarding all traffic from IP addresses used by multiple hosts, we isolated the timestamps for each host).

Kumar et al. examined IBR from the Witty worm to extract host uptimes. However, since Witty targeted a buffer overflow in network security products, the number of networks they could analyze was limited (inferring uptime for only about 800 machines) and not diverse (about a quarter of the machines were from only two institutions) [32]. Inferring properties from information extracted at the transport layer expands our coverage.

8.3 Identifying path changes

Detecting and analyzing path changes provides insight into Internet path stability [19,42], and outages [12,31,51]. Our goals with this case study are to explore an inference that: (1) requires successive measurements; (2) has an element of predictability (although IBR composition is erratic, TTL is predictable); and (3) shows how to use IBR to reduce the active probing required to infer changes (similar to [31,51]).

Method. We extend the technique of [12] to identify path changes from remote ASes to the darknet, which relies on the insight that the TTL of a received packet reflects the number of hops on the path to the darknet. If the path is unchanged, all packets from a host will have the same TTL. We calculate the number of hops by subtracting the TTL from the next highest power of 2 (a technique used in [13]), excluding any packets with a TTL less than 3 since they likely originate from traceroute and are not a predictable measure of hop count. When the number of hops from a source to the darknet increases or decreases, we infer a likely path change (similar to a previous technique for monitoring traffic at a CDN [51]). Note this method will not detect changes that result in the same length path (but through different routers).

For each IP address, we calculate for each 5-minute time bin, t, $\max_t$ and $\min_{t-1}$, the most and least number of hops taken at time t respectively. We consider a path to have changed if $\max_t > \max_{t-1}$ or if $\min_t < \min_{t-1}$. We expect most path changes to occur during a 5-minute bin, and not at time bin boundaries; our requirement for a change will identify changes that occur during a 5-minute bin (the time bin includes packets with the old TTL and the new TTL). This method should also account for a change in load balancing paths (the whole distribution shifts). The method will have some false positives due to NAT (when a new host, with a longer/short path starts transmitting) as well as false negatives.

To study changes affecting larger source granularities, e.g., a prefix or AS, for each time bin we also calculate the percentage of IP addresses that sent packets in that time bin as well as the previous one, and also indicated a path change. Using multiple sources from a prefix or AS increases our confidence that an event occurred. In particular, we can identify path changes affecting large portions of the address space (as opposed to the Internet edge).

Results. We are interested in paths that we can continually monitor, which we call *always-analyzable*. Section 6 showed that only countries and a few ASes send IBR to our darknets every minute. Table 7 confirms that few sources are always-analyzable; not shown is the significant overlap of such sources across datasets: 1300 ASes are in both `UCSD-13` and `MERIT-13`, and 1000 ASes are in both `UCSD-13` and `UCSD-12`. The `UCSD-13` data yields the best insight into path changes for transit/access ASes. Although large ASes (announcing a /16 or more) are more likely always-analyzable, half of the always-analyzable sources are small (announce less than a /16 block).

	UCSD-12	UCSD-13	UCSD-13 Partial	MERIT-13
IP addresses	2.5k	2.8k	2.4k	2.2k
/24 blocks	2.3k	2.6k	2.1k	2.0k
Prefixes	3.3k	3.6k	2.7k	2.9k
ASes	1.6k	1.7k	1.4k	1.4k
Countries	146	155	145	148

Table 7: Number of sources for which we can detect path changes throughout our measurement periods is consistent across datasets.

Validation. We validate our method using historical traceroutes from Ark nodes [6] located in always-detectable ASes in `UCSD-13`. The Ark infrastructure uses teams of about 20 nodes to send traceroutes to every routed /24 block over a span of 2-3 days [6]; thus, we can expect about one traceroute per minute from each Ark node to reach the darknet. Nine Ark nodes are in 8 always-detectable ASes, including five educational networks, two large transit providers, and a Regional Internet Registry.

We cannot validate all path changes from the hosts sending IBR, as we do not know when these hosts start sharing links to the darknet. However, AS-level path changes should be observable in both Ark data and IBR. We find our analysis of other IBR-transmitting IP addresses frequently corroborates path changes in traceroute data. Figure 11 reports, for events in KIST (ASN1237) and Purdue (AS17), the percentage of hosts in darknet data signaling a path change, and the periods of time (the colored) periods that a path change was observed from IPs in both darknet and traceroute data.

KIST had very few path changes (in both types of data). Figure 11a includes all traceroute-inferred path changes for KIST, and all but one path change in `UCSD-13`. Most traceroute-inferred path changes occur around the same time as the darknet-inferred changes. Traceroute reveals that the path change occurred in the core of the network. Further investigation of the KIST sources suggests that traffic from the darknet sources used multiple paths in the 8:00 to 8:10 time bins (during these time bins the hop count was 16 or 17; outside of the time bins the hop count was 16). For one of the IP addresses, it is possible to look at a 1-minute time bins. With this granularity all darknet-inferred changes align with traceroute-inferred changes.

Figure 11b shows many path changes over a six-day period for Purdue in both Ark (8.9k changes), and darknet data (1.3k 5 minute bins with changes). Several IP addresses produce evidence of frequent path changes. Before August 4, 2013, traceroutes sent by the Ark monitor to UCSD-NT used the same route out of Purdue, but after this date, traffic from the Ark node traversed multiple routes out of Purdue's network. A likely explanation is that some Purdue sources used stable routes, while others used flapping routes; on August 4, 2013 the Ark node switched to using the flapping routes.

It is future work to fully validate our method; but from these examples, we suspect our technique can provide strong evidence of paths changes to the darknet. At a high level, our results for path-change detectable ASes are consistent with previous studies of route persistence [19,42].

Discussion. Although IBR is an erratic data source, this example shows that it can provide insight into abnormal events and macroscopic dynamics. Our success with this case study is partially due to the aspect of IBR we are evaluating: the expectation that the initial TTL value remains the same is true regardless of the number of sources sending IBR or the volume of IBR, although in-

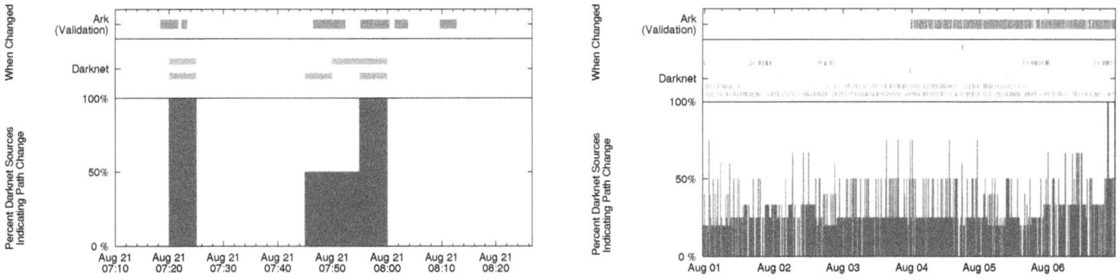

(a) KIST (b) Purdue

Figure 11: **Identifying path changes with IBR.** The top portion of each figure shows our validation data from Ark. The middle portion of each figure shades, for each source, the periods it inferred a path change. The bottom portion of each figure shows the percentage of darknet IP addresses signaling a path change. We identify the start of path change events at KIST, and route-flapping at Purdue.

creases in either would likely improve our coverage and accuracy. This path change detection method would work best in conjunction with other data sources. Like PlanetSeer and Hubble, passive traffic measurements such as IBR can help inform when and where active measurements would be most useful [31, 51]. IBR also provides features that traceroute and BGP data lack, e.g., no injected traffic required, and intra-AS visibility, respectively.

9. SUMMARY

We create a framework, and use case studies to apply the framework, to investigate the utility of Internet Background Radiation to support inference of a range of properties of networks across the global Internet. Using traffic from two large darknets, we carefully characterize it along dimensions applicable to macroscopic Internet measurements. We examine which networks send IBR, identify components that enable opportunistic network inferences, characterize the frequency and granularity of traffic sources, and analyze sensitivity to time of collection and position in the address space. Three case studies highlight the range of inferences possible with IBR, and show that IBR can supplement existing techniques by improving coverage and/or diversity of analyzable networks, and reducing measurement overhead. We also taxonomize 10 other potential inferences, and hope that our framework encourages additional consideration of the circumstances and properties for which unsolicited traffic is an appropriate data source for Internet research. This work demonstrates the applicability of IBR to many types of Internet measurement studies. More generally, this framework can serve as a template for evaluating the utility of other Internet measurement data sources.

10. ACKNOWLEDGEMENTS

We would like to thank Nevil Brownlee, Louis DeKoven, Kirill Levchenko, Brian Kantor and Cooper Nelson for their assistance in investigating IBR phenomena.

This research used resources of the National Energy Research Scientific Computing Center, a DOE Office of Science User Facility supported by the Office of Science of the U.S. Department of Energy under Contract No. DE-AC02-05CH11231. This work also used the Extreme Science and Engineering Discovery Environment (XSEDE), which is supported by National Science Foundation grant number ACI-1053575.

This work was supported by Department of Homeland Security Science and Technology Directorate grant FA8750-12-2-0314, cooperative agreement FA8750-12-2-0326, and NSF grant CNS-1228994.

11. REFERENCES

[1] 360 Total Security Software License and Service Agreement. www.360safe.com/totalsecurity/en/licence.html.

[2] Chapter 8. Remote OS Detection: Usage and Examples. nmap.org/book/osdetect-methods.html#osdetect-ts.

[3] Server queries. developer.valvesoftware.com/wiki/Server_queries.

[4] Xbox 360 network ports and router configurations for Xbox Live. support.xbox.com/en-US/xbox-360/networking/network-ports-used-xbox-live.

[5] Teredo Overview. technet.microsoft.com/en-us/library/bb457011.aspx, 2003.

[6] Archipelago Measurement Infrastructure. www.caida.org/projects/ark, 2006.

[7] Important: kernel security and bug fix update. www.redhat.com/archives/rhsa-announce/2012-July/msg00014.html, 2012.

[8] BIND remote denial of service. www.freebsd.org/security/advisories/FreeBSD-SA-13:07.bind.asc, 2013.

[9] Open Resolver Project, 2014. openresolverproject.org.

[10] Routeviews Prefix to AS mappings Dataset for IPv4 and IPv6. www.caida.org/data/routing/routeviews-prefix2as.xml, 2015.

[11] S. M. Bellovin. A Technique for Counting NATted Hosts. In *Internet Measurement Workshop (IMW)*, 2002.

[12] K. Benson, A. Dainotti, k. claffy, and E. Aben. Gaining Insight into AS-level Outages through Analysis of Internet Background Radiation. In *Traffic Monitoring and Analysis Workshop (TMA)*, 2013.

[13] R. Beverly. A Robust Classifier for Passive TCP/IP Fingerprinting. In *PAM*, 2004.

[14] N. Brownlee. One-way Traffic Monitoring with iatmon. In *Passive and Active Network Measurement Workshop (PAM)*, 2012.

[15] M. Casado, T. Garfinkel, W. Cui, V. Paxson, and S. Savage. Opportunistic Measurement: Extracting Insight from Spurious Traffic. In *HOTNETS*, 2005.

[16] W. Chen, Y. Huang, B. F. Ribeiro, K. Suh, H. Zhang, E. de Souza e Silva, J. F. Kurose, and D. F. Towsley. Exploiting the IPID field to infer network path and

end-system characteristics. In *Passive and Active Network Measurement Workshop (PAM)*, 2005.

[17] E. Chien. Downadup: Attempts at Smart Network Scanning. www.symantec.com/connect/blogs/downadup-attempts-smart-network-scanning, 2009.

[18] CIA. The World Factbook: Population.

[19] Í. Cunha, R. Teixeira, and C. Diot. Measuring and Characterizing End-to-End Route Dynamics in the Presence of Load Balancing. In *Passive and Active Network Measurement Conference (PAM)*, 2011.

[20] A. Dainotti, R. Amman, E. Aben, and k. claffy. Extracting Benefit from Harm: Using Malware Pollution to Analyze the Impact of Political and Geophysical Events on the Internet. *SIGCOMM Comput. Commun. Rev. (CCR)*, 42, Jan. 2012.

[21] A. Dainotti, K. Benson, A. King, k. claffy, E. Glatz, X. Dimitropoulos, P. Richter, A. Finamore, and A. Snoeren. Lost in Space: Improving Inference of IPv4 Address Space Utilization. Technical report, CAIDA, Oct 2014.

[22] A. Dainotti, K. Benson, A. King, k. claffy, M. Kallitsis, E. Glatz, and X. Dimitropoulos. Estimating Internet Address Space Usage through Passive Measurements. *SIGCOMM CCR*, 44(1), Dec. 2013.

[23] A. Dainotti, A. Pescapè, and K. Claffy. Issues and future directions in traffic classification. *IEEE Network*, 26(1):35–40, Jan 2012.

[24] A. Dainotti, C. Squarcella, E. Aben, k. claffy, M. Chiesa, M. Russo, and A. Pescapé. Analysis of Country-wide Internet Outages Caused by Censorship. In *Internet Measurement Conference (IMC)*, 2011.

[25] A. Dhamdhere and C. Dovrolis. Twelve Years in the Evolution of the Internet Ecosystem. *IEEE/ACM Transactions on Networking*, 19, Sep 2011.

[26] Z. Durumeric, M. Bailey, and J. A. Halderman. An Internet-Wide View of Internet-Wide Scanning. In *USENIX Security*, 2014.

[27] N. Falliere. Sality: Story of a Peer-to-Peer Viral Network. www.symantec.com/content/en/us/enterprise/media/security_response/whitepapers/sality_peer_to_peer_viral_network.pdf, 2011.

[28] J. Goubault-Larrecq and J. Olivain. Detecting Subverted Cryptographic Protocols by Entropy Checking. Technical Report LSV-06-13, Laboratoire Spécification et Vérification, ENS Cachan.

[29] J. Heidemann, Y. Pradkin, R. Govindan, C. Papadopoulos, G. Bartlett, and J. Bannister. Census and Survey of the Visible Internet. In *IMC*, 2008.

[30] V. Jacobson, R. Braden, and D. Borman. TCP Extensions for High Performance. RFC 1323 (Proposed Standard), May 1992.

[31] E. Katz-Bassett, H. V. Madhyastha, J. P. John, A. Krishnamurthy, D. Wetherall, and T. Anderson. Studying Black Holes in the Internet with Hubble. In *NSDI*, 2008.

[32] A. Kumar, V. Paxson, and N. Weaver. Exploiting Underlying Structure for Detailed Reconstruction of an Internet-scale Event. In *IMC*, 2005.

[33] Z. Li, A. Goyal, Y. Chen, and V. Paxson. Automating Analysis of Large-scale Botnet Probing Events. In *ACM Symposium on Information, Computer, and Communications Security (ASIACCS)*, 2009.

[34] Y. Liu and Y. Yang. Analysis of P2P Traffic Identification Methods. *Emerging Trends in Computing and Information Sciences*, 4(5), 2013.

[35] A. Loewenstern and A. Norberg. DHT Protocol. www.bittorrent.org/beps/bep_0005.html, Jan 2008.

[36] A. Lutu, M. Bagnulo, and O. Maennel. The BGP Visibility Scanner. In *Global Internet Symposium (GI)*, 2013.

[37] B. McDanel. TCP Timestamping - Obtaining System Uptime Remotely. seclists.org/bugtraq/2001/Mar/182, 2001.

[38] K. McNamee. Malware Analysis Report: New C&C Protocol for ZeroAccess/Sirefef. botnetlegalnotice.com/zeroaccess/files/Ex_14_Decl_Anselmi.pdf, 2012.

[39] D. Moore, C. Shannon, D. Brown, G. Voelker, and S. Savage. Inferring Internet Denial-of-Service Activity. *ACM Transactions on Computer Systems*, 24(2), May 2006.

[40] A. Norberg. uTorrent transport protocol. www.bittorrent.org/beps/bep_0029.html, June 2009.

[41] R. Pang, V. Yegneswaran, P. Barford, V. Paxson, and L. Peterson. Characteristics of Internet Background Radiation. In *IMC*, 2004.

[42] V. Paxson. End-to-end Routing Behavior in the Internet. In *ACM SIGCOMM*, 1996.

[43] M. Prince. The DDoS That Almost Broke the Internet. blog.cloudflare.com/the-ddos-that-almost-broke-the-internet, March 2013.

[44] M. Sargent, J. Czyz, M. Allman, and M. Bailey. On The Power and Limitations of Detecting Network Filtering via Passive Observation. In *PAM*, 2015.

[45] K. Schomp, T. Callahan, M. Rabinovich, and M. Allman. On Measuring the Client-side DNS Infrastructure. In *IMC*, 2013.

[46] The Bro Project. TCP Scan detection. bro.icir.org/sphinx/scripts/policy/misc/scan.bro.html, 2014.

[47] B. Van Nice. Drilling Down into DNS DDoS. www.nanog.org/sites/default/files/nanog63-dnstrack-vannice-ddos.pdf. NANOG 63, Feb 2015.

[48] E. Wustrow, M. Karir, M. Bailey, F. Jahanian, and G. Huston. Internet Background Radiation Revisited. In *Internet Measurement Conference (IMC)*, 2010.

[49] M. Zalewski. p0f v3: passive fingerprinter. lcamtuf.coredump.cx/p0f3/README, 2012.

[50] S. Zander, L. L. H. Andrew, and G. Armitage. Capturing Ghosts: Predicting the Used IPv4 Space by Inferring Unobserved Addresses. In *IMC*, 2014.

[51] M. Zhang, C. Zhang, V. Pai, L. Peterson, and R. Wang. PlanetSeer: Internet Path Failure Monitoring and Characterization in Wide-Area Services. In *Operating Systems Design and Implementation (OSDI)*, 2004.

Quantifying Interference between Measurements on the RIPE Atlas Platform

Thomas Holterbach
ETH Zürich
thomahol@ethz.ch

Cristel Pelsser
Internet Initiative Japan
cristel@iij.ad.jp

Randy Bush
Internet Initiative Japan
randy@psg.com

Laurent Vanbever
ETH Zürich
lvanbever@ethz.ch

ABSTRACT

Public measurement platforms composed of low-end hardware devices such as RIPE Atlas have gained significant traction in the research community. Such platforms are indeed particularly interesting as they provide Internet-wide measurement capabilities together with an ever growing set of measurement tools. To be scalable though, they allow for concurrent measurements between users. This paper answers a fundamental question for any platform user: Do measurements launched by others impact my results? If so, what can I do about it?

We measured the impact of multiple users running experiments in parallel on the RIPE Atlas platform. We found that overlapping measurements do interfere with each other in at least two ways. First, we show that measurements performed from and towards the platform can significantly increase timings reported by the probe. We found that increasing hardware CPU greatly helped in limiting interference on the measured timings. Second, we show that measurement campaigns can end up completely out-of-synch (by up to one hour), due to concurrent loads. In contrast to precision, we found that better hardware does not help.

1. INTRODUCTION

Public measurement platforms composed of many low-end devices or *probes*, such as RIPE Atlas [1], are increasingly used by researchers and network operators. In addition to measure network performance [2, 3, 4], these platforms are now used to map the Internet [5], detect routing attacks [6], routing anomalies [7] and censorship [8, 6].

To scale and be practical, measurement platforms schedule measurements in parallel, without providing feedback to the user. When put together with the limited hardware and software capabilities, this raises the question of measurement interferences. What is the impact of an increased load on the precision of measurements performed? Do the measurements performed by one participant impact the results obtained by others? If so, by how much? Can this have an impact on previous research results? This paper answers these questions empirically for the RIPE Atlas platform.

By measuring the interference between our own measurements (§3), we show that measurements do indeed interfere with each other, sometimes significantly. More particularly, we found that user-induced interferences can impact two aspects of measurements: *precision* and *synchrony*.

First, the precision of delay measurements (*e.g.*, using ping) performed either from or towards probes can be significantly impacted when other measurements are launched from or toward them (§4).

Second, user-induced interferences can heavily desynchronize experiments performed on multiple probes, even when launched at the same time (§5).

Our key findings are as follows:

- The precision of measurements performed *from* and *towards* the probe are impacted when other measurements use the probe at the same time. On older hardware, delays increase by more than 1 ms in the median case and by more than 7 ms for the 95th percentile (Table 2).
- Measurements are very quickly desynchronized when other measurements are run in parallel. Under heavy load, completion time may be delayed by close to 1 hour (Figure 8).
- Upgrading the probe hardware significantly improves precision levels, but does *not* help ensuring good synchronization levels (§5).
- Previous research results, as well as the RIPE Atlas historic dataset, may have been affected by interfering measurements. We also highlight two techniques to mitigate interferences in the future (§6).

Overall, our results show that measurement interferences should be systematically taken into account when analyzing results from public platforms. To ensure reproducibility, all our measurement and analysis tools are available online [9].

2. THE RIPE ATLAS PLATFORM

We now describe how Atlas works and highlight its increasing popularity among the academic community.

As of April 2015, RIPE Atlas is composed of over 6,700 public probes scattered in 197 countries. Three versions of the probes exist, differing only by their hardware. Version 1 and version 2 are identical except for the amount of RAM they have. Both are Lantronix XPort Pro with a 167MHz CPU, 8MB or 16MB of RAM, respectively and a 16MB flash. The version 3 probe is a revamped TP-Link TL-

IMC'15, October 28–30, 2015, Tokyo, Japan.

DOI: http://dx.doi.org/10.1145/2815675.2815710.

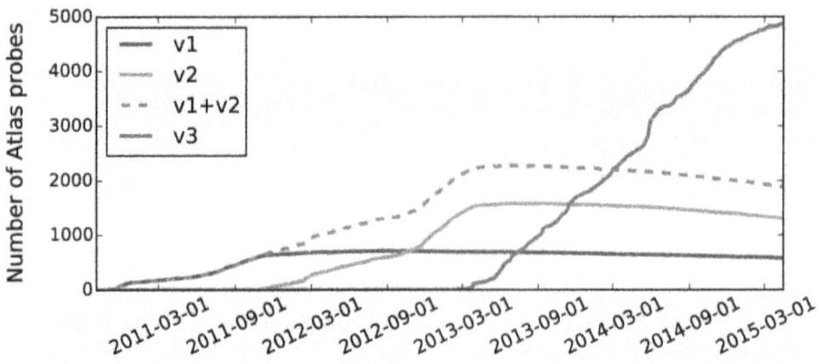

Figure 1: RIPE Atlas is composed of more than 6000 low-end probes which differ by their hardware: v1 and v2 probes are not powerful with respect to v3.

MR3020 router with a 400MHz CPU, 32MB of RAM and a 4MB NAND. The v3 probes are therefore more powerful.

Figure 1 depicts the evolution of the number of public probes per version since the platform inception. The number of v3 probes increased rapidly after they started to be distributed in 2013. While the number and proportion of v1 and v2 probes is decreasing, they remain non-negligible, accounting for 28.2% of the probes in April 2015.

RIPE Atlas uses credits to regulate the platform usage and schedules users' measurements concurrently. As of 2015, RIPE Atlas offers four[1] types of measures to its users: `ping`, `traceroute`, `DNS` and `SSL` [10]. In RIPE Atlas, a measurement is defined by a type, a frequency and set of probes. It can therefore refer to an arbitrary number of individual measurements performed from multiple probes. Users can also provide a start date and an end date. If none is provided, the measurement will start as soon as possible and has to be stopped manually. Measurements can be repeated or run only once (*one-off*). One-off measurements are near real-time if no start time is defined: users should expect results within 10 seconds [10].

RIPE Atlas regulates users load via a credit system. Users earn credits by hosting a probe and use them to perform measurements. RIPE's cost model is based on the resources each measurement needs. `traceroute` is the most expensive measurement, while `ping` is the cheapest. One-off measurements are also more expensive (twice more) than their scheduled counterparts as their arrival is not predictable.

RIPE Atlas uses basic scheduling strategies on each probe to handle concurrent load. The source code of the RIPE Atlas probes is based on `BusyBox` [11]. It has been adapted to improve the event management using the `libevent` library [12]. In addition, probes control the measurements frequency with `eperd`, a cron-like utility that can run measurements at regular intervals. One-off measurements are managed by the utility `eooqd`. Probes receive measurement requests from their controller with a *telnet* daemon. As several users can use a probe at the same time, it is essential to somehow schedule and limit users requests. In 2013, RIPE made the Atlas source code publicly available [13] but not yet the controller's.

Atlas probes are popular sources of measurements and are increasingly used in research. Since its inception, Atlas performed almost 30 million individual measurements[2] (Table 1). V3 probes hosted 2/3 of the measurements, while v1 and v2 probes hosted the rest. In March 2015, the user who used the most credits spent 83.3 million credits [14]. This is enough to perform more than 2,700,000 traceroutes. During the same month, the most used Atlas probe (a v1) provided 608,824 results [14], one every 4 seconds. Finally, the number of concurrent measurements is important. As an illustration, the platform was executing 592,000 concurrent individual measurements when we collected the statistics of Table 1.

	v1	v2	v3	Total
Total	3.1M	7M	19.7M	29.8M
In progress	58K	120K	414K	592K

Table 1: Overall, RIPE Atlas has hosted 29.8 million individual measurements. When we collected those results, 592,000 concurrent individual measurements were running on the platform.

An increasing number of research papers use RIPE Atlas. As an illustration, Machado *et al.* [15] used it to perform more than 3,000 traceroutes between a set of Atlas probes and a destination in Switzerland to see whether traffic stayed in the Schengen space. Fanou *et al.* [16] performed 1,108,709 traceroutes from 214 probes located in Africa to measure the impact of IXPs on interdomain routing in this region. Fiadino *et al.* [17] perfomed DNS requests for `*.whatsapp.net` from 600 Atlas probes to identify IP addresses hosting this service. Cicalese *et al.* [18] performed ping measurements from over 6000 probes located in 350 ASes in order to enumerate and geolocate IP-level anycast replicas.

Atlas probes are becoming popular destinations. Despite being designed for sourcing measurements, Atlas probes are increasingly used as targets by researchers [19, 20, 21, 16]. For example, Aben *et al.* [19] launched 7140 one-off traceroutes between a set of Atlas probes located in Sweden to infer topological properties. As the IP addresses of the Atlas probes are publicly available, users can target them from any possible sources (not necessarily from an Atlas probe). This enables users to perform hybrid measurement campaigns, with powerful machines as sources, and Atlas probes as destinations. Doing so, one can bypass the RIPE Atlas limitations (*e.g.*, frequency, credits cost) while keeping some of its interesting characteristics such as the large number of probes.

Some Atlas probes are more used than others. Due to their geographical position, IPv6 capability or a NAT gateway, some probes are more attractive than others. For instance, the distribution of probes per-country is highly skewed [22, 23]. While there are more than 1,200 Atlas probes in Germany, there are 29 countries with only one Atlas probe. The recent project `sbucket` [24] (supported by RIPE) aims at selecting probes based on spatial distribution rather than uniformly. Doing so would then to increase the load on isolated probes.

[1]`HTTP` measurements are possible but are restricted to researchers and other interested users on a case-by-case basis.

[2]As a measurement may involve a large number of probes, the number of individual measurements is more representative of the load of the platform.

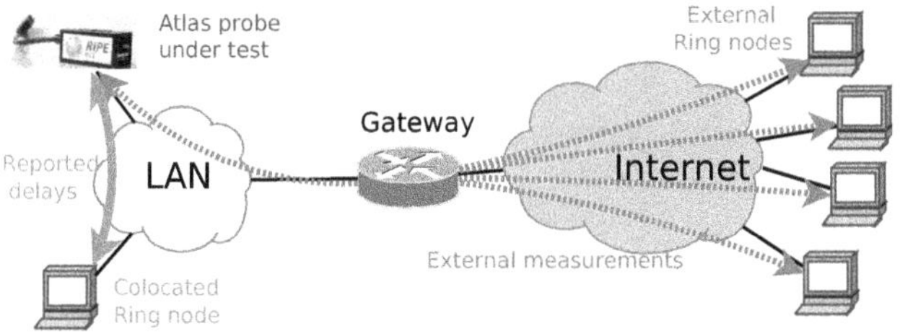

Figure 2: As opposed to traditional measurements which pass through the Internet (red arrows), the packets between the tested Atlas probe and its colocated Ring node (green arrow) always stay in the local network, thus preventing our measurements from being polluted by Internet variations.

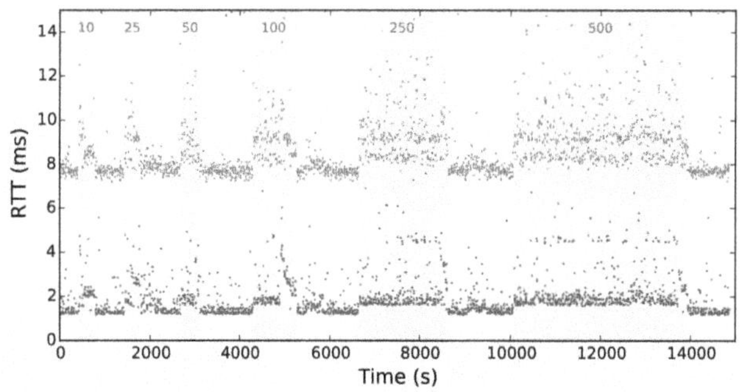

Figure 3: Delays measured *from* a v2 probe systematically increase when concurrent one-off traceroutes are launched on this probe.

3. QUANTIFYING INTERFERENCE

We describe how we quantify interference between measurements performed on a RIPE Atlas probe. We take the perspective of one user λ and one probe ρ and measure the effects on the results reported by ρ to λ when: *i)* ρ originates; or *ii)* is the target of concurrent measurements. In particular, we look at changes in the delay reported by ρ when concurrent one-off traceroutes are originated or when ρ is being used as ping destination. We use NL Ring nodes [25] as destinations (resp. as sources) of the pings sourced on (resp. destined to) ρ. We also look at changes in the completion time of one-off traceroute experiments performed on ρ.

We measure the delay reported by a probe using ping Delay-based measurements are indeed the most sensitive to concurrent load. In contrast, `traceroute`, `SSL`, and `DNS` output is less impacted by extra delay.

We also study the decrease in synchrony by measuring the completion time of one-off traceroutes performed on the probe.

...when increasing the number of concurrent measurements sourced from a probe To generate load on a probe, we launch an increasing number of one-off traceroutes from it using the REST API [26]. We use traceroute because it uses the most resources, as indicated by the higher cost. It is also one of the tools mostly used by researchers.

...when increasing the number of concurrent measurements targeting a probe The second technique we use to load a probe consists in gradually increasing the number of ICMP echo requests (800 bytes) targeted to it. We use a set of NL Ring nodes as sources. Each source sends 16 echo requests per second. We start with a single source. Every 2 minutes, we add a new source. We stop when there are 115 sources ($115 * 16 = 1840$ ping/s). While such frequencies are not common, experiments that use Atlas probes in a mesh-like fashion [16, 19, 20, 21] or that ping them from machines not limited in ping frequency may generate such a load. We use several Ring nodes as sources to mimic real experiments. To perform remote pings on multiple Ring nodes and collect the results, we built a tool [9] atop Scamper [27].

...and while preventing the effects from external factors We want to focus on the behavior of the probe and avoid network interferences. For each experiment, we measure the delay between the tested Atlas probe and a colocated Ring node in the same LAN (*i.e.* there is no IP hop between them). Because packets between the Atlas probe and its colocated Ring node always stay in the same LAN, we prevent our measurements from being polluted by Internet variations (Figure 2). We obtained these pairs of colocated Atlas probe and Ring node by a traceroute campaign between each Ring node and Atlas probes in the same AS. The results depicted in Table 2 all come from measurements done between an Atlas probe and its colocated NL Ring node.

4. DECREASED PRECISION

We now use our methodology (§3) to measure: *i)* the decrease in precision of delay-based measurements (this section); and *(ii)* the decrease in synchrony produced by concurrent measurements (§5). We performed all our measurements on multiple probes (at least two per version) to ensure conformity. As their number is not negligible and their decrease in precision and synchrony is serious, the next figures only focus on v2 probes.

Delays measured *from* the probe increase when concurrent measurements are launched *on* it. We launched ping measurements from the Atlas probe and towards eight random Ring nodes plus the colocated Ring node. The ping rate towards each destination is 9 ping/min, averaging 1.4 ping/s over all destinations. We increase the load on the probe by launching successively 10, 25, 50, 100, 250, and 500 one-off traceroutes.

Figure 3 shows the impact of the concurrent one-off traceroutes on the delay measured from a v2 probe. The blue points are RTTs between the Atlas probe and its colocated Ring node, while the red points are RTTs between the Atlas probe and another Ring node. The gray areas are the periods when one-off traceroutes are running. The number above each gray area is the number of one-off traceroutes executed. To quantify the impact, we compare the median, 95th percentile, and standard deviation of the ping measurements before the one-off traceroutes (the white area preceding the gray area) and during the one-off traceroutes execution time (gray area). The difference is reported in Table 2.

Delays measured from the probe systematically increase when one-off traceroutes are performed. Starting 100 one-off traceroutes increases the median delay of the concurrent pings by more than 1 ms. For v1 and v2 Atlas probes, the standard deviation is seriously impacted: +16.3 ms (v1) and +7.4 ms (v2). Atlas probes v3 show less effect, the median is only increased by 0.06 ms while the standard deviation is not impacted; this is due to v3 probes having more power. Sur-

impact on ping delay …	sourced on probe				destined to probe			
when increasing load …								
on probe		50th	95th	stdev		50th	95th	stdev
	(on : 100 traceroutes + 1.4 ping/s)				(on : 100 traceroutes, to : 9 ping/s)			
	v1	1.10 ms	7.30 ms	16.3 ms	v1	0.61 ms	0.72 ms	0.04 ms
	v2	1.20 ms	7.70 ms	7.40 ms	v2	0.50 ms	0.62 ms	0.02 ms
	v3	0.06 ms	0.10 ms	0.00 ms	v3	0.06 ms	0.05 ms	0.00 ms
towards probe		50th	95th	stdev		50th	95th	stdev
	(on : 9 ping/min, to : 400 ping/s)				(on* : 9 ping/min, to : 1000 ping/s)			
	v1	0.11 ms	1.90 ms	15.2 ms	v1	0.20 ms	5.40 ms	33.0 ms
	v2	0.22 ms	2.90 ms	3.90 ms	v2	0.45 ms	2.60 ms	1.10 ms
	v3	0.00 ms	0.04 ms	0.00 ms	v3	0.00 ms	0.00 ms	0.00 ms

Table 2: Quantification of interferences for v1, v2 and v3 probes. At the top, the probe is loaded by sourcing 100 one-off traceroutes. At the bottom, the load comes from incoming pings. Columns represent benchmarking measurements. On the left, we look at the impact of a load on the ping delay reported by the probe. On the right, pings are destined to the probe. With more powerful hardware, v3 probes are less sensitive to load than v1 and v2. *We used these pings to quantify the impact a load towards the probe produces on ping delay sourced on the probe (bottom-left).

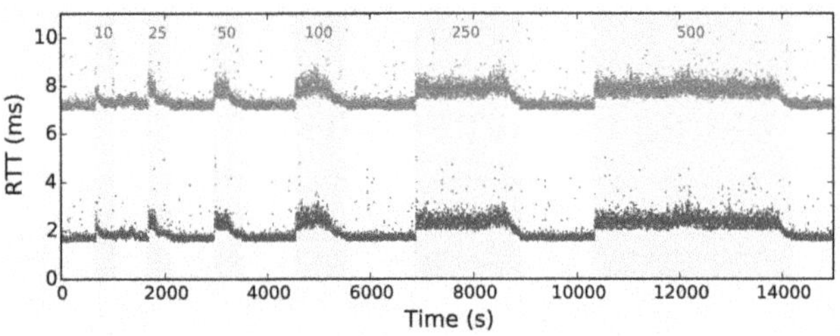

Figure 4: Delays measured *towards* a v2 probe systematically increase when concurrent one-off traceroutes are launched on the probe.

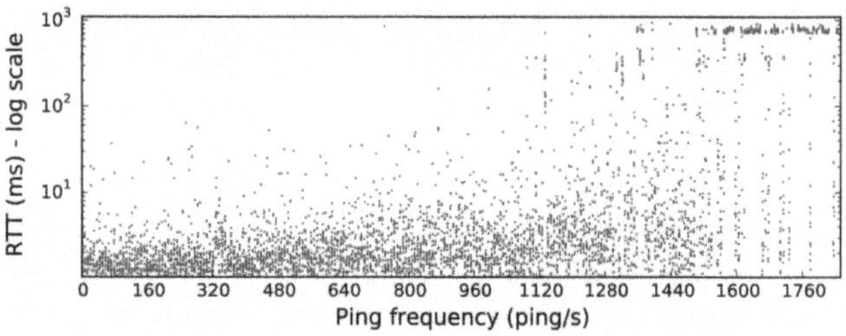

Figure 5: Delays measured *from* a v2 probe increase as the ping frequency targeting the probe increases.

prisingly, the number of one-off traceroutes does not change the magnitude of the impact but increases its duration: 10 one-off traceroutes impact as severely as 100 the concurrent ping measurements. As soon as the one-off traceroutes are done, RTTs go back to normal almost immediately.

Delays measured *towards* the probe increase when concurrent measurements are launched *on* it. We chose eight random Ring nodes plus the colocated Ring node and ping from them towards the Atlas probe with a frequency of 1 ping/s, summing up to a load of 9 ping/s. We then perform successively 10, 25, 50, 100, 250, and 500 one-off traceroutes from the Atlas probe.

Figure 4 shows the impact of the one-off traceroutes on the delay measured towards the Atlas probe. The blue points are the delays reported between the colocated Ring node and the Atlas probe while the red points are the delays reported between another Ring node and the Atlas probe. Again, gray indicates periods when one-off traceroutes are running.

The impact on pings targeting the probe is relatively lower (Table 2). When 100 one-off traceroutes are executed, the median of RTTs targeting a v2 Atlas probe increases by 0.5 ms. Despite the lower impact, we can easily see RTT shifts.

Delays measured *from* and *towards* a probe increase when it is used as a destination by concurrent measurements. We first launch pings from the Atlas probe towards its colocated Ring node with a frequency of 9 ping/min. We then use an increasing set of Ring nodes to target the probe with 800 bytes pings, each of them sending 16 ping/s (§3).

Figure 5 shows the impact on delay measured *from* the probe. Unlike with one-off traceroute measurements, the impact now increases with the number of pings directed towards the probe. When the frequency reaches 400 ping/s, the median delay reported by the probe increases by 0.22 ms, while the 95th percentile increases by 2.90 ms and the standard deviation by 3.90 ms. The probe becomes completely overloaded when the frequency reaches 1000 ping/s. This leads to very high delays (~1000 ms). Also, 10% of the pings are lost when the frequency becomes higher than 1280 ping/s. Here, the probe is the target of the load. Traffic is just sent to the probe, without involving the RIPE Atlas controller. We believe the inaccuracy increases progressively because the load per unit of time also increases. The controller cannot smooth the load by spreading it in time.

Figure 6 illustrates similar effects on the delays measured *towards* the probe. At the bottom of the figure, each box shows the inter-quartile range of RTTs between the colocated Ring node and the Atlas probe. The line in the box depicts the median value; the whiskers show the 1st and the 99th percentile, respectively. The top figure indicates the packet loss percentage. When reaching 1000 ping/s, the median RTT increases by 0.45 ms and the 95th percentile increases by 2.60 ms. As in Figure 5, when the frequency

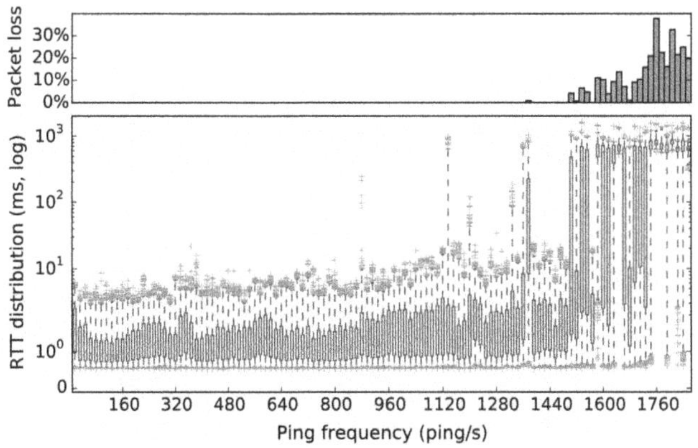

Figure 6: Delays measured *towards* a v2 probe increase as the pings frequency targeting this probe increases. Packet losses may appear if the ping frequency *towards* the probe becomes too high.

becomes even higher, the probe becomes completely overloaded. Reported delays skyrocket (~1000 ms) and some requests are lost.

Interference effects are compounded when combining source and destination load. So far, we have quantified separately the impact of using a probe as source or as destination. In reality, a probe may be used both as source and as destination at the same time. We could expect these interference effects to be additive, but our experiments show that *these effects are compounded.*

To quantify, we first start pings between an Atlas probe and its colocated Ring node (9 ping/min). We then start to flood the probe using the set of Ring nodes as described before. Finally, we start series of 25 one-off traceroutes. Figure 7 shows the results. The blue points are the measured delays between the probe and the colocated Ring node. The red vertical line indicates when we start to flood the probe with pings. The gray areas are the periods when one-off traceroutes are running. Before starting to flood the probe, we performed 25 one-off traceroutes in order to be able to compare the interference effects produced by these traceroutes with and without the ping flood. Each green point on the top indicates a traceroute success. The success rate of each one-off traceroute series is also mentioned.

When compounding source and destination load, delays measured from the probe increase even further. During the second series of one-off traceroutes, the standard deviation of the delay reported by the probe to the colocated Ring node is 30.8 ms and the 95th percentile is 23.9 ms. These values are far higher than the addition of the interference effects produced by a non-combined load on source and destination (Table 2). Success rate is also effected. 99% of the pings are lost during the last one-off traceroute series.

Key points. We observed significant interferences on delay measurements for v1 and v2 probes. These probes compose 28% percent of the platform. An important portion (34%) of the public experiments available result from experiments on v1 and v2 probes.

5. INCREASED ASYNCHRONY

We now study the impact of concurrent load on completion time. Atlas measurements are indeed scheduled over

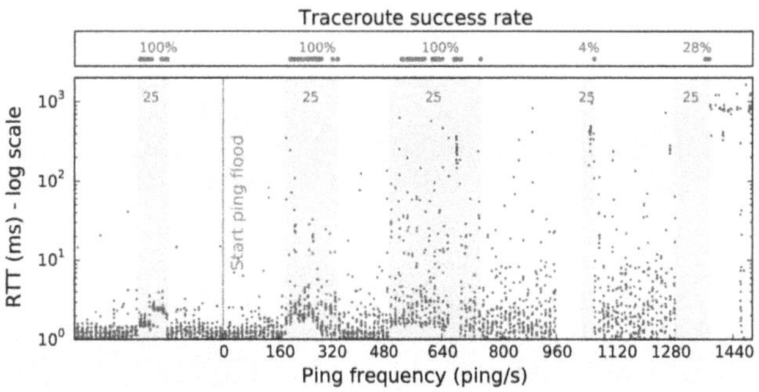

Figure 7: Increasing the source and destination load at the same time greatly increases the interference between measurements. One-off traceroutes take more time to execute, and worse, may fail. RTTs measured from the probe become higher.

time to limit the instantaneous load on a probe. When load increases, so does the completion time. We measure the time delta between when we request traceroute measurements and the time they finish.

Completion time significantly increases with the number of traceroutes. Figure 8 shows that the completion time may be 6.7 minutes (resp. 4.5 minutes) when requesting 50 one-off traceroutes on a v2 (resp. v3) probe. It takes up to 41 minutes with 500 one-off traceroutes on a v3 probes. All probe versions, including v3, are subject to a significant increase in completion time. Further experiments have shown completion times greater than one hour, even for v3 probes.

Completion time increases with the load *towards* the probe. In Figure 7, while the completion time for the first 25 one-off traceroutes takes up to 6.2 minutes, it takes up to 11.3 minutes for the second series of one-off traceroutes and up to 20.2 minutes for the third series. Sending 500 ping/s to a probe may then multiply the one-off traceroutes completion time by more than 3. When the ping frequency becomes too high, most of the traceroutes fail.

Key points Under load, requested measurements may be delayed, rendering the platform unsuitable to synchronized measurements. One could not ensure that pings or traceroutes start simultaneously on multiple probes. This is especially a problem when one wants to measure the effect of a single event from multiple vantage points, or an exogenous event. *This problem applies to all probe hardware—including the most powerful v3.*

6. DISCUSSIONS

We now describe the impact for researchers working with the platform (§6.1) as well as two solutions on how to mitigate interference in practice (§6.2).

6.1 Impact for researchers

On previous works. As described earlier, many research papers have used RIPE Atlas. Some of them relied on delay-based measurements [3, 4, 18, 28, 6, 16] which can be impacted by interferences. For instance, Rimondini *et al.* [3] used PELT [29], a changepoint detection algorithm, to detect shifts in RTTs and correlate them with routing changes. We mimicked such experiments on the RTTs of Figures 3 and 4 and detected a changepoint each time a one-off tracer-

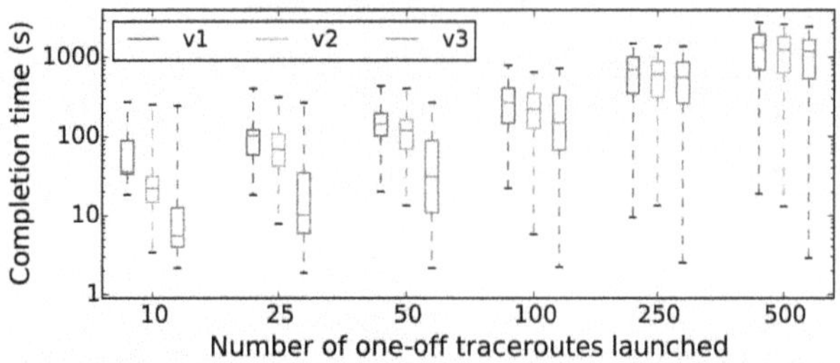

Figure 8: One-off traceroutes completion time is also impacted by concurrent measurements, independent of the hardware used. Results can be delayed by more than half an hour—making it impossible to perform synchronized experiments.

oute series starts and stops. Cicalese *et al.* [18] used the minimum value of ten successive RTTs to enumerate and geolocate IP-level anycast replicas. As a 1ms difference in latency measurements corresponds to a 100 km radius in geodesic distance, such studies may also be polluted by interference effects. An operator can use Atlas probes to measure the performance of her network. In this case, interference effects highlighted on the Figure 5 and 6 could wrongly trigger congestion alarms. Based on our results, any delay-based measurement obtained from v1 and v2 probes should be avoided if a precision below 15 ms is required.

On publicly available data. RIPE Atlas makes publicly available all the results collected with the platform since its inception in 2010 [30]. Researchers using these data should consider the impact of interferences. Especially for data collected before 2013—prior to v3 probes. We suggest researchers to be very careful when using publicly available delay measurements.

6.2 Solutions

Provide feedback to users with a measurement confidence index. A fundamental problem with Atlas is that the user has no visibility on the concurrent load of the platform. For that, we argue that RIPE can return a "confidence index" along with each result. The index would be function of the platform concurrent load. High (resp. low) load would lead to low (resp. high) confidence. Obviously, computing this metric should be done based on passive measurements to not stress the platform even more. We are currently working on calibrating such a metric using our measurements.

Enforce synchronization. While real-time is not a reasonable objective on shared platforms, more precise scheduling is achievable by maintaining a lower load on the probes and delaying upcoming measurements in favor of already scheduled events. Upon a measurement request, the user could then be informed of the exact timing of her experiment. Such an approach is however not possible if users do not all have the same privileges and some experiments can be preempted.

7. RELATED WORK

Other researchers have observed measurement interference and its impact on RTT. As an example, the effects virtualization can produce on measured delays have already been pointed out [31, 32]. As a number of large-scale platforms use VMs [33, 34, 25], tools such as [35] for PlanetLab, provide users with information about the state of these platforms and their nodes. In contrast, RIPE Atlas does not use virtualization and relies on a scheduler to share resources among users.

Gangam *et al.* [36] introduced heuristics to schedule a set of measurements between a set of nodes in order to avoid interference effects. However, this does not work when external measurements use Atlas probes as destinations.

Sanchez [37] *et al.* proposed a technique to coordinate experiments of a large-scale measurements platform in order to avoid undesired load on a network or a device. This solution is based on contracts, that give their holder specified rights over a set of resources for a limited period of time. In contrast, RIPE Atlas applies static rate limits for users and measurements. An user cannot run more than 100 simultaneous measurements, and the ping frequency is limited to one ping per minute.

Dasu [38] is a software-based measurement platform hosted by voluntary nodes located at the edge of the network. To enable finer-grained synchronization between a set of measurements (on the order of milliseconds), Dasu adopts a remote triggering execution model. In contrast, the one-off measurements provided by RIPE Atlas are launched as soon as possible (best-effort).

In [23], Bajpai *et al.* showed that RTTs from v1 and v2 probes to the first hop router are consistently higher than for v3 probes. They do not however study the relation between the measured delays and the load of the probes.

Mok *et al.* [39] proposed a technique to reduce packet sending time on low-end devices such as Atlas probes. This technique may be useful to counteract some of the interference effects we expose in this paper.

8. CONCLUSION

We presented the first measurement study of user-induced interferences on the RIPE Atlas platform. We found that measurements do interfere with each other. Delays reported from the probe increase and vary more when they compete with concurrent measurements. Measurement campaigns can further be arbitrary delayed, making it hard to perform simultaneous experiments from multiple probes.

Our findings also bring up new, non-trivial research questions: how can we design measurement platforms that provide more isolation between users, while still being efficient (*i.e.*, not requiring a global lock). We plan to explore this direction in the future.

9. ACKNOWLEDGMENTS

We wish to thank both the RIPE Atlas and the NLNOG RING support teams for accommodating our measurements and promptly replying to our questions.

10. REFERENCES

[1] RIPE NCC. RIPE Atlas. [Online]. Available: https://atlas.ripe.net

[2] S. Roy and N. Feamster, "Characterizing correlated latency anomalies in broadband access networks," in *ACM SIGCOMM 2013 (Poster Session)*, 2013.

[3] M. Rimondini, C. Squarcella, and G. Di Battista, "Towards an Automated Investigation of the Impact of BGP Routing Changes on Network Delay Variations," in *PAM*, 2014.

[4] G. Da Lozzo, G. Di Battista, and C. Squarcella, "Visual discovery of the correlation between bgp routing and round-trip delay active measurements," *Computing*, vol. 96, no. 1, pp. 67–77, 2014.

[5] A. Faggiani, E. Gregori, A. Improta, L. Lenzini, V. Luconi, and L. Sani, "A study on traceroute potentiality in revealing the internet as-level topology," in *IFIP Networking 2014*, 2014.

[6] A RIPE Atlas View of Internet Meddling in Turkey . [Online]. Available: https://labs.ripe.net/Members/emileaben/a-ripe-atlas-view-of-internet-meddling-in-turkey

[7] T. Yakimov, "Detecting routing anomalies with ripe atlas," april 2014.

[8] C. Anderson, P. Winter, and Roya, "Global network interference detection over the ripe atlas network," in *4th USENIX Workshop on Free and Open Communications on the Internet*, August 2014.

[9] [Online]. Available: https://github.com/nsg-ethz/atlas_interference

[10] RIPE Atlas - User-Defined Measurements. [Online]. Available: https://atlas.ripe.net/docs/udm/

[11] N. Wells, "Busybox: A swiss army knife for linux," *Linux J.*, vol. 2000, no. 78es, Oct. 2000.

[12] libevent - an event notification library. [Online]. Available: http://libevent.org/

[13] Releasing RIPE Atlas Measurements Source Code . [Online]. Available: https://labs.ripe.net/Members/philip_homburg/ripe-atlas-measurements-source-code

[14] Community Information, contributions, and hosts that stand out. [Online]. Available: https://atlas.ripe.net/get-involved/community/

[15] G. Machado, C. Tsiaras, and B. Stiller, "Schengen Routing: A Compliance Analysis," in *AIMS*, 2015.

[16] R. Fanou, F. Pierre, and E. Aben, "On the Diversity of Interdomain Routing in Africa," in *PAM*, 2015.

[17] P. Fiadino, M. Schiavone, and P. Casas, "Vivisecting whatsapp in cellular networks: Servers, flows, and quality of experience," in *TMA*, 2015.

[18] D. Cicalese, D. Joumblatt, D. Rossi, M.-O. Buob, J. Auge, and T. Friedman, "A fistful of pings: Accurate and lightweight anycast enumeration and geolocation," in *IEEE INFOCOM*, 04/2015 2015.

[19] Measuring Countries and IXPs with RIPE Atlas. [Online]. Available: https://labs.ripe.net/Members/emileaben/measuring-ixps-with-ripe-atlas

[20] How does the MENOG Region Measure up? [Online]. Available: https://labs.ripe.net/Members/mirjam/how-does-the-menog-region-measure-up

[21] Measuring Countries and IXPs in the SEE Region. [Online]. Available: https://labs.ripe.net/Members/emileaben/measuring-countries-and-ixps-in-the-see-region

[22] Percentage of connected probes per country. [Online]. Available: https://atlas.ripe.net/results/maps/density/

[23] V. Bajpai, S. J. Eravuchira, and J. Schönwälder, "Lessons learned from using the ripe atlas platform for measurement research," *SIGCOMM Comput. Commun. Rev.*, vol. 45, no. 3, pp. 35–42, Jul. 2015.

[24] RIPE-Atlas-sbucket. [Online]. Available: https://github.com/cod3monk/RIPE-Atlas-sbucket

[25] NLNOG Ring. [Online]. Available: https://ring.nlnog.net

[26] Creating Measurements with the RIPE Atlas Restful API. [Online]. Available: https://atlas.ripe.net/docs/measurement-creation-api/

[27] M. J. Luckie, "Scamper: a scalable and extensible packet prober for active measurement of the internet," in *IMC*, 2010.

[28] RIPE Atlas - Superstorm Sandy. [Online]. Available: https://labs.ripe.net/Members/emileaben/ripe-atlas-superstorm-sandy

[29] R. Killick and I. A. Eckley, "changepoint: An r package for changepoint analysis," *Journal of Statistical Software*, vol. 58, no. 3, pp. ??–??, 6 2014.

[30] RIPE Atlas - Public measurements. [Online]. Available: https://atlas.ripe.net/measurements/#!public

[31] J. Whiteaker, F. Schneider, and R. Teixeira, "Explaining packet delays under virtualization," *SIGCOMM Comput. Commun. Rev.*, vol. 41, 2009.

[32] N. Spring, L. Peterson, A. Bavier, and V. Pai, "Using planetlab for network research: Myths, realities, and best practices," *SIGOPS Oper. Syst. Rev.*, 2006.

[33] Planetlab, "Planetlab: An open platform for developing, deploying and accessing planetary-scale services," http://planet-lab.org.

[34] M-Lab, "Measurement lab," http://www.measurementlab.net.

[35] K. Park and V. S. Pai, "Comon: A mostly-scalable monitoring system for planetlab," *SIGOPS Oper. Syst. Rev.*, vol. 40, no. 1, pp. 65–74, Jan. 2006.

[36] S. Gangam and S. Fahmy, "Mitigating interference in a network measurement service," ser. IWQoS '11, 2011.

[37] M. A. Sánchez, F. E. Bustamante, B. Krishnamurthy, and W. Willinger, "Experiment coordination for large-scale measurement platforms," in *ACM SIGCOMM Workshop on C2B(I)D*, 2015.

[38] M. A. Sánchez, J. S. Otto, Z. S. Bischof, D. R. Choffnes, F. E. Bustamante, B. Krishnamurthy, and W. Willinger, "Dasu: Pushing experiments to the internet's edge," in *NSDI*, 2013.

[39] R. K. P. Mok, W. Li, and R. K. C. Chang, "Improving the packet send-time accuracy in embedded devices," in *PAM 2015*.

Examining How the Great Firewall Discovers Hidden Circumvention Servers

Roya Ensafi
Princeton University

David Fifield
UC Berkeley

Philipp Winter
Karlstad & Princeton University

Nick Feamster
Princeton University

Nicholas Weaver
UC Berkeley & ICSI

Vern Paxson
UC Berkeley & ICSI

ABSTRACT

Recently, the operators of the national censorship infrastructure of China began to employ "active probing" to detect and block the use of privacy tools. This probing works by passively monitoring the network for suspicious traffic, then actively probing the corresponding servers, and blocking any that are determined to run circumvention servers such as Tor.

We draw upon multiple forms of measurements, some spanning years, to illuminate the nature of this probing. We identify the different types of probing, develop fingerprinting techniques to infer the physical structure of the system, localize the sensors that trigger probing—showing that they differ from the "Great Firewall" infrastructure—and assess probing's efficacy in blocking different versions of Tor. We conclude with a discussion of the implications for designing circumvention servers that resist such probing mechanisms.

Categories and Subject Descriptors

C.2.0 [**General**]: Security and protection (e.g., firewalls); C.2.3 [**Network Operations**]: Network monitoring

General Terms

Measurement

Keywords

Active Probing, Deep Packet Inspection, Great Firewall of China, Censorship Circumvention, Tor

1. INTRODUCTION

Those in charge of the Chinese censorship apparatus spend considerable effort countering privacy tools. Among their most advanced techniques is what the Tor community terms "active probing": passively monitoring the network for suspicious traffic, actively probing the corresponding servers, and blocking those determined to run circumvention services such as Tor.

The phenomenon of active probing arose presumably in response to enhanced circumvention systems that better resist traditional forms of blocking. For example, instead of employing a protocol recognizable by deep packet inspection (DPI), some of these systems embed their traffic inside TLS streams. Barring any subtle "tells" in the circumvention system's communication, the censor cannot distinguish circumventing TLS from any other TLS, and thus cannot readily block the circumvention without incurring significant collateral damage. Active probing enables the censor to disambiguate the otherwise opaque traffic and once again obtain a measure of control over it.

Figure 1 illustrates the general scheme of active probing. The censor *acts like a user* and issues its own connections to a suspected circumvention server. If the server responds using a prohibited protocol, then the censor takes a blocking action, such as adding its IP address to a blacklist. If the circumvention server does not incorporate access control mechanisms or techniques to distinguish the censor's probes from normal user connections, the censor can reliably identify and block it.

The effectiveness of active probing is reflected in its diverse uses. As of September 2015, researchers have documented

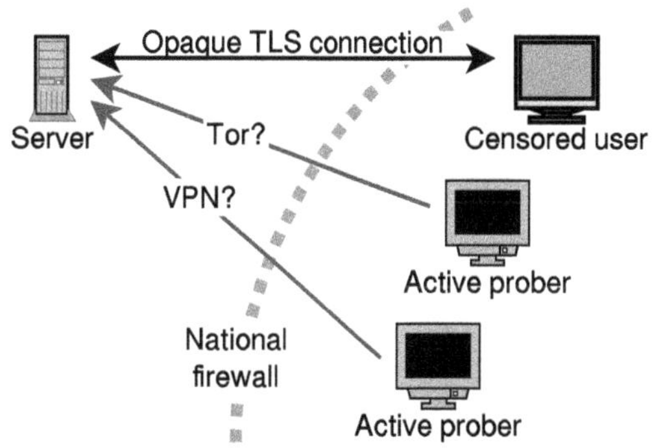

Figure 1: The firewall cannot determine, by mere inspection, whether the encrypted connection carries a prohibited circumvention protocol. Therefore it issues its own probes and observes how the server responds.

IMC'15, October 28–30, 2015, Tokyo, Japan.
Copyright is held by the owner/author(s). Publication rights licensed to ACM.
ACM 978-1-4503-3848-6/15/10 ...$15.00.
DOI: http://dx.doi.org/10.1145/2815675.2815690.

its use against Tor [32], SSH [20], and VPN protocols [21, 10], and here we document additional probing targets.

Through this work we aim to better understand the nature of active probing as conducted today against privacy tools and censorship circumvention systems. We seek to answer questions such as: What stimuli cause active probing? How long does it take until a server gets probed? What types of probes do we see, and from where do they originate? How effective is active probing? What does its operation reveal about ways to thwart it?

We consider only "reactive probing:" probing that is triggered by the observation of some stimulus. Censors could also conceivably employ "proactive probing" by scanning the Internet (on a particular port, say) without waiting for a stimulus, but we did not seek to study that. The only possible exception is in our examination of the logs of a server that began to receive active probes without our having instigated them—though the server's status as a Tor bridge may help explain that.

We draw upon a number of datasets from several vantage points, including some extensive longitudinal data, to examine these questions. Our work makes these contributions:

- We describe measurement infrastructure for studying active probing systems.
- We identify various probe types, including some previously undocumented, and chart their volume over time since their first appearance in our data in 2013. The vast majority originate from Chinese IP addresses.
- Using network protocol fingerprinting techniques, we infer the physical structure of the probing system.
- We localize the sensors that trigger active probes and show they are likely distinct from China's main censorship infrastructure, the "Great Firewall" (GFW).

We structure the rest of the paper as follows. Section 2 covers related work, followed by background in Section 3. Section 4 describes our datasets, and Section 5 delves into their analysis; Section 6 concludes.

2. RELATED WORK

Academia and civil society have spent significant efforts analyzing and circumventing the GFW, providing us with a comprehensive understanding of how it blocks IP addresses and TCP ports [7], DNS requests [1, 24], and HTTP requests [22, 3]; and the nature of its TCP processing [13].

McLachlan and Hopper [19] warned of the possibility of Tor bridge discovery by Internet scanning in 2009. The study of practical, in-the-wild "active probing" associated with Chinese censorship began in late 2011, when Nixon noticed suspicious entries in his SSH log files [20], including non-conformant payloads of seemingly random byte strings. Careful analysis revealed a pattern: these strange probes, which originated from IP addresses in China, were triggered by prior genuine SSH logins, by real users, from different Chinese IP addresses. In 2012, Wilde documented a similar phenomenon, this time targeting the Tor protocol [30]. Motivated by reports that China was blocking Tor bridges only minutes after their first use from within China, he investigated and observed the GFW performing active probing, triggered by observing a particular list of TLS cipher suites, the one offered by Tor clients. The probing took the form of TLS connections that attempted to establish Tor circuits. Wilde also observed "garbage" random binary probes like the ones seen by Nixon for SSH.

Later in 2012, Winter and Lindskog revisited Wilde's analysis using a server in Beijing [32]. They attracted probers over a period of 17 days and analyzed the probers' IP address distribution, how blocking was effected, and how long bridges remained blocked. They conjectured, but did not establish, that the GFW uses IP address hijacking to obtain its large pool of source IP addresses; that is, that the probing apparatus temporarily borrowed IP addresses that were otherwise allocated.

In 2013, reports suggested that the GFW had begun active probing against obfs2 [31], an obfuscation transport for Tor specifically designed to be difficult to detect by DPI. (A description of obfs2 appears in the next section.) The timing of these reports corresponds well with our own data.

A year later, Nobori and Shinjo discussed their experience with running a large VPN cluster for circumvention [21]. They likewise observed a pattern of connections from China shortly prior to blocking of a server. Other reports indicate that VPN services receive similar probing [10].

Our work aims to broaden the above perspectives, which have generally relied upon one-time measurements from single vantage points; and to illuminate the nature of active probing in greater depth, including its range of probing, response times, and system infrastructure.

3. BACKGROUND: CIRCUMVENTION PROTOCOLS

Active probing is a reaction against the increasing effectiveness of censorship circumvention. In this section we briefly describe Tor's place in the world of circumvention, and the obfuscated protocols ("transports") that cloak Tor traffic and make it more resistant to censorship. Three of these protocols—"vanilla" Tor, obfs2, and obfs3—underlie and motivate our experiments. More than that, though, these protocols tell a small part of the story of the global censorship arms race. In their technological advancement, one can see the correspondingly increasing sophistication of censors: starting from their ignorance of Tor, moving on to simple IP address-based blocking, then online detection of obfuscation, and now active probing.

3.1 Tor

Years ago, Tor found success in evading various types of censorship such as web site blocks. Censored users found they could treat the network as a simple proxy service with many access points (its anonymity properties being of secondary importance to these users). Despite this success, however, the unadorned "vanilla" Tor protocol is not particularly suited to circumvention. Once censors began looking for it, they found it easy to block. Tor's biggest weakness in this respect is its global public list of relays. A censor can simply download this list and add each IP address to a blacklist—and censors began to do exactly that.

In response to the blocking of its relays, the operators of the Tor network began to reserve a portion of new relays as secret, non-public "bridges." Unlike ordinary relays, bridges are not easily enumerable [6]. They are carefully distributed through rate-limited out-of-band channels such as email and

HTTPS, and only a few at a time. The goal is to make it possible for anyone to learn a few bridge addresses, while making it hard for anyone to learn them all. By design, learning many bridge addresses requires an attacker to control resources such as an abundance of IP addresses and email addresses, or the ability to solve CAPTCHAs.

Even using secret bridge relays, Tor remains vulnerable to detection by deep packet inspection (DPI). Tor uses TLS in a fairly distinctive way that causes it to stand out from other TLS-based protocols. Censors can inspect traffic looking for the "tells" that distinguish Tor from other forms of TLS, and block connections as they arise. After early efforts to make their use of TLS less conspicuous [28], the developers of Tor settled on a more sustainable strategy: wrapping the entire Tor TLS stream in another layer—a "pluggable transport" [29]—that assumes responsibility for protocol-level obfuscation. This model allows for independent innovation in circumvention, while leaving the core of Tor free to focus on its main purpose of anonymity.

3.2 Obfs2

The first pluggable transport was *obfs2* [25], introduced in 2012. It was designed as a simple, expedient workaround for DPI of the kind that was then occurring in Iran [4]. It provides a lightweight obfuscation layer around Tor's TLS, re-encrypting the entire stream with a separate key in a way that leaves no plaintext or framing information that can serve as a basis for blocking—the entire communication looks like a uniformly random byte stream in both directions. The simple scheme of obfs2 had immediate success. The protocol has a serious deficiency, though: it is possible to detect it completely passively and with high confidence. Essentially, obfs2 works by first sending a key, then sending ciphertext encrypted with that key. Therefore a censor can simply read the first few bytes of every TCP connection, treat them as a key, and speculatively decrypt the first few bytes that follow. If the decryption is meaningful (matching a TLS handshake, for example), then obfs2 is detected and the censor can terminate the connection.

We turned the weakness of obfs2 to our advantage. Its easy passive detectability, coupled with its lack of use for anything but circumvention (and active probing), meant that we could mine past network logs looking for obfs2 connection attempts. Later we will describe how we used obfs2 probes to seed a list of past prober IP addresses.

3.3 Obfs3

The follow-up protocol *obfs3* [26] was designed to remedy this critical flaw in obfs2. Its key innovation is a Diffie-Hellman negotiation that determines the keys to be used to encrypt the rest of the stream. (The key exchange is not as trivial as it may seem, because it, like the rest of the protocol, must be indistinguishable from randomness.) This enhancement in obfs3 deprives the censor of the simple, passive, reliable distinguisher it had for obfs2. The censor must either intercede in the key exchange (using a man-in-the-middle attack to learn the secret encryption keys), or settle for heuristic detection of random-looking streams. While either of these options may be problematic to implement, heuristic detection becomes entirely workable when combined with active probing. An initial, inaccurate test can identify potential obfs3 connections; then an active probe confirms or denies the suspicion.

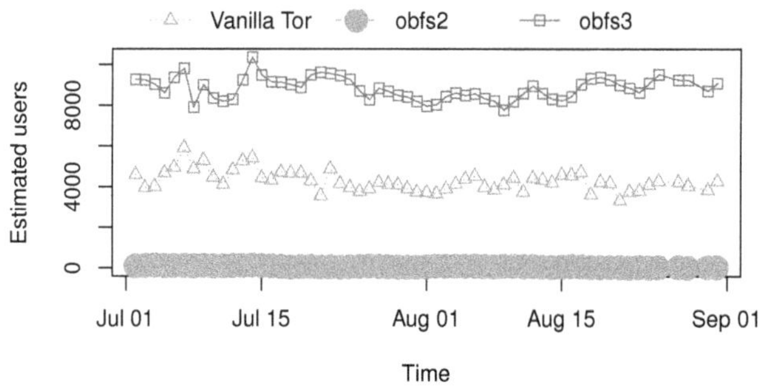

Figure 2: The estimated user numbers of the three transport protocols we study—vanilla Tor, obfs2, and obfs3—in July and August 2015. Obfs3 is the most popular protocol, followed by vanilla Tor. Obfs2 is superseded and sees practically no use any more.

3.4 Other Protocols

Though we limited the focus of our active experiments to Tor-related protocols, in the course of gathering data we incidentally found evidence of probing for other protocols, unrelated to Tor except that they also have to do with circumvention. The first of these probes, which we have labeled *AppSpot* in this paper, is an HTTPS-based check for domain fronting [8], a circumvention technique that disguises access to a proxy by making it appear to be access to an innocuous web page. In all of the examples we found, the probes checked whether a server is capable of fronting for Google App Engine at its domain `appspot.com`. The other probe we discovered we label *SoftEther*, because it resembles the client portion of the handshake of SoftEther VPN, the VPN software underlying the VPN Gate circumvention system [21]. Because we found these ancillary types of probe activity by accident, we make no claims to thoroughness in our coverage of them, and suggest that there may be other, yet unknown types of active probing to discover.

Our study focuses on vanilla Tor, obfs2, and obfs3, these being the commonly used protocols that remain vulnerable to active probing. There are other, newer protocols, including spiritual successors ScrambleSuit [33] and obfs4 [27], that have resistance to active probing as an explicit design criterion. Although they are gaining in popularity, they have not yet eclipsed obfs3. The key enhancement of these successor protocols is that they require the client, in its initial message, to prove knowledge of a server-specific secret (transmitted out of band). Put another way, mere knowledge of an IP address and port is not enough to confirm the existence of a circumvention server. As of this writing, obfs3 remains Tor's most-used transport, having around 8,000 simultaneous users on average, as shown in Figure 2. The obfs2 protocol is deprecated, no longer offered in the user interface, and its use is on the wane.

4. EXPERIMENTS

We base our results on several experiments, each resulting in a dataset that offers a distinct view into the behavior of active probing. The datasets cover different time ranges (see Table 1) and involve different setups. Table 2 summarizes the phenomena that each can illuminate, with each contributing at least one facet not covered by the others. We now describe each experiment in detail.

Dataset	Time span
Shadow	Dec 2014 – Feb 2015 (three months)
Sybil	Jan 29, 2015 – Jan 30, 2015 (20 hours)
Log	Jan 2010 – Aug 2015 (five years)
Counterprobe	Apr 22 – Apr 27 (six days)

Table 1: Timeline of our experiments. We created four datasets that span hours, days, months, and years.

	Shadow	Sybil	Log	Counter-probe
Probing rate		✓		
ISN patterns		✓		
TSval patterns	✓	✓	✓	
obfs2/3 blocking	✓		✓	
Tor bootstrapping	✓			
Probing types			✓	
Architecture			✓	✓
Topology				✓

Table 2: Observed phenomena and their visibility in our datasets.

4.1 Shadow Infrastructure

We built a "shadow infrastructure" of our own Tor clients and bridges for a controlled experiment of active probing over time. These clients and bridges were not actually used by any real users, but rather were dedicated exclusively to our own experimental purposes. The infrastructure tested vanilla Tor, obfs2, and obfs3 in equal measure, since active probing is known to target all three of these protocols. Figure 3 illustrates this setup.

We had six Tor clients within China: three in China Unicom, a large country-wide ISP; and three in CERNET, the Chinese Research and Education Network. (We chose CERNET because previous work suggested that censorship of CERNET might differ from the rest of China [7].) Outside of China, we ran six Tor bridges in Amazon's EC2 cloud. Two of the bridges ran vanilla Tor, two ran obfs2, and two ran obfs3. We assigned each of our six clients in China to a unique EC2 machine; the clients never contacted any bridge other than their own assigned one. Initially, all clients attempted to connect to their assigned bridge every 15 minutes. After one month, we changed this to five minutes after preliminary analysis showed that finer granularity in timing might be useful.

We also created a control group consisting of nine bridges (six in Amazon EC2, three in a US university) and a single client outside of China. We never connected to any of the control bridges from one of the clients within China; by comparing the traffic received by our "active" and control bridges, we can isolate general background scanning from active probing by the GFW. The three control bridges not hosted on EC2 allow us to determine whether the GFW treats EC2-hosted servers differently from others. The control client outside of China connects to all of the bridges. If our control client could not establish a Tor connection to one of the "active" bridges, we discarded the measurement we did from China for that bridge.

We took various steps to prevent our bridges from being discovered by any means other than active probing. We configured all of them to be *private bridges*, which means that

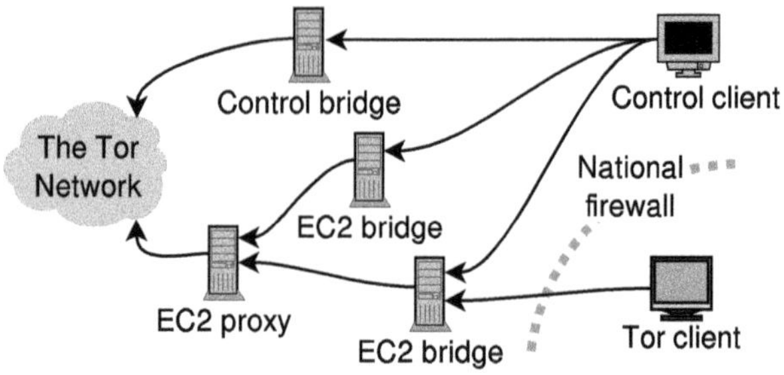

Figure 3: Experimental setup for the "Shadow" dataset.

they did not advertise themselves publicly, neither to the public Tor directory, nor to its database of secret bridges. As a result, no genuine Tor user should attempt to connect to one of our bridges. The bridges listened on random ports in the ephemeral range, to reduce the chance of their discovery by blind Internet scanning. Finally, we used another EC2 machine to proxy the communication between our Tor bridges and the first public Tor relay in a circuit. This extra proxy hop is to prevent another potential bridge-discovery attack, wherein a malicious Tor relay makes a list of all the IP addresses that connect to it (cf. [14, §III.D]).

4.2 Sybil Infrastructure

To obtain broader insight into the extent of the censor's active probing infrastructure, we designed another experiment to attract[1] many active probers in a short period of time.

We did so by constructing a "Sybil infrastructure," so named because it seemingly consisted of hundreds of distinct Tor servers. We used a virtual private server (VPS) in France and one in China. We ran a vanilla Tor bridge on the VPS in France and redirected the port range 30000–30600 to our Tor port using firewall port redirection. The actual Tor server ran on a separate port in the ephemeral range.

Then, from our VPS in China, we established Tor connections to every port in the port range in ascending order. This took approximately two hours, because we waited several seconds in between connection attempts. Since the GFW blocks by IP:port tuple, not just IP address [32], the GFW interpreted every single port in the range as a distinct Tor bridge and probed them separately. This experiment resulted in 622 active probing connections (and significantly more TCP connections, as we will discuss later) to the VPS in France.

4.3 Server Log Analysis

This dataset comes from the application logs of a server operated by one of the authors, some stretching back to January 2010. The server runs various common network services, including the three we use in the analysis: HTTP, HTTPS, and SSH. In addition to common networking ports, the server has hosted a Tor bridge since January 2011, an ordinary vanilla bridge without pluggable transports. By mining the application logs, we found that the server has been receiving active probes from China for over 2.5 years. An important difference in the Log experiment compared

[1]Our earlier analysis confirmed that simply establishing an initial TLS handshake with a server suffices to attract a prober.

to the others is that it is not the result of artificial activity to induce probing. Our server received its first probes in January 2013, slightly earlier than the first public reports of obfs2 probing [31]. On average, it has received dozens of probes every day since active probing began—though there are long stretches during which it received few probes.

This dataset provides an invaluable longitudinal perspective, though with the significant limitation that application logs do not record as much forensic information as we would like: they omit source ports and other transport-layer information, and usually truncate probe payloads (see below).

Data Types and Ranges.

The HTTP and HTTPS log go back to January 2010, before the earliest reports of active probing of any kind. The SSH log dates only to September 2014; probing of that port was already in effect at the beginning of the log. While application logs do not contain as much information as would, say, packet captures, they suffice in many cases to identify the type of probe and the prober's IP address. The HTTPS log is even superior to a packet capture in one respect: for TLS probes it contains the decrypted application data, which would not be accessible from a packet capture.

Along with the application logs, the system has full packet captures for ports 23, 80, and 443, between December 2014 and May 2015. The packet captures enable us to perform more detailed analysis on the network- and transport-layer features of probes. We opened port 23 (Telnet) specially during this period, and used it to host a multi-protocol honeypot server capable of responding to probes of various types (TLS, obfs2, and obfs3), and recording the protocol layers inside them. (To avoid inadvertently capturing potentially sensitive activity, we do not perform any packet capture or additional logging on the SSH and Tor ports.)

The server from which we gathered the Log data is a working server that performs a number of functions apart from simply absorbing active probes. In order to distinguish active probes from operational traffic, we used a form of conservative snowball sampling. We started by extracting incontrovertible probes; namely, obfs2 probes and non-protocol-conforming payloads that we could not otherwise explain, for example random binary garbage written to the HTTP port. (It is easy to detect obfs2, with negligible false positives, because of the protocol weakness described in Section 3.2. It requires only the first 20 bytes sent by the client.) We then made a list of the IP addresses that had sent those probes, and examined all other traffic they had sent at any point in time. Despite that the GFW's active probing rarely reuses source IP addresses, we occasionally found a new probe type. When we did, we added it to our list of known probes and repeated the process. In this way, we slowly expanded our universe of known active prober IP addresses, all the while checking manually to make sure we were not sweeping up non-probing traffic.

This conservative approach enabled us to find a variety of probing behaviors with few false positives, at the potential cost of missing some novel probes from IP addresses that did not also send a recognized probe type. This technique led to our discovery of the "AppSpot" and "SoftEther" probes, even though we seeded the process only with Tor-related probes. Except for a handful of manually excluded hosts (e.g., systems under our control), we did not consider the source IP address in deciding whether a log entry indicated a probe. Specifically, we did not employ IP geolocation to find probes emanating from China, though Figure 7 shows that the probes we found did in fact overwhelmingly come from China.

We found a small amount of non-probing traffic (e.g., ordinary HTTP requests for actual pages) from IP addresses that also sent a probes at some other time. The shortest separation between probe and non-probe was three weeks, and the longest was two years.

Limitations.

Our application logs have several limitations. The HTTP and HTTPS (Apache) log truncates at the first '\0', '\n', or '\r\n' sequence, and omits a leading '\n' (we account for this possibility when classifying probes). The SSH (OpenSSH) log truncates at the first '\0', '\r', or '\n', and has a hard limit of 100 bytes.

A significant effect of these limitations is that application logs will not record any Tor probes as such, not even when they are received by the HTTPS port, which removes the outer TLS layer. The first message that a Tor client sends after the TLS handshake is a `VERSIONS` cell, which happens to start with a '\0' byte, causing the payload to be truncated to a length of zero in the server log.

4.4 Counterprobing

Active probers seem to share their IP address pools with normal Internet users. To investigate this, we scanned some probers repeatedly using network diagnostic tools such as ping, traceroute, and Nmap. We started the first scan the moment a prober showed up. From then on, we repeated the scan hourly for 24 hours. Interestingly, the very first scan never yielded anything. The probers were unresponsive to all packets. Later scans, however, painted a different picture. In many cases, our port scans identified the IP addresses that were used for active probing just hours before as various versions of Windows and Linux. We found open ports used for file sharing, FTP, HTTP, RPC, and many other services typical for home users. This indicates that in many cases active probers share their address pools with Internet users. We were able to run a small number of counterprobes from a host within China, and the results matched those of simultaneous counterprobes from outside the country: prober IP addresses were initially unresponsive, but occasionally became responsive as disparate and seemingly ordinary Internet hosts.

With the previous experiments in hand, we then set out to develop tests to probe the architecture of the passive monitor that triggers the probes, and the active component responsible for sending them. A unidirectional three-packet sequence—SYN, ACK, and a Tor TLS client handshake packet—sent from a Chinese host suffices to trigger an active probe.

We built several tests and ran them from a Unicom host and a CERNET host to our EC2 infrastructure. These tests included a traceroute for the monitor; a fragmentation test that splits the request across multiple TCP packets to expose whether the passive detection maintains per-flow state; a SYN-ACK traceroute that uses TTL-limited packets to respond to probe requests; and a "milker" that repeatedly sends triggering requests to a Tor bridge.

Client	Succeeded	Failed	Total
CERNET vanilla	639 (12%)	4,490 (88%)	5,129
Unicom vanilla	90 (2%)	3,864 (98%)	3,954
CERNET obfs2	4,584 (98%)	81 (2%)	4,665
Unicom obfs2	4,153 (89%)	515 (11%)	4,668
CERNET obfs3	5,015 (98%)	95 (2%)	5,110
Unicom obfs3	3,402 (86%)	552 (14%)	3,954

Table 3: Connection success statistics for our clients in China. While vanilla Tor is mostly unreachable, obfuscation protocols are mostly reachable.

5. ANALYSIS

In this section, we study the following questions:

- Is active probing successful at discovering Tor bridges? (§ 5.1)
- What is the delay between a connection attempt to a Tor bridge and subsequent active probing of the bridge? (§ 5.2)
- Where in the network are the probes coming from? (§ 5.3)
- What types of probers do we see? (§ 5.4)
- Do active probers have "fingerprints" that distinguish them from normal clients? (§ 5.5)
- What is the underlying architecture of the probing system? (§ 5.6)

5.1 Effectiveness of Active Probing

To determine whether China's active probing infrastructure is effectively discovering and blocking Tor bridges, we analyzed the log files of our Tor clients inside China to see which connection attempts were successful in connecting to their assigned bridge. We consider a connection unblocked if the TCP handshake succeeded, because previous work showed that the Chinese censors block Tor bridges by dropping SYN-ACK segments [32]; if a bridge is blocked, it will be blocked at the TCP layer. We did this for each of the protocols supported by our clients and bridges: "vanilla" Tor, and the obfs2 and obfs3 obfuscation protocols.

Table 3 shows the results of this experiment. Our results show that obfs2 and obfs3 were almost always reachable for our clients both in CERNET and Unicom. This result is surprising because the Great Firewall has the ability to probe for obfs2 and obfs3 (Section 4.3). Vanilla Tor, on the other hand, is almost completely blocked. Figure 4 illustrates our attempts to connect to Tor bridges using vanilla Tor clients over time. We find that although Tor is mostly blocked, Tor clients succeed in connecting *roughly every 25 hours*. We believe that this reflects an implementation artifact of the GFW (e.g., many commercial firewalls "fail open" when their access control lists are being updated).

5.2 Delay Between Connection and Probing

We investigate how long it takes the Chinese censors to probe a Tor bridge after we initiate a connection to it. In 2011, Wilde observed that active probing occurred in 15-minute intervals [30], suggesting that the censors maintained a "probing queue" that was processed every 15 minutes. The

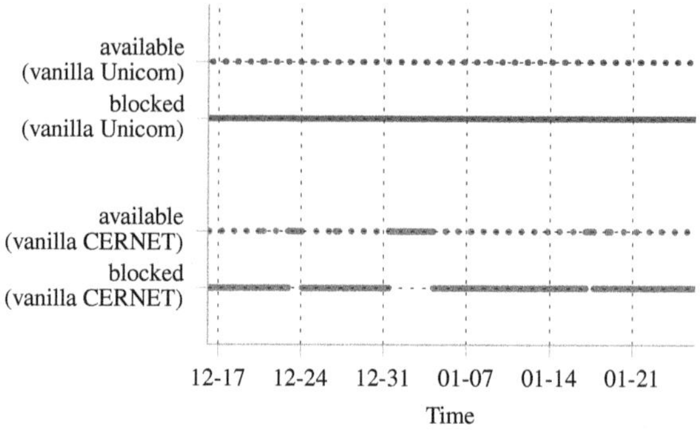

Figure 4: Successful Tor connections of our vanilla Tor clients in China over time. Every dot represents one connection attempt.

Sybil experiment helps us determine whether this is still the case. We calculated the time between when we established a connection to our Sybil node in France and when we observed the Chinese censors' subsequent probing connections. Figure 5 illustrates the results of this experiment. It shows the time difference in seconds (Y-axis) for every port (X-axis) on our decoy bridge. There are two interesting aspects. First, 56% of all probing connections arrived after less than one second (median 552 ms). We conclude that the Chinese censors have abandoned a 15-minute queue and now operate in real time. Second, there are several curious delay spikes where the Chinese censors took more than one minute to probe our bridge. We removed four outliers that had a probing delay above 800 seconds. Interestingly, all spikes decreased linearly until they reached the default of real-time probing.

Figure 6 shows a superset of the same data, but with the bridge port on the Y-axis and the absolute time on the X-axis. The line to the left consists of our decoy connections (red circles), which were quickly followed by probing connections (black crosses), which is basically the data shown in Figure 5. What Figure 5 did not show is the line to the right, a secondary "swarm" of probing connections. We captured these connections approximately 12 hours after our initial decoy connections (at which point our bridge was no longer running). The probers tried to connect several times, without success. Presumably, the Chinese censors were reconnecting to all bridges in order to verify whether they were still online.

5.3 Origin of the Probers

In total, we collected 16,083 unique prober IP addresses. There are 158 IP addresses in the Shadow dataset; 1,182 in the Sybil; and 14,912 in the Log. 111 of the addresses appear in two of the three datasets, and just one—202.108.181.70—appears in all three.

Prober IP addresses are rarely reused. Consider just the Log experiment: it recorded 16,464 probes carrying 15,249 distinct payloads; these probes were sent by 14,163 distinct IP addresses. 95% of addresses appear only once; another 4% appear twice. This lack of IP address reuse precludes simple blacklisting as a counter to active probing: a blacklisted prober IP is unlikely to be seen again. There is one clear outlier among probers, the aforementioned

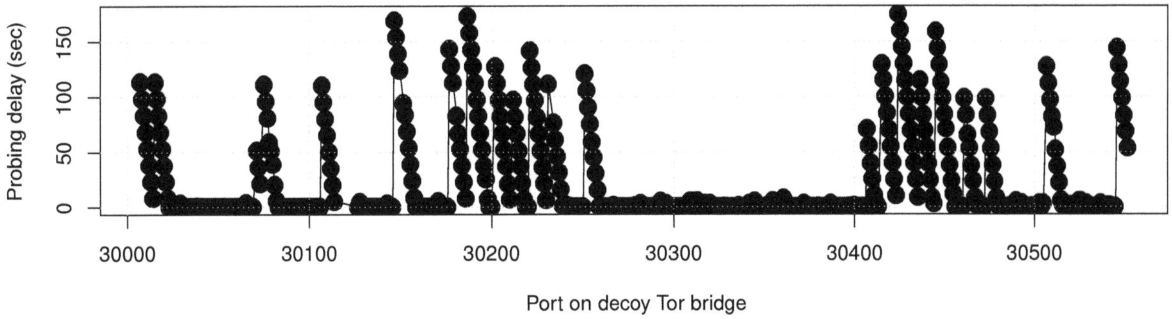

Figure 5: The time difference between decoy connections through our Sybil node and probing connections for every port on our Tor decoy bridge; the censors probe the ports on this bridge in rapidly ascending order. While the censors probed most ports immediately, some port ranges were only scanned significantly later.

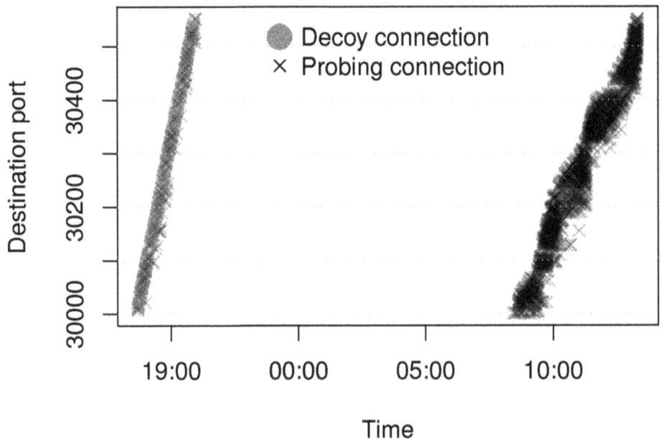

Figure 6: The arrival rate of probing connections. Decoy connections through our Sybil node are immediately followed by probing connections from the Chinese censors (the red circles and first set of black crosses are nearly on top of one another). After approximately 12 hours, the Chinese censors probed the same port range again.

Count	SOA
7,379	ns1.apnic.net
2,013	*none*
501–1,000	ns.jlccptt.net.cn, ns.zjnbptt.net.cn
201–500	ns.sdjnptt.net.cn, ns3.tpt.net.cn, soa, ns.sxtyptt.net.cn, ns.hbwhptt.net.cn, ns.bta.net.cn, ns.hazzptt.net.cn, hzdns.zjnetcom.com, dns.fz.fj.cn, nmdns.hh.nm.cn
101–200	ns.timeson.com.cn, dnssvr1.169ol.com, HNGTDNS2.hunan.unicom.com, HNGTDNS1.hunan.unicom.com, nmc1.ptt.js.cn, NS2.NET.EDU.CN, ns.dcb.ln.cn, ns1.jscnc.net, ns.yn.cninfo.net, ns1.ah.cnuninet.net, localhost.localdomain
1–100	*53 others*

Table 4: DNS Start of Authority of prober IP addresses.

202.108.181.70, which appears 248 times in the Log dataset. This special IP address has previously been associated with the GFW's active probing by Winter and Lindskog [32] and Majkowski [16]. We have observed it to send the obfs2, obfs3, and TLS probe types. It lies in AS4837, along with many other probers. No other prober IP address is in its /16 network.

Various measurements place the probing IP addresses almost entirely within China. Figure 7 shows the distribution of autonomous systems of prober IP addresses. Nearly every probe is from a Chinese AS. Table 4 shows the DNS Start of Authority (SOA) of the prober IP addresses. The most common SOA is ns1.apnic.net (Asia Pacific Network Information Centre, the regional Internet registry for the Asia Pacific region). The next most common SOAs are .cn domains and Chinese ISPs.

5.4 Probe Types

We categorized the probes we received into probe types. We discovered five distinct probe types across all four of our experiments, plus one "TLS" pseudo-type, as we describe below. Although the probes differ in important ways, they have in common the targeting of circumvention protocols. Section 5.5 describes how seemingly independent probes share low-level features (suggesting that they may originate from shared physical infrastructure), and highlights some of the features that may be useful for distinguishing active probers from genuine clients.

TLS.

The "TLS" probe type is a TLS client hello, one whose application payload we did observe, or one that did not match any more specific probe type. This was the case, for example, in the Log experiment when a TLS probe arrived at a plaintext port: the application log records the beginning of the TLS header but nothing else. "TLS" probes could have been one of our other known types—Tor, SoftEther, or Appspot—or something else entirely.

Tor.

The "Tor" probe type is a Tor `VERSIONS` cell received within a TLS connection. The probes we observed used a relatively obsolete "v2 handshake," superseded since 2011 [28]. This probe type is presumably aimed at the discovery of Tor bridges.

Obfs2.

The "obfs2" probe type is the client part of the handshake of obfs2. Recall that obfs2's handshake is intended to look

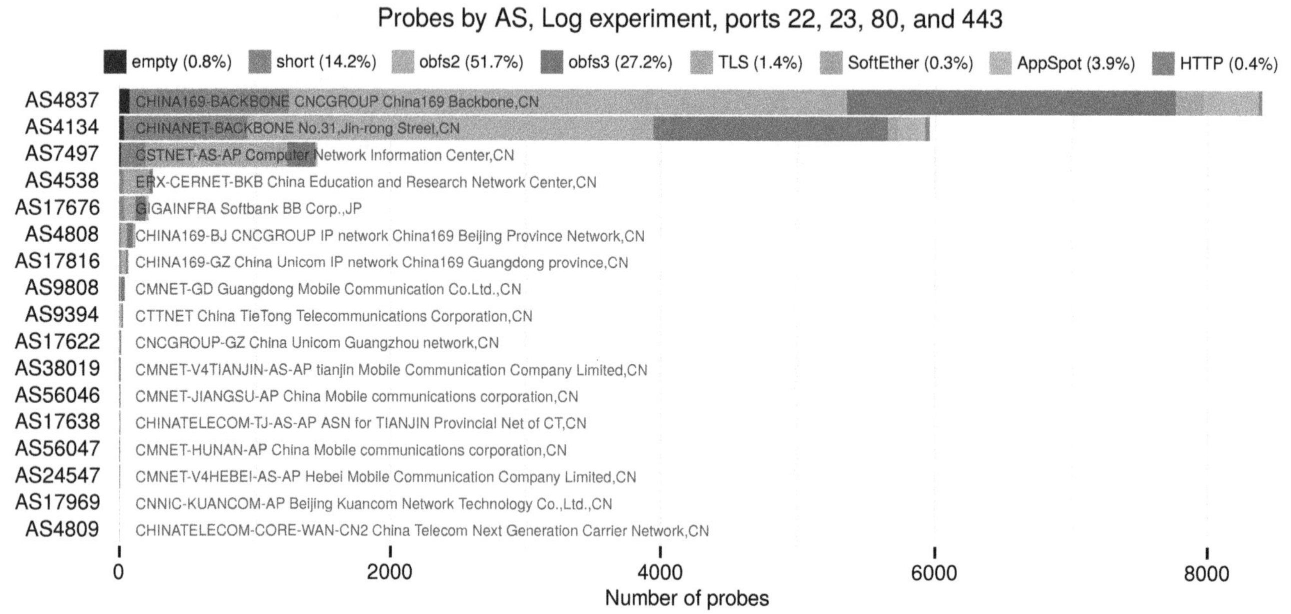

Figure 7: Three autonomous systems—AS4837, AS4134, and AS7497—account for 95% of probes observed in the Log experiment. We identified probing behavior by content, not by source address. Despite that, essentially all probes turn out to originate from China. All of the main ASes sent a variety of probe types; they do not appear to specialize. The most prolific prober, 202.108.181.70, lies in AS4837.

like a random bytestream; however its in-band key transmission makes it easy to identify, a great aid to our retrospective analysis. The first 20 bytes of a connection suffice to identify obfs2 with a negligible error rate.

Obfs3.

The "obfs3" probe type is an obfs3 client handshake message. By design, obfs3 is resistant to passive detection, which poses problems for our retroactive analysis. Though we have many samples of probes whose properties are consistent with obfs3—that is, they appear random, of length between 192 and 8,386 bytes, and are not obfs2—it is not possible to say with certainty that they are obfs3 probes (and not, for example, some other random-looking protocol). To test our guess that the probes were probably obfs3, for a short period (Feb. 3–19, 2015) we enabled an obfs3 listener on the multi-protocol honeypot running on the server of the Log experiment. The listener would complete the server half of the obfs3 handshake, and then log everything received within the encrypted channel. By participating in the handshake, we found that the probes we would have suspected of being obfs3 were, in fact, obfs3. We have therefore labeled all probes bearing such as signature "obfs3," even though it is confirmed to be the case only in a small fraction of cases.

SoftEther.

The "SoftEther" probe type is an HTTPS POST request: "`POST /vpnsvc/connect.cgi HTTP/1.1`". It resembles the first part of the client handshake of SoftEther VPN, the software that powers the VPN Gate circumvention system [21]. We discovered this probe type because it appeared many times in our HTTPS log; and we were able to observe it in detail (including its POST body) when it arrived on port 23 during the time we were running the multi-protocol honeypot listener. We further conjecture that some of the "TLS" probes that arrived at port 80 were in fact SoftEther probes, because they share a TCP timestamp sequence with other SoftEther probes. We first observed SoftEther probes in Aug. 2014. This is five months after the first active probes seen by the creators of VPN Gate, shortly after the release of their software [21].

AppSpot.

The "AppSpot" probe type is an HTTPS GET request with a special `Host` header:

```
GET / HTTP/1.1
Host: webncsproxyXX.appspot.com
```

The '`XX`' is a number that varies across probes. The `Host` header reveals that this probe type is likely intended to discover servers that are capable of providing access to Google App Engine through domain fronting [8]. When a typical web server receives a request with an alien `Host` header such as this, it will respond with its default document, or an error message. But when a Google server receives the request, it will forward the request to the web application running at `webncsproxyXX.appspot.com`. Circumventors can and do run various proxies on App Engine using precisely this technique. These probes would be useful for eliminating any gaps left in the GFW's near-total block of Google services. We observed this probe type only on port 443. Though originating from the same pool of IP addresses as the other probe types, this one seems somewhat independent, in its TLS fingerprint, the rate of its TCP timestamp counter (Figure 11c), and the temporal patterns in its activity (Figure 8).

We crawled `webncsproxyXX.appspot.com` for values of `XX` between 1 and 100. Some of them were instances of GoAgent (a circumvention tool based on App Engine), while others are instances of a web-based proxy. This probe type exists in a few variations. For a time, they probes switched from requesting `/` to requesting `/twitter.com`, which would have caused the `webncsproxy` application to retrieve the Twitter home page. In July 2015, AppSpot probes began to arrive in pairs separated by a few seconds and originating from different IP addresses. The second probe in a pair had a different set of header fields; it also had a similar `Host: webncsproxyXX.appspot.com` header, though the value of 'XX' was generally different from that of the first probe.

Figure 8 shows the complete probe history of the HTTP and HTTPS ports in the Log dataset. It is apparent that obfs2 and obfs3 are temporally related, and that "short" probes of less than 20 bytes also follow the same temporal pattern. The volume of TLS and SoftEther probes is much less than that of the other probe types. AppSpot appears to follow its own independent pattern. There are conspicuous lulls in probing behavior: between Dec. 2013 and Aug. 2014; between Feb. and Mar. 2015; and after May 2015. We do not know why probing nearly ceased during these periods.

5.5 Fingerprinting Active Probers

We now seek out telltale fingerprints in active probing: clues that may help distinguish probers from genuine clients, as well as clues as to how the probing infrastructure is implemented. We proceed layer by layer, starting with the IP layer and moving up through several application layers. Our analysis shows that despite there being a large number of probing IP addresses, there are likely only *a small number of independent processes* controlling them. In particular, our analysis of TCP initial sequence numbers and timestamps shows that shared state exists between disparate probing IP addresses.

IP Layer.

In 2014, anonymous researchers inferred the structure of a DNS-poisoning censor node by analyzing side channels in the IP TTL and IP ID [1]. Figure 9 shows the TTL distribution of all SYN segments we received from probers in our Sybil experiment. Five TTL values account for the overwhelming majority of observed TTLs. We did not, however, find any discernible patterns in the distribution of the IP ID field.

TCP Layer.

The TCP header is rich with potentially fingerprintable fields, particularly initial sequence numbers (ISNs), source ports, timestamps, and options. Patterns across TCP connections initiated by different IP addresses indicate that all the traffic originates from only a few processes (two in the Shadow dataset, one in the Sybil dataset, and about a dozen in the Log dataset). We analyzed in detail the TCP headers of SYN segments received in the Sybil experiment and found that they are all very similar.

TCP options: With respect to TCP options, all SYN segments:

- Employ an MSS of either 1400 (88% of probes), or 1460 (12%).

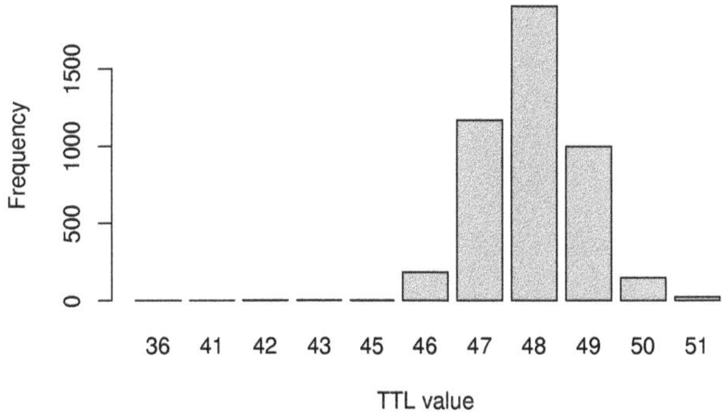

Figure 9: The TTL values in the SYN segments sent by probers. 99% of all observed TTL values are in between 45 and 51.

- Use window scaling of 7.
- Permit selective ACKs.
- Use the TCP timestamp option.
- Use the "no operation" option.

In particular, the OS identification tool p0f3 [35] yielded the following (truncated) signatures. The shaded part is identical in all three observed signatures.

`0:1460:mss*4,7:mss,sok,ts,nop,ws:df,id+:0` (1% of probes)
`0:1460:mss*20,7:mss,sok,ts,nop,ws:df,id+:0` (11% of probes)
`0:1400:mss*4,7:mss,sok,ts,nop,ws:df,id+:0` (88% of probes)

Initial sequence numbers: To protect TCP connections from off-path attackers, initial sequence numbers must not be guessable by an attacker. Modern operating systems use strong randomness to select ISNs. As a result, if all probing connections came from independent systems, we would expect no patterns in the distribution of ISNs.

We extracted the 32-bit ISNs of all SYN segments sent by probers. Figure 10 shows the ISN value on the Y-axis versus the time captured on the X-axis. To our surprise, the time series shows a striking, non-random pattern. Instead of uniformly distributed points over time, we see a "zigzag" pattern. ISNs increase until 2^{32} and then wrap around to 0. We conclude that the infrastructure derives ISNs from the current time.

The Sybil experiment induces a large amount of active probing over a short period of time—which was necessary for finding this ISN pattern. Our other experiments had too low a sample rate for the pattern to become apparent.

Source ports: We did not find any apparent patterns in the distribution of source ports. Interestingly, however, the source port distribution covers the entire 16-bit port range, including ports below 1024. This selection of ephemeral ports differs from that of standard operating systems, which typically only use port numbers above 1024.

TCP timestamps: We extracted the TSval from the TCP timestamp option [2] in all SYN segments sent by probers in the Shadow, Sybil, and Log experiments. Figure 11 illustrates the result. Though the SYN segments came from many different IP addresses, their timestamps form only a small number of distinct sequences (visible as straight lines in the graphs). We can characterize every line by its slope (i.e., its timestamp clock rate) and intercept (i.e., its system

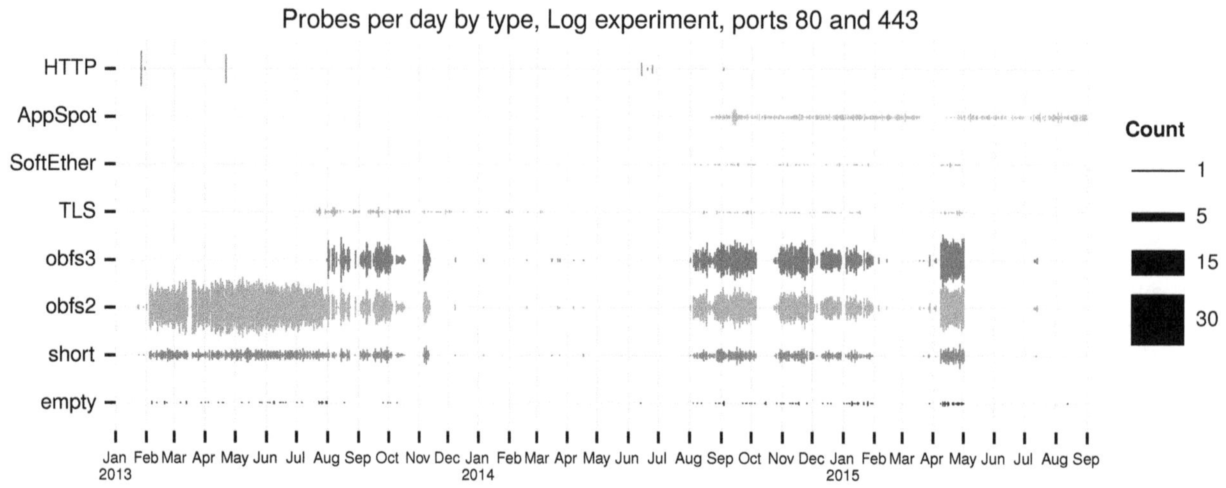

Figure 8: Probe types and volume of the HTTP and HTTPS ports in the Log experiment. The log file starts in Jan. 2011, but probes only began in 2013. The "HTTP," "AppSpot," and "SoftEther" rows are HTTPS requests to port 443; the others (including "TLS") are probes to port 80. The "short" probes are those that appear random, but are too short (< 20 bytes) for the obfs2 test. We believe that the "short" and "empty" probe types are actually truncated "obfs2" or "obfs3" probes. (Apache's log file truncates requests at the first '\0' or '\n' byte; a random byte string has about a 15% chance of being truncated in the first 20 bytes.) The "HTTP" row represents not probes, but ordinary requests for web pages on the server. They may be ordinary web users that happened to have an IP address that at another time sent some other type of probe; or they may be firewall operators web browsing from their probing infrastructure. (The requested pages were related to circumvention, which would be of interest to Chinese Internet users and firewall operators alike.) Two "HTTP" data points, at Aug. 2011, are not shown on the graph. They are from an IP address that would later send a "short" probe in May 2013.

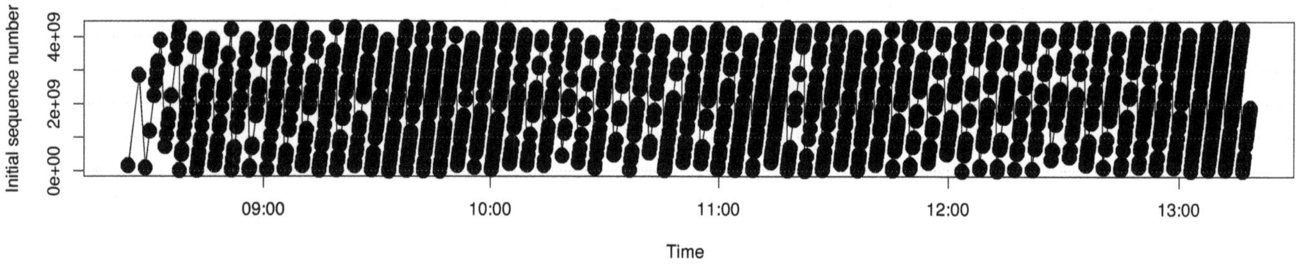

Figure 10: Initial sequence numbers of SYN segments sent by probers. Despite the probers coming from different IP addresses, a clear linear pattern manifests.

uptime). If all probes came from different physical systems, we would expect a larger number of distinct sequences.

SSL/TLS Layer.

The Tor protocol is encapsulated within TLS. The TLS protocol has many features that enable fingerprinting. We analyze the TLS "client hello," the first message sent by a client—or an active prober—after establishing a TCP connection. We used a TLS fingerprinting patch [15] for the passive network fingerprinting tool p0f [35]. We captured a total of 621 client hellos in the Sybil dataset. They all had the same TLS fingerprint: TLSv1.0, with a particular list of 11 cipher suites, support for the TLS session ticket extension, and support for compression.

To better understand how common this fingerprint is, we extracted the offered cipher suites of all Tor clients connecting to a Tor guard relay under our control.[2] Over a 24-hour period, we observed 236,101 client hellos, out of which only 67 used the cipher suites listed above.

Application Layer—Tor.

After the TLS handshake, a Tor client is supposed to send a `VERSIONS` cell [5, §4], in which it declares what versions of the Tor protocol it supports. After that there is further interaction before the establishment of a Tor circuit.

By inspecting the log files of a private Tor bridge, we found that probers send only the `VERSIONS` cell, and none of the other cells that would normally follow in order to establish a full Tor connection. After receiving a `VERSIONS` cell, our bridge, following the protocol specification, replied with a `NETINFO` cell, after which the probers abruptly closed the

[2]We extracted only the cipher suites and did not capture or store identifying information such as IP addresses.

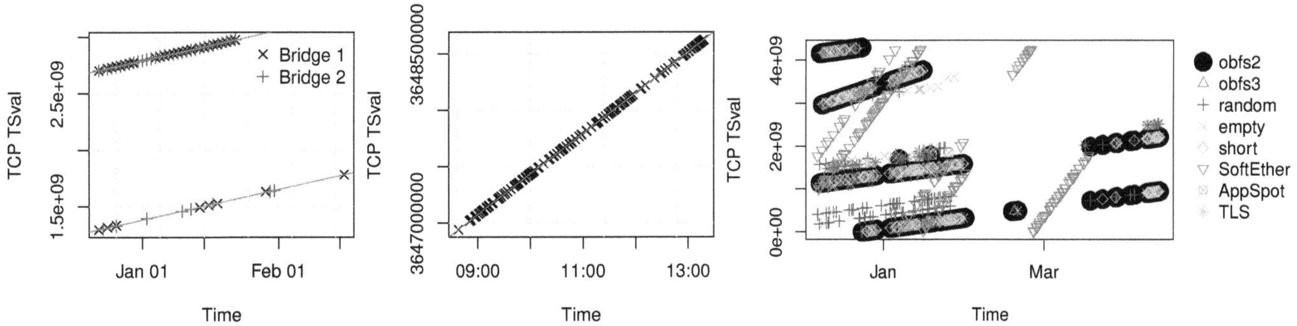

(a) Shadow experiment. (b) Sybil experiment. (c) Log experiment.

Figure 11: The TCP TSval value of SYN segments received by active probers.

connection. The probers' `VERSIONS` cell declares support for Tor protocol versions 1 and 2, which were superseded in Oct. 2011 [18], and are now only supported for backward compatibility (the current protocol version is 4). The fact that probers use such an old protocol version, suggests, to us, that the Tor probes were developed in 2011 or earlier, and not materially updated since. We briefly modified a Tor bridge to ignore connections that offered only versions 1 and 2 and found that such a bridge does not get blocked despite being probed. (This is unfortunately not a universally deployable defense against probing because there are still some old clients that support only old protocol versions, and ignoring their handshakes would cut them out of the network.)

Application Layer—obfs2.

The active probers' implementation of obfs2 conforms with the protocol specification: A 16-byte seed, an encrypted "magic" number, a padding length of 0–8,192 bytes, and random padding. The amount of random padding matches the declared padding length, except in a small number of cases when the TCP stream ended prematurely because of missing segments. The probers do not send anything in the encrypted payload layer inside the obfs2 obfuscation layer, even when communicating with an actual obfs2 server. In genuine use of Tor with obfs2, there is TLS within the obfs2 layer, but within the active probers' obfs2 there is no payload at all—the prober simply terminates the TCP connection. It seems that the mere existence of an obfs2 server is sufficient evidence for the censor.

Obfs2 clients should use fresh randomness for every connection. We were therefore surprised to find a few instances of duplicate obfs2 bytestreams. If two obfs2 streams have identical payloads, they must have had identical session keys and identical random padding. Out of 8,479 obfs2 probes received in the Log experiment, 56 (0.7%) were part of a pair having identical payloads. We did not find any payload that occurred more than twice. In every case, the paired probes came from different IP addresses, and arrived at nearly the same time, never more than five seconds apart. The probability that two independent obfs2 streams are identical is negligible; therefore the probers must share some state behind the scenes—at least a weak random number generator if not actually complete process state.

This apparent "state leakage" shows up in another way. Occasionally, an IP address that sent one half of a pair of identical obfs2 probes also sent, nearly simultaneously, a probe of some other type. Here is a sample from the Log experiment on port 80. Two different IP addresses sent the same obfs2 payload in the same second. One second later, one of the two additionally sent a TLS probe:

```
2014-08-29 15:44:01  60.216.143.31  obfs2  eef890766636...
2014-08-29 15:44:01  14.135.253.56  obfs2  eef890766636...
2014-08-29 15:44:02  14.135.253.56  tls    160301
```

Curiously, the active probers do more work to detect obfs2 than they strictly have to. Although the protocol does not require it, existing server implementations send their seed, magic number, and padding immediately upon receiving a TCP connection, without waiting the client's half of the handshake. A more stealthier active prober would open a TCP connection and simply listen. It would be able to detect current obfs2 servers without being so conspicuous.

Application Layer—obfs3.

In contrast to obfs2, the active probers' implementation of obfs3 differs from the specification in an interesting way that does not affect protocol semantics. The specification calls for each side to send 0–8,194 bytes of random padding, but in two chunks, each with a length that is a uniform random number between 0 and 4,097. Instead, the active probers send their padding all at once, in a single chunk of length between 0 and 8,194. It is therefore possible to fingerprint active probers in 50% of cases: if the first padding chunk is longer than 4,097 bytes, then the client is an active prober.

As with obfs2, we observe some duplicated probe payloads. Out of 4,493 obfs3 probes received, 82 (1.8%) share their exact payload with another. The elements of a pair arrive within a few seconds of one another. As with obfs2, there is no payload within the obfuscation layer.

Application Layer—SoftEther.

The SoftEther probe—an HTTPS POST request with a particular request body—matches one formerly sent by the genuine SoftEther VPN client. However, since July 2014, the genuine client has included a `Host` header containing the IP address of the VPN server. The active probers do not set this header, making them distinguishable.

There is another way to identify SoftEther probes. Although the SoftEther VPN protocol lacks documentation, in our experiments with version 4.15 we found that the client software always sends a GET request before sending its POST. The purpose of the GET request is to determine whether the server is SoftEther VPN and not some other HTTPS server. Because the active probers do not send the preceding GET request, we can distinguish them from legitimate clients.

The TLS fingerprint of the SoftEther probes differs strikingly from that of the actual SoftEther VPN client software, which has more and newer ciphersuites, and various extensions.

Application Layer—AppSpot.

The special `Host` header of the AppSpot probe type is a dead giveaway to its purpose of discovering servers capable of fronting access to Google App Engine. All the probes we saw carry a fairly distinctive and specific `User-Agent` string, which is probably spoofed, as the rest of the header is inconsistent with its purported version of Chromium. The declared version of the browser was originally released in Apr. 2014, and superseded just two weeks later by a new update. We found a small number of real web requests using this `User-Agent`, but the great majority were active probers. The first AppSpot probes arrived in Sep. 2014.

Among other header inconsistencies, the probes set the header `Accept-Encoding: identity`, which forces the server to send the response body uncompressed. We used this characteristic to weed out the small number of non-prober requests that happened to use the same `User-Agent` string—these requests, using a real Chromium browser, would have set `Accept-Encoding: gzip`, and the server would have compressed its response. We can therefore identify active probes in our server logs because the number of transferred bytes is greater than it should be.

The TLS signature of AppSpot probes entirely differs from that of the claimed version of Chromium. The probes almost certainly reflect use of a custom program that merely imitates a web browser.

5.6 Characteristics of the Probing System

We designed our Counterprobe experiment (Section 4.4) to illuminate multiple features of both the active probing sensors and its probing network. We find clear evidence that the sensor responsible for triggering probes operates in a single-sided fashion, meaning that it only considers unidirectional flows. Our experiments showed that an unacknowledged series of a SYN segment, followed by an ACK, and finally data (i.e., Tor's TLS client hello) suffices to trigger a probe. The following subsections discuss additional findings.

The sensor does not process stateless segments.

Some DPI sensors are stateless, i.e., they process TCP segments in isolation, without considering the TCP connection state. To learn if the active probing sensor is stateless, we set out to attract a probe in two ways: once after establishing a three-way handshake and once—on a different port—without prior handshake. The stateful data triggered a probe and the stateless did not. This matches our understanding of the behavior of the Great Firewall. However, it differs from the Great Cannon [17] that has been used to inject malicious JavaScript into web pages, which acts on naked packets.

The sensor does not seem to robustly reassemble TCP.

Next, we tried to establish if the sensor is reassembling TCP streams. In the first step, we sent the triggering data in a single TCP segment after establishing a TCP connection, which, as expected, attracted an active probe. In the next step, we split the triggering data across packets in 20 byte increments—again after establishing a TCP connection. The fragmented data did not trigger an active probe, which differs from the GFW [13].

This behavior was already observed by Winter and Lindskog [32, §5.2] in 2012. There are, however, reports stating that the active probing sensor used to reassemble TCP streams at some point [31].

Traceroute to the sensors.

We sent response-triggering packet trains with the TTL encoded in the port selection, and also performed a similar traceroute to locate the Great Firewall, from both a Unicom server and a CERNET server. Unicom's sensor appears to operate on the same link as the GFW, but the CERNET sensor appears one hop closer to our server.

Together, these three tests suggest that the active prober's sensor is distinct from both the RST-injecting portion of the Great Firewall and the sensor in the Great Cannon.

Inferring the physical infrastructure.

Section 5.5 suggests that there is clearly a substantial amount of centralization, as probes from a diverse range of IP addresses share both TCP timestamps and initial sequence number patterns. But what is the nature of the IP addresses from which the probes originate? We envision three possibilities:

1. A network of distributed proxies that simply forwards raw packets, and is centrally controlled by the active probing system.
2. A few centralized packet injection devices that extract the probed server's reply via passive monitoring.
3. A few centralized man-in-the-middle devices that selectively intercept traffic, temporarily hijacking end-system IP addresses, in a manner similar to the Great Cannon.

Our solution to distinguish these three possibilities was to deploy a system that responds to incoming probes with a series of TTL-limited packets, effectively acting as a traceroute. Our responses included:

- SYN-ACK packets, encoding the hop in the sequence number.
- UDP packets, encoding the hop in the IP ID field.
- UDP packets to the probe's source.
- SYN-ACK (with the hop encoded in both the port and sequence number) and UDP packets to the topologically next IP address.
- SYN-ACK and UDP packets to the topologically next subnet.

We triggered probes by sending requests from our server in China, and our responses were sent blindly, only capturing packet traces for a post-processing analysis.

The resulting traceroutes argue against the possibility of packet injection: a packet injecting system is unable to suppress the legitimate reply, and we would expect to see ICMP time exceeded packets corresponding to the answered ACKs. The only exception would be if the injector's author maintained a careful topology, ensuring that the injector never replied to an observed packet with too low a TTL to reach the real destination. Given that other Chinese systems, including the detectors in the Great Cannon and the Great Firewall's RST injector, do not perform such an analysis, we find it unlikely to believe that this system used packet injection.

For the same reason the traceroutes argue against a Great Cannon-type interceptor: the UDP and TCP traceroutes are consistent for both for the target IP address and the next IP address in sequence. In particular, note that the SYN-ACK is never answered early. To be consistent with the next IP address's topology, again the probing devices would need a deep understanding of the actual network.

For both cases, such a deep understanding of the network's topology would not significantly increase the system's stealth: It's already clear that the probes come from thousands of different IP addresses, and probing itself is not, by its nature, stealthy. Thus we believe, but cannot prove conclusively, that the system conducts its probes through a large, distributed proxy network.

6. CONCLUSION

Our work paints a detailed picture of active probing, the Great Firewall's newest weapon in the arms race of Internet censorship. Our results show that the system operates in real time, but regularly suspends for a short amount of time. It is capable of detecting the servers of at least five circumvention protocols and is upgraded regularly. We show that the system makes use of a vast amount of IP addresses, provide evidence that all these IP addresses are centrally controlled, and determine the location of the Great Firewall's sensors.

Future work could develop more circumvention strategies that can defeat active probing. Fortunately, users behind the GFW already have a number of working circumvention tools at their disposal, and other designs are in development. A family of techniques known variously as decoy routing [12], end-to-middle proxying [34, 9], and domain fronting [8] colocate the circumvention system's entry point with important network infrastructure, so that it cannot be easily blocked even if its address is known.

The obfuscation protocols ScrambleSuit [33] and its successor obfs4 [27] tread a different path by requiring clients to prove knowledge of a shared secret before responding. This technique is essentially port knocking at the application layer. Other proposals would add scanning resistance at the TCP layer [23] or the Tor protocol layer [11].

Our datasets, code, and auxiliary information are available online at `https://nymity.ch/active-probing/`.

Acknowledgments

This material is based upon work supported in part by the National Science Foundation under grant nos. #1223717, #1518918, #1540066, and #1518882. This work was also supported in part by funding from the Open Technology Fund through the Freedom2Connect Foundation and from the US Department of State, Bureau of Democracy, Human Rights and Labor. The opinions in this paper are those of the authors and do not necessarily reflect those of any funding agency or governmental organization.

7. REFERENCES

[1] Anonymous. Towards a comprehensive picture of the Great Firewall's DNS censorship. In *FOCI*. USENIX, 2014.

[2] David Borman, Bob Braden, Van Jacobson, and Richard Scheffenegger. TCP extensions for high performance. RFC 7323 (Proposed Standard), September 2014.

[3] Richard Clayton, Steven J. Murdoch, and Robert N. M. Watson. Ignoring the Great Firewall of China. In *PET*. Springer, 2006.

[4] Roger Dingledine. Obfsproxy: the next step in the censorship arms race. https://blog.torproject.org/blog/obfsproxy-next-step-censorship-arms-race, February 2012.

[5] Roger Dingledine and Nick Mathewson. Tor protocol specification. https://spec.torproject.org/tor-spec.

[6] Roger Dingledine and Nick Mathewson. Design of a blocking-resistant anonymity system. Technical report, The Tor Project, 2006.

[7] Roya Ensafi, Philipp Winter, Abdullah Mueen, and Jedidiah R. Crandall. Analyzing the Great Firewall of China over space and time. In *PETS*. De Gruyter Open, 2015.

[8] David Fifield, Chang Lan, Rod Hynes, Percy Wegmann, and Vern Paxson. Blocking-resistant communication through domain fronting. In *PETS*. De Gruyter Open, 2015.

[9] Amir Houmansadr, Giang T. K. Nguyen, Matthew Caesar, and Nikita Borisov. Cirripede: Circumvention infrastructure using router redirection with plausible deniability. In *CCS*, pages 187–200. ACM, 2011.

[10] Andrew Jacobs. China further tightens grip on the Internet. http://www.nytimes.com/2015/01/30/world/asia/china-clamps-down-still-harder-on-internet-access.html, 2015.

[11] George Kadianakis. Bridge client authorization based on a shared secret. https://gitweb.torproject.org/torspec.git/tree/proposals/190-shared-secret-bridge-authorization.txt, 2011.

[12] Josh Karlin, Daniel Ellard, Alden W. Jackson, Christine E. Jones, Greg Lauer, David P. Mankins, and W. Timothy Strayer. Decoy routing: Toward unblockable Internet communication. In *FOCI*. USENIX, 2011.

[13] Sheharbano Khattak, Mobin Javed, Philip D. Anderson, and Vern Paxson. Towards illuminating a censorship monitor's model to facilitate evasion. In *FOCI*. USENIX, 2013.

[14] Zhen Ling, Xinwen Fu, Wei Yu, Junzhou Luo, and Ming Yang. Extensive analysis and large-scale empirical evaluation of Tor bridge discovery. In *INFOCOM*. IEEE, 2012.

[15] Marek Majkowski. SSL fingerprinting for p0f. https://idea.popcount.org/2012-06-17-ssl-fingerprinting-for-p0f/, June 2012.

[16] Marek Majkowski. Fun with the Great Firewall. https://idea.popcount.org/2013-07-11-fun-with-the-great-firewall/, July 2013.

[17] Bill Marczak, Nicholas Weaver, Jakub Dalek, Roya Ensafi, David Fifield, Sarah McKune, Arn Rey, John Scott-Railton, and Ron Deibert. An analysis of China's "Great Cannon". In *FOCI*. USENIX, 2015.

[18] Nick Mathewson. Proposed version-3 link handshake for Tor. https://gitweb.torproject.org/torspec.git/tree/proposals/176-revising-handshake.txt, January 2011.

[19] Jon McLachlan and Nicholas Hopper. On the risks of serving whenever you surf: Vulnerabilities in Tor's blocking resistance design. In *WPES*. ACM, 2009.

[20] Leif Nixon. Some observations on the Great Firewall of China. https://www.nsc.liu.se/~nixon/sshprobes.html, 2011.

[21] Daiyuu Nobori and Yasushi Shinjo. VPN gate: A volunteer-organized public VPN relay system with blocking resistance for bypassing government censorship firewalls. In *NSDI*. USENIX, 2014.

[22] Jong Chun Park and Jedidiah R. Crandall. Empirical study of a national-scale distributed intrusion detection system: Backbone-level filtering of HTML responses in China. In *ICDCS*. IEEE, 2010.

[23] Rob Smits, Divam Jain, Sarah Pidcock, Ian Goldberg, and Urs Hengartner. BridgeSPA: Improving Tor bridges with single packet authorization. In *WPES*. ACM, 2011.

[24] Sparks, Neo, Tank, Smith, and Dozer. The collateral damage of Internet censorship by DNS injection. *SIGCOMM Computer Communication Review*, 42(3):21–27, 2012.

[25] The Tor Project. obfs2 (the twobfuscator). https://gitweb.torproject.org/pluggable-transports/obfsproxy.git/tree/doc/obfs2/obfs2-protocol-spec.txt.

[26] The Tor Project. obfs3 (the threebfuscator). https://gitweb.torproject.org/pluggable-transports/obfsproxy.git/tree/doc/obfs3/obfs3-protocol-spec.txt.

[27] The Tor Project. obfs4 (the obfourscator). https://gitweb.torproject.org/pluggable-transports/obfs4.git/tree/doc/obfs4-spec.txt.

[28] The Tor Project. TLSHistory. https://trac.torproject.org/projects/tor/wiki/org/projects/Tor/TLSHistory.

[29] The Tor Project. Tor: Pluggable transports. https://www.torproject.org/docs/pluggable-transports.html.en.

[30] Tim Wilde. Knock knock knockin' on bridges' doors. https://blog.torproject.org/blog/knock-knock-knockin-bridges-doors, 2012.

[31] Philipp Winter. #8591: GFW actively probes obfs2 bridges. https://bugs.torproject.org/8591, March 2013.

[32] Philipp Winter and Stefan Lindskog. How the Great Firewall of China is blocking Tor. In *FOCI*. USENIX, 2012.

[33] Philipp Winter, Tobias Pulls, and Juergen Fuss. ScrambleSuit: A polymorphic network protocol to circumvent censorship. In *WPES*. ACM, 2013.

[34] Eric Wustrow, Scott Wolchok, Ian Goldberg, and J. Alex Halderman. Telex: Anticensorship in the network infrastructure. In *USENIX Security Symposium*. USENIX, 2011.

[35] Michal Zalewski. p0f v3 (version 3.08b). http://lcamtuf.coredump.cx/p0f3/, 2014.

Characterizing Smartphone Usage Patterns from Millions of Android Users

Huoran Li, Xuan Lu, Xuanzhe Liu [‡]
Peking University
{lihuoran, luxuan, xzl}@pku.edu.cn

Tao Xie
University of Illinois Urbana-Champaign
taoxie@illinois.edu

Kaigui Bian
Peking University
bkg@pku.edu.cn

Felix Xiaozhu Lin
Purdue University
xzl@purdue.edu

Qiaozhu Mei
University of Michigan
qmei@umich.edu

Feng Feng
Wandoujia Lab
jackfeng@wandoujia.com

ABSTRACT

The prevalence of smart devices has promoted the popularity of mobile applications (a.k.a. apps) in recent years. A number of interesting and important questions remain unanswered, such as why a user likes/dislikes an app, how an app becomes popular or eventually perishes, how a user selects apps to install and interacts with them, how frequently an app is used and how much traffic it generates, etc. This paper presents an empirical analysis of app usage behaviors collected from millions of users of Wandoujia, a leading Android app marketplace in China. The dataset covers two types of user behaviors of using over 0.2 million Android apps, including (1) app management activities (i.e., installation, updating, and uninstallation) of over 0.8 million unique users and (2) app network traffic from over 2 million unique users. We explore multiple aspects of such behavior data and present interesting patterns of app usage. The results provide many useful implications to the developers, users, and disseminators of mobile apps.

Categories and Subject Descriptors

D.4.8 [**Operating Systems**]: Performance—*Measurement; Modeling and Prediction*; D.2.8 [**Software Engineering**]: Metrics—*complexity measures, performance measures*

General Terms

Performance, Measurement

Keywords

Android apps; app management; app popularity; app performance; app stores.

IMC'15, October 28–30, 2015, Tokyo, Japan.
© 2015 ACM. ISBN 978-1-4503-3848-6/15/10 ...$15.00.
DOI: http://dx.doi.org/10.1145/2815675.2815686.

1. INTRODUCTION

The release of iPhone in 2007 has opened a new era of mobile computing. Eight years later, smart devices such as iPhones and Android devices have played an indispensable role in our daily lives. The increasing popularity of mobile devices and apps has induced an evolution of software industry. The emergence of online marketplaces and platform APIs has been a game changer to developers, market intermediaries, and consumers, making them more and more willing to develop, disseminate, and use mobile apps rather than Web-based services [24].

The prevalence of mobile apps has also generated a huge volume of app usage data. Understanding user behaviors of using mobile apps is meaningful to all the stakeholders mentioned above. For example, marketplace operators can identify popular or problematic apps and provide effective app recommender systems; developers can understand why their apps are liked or disliked by the users and therefore improve the app design; end-users can have a better knowledge of how particular apps are consuming their time and bandwidth, and therefore optimize their decisions of selecting apps. Due to the lack of a sizable repository of such behavioral data, most of these important questions remain unanswered.

Previous studies have shown evidence about different users having different patterns of using mobile apps [19, 23, 7, 1]. Most of these studies were conducted using rather small behavior datasets, typically collected from a small number of student volunteers. The analyses also suffer from various selection biases introduced by college students.

Moreover, most behavioral signals were collected through a monitoring app voluntarily installed on the subjects' devices. Such a design is difficult to be applied by the variety of crowd due to the security and privacy concerns. As a result, very few studies could scale up to millions of users.

We present a comprehensive analysis of app usage behaviors collected from millions of Android users[1]. Our data comes from a leading Android app marketplace in China,

[1]All users involved in our dataset are anonymized by removing the identifiers. A sample of dataset has been released on DatCat. Researchers can search over DatCat by the title of this paper or directly access our server `http://45.56.95.4/description.html`. Contact the corresponding author: xzl@pku.edu.cn for technical issues.

called **Wandoujia**[2]. Similar to other app marketplace operators in China, such as Baidu, 360Safe, and Tencent, Wandoujia provides its own management app that facilitates users to search, browse, download, install, update, and uninstall apps. Once being launched, the Wandoujia management app runs as a background system-level service without requiring the "root" privilege. It also provides the user option to collect network activity information of each app on device, e.g., data traffic and access time under different networks.

The dataset that we study covers over 0.2 million (260,172) Android apps. The data mainly contains two types of user behaviors: (1) app management activities (i.e., installation, updating, and uninstallation) of over 0.8 million (8,112,145) unique users; (2) app network usage of 2 million (2,031,007) unique users. Based on this dataset, we conduct a ***systematic descriptive analysis*** that includes the distributions of app popularity, possible reasons of app selection, life cycles of abandoned apps, fine-grained network analysis of apps, and the impact of economic factors on app usage.

To the best of our knowledge, our work is the first descriptive analysis of millions of users of Android marketplaces. Although most users are Chinese, the usage patterns learned from the millions could generalize to other populations. Based on such a new dataset, we not only validate some conclusions from previous efforts, but also explore some new knowledge of user behaviors on app usage. The paper aims to answer the following questions:

- **How can we characterize the app popularity among millions of users?** Compared to previous studies that mainly investigated app popularity by downloads [17], we explore the app popularity from various aspects, including the monthly downloads of an app, the number of unique devices an app was installed on, the network traffic of an app, and the network access time of an app. Distributions of all these aspects comply with the Pareto principle [14], i.e., a small portion of apps account for substantial popularity. These findings can help marketplace operators and network providers improve their workloads for serving the most popular apps, and organize efficient caching or prefetching mechanisms to enable fast downloads and delivery of these popular apps.

- **How do mobile users choose and manage apps?** Compared to previous studies that usually examined the co-installed apps [24, 17], we further explore why the apps are installed and how soon they are likely to be uninstalled. We try to understand the possible reasons for co-installing apps, i.e., apps provided by the same **vendor/developer** or with similar **functionalities** are more likely to be installed together. We first study the uninstallation patterns of apps by devising a new metric called the *temporal installation/uninstallation ratio* to indicate how much an app is likely to be abandoned. These findings can help app marketplace operators improve their recommendation systems.

- **How do different apps perform in network activity?** Compared to previous studies [25, 24, 7], our network analysis is conducted at fine granularity. We study the network activities in terms of the data traffic and the access time under Wi-Fi and cellular, respectively. We further investigate where the network activity occurs (foreground or background). Besides identifying some "network intensive" apps, we find apps that may "suspiciously" keep continuous network connections or consume traffic at the background. For example, it is surprising that some tools, such as flashlight apps and namecard apps, generate unexpected background traffic against their main purposes. We are also surprised to find that a large number of apps keep long-lived TCP connections at the background after they are launched. These findings can help marketplace operators to locate some "*problematic*" apps, and help users choose alternative apps to reduce potential threats caused by these apps.

- **How do economic factors affect app selection and network usage?** Compared to previous studies that relied on free/paid apps to measure economic factors [23], our study is performed in a quite different way. Based on the hypothesis that the price of a device model can reflect the user's financial background, we classify users into different groups according to their device models. We make the first report on how device models impact the apps selection and data traffic, e.g., users with lower-end device models tend to use local or less network-intensive apps. Based on our findings, app marketplace operators can make more accurate app recommendations, and app developers can target specific user groups to optimize user experiences.

The remainder of this paper is organized as follows. Section 2 describes the dataset. Sections 3-6 describe the inferred app usage patterns in four aspects, app popularity patterns, management patterns, network patterns, and price-sensitive patterns, respectively. Section 7 summarizes the findings and implications to different stakeholders. Section 8 discusses the threats to validity. Section 9 makes comparisons with related work, and Section 10 concludes the paper.

2. DATASET

In this section, we briefly introduce the Wandoujia marketplace and describe the features of our dataset collected by the Wandoujia management app. To protect the user privacy and assure the ethnics of our research, we also discuss how the data is processed.

2.1 Wandoujia

Our data is from Wandoujia[3], a free Android app marketplace in China. Wandoujia was founded in 2009 and has grown to be a leading Android app marketplace. Like other marketplaces, third-party app developers can upload their apps to Wandoujia and get them published after authenticated. Compared to other marketplaces such as Google Play, apps on Wandoujia are all free, although some apps can still support "*in-app purchase*".

Users have two channels to access the Wandoujia marketplace, either from the Web portal, or from the Wandoujia management app. The Wandoujia management app is a native Android app, by which people can manage their apps,

[2]http://www.wandoujia.com

[3]Visit its official site via `http://www.wandoujia.com`.

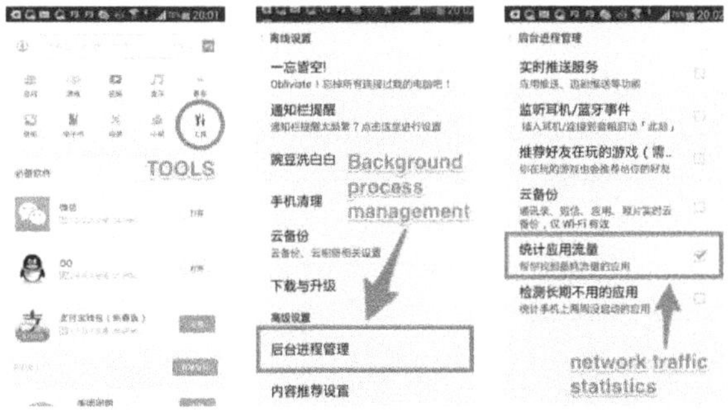

(a) (b) (c)

Figure 1: Screenshots of advanced settings in the Chinese version of the Wandoujia management app (the advanced settings is not supported in the current English version). *(a) is the homepage of the Wandoujia management app, where users can navigate to "settings" by clicking the text circled by red; (b) refers to the background management service setting, which is highlighted by the red rectangle; (c) is to toggle whether to allow Wandoujia to collect the data of network activities.*

e.g., downloading, searching, updating, and uninstalling apps. The logs of these management activities are all automatically recorded.

Beyond these basic features, the Wandoujia management app is developed with some advanced but optional features that can monitor and optimize a device. These features include network activity statistics, permission monitoring, content recommendation, etc. All features are developed upon Android system APIs and do not require "root" privilege. Users can decide whether to enable these features, as shown in Figure 1. However, these features are supported only in the Chinese version.

The Wandoujia management app is automatically launched and it works as a system-wide service after the device that installs the app starts up. The data collected on each device is uploaded to the Wandoujia server every day.

2.2 Data Collection

As of 2015, Wandoujia has over 250 million users. Each user is actually associated with a unique Android device, which could be either a smartphone or tablet computer. In the study of this paper, we collected one-month usage data from August 4, 2013 to September 2, 2013. The volume of our data set is 1.2 TB.

Our one-month dataset covers more than 0.2 million (260,172) Android apps. The data of user behaviors consists of two types: (1) the ***data of app management activities*** (i.e., installation, update, and uninstallation) (2) ***the data of app network usage*** (i.e., the traffic and access time per app).

2.2.1 App Management Activities

App management activities consist of downloading[4], updating, and uninstalling apps. When an app is installed or updated via the Wandoujia management app, its installation counter is automatically increased by one and a log entry of this activity is created. The logs of uninstallation via the Wandoujia management app are processed in a similar way. In the Wandoujia management app, collecting app management activities is always enabled.

In our one-month data, we collected the management activity logs from **8,112,145 unique users** (devices in fact). We denote the dataset as "**Universal User Set**". The logs of management activities are used to explore an app's popularity, and can implicitly reflect the app's quality.

2.2.2 Network Activities

When the advanced features are enabled, the Wandoujia management app collects daily network statistics of each app, if the app generates network connections either from Wi-Fi or cellular (2G/3G/LTE). However, if an app is never launched or generates no network connections, the app is not recorded in the network statistic logs.

To reduce the overhead of runtime monitoring, the Wandoujia management app does not record network details of each session of an app. Instead, it summarizes the total daily traffic and access time of an app by examining flows at the TCP level. The traffic and access time are captured for Wi-Fi and cellular, respectively.

In particular, the traffic and access time generated from **foreground** and **background** are treated separately. The Wandoujia management app determines whether an app is running at "foreground" by probing the Android system stack for every 2 seconds. In this way, the "foreground" access time can imply how long the user interacts with an app. The Wandoujia management app checks whether an app running at "background" every 2 minutes. If any network activity is detected during this interval, this app is regarded to be "online" and its "background" access time is increased by 2 minutes. Such time interval is reasonable to initiate and release a TCP connection.

In summary, the statistic of network activity provides 8 combinations of information, i.e., 2 ***metrics*** (access time and traffic) * 2 ***modes*** (Wi-Fi and Cellular) * 2 ***states*** (foreground and background).

As the statistic of network activity is an optional feature for end-users, the covered users are a subset of the "**Universal User Set**". We take into account only the users who successively contributed the statistics for more than 3 weeks. In our one-month dataset, the network activity covers **2,031,007** unique users. We denote such a dataset as "**Networked User Set**".

2.2.3 Device Models and Price

The Wandoujia management app also records the model information of each device, e.g., Samsung Galaxy Note 2, Google Nexus. We leverage the device models to classify users. Finally there are 12,091 different device models in total. Such a result implies the heavy fragmentation of Android devices. To better organize these models, we collected their listing price information when they were firstly put onto market.

2.3 User Privacy

We took a series of steps to preserve the privacy of involved users in our dataset. First, all raw data collected for this study was kept within the Wandoujia data warehouse

[4]In the Wandoujia management app, a pop-up of installation wizard is presented to users when an app is downloaded. So we treat "download" and "installation" equally.

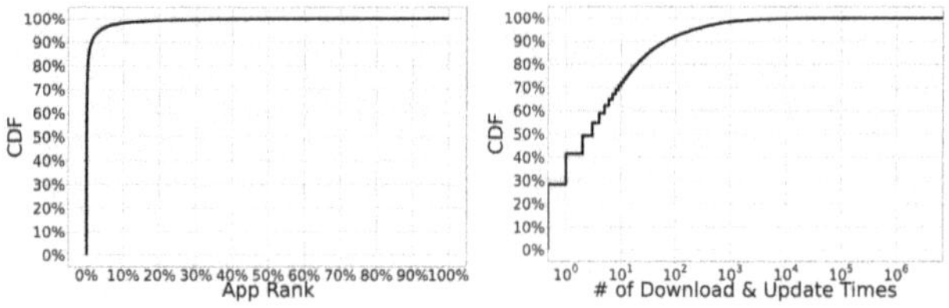

(a) Percentage of Downloads against App Rank (b) Downloads of an App

Figure 2: App Popularity by Downloads

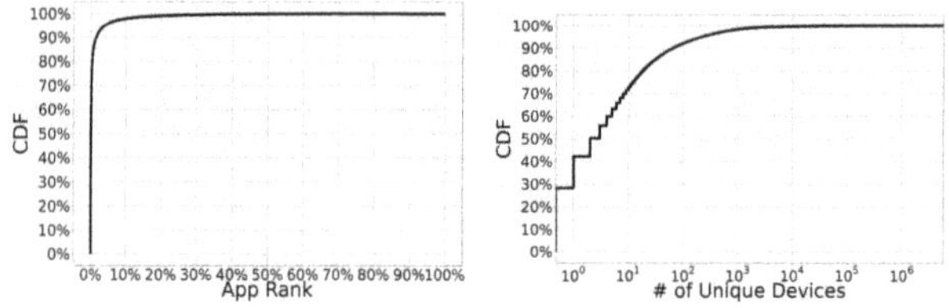

(a) Percentage of Unique Subscribers against App Rank (b) Unique Subscribers of an App

Figure 3: App Popularity by Unique Devices

servers (which live behind a company firewall). Second, our data collection logic and analysis pipelines were completely governed by three Wandoujia employees[5] to ensure compliance with the commitments of Wandoujia privacy stated in the *Term-of-Use* statements. Finally, the Wandoujia employees anonymized the user identifiers. The dataset includes only the aggregated statistics for the users covered by our study period.

3. APP POPULARITY

In this section, we make a **macro-level analysis** on app distribution. In most previous studies [17, 19], apps are usually ranked by their number of downloads on the marketplaces. To make a comprehensive analysis, we use four metrics: **(1) the number of downloads of the app; (2) the number of unique devices that download the app; (3) the aggregated data traffic generated by the app; (4) the aggregated access time that users interact with the app.** The former two metrics can indicate how many users an app has, and the latter two can indicate how much an app is really used.

3.1 Popularity by Downloads

First, we investigate the most intuitive metric of app popularity, i.e., the number of downloads of an app. Most app stores take the number of downloads (i.e., total, monthly, or weekly) as an indicator to rank app popularity. We then investigate the app downloads from the management activities of the **Universal User Set**. It is a common observation that people often update their installed apps. Hence, we compute total downloads of an app by aggregating its number of downloads and updates in our dataset.

Various evidence reports that the Pareto principle exists in networked application domains such as web content, audio, and video downloads [14], i.e., *20% of the objects account for 80% downloads.* Figure 2(a) shows that the cumulative distribution function (CDF) of the percentage of app downloads against the app ranking by downloads. The results show that the app downloads follow the Pareto principle. For example, 10% apps account for 96.2% downloads of all apps. Such finding validates a similar distribution of app downloads reported previously [17].

We also explore the distributions of downloads of each app. Figure 2(b) indicates that about 80% apps are downloaded or updated less than 10 times in our one-month dataset. A substantially large number of apps are downloaded, updated, or uninstalled only once. Such finding indicates a "*long-tail*" of apps that are rarely active.

[5]One co-author, Feng Feng, is a co-founder and current CTO of Wandoujia. He supervised the process of data collection and de-identification.

3.2 Popularity by Unique Subscribers

Although the number of downloads of an app is a natural indicator for popularity, it is also possible that some apps are frequently downloaded or updated due to "**fraud**" behavior. For example, apps can be downloaded and updated by automated programs to increase their ranks on marketplaces. To validate whether the "*mostly downloaded apps*" also have more users, we aggregate the **unique subscribers (devices)** that ever downloaded, updated, or uninstalled an app. Compared to the number of downloads of an app, each device is counted only once as a subscriber. Figure 3(a) shows that the CDF of the percentage of unique subscribers against app ranking by downloads. We can find that the distribution of subscribers of an app still complies with the Pareto principle, i.e., about 10% apps account for 95.1% users. In this way, we could conclude that **the more an app is downloaded, the more users it usually owns.**

Meanwhile, we explore how many users an app owns in Figure 3(b). It shows that about 80% apps have been installed, updated, or uninstalled by only less than 10 unique devices.

However, it is observed that some apps may have high downloads but rather limited users/devices. We find that one app used by only 4 unique subscribers has 973 downloads in one month. We further explore its download logs, and find that its downloading actions were all performed in a quite short interval (within two days). There are two possible reasons. One is that all of the 4 devices (subscribers) are testing devices used by the app developers. The other is that the app developers may purposely increase the downloads. **Although such kind of apps is rare, the number of their downloads may mislead end-users or even bring threats.**

3.3 Popularity by Network Traffic

Either downloads or unique devices of an app can just indicate that an app is downloaded and installed. However, we cannot judge whether the app is really used by users. Not surprisingly, **mobile users may never use an app after first launching it, but do not uninstall it either.** From the logs of the **Networked User Set**, an app cannot generate network logs if it is never launched by users. Hence, we employ the network activities to examine whether the app is really used. Although we may miss some apps that

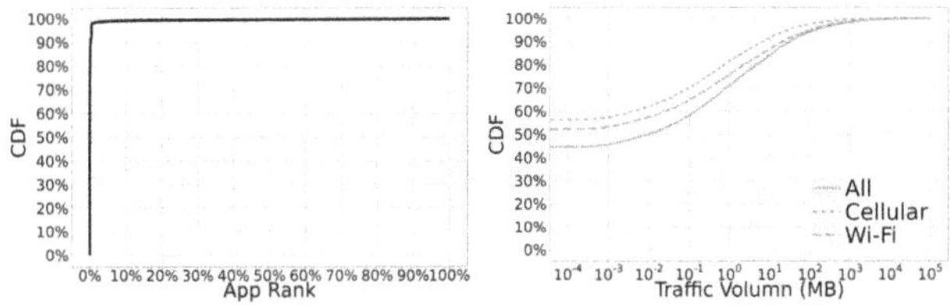

(a) Percentage of Traffic against App Rank (b) Traffic of an App

Figure 4: App Popularity by Data Traffic

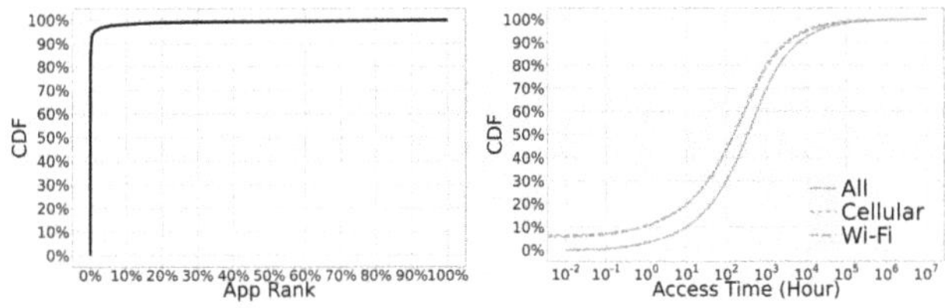

(a) Percentage of Access Time against App Rank (b) Access Time of an App

Figure 5: App Popularity by Access Time

are usually used offline, e.g., PDF readers or dictionaries, most of currently popular apps heavily rely on network and can be covered.

For better illustration, we distinguish *Wi-Fi*, *Cellular*, and *All (Wi-Fi + Cellular)* of each app. The data traffic comes from both foreground and background. In contrast, we take into account only the access time from foreground, because such time indicates how long users really interact with the app.

Figure 4(a) and Figure 5(a) illustrate the CDF of the percentage of aggregated traffic/access time of apps against app ranking by downloads, respectively. We can find that the Pareto principle still holds for the network activities of apps.

We also show the aggregated data traffic/access time of an app in Figure 4(b) and Figure 5(b), respectively. We can observe that about 97% apps consume less than 100 MB traffic volume in one month, and about 95% apps are used less than 100 hours.

3.4 Summary

From the preceding macro-level analysis of popularity, we can conclude that the app popularity generally complies with the Pareto principle in terms of downloads, unique users, data traffic, and access time. This finding not only validates results reported in previous studies [24, 17], but also helps marketplace operators and network providers identify the "real" popular apps that are frequently downloaded, updated, and used. To make the apps fast delivered to end-users, the marketplace operators can leverage this distribution to allocate resources for serving these apps, design efficient cache mechanisms, or quickly redirect user requests to the app providers. Knowing which apps are more adopted by users, network providers can provide better bandwidth, cache/prefetch contents to users, or explore value-added services such as advertisements to increase revenue.

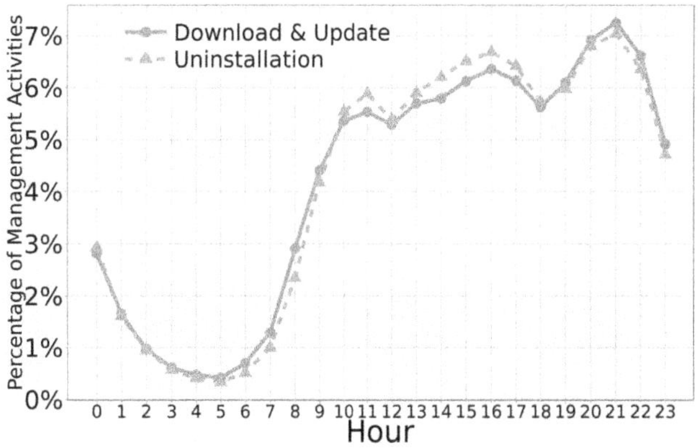

Figure 6: **Distribution of Diurnal App Management Activities.** Each point on the cureve represents the percentage of activities performed during the one-hour time interval against the total activities, during the whole day. ***For example, activities during 10:00 am-11:00 am account for about 6% of all activities.***

4. APP MANAGEMENT PATTERNS

In this section, we investigate how users manage their apps, e.g., which apps they often install and when they install these apps, which apps are more likely to be uninstalled, and why these apps are uninstalled by users.

4.1 Diurnal Management Patterns

App management activities include downloading, updating, and uninstalling apps. Exploring app management activities is motivated for various reasons. As app management activities are usually made manually, they can implicitly reflect the density and frequency of user interactions with the devices. For marketplace operators, this information can help them understand when a large number of concurrent user requests would arrive, so that the marketplace operators can optimize their servers for faster and more reliable network bandwidth. For app developers, they can leverage such information to publish the latest versions of apps at a proper time, to attract more downloads and updates.

We investigate the diurnal downloading, updating, and uninstallation distribution. We aggregate activities of downloading and updating an app, because they both reflect the users' interest towards this app. As shown in Figure 6, **the app management activities are "periodically" performed during a day**. The extent of app downloading and updating activities keeps growing from 6:00 am and reaches the first peak around 11:00 am. The downloading and updating activities decline slightly between 11:00 am to 12:00 pm. It is not very surprising because users may take lunch at this time. The same observation could be found between 4:00 pm to 6:00 pm, i.e., the time on the way back home or at dinner. We can also find that about 32% downloading and updating activities are performed during 7:00 pm to 11:00 pm, where they reach the maximum around 9:00 pm. Such distribution is quite consistent with human regularity. After 9:00 pm, the downloading and updating activities decline quite sharply, and reach the minimum around 5:00 am. However, at the midnight, downloading and updating activ-

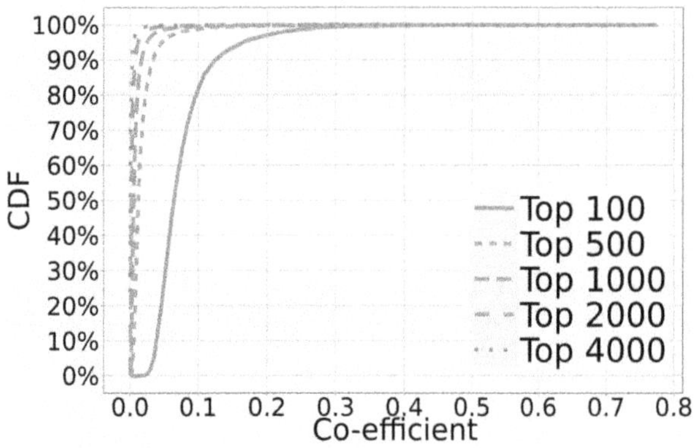

Figure 7: Coefficiency of installed apps.

ities occupy about 7% in total, implying that there are still a large number of active users.

Activities of uninstallating apps present a similar distribution to the ones of downloading/updating apps. However, knowing when users uninstall apps may be less meaningful, because the uninstallation activities do not have interactions with the marketplace operators or app providers.

4.2 App Selection Patterns

Knowing user interests and needs towards apps is useful. For marketplace operators, such information can help improve their recommendation systems. For app developers, such information can help improve their apps to work better with other co-installed apps, or explore potential collaboration opportunities with other developers. For network providers, such information can help them provide a more personalized data plan to bundle correlated apps and download them.

In fact, a lot of previous studies investigated how users select apps [24, 11, 19, 17], and some interesting findings were reported. From these studies, a common metric is to check the "cluster effect": which apps are more likely to be selected together. We adopt the same metric, but investigate it at two levels: the **micro-level** of co-installed apps, and the **meso-level** of correlated app categories.

From our previous analysis, substantial apps are rarely downloaded (less than 10 times or 10 devices), so we choose only the top 4,000 apps by their downloads. Each app is downloaded by at least 20 devices. To better explore the underlying reasons why apps are selected, we organize the apps into categories according to the classification system of Wandoujia. Table 1 summarizes the categories ordered by the number of apps. We also present the number of users and network summary of each category, which are used for analysis in Section 5.

4.2.1 Co-Installed Apps

We first study co-installed apps. Given two apps app_m and app_n, we employ the classical ***Jaccard Similarity Coefficient*** (denoted as λ) to measure the possibility how they are likely to be installed together. We denote the number of unique devices that install either app_m or app_n as $\mathbb{D}$ ($app_m \cup app_n$), and the number of unique devices that install both app_m and app_n as $\mathbb{D}$ ($app_m \cap app_n$). We then compute $\frac{\mathbb{D}(app_m \cap app_n)}{\mathbb{D}(app_m \cup app_n)}$.

Figure 7 shows the **Jaccard Similarity Coefficient** of the top-N apps, where N varies from 100 to 4,000. With the increasing the number of N, the CDF of λ indicates that there are a very small fraction of apps being co-installed together. The λ of 90% app pairs is lower than 0.1, if both app_m and app_n have 2,000 unique devices. Given the λ value of 0.1, app_m and app_n share only 200 unique devices. In contrast, we focus on the app pairs that take a higher value of λ, and explore **why these apps are more likely to be installed together**. We choose the pairs whose λ is more than 0.1. Rather than exploring the detailed textual descriptions of the apps, we focus on two properties *vendor* and *category*.

The *vendor* information of an app can reflect the developer, provider, or owner of the app. Usually, the naming rules of an Android app can reflect its vendor information. For example, the package `com.tencent.mm` can be processed by removing the general term "`com`" and the usage term "`mm`", and the vendor information "`tencent`" is extracted. By clustering the vendors, we find that **a number of co-installed apps with high λ value come from the same vendor**. For example, the pair of $<$ `360Safe` (a mobile anti-virus app used by 719,258 devices), `360 AppStore` (a marketplace app used by 560,600 devices) $>$ has the λ value of 0.358, and these two apps are both provided by Qihoo[6]. Furthermore, the **λ value could be much higher, if two apps developed by the same vendor belong to the same category**. For example, the pair of $<$ `MI Video` (a media player used by 54,217 devices), `MI Voice Assistant` (a voice assistant used by 75,221 devices)$>$ holds the λ value of 0.604, and the two apps are both provided by XIAOMI[7]; the pair of $<$ `WeChat` (used by 1,567,563 devices), `QQ` (used by 1,606,222 devices)$>$ holds the λ value of 0.7, and the two apps are provided by Tencent.

There are many possible reasons why apps from the same vendor are often co-installed. A vendor may focus on a specific application domain, e.g., Tencent is the largest messaging service provider in China. Tencent `QQ` is the most popular instant messaging app in China; `WeChat` not only supports instant messaging, but also provides social communication features such as content sharing. Another reason is that there might be "**in-app bundled installation**" in some apps. For example, when users install an app, the app's vendor may implicitly or explicitly recommend users to install other apps. For simple validation, we make field studies by selecting 50 apps from well-known app developers such as Qihoo, Baidu, and Tencent, and install them manually. 14 apps out of the 50 apps recommend installing other apps in their installation process, and 8 apps of these 14 "bundled" installations suggest apps provided by the same provider.

4.2.2 Correlation of App Categories

The *category* information of an app indicates the functionality and application domains of the app. We can infer the user needs and interests according to their selected app's category. Furthermore, knowing the correlations of app categories can suggest marketplace operators to organize apps

[6]Qihoo is one of the largest anti-virus software vendors in China.

[7]XIAOMI is one of the largest mobile phone manufacturers in China.

Table 1: Chosen Top Apps by Category.

App Category	Apps	Users (10^6 devices)	Downloads (10^6 times)	Traffic (GB)	Access-Time (10^7 hours)	*C*-Traffic	*C*-Time	*W*-Traffic	*W*-Time
GAME	1,227	3.87	15.15	13,669.71	0.38	2.98%	5.19%	0.76%	6.39%
NEWS_AND_READING	274	1.17	1.97	13,143.17	0.23	3.11%	2.91%	0.72%	3.95%
VIDEO	238	2.86	6.52	1,196,978.79	0.38	28.41%	1.42%	81.08%	10.54%
TOOL	227	3.84	9.43	77,329.87	0.68	15.63%	10.79%	4.40%	9.46%
SYSTEM_TOOL	217	3.37	7.54	34,012.16	0.25	3.05%	3.37%	2.17%	4.24%
SOCIAL	188	2.18	4.01	35,926.76	0.35	8.96%	4.77%	1.94%	5.66%
EDUCATION	172	1.68	2.98	13,893.55	0.34	1.46%	5.35%	0.87%	4.71%
LIFESTYLE	156	1.68	2.85	2,388.59	0.07	0.72%	1.00%	0.12%	1.06%
TRAVEL	111	1.62	2.75	8,182.24	0.03	0.78%	0.53%	0.52%	0.25%
PERSONALIZATION	104	1.49	3.68	7,426.38	0.86	0.85%	12.03%	0.46%	13.67%
FINANCE	99	0.32	0.50	382.60	0.02	0.13%	0.24%	0.02%	0.26%
COMMUNICATION	85	4.09	8.45	54,394.71	2.85	24.74%	49.01%	2.26%	35.26%
SHOPPING	78	1.57	3.00	21,808.51	0.07	3.16%	0.65%	1.32%	1.60%
PRODUCTIVITY	75	0.76	1.17	2,712.50	0.01	0.18%	0.17%	0.18%	0.26%
MOTHER_AND_BABY	48	0.10	0.15	525.72	0.01	0.07%	0.04%	0.03%	0.12%
MUSIC	43	2.33	3.39	49,540.12	0.17	5.66%	2.47%	3.08%	2.49%
SPORTS	27	0.31	0.36	61.40	0.00	0.02%	0.05%	0.00%	0.04%
IMAGE	23	0.14	0.17	801.64	0.00	0.06%	0.01%	0.05%	0.03%
TRAFFIC	14	0.10	0.12	78.10	0.00	0.02%	0.03%	0.00%	0.01%

The users, downloads, traffic, and access time are all computed by aggregating the data of each app in the category
The percentile of *W*-Traffic (*C*-Traffic) and *W*-Time (*C*-Time) refer to the data traffic and foreground access time over Wi-Fi (W) and cellular (C) network, respectively.

from different categories to enable the fast delivery of potentially co-installed apps to end-users.

Given two app categories M and N, we denote the number of unique devices that install an app either in M or N as $\mathbb{D}$ $(M \cup N)$, and the number of unique devices that install apps from both in M and N as $\mathbb{D}$ $(M \cap N)$. We then compute $\frac{\mathbb{D}(M \cup N)}{\mathbb{D}(M \cap N}$ to indicate how likely that the apps in M and N are installed together. We also take into account the special case, where M=N, indicating how many users install more than one app in this category.

Figure 8 shows the probability distribution that apps from different categories are selected together. The categories are sorted in the descending order of the number of apps. An immediate observation is that categories having more apps are more closely correlated. In addition, apps providing related functionalities are more likely to be selected together. For example, users may want to share a video from a video-player app to friends by employing a communication app (e.g., correlation between *COMMUNICATION* and *VIDEO* is 0.77), or use a viewer app to open a document that is received by an instant messenger app (e.g., correlation between *TOOL* and *COMMUNICATION is 0.88*).

It is not surprising that users may install more than one app in some categories. For example, in *GAME*, *TOOL*, and *COMMUNICATION*, the correlations are all more than 0.8. The result suggests that users have more interests and needs in these categories.

4.3 Uninstallation Patterns

We next to explore a question: **how an app is likely to be disliked or abandoned by users**. Such question is quite crucial to app developers, marketplace operators, and end-users. App developers can know how much their apps are not appreciated by users, so that they can find and fix problems in time to avoid user loss. Marketplace operators can improve their recommendation systems to filter unpopular, low-quality, or even malware apps. End-users can avoid downloads of frequently abandoned apps and potential threats.

For the question, the absolute number of unistallations of an app may not be a good indicator. For example, apps with high uninstallations may also have high downloads. So we compute the metric of *installation/uninstallation ratio*, denoted as $\Omega(app_i)$, to indicate how likely an app would be abandoned.

Given an app app_i, we first compute $\frac{\sum \mathbb{I}_{device_i}}{\sum \mathbb{U}_{devicei}}$, where $\sum \mathbb{I}_{device_i}$ and $\sum \mathbb{U}_{device_i}$ represent the number of devices that installed and uninstalled app_i, respectively. We extract all devices that appear in both installation and uninstallation logs of app_i from the **Universal User Set**. For each device, we order the app_i's installation and uninstallation log entries by their timestamps, in the form of $< I_{t1}, I_{t2}, ... >$ and $< U_{t1}, U_{t2}, ... >$. Here, t_i refers to the timestamp when the installation or uninstallation action was performed. In particular, an uninstallation action could not be used unless an installation action was made previously, i.e., $I_{ti} \prec U_{ti}$. Doing so assures that app_i is exactly uninstalled.

The lower value of $\Omega(app_i)$ an app holds, the higher likelihood it is abandoned. For better illustration, Figure 9(a) shows the scattered distribution of $\Omega(app_i)$ (denoted as "I/U ratio") of top 12,000 apps ranked by their downloads. The median value of Ω is about 7.46. The Ω of 80% apps' is less than 11. **In this way, Ω can exactly tell how much an app is actually abandoned by users.** However, $\Omega(app_i)$ is not a good signal to comprehensively reflect how much an app is disliked by users, because users may not always uninstall an app even if they do not need the app any longer.

To better understand the users' attitude towards apps, we evaluate the lifecycle of abandoned apps by combining the temporal information to Ω. Such evaluation is motivated by an intuition that an app is likely to be a disliked one if it is uninstalled shortly after installed. To this end, we compute the app's lifecyle by the timestamps of installation and uninstallation. We have two immediate observations. First, from Figure 9(b), if an app is exactly uninstalled, its lifecycle can be identified. **About 40% abandoned apps can "survive" for only less than one day, and about 93% abandoned apps can "survive" for less than a week.**

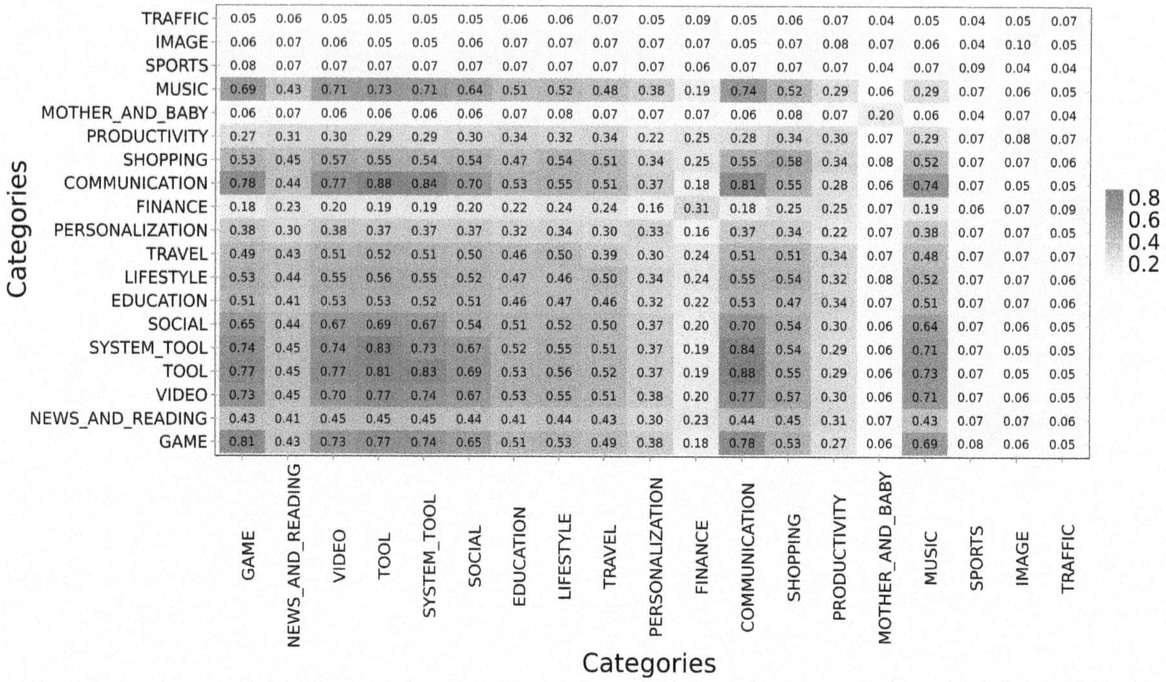

Figure 8: Heatmap of illustrating the relationship of co-installed app categories.

Second, from Figure 9(c), we can find **a positive correlation among Ω and lifecycle of abandoned apps**. In other words, apps with a lower Ω are more likely to be uninstalled within a shorter interval.

5. NETWORK ACTIVITY PATTERNS

Understanding network activities of apps is a highly interesting topic. Previous studies have already revealed some findings on network usage of apps, e.g., TCP flows on tier-1 network [24], or usage logs by field studies [20, 23]. In contrast, our study is performed at a much finer granularity. First, we distinguish daily data traffic and access time from Wi-Fi and cellular network, respectively. Second, we distinguish daily data traffic and access time from foreground and background, respectively.

Based on the granularity of network activities, our study aims to explore some findings not covered by previous efforts. End-users can know which apps are network-intensive, and result in more data traffic and battery life. In this way, end-users can identify "undesirable" apps, optimize improper network privilege, or even remove these apps. Marketplace operators can also detect some potentially problematic apps. App developers can fix possible bugs, and OS-vendors can patch to avoid threats. Network providers can leverage network behavior and suggest proper data plans for end-users.

5.1 Data Traffic Patterns

First, we identify "network-intensive" apps, i.e., apps that consume more data traffic than others. We aggregate apps by their categories and summarize the total traffic consumption (in GB) from Wi-Fi and cellular, respectively. As shown in Table 1, *VIDEO* apps are the most *"traffic-intensive"*. Apps from the *VIDEO* category consume 81.08% of Wi-Fi traffic and 28.41% cellular traffic against all apps. Interestingly, apps from *TOOL* and *SYSTEM_TOOL* consume a lot of data traffic. The apps in these two categories include apps of input method, anti-virus, app management, etc. Users heavily rely on these apps to manage, optimize, and personalize their devices.

We then classify data traffic into two dimensions: (1) Wi-Fi and cellular; (2) foreground and background. Such classification can provide us more insights of traffic consumption. We show the detailed summary in Table 2.

5.1.1 *Traffic of Wi-Fi and Cellular*

In most categories, it is not surprising that Wi-Fi accounts for more than **60%** in total traffic. In the categories of *VIDEO*, *TOOL*, *MUSIC*, *SYSTEM_TOOL*, *SHOPPING*, and *EDUCATION*, more than 80% data traffic is from Wi-Fi. A possible reason is that most of these apps are usually used in places with stable Wi-Fi connection, e.g., at home or cafe. The situation is quite different in *COMMUNICATION*. The traffic from cellular network accounts for about 39.9%. It is not surprising because users may use *COMMUNICATION* apps whenever a network connection is available.

5.1.2 *Traffic of Foreground and Background*

We then identify the foreground and background traffic of an app, respectively. Often, the foreground traffic is generated when users interact with the app. In an Android OS, a foreground app can be determined if the app is currently at the top of the activity stack. In contrast, the background traffic implies that the app is still connecting to network even users do not interact with it. From Table 2, the foreground traffic accounts for more than 60% in most categories. Foreground traffic accounts for about 50%

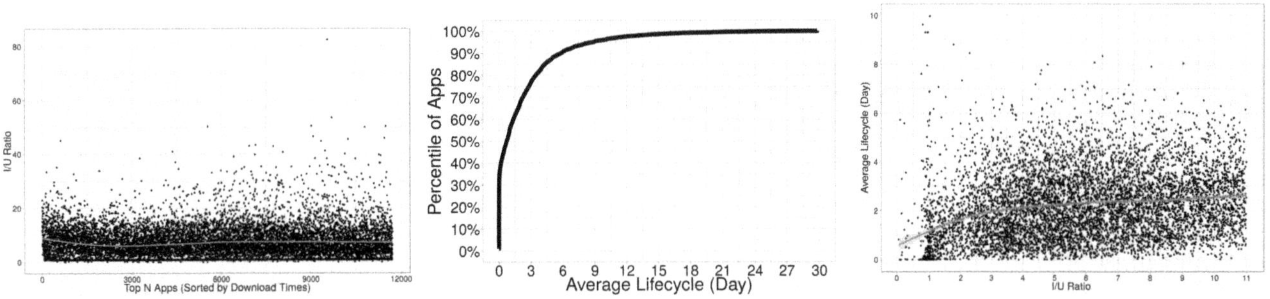

(a) Possibility of app abadonment (b) Lifecyle distribution of abandoned apps (c) Lifecycle of frequently abandoned apps

Figure 9: Lifecyle of abandoned app.

Table 2: Network Summary by App Category

App Category	*C*-Traffic (B)	*W*-Traffic (B)	*C*-Traffic (F)	*W*-Traffic (F)	*C*-Time (B)	*W*-Time (B)	*C*-Time (F)	*W*-Time (F)
VIDEO	0.81%	45.13%	1.28%	52.78%	42.62%	56.66%	0.10%	0.63%
TOOL	8.16%	39.13%	9.56%	43.14%	48.57%	50.42%	0.57%	0.43%
COMMUNICATION	12.42%	15.90%	27.48%	44.20%	48.01%	46.85%	3.15%	1.99%
MUSIC	4.35%	35.19%	5.67%	54.80%	49.23%	50.09%	0.36%	0.32%
SOCIAL	7.26%	20.65%	14.63%	57.47%	48.43%	50.41%	0.57%	0.59%
SYSTEM_TOOL	5.07%	51.57%	2.80%	40.55%	50.02%	49.48%	0.23%	0.26%
SHOPPING	3.29%	17.09%	9.42%	70.21%	43.34%	56.42%	0.08%	0.17%
EDUCATION	3.76%	39.38%	5.46%	51.40%	45.57%	52.83%	0.90%	0.69%
GAME	10.34%	43.11%	8.80%	37.74%	48.13%	51.34%	0.26%	0.28%
NEWS_AND_READING	5.91%	24.64%	14.83%	54.62%	43.43%	55.25%	0.60%	0.71%

W **and** ***C*** **refer to Wi-Fi and Cellular, respectively.**
B **refers to background and** ***F*** **refers to foreground.**

in four categories, i.e., *SYSTEM_TOOL* (43.35%), *GAME* (46.54%), *TOOL* (52.7%), and *VIDEO*(54.1%). **We infer that some apps in these categories keep consuming a large amount of traffic**, when users switch to use other apps, or the screen-off traffic occurs with device sleeping [9]. This observation draws our attention. Usually, *GAME* apps may embed some third-party advertisement libraries (ad-libs). Besides ad-libs, *VIDEO* apps may often prefetch content. Hence, the background traffic of these apps should be necessary. If we can find reasonable explanations for background traffic, we denote such behavior as "reasonable". For example, some management apps such as Wandoujia and anti-virus apps often need downloading or updating actions at background. Otherwise, we annotate an app with "unknown" if we can not judge whether the background traffic is really necessary. We manually check some top apps with high traffic consumptions to see whether these consumptions are reasonable. We find 14 apps that we are not quite clear why they need background network privilege[8]. For example, on average, an alarm clock app (`at.samsung.powersleep`) daily consumes about 13 MB cellular traffic and 156 MB Wi-Fi traffic at background for a user among about 300 users; a LED flashlight app (`com.chenlei.flashlightfree`) daily consumes about 7 MB cellular traffic and 5 MB Wi-Fi traffic at background for a user among about 20 users. Users may suffer from lots of unnecessary loss of background cellular data if they use these apps.

There are some reasons for producing background network activities. One reason is that ad libraries are widely used in a lot of apps, and may download and update advertisements according to user contexts. We simply validate such reason from two aspects. First, we crawl the user reviews of the 14 "suspicious" apps on Wandoujia, and check whether advertisement issues are reported. From user reviews, 3 out of 14 apps are found with complaints about advertisement. Second, by disassembling the `.apk` files and conducting program analysis, we find that 3 out of 14 apps include at least one of popular advertisement libraries published on AppBrain[9]. Although we are still not sure whether and how much these advertisement libraries consume background network, we believe such finding already brings awareness to end-users about the potential traffic loss.

Another reason is that the misuses or even malicious granting of network permissions. Since our current case analysis is manual, we plan to leverage our previously developed `WHYPER` tool [15] to further dig out "suspicious" apps by combining their permissions and descriptions.

In summary, the results show that **users may be unaware that the traffic is "silently but maybe unexpectedly" consumed at background.** It reminds users to alert or kill background network activities after launching these apps. Background network activities may lead to unnecessary data loss in a data plan, or imply some threats.

[8]We list these apps and their network activities on `http://www.sei.pku.edu.cn/~liuxzh/IMC2015/`

[9]http://www.appbrain.com/stats/libraries/ad. AppBrain is a well-known platform for Android users and developers.

5.2 Access Time Patterns

We then investigate the access time of network activities. Intuitively, access time may reflect two important insights. First, the foreground access time of an app indicates how long a user interacts with it. Therefore, such metric can imply how much the user likes or needs the app. Second, similar to background data traffic, background access time indicates how long an app connects to network when users do not interact with it. Therefore, the background access time can imply the "liveness" of the app after it is launched.

Similar to the study of data traffic, we first illustrate the access time distribution among app categories, as shown in Table 1. When exploring the foreground access time, it is not surprising that the *COMMUNICATION* apps account for 49% cellular time and 35.26% against all apps. It is also interesting to find that users spend a lot of time on *TOOL* (10.79% under cellular and 9.46% under Wi-Fi).

We investigate how much foreground and background account for network time, respectively. From Table 2, we are surprised to observe that foreground time accounts for only less than 2% (by aggregating W-Time(F) and C-Time(F)) in total network access time, whereas the background time occupies more than 98% (by aggregating W-Time(B) and C-Time(B)). In other words, **most apps still keep "long-and-live" TCP connection at background after being launched, although they are not used by users**. The background network time may be reasonable for apps that heavily rely on network, e.g., *COMMUNICATION*, and *SOCIAL*. For example, most of these apps require auto synchronization or notification. However, it hardly makes sense that many apps from other categories have continuous network connection at background. Although background network activities do not always reflect more data traffic, they still occupy network connections and may lead to unnecessary energy cost.

6. PRICE-SENSITIVE PATTERNS

The preceding measurements provide us information on some patterns of app selection and network usage. In this section, we further explore these patterns by classifying users, i.e., **how these patterns are influenced by the prices of devices**. Our goal is motivated by two concerns: **(1) do users with devices of different prices have different needs and interests in using apps? (2) if yes to (1), how much do the prices of devices matter?** In other words, we would like to investigate whether the user's usage patterns are price sensitive.

6.1 Device Model Clustering

We cluster users by their device models from the **Networked App Set**, that covers about 2 million users. We finally have 12,091 device models. We present the number of users of each device model in Figure 10. It is observed that 96% device models have less than 500 users. This number of users accounts for only less than 0.1% in our dataset. It demonstrates the heavy fragmentation of Android devices. Therefore, we take a set of *"popular"* device models, each of which has at least 500 users. We further manually check these device models and merge some duplicated device models. For example, GT 7100/7102/7108 all refer to Galaxy Note 2 with the same hardware specification, but customized by different network carriers such as China Mobile and China Unicom. In this way, we finally label 327 "popular" device models. Then, we categorize the 327 device models according to their on-market sale prices. Although the price of a device is cut down gradually after the device is sold, such categorization could still roughly reflect economic factors. We put each device model into one of five groups, which are numbered as 1-5 in Table 3.

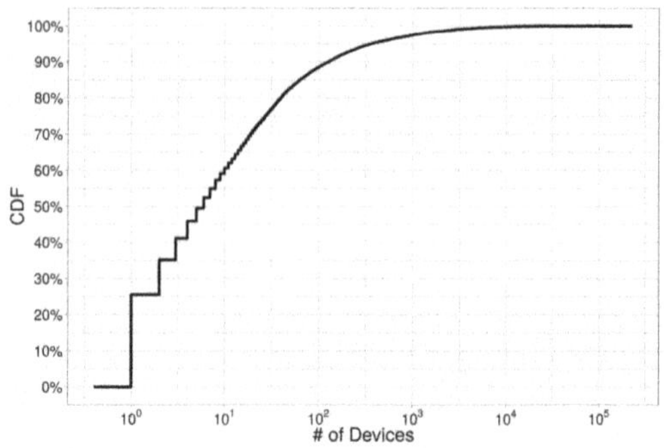

Figure 10: CDF for Number of Users of Device Models

6.2 Apps Used Among Groups

We investigate the number of used apps among different groups, and present the distribution in Figure 11. Note that we examine the apps from the **Networked User Set**, indicating that they are exactly used by users. An immediate observation is that **the higher price a device model has, the more apps are used on this device model**. Such finding might come from two reasons. First, the more expensive device models usually provide more powerful hardware specifications, e.g., faster CPU, larger RAM, and higher definition of screen. The computation power should motivate the users to install and use more apps. Second, more expensive device models usually come from more famous manufacturers, such as Samsung, Motorola, LG. Such observation is attributed to the fact that Android systems customized by these manufacturers may pre-load more apps than cheaper devices, and may lead to the problem of *"bloatware"*. We download the factory ROM files of some representative device models from ROMJD[10]. For example, the Samsung Galaxy Note 2 (Group 5) has 18 pre-installed apps that generate network activities, and the number on Galaxy S4 (Group 4) is 15. In contrast, Meizu M040 (Group 1) has only 9 pre-installed apps that generate network activities. Although we sample only some device models, the finding can support our hypothesis to some degree.

6.3 Network Activity Among Groups

Similar to the preceding analysis of network activities, we show the CDF of data traffic and access time from different groups in Figure 12. **We can find that the usage of Wi-Fi also tends to take a positive correlation with device model price**. In other words, the more expensive a device model is, the more Wi-Fi traffic its users tend to consume. However, **the situation is quite different for cellular traffic**. The differences of cellular traffic among Group 1-3 are quite marginal, where 80% users consume less than 150 MB cellular traffic in one month. From

[10]ROMJD is a website sharing Android ROM files. http://www.romjd.com/

Table 3: Device Model by On-Market Price

Group (price in Chinese Yuan)	# of Device Models	Typical Device Model	# of Covered Users
Group_1: 1,000-	57	HUAWEI-T8951, HUAWEI-C8812, Samsung SCH-I739	216,249
Group_2: 1,000-1,999	98	Motorola XT681,Meizu M040, Samsung GT-I9082	385,811
Group_3: 2,000-2,999	76	Xiaomi MI-1S, Xiaomi MI-2, Samsung GT-S7568, LG-P970	329,361
Group_4: 3,000-4,999	69	Samsung Galaxy S3, Nexus 4, HTC_One	517,262
Group_5: 5,000+	27	Samsung Galaxy Note 2, Galaxy S4, SCH-N719	378,504

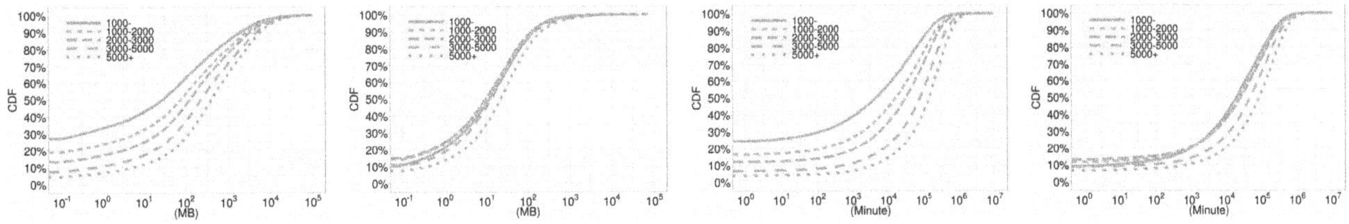

(a) Wi-Fi traffic volume (b) Cellular traffic volume (c) WiFi time (d) Cellular time

Figure 12: Network Activity Distribution among User Groups

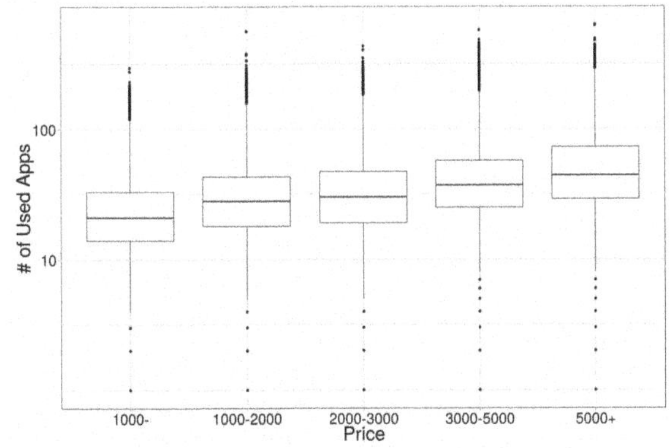

Figure 11: Number of App Usage Across Different Groups

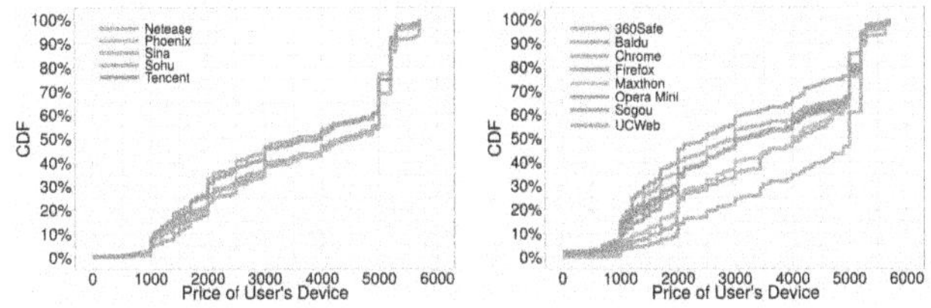

(a) News Reader Apps (b) Browser Apps

Figure 13: Similar App Preferences among User Groups

Group 4, the cellular traffic and the access time begin to increase. Users from Group 5 consume the most cellular traffic and the most access time. About 5% users from this group use about 1GB cellular traffic. There may be two possible reasons. First, as device models from Groups 4 and 5 are more powerful, their users tend to connect to the network and download more contents. Second, users from these two groups could be supposed to have better economic background, so they are likely to afford a higher-cost data plan to use.

6.4 User Interest on Similar Apps

To explore whether users' interests are affected by device prices, we study how users from different groups perform in selecting apps with the same or similar functionalities. We choose two typical types of networked apps: (1) **News Reader**: we choose 5 popular apps: `Netease, Sohu, Phoenix, Tencent`, and `Sina`; (2) **Browser:** we choose 8 popular browsers: `Chrome, FireFox, Opera, Maxthon, UCWeb, 360Safe, Baidu`, and `Sogou`. We show the foreground time against device models. Some preference tendencies could be found. For news reader apps, users from Groups 4 and 5 tend to use the `Netease` app, but users from Groups 1-3 tend to use the `Sohu` app. A similar finding could be found in **Browser**. Users from Groups 4 and 5 tend to use `Chrome`, but users from Group 1-3 tend to use `UCWeb` and `360safe`.

For better understanding the user preferences, we assume that the features and performance may impact users from different groups. First, users in Groups 1-3 may prefer local apps over international apps. For example, `UCWeb` and `360safe` are both developed by local app providers in China, and preferred over `Chrome`. Second, user interface designs may influence target user groups. For example, the `Tencent` news reader often embeds a video that fits the textual content browsed by users. Considering 42% of its users are from Group 3, we can suppose that users in this group are interested in watching videos instead of textual content. In contrast, users from Groups 4-5 seem to prefer to go through the textual content, so they prefer the `Netease` news reader. Third, some specific features might motivate different user preferences. For example, `Opera Mini` is said to save traffic by offloading computation onto cloud, and its 60% users are from Groups 1, 2, and 3. In summary, **such finding implies that device prices has impacts on app selection and usage, and reflect different user interests and needs.**

7. IMPLICATIONS

We have investigated the user behaviors and infer some patterns. In this section, we summarize our findings. We not only validate some findings that were reported in previous studies based on a smaller scale of users, but also identify

Table 4: Summary of Findings and Implications

Findings in Diverse Usage Patterns	Implications for Relevant Stakeholders
The popularity distribution of apps typically follows the "Pareto" effect. A large number of smartphone apps are with only quite few download count and subscriber devices, and contribute marginally to network usage. Such a finding has been mentioned in various previous studies [2, 5, 7, 17].	The **marketplace operators** can identify which apps are really popular and more frequently downloaded and used. The marketplace operators should put the `.apk` files of these popular apps "as close as possible" to end-users, e.g., by deploying Content Delivery Networks (CDN) servers. They can further design efficient mechanisms such as cache, prefetching, and large bandwidth to make these apps fast delivered. The apps that are downloaded by a limited number of devices in a short interval could alert marketplace operators and end-users for further examination.
Diurnal distribution of apps management is quite periodical during a day. Böhmer *et al.* [2] also reported some similar results.	The **marketplace operators** can better allocate resources such as server and bandwidth to adapt the downloading/updating requests. The **app developers** can publish their up-to-date app versions at proper time to attract more downloads.
It is not surprising that some apps are frequently installed together such as *COMMUNICATION* and *SOCIAL*. Apps that come from the same vendor or have similar functionalities are more likely to be installed together.	The **marketplace operators** can improve recommendation systems, e.g., cluster the frequently co-installed apps at a close location to allow end-users to fast download them. The **app developers** can leverage this knowledge to find "mutual-composition" opportunities and design some APIs, e.g., navigating to a *social networking* app from a *news reader* app to share content. Some co-installed apps come from the same vendors. The **end-users** can be cautious to avoid undesirable app downloads. The **advertisers** can deliver relevant ads in some apps. For example, earphone advertisers can focus on users who use *MUSIC* and *VIDEO* apps as they are correlated with *SHOPPING* apps.
An app's installation/uninstallation ratio performs a positive correlation to its lifecycle. Most "disliked" apps are likely to be uninstalled within 2 days.	The **marketplace operators** can know which apps are disliked and further explore why they are abandoned. The **end-users** can judge an app's popularity even without user reviews according to its installation/uninstallation ratio.
Some apps are more network intensive than others with similar functionalities. Similar findings were reported previously [16].	The **marketplace operators** can recommend end-users proper apps that have similar functionalities but better fit the users' data plan. The **network providers** can also leverage this knowledge and provide special data plan. For example, some network providers in China make special data-plan contract with *music* (such as Baidu Music (`com.ting.mp3.oemc.android`) and Kuwo Music (`cn.kuwo.player`)) and *video* apps (such as Youku (`com.cibn.tv`)), and users can pay for this data plan independently and enjoy unlimited cellular traffic to download video/audio files or enjoy them online.
Some apps may consume a large amount of traffic volume at background, but the behaviors might not be reasonable or necessary, e.g., the `flashlight` and `namecard` apps. Some apps are found using advertisement libraries.	Such findings can remind the **marketplace operators** to pay attention to these apps and warn the **end-users** and the **app developers**. The **OS-vendors** can benefit from our findings by preventing these apps from potential threats.
A lot of apps keep long-lived TCP connection when they are not "used" by users.	Background network connections would consume resources and energy, or even imply some malicious behaviors. Such a finding reminds that the **end-users** should periodically "clean up" their devices or terminate the threads of unused apps running at background.
Although fragmentation is quite severe in Android devices, most device models have only few users.	Such findings can suggest the **app developers** focus on mainstream devices and make their apps adaptive to them.
The app selection is diverse among users who take different device models. For example, lower-end device users prefer the `Opera` browser as it is said to save traffic.	The **marketplace operators** can recommend functionality-similar apps to users with different device models.
The network usage is diverse among different users who have different price levels of device models. Lower-end device users heavily rely on Wi-Fi. In contrast, higher-end devices are likely to use more cellular than lower-end device users.	Such findings can predict how much data plan a device will probably use based on the same or similar device models. In this way, the **marketplace operators** can recommend *end-users* different apps according to their own data plan. The **app developers** can also provide some features to adapt different users, e.g., making their apps prefetch contents under Wi-Fi network for the lower-end users.

In the left column, we summarize the findings from our study. In the right column, we suggest some implications for various stakeholders.

some new insights and suggest some implications. We list the findings and implications in Table 4.

8. THREATS TO VALIDITY

One potential limitation of our work is that the dataset is collected from a single app marketplace in China. This limitation may have introduced some biases caused by app marketplace specific policies, and some of our findings may not always hold in other app marketplaces. Care should be given to generalize our findings to another marketplace.

Another limitation is that the users under study are mainly Chinese, and the region differences should be considered. The same limitation also exists in most of previous studies that were conducted over users from a specific region, e.g., some states in USA [24]. To alleviate this issue, we conduct our study over millions of users. We believe that such scale of users could reduce the threats. In fact, our findings such as the Pareto principle of app popularity and user interests of co-installed apps have validated the findings from previous studies.

Because the analysis is done on one month of usage data, some of our findings may not generalize to a longer period of time. Mobile apps are updated very frequently, and some potential security threats of apps, e.g., overprivilege of network permissions, might be already fixed in their up-to-date versions. Meanwhile, we realize that one-month data is not sufficient to predict app quality in the latest Wandoujia marketplace. We plan to evaluate our findings based on a new half-year dataset and investigate how users and app usage evolve.

9. RELATED WORK

Understanding user behavior of mobile apps establishes a foundation for different stakeholders in the research community of mobile computing, e.g., app developers, network providers, marketplace operators, and OS vendors. A plethora of studies have been made from different perspectives.

Understanding User Behavior by Field Study. Given that collecting large-scale user data is hardly feasible for most studies, learning user behavior by field study is always a straightforward way. A lot of studies were performed over specific user groups. Rahmati *et al.* [19, 18] performed a four-month field study of the adoption and usage of smartphone-based services by 14 novice teenage users. Tossell *et al.* [23] applied a naturalistic and longitudinal logs-based approach to collect real usage data from 24 iPhone users in the wild. Sanzi *et al.* [20] collected data from 387 Android users in India, where users pay for cellular data consumed, with little prevalence of unlimited data plans. Falaki *et al.* [6] found that web browsing contributed over half of the traffic. Using detailed traces from 255 volunteer users, Falaki *et al.* [7] conducted a comprehensive study of smartphone use and found immense diversity of users, by characterizing intentional user activities. Lim *et al.* [12] made a questionnaire-based study to discover the diverse usages from about 4,800 users across 15 top GDP countries. Yan *et al.* [25] developed and deployed an app to collect usage logs from over 4,600 users to find their similar interests and explore mobile apps recommendation systems for smartphone apps. For a study closely to ours, Xu *et al.* [24] presented usage patterns by analyzing IP-level traces of thousands of users from a tier-1 cellular carrier in U.S. They identified traffic from distinct marketplace apps based on HTTP signatures and present aggregate results on their spatial and temporal prevalence, locality, and correlation.

Some field studies were made on specific apps. Böhmer *et al.* [2, 3] made a field study over three popular apps such as Angry Bird, Facebook, and Kindle. Patro *et al.* [16] deployed a multiplayer RPG app game and an education app, respectively, and collected diverse information to understand various factors affecting application revenues.

Mining App Marketplace Data. Some types of app related data like user reviews, star ratings, and like/dislike voting are publicly accessible. Chen *et al.* [4] presented AR-Miner to extract informative user reviews and group them using topic modeling. Fu *et al.* [8] presented WisCom, a system that can analyze tens of millions user ratings and comments in mobile app markets. Pestas *et al.* [17] monitored and mined four popular third-party Android app marketplaces and showed that the app popularity distribution deviates from commonly observed Zipf-like model.

Predicting Apps to Use. Some studies target predicting the "*to-be-used*" apps by collecting user logs. Shin *et al.* [22, 21] collected a wide range of smartphone information from 23 users, extracted and analyzed features related to app prediction. Liao *et al.* [11, 10] proposed a temporal-based app predictor to dynamically predict the apps which are most likely to be used. Montoliu *et al.* [13] presented a framework to discover places-of-interest from multimodal mobile phone sensory data. Do *et al.* [5] presented a framework for predicting where users will go and which app they are to use in the next ten minutes from the contextual information collected by smartphone sensors.

Compared to these studies, the major differences of our study include the unique dataset covering millions of users, some unique information such as app installation, uninstallation, and diverse network usage. Although Chinese users take up majority of all users, we believe that behavior patterns inferred from millions of users under study should be more generalized and comprehensive than those from volunteers. With our dataset, we also validate some results that were reported over smaller scale of users. For example, a small set of apps account for substantially a large portion of downloads [17] and unique users [24], some apps are more likely to be installed together [24, 6, 7], and some functionality-similar apps may vary in terms of performance [20]. However, besides using a different dataset collected from millions of users, our study explores uniquely new findings that were not covered previously:

1. First, we make comprehensive measurement of the app popularity from various aspects including downloads, users, and diverse network activities.

2. Second, we explore which apps are likely to be uninstalled and the lifecycle of the abandoned apps.

3. Third, beyond reporting the co-installation of apps, we further explore the possible reasons why these apps are selected together.

4. Fourth, we make a fine-granularity analysis of network activities to identify the "network-intensive" apps and "problematic" apps that consume traffic at background.

5. Finally, we study the economic factor by the price of device model, and explore how it impacts on user behaviors on apps usage.

10. CONCLUSION

We conducted a systematic descriptive analysis of a large collection of mobile app usage behaviors from millions of Android users. Interesting usage patterns are with respect to app popularity, app management, app selection, app abandonment, network usage, and so on. Our findings provide valuable implications for different stakeholders in the mobile app industry and in the research community of mobile computing.

This paper mainly focuses on the descriptive analysis of the data. Many findings of the analysis lead to interesting research questions that can be immediately explored. Such research tasks include predicting app quality and popularity, optimizing app performance, and improving app recommendations, etc. Development of these directions can directly improve the Wandoujia management app and benefit millions of users.

Acknowledgment

This work was supported by the National Basic Research Program (973) of China under Grant No. 2014CB347701, the Natural Science Foundation of China (Grant No. 61370020, 61421091, 61222203, 61572051, 61528201). Tao Xie's work was supported in part by National Science Foundation under grants no. CCF-1349666, CCF-1409423, CNS-1434582, CCF-1434590, CCF-1434596, CNS-1439481, and CNS-1513939. Qiaozhu Mei's work was supported in part by the National Science Foundation under grant no. IIS-1054199.

11. REFERENCES

[1] A. Apaolaza, S. Harper, and C. Jay. Understanding users in the wild. In *Proc. of W4A*, page 13, 2013.

[2] M. Böhmer, B. Hecht, J. Schöning, A. Krüger, and G. Bauer. Falling asleep with angry birds, Facebook and Kindle: a large scale study on mobile application usage. In *Proc. of MobileHCI*, pages 47–56, 2011.

[3] M. Böhmer and A. Krüger. A study on icon arrangement by smartphone users. In *Proc. of CHI*, pages 2137–2146, 2013.

[4] N. Chen, J. Lin, S. C. H. Hoi, X. Xiao, and B. Zhang. AR-miner: mining informative reviews for developers from mobile app marketplace. In *Proc. of ICSE*, pages 767–778, 2014.

[5] T. M. T. Do and D. Gatica-Perez. Where and what: Using smartphones to predict next locations and applications in daily life. *Pervasive and Mobile Computing*, 12:79–91, 2014.

[6] H. Falaki, D. Lymberopoulos, R. Mahajan, S. Kandula, and D. Estrin. A first look at traffic on smartphones. In *Proc. of IMC*, pages 281–287, 2010.

[7] H. Falaki, R. Mahajan, S. Kandula, D. Lymberopoulos, R. Govindan, and D. Estrin. Diversity in smartphone usage. In *Proc. of MobiSys*, pages 179–194, 2010.

[8] B. Fu, J. Lin, L. Li, C. Faloutsos, J. I. Hong, and N. M. Sadeh. Why people hate your app: making sense of user feedback in a mobile app store. In *Proc. of KDD*, pages 1276–1284, 2013.

[9] J. Huang, F. Qian, Z. M. Mao, S. Sen, and O. Spatscheck. Screen-off traffic characterization and optimization in 3g/4g networks. In *Proc. of IMC*, pages 357–364, 2012.

[10] Z. Liao, S. Li, W. Peng, P. S. Yu, and T. Liu. On the feature discovery for app usage prediction in smartphones. In *Proc. of ICDM*, pages 1127–1132, 2013.

[11] Z. Liao, Y. Pan, W. Peng, and P. Lei. On mining mobile apps usage behavior for predicting apps usage in smartphones. In *Proc. of CIKM*, pages 609–618, 2013.

[12] S. L. Lim, P. J. Bentley, N. Kanakam, F. Ishikawa, and S. Honiden. Investigating country differences in mobile app user study behavior and challenges for software engineering. *IEEE Transactions on Software Engineering*, 40(5):40–64, 2014.

[13] R. Montoliu, J. Blom, and D. Gatica-Perez. Discovering places of interest in everyday life from smartphone data. *Multimedia Tools Appl.*, 62(1):179–207, 2013.

[14] M. E. J. Newman. Power Laws, Pareto Distributions and Zipf's Law. *Contemporary Physics*, 46:323, 2005.

[15] R. Pandita, X. Xiao, W. Yang, W. Enck, and T. Xie. WHYPER: Towards automating risk assessment of mobile applications. In *USENIX Security*, pages 527–542, 2013.

[16] A. Patro, S. K. Rayanchu, M. Griepentrog, Y. Ma, and S. Banerjee. Capturing mobile experience in the wild: a tale of two apps. In *Proc. of CoNEXT*, pages 199–210, 2013.

[17] T. Petsas, A. Papadogiannakis, M. Polychronakis, E. P. Markatos, and T. Karagiannis. Rise of the planet of the apps: a systematic study of the mobile app ecosystem. In *Proc. of IMC*, pages 277–290, 2013.

[18] A. Rahmati, C. Tossell, C. Shepard, P. T. Kortum, and L. Zhong. Exploring iphone usage: the influence of socioeconomic differences on smartphone adoption, usage and usability. In *Proc. of MobileHCI*, pages 11–20, 2012.

[19] A. Rahmati and L. Zhong. Studying smartphone usage: Lessons from a four-month field study. *IEEE Trans. Mob. Comput.*, 12(7):1417–1427, 2013.

[20] A. A. Sani, Z. Tan, P. Washington, M. Chen, S. Agarwal, L. Zhong, and M. Zhang. The wireless data drain of users, apps, & platforms. *Mobile Computing and Communications Review*, 17(4):15–28, 2013.

[21] C. Shin and A. K. Dey. Automatically detecting problematic use of smartphones. In *Proc. of Ubicomp*, pages 335–344, 2013.

[22] C. Shin, J. Hong, and A. K. Dey. Understanding and prediction of mobile application usage for smart phones. In *Proc. of Ubicomp*, pages 173–182, 2012.

[23] C. Tossell, P. T. Kortum, A. Rahmati, C. Shepard, and L. Zhong. Characterizing web use on smartphones. In *Proc. of CHI*, pages 2769–2778, 2012.

[24] Q. Xu, J. Erman, A. Gerber, Z. M. Mao, J. Pang, and S. Venkataraman. Identifying diverse usage behaviors of smartphone apps. In *Proc. of IMC*, pages 329–344, 2011.

[25] B. Yan and G. Chen. Appjoy: personalized mobile application discovery. In *Proc. of MobiSys*, pages 113–126, 2011.

Offline Downloading in China: A Comparative Study

Zhenhua Li
Tsinghua University
Tencent Co. Ltd, China
lizhenhua1983@tsinghua.edu.cn

Christo Wilson
Northeastern University
Boston, MA, US
cbw@ccs.neu.edu

Tianyin Xu
University of California
San Diego, CA, US
tixu@cs.ucsd.edu

Yao Liu
State University of New York
Binghamton University
yaoliu@binghamton.edu

Zhen Lu
Tsinghua University
Beijing, China
luzhen02@gmail.com

Yinlong Wang
Tsinghua University
Tencent Co. Ltd, China
wangyinlong239@gmail.com

ABSTRACT

Although Internet access has become more ubiquitous in recent years, most users in China still suffer from low-quality connections, especially when downloading large files. To address this issue, hundreds of millions of China's users have resorted to technologies that allow for "*offline downloading*", where a proxy is employed to pre-download the user's requested file and then deliver the file at her convenience.

In this paper, we examine two typical implementations of offline downloading: the *cloud-based approach* and the *smart AP* (access point) *based approach.* Using a large-scale dataset collected from a major cloud-based system and comprehensive benchmarks of popular smart APs, we find that the two approaches are complementary while also being subject to distinct performance bottlenecks. Driven by these results, we design and implement a proof-of-concept middleware called ODR (Offline Downloading Redirector) to help users get rid of performance bottlenecks.

We feel that offline downloading has broad applicability to other areas of the world that lack broadband penetration. By deploying offline downloading technologies, coupled with our proposed ODR middleware, the Internet experiences for users in many parts of the world can be improved.

Categories and Subject Descriptors

C.2.1 [**COMPUTER-COMMUNICATION NETWORKS**]: Network Architecture and Design—*Store and forward networks*; C.2.5 [**COMPUTER-COMMUNICATION NETWORKS**]: Local and Wide-Area Networks—*Internet*; C.4 [**PERFORMANCE OF SYSTEMS**]: Design studies

General Terms

Design, Experimentation, Measurement, Performance

Keywords

Internet; offline downloading; DTN; cloud storage; smart AP

IMC'15, October 28–30, 2015, Tokyo, Japan.
© 2015 ACM. ISBN 978-1-4503-3848-6/15/10 ...$15.00.
DOI: http://dx.doi.org/10.1145/2815675.2815688.

1. INTRODUCTION

Although Internet access has become more ubiquitous in recent years, many users still suffer from low-quality (*i.e.,* low-bandwidth, intermittent, or restricted) network connections [54, 48, 71, 61, 51, 70]. In particular, there is a huge gap of high-speed, fixed broadband penetration between developed and developing countries. By the end of 2014, the penetration rate of fixed broadband access in the developed world has reached 27.5% with as high as 25 Mbps of download bandwidth [18]. On the other hand, the broadband penetration rate is merely 6.1% in the developing world with relatively limited, unstable download bandwidth [25].

This digital divide prevents many Internet users in developing countries from accessing the full wealth of data and services available online, especially those *large files* (*e.g.,* HD videos and large software) which require high-quality connections to download [45]. Researchers have studied various approaches to making the Internet more accessible, performant, and affordable, such as delay-tolerant networking (DTN) [17, 60]. Nevertheless, to date these technologies have not been widely deployed or evaluated in practice.

Modern China exemplifies both the promise and challenges of increasing Internet penetration [16]. In the last ten years, 46% of China's population has come online [36], and China is now home to world-class Internet companies like Tencent, Baidu, Alibaba, and Sina Weibo. However, the majority (over 72%) of China's Internet users have low-quality connections [38], due to low access bandwidth, unreliable/unstable data connection, and poor inter-connectivity between ISPs (a well-known problem in China known as the *ISP barrier*). The disparity between those who have access to high-speed, fixed broadband and those who do not is likely to increase over the next few years as more of China's rural population comes online.

To deal with the problems caused by low-quality Internet connections, hundreds of millions of China's users have resorted to technologies that allow for "*offline downloading*" of large files [44, 59, 42, 41, 10, 22, 1]. Offline downloading implements ideas from DTNs by outsourcing long downloads to a proxy, as demonstrated in Figure 1. Specifically, when a user wants to acquire a file, the user first *requests* a proxy to *pre-download* the file on her behalf (typically using an HTTP/FTP/P2P link via a low-quality network connection). The proxy may have access to faster, cheaper, or more reliable connectivity than the user, so it is better suited to downloading the file from the Internet. The user can then *fetch* the file from the proxy at a later point in time, when local network conditions are conducive to the task.

In this paper, we examine two implementations of offline downloading that are extremely popular in China [31, 33] (§ 2):

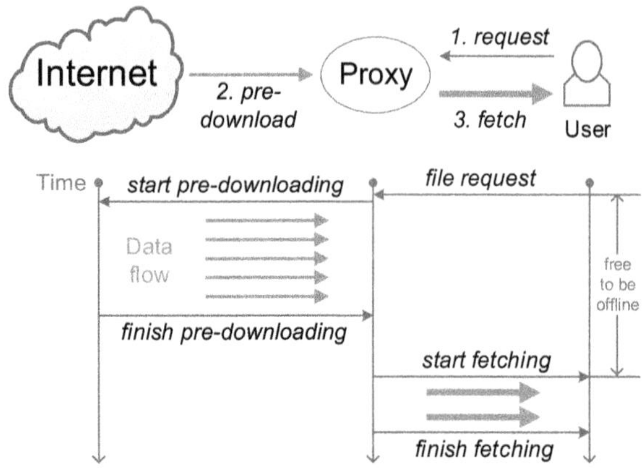

Figure 1: Basic working principle of offline downloading, as well as the corresponding timing diagram.

- *The cloud-based approach* leverages a geo-distributed, massive cloud storage pool as the proxy [59, 44, 72], which usually caches petabytes of files in a datacenter that is within or directly peered with the requesting user's ISP. This approach is adopted by Tencent Xuanfeng [41], Baidu CloudDisk [10], and Xunlei [42]. As it requires expensive cloud infrastructure for data storage and delivery, it is mostly operated by big Internet companies like Tencent and Baidu.
- *The smart AP based approach* relies on a local smart WiFi AP (access point, also known as home router) as the proxy. It is adopted by HiWiFi [21], MiWiFi [28], Newifi [30], *etc.* A traditional AP only forwards data for its connected end devices like laptops and smartphones. In contrast, a smart AP, if requested, also pre-downloads and caches data on an embedded/connected storage device (*e.g.,* an SD card, a USB flash drive, or a hard disk drive). The user can then fetch the requested file at her convenience once it is successfully pre-downloaded. This approach incurs almost zero infrastructure cost, but requires smart AP devices with redesigned hardware, OS, and application software.

Currently, there is a dispute over which approach better suits the best-effort Internet [3, 24]. This *selection dilemma* confuses the users of offline downloading services, especially those who have little expertise in Internet content delivery. The key argument lies in the performance of the two approaches, in terms of (pre-)downloading *speed*, *delay*, and *failure ratio*. Both approaches have advocates that express complaints in news media and marketing reports. However, all these disputes are either limited to one particular offline downloading service/product [59, 44, 6, 7, 8], or rely on oversimplified workloads and network environments [72, 39, 23, 4]. The former make it hard to form a general and unified view of the factors that may affect offline downloading performance, while the latter do not present comprehensive or objective results.

In this paper, we address the issue in a *quantitative* and *comparative* manner. First, we measure the workload characteristics of offline downloading (§ 3), based on a large-scale dataset collected from a major cloud-based system called Xuanfeng [41]. Our analysis of this dataset provides useful insights on the optimization of offline downloading services. Second, we identify the key performance bottlenecks of both approaches, based on the complete running logs of Xuanfeng (§ 4) and comprehensive benchmarks of three popular smart APs (§ 5). Some of our key results include:

1. *The users' fetching processes are often impeded.* The cloud-based approach can usually accelerate downloading by 7∼11 times, but performs *poorly* (*i.e.,* the user's fetching speed falls below 1 Mbps, or 125 KBps, and is thus unfit for HD-video streaming) once there is a bandwidth bottleneck in the network path between the cloud and the user. Specifically, a high portion (28%) of Xuanfeng users suffer from this bottleneck, which is mainly caused by cross-ISP data delivery, low user-side access bandwidth, or lack of cloud-side upload bandwidth. These users should utilize an additional smart AP to mitigate these impediments.
2. *The cloud's upload bandwidth is being overused.* The cloud-based approach is threatened by running out of its upload bandwidth due to *unnecessarily* sending *highly popular* files. A small percentage (0.84%) of highly popular files account for a large part (39%) of all downloads. As the user base grows, the cloud of Xuanfeng will have to reject more (>1.5%) users' fetching requests. Because the majority (87%) of requested files are hosted in peer-to-peer data swarms [47], many highly popular files can be directly downloaded by users with as good or greater performance than what is provided by cloud-based offline downloading services.
3. *Smart APs frequently fail during pre-downloading.* Although smart APs are immune to the above performance bottlenecks of the cloud-based approach, they frequently (42%) fail while pre-downloading *unpopular* files. This is mainly caused by insufficient seeds in a P2P data swarm and poor HTTP/FTP connections. Note that 36% of offline downloading requests are issued for unpopular files. Therefore, users who need to download unpopular files should choose the cloud-based approach, which is better at downloading unpopular files — the failure ratio (13%) is much lower owing to *collaborative caching* (refer to § 2.1) in the massive cloud storage pool.
4. *Smart APs can be slower due to hardware/filesystem restrictions.* Surprisingly, a smart AP's pre-downloading speed can be restricted by its hardware and filesystem. This is because some types of storage devices (*e.g.,* USB flash drive) and filesystems (*e.g.,* NTFS) do not fit the pattern of frequent, small data writes during the pre-downloading process. These smart APs would benefit from upgraded storage devices and/or alternate filesystems, so as to release the full potential of offline downloading.

Driven by these results, we design and implement a proof-of-concept middleware called ODR (Offline Downloading Redirector, available at *http://odr.thucloud.com*) to help users get rid of performance bottlenecks (§ 6). As illustrated in Figure 2, the basic idea of ODR is to adaptively redirect the user's file request to where the best performance is expected to be achieved, including the cloud (we use the Xuanfeng cloud in our implementation), the smart AP, the user's local device, or a combination. ODR's primary goal is to minimize the downloading time and failure ratio; its secondary goal is to minimize the upload bandwidth burden on the cloud.

ODR makes redirection decisions based on two types of information. First, after receiving an offline downloading request, ODR queries the content database of Xuanfeng to obtain the popularity information of the requested file. Then, ODR examines whether there is a potential bandwidth bottleneck by analyzing the user's IP address, access bandwidth, storage device, and so forth. Note that ODR requires no modification to existing cloud-based systems or smart AP devices. As a result, it is easy to deploy in practice.

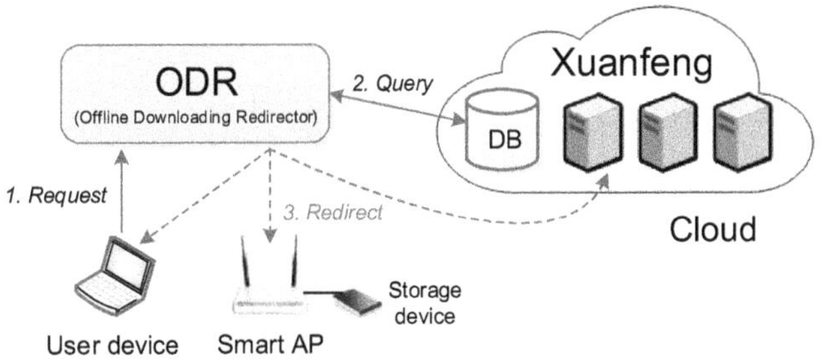

Figure 2: Basic working principle of ODR.

To validate the efficacy of ODR, we replay an unbiased sample of Xuanfeng users' offline downloading requests using a prototype ODR system. The evaluation results indicate that ODR is able to effectively overcome the performance bottlenecks. First, the percentage of impeded fetching processes is reduced from 28% to 9%. Second, the cloud's upload bandwidth burden is reduced by 35% and thus no fetching request will need to be rejected. Third, the percentage of smart APs' failures in pre-downloading unpopular files is reduced from 42% to 13%. Last, the hardware/filesystem restrictions on smart APs' pre-downloading speeds are almost completely avoided.

Finally, we feel that offline downloading has broad applicability to other areas of the world that lack broadband penetration. By deploying offline downloading technologies, coupled with our proposed ODR middleware, the Internet experiences for users in many parts of the world can be significantly improved.

2. SYSTEM OVERVIEW

This section provides an overview of the systems studied in this paper, including the cloud-based offline downloading system (Xuanfeng) and three popular smart AP systems.

2.1 Overview of Xuanfeng

Xuanfeng is a major provider of cloud-based offline downloading service in China, possessing over 30 million users at the moment (including a small portion of overseas users). Its service can be accessed via either a PC client (available from *http://xf.qq.com*) or a web-based portal (available at *http://lixian.qq.com/main.html*). The former access method is dominant due to its full-fledged functionality (supporting almost all the common file transfer protocols like HTTP/FTP and BitTorrent/eMule). In terms of business model, Xuanfeng exists as a value-added service of the Tencent company, *i.e.,* any registered Tencent user can access it freely. Baidu CloudDisk [10] and Xunlei [42] are the main competitors of Xuanfeng [1]. The former is also a free service, while the latter charges its users around $1.50 per month.

As depicted in Figure 3, the system architecture of the Xuanfeng cloud mainly consists of three clusters of servers: 1) *pre-downloading servers*, 2) *storage servers*, and 3) *uploading servers*, as well as a database (DB) for maintaining the metadata information of users and cached files. The total cloud storage space (spread across nearly 500 commodity servers) is nearly 2 PB at the moment, caching around 5 million files. The cached files are replaced in an LRU (least recently used) manner.

[1]Note that the configuration and engineering of Xunlei and Baidu CloudDisk may differ from those of Xuanfeng. Hence, their performance bottlenecks may also be different.

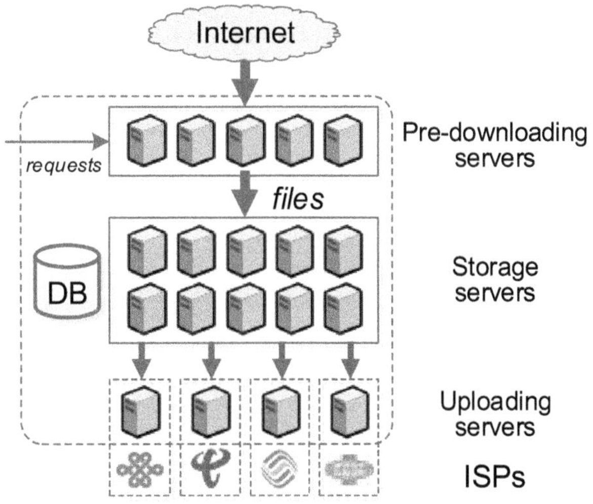

Figure 3: System architecture of the Xuanfeng cloud.

Collaborative caching. In the Xuanfeng cloud, all users' requested files are cached in a *collaborative* way. Specifically, every file is identified using the MD5 hash code of its content, which facilitates file-level deduplication across different users. Consequently, the vast majority (89%) of offline downloading requests can be instantly satisfied with cached files and then no pre-downloading bandwidth cost is incurred. Xuanfeng does not utilize chunk-level deduplication to avoid trading high chunking complexity for low (<1%) storage space savings. The low storage savings come from the fact that there do exist a few videos sharing a portion of frames/chunks.

When a user-requested file cannot be found in the cloud cache, Xuanfeng assigns a virtual machine (named a *pre-downloader*) to pre-download the file from the Internet. The Internet access bandwidth of a pre-downloader is around 20 Mbps (= 2.5 MBps), equivalent to the high-end, fixed broadband bandwidth in China.

Privileged network path. China has a different Internet topology from Europe and the US. Particularly, China has a simple AS topology with a small number of major ISPs; each ISP has a giant AS built on top of a nationwide backbone network [68]. As a consequence, the performance of cross-ISP data delivery is significantly degraded, a problem which is known as the *ISP barrier* [69, 49]. To accelerate users' fetching processes, Xuanfeng tries to construct *privileged network paths* between the cloud and users by deploying uploading servers within the four major ISPs: Unicom [15], Telecom [14], Mobile [13], and CERNET [12].

To construct a privileged network path, Xuanfeng always attempts to select an uploading server that resides in the same ISP as the fetching user, so that the ISP barrier is avoided. However, privileged path construction may fail in two cases: 1) The fetching user is not within any of the four major ISPs; 2) The fetching user is within one of the four major ISPs (say CERNET) but the uploading servers in CERNET have exhausted their upload bandwidth at that time. In either case, Xuanfeng would select an alternative uploading server that has the shortest network latency from the user.

Once a privileged network path is set up, Xuanfeng sets no limitation on the user's fetching speed, with maximum speeds reaching 50 Mbps (= 6.25 MBps). However, at some "peak" point, all the uploading servers may have exhausted their upload bandwidth. In this case, Xuanfeng temporarily rejects new fetching requests rather than degrade the speeds of active downloads.

Table 1: Hardware configurations of the three popular smart APs studied in this paper.

Smart AP	CPU	RAM	Storage Interface (and Device)	WiFi Protocol and Channel
HiWiFi (1S)	MT7620A @580 MHz	128 MB	an SD card interface	IEEE 802.11 b/g/n @2.4 GHz
MiWiFi	Broadcom4709 @1 GHz	256 MB	a USB 2.0 interface and an internal 1-TB SATA hard disk drive	IEEE 802.11 b/g/n/ac @2.4/5.0 GHz
Newifi	MT7620A @580 MHz	128 MB	a USB 2.0 interface	IEEE 802.11 b/g/n/ac @2.4/5.0 GHz

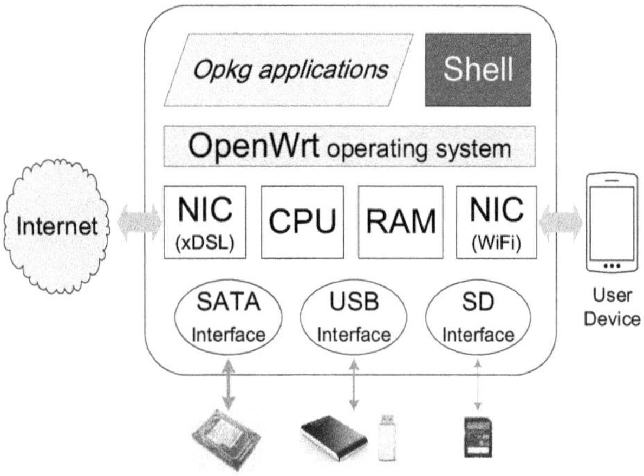

Figure 4: System architecture of a commerical smart AP. Note that a given smart AP device may not contain all potential storage device interfaces.

2.2 Overview of the Smart AP Systems

Though smart APs have only been on the market for around two years, they have quickly gained enormous popularity in China. HiWiFi, the first widely available smart AP device released in Mar. 2013 [20], is now striving towards 5 million sales [22]. Despite the late entry into the market (in May 2014), 100,000 MiWiFi devices were sold out in just 59 seconds [1].

As depicted in Figure 4, the system architecture of popular smart APs is essentially made up of three parts: 1) Basic hardware, including CPU, RAM, NIC (network interface card) for xDSL, NIC for WiFi, and the storage device interface(s); 2) The operating system (typically OpenWrt [34]); 3) Shell and the other applications.

Table 1 lists the hardware configurations of the three popular smart APs we examine in this study. Among them, MiWiFi has the best configuration in terms of CPU, RAM, storage device, and WiFi data transfer. Accordingly, MiWiFi costs more than $100, while HiWiFi and Newifi each costs around $20.

All the three popular smart APs utilize OpenWrt, a Linux-based embedded operating system. OpenWrt provides a fully writable filesystem and supports the lightweight Opkg package management system [35], which allows users to install any Opkg application. For instance, the three APs make use of wget and aria2 [9] to support HTTP/FTP and BitTorrent/eMule protocols. Also, a web interface is provided for users to specify offline downloading requests. In our benchmark experiments, we measure and record detailed performance of smart APs with Opkg tools/apps such as BASH, tcpdump, top, iostats, and scp.

3. WORKLOAD CHARACTERISTICS

To understand the workload characteristics of offline downloading, we study a large-scale dataset collected from Xuanfeng. We assume that the smart AP based offline downloading systems have similar workload characteristics to Xuanfeng, since most end users are not familiar with the technical details and cannot differentiate these services. The large-scale dataset contains the complete running logs of Xuanfeng during a whole week (Feb. 22–28, 2015), involving 4,084,417 offline downloading tasks, 783,944 users, and 563,517 unique files. Corresponding to the three stages of offline downloading (refer to Figure 1), the dataset is composed of the following three parts:

1. The trace of user requests (workload trace) records all the offline downloading requests issued by users. For each request, the logs record the user ID, IP address, access bandwidth (if available), request time, file type, file size, link to the original data source, and file transfer protocol;

2. The pre-downloading trace records the performance data of the proxy's pre-downloading user-requested files. It includes the start time, finish time, acquired file size, network traffic consumed, cloud cache hit status, average downloading speed, peak downloading speed, and success or failure for each pre-downloading process;

3. The fetching trace records the performance data of users' fetching processes from the proxy. It contains the user ID, IP address, access bandwidth (if available), start time, finish/pause time, acquired file size, network traffic consumed, average fetching speed, and peak fetching speed for each fetching process.

This section studies the first part of the dataset (*i.e.,* users' offline downloading requests). The second and third parts of the dataset will be examined in § 4 and § 5.

File type. In the workload trace, the majority (75%) of offline downloading requests are issued for videos; the other 15% are for software packages. The reason is intuitive: among all the requested files, videos are the largest in size, *i.e.,* the most time and traffic consuming to download, so users are more inclined to issue offline downloading requests for videos. This suggests that offline downloading systems should be mainly optimized for videos.

File size. As shown in Figure 5, the average size of requested files is 390 MB and the maximum size is 4 GB, which is consistent with our observation that most requested files are large videos. Nevertheless, we also find that up to 25% of requested files are smaller than 8 MB in size, most of which are demo videos, pictures, documents, and small software packages.

File transfer protocol. The majority (87%) of requested files are hosted in P2P data swarms, including BitTorrent (68%) and eMule (19%) swarms. The remaining 13% are hosted on HTTP or FTP servers. Thus, designers of offline downloading systems should pay special attention to P2P-based file transfer protocols.

Since P2P suffers from several technical shortcomings (*e.g.,* high dynamics and heterogeneities among end-user devices and network connections), it is often difficult for users to find peers (including both seeds and leechers) sharing the target files. As a result, the downloading efficacy of P2P can be poor and unpredictable. For

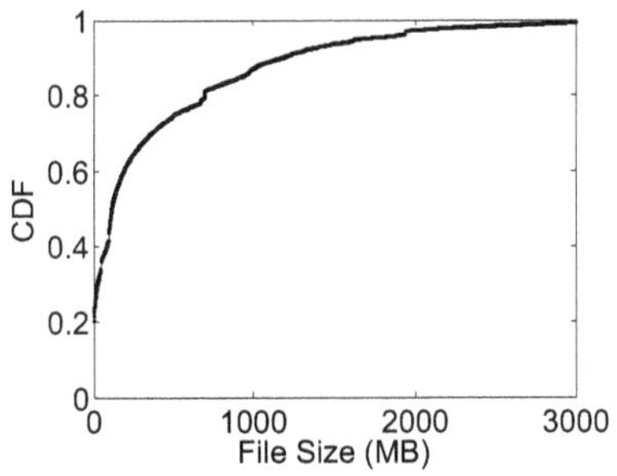

Figure 5: CDF of requested file size. Min size: 4 B, Median size: 115 MB, Average size: 390 MB, and Max size: 4 GB.

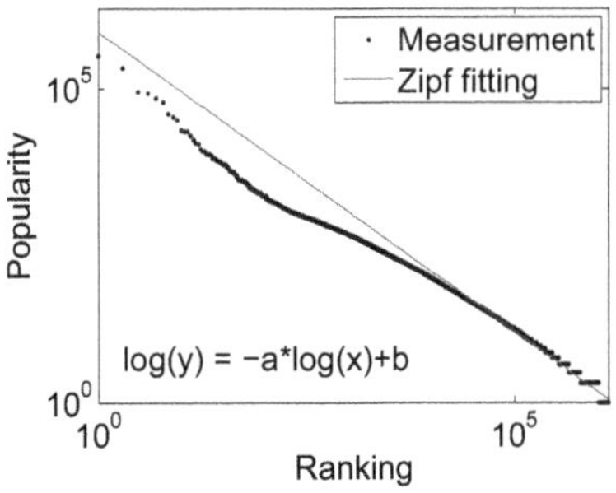

Figure 6: Popularity distribution of requested files — Zipf fitting. The average relative error of fitness is 15.3%.

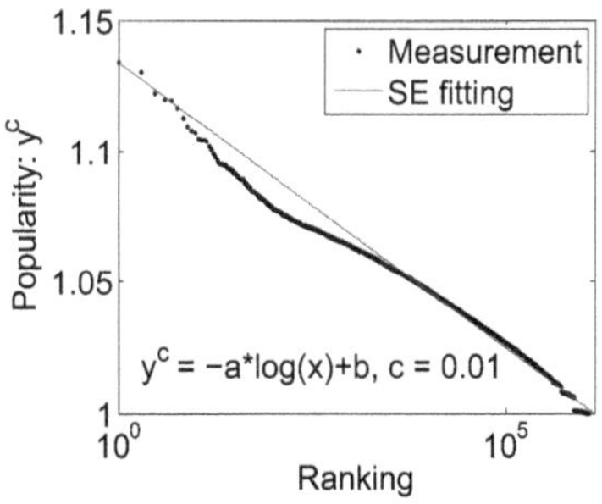

Figure 7: Popularity distribution of requested files — SE fitting. The average relative error of fitness is 13.7%.

this reason, users resort to offline downloading to obtain P2P files over the long run. On the contrary, HTTP and FTP servers are usually stable with more predictable performance, so online downloading is preferred. This explains the dominance of P2P in terms of file transfer protocol.

File popularity. As mentioned in § 2.1, Xuanfeng actively maintains a content database where every file is associated with a unique identifier (ID). The ID is the MD5 hash code of the complete file content. Hence, files are considered *identical* as long as they have the same ID. Figure 6 (in $\log(x)$ *vs.* $\log(y)$ style) and Figure 7 (in $\log(x)$ *vs.* y^c style) indicate that the popularity distribution of requested files is highly skewed, approximately following the well known Zipf model [46] or the SE (stretched exponential) model [56].

Let x denote the popularity ranking of a file, and y denote its popularity (according to the workload trace). Then, we have the following fitting equations:

$$\text{Zipf:} \quad log(y) = -a_1 \times log(x) + b_1,$$
$$\text{SE:} \quad y^c = -a_2 \times log(x) + b_2,$$

where $a_1 = 1.034$, $b_1 = 14.444$, $a_2 = 0.010$, $b_2 = 1.134$, and $c = 0.01$.

With regard to the average relative error of fitness, SE (13.7%) seems to be a better fit than Zipf (15.3%), especially for those small-ranking (*i.e.,* most popular) files. The reason why SE fits the measurement data better than Zipf can be mainly attributed to the *fetch-at-most-once* effect of P2P video files [55]. It is known that 75% of offline downloading requests are issued for videos and 87% of requested files are hosted in P2P data swarms. That is to say, P2P video files dominate the workload of Xuanfeng. Specifically, a given Xuanfeng user generally fetches a P2P video file for at most once, whereas web pages and other small documents are often fetched repeatedly [46]. Therefore, the access pattern of offline downloaded files deviates from the Zipf access pattern of web objects. The above finding complements the analysis of file popularity in previous studies of offline downloading [59, 72], which simply used the Zipf model to characterize the workload.

4. PERFORMANCE OF THE CLOUD-BASED SYSTEM

This section presents the performance of our representative cloud-based offline downloading system Xuanfeng, including both the pre-downloading and fetching phases. In addition, we analyze the end-to-end performance by combining the two phases.

4.1 Pre-downloading Performance

Pre-downloading speed. Figure 8 (the upper curve) plots the distribution of pre-downloading speeds in Xuanfeng. The median speed is merely 25 KBps, which indicates that half of the pre-downloading processes are quite slow. The average speed (69 KBps) is higher than the median speed, but is still far from satisfactory — keep in mind that, as mentioned in § 2.1, the access bandwidth of a pre-downloader is around 20 Mbps (= 2.5 MBps). 21% of the pre-downloading processes even have a speed close to 0 KBps, which is mostly caused by pre-downloading failures.

Pre-downloading delay. Figure 9 (the lower curve) plots the distribution of the pre-downloading delay in Xuanfeng (excluding the cache-hit cases where the pre-downloading delay is zero). The average delay is as high as 370 minutes, which is much longer than the length of a common movie (100∼120 minutes). Obviously, such long delay is unfit for continuous video streaming [63, 53]. Also, the average delay is much longer than the median delay (82 minutes), indicating that the pre-downloading delay of many requested files is extremely long.

Failure ratio. A *pre-downloading failure* occurs when the service gives up the pre-downloading attempt and notifies the requesting user of the failure. It is hard to theoretically define a failure if we allow the pre-downloading process to take infinite time. However, practical systems have to timeout the pre-downloading process if the expected completion time is not reasonable. In practice, Xuanfeng raises a pre-downloading failure for a requested file when *the corresponding pre-downloading progress stagnates for an hour*. This timeout rule is supported by our following observation in Xuanfeng: if the pre-downloading progress of a requested file stagnates for an hour, then this file can hardly be successfully pre-downloaded even if the timeout threshold is set to be one week.

The overall pre-downloading failure ratio of Xuanfeng is 8.7%. Note that if a user-requested file is already cached in the cloud storage pool, the pre-downloading is immediately successful. On the other hand, if we do not take the cache hit cases into account (*i.e.,* we assume that the cloud storage pool does not exist), the overall pre-downloading failure ratio will increase to 16.4%. This confirms the importance of the massive cloud storage pool as well as the collaborative caching mechanism (refer to § 2.1) in mitigating pre-downloading failures.

More importantly, we discover that the pre-downloading failure ratio correlates with the popularity of requested files, as shown in the scatter plot of Figure 10. For the purposes of this discussion, we define a file to be *unpopular* if it was downloaded less than 7 times per week. *Popular* files are downloaded 7–84 times per

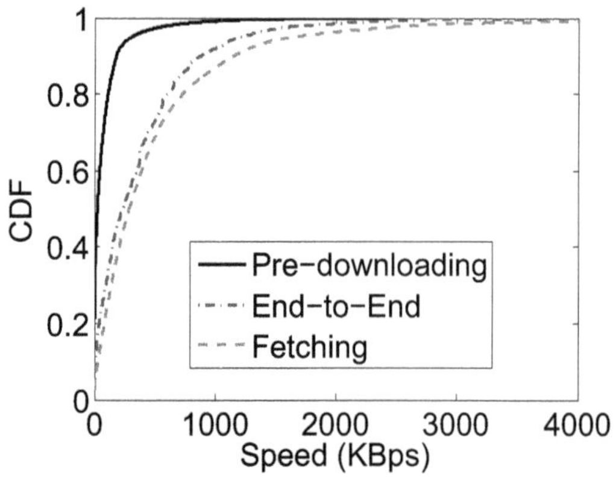

Figure 8: CDF of pre-downloading and fetching speeds in Xuanfeng. As for the pre-downloading speed (excluding the cache-hit cases), Min: 0 KBps, Median: 25 KBps, Average: 69 KBps, and Max: 2.37 MBps ($\approx$ 20 Mbps). As for the fetching speed, Min: 0 KBps, Median: 287 KBps, Average: 504 KBps, and Max: 6.1 MBps ($\approx$ 50 Mbps). As for the end-to-end speed, Min: 0 KBps, Median: 233 KBps, Average: 380 KBps, and Max: 6.1 MBps ($\approx$ 50 Mbps).

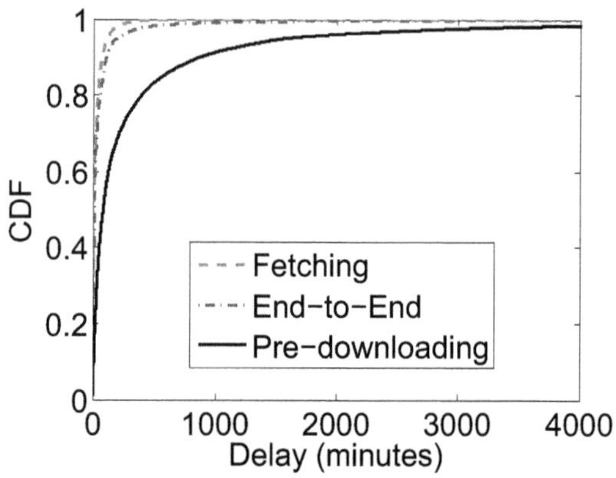

Figure 9: CDF of pre-downloading, fetching, and end-to-end delay in Xuanfeng. As for the pre-downloading delay (excluding the cache-hit cases), Min: 0 minute, Median: 82 minutes, Average: 370 minutes, and Max: 10071 minutes. As for the fetching delay, Min: 0 minute, Median: 7 minutes, Average: 27 minutes, and Max: 9724 minutes. As for the end-to-end delay, Min: 0 minute, Median: 10 minutes, Average: 68 minutes, and Max: 19553 minutes.

week, while *highly popular* files are downloaded greater than 84 times per week. Given these definitions, we find that 93.2% of files are unpopular while only 0.84% of files are highly popular. However, only 36% of offline downloading requests are issued for the 93.2% unpopular files, while 39% of requests are issued for the 0.84% highly popular files.

Network traffic cost. As discussed in § 3, only 13% of requested files are hosted in HTTP or FTP servers, while 87% are hosted in P2P data swarms. For HTTP and FTP, the pre-downloading traffic is slightly (typically 7%–10%) larger than the file size; the overhead mainly comes from HTTP, FTP, TCP, and IP packet headers. For P2P, its "tit-for-tat" policy [50] (*i.e.*, a peer that downloads data from others must upload data to others at the same time) causes the pre-downloading traffic to be considerably (50%–150%) larger than the file size. In the Xuanfeng system, we observe that the overall pre-downloading traffic is 196% of the total file size. That is to say, the overhead traffic is comparable to the file size.

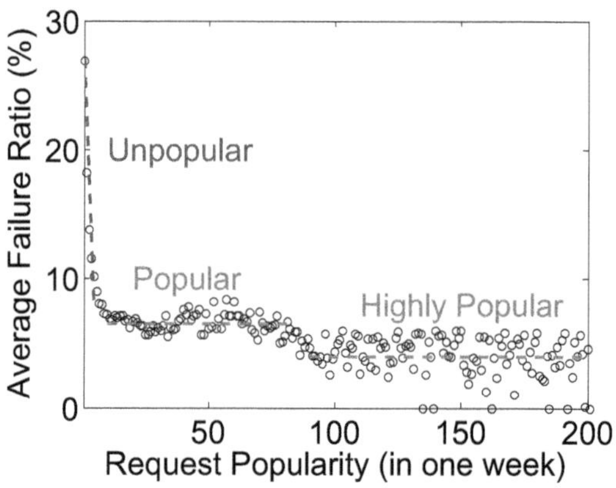

Figure 10: Request popularity *vs.* Pre-downloading failure ratio. Request popularity: [0, 7) $\rightarrow$ unpopular files, [7, 84] $\rightarrow$ popular files, and (84, MAX] $\rightarrow$ highly popular files.

4.2 Fetching Performance

Fetching speed. Figure 8 (the lower curve) shows the distribution of users' fetching speeds from the cloud. Owing to the privileged network paths constructed by Xuanfeng (refer to § 2.1), the median and average fetching speeds are as high as 287 KBps and 504 KBps. Given that the median and average pre-downloading speeds are merely 25 KBps and 69 KBps, Xuanfeng greatly improves *perceived* downloading speeds (by 7~11 times in terms of median and average speeds) for China's Internet users.

When videos are fetched from the proxy, Xuanfeng supports two different modes: a) *view-as-download* and b) *view-after-download*. According to Xuanfeng users' behaviors, most users tend to choose the former mode over the latter. Therefore, to facilitate users' real-time video playback in a continuous manner, a *bandwidth bottleneck* is recognized when the fetching speed falls below 125 KBps. The 125 KBps threshold corresponds with the typical 1 Mbps playback rate of large (HD) videos [57, 62].

Specifically, a high portion (28%) of fetching speeds are below 125 KBps. To explore why Xuanfeng exhibits poor performance during these fetching processes, we carefully examine the corresponding logs in the fetching trace, and find that the bandwidth bottleneck is mainly caused by three issues: 1) cross-ISP data delivery, 2) low user-side access bandwidth, and 3) lack of cloud-side upload bandwidth.

In detail, 9.6% of fetching processes are limited by the ISP barrier. For these fetching processes, the users' IP addresses do not belong to any of the four ISPs supported by Xuanfeng. Besides, around 10.8% of fetching processes are limited by low user-side access bandwidth [2] ($<$ 125 KBps). Additionally, there are 1.5% of fetching requests rejected by the cloud due to lack of upload bandwidth (refer to § 2.1). These rejected requests explain why the minimum observed fetching speed is 0 KBps. Finally, the remaining unmentioned portion ($= 28\% - 9.6\% - 10.8\% - 1.5\% = 6.1\%$) are owing to unknown reasons we have not figured out yet, possibly because of the network dynamics or system bugs.

[2]Some users of Xuanfeng did not report their access bandwidth. For these users, we use the peak fetching speed recorded in the fetching trace to approximate their access bandwidth.

Fetching delay. Figure 9 (the upper curve) shows the distribution of users' fetching delay. As a consequence of most users' high fetching speeds, the median fetching delay is as low as 7 minutes and the average fetching delay is merely 27 minutes. Given that the median and average pre-downloading delay is as high as 82 minutes and 370 minutes, Xuanfeng has significantly shortened *perceived* downloading delay (by 12∼14 times in terms of median and average fetching delay) for China's Internet users.

In summary, we find the first key performance bottleneck of offline downloading:

- *The cloud-based approach performs poorly once there is a bandwidth bottleneck in the privileged network path between the cloud and the user. This bottleneck is mainly caused by cross-ISP data delivery, low user-side access bandwidth, or lack of cloud-side upload bandwidth.*

Shortage of cloud bandwidth. In order to support high-speed fetching from the cloud to users' devices, Xuanfeng has purchased a total of 30 Gbps of upload bandwidth from the four major ISPs in China. In the 7th day of the measurement week, the peak cloud-side upload bandwidth burden exceeded 30 Gbps, as demonstrated in Figure 11. Consequently, a small portion (1.5%) of fetching requests were rejected by Xuanfeng. As the user base continues to grow, Xuanfeng will have to reject more fetching requests, which unfortunately harms the user experience.

On the other hand, if we look deeply into the usage of cloud bandwidth, we find that *the current cloud-side upload bandwidth burden is not all necessary.* We calculate the cloud-side bandwidth used for delivering (uploading) highly popular files based on the fetching trace, plotted as the lower, blue curve in Figure 11. We can see that, on average, nearly 40% of the cloud bandwidth is spent delivering highly popular files. The reason is that a small percentage (0.84%) of highly popular files account for a large part (39%) of all downloads, as discussed in § 4.1.

In fact, because the majority (87%) of requested files are hosted in P2P data swarms, many highly popular files can be directly downloaded by users with as good or greater performance than what the cloud provides [66, 64]. This is because P2P data sharing among end users can achieve the so-called "*bandwidth multiplier effect*" [66]. Specifically, by appropriately allocating a certain portion of cloud bandwidth (S_i) to a P2P data swarm i to seed the content, the Xuanfeng system can attain a higher aggregate content distribution bandwidth (D_i) by letting P2P users exchange data and distribute content among themselves. The ratio $\frac{D_i}{S_i}$ is referred to as the bandwidth multiplier for P2P data swarm i. The above observation and analysis lead to the second key performance bottleneck of offline downloading:

- *The cloud-based approach is threatened by running out of upload bandwidth due to unnecessarily sending highly popular files. As the user base continues to grow, the cloud will have to reject more (>1.5%) fetching requests.*

User-side network overhead. Xuanfeng minimizes the user-side network overhead, as its users only download requested files from the cloud and do not upload data to others. On average, a user's downloading traffic usage is slightly (7% – 10%) larger than the file size. This is especially useful for mobile P2P users with limited data plans or traffic caps. As mentioned in § 4.1, for an average P2P user to download a file from the corresponding data swarm, the total traffic usage is 196% of the total file size. Therefore, by resorting to Xuanfeng rather than the original data swarm, an average P2P user could achieve considerable traffic usage saving which is comparable to 86% – 89% of the total file size.

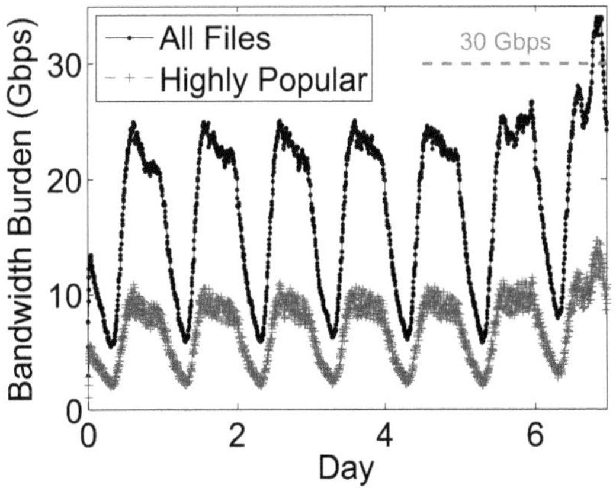

Figure 11: Cloud-side upload bandwidth burden of Xuanfeng in the measurement week (including those rejected fetching requests). The time interval is 5 minutes. Note that for the 1.5% of fetching requests rejected by Xuanfeng in the 7th day, their incurred cloud-side upload bandwidth burden (which did not really happen) is estimated by approximately taking their average fetching speed as 504 KBps (*i.e.,* , the average speed of all the real fetching processes in Xuanfeng, refer to Figure 8).

4.3 End-to-End Performance

Finally, we analyze the *end-to-end speed and delay* of offline downloading in Xuanfeng. For a complete offline downloading process, the end-to-end delay is the sum of pre-downloading delay and fetching delay, and the end-to-end speed is the size of the requested file divided by the end-to-end delay.

As illustrated in Figure 9, the CDF curve of end-to-end delay falls between the CDF curves of pre-downloading delay and fetching delay, which is within our expectation. More importantly, the distribution of end-to-end delay looks much closer to the distribution of fetching delay. This is because the vast majority (89%) of offline downloading requests can be instantly satisfied by the cloud cache and thus the corresponding pre-downloading delay is almost zero (refer to § 2.1). Similarly, Figure 8 indicates that the CDF curve of end-to-end speed falls between the CDF curves of pre-downloading speed and fetching speed, and the distribution of end-to-end speed is much closer to the distribution of fetching speed.

From the above observations, we conclude that even from an end-to-end perspective, the offline downloading service provided by Xuanfeng can effectively improve the *perceived experiences* for its users.

5. PERFORMANCE OF THE SMART APS

Now that we understand the dynamics and performance characteristics of Xuanfeng, we move on to examining smart AP based offline downloading. In this section, we report our benchmark methodology and the performance of the three most popular smart APs in China: HiWiFi, MiWiFi, and Newifi.

5.1 Methodology

To comprehensively measure the performance of the three popular smart APs (during Mar. 1–22, 2015), we randomly sample 1000 real offline downloading requests [3] issued by Unicom users

[3]Each selected request record should contain the user's access bandwidth information so that we can approximate the user's real network connection characteristics during our benchmarks.

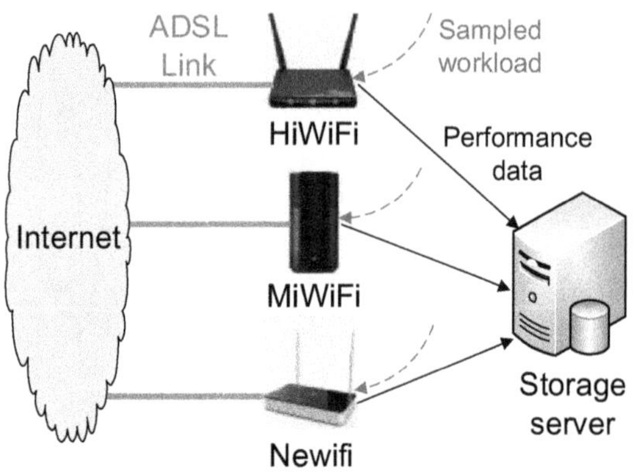

Figure 12: Our benchmark environment. For each smart AP, its embedded/connected storage device is not plotted to make the figure tidy.

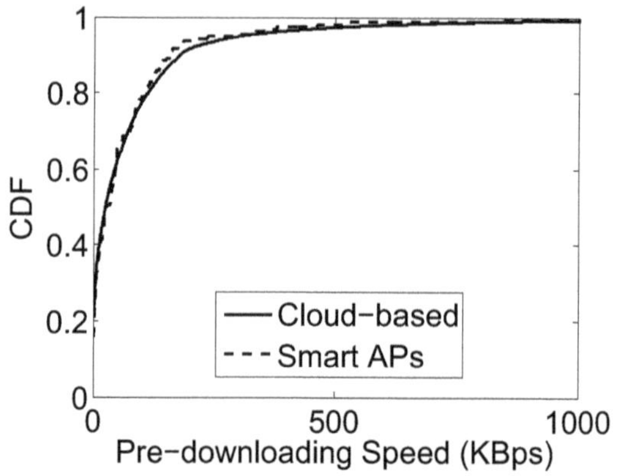

Figure 13: CDF of smart APs' pre-downloading speeds. Min: 0 KBps; Median: 27 KBps; Average: 64 KBps; Max: 2.37 MBps (≈ 20 Mbps) for HiWiFi and MiWiFi, and 0.93 MBps for Newifi. As a comparison, the CDF of cloud-based pre-downloading speeds is also plotted.

in the workload trace of Xuanfeng (refer to § 3). These sampled requests (which we refer to as the sampled workload) are restricted to Unicom users because our benchmark experiments are conducted by replaying the sampled workload with smart APs on Unicom network connections. On the other hand, the data sources of these sampled requests are located across various ISPs in China. For every request record, we ignore its user ID, IP address, and request time (since these factors cannot be reproduced in our benchmarks), but reuse the user's access bandwidth, as well as the file type, file size, link to the original data source, and file transfer protocol.

To replay the sampled workload using the three smart APs, we utilize three independent residential ADSL links provided by the Unicom ISP, each of which was used exclusively by one smart AP, as depicted in Figure 12. Each link has 20 Mbps (= 2.5 MBps) of Internet access bandwidth. When replaying an individual offline downloading request, we restrict the smart AP's pre-downloading speed within the recorded user access bandwidth, so as to approximate the real network connection status. We sequentially replay around 333 requests (request $i+1$ is replayed after request i completes or fails) on each smart AP and record the performance data.

HiWiFi uses an embedded 8-GB SD card (Max Write/Read Speed: 15 MBps/30 MBps) as the storage device. The SD card can only be formatted as FAT (otherwise, HiWiFi does not work). Newifi uses an external 8-GB USB flash drive (Max Write/Read Speed: 10 MBps/20 MBps) via a USB 2.0 interface. The USB flash drive is formatted as NTFS. Since both HiWiFi and Newifi have a small storage capacity, we remove requested files from the storage device after they are completely downloaded or the corresponding pre-downloading task failures (refer to § 4.1). At the same time, the performance data is aggregated into a storage server. MiWiFi uses its internal 1-TB SATA hard disk drive (5400 RPM, Max Write/Read Speed: 30 MBps/70 MBps). This hard disk drive has been formatted as EXT4 by the manufacturer, and it cannot be re-formatted to any other filesystem.

5.2 Benchmark Results

Since smart APs are located in the same LAN (local area network) as users, the performance of the fetching phase is seldom an issue except when multiple user devices are fetching from a smart AP at the same time. Specifically, a user can fetch from a smart AP by directly dumping from the AP's storage device or through a wired/WiFi LAN connection. Even the lowest WiFi fetching speed lies in 8∼12 MBps, which is higher than the maximum fetching speed (*i.e.,* 6.1 MBps) of Xuanfeng users. As a consequence, below we focus on the performance of the pre-downloading phase.

Pre-downloading failure ratio. The overall pre-downloading failure ratio of smart APs is 16.8%, which is higher than that of Xuanfeng (8.7%). More importantly, for unpopular files the pre-downloading failure ratio of smart APs is as high as 42%, significantly higher than that of Xuanfeng (13%). Note that according to the workload trace of Xuanfeng, 36% of offline downloading requests are issued for unpopular files. With these results, we discover the third key performance bottleneck of offline downloading:

- *Although smart APs are immune to the two bottlenecks of the cloud-based approach described in § 4, they frequently fail in pre-downloading unpopular files. In contrast, the cloud-based approach performs much better at downloading unpopular files since it benefits from the massive geo-distributed cloud storage pool.*

Further, we delve into the details of the pre-downloading failures of smart APs. Among the 168 (= 1000 × 16.8%) failures, the vast majority (145, 86%) were caused by insufficient seeds in a P2P data swarm. This explains why the pre-downloading failure ratio of unpopular files is especially high. Besides, a non-negligible part (17, 10%) were ascribed to poor HTTP/FTP connections, *i.e.,* the server at the other end failed to maintain a persistent/resumable download. The remainder (6, 4%) might be the result of system bugs in HiWiFi, MiWiFi and Newifi.

Pre-downloading speed and delay. As shown in Figure 13 and Figure 14, the pre-downloading speeds of smart APs are just a bit lower than those of Xuanfeng's pre-downloaders, and thus the pre-downloading delay of smart APs seems a bit longer than that of Xuanfeng. This is because smart APs work in a similar way as the pre-downloaders (*i.e.,* they also download files using HTTP, FTP and P2P protocols; refer to § 2.1), although their access bandwidths are generally lower than 20 Mbps (or 2.5 MBps, *i.e.,* a pre-downloader's access bandwidth).

However, one detail in Figure 13 and Figure 14 is worth discussing: the median pre-downloading speed of smart APs (27 KBps) is *higher* than that of Xuanfeng (25 KBps), but the average pre-downloading speed of smart APs (64 KBps) is *lower* than that of Xuanfeng (69 KBps). Accordingly, the median pre-downloading

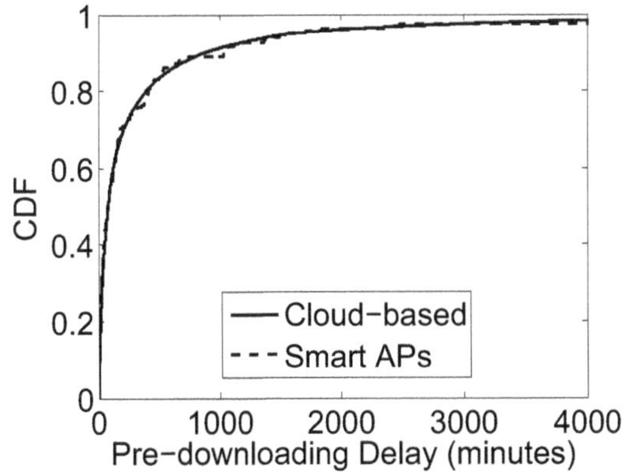

Figure 14: CDF of smart APs' pre-downloading delay. Min: 0 minutes; Median: 77 minutes; Average: 402 minutes; Max: 8297 minutes. As a comparison, the CDF of cloud-based pre-downloading delay is also plotted.

delay of smart APs (77 minutes) is *shorter* than that of Xuanfeng (82 minutes), but the average pre-downloading delay of smart APs (402 minutes) is *longer* than that of Xuanfeng (370 minutes). To demystify this counter-intuitive phenomenon, we examine the pre-downloading performance data of every task in the sampled workload and its original performance data in the pre-downloading trace. Surprisingly, we uncover the fourth key performance bottleneck of offline downloading:

- *A smart AP's pre-downloading speed can be restricted by its hardware and/or filesystem, since some types of storage devices and filesystems do not fit the pattern of frequent, small data writes during the pre-downloading process.*

In particular, among all the experimented storage devices, USB flash drive is the slowest. When Newifi uses the USB flash drive (in the NTFS format) as its storage device, the max pre-downloading speed is merely 0.93 MBps, much lower than that of HiWiFi and MiWiFi (2.37 MBps). This finding is basically consistent with Sundaresan *et al.* 's study results on broadband Internet performance in 2011, which also indicate that a user's home network equipment (including the home router of course, though smart APs did not exist in 2011) can significantly affect downloading performance [67].

To comprehensively understand the influence of hardware and filesystem on Newifi's pre-downloading speed, we replay the top-10 popular requests in the sampled workload on Newifi while setting no restriction on its pre-downloading speed (so the maximum speed should be nearly 2.37 MBps). We conducted replays with the USB flash drive formatted as FAT, NTFS, and EXT4, respectively, as well as with the USB flash drive replaced by a USB hard disk drive (5400 RPM, Max Write/Read Speed: 10 MBps/25 MBps). The resulting maximum pre-downloading speeds, as well as the corresponding iowait ratios, are listed in Table 2. We make three observations as follows:

- The NTFS filesystem severely harms Newifi's maximum pre-downloading speed, no matter whether the storage device is a USB flash drive or a USB hard disk drive. This is mainly attributed to the incompatibility between NTFS and Newifi's OpenWrt operating system (refer to § 2.2) which utilizes the EXT4 filesystem.
- When Newifi uses a USB flash drive as its storage device, FAT and EXT4 filesystems also appear to have degraded its maximum pre-downloading speed. The major reason should be the unsuitability of the USB flash drive on handling frequent, small data writes during pre-downloading. This is reflected by the high iowait ratios (66.3% and 55%) as shown in Table 2. Besides, we observe that the receiver-side TCP sliding window (the typical size is 14608 bytes) is almost full in most of the time during the pre-downloading process.
- When Newifi uses a USB hard disk drive, its maximum pre-downloading speed is considerably enhanced (compared with using a USB flash drive) even when the hard disk drive is formatted as NTFS. No matter which filesystem is used, the iowait ratio is relatively low.

Table 2: Max pre-downloading speeds and the corresponding iowait ratios for HiWiFi, MiWiFi, and Newifi, with different storage devices and filesystems.

Max pre-downloading speed (MBps)	FAT	NTFS	EXT4
HiWiFi + SD card	2.37	–	–
MiWiFi + SATA hard disk drive	–	–	2.37
Newifi + USB flash drive	**2.12**	**0.93**	**2.13**
Newifi + USB hard disk drive	2.37	**1.13**	2.37
iowait ratio	**FAT**	**NTFS**	**EXT4**
HiWiFi + SD card	42.1%	–	–
MiWiFi + SATA hard disk drive	–	–	29.7%
Newifi + USB flash drive	**66.3%**	15.1%	**55%**
Newifi + USB hard disk drive	42%	9.8%	17.4%

Based on the above observations, we suggest that Newifi-like smart APs upgrade their storage devices and/or change their default filesystems to more performant variants, so as to release the full potential of offline downloading. Currently, because Newifi only has a USB 2.0 interface (refer to Table 1), using a USB hard disk drive coupled with the EXT4 filesystem seems to be the best fit. On the other hand, if Newifi upgrades its storage interface to USB 3.0 in the future, using a USB 3.0 flash drive formatted as EXT4 might be a more cost-effective choice, given that a USB flash drive is usually much smaller and cheaper than a USB hard disk drive.

6. THE ODR MIDDLEWARE

Motivated by the study in § 4 and § 5, we design and implement a proof-of-concept middleware called ODR (Offline Downloading Redirector) to help users get rid of performance bottlenecks. We evaluate the performance of ODR using real-world workloads.

6.1 Design and Implementation

ODR is presented as a public web service to users available at *http://odr.thucloud.com*. It is implemented as a middleware independent of any specific cloud-based offline downloading system or smart AP, and thus can be deployed on any dedicated servers or virtual machines. ODR takes users' offline downloading requests, and adaptively decides in which way the requested files should be downloaded to achieve the best expected downloading experience.

Specifically, when a user wants to download a file from the Internet, she first accesses the web service of ODR (by opening the front web page) and inputs the HTTP/FTP/P2P link to the original data source. In addition, ODR asks for other auxiliary information including the user's IP address, access bandwidth, smart AP type, storage device and filesystem type [4]. All the aforementioned information is straightforward for common users, except the access

[4]ODR maintains a web cookie at the user side (if her web browser permits), so that the user does not need to repeatedly input the auxiliary information every time.

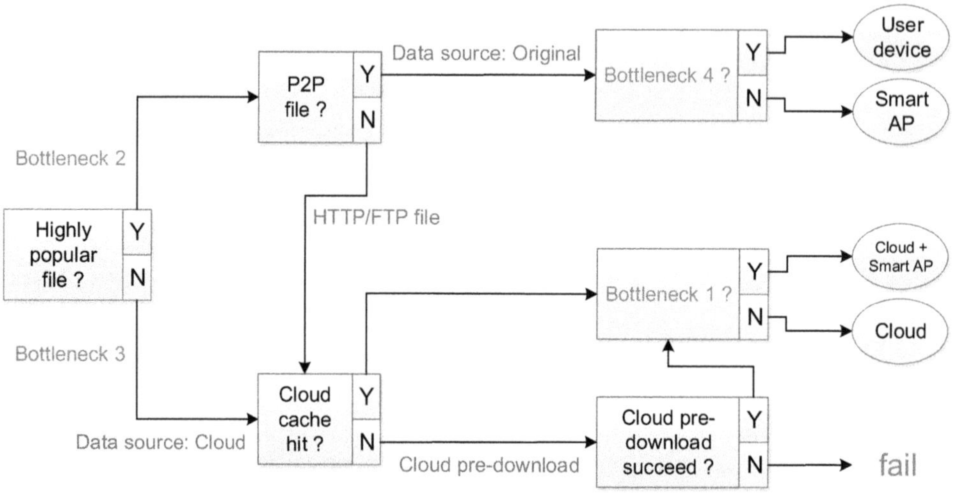

Figure 15: Workflow state transition diagram of ODR. "Y": Yes; "N": No. Bottleneck 1, Bottleneck 2, Bottleneck 3 and Bottleneck 4 denote the four performance bottlenecks of offline downloading mentioned in our key results (refer to § 1).

bandwidth. Fortunately, as the majority of China's Internet users have installed PC-assistant software such as Tencent PC Manager [37], Baidu Guard [11], and 360 Security Guard [2]. With simple instructions, ODR is able to guide users how to obtain the approximate value of access bandwidth with the PC-assistant software.

On receiving an offline downloading request, ODR firstly queries the content database to obtain the latest popularity statistics of the requested file. We use the Xuanfeng database in our implementation, while keep in mind that the performance of ODR would be further enhanced if it is able to use multiple cloud services (*e.g.*, Xuanfeng + Xunlei + Baidu CloudDisk) at once. ODR calculates the decisions based on the popularity of the file and the auxiliary information provided by the user. The decision is then returned to users via the front web page of the ODR service.

Figure 15 plots the state transition diagram of ODR's decision making process, which involves a series of conditions and branches as follows.

Handling highly popular files. First and foremost, users are concerned with the downloading success of a requested file. As the downloading failure ratio is tightly related with the popularity (refer to § 4.1 and § 5.2), ODR needs to examine whether the requested file is highly popular. If yes, the ODR is likely to be successful at downloading the file, and therefore we can make efforts to mitigate the cloud-side upload bandwidth burden (addressing Bottleneck 2 in Figure 15).

To deal with Bottleneck 2, if the highly popular file is hosted in a P2P data swarm, ODR suggests the user to directly download the file from its original data source (*i.e.*, the abundant peers sharing the file). On the contrary, if the highly popular file is hosted in an HTTP/FTP server, ODR would suggest the user to fall back on the cloud, so as to avoid making the HTTP/FTP server a bottleneck.

Further, to minimize the expected (pre-)downloading time, ODR considers the user-side access bandwidth, as well as the smart AP's storage device and filesystem type (addressing Bottleneck 4 in Figure 15). For example, when the user-side access bandwidth reaches 20 Mbps (= 2.5 MBps), if the smart AP uses a USB flash drive as its storage device or its storage device is formatted as NTFS, ODR would suggest the user to directly download the file using her local device (given that it is usually inconvenient for the user to change the storage device and filesystem of a smart AP during pre-downloading). On the other hand, when the user-side access bandwidth is below 0.93 MBps (refer to Table 2), ODR would suggest the user to utilize their smart AP.

Handling less popular files. When a requested file is not highly popular, the success of downloading is our primary concern (addressing Bottleneck 3 in Figure 15). To this end, ODR leverages the cloud storage pool to minimize the failure ratio of (pre-)downloading. Specifically, the downloading falls into the following two cases:

- *Case 1:* If the requested file is already cached in the cloud, ODR should further detect whether there is a bandwidth bottleneck between the cloud and the user by analyzing the user-side access bandwidth and ISP information [5] (addressing Bottleneck 1 in Figure 15). If the user-side access bandwidth is low (< 1 Mbps = 125 KBps) or the user is located in a different ISP other than the four ISPs supported by the cloud, ODR would suggest the user to leverage both the cloud and their smart AP to mitigate the impediments of Bottleneck 1 ("Cloud + Smart AP" in Figure 15, *i.e.*, the file should be first pre-downloaded by the smart AP from the cloud, and then fetched by the user from the smart AP). Otherwise, ODR suggests the user to fetch from the cloud.

- *Case 2:* If the requested file is not cached in the cloud, ODR suggests the user to first use the cloud for pre-downloading. After the file is successfully pre-downlo- aded by the cloud, the user will be notified, and then she can ask ODR again for further suggestions (either directly fetching from the cloud, or from the cloud to a smart AP and then to her local device). If the cloud fails to download the file, the user will be notified of a pre-downloading failure.

Note that ODR never delivers file contents by itself, which makes its operation lightweight in terms of bandwidth and traffic consumption. For our implementation, we rent a low-end virtual machine from Aliyun.com (a major cloud service provider in China) to host the entire ODR service. This virtual machine has a public

[5] The user's ISP information is obtained based on her IP address with the help of the APNIC service (*http://www.apnic.net*), a major service provider for IP address collecting/resolving in Asia Pacific.

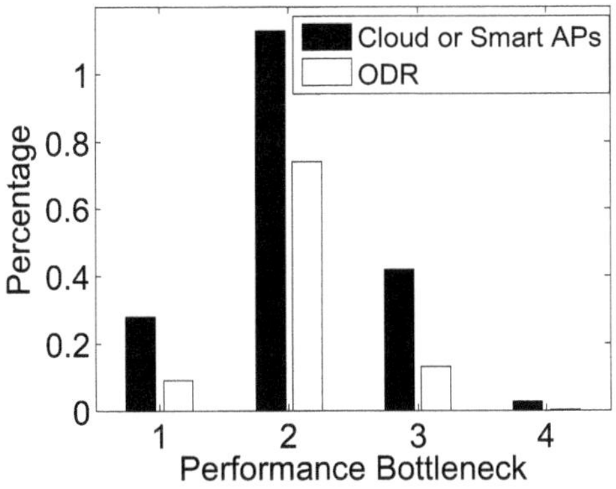

Figure 16: Benchmark performance of ODR, compared with Cloud (*i.e.,* the cloud-based approach) or Smart APs (*i.e.,* the smart AP based approach). Note that the Y-label of Bottleneck 2 is defined as $\frac{\text{Peak cloud bandwidth burden}}{\text{Purchased cloud bandwidth (30 Gbps)}}$.

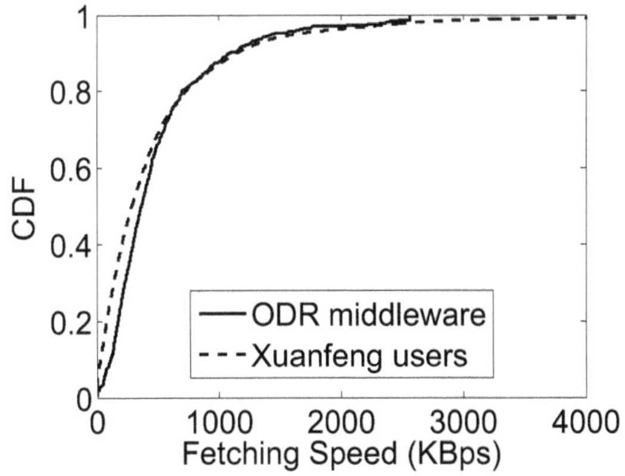

Figure 17: CDF of fetching speeds using ODR. Min: 0 KBps; Median: 368 KBps; Average: 509 KBps; Max: 2.37 MBps (≈ 20 Mbps). As a comparison, the CDF of cloud-based fetching speeds is also plotted.

IP address and 1 Mbps (= 125 KBps) of Internet access bandwidth. The monthly operation cost of ODR is merely $20.

Limitation. By proposing the ODR middleware, our major goal is to demonstrate the potential benefits for a hybrid approach that can effectively address the limitations of the two existing conventional approaches while inheriting their respective advantages. Therefore, the above design and implementation of ODR is basically a *coarse-grained* solution to optimize the offline downloading performance and overhead, where the optimization granularity is a whole offline downloading request/task.

ODR can further benefit from more fine-grained alternative optimization solutions at the chunk, TCP data flow, or sub-stream levels. For instance, a more dynamic solution proposed by Huang *et al.* [58] (*i.e.,* a buffer-based adaptive bit rate selection algorithm for video streaming) can be used instead of the current hard coded decision procedure of ODR. Moreover, a simple solution (called "mobile phone content pre-staging" [52]) that has been proposed in the past is to simply defer downloads to later times when the download bandwidth is better if the users are not particularly time sensitive. In addition, there are even standards efforts like Low Extra Delay Background Transport (LEDBAT, IETF RFC 6817 [27]) that seeks to utilize the available bandwidth on an end-to-end path while limiting the resulting penalty of delay increase on that path. ODR can learn from LEDBAT to further mitigate the cloud-side upload bandwidth burden.

6.2 Performance Evaluation

To evaluate the performance of ODR, we replay the sampled workload (refer to § 5.1) using the deployed ODR middleware during Mar. 23–Apr. 13, 2015. The environment is similar to that in Figure 12. For each smart AP, we use a common laptop (with Quad-core Intel i5 CPU @1.70 GHz, 4-GB RAM, and 7200-RPM 500-GB hard disk drive) as the user device. Figure 16 shows the overall performance results of ODR, compared with the performances of Xuanfeng and the three popular smart APs.

First, the percentage of impeded fetching processes (Bottleneck 1) is reduced from 28% to 9%. The remainder (9%) is mostly due to the intrinsic dynamics of the Internet. In detail, Figure 17 shows the fetching speed distribution using ODR. Compared with the fetching speed distribution of Xuanfeng, the median fetching speed is enhanced from 287 KBps to 368 KBps. Limited by our benchmark environment, the max fetching speed using ODR is 20 Mbps (= 2.5 MBps), which is lower than that in Xuanfeng (*i.e.,* 50 Mbps = 6.25 MBps). This is why the average fetching speed using ODR (509 KBps) is comparable to that of Xuanfeng (504 KBps).

With regard to Bottleneck 2, the cloud-side upload bandwidth burden under the sampled workload is reduced by 35%, which is attributable to the fact that the cloud no longer needs to deliver highly popular P2P files. If Xuanfeng had integrated ODR, its peak upload bandwidth burden could decrease from 34 Gbps (refer to Figure 11) to around 22 Gbps, and thus Xuanfeng would not need to reject any fetching request, given their current workload.

Further, the percentage of smart APs' failures in pre-downloading unpopular files (Bottleneck 3) is reduced from 42% to 13%. In addition, Bottleneck 4 (caused by unsuitable storage devices or filesystems) is almost completely avoided with the use of ODR.

In a nutshell, the integration of ODR into offline downloading services results in a marked reduction of performance bottlenecks, as well as considerable improvement on the quality of service.

Limitation. We acknowledge that ODR occasionally makes incorrect redirection decisions due to the inherent dynamics of Internet that may degrade performance. Fortunately, the percentage of such decisions is negligible (<1%) in our evaluation. Thus, we believe that the performance of ODR is acceptable in practice, especially given the significant advantages of the system.

7. RELATED WORK

This section reviews previous studies of offline downloading, including both the cloud and smart AP based approaches. We also discuss the hybrid approach which directly connects the smart AP to the cloud and compare it with our ODR. In addition, we describe a few offline downloading (based) services outside China. Finally, we briefly survey the state-of-the-art downloading techniques and compare them with offline downloading.

Cloud-based approach. With the proliferation of cloud-based services, a number of studies have investigated the design and implementation of cloud-based offline downloading systems and their performance measurements.

Huang *et al.* [59] presented the early-stage system design of Xuanfeng in 2011, which focuses on guaranteeing data health and accelerating the downloading speed of unpopular videos. However, perhaps due to the startup stage of the system at that time (with a relatively small user base), their study did not notice the two critical performance bottlenecks, *i.e.,* Bottleneck 1 and Bottleneck 2 uncovered in this paper.

Ao *et al.* [44] conducted a long-term measurement study of Xuanfeng in 2012, and predicted that the system would be short of cloud-side upload bandwidth in the near future. Complementary to their study, our work provides in-depth insights into the cloud-side upload bandwidth burden, and recognizes Bottleneck 2 — the root cause of cloud bandwidth shortage. Furthermore, our proposed ODR middleware can significantly reduce cloud-side bandwidth consumption by asking users to download highly popular P2P files directly from their data swarms.

Zhou *et al.* [72] made a theoretical analysis of offline downloading service models, including the cloud-based model and the peer-assisted model. They argue that the former can help scale with file population and the latter should be used to deal with popular files. An adaptive algorithm called AMS (Automatic Mode Selection) is proposed for selecting an appropriate model. Compared with AMS, ODR is more general and applicable: it requires no modification on the cloud side. Additionally, ODR is a deployed system rather than a theoretical algorithm.

Smart AP based approach. Since the history of smart APs is extremely short (just two years), we are not aware of any systematic study on their downloading performances. Most of the existing evaluations [6, 7, 8, 39, 23, 4] are based on simplified network environments and unrealistic workloads (*e.g.,* a few popular files). This is probably the reason why Bottleneck 3 in our study had not been discovered yet. Furthermore, Bottleneck 4 had never been identified in existing evaluations of smart APs.

Hybrid approach. HiWiFi, MiWiFi, and Newifi all provide hybrid solutions for offline downloading [19, 29, 32]. In these hybrid solutions, user-requested files are first downloaded by the cloud, and then the smart AP fetches the files from the cloud. That is to say, the downloading process always goes through the longest data flow: first from the Internet to the cloud, and then to the smart AP of the user.

In contrast, our ODR middleware adaptively selects the most efficient data flow for users to avoid performance bottlenecks. Therefore, ODR significantly outperforms the current hybrid approach by addressing the bottlenecks of both (cloud and smart AP based) approaches while also inheriting their advantages.

Offline downloading outside China. Besides those developing countries (as mentioned in § 1), developed countries can also benefit from offline downloading (based) services. For example, URL Droplet [40] and the Amazon Silk web browser [5] take advantage of the cloud to speed-up file transfers. The former employs the Dropbox cloud storage service to download and host files for its users; the latter utilizes Amazon's cloud servers to improve web page loading performance for Kindle Fire tablets and smartphones. On the other side, the smart AP based approach is adopted by the Linksys Smart WiFi Router [26] which is sold in the US.

State-of-the-art downloading techniques. Existing techniques for Internet file downloading mainly include the centralized Web-based (or client-server), the hierarchical CDN (*i.e.,* content delivery network like Akamai, L-3, and ChinaCache), the decentralized P2P, and the latest ICN (*i.e.,* information centric networking).

The Web-based technique is obviously subject to the intrinsic dynamics and heterogeneities of the Internet, particularly the single-point bottleneck of the Web server. By strategically deploying edge servers in numerous locations that are closer to users, the CDN technique effectively optimizes file downloading performance. Nevertheless, being a commercial service, CDN vendors typically only help to deliver files for *content providers* who pay for the service. On the contrary, the business model of offline downloading is the opposite of CDN, because it charges (or sometimes frees) its users, *i.e., content receivers*, for better downloading experiences.

As mentioned in § 3, the P2P technique is good at distributing popular files that are each shared by a number of users, but cannot guarantee the data availability or maintain a high speed for the downloads of unpopular files. This is why so many users have resorted to offline downloading for acquiring files that are originally hosted in P2P data swarms. In a word, offline downloading addresses the unstability and uncertainty of P2P under certain scenarios.

ICN, also known as CCN (content centric networking) or NDN (named data networking), is motivated by content receivers' interest in the network to achieve efficient and reliable data distribution [43], regardless of the properties of the original data sources. Specifically, ICN is featured by a number of desired functions, such as 1) in-network storage for caching, 2) decoupling content senders and receivers, 3) disruption tolerance, 4) multi-party communication through replication, 5) mobility and multi-homing, *etc.* It is easy to find that offline downloading fulfills at least the first three desired functions of ICN *in a real-world setting without breaking the current Internet architecture.* Further, we would like to explore whether and how offline downloading can enable the other functions of ICN.

8. CONCLUSION

In recent years, the Internet has gained enormous penetration all over the world. However, basic Internet services, like downloading (large) files, remains an issue in most developing countries as a consequence of low-quality network connections. To improve users' downloading experiences, offline downloading services have been proposed and widely deployed in China.

The idea of offline downloading is mainly embodied in two different types of approaches: (1) the cloud-based approach and (2) the smart AP based approach. Unfortunately, the two approaches are confusing to end users since they offer different strengths and weaknesses (the so-called "selection dilemma"). Our study addresses this dilemma with in-depth analysis of a large-scale cloud-based offline-downloading system, as well as comprehensive benchmark experiments of three popular smart APs. Our study shows that the two approaches are subject to distinct performance bottlenecks, while also being complementary to each other. Driven by the study, we build an ODR middleware to help users achieve the best expected performance.

In the future, we envision that offline downloading will become a widely used technology for enhancing the Internet experiences of users across both the developing world and the developed world. For example, people start to build a variety of useful Internet services on top of cloud-based offline downloading systems, such as cloud-based media converters (*e.g.,* Cloud Transcoder [65]) and cloud-accelerated web browsers (*e.g.,* QQ mobile web browser, UCWeb browser, and Amazon Silk web browser). Our study of offline downloading provides solid experiences and valuable heuristics for the developers of similar and relevant services.

9. ACKNOWLEDGEMENTS

This work is supported by the High-Tech Research and Development Program of China ("863 – China Cloud" Major Program) under grant 2015AA01A201, the China NSF under grant 61471217, the US NSF under grant CNS-1319019, the China Postdoctoral Science Fund under grant 2014M550735, and the CCF-Tencent Open Fund under grant AGR20150201.

We would like to thank our shepherd Vyas Sekar and the Tencent Xuanfeng team for their valuable help.

10. REFERENCES

[1] 100,000 MiWiFi smart AP devices are sold out in just 59 seconds. http://bbs.xiaomi.cn/thread-9658495-1-1.html.

[2] 360 Security Guard. http://www.360.cn/weishi.

[3] A Collection of the Best Offline Downloading Tools. http://jingyan.baidu.com/article/636f38bb295e9bd6b84610e9.html.

[4] A Comparison of Nine Smart APs. http://net.zol.com.cn/478/4788494.html.

[5] Amazon Silk web browser. http://amazonsilk.wordpress.com.

[6] An Evaluation Report of HiWiFi. http://news.mydrivers.com/1/279/279305_all.htm.

[7] An Evaluation Report of MiWiFi. http://www.geekpark.net/read/view/195133.

[8] An Evaluation Report of NewiFi. http://www.itbear.com.cn/n112446c93.aspx.

[9] aria2: The next generation download utility. http://aria2.sourceforge.net.

[10] Baidu CloudDisk offline downloading system. http://pan.baidu.com.

[11] Baidu Guard. http://anquan.baidu.com/weishi.

[12] CERNET (China Education and Research Network) ISP. http://www.cernet.edu.cn.

[13] China-Mobile ISP. http://www.10086.cn.

[14] China-Telecom ISP. http://www.chinatelecom.com.cn.

[15] China-Unicom ISP. http://www.chinaunicom.com.cn.

[16] China's Broadband Penetration Is Increasingly Lagging Behind Developed Nations, Says MIIT's Research Head. http://techcrunch.com/2013/03/21/china-broadband-laggin.

[17] Delay-tolerant networking (DTN) Wiki page. http://en.wikipedia.org/wiki/Delay-tolerant_networking.

[18] FCC raises broadband definition to 25Mbps, Chairman mocks ISPs. http://www.extremetech.com/mobile/198583-fcc-raises-broadband-definition-to-25mbps-chairman-mocks-isps.

[19] HiWiFi APPs. http://bbs.hiwifi.com/thread-22663-1-1.html.

[20] HiWiFi Introduction and History. http://www.hiwifi.com/about.

[21] HiWiFi smart AP. http://www.hiwifi.com.

[22] HiWiFi smart AP is striving towards 5,000,000 sales. http://www.pcpop.com/doc/1/1002/1002782.shtml.

[23] HiWiFi vs. Newifi: A Benchmark Test. http://test.smzdm.com/pingce/p/20574.

[24] How to Offline Download? Which is the Best Offline Downloading Tool? http://jingyan.baidu.com/article/a65957f4fe63c424e67f9b92.html.

[25] Key ICT indicators for developed and developing countries and the world (totals and penetration rates). http://www.itu.int/en/ITU-D/Statistics/Documents/statistics/2014/ITU_Key_2005-2014_ICT_data.xls.

[26] Linksys Smart WiFi Router. http://www.linksys.com/en-us/smartwifi.

[27] Low Extra Delay Background Transport (LEDBAT), IETF RFC 6817. http://datatracker.ietf.org/doc/rfc6817.

[28] MiWiFi smart AP. http://www.miwifi.com.

[29] MiWiFi: System Options. http://www.mi.com/miwifi#op.

[30] Newifi smart AP. http://www.newifi.com.

[31] Offline Downloading: the Baidu Wikipedia page. http://baike.baidu.com/view/2718066.htm.

[32] Offline Downloading with Newifi and Xunlei. http://jingyan.baidu.com/article/3d69c5517049e1f0cf02d7a4.html.

[33] Offline (movie) Downloading for MiWiFi. http://www.mi.com/miwifi/movie-download.

[34] OpenWrt operating system. http://openwrt.org.

[35] Opkg (Open PacKaGe Management) web site. https://code.google.com/p/opkg.

[36] Statistics of China Internet Users. http://www.internetlivestats.com/internet-users/china.

[37] Tencent PC Manager. http://guanjia.qq.com.

[38] The State of Broadband 2014 – A Report by the Broadband Commission. http://www.broadbandcommission.org/documents/reports/bb-annualreport2014.pdf.

[39] Three Faults of HiWiFi. http://digi.tech.qq.com/a/20131112/002037.htm.

[40] URL Droplet offline downloading system. http://www.urldroplet.com.

[41] Xuanfeng offline downloading system. http://xf.qq.com.

[42] Xunlei offline downloading system. http://lixian.xunlei.com.

[43] Bengt Ahlgren, Christian Dannewitz, Claudio Imbrenda, Dirk Kutscher, and Börje Ohlman. A Survey of Information-Centric Networking. *IEEE Communications Magazine*, 50(7):26–36, 2012.

[44] Naixiang Ao, Yingying Xu, Changjia Chen, and Yuchun Guo. Offline Downloading: A Non-Traditional Cloud-Accelerated and Peer-Assisted Content Distribution Service. In *Proc. of the International Conference on Cyber-Enabled Distributed Computing and Knowledge Discovery (CyberC)*, pages 81–88. IEEE, 2012.

[45] Zachary S Bischof, Fabián E Bustamante, and Rade Stanojevic. Need, Want, Can Afford ĺC Broadband Markets and the Behavior of Users. In *Proc. of the 14th ACM Internet Measurement Conference (IMC)*, pages 73–86. ACM, 2014.

[46] Lee Breslau, Pei Cao, Li Fan, Graham Phillips, and Scott Shenker. Web Caching and Zipf-like Distributions: Evidence and Implications. In *Proc. of the 18th Annual Joint Conference of the IEEE Computer and Communications Societies (INFOCOM)*, pages 126–134. IEEE, 1999.

[47] Guihai Chen and Zhenhua Li. *Peer-to-Peer Network: Structure, Application and Design*. Tsinghua University Press, 2007.

[48] Marshini Chetty, Srikanth Sundaresan, Sachit Muckaden, Nick Feamster, and Enrico Calandro. Measuring Broadband Performance in South Africa. In *Proc. of the 4th Annual Symposium on Computing for Development (DEV), Rondebosch Cape Town, South Africa*. ACM, 2013.

[49] David Choffnes and Fabián E Bustamante. Taming the Torrent: A Practical Approach to Reducing Cross-ISP Traffic in Peer-to-Peer Systems. *ACM SIGCOMM Computer Communication Review (CCR)*, 38(4):363–374, 2008.

[50] Bram Cohen. Incentives Build Robustness in BitTorrent. In *Proc. of the 1st Workshop on Economics of Peer-to-Peer Systems*, pages 68–72, 2003.

[51] Amal Fahad, Zhuan Chen, Kai Shen, Jeffrey Bigham, and Assmaa Fahad. An Evaluation of Web Acceleration Techniques for the Developing World. In *Proc. of the 6th USENIX/ACM Workshop on Networked Systems for Developing Regions (NSDR), Boston, MA*, 2012.

[52] Alessandro Finamore, Marco Mellia, Zafar Gilani, Konstantina Papagiannaki, Vijay Erramilli, and Yan Grunenberger. Is There a Case for Mobile Phone Content Pre-staging? In *Proc. of the 9th ACM Conference on emerging Networking EXperiments and Technologies (CoNEXT)*, pages 321–326. ACM, 2013.

[53] Aditya Ganjam, Junchen Jiang, Xi Liu, Vyas Sekar, Faisal Siddiqi, Ion Stoica, Jibin Zhan, and Hui Zhang. C3: Internet-Scale Control Plane for Video Quality Optimization. In *Proc. of the 12th USENIX Symposium on Networked Systems Design and Implementation (NSDI)*, 2015.

[54] Sarthak Grover, Mi Seon Park, Srikanth Sundaresan, Sam Burnett, Hyojoon Kim, Bharath Ravi, and Nick Feamster. Peeking Behind the NAT: An Empirical Study of Home Networks. In *Proc. of the 13th ACM Internet Measurement Conference (IMC)*, pages 377–390. ACM, 2013.

[55] Krishna P Gummadi, Richard J Dunn, Stefan Saroiu, Steven D Gribble, Henry M Levy, and John Zahorjan. Measurement, Modeling, and Analysis of a Peer-to-Peer File-sharing Workload. *ACM SIGOPS Operating Systems Review (OSR)*, 37(5):314–329, 2003.

[56] Lei Guo, Enhua Tan, Songqing Chen, Zhen Xiao, and Xiaodong Zhang. The Stretched Exponential Distribution of Internet Media Access Patterns. In *Proc. of the 27th ACM Symposium on Principles of Distributed Computing (PODC)*, pages 283–294. ACM, 2008.

[57] Te-Yuan Huang, Nikhil Handigol, Brandon Heller, Nick McKeown, and Ramesh Johari. Confused, Timid, and Unstable: Picking a Video Streaming Rate is Hard. In *Proc. of the 12th ACM Internet Measurement Conference (IMC)*, pages 225–238. ACM, 2012.

[58] Te-Yuan Huang, Ramesh Johari, Nick McKeown, Matthew Trunnell, and Mark Watson. A Buffer-Based Approach to Rate Adaptation: Evidence from a Large Video Streaming Service. In *Proc. of the 2014 ACM Conference on Communication Architectures, Protocols and Applications (SIGCOMM)*, pages 187–198. ACM, 2014.

[59] Yan Huang, Zhenhua Li, Gang Liu, and Yafei Dai. Cloud Download: Using Cloud Utilities to Achieve High-quality Content Distribution for Unpopular Videos. In *Proc. of the 19th ACM International Conference on Multimedia (MM)*, pages 213–222. ACM, 2011.

[60] Sibren Isaacman and Margaret Martonosi. Low-Infrastructure Methods to Improve Internet Access for Mobile Users in Emerging Regions. In *Proc. of the 20th International Conference on World Wide Web (WWW)*, pages 473–482. ACM, 2011.

[61] David Johnson, Elizabeth Belding, and Consider Mudenda. Kwaabana: File Sharing for Rural Networks. In *Proc. of the 4th Annual Symposium on Computing for Development (DEV), Rondebosch Cape Town, South Africa*. ACM, 2013.

[62] Shunmuga Krishnan and Ramesh Sitaraman. Video Stream Quality Impacts Viewer Behavior: Inferring Causality Using Quasi-Experimental Designs. *IEEE/ACM Transactions on Networking (TON)*, 21(6):2001–2014, 2013.

[63] Zhenhua Li, Jiannong Cao, and Guihai Chen. ContinuStreaming: Achieving High Playback Continuity of Gossip-based Peer-to-Peer Streaming. In *Proc. of the 22nd IEEE International Parallel and Distributed Processing Symposium (IPDPS)*, pages 1–12. IEEE, 2008.

[64] Zhenhua Li, Yan Huang, Gang Liu, Fuchen Wang, Yunhao Liu, Zhi-Li Zhang, and Yafei Dai. Challenges, Designs, and Performances of Large-Scale Open-P2SP Content Distribution. *IEEE Transactions on Parallel and Distributed Systems (TPDS)*, 24(11):2181–2191, 2013.

[65] Zhenhua Li, Yan Huang, Gang Liu, Fuchen Wang, Zhi-Li Zhang, and Yafei Dai. Cloud Transcoder: Bridging the Format and Resolution Gap between Internet Videos and Mobile Devices. In *Proc. of the 22nd SIGMM Workshop on Network and Operating System Support for Digital Audio and Video (NOSSDAV)*, pages 33–38. ACM, 2012.

[66] Zhenhua Li, Tieying Zhang, Yan Huang, Zhi-Li Zhang, and Yafei Dai. Maximizing the Bandwidth Multiplier Effect for Hybrid Cloud-P2P Content Distribution. In *Proc. of the 20th IEEE/ACM International Workshop on Quality of Service (IWQoS)*, pages 1–9. IEEE, 2012.

[67] Srikanth Sundaresan, Walter De Donato, Nick Feamster, Renata Teixeira, Sam Crawford, and Antonio Pescapè. Broadband Internet Performance: A View From the Gateway. *ACM SIGCOMM Computer Communication Review (CCR)*, 41(4):134–145, 2011.

[68] Ye Tian, Ratan Dey, Yong Liu, and Keith Ross. Topology Mapping and Geolocating for China's Internet. *IEEE Transactions on Parallel and Distributed Systems (TPDS)*, 24(9):1908–1917, 2013.

[69] Haiyong Xie, Richard Yang, Arvind Krishnamurthy, Yanbin Grace Liu, and Abraham Silberschatz. P4P: Provider Portal for Applications. *ACM SIGCOMM Computer Communication Review (CCR)*, 38(4):351–362, 2008.

[70] Yasir Zaki, Jay Chen, Thomas Pötsch, Talal Ahmad, and Lakshminarayanan Subramanian. Dissecting Web Latency in Ghana. In *Proc. of the 14th ACM Internet Measurement Conference (IMC)*, pages 241–248. ACM, 2014.

[71] Mariya Zheleva, Paul Schmitt, Morgan Vigil, and Elizabeth Belding. The Increased Bandwidth Fallacy: Performance and Usage in Rural Zambia. In *Proc. of the 4th Annual Symposium on Computing for Development (DEV), Rondebosch Cape Town, South Africa*. ACM, 2013.

[72] Yipeng Zhou, Zhengjia Fu, Dah-Ming Chiu, and Yan Huang. An Adaptive Cloud Downloading Service. *IEEE Trans. on Multimedia (TMM)*, 15(4):802–810, 2013.

In and Out of Cuba

Characterizing Cuba's Connectivity

Zachary S. Bischof John P. Rula Fabian E. Bustamante
Northwestern University

ABSTRACT

The goal of our work is to characterize the current state of Cuba's access to the wider Internet. This work is motivated by recent improvements in connectivity to the island and the growing commercial interest following the ease of restrictions on travel and trade with the US. In this paper, we profile Cuba's networks, their connections to the rest of the world, and the routes of international traffic going to and from the island. Despite the addition of the ALBA-1 submarine cable, we find that round trip times to websites hosted off the island remain very high; pings to popular websites frequently took over 300 ms. We also find a high degree of path asymmetry in traffic to/from Cuba. Specifically, in our analysis we find that traffic going out of Cuba typically travels through the ALBA-1 cable, but, surprisingly, traffic on the reverse path often traverses high-latency satellite links, adding over 200 ms to round trip times. Last, we analyze queries to public DNS servers and SSL certificate requests to characterize the availability of network services in Cuba.

Categories and Subject Descriptors

C.2.4 [**Computer Communication Networks**]: [Network Protocols]; C.4 [**Performance of Systems**]: [Measurement techniques]

Keywords

Developing countries; Measurement; Performance; Satellite

1. INTRODUCTION

It may have taken 54 years, but change is coming to Cuba. Last December, the US government announced plans to restore relations with Cuba and ease restrictions on travel and trade. It took little time for American businesses – from the obvious tourist sector to telephony and video streaming services – to start scouting opportunities. In February, IDT Corp reached an agreement with the Empresa de Telecomunicaciones de Cuba, S.A. (ETECSA) to provide direct international long distance telephony between the USA and Cuba [16]. The same month, Netflix announced their plan to offer their video streaming service and two months later Airbnb brought their sharing economy to the island [3].

Despite the promising news, the state of Cuban infrastructure, particularly in the computing and network segment, pose no small challenges to these plans. Today, less than 5% of the population have their own fixed-line Internet connection [18] and only an estimated 25% of the population are able to get online [9]. Those that are actually connected experience very poor performance. Ookla's NetIndex, for instance, ranks Cuba among the *worst ten countries* in terms of average bandwidth – 197th out of 202 – with a measured broadband download speed of 1.67 Mbps. An even bigger barrier to Internet access is cost with services that are prohibitively expensive for much of the population. While the average monthly income in Cuba is around $20 a month, paying by the hour at an Internet cafe can cost about $5 per hour [19]. A broadband subscription is even more expensive with private subscription plans costing about 386% of the gross national income per capita [6].

Recent years have brought some progress in connecting Cubans to the rest of the Internet and the recent commercial interest may help speed up the process. In February of 2011, Cuba completed its first undersea fiber-optic cable, ALBA-1 (640 Gbps), with landings in Jamaica and Venezuela. The US government has also set the promotion of Internet access in the island as one of their top priorities [17] and the US Department of Defense stated plans to build a submarine cable between Florida and the Guantanamo Bay Naval Base in Cuba and to eventually extend it to the rest of Cuba [15].

Our goal is to characterize the current state of Cuba's access to the wider Internet. We collected and analyzed two months of measurements (March and April of 2015) with probes going in and out of Cuba launched from 50 RIPE Atlas [13] nodes and our 6,000 Namehelp [12] clients. Our analysis validates some of the anecdotal evidence on the limited connectivity of the island. Though bandwidth capacity to the country is severely limited, we find that end-to-end latency is a key bottleneck in international network traffic with a large number of paths traversing high-latency satellite links despite the availability of ALBA-1. Interestingly, we find that many of the high RTT measurements are linked to high degrees of path asymmetry in traffic to/from Cuba. Specifically, most traffic going out of Cuba travels through the ALBA-1 submarine cable,

IMC'15, October 28–30, 2015, Tokyo, Japan.

ACM 978-1-4503-3848-6/15/10 ...$15.00.
DOI: http://dx.doi.org/10.1145/2815675.2815718.

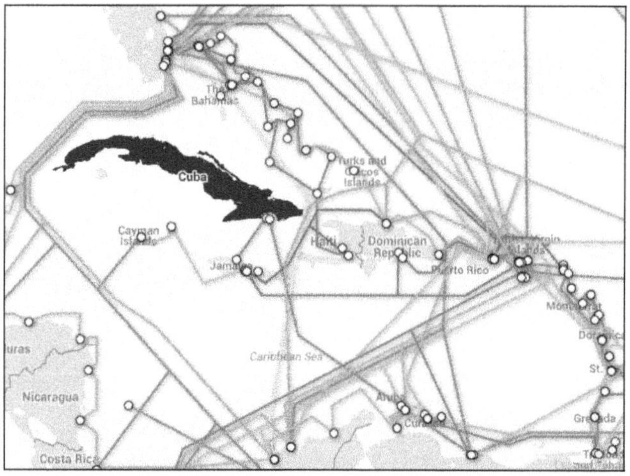

Figure 1: Map of submarine cables in the Caribbean. (Source: `http://www.submarinecablemap.com/`)

but on the reverse path, responses often traverse satellite links, typically adding over 200 ms of additional end-to-end latency. We also survey a number of popular network services, such as public DNS and web services, checking their availability in Cuba, finding that some services appear to be blocking users in the island.

The rest of the paper is organized as follows. In Sec. 2 we discuss the state of Internet connectivity in Cuba. Section 3 describes the datasets that we use for our analysis. We then discuss the domestic and international connectivity of Cuba's networks in Sec. 4 and look at how routing through these connections affects performance in Sec. 5. In Sec. 6, we discuss our preliminary findings on the availability of network services in Cuba before concluding in Sec. 7.

2. BACKGROUND

Although Cubans have been able to legally acquire a computer since 2008 [8], getting access to the Internet has remained a challenge. Network availability has been problematic for such a long time that several makeshift "offline Internets" have appeared, with individuals and companies sharing or selling content downloaded from the Internet (e.g., films, TV shows, magazines, news articles, or applications) via USB flash drives or CDs – a popular service known as "El paquete" [18].

Things have been changing, if slowly. In early 2011, Alcatel-Lucent began work on a submarine fiber-optic cable, named ALBA-1, with landing points in Ocho Rios, Jamaica; Siboney, Cuba; and La Guaira, Venezuela [1]. Estimates suggested that this link would increase capacity to the island by a factor of 3,000.

Prior to this, all traffic was routed to and from the island via satellite links. These satellites are located in geosynchronous orbit, at a distance of about 36,000 km from the equator. Sending a single packet from the Earth's surface to the satellite and back to Earth takes approximately $2 \times 36,000\ km/c = 240\ ms$ where c is the speed of light. Traversing a satellite link on both the forward and reverse path would add approximately 480 ms to RTT measurements.

The ALBA-1 cable was not actually activated until two years later, in January 2013 [11]. Even after the addition of ALBA-1, Cuba's connectivity to the rest of the Internet remains relatively poor, even compared to other Caribbean islands. Figure 1 shows a map of the submarine cables in the region. Despite the large number of cables in the surrounding area, Cuba is one of the least connected countries in the region, with a number of submarine cables detouring around the island in order to reach their destination.

Affordability remains a problem, with a broadband subscription costing close to 4x the gross national income per capita [6], but in March of 2015, the Cuban government approved the first public Wi-Fi hub in Havana [2] potentially improving citizens' (and visitors') access to the Internet.

3. DATASETS

To characterize the current state of Cuba's connections to the rest of the Internet we collected measurements over a two month period (March and April, 2015). Probes going in and out of Cuba were launched from RIPE Atlas [13] nodes and our Namehelp [12] clients. The following paragraphs describe our datasets in more detail.

RIPE Atlas probes. The RIPE Atlas data was collected from approximately 50 probes across North and South America. One probe was located in Cuba (the only available one) and approximately half of rest were located on other islands throughout the Caribbean, including the Dominican Republic, Jamaica, Puerto Rico, Saint Barthélemy, Saint Kitts and Nevis, Guadeloupe, Trinidad and Tobago, Martinique, and Grenada. The rest of the probes were located in the US, Mexico, Venezuela, and Brazil. Most of our analysis in this paper focuses on the measurements collected from the Atlas probe located in Havana, Cuba.

The RIPE Atlas API allows us to schedule ping and traceroute measurements, issue DNS queries, and fetch SSL certificates on each of these nodes. We measured the routes between each vantage point by running traceroutes between all pairs of our selected RIPE Atlas probes. Additionally, the RIPE Atlas probe in Cuba ran traceroute measurements to every Namehelp endhost. To test the availability of network services in Cuba, we had the Atlas probe in Havana fetch SSL certificates for popular websites that supported HTTPS. We also measured DNS performance to the probes' configured DNS server and to a number of public DNS services. We compared the results of these tests to other requests issued simultaneously from the other 49 Atlas probes. These measurements are discussed in greater detail in Sec. 6.

Namehelp clients. In addition to the RIPE Atlas data, we also leveraged 6,000 endhosts running Namehelp, with presence in over 600 networks across 78 countries. Namehelp is a tool based on the popular DNS benchmark utility, *namebench*, that aims to both provide a comparative evaluation of DNS services and act as a DNS proxy to improve CDN mappings. [1]

Namehelp is also able to conduct controlled network measurements, such as **`ping`**, **`traceroute`**, or **`wget`**. For this dataset, Namehelp clients ran hourly traceroute measurements to prefixes located in Cuba. While running these traceroutes, Namehelp did not run any other network measurements simultaneously. By combining this data with

[1] http://aqualab.cs.northwestern.edu/projects/namehelp

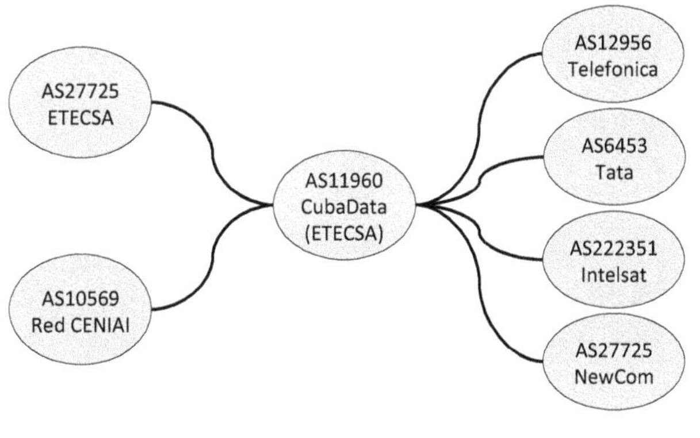

Figure 2: AS map of Cuba's networks and their connections.

Autonomous System	# of IPv4 prefixes	# of IPv6 prefixes
AS11960 CubaData (ETECSA)	2	1
AS27725 ETECSA	20	0
AS10569 Red CENIAI	1	1

Table 1: Number of IPv4 and IPv6 prefixes in each Cuban network.

the traceroute measurements of the Atlas probe in Havana, we were able to construct the forward and reverse path between Namehelp users and this Atlas probe.

4. CONNECTIVITY

In this section, we briefly describe the structure of Cuba's networks and its connectivity to the global Internet. According to Prefix WhoIs, there are a total of three Autonomous Systems (ASes) in Cuba, two of which (AS11960 and AS27725) are operated by ETECSA, a government-owned telecommunications service provider. The third AS (AS10569) is operated by Centro de Intercambio Automatizado de Informacion (CENIAI). All international traffic to and from the island flows through AS11960. Table 1 lists the number of IPv4 and IPv6 prefixes in each of the Cuban ASes.

Using the traceroute measurements launched from Namehelp clients targeting each prefix in Cuba [4, 5], we created the AS map in Figure 2, which describes how these three networks are connected to each other and to the rest of the Internet (via the four ASes listed on the right side of the diagram). Before reaching Cuba, all of our traceroute measurements traversed one of four networks: Tata's, Telefonica's, NewCom's, or the Intelsat's network. Traffic that travels through Tata's (AS6453) or Telefonica's (AS12956) networks appears to travel to Cuba via the ALBA-1 submarine cable as it leaves those networks. Paths that reach Cuba via Intelsat's (AS222351) or Newcom's (AS27725) networks are reaching the island via satellite.

In AS11960, we found that one of the IPv4 prefixes (200.13.144.0/21) hosts a small number of domains, including cubacel.cu, a website for ETECSA. The remaining IPv4 and IPv6 prefixes are part of the Cuban Internet Exchange Point (IXP). All of our measurements into and out of Cuba flow through this IXP.

In AS27725, a number of prefixes are assigned to governmental and educational organizations. After analyzing traceroutes from Namehelp users to the island, we found that of the 20 IPv4 prefixes in AS27725, 15 of the prefixes appeared to be consistently routed over the ALBA-1 cable on both the forward and reverse paths. Looking at the forward paths going into Cuba, it is clear that traceroutes to these prefixes did not travel through either Intelsat's or NewCom's networks (satellite link). Considering that the end-to-end RTT was always less than 200 ms, it is also clear that the reverse path did not traverse the satellite link as this would have added over 230 ms.

The five remaining prefixes were frequently routed asymmetrically; traffic traveling out of the country went through the ALBA-1 cable into either Tata's or Telefonica's network, while incoming traffic was, in the majority of cases, routed through one of the satellite networks.

Using a list of popular Cuban websites [7], we also looked at where websites under the .cu TLD were hosted geographically. Of the websites ending with .cu that we were able to successfully resolve, about 80% were located in the island. Cuban websites that were located outside of Cuba were typically in the US, France, Venezuela, or Canada. Of the listed websites that were hosted in Cuba, about 60% were located in a single prefix, 190.91.112.0/20. Domains that were hosted in other Cuban prefixes were typically government websites, in the prefix assigned to the respective government organization.

5. PERFORMANCE

With an understanding of the island connectivity, we now look at how the routing of international traffic to and from Cuba affects end-to-end RTT performance. We start by looking at individual cases where asymmetry is causing a significant increase in RTT, before discussing how frequently this issue occurs across all measurements in our global dataset.

5.1 Case studies

As we mentioned in the previous section, we found a high degree of path asymmetry in Cuban international traffic. Unfortunately, since there is only one available probe in Cuba, we are only able to verify the outgoing path from a single prefix. However, based on RTT measurements, this asymmetry appears to apply to the prefixes that route incoming traffic via the satellite networks.

We compute the AS path for each traceroute in our dataset using the methodology presented in Chen et. al. [5]. We then match traceroutes with opposite source and destination IP address to get the forward and reverse path and calculate the asymmetry of the path [10, 14].

Figure 3 shows one example of path asymmetry to/from Cuba. In this case, traceroutes were run simultaneously by Atlas nodes in Havana, Cuba and Miami, Florida (in NTT's network), with each node targeting the other.

We start with the traceroute launched by the Atlas node in Cuba, shown on the top half of Figure 3. RTT measurements to the edge of the Cuban IXP were very low, typically taking less than 3 ms. The first jump in latency occurs as the traceroute leaves AS12956 and enters Telefonica's transit network. Though we were unable to verify the exact location of this hop, we believe that it likely located in Venezuela; the only other landing of the ALBA-1 submarine is located in Jamaica and is reportedly intended to be a backup. The next hop is still in Telefonica's network, but there is another

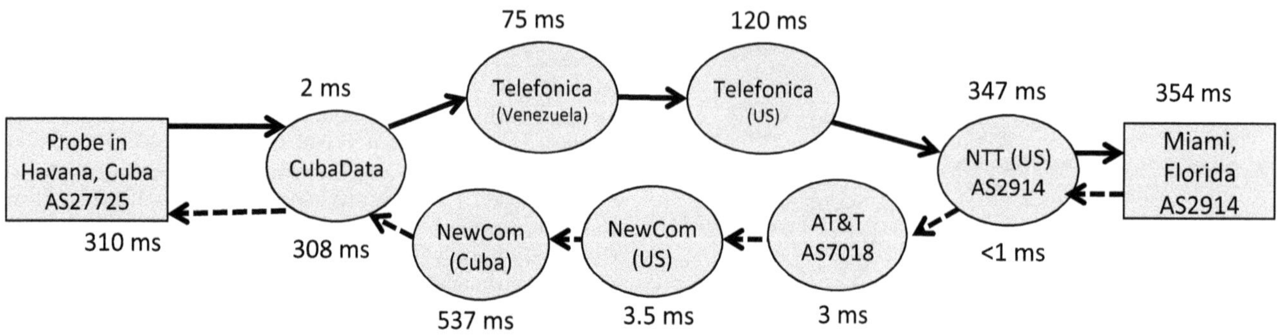

Figure 3: Forward and reverse paths between RIPE Atlas nodes in Havana, Cuba and Miami, Florida. The solid arrows and latency measurements on the top of the figure represent the forward path (Cuba to US) while the dotted arrow and latency measurements on the bottom are from the reverse path (US to Cuba). The numbers above and below each network represent the RTT to each hop. Note that hops with similar RTTs in the same AS have been omitted. As a result, the diagram is not representative of the total number of end-to-end hops.

significant jump in RTT. Based on traceroute measurements to this router's IP address from Atlas probes in the US, this hop appears to be near Washington DC; the Atlas probe with the shortest latency to this probe (less than 1 ms) was located in the DC metropolitan area.

Once the traceroute from Cuba to Miami had a high enough TTL to reach a router in NTT's network, RTT suddenly increases by over 200 ms. Based on the router's hostname, the router is located near Ashburn, Virginia, and is likely within 60 km of the previous hop. In fact, once the TTL was high enough to leave Telefonica's network, RTT was never below 345 ms.

The reason for this sudden jump in latency becomes clear when examining the reverse path. The dashed arrows and RTTs on the bottom of Figure 3 summarize the output of the traceroute initiated by the probe in NTT's network. Instead of routing through Telefonica's network, probes from the Atlas node in Miami are being routed to Cuba via AT&T's transit network to NewCom's network, traversing the satellite link to the island. Interestingly, the RTT actually reaches its highest point once the path arrives at the NewCom's base station in Cuba. At this point, packets must travel over the satellite link in both directions (which must take at least 477 ms). Once the TTL is high enough to reach the Cuban network, RTT drops by over 200 ms, as the traceroute responses are now returning via the submarine cable.

Although this example only covers a single forward and reverse path between Atlas probes in Cuba and Florida, the sudden jumps in latency and path asymmetry were both common when measuring between Cuba and the US. In our analysis of paths between the Atlas node in Cuba and Namehelp users in the US, we found that all paths going out of Cuba traversed the submarine cable and 92% of paths going into Cuba traversed a satellite link.

This issue also appeared frequently on paths to popular websites. Figure 4 summarizes the path of a traceroute from the Atlas probe in Cuba to google.com. Despite the fact that we were unable to run traceroutes along the reverse path (from Google's network to Cuba), the forward path is very similar to the example in Figure 3; after leaving Telefonica's network, latency suddenly jumps by 220 ms.

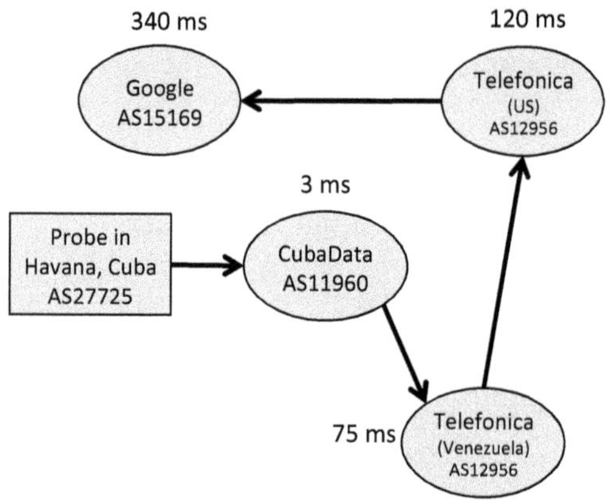

Figure 4: Traceroute from Atlas probe in Cuba to google.com. The latencies represent the RTT at each hop. Hops with similar RTT in the same AS have been omitted.

Based on the hostname of the Google server targeted by the Atlas node in Cuba, the server appeared to be located near Dallas-Fort Worth, Texas. Ping measurements from Atlas probes in the DC area (near the last hop in Telefonica's network) to the same Google server took less than 35 ms. However, between Telefonica's network and the destination, RTT increases by 220 ms. Given the similarity to the previous example, we believe that this sudden increase is also a result of the reverse path being routed to Cuba via a high latency satellite link. We observed this same trend for all of the other top sites included in our tests (i.e., Yahoo, Wikipedia, Facebook, Twitter, and Reddit).

5.2 Wider impact

We now summarize the paths between our population of Namehelp users and the Atlas probe in Cuba. Using the Atlas node in Havana, we launched traceroutes targeting

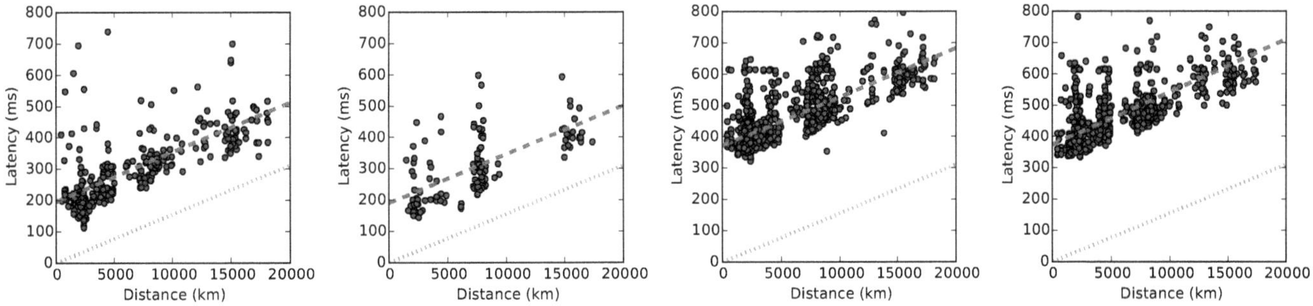

(a) Tata (AS6453)
$y = 0.0158x + 196$

(b) Telefonica (AS12956)
$y = 0.0156x + 190$

(c) Intelsat (AS22351)
$y = 0.0155x + 372$

(d) NewCom (AS32034)
$y = 0.0168x + 374$

Figure 5: RTT from Namehelp users to prefixes in Cuba by distance. Paths are split across figures based on the network immediately prior to CubaData (AS11960). Traffic through Tata's and Telefonica's network reach Cuba via the ALBA-1 submarine cable while IntelSat and NewCom use satellite connections. The equation below each figure represents the linear regression between distance and RTT.

each Namehelp user in our dataset. We found that all traceroutes launched by this probe and targeting the IPs of Namehelp users would leave the country via either Tata's and Telefonica's network, avoiding the high-latency satellite connections.

However, the reverse path (going into Cuba) was not as consistent. For each traceroute measurement from Namehelp, we identified the last AS hop that appeared before entering the Cuban IXP network (AS11960). We then calculated the approximate distance between the Namehelp user and the Atlas node using MaxMind's GeoIP database to map users' IP addresses to geographic locations. Finally, we grouped measurements according to the last AS seen before entering Cuba.

Figure 5 shows the relationship between RTT and distance, grouped by the last AS before entering Cuba. The gray dotted line represents the RTT of light moving through a cable of length x (assuming that light is moving through the medium at $c/2$). The green dashed line represents the linear regression between distance and latency for each group of vantage points. Below each figure, we also include the equation of the linear regression. We find that the slope of the linear regression of measurements that travel through satellite networks is similar to that of the measurements traversing the submarine cable, but is approximately 180 ms higher.

Despite the fact that approximately 40% of the Earth's surface should be able to communicate directly with satellites in geostationary orbit, we were unable to find any satellite base stations outside of North America in either of the satellite networks. As a result, packets headed to Cuba had to first be routed to North America and *then* to Cuba over a satellite connection.

For example, packets originating in Europe had to first traverse an intercontinental submarine cable before traversing a satellite link, even though some countries should be within the satellite's serviceable area. The slopes of the linear regression lines are thus roughly consistent across each group of users, and similar to the slope of the estimated speed of light through a fiber cable. The difference in the y-intercept of the regression lines in Figs. 5a and 5b when compared to Figs. 5c and 5d is a result of traversing a satellite link.

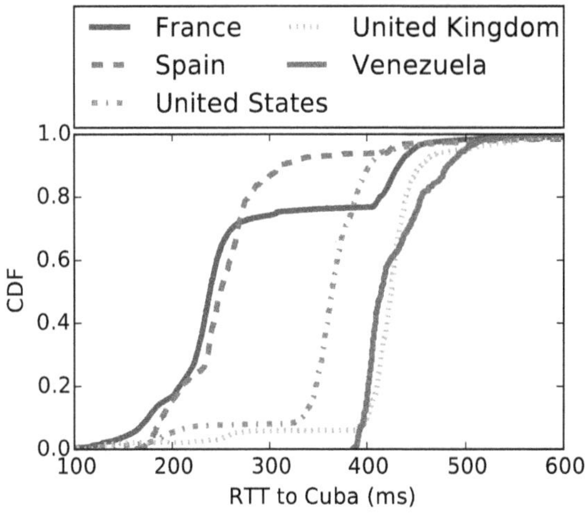

Figure 6: CDFs of the RTT to Cuba, as measured by users in each country.

We also looked for trends between the origin of the traceroute measurement and which network was used to reach Cuba. We found that RTT could vary widely between countries, even those in the same region, due to differences in routing. In some cases, vantage points that were in countries much further away from Cuba (e.g., in Europe) would have significantly lower RTTs than those in North and South America.

Figure 6 shows the CDF of RTTs for users in France, Spain, the US, the UK, and Venezuela. Latency measurements from Namehelp users in France and Spain had the lowest median latencies of all subpopulations in our dataset, nearly half that of the median latency of users in the UK. Despite the fact that users in the US and Venezuela are much closer to Cuba, their RTTs were much higher. This difference is due to the fact that most users in France and Spain are routed to Cuba through Telefonica's transit network, and were sent via the ALBA-1 submarine cable instead of satellite networks. In total, 77% of routes to Cuba from France and 94% of routes from Spain were routed over the ALBA-1 submarine cable in both directions.

In contrast to previously reported networking performance issues in developing countries, such as Ghana [20] and Zambia [21], Cuba presents an interesting case in that at least part of the performance issues can be attributed to asymmetric routing and could be addressed via changes to routing policy.

6. NETWORK SERVICE AVAILABILITY

We also survey a number of popular network services and websites, checking their availability in Cuba. To test website availability, we issued SSL certificate requests from our set of 50 Atlas probes in North and South America to 4,434 domains supporting HTTPS from the top 10,000 most popular websites.[2] While we would have liked to test the availability of any website, the RIPE Atlas API does not support general HTTP tests. For every site, if the request succeeded (replied with a valid certificate), we removed it from our list. If the request failed, we tried four more times before labeling the site as "unavailable". The experiment ran between August 31st and September 4th, 2015.

We found that, while most of the sites replied with a valid certificate, requests from the Atlas probe in Cuba timed out consistently across all five tests for 111 (2.5%) of sites. Nearly every other Atlas probe was able to successfully retrieve a valid SSL certificate from these domains. Most of the "unavailable" websites in Cuba fall into a few categories, such as finance-related (e.g., paypal.com, bankofamerica.com, capitalone.com, and usbank.com), ad network (e.g., adcash.com, adnetworkperformance.com, and tradeadexchange.com), computer hardware (e.g., dell.com and seagate.com), and adult content. A few of these sites were registered by the same entity but provided different services or different TLDs (e.g., capitalone.com and capitaloneinvesting.com, blizzard.com and battle.net, and the multiple TLDs of cam4.com), hinting at a parent company policy. Table 2 list the percentage of websites per category, along with a few examples.

We also found that many of the same sites we labeled as unavailable in Cuba also timed out when requested from Atlas probes in other US-sanctioned countries. Specifically, 51 of the 111 (46%) domains timed out when requests originated from a probe in Sudan.

Beyond websites, we surveyed the availability of public DNS services in Cuba and found all of those tested to be reachable. A first analysis showed as if some services were unavailable; however, the result was due to the Recursion Desired (RD) flag of the request being unset by default in the Atlas probe while many of the DNS servers are configured to ignore requests with RD unset or respond with an empty answer. We diagnosed the issue by comparing our results with those of dig, which sets RD by default.

7. CONCLUSION

We have started to characterize the state of Cuba's access to the wider Internet. Our work is motivated by recent improvements in connectivity to the island and the growing commercial interest following the ease of restrictions on travel and trade with the US. This paper reports on some of our early findings, including high RTTs to websites hosted off the island, even after the addition of ALBA-1, a high degree of path asymmetry in traffic to/from the island that partially traverse high-latency satellite links, and several web services that return invalid responses to requests originating from the island. We plan to make a periodic status report on the state of the Internet in Cuba and the associated data available to the research community.

[2]As ranked by Alexa `alexa.com`

Acknowledgements

This work was supported in part by the National Science Foundation through Awards CNS 1211375 and CNS 1218287.

8. REFERENCES

[1] Venezuela-Cuba undersea cable link work starts. `http://www.bbc.com/news/world-latin-america-12260410`, January 2011.

[2] Cuba approves first public wi-fi hub in Havana. `http://www.bbc.com/news/technology-31905794`, March 2015.

[3] The thrill of the law. *The Economist*, April 11 2015.

[4] Z. S. Bischof, J. S. Otto, and F. E. Bustamante. Distributed Systems and Natural Disasters: BitTorrent As a Global Witness. In *Proc. of CoNEXT SWID*, 2011.

[5] K. Chen, D. R. Choffnes, R. Potharaju, Y. Chen, F. E. Bustamante, D. Pei, and Y. Zhao. Where the sidewalk ends: Extending the Internet AS graph using traceroutes from P2P users. In *Proc. ACM CoNEXT*, 2009.

[6] C. Dewey. In Cuba, connecting to the Internet costs four times the average annual salary. `http://www.washingtonpost.com/blogs/worldviews/wp/2013/10/08/in-cuba-connecting-to-the-internet-costs-four-times-the-average-annual-salary/`.

[7] DomainTyper. Top websites with .cu. `https://domaintyper.com/top-websites/most-popular-websites-with-cu-domain`.

[8] M. Frank. Cuba lifts ban on computer and DVD player sales. `http://www.reuters.com/article/2008/03/13/us-cuba-reforms-idUSN1329909720080313`, March 2008.

[9] ITU. Statistics. `http://www.itu.int/en/ITU-D/Statistics/Pages/stat/default.aspx`, 2014.

[10] E. Katz-Bassett, H. V. Madhyastha, V. K. Adhikari, C. Scott, J. Sherry, P. Van Wesep, T. Anderson, and A. Krishnamurthy. Reverse traceroute. In *Proc. of USENIX NSDI*, 2010.

[11] D. Madory. Mystery cable activated in Cuba. `http://research.dyn.com/2013/01/cuban-mystery-cable-activated/`, January 2013.

[12] J. S. Otto, M. A. Sánchez, J. P. Rula, and F. E. Bustamante. Content delivery and the natural evolution of DNS: Remote DNS trends, performance issues and alternative solutions. In *Proc. of IMC*, 2012.

[13] RIPE NCC. RIPE Atlas. `http://atlas.ripe.net`.

[14] M. A. Sánchez, J. S. Otto, Z. S. Bischof, D. R. Choffnes, F. E. Bustamante, B. Krishnamurthy, and W. Willinger. Dasu: Pushing experiments to the Internet's edge. In *Proc. of USENIX NSDI*, 2013.

Category	Examples	% of sites
Advertising and marketing	adcash.com	11.7
Adult content	xhamster.com	28.9
Communication and social	lovoo.com	2.7
Computers	adobe.com, dell.com, tinyurl.com	15.3
Employment	shine.com	1.8
Financial	paypal.com, citi.com	17.1
Gaming	blizzard.com, secondlife.com	5.4
Online commerce and services	eventbrite.com	8.1
News	moneycontrol.com	5.4
Travel	priceline.com	3.6

Table 2: Percent of websites by category for which SSL certificate requests from Cuba consistently failed.

[15] J. Sutton. U.S. to establish cable link to Guantanamo base in two years. http://in.reuters.com/article/2013/09/20/usa-guantanamo-cable-idINDEE98J0F020130920, September 2013.

[16] S. Varadhan. IDT Corp to provide long distance telephony between U.S. and Cuba. http://reut.rs/1EZDxFT, February 2015.

[17] K. Vyas. U.S. sets a goal in Cuba: Open Internet. http://www.wsj.com/articles/u-s-sets-a-priority-in-cuba-open-internet-1421792275.

[18] J. Watts. Cuba's 'offline internet': no access, no power, no problem. http://www.theguardian.com/world/2014/dec/23/cuba-offline-internet-weekly-packet-external-hard-drives, December 2014.

[19] S. Wills. Cuba's Internet: It's Bad, But It Might Get Better. http://abcnews.go.com/ABC_Univision/internet-cuba-facts-myths-web-access/story?id=19895951.

[20] Y. Zaki, J. Chen, T. Pötsch, T. Ahmad, and L. Subramanian. Dissecting web latency in ghana. In *Proc. of IMC*, 2014.

[21] M. Zheleva, P. Schmitt, M. Vigil, and E. Belding. The increased bandwidth fallacy: performance and usage in rural Zambia. In *Proc. of ACM DEV*, 2013.

Peeking Beneath the Hood of Uber

Le Chen
Northeastern University
Boston, MA
leonchen@ccs.neu.edu

Alan Mislove
Northeastern University
Boston, MA
amislove@ccs.neu.edu

Christo Wilson
Northeastern University
Boston, MA
cbw@ccs.neu.edu

ABSTRACT

Recently, Uber has emerged as a leader in the "sharing economy". Uber is a "ride sharing" service that matches willing drivers with customers looking for rides. However, unlike other open marketplaces (e.g., AirBnB), Uber is a black-box: they do not provide data about supply or demand, and prices are set dynamically by an opaque "surge pricing" algorithm. The lack of transparency has led to concerns about whether Uber artificially manipulate prices, and whether dynamic prices are fair to customers and drivers.

In order to understand the impact of surge pricing on passengers and drivers, we present the first in-depth investigation of Uber. We gathered four weeks of data from Uber by emulating 43 copies of the Uber smartphone app and distributing them throughout downtown San Francisco (SF) and midtown Manhattan. Using our dataset, we are able to characterize the dynamics of Uber in SF and Manhattan, as well as identify key implementation details of Uber's surge price algorithm. Our observations about Uber's surge price algorithm raise important questions about the fairness and transparency of this system.

Categories and Subject Descriptors

H.3.5 [**Online Information Services**]: Commercial services, Web-based services

Keywords

Uber; Surge Pricing; Sharing Economy; Algorithm Auditing

1. INTRODUCTION

Recently, there has been an explosion of services that facilitate the so-called "sharing economy". Websites like AirBnB, Care.com, TaskRabbit, and Fiverr allow individuals to advertise their services and set their own schedules without the necessity of working for a company. Typically, these websites function as marketplaces where participants set their own prices and choose who to accept jobs from. By acting as open platforms, these websites are poised to unlock the productive potential of millions of people.

Uber has emerged as a leader in the sharing economy. Uber is a "ride sharing" service that matches willing drivers (i.e., anyone with a car) with customers looking for rides. Uber charges passengers based on time and distance of travel; however, during times of high demand, Uber uses a "surge multiplier" to increase prices. Uber provides two justifications for surge pricing [11]: first, it reduces demand by pricing some customers out of the market, thus reducing the wait times for the remaining customers. Second, surge pricing increases profits for drivers, thus incentivizing more people to drive during times of high demand. Uber's business model has become so widely emulated that the media now refers to the "Uberification" of services [4].

While Uber has become extremely popular, there are also concerns about the fairness, efficacy, and disparate impact of surge pricing. The key difference between Uber and other sharing economy marketplaces is that Uber is a black-box: they do not provide data about supply and demand, and surge multipliers are set by an opaque algorithm. This lack of transparency has led to concerns that Uber may artificially manipulate surge prices to increase profits [25], as well as apprehension about the fairness of surge pricing [10]. These concerns were exacerbated when Uber was forced to publicly apologize and refund rides after prices surged during Hurricane Sandy [16] and the Sydney hostage crisis [19].

In order to understand the impact of surge pricing on passengers and drivers, we present the first in-depth investigation of Uber. We gather four weeks of data from Uber by emulating 43 copies of the Uber smartphone app and distributing them in a grid throughout downtown San Francisco (SF) and midtown Manhattan. By carefully calibrating the GPS coordinates reported by each emulated app, we are able to collect high-fidelity data about surge multipliers, estimated wait times (EWTs), car supply, and passenger demand for all types of Ubers (e.g., UberX, UberBLACK, *etc.*). We validate our methodology using ground-truth data on New York City (NYC) taxicabs.

Using our dataset, we are able to characterize the dynamics of Uber in SF and Manhattan. As expected, supply and demand show daily patterns that peak around rush hours. However, we also observe differences between these cities: although SF has many more Ubers than Manhattan, it also surges much more often. Surge prices are extremely noisy: the majority of surges last less than five minutes. Finally, by analyzing the movements and actions of Uber drivers, we

IMC'15, October 28–30, 2015, Tokyo, Japan.

ACM 978-1-4503-3848-6/15/10 ...$15.00.
DOI: http://dx.doi.org/10.1145/2815675.2815681 .

show that surge prices have a small, positive effect on vehicle supply, and a large, negative impact on passenger demand.

Additionally, our measured data enables us to identify key implementation details of Uber's surge price algorithm. Based on our understanding of Uber's algorithm, we make the following observations:

- Uber has manually divided cities into "surge areas" with independent surge prices. Prices update every 5 minutes and show high correlation with supply, demand, and estimated wait time over the previous 5-minute interval. This suggests that surge prices are set algorithmically, not manually, and that the algorithm is quite responsive.
- However, as April 2015, Uber began serving surge prices to users that do not always match the prices returned by the Uber API. Furthermore, surge prices were no longer uniform for users, even if they were in the same surge area at the same time. We reported this finding to Uber, and their engineers confirmed that this behavior was caused by a bug in their system.
- Although we show that surge prices cannot be forecast in advance, given knowledge of the surge pricing algorithm, we demonstrate how passengers can significantly reduce surge prices 10-20% of the time by exploiting differences between surge areas.

Our observations about Uber's surge price algorithm raise important questions about fairness and transparency. For example, users may receive dramatically different prices due to small changes in geolocation. Furthermore, the vague, changing aspects of the algorithm impacts drivers' ability to predict fares. Finally, the black-box nature of Uber's system makes it vulnerable to exploitation by passengers (as we show), or possibly by colluding groups of drivers [2].

Outline. We begin in §2 by introducing Uber. In §3, we present and validate our data collection methodology. In §4, we characterize supply and demand on Uber, and analyze Uber's surge pricing algorithm in §5. Based on these findings, we present a strategy for avoiding surge prices in §6, followed by related work and discussion in §7 and §8.

2. BACKGROUND

In this section, we briefly introduce Uber, surge pricing, and technical details about the Uber service.

Uber. Founded in 2009, Uber is a "ride sharing" service that connects people who need transportation with a crowd-sourced pool of drivers. Unlike typical transportation providers, Uber does not own any vehicles or directly hire drivers. Instead, Uber drivers are independent contractors (known as "partners") who use their own vehicles and set their own schedules. As of May 2015, Uber is available in 200 cities in 57 countries[1], and claims to have 160K active drivers in the U.S. alone [15].

Uber provides a platform that connects passengers to drivers in real-time. Drivers use the Uber *Partner app* on their smartphone to indicate their willingness to accept fares. Passengers use the Uber *Client app* to determine the availability of rides and get estimated prices. Uber's system routes passenger requests to the nearest driver, and automatically charges passengers' credit cards at the conclusion

[1]`https://www.uber.com/cities`

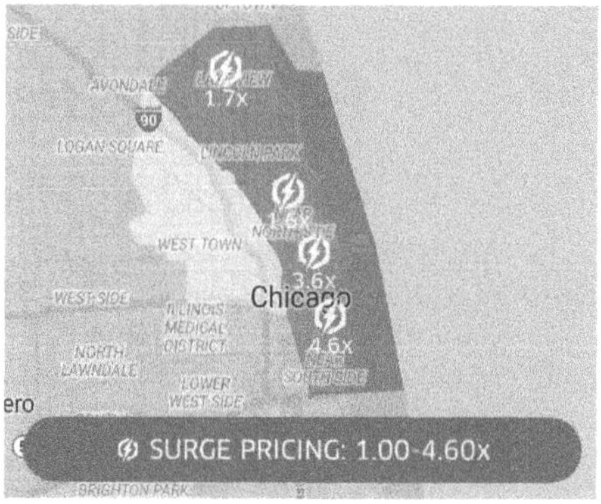

Figure 1: Screenshot of the Uber Partner app.

of each trip. Uber retains 20% of each fare and pays the rest to drivers.

Depending on location, Uber offers a variety of different services. UberX and UberXL are basic sedans and SUVs that compete with traditional taxis, while UberBLACK and UberSUV are luxury vehicles that compete with limousines. UberFAMILY is a subset of UberX and UberXL cars equipped with car seats, while UberWAV refers to wheelchair accessible vehicles. UberT allows users to request traditional taxis from within the Uber app. UberPOOL allows passengers to save money via carpooling, i.e., Uber will assign multiple passengers to each vehicle. UberRUSH is a delivery service where Uber drivers agree to courier packages on behalf of customers.

Surge Pricing. Uber's fare calculation changes depending on local transportation laws. It typically incorporates a minimum base fare, cost per mile, cost per minute, and fees, tolls, and taxes. The base fare and distance/time charges vary depending on the type of vehicle (e.g., UberX vs. UberBLACK).

In 2012, Uber introduced a dynamic component to pricing known as the *surge multiplier*. As the name suggests, fare prices are multiplied by the surge multiplier; typically the multiplier is 1, but during times of high demand it increases. Uber has stated that there are two goals of this system: *first*, higher profits may increase supply by incentivizing drivers to come online. *Second*, higher prices may reduce demand by discouraging price-elastic customers.

Little is known about Uber's surge price algorithm, or whether the system as a whole is successful at addressing supply/demand imbalances. As shown in Figure 1, surge multipliers vary based on location, and recent measurements suggest that Uber updates the multipliers every 3-5 minutes [6]. Uber has a patent pending on the surge price algorithm, which states that features such as car supply, passenger demand, weather, and road traffic may be used in the calculation [23].

Passenger's Perspective. Uber's apps provide different information to passengers and drivers. The Client app displays a map with the eight closest cars to the user (based on the smartphone's geolocation), and the Estimated Wait Time (EWT) for a car. The app provides separate eight-car inventories and EWTs for each type of Uber. Users are not shown the surge multiplier until they attempt to request a car (and only if it is >1). Although the app initially assumes that the user's current location is their pickup point, the user may move the map to choose a different pickup point. This new location may have a different EWT and/or surge multiplier than the original location.

Driver's Perspective. In contrast to the Client app, the Partner app displays very different information to drivers. As shown in Figure 1, the centerpiece of the Partner app is a map with colored polygons indicating areas of surge. Unlike the Client app, the locations of other cars are not shown. In theory, this map allows drivers to locate areas of high demand where they can earn more money. In practice, drivers often use the Partner and Client apps concurrently, to see the exact locations of competing drivers [3]. The Partner app's map also suggests that Uber calculates discreet surge multipliers for different geographic areas. We empirically derive these *surge areas* in § 5.

3. METHODOLOGY

There are three high-level goals of this study. *First*, we aim to understand the overall dynamics of the Uber service. *Second,* we want to determine how Uber calculates surge multipliers. *Third*, we want to understand whether surge pricing is effective at mitigating supply/demand imbalances. To answer these questions, we need detailed data about Uber (e.g., supply of cars, surge multipliers, *etc.*) across time and geography.

In this section, we discuss our approach for collecting data from Uber. We begin by motivating San Francisco (SF) and Manhattan as the regions for our study. Next, we discuss our methodology for collecting data from the Uber Client app, and how we calibrated our measurement apparatus. Finally, we validate our methodology using simulations driven by ground-truth data on all taxi rides in NYC in 2013.

3.1 Selecting Locations

In this study, we focus on the dynamics of Uber in SF and Manhattan. As we discuss in §3.2 and §3.3, there are practical issues that force us to constrain our data collection to relatively small geographic regions. Furthermore, not all regions are viable or interesting: Uber does not offer service everywhere, and many places will have few cars and passengers (i.e., rural areas).

We chose to focus on SF and Manhattan for four reasons. *First*, San Francisco and New York City have the 2nd and 3rd largest populations of Uber drivers in the U.S. (Los Angeles has the largest population) [15]. *Second*, SF was Uber's launch city, and recent measurements suggest that it accounted for 71% of all "taxi" rides in the city in 2014 (the highest percentage of any U.S. city; Uber accounted for 29% of all rides in NYC during 2014) [27]. *Third*, SF and NYC are very different cities in terms of culture and access to public transportation, which may lead to interesting differences in the dynamics of Uber.

Fourth and finally, Manhattan is a useful location to measure Uber because there also exists a publicly available dataset of all taxi rides in NYC for 2013 [22]. We leverage this data in §3.5 to validate the accuracy of our Uber measurement methodology.

3.2 The Uber API

Now that we have chosen locations, the next step is to collect data from Uber in these two areas. Like many modern web services, Uber provides an HTTP-based API for third-party developers to retrieve information about the state of the service. In our case, the `estimates/price` and `estimates/time` endpoints are most useful. The former takes longitude and latitude as input, and returns a JSON-encoded list of price estimates (including surge multipliers) for all car types available at the given location. The latter is similar, except it returns EWTs. Uber imposes a rate limit of 1,000 API requests per hour per user account.

While data from the Uber API is useful, it is not sufficient for this study, since it does not include information about car supply or passenger demand. Thus, we only rely on API data for specific experiments in §5.

3.3 Collecting Data from the Uber App

To overcome the shortcomings of the Uber API, we leverage the Uber Client app. After a user opens the app and authenticates with Uber, the app sends `pingClient` messages to Uber's server every 5 seconds. Each ping includes the user's geolocation, and the server responds with a JSON-encoded list of information about all available car types at the user's location. For each car type, the nearest eight cars, EWT, and surge multiplier are given. Each car is represented by a unique ID, its current geolocation, and a path vector that traces the recent movements of the car.

To gather this data, we wrote a script that emulates the exact behavior of the Client app. Our script logs-in to Uber, sends `pingClient` messages every 5 seconds, and records the responses. By controlling the latitude and longitude sent by the script, we can collect data from arbitrary locations. We created 43 Uber accounts (each account requires a credit card to create), giving us the ability to "blanket" a small geographic area with measurement points. To simplify our discussion, we refer to these 43 measurement points as "clients".

While we were collecting data we never encountered rate limits or had our accounts banned. This indicates that we very likely were not detected by Uber. Although it is possible that Uber detected our clients and fed them false data, it is much more plausible that Uber would have simply banned our clients if they were concerned about our measurements.

Measuring Demand and Supply. Using the data returned by `pingClient`, we can approximate the aggregate supply and demand within our measurement region. To measure *supply*, we can simply count the total number of unique cars observed across all measurement points; each of these cars represents a driver who is looking to provide a ride. To measure *demand*, we can measure the aggregate number of cars that go *offline* (disappear) between responses; one of the reasons a car may go offline is because it picked up a rider (we discuss other potential reasons, and how we handle them, below).

Limitations. Although `pingClient` returns more information than the Uber API, there are still four limitations that we must address. *First*, clients only receive information about the eight closest cars. Thus, to measure the overall supply of vehicles in a geographic area, we must position the 43 clients such that they completely cover the area. This situation is further complicated by the fact that each client's visibility changes as the density of Uber cars fluctuates (e.g., cars are dense during rush hour but sparse at 4am). In §3.4, we perform calibration experiments to determine the appropriate distance to space our clients.

Second, the demand we are able to estimate from our data is *fulfilled demand*, i.e., the number of cars that pick up passengers. Uber does not provide public data about *quantity demanded*, i.e., the number of passengers that request rides. The difference between fulfilled and quantity demand is that some passengers may request a ride but not receive one due to supply shortages. Thus, in this study, when we refer to "demand", we are talking about fulfilled demand.

Third, our measurement of demand may overestimate the true demand because there are three reasons why a car might disappear between one response and the next: 1) the car drives outside our measurement area, 2) the driver accepts a ride request, or 3) the driver goes offline. We can disambiguate case 1 since the Client data includes the path vector for each car. Although we cannot disambiguate cases 2 and 3, we can still use car disappearances as an upper-bound on the fulfilled demand within the measurement area.

Fourth, data from the Client app does not allow us to track individual Uber drivers over time. Although each car is assigned a unique ID, these IDs are randomized each time a car comes online. Unfortunately, there is no way to overcome this limitation, and thus none of our experiments rely on tracking individual drivers.

Phantom Cars. Several press articles claim that Uber's Client app does not display data about actual Uber cars; instead, they claim that the cars are "phantoms" designed to give customers the illusion of supply [26]. Uber has publicly disputed these claims [5,32], explaining that the data shown in the Client app is as accurate as possible, given practical constraints like the accuracy of smartphone GPS measurements. Furthermore, Uber stated that car locations may be slightly perturbed to protect drivers' safety. We have not observed any evidence in our data to suggest that the cars are phantoms; on the contrary, the cars in our data exhibit all the hallmarks of human activity, such as diurnal activity patterns (see §4). If Uber does present phantom cars, it is likely that they only do so in rural areas with low supply, rather than in major cities like Manhattan and SF.

Uber Driver App. As shown in Figure 1, the Driver app also includes useful information (i.e., the surge map). However, only registered Uber drivers may log in to the Driver app. We attempted to sign-up as an Uber driver, but unfortunately Uber requires that drivers sign a document prohibiting data-collection from the Driver app. We opted not to sign this agreement. Instead, in §5, we reconstruct the surge map based on data from the Uber API.

Ethics. While conducting this study, we were careful to collect data in an ethical manner. *First*, we do not collect any personal information about any Uber users or drivers. We discussed our study with the Chair of our University's Institutional Review Board (IRB); she evaluated it as not being subject to IRB review because we did not collect personal information or impact any user's environment.

Second, we minimize our impact on Uber users and drivers. Before we began our data collection, we conducted an experiment to see if our measurements would impact Uber users by artificially raising the surge price. Fully discussed below, our results strongly suggests that our measurements have no impact on the surge multiplier. Moreover, at no point in this study did we actually request rides from any Uber driver, and drivers are not able to observe our measurement clients in the Driver app.

Third, we minimized our impact on Uber itself by collecting just the data we need to perform the study. The overall effect of our measurements was the same as 43 extra users running the Uber Client app. Given that Uber claims millions of users worldwide, we believe this is a worthwhile tradeoff in order to conduct this research.

Other Ride-Sharing Services. Although we attempted to collect data from other ride sharing services, these efforts were not successful. Lyft implements "prime time" pricing, but this data is only available *after* a user requests a ride. Thus, there was no ethical way for us to collect this data. Sidecar does not implement surge pricing; instead, drivers set their own rates based on time and distance. These additional variables make it difficult to systematically collect price information.

3.4 Calibration

The next step in our methodology is determining the locations for our 43 clients in SF and Manhattan. This step is crucial; on one hand, if we distribute the clients sparsely, we may only observe a subset of cars and thus underestimate supply and demand (recall that `pingClient` responses from Uber only contain the closest eight cars to each client). On the other hand, if the clients are too close together, the cars they observe will overlap, and we will fail to observe supply and demand over a sufficiently large geographic area.

To determine the appropriate placement of our 43 clients, we conducted a series of experiments between December 2013 and February 2014. In our first experiment, we chose a random location in Manhattan and placed all 43 clients there for one hour. We then repeated this test over several days with different random locations around Manhattan and SF. The results of these experiments reveal two important details about Uber: *first*, during each test, all 43 clients observed exactly the same vehicles, surge multipliers, and EWTs. This strongly suggests that the data received from `pingClient` is deterministic.

Second, when the clients were placed in areas where we would not expect to see surge (e.g., residential neighborhoods at 4 a.m.), all 43 clients recorded surge multipliers of 1 for the entire hour. This strongly suggests that our measurement methodology does not *induce* surges. As we show in Figure 8, fulfilled demand in midtown Manhattan peaks around 100 rides per hour, so 43 clients is a significant enough number that we would expect surge to increase if the algorithm took "views" into account.

The goal of our next experiment is to measure the *visibility radius* of clients. Intuitively, this is the distance from a client to the furthest of the eight cars returned by `pingClient`.

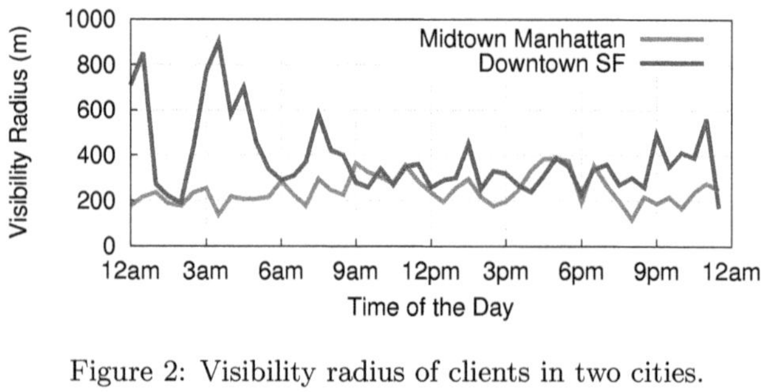

Figure 2: Visibility radius of clients in two cities.

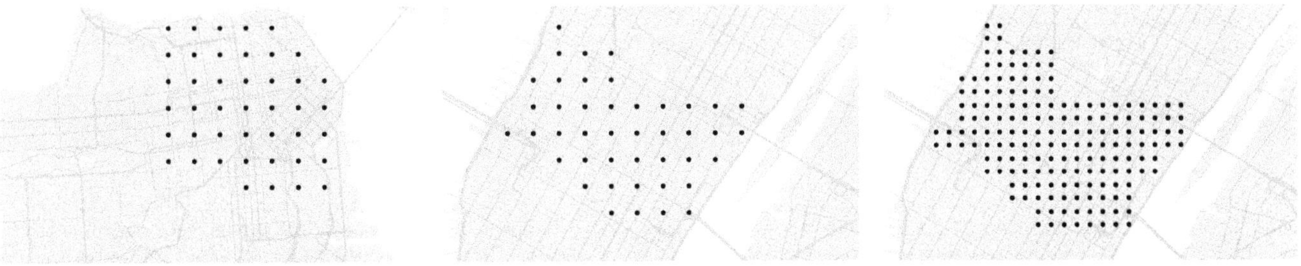

(a) Uber in downtown SF. (b) Uber in midtown Manhattan. (c) Taxis in midtown Manhattan.

Figure 3: Locations of our Uber and taxi measurement points in SF and Manhattan.

Once we know the visibility radius in SF and Manhattan, we can determine the placement of our 43 clients.

To calculate the visibility radius, we conduct the following experiment. We 1) place 4 clients, denoted as $C = \{c_1, c_2, c_3, c_4\}$, at the same geolocation; 2) each of the clients "walks" 20 meters Northeast, Northwest, Southeast and Southwest (respectively) every 5 seconds; 3) the experiment halts when $|\bigcap_c V_c| = 0$, where V_{c_i} is the set of cars observed by client c_i; 4) record the distance D_c from each $c \in C$ to the starting point. Given this information, we calculate the visibility radius r (consider a 45°-45°-90° triangle where r is the leg and D_c is the hypotenuse) as:

$$r = \frac{1}{4} \sum_c \frac{D_c}{\sqrt{2}} \approx 0.1768 \times \sum_c D_c$$

Figure 2 shows the measured radii in meters when the clients were placed in downtown SF and midtown Manhattan. We chose these specific locations because they are the "hearts" of these cities, and thus they are likely to have the highest densities of Uber cars. As expected, the visibility radius changes throughout the day, with the most obvious difference being night/day in SF. There are also differences between the cities: the average radius is 247 ± 2.6 meters in Manhattan, versus 387 ± 6.8 meters in SF.[2]

In the end, we chose 200 meters as the radius for our data collection in midtown Manhattan, and 350 meters in downtown SF. These values represent a conscientious tradeoff between obtaining complete coverage of supply/demand and covering a large overall geographic area. Figures 3a and 3b depict the exact positions where we placed our clients in SF and Manhattan.[3]

3.5 Validation

Our final step is to validate our measurement methodology. The fundamental challenge is that we do not have ground-truth information about supply and demand on Uber; we attempt to mitigate this through careful placement of our clients, but the key challenge is having confidence that we will observe the vast majority of cars.

To address this issue, we constructed an Uber simulator powered by ground-truth data on NYC taxis [22]. The NYC taxi data includes timestamped, geolocated pickup and dropoff points for all taxi rides in NYC in 2013. Each taxi is assigned a unique ID, so its location can be tracked over time. Our simulator takes the taxi data as input, and plays the rides back in real-time. Since the taxi data only includes pickup and dropoff points, the simulator "drives" each taxi in a straight-line from point-to-point. We assume that a taxi has gone "offline" if it is idle for more than 3 hours (this filter only removes 5% of taxi sessions in the data).

We built an API in our simulator that offers the same functionality as Uber's `pingClient`: it returns the eight closest taxis to a given geolocation. Just as with Uber, the ID for each taxi is randomized each time it becomes available. Given this API, we used our methodology from §3.3 and §3.4 to measure the supply and demand of taxis over time. If the measured values from the simulator's API are similar to the ground-truth values, we can confidently say that our methodology will also collect accurate data from Uber.

Calibration. To make our simulation fair, we calibrated it by using four taxi clients to determine the visibility radius for taxis in midtown NYC (see §3.4). Taxis are much denser than Ubers in this area, so r = 100 meters is commensurately smaller. Figure 3c shows the locations of our 172 taxi clients; compared to Uber clients, it takes 300% more taxi clients to cover midtown.

Results. Using our taxi clients, we measured the supply and demand of taxis in the simulator between April 4–11, 2013. We chose these dates because they correspond to the same month and week of our Uber measurements (except in 2013 versus 2015, see §4).

As we discuss in §3.3, neither Uber nor our simulator return direct information about demand. Instead, we assume that cars that 1) disappear from the measured data, and 2) were not driving near the outer edge of the measurement polygon were booked by a passenger.[4] We refer to these events as *deaths*.

Figure 4 plots the measured and ground-truth taxi supply and demand per 5-minute interval. The two lines are almost indistinguishable since our taxi clients capture 97% of cars and 95% of deaths. The results provide strong evidence that our measurement methodology captures most of Uber's supply and demand.

4. ANALYSIS

In this section, we analyze supply, demand, and wait times on Uber. We begin by briefly introducing our datasets and how we cleaned them. Next, we examine how the dynamics of Uber change over time and spatially across cities. We

[2]Throughout this study, we present the 95% confidence interval (CI) of the mean value.

[3]All map images used in this paper are ©2015 Google.

[4]Restriction (2) is conservative: cars near the edge of the measurement area may disappear because they were booked, or because they drove outside the measurement polygon.

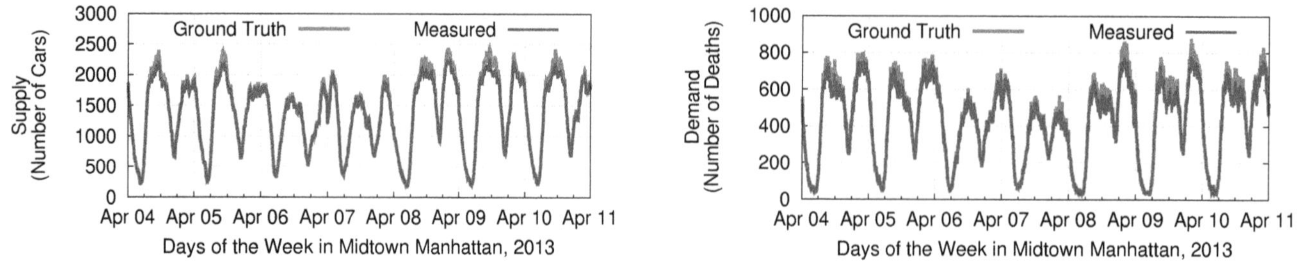

Figure 4: Measured and ground-truth supply (left) and demand (right) of taxis in midtown Manhattan.

focus the majority of our analysis on UberX, since (as we will show) they are the most common type of Uber by a large margin. We defer detailed analysis of surge multipliers and the surge pricing algorithm to §5.

4.1 Data Collection and Cleaning

For this study, we collected data from 43 clients placed in midtown Manhattan and downtown SF between April 3rd–17th (391 GB of data containing 9.3M samples) and April 18th–May 2nd (605 GB of data, 9.4M samples), respectively. Data was collected using the Uber client methodology described in §3.3. The locations of our clients are shown in Figures 3a and 3b. We also collected more limited datasets from the Uber API, as well as client data between December 27th, 2014–March 1st, 2015; we use this data in §5.

Before proceeding with analysis, our data must be cleaned to remove outliers. Figure 5 shows the *lifespan* of UberX cars in our dataset, measured as the time delta during which we observe a car's ID. Problematically, ~50% of UberXs have a lifespan of zero, i.e., we only observe them in a single `pingClient` response. We refer to these cars as being *short-lived*, and observe similar trends for other types of Ubers.

The obvious question is: what is the cause of short-lived cars? Fortunately, we discovered that short-lived cars are an easily understood artifact of our measurement methodology. We examined the GPS coordinates of all short-lived cars, and found that 80% of them are *outsiders*: they are $> r$ meters away from the nearest client in our measurement polygon. Figure 6 plots the distances of short-lived *insiders* (those within the measurement polygon), and shows that 100% of them are $< r$ meters from the polygon boundary.

These results reveal that short-lived cars are due to the fact that `pingClient` only returns information about the eight nearest cars. Cars that are outside the measurement polygon, or $< r$ meters from its edge, may only be observed by a single client. These cars may get pushed out of `pingClient` responses by closer vehicles, or the car may only briefly be near our measurement area. In contrast, cars well-within the boundaries can potentially be observed by many clients, even as they drive around. Thus, we can safely filter short-lived cars from our dataset, and focus in the remainder of the paper only on cars that are driving within the bounds of our measurement area.

Car Lifespan. Figure 7 shows the lifespans of Ubers after removing short-lived cars. We observe similar trends in Manhattan and SF: ~90% of low-priced Ubers (X, XL, FAMILY, and POOL) live for <10 minutes, while ~65% of high-priced Ubers (BLACK and SUV) live for <10 minutes. There are two possible reasons for this observation: first, demand for low-priced Ubers may be higher than for expensive Ubers. Second, as we show in §4.2, low-priced Ubers greatly outnumber high-priced Ubers, so there may simply be more churn amongst the former due to their greater prevalence.

4.2 Dynamics Over Time

Next, we examine how supply, demand, surge multiplier, and EWT vary over time. We calculate supply by counting all the unique car IDs observed by our 43 clients during each 5-minute interval. Demand is the number of cars that disappear during each 5-minute interval (excluding cars that drive outside the measurement area). Surge multiplier and EWT are averaged across each 5-minute interval and all 43 clients. We explain why we chose 5-minute intervals in §5.

Note that our measurements for supply and demand are approximations. As shown in §3.5, our methodology may miss some cars, leading us to slightly underestimate supply. Similarly, we cannot disambiguate cars that pickup a passenger from cars that simply go offline. Thus, our demand numbers are an upper-bound. Finally, a driver that repeatedly goes online and offline during a 5-minute interval will appear as multiple unique cars to us, since cars are assigned a fresh ID each time they come online.

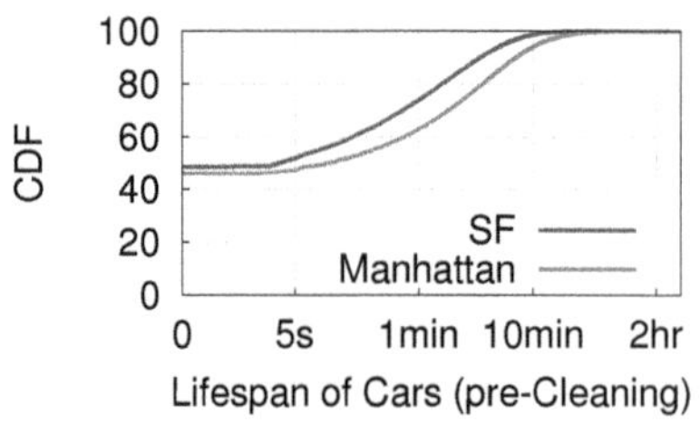

Figure 5: Lifespan of UberX cars in Manhattan and SF before data cleaning.

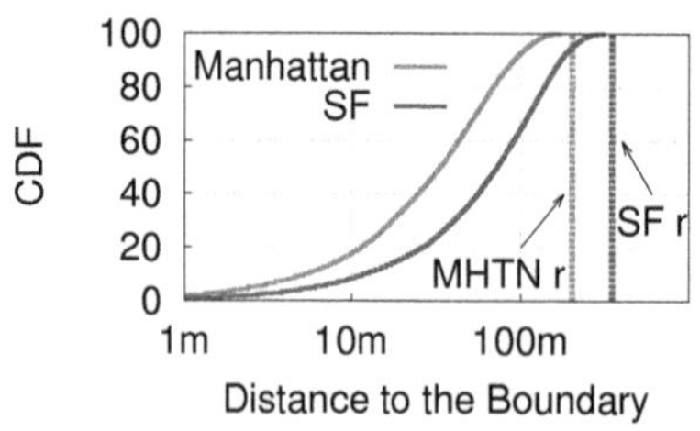

Figure 6: Distance of short-lived insiders to the boundary.

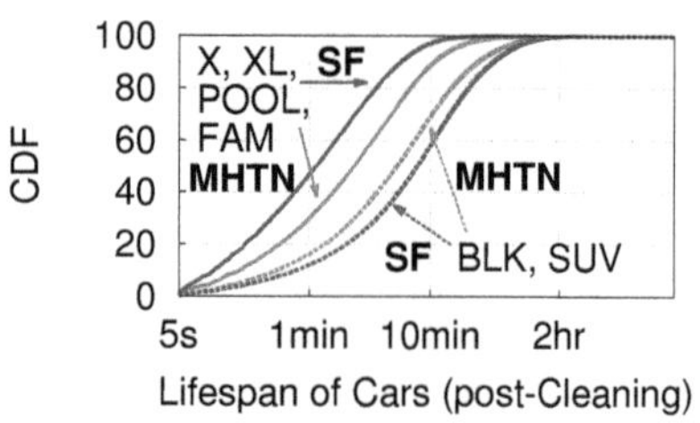

Figure 7: Lifespan of different types of Uber cars after data cleaning.

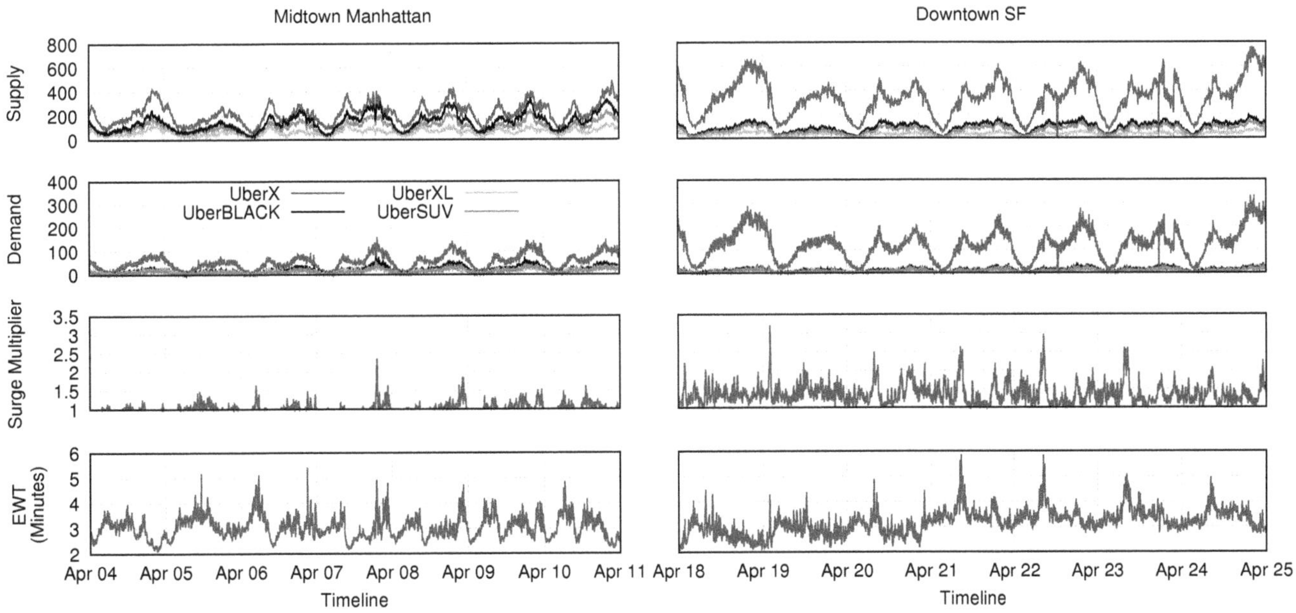

Figure 8: Supply, demand, surge multiplier, and EWT over time for midtown Manhattan and downtown SF. Surge multiplier and estimated wait time (EWT) are only shown for UberX. Diurnal patterns are observed in supply and demand, but the characteristics of the surge multiplier show less predictability.

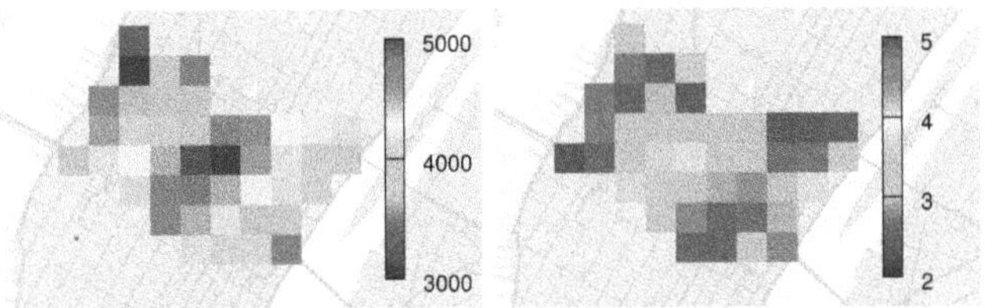

(a) Avg. Number of Cars (b) Avg. EWT (Minutes)

Figure 9: Heatmaps for UberX cars in Manhattan.

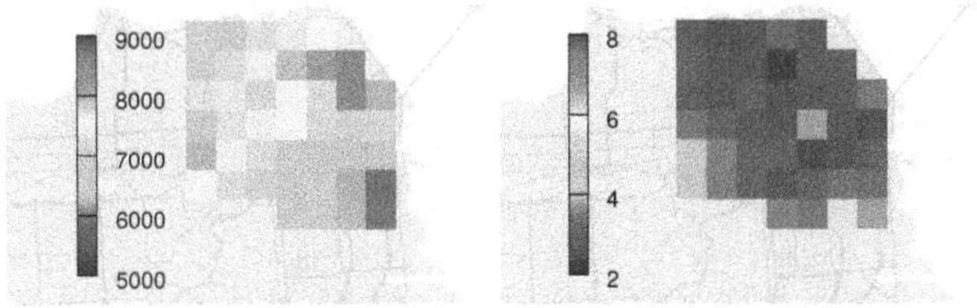

(a) Avg. Number of Cars (b) Avg. EWT (Minutes)

Figure 10: Heatmaps for UberX cars in SF.

Unsurprisingly, Figure 8 shows that Uber exhibits regular daily trends: all four quantities peak during the day and decline at night. We also observe that supply, demand, and EWT have local peaks during morning and afternoon rush hour.[5] Rush hour peaks are less prominent for surge pricing, and we show in §5 that surge pricing is extremely noisy.

Both cities exhibit the same rank ordering of Uber types. UberXs are most prevalent, followed by UberBLACK, UberSUV, and UberXL. Both cities also have other types of Ubers (e.g., UberRUSH, UberFAMILY, *etc.*), however there are only 4 cars of these types on the road on average. Manhattan does have a significant number of UberT's, but these are not interesting in our context since they are not subject to surge pricing (recall that UberT corresponds to an ordinary taxi). Comparing the NYC taxi data in Figure 4 to Figure 8 we see that there are an order of magnitude more taxis in midtown Manhattan than all Ubers combined.

Despite their similarities, Figure 8 also reveals differences between Manhattan and SF. In our measurement region, SF has 58% more Ubers overall than Manhattan, mostly due to the large amount of UberXs in SF. The relative dearth of Ubers in Manhattan may be due to greater availability of taxis and better public transport. However, Manhattan has more UberXLs, UberBLACKs, and UberSUVs than SF.

Manhattan and SF also exhibit different surge pricing characteristics. As shown in Figure 8, downtown SF *surges* (i.e., surge >1) more frequently than midtown Manhattan. Surge multipliers are also tend to be higher in SF: $1.36 \pm 1 \times 10^{-4}$ on average versus $1.07 \pm 7 \times 10^{-5}$ in Manhattan. In midtown Manhattan, surge tends to increase starting at 3pm through evening rush hour Monday–Thursday. On the weekends, surge tends to peak between noon and 3pm, likely due to the influx of tourists. In SF, surge peaks at around 2.0 during morning rush hour (6am–9am) Monday–Friday. Surge also has a localized peak at 2am every night (but especially on weekends, reaching up to 3.0), which is "last call" throughout California.

Although Figure 8 focuses on surge multipliers of UberX, other types of Ubers exhibit similar trends. A recent report estimated that Uber accounts for 71% of "taxi" rides in SF versus 29% in NYC [27], so it is possible that this difference in demand explains the differences in surge characteristics. We defer in-depth discussion of surge pricing to §5.

We also observe that Uber offers expedient service in both cities. Average EWT for an UberX in midtown Manhattan

[5]Note that the y-axes of supply and demand have different scales.

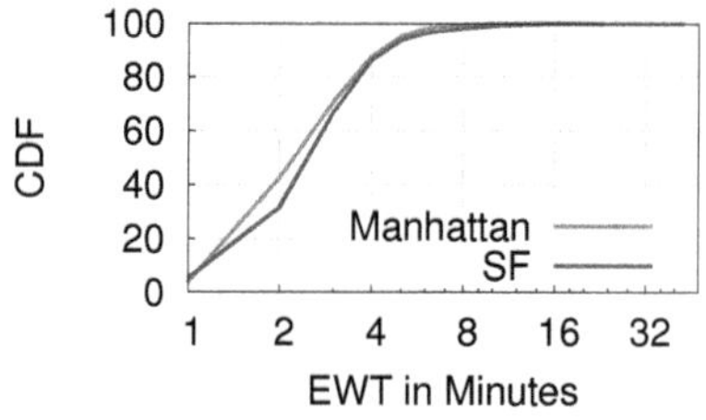

Figure 11: Distribution of EWTs for UberXs.

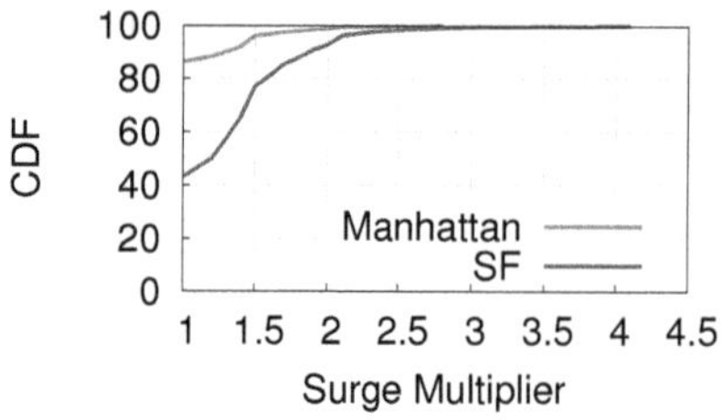

Figure 12: Distribution of surge multipliers for UberXs.

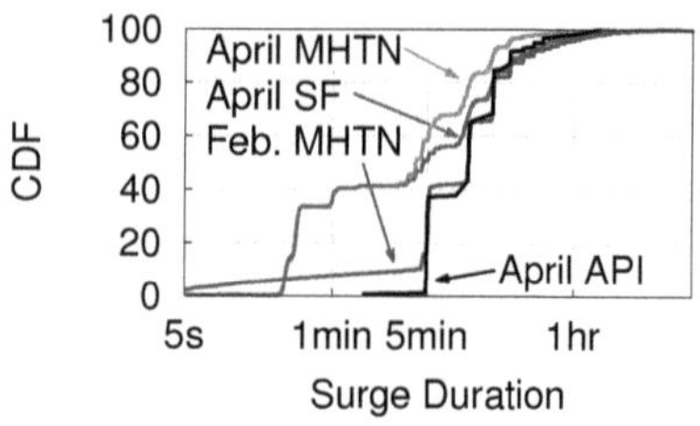

Figure 13: Duration of surges for UberXs.

is $3.0 \pm 2 \times 10^{-4}$ minutes, and $3.1 \pm 2 \times 10^{-4}$ minutes in downtown SF. In both cities, average EWT never exceeds six minutes. We observe similar trends for other types of Ubers, although rarer types (e.g., UberFAMILY) typically have slightly longer EWTs.

4.3 Spatial Dynamics and EWT

Next, we investigate the spatial dynamics of Uber. Figures 9(a) and 10(a) show the average number of unique UberX IDs seen per day by each of our 43 clients.[6] Since each square in these figures is an average, each one has a different confidence interval; the min and max CI for cars in Manhattan are ± 103 and ± 205 cars, respectively. The min and max CI for cars SF is are ± 170 and ± 250. As one might expect, the distribution of cars in both cities is skewed towards commercial and tourist locations. In Manhattan, UberXs congregate between Times Square and 5th Avenue. In SF, UberXs are densest in Russian Hill, Telegraph Hill, the Embarcadero, and the Financial District (upper-right corner of Figure 10(a)), as well as around the University of California, San Francisco (UCSF, lower-left corner).

In contrast, Figures 9(b) and 10(b) depict the distribution of EWTs across space. Each square is the average EWT for UberXs measured every five seconds over two weeks. The min and max CI for Manhattan are $\pm 6 \times 10^{-6}$ and $\pm 2 \times 10^{-4}$ minutes, respectively; the min and max CI for SF are $\pm 7 \times 10^{-7}$ and $\pm 4 \times 10^{-5}$. We observe that there is a complex relationship between car density and EWT. In some cases, locations with low car density have commensurately higher EWTs (e.g., the lower-right corners in Figures 9(b) and 10(b)), suggesting that these areas are under-supplied. However, we also observe under-supply in several areas with high car density (e.g., Times Square and UCSF). This complex interplay between supply and demand supports Uber's case for implementing dynamic pricing.

Figure 11 presents the overall distribution of EWTs in Manhattan and SF for UberXs. 87% of the time, the wait for an UberX is ≤4 minutes. However, there are rare instances of severe supply/demand imbalance when EWT can go as high as 43 minutes. Note that our EWT data comes from the hearts of Manhattan and SF, and may not be representative for suburban areas.

5. SURGE PRICING

Now that we have an understanding of supply and demand on Uber, we turn our attention to surge pricing. Surge pricing is one of Uber's most controversial features [19,24], and thus it warrants special attention. We begin by analyzing the basic characteristics of surge pricing. Next, we use our measured data to extrapolate how Uber updates surge prices over time and geography, and explore the features that Uber uses when calculating surge. Finally, we examine the impact of surge pricing on car supply and passenger demand.

5.1 The Cost of Surges

We begin by answering the questions: *how often and how much does it surge on Uber?* Figure 12 presents the distribution of surge multipliers for UberXs over two weeks. We observe that Manhattan and SF have drastically different characteristics: 86% of the time there is no surge in Manhattan, versus 43% of the time in SF. Furthermore, the maximum surge multiplier we observe in Manhattan is 2.8, versus 4.1 in SF. In both cities, the surge multiplier is ≤1.5 during the majority of surges.

The results in Figure 12 reveal that prices surge on Uber a large fraction of the time (in SF, it's surging the *majority* of the time). Although most of the time the multiplier makes UberXs 25-50% more expensive, there are times (especially in SF) when the multiplier can double, triple, or even quadruple prices.

5.2 Surge Duration and Updates

Next, we answer the question: *how long do surges last?* Figure 13 plots the duration of surges for UberXs over two weeks. We define the duration of a surge as the continuous length of time when the multiplier is >1.

When we first began collecting data from Uber in February 2015, we observed that 90% of surges had durations that were a multiple of 5 minutes. This is shown by the stair-step pattern in the "Feb. Manhattan" line in Figure 13. We also measured surge durations using the Uber API in April 2015,

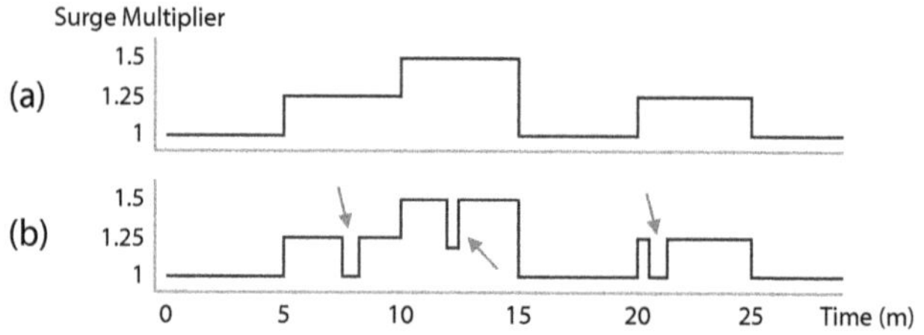

Figure 14: Examples of surge over time as seen from (a) the API and (b) the Client app. Although surge is recalculated every 5 minutes in both cases, clients also observe surge jitters for 20-30 seconds (red arrows).

[6]Note that these numbers are strict upper-bounds on the true number of UberX cars, since IDs are randomized each time a car comes online.

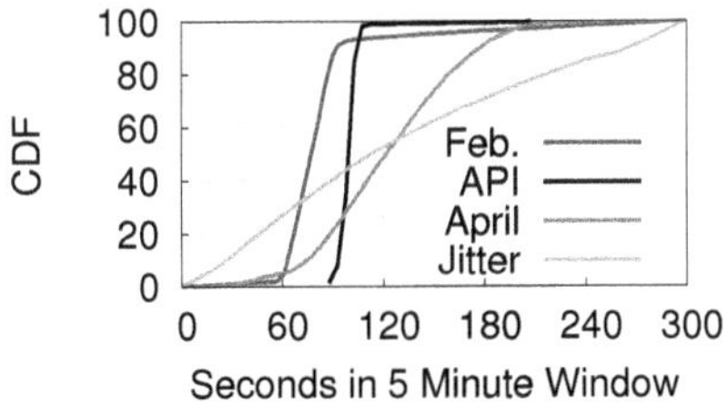

Figure 15: Moment when surge changes during each interval.

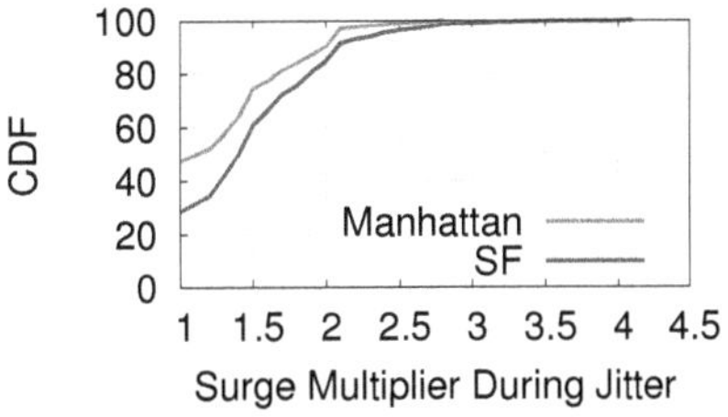

Figure 16: Distribution of surge multipliers seen during times of jitter.

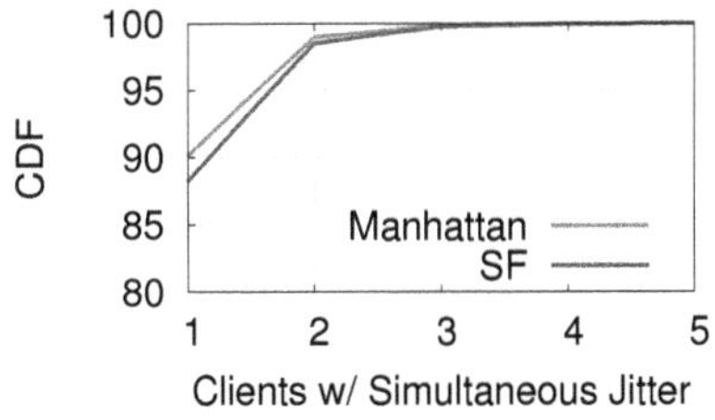

Figure 17: Fraction of clients that observe jitter at the same time.

and observed the same 5-minute pattern. In both of these cases, ~40% of surges last 5 minutes, and ~20% last 10 minutes. Less than 10% of surges last more than 20 minutes.

Strangely, the behavior of the surge price algorithm changed in April 2015. As shown by the two "April" lines in Figure 13, 40% of surges are now less than 1 minute long. The remaining 60% of surges still loosely follow the 5-minute stair-step pattern.

There are two takeaways from Figure 13. First, under normal circumstances, Uber appears to update surge prices on a 5-minute clock (we discuss jitter in greater detail below). Second, the vast majority of surges are short-lived, which suggests that savvy Uber passengers should "wait-out" surges rather than pay higher prices.

Figure 14 illustrates how Uber updates surge multipliers. Figure 14(a) shows the datastream from the API (and what clients observed, prior to April 2015): surge changes at regular 5-minute intervals. Figure 14(b) shows the behavior of `pingClient` responses as of April 2015: surge multipliers are still updated on a 5-minute clock, but within each interval there may be brief periods of jitter. Jitter breaks up a 5-minute surge interval into three separate components, which explains why we observe many surge durations less than 1 minute long in Figure 13. These two processes are the same in Manhattan and SF, and for all types of Ubers.

Timing. Figure 15 examines the fine-grained timing of surge updates. We chose one day of data in February and April, divided time into 5-minute intervals starting at 12:00am, and calculated the exact moment in each interval when surge changed due to the clock and jitter. We observe that the old client-update and the current API-update mechanisms are extremely regular: updates occur during a 35-second range in each interval. The new client-update mechanism is less precise: updates occur during a 2-minute range in each interval. Jitters are distributed almost uniformly throughout the interval, which suggests that jitter is driven by a stochastic or non-deterministic process.

Jitter. Next, we examine the behavior of jitter. In our data, 90% of jitter events last 20-30 seconds, and 100% are less than 1 minute. Furthermore, during jitter, we observe that the surge multiplier is equal to the multiplier from the *previous* 5-minute interval. Because most surges only last 5 minutes, this means that jitter causes the surge multiplier to drop 74% of the time in Manhattan, and 64% of the time in SF. As shown in Figure 16, in 30-50% of jitter events the surge multiplier drops to 1, depending on location. Thus, jitter almost always reduces prices for passengers, if they are lucky enough to request a car during the brief window when the low multiplier is available.

Jitter also deviates from the 5-minute surge intervals in another key way. As we demonstrate in the next section, the 5-minute surge intervals are uniform over specific geographic regions. However, jitter occurs on a per-client basis. Figure 17 plots the number of our clients that observed jitter at the same moment in time (recall, we have 43 total clients). We see that ~90% of jitter events are only observed by a single client, and none are observed by more than 5 clients simultaneously.

In August 2015, we contacted Uber to make them aware of our findings. They were very concerned about the presence of jitter in the datastream, and the implication that customers were receiving inconsistent surge multipliers. We provided log data to Uber's engineers, and they quickly determined that jitter was being caused by a consistency bug in their system. The manifestation of this bug was that random customers could receive stale surge multipliers. This precisely coincides with our observations that jitter appeared at random times for random clients, and that the surge multiplier during jitter was equal to multiplier from the previous 5-minute window. As of this writing, Uber is fixing the bug and restoring consistency for all customers.

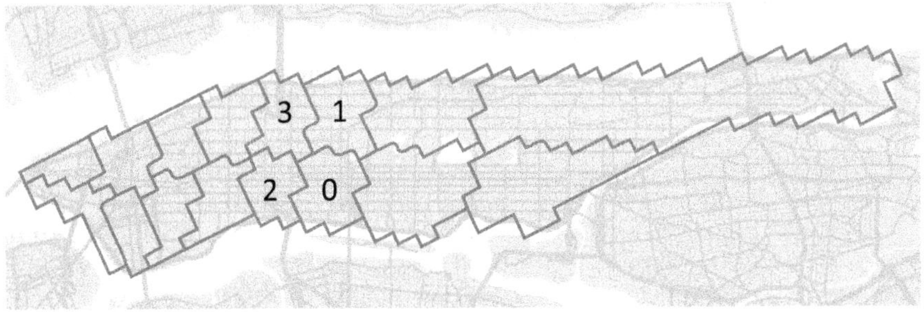

Figure 18: Surge areas in in Manhattan.

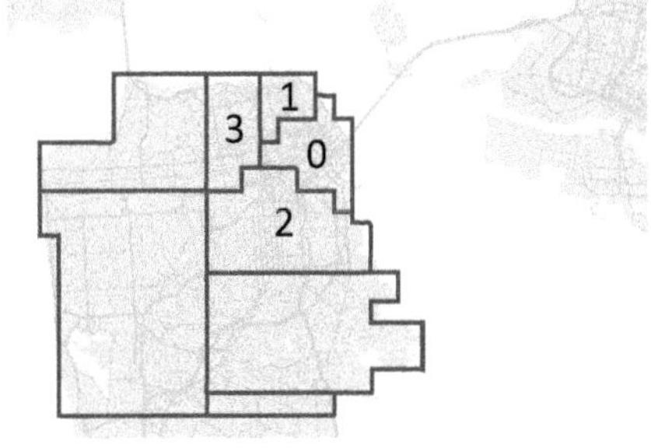

Figure 19: Surge areas in SF.

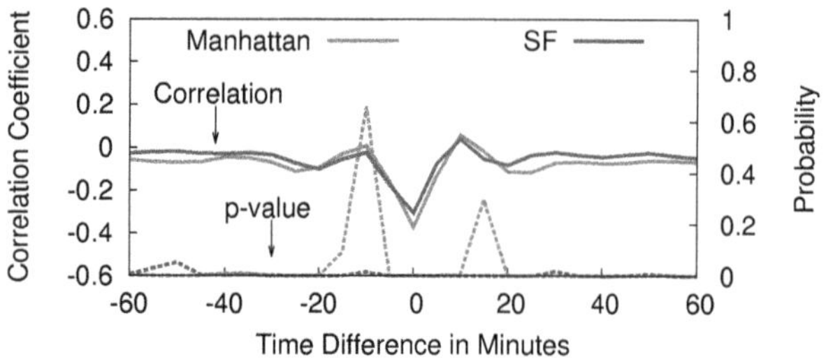

Figure 20: (Supply - Demand) vs. Surge for UberX.

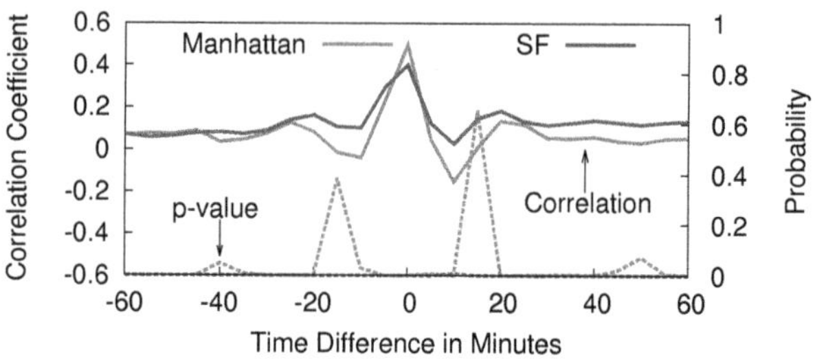

Figure 21: EWT vs. Surge for UberX.

5.3 Surge Areas

Next, we answer the question: *how do surge prices vary by location?* Intuitively, it is clear that surge must vary geographically: a rural location is very different than Times Square.

To answer this question, we used the Uber API to query surge prices throughout Manhattan and SF over the course of eight days. During these tests, we queried data from adjacent locations that obey our visibility radius constraints (see §3.4). Fortunately, since we know that surge prices only change every 5 minutes (and the API does not contain jitter), this enabled us to scale up our measurements to large geographic areas.

Using this data, we looked for clusters of adjacent locations that *always* had equal surge multipliers. Figures 18 and 19 show the regions of Manhattan and SF where the surge multipliers are always in lock-step. These figures reveal the granularity of Uber's surge price algorithm: Uber partitions cities into *surge areas* and computes multipliers independently for each area. The numbered areas correspond to the locations where we collected client data (see Figures 3a and 3b). Given the odd shape of some regions, it is likely that Uber defines surge areas manually. Note that there are some areas where we did not observe sufficient surging samples during our measurements (e.g., Upper Manhattan and Washington Heights); in these cases we cannot isolate individual surge areas, so it is possible these large areas may be composed of several smaller areas.

5.4 Algorithm Features and Forecasting

Next, we investigate the question: *what features does Uber use to calculate surge prices?* Uber has a pending patent that lists potential features [23], but it is unclear what features are truly used in the calculation.

To answer this question, we examine the cross correlation between observed supply, demand, and EWT versus surge price. In these tests, we treat each feature as a continuous time series. For surge, the time series is simply the observed surge multipliers during each 5-minute interval (we discard jitters since they are unpredictable). For supply, demand, and EWT we construct corresponding time series by averaging each quantity over the 5-minute window. We construct independent time series for the four areas in Manhattan and SF where we collect client data, since each area has its own surge characteristics. As before, we focus on UberXs.

Although we examined many possible correlations between these features (such as supply and surge, demand and surge, supply-demand ratio and surge, *etc.*), we obtained the strongest results when comparing *(average supply - average demand)* and *average EWT* to surge. Figure 20 shows the cross correlation (and p-value) between supply/demand difference and surge price. The correlation coefficient at time shift Δt is computed using surge at time t and feature values in the interval $[t + \Delta t - 5, t + \Delta t)$. We observe a relatively strong negative correlation when $-10 \leq \Delta t \leq 10$, which indicates that the surge multiplier rises when supply/demand difference shrinks. It appears that Uber's goal is to maintain a certain amount of slack in their car supply: when demand approaches available supply, surge pricing is instituted to increase supply and reduce demand. Figure 20 also reveals that Uber's surge pricing algorithm is quite responsive, since the correlation is strongest when $\Delta t = 0$.

Figure 21 shows the cross correlation between average EWT and surge price. In this case, we see a relatively strong positive correlation at $\Delta t = 0$, i.e., EWT and surge price increase at the same time. This result also makes sense: if surge increases during times of strained supply, then the wait times for cars should also increase.

Forecasting. Given that we observe correlations between supply, demand, EWT, and surge prices, this raises a new question: *can future surge prices be forecast?* To answer this question, we fitted three linear regression models that take the current supply/demand difference, EWT, and surge multiplier for UberXs as input, and predict the surge multiplier in the next 5-minute interval. As before, we filter jitter out of the time series. We also evaluated models that accept historical data (e.g., samples from previous 5-minute intervals), but this resulted in worse predictive performance.

Table 1 presents the overall R^2 scores for three linear regression models evaluated on two weeks of UberX data. We fitted separate models for all four surge areas in Manhattan and SF (see Figures 18–19), but in the interest of space we present the average R^2 scores in Table 1. In all three models,

City	Raw				Threshold				Rush			
	θ_{sd_diff}	θ_{ewt}	θ_{prev_surge}	R^2	θ_{sd_diff}	θ_{ewt}	θ_{prev_surge}	R^2	θ_{sd_diff}	θ_{ewt}	θ_{prev_surge}	R^2
NY	0.02	0.03	0.13	0.37	0.01	0.12	0.25	0.43	-0.01	0.26	0.33	0.43
SF	0.01	0.34	0.45	0.40	0.01	0.23	0.43	0.43	0.01	0.20	0.43	0.57

Table 1: Estimated Parameters and R^2 scores of linear regression in Manhattan and SF

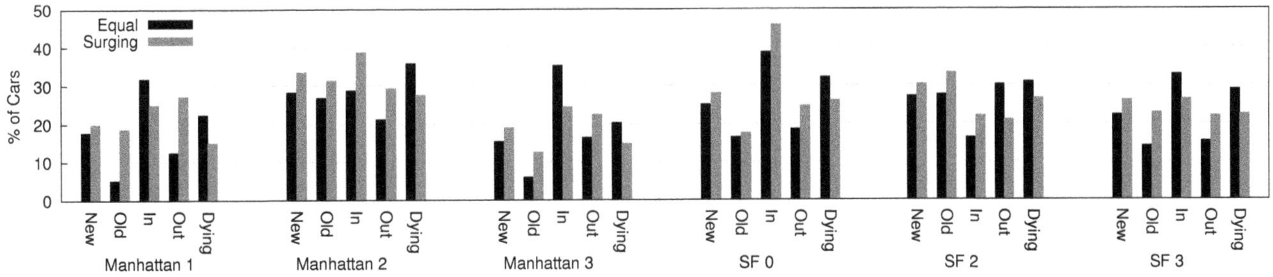

Figure 22: Transition probabilities of UberXs when all areas have equal surge, and when one area is surging.

we remove time intervals when the surge multiplier equals 1 from the data[7] before fitting, since this would make the prediction task too easy (e.g., you could achieve 86% accuracy in Manhattan by always predicting that the surge multiplier will be 1, see §5.1).

We also provide the parameters learned in the linear regression models in Table 1. Note that the learned parameters do not represent the relative importances of the variables; they are simply the slopes of the fitting surfaces.

Unfortunately, even with our large corpus of data, forecasting surge multipliers is an extremely difficult task. The *Raw* model in Table 1 is the most permissive of our three models: it was fitted and evaluated on the entire time series. We see that it has the worst performance, which suggests that either we are missing some key data that is used in Uber's surge calculation, or surge pricing is simply very noisy. The *Threshold* model improves performance by being more restrictive: it only attempts to predict the surge at time t if surge was >1 at $t-1$. We instituted this filter because surge cannot go below 1, i.e., we know less about the state of the system when surge is 1 than when surge is >1.

Finally, the *Rush* model is the most restrictive: it was fitted and evaluated on the subset of data corresponding to rush hours (6am–10am and 4pm–8pm). Although the performance of the Rush model clearly benefits from the predictable characteristics of rush hour traffic (see §4.2), it does not perform uniformly better than the more general Threshold model.

In summary, our forecasting results demonstrate that it is very difficult to predict surge multipliers, even with large amounts of supply and demand data. None of our models exhibits strong predictive performance in absolute terms (i.e., $R^2 \geq 0.9$). This suggests that Uber relies on non-public data to calculate surge prices, and motivates us to examine alternative strategies for obtaining lower prices in §6.

5.5 Impact of Surge on Supply and Demand

The final question that we address in this section is: *what is the impact of surge prices on supply and demand?* Uber has stated that the goals of surge pricing are to increase supply and intentionally reduce demand, and they claim that the system increased the number of drivers by 70-80% after it was introduced [11]. However, it is unclear if and how surge pricing continues to impact supply and demand, now that drivers and passengers have acclimated to the system. Furthermore, recent measurements of Uber suggest that surge pricing redistributes existing supply, rather than encouraging new drivers to come online [6], but these observations have not been verified at-scale.

To answer these questions, we treat the cars in our data as state-machines, and examine how they transition between states when there is and is not surge. At a high-level, we divide time into 5-minute intervals, and compare the states of cars at the beginning and end of each interval. Cars that appear for the first time in interval t are placed in the initial, **new** state, while cars that disappear go into the terminal **dying** state. Cars that start and end in surge area a are **old**. Finally, cars may transition into states that are relative to surge areas, e.g., a car that moves from area a_i to area a_j during t is placed in the move-**in** state relative to a_j, and the move-**out** state relative to a_i.

Based on this model, we examine the behavior of cars during times when all four surge areas have the *same* surge multipliers (in Manhattan and SF, respectively), and times when a single area has a surge multiplier that is at least 0.2 *higher* than its neighboring areas (again, excluding jitter) in the immediately proceeding interval. Intuitively, the former case captures times when there is no monetary incentive for drivers to choose one area over another, while in the latter case there is a monetary incentive to relocate to the surging area.

Figure 22 shows the probability of cars in specific surge areas being in each of our five states. The black bars show the probabilities when all areas have equal surge multipliers, while red corresponds to times when the given area has a multiplier that is at least 0.2 higher than its neighbors. For example, the Manhattan Area 1 "New" bars show that 18% of new cars appear in the area when surge is equal in all four Manhattan areas, whereas 20% of cars appear in the area when it has higher surge than its neighbors. We omit results for two areas because they rarely had higher surge prices than their neighbors.

Results. First, we examine the impact of surge pricing on the behavior of **new** cars. In all six areas, we observe that the fraction of **new** cars increases when that area has higher surge than its neighbors. Although this effect is not large (3.7% on average), it is consistent. This suggests that surge pricing is effective at drawing drivers onto the roads.

Second, we examine the impact of surge on the distribution of existing supply. In five areas, we observe that the fraction of cars that move **out** of an area increases when it is surging. This is the opposite result of what we expected. Furthermore, in three areas (Manhattan 2, SF 0, and SF 2) we observe more cars moving **in** during times of surge, while

[7]The two exceptions to this data cleaning rule are intervals where surge=1 directly preceding or proceeding an interval where surge>1.

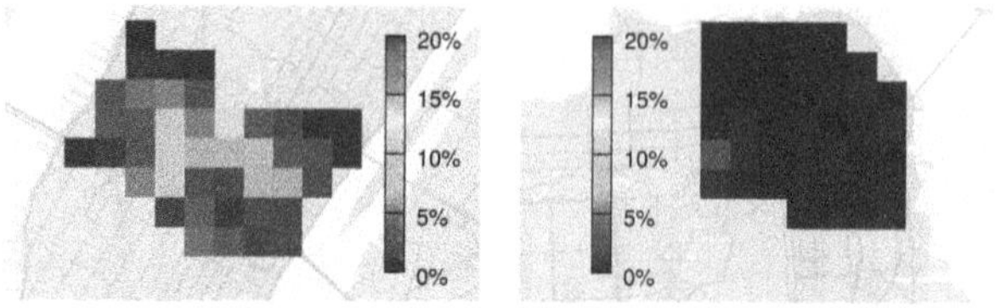

(a) Manhattan (b) SF

Figure 23: Fraction of the time when passengers would receive lower surge prices on UberXs by walking to an adjacent area.

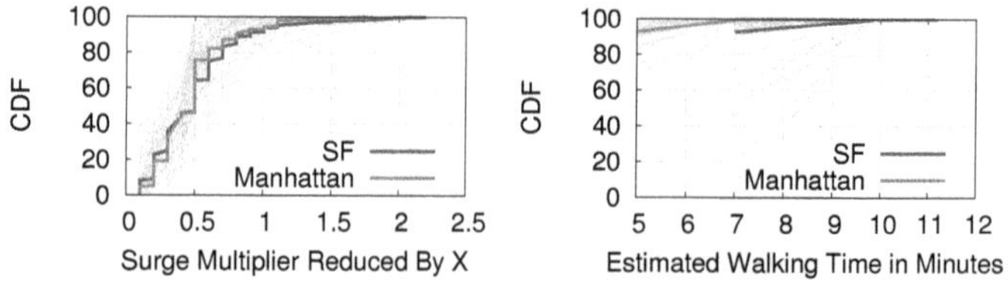

(a) Surge reduced. (b) Walking time.

Figure 24: Amount that surge is reduced and walking time needed when passengers walk to an adjacent area.

in three other areas (Manhattan 1, Manhattan 3, and SF 3) we observe less cars moving **in** during surges. This result is inconclusive, and also unexpected: we assumed that cars would flock to the surging area.

Third and finally, we examine the impact of surge on passenger demand. In all six areas, the fraction of **old** cars increases while **dying** cars decrease within the surging area. Both of these observations point to reduced demand within the surging area.

Discussion. The results in Figure 22 paint a complex picture of surge pricing's impact on supply and demand. On one hand, surge does seem to have a small effect on attracting new cars. On the other hand, it also appears to have a larger, negative effect on demand, which causes cars to either become idle or leave the surge area. Although we cannot say with certainty why surge has such a large, negative effect on demand, one possibility is that customers have learned that surges tend to have short duration (see Figure 13), and thus they choose to wait for 5 minutes before requesting a ride. Another possibility is that surging areas may be impacted by adverse traffic conditions, which prevents drivers from flocking to them.

To make the surge pricing algorithm more effective, we propose that Uber alter the algorithm to update surge prices more smoothly. For example, rather than oscillating between periods of no and high-surge, Uber could use a weighted moving average to smooth the price changes over time. This would make surge price changes more predictable and less dramatic, which may encourage driver flocking, as well as discourage sudden, temporary drops in customer demand. Another alternative would be for Uber to adopt Sidecar's pricing approach, in which drivers set their own prices independently. This free-market approach obviates the need for a complex, opaque algorithm and empowers customers to accept or decline fares at will.

6. AVOIDING SURGE PRICING

In the previous section, we show that short-term surge prices cannot be forecast, even with large amounts of data directly from Uber. This is disappointing, since forecasting short-term changes in surge prices would be a useful capability for drivers and passengers.

In this section, we propose an alternative method that passengers can use to obtain lower prices from Uber. Since we cannot forecast surges, this means that only the price information during the current 5-minute surge interval is reliable. Thus, our goal is to locate the lowest price car for the passenger given their current location and the instantaneous surge prices.

Our Approach. Our key insight is to leverage our knowledge of surge areas. Suppose a user observes that the surge multiplier at their current location is m', and there are a set of adjacent surge areas A. We can use the Uber API to query the surge multiplier m_a and EWT e_a for each $a \in A$, as well as the walking time w_a to each area. If $m_a < m'$ and $w_a \leq e_a$ for some a, then this means the user could reserve an Uber immediately at a lower price, and walk to the pickup point in the adjacent area before the car arrives. Startups have proposed similar approaches to avoiding surge prices [30], however their techniques do not leverage precise knowledge of surge areas, or take EWTs into account.

Results. To demonstrate the feasibility of our approach, we plot Figure 23, which shows the percentage of time that each of our 43 measurement clients could have obtained a cheaper UberX using our approach. We assume that people can walk 83 meters per minute (i.e., 5km/hour). We also assume that, for our technique to be implemented in practice, it would need to rely on data from the Uber API. Thus, surge prices change every 5 minutes and there is no jitter, but EWTs may change moment to moment.

In Manhattan, we see that users around Times Square would have been able to request cheaper cars 10-20% of the time, depending on the user's precise location. In contrast, users in SF would not generally benefit from our approach; only users at UCSF would be able to save money 2% of the time. Our approach works better in Manhattan for two reaons: first, the surge areas in Manhattan are smaller, so it is more feasible for users to walk from one area to another in only a few minutes (50% of EWTs on Uber are less than 3 minutes, see Figure 11). Second, the surge areas in SF tend to be more correlated than those in Manhattan, i.e., it's rare for one area in downtown SF to have significantly higher surge than all the others.

Figure 24(a) shows how much surge multipliers are reduced when users reserve Ubers using our approach. The faded lines correspond to our 43 clients in Manhattan and SF, while the solid lines are the combined results. We see that our approach brings substantial savings: in more than 50% of cases, surge multipliers are reduced by at least 0.5, i.e., a 50% savings or more.

Figure 24(b) shows how many minutes users would need to walk while using our approach. In all cases, users walk for less than 7 and 9 minutes to meet the car in the adjacent surge area in Manhattan and SF, respectively. Note that the surge areas in SF are larger than those in Manhattan, so the shortest walks in SF are 7 minutes long, versus 5 minutes in Manhattan. Overall, these walking times are quite reasonable, given the dramatic savings that this strategy enables.

7. RELATED WORK

Uber. Recently, researchers have begun to take an interest in Uber. Salnikov et al. compared 2013 NYC taxi and Uber API data to reveal when and where taxis are cheaper than Ubers [31]. In [6], Diakopoulos tracked surge prices via the Uber API in multiple locations around Washington D.C., and identified the same 5-minute surge update behavior that we observed, as well as a positive correlation between EWT and surge prices. Lee et al. surveyed the attitudes of Uber and Lyft drivers towards algorithmically directed work, surge pricing, and the driver-review system [18].

Auditing Algorithms. There is a growing body of literature that aims to understand the algorithms that impact people's daily lives. [7,8] examined user perceptions of algorithmically curated content in the Facebook News Feed. [14] determined the features used by Google Search to personalize content, while [13,20,21] measure price discrimination and steering on e-commerce sites. [1,12,17] investigate online tracking techniques. Most disturbingly, [9,29] revealed the existence of racial discrimination on AirBnB and Google Ads.

8. CONCLUDING DISCUSSION

In this paper, we present the first in-depth analysis of Uber. We leverage four weeks of data collected from Uber's smartphone app and official API that covers midtown Manhattan and downtown SF. In total, we collected 2.1 TB of data on supply, demand, EWTs, and surge prices for Uber vehicles. We validate the fidelity of our methodology using ground-truth information about all taxi rides in NYC in 2013.

Our results reveal high-level characteristics about Uber's service and the impact of surge pricing. We observe that SF has 3× more surges than Manhattan even though SF also has a much greater supply of cars. Furthermore, surge pricing is noisy: the majority of surges last less than 10 minutes. Finally, we observe that on a micro-scale, surge prices have a strong, negative impact on passenger demand, and a weak, positive impact on car supply. However, it is possible that different effects may occur at the macro-scale (i.e., a whole city).

Algorithmic Transparency. Using our measured data, we are able to infer some implementation details of Uber's surge pricing algorithm. Uber has divided cities up into discrete areas, and surge prices are updated in each area independently on a 5-minute clock. Our correlation analysis suggests that average estimated wait times, and the difference between supply and demand, are used to calculate surge multipliers.

Our investigation uncovered a bug in Uber's systems that was causing some customers to randomly receive out-of-data surge price information. To Uber's credit, after we informed them of this issue, they acted quickly to fix the bug. However, the existence of this "jitter" bug serves as a cautionary tale: as the complexity of algorithmic systems increases, they are more likely to exhibit unintended behaviors. Just as white-hat security research is critical for helping companies identify and patch software vulnerabilities, algorithmic audits [28] are a vital tool for identifying problematic behaviors exhibited by algorithmic systems.

We argue that Uber's reliance on discrete surge areas introduces unfairness into their system: two users standing a few meters apart may unknowingly receive dramatically different surge multipliers. For example, 20% of the time in Times Square, customers can save 50% or more by being in an adjacent surge area.

Lastly, we argue that Uber's reliance on black-box algorithms makes their system more vulnerable to manipulation than other online marketplaces. The forces at play on markets like eBay and AirBnB are well understood: the supply of goods is transparent, and prices are set by competing individuals. In contrast, Uber does not provide data about supply and demand, and the pricing algorithm is opaque. This leads to situations where, once the algorithm is known, it can be manipulated. For example, we show in §6 that users can obtain lower prices by exploiting differences between surge areas. Meanwhile, Uber drivers discuss strategies for inducing surges by colluding to artificially decrease supply [2]. Although we were unable to detect collusion in our dataset, our inability to track drivers over time limits our ability to detect this attack.

Acknowledgements

We thank the anonymous reviewers for their helpful comments. This research was supported in part by NSF grants CNS-1054233, CNS-1319019, and CHS-1408345. Any opinions, findings, and conclusions or recommendations expressed in this material are those of the authors and do not necessarily reflect the views of the NSF.

9. REFERENCES

[1] G. Acar, C. Eubank, S. Englehardt, M. Juarez, A. Narayanan, and C. Diaz. The Web Never Forgets: Persistent Tracking Mechanisms in the Wild. *CCS*, 2014.

[2] Anonymous. Uber Brotherhood, and a Few Sisters Too. Confessions of an Uber Driver Blog, 2014. `http://bit.ly/SVv4RE`.

[3] Anonymous. Empty Promises. Confessions of an Uber Driver Blog, 2015. `http://bit.ly/1c4JZmZ`.

[4] M. Boland. Apple Pay's Real Killer App: The Uber-ification of Local Services. Huffington Post, 2015. `http://huff.to/1IxEE3M`.

[5] L. Clark. Uber denies researchers' 'phantom cars' map claim. Wired, 2015. `http://www.wired.co.uk/news/archive/2015-07/28/uber-cars-always-in-real-time`.

[6] N. Diakopoulos. How Uber surge pricing really works. The Washington Post, 2015. `http://wapo.st/1yBf3EO`.

[7] M. Eslami, A. Aleyasen, K. Karahalios, K. Hamilton, and C. Sandvig. FeedVis: A Path for Exploring News Feed Curation Algorithms. *CSCW*, 2015.

[8] M. Eslami, A. Rickman, K. Vaccaro, A. Aleyasen, A. Vuong, K. Karahalios, K. Hamilton, and C. Sandvig. "I always assumed that I wasn't really that close to [her]": Reasoning about invisible algorithms in the news feed. *CHI*, 2015.

[9] B. G. Edelman and M. Luca. Digital Discrimination: The Case of Airbnb.com. *SSRN*, 2014.

[10] A. Griswold. Does Uber's Surge Pricing Take Unfair Advantage of Drunk People? Slate, 2014. http://slate.me/10s0zXH.

[11] B. Gurley. A Deeper Look at Uber's Dynamic Pricing Model. Above the Crowd, 2014. http://bit.ly/1fmNgI1.

[12] S. Guha, B. Cheng, and P. Francis. Challenges in Measuring Online Advertising Systems. *IMC*, 2010.

[13] A. Hannak, G. Soeller, D. Lazer, A. Mislove, and C. Wilson. Measuring Price Discrimination and Steering on E-commerce Web Sites. *IMC*, 2014.

[14] A. Hannak, P. Sapiezyński, A. M. Kakhki, B. Krishnamurthy, D. Lazer, A. Mislove, and C. Wilson. Measuring Personalization of Web Search. *WWW*, 2013.

[15] J. V. Hall and A. B. Krueger. An Analysis of the Labor Market for Uber's Driver-Partners in the United States. *Princeton Working Paper 587*, 2015.

[16] D. Kedmey. This is How Uber's 'Surge Pricing' Works. Time, 2014. http://time.com/3633469/uber-surge-pricing/.

[17] M. Lecuyer, G. Ducoffe, F. Lan, A. Papancea, T. Petsios, R. Spahn, A. Chaintreau, and R. Geambasu. XRay: Enhancing the Web's Transparency with Differential Correlation. *USENIX Security*, 2014.

[18] M. K. Lee, D. Kusbit, E. Metsky, and L. Dabbish. Working with Machines: The Impact of Algorithmic and Data-Driven Management on Human Workers. *CHI*, 2015.

[19] E. Mazza. Uber Raises Fares During Sydney Hostage Crisis, Then Offers Free Rides. The Huffington Post, 2014. http://huff.to/18W6ybk.

[20] J. Mikians, L. Gyarmati, V. Erramilli, and N. Laoutaris. Detecting Price and Search Discrimination on the Internet. *HotNets*, 2012.

[21] J. Mikians, L. Gyarmati, V. Erramilli, and N. Laoutaris. Crowd-assisted Search for Price Discrimination in E-Commerce: First results. *CoNEXT*, 2013.

[22] A. Monroy-Hernández. NYC Taxi Trips. GitHub, 2014. http://www.andresmh.com/nyctaxitrips/.

[23] K.M. Novak and T.C. Kalanick. System and method for dynamically adjusting prices for services. US Patent App. 13/828,481, 2013.

[24] I. Oh. Uber Will Stop Charging Ridiculous Prices During Emergencies. Huffington Post, 2014. http://huff.to/1qJLs5c.

[25] B. Popper. Uber kept new drivers off the road to encourage surge pricing and increase fares. The Verge, 2014. http://bit.ly/1hoPgU8.

[26] A. Rosenblat. Uber's Phantom Cabs. Motherboard, 2015. http://motherboard.vice.com/read/ubers-phantom-cabs.

[27] B. Stone. Uber is Winning Over Americans' Expense Accounts. Bloomberg, 2015. http://bloom.bg/1IFZ0p7.

[28] C. Sandvig, K. Hamilton, K. Karahalios, and C. Langbort. Auditing algorithms: Research methods for detecting discrimination on internet platforms. *Proceedings of "Data and Discrimination: Converting Critical Concerns into Productive Inquiry", a preconference at the 64th Annual Meeting of the International Communication Association*, 2014.

[29] L. Sweeney. Discrimination in Online Ad Delivery. *SSRN*, 2013.

[30] T. Schmidt. SurgeProtector. iTunes App Store, 2014. http://apple.co/1GxhDMU.

[31] V. Salnikov, R. Lambiotte, A. Noulas, and C. Mascolo. OpenStreetCab: Exploiting Taxi Mobility Patterns in New York City to Reduce Commuter Costs. *CoRR*, abs/1503.03021, 2015.

[32] M. Wilson. Uber Fudges the Position of Local Drivers, But They've Got a Pretty Good Reason Why. Fast Company, 2015. http://www.fastcodesign.com/3049169/uber-fudges-the-position-of-local-drivers-but-theyve-got-a-pretty-good-reason-why?utm_content.

Temporal and Spatial Classification of Active IPv6 Addresses

David Plonka
Akamai Technologies
plonka@akamai.com

Arthur Berger
Akamai Technologies
Massachusetts Institute of Technology
arthur@akamai.com

ABSTRACT

There is striking volume of World-Wide Web activity on IPv6 today. In early 2015, one large Content Distribution Network handles 50 billion IPv6 requests per day from hundreds of millions of IPv6 client addresses; billions of unique client addresses are observed per month. Address counts, however, obscure the number of hosts with IPv6 connectivity to the global Internet. There are numerous address assignment and subnetting options in use; privacy addresses and dynamic subnet pools significantly inflate the number of active IPv6 addresses. As the IPv6 address space is vast, it is infeasible to comprehensively probe every possible unicast IPv6 address. Thus, to survey the characteristics of IPv6 addressing, we perform a year-long passive measurement study, analyzing the IPv6 addresses gleaned from activity logs for all clients accessing a global CDN.

The goal of our work is to develop flexible classification and measurement methods for IPv6, motivated by the fact that its addresses are not merely more numerous; they are different in kind. We introduce the notion of classifying addresses and prefixes in two ways: *(1) temporally*, according to their instances of activity to discern which addresses can be considered stable; *(2) spatially*, according to the density or sparsity of aggregates in which active addresses reside. We present measurement and classification results numerically and visually that: provide details on IPv6 address use and structure in global operation across the past year; establish the efficacy of our classification methods; and demonstrate that such classification can clarify dimensions of the Internet that otherwise appear quite blurred by current IPv6 addressing practices.

1. INTRODUCTION

In 2015, we are in an era of production-quality, simultaneous operation of the Internet protocol versions 4 (IPv4) and 6 (IPv6). IPv6 traffic volumes have reportedly doubled in the past year, and globally over 6% of clients having IPv6 connectivity [2, 27, 36]. In the fourth quarter of 2014, a significant proportion of World-Wide Web (WWW) clients used IPv6 to access content that is available over both IPv6 and IPv4 via a global Content Distribution Network (CDN): 70% for Verizon Wireless, 30% for AT&T, and 27% for Comcast [4].

In this work, we study populations of active IPv6 addresses, *i.e.*, those observed to exchange traffic rather than merely allocated or assigned. Like most censuses, ours involves counting members of groups or *classes*. IP addresses can be classified with respect to various dimensions. Historically, the initial IPv4 address "classes" were determined *a priori* as classes A, B, C, *etc.* Following the introduction of classless inter-domain routing (CIDR), addresses would more naturally be classified based on flexible aggregates in routing tables, such as that of their Border Gateway Protocol (BGP) prefix. Addresses can also be classified based on reserved and special-use prefixes, *e.g.*, RFC1918 and multicast. However, operational needs have led to a broader notion of address class, even if not referred to as "class" *per se*, nor are classes mutually exclusive. Some example IPv4 address classifications of recent interest are based on client reputation, geolocation, assignment to a common network element (*e.g.*, router aliases), anycast, and proxy.

Most of these classes pertain to both IPv4 and IPv6 addresses. However, two dimensions are more significant with IPv6, and are the focus of this paper. The first we call "temporal" and is primarily motivated by the popularity of host privacy extensions whereby the vast majority of IPv6 addresses are used for short periods, *e.g.*, 24 hours or less, and in all likelihood will never be used again. The second we call "spatial" and pertains to the vastly greater number of possible areas (prefixes) and positions (addresses) in the IPv6 address space. Whereas scanning the full IPv4 address space is now routine, this is not feasible for IPv6. We need other techniques to discover "where the action is." IPv6, also, allows greater freedom in the use of the subnet prefix. We find a variety of practices employed by different network operators. Our goal is to detect the different types of IPv6 addresses in active use, with particular interest in (a) discriminating *stable*, persistent addresses from *ephemeral*, short-lived addresses and (b) discovering

IMC '15, October 28–30, 2015, Tokyo, Japan

ACM 978-1-4503-3848-6/15/10...$15.00
DOI: http://dx.doi.org/10.1145/2815675.2815678

how addresses are arranged in the address space, thereby forming *sparse* and *dense* regions.

There are numerous applications of temporal and spatial address classification. Examples include: selecting targets for active measurements, *e.g.,* traceroutes, vulnerability scans, and reachability surveys; informing data retention policy to prevent resource exhaustion, *e.g.,* when encountering many ephemeral addresses or prefixes; informing host reputation and access control, *e.g.,* to mitigate network abuse; identifying homogeneous address aggregates, *e.g.,* for IP geolocation; and detecting changes in network operation or estimating Internet usage over time.

This paper makes the following contributions:
(1) We present census results based on a large-scale, longitudinal, passive IPv6 measurement study of *active addresses* used by WWW clients in 133 countries and over four thousand autonomous systems. *(2)* We introduce a *temporal* classification technique for IPv6 addresses based on observation of address activity over time. *(3)* We introduce a complementary *spatial* classification technique for IPv6 addresses based on measurement of the sparsity or density of the address prefixes in which they reside. *(4)* We evaluate the temporal and spatial classifiers by utilizing them *in situ,* and show results of the classification of billions of active IPv6 addresses.

In addition, we introduce the Multi-Resolution Aggregate (MRA) plot, a tool for examining a set of numbers in a very sparsely populated number space, inspired by the work of Kohler *et al.* [28] and make available the plot data for any or all of the IPv6 BGP prefixes across the year under study. [3] MRA plots show structural detail and allow address space exploration without necessarily identifying specific addresses or blocks by number.

Highlights of our results include, as of early 2015:

- When autonomous systems (ASNs) are ranked by their WWW client address counts, the top 5 ASNs represent 85% of active /64 prefixes ("/64s") and 59% of all active addresses. Of these ASNs, 2 are U.S.-based mobile carriers, *i.e.,* wireless Internet Service Providers (ISP); the others are a European, an American, and a Japanese ISP.
- Although the vast majority of IPv6 clients use native transport, 6to4 tunneling is still common. If not segregated in measurement, the ASNs hosting 6to4 relays would be amongst the top 5 ASNs.
- 74% of the 153 million of the /64s observed as active during both of two weeks separated by 6 months are associated with just 1 ASN.
- Despite the vast IPv6 unicast address space and generous allocations to networks, many /64s are *reused, i.e.,* assigned to different users over time, certainly within a week.
- Of 1.81 million addresses observed as *stable* across 1 year, over half a million are associated with two mobile carriers which, in apparent contradiction, use *dynamic* values in network identifiers. Further investigation shows that many mobile devices simultaneously use the same fixed interface identifier. Combined with dynamic /64 assignment, this can result in an IPv6 address being reused by a different subscriber on a short timescale, *e.g.,* within days.
- While privacy addressing is common and brings randomness and sparsity to address values, there are many dense regions of IPv6 address space where addresses are well-ordered and tightly-packed. 49% of active IPv6 ASNs have BGP prefixes containing such regions, *e.g.,* /112 prefixes (64K address blocks) containing multiple active WWW client addresses. These blocks are natural targets if future, active scanning or probing is intended.

The remainder of this paper is organized as follows. In Section 2, we discuss related prior work. In Section 3, we give a brief introduction to IPv6 addresses. In Section 4, we describe the data used in our empirical study. In Section 5, we present our IPv6 address classification methods. In Section 6, we present and discuss results of our temporal and spatial classifications. In Section 7, we propose future work based on our results, and subsequently conclude.

2. RELATED WORK

To our knowledge, our temporal classifier does not have a precedent in the research literature. The temporal characteristics of IPv4 addresses, however, became topical as scalability concerns arose with the Internet's exponential growth in the 1990s. Carpenter *et al.* comment on this in RFC 2101 [10]. With respect to IPv6, Malone's work [30] is similar to ours in that they also study active IPv6 addresses. They develop a technique intended to classify short-lived privacy addresses by examining only the address itself, but its accuracy is limited by design, expected to identify approximately 73% of all privacy addresses. Since it is very challenging to detect randomness in short strings, *e.g.,* 63 bits of an IPv6 address, we take the complementary approach and identify those addresses that are stable and, thus, almost certainly *not* privacy addresses. In the end, Malone speculates that "[accuracy] might be improved accounting for the times addresses are observed and spatially/temporally adjacent addresses," which seems exactly the notion at which we arrive independently, inspiring the strategies that we develop here.

Development of our spatial classifier is largely informed by the prior work of two teams: Cho *et al.* and Kohler *et al.* Cho *et al.* [12] introduce *aguri,* a traffic profiler that employs automatic aggregation based on addresses' and prefixes' observed traffic volume. As in their work, we find their PATRICIA/radix tree-based aggregation useful in dealing with resource constraints, however, we use it to discover *address structure.* We do this by aggregating to a threshold that is either (a) a percentage of total addresses or (b) a prefix density, rather than a percentage of total traffic volume. This aggregation method is useful because it generalizes to other metrics.

Kohler *et al.* [28] investigate the structure of the IPv4 address space based on passive traffic analysis. In a broad sense, our IPv6 investigation is similar and we employ two of their metrics as-is: active aggregate counts and aggregate population distributions. IPv6 addresses, however, present different challenges and opportunities to discern structure, so we develop new IPv6-specific metrics. Our work also differs in that we apply those metrics to classify addresses rather than to evaluate mathematical characterizations of the address space.

Dainotti *et al.* [16] investigate IPv4 address space usage by attempting to identify active and inactive /24 address-blocks using passive measurement. Our census of WWW client addresses similarly employs passive means, but we count aggregates of every possible prefix length. Also, because we determine address activity from the complete logs of all clients' successful WWW transactions with a large CDN, we eschew complications introduced by spoofed addresses. While they propose that their method could potentially apply to measuring IPv6 address space usage, they do not discuss how it might treat persistent versus ephemeral addresses nor if it could count addresses in "small" address-blocks, *e.g.,* smaller than /64 prefixes. Our method would likely complement theirs, if applied to IPv6.

In 2012, Barnes *et al.* [8, 13] evaluated methods to map the vast IPv6 address space by probes in order to discover active addresses. Our work shares that goal but benefits from increased IPv6 activity and content-accessibility that make passive methods viable. The stable addresses and dense address regions that we identify are feasible targets for active scans or probes, thus our method may repair or complement target selection heuristics employed in their early survey. Still, like Barnes *et al.*, our work is guided by operator practice with respect to IPv6 addressing.

There are a number of studies in the literature that measure and report on the deployment and adoption of IPv6. Recent examples of such work are those of Colitti *et al.* [14] and Czyz *et al.* [15] Our work differs in that we measure IPv6 by counting active addresses and prefixes, rather than by counting advertised prefixes or traffic hits and bytes. Each have different biases with respect to estimating usage. Internet-wide surveys of active IPv6 addresses are scarce in the literature, *e.g.,* Malone [30] circa 2008. However, Huston and Michaelson [26, 27], perform a significant ongoing measurement study involving IPv6 addresses; they observe activity by opportunistically running "interactive" advertisements that are crafted to elicit connection attempts from WWW clients to their own measurement service via both IPv4 and IPv6. Our study is limited to IPv6, but seems to offer different advantages. They observe the IPv4/IPv6 address pairs associated with WWW clients. We observe significantly more activity from mobile carriers, where the ads rarely run, and activity in a larger set of ASNs [32, 25].

3. IPV6 ADDRESSES

Here we present a brief introduction to IPv6 address assignment. An IPv6 address consists of a leading network identifier, *a.k.a.* subnet prefix, portion followed by an interface identifier (IID) portion. The network identifier is used to route traffic destined for this address to its Local Area Network (LAN) and the IID makes a host interface's address unique on its local network segment. While superficially similar to the network and host identifier portions of IPv4 addresses, the vast IPv6 address space allows much more freedom.

There are many IPv6 addressing schemes and network operators are reminded to treat interface identifiers as semantically opaque [11]. In this work, however, we utilize address content, including IID, as a basis for classification and find correspondences with a variety of standards-defined address types. For instance, administrators have the option to use a /64 network prefix and a rather large IID, *i.e.,* 64 bits [22], or a larger network prefix, *e.g.,* /127, and a smaller IID, *e.g.,* only 1 bit [17, 29]. In the former case, with stateless address auto-configuration (SLAAC), the host chooses a 64-bit IID suffix for itself. Consider the sample addresses in Figure 1. In increasing order of complexity, these addresses appear to be: *(i)* an address with fixed IID value (`::103`), *(ii)* an address with a structured value in the low 64 bits (perhaps a subnet distinguished by `::10`), *(iii)* a SLAAC address with EUI-64 Ethernet-MAC-based IID, and *(iv)* a SLAAC privacy address with a pseudorandom IID.

```
2001:db8:10:1::103
2001:db8:167:1109::10:901
2001:db8:0:1cdf:21e:c2ff:fec0:11db
2001:db8:4137:9e76:3031:f3fd:bbdd:2c2a
```

Figure 1: Sample IPv6 addresses in presentation format with the low 64 bits shown bold.

The first two addresses are similar to those created by traditional addressing schemes used in IPv4 while the latter two use standard IPv6-specific addresses schemes: EUI-64 [39] and privacy addresses [33], respectively. [1] Since one might reasonably expect these interface identifiers to be difficult to distinguish merely by their content, we employ temporal analysis to discriminate these from, at least, privacy addresses.

A number of transition mechanisms aid concurrent operation of IPv6 with IPv4 and affect IPv6 addresses themselves. These include: 6to4 relays [23] and Teredo [24], which employ global reserved prefixes; and ISATAP [38] which embeds IPv4 addresses in the IPv6 IID. Finally, there are additional *ad hoc* schemes by which an IPv6 address contains an embedded IPv4 address, *e.g.,* those used for some router and dual-stack host interfaces. This is typically a convenience rather than a requirement.

4. EMPIRICAL DATA

Our study requires data sources containing IPv6 addresses which are active, that is, addresses that exchange globally-routed Internet traffic.

4.1 WWW Client Addresses

We primarily rely on aggregated logs of WWW server activity in this study. These aggregated logs contain hit counts per client IP address. We select only the client IP addresses from log entries that represent successfully handled requests, thus avoiding spoofed sources. The aggregation interval is 24 hours, for 55,000 of the CDN's IPv6-capable servers, and is processed roughly by the end of

[1] Other IPv6 address schemes by which interface identifiers are generated include: Cryptographically Generated Addresses [5, 7], Hash-Based Addresses [6], and stable privacy addresses [20].

the subsequent day. Note that the aggregation does not include the timestamp from the individual log lines, used in separate processing for the CDN's customers. Instead, we use the time epoch of the completion of processing of the aggregated logs. Our stability analysis, described in Section 5, uses a heuristic to accommodate this timestamp slew.

In March 2015, the dataset contains IPv6 addresses in 6,872 BGP prefixes originating from 4,420 ASNs (46% of those advertising IPv6 prefixes). These figures are an increase from March 2014 when there were 5,531 BGP prefixes originating from 3,842 ASNs (40%). Alas, we certainly do not see traffic from all the world's WWW client addresses at this observation point, and our stability analysis shows that some specific long-lived active IPv6 addresses, *e.g.,* EUI-64, return as WWW clients only infrequently.

Table 1 summarizes the IPv6 WWW client address activity observed across a year at 6 month intervals, March 2014 through March 2015; we report both daily and weekly counts. With daily counts, fewer ephemeral privacy addresses are observed, while with weekly counts there is increased opportunity to observe activity of WWW clients that visit the CDN less frequently than daily.

In Table 1, by March 2015, we see that the address count increased to over 318 million observed daily and over 1.8 billion observed in a week's time. Correspondingly, 121 million /64 prefixes are observed daily and 307 million /64 prefixes in a week's time.

We are careful to separate client addresses involving some IPv6 transition mechanisms from addresses involved in "native" IPv6 end-to-end transport; this is because those transition mechanisms' addresses would skew results. Specifically, we cull addresses associated with the early IPv6 transition mechanisms, *i.e.,* Teredo, ISATAP, and 6to4. Of these, only 6to4 still shows significant use. These 3 particular transition mechanisms' addresses are easily classified, do not involve native, end-to-end IPv6 transport, and are, thus, not the focus of our classifiers. Once removed the remaining "Other" addresses in Table 1 account for over 90% of the active addresses observed. These "Other" addresses are subjects for the classifiers we introduce in Section 5 and are those for which we report results unless otherwise noted. These addresses intentionally include those of transition mechanisms such as 464-XLAT [31] and DS-Lite [18, 9], *e.g.,* used by large mobile carriers involving native, end-to-end IPv6 transport.

Lastly, in Table 1, EUI-64 addresses are reported. These are those addresses in which we detect the 16-bit value `ff:fe` at the prescribed position when the EUI-64 IID is based on an Ethernet MAC address. [39] Some of these have invalid or duplicate MAC addresses, *e.g.,* MAC address `00:11:22:33:44:56` is the most prevalent and just in one mobile carrier's network. Others are likely false positives, *e.g.,* privacy addresses where the likelihood of being mislabelled as EUI-64 is 1 in 2^{16}, or less than $30,000$ of 1.8 billion addresses. We consider these an inconsequential subset of the 16.2 million EUI-64 addresses in Table 1, March 17-23, 2015.

4.2 Router Addresses

In addition to periodic collection of active WWW client addresses, we also collect a set of IPv6 addresses that were the source addresses of ICMP "Time Exceeded" responses to our TTL-limited probes, similar to those generated by the *traceroute* tool. Based on collection in February 2015, this dataset consists of 3.2 million addresses that appear to be assigned to router interfaces. Three types of probe targets were used: *(1)* addresses of IPv6 recursive DNS servers, as observed by our authoritative DNS servers, *(2)* addresses of the CDN's servers in approximately 500 locations world-wide, and *(3)* a selection of about 18 million WWW client addresses assembled since 2013, including a subset (12 million) of those addresses identified as stable in March and September, 2014 (Those reported in Table 2a in Section 6.) This dataset is used to identify additional dense prefixes as reported in Table 3 with the expectation that areas of the address space containing WWW clients differ from those containing routers.

5. ANALYSIS METHOD

5.1 Temporal Classification

Our temporal methods of IPv6 address classification are intended to determine address lifetime, primarily to separate those client addresses that are persistent or stable from those that are perhaps not. We refer to this as *stability* analysis. Let's first consider a simple notion of stability. If one periodically logs sets of active addresses at some interval, *e.g.,* 6 months, it is easy to find which sets have addresses in common. For instance, if address *x* is observed as active in March 2015 as well as a year earlier, in March 2014, it can be considered stable. Our stability classes are named according to the length of time across which stability has been assessed. Thus we would say address *x* is "1 year stable," when sampled across the past 1 year, and is classified as "1y-stable (-1y)." If *x* is observed in March 2015 and also 6 months earlier, in September 2014, it would also be classified as "6m-stable (-6m)." This notion of stability generalizes to prefixes of any length, not just full addresses; we similarly assess the stability of /64 prefixes extracted from the full addresses.

Since we wish to perform stability analysis on an ongoing basis, consider a slightly more complicated notion of stability. Let's define more granular classes of stability, *e.g.,* daily. Definition: "*n*d-stable" is the class of addresses for which there exist observations of activity on two different days with an intervening time period of at least $n-1$ days. For example, a given address seen on March 17 and again on March 18 (for which there are no intervening days) is said to be "1d-stable." Likewise, an address seen on March 17 and on March 19 (for which there is one intervening day) is said to be "2d-stable." Note that since March 17 and March 19 have *at least* zero intervening days, then an address seen on these two days is also "1d-stable," besides being "2d-stable;" the classes are *not* mutually exclusive. More generally, an address that is "*n*d-stable" is also "$(n-1)$d-stable."

Since a measurement study of client IP addresses that access a given service will typically capture only a portion

Characteristic	Mar 17, 2014	Sep 17, 2014	Mar 17, 2015
Teredo addresses	1.98K (0.00%)	3.28K (0.00%)	20.1K (0.01%)
ISATAP addresses	90.2K (0.06%)	101K (0.04%)	133K (0.04%)
6to4 addresses	12.8M (7.97%)	12.5M (5.90%)	13.9M (4.19%)
Other addresses	**149M (92.0%)**	**199M (94.1%)**	**318M (95.8%)**
Other /64 prefixes	**61.4M**	**82.9M**	**121M**
ave. addrs per /64	2.41	2.40	2.63
EUI-64 addr (!6to4)	3.13M (1.94%)	3.66M (1.73%)	4.49M (1.35%)
EUI-64 IIDs (MACs)	2.85M	3.23M	3.81M

(a) Address characteristics per day

Characteristic	Mar 17-23, 2014	Sep 17-23, 2014	Mar 17-23, 2015
Teredo addresses	15.1K (0.00%)	24.5K (0.00%)	131K (0.01%)
ISATAP addresses	210K (0.02%)	238K (0.02%)	346K (0.02%)
6to4 addresses	64.9M (7.22%)	78.3M (6.34%)	64.2M (3.43%)
Other addresses	**833M (92.8%)**	**1.17B (94.9%)**	**1.80B (96.5%)**
Other /64 prefixes	**157M**	**207M**	**307M**
ave. addrs per /64	5.32	5.64	5.88
EUI-64 addr (!6to4)	8.88M (0.99%)	13.1M (1.06%)	16.2M (0.866%)
EUI-64 IIDs (MACs)	6.12M	8.16M	9.74M

(b) Address characteristics per week

Table 1: Active IPv6 WWW client address characteristics: March 2014 through March 2015.

of the addresses' total Internet activity, and since that service may be accessed infrequently, even a long-lived client address, *e.g.,* using EUI-64, may appear to be ephemeral. Thus, we will simply label such addresses as "not stable," meaning only that we do not know that address to be stable. Stability classification relies on, and is limited by, the opportunity for observation of activity from given vantage points.

In our daily stability analysis, we employ a sliding 15-day window centered on the day of observation and spanning 7 days prior through 7 days following. In such context, a 3d-stable address might be classified as "3d-stable (-7d,+7d)." For stability results herein, "(-7d,+7d)" is implied unless otherwise noted. Figure 5 in Section 6 shows the numbers of active addresses and /64s observed on each day as well as the subset in common between those also observed on the reference day (March 17 or March 23, 2015).

5.2 Spatial Classification

Our spatial methods of IPv6 address classification and prefix characterization are intended to both assess the proximity of addresses and prefixes and to visualize the address blocks in which they are contained. We develop two related metrics for use with IPv6: Multi-Resolution Aggregate (MRA) Count Ratios and Prefix Density, and a complementary visualization technique, the MRA plot. In the following, prefixes are characterized structurally, then addresses therein are classified according to the densities of their containing, non-overlapping sub-prefixes.

5.2.1 Multi-Resolution Aggregate Count Ratios

Our metric MRA Count Ratio is a generalization of a metric introduced by Kohler *et al.* With 128 bit addresses and IPv6 presentation format using hexadecimal characters, network operators have great flexibility to use segments of the address for internal purposes; *e.g.,* 16 bit and 4 bit segments are commonly used for subnetting. (See [21] and [35] for recommended operational guidelines.) Here we present an informal, high-level understanding of MRA ratios and an optional, formal definition. The latter is unnecessary for a general introduction.

• *Informally,* to the trained eye, MRA plots expose structure amongst prefixes populating the vast IPv6 address space. In the following MRA plots, the height indicates how much that segment of the address is relevant to grouping a set of addresses into areas of the address space. Addresses aggregated further to the left (high order bits) are more distant from each other; addresses aggregated to the right are close to one another. MRA ratios for a set of addresses, when plotted, expose the density (or sparsity) of each segment of the addresses, whether bits, characters, or colon-separated segments.

• *Formally,* Kohler *et al.* introduce the metric of active aggregate (prefix) counts, and their ratio. Given N addresses, they can be grouped into prefixes of various sizes. For a given prefix size, say $/p$, there is a (smallest) set of prefixes of size $/p$ that contains (covers) all N addresses. At one extreme, each IPv6 address is in its own $/128$ prefix, at the other extreme the single $/0$ prefix contains all of the addresses. Let the "active aggregate count" n_p be the number of $/p$ prefixes that covers the given set of addresses. By definition $n_p = 1$ for $p = 0$ and $n_p = N$ for $p = 128$. Often a more convenient metric is the *ratio* of active aggregate counts, $\gamma_p \equiv n_{p+1}/n_p$. The range of γ_p is 1 to 2. As an example, suppose that a set of addresses is covered by 100 prefixes of size $/56$, $n_{56} = 100$. Now, consider one of these $/56$ prefixes and what can happen when it is partitioned in two $/57$ prefixes. Either all of the addresses in the $/56$ are in one of the $/57$ prefixes, or there is at least one address in each of the two $/57$ prefixes. If the former pertains for *all* of the $/56$ prefixes then the ratio n_{57}/n_{56} would be 1, and if the latter pertains for all, the ratio would be 2. Typically, the former pertains for some and the latter for others, in which case the ratio is between 1 and 2. Now, to examine 4-bit address segments, for instance, it is convenient to compute ratios of active aggregate counts where the mask has been incremented by values larger than 1 bit. Note that 4 bits is one hexadecimal character and 16 bits is a series of 4 hexadecimal characters that, when aligned, are colon-delimited in IPv6 presentation format; these are convenient segment sizes in IPv6 that are not convenient in IPv4 due to presentation format being in base 10. We consider the somewhat more general "MRA count ratio" $\gamma_p^k \equiv n_{p+k}/n_p$, where canonically p is a multiple of k, and k is 1, 4, 8, or 16. The range of γ_p^k is 1 to 2^k. Note: The definition of the ratios implies that, for given resolution (k), the product of the ratios is the total number of addresses in the set.

Sample MRA plots are shown in Figure 2, annotated with sample addresses (inset) and arrows marking features to aid the reader's interpretation. In Figure 2a, consider the

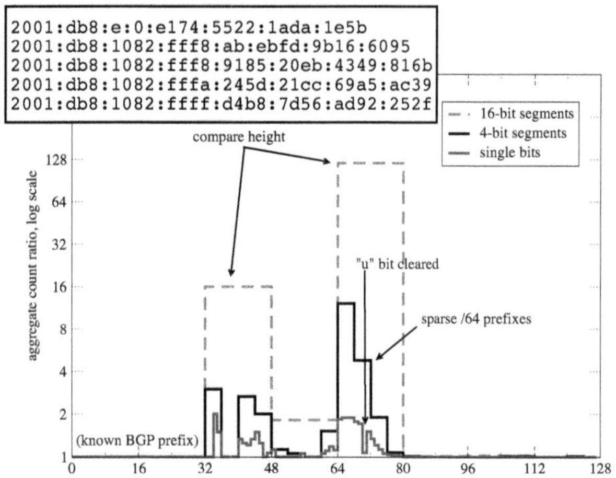

(a) US university

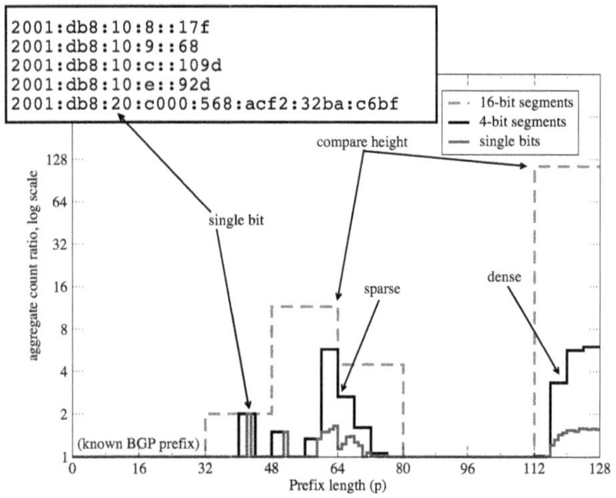

(b) JP telco

Figure 2: Sample MRA plots for active IPv6 client addresses (a) a university prefix with 7.22K addresses and (b) a telco prefix with 12.8K addresses.

portion of the plot for the "single bits" (blue) line at $x >= 64$. This portion of the plot initially approximates 2, then slopes downward to the right, but with a drop to 1 at a particular bit: this is the signature of a scenario where each /64 contains many addresses and where, within each prefix, the majority of the addresses have IIDs determined by the end host according to the pseudorandom privacy extension as specified in RFC 4941 [33].

• *Details on the signature for privacy extension:* Consider one of the /64 prefixes. Given that the 65th bit is chosen randomly, and that there are many addresses in the /64 prefix, *e.g.*, x addresses, then it is very likely (probability = $1-(1/2)^{x-1}$) that at least one of the addresses will have a 0 for the 65th bit and, likewise, that at least one of the addresses will have a 1. Thus the ratio n_{65}/n_{64} for this prefix is very likely to be 2. If this pertains for all /64 prefixes, the ratio for the whole set of addresses will also be 2. In turn, given that each /65 prefix also has a large number of addresses, the above logic repeats, and thus we expect the ratio to remain close to 2. However, as we continue to split prefixes in half, each prefix has a decreasing number of addresses and an increasing chance that those addresses will all have the same next bit. Once they are all the same, the ratio for such prefixes will be 1 and the overall ratio will begin to decline from 2. Moreover, even if the original set contained a billion addresses, it would still be very sparse in the space of 2^{64} possible IIDs. As we continue to consider ever smaller prefixes, eventually, each will contain just one pseudorandom-IID address, and the overall ratio will flat line at 1. In the presented plot, this occurs at about the 80th bit. Finally, as a defining feature of the present scenario, note that the ratio drops to almost 1 at the 71st bit, shown at 70 on the horizontal axis. This is consistent with end hosts that determine the IID according to RFC 4941, which specifies that the "u" bit be set to 0, meaning that an IID is not necessarily universally unique, as opposed to a MAC address.

Now consider Figure 2b in contrast to Figure 2a. These two organizations appear to have significantly different address assignment policies. In Figure 2b, we see a prominence between bits 112 and 128. This indicates that there are many active addresses that differ in only those least-significant bits, *i.e.*, addresses are clustered within smaller prefixes, and thus such prefixes are more dense address blocks.

If one were interested in searching for additional active IPv6 addresses, these denser address blocks would be natural targets. A /112 prefix covers 2^{16} addresses, the same as a /16 in IPv4, and is easily scanned, whereas scanning across a /64 is not practical.

Now consider Figure 2a with respect to the plotted ratios for 4-bit segments, *a.k.a. nybbles*, in the plot (black line). Here we consider changes on a per-nybble, hexadecimal character basis. This provides a more aggregated view, summarizing details of changes on a per-bit basis. Our first-order interest is network operator practice with respect to subnetting. In particular, we assume this network subnets their /32 BGP prefix, so we consider segments of the address down to the /64, *i.e.*, across the canonical network identifier. The jump up for the plot at 32 indicates that addresses have differing (character) values at that nybble, but not, in turn, at the subsequent nybble at 36. The subsequent two nybbles could also be used to discriminate many addresses, and then much less so for the subsequent three nybbles. In contrast to Figure 2a, note that the addresses in Figure 2b have many different (character) values in the last nybble within network portion of the address at 60.

While this introduction to Multi-Resolution Aggregation ratio focused on visual recognition of IPv6 features in MRA plots, the underlying x, y values offer a convenient basis to classify prefixes, and the addresses therein. While defining MRA-based address classes is left for future work, we begin by developing spatial classification by identifying dense prefixes.

5.2.2 Prefix Density

Kohler *et al.* [28] introduces the metric of the number of active addresses in a prefix, and examine the distribution of this number across prefixes of a given size. They consider IPv4 and are interested in how well their models match with measurements, commenting, "aggregate population distributions are the most effective test we have found to differentiate address structures."

We plot the aggregate population complementary cumulative distribution function for all IPv6 addresses and /64 prefixes active during a 7-day period in Figure 3. For the curve showing the 112-aggregate of addresses (the lowest curve), only 10^{-5} of the /112 prefixes contained 10 or more observed addresses; for the 48-aggregate of addresses, fewer than one in ten of the /48 prefixes contained 10 or more observed addresses, hence, a few prefixes must contain most of the addresses. Approximately 10^{-4} of the 48-aggregate of addresses contain 10^5 or more addresses, which clearly illustrates the sparsity of the IPv6 address space and the concentration of observed addresses in a small subset of prefixes.

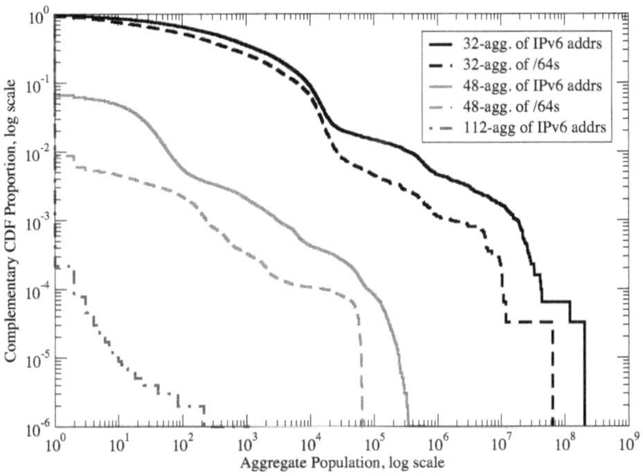

Figure 3: Aggregate population distributions for 1.87B IPv6 addresses, 358M /64s, March 17-23, 2015.

Kohler's aggregate population considers the observed *count* of addresses in a prefix. A related measure is obtained by dividing that observed count by the number of addresses spanned by the prefix, yielding the *percentage* of the addresses of the prefix that were observed.

Cho *et al.* [12] use a percentage as a criterion in an aggregation-based traffic profiler, *however,* their percentage is obtained by dividing an observed count by a total observed count across all prefixes. In their implementation, prefixes are nodes in an *aguri tree,* with observed addresses added as leaf nodes. Aggregation is kind of "pruning," and is performed by aggregating a node's count to its parent (and removing that node), unless that node's count meets or exceeds a target minimum percentage.

Consider an IP network prefix such as `2000::/3` or `2001:db8::/32`. A prefix might contain "addresses of interest" by arbitrary criterion, *e.g.,* addresses for which activity was observed. A simple notion of a prefix's *density,* then, is the fraction of its addresses that are active. Both the prefix and its addresses can be said to have a density of *d*. where *d* is a fraction with a value greater than 0 and less than or equal to 1.

If we restrict desired minimum densities to the fraction $n/2^{p'}$, where p' is a number of bits in the range 0 through 128, there is a simpler solution that does not require base-10 math with large numbers, *i.e.,* greater than 64 bits. We use this restriction, and choose densities based on two parameters: n and p, where $p = 128 - p'$.

Now, let's define our spatial address classes based on prefix density. Definition: "n@/p-dense" is the class of prefixes of length p that contain at least n addresses for which there exist observations of activity. It is also the class of those addresses contained therein. For example, let's say the IPv6 addresses `2001:db8::1` and `2001:db8::4` are both active, but no others. If the desire is to identify /112 prefixes that are dense, then `2001:db8::/112` is the sole 2@/112-dense prefix. There is also one 2@/125-dense prefix, but no 2@/126-dense prefixes.

5.2.3 Computing Dense Prefixes

We would like to identify the dense prefixes based on observed active addresses. We start by choosing a desired minimum density, and then compute the set of dense prefixes, if any.

Given a set of IP addresses and a desired minimum density, we compute a corresponding set of prefixes that *(a)* contain a subset of those addresses, *(b)* have the desired density, and *(c)* have prefix length up to 127. The dense subset are the least-specific, non-overlapping prefixes that are dense, *i.e.,* contain the requisite fraction of addresses.

One way to implement this "densification" is inspired by Cho *et al.* and uses their aguri tree, [12] (a base-2 radix tree, *a.k.a.,* PATRICIA trie) augmented with a new "densify" operation that works as follows:

(1) Populate the tree by adding each of the addresses with a count of 1. If dense prefixes of just that one length are desired, add each address with a "/*p*" and skip to step *3.* [2]

(2) Perform a post-order traversal of the tree; when visiting a node that has children and the sum of counts for the current node and its children would make the current node's prefix of the desired density, aggregate the node's children into the current node, by accumulating the count and removing the children.

(3) Now the least-specific dense prefixes, of at least the desired length p (if specified), are nodes in the tree. However, addresses in sparse regions remain unaggregated, so they are present as well, *e.g.,* /128s. To report only the dense prefixes, perform an in-order traversal, skipping those with a count that is less than n, *e.g.,* 2, and print others as they are dense prefixes.

An example of this process, implemented using an enhanced aguri tree, is shown in Figure 4. The result is that we identify one dense prefix (`2001:db8:10:1::/125`) and two sparse prefixes (a /66 and /68).

[2]When prefixes of just one length are desired, the aguri tree is unnecessary; it is just accumulating counts and sorting output. An alternative is to print addresses in a fixed-width 32-character hex format, one per line, and use: `sort [-m] |cut -c1-$((p/4)) |uniq -c` [1]

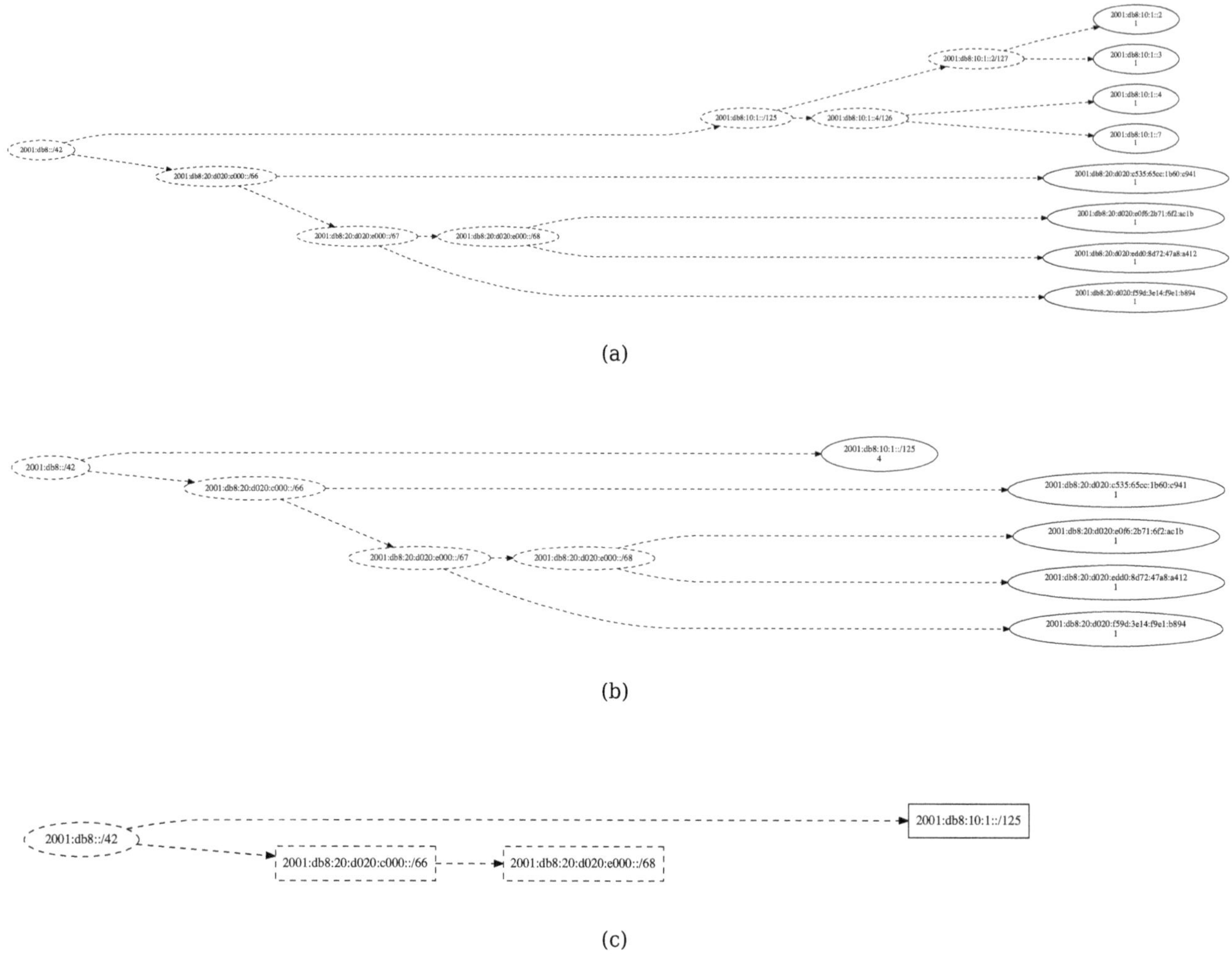

Figure 4: A 3-step method to identify dense (and sparse) prefixes using a binary PATRICIA tree: (a) First, an aguri tree is populated with 8 active addresses, *i.e.*, /128 prefixes, shown as nodes with solid lines, each with a count of 1; internal nodes are shown dashed. (b) Next, the tree is "densified" to a density of $2/2^{24}$ (at least 2@/104-dense) during a post-order traversal; addresses are aggregated to their parent nodes for dense prefixes, with their respective counts accumulated there, while addresses in sparse prefixes remain unaggregated. (c) Lastly, the contents of pruned tree are reported: one dense /125 prefix, shown solid, and two sparse prefixes, shown dashed; here, we simply skip reporting the unaggregated addresses (having a count of 1) in sparse regions during traversal.

6. RESULTS

6.1 Temporal Classification

Table 2 summarizes the temporal classifications for the "Other" addresses in Table 1 of Section 4.

Based on our temporal classification method as described in Section 5.1, Figure 5 shows stability of active addresses and /64 prefixes observed on March 17 and 23, 2015, by 15-day sliding window. Consider the values for "March 17 active" (red) in Figure 5a. Here we see that about 320 million WWW client IPv6 addresses were observed on March 17. Of those addresses, about 75 million were also seen the previous day, about 20 million the day before that, about 10 million the day before that, and so on, in stepwise fashion. The same is true, approximately symmetrically, for the days following March 17. Ultimately, this assessment yields 30.1 million 3d-stable addresses (9.44%), as listed in the "Mar 17, 2015" column of Table 2a.

Now consider the corresponding stability of /64 prefixes shown in Figure 5b. A larger proportion of /64 prefixes are stable than that of full addresses: 109 million 3d-stable /64s (89.8%), as listed in the "Mar 17, 2015" column of Table 2b. (The upper limit on the number stable addresses is the number of stable /64s, or stable prefixes of any length.)

See Tables 2c and 2d for the stability results of addresses and /64s, respectively, over a week's time. For each of the seven days, the 3d-stable addresses are determined, and the table reports the count of the unique 3d-stable addresses seen over those days. Likewise for the "not 3d-stable."

On examining the values highlighted (bold) in Table 2, we make two notes: *(a)* in a relative sense, there are not

addr class	Mar 17, 2014	Sep 17, 2014	Mar 17, 2015
3d-stable	13.7M (9.22%)	13.6M (6.84%)	30.1M (9.44%)
not 3d-stable	134M (90.8%)	185M (93.2%)	288M (90.6%)
6m-stable (-6m)		588K (.296%)	1.08M (.340%)
1y-stable (-1y)			328K (.103%)

(a) Stability of IPv6 addresses per day

/64 class	Mar 17, 2014	Sep 17, 2014	Mar 17, 2015
3d-stable	55.8M (91.0%)	74.6M (89.9%)	**109M (89.8%)**
not 3d-stable	5.53M (9.01%)	8.33M (10.1%)	12.3M (10.2%)
6m-stable (-6m)		23.4M (28.2%)	32.4M (26.7%)
1y-stable (-1y)			21.8M (18.0%)

(b) Stability of /64 prefixes per day

addr class	Mar 17-23, 2014	Sep 17-23, 2014	Mar 17-23, 2015
3d-stable	37.0M (4.44%)	34.0M (2.91%)	69.0M (3.82%)
not 3d-stable	796M (95.6%)	1.13B (97.1%)	1.74B (96.2%)
6m-stable (-6m)		3.25M (.280%)	3.66M (.202%)
1y-stable (-1y)			**1.81M (.100%)**

(c) Stability of IPv6 addresses per week

/64 class	Mar 17-23, 2014	Sep 17-23, 2014	Mar 17-23, 2015
3d-stable	131M (83.7%)	169M (81.8%)	**246M (80.3%)**
not 3d-stable	25.5M (16.3%)	37.7M (18.2%)	60.6M (19.7%)
6m-stable (-6m)		120M (58.1%)	**153M (49.9%)**
1y-stable (-1y)			**116M (37.8%)**

(d) Stability of /64 prefixes per week

Table 2: Stability of active IPv6 WWW client address and prefix counts, not 6to4 or Teredo, March 2015.

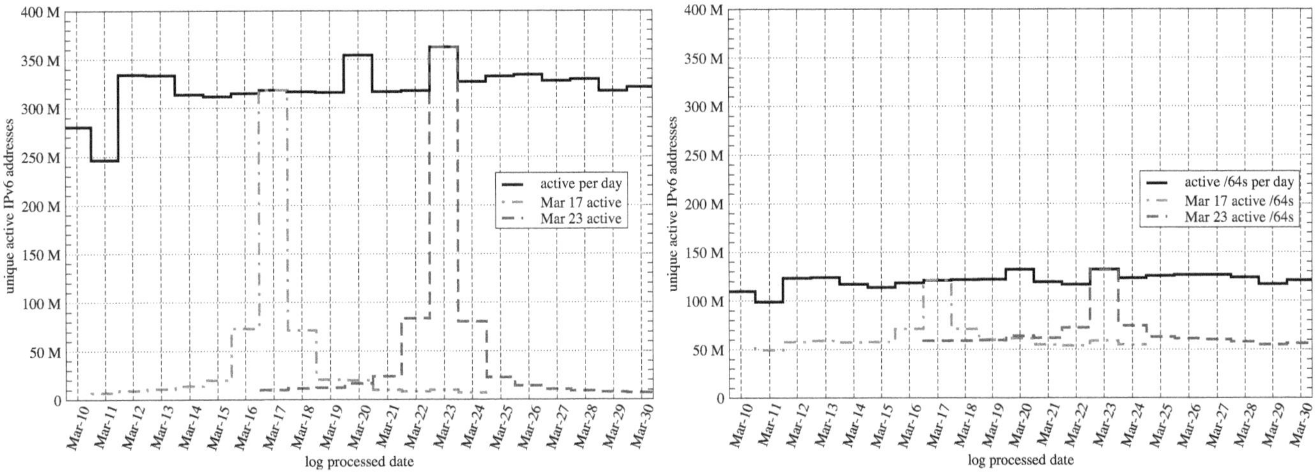

(a) IPv6 address stability (b) /64 prefix stability

Figure 5: Stability study of active IPv6 WWW client addresses and prefixes observed per day, March 2015.

many very long-lived WWW client IPv6 addresses, only 1.81 million (0.1%) observed over the course of a year; and *(b)*, there are many long-lived /64 prefixes for active WWW clients: 153 million 6m-stable /64s, and even 116 million 1y-stable /64s. Consider Figure 6a, where we plot the CCDF of various counts by ASN. We see that a single ASN accounts for over 100 million /64s (dashed black) as observed across 6 months, indicating that most long-lived /64s (dashed blue) are in only a few networks. We explore this further in Section 6.2.1.

6.1.1 *Discussion of Temporal Results*

One motivation for identifying 3d-stable addresses is the proposal that they'd make reliable targets for active probing to discover network infrastructure. We tested this hypothesis by randomly selecting 3.18 million 3d-stable active WWW client IPv6 addresses as targets for TTL-limited probes and then performed 52.6 million traces to them from 20 geographically-diverse source locations. We received a response from 10.9% of the targets target versus only 0.312% of targets selected randomly from *all* active WWW client IPv6 addresses, *i.e.,* not just the stable ones. While also likely useful to trace toward ephemeral WWW client address targets, we discover the last hop routers and the diameter of the IPv6 Internet only if the target responds. Thus, we find that stable client addresses are clearly useful as targets in subsequent active measurements.

As for the "not 3d-stable" addresses, we expect that the vast majority are hosts using a privacy-extension IID, as the default timeout is 24 hours. [33] However, other types of addresses are present as well. Note that, although the IID of EUI-64 addresses is static, the subnet prefix can vary, as when the device is moved between networks, or when a given operator implements a policy of assigning another subnet prefix each time the device connects to the network. (See Section 6.2.1 for further discussion.) We investigated EUI-64 addresses in the Sept. 17-23, 2014 dataset that were classified as "not 3d-stable." In 62% of them, the IID appeared in more than one address. Also, for 14% of them, the IID also appeared in an address that was classified as 3d-stable.

While the temporal class "3d-stable (-7d,+7d)" is useful when applied to target selection for active measurements, more research is warranted in order to determine what specific temporal classes may be most useful, *e.g.*, varying the number of days or the sliding window size, and in combination with addressing practices.

One wonders whether or not any of our counts of active or stable /64s could be an approximate lower-bound on the actual number of subscribers or instances of IPv6-capable Internet connections in the world today. Consider the highlighted (bold) counts in Table 2d; is the 116 million 1y-stable /64s observed March, 2015, a reasonable lower-bound? We discuss this in the forthcoming Section 7, but first, we address spatial classification results in order to better understand how network identifiers such as /64 prefixes are assigned by ISPs.

6.2 Spatial Classification

6.2.1 Multi-Resolution Aggregate Count Ratio

Here we turn to results based on MRA plots that we introduced in Section 5.2.1. With myriad possible address populations for which to produce MRA plots but limited space, a data-driven exploration methodology that directs our attention to ASNs and prefixes of interest is called for. To this end, we first examine Figures 6a and 6b, distributions of aggregate counts across all active IPv6 ASNs and BGP prefixes.

Consider Figure 6b. This is a set of box plots, each showing the distribution of aggregation ratios across all IPv6 BGP prefixes for each of the 16-bit segments of each prefixes' set of active IPv6 addresses. Unlike a typical box plot showing just the median, middle 50, and whiskers to, say, the 1st and 99th percentiles, these also show middle 90% and whiskers extend to the absolute maximum, as annotated. Overall, we can see that most aggregation takes place across the three 16-bit segments between bits 32 and 80. We also see that about 20% of the prefixes (the 75th through 95th percentiles (transparent portion of the box) have significant aggregation in the 112-128 bit segment, thus we include an MRA plot for just such a prefix in Figure 7e.

In Figure 6a, by the solid black line near the lower right-hand corner, we see that there is an exceptional ASN with 500 million active addresses in a week's time, thus we include its MRA plot as Figure 7c. This happens to be the ASN of the prefix with the highest aggregation in the 48-64 bit segment in Figure 6b.

Figures 7a through 7f are the resulting selected MRA plots for active WWW client addresses observed March 17-23, 2015. Let's tour the active IPv6 address space through these plots, discovering their features of interest. Coincidentally, the networks represented in these plots happen also to be diversely located in the world. Figure 7a is the MRA plot for all active WWW client addresses observed in the entire IPv6 unicast address space, the proverbial "30,000-foot view." The 0-32 bit segment is roughly governed by the Regional Internet Registries (RIRs) via their allocations and assignments to ISPs and end users (though some allocations are much larger than a /32), and remaining bits down to /64 are within the area that a network operator uses for subnetting in routing protocols. Figure 7a shows that there is greater use of the bit space

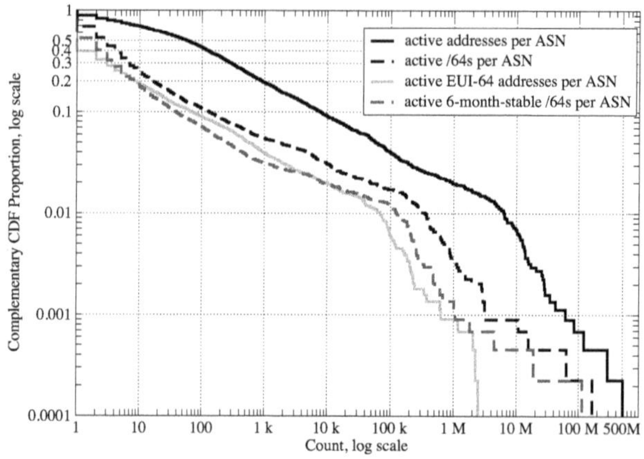

(a) Distribution of active addrs and /64 counts, 4.42K ASNs

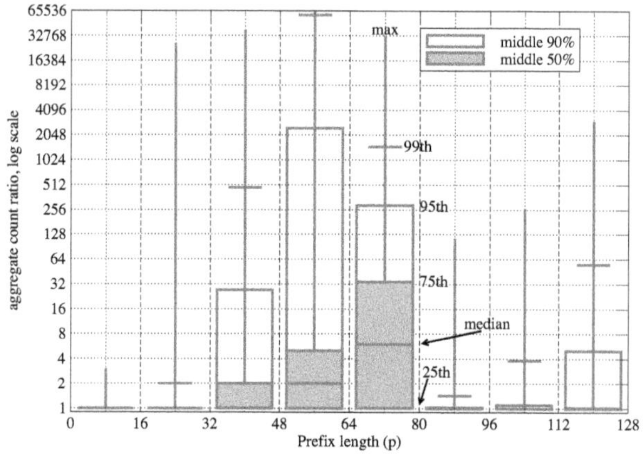

(b) 16-bit segment agg. distributions, 6.87K BGP prefixes

Figure 6: Distribution plots for active IPv6 addresses observed during 7 days, March 17-23, 2015.

in the 32-64 range than the 0-32, with the greatest use of a 16-bit segment in the 32-48 bit range. Within the 16-32 bit range, the RIRs partition more frequently by the higher-order bits, while in the 32-48 bit range, network operators partition more frequently by the lower-order bits. Lastly, the 64-128 bit segment is clearly different, as expected given the prevalence of ephemeral addresses presumably due to SLAAC and privacy addressing. While we can't see fine details at this level, prefix aggregation here happens near bit position 64; this is because this segment is mostly sparsely populated with random values such that the majority of hosts' addresses share at most short runs of leading bits of their IIDs in common with other active addresses in their /64.

Figure 7b is the MRA plot for 6to4 clients. Here we witness the significant difference between IPv6 and IPv4 aggregation. For addresses in the /16 prefix reserved for 6to4, IPv4 addresses are embedded in bits 16 through 48, as is clearly evident in the plot. The single bits ratios plotted (blue) in the 16-48 segment are similar to those Kohler *et al.* studied years ago and plot in [28]. This 32-bit IPv4

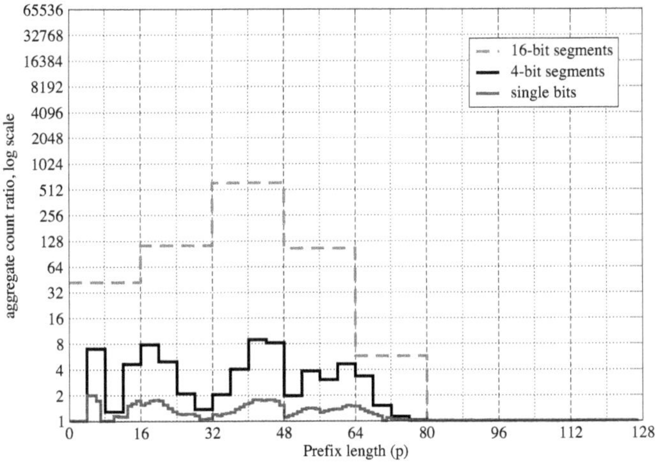

(a) All: 1.81B active IPv6 client addrs, not 6to4 or Teredo

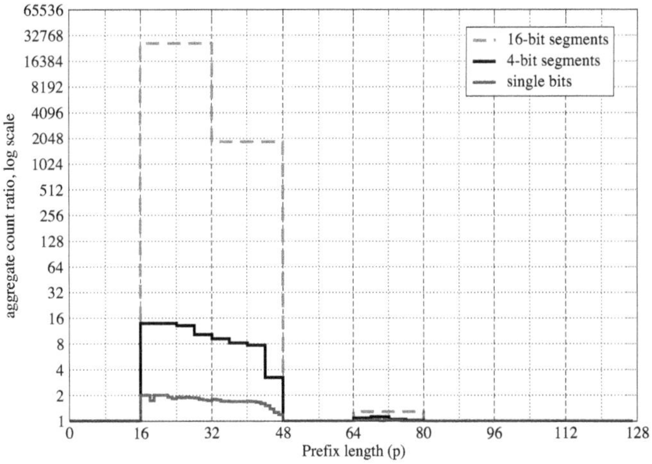

(b) 6to4: 64.2M active IPv6 (49.3M IPv4) client addresses

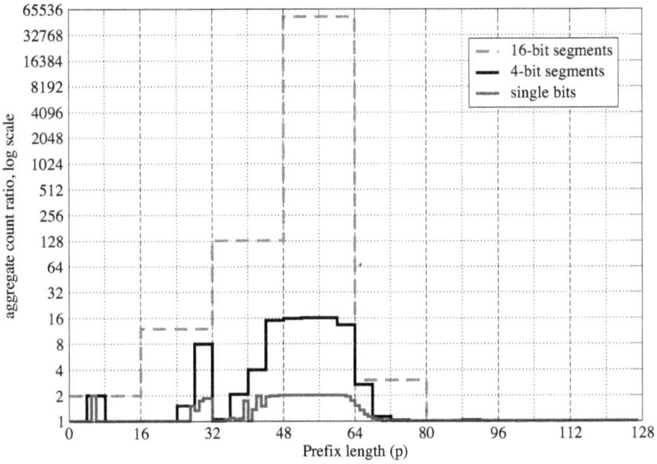

(c) US mobile: 510M active IPv6 client addrs, 167M /64s

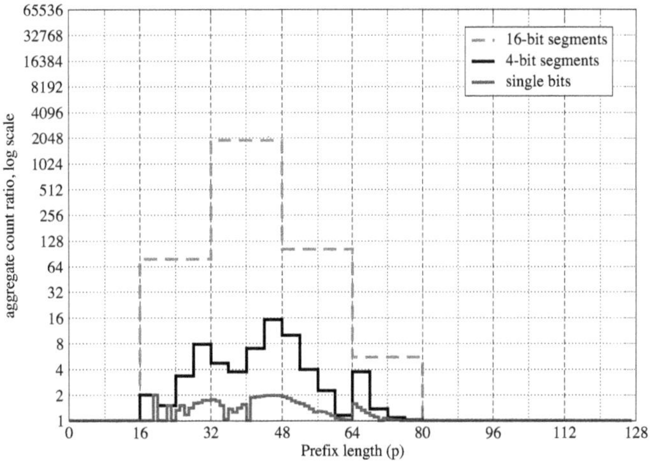

(d) EU ISP prefix: 86.2M active IPv6 client addrs, 15.5M /64s

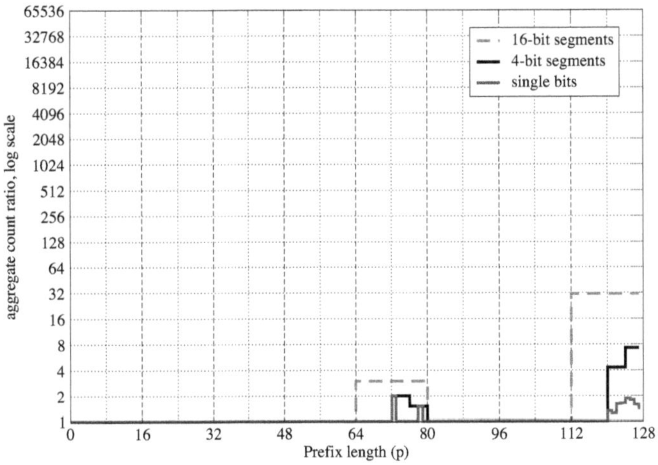

(e) EU univ. dept. prefix: 94 active IPv6 client addrs, 1 /64

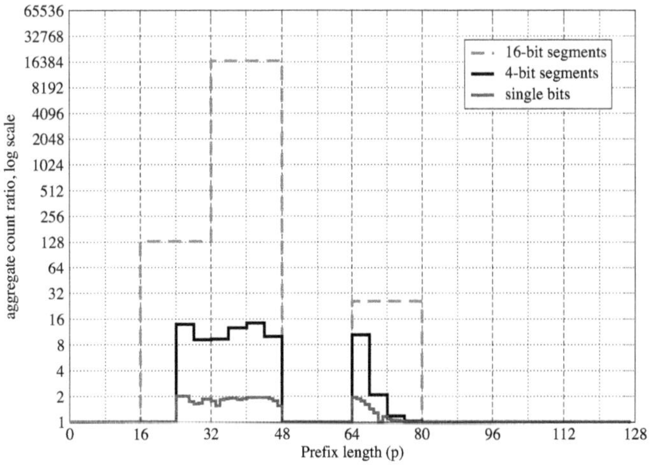

(f) JP ISP prefix: 57.0M active IPv6 client addrs, 2.18M /64s

Figure 7: Multi-Resolution Aggregate (MRA) plots for active IPv6 addresses observed during 7 days, March 17-23, 2015.

address segment has much higher aggregation than any similar segments of IPv6 in Figure 7a.

Figure 7c is the MRA plot for a U.S.-based mobile carrier. Its most unusual feature is that the 44-64 bit segment is nearly 100% utilized when observed over one week's time. This is evidenced by the 16-bit segments value (dashed red) and the 4-bits segments value (black) nearly reaching their maximum possible heights of 64K and 16, respectively. By experiment as a subscriber, we know that user equipment (UE) in this mobile service receives a different /64 prefix on each association, and by comparison to the same plot over only 1 day (not shown), we can deduce that this network seems to dynamically assign /64s from pools of addresses in this 44-64 bit segment. This dynamic assignment has consequences when trying to estimate subscribers because it can cause the count of active /64s observed to over-represent the number of subscribers. Corroborating evidence for a dynamic address component in the 44-64 bit segment is that this carrier's BGP advertisements consist of over 400 /44 prefixes. The MRA plot for another top mobile carrier that advertises tens of /40 prefixes (not shown due to limited space) is strikingly similar.

Next, let's consider the MRA plots of a European ISP, in Figure 7d, and a Japanese ISP, in Figure 7f, for one of each of their advertised BGP prefixes. The careful observer will note that the prefixes are at least of size 19 and 24 bits, respectively, as evidenced by the left-most of the single bits (blue) values. Their numbers of active addresses are similar and both sets appear to primarily consist of privacy addresses, sparsely distributed in the 64-128 bit segment. However, the leading 64-bit portions (left side) of the plots differ starkly, suggesting very different address plans are in use. Most notably, in Figure 7d, the 40-64 bit segment is populated with many values over a week's time, with heavier usage of the higher order bits of this range. Note that bit 40 seems to be constant and that there is a subtle perturbation in the single bits (blue) aggregation ratios at position 56. After examining the distribution (not shown) of values in bits 40-55, we posit that this segment contains an oft-changing, pseudorandom 15-bit number beginning at bit 41. This is followed by an 8-bit value in bits 56-63 of unknown construction, with all 256 possible values observed, but non-uniform and most often 0x00 or 0x01. By contrast, in Figure 7f, the 48-64 bit segment exhibits seemingly no aggregation, suggesting that each /48 has the same 16-bit value in every address it contains. Further, by examining the distribution (not shown) of /64 counts per IID (or Ethernet MAC address) for the JP ISP's 185K active EUI-64 addresses, we see that 99.6% of them were observed in just one /64 in a week's time; this figure is 67.4% for the EU ISP. We discuss a reason for this in Section 6.2.3.

Figure 7e is the MRA plot for one /64 prefix for one department at a European university. We selected it for consideration because it contains multiple 2@/112-dense prefixes, identified in the forthcoming results in Section 6.2.2. Consequently, the structure shown is markedly different from other plots. The WWW client addresses are densely packed, as evidenced by the values at all resolutions (dashed red, black, and blue) being most prominent in the 112-128 bit segment; this indicates that these client addresses are numerically close together, as one might expect, *e.g.* when assigning static addresses to hosts or when assigning addresses via DHCP. There don't appear to be any SLAAC addresses, which require a 64-bit network identifier. Aggregation seen in the 72-80 bit range and none in bits 80-120 suggests network identifier lengths are between 80 and 120.

6.2.2 Dense Prefixes and Addresses

Density Class	Dense Prefixes	Router Addresses	Possible Addresses	Router Address Density
2 @ /124	43.1K	116K	689K	0.1678459119
3 @ /120	8.28K	81.0K	**2.12M**	0.0382372758
2 @ /120	64.2K	193K	16.4M	0.0117351137
2 @ /116	207K	568K	852M	0.0006670818
64 @ /112	187	41.2K	12.3M	0.0033593815
32 @ /112	509	54.8K	33.4M	0.0016417438
16 @ /112	3.06K	105K	201M	0.0005259994
8 @ /112	21.5K	290K	1.41B	0.0002057970
4 @ /112	101K	681K	6.63B	0.0001026403
2 @ /112	367K	1.29M	24.1B	0.0000534072
2 @ /108	289K	1.72M	303B	0.0000056895
2 @ /104	108K	1.84M	1.81T	0.0000010171

Table 3: Dense prefixes identified at various densities for 3.2M router addresses collected February 2015.

Table 3 summarizes the dense prefixes discovered, by the method described in Section 5.2.3, using the router addresses dataset described in Section 4. Here we perform a limited search of the parameter space to determine what combinations of n and p (where n is the number of hosts that must be observed within a prefix of length p for the prefix to be considered dense) yield a reasonable number of targets for active measurements. As we see, manipulating these two parameters gives significant control over the prefixes classified as dense and, therefore, the number of possible target addresses that result.

Finally, for active WWW client addresses observed March 17, 2015, we identify 128 thousand 2@/112-dense prefixes and 1.38 million WWW client addresses contained therein. This yields 8.39 billion possible target addresses. Given that it is feasible to survey the entire IPv4 address space space by active probing in only minutes [19], we propose that it is similarly feasible to survey these dense regions of the IPv6 address space. Other IPv6 address datasets could yield additional sets of dense prefixes to survey.

6.2.3 Discussion of Spatial Classification

To evaluate the interpretation of our MRA plots, we contacted operators pertaining to networks in Figure 7 and received the following information. *(1)* The high utilization of the 40 - 64 bit address segment in Figure 7c coincides with their subscribers being assigned /64s, *e.g.*, by least recently used, from a pool sized according to the connection capacity of a gateway. Thus the /64s are reused by other subscribers. Our results suggest this reuse can occur in just days. *(2)* The university of Figure 2a provided us with their full IPv6 address plan, and the implication from the figure that we observe only 3 hex character values matches their address plan. Two of these indicate "customer networks" and "large customer networks," which are the portions of their prefix that one would expect to see WWW clients.

After we posited that the IP addresses plotted in Figure 7d contain a pseudorandom value in the network identifier, we learned that a European ISP does just that. As a supposed privacy-enhancing feature, they allow service subscribers to have their IP addresses' network identifier changed on demand, at the press of a button [37].

Regarding the subnet shown in Figure 7d, we found a pertinent IPv6 address allocation plan available on the web; this indicates the university to which the containing /48 is assigned. Furthermore, we found that *every* active address had an `ip6.arpa` PTR record in the DNS and, thus, were able to collect names for each of these hosts of which 92 began with "`dhcpv6-`." This is evidence that the department uses a single /64 to provide IPv6 addresses to a set of about 100 active hosts.

We evaluate the application of our dense prefix results by performing `ip6.arpa` PTR queries for the 2.12 million possible addresses prefixes of the 3@/120-dense class, highlighted (bold) in Table 3. This yielded an additional 47K domain names more than performing queries for just the active WWW client addresses. (DNS names are valuable hints to IP geolocation software because domain names sometimes contain physical location information; this is especially true for routers. [34])

Overall, although our results are based on only a few months of data across a year-long period, we claim they demonstrate that both temporal and spatial address classifications can reasonably be performed at large scale, and that the results are useful in choosing targets for active measurements and in discovering network-specific addressing practices.

7. DISCUSSION AND FUTURE WORK

7.1 Counting IPv6

If one assumes a 1:1 correspondence between /64 prefixes and IPv6 subscribers or "user connections," the numbers of /64 prefixes are candidate surrogates for IPv6 "user" counts. However, this assumption is rather crude. It is difficult to say whether numbers of active and stable /64 prefixes are low or high estimates. Some networks employ addressing schemes which cause the count of /64s (active or stable) to overestimate the number of subscribers, *e.g.,* the U.S. mobile carrier in Figure 7c. Other networks use a plan by which the number of active /64s seems a reasonable estimate of active subscribers, *e.g.,* the Japanese ISP in Figure 7f. Still other networks place many users in the same /64, or more specific subnet, causing the count of active /64s to underestimate the number of user connections, *e.g.,* the network in Figure 7e. Evidence shows that the number active /64s observed in a week's time can miscount IPv6 WWW client devices by a *factor of 100* in either direction.

This challenging situation leads us to conclude that estimating IPv6 user or device counts should be informed by addressing practice on a per-network or per-prefix basis. This likely requires either inside information from network operators, or a reliable measurement method to determine addressing practices from outside. We've had success in reverse engineering addressing practice by examining the network identifiers of EUI-64 addresses over time. These persistent, unique IIDs serve as guides that help find our way in areas of the IPv6 address space.

7.2 Longest Stable Prefixes

Having achieved some success reverse engineering network structure "manually," as just described, we propose that one could automatically discover stable portions of network identifiers, defined as the set of *longest stable prefixes* in a dataset recording many address observations over time. By combining aspects of our temporal and spatial classification techniques, we claim that it is possible to identify a set of such prefixes, perhaps without relying on inspection of addresses with long-lived IIDs, *e.g.,* EUI-64. These longest stable prefixes are likely to be significant aggregates within a network's routing tables, thus this presents a passive means by which one might glean a network's address plan. We've begun to explore this prospect and it is a focus of our future work.

8. CONCLUSION

In this paper, we present a methodology to classify IPv6 addresses. We employ two techniques: *(1)* temporal analysis to determine prefix and address stability over time, and *(2)* spatial analysis to determine the structure in which prefixes and addresses are contained. We develop classifiers and demonstrate their efficacy in an empirical study of active IPv6 addresses observed at a large CDN across a year's time, involving billions of WWW client addresses. The results of our analyses expose operator addressing practices that impact the interpretation of Internet measurements. Finally, we propose that the classifications we develop are applicable, and likely necessary, to comprehensively survey or census the IPv6 Internet by passive and active means.

Acknowledgments

We thank Cameron Byrne, Dale Carder, Jon Crowcroft, Paweł Foremski, Jan Galkowski, Steve Hoey, Geoff Huston, Jeff Kline, Liz Krznarich, David Malone, George Michaelson, Keung-Chi "KC" Ng, and Erik Nygren for their helpful comments and assistance.

9. REFERENCES

[1] GNU core utilities. `http://www.gnu.org/software/coreutils/`, 2003.

[2] Google IPv6 Statistics. `http://www.google.com/intl/en/ipv6/statistics.html`, 2015.

[3] Sample IPv6 Active WWW Client Address Aggregate Counts Data. `http://www.akamai.com/technical-publications/`, October 2015.

[4] State of the Internet: IPv6 Adoption Trends by Country and Network. `http://www.stateoftheinternet.com/ipv6`, April 2015.

[5] T. Aura. Cryptographically Generated Addresses (CGA). IETF RFC 3972, March 2005.
[6] M. Bagnulo. Hash-Based Addresses (HBA). IETF RFC 5535, June 2009.
[7] M. Bagnulo and J. Arkko. Support for Multiple Hash Algorithms in Cryptographically Generated Addresses (CGAs). IETF RFC 4982, July 2007.
[8] R. Barnes, R. Altmann, and D. Kerr. Mapping the Great Void: Smarter scanning for IPv6. http://www.caida.org/workshops/isma/1202/slides/aims1202_rbarnes.pdf, Feb 2012.
[9] F. Brockners, S. Gundavelli, S. Seicher, and D. Ward. Gateway-Initiated Dual-Stack Lite Deployment. IETF RFC 6674, July 2012.
[10] B. Carpenter, J. Crowcroft, and Y. Rekhter. IPv4 Address Behaviour Today. IETF RFC 2101, February 1997.
[11] B. Carpenter and S. Jiang. Significance of IPv6 Interface Identifiers. IETF RFC 7136, February 2014.
[12] K. Cho, R. Kaizaki, and A. Kato. Aguri: An Aggregation-Based Traffic Profiler. In *Proceedings of the Workshop on Quality of Future Internet Services (QofIS '01)*, Coimbra, Portugal, September 2001.
[13] k. claffy. The 4th Workshop on Active Internet Measurements (AIMS-4) Report. *ACM SIGCOMM Computer Communication Review (CCR)*, 42(3):34–38, Jul 2012.
[14] L. Colitti, S. H. Gunderson, E. Kline, and T. Refice. Evaluating IPv6 Adoption in the Internet. In *PAM*, pages 141–150, 2010.
[15] J. Czyz, M. Allman, J. Zhang, S. Iekel-Johnson, E. Osterweil, and M. Bailey. Measuring IPv6 Adoption. *SIGCOMM Computer Communication Review*, 44(4):87–98, August 2014.
[16] A. Dainotti, K. Benson, A. King, k. claffy, M. Kallitsis, E. Glatz, and X. Dimitropoulos. Estimating Internet Address Space Usage Through Passive Measurements. *ACM SIGCOMM Computer Communication Review (CCR)*, 44(1):42–49, Jan 2014.
[17] R. Droms, J. Bound, B. Volz, T. Lemon, C. Perkins, and M. Carney. Dynamic Host Configuration Protocol for IPv6 (DHCPv6). IETF RFC 3315, July 2003.
[18] A. Durand, R. Droms, J. Woodyatt, and Y. Lee. Dual-Stack Lite Broadband Deployments Following IPv4 Exhaustion. IETF RFC 6333, August 2011.
[19] Z. Durumeric, E. Wustrow, and J. A. Halderman. ZMap: Fast Internet-Wide Scanning and its Security Applications. In *Proceedings of the 22nd USENIX Security Symposium*, August 2013.
[20] F. Gont. A Method for Generating Semantically Opaque Interface Identifiers with IPv6 Stateless Address Autoconfiguration (SLAAC). IETF RFC 7217, April 2014.
[21] C. Grundemann, A. Hughes, and O. Delo. Best Current Operational Practices - IPv6 Subnetting. http://bcop.nanog.org/images/6/62/BCOP-IPv6_Subnetting.pdf, 2011.
[22] R. Hinden and S. Deering. IP Version 6 Addressing Architecture. IETF RFC 4291, February 2006.
[23] C. Huitema. An Anycast Prefix for 6to4 Relay Routers. IETF RFC 3068, June 2001.
[24] C. Huitema. Teredo: Tunneling IPv6 over UDP through Network Address Translations (NATs). IETF RFC 4380, February 2006.
[25] G. Huston. Personal correspondence, April 2015.
[26] G. Huston and G. Michaelson. Measuring IPv6. http://www.potaroo.net/presentations/2013-05-16-ipv6-measurement.pdf, May 2013.
[27] G. Huston and G. Michaelson. March 2015 Update on Measuring IPv6. http://www.potaroo.net/presentations/2015-03-22-ipv6-stats.pdf, March 2015.
[28] E. Kohler, J. Li, V. Paxson, and S. Shenker. Observed Structure of Addresses in IP Traffic. In *Internet Measurement Workshop*, pages 253–266, 2002.
[29] M. Kohno, B. Nitzan, R. Bush, Y. Matsuzaki, L.Colitti, and T. Narten. Using 127-Bit IPv6 Prefixes on Inter-Router Links. IETF RFC 6164, April 2011.
[30] David Malone. Observations of IPv6 Addresses. In *Passive and Active Network Measurement, 9th International Conference, PAM 2008, Cleveland, OH, USA, April 29-30, 2008. Proceedings*, pages 21–30, 2008.
[31] M. Mawatari, M. Kawashima, and C. Byrne. 464XLAT: Combination of Stateful and Stateless Translation. IETF RFC 6877, April 2013.
[32] G. Michaelson. Personal conversation, July 2014.
[33] T. Narten, R. Draves, and S. Krishnan. Privacy Extensions for Stateless Address Autoconfiguration in IPv6. IETF RFC 4941, September 2007.
[34] V. N. Padmanabhan and L. Subramanian. An Investigation of Geographic Mapping Techniques for Internet Tools. In *Proceedings of ACM SIGCOMM 2001*, San Diego, CA, August 2001.
[35] SURFnet. Preparing an IPv6 Address Plan. http://www.ripe.net/lir-services/training/material/IPv6-for-LIRs-Training-Course/Preparing-an-IPv6-Addressing-Plan.pdf, September 2013.
[36] Akamai Technologies. State Of The Internet Q3 2014 Report. http://www.akamai.com/dl/akamai/akamai-soti-q314.pdf, 2014.
[37] Deutsche Telekom. Deutsche Telekom offers anonymous surfing with IPv6. https://www.telekom.com/media/company/93184, Nov 2011.
[38] F. Templin, T. Gleeson, and D. Thaler. Intra-Site Automatic Tunnel Addressing Protocol (ISATAP). IETF RFC 5214, March 2008.
[39] S. Thompson, T. Narten, and T. Jinmei. IPv6 Stateless Address Autoconfiguration. IETF RFC 4862, September 2007.

Are We One Hop Away from a Better Internet?

Yi-Ching Chiu*, Brandon Schlinker*, Abhishek Balaji Radhakrishnan,
Ethan Katz-Bassett, Ramesh Govindan
Department of Computer Science, University of Southern California

ABSTRACT

The Internet suffers from well-known performance, reliability, and security problems. However, proposed improvements have seen little adoption due to the difficulties of Internet-wide deployment. We observe that, instead of trying to solve these problems in the general case, it may be possible to make substantial progress by focusing on solutions tailored to the paths between popular content providers and their clients, which carry a large share of Internet traffic.

In this paper, we identify one property of these paths that may provide a foothold for deployable solutions: they are often very short. Our measurements show that Google connects directly to networks hosting more than 60% of end-user prefixes, and that other large content providers have similar connectivity. These direct paths open the possibility of solutions that sidestep the headache of Internet-wide deployability, and we sketch approaches one might take to improve performance and security in this setting.

Categories and Subject Descriptors

C.2.1 [**Network Architecture and Design**]: Network topology; C.2.5 [**Local and Wide-Area Networks**]: Internet

Keywords

Measurements; Internet topology

1. INTRODUCTION

Internet routing suffers from a range of problems, including slow convergence [25, 43], long-lasting outages [23], circuitous routes [41], and vulnerability to IP spoofing [6] and prefix hijacking [44]. The research and operations communities have responded with a range of proposed fixes [7,22,24,30,31]. However, proposed solutions to these well-known problems have seen little adoption [28, 33, 35].

One challenge is that some proposals require widespread adoption to be effective [6, 22, 28]. Such solutions are hard to deploy, since they require updates to millions of devices across tens of thousands of networks. A second challenge is that the goal is often an approach that works in the general case, applicable equally to any Internet path, and it may be difficult to design such general solutions.

We argue that, instead of solving problems for arbitrary paths, we can think in terms of solving problems for an arbitrary byte, query, or dollar, thereby putting more focus on paths that carry a higher volume of traffic. Most traffic concentrates along a small number of routes due to a number of trends: the rise of Internet video had led to Netflix and YouTube alone accounting for nearly half of North American traffic [2], more services are moving to shared cloud infrastructure, and a small number of mobile and broadband providers deliver Internet connectivity to end-users. This skewed distribution means that an approach to improving routing can have substantial impact even if it only works well over these important paths. Further, it may be possible to take advantage of properties of these paths, of the traffic along them, or of the providers using them, in order to develop tailored approaches that provide increased benefit in these scenarios.

This paper focuses on one attribute of these high traffic routes: they are very short. Our measurements show that, whereas the average path on the Internet traverses 1-2 intermediate transit ASes, most paths from a large content provider, Google, go directly from Google's network into the client's network.

While previous results suggested that the Internet has been "flattening" in this manner [20, 26], our results are novel in a number of ways. First, whereas previous work observed flattening in measurements sampling a small subset of the Internet, we quantify the full degree of flattening for a major content provider. Our measurements cover paths to 3.8M /24 prefixes–all of the prefixes observed to request content from a major CDN–whereas earlier work measured from only 50 [20] or 110 [26] networks. Peering links, especially of content providers like Google, are notoriously hard to uncover, with previous work projecting that traditional measurement techniques miss 90% of these links [34]. Our results support a similar conclusion to this projection: Whereas a previous study found up to 100 links per content provider across years of measurements [40] and CAIDA's analysis lists 184 Google peers [3], our analysis uncovers links from Google to over 5700 peers.

Second, we show that, from the same content provider, popular paths serving high volume client networks tend to be shorter than paths to other networks. Some content providers even host servers in other networks [9], which in effect shortens paths further.

Third, in addition to quantifying Google's connectivity, we provide context. We show that ASes that Google does not peer with often have a local geographic footprint and low query volumes. In addition, our measurements for other providers suggest that Microsoft has short peering paths similar to Google, whereas Amazon relies on Tier 1 and other providers for much of its routing.

*These authors contributed equally to this work.

IMC'15, October 28–30, 2015, Tokyo, Japan.
© 2015 ACM. ISBN 978-1-4503-3848-6/15/10 ...$15.00.
DOI: http://dx.doi.org/10.1145/2815675.2815719.

We conclude by asking whether it might be possible to take advantage of short paths–in particular those in which the content provider peers directly with the client network–to make progress on long-standing routing problems. Is it easier to make progress in this setting that, while limited, holds for much of our web activity?

- The need to work over paths that span multiple administrative boundaries caused, for example, our previous route reliability work to require complex lockstep coordination among thousands of networks [22]. Is coordination simplified when all concerned parties already have a peering relationship?
- The source and destination of traffic have direct incentive to guarantee the quality of the route between them, but intermediate networks lack visibility into end-to-end issues. With direct paths that bypass intermediate transit providers, can we design approaches that use the natural incentives of the source and destination–especially of large content providers–to deploy improvements?
- Some solutions designed to apply universally provide little benefit over simpler but less general techniques in likely scenarios [28]. Given the disproportionate role of a small number of providers, can we achieve extra benefit by tailoring our approaches to apply to these few important players?

We have not answered these questions, but we sketch problems where short paths might provide a foothold for a solution. We hope this paper will encourage the community to take advantage of the short paths of popular services to sidestep hurdles and improve Internet routing.

2. DATASETS AND DATA PROCESSING

Our measurement goal is to assess the AS path lengths between popular content providers and consumers of content. We use collections of traceroutes as well as a dataset of query volumes to estimate the importance of different paths.

Datasets. To assess paths from users to popular content, we use: (1) traceroutes from PlanetLab to establish a baseline of path lengths along arbitrary (not necessarily popular) routes; (2) a CDN log capturing query volumes from end users around the world; (3) traceroutes from popular cloud service providers to prefixes around the world; and (4) traceroutes from RIPE Atlas probes around the world to popular cloud and content providers.

Traceroutes from PlanetLab. A day of iPlane traceroutes from April 2015 [29], which contains traceroutes from all PlanetLab sites to 154K BGP prefixes. These traceroutes represent the view of routing available from an academic testbed.

End-User Query Volumes. Aggregated and anonymized queries to a large CDN, giving (normalized) aggregate query count per /24 client prefix in one hour in 2013 across all of the CDN's globally distributed servers. The log includes queries from 3.8M client prefixes originated by 37496 ASes. The set has wide coverage, including clients in every country in the world, according to MaxMind's geolocation database [1].

While the exact per prefix volumes would vary across provider and time, we expect that the trends shown by our results would remain similar. To demonstrate that our CDN log has reasonable query distributions, we compare it with a similar Akamai log from 2014 (Fig. 21 in [16]). The total number of /24 prefixes requesting content in the Akamai log is 3.76M, similar to our log's 3.8M prefixes. If V_n^C and V_n^A are the percentage of queries from the top n prefixes in our CDN dataset and in Akamai's dataset, respectively, then $|V_n^C - V_n^A| < 6\%$ across all n. The datasets are particularly similar when it comes to the contribution of the most active client prefixes: $|V_n^C - V_n^A| < 2\%$ for $n \leq 100{,}000$, which accounts for $\approx$31% of the total query volume.

Traceroutes from the cloud. In March and August/September 2015, we issued traceroutes from Google Compute Engine (GCE) [Central US region], Amazon EC2 (EC2) [Northern Virginia region], and IBM SoftLayer [Dallas DAL06 datacenter] to all 3.8M prefixes in our CDN trace and all 154K iPlane destinations. For each prefix in the CDN log, we chose a target IP address from a 2015 ISI hitlist [15] to maximize the chance of a response. We issued the traceroutes using Scamper [27], which implements best practices like Paris traceroute [5].

Traceroutes from RIPE Atlas. The RIPE Atlas platform includes small hardware probes hosted in thousands of networks around the world. In April 2015, we issued traceroutes from Atlas probes in approximately 1600 ASes around the world towards our cloud VMs and a small number of popular websites.

Processing traceroutes to obtain AS paths. Our measurements are IP-level traceroutes, but our analysis is over AS-level paths. Challenges exist in converting IP-level paths to AS paths [32]; we do not innovate on this front and simply adopt widely-used practices.

First, we remove any unresponsive hops, private IP addresses, and IP addresses associated with Internet Exchange Points (IXPs).[1]

Next, we use a dataset from iPlane [29] to convert the remaining IP addresses to the ASes that originate them, and we remove any ASes that correspond to IXPs. If the iPlane data does not include an AS mapping for an IP address, we insert an unknown AS indicator into the AS path. We remove one or more unknown AS indicators if the ASes on both sides of the unknown segment are the same, or if a single unknown hop separates two known ASes. After we apply these heuristics, we discard paths that still contains unknown segments. We then merge adjacent ASes in a path if they are siblings or belong to the same organization, using existing organization lists [8], since these ASes are under shared administration.[2]

Finally, we exclude paths that do not reach the destination AS. For our traceroutes from the cloud, we are left with paths to 3M of the 3.8M /24 prefixes.

3. INTERNET PATH LENGTHS

How long are Internet paths? In this section, we demonstrate that the answer depends on the measurements used. We show that most flows from some popular web services to clients traverse at most one inter-AS link (or one *hop*), whereas traditional measurement datasets result in longer paths.

3.1 Measuring paths from the cloud

Paths from the cloud are short. As a baseline, we use our set of traceroutes from PlanetLab to iPlane destinations, as traceroutes from academic testbeds are commonly used in academic studies.

[1] We filter IXPs because they simply facilitate connectivity between peers. We use two CAIDA supplementary lists [3, 21] to identify ASes and IPs associated with IXPs.

[2] We compared the AS paths inferred by our approach with those inferred by a state-of-the-art approach designed to exclude paths with unclear AS translations [12], generating the results in our paper using both approaches. The minor differences in the output of the two approaches do not impact our results meaningfully, and so we only present results from our approach.

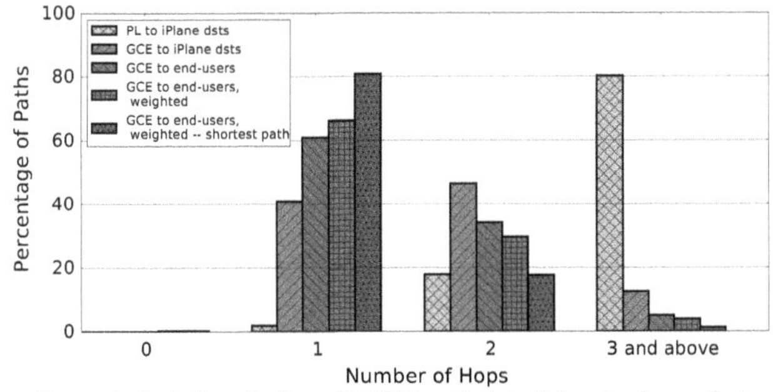

Figure 1: Paths lengths from GCE/PlanetLab to iPlane/end-user dest.

Figure 1 shows that only 2% of paths from PlanetLab are one hop to the destination, and the median path is between two and three AS hops.[3] However, there is likely little traffic between the networks hosting PlanetLab sites (mostly universities) and most prefixes in the iPlane list, so these longer paths may not carry much traffic.

Instead, traffic is concentrated on a small number of links and paths from a small number of sources. For example, in 2009, 30% of traffic came from 30 ASes [26]. At a large IXP, 10% of links contribute more than 70% of traffic [38]. In contrast, many paths and links are relatively unimportant. At the same IXP, 66% of links combined contributed less than 0.1% of traffic [37].

To begin answering what paths look like for one of these popular source ASes, we use our traceroutes from GCE, Google's cloud offering, to the same set of iPlane destinations. We use GCE traceroutes as a view of the routing of a major cloud provider for a number of reasons. First, traceroutes *from* the cloud give a much broader view than traceroutes *to* cloud and content providers, since we can measure outward to all networks rather than being limited to the relatively small number where we have vantage points. Second, we are interested in the routing of high-volume services. Google itself has a number of popular services, ranging from latency-sensitive properties like Search to high-volume applications like YouTube. GCE also hosts a number of third-party tenants operating popular services which benefit from the interdomain connectivity Google has established for its own services. For the majority of these services, most of the traffic flows in the outbound direction. Third, Google is at the forefront of the trends we are interested in understanding, maintaining open peering policies around the world, a widespread WAN [20], a cloud offering, and ISP-hosted front end servers [9]. Fourth, some other cloud providers that we tested filter traceroutes (§3.4 discusses measurements from Amazon and SoftLayer, which also do not filter). Finally, our previous work developed techniques that allow us to uncover the locations of Google servers and the client-to-server mapping [9], enabling some of the analysis later in this paper.

Compared to PlanetLab paths towards iPlane destinations, GCE paths are much shorter: 87% are at most two hop, and 41% are one hop, indicating that Google peers directly with the ASes originating the prefixes. Given the popularity of Google services in particular and cloud-based services in general, these short paths may better represent today's Internet experience.

However, even some of these paths may not reflect real traffic, as some iPlane prefixes may not host Google clients. In the rest of this section and §3.3, we capture differences in Google's and GCE's paths toward iPlane destinations and end-users.

[3]In addition to using PlanetLab, researchers commonly use BGP route collectors to measure paths. A study of route collector archives from 2002 to 2010 found similar results to the PlanetLab traceroutes, with the average number of hops *increasing* from 2.65 to 2.90 [14].

Paths from the cloud to end-users are even shorter. In order to understand the paths between the cloud and end-users, we analyze 3M traceroutes from GCE to client prefixes in our CDN trace (§2). We assume that, since these prefixes contain clients of one CDN, most of them host end-users likely to use other large web services like Google's. As seen in Figure 1, 61% of the prefixes have one hop paths from GCE, meaning their origin ASes peer directly with Google, compared to 41% of the iPlane destinations.

Prefixes with more traffic have shorter paths. The preceding analysis considers the distribution of AS hops across prefixes, but the distribution across queries/requests/flows/bytes may differ, as per prefix volumes vary. For example, in our CDN trace, the ratio between the highest and lowest per prefix query volume is 8.7M:1. To approximate the number of AS hops experienced by queries, the *GCE to end-users, weighted* line in Figure 1 weights each of the 3M prefixes by its query volume in our CDN trace (§2), with over 66% of the queries coming from prefixes with a one hop path.

While our quantitative results would differ with a trace from a different provider, we believe that qualitative differences between high and low volume paths would hold. The dataset has limitations: the trace is only one hour, so suffers time-of-day distortions, and prefix weights are representative of the CDN's client distribution but not necessarily Google's client distribution. However, the dataset suffices for our purposes: precise ratios are not as important as the trends of how paths with no/low traffic differ from paths with high traffic, and a prefix that originates many queries in this dataset is more likely to host users generating many queries for other services.

Path lengths to a single AS can vary. We observed traceroutes traversing paths of different lengths to reach different prefixes within the same destination AS. Possible explanations for this include: (1) traffic engineering by Google, the destination AS, or a party in between; and (2) split ASes, which do not announce their entire network at every peering, often due to lack of a backbone or a capacity constraint. Of 17,905 ASes that had multiple traceroutes in our dataset, 4876 ASes had paths with different lengths. Those 4876 ASes contribute 72% of the query volume in our CDN trace, with most of the queries coming from prefixes that have the shortest paths for the ASes. The *GCE to end-users weighted, shortest path* bars in Figure 1 show how long paths would be if all traffic took the shortest observed path to its destination AS. With this hypothetical routing, 80% of queries traverse only one hop.

Path lengths vary regionally. Peering connectivity can also vary by region. For example, overall, 10% of the queries in our CDN log come from end users in China, 25% from the US, and 20% from Asia-Pacific excluding China. However, China has longer paths and less direct peering, so 27% of the 2 hop paths come from China, and only 15% from the US and 10% from Asia-Pacific.

3.2 Google's Peers (and Non-Peers)

In our traceroutes from GCE, we observed Google peering with 5083 ASes (after merging siblings).[4,5] Since a primary reason to peer is to reduce transit costs, we first investigate the projected query volume of ASes that do and do not peer with Google. We form a flow graph by combining the end-user query volumes from our CDN trace with the AS paths defined by our GCE traceroutes. So, for example, the total volume for an AS will have both the queries from that AS's prefixes and from its customer's prefixes if traceroutes to the customer went via the AS. We group the ASes into buckets based on this aggregated query volume.

[4]For the interested reader, Google publishes its peering policy and facilities list at `http://peering.google.com` and in PeeringDB.
[5]Some of these peers may be using remote peering [10].

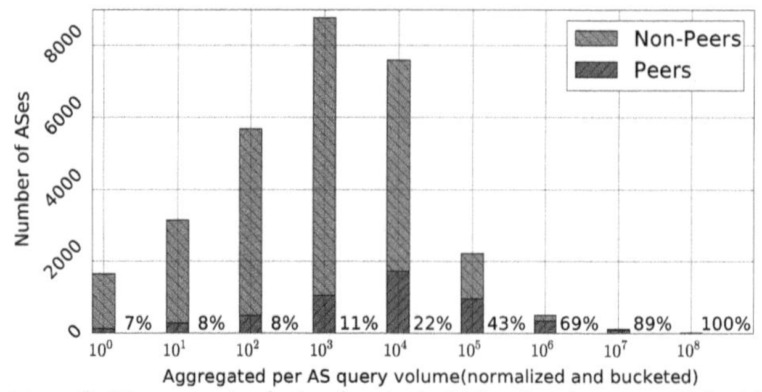

Figure 2: How many (and what fraction) of ASes Google peers with by AS size. AS size is the number of queries that flow through it, given paths from GCE to end-user prefixes and per prefix query volumes in our CDN trace. Volumes are normalized and bucketed by powers of 10.

Figure 2 shows the number of ASes within each bucket that do / do not peer with Google in our traceroutes. As expected, Google peers with a larger fraction of higher volume ASes. And while there are still high volume ASes that do not peer with Google, most ASes that do not peer are small in terms of traffic volume and, up to the limitations of public geolocation information, geographic footprint. We used MaxMind to geolocate the prefixes that Google reaches via a single intermediate transit provider, then grouped those prefixes by origin AS. Of 20,946 such ASes, 74% have all their prefixes located within a 50 mile diameter.[6] However, collectively these ASes account for only 4% of the overall query volume.

Peering is increasing over time. We evaluated how Google's visible peering connectivity changed over time by comparing our March 2015 traces with an additional measurement conducted in August 2015. In August, we observed approximately 700 more peerings than the 5083 we measured in March. While some of these peerings may have been recently established, others may have been previously hidden from our vantage point, possibly due to traffic engineering. These results suggest that a longitudinal study of cloud connectivity may provide new insights.

3.3 Estimating paths to a popular service

The previous results measured the length of paths from Google's GCE cloud service towards end-user prefixes. However, these paths may not be the same as the paths from large web properties such as Google Search and YouTube for at least two reasons. First, Google and some other providers deploy front-end servers inside some end-user ASes [9], which we refer to as *off-net* servers. As a result, some client connections terminate at off-nets hosted in other ASes than where our GCE traceroutes originate. Second, it is possible that Google uses different paths for its own web services than it uses for GCE tenants. In this section, we first describe how we estimate the path length from end-users to `google.com`, considering both of these factors. We then validate our approach. Finally, we use our approach to estimate the number of AS hops from end-users to `google.com` and show that some of the paths are shorter than our GCE measurements above.

Estimating AS Hops to Google Search: First, we use EDNS0 client-subnet queries to resolve `google.com` for each /24 end-user prefix, as in our previous work [9]. Each query returns a set of server IP addresses for that end-user prefix to use. Next, we translate the server addresses into ASes as described in §2. We discard any end-user prefix that maps to servers in multiple ASes, leaving a set of prefixes directed to servers in Google's AS and a set of prefixes directed to servers in other ASes.

[6]Geolocation errors may distort this result, although databases tend to be more accurate for end-user prefixes like the ones in question.

Table 1: Estimated vs. measured path lengths from Atlas to `google.com`

Type	Count	no error	error ≤ 1 hop
all paths	1,409	81.26%	97.16%
paths to on-nets	1,120	80.89%	98.21%
paths to off-nets	289	82.70%	93.08%
paths w/ ≤ 1 hop	925	86.05%	97.62%

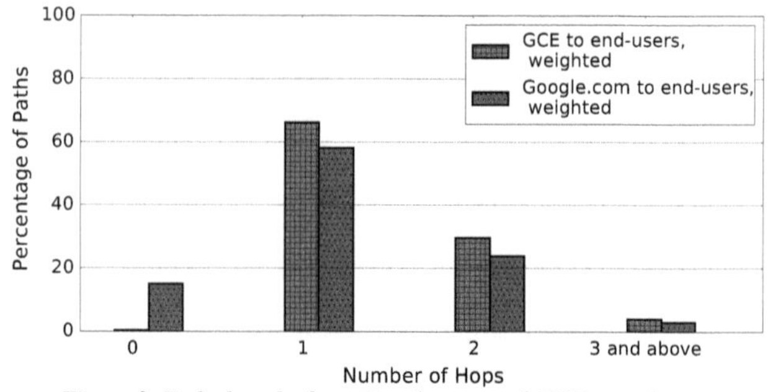

Figure 3: Paths lengths from Google.com and GCE to end-users

For end-user prefixes directed towards Google's AS, we estimate the number of AS hops to `google.com` as equal to the number of AS hops from GCE to the end-user prefix, under the assumption, which we will later validate, that Google uses similar paths for its cloud tenants and its own services. For all other traces, we build a graph of customer/provider connectivity in CAIDA's AS relationship dataset [3] and estimate the number of AS hops as the length of the shortest path between the end-user AS and the off-net server's AS.[7] Since off-net front-ends generally serve only clients in their customer cone [9] and public views such as CAIDA's should include nearly all customer/provider links that define these customer cones [34], we expect these paths to usually be accurate.

Validating Estimated AS Hops: To validate our methodology for estimating the number of AS hops to `google.com`, we used traceroutes from 1409 RIPE Atlas probes[8] to `google.com` and converted them to AS paths. We also determined the AS hosting the Atlas probe and estimated the number of AS hops from it to `google.com` as described above.[9]

For the 289 ground-truth traces directed to off-nets, we calculate the difference between the estimated and measured number of AS hops. For the remaining 1120 traces that were directed to front-ends within Google's network, we may have traceroutes from GCE to multiple prefixes in the Atlas probe's AS. If their lengths differed, we calculate the difference between the Atlas-measured AS hops and the GCE-measured path with the closest number of AS hops.

Table 1 shows the result of our validation: overall, 81% of our estimates have the same number of AS hops as the measured paths, and 85% in cases where the number of hops is one (front-end AS peers with client AS). We conclude that our methodology is accurate enough to estimate the number of AS hops for all clients to `google.com`, especially for the short paths we are interested in.

Off-net front-ends shorten some paths even more. Applying our estimation technique to the full set of end-user prefixes, we arrive at the estimated AS hop distribution shown in the *Google.com to end-users, weighted* line in Figure 3.

The estimated paths between `google.com` and end-user prefixes are shorter overall than the traces from GCE, with 73% of queries coming from ASes that either peer with Google, use off-nets hosted in their providers, or themselves host off-nets. For clients served by off-nets, the front-end to back-end portions of their connections also

[7]If the end-user AS and off-net AS are the same, the length is zero.

[8]The rest of the 1600 traceroutes failed.

[9]We are unable to determine the source IP address for some Atlas probes and thus make estimations at the AS level.

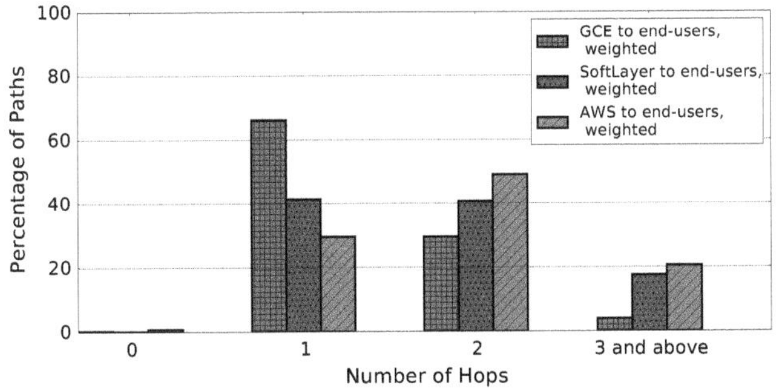

Figure 4: Paths lengths from different cloud platforms to end-users.

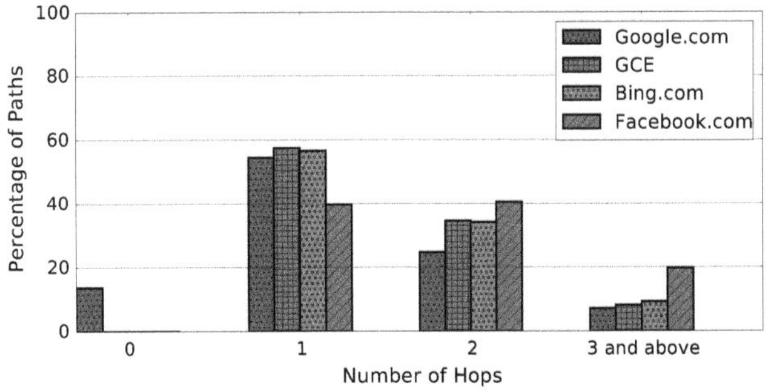

Figure 5: Path lengths from RIPE Atlas nodes to content and cloud[11]

cross domains, starting in the hosting AS and ending in a Google datacenter. The connection from the client to front-end likely plays the largest role in client-perceived performance, since Google has greater control of, and can apply optimizations to, the connection between the front-end and back-end [17]. Still, we evaluated that leg of the split connection by issuing traceroutes from GCE to the full set of Google off-nets [9]. Our measurements show that Google has a direct connection to the hosting AS for 62% of off-nets, and there was only a single intermediate AS for an additional 34%.

3.4 Paths to Other Popular Content

In this section, we compare measurements of Google and other providers. First, in Figure 4, we compare the number of AS hops (weighted by query volume) from GCE to the end-user prefixes to the number of AS hops to the same targets from two other cloud providers. While SoftLayer and AWS each have a substantial number of one hop paths, both are under 42%, compared to well over 60% for GCE. Still, the vast majority of SoftLayer and AWS paths have two hops or less. Our measurements and related datasets suggest that these three cloud providers employ different strategies from each other: Google peers widely, with 5083 next hop ASes in our traceroutes, and only has 5 providers in CAIDA data [3], using routes through those providers to reach end users responsible for 10% of the queries in our CDN trace; Amazon only has 756 next hop ASes, but uses 20 providers for routes to 50% of the end user queries; and SoftLayer is a middle ground, with 1986 next hops and 11 providers it uses to reach end users with 47% of the queries.

We anticipate that some other large content providers are building networks similar to Google's to reduce transit costs and improve quality of service for end-users. Since we cannot issue traceroutes from within these providers' networks towards end-users,[10] we use traceroutes from RIPE Atlas vantage points towards the providers. We execute traceroutes from a set of Atlas probes towards `facebook.com` and Microsoft's `bing.com`. We calibrate these results with our earlier ones by comparing to traceroutes from the Atlas probes towards `google.com` and our GCE instance.

Figure 5 shows the number of AS hops to each destination.[11] The AS hop distribution to `bing.com` is nearly identical to the AS hop distribution to GCE. Paths to `bing.com` are longer than paths to `google.com`, likely because Microsoft does not have an extensive set of off-net servers like Google's. Facebook trails the pack, with just under 40% of paths to `facebook.com` having 1 AS hop.

Summary. *Path lengths for popular services tend to be much shorter than random Internet paths. For instance, while only 2% of PlanetLab paths to iPlane destinations are one hop, we estimate that 73% of queries to* `google.com` *go directly from the client AS to Google.*

[10]Microsoft's Azure Cloud appears to block outbound traceroutes.

[11]The percentages are of total Atlas paths, not weighted.

4. CAN SHORT PATHS BE BETTER PATHS?

Our measurements suggest that much of the Internet's popular content flows across at most one interdomain link on its path to clients. In this section, we argue that these direct connections may represent an avenue to making progress on long-standing Internet routing problems. Within the confines of this short paper, we do not develop complete solutions. Instead, we sketch where and why progress may be possible, starting with general arguments about why short paths may help, and then continuing with particular problems where short paths may yield deployable solutions. We hope this paper serves as a spark for future work in this area.

4.1 Short paths sidestep existing hurdles

Paths to popular content will continue to shorten. Competitive pressures and the need to ensure low latency access to popular content will continue to accelerate this trend. Services are moving to well-connected clouds; providers are building out serving infrastructure [9, 18]; and peering is on the rise [11, 37]. The rise of video [2] and interactive applications suggests that providers will continue to seek peering and distributed infrastructure to reduce costs and latency. Because traffic is concentrating along short paths, solutions tailored for this setting can have impact, even if they do not work as well for or do not achieve deployment along arbitrary Internet paths.

One-hop paths only involve invested parties. The performance of web traffic depends on the intra- and inter-domain routing decisions of every AS on the path. The source and destination have incentives to improve performance, as it impacts their quality of experience and revenue. Transit ASes in the middle are not as directly invested in the quality of the route. In comparison, one-hop paths bypass transit, and the only ASes are senders and receivers with motivation to improve routing.

Internet protocols support communication between neighbors. An AS can use MEDs, selective advertisements, and BGP communities to express policy that may impact the routing of neighbors. ASes are willing to work together [41] using these mechanisms. However, the mechanisms generally only allow communication to neighbors: MEDs and communities usually do not propagate past one hop [36], and selective advertising only controls which neighbors receive a route. This limitation leaves ASes with almost no ability to affect the routing past their immediate neighbors,[12] but one-hop paths only consist of immediate neighbors.

[12]Some ASes offer communities to influence route export.

4.2 Short paths can simplify many problems

Joint traffic engineering. BGP does not support the negotiation of routing and traffic engineering between autonomous systems. Instead, network operators *hint* via MEDs and prepending, to indicate to neighbor ASes their preferences for incoming traffic. The coarse granularity of these hints and the lack of mechanisms to mutually optimize across AS boundaries result in paths with inflated latencies [41].

Prior work proposed the joint optimization of routing between neighboring ASes [31]. Yet such protocols become more complex when they must be designed to optimize paths that traverse intermediate ASes [30], to the point that it is unclear what fairness and performance properties they guarantee. In comparison, one-hop paths between provider and end-user ASes reduce the need for complicated solutions, enabling direct negotiation between the parties that benefit the most. Since the AS path is direct and does not involve the rest of the Internet, it may be possible to use channels or protocols outside, alongside, or instead of BGP, without requiring widespread adoption of changes.

Preventing spoofed traffic. Major barriers exist to deploying effective spoofing prevention. First, filters are only easy to deploy correctly near the edge of the Internet [6]. Second, existing approaches do not protect the AS deploying a filter, but instead prevent that AS from originating attacks on others. As a result, ASes lack strong incentives to deploy spoofing filters [6].

The short paths on today's Internet create a setting where it may be possible to protect against spoofing attacks for large swaths of the Internet by sidestepping the existing barriers. A cloud provider like Google that connects directly to most origins should know valid source addresses for traffic over any particular peering and be able to filter spoofed traffic, perhaps using strict uRPF filters. The direct connections address the first barrier by removing the routing complexity that complicates filter configuration, essentially removing the core of the Internet from the path entirely. The cloud provider is the destination,[13] removing the second barrier as it can protect itself by filtering spoofed traffic over many ingress links. While these mechanisms do not prevent all attacks,[14] they reduce the attack surface and may be part of a broader solution.

Limiting prefix hijacks. Prefix origins can be authenticated with the RPKI, now being adopted, but it does not enable authentication of the non-origin ASes along a path [28]. So, a provider having direct paths does not on its own prevent other ASes from hijacking the provider's prefixes via longer paths. While RPKI plus direct paths are not a complete solution by themselves, we view them as a potential building block towards more secure routing. If an AS has authenticated its prefix announcements–especially an important content provider or set of end users–it seems reasonable for direct peers to configure preferences to prefer one-hop, RPKI-validated announcements over competing advertisements.

Speeding route convergence. BGP can experience delayed convergence [25], inspiring general clean-slate alternatives such as HLP [42] and simpler alternatives with restricted policies that have better convergence properties [39]. Our findings on the flattening of the path distribution may make the latter class of solutions appealing. Specifically, it may suffice to deploy restricted policies based on BGP next-hop alone [39] for one-hop neighbors. In this as well, the incentive structure is just right: delayed route failovers can disrupt popular video content, so the content provider wants to ensure fast failover to improve the user's quality of experience.

[13] Most cloud and content providers are stub networks.

[14] An attacker can still spoof as a cloud provider in a reflection attack.

Avoiding outages. The Internet is susceptible to long-lasting partial outages in transit ASes [23]. The transit AS lacks visibility into end-to-end connections, so it may not detect a problem, and the source and destination lack visibility into or control over transit ASes, making it difficult to even discern the location of the problem [24]. With a direct path, an AS has much better visibility and control over its own routing to determine and fix a local problem, or it can know the other party–also invested in the connection–is to blame. Proposals exist to enable coordination between providers and end-user networks [19], and such designs could enable reactive content delivery that adapts to failures and changes in capacity.

5. RELATED WORK

Previous work observed a trend towards flattening and the centrality of content using active measurements [20], passive monitoring [4, 26], and modeling [13]. Our work extends this observation by measuring to and from a much larger number of networks. Earlier work showed advantages to allowing direct negotiation between neighbors [31] and CDNs and access ISPs [19], similar to approaches we imagine over direct paths. Work showing the benefits to BGP policy based only on the next hop [39] helps demonstrate the potential of such approaches. Similarly, ARROW posited that many routing problems can be lessened by tunneling to a network that offers reliable transit, and that the flattening Internet means that one tunnel is often enough [35]. Our work relies on a similar observation but an even flatter Internet.

6. CONCLUSIONS

As large content and cloud providers have been building out content distribution infrastructure and engaging in direct peering, many clients are one AS hop away from important content. This trend towards one-hop paths for important content will likely accelerate, driven by competitive pressures, and by the need to reduce latency for improved user experience. The trend suggests that, in a departure from the current focus on general solutions, interdomain routing and traffic management techniques may benefit from optimizing for the common case of one-hop paths, a regime where simpler, deployable solutions may exist.

7. ACKNOWLEDGMENTS

We would like to thank the anonymous reviewers for their valuable feedback. We also thank David Choffnes for running Sidewalk Ends AS-path conversion for our traces, Matthew Luckie for help with Scamper, Matt Calder for RIPE Atlas measurements, and Jitendra Padhye and Ratul Mahajan for helpful conversations. We thank Google for a Faculty Research Award and for a Cloud Credits Award. This work was supported in part by the National Science Foundation grants CNS-1351100 and CNS-1413978.

8. REFERENCES

[1] MaxMind GeoLite Database. `http://dev.maxmind.com/geoip/legacy/geolite/`.

[2] Sandvine global Internet phenomena report, 2014.

[3] The CAIDA AS relationships dataset. `http://www.caida.org/data/as-relationships/`, cited February 2015.

[4] B. Ager, W. Mühlbauer, G. Smaragdakis, and S. Uhlig. Web content cartography. IMC '11.

[5] B. Augustin, X. Cuvellier, B. Orgogozo, F. Viger, T. Friedman, M. Latapy, C. Magnien, and R. Teixeira. Avoiding Traceroute anomalies with Paris Traceroute. IMC '06.

[6] R. Beverly, A. Berger, Y. Hyun, and k. claffy. Understanding the efficacy of deployed Internet source address validation filtering. IMC '09.
[7] K. Butler, T. R. Farley, P. McDaniel, and J. Rexford. A survey of BGP security issues and solutions. *Proceedings of the IEEE*, January 2010.
[8] X. Cai, J. Heidemann, B. Krishnamurthy, and W. Willinger. An organization-level view of the Internet and its implications (extended). Technical report, USC/ISI TR, June 2012.
[9] M. Calder, X. Fan, Z. Hu, E. Katz-Bassett, J. Heidemann, and R. Govindan. Mapping the expansion of Google's serving infrastructure. IMC '13.
[10] I. Castro, J. C. Cardona, S. Gorinsky, and P. Francois. Remote peering: More peering without Internet flattening. CoNEXT '14.
[11] N. Chatzis, G. Smaragdakis, A. Feldmann, and W. Willinger. There is more to IXPs than meets the eye. *ACM SIGCOMM CCR*, October 2013.
[12] K. Chen, D. R. Choffnes, R. Potharaju, Y. Chen, F. E. Bustamante, D. Pei, and Y. Zhao. Where the sidewalk ends: Extending the Internet AS graph using traceroutes from P2P users. CoNEXT '09.
[13] A. Dhamdhere and C. Dovrolis. The Internet is flat: Modeling the transition from a transit hierarchy to a peering mesh. CoNEXT '10.
[14] B. Edwards, S. Hofmeyr, G. Stelle, and S. Forrest. Internet topology over time. *arXiv preprint*, 2012.
[15] X. Fan and J. Heidemann. Selecting representative IP addresses for Internet topology studies. IMC '10.
[16] M. T. Fangfei Chen, Ramesh K. Sitaraman. End-user mapping: Next generation request routing for content delivery. SIGCOMM '15.
[17] T. Flach, N. Dukkipati, A. Terzis, B. Raghavan, N. Cardwell, Y. Cheng, A. Jain, S. Hao, E. Katz-Bassett, and R. Govindan. Reducing web latency: The virtue of gentle aggression. SIGCOMM '13.
[18] A. Flavel, P. Mani, D. Maltz, N. Holt, J. Liu, Y. Chen, and O. Surmachev. FastRoute: A scalable load-aware anycast routing architecture for modern CDNs. NSDI '15.
[19] B. Frank, I. Poese, Y. Lin, G. Smaragdakis, A. Feldmann, B. Maggs, J. Rake, S. Uhlig, and R. Weber. Pushing CDN-ISP collaboration to the limit. *ACM SIGCOMM CCR*, July 2013.
[20] P. Gill, M. Arlitt, Z. Li, and A. Mahanti. The flattening Internet topology: Natural evolution, unsightly barnacles or contrived collapse? PAM '08.
[21] V. Giotsas, M. Luckie, B. Huffaker, and k. claffy. Inferring complex AS relationships. IMC '14.
[22] J. P. John, E. Katz-Bassett, A. Krishnamurthy, T. Anderson, and A. Venkataramani. Consensus routing: The Internet as a distributed system. NSDI '08.
[23] E. Katz-Bassett, H. V. Madhyastha, J. P. John, A. Krishnamurthy, D. Wetherall, and T. Anderson. Studying black holes in the Internet with Hubble. NSDI '08.
[24] E. Katz-Bassett, C. Scott, D. R. Choffnes, I. Cunha, V. Valancius, N. Feamster, H. V. Madhyastha, T. Anderson, and A. Krishnamurthy. LIFEGUARD: Practical repair of persistent route failures. SIGCOMM '12.
[25] C. Labovitz, A. Ahuja, A. Bose, and F. Jahanian. Delayed Internet routing convergence. SIGCOMM '00.
[26] C. Labovitz, S. Iekel-Johnson, D. McPherson, J. Oberheide, and F. Jahanian. Internet inter-domain traffic. SIGCOMM '10.
[27] M. Luckie. Scamper: A scalable and extensible packet prober for active measurement of the Internet. IMC '10.
[28] R. Lychev, S. Goldberg, and M. Schapira. BGP security in partial deployment: Is the juice worth the squeeze? SIGCOMM '13.
[29] H. V. Madhyastha, T. Isdal, M. Piatek, C. Dixon, T. Anderson, A. Krishnamurthy, and A. Venkataramani. iPlane: An information plane for distributed services. OSDI '06.
[30] R. Mahajan, D. Wetherall, and T. Anderson. Mutually controlled routing with independent ISPs. NSDI '07.
[31] R. Mahajan, D. Wetherall, and T. Anderson. Negotiation-based routing between neighboring ISPs. NSDI '05.
[32] Z. M. Mao, J. Rexford, J. Wang, and R. H. Katz. Towards an accurate AS-level Traceroute tool. SIGCOMM '03.
[33] J. Mirkovic and E. Kissel. Comparative evaluation of spoofing defenses. *IEEE Transactions on Dependable and Secure Computing*, March 2011.
[34] R. Oliveira, D. Pei, W. Willinger, B. Zhang, and L. Zhang. The (in)completeness of the observed Internet AS-level structure. *IEEE/ACM Transactions on Networking*, February 2010.
[35] S. Peter, U. Javed, Q. Zhang, D. Woos, T. Anderson, and A. Krishnamurthy. One tunnel is (often) enough. SIGCOMM '14.
[36] B. Quoitin and O. Bonaventure. A survey of the utilization of the BGP community attribute. Internet-Draft draft-quoitin-bgp-comm-survey-00, February 2002.
[37] P. Richter, G. Smaragdakis, A. Feldmann, N. Chatzis, J. Boettger, and W. Willinger. Peering at peerings: On the role of IXP route servers. IMC '14.
[38] M. A. Sanchez, F. E. Bustamante, B. Krishnamurthy, W. Willinger, G. Smaragdakis, and J. Erman. Inter-domain traffic estimation for the outsider. IMC '14.
[39] M. Schapira, Y. Zhu, and J. Rexford. Putting BGP on the right path: A case for next-hop routing. HotNets '10.
[40] Y. Shavitt and U. Weinsberg. Topological trends of Internet content providers. SIMPLEX '12.
[41] N. Spring, R. Mahajan, and T. Anderson. The causes of path inflation. SIGCOMM '03.
[42] L. Subramanian, M. Caesar, C. T. Ee, M. Handley, M. Mao, S. Shenker, and I. Stoica. HLP: A next generation inter-domain routing protocol. SIGCOMM '05.
[43] F. Wang, Z. M. Mao, J. Wang, L. Gao, and R. Bush. A measurement study on the impact of routing events on end-to-end Internet path performance. SIGCOMM '06.
[44] Z. Zhang, Y. Zhang, Y. C. Hu, Z. M. Mao, and R. Bush. iSPY: detecting IP prefix hijacking on my own. SIGCOMM '08.

Analyzing the Performance of an Anycast CDN

Matt Calder*,†, Ashley Flavel†, Ethan Katz-Bassett*, Ratul Mahajan†, and Jitendra Padhye†

†Microsoft *University of Southern California

ABSTRACT

Content delivery networks must balance a number of trade-offs when deciding how to direct a client to a CDN server. Whereas DNS-based redirection requires a complex global traffic manager, anycast depends on BGP to direct a client to a CDN front-end. Anycast is simple to operate, scalable, and naturally resilient to DDoS attacks. This simplicity, however, comes at the cost of precise control of client redirection. We examine the performance implications of using anycast in a global, latency-sensitive, CDN. We analyze millions of client-side measurements from the Bing search service to capture anycast versus unicast performance to nearby front-ends. We find that anycast usually performs well despite the lack of precise control but that it directs roughly 20% of clients to a suboptimal front-end. We also show that the performance of these clients can be improved through a simple history-based prediction scheme.

Categories and Subject Descriptors

C.2.5 [**Computer-Communication Networks**]: Local and Wide-Area Networks—Internet; C.4 [**Performance of Systems**]: Measurement techniques

Keywords

Anycast; CDN; Measurement;

1. INTRODUCTION

Content delivery networks are a critical part of Internet infrastructure. CDNs deploy front-end servers around the world and direct clients to nearby, available front-ends to reduce bandwidth, improve performance, and maintain reliability. We will focus on a CDN architecture which directs the client to a nearby front-end, which terminates the client's TCP connection and relays requests to a backend server in a data center. The key challenge for a CDN is to map each client to the right front-end. For latency-sensitive services such as search results, CDNs try to reduce the client-perceived latency by mapping the client to a nearby front-end.

CDNs can use several mechanisms to direct the client to a front-end. The two most popular mechanisms are DNS and anycast. DNS-based redirection was pioneered by Akamai. It offers fine-grained and near-real time control over client-front-end mapping, but requires considerable investment in infrastructure and operations [35].

IMC'15, October 28–30, 2015, Tokyo, Japan.

ACM 978-1-4503-3848-6/15/10 ...$15.00.
DOI: http://dx.doi.org/10.1145/2815675.2815717.

Some newer CDNs like CloudFlare rely on anycast [1], announcing the same IP address(es) from multiple locations, leaving the client-front-end mapping at the mercy of Internet routing protocols. Anycast offers only minimal control over client-front-end mapping and is performance agnostic by design. However, it is easy and cheap to deploy an anycast-based CDN – it requires no infrastructure investment, beyond deploying the front-ends themselves. The anycast approach has been shown to be quite robust in practice [23].

In this paper, we aim to answer the questions: Does anycast direct clients to nearby front-ends? What is the performance impact of poor redirection, if any? To study these questions, we use data from Bing's anycast-based CDN [23]. We instrumented the search stack so that a small fraction of search response pages carry a JavaScript beacon. After the search results display, the JavaScript measures latency to four front-ends– one selected by anycast, and three nearby ones that the JavaScript targets. We compare these latencies to understand anycast performance and determine potential gains from deploying a DNS solution.

Our results paint a mixed picture of anycast performance. For most clients, anycast performs well despite the lack of centralized control. However, anycast directs around 20% of clients to a suboptimal front-end. When anycast does not direct a client to the best front-end, we find that the client usually still lands on a nearby alternative front-end. We demonstrate that the anycast inefficiencies are stable enough that we can use a simple prediction scheme to drive DNS redirection for clients underserved by anycast, improving performance of 15%-20% of clients. Like any such study, our specific conclusions are closely tied to the current front-end deployment of the CDN we measure. However, as the first study of this kind that we are aware of, the results reveal important insights about CDN performance, demonstrating that anycast delivers optimal performance for most clients.

2. CLIENT REDIRECTION

A CDN can direct a client to a front-end in multiple ways.

DNS: The client will fetch a CDN-hosted resource via a hostname that belongs to the CDN. The client's local DNS resolver (LDNS), typically configured by the client's ISP, will receive the DNS request to resolve the hostname and forward it to the CDN's authoritative nameserver. The CDN makes a performance-based decision about what IP address to return based on which LDNS forwarded the request. DNS redirection allows relatively precise control to redirect clients on small timescales by using small DNS cache TTL values.

Since a CDN must make decisions at the granularity of LDNS rather than client, DNS-based redirection faces some challenges. An LDNS may be distant from the clients that it serves or may serve clients distributed over a large geographic region, such that there is no good single redirection choice an authoritative resolver can make. This situation is very common with public DNS resolvers such as Google Public DNS and OpenDNS, which serve large, geographically disparate sets of clients [17]. A proposed solution to this issue is the EDNS client-subnet-prefix standard (ECS) which allows a portion of the client's actual IP address to be forwarded

to the authoritative resolver, allowing per-prefix redirection decisions [21].
Anycast: Anycast is a routing strategy where the same IP address is announced from many locations throughout the world. Then BGP routes clients to one front-end location based on BGP's notion of best path. Because anycast defers client redirection to Internet routing, it offers operational simplicity. Anycast has an advantage over DNS-based redirection in that each client redirection is handled independently – avoiding the LDNS problems described above.

Anycast has some well-known challenges. First, anycast is unaware of network performance, just as BGP is, so it does not react to changes in network quality along a path. Second, anycast is unaware of server load. If a particular front-end becomes overloaded, it is difficult to gradually direct traffic away from that front-end, although there has been recent progress in this area [23]. Simply withdrawing the route to take that front-end offline can lead to cascading overloading of nearby front-ends. Third, anycast routing changes can cause ongoing TCP sessions to terminate and need to be restarted. In the context of the Web, which is dominated by short flows, this does not appear to be an issue in practice [31, 23]. Many companies, including Cloudflare, CacheFly, Edgecast, and Microsoft, run successful anycast-based CDNs.
Other Redirection Mechanisms: Whereas anycast and DNS direct a client to a front-end before the client initiates a request, the response from a front-end can also direct the client to a different server for other resources, using, for example, HTTP status code 3xx or manifest-based redirection common for video [4]. These schemes add extra RTTs, and thus are not suitable for latency-sensitive Web services such as search. We do not consider them further in this paper.

3. METHODOLOGY

Our goal is to answer two questions: **1)** How effective is anycast in directing clients to nearby front-ends? And **2)** How does anycast performance compare against the more traditional DNS-based unicast redirection scheme? We experiment with Bing's anycast-based CDN to answer these questions. The CDN has dozens of front end locations around the world, all within the same Microsoft-operated autonomous system. We use measurements from real clients to Bing CDN front-ends using anycast and unicast. In § 4, we compare the size of this CDN to others and show how close clients are to the front ends.

3.1 Routing Configuration

All test front-ends locations have both anycast and unicast IP addresses.
Anycast: Bing is currently an anycast CDN. All production search traffic is current served using anycast from all front-ends.

Unicast: We also assign each front-end location a unique /24 prefix which does not serve production traffic. Only the routers at the closest peering point to that front-end announce the prefix, forcing traffic to the prefix to ingress near the front-end rather than entering Microsoft's backbone at a different location and traversing the backbone to reach the front-end. This routing configuration allows the best head-to-head comparison between unicast and anycast redirection, as anycast traffic ingressing at a particular peering point will also go to the closest front-end.

3.2 Data Sets

We use both passive and active measurements in our study, as discussed below.

3.2.1 Passive Measurements

Bing server logs provide detailed information about client requests for each search query. For our analysis we use the client IP address, location, and what front-end was used during a particular request. This data set was collected on the first week of April 2015 and represents many millions of queries.

3.2.2 Active Measurements

To actively measure CDN performance from the client, we inject a JavaScript beacon into a small fraction of Bing Search results. After the results page has completely loaded, the beacon instructs the client to fetch four test URLs. These URLs trigger a set of DNS queries to our authoritative DNS infrastructure. The DNS query results are randomized front-end IPs for measurement diversity, which we discuss more in § 3.3.

The beacon measures the latency to these front-ends by downloading the resources pointed to by the URLs, and reports the results to a backend infrastructure. Our authoritative DNS servers also push their query logs to the backend storage. Each test URL has a globally unique identifier, allowing us to join HTTP results from the client side with DNS results from the server side [34].

The JavaScript beacon implements two techniques to improve quality of measurements. First, to remove the impact of DNS lookup from our measurements, we first issue a warm-up request so that the subsequent test will use the cached DNS response. While DNS latency may be responsible for some aspects of poor Web-browsing performance [5], in this work we are focusing on the performance of paths between client and front-ends. We set TTLs longer than the duration of the beacon. Second, using JavaScript to measure the elapsed time between the start and end of a fetch is known to not be a precise measurement of performance [32], whereas the W3C Resource Timing API [29] provides access to accurate resource download timing information from compliant Web browsers. The beacon first records latency using the primitive timings. Upon completion, if the browser supports the resource timing API, then the beacon substitutes the more accurate values.

We study measurements collected from many millions of search queries over March and April 2015. We aggregated client IP addresses from measurements into /24 prefixes because they tend to be localized [27]. To reflect that the number of queries per /24 is heavily skewed across prefixes [35], for both the passive and active measurements, we present some of our results weighting the /24s by the number of queries from the prefix in our corresponding measurements.

3.3 Choice of Front-ends to Measure

The main goal of our measurements is to compare the performance achieved by anycast with the performance achieved by directing clients to their best performing front-end. Measuring from each client to every front-end would introduce too much overhead, but we cannot know a priori which front-end is the best choice for a given client at a given point in time.

We use three mechanisms to balance measurement overhead with measurement accuracy in terms of uncovering the best performing choices and obtaining sufficient measurements to them. First, for each LDNS, we consider only the ten closest front-ends to the LDNS (based on geolocation data) as candidates to consider returning to the clients of that LDNS. Recent work has show that LDNS is a good approximation of client location: excluding 8% of demand from public resolvers, only 11-12% of demand comes from clients who are further than 500km from their LDNS [17]. In Figure 1, we will show that our geolocation data is sufficiently accurate that the best front-ends for the clients are generally within that set. Second,

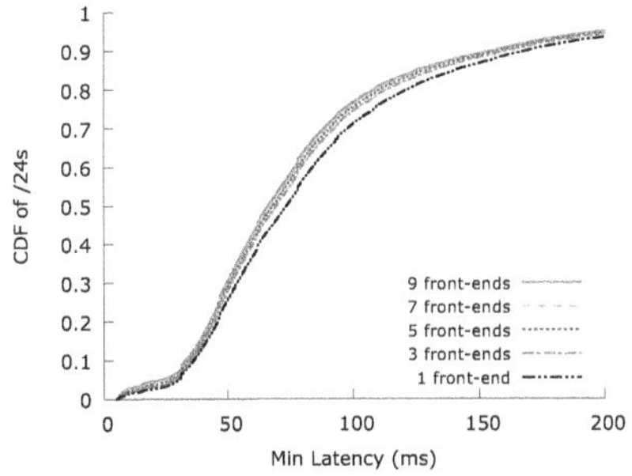

Figure 1: Diminishing returns of measuring to additional front-ends. The close grouping of lines for the 5th+ closest front-ends suggests that measuring to additional front-ends provides negligible benefit.

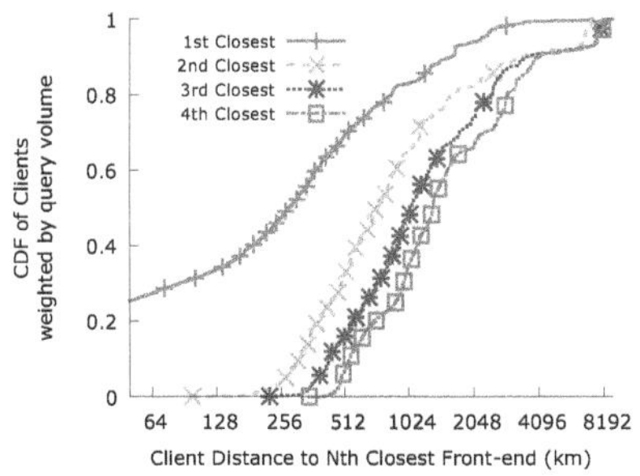

Figure 2: Distances in kilometers (log scale) from volume-weighted clients to nearest front-ends.

to further reduce overhead, each beacon only makes four measurements to front-ends: (a) a measurement to the front-end selected by anycast routing; (b) a measurement to the front-end judged to be geographically closest to the LDNS; and (c-d) measurements to two front-ends randomly selected from the other nine candidates, with the likelihood of a front-end being selected weighted by distance from the client LDNS (e.g. we return the 3rd closest front-end with higher probability than the 4th closest front-end). Third, for most of our analysis, we aggregate measurements by /24 and consider distributions of performance to a front-end, so our analysis is robust even if not every client measures to the best front-end every time.

To partially validate our approach, Figure 1 shows the distribution of minimum observed latency from a client /24 to a front-end. The labeled *N*th line includes latency measurements from the nearest *N* front-ends to the LDNS. The results show decreasing latency as we initially include more front-ends, but we see little decrease after adding five front-ends per prefix, for example. So, we do not expect that minimum latencies would improve for many prefixes if we measured to more than the nearest ten front-ends that we include in our beacon measurements.

4. CDN SIZE AND GEO-DISTRIBUTION

The results in this paper are specific to Bing's anycast CDN deployment. In this section we characterize the size of the deployment, showing that our deployment is of a similar scale–a few dozens of front-end server locations–to most other CDNs and in particular most anycast CDNs, although it is one of the largest deployments within that rough scale. We then measure what the distribution of these dozens of front-end locations yields in terms of the distance from clients to the nearest front-ends. Our characterization of the performance of this CDN is an important first step towards understanding anycast performance. An interesting direction for future work is to understand how to extend these performance results to CDNs with different numbers and locations of servers and with different interdomain connectivity [18].

We compare our CDN to others based on the number of server locations, which is one factor impacting CDN and anycast performance. We examine 21 CDNs and content providers for which there is publicly available data [3]. Four CDNs are extreme outliers. ChinaNetCenter and ChinaCache each have over 100 locations in China. Previous research found Google to have over 1000 locations worldwide [16], and Akamai is generally known to have over 1000 as well [17]. While this scale of deployment is often the popular image of a CDN, it is in fact the exception. Ignoring the large Chinese deployments, the next largest CDNs we found public data for are CDNetworks (161 locations) and SkyparkCDN (119 locations). The remaining 17 CDNs we examined (including ChinaNetCenter's and ChinaCache's deployments outside of China) have between 17 locations (CDNify) and 62 locations (Level3). In terms of number of locations and regional coverage, the Bing CDN is most similar to Level3 and MaxCDN. Well-known CDNs with smaller deployments include Amazon CloudFront (37 locations), CacheFly (41 locations), CloudFlare (43 locations) and EdgeCast (31 locations). CloudFlare, CacheFly, and EdgeCast are anycast CDNs.

To give some perspective on the density of front-end distribution, Figure 2 shows the distance from clients to nearest front-ends, weighted by client Bing query volumes. The median distance of the nearest front-end is 280 km, of the second nearest is 700 km, and of fourth nearest is 1300 km.

5. ANYCAST PERFORMANCE

We use measurements to estimate the performance penalty anycast pays in exchange for simple operation. Figure 3 is based on millions of measurements, collected over a period of a few days, and inspired us to take on this project.

As explained in § 3, each execution of the JavaScript beacon yields four measurements, one to the front-end that anycast selects, and three to nearby unicast front-ends. For each request, we find the latency difference between anycast and the lowest-latency unicast front-end. Figure 3 shows the fraction of requests where anycast performance is slower than the best of the three unicast front-ends. Most of the time, in most regions, anycast does well, performing as well as the best of the three nearby unicast front-ends. However, anycast is at least 25ms slower for 20% of requests, and just below 10% of anycast measurements are 100ms or more slower than the best unicast for the client.

This graph suggests possible benefits in using DNS-based redirection for some clients, with anycast for the rest. Note that this is not an upper bound: to derive that, we would have to poll all front-ends in each beacon execution, which is too much overhead. There is also no guarantee that a deployed DNS-based redirection system will be able to achieve the performance improvement seen in Figure 3 – to do so the DNS-based redirection system would have to be practically clairvoyant. Nonetheless, this result was sufficiently tantalizing for us to study anycast performance in more detail, and seek ways to improve it.

Examples of poor anycast routes: A challenge in understanding anycast performance is figuring out why clients are being directed to distant or poor performing edges front-ends. To troubleshoot, we used the RIPE Atlas [2] testbed, a network of over 8000 probes predominantly hosted in home networks. We issued traceroutes from Atlas probes hosted within the same ISP-metro area pairs where we have observed clients with poor performance. We observe in our analysis that many instances fall into one of two cases. 1) BGP's lack of insight into the underlying topology causes anycast

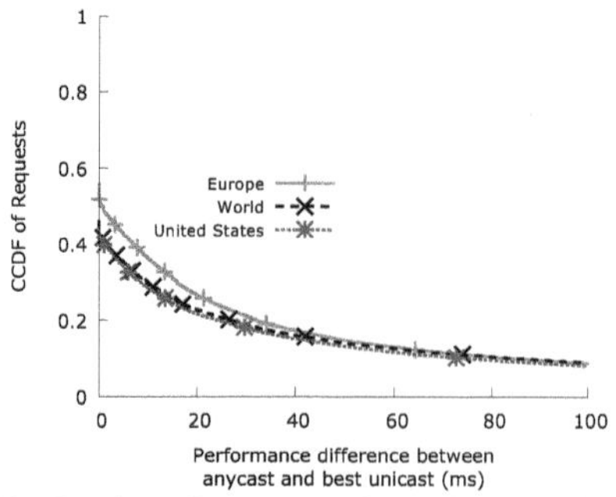

Figure 3: The fraction of requests where the best of three different unicast front-ends out-performed anycast.

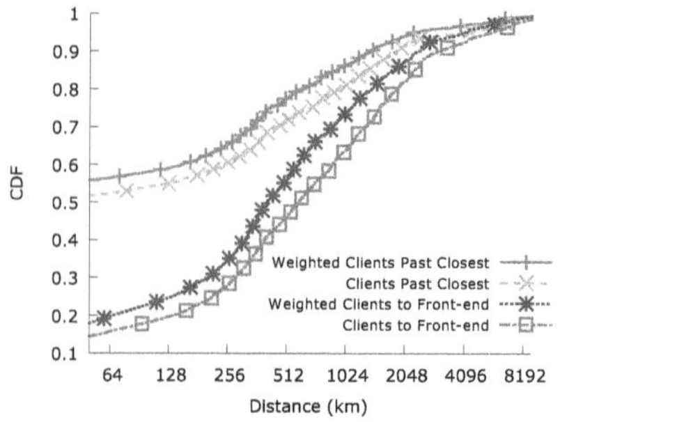

Figure 4: The distance in kilometers (log scale) between clients and the anycast front-ends they are directed to.

to make suboptimal choices and 2) intradomain routing policies of ISPs select remote peering points with our network.

In one interesting example, a client was roughly the same distance from two border routers announcing the anycast route. Anycast chose to route towards router A. However, internally in our network, router B is very close to a front-end C, whereas router A has a longer intradomain route to the nearest front-end, front-end D. With anycast, there is no way to communicate [39] this internal topology information in a BGP announcement.

Several other examples included cases where a client is nearby a front-end but the ISP's internal policy chooses to hand off traffic at a distant peering point. Microsoft intradomain policy then directs the client's request to the front-end nearest to the peering point, not to the client. Some examples we observed of this was an ISP carrying traffic from a client in Denver to Phoenix and another carrying traffic from Moscow to Stockholm. In both cases, direct peering was present at each source city.

Intrigued by these sorts of case studies, we sought to understand anycast performance quantitatively. The first question we ask is whether anycast performance is poor simply because it occasionally directs clients to front-ends that are geographically far away, as was the case when clients in Moscow went to Stockholm.

Does anycast direct clients to nearby front-ends? In a large CDN with presence in major metro areas around the world, most ISPs will see BGP announcements for front-ends from a number of different locations. If peering among these points is uniform, then the ISP's least cost path from a client to a front-end will often be the geographically closest. Since anycast is not load or latency aware, geographic proximity is a good indicator of expected performance.

Figure 4 shows the distribution of the distance from client to anycast front-end for all clients in one day of production Bing traffic. One line weights clients by query volume. Anycast is shown to perform 5-10% better at all percentiles when accounting for more active clients. We see that about 82% of clients are directed to a front-end within 2000 km while 87% of client volume is within 2000 km.

The second pair of lines in Figure 4, labeled "Past Closest", shows the distribution of the difference between the distance from a client to its closest front-end and the distance from the client to the front-end anycast directs to. About 55% of clients and weighted clients have distance 0, meaning they are directed to the nearest front-end. Further, 75% of clients are directed to a front-end within around 400 km and 90% are within 1375 km of their closest. This supports the idea that, with a dense front-end deployment such as is achievable in North America and Europe, anycast directs most clients to a relatively nearby front-end that should be expected to deliver good performance, even if it is not the closest.

From a geographic view, we found that around 10-15% of /24s are directed to distant front-ends, a likely explanation for poor performance.[1] Next we examine how common these issues are from day-to-day and how long issues with individual networks persist.

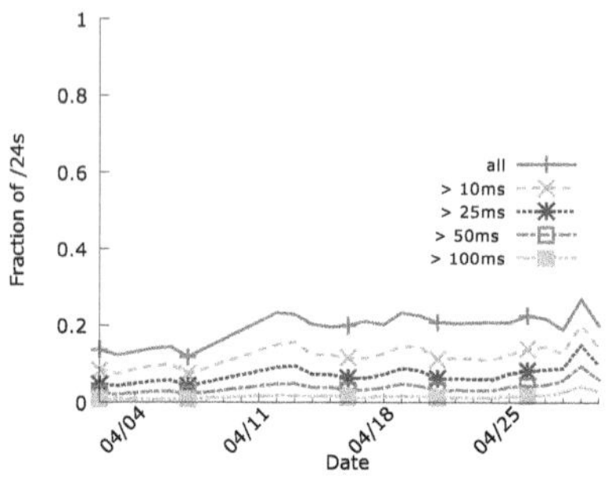

Figure 5: Daily poor-path prevalence during April 2015 showing what fraction of client /24s see different levels of latency improvement over anycast when directed to their best performing unicast front-end.

Is anycast performance consistently poor? We first consider whether significant fractions of clients see consistently poor performance with anycast. At the end of each day, we analyzed all collected client measurements to find prefixes with room for improvement over anycast performance. For each client /24, we calculate the median latency between the prefix and each measured unicast front-end and anycast.

Figure 5 shows the prevalence of poor anycast performance each day during April 2015. Each line specifies a particular minimum latency improvement, and the figure shows the fraction of client /24s each day for which some unicast front-end yields at least that improvement over anycast. On average, we find that 19% of prefixes see some performance benefit from going to a specific unicast front-end instead of using anycast. We see 12% of clients with 10ms or more improvement, but only 4% see 50ms or more.

Poor performance is not limited to a few days–it is a daily concern. We next examine whether the same client networks experience recurring poor performance. How long does poor performance persist? Are the problems seen in Figure 5 always due to the same problematic clients?

Figure 6 shows the duration of poor anycast performance during April 2015. For the majority of /24s categorized as having poor-performing paths, those poor-performing paths are short-lived. Around 60% appear for only one day over the month. Around 10% of /24s show poor performance for 5 days or more. These days are not necessarily consecutive. We see that only 5% of /24s see continuous poor performance over 5 days or more.

These results show that while there is a persistent amount of poor anycast performance over time, the majority of problems only last

[1] No geolocation database is perfect. A fraction of very long client-to-front-end distances may be attributable to bad client geolocation data.

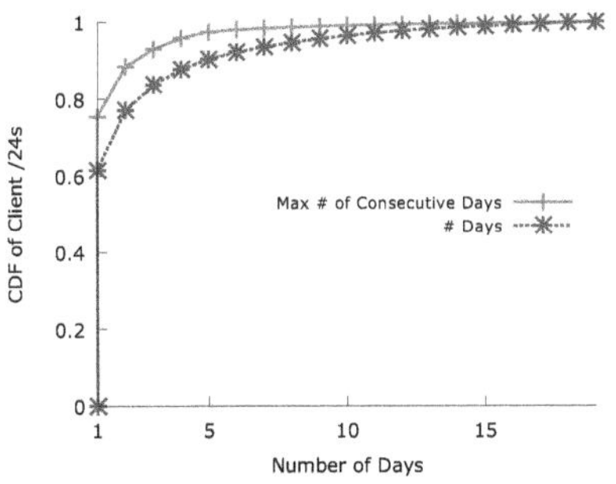

Figure 6: Poor path duration across April 2015. We consider poor anycast paths to be those with any latency inflation over a unicast front-end.

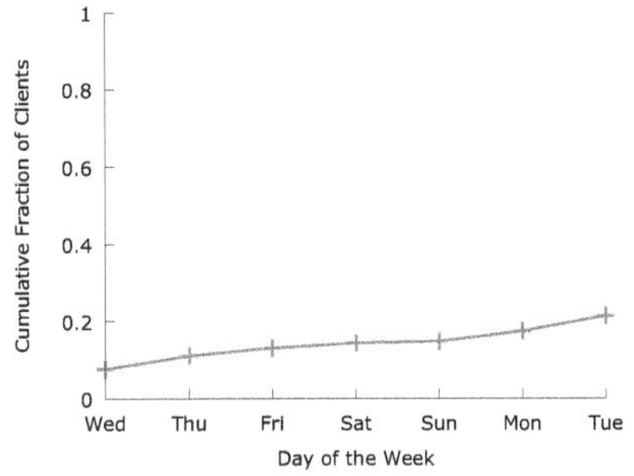

Figure 7: The cumulative fraction of clients that have changed front-ends at least once by different points in a week

for a single day. Next we look at how much of poor performance can be attributed to clients frequently switching between good and poor performing front-ends.

Front-end Affinity: Recurrent front-end selection changes for user over time may indicate route stability issues which can lead to anycast performance problems. We refer to how "attached" particular clients are to a front-end as *front-end affinity*. In this section, we analyze our passive logs.

Figure 7 shows the cumulative fraction of clients that have switched front-ends at least once by that time of the week. Within the first day, 7% of clients landed on multiple front-ends. An additional 2-4% clients see a front-end change each day until the weekend, where there is very little churn, less than .5%. This could be from network operators not pushing out changes during the weekend unless they have to. From the weekend to the beginning of the week, the amount of churn increases again to 2-4% each day. Across the entire week, 21% of clients landed on multiple front-ends, but the vast majority of clients were stable. We discuss potential solutions to this more at the end of §6. We observe that the number of client front-end switches is slightly higher in a one day snapshot compared to the 1.1-4.7% reported in previous work on DNS instance-switches in anycast root nameservers [20, 33]. A likely contributing factor is that our anycast deployment is around 10 times larger than the number of instances present in K root name server at the time of that work.

Figure 8 shows the change in the client-to-front-end distance when the front-end changes. This shows that when the majority of clients switch front-ends, it is to a nearby front-end. This makes sense given the CDN front-end density in North America and Europe. The median change in distance from front-end switches is 483 km while 83% are within 2000 km.

We saw in this section that most clients show high front-end-affinity, that is, they continue going to the same front-end over time. For the clients that do switch front-ends, there is a long tail of distance between a client and switched pairs of front-ends.

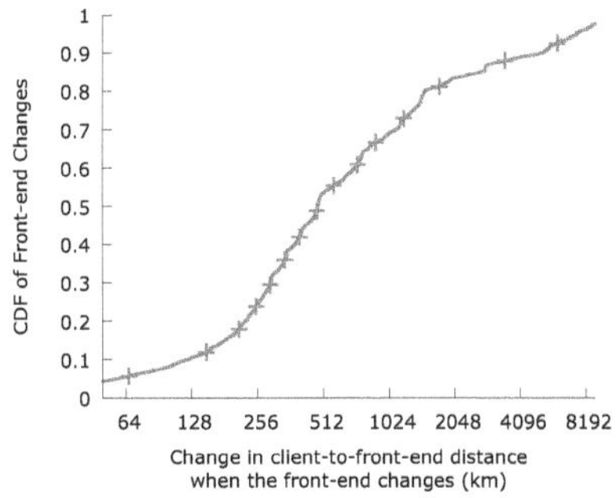

Figure 8: The distribution of change in client-to-front-end distance (log scale) when when the front-end changes, for the 7% of clients that change front-end throughout a day.

6. ADDRESSING POOR PERFORMANCE

The previous section showed that anycast often achieves good performance, but sometimes suffers significantly compared to unicast beacon measurements. However, the ability for unicast to beat anycast in a single measurement does not guarantee that this performance is predictable enough to be achievable if a system has to return a single unicast front-end to a DNS query. If a particular front-end outperformed anycast in the past for a client, will it still if the system returns that front-end next time? Additionally, because of DNS's design, the system does not know which client it is responding to, and so its response applies either to all clients of an LDNS or all clients in a prefix (if using ECS). Can the system reliably determine front-ends that will perform well for the set of clients?

We evaluate to what degree schemes using DNS and ECS can improve performance for clients with poor anycast performance. We evaluate (in emulation based on our real user measurements) a prediction scheme that maps from a client group (clients of an LDNS or clients within an ECS prefix) to its predicted best front-end. It updates its mapping every *prediction interval*, set to one day in our experiment.[2] The scheme chooses to map a client group to the lowest latency front-end across the measurements for that group, picking either the anycast address or one of the unicast front-ends. We evaluate two *prediction metrics* to determine the latency of a front-end, 25th percentile and median latency from that client group to that front-end. We choose lower percentiles, as analysis of client data showed that higher percentiles of latency distributions are very noisy (we omit detailed results due to lack of space). This noise makes prediction difficult, as it can result in overlapping performance between two front-ends. The 25th percentile and median have lower coefficient of variation, indicating less variation and more stability. Our initial evaluation showed that both 25th percentile and median show very similar performance as *prediction metrics*, so we only present results for 25th percentile.

We emulate the performance of such a prediction scheme using our existing beacon measurements. We base the predictions on one day's beacon measurements. For a given client group, we select among the front-ends with 20+ measurements from the clients.

We evaluate the performance of the prediction scheme by comparing against the performance observed in next day's beacon measurements. We compare 50th and 75th anycast performance for the group to 50th and 75th performance for the predicted front-end. The Bing team routinely uses 75% percentile latency as an internal benchmarks for a variety of comparisons. Next, we evaluate prediction using both ECS and LDNS client grouping.

[2] We cannot make predictions at finer timescales, as our sampling rate was limited due to engineering issues.

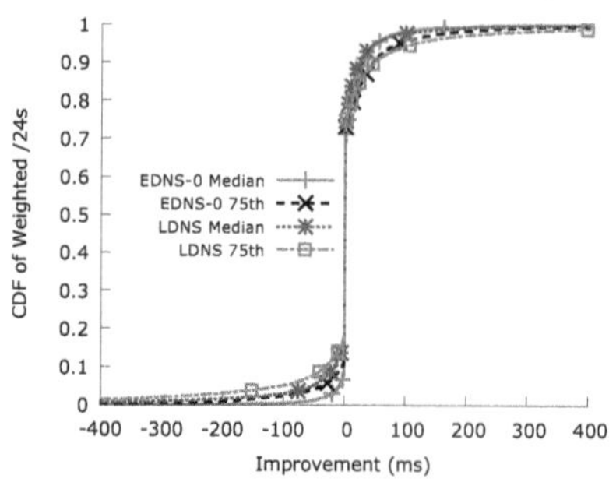

Figure 9: Improvement over anycast from making LDNS or ECS-based decisions with prediction using 25th percentile prediction metric. Negative x-axis values show where anycast was better than our prediction. Values at 0 show when we predicted anycast was the best performing. Positive x-axis values show our improvement.

Prediction using EDNS client-subnet-prefix: The ECS extension [21] enables precise client redirection by including the client's prefix in a DNS request. Our prediction scheme is straightforward: we consider all beacon measurements for a /24 client network and choose the front-end according to the *prediction metrics*.

The "EDNS-0" lines in Figure 9 depict, as a distribution across clients weighted by query volume, the difference between performance to the predicted front-end (at the 50th and 75th percentile) and the performance to the anycast-routed front-end (at the same percentiles). Most clients see no difference in performance, in most cases because prediction selected the anycast address. For the nearly 40% of queries-weighted prefixes we predict to see improvement over anycast, only 30% see a performance improvement over anycast, while 10% of weighted prefixes see worse performance than they would with anycast.

LDNS-based prediction: Traditionally, DNS-based redirection can only make decisions based on a client's LDNS. In this section, we estimate to what degree LDNS granularity can achieve optimal performance when anycast routing sends clients to suboptimal servers. We construct a latency mapping from LDNS to each measured edge by assigning each front-end measurement made by a client to the client's LDNS, which we can identify by joining our DNS and HTTP logs based on the unique hostname for the measurement. We then consider all beacon measurements assigned to an LDNS and select the LDNS's best front-end using the *prediction metrics*. In the page loads in our experiment, public DNS resolvers made up a negligible fraction of total LDNS traffic so their wide user base have an insignificant impact on results.

The "LDNS" lines in Figure 9 show the fraction of /24 client networks that can be improved from using prediction of performance based on an LDNS-based mapping. While we see improvement for around 27% of weighted /24s, we also pay a penalty where our prediction did poorly for around 17% of /24s.

Our results demonstrate that traditional and recent DNS techniques can improve performance for many of the clients who experience suboptimal anycast routing. We are also considering a hybrid approach that combines anycast with DNS-based redirection. The key idea is to use DNS-based redirection for a small subset of poor performing clients, while leaving others to anycast. Such a hybrid approach may outperform DNS redirection for clients not well represented by their LDNS, and it may be more scalable.

7. RELATED WORK

Most closely related to our work is from Alzoubi et al. [9, 8]. They describe a load-aware anycast CDN architecture where ingress routes from a CDN to a large ISP are managed by an ISP's centralized route controller. Unlike our work, they do not examine the end-to-end application performance comparison between DNS redirection and anycast. Follow up work focuses on handling anycast TCP session disruption due to BGP path changes [7]. Our work is also closely related to FastRoute [23], a system for load balancing within an anycast CDN, but it does not address performance issues around redirection. There has been a good deal of work on improving and evaluating general CDN performance [37, 24, 36, 6, 35, 25]. The majority of previous work on anycast performance has focused on DNS. There has been significant attention to anycast DNS from the network operations community [13, 15, 14, 28, 19, 12, 20] but less so for TCP and anycast [31]. Sarat et al. examined the performance impact of anycast on DNS across different anycast configurations [38]. Fan et al. [22] present new methods to identify and characterize anycast nodes. There are several pieces of work describing deployment of anycast services [30, 10, 11, 26].

Akamai recently published a study on DNS-based redirection [17]. The authors showed that the majority of clients are nearby their LDNS, enabling DNS-based redirection to perform well. However, they also show that a significant number of clients are far from their LDNS, and that some LDNS serve clients spread over large geographic regions. The paper describes Akamai's adoption of ECS-based redirection for clients of public DNS resolvers, showing impressive performance improvements for these clients versus LDNS-based redirection. However, public resolvers only make up a small fraction of global DNS traffic. Clients using their ISPs' LDNS cannot benefit unless the ISPs enable ECS and the CDN supports ECS requests from the LDNS. Since anycast works well for many clients, we see benefit in a hybrid approach that chooses whether to use DNS redirection or anycast based on measurements of which works better for the LDNS and whether the LDNS supports ECS.

8. CONCLUSION

In this paper we studied the performance of a large anycast-based CDN, and evaluated whether it could be improved by using a centralized, DNS-based solution. We found that anycast usually performs well despite the lack of precise control, but that it directs $\approx$ 20% of clients to a suboptimal front-end. We demonstrated that a simple prediction scheme may allow DNS redirection to improve performance for some of the clients that see poor anycast performance.

Acknowledgements

We gratefully acknowledge Nick Holt and Daniel Gicklhorn for their support of this work. Matt Calder and Ethan Katz-Bassett were partially supported by the U.S. National Science Foundation grant numbers CNS-1351100 and CNS-1413978.

9. REFERENCES

[1] CloudFlare. `https://www.cloudflare.com/`.

[2] RIPE Atlas. `https://atlas.ripe.net/`.

[3] USC CDN Coverage. `http://usc-nsl.github.io/cdn-coverage`.

[4] V. K. Adhikari, Y. Guo, F. Hao, V. Hilt, and Z.-L. Zhang. Tale of Three CDNs: An Active Measurement Study of Hulu and its CDNs. In *IEEE Global Internet Symposium '12*.

[5] B. Ager, W. Mühlbauer, G. Smaragdakis, and S. Uhlig. Comparing DNS Resolvers in the Wild. In *IMC '10*.

[6] B. Ager, W. Mühlbauer, G. Smaragdakis, and S. Uhlig. Web Content Cartography. In *IMC '11*.

[7] Z. Al-Qudah, S. Lee, M. Rabinovich, O. Spatscheck, and J. Van der Merwe. Anycast-aware Transport for Content Delivery Networks. In *WWW '09*.

[8] H. A. Alzoubi, S. Lee, M. Rabinovich, O. Spatscheck, and J. Van Der Merwe. A Practical Architecture for an Anycast CDN. *ACM Transactions on the Web (TWEB) '11*.

[9] H. A. Alzoubi, S. Lee, M. Rabinovich, O. Spatscheck, and J. Van der Merwe. Anycast CDNs Revisited. In *WWW '08*.

[10] H. Ballani and P. Francis. Towards a Global IP Anycast Service. In *SIGCOMM '05*.

[11] H. Ballani, P. Francis, and S. Ratnasamy. A Measurement-based Deployment Proposal for IP Anycast. In *IMC '06*.

[12] P. Barber, M. Larson, and M. Kosters. Traffic Source Analysis of the J Root Anycast Instances. NANOG 39. February, '07.

[13] P. Barber, M. Larson, M. Kosters, and P. Toscano. Life and Times of J-ROOT. NANOG 32. October, '04.

[14] P. Boothe and R. Bush. Anycast Measurements Used To Highlight Routing Instabilities. NANOG 35. October, '05.

[15] P. Boothe and R. Bush. DNS Anycast Stability. *19th APNIC, '05*.

[16] M. Calder, X. Fan, Z. Hu, E. Katz-Bassett, J. Heidemann, and R. Govindan. Mapping the Expansion of Google's Serving Infrastructure. In *IMC '13*.

[17] F. Cheng, R. K. Sitaraman, and M. Torres. End-user mapping: Next Generation Request Routing for Content Delivery. In *SIGCOMM '15*.

[18] Y. Chiu, B. Schlinker, A. B. Radhakrishnan, E. Katz-Bassett, and R. Govindan. Are We One Hop Away from a Better Internet? In *IMC '15*.

[19] L. Coletti. Effects of Anycast on K-root Performance. NANOG 37. June, '06.

[20] L. Colitti, E. Romijn, H. Uijterwaal, and A. Robachevsky. Evaluating the Effects of Anycast on DNS Root Name Servers. *RIPE document RIPE-393, '06*.

[21] C. Contavalli, W. van der Gaast, D. Lawrence, and W. Kumari. Client Subnet in DNS Requests. IETF Draft draft-vandergaast-edns-client-subnet-02, July 2015.

[22] X. Fan, J. Heidemann, and R. Govindan. Evaluating Anycast in the Domain Name System. In *INFOCOM '13*.

[23] A. Flavel, P. Mani, D. Maltz, N. Holt, J. Liu, Y. Chen, and O. Surmachev. FastRoute: A Scalable Load-Aware Anycast Routing Architecture for Modern CDNs. In *NSDI '15*.

[24] B. Frank, I. Poese, Y. Lin, G. Smaragdakis, A. Feldmann, B. Maggs, J. Rake, S. Uhlig, and R. Weber. Pushing CDN-ISP Collaboration to the Limit. *SIGCOMM CCR '14*.

[25] M. J. Freedman, E. Freudenthal, and D. Mazieres. Democratizing Content Publication with Coral. In *NSDI '04*.

[26] M. J. Freedman, K. Lakshminarayanan, and D. Mazières. OASIS: Anycast for Any Service. In *NSDI '06*.

[27] M. J. Freedman, M. Vutukuru, N. Feamster, and H. Balakrishnan. Geographic Locality of IP Prefixes. In *IMC '05*.

[28] J. Hiebert, P. Boothe, R. Bush, and L. Lynch. Determining the Cause and Frequency of Routing Instability with Anycast. In *AINTEC '06*.

[29] A. Jain, J. Mann, Z. Wang, and A. Quach. W3C Resource Timing Working Draft. http://www.w3.org/TR/resource-timing/, July 2015.

[30] D. Katabi and J. Wroclawski. A Framework For Scalable Global IP-anycast (GIA). *SIGCOMM CCR '00*.

[31] M. Levine, B. Lyon, and T. Underwood. Operation Experience with TCP and Anycast. NANOG 37. June, '06.

[32] W. Li, R. K. Mok, R. K. Chang, and W. W. Fok. Appraising the Delay Accuracy In Browser-based Network Measurement. In *IMC '13*.

[33] Z. Liu, B. Huffaker, M. Fomenkov, N. Brownlee, et al. Two Days in the Life of the DNS Anycast Root Servers. In *PAM '07*.

[34] Z. M. Mao, C. D. Cranor, F. Douglis, M. Rabinovich, O. Spatscheck, and J. Wang. A Precise and Efficient Evaluation of the Proximity Between Web Clients and Their Local DNS Servers. In *USENIX ATC '02*.

[35] E. Nygren, R. K. Sitaraman, and J. Sun. The Akamai Network: A Platform for High-performance Internet Applications. *SIGOPS '10*.

[36] J. S. Otto, M. A. Sánchez, J. P. Rula, and F. E. Bustamante. Content Delivery and the Natural Evolution of DNS: Remote DNS Trends, Performance Issues and Alternative Solutions. In *IMC '12*.

[37] I. Poese, B. Frank, B. Ager, G. Smaragdakis, S. Uhlig, and A. Feldmann. Improving Content Delivery with PaDIS. *Internet Computing, IEEE '12*.

[38] S. Sarat, V. Pappas, and A. Terzis. On the Use of Anycast in DNS. In *ICCCN '06*.

[39] N. Spring, R. Mahajan, and T. Anderson. The Causes of Path Inflation. In *SIGCOMM '03*.

Author Index

www.ingramcontent.com/pod-product-compliance
Ingram Content Group UK Ltd.
Pitfield, Milton Keynes, MK11 3LW, UK
UKHW051416290926
15471UKWH00009B/1629

9 781450 341011